FINANCIAL ACCOUNTING
A Business Perspective

FINANCIAL ACCOUNTING
A Business Perspective

Tenth Edition

Roger H. Hermanson, Ph.D., CPA
Regents Professor Emeritus of Accounting
Ernst & Young–J. W. Holloway Memorial Professor Emeritus
Georgia State University

James Don Edwards, Ph.D., D.H.C., CPA
J. M. Tull Professor Emeritus of Accounting
Terry College of Business
University of Georgia

Jefferson P. Williams, M.Acc., M.A., CPA
Ross School of Business
University of Michigan

TEXTBOOK\MEDIA

- Select textbooks since 2004
- Unique student options
- Uniquely affordable prices

FINANCIAL ACCOUNTING: A BUSINESS PERSPECTIVE, Tenth Edition

Copyright 2013 by Hermanson and Edwards. Published by Textbook Media Press, 2013

Previous editions © 2005 Freeload Press, © 2002 by Authors Academic Press, © 1998 by The McGraw-Hill Companies, Inc., and © 1980, 1983, 1986, 1987, 1989, 1992, and 1995 by Richard D. Irwin, a Times Mirror Higher Education Group, Inc. company.

For more information contact Textbook Media Press, 1808 Dayton Avenue, St. Paul, MN 55104

ISBN 1-930789-79-3

Textbook Media Press is a Minnesota-based educational publisher. We deliver textbooks and supplements with the quality that instructors expect, while providing students with unique media options at uniquely affordable prices. **All our publications are 100% made in the U.S.A.**

About the Authors

Professor Roger H. Hermanson, Ph.D., CPA

Regents Professor Emeritus of Accounting and Ernst & Young–J. W. Holloway Memorial Professor Emeritus at Georgia State University. He received his doctorate at Michigan State University in 1963 and is a CPA in Georgia. Professor Hermanson taught and later served as chairperson of the Division of Accounting at the University of Maryland. He has authored or coauthored approximately one-hundred articles for professional and scholarly journals and has coauthored numerous editions of several textbooks, including *Accounting Principles, Financial Accounting, Survey of Financial and Managerial Accounting, Auditing Theory and Practice, Principles of Financial and Managerial Accounting,* and *Computerized Accounting with Peachtree Complete III.* He also has served on the editorial boards of the *Journal of Accounting Education, New Accountant, Accounting Horizons,* and *Management Accounting.* Professor Hermanson has served as coeditor of the Trends in Accounting Education column for *Management Accounting.* He has held the office of vice president of the American Accounting Association and served on its executive committee. He was also a member of the Institute of Management Accountants, the American Institute of Certified Public Accountants, and the Financial Executives Institute.

Professor Hermanson has been awarded two excellence in teaching awards, a doctoral fellow's award, and a Distinguished Alumni Professor award; and he was selected as the Outstanding Faculty Member for 1985 by the Federation of Schools of Accountancy. He has served as a consultant to many companies and organizations. In 1990, Professor Hermanson was named Accounting Educator of the Year by the Georgia Society of CPAs. His wife's name is Dianne, and he has two children, Dana and Susan, both of whom are accounting professors.

Professor James Don Edwards, Ph.D., D.H.C., CPA

J. M. Tull Professor Emeritus of Accounting in the Terry College of Business at the University of Georgia. He is a graduate of Louisiana State University and has been inducted into the Louisiana State University Alumni Federation's Hall of Distinction. He received his M.B.A. from the University of Denver and his Ph.D. from the University of Texas and is a CPA in Texas and Georgia. He has served as a professor and chairman of the Department of Accounting and Financial Administration at Michigan State University, a professor and dean of the Graduate School of Business Administration at the University of Minnesota, and a Visiting Scholar at Oxford University in Oxford, England.

Professor Edwards is a past president of the American Accounting Association and a past national vice president and executive committee member of the Institute of Management Accountants. He has served on the board of directors of the American Institute of Certified Public Accountants and as chairman of the Georgia State Board of Accountancy. He was an original trustee of the Financial Accounting Foundation, the parent organization of the FASB, and a member of the Public Review Board of Arthur Andersen & Co.

He has published in *The Accounting Review, The Journal of Accountancy, The Journal of Accounting Research, Management Accounting,* and *The Harvard Business History Review.* He is also the author of *History of Public Accounting in the United States.* He has served on various American Institute of Certified Public Accountants committees and boards, including the Objectives of Financial Statements Committee, Standards of Professional Conduct Committee, and the CPA Board of Examiners. He was the managing editor of the centennial issue of *The Journal of Accountancy.*

In 1974, Beta Alpha Psi, the National Accounting Fraternity, selected Professor Edwards for its first annual Outstanding Accountant of the Year award. This selection is made from industry, government, and educational leaders. In 1975, he was selected by the American Accounting Association as its Outstanding Educator.

He has served the AICPA as president of the Benevolent Fund, chairman of the Awards Committee, member of the Professional Ethics Committee and Program for World Congress of Accountants. He was on the Education Standards Committee of the International Federation of Accountants and the Committee on Planning for the Institute of Management Accountants. He was the director of the Seminar for Management Accountants–Financial Reporting for the American Accounting Association. He is also a member of the Financial Executives Institute.

He received the 1993 AICPA Gold Medal Award, the highest award given by the Institute. A Doctor Honoris Causa (Honorary Doctorate) from the University of Paris was awarded to him in 1994. He is the first accountant to receive this distinction in France. The Academy of Accounting Historians awarded him the 1994 Hourglass Award which is the highest international honor in the field of Accounting History. He was inducted into the Ohio State University Accounting Hall of Fame in 2001. His wife's name is Clara, and he has one son, Jim.

Jefferson P. Williams, M.Acc., M.A., CPA

Jeff Williams is a Lecturer of Accounting at the Stephen M. Ross School of Business at the University of Michigan. He teaches financial accounting at the undergraduate and at the graduate levels. Mr. Williams also teaches federal taxation at the graduate level.

He received his Bachelor of Science and Master of Accountancy degrees from the University of Tennessee and his Master of Arts Degree from the University of Michigan.

Prior to his teaching career, Mr. Williams worked as a CPA in the states of Tennessee and South Carolina. His practice focused on audit and assurance services and valuation services. He and his wife, Debbie, are the parents of five children and live in Ann Arbor, Michigan.

Preface

Philosophy and Purpose

Imagine that you have graduated from college without taking an accounting course. You are employed by a company as a sales person, and you eventually become the sales manager of a territory. While attending a sales managers' meeting, financial results are reviewed by the Vice President of Sales and terms such as gross margin percentage, cash flows from operating activities, and LIFO inventory methods are being discussed. The Vice President eventually asks you to discuss these topics as they relate to your territory. You try to do so, but it is obvious to everyone in the meeting that you do not know what you are talking about.

Financial accounting principles courses teach you the "language of business" so you understand terms and concepts used in business decisions. If you understand how accounting information is prepared, you will be in an even stronger position when faced with a management decision based on accounting information.

We wrote this text to give you an understanding of how to use accounting information to analyze business performance and make business decisions. The text takes a business perspective. We use the annual reports of **real** companies to illustrate many of the accounting concepts. You are familiar with many of the companies we use, such as Wal-Mart Stores, The Home Depot, and Coca-Cola Company.

Gaining an understanding of accounting terminology and concepts, however, is not enough to ensure your success. You also need to be able to find information on the internet, analyze various business situations, work effectively as a member of a team, and communicate your ideas clearly. This text was developed to help you develop these skills.

Curriculum Concerns

Significant changes have been recommended for accounting education. Some parties have expressed concern that recent accounting graduates do not possess the necessary set of skills to succeed in an accounting career. The typical accounting graduate seems unable to successfully deal with complex and unstructured "**real world**" accounting problems and generally lacks communication and interpersonal skills. One recommendation is the greater use of active learning techniques in a reenergized classroom environment. The traditional lecture and structured problem solving method approach would be supplemented or replaced with a more informal classroom setting dealing with cases, simulations, and group projects. Both inside and outside the classroom, there would be two-way communication between (1) professor and student and (2) student and student. Study groups would be formed so that students could tutor other students. The purposes of these recommendations include enhancing students' critical thinking skills, written and oral communication skills, and interpersonal skills.

One of the most important benefits you can obtain from a college education is that you "learn how to learn." The concept that you gain all of your learning in school and then spend the rest of your life applying that knowledge is not valid. Change is occurring at an increasingly rapid pace. You will probably hold many different jobs during your career, and you will probably work for many different companies. Much of the information you learn in college will be obsolete in just a few years. Therefore, you will be expected to engage in life-long learning. Memorizing is much less important than learning how to think critically.

With this changing environment in mind, we have developed a text that will lend itself to developing the skills that will lead to success in your future career in business. The section at the end of each chapter titled, "Beyond the Numbers—Critical Thinking," provides the opportunity for you to address unstructured case situations, the analysis of real companies' financial situations, ethics cases, and team projects. Each chapter also includes one or two **Internet projects** in the section titled "Using the Internet—A View of the Real World." For many of these items, you will use written and oral communication skills in presenting your results.

Objectives and Overall Approach of the Tenth Edition

The Accounting Education Change Commission (AECC) made specific recommendations regarding teaching materials and methods used in the first-year accounting course. As a result, significant changes are taking place in that course at many universities. The AECC states:

The first course in accounting can significantly benefit those who enter business, government, and other organizations, where decision-makers use accounting information. These individuals will be better prepared for their responsibilities if they understand the role of accounting information in decision-making by managers, investors, government regulators, and others. All organizations have accountability responsibilities to their constituents, and accounting, properly used, is a powerful tool in creating information to improve the decisions that affect those constituents.[1]

One of the purposes of the first course should be to recruit accounting majors. To help accomplish this, the text has a section preceding each chapter entitled, "Careers in Accounting."

We retained a solid coverage of accounting that serves business students well regardless of the majors they select. Those who choose not to major in accounting, which is a majority of those taking this course, will become better users of accounting information because they will know something about the preparation of that information.

Approach and Organization

Business Emphasis

Without actual business experience, business students sometimes lack a frame of reference in attempting to apply accounting concepts to business transactions. We seek to involve the business student more in real world business applications as we introduce and explain the subject matter.

- **"An Accounting Perspective: Business Insight"** boxes throughout the text provide examples of how companies featured in text examples use accounting information every day, or they provide other useful information.

- **"Accounting Perspective: Uses of Technology"** boxes throughout the text demonstrate how technology has affected the way accounting information is prepared, manipulated, and accessed.

- Some chapters contain **"A Broader Perspective."** These situations, taken from annual reports of real companies and from articles in current business periodicals such as *Accounting Today,* and *Management Accounting,* relate to subject

matter discussed in that chapter or present other useful information. These real world examples demonstrate the business relevance of accounting.

- Real world questions and real world business decision cases are included in almost every chapter.

- The Annual Report Appendix included with this text contains significant portions of the annual report of Wal-Mart Stores, Inc. Many of the real world questions and business decision cases are based on this annual report.

- Numerous illustrations adapted from *Accounting Trends & Techniques* show the frequency of use in business of various accounting techniques. Placed throughout the text, these illustrations give students real world data to consider while learning about different accounting techniques.

- Throughout the text we have included numerous references to the annual reports of many companies.

- Most of the chapters contain a section entitled, "Analyzing and Using the Financial Results." This section discusses and illustrates a ratio or other analysis technique that pertains to the content of the chapter. For instance, this section in Chapter 4 discusses the current ratio as it relates to a classified balance sheet.

- Most of the chapters contain end-of-chapter questions, exercises, or business decision cases that require the student to refer to the Annual Report Appendix and answer certain questions. As stated earlier, this appendix is included with the text and contains significant portions of the annual report of Wal-Mart Stores, Inc.

- Each chapter contains a section entitled, "Beyond the Numbers—Critical Thinking." This section contains business decision cases, annual report analysis problems, writing assignments based on the Ethical Perspective and Broader Perspective boxes, group projects, and Internet projects.

Pedagogy

Students often come into accounting principles courses feeling anxious about learning the subject matter. Recognizing this apprehension, we studied ways to make learning easier and came up with some helpful ideas on how to make this edition work even better for students.

- Improvements in the text's content reflect feedback from adopters, suggestions by reviewers, and a serious study of the learning process itself by

---

[1]Accounting Education Change Commission, *Position Statement No. Two,* "The First Course in Accounting" (Torrance, CA, June 1992), pp. 1–2.

the authors and editors. New subject matter is introduced only after the stage has been set by transitional paragraphs between topic headings. These paragraphs provide students with the reasons for proceeding to the new material and explain the progression of topics within the chapter.

- The Introduction contains a section entitled "How to Study the Chapters in This Text," which should be very helpful to students.

- Each chapter has an "Understanding the Learning Objectives" section. These "summaries" enable the student to determine how well the Learning Objectives were accomplished. We were the first authors (1974) to ever include Learning Objectives in an accounting text. These objectives have been included at the beginning of the chapter, as marginal notes within the chapter, at the end of the chapter, and in supplements such as the Test Bank, Instructors' Resource Guide, Computerized Test Bank, and Study Guide. The objectives are also indicated for each exercise and problem.

- Demonstration problems and solutions are included for each chapter, and a different one appears for each chapter in the Study Guide. These demonstration problems help students to assess their own progress by showing them how problems that focus on the topic(s) covered in the chapter are worked before students do assigned homework problems.

- Key terms are printed in another color for emphasis. End-of-chapter glossaries contain the definition and the page number where the new term was first introduced and defined. Students can easily turn back to the original discussion and study the term's significance in context with the chapter material.

- Each chapter includes a "Self-Test" consisting of true-false and multiple-choice questions. The answers and explanations appear at the end of the chapter. These self-tests are designed to determine whether the student has learned the essential information in each chapter.

- In the margin beside each exercise and problem, we have included a description of the requirements and the related Learning Objective(s). These descriptions let students know what they are expected to do in the problem.

- Throughout the text we use examples taken from everyday life to relate an accounting concept being introduced or discussed to students' experiences.

Ethics

There is no better time to emphasize high ethical standards to students. This text includes many items throughout the text entitled, "An Ethical Perspective." These items present situations in which students are likely to find themselves throughout their careers. They range from resisting pressure by a superior or a client to do the wrong thing to deciding between alternative corporate behaviors that have environmental and profit consequences.

End-of-Chapter Materials

Describing teaching methods, the AECC stated, "Teachers . . . should place a priority on their interaction with students and on interaction among students. Students' involvement should be promoted by methods such as cases, simulations, and group projects. . . ."[2] A section entitled **"Beyond the Numbers—Critical Thinking"** at the end of every chapter is designed to implement these recommendations. **Business Decision Cases** require critical thinking in complex situations often based on real companies. The **Annual Report Analysis** section requires analyzing annual reports and interpreting the results in writing. The **Ethics Cases** require students to respond in writing to situations they are likely to encounter in their careers. These cases do not necessarily have one right answer. The **Group Projects** for each chapter teach students how to work effectively in teams, a skill that was stressed by the AECC and is becoming increasingly necessary for success in business. The **Internet Projects** teach students how to retrieve useful information from the Internet.

A team approach can also be introduced in the classroom using the regular exercises and problems in the text. Teams can be assigned the task of presenting their solutions to exercises or problems to the rest of the class. Using this team approach in class can help reenergize the classroom by creating an active, informal environment in which students learn from each other. (Two additional group projects are described in the Instructor's Resource Guide. These projects are designed to be used throughout the semester or quarter.)

We have included a vast amount of other resource materials for each chapter *within* the text from which the instructor may draw: (1) one of the largest selections of end-of-chapter questions, exercises, and problems available; (2) several comprehensive review problems that allow students to review all major concepts covered to that point; and (3) from one to three business decision cases per chapter. Other key features regarding end-of-chapter material follow.

- A uniform chart of accounts appears in a separate file you can download. This uniform chart of accounts is used consistently throughout the first 11 chapters. We believe students will benefit from using the same chart of accounts for all homework problems in those chapters.

[2] Ibid, p. 2.

- Some of the end-of-chapter problem materials (questions, exercises, problems, business decision cases, other "Beyond the Numbers" items, and comprehensive review problems) have been updated. Each exercise and problem is identified with the learning objective(s) to which it relates.

- All end-of-chapter exercises and problems have been traced back to the chapters to ensure that nothing is asked of a student that does not appear in the book. This feature was a strength of previous editions, ensuring that instructors could confidently assign problems without having to check for applicability. Also, we took notes while teaching from the text and clarified problem and exercise instructions that seemed confusing to our students.

Supplements for the Instructor

A complete package of supplemental teaching aids contains all you need to efficiently and effectively teach the course.

Instructor's Resource Guide   This guide contains sample syllabi for both semester- and quarter-based courses. Each chapter contains: (1) a summary of major concepts; (2) learning objectives from the text; (3) space for the instructor's own notes; (4) an outline of the chapter with an indication of when each exercise can be worked; and (5) detailed lecture notes that also refer to specific end-of-chapter exercise and problem materials illustrating these concepts. Also included are (6) a summary of the estimated time, learning objective(s), level of difficulty, and content of each exercise and problem that is useful in deciding which items to cover in class or to assign as homework. The Instructor's Resource Guide for Chapter 17 contains a case study based on Hasbro, Inc. This company is one of the world's leading manufacturer and marketer of toys, games, puzzles, and infant care products. You may want to assign this case as a special project to individuals or to teams. The results of the analysis, with recommendations, could then be presented to the class. The Instructor's Resource Guide is provided to adopters in both Word and PDF formats.

Solutions Manual   The solutions manual contains suggested discussion points for each ethics case as well as detailed answers to questions, exercises, two series of problems, business decision cases, most "Beyond the Numbers" items, comprehensive review problems, and some group projects. The Solutions Manual is provided to adopters in both Word and PDF files.

Test Bank   The test bank contains approximately 3,000 questions and problems to choose from in preparing examinations. This test bank contains true-false questions, multiple-choice questions, and short problems for each chapter. Questions and problems are *classified by the learning objective* to which they relate. The Test Bank is provided to adopters in both Word and PDF files. A computer test bank version is also available for selecting questions and printing exams.

PowerPoint Slides   An average of 26 PowerPoint slides exist for each chapter. These slides illustrate the most important points in the chapter. They can be used as a basis for classroom lectures and/or discussions.

Supplements for the Student

In addition to the text, the package of support items for the student includes the following:

Study Guide   Included for each chapter are learning objectives, a reference outline, a chapter review, and an additional demonstration problem and solution. If students use the study guide throughout the course, their knowledge of accounting will be enhanced significantly. The study guide is a valuable learning tool in that it includes matching, true-false, and multiple-choice questions, completion questions, and exercises. Solutions to all exercises and questions are also included. The Study Guide is available to students in online or PDF format. It can be purchased at the publisher's website (www.textbookmedia.com).

Check Figures   Check figures are available in a separate file at the end of the text. They show key amounts that students can check to see if they are on the right track when working the Exercises and Problems.

Working Papers   A set of working papers is available for completing assigned exercises, problems, business decision cases, other "Beyond the Numbers" items, and comprehensive review problems. The Working Papers are customized for each exercise and problem in each chapter. They can be purchased at the publisher's website (www.textbookmedia.com).

We are indebted to all our previous coauthors who have contributed to the project in the past, especially R. F. "Sully" Salmonson who worked on many of the early editions.

Roger H. Hermanson
James Don Edwards
Jefferson P. Williams

Acknowledgments

The development of all ten editions of *Financial Accounting: A Business Perspective* was an evolving and challenging process. Significant changes are taking place in the first course in accounting in schools across the country, and the authors and publisher worked hard throughout the development of this text to stay on top of those changes. Recent editions are the product of extensive market research including interviews with adopters and nonadopters and comprehensive reviews by faculty. In particular, we are grateful to the following individuals for their valuable contributions and suggestions.

Survey Participants

Diane Adcox
University of North Florida–Jacksonville

Sue Atkinson
Tarleton State University

Ed Bader
Holy Family College

Keith Baker
Oglethorpe University

C. Richard Baker
Fordham University

Audrie Beck
The American University

Joe Bentley
Bunker Hill Community College

Lucille Berry
Webster University

Robert Bricker
Case Western Reserve

William Brosi
Delhi College

Doug Brown
Eastern Montana College

Stuart Brown
Bristol Community College

Janice Buddinseck
Wagner College

Kurt Buerger
Anglo State University

Robert Cantwell
University of Phoenix–Utah

Bruce Cassel
Dutchess Community College

Stan Chu
Borough of Manhattan Community College

Bruce Collier
University of Texas–El Paso

Rosalind Cranor
Virginia Polytech Institute

James Crockett
University of Southern Mississippi

Lee Daugherty
Lorain County Community College

Mary Davis
University of Maryland

Frances Engel
Niagra University

J. Michael Erwin
University of Tennessee

Ali Fekrat
Georgetown University

Bill Felty
Lindenwood College

Clyde J. Galbraith
West Chester University

Susan D. Garr
Wayne State University

John Gercio
Loyola College

Martin Ginsberg
Rockland Community College

Earl Godfrey
Gardner-Webb College

Thomas Grant
Kutztown University

Paul W. Greenough
Assumption College

Roy Gross
Dutchess Community College

Vincent D. R. Guide
Clemson University

Pat Haggerty
Lansing Community College

Paul Hajja
Rivier College

Joh Haney
Lansing Community College

Thomas D. Harris
Indiana State University

Dennis Hart
Manchester Community College

Brenda Hartman
Tomball College

Mary Hatch
Thomas College

Margaret Hicks
Howard University

Patricia H. Holmes
Des Moines Area Community College

Anita Hope
Tarrant County Junior College

Andrew Jackson
Central State University

Donald W. Johnson, Sr.
Siena College

Glenn L. Johnson
Washington State University

Richard W. Jones
Lamar University

Ed Kerr
Bunker Hill Community College

David Kleinerman
Roosevelt University

Jane Konditi
Northwood University

Nathan J. Kranowski
Radford University

Michael Kulper
Santa Barbara Community College

Michael R. Lane
Nassau Community College

Judy Laux
Colorado College

Linda Lessing
SUNY–Farmingdale

Bruce McClane
Hartnell College

Melvin T. McClure
University of Maine

T. J. McCoy
Middlesex Community College

J. Harrison McCraw
West Georgia College

James E. McKinney
Valdosta State

B. J. Michalek
La Roche College

Andrew Miller
Hudson Valley Community College

Cheryl E. Mitchum
Virginia State University

Susan Moncada
Indiana State University

Susan Mulhern
Rivier College

Lee H. Nicholas
University of Southern Iowa

Kristine N. Palmer
Longwood College

Lynn M. Paluska
Nassau Community College

Seong Park
University of Tennessee–Chattanooga

Vikki Passikoff
Dutchess Community College

Barb Pauer
W. Wisconsin Tech Institute

Doug Pfister
Lansing Community College

Sharyll A. Plato
University of Central Oklahoma

Patricia P. Polk
University of Southern Mississippi

Harry Purcell
Ulster Community College

T. J. Regan
Middlesex County College

Ruthie G. Reynolds
Howard University

E. Barry Rice
Loyola College in Maryland

Cheryl Rumler
Monroe County Community College

Francis Sake
Mercer County Community College

Jackie Sanders
Mercer County Community College

Alex J. Sannella
Rutgers University

Thomas Sears
Hartwich College

John Sedensky
Newbury College

Sarah H. Smith
Cedarville College

John Snyder
Mohawk Valley Community College

Leonard E. Stokes
Siena College

Janice Stoudemire
Midlands Technical College–Airport Campus

Marty Stub
DeVry Institute–Chicago

Barbara Sturdevant
Delhi College

William N. Sullivan
Assumption College

Norman A. Sunderman
Angelo State University

Janice M. Swanson
Southern Oregon State College

Norman Swanson
Greenville College

Audrey G. Taylor
Wayne State University

Kayla Tessler
Oklahoma City Community College

Julia Tiernan
Merrimack College

John Vaccaro
Bunker Hill Community College

Al Veragraziano
Santa Barbara Community College

David Wagaman
Kutztown University

Karen Walton
John Carroll University

Linda Wanacott
Portland Community College

Jim Weglin
North Seattle Community College

David P. Weiner
University of San Francisco

L.K. Williams
Morehead State University

Marge Zolldi
Husson College

Reviewers

Lucille Berry
Webster University

Elizabeth L. Boudreau
Newbury College

Wayne G. Bremser
Villanova University

Fred Dial
Stephen F. Austin State University

Larry Falcetto
Emporia State University

Katherine Beal Frazier
North Carolina State University

Al L. Hartgraves
Emory University

Martin G. Jagels
University of South Carolina

Emel Kahya
Rutgers University

Emogene W. King
Tyler Junior College

Jane Konditi
Northwood University

Charles Konkol
University of Wisconsin–Milwaukee

William Lawler
Tomball College

Keith R. Leeseberg
Manatee Junior College–Bradenton

Susan Moncada
Indiana State University

Lee H. Nicholas
University of Northern Iowa

Douglas R. Pfister
Lansing Community College

Patricia P. Polk
University of Southern Mississippi

Richard Rand
Tennessee Technical University

Ruthie G. Reynolds
Howard University

Marilyn Rholl
Lane Community College

E. Berry Rice
Loyola College in Maryland

William Richardson
University of Phoenix

Douglas Sharp
Wichita State University

Janet Stoudemire
Midlands Technical College–Airport Campus

Marilyn Young
Tulsa Junior College–Southeast

Annotations Authors

Diane Adcox
Instructor of Accounting
University of North Florida–Jacksonville

C. Sue Cook
Tulsa Junior College

Alan B. Cryzewski
Indiana State University

Patricia H. Holmes, CPA (Coordinator)
Des Moines Area Community College

Donald W. Johnson, Sr.
Siena College

Linda Lessing
SUNY at Farmingdale

Cheryl E. Mitchem (Coordinator)
Virginia State University

Lee H. Nicholas
University of Northern Iowa

Lynn Mazzola Paluska
Nassau Community College

Benjamin Shlaes, CPA (Coordinator)
Des Moines Area Community College

Margaret Skinner
SUNY at New Paltz

Leonard F. Stokes III, CPA
Siena College

Kathy J. Tam, CPA
Tulsa Junior College

Former Coauthors

R. F. Salmonson (Deceased)
Michigan State University

Ray H. Garrison (Retired)
Brigham Young University

Gayle L. Rayburn (Retired)
S. W. Missouri State University

Donald R. Herrmann
Baylor University

Keith F. Sellers
Fort Lewis College

Wayne B. Thomas
University of Oklahoma

T. Sterling Wetzel
Oklahoma State University–Stillwater

Contents in Brief

Table of Contents

Careers in Accounting:
Tax Specialist   98

Chapter Three
Adjustments for Financial Reporting   99

Careers in Accounting:
Information Systems   132

Chapter Four
Completing the Accounting Cycle   133

Careers in Accounting:
Accounting Professor   176

Chapter Five
Accounting Theory   177

Careers in Accounting:
A Career as a CEO   212

Chapter Six
Merchandising Transactions: Introduction to Inventories and the Classified Income Statement   213

Careers in Accounting:
Career Opportunities   256

Chapter Seven
**Measuring and Reporting
Inventories   257**

PART III   Management's Perspectives in Accounting for Resources

Careers in Accounting:
Forensic Accounting   306

Chapter Eight
Control of Cash   307

Careers in Accounting:
Litigation Support   344

Chapter Nine
Receivables and Payables   345

Careers in Accounting:
Plant Assets   384

Chapter Ten
Property, Plant, and Equipment   385

Careers in Accounting:
Financial Analyst 496

Chapter Thirteen
Corporations: Paid-in Capital, Retained Earnings, Dividends, and Treasury Stock 497

Careers in Accounting:
Business Acquisitions 540

Chapter Fourteen
Stock Investments 541

The Accounting Environment

You have embarked on the challenging and rewarding study of accounting—an old and time-honored discipline. History indicates that all developed societies require certain accounting records. Record keeping in an accounting sense is thought to have begun about 4000 B.C.

The record keeping, control, and verification problems of the ancient world had many characteristics similar to those we encounter today. For example, ancient governments also kept records of receipts and disbursements and used procedures to check on the honesty and reliability of employees.

A study of the evolution of accounting suggests that accounting processes have developed primarily in response to business needs. Also, economic progress has affected the development of accounting processes. History shows that the higher the level of civilization, the more elaborate the accounting methods.

The emergence of double-entry bookkeeping was a crucial event in accounting history. In 1494, a Franciscan monk, Luca Pacioli, described the double-entry Method of Venice system in his text called *Summa de Arithmetica, Geometric, Proportion et Proportionalite* (Everything about Arithmetic, Geometry, and Proportion). Many consider Pacioli's *Summa* to be a reworked version of a manuscript that circulated among teachers and pupils of the Venetian school of commerce and arithmetic.

Since Pacioli's days, the roles of accountants and professional accounting organizations have expanded in business and society. As professionals, accountants have a responsibility for placing public service above their commitment to personal economic gain. Complementing their obligation to society, accountants have analytical and evaluative skills needed in the solution of ever-growing world problems. The special abilities of accountants, their independence, and their high ethical standards permit them to make significant and unique contributions to business and areas of public interest.

You probably will find that of all the business knowledge you have acquired or will learn, the study of accounting will be the most useful. Your financial and

After studying this chapter, you should be able to:

1. Define accounting.

2. Describe the functions performed by accountants.

3. Describe employment opportunities in accounting.

4. Differentiate between financial and managerial accounting.

5. Identify several organizations that have a role in the development of financial accounting standards.

economic decisions as a student and consumer involve accounting information. When you file income tax returns, accounting information helps determine your taxes payable. Understanding the discipline of accounting also can influence many of your future professional decisions. You cannot escape the effects of accounting information on your personal and professional life.

Every profit-seeking business organization that has economic resources, such as money, machinery, and buildings, uses accounting information. For this reason, accounting is called the *language of business*. Accounting also serves as the language providing financial information about not-for-profit organizations such as governments, churches, charities, fraternities, and hospitals. However, this text concentrates on accounting for business firms.

The accounting system of a profit-seeking business is an information system designed to provide relevant financial information on the resources of a business and the effects of their use. Information is relevant if it has some impact on a decision that must be made. Companies present this relevant information in their financial statements. In preparing these statements, accountants consider the users of the information, such as owners and creditors, and decisions they make that require financial information.

As a background for studying accounting, this Introduction defines accounting and lists the functions accountants perform. In addition to surveying employment opportunities in accounting, it differentiates between financial and managerial accounting. Because accounting information must conform to certain standards, we discuss several prominent organizations contributing to these standards. As you continue your study of accounting in this text, accounting—the language of business—will become your language also. You will realize that you are constantly exposed to accounting information in your everyday life.

Accounting Defined

<table>
<tr><td>**Objective 1**
Define accounting.</td><td>The American Accounting Association—one of the accounting organizations discussed later in this Introduction—defines accounting as *"the process of identifying, measuring, and communicating economic information to permit informed judgments and decisions by the users of the information."*[1] This information is primarily financial—stated in money terms. Accounting, then, is a measurement and communication process used to report on the activities of profit-seeking business organizations and not-for-profit organizations. As a measurement and communication process for business, accounting supplies information that permits informed judgments and decisions by users of the data.</td></tr>
</table>

The accounting process provides financial data for a broad range of individuals whose objectives in studying the data vary widely. Bank officials, for example, may study a company's financial statements to evaluate the company's ability to repay a loan. Prospective investors may compare accounting data from several companies to decide which company represents the best investment. Accounting also supplies management with significant financial data useful for decision making.

Reliable information is necessary before decision makers can make a sound decision involving the allocation of scarce resources. Accounting information is valuable because decision makers can use it to evaluate the financial consequences of various alternatives. Accountants eliminate the need for a crystal ball to estimate the future. They can reduce uncertainty by using professional judgment to quantify the future financial impact of taking action or delaying action.

Although accounting information plays a significant role in reducing uncertainty within the organization, it also provides financial data for persons outside the company. This information tells how management has discharged its responsibility for protecting and managing the company's resources. Stockholders have the right to know how a

---

[1]American Accounting Association, *A Statement of Basic Accounting Theory* (Evanston, Ill., 1966), p. 1.

company is managing its investments. In fulfilling this obligation, accountants prepare financial statements such as an income statement, a statement of retained earnings, a balance sheet, and a statement of cash flows. In addition, they prepare tax returns for federal and state governments, as well as fulfill other governmental filing requirements.

Accounting is often confused with bookkeeping. Bookkeeping is a mechanical process that records the routine economic activities of a business. Accounting includes bookkeeping but goes well beyond it in scope. Accountants analyze and interpret financial information, prepare financial statements, conduct audits, design accounting systems, prepare special business and financial studies, prepare forecasts and budgets, and provide tax services.

Specifically the accounting process consists of the following groups of functions (see Illustration 0.1):

Objective 2
Describe the functions performed by accountants.

1. Accountants *observe* many events (or activities) and *identify* and *measure* in financial terms (dollars) those events considered evidence of economic activity. (Often, these three functions are collectively referred to as *analyze*.) For instance, the purchase and sale of goods and services are economic events.
2. Next, the economic events are *recorded, classified* into meaningful groups, and *summarized.*
3. Accountants *report* on economic events (or business activity) by preparing financial statements and special reports. Often accountants *interpret* these statements and reports for various groups such as management, investors, and creditors. Interpretation may involve determining how the business is performing compared to prior years and other similar businesses.

Employment Opportunities in Accounting

During the last half-century, accounting has gained the same professional status as the medical and legal professions. Today, the accountants in the United States number well over a million. In addition, several million people hold accounting-related positions. Typically, accountants provide services in various branches of accounting. These include public accounting, management (industrial) accounting, governmental or other not-for-profit accounting, and higher education. The demand for accountants will likely increase dramatically in the future. This increase is greater than for any other profession. You may want to consider accounting as a career.

Objective 3
Describe employment opportunities in accounting.

Public accounting firms   Offer professional accounting and related services for a fee to companies, other organizations, and individuals. An accountant may become a Certified Public Accountant (CPA) by passing an examination prepared and graded by the American Institute of Certified Public Accountants (AICPA). The exam is administered by computer. In addition to passing the exam, CPA candidates must meet other requirements, which include obtaining a state license. These requirements vary by state. A number of states require a CPA candidate to have completed specific accounting courses and earned a certain number of college credits (five years of study in many states); worked a certain number of years in public accounting, industry, or government; and lived in that state a certain length of time before taking the CPA examination. Five years of course work are required to become a member of the AICPA.

Public Accounting

After a candidate passes the CPA examination, some states (called one-tier states) insist that the candidate meet all requirements before the state grants the CPA certificate and license to practice. Other states (called two-tier states) issue the CPA certificate immediately after the candidate passes the exam. However, these states issue the license to practice only after all other requirements have been met. CPAs who want

Illustration 0.1   Functions Performed by Accountants.

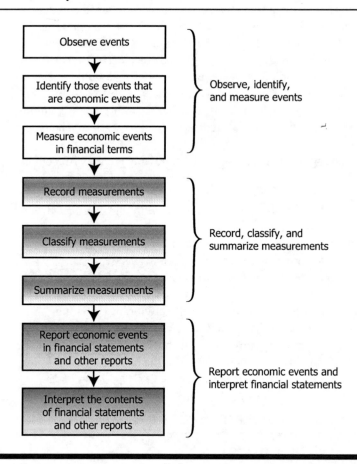

to renew their licenses to practice must stay current through continuing professional education programs and must prove that they have done so. No one can claim to be a CPA and offer the services normally provided by a CPA unless that person holds an active license to practice.

The public accounting profession in the United States consists of the Big Four international CPA firms, several national firms, many regional firms, and numerous local firms. The Big Four firms include Deloitte & Touche, Ernst & Young, KPMG, and PricewaterhouseCoopers. At all levels, these public accounting firms provide auditing, tax, and, for nonaudit clients, management advisory (or consulting) services.

Auditing   A business seeking a loan or attempting to have its securities traded on a stock exchange usually must provide financial statements to support its request. Users of a company's financial statements are more confident that the company is presenting its statements fairly when a CPA has audited the statements. For this reason, companies hire CPA firms to conduct examinations (independent audits) of their accounting and related records. Independent auditors of the CPA firm check some of the company's records by contacting external sources. For example, the accountant may contact a bank to verify the cash balances of the client. After completing a company audit, independent auditors give an independent auditor's opinion or report. (For an example of an auditor's opinion, see Wal-Mart Stores, Inc. annual report in the Annual Report Appendix at the end of the text.) This report states whether the company's financial statements fairly (equitably) report the economic performance and financial condition of the business. As you will learn in the next section, auditors within a business also conduct audits, which are not independent audits. Currently auditing standards are established by the Public Company Accounting Oversight Board.

In 2002 The Sarbanes-Oxley Act was passed. The Act was passed as one result of the large losses to the employees and investors from accounting fraud situations involving companies such as Enron and WorldCom. The Act created the Public Company Accounting Oversight Board. The Board consists of five members appointed and overseen by the Securities and Exchange Commission. The Board oversees and investigates the audits and auditors of public companies and can sanction both firms and individuals for violations of laws, regulations, and rules. The Chief Executive Officer and Chief Financial Officer of a public company must now certify the company's financial statements. Corporate audit committees, rather than the corporate management, are now responsible for hiring, compensating, and overseeing the external auditors.

Tax Services   CPAs often provide expert advice on tax planning and preparing federal, state, and local tax returns. The objective in preparing tax returns is to use legal means to minimize the taxes paid. Almost every major business decision has a tax impact. Tax planning helps clients know the tax effects of each financial decision.

Management Advisory (or Consulting) Services   Before Sarbanes-Oxley, management advisory services were the fastest growing service area for most large and many smaller CPA firms. Management frequently identifies projects for which it decides to retain the services of a CPA. However, the Sarbanes-Oxley Act specifically prohibits providing certain types of consulting services to a publicly-held company by its external auditor. These services include bookkeeping, information systems design and implementation, appraisals or valuation services, actuarial services, internal audits, management and human resources services, broker/dealer and investment services, and legal or expert services related to audit services. Accounting firms can perform many of these services for publicly held companies they do not audit. Other services not specifically banned are allowed if pre-approved by the company's audit committee.

> **Management (or Industrial) Accounting**

In contrast to public accountants, who provide accounting services for many clients, **management accountants** provide accounting services for a single business. In a company with several management accountants, the person in charge of the accounting activity is often the **controller** or **chief financial officer.**

Management accountants may or may not be CPAs. If management accountants pass an examination prepared and graded by the Institute of Certified Management Accountants (ICMA) and meet certain other requirements, they become **Certified Management Accountants (CMAs).** The ICMA is an affiliate of the Institute of Management Accountants, an organization primarily consisting of management accountants employed in private industry.

A career in management accounting can be very challenging and rewarding. Many management accountants specialize in one particular area of accounting. For example, some may specialize in measuring and controlling costs, others in budgeting (the development of plans for future operations), and still others in financial accounting and reporting. Many management accountants become specialists in the design and installation of computerized accounting systems. Other management accountants are **internal auditors** who conduct **internal audits.** They ensure that the company's divisions and departments follow the policies and procedures of management. This last group of management accountants may earn the designation of **Certified Internal Auditor (CIA).** The Institute of Internal Auditors (IIA) grants the CIA certificate to accountants after they have successfully completed the IIA examination and met certain other requirements.

> **Governmental and Other Not-for-Profit Accounting**

Many accountants, including CPAs, work in **governmental and other not-for-profit accounting.** They have essentially the same educational background and training as accountants in public accounting and management accounting.

Governmental agencies at the federal, state, and local levels employ governmental accountants. Often the duties of these accountants relate to tax revenues and expenditures.

For example, Internal Revenue Service employees use their accounting backgrounds in reviewing tax returns and investigating tax fraud. Government agencies that regulate business activity, such as a state public service commission that regulates public utilities (e.g., telephone company, electric company), usually employ governmental accountants. These agencies often employ governmental accountants who can review and evaluate the utilities' financial statements and rate increase requests. Also, FBI agents trained as accountants find their accounting backgrounds useful in investigating criminals involved in illegal business activities, such as drugs or gambling.

Not-for-profit organizations, such as churches, charities, fraternities, and universities, need accountants to record and account for funds received and disbursed. Even though these agencies do not have a profit motive, they should operate efficiently and use resources effectively.

Higher Education

Approximately 10,000 accountants are employed in higher education. The activities of these **academic accountants** include teaching accounting courses, conducting scholarly and applied research and publishing the results, and performing service for the institution and the community. Faculty positions exist in two-year colleges, four-year colleges, and universities with graduate programs. A significant shortage of accounting faculty has developed due to the retirement beginning in the late 1990s of many faculty members. Starting salaries will continue to rise significantly because of the shortage. You may want to talk with some of your professors about the advantages and disadvantages of pursuing an accounting career in higher education.

A section preceding each chapter, entitled "Careers in Accounting", describes various accounting careers. You might find one that you would like to pursue.

Financial Accounting versus Managerial Accounting

Objective 4
Differentiate between financial and managerial accounting.

An accounting information system provides data to help decision makers both outside and inside the business. Decision makers outside the business are affected in some way by the performance of the business. Decision makers inside the business are responsible for the performance of the business. For this reason, accounting is divided into two categories: financial accounting for those outside and managerial accounting for those inside.

Financial Accounting

Financial accounting information appears in financial statements that are intended primarily for external use (although management also uses them for certain internal decisions). Stockholders and creditors are two of the outside parties who need financial accounting information. These outside parties decide on matters pertaining to the entire company, such as whether to increase or decrease their investment in a company or to extend credit to a company. Consequently, financial accounting information relates to the company as a whole, while managerial accounting focuses on the parts or segments of the company.

Management accountants in a company prepare the financial statements. Thus, management accountants must be knowledgeable concerning financial accounting and reporting. The financial statements are the representations of management, not the CPA firm that performs the audit.

The external users of accounting information fall into six groups; each has different interests in the company and wants answers to unique questions. The groups and some of their possible questions are:

1. **Owners and prospective owners.** Has the company earned satisfactory income on its total investment? Should an investment be made in this company? Should the present investment be increased, decreased, or retained at the same level? Can the company install costly pollution control equipment and still be profitable?

2. **Creditors and lenders.** Should a loan be granted to the company? Will the company be able to pay its debts as they become due?
3. **Employees and their unions.** Does the company have the ability to pay increased wages? Is the company financially able to provide long-term employment for its workforce?
4. **Customers.** Does the company offer useful products at fair prices? Will the company survive long enough to honor its product warranties?
5. **Governmental units.** Is the company, such as a local public utility, charging a fair rate for its services?
6. **General public.** Is the company providing useful products and gainful employment for citizens without causing serious environmental problems?

General-purpose financial statements provide much of the information needed by external users of financial accounting. These **financial statements** are formal reports providing information on a company's financial position, cash inflows and outflows, and the results of operations. Many companies publish these statements in annual reports. (See Wal-Mart Stores, Inc. annual report in the Annual Report Appendix.) The **annual report** also contains the independent auditor's opinion as to the fairness of the financial statements, as well as information about the company's activities, products, and plans.

Financial accounting information is historical in nature, reporting on what has happened in the past. To facilitate comparisons between companies, this information must conform to certain accounting standards or principles called **generally accepted accounting principles (GAAP).** These generally accepted accounting principles for businesses or governmental organizations have developed through accounting practice or been established by an authoritative organization. We describe several of these authoritative organizations in the next major section of this Introduction.

Managerial accounting information is for internal use and provides special information for the managers of a company. The information managers use may range from broad, long-range planning data to detailed explanations of why actual costs varied from cost estimates. Managerial accounting information should:

Managerial Accounting

1. Relate to the part of the company for which the manager is responsible. For example, a production manager wants information on costs of production but not of advertising.
2. Involve planning for the future. For instance, a budget would show financial plans for the coming year.
3. Meet two tests: the accounting information must be useful (relevant) and must not cost more to gather and process than it is worth.

Managerial accounting generates information that managers can use to make sound decisions. The four major types of internal management decisions are:

1. **Financial decisions**—deciding what amounts of capital (funds) are needed to run the business and whether to secure these funds from owners (stockholders) or creditors. In this sense, *capital* means money used by the company to purchase resources such as machinery and buildings and to pay expenses of conducting the business.
2. **Resource allocation decisions**—deciding how the total capital of a company is to be invested, such as the amount to be invested in machinery.
3. **Production decisions**—deciding what products are to be produced, by what means, and when.
4. **Marketing decisions**—setting selling prices and advertising budgets; determining the location of a company's markets and how to reach them.

Development of Financial Accounting Standards

Several organizations are influential in the establishment of generally accepted account-ing principles (GAAP) for businesses or governmental organizations. These are the American Institute of Certified Public Accountants, the Financial Accounting Standards Board, the Governmental Accounting Standards Board, the Securities and Exchange Commission, the American Accounting Association, the Financial Executives Institute, and the Institute of Management Accountants. Each organization has contributed in a different way to the development of GAAP.

American Institute of Certified Public Accountants (AICPA)

The American Institute of Certified Public Accountants (AICPA) is a professional organization of CPAs. Many of these CPAs are in public accounting practice. Until recent years, the AICPA was the dominant organization in the development of accounting standards. In a 20-year period ending in 1959, the AICPA Committee on Accounting Procedure issued 51 *Accounting Research Bulletins* recommending certain principles or practices. From 1959 through 1973, the committee's successor, the **Accounting Principles Board (APB),** issued 31 numbered *Opinions* that CPAs generally are required to follow. Through its monthly magazine, the *Journal of Accountancy,* its research division, and its other divisions and committees, the AICPA continues to influence the development of accounting standards and practices. Two of its committees—the Accounting Standards Committee and the Auditing Standards Committee—are particularly influential in providing input to the Financial Accounting Standards Board (the current rule-making body) and to the Securities and Exchange Commission and other regulatory agencies.

Financial Accounting Standards Board (FASB)

In 1973, an independent, seven-member, full-time **Financial Accounting Standards Board (FASB)** replaced the Accounting Principles Board. The FASB has issued numer-ous *Statements of Financial Accounting Standards.* The old *Accounting Research Bulletins* and *Accounting Principles Board Opinions* are still effective unless specifi-cally superseded by a Financial Accounting Standards Board Statement. The FASB is the *private sector* organization now responsible for the development of new financial accounting standards.

All current accounting and reporting standards are compiled by the FASB in its *FASB Accounting Standards Codification*™.

Governmental Accounting Standards Board (GASB)

In 1984, the **Governmental Accounting Standards Board (GASB)** was established with a full-time chairperson and four part-time members. The GASB issues statements on accounting and financial reporting in the governmental area. This organization is the *private sector* organization now responsible for the development of new govern-mental accounting concepts and standards. The GASB also has the authority to issue interpretations of these standards.

Securities and Exchange Commission (SEC)

Created under the Securities and Exchange Act of 1934, the **Securities and Exchange Commission (SEC)** is a government agency that administers important acts dealing with the interstate sale of securities (stocks and bonds). The SEC has the authority to prescribe accounting and reporting practices for companies under its jurisdiction. This includes virtually every major U.S. business corporation. Instead of exercising this power, the SEC has adopted a policy of working closely with the accounting profession, especially the FASB, in the development of accounting standards. The SEC indicates to the FASB the accounting topics it believes the FASB should address.

Consisting largely of accounting educators, the **American Accounting Association (AAA)** has sought to encourage research and study at a theoretical level into the concepts, standards, and principles of accounting. One of its journals, *The Accounting Review,* carries many articles reporting on scholarly accounting research. Another quarterly journal, *Accounting Horizons,* reports on more practical matters directly related to accounting practice. A third journal, *Issues in Accounting Education,* contains articles relating to accounting education matters. Students may join the AAA as associate members by contacting the American Accounting Association, 5717 Bessie Drive, Sarasota, Florida 34233.

| American Accounting Association (AAA) |

The **Financial Executives International** is an organization established in 1931 whose members are primarily financial policy-making executives. Many of its members are chief financial officers (CFOs) of very large corporations. The role of the CFO has evolved in recent years from number cruncher to strategic planner. These CFOs have played a major role in restructuring American businesses. Slightly more than 14,000 financial officers, representing approximately 7,000 companies in the United States, Canada, and Japan, are members of the FEI. Through its Committee on Corporate Reporting (CCR) and other means, the FEI is very effective in representing the views of the private financial sector to the FASB and to the Securities and Exchange Commission and other regulatory agencies.

| Financial Executives International (FEI) |

The **Institute of Management Accountants** (formerly the National Association of Accountants) is an organization with approximately 70,000 members, consisting of management accountants in private industry, CPAs, and academics. The primary focus of the organization is on the use of management accounting information for internal decision making. However, management accountants prepare the financial statements for external users. Thus, through its Management Accounting Practices (MAP) Committee and other means, the IMA provides input on financial accounting standards to the Financial Accounting Standards Board and to the Securities and Exchange Commission and other regulatory agencies.

| Institute of Management Accountants (IMA) |

Many other organizations such as the Chartered Financial Analyst Institute (composed of investment advisors and investors), the Securities Industry and Financial Markets Association (composed of investment bankers), and CPA firms have committees or task forces that respond to Exposure Drafts of proposed FASB Statements. Their reactions are in the form of written statements sent to the FASB and testimony given at FASB hearings. Many individuals also make their reactions known to the FASB.

| Other Organizations |

Ethical Behavior of Accountants

Several accounting organizations have codes of ethics governing the behavior of their members. For instance, both the American Institute of Certified Public Accountants and the Institute of Management Accountants have formulated such codes. Many business firms have also developed codes of ethics for their employees to follow.

Ethical behavior involves more than merely making sure you are not violating a code of ethics. Most of us sense what is right and wrong. Yet get-rich-quick opportunities can tempt many of us. Almost any day, newspaper headlines reveal public officials and business leaders who did not do the right thing. Greed won out over their sense of right and wrong. These individuals followed slogans such as: "Get yours while the getting is good"; "Do unto others before they do unto you"; and "You have done wrong only if you get caught." More appropriate slogans might be: "If it seems too good to be true, it usually is"; "There are no free lunches"; and the Golden Rule, "Do unto others as you would have them do unto you."

An accountant's most valuable asset is an honest reputation. Those who take the *high road* of ethical behavior receive praise and honor; they are sought out for their advice and services. They also like themselves and what they represent. Occasionally, accountants do take the *low road* and suffer the consequences. They sometimes find their names mentioned in *The Wall Street Journal* and news programs in an unfavorable light, and former friends and colleagues look down on them. Some of these individuals are removed from the profession. Fortunately, the accounting profession has many leaders who have taken the high road, gained the respect of friends and colleagues, and become role models for all of us to follow.

Many chapters in the text include an ethics case entitled, "An Ethical Perspective." We know you will benefit from thinking about the *situational ethics* in these cases. Often you will not have much difficulty in determining "right and wrong." Instead of making the cases "close calls," we have attempted to include situations business students might actually encounter in their careers.

Critical Thinking and Communication Skills

Accountants in practice and business executives have generally been dissatisfied with accounting graduates' ability to think critically and to communicate their ideas effectively. The Accounting Education Change Commission has recommended that changes be made in the education of accountants to remove these complaints.

To address these concerns, we have included a section at the end of each chapter entitled, "Beyond the Numbers—Critical Thinking." In that section, you are required to work relatively unstructured business decision cases, analyze "real world" annual report data, write about situations involving ethics, and participate in group projects. Most of the other end-of-chapter materials also involve analysis and written communication of ideas.

In some of the cases, analyses, ethics situations, and group projects, you are asked to write a memorandum regarding the situation. In writing such a memorandum, identify your role (auditor, consultant), the audience (management, stockholders, and creditors), and the task (the specific assignment). Present your ideas clearly and concisely.

The purpose of the group projects is to assist you in learning to listen to and work with others. These skills are important in succeeding in the business world. Team players listen to the views of others and work cohesively with them to achieve group goals.

Internet Skills

The internet is an important tool for accounting researchers and practitioners. It is important for accountants and students to be able to use the internet to find relevant information. Thus, each chapter contains approximately two internet projects related to accounting. Your instructor might assign some of these, or you could pursue them on your own.

How to Study the Chapters in This Text

In studying each chapter:

1. Begin by reading the learning objectives at the beginning of each chapter.
2. Read "Understanding the Learning Objectives" at the end of the chapter for a preview of the chapter content.

3. Read the chapter content. Notice that the learning objectives appear in the margins at the appropriate places in the chapter. Each exercise at the end of the chapters identifies the learning objective(s) to which it pertains. If you learn best by reading about a concept and then working a short exercise that illustrates that concept, work the exercises as you read the chapter.
4. Reread "Understanding the Learning Objectives" to determine if you have achieved each objective.
5. Study the New Terms to see if you understand each term. If you do not understand a certain term, refer to the page indicated to read about the term in its original context.
6. Take the Self-Test and then check your answers with those at the end of the chapter.
7. Work the Demonstration Problem to further reinforce your understanding of the chapter content. Then, compare your solution to the correct solution that follows immediately.
8. Look over the questions at the end of the chapter and think out an answer to each one. If you cannot answer a particular question, refer back into the chapter for the needed information.
9. Work at least some of the exercises at the end of the chapter.
10. Work the Problems assigned by your instructor, using the forms available. They can be downloaded from the publisher's website (www.textbookmedia.com).
11. Study the items in the "Beyond the Numbers—Critical Thinking" section and the "Using the Internet—A View of the Real World" section at the end of each chapter to relate what you have learned to real-world situations.
12. Work the Study Guide for the chapter. The Study Guide is a supplement that contains (for each chapter) Learning Objectives; Reference Outline; Chapter Review; Demonstration Problem and Solution (different from the one in the text); Matching, Completion, True-False, and Multiple-Choice Questions; and Solutions to all Questions and Exercises in the Study Guide. The Study Guide can be downloaded from the publisher's website (www.textbookmedia.com).

If you perform each of these steps for each chapter, you should do well in the course. Remember that a knowledge of accounting will serve you well regardless of the career you pursue.

Careers in Accounting

A Career as an Entrepreneur

When today's college students are polled about their long-term career choice, a surprisingly large number respond that they wish to someday own and manage their own business. In fact, the aspiration to start a business, to be an entrepreneur, is nearly universal. It is widely acknowledged that a degree in accounting offers many advantages to a would-be entrepreneur. In fact, if you ask owners of small businesses which skill they wish they had more expertise in, they will very frequently reply "accounting." No matter what the business may be, the owner and/or manager must be able to understand the accounting and financial consequences of business decisions.

Most successful entrepreneurs have learned that it takes a lot more than a great marketing idea or product innovation to make a successful business. There are many steps involved before an idea becomes a successful and rewarding business. Entrepreneurs must be able to raise capital, either from banks or investors. Once a business has been launched, the entrepreneur must be a manager – a manager of people, inventory, facilities, customer relationships, and relationships with the very banks and investors that provided the capital. Business owners quickly learn that in order to survive they need to be well-rounded, savvy individuals who can successfully manage these diverse relationships. An accounting education is ideal for providing this versatile background.

In addition to providing a good foundation for entrepreneurship in any business, an accounting degree offers other ways of building your own business. For example, a large percentage of public accountants work as sole proprietors – building and managing their own professional practices. This can be a very rewarding career, working closely with individuals and small businesses. One advantage of this career is that you can establish your practice in virtually any location, ranging from large cities to rural settings. Finally, many accountants who have gained specialized expertise and experience in a particular field start their own practices as consultants. Expertise such as this, which may be in a field outside of traditional accounting practice, can generate billing rates well in excess of $100 an hour.

1

Accounting and Its Use in Business Decisions

The Introduction to this text provided a background for your study of accounting. Now you are ready to learn about the forms of business organizations and the types of business activities they perform. This chapter presents the financial statements used by businesses. These financial statements show the results of decisions made by management. Investors, creditors, and managers use these statements in evaluating management's past decisions and as a basis for making future decisions.

In this chapter, you also study the accounting process (or accounting cycle) that accountants use to prepare those financial statements. This accounting process uses financial data such as the records of sales made to customers and purchases made from suppliers. In a systematic manner, accountants analyze, record, classify, summarize, and finally report these data in the financial statements of businesses. As you study this chapter, you will begin to understand the unique, systematic nature of accounting—the language of business.

Forms of Business Organizations

Accountants frequently refer to a business organization as an *accounting entity* or a *business entity*. A business entity is any business organization, such as a hardware store or grocery store, that exists as an economic unit. For accounting purposes, each business organization or **entity** has an existence separate from its owner(s), creditors, employees, customers, and other businesses.[1] This separate existence of the business organization is known as the **business entity concept**. Thus, in the accounting records of the business entity, the activities of each business should be kept separate from the activities of other businesses and from the personal financial activities of the owner(s).

Learning Objectives

After studying this chapter, you should be able to:

1. Identify and describe the three basic forms of business organizations.

2. Distinguish among the three types of activities performed by business organizations.

3. Describe the content and purposes of the income statement, statement of retained earnings, balance sheet, and statement of cash flows.

4. State the basic accounting equation and describe its relationship to the balance sheet.

---

[1]When first studying any discipline, students encounter new terms. Usually these terms are set in boldface color and defined at their first occurrence. The boldface color terms are also listed and defined at the end of each chapter (see pages 34–35 in this chapter). After the definition of the term in the term list, a page number in parentheses indicates where the term is discussed in the chapter.

(continued)

Assume, for example, that you own two businesses, a physical fitness center and a horse stable. According to the business entity concept, you would consider each business as an independent business unit. Thus, you would normally keep separate accounting records for each business. Now assume your physical fitness center is unprofitable because you are not charging enough for the use of your exercise equipment. You can determine this fact because you are treating your physical fitness center and horse stable as two separate business entities. You must also keep your personal financial activities separate from your two businesses. Therefore, you cannot include the car you drive only for personal use as a business activity of your physical fitness center or your horse stable. However, the use of your truck to pick up feed for your horse stable is a business activity of your horse stable.

As you will see shortly, the business entity concept applies to the three forms of businesses—single proprietorships, partnerships, and corporations. Thus, for accounting purposes, all three business forms are separate from other business entities and from their owner(s). Since most large businesses are corporations, we use the corporate approach in this text and include only a brief discussion of single proprietorships and partnerships.

Single Proprietorship

Objective 1
Identify and describe the three basic forms of business organizations.[2]

A **single proprietorship** (or "sole proprietorship") is an unincorporated business owned by an individual and often managed by that same person. Single proprietors include physicians, lawyers, electricians, and other people in business for themselves. Many small service businesses and retail establishments are also single proprietorships. No legal formalities are necessary to organize such businesses, and usually business operations can begin with only a limited investment.

In a single proprietorship, the owner is solely responsible for all debts of the business. For accounting purposes, however, the business is a separate entity from the owner. Thus, single proprietors must keep the financial activities of the business, such as the receipt of fees from selling services to the public, separate from their personal financial activities. For example, owners of single proprietorships should not enter the cost of personal houses or car payments in the financial records of their businesses.

Partnership

A **partnership** is an unincorporated business owned by two or more persons associated as partners. Often the same persons who own the business also manage the business. Many small retail establishments and professional practices, such as dentists, physicians, attorneys, and many CPA firms, are partnerships.

A partnership begins with a verbal or written agreement. A written agreement is preferable because it provides a permanent record of the terms of the partnership. These terms include the initial investment of each partner, the duties of each partner, the means of dividing profits or losses between the partners each year, and the settlement after the death or withdrawal of a partner. Each partner may be held liable for all the debts of the partnership and for the actions of each partner within the scope of the business. However, as with the single proprietorship, for accounting purposes, the partnership is a separate business entity.

Corporation

A **corporation** is a business incorporated under the laws of a state and owned by a few stockholders or by thousands of stockholders. Almost all large businesses and many small businesses are incorporated.

The corporation is unique in that it is a separate legal business entity. The owners of the corporation are **stockholders**, or **shareholders**. They buy shares of stock, which are units of ownership, in the corporation. Should the corporation fail, the

---

[2]After reading a portion of text material that covers a certain learning objective, some students immediately want to work an exercise that illustrates that material. The exercises at the end of each chapter are labeled with the learning objective to which they pertain. For instance, turn to pages 37–43 to see which learning objective(s) each exercise covers in Chapter 1. Also, "Reinforcing Problems," referring to specific exercises or problems that relate to the concepts being discussed, are mentioned in the margin of the text (e.g., see page 15).

owners would only lose the amount they paid for their stock. The corporate form of business protects the personal assets of the owners from the creditors of the corporation.[3]

Stockholders do not directly manage the corporation. They elect a board of directors to represent their interests. The board of directors selects the officers of the corporation, such as the president and vice presidents, who manage the corporation for the stockholders.

Accounting is necessary for all three forms of business organizations, and each company must follow generally accepted accounting principles (GAAP). Since corporations have such an important impact on our economy, we use them in this text to to illustrate basic accounting principles and concepts.

BUSINESS INSIGHT Although corporations constitute about 17% of all business organizations, they account for almost 90% of all sales volume. Single proprietorships constitute about 75% of all business organizations but account for less than 10% of sales volume.

An Accounting Perspective

Types of Activities Performed by Business Organizations

The forms of business entities discussed in the previous section are classified according to the type of ownership of the business entity. Business entities can also be grouped by the type of business activities they perform—service companies, merchandising companies, and manufacturing companies. Any of these activities can be performed by companies using any of the three forms of business organizations.

1. **Service companies** perform services for a fee. This group includes accounting firms, law firms, and dry cleaning establishments. The early chapters of this text describe accounting for service companies.
2. **Merchandising companies** purchase goods that are ready for sale and then sell them to customers. Merchandising companies include auto dealerships, clothing stores, and supermarkets. We begin the description of accounting for merchandising companies in Chapter 6.
3. **Manufacturing companies** buy materials, convert them into products, and then sell the products to other companies or to the final consumers. Manufacturing companies include steel mills, auto manufacturers, and clothing manufacturers.

All of these companies produce financial statements as the final end product of their accounting process. These financial statements provide relevant financial information both to those inside the company—management—and to those outside the company—creditors, stockholders, and other interested parties. The next section introduces four common financial statements—the income statement, the statement of retained earnings, the balance sheet, and the statement of cash flows.

Financial Statements of Business Organizations

Business entities may have many objectives and goals. For example, one of your objectives in owning a physical fitness center may be to improve *your* physical fitness. However, the two primary objectives of every business are profitability and solvency.

---

[3]When individuals seek a bank loan to finance the formation of a small corporation, the bank often requires those individuals to sign documents making them personally responsible for repaying the loan if the corporation cannot pay. In this instance, the individuals can lose their original investments plus the amount of the loan they are obligated to repay.

Profitability is the ability to generate income. **Solvency** is the ability to pay debts as they become due. Unless a business can produce satisfactory income and pay its debts as they become due, the business cannot survive to realize its other objectives.

There are four basic financial statements. Together they present the profitability and strength of a company. The financial statement that reflects a company's profitability is the **income statement**. The **statement of retained earnings** shows the change in retained earnings between the beginning and end of a period (e.g., a month or a year). The **balance sheet** reflects a company's solvency and financial position. The **statement of cash flows** shows the cash inflows and outflows for a company over a period of time. The headings and elements of each statement are similar from company to company. You can see this similarity in the financial statements of actual companies in the appendix of this textbook.

The Income Statement

The **income statement**, sometimes called an earnings statement, reports the profitability of a business organization for a *stated period of time*. In accounting, we measure profitability for a period, such as a month or year, by comparing the revenues earned with the expenses incurred to produce these revenues. **Revenues** are the inflows of assets (such as cash) resulting from the sale of products or the rendering of services to customers. We measure revenues by the prices agreed on in the exchanges in which a business delivers goods or renders services. **Expenses** are the costs incurred to produce revenues. Expenses are measured by the assets surrendered or consumed in serving customers. If the revenues of a period exceed the expenses of the same period, **net income** results. Thus,

$$\text{Net income} = \text{Revenues} - \text{Expenses}$$

Net income is often called the *earnings* of the company. When expenses exceed revenues, the business has a **net loss**, and it has operated unprofitably.

In Illustration 1.1, Part A shows the income statement of Metro Courier, Inc., for July 2012. This California corporation performs courier delivery services of documents and packages in San Diego.

Metro's income statement for the month ended July 31, 2012, shows that the revenues (or delivery fees) generated by serving customers for July totaled $5,700. Expenses for the month amounted to $3,600. As a result of these business activities, Metro's net income for July was $2,100. To determine its net income, the company subtracts its expenses of $3,600 from its revenues of $5,700. Even though corporations are taxable entities, we ignore corporate income taxes at this point.

The Statement of Retained Earnings

One purpose of the *statement of retained earnings* is to connect the income statement and the balance sheet. The **statement of retained earnings** explains the changes in retained earnings between two balance sheet dates. These changes usually consist of the addition of net income (or deduction of net loss) and the deduction of dividends.

Dividends are the means by which a corporation rewards its stockholders (owners) for providing it with investment funds. A **dividend** is a payment (usually of cash) to the owners of the business; it is a distribution of income to owners rather than an expense of doing business. Corporations are not required to pay dividends and, because dividends are not an expense, they do not appear on the income statement.

The effect of a dividend is to reduce cash and retained earnings by the amount paid out. Then, the company no longer retains a portion of the income earned but passes it on to the stockholders. Receiving dividends is, of course, one of the primary reasons people invest in corporations.

The statement of retained earnings for Metro Courier, Inc., for July 2012 is relatively simple (see Part B of Illustration 1.1). Organized on June 1, Metro did not earn any revenues or incur any expenses during June. So Metro's beginning retained earnings balance on July 1 is zero. Metro then adds its $2,100 net income for July.

Illustration 1.1

A. Income Statement

METRO COURIER, INC.

Income Statement

For the Month Ended July 31, 2012

Revenues:

Service revenue		$	5,700

Expenses:

Salaries expense	$	2,600		
Rent expense		400		
Gas and oil expense		600		
Total expenses				3,600
Net income			$	2,100

B. Statement of Retained Earnings

METRO COURIER, INC.

Statement of Retained Earnings

For the Month Ended July 31, 2012

Retained earnings, July 1		-0-
Add: Net income for July		2,100
Retained earnings, July 31	$	2,100

C. Balance Sheet

METRO COURIER, INC.

Balance Sheet

July 31, 2012

Assets			Liabilities and Stockholder's Equity		
Cash	$	15,500	Liabilities:		
Account receivables		700	Accounts payable	$	600
Trucks		20,000	Notes payable		6,000
Office equipment		2,500	Total liabilities	$	6,600
			Stockholders equity:		
			Capital stock	$	30,000
			Retained earnings		2,100
			Total stockholders' equity	$	32,100
Total assets	$	38,700	Total liabilities and stockholders' equity	$	38,700

Since Metro paid no dividends in July, the $2,100 would be the ending balance of retained earnings.

Next, Metro carries this $2,100 ending balance in retained earnings to the balance sheet (Part C). If there had been a net loss, it would have deducted the loss from the beginning balance on the statement of retained earnings. For instance, if during the next month (August) there is a net loss of $500, the loss would be deducted from the beginning balance in retained earnings of $2,100. The retained earnings balance at the end of August would be $1,600.

Dividends could also have affected the Retained Earnings balance. To give a more realistic illustration, assume that (1) Metro Courier, Inc.'s, net income for August was actually $1,500 (revenues of $5,600 less expenses of $4,100) and (2) the company declared and paid dividends of $1,000. Then, Metro's statement of retained earnings for August would be:

Reinforcing Problem
P1-3A Prepare income statement.

METRO COURIER, INC.
Statement of Retained Earnings
For the Month Ended August 31, 2012

Retained earnings, August 1...	$2,100
Add: Net income for August...	1,500
Total..	$3,600
Less: Dividends..	1,000
Retained earnings, August 31...	$2,600

The Balance Sheet

The **balance sheet**, sometimes called the *statement of financial position,* lists the company's assets, liabilities, and stockholders' equity (including dollar amounts) as of a specific moment in time. That specific moment is the close of business on the date of the balance sheet. Notice how the heading of the balance sheet differs from the headings on the income statement and statement of retained earnings. A balance sheet is like a photograph; it captures the financial position of a company at a particular *point* in time. The other two statements that we have seen thus far are for a *period* of time. As you study about the assets, liabilities, and stockholders' equity contained in a balance sheet, you will understand why this financial statement provides information about the solvency of the business.

Assets are things of value owned by the business. They are also called the *resources* of the business. Examples include cash, machines, and buildings. Assets have value because a business can use or exchange them to produce the services or products of the business. In Part C of Illustration 1.1, the assets of Metro Courier, Inc., amount to $38,700. Metro's assets consist of cash, **accounts receivable** (amounts due from customers for services previously rendered), trucks, and office equipment.

Liabilities are the debts owed by a business. Typically, a business must pay its debts by certain dates. A business incurs many of its liabilities by purchasing items on credit. Metro's liabilities consist of **accounts payable** (amounts owed to suppliers for previous purchases) and **notes payable** (written promises to pay a specific sum of money) totaling $6,600.[4]

Metro Courier, Inc., is a corporation. The owners' interest in a corporation is referred to as **stockholders' equity**. Metro's stockholders' equity consists of (1) $30,000 received for shares of capital stock and (2) retained earnings of $2,100. **Capital stock** shows the amount of the owners' investment in the corporation. **Retained earnings** generally consists of the accumulated net income of the corporation minus dividends distributed to stockholders. We discuss these items later in the text. At this point, simply note that the balance sheet heading includes the name of the organization and the title and date of the statement. Notice also that the dollar amount of the total assets is equal to the claims on (or interest in) those assets. The balance sheet shows these claims under the heading "Liabilities and Stockholders' Equity."

The Statement of Cash Flows

Management is interested in the cash inflows to the company and the cash outflows from the company because these determine the company's cash it has available to pay its bills when due. The **statement of cash flows** shows the cash inflows and cash outflows from operating, investing, and financing activities. *Operating activities* generally include the cash effects of transactions and other events that enter into the determination of net income. *Investing activities* generally include business transactions involving the acquisition or disposal of long-term assets such as land, buildings, and equipment. *Financing activities* generally include the cash effects of transactions and other events involving creditors and owners (stockholders).

Chapter 16 describes the statement of cash flows in detail. Our purpose here is to merely introduce this important financial statement. Normally, a firm prepares a statement of cash flows for the same time period as the income statement. The following statement, however, shows the cash inflows and outflows for Metro Courier, Inc., since it was formed on June 1, 2012. Thus, this cash flow statement is for two months.

---

[4]Most notes bear interest, but in this chapter we assume that all notes bear no interest. Interest is an amount paid by the borrower to the lender (in addition to the amount of the loan) for use of the money over time

METRO COURIER, INC.
Statement of Cash Flows
For the Two-Month Period Ended July 31, 2012

Cash flows from operating activities:		
Net income	$2,100	
Adjustments to reconcile net income to net cash provided by operating activities:		
Increase in accounts receivable	(700)	
Increase in accounts payable..	600	
Net cash provided by operating activities		$2,000
Cash flows from investing activities:		
Purchase of trucks	$(20,000)	
Purchase of office equipment..	(2,500)	
Net cash used by investing activities....................................		(22,500)
Cash flows from financing activities:		
Proceeds from notes payable......................................	$6,000	
Proceeds from sale of capital stock...............................	30,000	
Net cash provided by financing activities		36,000
Net increase in cash		$15,500

At this point in the course, you need to understand what a statement of cash flows is rather than how to prepare it. We do not ask you to prepare such a statement until you have studied Chapter 16.

The income statement, the statement of retained earnings, the balance sheet, and the statement of cash flows of Metro Courier, Inc., show the results of management's past decisions. They are the end products of the accounting process, which we explain in the next section. These financial statements give a picture of the solvency and profitability of the company. The accounting process details how this picture was made. Management and other interested parties use these statements to make future decisions. Management is the first to know the financial results; then, it publishes the financial statements to inform other users. The most recent financial statements for most publicly-held companies can be found on their websites under "Investor Relations" or some similar heading.

The Financial Accounting Process

In this section, we explain the accounting equation—the framework for the entire accounting process. Then, we show you how to recognize a business transaction and describe underlying assumptions that accountants use to record business transactions. Next, you learn how to analyze and record business transactions.

In the balance sheet presented in Illustration 1.1 (Part C), the total assets of Metro Courier, Inc., were equal to its total liabilities and stockholders' equity. This equality shows that the assets of a business are equal to its equities; that is,

The Accounting Equation

Assets = Equities

Assets were defined earlier as the things of value owned by the business, or the economic resources of the business. **Equities** are all claims to, or interests in, assets. For example, assume that you purchased a new company automobile for $15,000 by investing $10,000 in your own corporation and borrowing $5,000 in the name of the corporation from a bank. Your equity in the automobile is $10,000, and the bank's equity is $5,000. You can further describe the $5,000 as a liability because you owe the bank $5,000. If your business is a corporation, you can describe your $10,000 equity as stockholders' equity or interest in the asset. Since the owners in a corporation are stockholders, the basic **accounting equation** becomes:

Objective 4
State the basic accounting equation and describe its relationship to the balance sheet.

Assets (A) = Liabilities (L) + Stockholders' equity (SE)

From Metro's balance sheet in Illustration 1.1 (Part C), we can enter in the amount of its assets, liabilities, and stockholders' equity:

$$A = L + SE$$
$$\$38,700 = \$6,600 + \$32,100$$

Remember that someone must provide assets or resources—either a creditor or a stockholder. Therefore, this equation must always be in balance.

You can also look at the right side of this equation in another manner. The liabilities and stockholders' equity show the sources of an existing group of assets. Thus, liabilities are not only claims against assets but also sources of assets.

Together, creditors and owners provide all the assets in a corporation. The higher the proportion of assets provided by owners, the more solvent the company. However, companies can sometimes improve their profitability by borrowing from creditors and using the funds effectively. As a business engages in economic activity, the dollar amounts and composition of its assets, liabilities, and stockholders' equity change. *However, the equality of the basic accounting equation always holds.*

Reinforcing Problem
E1-4 Compute retained earnings and total assets at beginning of year.

Analysis of Transactions

Objective 5
Using the underlying assumptions or concepts, analyze business transactions and determine their effects on items in the financial statements.

An accounting **transaction** is a business activity or event that causes a measurable change in the accounting equation, Assets = Liabilities + Stockholders' equity. An exchange of cash for merchandise is a transaction. The exchange takes place at an agreed price that provides an objective measure of economic activity. For example, the objective measure of the exchange may be $5,000. These two factors—evidence and measurement—make possible the recording of a transaction. Merely placing an order for goods is not a recordable transaction because no exchange has taken place.

A *source document* usually supports the evidence of the transaction. A **source document** is any written or printed evidence of a business transaction that describes the essential facts of that transaction. Examples of source documents are receipts for cash paid or received, checks written or received, bills sent to customers for services performed or bills received from suppliers for items purchased, cash register tapes, sales tickets, and notes given or received. We handle source documents constantly in our everyday life. Each source document initiates the process of recording a transaction.

Underlying Assumptions or Concepts   In recording business transactions, accountants rely on certain underlying assumptions or concepts. Both preparers and users of financial statements must understand these assumptions:

1. **Business entity concept (or accounting entity concept).** Data gathered in an accounting system relate to a specific business unit or **entity**. The business entity concept assumes that each business has an existence separate from its owners, creditors, employees, customers, other interested parties, and other businesses.
2. **Money measurement concept.** Economic activity is initially recorded and reported in a common monetary unit of measure—the dollar in the United States. This form of measurement is known as *money measurement*.
3. **Exchange-price (or cost) concept (principle).** Most of the amounts in an accounting system are the objective money prices determined in the exchange process. As a result, we record most assets at their acquisition cost. **Cost** is the sacrifice made or the resources given up, measured in money terms, to acquire some desired thing, such as a new truck (asset).
4. **Going-concern (continuity) concept.** Unless strong evidence exists to the contrary, accountants assume that the business entity will continue operations into the indefinite future. Accountants call this assumption the *going-concern or continuity* concept. Assuming that the entity will continue indefinitely allows accountants to value long-term assets, such as land, at cost on the balance sheet since they are to be used rather than sold. Market values of these assets would be relevant only if they were for sale. For instance, accountants would still

record land purchased in 1988 at its cost of $100,000 on the December 31, 2012, balance sheet even though its market value has risen to $300,000.

5. **Periodicity (time periods) concept.** According to the *periodicity (time periods)* concept or assumption, an entity's life can be meaningfully subdivided into time periods (such as months or years) to report the results of its economic activities.

Now that you understand business transactions and the five basic accounting assumptions, you are ready to follow some business transactions step by step. To begin, we divide Metro's transactions into two groups: (1) transactions affecting only the balance sheet in June, and (2) transactions affecting the income statement and/or the balance sheet in July. Note that we could also classify these transactions as operating, investing, or financing activities, as shown in the statement of cash flows on page 19.

Transactions Affecting Only the Balance Sheet   Since each transaction affecting a business entity must be recorded in the accounting records, analyzing a transaction before actually recording it is an important part of financial accounting. An error in transaction analysis results in incorrect financial statements.

Reinforcing Problem
E1-5 Analyze transactions.

To illustrate the analysis of transactions and their effects on the basic accounting equation, the activities of Metro Courier, Inc., that led to the statements in Illustration 1.1 follow. The first set of transactions (for June), 1a, 2a, and so on, are repeated in the summary of transactions, Illustration 1.2 (Part A) on page 26. The second set of transactions (for July) (1b–6b) are repeated in Illustration 1.3 (Part A) on page 28.

Note to the Student
Choose a business you would like to start. Develop several transactions for your business and then describe the influence of those transactions on the financial statements.

1a. Owners Invested Cash   When Metro Courier, Inc., was organized as a corporation on June 1, 2012, the company issued shares of capital stock for $30,000 cash to Ron Chaney, his wife, and their son. This transaction increased assets (cash) of Metro by $30,000 and increased equities (the capital stock element of stockholders' equity) by $30,000. Consequently, the transaction yields the following basic accounting equation:

Trans-action	Explanation	Cash	Accounts Receiv-able	Trucks	Office Equip-ment	=	Accounts Payable	Notes Payable	+	Capital Stock
	Beginning balances	$ -0-	$ -0-	$ -0-	$ -0-	=	$ -0-	$ -0-		$ -0-
1a	Stockholders invested cash	30,000								30,000
	Balance after transaction	$ 30,000								$ 30,000

Assets = Liabilities + Stockholders' Equity

Increased by $30,000   Increased by $30,000

2a. Borrowed Money   The company borrowed $6,000 from Chaney's father. Chaney signed the note for the company. The note bore no interest, and the company promised to repay (recorded as a *note payable*) the amount borrowed within one year. After including the effects of this transaction, the basic accounting equation is:

Trans-action	Explanation	Cash	Accounts Receiv-able	Trucks	Office Equip-ment	=	Accounts Payable	Notes Payable	+	Capital Stock
	Balances before transaction	$ 30,000	$ -0-	$ -0-	$ -0-	=	$ -0-	$ -0-		$ 30,000
2a	Borrowed money	6,000						6,000		
	Balance after transaction	$ 36,000				=		$ 6,000	+	$ 30,000

Assets = Liabilities + Stockholders' Equity

Increased by $6,000   Increased by $6,000

Illustration 1.2

A. Summary of Transactions

METRO COURIER, INC.
Summary of Transactions
Month of June 2012

Trans-action	Explanation	Cash	Accounts Receivable	Trucks	Office Equipment	=	Accounts Payable	Notes Payable	+	Capital Stock
				Assets		=	Liabilities		+	Stockholders' Equity
	Beginning balances	$ -0-	$ -0-	$ -0-	$ -0-	=	$ -0-	$ -0-		$ -0-
1a	Stockholders invested cash	30,000								30,000
		$ 30,000				=				$ 30,000
2a	Borrowed money	6,000						6,000		
		$ 36,000				=		$ 6,000	+	$ 30,000
3a	Purchased trucks and office equipment for cash	(21,500)		20,000	1,500					
		$ 14,500		$ 20,000	$ 1,500	=		$ 6,000	+	$ 30,000
4a	Purchased office equipment on account				1,000		1,000			
		$ 14,500		$ 20,000	$ 2,500	=	$ 1,000	$ 6,000	+	$ 30,000
5a	Paid an account payable	(1,000)					(1,000)			
	End-of-month balances	$ 13,500	$ -0-	$ 20,000	$ 2,500	=	$ -0-	$ 6,000	+	$ 30,000

B. Balance Sheet

METRO COURIER, INC.
Balance Sheet
June 30, 2012

Assets		Liabilities and Stockholders' Equity	
Cash	$ 13,500	Liabilities:	
Trucks	20,000	Notes Payable	$ 6,000
Office equipment	2,500	Total Liabilities	$ 6,000
		Stockholders' equity:	
		Capital stock	30,000
Total assets	$ 36,000	Total liabilities and stockholders' equity	$ 36,000

Illustration 1.2, Part A, is a *summary of transactions* prepared in accounting equation form for June. A **summary of transactions** is a teaching tool used to show the effects of transactions on the accounting equation. Note that the stockholders' equity has remained at $30,000. This amount changes as the business begins to earn revenues or incur expenses. You can see how the totals at the bottom of Part A of Illustration 1.2 tie into the balance sheet shown in Part B. The date on the balance sheet is June 30, 2012. These totals become the beginning balances for July 2012.

Thus far, all transactions have consisted of exchanges or acquisitions of assets either by borrowing or by owner investment. We used this procedure to help you focus on the accounting equation as it relates to the balance sheet. However, people do not form a business only to hold existing assets. They form businesses so their assets can generate greater amounts of assets. Thus, a business increases its assets by providing goods or services to customers. The results of these activities appear in the income statement. The section that follows shows more of Metro's transactions as it began earning revenues and incurring expenses.

Reinforcing Problems
E1-6 Analyze transactions.
E1-7 Determine effect of
transactions on stockholders'
equity.

Transactions Affecting the Income Statement and/or Balance Sheet

To survive, a business must be profitable. This means that the revenues earned by pro-viding goods and services to customers must exceed the expenses incurred.

In July 2012, Metro Courier, Inc., began selling services and incurring expenses. The explanations of transactions that follow allow you to participate in this process and learn the necessary accounting procedures.

1b. Earned Service Revenue and Received Cash   As its first transaction in July, Metro performed delivery services for customers and received $4,800 cash. This transac-tion increased an asset (cash) by $4,800. Stockholders' equity (retained earnings) also increased by $4,800, and the accounting equation was in balance.

The $4,800 is a revenue earned by the business and, as such, increases stockholders' equity (in the form of retained earnings) because stockholders prosper when the busi-ness earns profits. Likewise, if the corporation sustains a loss, the loss would reduce retained earnings.

Revenues increase the amount of retained earnings, while expenses and dividends decrease them. (In this first chapter, we show all of these items as immediately affect-ing retained earnings. In later chapters, the revenues, expenses, and dividends are accounted for separately from retained earnings during the accounting period and are transferred to retained earnings only at the end of the accounting period as part of the closing process described in Chapter 4.) The effects of this $4,800 transaction on the financial position of Metro are:

Trans-action	Explanation	Cash	Accounts Receiv-able	Trucks	Office Equip-ment	=	Accounts Payable	Notes Payable	+	Capital Stock	Retained Earnings
					Assets	=	Liabilities		+	Stockholders' Equity	
	Beginning balances (Illustration 1.2)	$13,500	$ -0-	$20,000	$2,500	=	$ -0-	$ 6,000		$ 30,000	$ -0-
1b	Earned service revenue and received cash	4,800									4,800
	Balances after transaction	$18,300		$20,000	$2,500	=		$ 6,000	+	$ 30,000	$ 4,800

Increased by $4,800   Increased by $4,800

Metro would record the increase in stockholders' equity brought about by the rev-enue transaction as a separate account, retained earnings. This does not increase capital stock because the Capital Stock account increases only when the company issues shares of stock. The expectation is that revenue transactions will exceed expenses and yield net income. If net income is not distributed to stockholders, it is in fact retained. Later chapters show that because of complexities in handling large numbers of transactions, revenues and expenses affect retained earnings only at the end of an accounting period. The preceding procedure is a shortcut used to explain why the accounting equation remains in balance.

2b. Service Revenue Earned on Account (for Credit)   Metro performed courier delivery services for a customer who agreed to pay $900 at a later date. The company granted credit rather than requiring the customer to pay cash immediately. This is called earning revenue *on account*. The transaction consists of exchanging services for the customer's promise to pay later. This transaction is similar to the preceding transaction in that stockholders' equity (retained earnings) increases because the company has earned revenues. However, the transaction differs because the company has not received cash. Instead, the company has received another asset, an *account receivable*. As noted earlier, an account receivable is the amount due from a customer for goods or services already provided. The company has a legal right to collect from the customer in the future. Accounting recognizes such claims as assets. The accounting equation, including this $900 item, is as follows:

Trans-action	Explanation	Cash	Accounts Receiv-able	Trucks	Office Equip-ment	=	Accounts Payable	Notes Payable	+	Capital Stock	Retained Earnings
	Balances before transaction	$ 18,300		$ 20,000	$ 2,500	=		$ 6,000		$ 30,000	$ 4,800
2b	Earned service revenue on account		$ 900								900
	Balances after transaction	$ 18,300	$ 900	$ 20,000	$ 2,500	=		$ 6,000	+	$ 30,000	$ 5,700

(Assets = Liabilities + Stockholders' Equity)

Increased by $900 (Accounts Receivable)

Increased by $900 (Retained Earnings)

3b. Collected Cash on Accounts Receivable   Metro collected $200 on account from the customer in transaction 2b. The customer will pay the remaining $700 later. This transaction affects only the balance sheet and consists of giving up a claim on a customer in exchange for cash. The transaction increases cash by $200 and decreases accounts receivable by $200. Note that this transaction consists solely of a change in the composition of the assets. When the company performed the services, it recorded the revenue. Therefore, the company does not record the revenue again when collecting the cash.

Trans-action	Explanation	Cash	Accounts Receiv-able	Trucks	Office Equip-ment	=	Accounts Payable	Notes Payable	+	Capital Stock	Retained Earnings
	Balances before transaction	$ 18,300	$ 900	$ 20,000	$ 2,500	=		$ 6,000		$ 30,000	$ 5,700
3b	Collected cash on account	$ 200	(200)								
	Balances after transaction	$ 18,500	$ 700	$ 20,000	$ 2,500	=		$ 6,000	+	$ 30,000	$ 5,700

(Assets = Liabilities + Stockholders' Equity)

Increased by $200 (Cash)   Decreased by $200 (Accounts Receivable)

4b. Paid Salaries   Metro paid employees $2,600 in salaries. This transaction is an exchange of cash for employee services. Typically, companies pay employees for their services after they perform their work. Salaries (or wages) are costs companies incur to produce revenues, and companies consider them an expense. Thus, the accountant treats the transaction as a decrease in an asset (cash) and a decrease in stockholders' equity (retained earnings) because the company has incurred an expense. Expense transactions reduce net income. Since net income becomes a part of the retained earnings balance, expense transactions also reduce the retained earnings.

Trans-action	Explanation	Assets				=	Liabilities		+	Stockholders' Equity	
		Cash	Accounts Receiv-able	Trucks	Office Equip-ment	=	Accounts Payable	Notes Payable +		Capital Stock	Retained Earnings
	Balances before transaction	$ 18,500	$ 700	$ 20,000	$ 2,500	=		$ 6,000		$ 30,000	$ 5,700
4b	Paid salaries	(2,600)									(2,600)
	Balances after transaction	$ 15,900	$ 700	$ 20,000	$ 2,500	=		$ 6,000	+	$ 30,000	$ 3,100

Decreased by $2,600

Decreased by $2,600

5b. Paid Rent In July, Metro paid $400 cash for office space rental. This transaction causes a decrease in cash of $400 and a decrease in retained earnings of $400 because of the incurrence of rent expense.

Transaction 5b has the following effects on the amounts in the accounting equation:

Trans-action	Explanation	Assets				=	Liabilities		+	Stockholders' Equity	
		Cash	Accounts Receiv-able	Trucks	Office Equip-ment	=	Accounts Payable	Notes Payable	+	Capital Stock	Retained Earnings
	Balances before transaction	$ 15,900	$ 700	$ 20,000	$ 2,500	=		$ 6,000		$30,000	$ 3,100
5b	Paid rent	(400)									(400)
	Balances after transaction	$ 15,500	$ 700	$ 20,000	$ 2,500	=		$ 6,000	+	$30,000	$ 2,700

Decreased by $400

Decreased by $400

6b. Received Bill for Gas and Oil Used At the end of the month, Metro received a $600 bill for gas and oil consumed during the month. This transaction involves an increase in accounts payable (a liability) because Metro has not yet paid the bill and a decrease in retained earnings because Metro has incurred an expense. Metro's accounting equation now reads:

Trans-action	Explanation	Assets				=	Liabilities		+	Stockholders' Equity	
		Cash	Accounts Receiv-able	Trucks	Office Equip-ment	=	Accounts Payable	Notes Payable	+	Capital Stock	Retained Earnings
	Balances before transaction	$ 15,500	$ 700	$ 20,000	$ 2,500	=		$ 6,000		$ 30,000	$ 2,700
6b	Received bill for gas and oil used						$ 600				(600)
	Balance after transaction	$ 15,500	$ 700	$ 20,000	$ 2,500	= $	600	$ 6,000	+	$ 30,000	$ 2,100

Increased by $600

Decreased by $600

Summary of Balance Sheet and Income Statement Transactions   Part A of Illustration 1.3 summarizes the effects of all the preceding transactions on the assets, liabilities, and stockholders' equity of Metro Courier, Inc., in July. The beginning balances are the ending balances in Part A of Illustration 1.2. The summary shows subtotals after each transaction; these subtotals are optional and may be omitted. Note how the accounting equation remains in balance after each transaction and at the end of the month.

The ending balances in each of the columns in Part A of Illustration 1.3 are the dollar amounts in Part B and those reported earlier in the balance sheet in Part C of Illustration 1.1. The itemized data in the Retained Earnings column are the revenue and expense items in Part C of Illustration 1.3 and those reported earlier in the income statement in Part A of Illustration 1.1. The beginning balance in the Retained Earnings column ($–0–) plus net income for the month ($2,100) is equal to the ending balance in retained earnings ($2,100) shown earlier in Part B of Illustration 1.1. Remember that the financial statements are not an end in themselves, but are prepared to assist users of those statements to make informed decisions. Throughout the text we show how people use accounting information in decision making.

Dividends Paid to Owners (Stockholders)   Stockholders' equity is (1) increased by capital contributed by stockholders and by revenues earned through operations and (2) decreased by expenses incurred in producing revenues. The payment of cash or other assets to stockholders in the form of dividends also reduces stockholders' equity. Thus, if the owners receive a cash dividend, the effect would be to reduce the retained earnings part of stockholders' equity; the amount of dividends is not an expense but is instead a distribution of income.

> **Objective 6**
> Prepare an income statement, a statement of retained earnings, and a balance sheet.

Reinforcing Problems
E1-8 Analyze transactions.
E1-9 Identify transactions that decrease retained earnings.
E1-10 Prepare income statement.
E1-11 Prepare statement of retained earnings.
E1-12 Prepare balance sheet.

James Stevens was taking an accounting course at State University. Also, he was helping companies find accounting systems that would fit their information needs. He advised one of his clients to acquire a software computer package that could record the business transactions and prepare the financial statements. The licensing agreement with the software company specified that the basic charge for one site was $4,000 and that $1,000 must be paid for each additional site where the software was used.

James was pleased that his recommendation to acquire the software was followed. However, he was upset that management wanted him to install the software at eight other sites in the company and did not intend to pay the extra $8,000 due the software company. A member of management stated, "The software company will never know the difference and, besides, everyone else seems to be pirating software. If they do find out, we will pay the extra fee at that time. Our expenses are high enough without paying these unnecessary costs." James believed he might lose this client if he did not do as management instructed.

A Broader Perspective

State University

USES OF TECHNOLOGY   Accountants and others can access the home pages of companies to find their annual reports and other information, home pages of CPA firms to find employment opportunities and services offered, and home pages of government agencies, universities, and any other agency that has established a home page. No doubt, you have spent many hours on the internet and know that you can discover all kinds of interesting information about almost anything. We have included some Internet Projects at the end of the chapters to give you some experience at "surfing the net" for accounting applications.

An Accounting Perspective

Illustration 1.3

A. Summary of Transactions

METRO COURIER, INC.
Summary of Transactions
Month of July 2012

Trans-action	Explanation		Cash	Accounts Receiv-able	Trucks	Office Equip-ment	=	Accounts Payable	Notes Payable +	Capital Stock	Retained Earn-ings
	Beginning balances (Illustration 1.2)	$	13,500	$ -0-	$ 20,000	$ 2,500	=	$ -0-	$ 6,000 +	$ 30,000	$ -0-
1b	Earned service revenue and received cash		4,800								4,800
		$	18,300		$ 20,000	$ 2,500	=		$ 6,000 +	$ 30,000	$ 4,800
2b	Earned service revenue on account			900							900
		$	18,300	$ 900	$ 20,000	$ 2,500	=		$ 6,000 +	$ 30,000	$ 5,700
3b	Collected cash on account		200	(200)							
		$	18,500	$ 700	$ 20,000	$ 2,500	=		$ 6,000 +	$ 30,000	$ 5,700
4b	Paid salaries		(2,600)								(2,600)
		$	15,900	$ 700	$ 20,000	$ 2,500	=		$ 6,000 +	$ 30,000	$ 3,100
5b	Paid rent		(400)								(400)
		$	15,500	$ 700	$ 20,000	$ 2,500	=		$ 6,000 +	$ 30,000	$ 2,700
6b	Received bill for gas and oil used							600			(600)
	End-of-month balances	$	15,500	$ 700	$ 20,000	$ 2,500	=	$ 600	$ 6,000 +	$ 30,000	$ 2,100

$38,700 $6,600 $32,100

B. Balance Sheet

METRO COURIER, INC.
Balance Sheet
July 31, 2012

Assets

Cash	$ 15,500
Accounts receivable	700
Trucks	20,000
Office equipment	2,500
Total assets	$ 38,700

Liabilities and Stockholders'

Liabilities:		
Accounts payable	$	600
Notes payable		6,000
Total liabilities	$	6,600
Stockholders' equity		
Capital stock	$	30,000
Retained earnings		2,100
Total stockholders' equity	$	32,100
Total liabilities and stockholders' equity	$	38,700

C. Income Statement

METRO COURIER, INC.
Income Statement
For the Month Ended July 31, 2012

Revenues:		
Service revenue	$	5,700
Expenses:		
Salaries expense	$ 2,600	
Rent expense	400	
Gas & oil expense	600	
Total expenses		3,600
Net income	$	2,100

Analyzing and Using The Financial Results— The Equity Ratio

The two basic sources of equity in a company are stockholders and creditors; their combined interests are called *total equities*. To find the **equity ratio,** divide stockholders' equity by total equities or total assets, since total equities equals total assets. In formula format:

$$\text{Equity ratio} = \frac{\text{Stockholders' equity}}{\text{Total equities}}$$

Objective 7
Analyze and use the financial results—the equity ratio.

The higher the proportion of equities (or assets) supplied by the owners, the more solvent the company. However, a high portion of debt may indicate higher profitability because quite often the interest rate on debt is lower than the rate of earnings realized from using the proceeds of the debt.

An example illustrates this concept: Suppose that a company with $100,000 in assets could have raised the funds to acquire those assets in these two ways:

Reinforcing Problem
E1-13 Calculate equity ratios for Merck & Co., Inc.

Case 1

| Assets | $100,000 | Liabilities | $20,000 |
| | | Stockholders' equity | $80,000 |

Case 2

| Assets | $100,000 | Liabilities | $80,000 |
| | | Stockholders' equity | $20,000 |

When a company suffers operating losses, its assets decrease. In Case 1, the assets would have to shrink by 80% before the liabilities would equal the assets. In Case 2, the assets would have to shrink only 20% before the liabilities would equal the assets. When the liabilities exceed the assets, the company is said to be insolvent. Therefore, creditors are safer in Case 1 and will more readily lend money to the company.

However, if funds borrowed at 10% are used to produce earnings at a 20% rate, Case 2 is preferable in terms of profitability. Therefore, owners are better off in Case 2 if the borrowed funds can earn more than they cost.

Next, we examine the recent equity ratios of some actual companies:

Name of Company	Stockholders' Equity ($ millions)	Total Equities ($ millions)	Equity Ratio
Johnson & Johnson	$56,579	$102,908	55.0%
3M Corporation	15,663	30,156	51.9
General Electric Company	118,936	751,216	15.8

As you can see from the preceding data, the equity ratios of actual companies vary widely. Companies such as Johnson & Johnson and 3M Corporation employ a higher proportion of stockholders' equity (a lower proportion of debt) than GE in an effort to have stronger balance sheets (more solvency). GE employs a greater proportion of debt, possibly in an attempt to increase profitability. Every company must strike a balance between solvency and profitability to ensure long-run survival. The correct balance between proportions of stockholder and creditor equities depends on the industry, general business conditions, and management philosophy.

Chapter 1 has introduced two important components of the accounting process—the accounting equation and the business transaction. In Chapter 2, you learn about debits and credits and how accountants use them in recording transactions. Understanding how data are accumulated, classified, and reported in financial statements helps you understand how to use financial statement data in making decisions.

Johnson & Johnson
The world's largest manufacturer of health care products, sells products in more than 150 countries.

3M Corporation
One of the world's leading manufacturing companies, produces abrasives, automotive fasteners, specialty films and chemicals, tapes (Scotch tape), electrical/electronic connectors, and imaging and medical products.

General Electric Company
One of the most successful U.S. companies, sells products and services to industries such as aerospace, appliances, industrial and power systems, medical systems, and plastics.

An Accounting Perspective	**USES OF TECHNOLOGY** When you apply for your first job after graduation, prospective employers will expect you to know how to use a PC to perform many tasks. Therefore, before you graduate you should be able to use word processing, spreadsheet, and database software. You should be able to use the Internet to find useful information. In many universities, you can learn these skills in courses taken for credit. If your school does not offer credit courses, take noncredit courses or attend a training center.

Understanding the Learning Objectives

Objective 1
Identify and describe the three basic forms of business organizations.

- A single proprietorship is an unincorporated business owned by an individual and often managed by that individual.
- A partnership is an unincorporated business owned by two or more persons associated as partners and is often managed by them.
- A corporation is a business incorporated under the laws of a state and owned by a few stockholders or by thousands of stockholders.

Objective 2
Distinguish among the three types of activities performed by business organizations.

- Service companies perform services for a fee.
- Merchandising companies purchase goods that are ready for sale and then sell them to customers.
- Manufacturing companies buy materials, convert them into products, and then sell the products to other companies or to final customers.

Objective 3
Describe the content and purposes of the income statement, statement of retained earnings, balance sheet, and the statement of cash flows.

- The income statement reports the revenues and expenses of a company and shows the profitability of that business organization for a stated period of time.
- The statement of retained earnings shows the change in retained earnings between the beginning of the period (e.g., a month) and its end.
- The balance sheet lists the assets, liabilities, and stockholders' equity (including dollar amounts) of a business organization at a specific moment in time.
- The statement of cash flows shows the cash inflows and cash outflows for a company for a stated period of time.

Objective 4
State the basic accounting equation and describe its relationship to the balance sheet.

- The accounting equation is Assets = Liabilities + Stockholders' equity.
- The left side of the equation represents the left side of the balance sheet and shows things of value owned by the business.
- The right side of the equation represents the right side of the balance sheet and shows who provided the funds to acquire the things of value (assets).

Objective 5
Using the underlying assumptions or concepts, analyze business transactions and determine their effects on items in the financial statements.

- Some transactions affect only balance sheet items: assets (such as cash, accounts receivable, and equipment), liabilities (such as accounts payable and notes payable), and stockholders' equity (capital stock). Other transactions affect both balance sheet items and income statement items (revenues, expenses, and eventually retained earnings).
- Illustrations 1.2 (Part A) and 1.3 (Part A) show the effects of business transactions on the accounting equation.

- The income statement appears in Illustrations 1.1 (Part A) and 1.3 (Part C).
- The statement of retained earnings appears in Illustration 1.1 (Part B).
- The balance sheet appears in Illustrations 1.1 (Part C) and 1.3 (Part B).

> **Objective 6**
> Prepare an income statement, a statement of retained earnings, and a balance sheet.

- The equity ratio is the stockholders' equity divided by total equities (or total assets).
- The equity ratio shows the percentage that assets would have to shrink before a company would become insolvent (liabilities exceed assets).

> **Objective 7**
> Analyze and use the financial results—the equity ratio.

A Comparison of Corporate Accounting with Accounting for a Sole Proprietorship and a Partnership

APPENDIX

Some textbook authors use a sole proprietorship and a partnership form of business ownership to illustrate accounting concepts and practices. In a survey of users and nonusers of our text, we learned that the majority preferred the corporate approach because most students will probably work for or invest in corporations. Also, many small businesses operate as corporations because of the investors' desire for limited liability.

This appendix briefly describes the differences in accounting for these three forms of business ownership. The major difference is in the stockholders' equity or owner's equity section of the balance sheet.

As you learned in this chapter, the stockholders' equity section of the balance sheet for a corporation consists of capital stock and retained earnings. The owner's equity section of the balance sheet for a sole proprietorship consists only of the owner's capital account. The owners' equity section of a partnership is similar to that of a single proprietorship except that it shows a capital account and its balance for each partner.

Corporation		Sole Proprietorship		Partnership	
Stockholders' equity:		Owner's equity:		Partners' capital:	
Capital		John Smith,		John Smith,	
stock	$100,000	Capital	$150,000	Capital	$75,000
Retained				Sam Jones,	
earnings	50,000			Capital	75,000
Total	$150,000		$150,000		$150,000

The stockholders' equity section of a corporate balance sheet can become more complex as you will see later in the text. However, the items in the owner's equity section of the balance sheets of a sole proprietorship and a partnership always remain as just shown. In a sole proprietorship, the owner's capital balance consists of the owner's investments in the business, plus cumulative net income since the beginning of the business, less any amounts withdrawn by the owner. Thus, all of the amounts in the various stockholders' equity accounts for a corporation are in the owner's capital account in a single proprietorship. In a partnership, each partner's capital account balance consists of that partner's investments in the business, plus that partner's cumulative share of net income since that partner became a partner, less any amounts withdrawn by that partner.

The Dividends account in a corporation is similar to an owner's drawing account in a single proprietorship. These accounts both show amounts taken out of the business by the owners. In a partnership, each partner has a drawing account. Accountants treat asset, liability, revenue, and expense accounts similarly in all three forms of organization.

Demonstration Problem

On June 1, 2012, Green Hills Riding Stable, Incorporated, was organized. The following transactions occurred during June:

June	1	Shares of capital stock were issued for $10,000 cash.
	4	A horse stable and riding equipment were rented (and paid for) for the month at a cost of $1,200.
	8	Horse feed for the month was purchased on credit, $800.
	15	Boarding fees of $3,000 for June were charged to those owning horses boarded at the stable. (Fee is due on July 10.)
	20	Miscellaneous expenses of $600 were paid.
	29	Land was purchased from a savings and loan association by borrowing $40,000 on a note from that association. The loan is due to be repaid in five years. Interest payments are due at the end of each month beginning July 31.
	30	Salaries of $700 for the month were paid.
	30	Riding and lesson fees were billed to customers in the amount of $2,800. (Fees are due on July 10.)

Required
a. Prepare a summary of the preceding transactions. Use columns headed Cash, Accounts Receivable, Land, Accounts Payable, Notes Payable, Capital Stock, and Retained Earnings. Determine balances after each transaction to show that the basic accounting equation is in balance.
b. Prepare an income statement for June 2012.
c. Prepare a statement of retained earnings for June 2012.
d. Prepare a balance sheet as of June 30, 2012.

Solution to Demonstration Problem

a.

GREEN HILLS RIDING STABLE, INCORPORATED
Summary of Transactions
Month of June 2012

| | | Assets | | | = | Liabilities | | + | Stockholders' Equity | |
		Cash	Accounts Receivable	Land		Accounts Payable	Notes Payable	+	Capital Stock	Retained Earnings
Date	Explanation									
June 1	Capital stock issued	$ 10,000			=				$ 10,000	
4	Rent expense	(1,200)								$ (1,200)
		$ 8,800			=			+	$ 10,000	$ (1,200)
8	Feed expense					$ 800				(800)
		$ 8,800			=	$ 800		+	$ 10,000	$ (2,000)
15	Boarding fees		$ 3,000							3,000
		$ 8,800	$ 3,000		=	$ 800		+	$ 10,000	$ 1,000
20	Miscellaneous expenses	(600)								(600)
		$ 8,200	$ 3,000		=	800		+	$ 10,000	$ 400
29	Purchased land by borrowing			$ 40,000			$ 40,000			
		$ 8,200	$ 3,000	$ 40,000	=	$ 800	$ 40,000	+	$ 10,000	$ 400
30	Salaries paid	(700)								(700)
		$ 7,500	$ 3,000	$ 40,000	=	$ 800	$ 40,000	+	$ 10,000	$ (300)
30	Riding and lesson fees billed		2,800							2,800
		$ 7,500	$ 5,800	$ 40,000		$ 800	$ 40,000	+	$ 10,000	$ 2,500

b.   **GREEN HILLS RIDING STABLE, INCORPORATED**
Income Statement
For the Month Ended June 30, 2012

Revenues:
Horse boarding fees revenue	$ 3,000	
Riding and lesson fee revenue	2,800	
Total revenues		$ 5,800

Expenses:
Rent expense	$ 1,200	
Feed expense	800	
Salaries expense	700	
Miscellaneous expense	600	
Total expenses		3,300
Net income		$ 2,500

c.   **GREEN HILLS RIDING STABLE, INCORPORATED**
Statement of Retained Earnings
For the Month Ended June 30, 2012

Retained earnings, June 1	$ -0-
Add: Net income for June	2,500
Total	$ 2,500
Less: Dividends	-0-
Retained earnings, June 30	$ 2,500

d.

GREEN HILLS RIDING STABLE, INCORPORATED
Balance Sheet
June 30, 2012

Assets

Cash		$ 7,500
Accounts receivable		5,800
Land		40,000
Total assets		$ 53,300

Liabilities and Stockholders' Equity

Liabilities:		
Accounts payable		$ 800
Noted payable		40,000
Total liabilities		$ 40,800
Stockholders' equity:		
Capital stock	$ 10,000	
Retained earnings	2,500	
Total stockholders' equity		$ 12,500
Total liabilities and stockholders' equity		$ 53,300

New Terms

Accounting equation Assets = Equities; or Assets = Liabilities + Stockholders' equity. *19*

Accounts payable Amounts owed to suppliers for goods or services purchased on credit. *18*

Accounts receivable Amounts due from customers for services already provided. *18*

Assets Things of value owned by the business. Examples include cash, machines, and buildings. To their owners, assets possess service potential or utility that can be measured and expressed in money terms. *18*

Balance sheet Financial statement that lists a company's assets, liabilities, and stockholders' equity (including dollar amounts) as of a specific moment in time. Also called a *statement of financial position. 16, 18*

Business entity concept (or accounting entity concept) The separate existence of the business organization. *13, 20*

Capital stock The title given to an equity account showing the investment in a business corporation by its stockholders. *18*

Continuity See *going-concern concept. 20*

Corporation Business incorporated under the laws of one of the states and owned by a few stockholders or by thousands of stockholders. *14*

Cost Sacrifice made or the resources given up, measured in money terms, to acquire some desired thing, such as a new truck (asset). *20*

Dividend Payment (usually of cash) to the owners of a corporation; it is a distribution of income to owners rather than an expense of doing business. *16*

Entity A business unit that is deemed to have an existence separate and apart from its owners, creditors, employees, customers, other interested parties, and other businesses, and for which accounting records are maintained. *13*

Equities Broadly speaking, all claims to, or interests in, assets; includes liabilities and stockholders' equity. *19*

Equity ratio A ratio found by dividing stockholders' equity by total equities (or total assets). *29*

Exchange-price (or cost) concept (principle) The objective money prices determined in the exchange process are used to record most assets. *20*

Expenses Costs incurred to produce revenues, measured by the assets surrendered or consumed in serving customers. *16*

Going-concern (continuity) concept The assumption by the accountant that unless strong evidence exists to the contrary, a business entity will continue operations into the indefinite future. *20*

Income statement Financial statement that shows the revenues and expenses and reports the profitability of a business organization for a stated period of time. Sometimes called an *earnings statement. 16*

Liabilities Debts owed by a business—or creditors' equity. Examples: notes payable, accounts payable. *18*

Manufacturing companies Companies that buy materials, convert them into products, and then sell the products to other companies or to final customers. *15*

Merchandising companies Companies that purchase goods ready for sale and sell them to customers. *15*

Money measurement concept   Recording and reporting economic activity in a common monetary unit of measure such as the dollar. *20*

Net income   Amount by which the revenues of a period exceed the expenses of the same period. *16*

Net loss   Amount by which the expenses of a period exceed the revenues of the same period. *16*

Notes payable   Amounts owed to parties who loan the company money after the owner signs a written agreement (a note) for the company to repay each loan. *18*

Partnership   An unincorporated business owned by two or more persons associated as partners. *14*

Periodicity (time periods) concept   An assumption that an entity's life can be meaningfully subdivided into time periods (such as months or years) for purposes of reporting its economic activities. *21*

Profitability   Ability to generate income. The income statement reflects a company's profitability. *16*

Retained earnings   Accumulated net income less dividend distributions to stockholders. *18*

Revenues   Inflows of assets (such as cash) resulting from the sale of products or the rendering of services to customers. *16*

Service companies   Companies (such as accounting firms, law firms, or dry cleaning establishments) that perform services for a fee. *15*

Single proprietorship   An unincorporated business owned by an individual and often managed by that individual. *14*

Solvency   Ability to pay debts as they become due. The balance sheet reflects a company's solvency. *16*

Source document   Any written or printed evidence of a business transaction that describes the essential facts of that transaction, such as receipts for cash paid or received. *20*

Statement of cash flows   Financial statement showing cash inflows and outflows for a company over a period of time. *16, 18*

Statement of retained earnings   Financial statement used to explain the changes in retained earnings that occurred between two balance sheet dates. *16*

Stockholders' equity   The owners' interest in a corporation. *18*

Stockholders or shareholders   Owners of a corporation; they buy shares of stock, which are units of ownership, in the corporation. *14*

Summary of transactions   Teaching tool used in Chapter 1 to show the effects of transactions on the accounting equation. *23*

Transaction   A business activity or event that causes a measurable change in the items in the accounting equation, Assets = Liabilities + Stockholders' equity. *20*

Self-Test

True-False
Indicate whether each of the following statements is true or false.

1. The three forms of business organizations are single proprietorship, partnership, and trust.
2. The three types of business activity are service, merchandising, and manufacturing.
3. The income statement shows the profitability of the company and is dated as of a particular date, such as December 31, 2012.
4. The statement of retained earnings shows both the net income for the period and the beginning and ending balances of retained earnings.
5. The balance sheet contains the same major headings as appear in the accounting equation.

Multiple-Choice
Select the best answer for each of the following questions.

1. The ending balance in retained earnings is shown in the:
   a. Income statement.
   b. Statement of retained earnings.
   c. Balance sheet.
   d. Both (b) and (c).
2. Which of the following is *not* a correct form of the accounting equation?
   a. Assets = Equities.
   b. Assets = Liabilities + Stockholders' equity.
   c. Assets – Liabilities = Stockholders' equity.
   d. Assets + Stockholders' equity = Liabilities.
3. Which of the following is *not* one of the five underlying assumptions or concepts mentioned in the chapter?
   a. Exchange-price concept.
   b. Inflation accounting concept.
   c. Business entity concept.
   d. Going-concern concept.

4. When the stockholders invest cash in the business, what is the effect?
   a. Liabilities increase and stockholders' equity increases.
   b. Both assets and liabilities increase.
   c. Both assets and stockholders' equity increase.
   d. None of the above.

5. When services are performed on account, what is the effect?
   a. Both cash and retained earnings decrease.
   b. Both cash and retained earnings increase.
   c. Both accounts receivable and retained earnings increase.
   d. Accounts payable increases and retainedearnings decreases.

Now turn to page 46 to check your answers.

Questions

1. Accounting has often been called the language of business. In what respects would you agree with this description? How might you argue that this description is deficient?

2. Define asset, liability, and stockholders' equity.

3. How do liabilities and stockholders' equity differ? How are they similar?

4. How do accounts payable and notes payable differ? How are they similar?

5. Define revenues. How are revenues measured?

6. Define expenses. How are expenses measured?

7. What is a balance sheet? On what aspect of a business does the balance sheet provide information?

8. What is an income statement? On what aspect of a business does this statement provide information?

9. What information does the statement of retained earnings provide?

10. Identify the three types of activities shown in a statement of cash flows.

11. What is a transaction? What use does the accountant make of transactions? Why?

12. What is the accounting equation? Why must it always balance?

13. Give an example from your personal life that illustrates your use of accounting information in reaching a decision.

14. You have been elected to the governing board of your church. At the first meeting you attend, mention is made of building a new church. What accounting information would the board need in deciding whether or not to go ahead?

15. A company purchased equipment for $2,000 cash. The vendor stated that the equipment was worth $2,400. At what amount should the equipment be recorded?

16. What is meant by money measurement?

17. Of what significance is the exchange-price (or cost) concept? How is the cost to acquire an asset determined?

18. What effect does the going-concern (continuity) concept have on the amounts at which long-term assets are carried on the balance sheet?

19. Of what importance is the periodicity (time periods) concept to the preparation of financial statements?

20. Describe a transaction that would:
   a. Increase both an asset and capital stock.
   b. Increase both an asset and a liability.
   c. Increase one asset and decrease another asset.
   d. Decrease both a liability and an asset.
   e. Increase both an asset and retained earnings.
   f. Decrease both an asset and retained earnings.
   g. Increase a liability and decrease retained earnings.

21. Identify the causes of increases and decreases in stockholders' equity.

22. **Real World Question** Refer to the 2011 financial statements of Wal-Mart Stores, Inc., in the Annual Report Appendix at the back of the text. What were the net income or loss amounts in the latest three years? Discuss the meaning of the changes after reading management's discussion and analysis of financial condition and results of operations.

23. **Real World Question** Refer to the financial statements of Wal-Mart Stores, Inc., in the Annual Report Appendix. Has the solvency of the company improved from one year to the next? Discuss.

Exercises

Match the descriptions in Column B with the appropriate terms in Column A.

Column A	**Column B**
1. Corporation.	**a.** An unincorporated business owned by an individual.
2. Merchandising company.	**b.** The form of organization used by most large businesses.
3. Partnership.	**c.** Buys raw materials and converts them into finished products.
4. Manufacturing company.	**d.** Buys goods in their finished form and sells them to
5. Service company.	customers in that same form.
6. Single proprietorship.	**e.** An unincorporated business with more than one owner.
	f. Performs services for a fee.

Assume that retained earnings increased by $3,600 from June 30, 2011, to June 30, 2012. A cash dividend of $300 was declared and paid during the year.

Exercise 1-2
Compute net income
and revenue (L.O. 3)

a. Compute the net income for the year.
b. Assume expenses for the year were $9,000. Compute the revenue for the year.

On December 31, 2012, Perez Company had assets of $150,000, liabilities of $97,500, and capital stock of $30,000. During 2013, Perez earned revenues of $45,000 and incurred expenses of $33,750. Dividends declared and paid amounted to $3,000.

a. Compute the company's retained earnings on December 31, 2012.
b. Compute the company's retained earnings on December 31, 2013.

At the start of the year, a company had liabilities of $50,000 and capital stock of $150,000. At the end of the year, retained earnings amounted to $135,000. Net income for the year was $45,000, and $15,000 of dividends were declared and paid. Compute retained earnings and total assets at the beginning of the year.

Exercise 1-4
Compute retained
earnings and total
assets at beginning
of year (L.O. 3, 4)

For each of the following events, determine if it has an effect on the specific items (such as cash) in the accounting equation. For the events that do have an effect, present an analysis of the transaction showing its two sides or dual nature.

a. Purchased equipment for cash, $12,000.
b. Purchased a truck for $40,000, signed a note (with no interest) promising payment in 10 days.
c. Paid $1,600 for the current month's utilities.
d. Paid for the truck purchased in (b).
e. Employed Mary Childers as a salesperson at $1,200 per month. She is to start work next week.
f. Signed an agreement with a bank in which the bank agreed to lend the company up to $200,000 any time within the next two years.

Bradley Company, engaged in a courier service business, completed the following selected transactions during July 2012:

Exercise 1-6
Indicate effect of
transactions on items
in the accounting
equation (L.O. 4, 5)

a. Purchased office equipment on account.
b. Paid an account payable.
c. Earned service revenue on account.
d. Borrowed money by signing a note at the bank.
e. Paid salaries for month to employees.
f. Received cash on account from a charge customer.
g. Received gas and oil bill for month.
h. Purchased delivery truck for cash.
i. Declared and paid a cash dividend.

Using a tabular form similar to Illustration 1.3 (Part A), indicate the effect of each transaction on the accounting equation using (+) for increase and (–) for decrease. No dollar amounts are needed, and you need not fill in the Explanation column.

Exercise 1-7
Determine effect of transactions on stockholders' equity (L.O. 5)

Indicate the amount of change (if any) in the stockholders' equity balance based on each of the following transactions:

a. The stockholders invested $100,000 cash in the business by purchasing capital stock.
b. Land costing $40,000 was purchased by paying cash.
c. The company performed services for a customer who agreed to pay $18,000 in one month.
d. Paid salaries for the month, $12,000.
e. Paid $14,000 on an account payable.

Exercise 1-8
Analyze transactions (L.O. 5)

Give examples of transactions that would have the following effects on the items in a firm's financial statements:

a. Increase cash; decrease some other asset.
b. Decrease cash; increase some other asset.
c. Increase an asset; increase a liability.
d. Decrease retained earnings; decrease an asset.
e. Increase an asset other than cash; increase retained earnings.
f. Decrease an asset; decrease a liability.

Exercise 1-9
Identify transactions that decrease retained earnings (L.O. 5)

Which of the following transactions results in a decrease in retained earnings? Why?

a. Employees were paid $20,000 for services performed during the month.
b. $175,000 was paid to acquire land.
c. Paid an $18,000 note payable. No interest was involved.
d. Paid a $200 account payable.

Exercise 1-10
Prepare income statement (L.O. 6)

Assume that the following items were included in the Retained Earnings column in the summary of transactions for Cinck Company for July 2012:

Salaries expense	$120,000
Service revenue	300,000
Gas and oil expense	27,000
Rent expense	48,000
Dividends paid	40,000

Prepare an income statement for July 2012.

Exercise 1-11
Prepare statement of retained earnings (L.O. 6)

Given the following facts, prepare a statement of retained earnings for Brindle Company, a tanning salon, for August 2012:

Balance in retained earnings at end of July, $188,000.
Dividends paid in August, $63,600.
Net income for August, $72,000.

Exercise 1-12
Prepare balance sheet (L.O. 6)

The column totals of a summary of transactions for Speedy Printer Repair, Inc., as of December 31, 2012, were as follows:

Accounts payable	$60,000
Accounts receivable	90,000
Capital stock	100,000
Cash	40,000
Land	80,000
Building	50,000
Equipment	30,000
Notes payable	20,000
Retained earnings	?

Prepare a balance sheet. We have purposely listed the accounts out of order.

Merck & Co, Inc. is a world leader in the discovery, development, manufacture and market-ing of a broad range of human and animal health products. The company, which has 94,000 employees, spends over $10 billion every year on the research and development of new drugs. As of the end of 2010, its 3.1 billion shares are valued in the stock market for a total of $111 billion. Given the following data for Merck (in millions), calculate the equity ratios for 2010 and 2009. Then comment on the results.

Exercise 1-13
Calculate the
equity ratios
for Merck & Co.
(L.O. 7)

	2010	**2009**
Stockholders' equity	$54,376	$59,058
Total equities	$105,781	$112,314

Problems

Lakewood Personal Finance Company, which provides financial advisory services, engaged in the following transactions during May 2012:

Problem 1-1
Prepare summary
of transactions
(L.O. 4, 5)

May	1	Received $300,000 cash for shares of capital stock issued when company was organized.
	2	The company borrowed $40,000 from the bank on a note.
	7	The company bought $182,400 of computer equipment for cash.
	11	Cash received for services performed to date was $15,200.
	14	Services performed for a customer who agreed to pay within a month were $10,000.
	15	Employee wages were paid, $13,200.
	19	The company paid $14,000 on the note to the bank.
	31	Interest paid to the bank for May was $140. (Interest is an expense, which reduces retained earnings.)
	31	The customer of May 14 paid $3,200 of the amount owed to the company.
	31	An order was received from a customer for services to be rendered next week, which will be billed at $12,000.

Prepare a summary of transactions (see Part A of Illustration 1.3). Use money columns headed *Required* Cash, Accounts Receivable, Equipment, Notes Payable, Capital Stock, and Retained Earnings. Determine balances after each transaction to show that the accounting equation balances.

Reliable Lawn Care Service, Inc., a company that takes care of lawns and shrubbery of personal residences, engaged in the following transactions in April 2012:

Problem 1-2
Prepare summary
of transactions and
balance sheet
(L.O. 4-6)

Apr.	1	The company was organized and received $400,000 cash from the owners in exchange for capital stock issued.
	4	The company bought equipment for cash, $101,760.
	9	The company bought additional mowing equipment that cost $9,120 and agreed to pay for it in 30 days.
	15	Cash received for services performed to date was $3,840.
	16	Amount due from a customer for services performed totaled $5,280.
	30	Of the receivable (see April 16), $3,072 was collected in cash.
	30	Miscellaneous operating expenses of $6,240 were paid during the month.
	30	An order was placed for miscellaneous equipment costing $28,800.

a. Prepare a summary of transactions (see Part A of Illustration 1.3). Use money columns headed Cash, Accounts Receivable, Equipment, Accounts Payable, Capital Stock, and Retained Earnings. Determine balances after each transaction to show that the basic accounting equation balances.
 Required

b. Prepare a balance sheet as of April 30.

Problem 1-3
Prepare income statement, statement of retained earnings, and balance sheet (L.O. 6)

Analysis of the transactions of the Moonlight Drive-In Theater for June 2012 disclosed the following:

Ticket revenue	$180,000
Equipment rent expense	50,000
Film rent expense	53,400
Concession revenue	29,600
Advertising expense	18,600
Salaries expense	60,000
Utilities expense	14,100
Cash dividends declared and paid	12,000

Balance sheet amounts at June 30 include the following:

Cash	$140,000
Land	148,000
Accounts payable	87,600
Capital stock	114,000
Retained earnings as of June 1, 2012	84,900

Required ➡

a. Prepare an income statement for June 2012.
b. Prepare a statement of retained earnings for June 2012.
c. Prepare a balance sheet as of June 30, 2012.
d. How solvent does this company appear to be?

Problem 1-4
Prepare income statement, statement of retained earnings, and balance sheet (L.O. 4-6)

Little Folks Baseball, Inc., was formed by a group of parents to meet a need for a place for kids to play baseball. At the beginning of its second year of operations, its balance sheet appeared as follows:

LITTLE FOLKS BASEBALL, INC.
Balance Sheet
April 30, 2012
Assets

Cash		$ 56,000
Accounts Receivable		80,000
Land		600,000
Total assets		$ 736,000

Liabilities and Stockholders' Equity

Liabilities:		
Accounts payable		$ 64,000
Stockholders' Equity:		
Capital stock	$ 400,000	
Retained earnings	272,000	672,000
Total liabilities and stockholders' equity		$ 736,000

The summarized transactions for May 2012 are as follows:
a. Issued additional capital stock for cash, $200,000.
b. Collected $80,000 on accounts receivable.
c. Paid $64,000 on accounts payable.
d. Received membership fees from parents (nonrefundable): in cash, $260,000; and on account, $120,000.
e. Incurred operating expenses: for cash, $60,000; and on account, $160,000.
f. Paid dividends of $16,000.
g. Purchased more land for cash, $96,000.
h. Placed an order for new equipment expected to cost $120,000.

Required ➡

a. Prepare a summary of transactions (see Part A of Illustration 1.3) using column headings as given in the balance sheet. Determine balances after each transaction.
b. Prepare an income statement for May 2012.
c. Prepare a statement of retained earnings for May 2012.
d. Prepare a balance sheet as of May 31, 2012.

The balance sheets for May 31, 2012, and April 30, 2012, and the income statement for May of the Target-Line Golf Driving Range follow. (Common practice is to show the most recent period first.)

Problem 1-5
State causes of
balance sheet
changes (L.O. 3, 6)

TARGET-LINE GOLF DRIVING RANGE
Comparative Balance Sheet

	May 31, 2012	April 30, 2012
Assets		
Cash	$ 56,400	$ 46,800
Land	163,200	144,000
Total assets	$ 219,600	$ 190,800
Liabilities and Stockholders' Equity		
Accounts payable	$ 18,000	$ 27,600
Capital stock	144,000	144,000
Retained earnings	57,600	19,200
Total liabilities and stockholders' equity	$ 219,600	$ 190,800

TARGET-LINE GOLF DRIVING RANGE
Income Statement
For the Month Ended May 31, 2012

Revenues:		
Service revenue		$ 64,000
Expenses:		
Salaries expense	$ 16,000	
Equipment rental expense	9,600	25,600
Net income		$ 38,400

All revenues earned are on account.

State the probable cause(s) of the change in each of the balance sheet accounts from April 30 to May 31, 2012.

 Required

Alternate Problems

Preston Auto Paint Company had the temporary free use of an old building and completed the following transactions in September 2012:

Problem 1-1A
Prepare summary
of transactions
(L.O. 4, 5)

Sept.
1   The company was organized and received $100,000 cash from the issuance of capital stock.

5   The company bought painting and sanding equipment for cash at a cost of $25,000.

7   The company painted the auto fleet of a customer who agreed to pay $8,000 in one week. The customer furnished the special paint.

14   The company received the $8,000 from the transaction of September 7.

20   Additional sanding equipment that cost $2,800 was acquired today; payment was postponed until September 28.

28   $2,400 was paid on the liability incurred on September 20.

30   Employee salaries for the month, $2,200, were paid.

30   Placed an order for additional painting equipment advertised at $20,000.

Required   Prepare a summary of transactions (see Part A of Illustration 1.3) for the company for these transactions. Use money columns headed Cash, Accounts Receivable, Equipment, Accounts Payable, Capital Stock, and Retained Earnings. Determine balances after each transaction to show that the basic accounting equation balances.

Problem 1-2A
Prepare summary
of transactions and
balance sheet
(L.O. 4-6)

Quick-Start Home Repair Company completed the following transactions in June 2012:

June   1   The company was organized and received $200,000 cash from the issuance of capital stock.

          4   The company paid $48,000 cash for a truck.

          7   The company borrowed $10,000 from its bank on a note.

          9   Cash received for repair services performed was $4,500.

        12   Expenses of operating the business so far this month were paid in cash, $3,400.

        18   Repair services performed for a customer who agreed to pay within a month amounted to $5,400.

        25   The company paid $4,065 on its loan from the bank, including $4,050 of principal and $15 of interest. (The principal is the amount of the loan. Interest is an expense, which reduces retained earnings.)

        30   Miscellaneous expenses incurred in operating the business from June 13 to date were $3,825 and were paid in cash.

        30   An order (contract) was received from a customer for repair services to be performed tomorrow, which will be billed at $3,000.

Required   a. Prepare a summary of transactions (see Part A of Illustration 1.3). Include money columns for Cash, Accounts Receivable, Trucks, Notes Payable, Capital Stock, and Retained Earnings. Determine balances after each transaction to show that the basic accounting equation balances.

             b. Prepare a balance sheet as of June 30, 2012.

Problem 1-3A
Prepare income
statement (L.O. 6)

Following are summarized transaction data for Luxury Apartments, Inc., for the year ending June 30, 2012. The company owns and operates an apartment building.

Rent revenue from building owned	$150,000
Building repairs	2,870
Building cleaning, labor cost	3,185
Property taxes on the building	4,000
Insurance on the building	1,225
Commissions paid to rental agent	5,000
Legal and accounting fees (for preparation of tenant leases)	1,260
Utilities expense	8,225
Cost of new awnings (installed on June 30, will last 10 years)	5,000

Of the $150,000 rent revenue, $5,000 was not collected in cash until July 5, 2012.

Required   Prepare an income statement for the year ended June 30, 2012.

Problem 1-4A
Prepare summary of
transactions, income
statement, statement
of retained earnings,
and balance sheet
(L.O. 4-6)

The following data are for Central District Parking Corporation:

CENTRAL DISTRICT PARKING CORPORATION
Balance Sheet
October 1, 2012

Assets

Cash	$ 344,000
Accounts Receivable	18,000
Total assets	$ 362,000

Liabilities and Stockholders' Equity

Accounts payable	$ 94,000
Capital stock	232,000
Retained earnings	36,000
Total liabilities and stockholders' equity	$ 362,000

The summarized transactions for October 2012 are as follows:

Oct.   1   The accounts payable owed as of September 30 ($94,000) were paid.
        1   The company paid rent for the premises for October, $19,200.
        7   The company received cash of $4,200 for parking by daily customers during the week.
        10   The company collected $14,400 of the accounts receivable in the balance sheet at September 30.
        14   Cash receipts for the week from daily customers were $6,600.
        15   Parking revenue earned but not yet collected from fleet customers was $6,000.
        16   The company paid salaries of $2,400 for the period October 1–15.
        19   The company paid advertising expenses of $1,200 for October.
        21   Cash receipts for the week from daily customers were $7,200.
        24   The company incurred miscellaneous expenses of $840. Payment will be due November 10.
        31   Cash receipts for the last 10 days of the month from daily customers were $8,400.
        31   The company paid salaries of $3,000 for the period October 16–31.
        31   Billings to monthly customers totaled $21,600 for October.
        31   Paid cash dividends of $24,000.

a. Prepare a summary of transactions (see Part A of Illustration 1.3) using column headings as given in the preceding balance sheet. Determine balances after each transaction.

b. Prepare an income statement for October 2012.

c. Prepare a statement of retained earnings for October 2012.

d. Prepare a balance sheet as of October 31, 2012.

Required

The following balance sheets for June 30, 2012, and May 31, 2012, and the income statement for June are for Beach Camping Trailer Storage, Inc. (Common practice is to show the most recent period first.)

Problem 1-5A
State causes of balance sheet changes
(L.O. 3, 6)

BEACH CAMPING TRAILER STORAGE, INC.
Comparative Balance Sheet

	June 30, 2012	May 31, 2012
Assets		
Cash	$ 52,000	$ 60,000
Accounts receivable	24,000	-0-
Land	36,000	36,000
Total assets	$ 112,000	$ 96,000
Liabilities and Stockholders' Equity		
Accounts payable	$ 18,000	$ 24,000
Capital stock	60,000	60,000
Retained earnings	34,000	12,000
Total liabilities and stockholders' equity	$ 112,000	$ 96,000

BEACH CAMPING TRAILER STORAGE, INC.
Income Statement
For the Month Ended June 30, 2012

Revenues:		
Service revenue		$ 100,000
Expenses:		
Salaries expense	$ 48,000	
Supplies bought and used	24,000	72,000
Net income		$ 28,000

A cash dividend of $6,000 was declared and paid in June.

State the probable causes of the changes in each of the balance sheet accounts from May 31 to June 30, 2012.

 Required

Beyond the Numbers—Critical Thinking

Business Decision Case 1-1
Identify information needed to make decision (L.O. 3)

Upon graduation from high school, Jim Crane went to work for a builder of houses and small apartment buildings. During the next six years, Crane earned a reputation as an excellent employee—hardworking, dedicated, and dependable—in the light construction industry. He could handle almost any job requiring carpentry, electrical, or plumbing skills.

Crane then decided to go into business for himself under the name Jim's Fix-It Shop, Inc. He invested cash, some power tools, and a used truck in his business. He completed many repair and remodeling jobs for homeowners and apartment owners. The demand for his services was so large that he had more work than he could handle. He operated out of his garage, which he had converted into a shop, adding several new pieces of power woodworking equipment.

Now, two years after going into business for himself, Crane must decide whether to continue in his own business or to accept a position as construction supervisor for a home builder. He has been offered an annual salary of $50,000 and a package of fringe benefits (medical and hospitalization insurance, pension contribution, vacation and sick pay, and life insurance) worth approximately $8,000 per year. The offer is attractive to Crane. But he dislikes giving up his business since he has thoroughly enjoyed being his own boss, even though it has led to an average workweek well in excess of the standard 40 hours.

Required

Suppose Crane comes to you for assistance in gathering the information needed to help him make a decision. He brings along the accounting records that have been maintained for his business by an experienced accountant. Using logic and your own life experiences, indicate the nature of the information Jim needs if he is to make an informed decision. Pay particular attention to the information likely to be found in his business accounting records. Does the accounting information available enter directly into the decision? Write a memorandum to Jim describing the information he will need to make an informed decision. The memo's headings should include Date, To, From, and Subject. (See the format in Group Project 1–5 below.)

Annual Report Analysis 1-2
Comment on solvency of Dell, Inc. (L.O. 7)

Recall that in this chapter we showed that the equity ratio is calculated by dividing stockholders' equity by total equities (or total assets). Another format for analyzing solvency is to divide total debt by total equities. This latter calculation tells the proportion of assets financed by debt rather than the proportion of assets financed by stockholders' equity. These two ratios are complements and must add to 100%. Thus, if 25% of assets were financed by debt, 75% were financed by stockholders' equity.

Using the following historical data from Dell, Inc., calculate the "total-debt-to-total-equities" ratio for each year.

	2010	2009	2008	2007	2006	2005	2004
Total Liabilities (in millions)	$30,833	$28,011	$22,229	$23,732	$21,196	$18,980	$16,730
Total Stockholders' Equity	7,766	5,641	4,271	3,735	4,328	4,129	6,485

Study these amounts and comment on the solvency of the company. Is there a trend in the company's solvency over time? Dell, Inc. has experienced growth in stockholders' equity during the past six years, but has also increased liabilities significantly. Could of Dell, Inc. have grown this much without increasing liabilities?

Annual Report Analysis 1-3
Answer questions about Wal-Mart's annual report

Look at the annual report of Wal-Mart Stores, Inc., in the Annual Report Appendix. In that report you will find a letter outlining Management's responsibilities concerning the financial statements, as well as the reports of the independent auditors.

 Write answers to the following questions:

1. Who is responsible for preparing the financial statements?
2. Of what importance is the internal audit?
3. What is the role of the audit committee?
4. Why are no officers or employees on the audit committee?

5. What is the responsibility of the external independent auditor?
6. Does the independent auditor have absolute assurance that the financial statements are free of material misstatement?
7. To what extent does the independent auditor examine evidence?

<table>
<tr><td>

Refer to "An Ethical Perspective" on page 27. Write a short essay discussing the alternatives James Stevens could pursue and the likely outcomes of those alternatives. Which of the alternatives you have discussed would you recommend?

</td><td>

Ethics Case—Writing Experience 1-4

</td></tr>
</table>

In teams of two or three students, interview a businessperson in your community. Ask how that person uses accounting information in making business decisions and obtain specific examples. Each team should write a memorandum to the instructor summarizing the results of the interview. Information contained in the memo should include:

Group Project 1-5
Interview a businessperson

> Date:
> To:
> From:
> Subject:

> Content of the memo must include the name and title of the person interviewed, name of the company, date of the interview, examples of the use of accounting information for decision making, and any other pertinent information.

With a team composed of one or two other students, conceive of a business that you would like to form after graduation. Then describe approximately 15–20 transactions that the business might undertake in its first month of operations. Prepare a summary of transactions showing how each transaction affects the accounting equation. Identify each asset, liability, and stockholders' equity item in your summary of transactions. For instance, instead of grouping all assets in one number, show cash, accounts receivable, and so on in your accounting equation.

Group Project 1-6
Analyze transactions for a business

With a team of one or two other students and using library sources, write a paper on the American Institute of Certified Public Accountants, their services to members, and their activities. Be careful to cite sources for your information. Direct quotes should be labeled as such and should be single-spaced and indented if relatively long or in quote marks and not indented if relatively short. To quote without giving the source is plagiarism and should be avoided at all costs.

Group Project 1-7
Perform library research

Using the Internet—A View of the Real World

Visit the following website for Nokia:
> **http://www.nokia.com**

Write a short paper describing company information, products and services, and support available for their products.

Internet Project 1-8
Investigate company information

Visit the following website for Ford Motor Company:
> **http://www.ford.com**

When the web page appears, search for Investor Information and then locate the Ford Motor Company Annual Report. Based on your investigation, write a short paper describing the general content of the annual report.

Internet Project 1-9
Examine an annual report

Answers to Self-Test

True-False

1. **False**. Corporation, not trust, is the third form.
2. **True**. The accounting for all three of these is covered in this text.
3. **False**. The income statement is dated using a period of time, such as "For the Year Ended December 31, 2012."

4. **True** In addition, the statement of retained earnings shows dividends declared.
5. **True** Both show assets, liabilities, and stockholders' equity.

Multiple-Choice

1. **d.** The ending balance in retained earnings is shown in both the statement of retained earnings and in the balance sheet.
2. **d.** This form of the equation would not balance.
3. **b.** The inflation accounting concept was not one of the ones discussed. The other two were the money measurement concept and the periodicity concept.

4. **c.** When the stockholders invest cash, assets and stockholders' equity increase.
5. **c.** The performance of services on account increases both accounts receivable and retained earnings.

Careers in Accounting

Salary Potential of Accountants

Selecting a major represents much more than the choice of courses a student takes in college. To a significant degree, the student's major, along with academic performance, will determine the career paths available upon graduation. Few professionals would recommend a specific career choice based solely on salaries. However, as students select their major and map out their career path, it is important that they make informed decisions with respect to the potential financial rewards of the various options. Outlined below is information on selected salaries for many accounting-related careers. These salaries, current as of 2011, should be viewed only as guidelines. Salaries at all levels can vary significantly between locations. Also, one should add 10 to 15 percent to the listed salary for professional certifications (such as the CPA) or for a graduate degree (Masters of Accounting or MBA).

Salaries for Public Accounting, Non-Partners

Position	Salary Range
Large CPA Firms:	
Starting Salaries	$50,000–$61,250
Salary between 1–3 years	$56,250–$72,500
Manager/Director	$83,250–$167,250
Small CPA Firms:	
Starting Salaries	$41,500–$50,250
Salary between 1–3 years	$46,250–$58,250
Manager/Director	$70,500–$116,500

Salaries for Corporate Accounting – Large Corporations

Position	Salary Range
Chief Financial Officer/Treasurer	$268,000–$395,500
Vice President, Finance	$212,000–$328,750
Director of Finance	$140,500–$206,750
Director of Accounting	$133,500–$183,250
Controller	$132,750–$175,250
Assistant Controller	$101,750–$135,750
Tax Director	$138,250–$224,500
Tax Manager	$97,750–$136,000
Audit Director	$152,750–$231,000
General Accounting–Manager	$73,750–$100,000
General Accounting–1-3 years experience	$45,750–$59,500
General Accounting–starting salary	$38,500–$47,750

Students interested in a career in accounting and finance can find detailed information for these and many other accounting related careers at Robert Half (www.roberthalf.com). Also, accounting professors are generally familiar with starting salaries and job opportunities for accounting graduates, so you may want to address more specific questions about potential careers and salaries with them.

Recording Business Transactions

In Chapter 1, we illustrated the income statement, statement of retained earnings, balance sheet, and statement of cash flows. These statements are the end products of the financial accounting process, which is based on the accounting equation. The financial accounting process quantifies past management decisions. The results of these decisions are communicated to users—management, creditors, and investors—and serve as a basis for making future decisions.

The raw data of accounting are the business transactions. We recorded the transactions in Chapter 1 as increases or decreases in the assets, liabilities, and stockholders' equity items of the accounting equation. This procedure showed you how various transactions affected the accounting equation. When working through these sample transactions, you probably suspected that listing all transactions as increases or decreases in the transactions summary columns would be too cumbersome in practice. Most businesses, even small ones, enter into many transactions every day. Chapter 2 teaches you how to actually record business transactions in the accounting process.

To explain the dual procedure of recording business transactions with debits and credits, we introduce you to some new tools: the T-account, the journal, and the ledger. Using these tools, you can follow a company through its various business transactions. Like accountants, you can use a trial balance to check the equality of your recorded debits and credits. This is the double-entry accounting system that the Franciscan monk, Luca Pacioli, described centuries ago. Understanding this system enables you to better understand the content of financial statements so you can use the information provided to make informed business decisions.

The Account and Rules of Debit and Credit

A business may engage in thousands of transactions during a year. An accountant classifies and summarizes the data in these transactions to create useful information.

Learning Objectives

After studying this chapter, you should be able to:

1. Use the account as the basic classifying and storage unit for accounting information.

2. Express the effects of business transactions in terms of debits and credits to different types of accounts.

3. List the steps in the accounting cycle.

4. Record the effects of business transactions in a journal.

5. Post journal entries to the accounts in the ledger. (continued)

(continued)

Objectives

6. Prepare a trial balance to test the equality of debits and credits in the journalizing and posting process.

7. Analyze and use the financial results—horizontal and vertical analyses.

The Account

Objective 1
Use the account as the basic classifying and storage unit for accounting information.

Note to the Student
Give an example of a business you would like to start or in which you are presently working. Develop typical transactions of the business and analyze these transactions.

The T-Account

Steps in Recording Business Transactions

Look at Illustration 2.1 to see the steps in recording and posting the effects of a business transaction. Note that source documents provide the evidence that a business transaction occurred. These source documents include such items as bills received from suppliers for goods or services received, bills sent to customers for goods sold or services performed, and cash register tapes. The information in the source document serves as the basis for preparing a journal entry. Then a firm posts (transfers) that information to accounts in the ledger.

You can see from Illustration 2.1 that after you prepare the journal entry, you post it to the accounts in the ledger. However, before you can record the journal entry, you must understand the rules of debit and credit. To teach you these rules, we begin by studying the nature of an account.

Fortunately, most business transactions are repetitive.   This makes the task of accountants somewhat easier because they can classify the transactions into groups having common characteristics. For example, a company may have thousands of receipts or payments of cash during a year. As a result, a part of every cash transaction can be recorded and summarized in a single place called an *account.*

An **account** is a part of the accounting system used to classify and summarize the increases, decreases, and balances of each asset, liability, stockholders' equity item, dividend, revenue, and expense. Firms set up accounts for each different business element, such as cash, accounts receivable, and accounts payable. Every business has a Cash account in its accounting system because knowledge of the amount of cash on hand is useful information.

Accountants may differ on the account title (or name) they give the same item. For example, one accountant might name an account Notes Payable and another might call it Loans Payable. Both account titles refer to the amounts borrowed by the company. The account title should be logical to help the accountant group similar transactions into the same account. Once you give an account a title, you must use that same title throughout the accounting records.

The number of accounts in a company's accounting system depends on the information needs of those interested in the business. The main requirement is that each account provides information useful in making decisions. Thus, one account may be set up for all cash rather than having a separate account for each form of cash (coins on hand, currency on hand, and deposits in banks). The amount of cash is useful information; the form of cash often is not.

To illustrate recording the increases and decreases in an account, texts use the T-account, which looks like a capital letter T. The name of the account, such as Cash, appears across the top of the T. We record increases on one side of the vertical line of the T and decreases on the other side. A T-account appears as follows:

Title of Account

An Accounting Perspective

BUSINESS INSIGHT Have you ever considered starting your own business? If so, you'll need to understand accounting to successfully run your business. To know how well your business is doing, you must understand and analyze financial statements. Accounting information also tells you why you are performing as reported. If you are in business to sell or develop a certain product or perform a specific service, you cannot operate profitably or consider expanding unless you base your business decisions on accounting information.

Illustration 2.1   The Steps in Recording and Posting the Effects of a Business Transaction

In Chapter 1, you saw that each business transaction affects at least two items. For example, if you—an owner—invest cash in your business, the company's assets increase and its stockholders' equity increases. This result was illustrated in the summary of transactions in Illustration 1.3. In the following sections, we use debits and credits and the double-entry procedure to record the increases and decreases caused by business transactions.

Accountants use the term **debit** instead of saying, "Place an entry on the left side of the T-account." They use the term **credit** for "Place an entry on the right side of the T-account." Debit (abbreviated Dr.) simply means left side; credit (abbreviated Cr.) means right side.[1] Thus, for all accounts a debit entry is an entry on the left side, while a credit entry is an entry on the right side.

Objective 2
Express the effects of business transactions in terms of debits and credits to different types of accounts.

Any Account

Left, or debit, side	Right, or credit, side

After recognizing a business event as a business transaction, we analyze it to determine its increase or decrease effects on the assets, liabilities, stockholders' equity items, dividends, revenues, or expenses of the business. Then we translate these increase or decrease effects into debits and credits.

In each business transaction we record, the total dollar amount of debits must equal the total dollar amount of credits. When we debit one account (or accounts) for $100, we must credit another account (or accounts) for a total of $100. The accounting requirement that each transaction be recorded by an entry that has equal debits and credits is called **double-entry procedure**, or *duality*. This double-entry procedure keeps the accounting equation in balance.

The dual recording process produces two sets of accounts—those with debit balances and those with credit balances. The totals of these two groups of accounts must be equal. Then, some assurance exists that the arithmetic part of the transaction recording process has been properly carried out. Now, let us actually record business transactions in T-accounts using debits and credits.

Double-Entry Procedure

Note to the Student
Debit and credit are directional signals. The limited meaning of debit is to record the amount on the left side of the account; the limited meaning of credit is to record the amount on the right side of the account.

Recording Changes in Assets, Liabilities, and Stockholders' Equity

While recording business transactions, remember that the foundation of the accounting process is the following basic accounting equation:

$$\text{Assets} = \text{Liabilities} + \text{Stockholders' Equity}$$

Recording transactions into the T-accounts is easier when you focus on the equal sign in the accounting equation. Assets, which are on the left of the equal sign,

---

[1]The abbreviations "Dr." and "Cr." are based on the Latin words "*debere*" and "*credere*." A synonym for *debit* an account is *charge* an account.

increase on the left side of the T-accounts. Liabilities and stockholders' equity, to the right of the equal sign, increase on the right side of the T-accounts. You already know that the left side of the T-account is the debit side and the right side is the credit side. So you should be able to fill in the rest of the rules of increases and decreases by deduction, such as:

Reinforcing Problem
E2-1 Indicate rules of debit and credit.

To summarize:

1. Assets *increase* by debits (left side) to the T-account and *decrease* by credits (right side) to the T-account.
2. Liabilities and stockholders' equity *decrease* by debits (left side) to the T-account and *increase* by credits (right side) to the T-account.

Applying these two rules keeps the accounting equation in balance. Now we apply the debit and credit rules for assets, liabilities, and stockholders' equity to business transactions.

Assume a corporation issues shares of its capital stock for $10,000 in transaction 1. (Note the figure in parentheses is the number of the transaction and ties the two sides of the transaction together.) The company records the receipt of $10,000 as follows:

(Dr.)	Cash	(Cr.)	(Dr.)	Capital Stock	(Cr.)
(1)	10,000			(1)	10,000

This transaction increases the asset, cash, which is recorded on the left side of the Cash account. Then, the transaction increases stockholders' equity, which is recorded on the right side of the Capital Stock account.

Assume the company borrowed $5,000 from a bank on a note (transaction 2). A **note** is an unconditional written promise to pay to another party (the bank) the amount owed either when demanded or at a specified date, usually with interest at a specified rate. The firm records this transaction as follows:

(Dr.)	Cash	(Cr.)	(Dr.)	Notes Payable	(Cr.)
(1)	10,000			(2)	5,000
(2)	5,000				

Observe that liabilities, Notes Payable, increase with an entry on the right (credit) side of the account.

Reinforcing Problem
E2-6 Explain sets of debits and credits.

Recording Changes in Revenues and Expenses   In Chapter 1, we recorded the revenues and expenses directly in the Retained Earnings account. However, this is not done in practice because of the volume of revenue and expense transactions. Instead, businesses treat the expense accounts as if they were subclassifications of the debit side of the Retained Earnings account, and the revenue accounts as if they were subclassifications of the credit side. Since firms need the amounts of revenues and expenses to prepare the income statement, they keep a separate account for each type of revenue and expense. The recording rules for revenues and expenses are:

- Record increases in revenues on the right (credit) side of the T-account and decreases on the left (debit) side. The reasoning behind this rule is that revenues increase retained earnings, and increases in retained earnings are recorded on the right side.
- Record increases in expenses on the left (debit) side of the T-account and decreases on the right (credit) side. The reasoning behind this rule is that expenses decrease retained earnings, and decreases in retained earnings are recorded on the left side.

To illustrate these rules, assume the same company received $1,000 cash from a customer for services rendered (transaction 3). The Cash account, an asset, increases on the left (debit) side of the T-account; and the Service Revenue account, an increase in retained earnings, increases on the right (credit) side.

(Dr.)	Cash	(Cr.)	(Dr.)	Service Revenue	(Cr.)
(1)	10,000			**(3)**	**1,000**
(2)	5,000				
(3)	**1,000**				

Now assume this company paid $600 in salaries to employees (transaction 4). The Cash account, an asset, decreases on the right (credit) side of the T-account; and the Salaries Expense account, a decrease in retained earnings, increases on the left (debit) side.[2]

(Dr.)	Cash		(Cr.)	(Dr.)	Salaries Expense	(Cr.)
(1)	10,000	**(4)**	**600**	**(4)**	**600**	
(2)	5,000					
(3)	1,000					

Recording Changes in Dividends   Since dividends decrease retained earnings, increases appear on the left side of the Dividends account and decreases on the right side. Thus, the firm records payment of a $2,000 cash dividend (transaction 5) as follows:

(Dr.)	Cash		(Cr.)	(Dr.)	Dividends[3]	(Cr.)
(1)	10,000	(4)	600	**(5)**	**2,000**	
(2)	5,000	**(5)**	**2,000**			
(3)	1,000					

At the end of the accounting period, the accountant transfers any balances in the expense, revenue, and Dividends accounts to the Retained Earnings account. This transfer occurs only after the information in the expense and revenue accounts has been used to prepare the income statement. We discuss and illustrate this step in Chapter 4.

To determine the balance of any T-account, total the debits to the account, total the credits to the account, and subtract the smaller sum from the larger. If the sum of the debits exceeds the sum of the credits, the account has a **debit balance**. For example, the following Cash account uses information from the preceding transactions. The account has a debit balance of $13,400, computed as total debits of $16,000 less total credits of $2,600.

> **Determining the Balance of an Account**

---

[2]Certain deductions are normally taken out of employees' pay for social security taxes, federal and state withholding, and so on. Those deductions are ignored here.

[3]As we illustrate later in the text, some companies debit dividends directly to the Retained Earnings account rather than to a Dividends account.

(Dr.)		Cash		(Cr.)
(1)	10,000	(4)		600
(2)	5,000	(5)		2,000
(3)	1,000			
	16,000			2,600
Dr. bal	13,400			

If, on the other hand, the sum of the credits exceeds the sum of the debits, the account has a **credit balance**. For instance, assume that a company has an Accounts Payable account with a total of $10,000 in debits and $13,000 in credits. The account has a credit balance of $3,000, as shown in the following T-account:

(Dr.)	Accounts Payable	(Cr.)
10,000		7,000
		6,000
10,000		13,000
	Cr. bal	3,000

Normal Balances　　Since debits increase asset, expense, and Dividend accounts, they normally have debit (or left-side) balances. Conversely, because credits increase liability, capital stock, retained earnings, and revenue accounts, they normally have credit (or right-side) balances.

The following chart shows the normal balances of the seven accounts we have used:

	Normal Balances	
Types of Accounts	Debit	Credit
Assets	X	
Liabilities		X
Stockholders' Equity		
Capital Stock		X
Retained earnings		X
Dividends	X	
Expenses	X	
Revenues		X

Rules of Debit and Credit Summarized

At this point, you should memorize the six rules of debit and credit. Later, as you proceed in your study of accounting, the rules will become automatic. Then, you will no longer ask yourself, "Is this increase a debit or credit?"

Asset accounts increase on the debit side, while liability and stockholders' equity accounts increase on the credit side. When the account balances are totaled, they conform to the following independent equations:

Assets = Liabilities + Stockholders' Equity
Debits = Credits

The arrangement of these two formulas gives the first three rules of debit and credit:

1. Increases in asset accounts are debits; decreases are credits.
2. Decreases in liability accounts are debits; increases are credits.
3. Decreases in stockholders' equity accounts are debits; increases are credits.

Illustration 2.2   Rules of Debit and Credit

Assets	=	Liabilities	+	Stockholders' Equity

Asset Accounts	=	Liability Accounts	+	Stockholders' Equity Account(s) (Capital Stock and Retained Earnings)	
Debit*	Credit	Debit	Credit*	Debit	Credit*
+ Debit for increase	− Credit for decrease	− Debit for decrease	+ Credit for increase	− Debit for decrease	+ Credit for increase

Debits	Credits	Expense Accounts and Dividends Account		Revenue Accounts	
		Debit*	Credit	Debit	Credit*
1. Increase assets. 2. Decrease liabilities. 3. Decrease stockholders' equity. 4. Decrease revenues. 5. Increase expenses. 6. Increase dividends.	1. Decreases assets. 2. Increase liabilities. 3. Increase stockholders' equity. 4. Increase revenues. 5. Decrease expenses. 6. Decrease dividends.	+ Debit for increase	− Credit for decrease	− Debit for decrease	+ Credit for increase

* Normal balance

The debit and credit rules for expense and Dividends accounts and for revenue accounts follow logically if you remember that expenses and dividends are decreases in stockholders' equity and revenues are increases in stockholders' equity. Since stockholders' equity accounts decrease on the debit side, expense and Dividend accounts increase on the debit side. Since stockholders' equity accounts increase on the credit side, revenue accounts increase on the credit side. The last three debit and credit rules are:

4. Decreases in revenue accounts are debits; increases are credits.
5. Increases in expense accounts are debits; decreases are credits.
6. Increases in Dividends accounts are debits; decreases are credits.

In Illustration 2.2, we depict these six rules of debit and credit. Note first the treatment of expense and Dividends accounts as if they were subclassifications of the debit side of the Retained Earnings account. Second, note the treatment of the revenue accounts as if they were subclassifications of the credit side of the Retained Earnings account. Next, we discuss the accounting cycle and indicate where steps in the accounting cycle are discussed in Chapters 2 through 4.

The Accounting Cycle

The **accounting cycle** is a series of steps performed during the accounting period (some throughout the period and some at the end) to analyze, record, classify, summarize, and report useful financial information for the purpose of preparing financial statements. Before you can visualize the eight steps in the accounting cycle, you must be able to recognize a business transaction. **Business transactions** are measurable events that affect the financial condition of a business. For example, assume that the owner of a business spilled a pot of coffee in her office or broke her leg while skiing. These two events may briefly interrupt the operation of the business. However, they are not measurable in terms that affect the solvency and profitability of the business.

Business transactions can be the exchange of goods for cash between the business and an external party, such as the sale of a book, or they can involve paying

> **Objective 3**
> List the steps in the accounting cycle.

salaries to employees. These events have one fundamental criterion: They must have caused a measurable change in the amounts in the accounting equation, Assets = Liabilities + Stockholders' Equity. The evidence that a business event has occurred is a source document such as a sales ticket, check, and so on. Source documents are important because they are the ultimate proof of business transactions.[4]

After you have determined that an event is a measurable business transaction and have adequate proof of this transaction, mentally analyze the transaction's effects on the accounting equation. You learned how to do this in Chapter 1. This chapter and Chapters 3 and 4 describe the other steps in the accounting cycle. The eight steps in the accounting cycle and the chapters that discuss them are:

Performed throughout the accounting period

1. Analyze transactions by examining source documents (Chapters 1 and 2).
2. Journalize transactions in the journal (Chapter 2).
3. Post journal entries to the accounts in the ledger (Chapter 2).

Performed only at end of the accounting period.

4. Prepare a trial balance of the accounts (Chapter 2) and complete the work sheet (Chapter 4). (This step includes adjusting entries from Chapter 3.)
5. Prepare financial statements (Chapter 4).
6. Journalize and post adjusting entries (Chapters 3 and 4).
7. Journalize and post closing entries (Chapter 4).
8. Prepare a post-closing trial balance (Chapter 4).

This listing serves as a preview of what you will study in Chapters 2–4. Notice that firms perform the last five steps at the end of the accounting period. Step 5 precedes steps 6 and 7 because management needs the financial statements at the earliest possible date. After the statements have been delivered to management, the adjusting and closing entries can be journalized and posted. In Illustration 2.3, we diagram the eight steps in the accounting cycle.

You can perform many of these steps on a computer with an accounting software package. However, you must understand a manual accounting system and all of the steps in the accounting cycle to understand what the computer is doing. This understanding removes the mystery of what the computer is doing when it takes in raw data and produces financial statements.

The Journal

Objective 4
Record the effects of business transactions in a journal.

In explaining the rules of debit and credit, we recorded transactions directly in the accounts. Each ledger (general ledger) account shows only the increases and decreases in that account. Thus, all the effects of a single business transaction would not appear in any one account. For example, the Cash account contains only data on changes in cash and does not show how the cash was generated or how it was spent. To have a permanent record of an entire transaction, the accountant uses a book or record known as a *journal*.

A **journal** is a chronological (arranged in order of time) record of business transactions. A *journal entry* is the recording of a business transaction in the journal. A **journal entry** shows all the effects of a business transaction as expressed in debit(s) and credit(s) and may include an explanation of the transaction. *A transaction is entered in a journal before it is entered in ledger accounts.* Because each transaction is initially recorded in a journal rather than directly in the ledger, a journal is called a *book of original entry*.

The General Journal

A business usually has more than one journal. Chapter 4 briefly describes several special journals. In this chapter, we use the basic form of journal, the general journal. As shown in Illustration 2.4, a general journal contains the following columns:

---

[4]Many companies send and receive source documents electronically, rather than on paper. In such an electronic computer environment, source documents might exist only in the computer databases of the two parties involved in the transaction.

Illustration 2.3 Steps in the Accounting Cycle

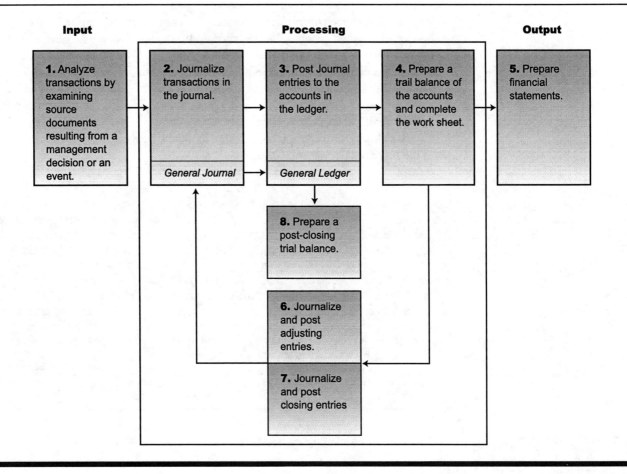

Illustration 2.4 General Journal

MICROTRAIN COMPANY
General Journal

Date		Account Titles and Explanation	Post. Ref.	Debit	Credit
2012 Nov.	28	Cash	100	5 0 0 0 0	
		Capital Stock	300		5 0 0 0 0
		Stockholders invested $50,000 cash in business.			

1. **Date column.** The first column on each journal page is for the date. For the first journal entry on a page, this column contains the year, month, and day (number). For all other journal entries on a page, this column contains only the day of the month, until the month changes.

2. **Account Titles and Explanation column.** The first line of an entry shows the account debited. The second line shows the account credited. Notice that we indent the credit account title to the right. For instance, in Illustration 2.4 we show the debit to the Cash account and then the credit to the Capital Stock account. Any necessary explanation of a transaction appears on the line(s) below the credit entry and is indented halfway between the accounts debited and credited. A journal entry explanation should be concise and yet complete enough

Reinforcing Problems
E2-2 Prepare journal entries
E2-3 Prepare journal entries

to describe fully the transaction and prove the entry's accuracy. When a journal entry is self-explanatory, we omit the explanation.

3. **Posting Reference column.** This column shows the account number of the debited or credited account. For instance, in Illustration 2.4, the number 100 in the first entry means that the Cash account number is 100. No number appears in this column until the information has been posted to the appropriate ledger account. We discuss posting later in the chapter.

4. **Debit column.** In the debit column, the amount of the debit is on the same line as the title of the account debited.

5. **Credit column.** In the credit column, the amount of the credit is on the same line as the title of the account credited.

An Accounting Perspective	**USES OF TECHNOLOGY** Preparing journal entries in a computerized system is different than in a manual system. The computer normally asks for the number of the account to be debited. After you type the account number, the computer shows the account title in its proper position. The cursor then moves to the debit column and waits for you to enter the amount of the debit. Then it asks if there are more debits. If not, the computer prompts you for the account number of the credit. After you type the account number, the computer supplies the account name of the credit and enters the same amount debited as the credit. When there is more than one credit, you can override the amount and enter the correct amount. Then you would enter the other credit in the same way. If your debits and credits are not equal, the computer warns you and makes you correct the error. You can supply an explanation for the entry from a standard list or type it in. As you enter the journal entries, the computer automatically posts them to the ledger accounts. At any time, you can have the computer print a trial balance.

Functions and Advantages of a Journal

A summary of the functions and advantages of using a journal follows:

The journal—

1. Records transactions in chronological order.
2. Shows the analysis of each transaction in debits and credits.
3. Supplies an explanation of each transaction when necessary.
4. Serves as a source for future reference to accounting transactions.
5. Eliminates the need for lengthy explanations from the accounts.
6. Makes possible posting to the ledger at convenient times.
7. Assists in maintaining the ledger in balance because the debit(s) must always equal the credit(s) in each journal entry.
8. Aids in tracing errors when the ledger is not in balance.

Reinforcing Problem
P2-1A Prepare journal entries.

The Ledger

A **ledger** (general ledger) is the complete collection of all the accounts of a company. The ledger may be in loose-leaf form, in a bound volume, or in computer memory.

Accounts fall into two general groups: (1) *balance sheet accounts* (assets, liabilities, and stockholders' equity) and (2) *income statement accounts* (revenues and expenses). The terms *real accounts* and *permanent accounts* also refer to balance sheet accounts. Balance sheet accounts are **real accounts** because they are not subclassifications or subdivisions of any other account. They are **permanent accounts** because their balances are not transferred (or closed) to any other account at the end of the accounting period. Income statement accounts and the Dividends account are **nominal accounts** because they are merely subclassifications of the stockholders' equity accounts. *Nominal* literally means "in name only." Nominal accounts are also called **temporary accounts** because they temporarily contain revenue, expense, and dividend information that is transferred (or closed) to the Retained Earnings account at the end of the accounting period.

The **chart of accounts** is a complete listing of the titles and numbers of all the accounts in the ledger. The chart of accounts can be compared to a table of contents. The groups of accounts usually appear in this order: assets, liabilities, stockholders' equity, dividends, revenues, and expenses.

Individual accounts are in sequence in the ledger. Each account typically has an identification number and a title to help locate accounts when recording data. For example, a company might number asset accounts, 100–199; liability accounts, 200–299; stockholders' equity accounts and Dividends account, 300–399; revenue accounts, 400–499; and expense accounts, 500–599. We use this numbering system in this text. The uniform chart of accounts used in the first 11 chapters appears in a separate file at the end of the text. You should print that file and keep it handy for working certain problems and exercises. Companies may use other numbering systems. For instance, sometimes a company numbers its accounts in sequence starting with 1, 2, and so on. The important idea is that companies use some numbering system.

Now that you understand how to record debits and credits in an account and how all accounts together form a ledger, you are ready to study the accounting process in operation.

The Accounting Process in Operation

MicroTrain Company is a small corporation that provides on-site microcomputer software training using the clients' equipment. The company offers beginning through advanced training with convenient scheduling. A small fleet of trucks transports personnel and teaching supplies to the clients' sites. The company rents a building and is responsible for paying the utilities.

We illustrate the capital stock transaction that occurred to form the company (in November) and the first month of operations (December). The accounting process used by this company is similar to that of any small company. The ledger accounts used by MicroTrain Company are:

	Acct. No.	Account Title	Description
Assets	100	Cash	Bank deposits and cash on hand.
	103	Accounts Receivable	Amounts owed to the company by customers.
	107	Supplies on Hand	Items such as paper, envelopes, writing materials, and other materials used in performing training services for customers or in doing administrative and clerical office work.
	108	Prepaid Insurance	Insurance policy premiums paid in advance of the periods for which the insurance coverage applies.
	112	Prepaid Rent	Rent paid in advance of the periods for which the rent payment applies.
	150	Trucks	Trucks used to transport personnel and training supplies to clients' locations.
Liabilities	200	Accounts Payable	Amounts owed to creditors for items purchased from them.
	216	Unearned Service Fees	Amounts received from customers before the training services have been performed for them.
Stockholders' equity	300	Capital Stock	The stockholders' investment in the business.
	310	Retained Earnings	The earnings retained in the business.
Dividends	320	Dividends	The amount of dividends declared to stockholders.
Revenues	400	Service Revenue	Amounts earned by performing training services for customers.
Expenses	505	Advertising Expense	The cost of advertising incurred in the current period.
	506	Gas and Oil Expense	The cost of gas and oil used in trucks in thecurrent period.
	507	Salaries Expense	The amount of salaries incurred in the current period.
	511	Utilities Expense	The cost of utilities incurred in the current period.

Notice the gaps left between account numbers (100, 103, 107, etc.). These gaps allow the firm to later add new accounts between the existing accounts.

The Recording of Transactions and Their Effects on the Accounts

To begin, a transaction must be *journalized*. **Journalizing** is the process of entering the effects of a transaction in a journal. Then, the information is transferred, or posted, to the proper accounts in the ledger. **Posting** is the process of recording in the ledger accounts the information contained in the journal. We explain posting in more detail later in the chapter.

In the following example, notice that each business transaction affects two or more accounts in the ledger. Also note that the transaction date in both the general journal and the general ledger accounts is the same. In the ledger accounts, the date used is the date that the transaction was recorded in the general journal, even if the entry is not posted until several days later. Our example shows the journal entries posted to T-accounts. In practice, firms post journal entries to ledger accounts, as we show later in the chapter.

Accountants use the *accrual basis of accounting*. Under the **accrual basis of accounting**, they recognize revenues when the company makes a sale or performs a service, regardless of when the company receives the cash. They recognize expenses as incurred, whether or not the company has paid out cash. Chapter 3 discusses the accrual basis of accounting in more detail.

In the following MicroTrain Company example, transaction 1 increases (debits) Cash and increases (credits) Capital Stock by $50,000. First, MicroTrain records the transaction in the general journal; second, it posts the entry to the accounts in the general ledger.

Transaction 1: Nov. 28, 2012 Stockholders invested $50,000 and formed MicroTrain Company.

General Journal

Date		Account Titles and Explanation	Post. Ref.	Debit	Credit
2012					
Nov.	28	Cash	100	5 0 0 0 0	
		Capital Stock	300		5 0 0 0 0
		Stockholders invested $50,000 cash in business.			

General Ledger

	Cash				Capital Stock	
(Dr.)	Acct. No. 100	*(Cr.)*		*(Dr.)*	Acct. No. 300	*(Cr.)*
2012					2012	
Nov. 28	50,000				Nov. 28	50,000

No other transactions occurred in November. The company prepares financial statements at the end of each month. Illustration 2.5 shows the company's balance sheet at November 30, 2012.

The balance sheet reflects ledger account balances as of the close of business on November 30, 2012. These closing balances are the beginning balances on December 1, 2012. The ledger accounts show these closing balances as beginning balances (Beg. bal.).

Now assume that in December 2012, MicroTrain Company engaged in the following transactions. We show the proper recording of each transaction in the journal and then in the ledger accounts (in T-account form), and describe the effects of each transaction.

Illustration 2.5 Balance Sheet

MICROTRAIN COMPANY
Balance Sheet
November 30, 2012

Assets		Liabilities and Stockholders' Equity	
Cash	$50,000	Stockholders' equity:	
		Capital stock	$50,000
		Total liabilities and stockholders'	
Total Assets	$50,000	equity	$50,000

Transaction 2: Dec. 1   Paid cash for four small trucks, $40,000.
General Journal

Date		Account Titles and Explanation	Post. Ref.	Debit	Credit
2012 Dec.	1	Trucks	150	4 0 0 0 0	
		Cash	100		4 0 0 0 0
		To record the purchase of four trucks.			

General Ledger
Trucks
(Dr.)   Acct. No. 150   (Cr.)

2012
Dec. 1   **40,000**

Cash
(Dr.)   Acct. No. 100   (Cr.)

2012
Dec. 1 Beg. bal.   50,000 | **Dec. 1**   **40,000**

Reinforcing Problem
E2-4 Prepare journal entries.

Transaction 3: Dec. 1   Paid cash for insurance on the trucks to cover a one-year period from this date.
General Journal

Date		Account Titles and Explanation	Post. Ref.	Debit	Credit
2012 Dec.	1	Prepaid Insurance	108	2 4 0 0	
		Cash	100		2 4 0 0
		Purchased truck insurance to cover a one-year period.			

General Ledger
Prepaid Insurance
(Dr.)   Acct. No. 108   (Cr.)

2012
Dec. 1   **2,400**

Cash
(Dr.)   Acct. No. 100   (Cr.)

2012
Dec. 1 Beg. Bal.   50,000 | 2012
Dec. 1   40,000
Dec. 1   2,400

Effects of Transaction
An asset, prepaid insurance, increases (debited); and an asset, cash, decreases (credited) by $2,400. The debit is to Prepaid Insurance rather than Insurance Expense because the policy covers more than the current accounting period of December (insurance policies are usually paid one year in advance). As you will see in Chapter 3, prepaid items are expensed as they are used. If this insurance policy was only written for December, the entire $2,400 debit would have been to Insurance Expense.

Transaction 4: Dec. 1   Rented a building and paid $1,200 to cover a three-month period from this date.

General Journal

Date		Account Titles and Explanation	Post. Ref.	Debit	Credit
2012					
Dec.	1	Prepaid Rent	112	1 2 0 0	
		Cash	100		1 2 0 0
		Paid three months' rent on a building.			

General Ledger

Prepaid Rent

(Dr.)	Acct. No. 112	(Cr.)
2012		
Dec. 1	**1,200**	

Cash

(Dr.)		Acct. No. 100	(Cr.)
2012		2012	
Dec. 1 Beg. Bal.	50,000	Dec. 1	40,000
		Dec. 1	2,400
		Dec. 1	**1,200**

Effects of Transaction
An asset, prepaid rent, increases (debited); and another asset, cash, decreases (credited) by $1,200. The debit is to Prepaid Rent rather than Rent Expense because the payment covers more than the current month. If the payment had just been for December, the debit would have been to Rent Expense.

Transaction 5: Dec. 4   Purchased $1,400 of training supplies on account to be used over the next several months.

General Journal

Date		Account Titles and Explanation	Post. Ref.	Debit	Credit
2012					
Dec.	4	Supplies on Hand	107	1 4 0 0	
		Accounts Payable	200		1 4 0 0
		To record the purchases of training supplies for future use.			

General Ledger

Supplies on Hand

(Dr.)	Acct. No. 107	(Cr.)
2012		
Dec. 4	**1,400**	

Accounts Payable

(Dr.)	Acct. No. 200	(Cr.)
	2012	
	Dec. 4	**1,400**

Effects of Transaction
An asset, supplies on hand, increases (debited); and a liability, accounts payable, increases (credited) by $1,400. The debit is to Supplies on Hand rather than Supplies Expense because the supplies are to be used over several accounting periods.

Reinforcing Problem
E2-5 Show entries using journal entries and T-accounts.

In each of the three preceding entries, we debited an asset rather than an expense. The reason is that the expenditure applies to (or benefits) more than just the current accounting period. Whenever a company will not fully use up an item such as insurance, rent, or supplies in the period when purchased, it usually debits an asset. In practice, however, sometimes the expense is initially debited in these situations.

Companies sometimes buy items that they fully use up within the current accounting period. For example, during the first part of the month a company may buy supplies that it intends to consume fully during that month. If the company fully consumes the supplies during the period of purchase, the best practice is to debit Supplies Expense at the time of purchase rather than Supplies on Hand. This same advice applies to insurance and rent. If a company purchases insurance that it fully consumes during the current period, the company should debit Insurance Expense at the time of purchase rather than Prepaid Insurance. Also, if a company pays rent that applies only to the current period, Rent Expense should be debited at the time of purchase rather than Prepaid Rent. As illustrated in Chapter 3, following this advice simplifies the procedures at the end of the accounting period.

Transaction 6: Dec. 7   Received $4,500 from a customer in payment for future training services.

General Journal

Date	Account Titles and Explanation	Post. Ref.	Debit	Credit
2012 Dec. 7	Cash	100	4 5 0 0	
	Unearned Service Fees	216		4 5 0 0
	To record the receipt of cash from a customer in payment			
	for future training services.			

General Ledger
Cash

(Dr.)	Acct. No. 100		(Cr.)
2012		2012	
Dec. 1 Beg Bal. 50,000		Dec. 1	40,000
Dec. 7	**4,500**	Dec. 1	2,400
		Dec. 1	1,200

Unearned Service Fees

(Dr.)	Acct. No. 216	(Cr.)
	2012	
	Dec. 7	**4,500**

Effects of Transaction
An asset, cash, increases (debited); and a liability, unearned service revenue, increases (credited) by $4,500. The credit is to Unearned Service Fees rather than Service Revenue because the $4,500 applies to more than just the current accounting period. Unearned Service Fees is a liability because, if the services are never performed, the $4,500 will have to be refunded. If the payment had been for services to be provided in December, the credit would have been to Service Revenue.

Transaction 7: Dec. 15   Performed training services for a customer for cash, $5,000.

General Journal

Date	Account Titles and Explanation	Post. Ref.	Debit	Credit
2012 Dec. 15	Cash	100	5 0 0 0	
	Service Revenue	400		5 0 0 0
	To record the receipt of cash for performing training			
	services for a customer.			

General Ledger
Cash

(Dr.)	Acct. No. 100		(Cr.)
2012		2012	
Dec. 1 Beg Bal. 50,000		Dec. 1	40,000
Dec. 7	4,500	Dec. 1	2,400
Dec. 15	**5,000**	Dec. 1	1,200

Service Revenue

(Dr.)	Acct. No. 400	(Cr.)
	2012	
	Dec. 15	**5,000**

Effects of Transaction
An asset, cash, increases (debited); and a revenue, service revenue, increases (credited) by $5,000.

General Journal

Date		Account Titles and Explanation	Post. Ref.	Debit	Credit
2012 Dec.	17	Accounts Payable	200	1 4 0 0	
		Cash	100		1 4 0 0
		Paid the account payable arising from the purchase of			
		Supplies on December 4.			

General Ledger

Accounts Payable

(Dr.)	Acct. No. 200	(Cr.)
2012 **Dec. 17** **1,400**	2012 Dec. 4 1,400	

Effects of Transaction
A liability, accounts payable, decreases (debited); and an asset, cash, decreases (credited) by $1,400.

Cash

(Dr.)		Acct. No. 100	(Cr.)
2012 Dec. 1 Beg Bal. 50,000		2012 Dec. 1 40,000	
Dec. 7 4,500		Dec. 1 2,400	
Dec. 15 5,000		Dec. 1 1,200	
		Dec 17 1,400	

General Journal

Date		Account Titles and Explanation	Post. Ref.	Debit	Credit
2012 Dec.	20	Accounts Receivable	103	5 7 0 0	
		Service Revenue	400		5 7 0 0
		To record the performance of training services on account			
		for which a customer was billed.			

General Ledger
Accounts Receivable

(Dr.)	Acct. No. 103	(Cr.)
2012 **Dec. 20 5,700**		

Effects of Transaction
An asset, accounts receivable, increases (debited); and a revenue, service revenue, increases (credited) by $5,700.

Service Revenue

(Dr.)	Acct. No. 400	(Cr.)
		2012 Dec. 15 5,000
		Dec. 20 5,700

Transaction 10: Dec. 24 Received a bill for advertising in a local newspaper in December, $50.

General Journal

Date		Account Titles and Explanation	Post. Ref.	Debit	Credit
2012 Dec.	24	Advertising Expense	505	5 0	
		Accounts Payable	200		5 0
		Received a bill for advertising for the month of December.			

General Ledger

Advertising Expense

(Dr.)	Acct. No. 505	(Cr.)
2012 **Dec. 24**	**50**	

Accounts Payable

(Dr.)		Acct. No. 200		(Cr.)
2012 Dec.	17	1,400	2012 Dec. 4	1,400
			Dec. 24	**50**

Effects of Transaction

An expense, advertising expense, increases (debited); and a liability, accounts payable, increases (credited) by $50. The reason for debiting an expense rather than an asset is because all the cost pertains to the current accounting period, the month of December. Otherwise, Prepaid Advertising (an asset) would have been debited.

Transaction 11: Dec. 26 Received $500 on accounts receivable from a customer.

General Journal

Date		Account Titles and Explanation	Post. Ref.	Debit	Credit
2012 Dec.	26	Cash	100	5 0 0	
		Accounts Receivable	103		5 0 0
		Received $500 from a customer on accounts receivable			

General Ledger

Cash

(Dr.)			Acct. No. 100		(Cr.)
2012			2012		
Dec.	1 Beg Bal.	50,000	Dec.	1	40,000
Dec.	7	4,500	Dec.	1	2,400
Dec.	15	5,000	Dec.	1	1,200
Dec. 26		**500**	Dec.	17	1,400

Accounts Receivable

(Dr.)		Acct. No. 103		(Cr.)
2012 Dec.	20	5,700	2012 **Dec. 26**	**500**

Effects of Transaction

One asset, cash, increases (debited); and another asset, accounts receivable, decreases (credited) by $500.

Transaction 12: Dec. 28   **Paid salaries of $3,600 to training personnel for the first four weeks of December.**
(Payroll and other deductions are to be ignored since they have not yet been discussed.)

General Journal

Date		Account Titles and Explanation	Post. Ref.	Debit	Credit
2012 Dec.	28	Salaries Expense	507	3 6 0 0	
		Cash	100		3 6 0 0
		Paid training personnel salaries for the first four weeks of			
		December.			

General Ledger

Salaries Expense

(Dr.)	Acct. No. 507	(Cr.)
2012		
Dec. 28	**3,600**	

Effects of Transaction
An expense, salaries expense, increases (debited); and an asset, cash, decreases (credited) by $3,600.

Cash

(Dr.)		Acct. No. 100		(Cr.)
2012			2012	
Dec. 1	50,000		Dec. 1	40,000
Dec. 7	4,500		Dec. 1	2,400
Dec. 15	5,000		Dec. 1	1,200
Dec. 26	500		Dec. 17	1,400
			Dec. 28	**3,600**

Transaction 13: Dec. 29   **Received and paid the utilities bill for December, $150.**

General Journal

Date		Account Titles and Explanation	Post. Ref.	Debit	Credit
2012 Dec.	29	Utilities Expense	511	1 5 0	
		Cash	100		1 5 0
		Paid the utilities bill for December.			

General Ledger

Utilities Expense

(Dr.)	Acct. No. 511	(Cr.)
2012		
Dec. 29	**150**	

Effects of Transaction
An expense, utilities expense, increases (debited); and an asset, cash, decreases (credited) by $150.

Cash

(Dr.)		Acct. No. 100		(Cr.)
2012			2012	
Dec. 1	50,000		Dec. 1	40,000
Dec. 7	4,500		Dec. 1	2,400
Dec. 15	5,000		Dec. 1	1,200
Dec. 26	500		Dec. 17	1,400
			Dec. 28	3,600
			Dec. 29	**150**

Transaction 14: Dec. 30 Received a bill for gas and oil used in the trucks for December, $680.

General Journal

Date	Account Titles and Explanation	Post. Ref.	Debit	Credit
2012 Dec. 30	Gas and Oil Expense	506	6 8 0	
	Accounts Payable	200		6 8 0
	Received a bill for gas and oil used in the trucks for			
	December.			

General Ledger

Gas and Oil Expense

(Dr.)	Acct. No. 506	(Cr.)
2012 Dec. 30 680		

Effects of Transaction

An expense, gas and oil expense, increases (debited); and a liability, accounts payable, increases (credited) by $680.

Accounts Payable

(Dr.)		Acct. No. 200		(Cr.)
2012 Dec. 17 1,400		2012 Dec. 4 1,400		
		Dec. 24 50		
		Dec. 30 680		

Transaction 15: Dec. 31   A dividend of $3,000 was paid to stockholders.

General Journal

Date	Account Titles and Explanation	Post. Ref.	Debit	Credit
2012 Dec. 31	Dividends	320	3 0 0 0	
	Cash	100		3 0 0 0
	Dividends were paid to stockholders.			

General Ledger

Dividends

(Dr.)	Acct. No. 320	(Cr.)
2012 Dec. 31 3,000		

Effects of Transaction

The Dividends account increases (debited); and an asset, cash, decreases (credited) by $3,000.

Cash

(Dr.)		Acct. No. 100		(Cr.)
2012		2012		
Dec. 1 Beg Bal. 50,000		Dec. 1 40,000		
Dec. 7 4,500		Dec. 1 2,400		
Dec. 15 5,000		Dec. 1 1,200		
Dec. 26 500		Dec. 17 1,400		
		Dec. 28 3,600		
		Dec. 29 150		
		Dec. 31 3,000		

Transaction 15 concludes the analysis of the MicroTrain Company transactions. The next section discusses and illustrates posting to ledger accounts and cross-indexing.

An Accounting Perspective

USES OF TECHNOLOGY The concept of the Internet dates to the 1960s when the military tied together several computers forming a 'network' that allowed users to communicate with each other instantaneously on their computers over many miles. Then universities and scientific institutions connected to the network to meet their research and communication needs. More and more organizations hooked up to the network over time. Today many companies seek customers and employees over the Internet. Students and faculty use the Internet to perform research, communicate with their colleagues (using e-mail), and search distant libraries. Accountants in practice are heavy users of the Internet to locate company data, tax regulations, and almost any other information they need. You will find that learning to use the Internet is essential to your future success, and using the Internet can be fun.

The Use of Ledger Accounts

Posting to Ledger Accounts

Objective 5
Post journal entries to the accounts in the ledger.

A journal entry is like a set of instructions. The carrying out of these instructions is known as posting. As stated earlier, posting is recording in the ledger accounts the information contained in the journal. A journal entry directs the entry of a certain dollar amount as a debit in a specific ledger account and directs the entry of a certain dollar amount as a credit in a specific ledger account. Earlier, we posted the journal entries for MicroTrain Company to T-accounts. In practice, however, companies post these journal entries to ledger accounts.

Using a new example, Jenks Company, we illustrate posting to ledger accounts. Later, we show you how to post the MicroTrain Company journal entries to ledger accounts.

In Illustration 2.6, the first journal entry for the Jenks Company directs that $10,000 be posted in the ledger as a debit to the Cash account and as a credit to the Capital Stock account. We post the debit in the general ledger Cash account by using the following procedure: Enter in the Cash account the date, a short explanation, the journal designation ("G" for general journal) and the journal page number from which the debit is posted, and the $10,000 in the Debit column. Then, enter the number of the account to which the debit is posted in the Posting Reference column of the general journal. Post the credit in a similar manner but as a credit to Account No. 300. The arrows in Illustration 2.6 show how these amounts were posted to the correct accounts.

Illustration 2.6 shows the ledger account. In contrast to the two-sided T- account format shown so far, the three-column format has columns for debit, credit, and balance. The three-column form has the advantage of showing the balance of the account after each item has been posted. In addition, in this chapter, we indicate whether each balance is a debit or a credit. In later chapters and in practice, the nature of the balance is usually not indicated since it is understood. Also, notice that we give an explanation for each item in the ledger accounts. Often accountants omit these explanations because each item can be traced back to the general journal for the explanation.

Posting is always from the journal to the ledger accounts. Postings can be made (1) at the time the transaction is journalized; (2) at the end of the day, week, or month; or (3) as each journal page is filled. The choice is a matter of personal taste. When posting the general journal, the date used in the ledger accounts is the date the transaction was recorded in the journal, not the date the journal entry was posted to the ledger accounts.

Cross-Indexing (Referencing)

Frequently, accountants must check and trace the origin of their transactions, so they provide cross-indexing. Cross-indexing is the placing of (1) the account number of the ledger account in the general journal and (2) the general journal page number in the ledger account. As shown in Illustration 2.6, the account number of the ledger account

Illustration 2.6   General Journal and General Ledger; Posting and Cross-Indexing

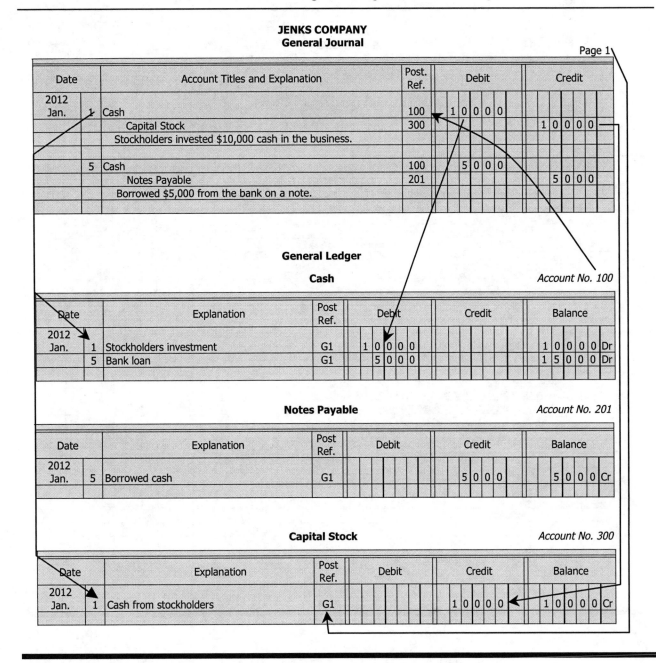

to which the posting was made is in the Posting Reference column of the general journal. Note the arrow from Account No. 100 in the ledger to the 100 in the Posting Reference column beside the first debit in the general journal. Accountants place the number of the general journal page from which the entry was posted in the Posting Reference column of the ledger account. Note the arrow from page 1 in the general journal to G1 in the Posting Reference column of the Cash account in the general ledger. The notation "G1" means general journal, page 1. The date of the transaction also appears in the general ledger. Note the arrows from the date in the general journal to the dates in the general ledger.

Cross-indexing aids the tracing of any recorded transaction, either from general journal to general ledger or from general ledger to general journal. Normally, they place cross-reference numbers in the Posting Reference column of the general journal when

Illustration 2.7   General Journal (after posting)

MICROTRAIN COMPANY
General Journal

Page 1

Date	Account Titles and Explanation	Post. Ref.	Debit	Credit
2012 Nov. 28	Cash	100*	5 0 0 0 0	
	Capital Stock	300		5 0 0 0 0
	Stockholders invested $50,000 cash in the business.			
Dec 1	Truck	150	4 0 0 0 0	
	Cash	100		4 0 0 0 0
	To record the purchase of four trucks.			
1	Prepaid Insurance	108	2 4 0 0	
	Cash	100		2 4 0 0
	Purchased truck insurance to cover a one-year period.			
1	Prepaid Rent	112	1 2 0 0	
	Cash	100		1 2 0 0
	Paid three months' rent on a building.			
4	Supplies on Hand	107	1 4 0 0	
	Accounts Payable	200		1 4 0 0
	To record the purchase of training supplies for future use.			
7	Cash	100	4 5 0 0	
	Unearned Service Fees	216		4 5 0 0
	To record the receipt of cash from a customer in payment for future training services.			
15	Cash	100	5 0 0 0	
	Service Revenue	400		5 0 0 0
	To record the receipt of cash for performing training services for a customer.			
17	Accounts Payable	200	1 4 0 0	
	Cash	100		1 4 0 0
	Paid the account payable arising from the purchase of supplies on December 4.			

* These postings references would be entered only after each amount has been posted.

the entry is posted. If this practice is followed, the cross-reference numbers indicate that the entry has been posted.

To understand the posting and cross-indexing process, trace the entries from the general journal to the general ledger. The ledger accounts need not contain explanations of all the entries, since any needed explanations can be obtained from the general journal.

Posting and Cross-Indexing—An Illustration

Look at Illustration 2.7 to see how all the November and December transactions of MicroTrain Company presented on pages 60–67 would be journalized. As shown in Illustration 2.7, you skip a line between journal entries to show where one journal entry ends and another begins. This procedure is standard practice among accountants. Note that no dollar signs appear in journals or ledgers. When amounts are in even dollar amounts, accountants leave the cents column blank or use zeros or a dash. When they

Illustration 2.7   (concluded)

General Journal

Page 2

Date		Account Titles and Explanation	Post. Ref.	Debit	Credit
2012 Dec.	20	Accounts Receivable	103	5 7 0 0	
		Service Revenue	400		5 7 0 0
		To record the performance of training services on account			
		for which a customer was billed.			
	24	Advertising Expense	505	5 0	
		Accounts Payable	200		5 0
		Received a bill for advertising for the month of December.			
	26	Cash	100	5 0 0	
		Accounts Receivable	103		5 0 0
		Received $500 from a customer on accounts receivable.			
	28	Salaries Expense	507	3 6 0 0	
		Cash	100		3 6 0 0
		Paid training personnel salaries for the first four weeks			
		of December.			
	29	Utilities Expense	511	1 5 0	
		Cash	100		1 5 0
		Paid the utilities bill for December.			
	30	Gas and Oil Expense	506	6 8 0	
		Accounts Payable	200		6 8 0
		Received a bill for gas and oil used in the trucks for			
		December.			
	31	Dividends	320	3 0 0 0	
		Cash	100		3 0 0 0
		Dividends were paid to stockholders.			

use lined accounting work papers, commas or decimal points are not needed to record an amount. When they use unlined paper, they add both commas and decimal points.

Next, observe Illustration 2.8, the three-column general ledger accounts of MicroTrain Company after the journal entries have been posted. Each ledger account would appear on a separate page in the ledger. Trace the postings from the general journal to the general ledger to make sure you know how to post journal entries.

All the journal entries illustrated so far have involved one debit and one credit; these journal entries are called **simple journal entries**. Many business transactions, however, affect more than two accounts. The journal entry for these transactions involves more than one debit and/or credit. Such journal entries are called **compound journal entries**.

Compound Journal Entries

As an illustration of a compound journal entry, assume that on January 2, 2013, MicroTrain Company purchased $8,000 of training equipment from Wilson Company.

Illustration 2.8   General Ledger – Extended Illustration

MICROTRAIN COMPANY
General Ledger
                                                                            Page 1

Cash   *Account No. 100*

Date		Explanation	Post Ref.	Debit	Credit	Balance
2012 Dec.	1	Beginning balance*				5 0 0 0 0 Dr
	1	Trucks	G1		4 0 0 0 0	1 0 0 0 0 Dr
	1	Prepaid insurance	G1		2 4 0 0	7 6 0 0 Dr
	1	Prepaid rent	G1		1 2 0 0	6 4 0 0 Dr
	7	Unearned service fees	G1	4 5 0 0		1 0 9 0 0 Dr
	15	Service revenue	G1	5 0 0 0		1 5 9 0 0 Dr
	17	Paid account payable	G1		1 4 0 0	1 4 5 0 0 Dr
	26	Collected account receivable	G2	5 0 0		1 5 0 0 0 Dr
	28	Salaries	G2		3 6 0 0	1 1 4 0 0 Dr
	29	Utilities	G2		1 5 0	1 1 2 5 0 Dr
	31	Dividends	G2		3 0 0 0	8 2 5 0 Dr

Accounts Receivable   *Account No. 103*

Date		Explanation	Post Ref.	Debit	Credit	Balance
2012 Dec.	20	Service revenue	G2	5 7 0 0		5 7 0 0 Dr
	26	Collections	G2		5 0 0	5 2 0 0 Dr

Prepaid Insurance   *Account No. 108*

Date		Explanation	Post Ref.	Debit	Credit	Balance
2012 Dec.	1	One-year policy on trucks	G1	2 4 0 0		2 4 0 0 Dr

Prepaid Insurance   *Account No. 108*

Date		Explanation	Post Ref.	Debit	Credit	Balance
2012 Dec.	1	One-year policy on trucks	G1	2 4 0 0		2 4 0 0 Dr

*Beginning balances result from carrying forward balances from a preceding page for this account. The Cash account, for example, is likely to use page after page over a period since so many transactions involve cash. This particular beginning balance came from the stockholders' investments in November. Often no explanation is included in the Explanation column since explanations may be found in the general journal or are not relevant.

Illustration 2.8   (continued)

General Ledger   Page 1

Prepaid Rent   *Account No. 112*

Date		Explanation	Post Ref.	Debit	Credit	Balance
2012 Dec.	1	Three-month payment	G1	1 2 0 0		1 2 0 0 Dr

Trucks   *Account No. 150*

Date		Explanation	Post Ref.	Debit	Credit	Balance
2012 Dec.	1	Paid cash	G1	4 0 0 0 0		4 0 0 0 0 Dr

Accounts Payable   *Account No. 200*

Date		Explanation	Post Ref.	Debit	Credit	Balance
2012 Dec.	4	Supplies	G1		1 4 0 0	1 4 0 0 Cr
	17	Paid for supplies	G1	1 4 0 0		- 0 -
	24	Advertising	G2		5 0	5 0 Cr
	30	Gas and oil	G2		6 8 0	7 3 0 Cr

Unearned Service Fees   *Account No. 216*

Date		Explanation	Post Ref.	Debit	Credit	Balance
2012 Dec.	7	Received cash	G1		4 5 0 0	4 5 0 0 Cr

Capital Stock   *Account No. 300*

Date		Explanation	Post Ref.	Debit	Credit	Balance
2012 Dec.	1	Beginning balance				5 0 0 0 0 Cr

Illustration 2.8   (continued)

General Ledger   Page 3

Dividends   *Account No. 320*

Date	Explanation	Post Ref.	Debit	Credit	Balance
2012 Dec. 31	Cash	G2	3 0 0 0		3 0 0 0 Dr

Service Revenue   *Account No. 400*

Date	Explanation	Post Ref.	Debit	Credit	Balance
2012 Dec. 15	Cash	G1		5 0 0 0	5 0 0 0 Cr
20	On account	G2		5 7 0 0	1 0 7 0 0 Cr

Advertising Expense   *Account No. 505*

Date	Explanation	Post Ref.	Debit	Credit	Balance
2012 Dec. 24	On account	G2	5 0		5 0 Dr

Gas and Oil Expense   *Account No. 506*

Date	Explanation	Post Ref.	Debit	Credit	Balance
2012 Dec. 30	On account	G2	6 8 0		6 8 0 Dr

Salaries Expense   *Account No. 507*

Date	Explanation	Post Ref.	Debit	Credit	Balance
2012 Dec. 28	Cash paid	G2	3 6 0 0		3 6 0 0 Dr

Utilities Expense   *Account No. 511*

Date	Explanation	Post Ref.	Debit	Credit	Balance
2012 Dec. 29	Cash paid	G2	1 5 0		1 5 0 Dr

Illustration 2.9   Trial Balance

MICROTRAIN COMPANY
Trial Balance
December 31, 2012

Acct. No.	Account Title	Debits	Credits
100	Cash	$ 8,250	
103	Accounts Receivable	5,200	
107	Supplies on Hand	1,400	
108	Prepaid Insurance	2,400	
112	Prepaid Rent	1,200	
150	Trucks	40,000	
200	Accounts Payable		$ 730
216	Unearned Service Fees		4,500
300	Capital Stock		50,000
320	Dividends	3,000	
400	Service Revenue		10,700
505	Advertising Expense	50	
506	Gas and Oil Expense	680	
507	Salaries Expense	3,600	
511	Utilities Expense	150	
		$65,930	$65,930

MicroTrain paid $2,000 cash with the balance due on March 3, 2013. The general journal entry for MicroTrain Company is:

			Debit	Credit
2013				
Jan.	2	Equipment	8,000	
		Cash		2,000
		Accounts Payable		6,000
		Training equipment purchased from Wilson Company.		

Note that the firm credits two accounts, Cash and Accounts Payable, in this one entry. However, the dollar totals of the debits and credits are equal.

The Trial Balance

Objective 6
Prepare a trial balance to test the equality of debits and credits in the journalizing and posting process.

Periodically, accountants use a *trial balance* to test the equality of their debits and credits. A **trial balance** is a listing of the ledger accounts and their debit or credit balances to determine that debits equal credits in the recording process. The accounts appear in this order: assets, liabilities, stockholders' equity, dividends, revenues, and expenses. Within the assets category, the most liquid (closest to becoming cash) asset appears first and the least liquid appears last. Within the liabilities, those liabilities with the shortest maturities appear first. Study Illustration 2.9, the trial balance for MicroTrain Company. Note the listing of the account numbers and account titles on the left, the column for debit balances, the column for credit balances, and the equality of the two totals.

When the trial balance does not balance, try retotaling the two columns. If this step does not locate the error, divide the difference in the totals by 2 and then by 9. If the difference is divisible by 2, you may have transferred a debit-balanced account to the trial balance as a credit, or a credit-balanced account as a debit. When the difference is divisible by 2, look for an amount in the trial balance that is equal to one-half of the difference. Thus, if the difference is $800, look for an account with a balance of $400 and see if it is in the wrong column.

If the difference is divisible by 9, you may have made a transposition error in transferring a balance to the trial balance or a slide error. A transposition error occurs when two digits are reversed in an amount (e.g., writing 753 as 573 or 110 as 101). A

An Ethical Perspective

Financial Deals, Inc.

Larry Fisher was captain of the football team at Prestige University. Later, he earned a master's degree in business administration with a concentration in accounting.

Upon graduation, Larry accepted a position with Financial Deals, Inc., in the accounting and finance division. At first, things were going smoothly. He was tall, good looking, and had an outgoing personality. The president of the company took a liking to him. However, Larry was somewhat bothered when the president started asking him to do some things that were slightly unethical. When he protested mildly, the president said, 'Come on, son, this is the way the business world works. You have great potential if you don't let things like this get in your way.'

As time went on, Larry was asked to do things that were more unethical, and finally he was performing illegal acts. When he resisted, the president appealed to his loyalty and asked him to be a team player. The president also promised Larry great wealth sometime in the future. Finally, when he was told to falsify some financial statements by making improper entries and to sign some documents containing material errors, the president supported his request by stating, 'You are in too deep now to refuse to cooperate. If I go down, you are going with me.' Through various company schemes, Larry had convinced some friends and relatives to invest about $10 million. Most of this would be lost if the various company schemes were revealed.

Larry could not sleep at night and began each day with a pain in his stomach and by becoming physically ill. He was under great strain and believed that he could lose his mind. He also heard that the president had a shady past and could become violent in retaliating against his enemies. If Larry blows the whistle, he believes he will go to prison for his part in the schemes. (Note: This scenario is based on an actual situation with some facts changed to protect the guilty.)

slide error occurs when you place a decimal point incorrectly (e.g., $1,500 recorded as $15.00). Thus, when a difference is divisible by 9, compare the trial balance amounts with the general ledger account balances to see if you made a transposition or slide error in transferring the amounts.

If you still cannot find the error, it may be due to one of the following causes:

Reinforcing Problems
E2-7 Prepare a trial balance.
E2-8 Prepare journal entries.
E2-9 Post journal entries in E2-8 to T-accounts.
E2-10 Prepare a trial balance using accounts in E2-9.
E2-11 Determine trial balance errors.

1. Failing to post part of a journal entry.
2. Posting a debit as a credit, or vice versa.
3. Incorrectly determining the balance of an account.
4. Recording the balance of an account incorrectly in the trial balance.
5. Omitting an account from the trial balance.
6. Making a transposition or slide error in the accounts or the journal.

Usually, you should work backward through the steps taken to prepare the trial balance. Assuming you have already retotaled the columns and traced the amounts appearing in the trial balance back to the general ledger account balances, use the following steps: Verify the balance of each general ledger account, verify postings to the general ledger, verify general journal entries, and then review the transactions and possibly the source documents.

The equality of the two totals in the trial balance does not necessarily mean that the accounting process has been error-free. Serious errors may have been made, such as failure to record a transaction, or posting a debit or credit to the wrong account. For instance, if a transaction involving payment of a $100 account payable is never recorded, the trial balance totals still balance, but at an amount that is $100 too high. Both cash and accounts payable would be overstated by $100.

Reinforcing Problem
P2-4A Prepare journal entries, post to ledger accounts, and prepare a trial balance.

You can prepare a trial balance at any time—at the end of a day, a week, a month, a quarter, or a year. Typically, you would prepare a trial balance before preparing the financial statements.

USES OF TECHNOLOGY The computers of persons in a given department or building are frequently connected in a Local Area Network (LAN). These persons can then access simultaneously the programs and databases stored in the LAN and can communicate with all other persons in the LAN through electronic mail. A more advanced type of computer network is called Client/Server Computing. Under this structure, any computer in the network can be used to update the information stored elsewhere in the network. For example, accounting information stored in one computer could be updated by authorized persons from a number of other computers in the system. The use of networks is designed to improve efficiency and to reduce software and hardware costs.

An Accounting Perspective

Analyzing and Using the Financial Results— Horizontal and Vertical Analyses

The calculation of dollar and/or percentage changes from one year to the next in an item on financial statements is **horizontal analysis**. For instance, in the following data taken from the 2010 annual report of Hewlett-Packard Company, the amount of inventory increased by $338 million from October 31, 2009, to October 31, 2010. This amount represented a 6% increase. To find the amount of the increase or decrease, subtract the 2009 amount from the 2010 amount. To find the percentage change, divide the increase or decrease by the 2009 amount.

Objective 7
Analyze and use the financial results - horizontal and vertical analyses.

Knowing the dollar amount and percentage of change in an amount is much more meaningful than merely knowing the amount at one point in time. By analyzing the data, we can see that cash and cash equivalents declined in 2010. Their decline at least partially explains the increases in some of the other current assets. We can also see that the company invested in property, plant and equipment. Any terms in Hewlett-Packard's list of assets that you do not understand are explained in later chapters. At this point, all we want you to understand is the nature of horizontal and vertical analyses.

Vertical analysis shows the percentage that each item in a financial statement is of some significant total such as total assets or sales. For instance, in the Hewlett-Packard data we can see that cash and cash equivalents were 11.6% of total assets as of October 31, 2009, and had declined to 8.8% of total assets by October 31, 2010. Total current assets (cash plus other amounts that will become cash or be used up within one year) increased from 45.8% of total assets to 43.5% during 2010. Long-term investments and other non-current assets accounted for 9.8% of total assets as of October 31, 2010.

	2010	2009	Increase or (Decrease) 2010 over 2009 Dollars	Percent	Percent of Total Assets October 31 2010	2009
Assets (in millions)						
Current assets:						
Cash and cash equivalents	$10,929	$13,279	$ (2,350)	−18%	8.8%	11.6%
Short-term investments	5	55	(50)	91%	0.0%	0.1%
Accounts receivable	21,467	19,212	2,255	12%	17.2%	16.7%
Inventory	6,466	6,128	338	6%	5.2%	5.3%
Other current assets	15,317	13,865	1,452	10%	12.3%	12.1%
Total cuurent assets	$ 54,184	$ 52,539	$ 1,645	3%	43.5%	45.8%
Property, plant and equipment:						
Property, plant and equipment, net	58,094	50,971	7,123	14%	46.7%	44.4%
Long-term investments and						
other non-current assets	12,225	11,289	936	8%	9.8%	9.8%
Total assets	$124,503	$114,799	$ 9,704	8%	100.0%	100.0%

Hewlett-Packard Company
Hewlett-Packard Company designs, manufactures, and services products and systems for measurement, computation and communications.

Reinforcing Problem
E2-12 Perform horizontal and vertical analyses on Wal-Mart Stores, Inc., assets and comment.

Management performs horizontal and vertical analyses along with other forms of analysis to help evaluate the wisdom of its past decisions and to plan for the future. Other data would have to be examined before decisions could be made regarding the assets shown. For instance, if you discovered the liabilities that would have to be paid within a short time by Hewlett-Packard were more than $30 billion, you might conclude that the company is short of cash even though current assets increased substantially during 2010. We illustrate horizontal and vertical analyses to a much greater extent later in the text.

An Accounting Perspective	**BUSINESS INSIGHT** Many companies have been restructuring their organizations and reducing the number of employees to cut expenses. General Motors, AT&T, IBM, and numerous other companies have taken this action. One could question whether companies place as much value on their employees as in the past. In previous years it was common to see the following statement in the annual reports of companies: 'Our employees are our most valuable asset.' Companies are not permitted to show employees as assets on their balance sheets. Do you think they should be allowed to do so?

What you have learned in this chapter is basic to your study of accounting. The entire process of accounting is based on the double-entry concept. Chapter 3 explains that adjustments bring the accounts to their proper balances before accurate financial statements are prepared.

Understanding the Learning Objectives

Objective 1
Use the account as the basic classifying and storage unit for accounting information.

- An account is a storage unit used to classify and summarize money measurements of business activities of a similar nature.
- A firm sets up an account whenever it needs to provide useful information about a particular business item to some party having a valid interest in the business.

Objective 2
Express the effects of business transactions in terms of debits and credits to different types of accounts.

- A T-account resembles the letter T.
- Debits are entries on the left side of a T-account.
- Credits are entries on the right side of a T-account.
- Debits increase asset, expense, and Dividends accounts.
- Credits increase liability, stockholders' equity, and revenue accounts.

Objective 3
List the steps in the accounting cycle.

- Analyze transactions by examining source documents.
- Journalize transactions in the journal.
- Post journal entries to the accounts in the ledger.
- Prepare a trial balance of the accounts and complete the work sheet.
- Prepare financial statements.
- Journalize and post adjusting entries.
- Journalize and post closing entries.
- Prepare a post-closing trial balance.
- A journal contains a chronological record of the transactions of a business.
- An example of a general journal is shown in Illustration 2.7.

Objective 4
Record the effects of business transactions in a journal.

- Journalizing is the process of entering a transaction in a journal.

- Posting is the process of transferring information recorded in the journal to the proper places in the ledger.
- Cross-indexing is the placing of (1) the account number of the ledger account in the general journal and (2) the general journal page number in the ledger account.
- An example of cross-indexing appears in Illustration 2.6.
- A trial balance is a listing of the ledger accounts and their debit or credit balances.
- If the trial balance does not balance, an accountant works backward to discover the error.
- A trial balance is shown in Illustration 2.9.

- Horizontal analysis involves calculating the dollar and/or percentage changes in an item from one year to the next.
- Vertical analysis shows the percentage that each item in a financial statement is of some significant total.

Objective 5
Post journal entries to the accounts in the ledger.

Objective 6
Prepare a trial balance to test the equality of debits and credits in the journalizing and posting process.

Objective 7
Analyze and use the financial results - horizontal and vertical analyses.

Demonstration Problem

Green Hills Riding Stable, Incorporated, had the following balance sheet on June 30, 2012:

GREEN HILLS RIDING STABLE, INCORPORATED
Balance Sheet
June 30, 2012

Assets

Cash		$ 7,500
Accounts receivable		5,400
Land		40,000
Total assets		$ 52,900

Liabilities and Stockholders' Equity

Liabilities:		
Accounts payable		$ 800
Notes payable		40,000
Total liabilities		$ 40,800
Stockholders' equity:		
Capital stock	$ 10,000	
Retained earnings	2,100	
Total stockholders' equity		12,100
Total liabilities and stockholders' equity		$52,900

Transactions for July 2012 were as follows:

July	1	Additional shares of capital stock were issued for $25,000 cash.
	1	Paid for a prefabricated building constructed on the land at a cost of $24,000.
	8	Paid the accounts payable of $800.
	10	Collected the accounts receivable of $5,400.
	12	Horse feed to be used in July was purchased on credit for $1,100.
	15	Boarding fees for July were charged to customers in the amount of $4,500. (This amount is due on August 10.)
	24	Miscellaneous expenses of $800 for July were paid.
	31	Paid interest expense on the notes payable of $200.
	31	Salaries of $1,400 for the month were paid.
	31	Riding and lesson fees for July were billed to customers in the amount of $3,600. (They are due on August 10.)
	31	Paid a $1,000 dividend to the stockholders.

a. Prepare the journal entries to record the transactions for July 2012.

Required ➲

b. Post the journal entries to the ledger accounts after entering the beginning balances in those accounts. Insert cross-indexing references in the journal and ledger. Use the following chart of accounts:

100	Cash	320	Dividends
103	Accounts Receivable	402	Horse Boarding Fees Revenue
130	Land	404	Riding and Lesson Fees Revenue
140	Buildings	507	Salaries Expense
200	Accounts Payable	513	Feed Expense
201	Notes Payable	540	Interest Expense
300	Capital Stock	568	Miscellaneous Expense
310	Retained Earnings		

c. Prepare a trial balance.

Solution to Demonstration Problem

a.

GREEN HILLS RIDING STABLE, INCORPORATED
General Journal

Page 1

Date		Account Titles and Explanation	Post. Ref.	Debit	Credit
2012 July	1	Cash	100	2 5 0 0 0	
		Capital Stock	300		2 5 0 0 0
		Additional capital stock issued.			
	1	Buildings	140	2 4 0 0 0	
		Cash	100		2 4 0 0 0
		Paid for building.			
	8	Account Payable	200	8 0 0	
		Cash	100		8 0 0
		Paid accounts payable.			
	10	Cash	100	5 4 0 0	
		Accounts Receivable	103		5 4 0 0
		Collected accounts receivable.			
	12	Feed Expense	513	1 1 0 0	
		Accounts Payable	200		1 1 0 0
		Purchased feed on account			
	15	Accounts Receivable	103	4 5 0 0	
		Horse Boarding Fee Revenue	402		4 5 0 0
		Billed boarding fees for July.			
	24	Miscellaneous Expense	568	8 0 0	
		Cash	100		8 0 0
		Paid miscellaneous expenses for July.			
	31	Interest Expense	540	2 0 0	
		Cash	100		2 0 0
		Paid interest			
	31	Salaries Expense	507	1 4 0 0	
		Cash	100		1 4 0 0
		Paid salaries for July.			
	31	Accounts Receivable	103	3 6 0 0	
		Riding and Lesson Fee Revenue	404		3 6 0 0
		Billed riding and lesson fees for July.			
	31	Dividends	320	1 0 0 0	
		Cash	100		1 0 0 0
		Paid a dividend to stockholders.			

b.

GREEN HILLS RIDING STABLE, INCORPORATED
General Ledger

Page 1

Land

Account No. 100

Date		Explanation	Post Ref.	Debit	Credit	Balance
2012 June	30	Balance				7 5 0 0 0 Dr
July	1	Stockholders' investment	G1	2 5 0 0 0		3 2 5 0 0 Dr
	1	Buildings	G1		2 4 0 0 0	8 5 0 0 Dr
	8	Accounts payable	G1		8 0 0	7 7 0 0 Dr
	10	Accounts receivable	G1	5 4 0 0		1 3 1 0 0 Dr
	24	Miscellaneous expense	G1		8 0 0	1 2 3 0 0 Dr
	31	Interest expense	G1		2 0 0	1 2 1 0 0 Dr
	31	Salaries expense	G1		1 4 0 0	1 0 7 0 0 Dr
	31	Dividends	G1		1 0 0 0	9 7 0 0 Dr

Accounts Receivable

Account No. 103

Date		Explanation	Post Ref.	Debit	Credit	Balance
2012 June	30	Balance				5 4 0 0 Dr
July	10	Cash	G1		5 4 0 0	- 0 -
	15	Horse boarding fees	G1	4 5 0 0		4 5 0 0 Dr
	31	Riding and lessons fees	G1	3 6 0 0		8 1 0 0 Dr

Land

Account No. 130

Date		Explanation	Post Ref.	Debit	Credit	Balance
2012 June	30	Balance				4 0 0 0 0 Dr

Buildings

Account No. 140

Date		Explanation	Post Ref.	Debit	Credit	Balance
2012 July	1	Cash	G1	2 4 0 0 0		2 4 0 0 0 Dr

Accounts Payable

Account No. 200

Date		Explanation	Post Ref.	Debit	Credit	Balance
2012 June	30	Balance				8 0 0 Cr
July	8	Cash	G1	8 0 0		- 0 -
	12	Feed expense	G1		1 1 0 0	1 1 0 0 Cr

General Ledger (continued)

Notes Payable

Account No. 201

Date		Explanation	Post Ref.	Debit	Credit	Balance
2012 June	30	Balance				4 0 0 0 0 Cr

Capital Stock

Account No. 300

Date		Explanation	Post Ref.	Debit	Credit	Balance
2012 June	30	Balance				1 0 0 0 0 Cr
July	1	Cash	G1		2 5 0 0 0	3 5 0 0 0 Cr

Retained Earnings

Account No. 310

Date		Explanation	Post Ref.	Debit	Credit	Balance
2012 June	30	Balance				2 1 0 0 Cr

Dividends

Account No. 320

Date		Explanation	Post Ref.	Debit	Credit	Balance
2012 July	31	Cash	G1	1 0 0 0		1 0 0 0 Dr

Horse Boarding Fee Revenue

Account No. 402

Date		Explanation	Post Ref.	Debit	Credit	Balance
2012 July	15	Accounts receivable	G1		4 5 0 0	4 5 0 0 Cr

Riding and Lesson Fee Revenue

Account No. 404

Date		Explanation	Post Ref.	Debit	Credit	Balance
2012 July	31	Accounts receivable	G1		3 6 0 0	3 6 0 0 Cr

General Ledger (concluded)

Salaries Expense

Account No. 507

Date		Explanation	Post Ref.	Debit	Credit	Balance
2012 July	31	Cash	G1	1 4 0 0		1 4 0 0 Dr

Feed Expense

Account No. 513

Date		Explanation	Post Ref.	Debit	Credit	Balance
2012 July	12	Accounts payable	G1	1 1 0 0		1 1 0 0 Dr

Interest Expense

Account No. 540

Date		Explanation	Post Ref.	Debit	Credit	Balance
2012 July	31	Cash	G1	2 0 0		2 0 0 Dr

Miscellaneous Expense

Account No. 568

Date		Explanation	Post Ref.	Debit	Credit	Balance
2012 July	24	Cash	G1	8 0 0		8 0 0 Dr

c.

GREEN HILLS RIDING STABLE, INCORPORATED
Trial Balance
July 31, 2012

Acct. No.	Account Title	Debits	Credits
100	Cash	$ 9,700	
103	Accounts Receivable	8,100	
130	Land	40,000	
140	Buildings	24,000	
200	Accounts Payable		$ 1,100
201	Notes Payable		40,000
300	Capital Stock		35,000
310	Retained Earnings		2,100
320	Dividends	1,000	
402	Horse Boarding Fee Revenue		4,500
404	Riding and Lesson Fee Revenue		3,600
507	Salaries Expense	1,400	
513	Feed Expense	1,100	
540	Interest Expense	200	
568	Miscellaneous Expense	800	
		$86,300	$86,300

New Terms

Account   A part of the accounting system used to classify and summarize the increases, decreases, and balances of each asset, liability, stockholders' equity item, dividend, revenue, and expense. The three-column account is normally used. It contains columns for debit, credit, and balance. *50*

Accounting cycle   A series of steps performed during the accounting period (some throughout the period and some at the end) to analyze, record, classify, summarize, and report useful financial information for the purpose of preparing financial statements. *55*

Accrual basis of accounting   Recognizes revenues when sales are made or services are performed, regardless of when cash is received. Recognizes expenses as incurred, whether or not cash has been paid out. *60*

Business transactions   Measurable events that affect the financial condition of a business. *55*

Chart of accounts   The complete listing of the account titles and account numbers of all of the accounts in the ledger; somewhat comparable to a table of contents. *59*

Compound journal entry   A journal entry with more than one debit and/or credit. *71*

Credit   The right side of any account; when used as a verb, to enter a dollar amount on the right side of an account; credits increase liability, stockholders' equity, and revenue accounts and decrease asset, expense, and Dividends accounts. *51*

Credit balance   The balance in an account when the sum of the credits to the account exceeds the sum of the debits to that account. *54*

Cross-indexing   The placing of (1) the account number of the ledger account in the general journal and (2) the general journal page number in the ledger account. *68*

Debit   The left side of any account; when used as a verb, to enter a dollar amount on the left side of an account; debits increase asset, expense, and Dividends accounts and decrease liability, stockholders' equity, and revenue accounts. *51*

Debit balance   The balance in an account when the sum of the debits to the account exceeds the sum of the credits to that account. *53*

Double-entry procedure   The accounting requirement that each transaction must be recorded by an entry that has equal debits and credits. *51*

Horizontal analysis   The calculation of dollar and/or percentage changes in an item on the financial statements from one year to the next. *77*

Journal   A chronological (arranged in order of time) record of business transactions; the simplest form of journal is the two-column general journal. *56*

Journal entry   Shows all of the effects of a business transaction as expressed in debit(s) and credit(s) and may include an explanation of the transaction. *56*

Journalizing   A step in the accounting recording process that consists of entering the effects of a transaction in a journal. *60*

Ledger   The complete collection of all of the accounts of a company; often referred to as the *general ledger*. *58*

Nominal accounts   See temporary accounts.

Note   An unconditional written promise to pay to another party the amount owed either when demanded or at a certain specified date. *52*

Permanent accounts (real accounts)   Balance sheet accounts; their balances are not transferred (or closed) to any other account at the end of the accounting period. *58*

Posting   Recording in the ledger accounts the information contained in the journal. *60, 68*

Real accounts   See *permanent accounts.*

Simple journal entry   An entry with one debit and one credit. *71*

T-account   An account resembling the letter T, which is used for illustrative purposes only. Debits are entered on the left side of the account, and credits are entered on the right side of the account. *50*

Temporary accounts (nominal accounts)   They temporarily contain the revenue, expense, and dividend information that is transferred (or closed) to a stockholders' equity account (Retained Earnings) at the end of the accounting period. *59*

Trial balance   A listing of the ledger accounts and their debit or credit balances to determine that debits equal credits in the recording process. *75*

Vertical analysis   Shows the percentage that each item in a financial statement is of some significant total such as total assets or sales. *77*

Self-Test

True-False

Indicate whether each of the following statements is true or false.

1. All of the steps in the accounting cycle are performed only at the end of the accounting period.
2. A transaction must be journalized in the journal before it can be posted to the ledger accounts.
3. The left side of any account is the credit side.
4. Revenues, liabilities, and Capital Stock accounts are increased by debits.
5. The Dividends account is increased by debits.
6. If the trial balance has equal debit and credit totals, it cannot contain any errors.

Multiple-Choice

Select the best answer for each of the following questions.

1. When the stockholders invest cash in the business:
   a. Capital Stock is debited and Cash is credited.
   b. Cash is debited and Dividends is credited.
   c. Cash is debited and Capital Stock is credited.
   d. None of the above.
2. Assume that cash is paid for insurance to cover a three-year period. The recommended debit and credit are:
   a. Debit Insurance Expense, credit Cash.
   b. Debit Prepaid Insurance, credit Cash.
   c. Debit Cash, credit Insurance Expense.
   d. Debit Cash, credit Prepaid Insurance.
3. A company received cash from a customer in payment for future delivery services. The correct debit and credit are:
   a. Debit Cash, credit Unearned Delivery Fees.
   b. Debit Cash, credit Delivery Fee Revenue.
   c. Debit Accounts Receivable, credit Delivery Fee Revenue.
   d. None of the above.
4. A company performed delivery services for a customer for cash. The correct debit and credit are:
   a. Debit Cash, credit Unearned Delivery Fees.
   b. Debit Cash, credit Delivery Fee Revenue.
   c. Debit Accounts Receivable, credit Delivery Fee Revenue.
   d. None of the above.
5. A cash dividend of $500 was declared and paid to stockholders. The correct journal entry is:

   a. Capital Stock   500
   　　　Cash   500
   b. Cash   500
   　　　Dividends   500
   c. Dividends   500
   　　　Cash   500
   d. Cash   500
   　　　Capital Stock   500

Now turn to page 96 to check your answers.

Questions

1. Describe the steps in recording and posting the effects of a business transaction.
2. Give some examples of source documents.
3. Define an account. What are the two basic forms (styles) of accounts illustrated in the chapter?
4. What is meant by the term *double-entry procedure,* or duality?
5. Describe how you would determine the balance of a T-account.
6. Define debit and credit. Name the types of accounts that are:
   a. Increased by a debit.
   b. Decreased by a debit.
   c. Increased by a credit.
   d. Decreased by a credit.
   Do you think this system makes sense? Can you conceive of other possible methods for recording changes in accounts?
7. Which of the steps in the accounting cycle are performed throughout the accounting period?
8. Which of the steps in the accounting cycle are performed only at the end of the accounting period?
9. Why are expense and revenue accounts used when all revenues and expenses could be shown directly in the Retained Earnings account?

10. What is the purpose of the Dividends account and how is it increased?

11. Are the following possibilities conceivable in an entry involving only one debit and one credit? Why?
    a. Increase a liability and increase an expense.
    b. Increase an asset and decrease a liability.
    c. Increase a revenue and decrease an expense.
    d. Decrease an asset and increase another asset.
    e. Decrease an asset and increase a liability.
    f. Decrease a revenue and decrease an asset.
    g. Decrease a liability and increase a revenue.

12. Describe the nature and purposes of the general journal. What does journalizing mean? Give an example of a compound entry in the general journal.

13. Describe a ledger and a chart of accounts. How do these two compare with a book and its table of contents?

14. Describe the act of posting. What difficulties could arise if no cross-indexing existed between the general journal and the ledger accounts?

15. Which of the following cash payments would involve the immediate recording of an expense? Why?
    a. Paid vendors for office supplies previously purchased on account.
    b. Paid an automobile dealer for a new company auto.

    c. Paid the current month's rent.
    d. Paid salaries for the last half of the current month.

16. What types of accounts appear in the unadjusted trial balance? What are the purposes of this trial balance?

17. You have found that the total of the Debits column of the trial balance of Burns Company is $200,000, while the total of the Credits column is $180,000. What are some possible causes of this difference? If the difference between the columns is divisible by 9, what types of errors are possible?

18. Store equipment was purchased for $2,000. Instead of debiting the Store Equipment account, the debit was made to Delivery Equipment. Of what help will the trial balance be in locating this error? Why?

19. A student remembered that the side toward the window in the classroom was the debit side of an account. The student took an examination in a room where the windows were on the other side of the room and became confused and consistently reversed debits and credits. Would the student's trial balance have equal debit and credit totals? If there were no existing balances in any of the accounts to begin with, would the error prevent the student from preparing correct financial statements? Why?

Exercises

Exercise 2-1
Indicate rules of debit and credit (L.O. 1, 2)

A diagram of the various types of accounts follows. Show where pluses (+) or minuses (−) should be inserted to indicate the effect debits and credits have on each account.

Asset Accounts		= Liability Accounts		+	Stockholders' Equity Accounts	
Debit	Credit	Debit	Credit		Debit	Credit

		Expense Accounts and Dividends Account		Revenue Accounts	
		Debit*	Credit	Debit	Credit*

Exercise 2-2
Prepare journal entries (L.O. 4)

Prepare the journal entry required for each of the following transactions:

a. Cash was received for services performed for customers, $1,200.
b. Services were performed for customers on account, $4,200.

Exercise 2-3
Prepare journal entries (L.O. 4)

Prepare the journal entry required for each of the following transactions:

a. Capital stock was issued for $100,000.
b. Purchased machinery for cash, $30,000.

Prepare the journal entry required for each of the following transactions:

a. Capital stock was issued for $200,000 cash.
b. A $30,000 loan was arranged with a bank. The bank increased the company's checking account by $30,000 after management of the company signed a written promise to return the $30,000 in 30 days.
c. Cash was received for services performed for customers, $700.
d. Services were performed for customers on account, $1,200.

Exercise 2-4
Prepare journal
entries (L.O. 4)

For each of the following unrelated transactions, give the journal entry to record the transaction. Then show how the journal entry would be posted to T-accounts. You need not include explanations or account numbers.

a. Capital stock was issued for $100,000 cash.
b. Salaries for a period were paid to employees, $24,000.
c. Services were performed for customers on account, $40,000.

Exercise 2-5
Show entries using
journal entries
and T-accounts
(L.O. 4, 5)

Explain each of the sets of debits and credits in these accounts for Tuxedos, Inc., a company that rents wedding clothing and accessories. There are 10 transactions to be explained. Each set is designated by the small letters to the left of the amount. For example, the first transaction is the issuance of capital stock for cash and is denoted by the letter (*a*).

Exercise 2-6
Explain sets of debits
and credits
(L.O. 1-5)

Cash				Dividends	
(a)	200,000	(b)	150,000	(e)	1,000
(d)	1,800	(e)	1,000		
		(f)	600		
		(g)	2,000		
		(i)	30,000		
Bal.	18,200				

Accounts Receivable				Service Revenue	
(c)	1,800	(d)	1,800	(c)	1,800
(j)	12,000			(j)	12,000
Bal.	12,000			Bal.	13,800

Supplies on Hand		Rent Expense	
(b)	150,000	(f)	600
(i)	30,000		
Bal.	180,000		

Accounts Payable		Delivery Expense	
	(h) 800	(h)	800

Capital Stock		Salaries Expense	
	(a) 200,000	(g)	2,000

Assume the ledger accounts given in Exercise 2–6 are those of Tuxedos, Inc., as they appear at December 31, 2012. Prepare the trial balance as of that date.

Exercise 2-7
Prepare trial balance
(L.O. 6)

Exercise 2-8
Prepare journal
entries(L.O. 4)

Prepare journal entries to record each of the following transactions for Sanchez Company. Use the letter of the transaction in place of the date. Include an explanation for each entry.

    a. Capital stock was issued for cash, $300,000.
    b. Purchased trucks by signing a note bearing no interest, $210,000.
    c. Earned service revenue on account, $4,800.
    d. Collected the account receivable resulting from transaction (c), $4,800.
    e. Paid the note payable for the trucks purchased, $210,000.
    f. Paid utilities for the month in the amount of $1,800.
    g. Paid salaries for the month in the amount of $7,500.
    h. Incurred supplies expenses on account in the amount of $1,920.
    i. Purchased another truck for cash, $48,000.
    j. Performed delivery services on account, $24,000.

Exercise 2-9
Post journal entries to
T-accounts(L.O. 5)

Using the data in Exercise 2–8, post the entries to T-accounts. Write the letter of the transaction in the account before the dollar amount. Determine a balance for each account.

Exercise 2-10
Prepare trial balance
(L.O. 6)

Using your answer for Exercise 2–9, prepare a trial balance. Assume the date of the trial balance is March 31, 2012.

Exercise 2-11
Determine trial balance
errors(L.O. 6)

John Adams owns and manages a bowling center called Strike Lanes. He also maintains his own accounting records and was about to prepare financial statements for the year 2012. When he prepared the trial balance from the ledger accounts, the total of the debits column was $435,000, and the total of the credits column was $425,000. What are the possible reasons why the totals of the debits and credits are out of balance? How would you normally proceed to find an error if the two trial balance columns do not agree?

Exercise 2-12
Perform horizontal and
vertical analysis and
comment on Wal-Mart's
current assets (L.O. 7)

Refer to the Consolidated Balance Sheets of Wal-Mart Stores, Inc., in the Annual Report Appendix located in the back of this text. Perform both horizontal and vertical analysis on each of Wal-Mart's current asset accounts, treating total current assets as a significant total for vertical analysis. Comment on the results.

Note: While you can certainly do this exercise with a calculator, computer spreadsheets such as Excel are ideal for this type of analysis.

Problems

Problem 2-1
Prepare journal entries
(L.O.4)

The transactions of Lightning Package Delivery Company for March 2012 follow:

Mar.
    1 The company was organized and issued capital stock for $300,000 cash.
    2 Paid $6,000 as the rent for March on a completely furnished building.
    5 Paid cash for delivery trucks, $180,000.
    6 Paid $4,000 as the rent for March on two forklift trucks.
    9 Paid $2,200 for supplies received and used in March.
    12 Performed delivery services for customers who promised to pay $27,000 at a later date.
    20 Collected cash of $4,500 from customers on account (see March 12 entry).
    21 Received a bill for $1,200 for advertising in the local newspaper in March.
    27 Paid cash for gas and oil consumed in March, $450.
    31 Paid $2,400 salaries to employees for March.
    31 Received an order for services at $12,000. The services will be performed in April.
    31 Paid cash dividend, $1,000.

Required

Prepare the journal entries required to record these transactions in the general journal of the company.

Economy Laundry Company had the following transactions in August 2012:

Problem 2-2
Record transactions in
journal, post to
T-accounts,
and prepare trial
balance
(L.O. 4-6)

Aug. 1 Issued capital stock for cash, $150,000.
3 Borrowed $40,000 from the bank on a note.
4 Purchased cleaning equipment for $25,000 cash.
6 Performed services for customers who promised to pay later, $16,000.
7 Paid this month's rent on a building, $2,800.
10 Collections were made for the services performed on August 6, $3,200.
14 Supplies were purchased on account for use this month, $3,000.
17 A bill for $400 was received for utilities for this month.
25 Laundry services were performed for customers who paid immediately, $22,000.
31 Paid employee salaries, $6,000.
31 Paid cash dividend, $2,000.

a. Prepare journal entries for these transactions.

➤ *Required*

b. Post the journal entries to T-accounts. Enter the account number in the Posting Reference column of the journal as you post each amount. Use the following account numbers:

Acct. No.	Account Title
100	Cash
103	Accounts Receivable
170	Equipment
200	Accounts Payable
201	Notes Payable
300	Capital Stock
320	Dividends
400	Service Revenue
507	Salaries Expense
511	Utilities Expense
515	Rent Expense
518	Supplies Expense

c. Prepare a trial balance as of August 31, 2012.

Clean-Sweep Janitorial, Inc., a company providing janitorial services, was organized July 1, 2012. The following account numbers and titles constitute the chart of accounts for the company:

Problem 2-3
Prepare ledger
accounts, journalize
transactions,
post to ledger
accounts, and prepare
trial balance (L.O. 4-6)

Acct. No.	Account Title
100	Cash
103	Accounts Receivable
150	Trucks
160	Office Equipment
170	Equipment
200	Accounts Payable
201	Notes Payable
300	Capital Stock
310	Retained Earnings
320	Dividends
400	Service Revenue
506	Gas and Oil Expense
507	Salaries Expense
511	Utilities Expense
512	Insurance Expense
515	Rent Expense
518	Supplies Expense

July 1 The company issued $600,000 of capital stock for cash.
5 Office space was rented for July, and $5,000 was paid for the rental.
8 Desks and chairs were purchased for the office on account, $28,800.
10 Equipment was purchased for $50,000; a note was given, to be paid in 30 days.
15 Purchased trucks for $150,000, paying $120,000 cash and giving a 60-day note to the dealer for $30,000.

➤ *Transactions*

July   18 Paid for supplies received and already used, $2,880.
       23 Received $17,280 cash as service revenue.
       27 Insurance expense for July was paid, $4,500.
       30 Paid for gasoline and oil used by the truck in July, $576.
       31 Billed customers for janitorial services rendered, $40,320.
       31 Paid salaries for July, $51,840.
       31 Paid utilities bills for July, $5,280.
       31 Paid cash dividends, $9,600.

Required ➡ **a.** Prepare general ledger accounts for all of these accounts except Retained Earnings. The Retained Earnings account has a beginning balance of zero and maintains this balance throughout the period.
b. Journalize the transactions given for July 2012 in the general journal.
c. Post the journal entries to ledger accounts.
d. Prepare a trial balance as of July 31, 2012.

Problem 2-4
Prepare journal entries, post to three-column ledger accounts, and prepare trial balance (L.O. 4-6)

Trim Lawn, Inc., is a lawn care company. Thus, the company earns its revenue from sending its trucks to customers' residences and certain commercial establishments to care for lawns and shrubbery. Trim Lawn's trial balance at the end of the first 11 months of the year follows:

TRIM LAWN, INC.
Trial Balance
November 30, 2012

Acct. No.	Account Title	Debits	Credits
100	Cash	$ 63,740	
103	Accounts Receivable	88,600	
150	Trucks	102,900	
160	Office Furniture	8,400	
200	Accounts Payable		$ 33,600
300	Capital Stock		30,000
310	Retained Earnings, January 1, 2012		30,540
400	Service Revenue		371,010
505	Advertising Expense	18,300	
506	Gas and Oil Expense	21,900	
507	Salaries Expense	65,850	
511	Utilities Expense	2,310	
515	Rent Expense	15,000	
518	Supplies Expense	75,600	
531	Entertainment Expense	2,550	
		$465,150	$465,150

Transactions ➡ Dec.   2 Paid rent for December, $3,000.
       5 Paid the accounts payable of $33,600.
       8 Paid advertising for December, $1,500.
       10 Purchased a new office desk on account, $1,050.
       13 Purchased $240 of supplies on account for use in December.
       15 Collected cash from customers on account, $75,000.
       20 Paid for customer entertainment, $450.
       24 Collected an additional $6,000 from customers on account.
       26 Paid for gasoline used in the trucks in December, $270.
       28 Billed customers for services rendered, $79,500.
       30 Paid for more December supplies, $12,000.
       31 Paid December salaries, $15,300.
       31 Paid a $4,000 cash dividend. (The Dividends account is No. 320.)

a. Open three-column general ledger accounts for each of the accounts in the trial balance under the date of December 1, 2012. Place the word *Balance* in the explanation space of each account. Also open an account for Dividends, No. 320.

b. Prepare entries in the general journal for the preceding transactions for December 2012.

c. Post the journal entries to three-column general ledger accounts.

d. Prepare a trial balance as of December 31, 2012.

 Required

Marc Miller prepared the following trial balance from the ledger of the Quick-Fix TV Repair Company. The trial balance did not balance.

Problem 2-5
Prepare corrected trial balance (L.O. 6)

QUICK-FIX REPAIR COMPANY
Trial Balance
December 31, 2012

Acct. No.	Account Title	Debits	Credits
100	Cash	$ 69,200	
103	Accounts Receivable	60,800	
160	Office Furniture	120,000	
172	Office Equipment	48,000	
200	Accounts Payable		$ 32,400
300	Capital Stock		180,000
310	Retained Earnings		80,000
320	Dividends	28,800	
400	Service Revenue		360,000
507	Salaries Expense	280,000	
515	Rent Expense	40,000	
568	Miscellaneous Expense	7,200	
		$654,000	$652,400

The difference in totals in the trial balance caused Miller to carefully examine the company's accounting records. In searching back through the accounting records, Miller found that the following errors had been made:

1. One entire entry that included a $10,000 debit to Cash and a $10,000 credit to Accounts Receivable was never posted.
2. In computing the balance of the Accounts Payable account, a credit of $3,200 was omitted from the computation.
3. In preparing the trial balance, the Retained Earnings account balance was shown as $80,000. The ledger account has the balance at its correct amount of $83,200.
4. One debit of $2,400 to the Dividends account was posted as a credit to that account.
5. Office equipment of $12,000 was debited to Office Furniture when purchased.

Prepare a corrected trial balance for the Quick-Fix TV Repair Company as of December 31, 2012. Also, write a description of the effect(s) of each error.

 Required

Alternate Problems

Speedy Laundry Company, Inc., entered into the following transactions in August 2012:

Problem 2-1A
Prepare journal enries (L.O. 4)

Aug. 1 Received cash for capital stock issued to owners, $400,000.
   3 Paid rent for August on a building and laundry equipment rented, $3,000.
   6 Performed laundry services for $2,000 cash.
   8 Secured an order from a customer for laundry services of $7,000. The services are to be performed next month.
   13 Performed laundry services for $6,300 on account for various customers.
   15 Received and paid a bill for $430 for supplies used in operations.
   23 Cash collected from customers on account, $2,600.
   31 Paid $2,400 salaries to employees for August.
   31 Received the electric and gas bill for August, $385, but did not pay it at this time.
   31 Paid cash dividend, $1,000.

Required   Prepare journal entries for these transactions in the general journal.

Problem 2-2A
Record transactions in journal, post to T-accounts, and prepare trial balance (L.O. 4-6)

The transactions listed below are those of Reliable Computer Repair, Inc., for April 2012:

Apr. 1 Cash of $500,000 was received for capital stock issued to the owners.
      3 Rent was paid for April, $3,500.
      6 Trucks were purchased for $56,000 cash.
      7 Office equipment was purchased on account from Wagner Company for $76,800.
     14 Salaries for first two weeks were paid, $12,000.
     15 $28,000 was received for services performed.
     18 An invoice was received from Roger's Gas Station for $400 for gas and oil used during April.
     23 A note was arranged with the bank for $80,000. The cash was received, and a note promising to return the $80,000 on May 30, 2012, was signed.
     29 Purchased trucks for $73,600 by signing a note.
     30 Salaries for the remainder of April were paid, $14,400.

Required

a. Prepare journal entries for these transactions.
b. Post the journal entries to T-accounts. Enter the account number in the Posting Reference column of the journal as you post each amount. Use the following account numbers:

Acct. No.	Account Title
100	Cash
150	Trucks
172	Office Equipment
200	Accounts Payable
201	Notes Payable
300	Capital Stock
400	Service Revenue
506	Gas and Oil Expense
507	Salaries Expense
515	Rent Expense

c. Prepare a trial balance as of April 30, 2012.

Problem 2-3A
Prepare ledger accounts, journalize transactions, post to ledger accounts, and prepare trial balance (L.O. 4-6)

Rapid Pick Up & Delivery, Inc., was organized January 1, 2012. Its chart of accounts is as follows:

Acct. No.	Account Title
100	Cash
103	Accounts Receivable
150	Trucks
160	Office Furniture
172	Office Equipment
200	Accounts Payable
201	Notes Payable
300	Capital Stock
310	Retained Earnings
400	Service Revenue
506	Gas and Oil Expense
507	Salaries Expense
511	Utilities Expense
512	Insurance Expense
515	Rent Expense
530	Repairs Expense

Transactions

Jan. 1 The company received $560,000 cash and $240,000 of office furniture in exchange for $800,000 of capital stock.
      2 Paid garage rent for January, $6,000.
      4 Purchased computers on account, $13,200.
      6 Purchased delivery trucks for $280,000; payment was made by giving cash of $150,000 and a 30-day note for the remainder.

Jan	12	Purchased insurance for January on the delivery trucks. The cost of the policy, $800, was paid in cash.
	15	Received and paid January utilities bills, $960.
	15	Paid salaries for first half of January, $3,600.
	17	Cash received for delivery services to date amounted to $1,800.
	20	Received bill for gasoline purchased and used in January, $180.
	23	Purchased delivery trucks for cash, $108,000.
	25	Cash sales of delivery services were $2,880.
	27	Purchased a copy machine on account, $3,600.
	31	Paid salaries for last half of January, $4,800.
	31	Sales of delivery services on account amounted to $11,400.
	31	Paid for repairs to a delivery truck, $1,120.

a. Prepare general ledger accounts for all these accounts except Retained Earnings. The Retained Earnings account has a beginning balance of zero and maintains this balance throughout the period.

b. Journalize the transactions given for January 2012 in the general journal.

c. Post the journal entries to ledger accounts.

d. Prepare a trial balance as of January 31, 2012.

 Required

The trial balance of California Tennis Center, Inc., at the end of the first 11 months of its fiscal year follows:

Problem 2-4A
Prepare journal entries, post to ledger accounts, and prepare trial balance(L.O. 4-6)

CALIFORNIA TENNIS CENTER, INC.
Trial Balance
November 30, 2012

Acct. No.	Account Title	Debits	Credits
100	Cash	$71,180	
103	Accounts Receivable	81,750	
130	Land	60,000	
200	Accounts Payable		$18,750
201	Notes Payable		15,000
300	Capital Stock		50,000
310	Retained Earnings, January 1, 2012		53,700
413	Membership and Lesson Revenue		202,500
505	Advertising Expense	21,000	
507	Salaries Expense	66,000	
511	Utilities Expense	2,100	
515	Rent Expense	33,000	
518	Supplies Expense	2,250	
530	Repairs Expense	1,500	
531	Entertainment Expense	870	
540	Interest Expense	300	
		$339,950	$339,950

Dec.	1	Paid building rent for December, $4,000.
	2	Paid vendors on account, $18,000.
	5	Purchased land for cash, $10,000.
	7	Sold memberships on account for December, $27,000.
	10	Paid the note payable of $15,000, plus interest of $150.
	13	Cash collections from customers on account, $36,000.
	19	Received a bill for repairs, $225.
	24	Paid the December utilities bill, $180.
	28	Received a bill for December advertising, $1,650.
	29	Paid the equipment repair bill received on the 19th, $225.
	30	Gave tennis lessons for cash, $4,500.
	30	Paid salaries, $6,000.
	30	Sales of memberships on account since December 7, $18,000 (for the month of December).
	30	Costs paid in entertaining customers in December, $350.
	30	Paid dividends of $1,500. (The Dividends account is No. 320.)

Transactions

Required

a. Open three-column general ledger accounts for each of the accounts in the trial balance. Place the word Balance in the explanation space and enter the date December 1, 2012, on this same line. Also open an account for Dividends, No. 320.

b. Prepare entries in the general journal for the transactions during December 2012.

c. Post the journal entries to ledger accounts.

d. Prepare a trial balance as of December 31, 2012.

Problem 2-5A
Prepare corrected trial balance(L.O. 6)

Bill Baxter prepared a trial balance for Special Party Rentals, Inc., a company that rents tables, chairs, and other party supplies. The trial balance did not balance. The trial balance he prepared was as follows:

SPECIAL PARTY RENTALS, INC.
Trial Balance
December 31, 2012

Acct. No.	Account Title	Debits	Credits
100	Cash	$ 74,000	
103	Accounts Receivable	50,800	
170	Equipment	160,000	
200	Accounts Payable		$ 34,000
300	Capital Stock		130,000
310	Retained Earnings		44,000
320	Dividends	16,000	
400	Service Revenue		432,000
505	Advertising Expense	1,200	
507	Salaries Expense	176,000	
511	Utilities Expense	44,800	
515	Rent Expense	64,000	
		$ 586,800	$ 640,000

In trying to find out why the trial balance did not balance, Baxter discovered the following errors:

1. Equipment was understated (too low) by $12,000 because of an error in addition in determining the balance of that account in the ledger.

2. A credit of $4,800 to Accounts Receivable in the journal was not posted to the ledger account at all.

3. A debit of $16,000 for a semiannual dividend was posted as a credit to the Capital Stock account.

4. The balance of $12,000 in the Advertising Expense account was entered as $1,200 in the trial balance.

5. Miscellaneous Expense (Account No. 568), with a balance of $3,200, was omitted from the trial balance.

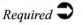 *Required*

Prepare a corrected trial balance as of December 31, 2012. Also, write a description of the effect(s) of each error.

Beyond the Numbers—Critical Thinking

Business Decision Case 2-1
Prepare journal entries, post to T-accounts, and judge profitability (L.O. 4, 5)

John Jacobs lost his job as a carpenter with a contractor when a recession hit the construction industry. Jacobs had been making $50,000 per year. He decided to form his own company, Jacobs Corporation, and do home repairs.

The following is a summary of the transactions of the business during the first three months of operations in 2012:

Jan.   15   Stockholders invested $40,000 in the business.

Feb.   25   Received payment of $4,400 for remodeling a basement into a recreation room. The homeowner purchased all of the building materials.

Mar.   5   Paid cash for an advertisement that appeared in the local newspaper, $150.

Apr.   10   Received $7,000 for converting a room over a garage into an office for a college
              professor. The professor purchased all of the materials for the job.
        11   Paid gas and oil expenses for automobile, $900.
        12   Miscellaneous business expenses were paid, $450.
        15   Paid dividends of $2,000.

a. Prepare journal entries for these transactions.
b. Post the journal entries to T-accounts.
c. How profitable is this new venture? Should Jacobs stay in this business?

Refer to the Annual Report of Wal-Mart Stores, Inc. in the Annual Report Appendix. Perform
horizontal and vertical analyses of the liabilities and stockholder's equity sections of the balance
sheets for the two most recent years shown. Horizontal analysis involves showing the dollar
amount and percentage increase or decrease of the latest year over the preceding year amounts.
Vertical analysis involves showing the percentage of total liabilities and stockholder's equity
that each account represents as of the balance sheet dates. Write comments on any important
changes between the two years that are evidence of decisions made by management.

**Annual Report
Analysis 2-2**
Perform horizontal and
vertical analyses and
comment (L.O. 7)

In The Home Depot's recent Annual Report, the following passages appear:

**Annual Report
Analysis 2-3**

The primary key to our success is our 39,000 employees who wear those orange aprons you see in
our stores.

    Few great achievements—in business or in any aspect of life—are reached and sustained without
the support and involvement of large numbers of people committed to shared values and goals they
deem worthy. Indeed, one need look no further than the business section of the morning newspaper
to read of how yet another 'blue chip' American business, entrenched in and isolated by its own
bureaucracy, has lost the support of its employees and customers. . .

    Frankly, the biggest difference between The Home Depot and our competitors is not the products
on our shelves, it's our people and their ability to forge strong bonds of loyalty and trust with our
customers. . .

    . . . Contrary to conventional management wisdom, those at the top of organization charts are
not the source of all wisdom. Many of our best ideas come from the people who work on the sales
floor. We encourage our employees to challenge senior management directives if they feel strongly
enough about their dissenting opinions. . .

    . . . We want our people to be themselves and to be bold enough to apply their talents as
individuals. Certainly, people can often perceive great risk acting this way. Thus, we go to great lengths
to empower our employees to be mavericks, to express differences of opinion without fear of being
fired or demoted. . . We do everything we can to make people feel challenged and inspired at work
instead of being threatened and made to feel insecure. An organization can, after all, accomplish
more when people work together instead of against each other.

Write answers to the following questions:

☛ *Required*

a. Do you think The Home Depot management regards its employees more as expenses or
assets? Explain.
b. What does The Home Depot regard as its most valuable asset? Explain your answer.
c. Is The Home Depot permitted to list its human resources as assets on its balance sheet?
Why or why not?
d. Could its philosophy regarding its employees be the major factor in its outstanding
financial performance? Explain.

Refer to "An Ethical Perspective" on page 76. Write out the answers to the following questions:

**Ethics Case—Writing
Experience 2-4**

a. What motivated Larry to go along with unethical and illegal actions? Explain.
b. What are Larry's options now? List each possibility.
c. What would you do if you were Larry? Describe in detail.
d. What do you think the real Larry did? Describe in detail.

Group Project 2-5
Interview a new staff member at a CPA firm

In teams of two or three students, interview in person or by speakerphone a new staff member who has worked for a CPA firm for only one or two years. Seek information on the advantages and disadvantages of working for a CPA firm. Also, inquire about the nature of the work and the training programs offered by the firm for new employees. As a team, write a memorandum to the instructor summarizing the results of the interview. The heading of the memorandum should contain the date, to whom it is written, from whom, and the subject matter.

Group Project 2-6
Perform library research

With one or two other students and using library resources, write a report on the life of Luca Pacioli, sometimes referred to as the father of accounting. Pacioli was a Franciscan monk who wrote a book on double-entry accounting in 1494. Be careful to cite sources and treat direct quotes properly. (If you do not know how to do this, ask your instructor.)

Using the Internet—A View of the Real World

Internet Project 2-8
Check on Job Openings

Visit the following website:
http://www.roberthalf.com
Click on Search Jobs. Read the information and write a memo to your instructor about your search and what you learned about certain jobs in accounting.

Internet Project 2-9
Check on Securities and Exchange Commission

Visit the following website:
http://www.sec.gov
Investigate this site for anything of interest. Write a memo to your instructor about your search.

Answers to Self-Test

True-False

1. **False**. Only the last five steps are performed at the end of the period. The first three steps are performed throughout the accounting period.
2. **True**. The journal is the book of original entry. Any amounts appearing in a ledger account must have been posted from the journal.
3. **False**. The left side of any account is the debit side.
4. **False**. These accounts are all increased by credits.
5. **True**. Since dividends reduce stockholders' equity, the Dividends account is increased by debits.
6. **False**. An entire journal entry may not have been posted, or a debit or credit might have been posted to the wrong account.

Multiple-Choice

1. **c.** An asset, Cash, is increased by a debit, and the Capital Stock account is increased by a credit.
2. **b.** Since the insurance covers more than the current accounting period, an asset is debited instead of an expense. The credit is to Cash.
3. **a.** The receipt of cash before services are performed creates a liability, Unearned Delivery

Fees. To increase a liability, it is credited. Cash is debited to increase its balance.
4. **b.** Cash is increased by the debit, and Delivery Service Revenue is increased by the credit.
5. **c.** Dividends is increased by the debit, and Cash is decreased by the credit.

Careers in Accounting

A Career As A Tax Specialist

While most students are aware that accountants frequently assist their clients with tax returns and other tax issues, few are aware of the large number of diverse and challenging careers available in the field of taxation. Nearly all public accounting firms, ranging from the "Big 4" international firms to the sole practitioner, generate a significant portion of their fees through tax compliance, planning and consulting. With over 115 million individual tax returns filed every year, it is not surprising that many individuals and most businesses need assistance in dealing with the incredibly complex U.S. and international tax laws. This complexity also provides tremendous tax planning opportunities. As a tax specialist, you will show individual clients how to reduce their taxes while simultaneously helping them make decisions about investing, buying a house, funding their children's education, and planning their retirement. For your business clients, careful planning and structuring of business investments and transactions can save millions of dollars in taxes. In fact, it is safe to say that very few significant business transactions take place without the careful guidance of a tax specialist.

A career in taxation is by no means limited to public accounting. Because there are so many types of taxes impacting so many aspects of our lives, tax specialists act as consultants in a large number of fields. For example, many companies offer deferred compensation or stock bonus plans to their executives. Nearly all companies provide some sort of pension or other retirement plan for their employees, as well as health care benefits. Significant tax savings can be generated for both the company and their employees if these benefits are structured correctly. In response to the amazing complexity of our tax laws, many schools offer masters degrees specializing in tax. Such a degree is not required to specialize in tax, but does offer students a significant advantage if they want to pursue a career in taxation. In a recent survey of 1,400 chief financial officers, the top two responses to the question "which one of the following areas of specialization would you recommend to someone just beginning his or her career in accounting?" were personal financial planning and tax accounting. These responses reflect the indisputable fact that as the U.S.demographic includes more wealthy, and older, Americans than ever before, professional tax guidance will be in ever-increasing demand.

The career paths outlined above do not nearly cover all of the many professional options available to tax specialists. For example, are you concerned that a traditional tax accounting job may be too tame for you? Special agents of the IRS routinely participate in criminal investigations and arrests, working closely with other federal law enforcement agencies. Are you interested in law? Accounting offers an ideal undergraduate degree for aspiring business and tax attorneys. If you think you may be interested in a career as a tax specialist, be sure to consult with one of your school's tax professors about the many job opportunities this field provides.

3

Adjustments for Financial Reporting

Chapters 1 and 2 introduced the accounting process of analyzing, classifying, and summarizing business transactions into accounts. You learned how these transactions are entered into the journal and posted to the ledger accounts. You also know how to use the trial balance to test the equality of debits and credits in the journalizing and posting process. The purpose of the accounting process is to produce accurate financial statements so they may be used for making sound business decisions. At this point in your study of accounting, you are concentrating on three financial statements—the income statement, the statement of retained earnings, and the balance sheet. Detailed coverage of the statement of cash flows appears in Chapter 16.

When you began to analyze business transactions in Chapter 1, you saw that the evidence of the transaction is usually a source document. It is any written or printed evidence that describes the essential facts of a business transaction. Examples are receipts for cash paid or received, checks written or received, bills sent to customers, or bills received from suppliers. The giving, receiving, or creating of source documents triggered the journal entries made in Chapter 2.

The journal entries we discuss in this chapter are *adjusting entries*. The arrival of the end of the accounting period triggers adjusting entries. Accountants use adjusting entries to bring accounts to their proper balances before preparing financial statements. In this chapter, you learn the difference between the cash basis and the accrual basis of accounting. Then you learn about the classes and types of adjusting entries and how to prepare them.

Cash versus Accrual Basis Accounting

Professionals such as physicians and lawyers and some relatively small businesses may account for their revenues and expenses on a cash basis. The **cash basis of accounting** recognizes revenues when cash is received and recognizes expenses

Learning Objectives

After studying this chapter, you should be able to:

1. Describe the basic characteristics of the cash basis and the accrual basis of accounting.

2. Identify the reasons why adjusting entries must be made.

3. Identify the classes and types of adjusting entries.

4. Prepare adjusting entries.

5. Determine the effects of failing to prepare adjusting entries.

6. Analyze and use the financial resultsÑtrend percentages.

Illustration 3.1   Cash Basis and Accrual Basis of Accounting Compared

	Cash Basis	Accrual Basis
Revenues are recognized	As cash is received	As earned (goods are delivered or services are performed)
Expenses are recognized	As cash is paid	As incurred to produce revenues

when cash is paid out. For example, under the cash basis, a company would treat services rendered to clients in 2012 for which the company collected cash in 2013 as 2013 revenues. Similarly, under the cash basis, a company would treat expenses incurred in 2012 for which the company disbursed cash in 2013 as 2013 expenses. Under the "pure" cash basis, even the purchase of a building would be debited to an expense. However, under the "modified" cash basis, the purchase of long-lived assets (such as a building) would be debited to an asset and depreciated (gradually charged to expense) over its useful life. Normally the "modified" cash basis is used by those few individuals and small businesses that use the cash basis.

Because the cash basis of accounting does not match expenses incurred and revenues earned, it is generally considered theoretically unacceptable. The cash basis is acceptable in practice only under those circumstances when it approximates the results that a company could obtain under the accrual basis of accounting. Companies using the cash basis do not have to prepare any adjusting entries unless they discover they have made a mistake in preparing an entry during the accounting period. Under certain circumstances, companies may use the cash basis for income tax purposes.

Throughout the text we use the accrual basis of accounting, which matches expenses incurred and revenues earned, because most companies use the accrual basis. The **accrual basis of accounting** recognizes revenues when sales are made or services are performed, regardless of when cash is received. Expenses are recognized as incurred, whether or not cash has been paid out. For instance, assume a company performs services for a customer on account. Although the company has received no cash, the revenue is recorded at the time the company performs the service. Later, when the company receives the cash, no revenue is recorded because the company has already recorded the revenue. Under the accrual basis, adjusting entries are needed to bring the accounts up to date for unrecorded economic activity that has taken place. In Illustration 3.1, we show when revenues and expenses are recognized under the cash basis and under the accrual basis.

The Need for Adjusting Entries

The income statement of a business reports all revenues earned and all expenses incurred to generate those revenues during a given period. An income statement that does not report all revenues and expenses is incomplete, inaccurate, and possibly misleading. Similarly, a balance sheet that does not report all of an entity's assets, liabilities, and stockholders' equity at a specific time may be misleading. Each adjusting entry has a dual purpose: (1) to make the income statement report the proper revenue or expense and (2) to make the balance sheet report the proper asset or liability. Thus, every adjusting entry affects at least one income statement account and one balance sheet account.

Since those interested in the activities of a business need timely information, companies must prepare financial statements periodically. To prepare such statements,

Illustration 3.2   Summary-Fiscal Year Ending by Month

January	26
February	7
March	17
April	8
May	16
June	33
July	8
August	14
September	37
October	14
November	10
Subtotal	**190**
December	310
Total Companies	**500**

Source: American Institute of Certified Public Accountants, *Accounting Trends & Techniques* (New York: AICPA, 2010) p39.

the accountant divides an entity's life into time periods. These time periods are usually equal in length and are called *accounting periods*. An **accounting period** may be one month, one quarter, or one year. An **accounting year**, or fiscal year, is an accounting period of one year. A **fiscal year** is any 12 consecutive months. The fiscal year may or may not coincide with the **calendar year**, which ends on December 31. As we show in Illustration 3.2, more than half of the companies surveyed have fiscal years that coincide with the calendar year. Companies in certain industries often have a fiscal year that differs from the calendar year. For instance many retail stores end their fiscal year on January 31 to avoid closing their books during their peak sales period. Other companies select a fiscal year ending at a time when inventories and business activity are lowest.

Periodic reporting and the matching principle necessitate the preparation of *adjusting entries*. **Adjusting entries** are journal entries made at the end of an accounting period or at any time financial statements are to be prepared to bring about a proper *matching* of revenues and expenses. The **matching principle** requires that expenses incurred in producing revenues be deducted from the revenues they generated during the accounting period. The matching principle is one of the underlying principles of accounting. This matching of expenses and revenues is necessary for the income statement to present an accurate picture of the profitability of a business. Adjusting entries reflect unrecorded economic activity that has taken place but has not yet been recorded. Why has the company not recorded this activity by the end of the period? One reason is that it is more convenient and economical to wait until the end of the period to record the activity. A second reason is that no source document concerning that activity has yet come to the accountant's attention.

Adjusting entries bring the amounts in the general ledger accounts to their proper balances before the company prepares its financial statements. That is, adjusting entries convert the amounts that are actually in the general ledger accounts to the amounts that should be in the general ledger accounts for proper financial reporting. To make this conversion, the accountants analyze the accounts to determine which need adjustment. For example, assume a company purchased a three-year insurance policy costing $600 at the beginning of the year and debited $600 to Prepaid Insurance. At year-end, the company should remove $200 of the cost from the asset and record it as an expense. Failure to do so misstates assets and net income on the financial statements.

Companies continuously receive benefits from many assets such as prepaid expenses (e.g., prepaid insurance and prepaid rent). Thus, an entry could be made daily to record the expense incurred. Typically, firms do not make the entry until

Note to the Student
Every adjusting entry impacts both a balance sheet and an income statement account. Therefore, every adjusting entry impacts net income. This is not true of all journal entries made during the accounting period.
Think of some examples of journal entries that do affect net income and some that do not.

Reinforcing Problem
Business Decision Case 3-1 Explain why adjusting entries are made and which accounts need adjustment.

Reinforcing Problem
E3-2 Answer multiple-choice questions concerning the accounting period and why adjusting entries must be made.

Illustration 3.3   Two Classes and Four Types of Adjusting Entries

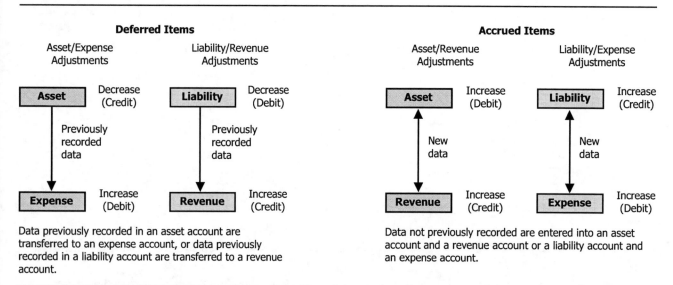

Deferred Items

Asset/Expense Adjustments	Liability/Revenue Adjustments

Asset — Decrease (Credit)

Previously recorded data

Expense — Increase (Debit)

Liability — Decrease (Debit)

Previously recorded data

Revenue — Increase (Credit)

Data previously recorded in an asset account are transferred to an expense account, or data previously recorded in a liability account are transferred to a revenue account.

Accrued Items

Asset/Revenue Adjustments	Liability/Expense Adjustments

Asset — Increase (Debit)

New data

Revenue — Increase (Credit)

Liability — Increase (Credit)

New data

Expense — Increase (Debit)

Data not previously recorded are entered into an asset account and a revenue account or a liability account and an expense account.

financial statements are to be prepared. Therefore, if monthly financial statements are prepared, monthly adjusting entries are required. By custom, and in some instances by law, businesses report to their owners at least annually. Accordingly, adjusting entries are required at least once a year. Remember, however, that the entry transferring an amount from an asset account to an expense account should transfer only the asset cost that has expired.

An Accounting Perspective

USES OF TECHNOLOGY   Accounting software has been designed that allows computers to automatically enter adjusting entries on a regular basis so that up-to-date financial statements can be printed at almost any time without prior notice. Computers are fed the facts concerning activities that would normally result in adjusting entries and instructed to seek any necessary information from their own databases or those of other computers to continually adjust the accounts.

Classes and Types of Adjusting Entries

Objective 3
Identify the classes and types of adjusting entries.

Adjusting entries fall into two broad classes: deferred (meaning to postpone or delay) items and accrued (meaning to grow or accumulate) items. **Deferred items** consist of adjusting entries involving data previously recorded in accounts. These entries involve the transfer of data already recorded in asset and liability accounts to expense and revenue accounts, respectively. **Accrued items** consist of adjusting entries relating to activity on which no data have been previously recorded in the accounts. These entries involve the initial, or first, recording of assets and liabilities and the related revenues and expenses (see Illustration 3.3).

Deferred items consist of two types of adjusting entries: asset/expense adjustments and liability/revenue adjustments. For example, prepaid insurance and prepaid rent are assets until they are used up; then they become expenses. Also, unearned revenue is a liability until the company renders the service; then the unearned revenue becomes earned revenue.

Accrued items consist of two types of adjusting entries: asset/revenue adjustments and liability/expense adjustments. For example, assume a company performs a service for a customer but has not yet billed the customer. The accountant records this

Illustration 3.4   Trial Balance

MICROTRAIN COMPANY
Trial Balance
December 31, 2012

Acct. No.	Account Title	Debits	Credits
100	Cash	$ 8,250	
103	Accounts Receivable	5,200	
107	Supplies on Hand	1,400	
108	Prepaid Insurance	2,400	
112	Prepaid Rent	1,200	
150	Trucks	40,000	
200	Accounts Payable		$ 730
216	Unearned Service Fees		4,500
300	Capital Stock		50,000
320	Dividends	3,000	
400	Service Revenue		10,700
505	Advertising Expense	50	
506	Gas and Oil Expense	680	
507	Salaries Expense	3,600	
511	Utilities Expense	150	
		$65,930	$65,930

transaction as an asset in the form of a receivable and as revenue because the company has earned a revenue. Also, assume a company owes its employees salaries not yet paid. The accountant records this transaction as a liability and an expense because the company has incurred an expense.

In this chapter, we illustrate each of the four types of adjusting entries: asset/expense, liability/revenue, asset/revenue, and liability/expense. Look at Illustration 3.4, the trial balance of the MicroTrain Company at December 31, 2012. As you can see, MicroTrain must adjust several accounts before it can prepare accurate financial statements. The adjustments for these accounts involve data already recorded in the company's accounts.

In making adjustments for MicroTrain Company, we must add several accounts to the company's chart of accounts shown in Chapter 2 on page 59. These new accounts are:

Reinforcing Problem
E3-3 Answer multiple-choice questions that differentiate between deferred and accrued items.

Type of Account	Acct. No.	Account Title	Description
Asset	121	Interest Receivable	The amount of interest earned but not yet received.
Contra asset*	151	Accumulated Depreciation—Trucks	The total depreciation expense taken on trucks since the acquisition date. The balance of this account is deducted from that of Trucks on the balance sheet.
Liability	206	Salaries Payable	The amount of salaries earned by employees but not yet paid by the company.
Revenue	418	Interest Revenue	The amount of interest earned in the current period.
Expenses	512	Insurance Expense	The cost of insurance incurred in the current period.
	515	Rent Expense	The cost of rent incurred in the current period.
	518	Supplies Expense	The cost of supplies used in the current period.
	521	Depreciation Expense—Trucks	The portion of the cost of the trucks assigned to expense during the current period.

*Accountants deduct the balance of a contra asset from the balance of the related asset account on the balance sheet. We explain the reasons for using a contra asset account later in the chapter.

Now you are ready to follow as MicroTrain Company makes its adjustments for deferred items. If you find the process confusing, review the beginning of this chapter so you clearly understand the purpose of adjusting entries.

<table>
<tr><td>**An Accounting Perspective**</td><td>**USES OF TECHNOLOGY** Today, it is difficult to name a publicly owned company that does not provide an extensive website. In fact, websites have become an important link between companies and their investors. Most websites will have a link titled "investor relations" or merely "company information" which provides a wealth of financial information ranging from audited financial statements to charts of the company's stock prices. As an example, check out the Gap, Inc's website at:

http://www.gapinc.com

Browse the Gap site and see for yourself the comprehensiveness of the financial information available there.</td></tr>
</table>

Adjustments for Deferred Items

Objective 4
Prepare adjusting entries.

This section discusses the two types of adjustments for deferred items: asset/expense adjustments and liability/revenue adjustments. In the asset/expense group, you learn how to prepare adjusting entries for prepaid expenses and depreciation. In the liability/revenue group, you learn how to prepare adjusting entries for unearned revenues.

Asset/Expense Adjustments— Prepaid Expenses and Depreciation

MicroTrain Company must make several asset/expense adjustments for prepaid expenses. A **prepaid expense** is an asset awaiting assignment to expense, such as prepaid insurance, prepaid rent, and supplies on hand. Note that the nature of these three adjustments is the same.

Prepaid Insurance   When a company pays an insurance policy premium in advance, the purchase creates the asset, *prepaid insurance*. This advance payment is an asset because the company will receive insurance coverage in the future. With the passage of time, however, the asset gradually expires. The portion that has expired becomes an expense. To illustrate this point, recall that in Chapter 2, MicroTrain Company purchased for cash an insurance policy on its trucks for the period December 1, 2012, to November 30, 2013. The journal entry made on December 1, 2012, to record the purchase of the policy was:

2012				
Dec.	1	Prepaid Insurance	2,400	
		Cash		2,400
		Purchased truck insurance to cover a one-year period.		

The two accounts relating to insurance are Prepaid Insurance (an asset) and Insurance Expense (an expense). After posting this entry, the Prepaid Insurance account has a $2,400 debit balance on December 1, 2012. The Insurance Expense account has a zero balance on December 1, 2012, because no time has elapsed to use any of the policy's benefits.

(Dr.)	**Prepaid Insurance**	(Cr.)	(Dr.)	**Insurance Expense**	(Cr.)
2012			2012		
Dec. 1			Dec. 1		
Bal.	2,400		Bal.	-0-	

By December 31, 2012, one month of the year covered by the policy has expired. Therefore, part of the **service potential** (or benefit obtained from the asset) has expired. The asset now provides less future services or benefits than when the company acquired it. We recognize this reduction by treating the cost of the services received from the asset as an expense. For the MicroTrain Company example, the service received was one month of insurance coverage. Since the policy provides the same services for every month of its one-year life, we assign an equal amount ($200) of cost to each month. Thus, MicroTrain charges $\frac{1}{12}$ of the annual premium to Insurance Expense on December 31, 2012. The adjusting journal entry is:

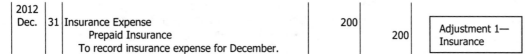

2012					
Dec.	31	Insurance Expense	200		Adjustment 1—
		Prepaid Insurance		200	Insurance
		To record insurance expense for December.			

After posting these two journal entries, the accounts in T-account format appear as follows:

Reinforcing Problem
E3-4 Prepare and post adjusting entry for insurance.

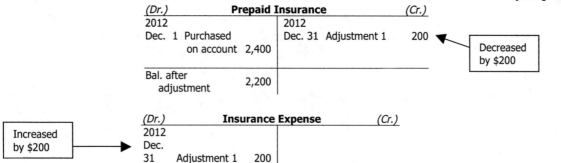

In practice, accountants do not use T-accounts. Instead, they use three-column ledger accounts that have the advantage of showing a balance after each transaction. After posting the preceding two entries, the three-column ledger accounts appear as follows:

Prepaid Insurance   *Account No. 108*

Date		Explanation	Post Ref.	Debit	Credit	Balance
2012						
Dec.	1	Purchased on Account	G1	2 4 0 0		2 4 0 0 Dr.
	31	Adjustment	G3*		2 0 0	2 2 0 0 Dr.

Insurance Expense   *Account No. 512*

Date		Explanation	Post Ref.	Debit	Credit	Balance
2012						
Dec.	31	Adjustment	G3*	2 0 0		2 0 0 Dr.

*Assumed page number.

Before this adjusting entry was made, the entire $2,400 insurance payment made on December 1, 2012, was a prepaid expense for 12 months of protection. So on December 31, 2012, one month of protection had passed, and an adjusting entry transferred $200 of the $2,400 ($2,400/12 = $200) to Insurance Expense. On the income statement for the year ended December 31, 2012, MicroTrain reports one month of insurance expense, $200, as one of the expenses it incurred in generating that year's revenues. It reports the remaining amount of the prepaid expense, $2,200, as an asset on the balance sheet. The $2,200 prepaid expense represents 11 months of insurance protection that remains as a future benefit.

Note to the Student
What would the adjustment be if the transaction had been recorded initially as an expense? What is the net result on the financial statements?

Prepaid Rent   Prepaid rent is another example of the gradual consumption of a previously recorded asset. Assume a company pays rent in advance to cover more than one accounting period. On the date it pays the rent, the company debits the prepayment to the Prepaid Rent account (an asset account). The company has not yet received benefits resulting from this expenditure. Thus, the expenditure creates an asset.

We measure rent expense similarly to insurance expense. Generally, the rental contract specifies the amount of rent per unit of time. If the prepayment covers a three-month rental, we charge one-third of this rental to each month. Notice that the amount charged is the same each month even though some months have more days than other months.

For example, MicroTrain Company paid $1,200 rent in advance on December 1, 2012, to cover a three-month period beginning on that date. The journal entry would be:

Reinforcing Problems
E3-5 Prepare adjusting entry for rent.
E3-6 Determine date and entry for rent paid.

2012				
Dec.	1	Prepaid Rent	1,200	
		Cash		1,200
		Paid three months' rent on a building.		

Note to the Student
How could the rent payment have been recorded such that no adjusting entry is required at December 31?

The two accounts relating to rent are Prepaid Rent (an asset) and Rent Expense. After this entry is posted, the Prepaid Rent account has a $1,200 balance and the Rent Expense account has a zero balance because no part of the rent period has yet elapsed.

(Dr.)	**Prepaid Rent**	(Cr.)	(Dr.)	**Rent Expense**	(Cr.)
2012			2012		
Dec. 1			Dec. 1		
Bal. Cash Paid	1,200		Bal.	-0-	

On December 31, 2012, MicroTrain must prepare an adjusting entry. Since one third of the period covered by the prepaid rent has elapsed, it charges one-third of the $1,200 of prepaid rent to expense. The required adjusting entry is:

Adjustment 2— Rent	2012				
	Dec.	31	Rent Expense	400	
			Prepaid Rent		400
			To record rent expense for December		

After posting this adjusting entry, the T-accounts appear as follows:

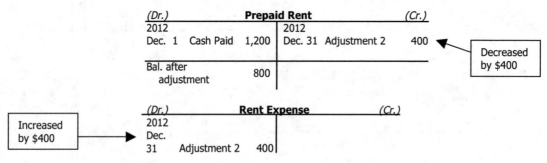

The $400 rent expense appears in the income statement for the year ended December 31, 2012. MicroTrain reports the remaining $800 of prepaid rent as an asset in the balance sheet on December 31, 2012. Thus, the adjusting entries have accomplished their purpose of maintaining the accuracy of the financial statements.

Supplies on Hand   Almost every business uses supplies in its operations. It may classify supplies simply as supplies (to include all types of supplies), or more specifically as office supplies (paper, stationery, pencils), selling supplies (gummed tape, string, paper bags, cartons, wrapping paper), or training supplies (transparencies, training manuals). Frequently, companies buy supplies in bulk. These supplies are an asset until the company uses them. This asset may be called *supplies on hand* or *supplies inventory.* Even though these terms indicate a prepaid expense, the firm does not use *prepaid* in the asset's title.

On December 4, 2012, MicroTrain Company purchased supplies for $1,400 and recorded the transaction as follows:

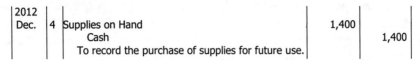

2012					
Dec.	4	Supplies on Hand	1,400	
		Cash		1,400
		To record the purchase of supplies for future use.		

MicroTrain's two accounts relating to supplies are Supplies on Hand (an asset) and Supplies Expense. After this entry is posted, the Supplies on Hand account shows a debit balance of $1,400 and the Supplies Expense account has a zero balance as shown in the following T-accounts:

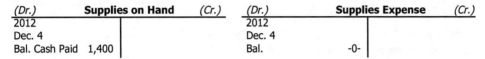

(Dr.)	**Supplies on Hand**	*(Cr.)*	*(Dr.)*	**Supplies Expense**	*(Cr.)*
2012			2012		
Dec. 4			Dec. 4		
Bal. Cash Paid 1,400			Bal.	-0-	

An actual physical inventory (a count of the supplies on hand) at the end of the month showed only $900 of supplies on hand. Thus, the company must have used $500 of supplies in December. An adjusting journal entry brings the two accounts pertaining to supplies to their proper balances. The adjusting entry recognizes the reduction in the asset (Supplies on Hand) and the recording of an expense (Supplies Expense) by transferring $500 from the asset to the expense. According to the physical inventory, the asset balance should be $900 and the expense balance, $500. So MicroTrain makes the following adjusting entry:

2012					
Dec.	31	Supplies Expense	500		Adjustment 3—Supplies
		Supplies on Hand		500	
		To record supplies used during December.			

After posting this adjusting entry, the T-accounts appear as follows:

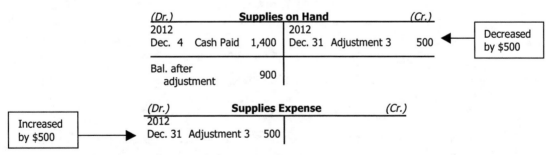

(Dr.)	**Supplies on Hand**		*(Cr.)*	
2012			2012	
Dec. 4 Cash Paid 1,400			Dec. 31 Adjustment 3 500	Decreased by $500
Bal. after adjustment 900				

(Dr.)	**Supplies Expense**	*(Cr.)*
2012		
Dec. 31 Adjustment 3 500		

Increased by $500

The entry to record the use of supplies could be made when the supplies are issued from the storeroom. However, such careful accounting for small items each time they are issued is usually too costly a procedure.

Accountants make adjusting entries for supplies on hand, like for any other prepaid expense, before preparing financial statements. Supplies expense appears in the income statement. Supplies on hand is an asset in the balance sheet.

Sometimes companies buy assets relating to insurance, rent, and supplies knowing that they will use them up before the end of the current accounting period (usually one month or one year). If so, an expense account is usually debited at the time of purchase rather than debiting an asset account. This procedure avoids having to make an adjusting entry at the end of the accounting period. Sometimes, too, a company debits an expense even though the asset will benefit more than the current period. Then, at the end of the accounting period, the firm's adjusting entry transfers some

Note to the Student
Suppose the company fails to make the required adjusting entry for supplies expense. What are the net effects on the year-end financial statements?

Reinforcing Problem
E3-7 Prepare entries for purchase of supplies and adjustment at year-end.

of the cost from the expense to the asset. For instance, assume that on January 1, a company paid $1,200 rent to cover a three-year period and debited the $1,200 to Rent Expense. At the end of the year, it transfers $800 from Rent Expense to Prepaid Rent. To simplify our approach, we will consistently debit the asset when the asset will benefit more than the current accounting period.

Depreciation   Just as prepaid insurance and prepaid rent indicate a gradual using up of a previously recorded asset, so does depreciation. However, the overall time involved in using up a depreciable asset (such as a building) is much longer and less definite than for prepaid expenses. Also, a prepaid expense generally involves a fairly small amount of money. Depreciable assets, however, usually involve larger sums of money.

A **depreciable asset** is a manufactured asset such as a building, machine, vehicle, or piece of equipment that provides service to a business. In time, these assets lose their utility because of (1) wear and tear from use or (2) obsolescence due to technological change. Since companies gradually use up these assets over time, they record depreciation expense on them. **Depreciation expense** is the amount of asset cost assigned as an expense to a particular period. The process of recording depreciation expense is called **depreciation accounting.** The three factors involved in computing depreciation expense are:

Note to the Student
Depreciation accounting requires the use of estimates in the accounting process. How might these estimates affect the accuracy and credibility of the financial statements?

1. **Asset cost**. The asset cost is the amount that a company paid to purchase the depreciable asset.
2. **Estimated useful life.** The **estimated useful life** of an asset is the estimated time that a company can use the asset. Useful life is an estimate, not an exact measurement, that a company must make in advance. However, sometimes the useful life is determined by company policy (e.g., keep a fleet of automobiles for three years).
3. **Estimated salvage value.** The **estimated salvage value (scrap value)** is the amount that the company can probably sell the asset for at the end of its estimated useful life.

Note to the Student
Why is depreciation an allocation process and not a valuation process even if the end result refers to a book value or carrying value?

Accountants use different methods for recording depreciation. The method illustrated here is the *straight-line method.* We discuss other depreciation methods in Chapter 10. Straight-line depreciation assigns the same amount of depreciation expense to each accounting period over the life of the asset. The **depreciation formula (straight-line)** to compute straight-line depreciation for a one-year period is:

$$\frac{\text{Annual}}{\text{depreciation}} = \frac{\text{Asset cost} - \text{Estimated salvage value}}{\text{Estimated years of useful life}}$$

To illustrate the use of this formula, recall that on December 1, MicroTrain Company purchased four small trucks at a cost of $40,000. The journal entry was:

2012				
Dec.	1	Trucks	40,000	
		Cash		40,000
		To record the purchase of four trucks.		

The estimated salvage value for each truck was $1,000, so MicroTrain estimated the total salvage value for all four trucks at $4,000. The company estimated the useful life of each truck to be four years. Using the straight-line depreciation formula, MicroTrain calculated the annual depreciation on the trucks as follows:

$$\text{Annual depreciation} = \frac{\$40,000 - \$4,000}{4 \text{ years}} = \$9,000$$

The amount of depreciation expense for one month would be $\frac{1}{12}$ of the annual amount. Thus, depreciation expense for December is $9,000 ÷ 12 = $750.

The difference between an asset's cost and its estimated salvage value is an asset's **depreciable amount.** To satisfy the matching principle, the firm must allocate the depreciable amount as an expense to the various periods in the asset's useful life. It does this by debiting the amount of depreciation for a period to a depreciation expense account and crediting the amount to an accumulated depreciation account. MicroTrain's depreciation on its delivery trucks for December is $750. The company records the depreciation as follows:

Reinforcing Problem
E3-8 Prepare adjusting entry for depreciation.

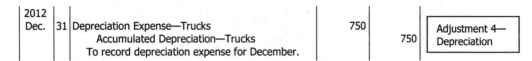

After posting the adjusting entry, the T-accounts appear as follows:

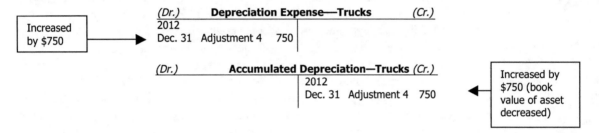

MicroTrain reports depreciation expense in its income statement. And it reports accumulated depreciation in the balance sheet as a deduction from the related asset.

The **accumulated depreciation account** is a contra asset account that shows the total of all depreciation recorded on the asset *from the date of acquisition up through the balance sheet date.* A **contra asset account** is a deduction from the asset to which it relates in the balance sheet. The purpose of a contra asset account is to reduce the original cost of the asset down to its remaining undepreciated cost or book value. The *accumulated depreciation account* does not represent cash that is being set aside to replace the worn out asset. The *undepreciated cost of the asset* is the debit balance in the asset account (original cost) minus the credit balance in the accumulated depreciation contra account. Accountants also refer to an asset's cost less accumulated depreciation as the **book value** (or net book value) of the asset. Thus, book value is the cost not yet allocated to an expense. In the previous example, the book value of the equipment after the first month is:

Cost	$40,000
Less: Accumulated depreciation	750
Book value (or cost not yet allocated to as an expense)	$39,250

MicroTrain credits the depreciation amount to an accumulated depreciation account, which is a contra asset, rather than directly to the asset account. Companies use contra accounts when they want to show statement readers the original amount of the account to which the contra account relates. For instance, for the asset Trucks, it is useful to know both the original cost of the asset and the total accumulated depreciation amount recorded on the asset. Therefore, the asset account shows the original cost. The contra account, Accumulated Depreciation—Trucks, shows the total amount of recorded depreciation from the date of acquisition. By having both original cost and the accumulated depreciation amounts, a user can estimate the approximate percentage of the benefits embodied in the asset that the company has consumed. For instance, assume the accumulated depreciation amount is about three-fourths the cost of the asset. Then, the benefits would be approximately three-fourths consumed, and the company may have to replace the asset soon.

Thus, to provide more complete balance sheet information to users of financial statements, companies show both the original acquisition cost and accumulated depreciation. In the preceding example for adjustment 4, the balance sheet at December 31, 2012, would show the asset and contra asset as follows:

Assets

Trucks	$40,000
Less: Accumulated Depreciation	750
	$39,250

As you may expect, the accumulated depreciation account balance increases each period by the amount of depreciation expense recorded until the remaining book value of the asset equals the estimated salvage value.

Liability/Revenue Adjustments— Unearned Revenues

Reinforcing Problems
E3-9 Prepare entries for receipt of subscription fees and adjustment at year-end.
E3-10 Prepare entries for receipt of ticket fees, adjustment for earning revenues, and refund of fees.

A liability/revenue adjustment involving unearned revenues covers situations in which a customer has transferred assets, usually cash, to the selling company before the receipt of merchandise or services. Receiving assets before they are earned creates a liability called unearned revenue. The firm debits such receipts to the asset account Cash and credits a liability account. The liability account credited may be Unearned Fees, Revenue Received in Advance, Advances by Customers, or some similar title. The seller must either provide the services or return the customer's money. By performing the services, the company earns revenue and cancels the liability.

Companies receive advance payments for many items, such as training services, delivery services, tickets, and magazine or newspaper subscriptions. Although we illustrate and discuss only advanced receipt of training fees, firms treat the other items similarly.

Unearned Service Fees   On December 7, MicroTrain Company received $4,500 from a customer in payment for future training services. The firm recorded the following journal entry:

2012					
Dec.	7	Cash		4,500	
		Unearned Service Fees			4,500
		To record the receipt of cash from a customer in payment for future training services.			

The two T-accounts relating to training fees are Unearned Service Fees (a liability) and Service Revenue. These accounts appear as follows on December 31, 2012 (before adjustment):

(Dr.)	**Unearned Service Fees**	(Cr.)
	2012	
	Dec. 7 Cash received in advance	4,500

(Dr.)	**Service Revenue**	(Cr.)
	2012	
	Bal. before adjustment	10,700*

*The $10,700 balance came from transactions discussed in Chapter 2.

The balance in the Unearned Service Fees liability account established when MicroTrain received the cash will be converted into revenue as the company performs the training services. Before MicroTrain prepares its financial statements, it must make an adjusting entry to transfer the amount of the services performed by the company from a liability account to a revenue account. If we assume that MicroTrain earned one-third of the $4,500 in the Unearned Service Fees account by December 31, then the company transfers $1,500 to the Service Revenue account as follows:

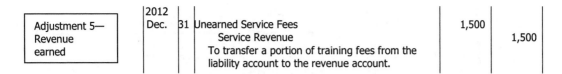

| Adjustment 5—
Revenue
earned | 2012
Dec. 31 | Unearned Service Fees
    Service Revenue
    To transfer a portion of training fees from the
    liability account to the revenue account. | 1,500 | 1,500 |

After posting the adjusting entry, the T-accounts would appear as follows:

MicroTrain reports the service revenue in its income statement for 2012. The company reports the $3,000 balance in the Unearned Service Fees account as a liability in the balance sheet. In 2013, the company will likely earn the $3,000 and transfer it to a revenue account.

If MicroTrain does not perform the training services, the company would have to refund the money to the training service customers. For instance, assume that MicroTrain could not perform the remaining $3,000 of training services and would have to refund the money. Then, the company would make the following entry:

| Unearned Service Fees
    Cash
    To record the refund of unearned training fees. | 3,000 | 3,000 |

Thus, the company must either perform the training services or refund the fees. This fact should strengthen your understanding that unearned service fees and similar items are liabilities.

Accountants make the adjusting entries for deferred items for data already recorded in a company's asset and liability accounts. They also make adjusting entries for accrued items, which we discuss in the next section, for business data not yet recorded in the accounting records.

BUSINESS INSIGHT According to the National Association of Colleges and Employers (NACE), the average salary offer to an accounting major in 2011 was $50,700, up 5.9% over 2010, and each year tends to increase. According to its most recent survey, the market for accounting graduates remains brisk. In fact, accounting majors received the most job offers of all 2011 graduates with bachelor's degrees. Current information on salaries and the job market for accountants and accounting majors can be found at:

http://www.naceweb.org

You may want to check out this website which has an entire section for students.

An Accounting Perspective

Adjustments for Accrued Items

Accrued items require two types of adjusting entries: asset/revenue adjustments and liability/expense adjustments. The first group—asset/revenue adjustments—involves accrued assets; the second group—liability/expense adjustments—involves accrued liabilities.

Asset/Revenue Adjustments— Accrued Assets

Accrued assets are assets, such as interest receivable or accounts receivable, that have not been recorded by the end of an accounting period. These assets represent rights to receive future payments that are not due at the balance sheet date. To present an accurate picture of the affairs of the business on the balance sheet, firms recognize these rights at the end of an accounting period by preparing an adjusting entry to correct the account balances. To indicate the dual nature of these adjustments, they record a related revenue in addition to the asset. We also call these adjustments **accrued revenues** because the revenues must be recorded.

Interest Revenue   Savings accounts literally earn interest moment by moment. Rarely is payment of the interest made on the last day of the accounting period. Thus, the accounting records normally do not show the interest revenue earned but not yet received (which affects the total assets owned by the investor), unless the company makes an adjusting entry. The adjusting entry at the end of the accounting period debits a receivable account (an asset) and credits a revenue account to record the interest earned and the asset owned.

For example, assume MicroTrain Company has some money in a savings account. On December 31, 2012, the money on deposit has earned one month's interest of $600, although the company has not received the interest. An entry must show the amount of interest earned by December 31, 2012, as well as the amount of the asset, interest receivable (the right to receive this interest). The entry to record the accrual of revenue is:

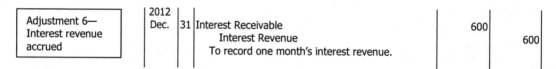

| Adjustment 6— Interest revenue accrued | 2012 Dec. | 31 | Interest Receivable
     Interest Revenue
     To record one month's interest revenue. | 600 | 600 |

The T-accounts relating to interest would appear as follows:

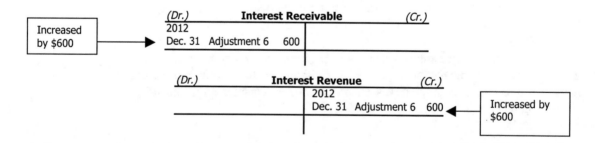

MicroTrain reports the $600 debit balance in Interest Receivable as an asset in the December 31, 2012, balance sheet. This asset accumulates gradually with the passage of time. The $600 credit balance in Interest Revenue is the interest earned during the month. Recall that in recording revenue under accrual basis accounting, it does not matter whether the company *collects* the actual cash during the year or not. It reports the interest revenue *earned* during the accounting period in the income statement.

Unbilled Training Fees   A company may perform services for customers in one accounting period while it bills for the services in a different accounting period.

MicroTrain Company performed $1,000 of training services on account for a client at the end of December. Since it takes time to do the paper work, MicroTrain

Reinforcing Problems
E3-11 Prepare adjusting entry for accrued legal services revenue.
E3-12 Prepare adjusting entry for accrued interest.

will bill the client for the services in January. The necessary adjusting journal entry at December 31, 2012, is:

	2012				
Adjustment 7— Unbilled revenues	Dec.	31	Accounts Receivable (or Service Fees Receivable)	1,000	
			Service Revenue		1,000
			To record unbilled training services performed in December.		

After posting the adjusting entry, the T-accounts appear as follows:

(Dr.)	Accounts Receivable		(Cr.)
2012			
Previous bal.	5,200*		
Dec. 31 Adjustment 7	1,000		
Bal. after adjustment	6,200		

*This previous balance came from transactions discussed in Chapter 2.

(Dr.)	Service Revenue		(Cr.)
	2012		
	Bal. before adjustment	10,700	
	Dec. 31 Adjustment 5— previously unearned revenue.	1,500	
	Dec. 31 Adjustment 7	1,000	
	Bal. after both adjustments	13,200	

Increased by $1,000

Note to the Student
Which accounting period should be associated with the training services performed? Should it be the period in which the actual service was performed, or the period in which the bill was sent out and presumably collected?

The service revenue appears in the income statement; the asset, accounts receivable, appears in the balance sheet.

Accrued liabilities   are liabilities not yet recorded at the end of an accounting period. They represent obligations to make payments not legally due at the balance sheet date, such as employee salaries. At the end of the accounting period, the company recognizes these obligations by preparing an adjusting entry including both a liability and an expense. For this reason, we also call these obligations **accrued expenses**.

Salaries   The recording of the payment of employee salaries usually involves a debit to an expense account and a credit to Cash. Unless a company pays salaries on the last day of the accounting period for a pay period ending on that date, it must make an adjusting entry to record any salaries incurred but not yet paid.

MicroTrain Company paid $3,600 of salaries on Friday, December 28, 2012, to cover the first four weeks of December. The entry made at that time was:

2012					
Dec.	28	Salaries Expense		3,600	
		Cash			3,600
		Paid training employee salaries for the first four weeks of December.			

Assuming that the last day of December 2012 falls on a Monday, this expense account does not show salaries earned by employees for the last day of the month. Nor does any account show the employer's obligation to pay these salaries. The T-accounts pertaining to salaries appear as follows before adjustment:

(Dr.)	Salaries Expense	(Cr.)		(Dr.)	Salaries Payable	(Cr.)
2012					2012	
Dec. 28	3,600				Dec. 28 Bal.	-0-

Liability/Expense Adjustments— Accrued Liabilities

Real World Example
In Europe, all companies that produce or sell products are responsible for the recycling or disposal of the resulting waste in the future. In February 2010, the Securities and Exchange Commission issued an interpretive release, *Commission Guidance Regarding Disclosure Related to Climate Change* (Release Nos. 33-9106 ; 34-61469; FR-82) to provide U.S. companies with guidance as to how to disclose potential future costs and liabilities due to climate change and legislative and regulatory developments.

Reinforcing Problem
E3-13 Prepare adjusting entry for accrued salaries.

A Broader Perspective

A Huge Adjusting Entry

A very significant example of a liability/expense adjustment became prominent in 1990. Many companies pay for retired employees' medical benefits. Before the 1990s, companies waited until they actually paid the benefits before recognizing an expense. Thus, they debited an expense and credited Cash when they paid the benefits. However, a rule passed by the Financial Accounting Standards Board in December 1990 requires that companies prepare an adjusting entry to account for the unfunded and unrecognized postretirement obligation and the related expense on the accrual basis.* The adjusting entry results in a debit to an expense and a credit to a liability.

Making this adjusting entry significantly reduced the reported earnings of many large companies by about 33% in 1992. The total net worth of approximately 60 of the largest U.S. companies shrunk by about $100 billion in 1992 as a result of this change. For instance, the net worth of General Motors Corporation declined by roughly 80% in 1992 as the result of recording this $20.72 billion expense on the accrual basis. Some companies have already reduced their retirees' medical benefits to minimize the future impact on earnings. Many companies reduced their retirees' medical benefits to minimize the future impact on earnings.

Typical of the disclosure made in annual reports regarding postretirement benefits is the following taken from the 1992 annual report of Waste Management, Inc. This company provides comprehensive environmental, waste management, and related services to industry, government, and consumers.

The Company and its principal subsidiaries adopted Statement of Financial Accounting Standards No. 106, 'Employers' Accounting for Postretirement Benefits Other Than Pensions' ('FAS 106') on the immediate recognition basis, effective as of January 1, 1992. This new Standard requires that the expected cost of future benefits be charged to expense during the years in which the employees render service. Previously, the Company recognized these costs, which relate primarily to health care costs and were not material, on a cash basis.

The cumulative effect of this accounting change was to decrease income for 1992 by $77,837,000 ($36,579,000, or $.07 per share, after tax and minority interest), representing the amount of the unfunded obligation measured as of January 1, 1992.

*Financial Accounting Standards Board, Statement of Financial Accounting Standards No. 106, 'Employers 'Accounting for Postretirement Benefits Other Than Pensions' (Norwalk, Conn., 1990).

Real World Example
During the most recent recession, many companies reduced their workforces and accrued losses amounting to billions of dollars. This reduction activity resulted in recording losses and created an offsetting liability. Once management has made the decision and has a plan, accruing losses is in accordance with the matching principle under GAAP. What is the nature of the losses that these companies probably experience when they reduce their workforces?

Reinforcing Problems
E3-14 Determine effect on net income from failing to record adjusting entries.
E3-15 Show the effects of failing to recognize indicated adjustments.

If salaries are $3,600 for four weeks, they are $900 per week. For a five-day workweek, daily salaries are $180. MicroTrain makes the following adjusting entry on December 31 to accrue salaries for one day:

Adjustment 8—
Accrued salaries

2012				
Dec.	31	Salaries Expense	180	
		Salaries Payable		180
		To accrue one day's salaries that were earned but not paid.		

After adjustment, the two T-accounts involved appear as follows:

(Dr.)	Salaries Expense		(Cr.)
2012			
Dec. 28 Bal.	3,600		
Dec. 31 Adjustment 8	180		
Bal. after adjustment	3,780		

(Dr.)	Salaries Payable		(Cr.)
	2012		
	Dec. 31 Adjustment 8	180	

Increased by $180

Illustration 3.5   Effects of Failure to Recognize Adjustments

	Failure to Recognize	Effect on Net Income	Effect on Balance Sheet Items
1.	Consumption of the benefits of an asset (prepaid expense)	Overstates net income	Overstates assets Overstates retained earnings
2.	Earning of previously unearned revenues	Understates net income	Overstates liabilities Understates retained earnings
3.	Accrual of assets	Understates net income	Understates assets Understates retained earnings
4.	Accrual of liabilities	Overstates net income	Understates liabilities Overstates retained earnings

The debit in the adjusting journal entry brings the month's salaries expense up to its correct $3,780 amount for income statement purposes. The credit to Salaries Payable records the $180 salary liability to employees. The balance sheet shows salaries payable as a liability.

Another example of a liability/expense adjustment is when a company incurs interest on a note payable. The debit would be to Interest Expense, and the credit would be to Interest Payable. We discuss this adjustment in Chapter 9.

Effects of Failing to Prepare Adjusting Entries

Failure to prepare proper adjusting entries causes net income and the balance sheet to be in error. You can see the effect of failing to record each of the major types of adjusting entries on net income and balance sheet items in Illustration 3.5.

Using MicroTrain Company as an example, this chapter has discussed and illustrated many of the typical entries that companies must make at the end of an accounting period. Later chapters explain other examples of adjusting entries.

Analyzing and Using the Financial Results— Trend Percentages

It is sometimes more informative to express all the dollar amounts as a percentage of one of the amounts in the base year rather than to look only at the dollar amount of the item in the financial statements. You can calculate **trend percentages** by dividing the amount for each year for an item, such as net income or net sales, by the amount of that item for the base year:

$$\text{Trend percentage} = \frac{\text{Current year amount}}{\text{Base year amount}}$$

To illustrate, Wal-Mart Stores, Inc., and its subsidiaries reported the following net income for the years ended January 31, 2001, through 2011. The last column expresses these dollar amounts as a percentage of the 2001 amount. For instance, we would calculate the 105% for 2002 as:

$$\left[\left(\frac{\$6,592,000}{\$6,295,000} \right) \times 100 \right]$$

Real World Example
The companies, such as General Motors, that took huge write-offs in the 1990s to account for post retirement benefits on an accrual basis may have been too conservative by taking too much of a write-off. If so, many of these companies could reverse some of these charges in the next few years, which could serve to cushion profits in the future. "Write-Offs May Become 'Write-Ons'," The Wall Street Journal, Monday, December 30, 1996, p. C1.

Objective 5
Determine the effects of failing to prepare adjusting entries.

Objective 5
Analyze and use the financial results—calculate trend percentages.

WalMart
Wal-Mart Stores, Inc., is a mass consumer goods merchandiser, operating 3,804 Walmart stores in the U.S., 4,557 Walmart stores internationally, and 609 Sam's Clubs as of the end of 2010.

	Dollar Amount of Net Income (millions)	Percentage of 2001 Net Income
2001	$6,295	100%
2002	6,592	105
2003	7,955	126
2004	9,054	144
2005	10,267	163
2006	11,231	178
2007	11,284	179
2008	12,731	202
2009	13,381	213
2010	14,370	228
2011	16,389	260

Examining the trend percentages, we can see that Wal-Mart's net income has increased steadily over the 10-year period. The 2011 net income is more than two-and-a-half times as much as the 2001 amount. This is the kind of performance that management and stockholders seek. Sam Walton started and built this company; when he died in 1993, he was one of the world's richest individuals. Walton spent considerable time at his stores talking with employees and customers. Wal-Mart currently is considered to be one of the greatest success stories in American business.

In the first three chapters of this text, you have learned most of the steps of the accounting process. Chapter 4 shows the final steps in the accounting cycle.

An Accounting Perspective

USES OF TECHNOLOGY The Internet sites of the Big-4 accounting firms are as follows:

Ernst & Young	http://www.ey.com
Deloitte Touche Tohmatsu	http://www.deloitte.com
KPMG	http://www.kpmg.com
PricewaterhouseCoopers	http://www.pwc.com

You might want to visit these sites to learn more about a possible career in accounting.

Understanding the Learning Objectives

Objective 1
Describe the basic characteristics of the cash basis and the accrual basis of accounting.

- The cash basis of accounting recognizes revenues when cash is received and recognizes expenses when cash is paid out.
- The accrual basis of accounting recognizes revenues when sales are made or services are performed, regardless of when cash is received; expenses are recognized as incurred, whether or not cash has been paid out.
- The accrual basis is more generally accepted than the cash basis because it provides a better matching of revenues and expenses.

Objective 2
Identify the reasons why adjusting entries must be made.

- Adjusting entries convert the amounts that are actually in the accounts to the amounts that should be in the accounts for proper periodic financial reporting.
- Adjusting entries reflect unrecorded economic activity that has taken place but has not yet been recorded.

- Deferred items consist of adjusting entries involving data previously recorded in accounts. Adjusting entries in this class normally involve moving data from asset and liability accounts to expense and revenue accounts. The two types of adjustments within this deferred items class are asset/expense adjustments and liability/revenue adjustments.

- Accrued items consist of adjusting entries relating to activity on which no data have been previously recorded in the accounts. These entries involve the initial recording of assets and liabilities and the related revenues and expenses. The two types of adjustments within this accrued items class are asset/revenue adjustments and liability/expense adjustments.

- This chapter illustrates entries for deferred items and accrued items.

- Failure to prepare adjusting entries causes net income and the balance sheet to be in error.

- For a particular item such as sales or net income, select a base year and express all dollar amounts in other years as a percentage of the base year dollar amount.

Objective 3
Identify the classes and types of adjusting entries.

Objective 4
Prepare adjusting entries.

Objective 5
Determine the effects of failing to prepare adjusting entries.

Objective 6
Analyze and use the financial results—calculate trend percentages.

Demonstration Problem

Among other items, the trial balance of Korman Company for December 31, 2012, includes the following account balances:

	Debits	Credits
Supplies on Hand	$ 6,000	
Prepaid Rent	25,200	
Buildings	200,000	
Accumulated Depreciation—Buildings		$33,250
Salaries Expense	124,000	
Unearned Delivery Fees		4,000

1. Some of the supplies represented by the $6,000 balance of the Supplies on Hand account have been consumed. An inventory count of the supplies actually on hand at December 31 totaled $2,400.
2. On May 1 of the current year, a rental payment of $25,200 was made for 12 months' rent; it was debited to Prepaid Rent.
3. The annual depreciation for the buildings is based on the cost shown in the Buildings account less an estimated salvage value of $10,000. The estimated useful lives of the buildings are 40 years each.
4. The salaries expense of $124,000 does not include $6,000 of unpaid salaries earned since the last payday.
5. The company has earned one-fourth of the unearned delivery fees by December 31.
6. Delivery services of $600 were performed for a customer, but a bill has not yet been sent.

 Additional data

Required

a. Prepare the adjusting journal entries for December 31, assuming adjusting entries are prepared only at year-end.

b. Based on the adjusted balance shown in the Accumulated Depreciation—Buildings account, how many years has Korman Company owned the building?

Solution to Demonstration Problem

a.

KORMAN COMPANY
General Journal

Date		Account Titles and Explanation	Post. Ref.	Debit	Credit
2012 Dec.	31	Supplies Expense		3 6 0 0	
		Supplies on Hand			3 6 0 0
		To record supplies expense ($6,000 - $2,400).			
	31	Rent Expense		1 6 8 0 0	
		Prepaid Rent			1 6 8 0 0
		To record rent expense ($25,200 X 8/12).			
	31	Depreciation Expense—Buildings		4 7 5 0	
		Accumulated Depreciation—Buildings			4 7 5 0
		To record depreciation ($200,000 - $10,000 / 40 years).			
	31	Salaries Expense		6 0 0 0	
		Salaries Payable			6 0 0 0
		To record accrued salaries.			
	31	Unearned Delivery Fees		1 0 0 0	
		Service Revenue			1 0 0 0
		To record delivery fees earned.			
	31	Accounts Receivable		6 0 0	
		Service Revenue			6 0 0
		To record delivery fees earned.			

b. Eight years; computed as:

$$\frac{\text{Total accumulated depreciation}}{\text{Annual depreciation expense}} = \frac{\$33,250 + \$4,750}{\$4,750} = 8$$

New Terms

Accounting period   A time period normally of one month, one quarter, or one year into which an entity's life is arbitrarily divided for financial reporting purposes. *101*

Accounting year   An accounting period of one year. The accounting year may or may not coincide with the calendar year. *101*

Accrual basis of accounting   Recognizes revenues when sales are made or services are performed, regardless of when cash is received. Recognizes expenses as incurred, whether or not cash has been paid out. *100*

Accrued assets and liabilities   Assets and liabilities that exist at the end of an accounting period but have not yet been recorded; they represent rights to receive, or obligations to make, payments that are not legally due at the balance sheet date. Examples are accrued fees receivable and salaries payable. *112, 113*

Accrued items   Adjusting entries relating to activity on which no data have been previously recorded in the accounts. Also, see *accrued assets and liabilities. 102*

Accrued revenues and expenses   Other names for accrued assets and liabilities. *112, 113*

Accumulated depreciation account   A contra asset account that shows the total of all depreciation recorded on the asset up through the balance sheet date. *109*

Adjusting entries   Journal entries made at the end of an accounting period to bring about a proper matching of revenues and expenses; they reflect economic activity that has taken place but has not yet been recorded. Adjusting entries are made to bring the accounts to their proper balances before financial statements are prepared. *101*

Book value   For depreciable assets, book value equals cost less accumulated depreciation. *109*

Calendar year   The normal year, which ends on December 31. *101*

Cash basis of accounting   Recognizes revenues when cash is received and recognizes expenses when cash is paid out. *99*

Contra asset account   An account shown as a deduction from the asset to which it relates in the balance sheet; used to reduce the original cost of the asset down to its remaining undepreciated cost or book value. *109*

Deferred items   Adjusting entries involving data previously recorded in the accounts. Data are transferred from asset and liability accounts to expense and revenue accounts. Examples are prepaid expenses, depreciation, and unearned revenues. *102*

Depreciable amount   The difference between an asset's cost and its estimated salvage value. *109*

Depreciable asset   A manufactured asset such as a building, machine, vehicle, or equipment on which depreciation expense is recorded. *108*

Depreciation accounting   The process of recording depreciation expense. *108*

Depreciation expense   The amount of asset cost assigned as an expense to a particular time period. *108*

Depreciation formula (straight-line): *108*

$$\text{Annual depreciation expense} = \frac{\text{Asset cost} - \text{Estimated salvage value}}{\text{Estimated years of useful life}}$$

Estimated salvage value (scrap value)   The amount that the company can probably sell the asset for at the end of its estimated useful life. *108*

Estimated useful life   The estimated time periods that a company can make use of the asset. *108*

Fiscal year   An accounting year of any 12 consecutive months that may or may not coincide with the calendar year. For example, a company may have an accounting, or fiscal, year that runs from April 1 of one year to March 31 of the next. *101*

Matching principle   An accounting principle requiring that expenses incurred in producing revenues be deducted from the revenues they generated during the accounting period. *101*

Prepaid expense   An asset awaiting assignment to expense. An example is prepaid insurance. Assets such as cash and accounts receivable are not prepaid expenses. *104*

Service potential   The benefits that can be obtained from assets. The future services that assets can render make assets "things of value" to a business. *105*

Trend percentages   Calculated by dividing the amount of an item for each year by the amount of that item for the base year. *115*

Unearned revenue   Assets received from customers before services are performed for them. Since the revenue has not been earned, it is a liability, often called *revenue received in advance* or *advances by customers. 110*

Self-Test

True-False
Indicate whether each of the following statements is true or false:
1. Every adjusting entry affects at least one income statement account and one balance sheet account.
2. All calendar years are also fiscal years, but not all fiscal years are calendar years.

3. The accumulated depreciation account is an asset account that shows the amount of depreciation for the current year only.
4. The Unearned Delivery Fees account is a revenue account.
5. If all of the adjusting entries are not made, the financial statements are incorrect.

Multiple-Choice
Select the best answer for each of the following questions.
1. An insurance policy premium of $1,200 was paid on September 1, 2012, to cover a one-year period from that date. An asset was debited on that date. Adjusting entries are prepared once a year, at year-end. The necessary adjusting entry at the company's year-end, December 31, 2012, is:

   a. Prepaid Insurance 400
       Insurance Expense 400
   b. Insurance Expense 800
       Prepaid Insurance 800
   c. Prepaid Insurance 800
       Insurance Expense 800
   d. Insurance Expense 400
       Prepaid Insurance 400

2. The Supplies on Hand account has a balance of $1,500 at year-end. The actual amount of supplies on hand at the end of the period was $400. The necessary adjusting entry is:

   a. Supplies Expense 1,100
       Supplies on Hand 1,100
   b. Supplies Expense 400
       Supplies on Hand 400
   c. Supplies on Hand 1,100
       Supplies Expense 1,100
   d. Supplies on Hand 400
       Supplies Expense 400

3. A company purchased a truck for $20,000 on January 1, 2012. The truck has an estimated salvage value of $5,000 and is expected to last five years. Adjusting entries are prepared only at year-end. The necessary adjusting entry at December 31, 2012, the company's year-end, is:

   a. Depreciation Expense—Trucks 4,000
       Accumulated Depreciation—Trucks 4,000
   b. Depreciation Expense—Trucks 3,000
       Trucks 3,000
   c. Depreciation Expense—Trucks 3,000
       Accumulated Depreciation—Trucks 3,000
   d. Accumulated Depreciation Trucks 3,000
       Depreciation Expense—Trucks 3,000

4. A company received cash of $24,000 on October 1, 2012, as subscriptions for a one-year period from that date. A liability account was credited when the cash was received. The magazine is to be published by the company and delivered to subscribers each month. The company prepares adjusting entries at the end of each month because it prepares financial statements each month. The adjusting entry the company would make at the end of each of the next 12 months would be:

   a. Unearned Subscription Fees 6,000
       Subscription Fee Revenue 6,000
   b. Unearned Subscription Fees 2,000
       Subscription Fee Revenue 2,000
   c. Unearned Subscription Fees 18,000
       Subscription Fee Revenue 18,000
   d. Subscription Fee Revenue 2,000
       Unearned Subscription Fees 2,000

5. When a company earns interest on a note receivable or on a bank account, the debit and credit are as follows:

	Debit	Credit
a.	Accounts Receivable	Interest Revenue
b.	Interest Receivable	Interest Revenue
c.	Interest Revenue	Accounts Receivable
d.	Interest Revenue	Interest Receivable

6. If $3,000 has been earned by a company's workers since the last payday in an accounting period, the necessary adjusting entry would be:
   a. Debit an expense and credit a liability.
   b. Debit an expense and credit an asset.
   c. Debit a liability and credit an asset.
   d. Debit a liability and credit an expense.

Now turn to page 131 to check your answers.

Questions

1. Which events during an accounting period trigger the recording of normal journal entries? Which event triggers the making of adjusting entries?
2. Describe the difference between the cash basis and accrual basis of accounting.
3. Why are adjusting entries necessary? Why not treat every cash disbursement as an expense and every cash receipt as a revenue when the cash changes hands?
4. "Adjusting entries would not be necessary if the 'pure' cash basis of accounting were followed (assuming no mistakes were made in recording cash transactions as they occurred). Under the cash basis, receipts that are of a revenue nature are considered revenue when received, and expenditures that are of an expense nature are considered expenses when paid. It is the use of the accrual basis of accounting, where an effort is made to match expenses incurred against the revenues they create, that makes adjusting entries necessary." Do you agree with this statement? Why?
5. Why don't accountants keep all the accounts at their proper balances continuously throughout the period so that adjusting entries would not have to be made before financial statements are prepared?
6. What is the fundamental difference between deferred items and accrued items?
7. Identify the types of adjusting entries included in each of the two major classes of adjusting entries.
8. Give an example of a journal entry for each of the following:
   a. Equal growth of an expense and a liability.
   b. Earning of revenue that was previously recorded as unearned revenue.
   c. Equal growth of an asset and a revenue.
   d. Increase in an expense and decrease in an asset.
9. A fellow student makes the following statement: "You can easily tell whether a company is using the cash or accrual basis of accounting. When an amount is paid for future rent or insurance services, a firm that is using the cash basis debits an expense account while a firm that is using the accrual basis debits an asset account." Is the student correct?
10. You notice that the Supplies on Hand account has a debit balance of $2,700 at the end of the accounting period. How would you determine the extent to which this account needs adjustment?
11. Some assets are converted into expenses as they expire and some liabilities become revenues as they are earned. Give examples of asset and liability accounts for which this statement is true. Give examples of asset and liability accounts to which the statement does not apply.
12. Give the depreciation formula to compute straight-line depreciation for a one-year period.
13. What does the term *accrued liability* mean?
14. What is meant by the term *service potential?*
15. When assets are received before they are earned, what type of an account is credited? As the amounts are earned, what type of account is credited?
16. What does the word *accrued* mean? Is there a conceptual difference between interest payable and accrued interest payable?
17. Matching expenses incurred with revenues earned is more difficult than matching expenses paid with revenues received. Do you think the effort is worth while?
18. Refer to "A Broader Perspective" on page 114. What type of adjusting entry is involved? How do you think the managements of some companies might react to having to record postretirement benefits in this way?

19. **Real World Question** Refer to the financial statements of Wal-Mart Stores, Inc., in the Annual Report Appendix. Approximately what percentage of the depreciable assets under property, plant, and equipment has been depreciated as of the end of the most recent year shown?

Exercises

Exercise 3-1
Answer multiple-choice
questions (L.O. 1)

Select the correct response for each of the following multiple-choice questions:

1. The cash basis of accounting:
   a. Recognizes revenues when sales are made or services are rendered.
   b. Recognizes expenses as incurred.
   c. Is typically used by some relatively small businesses and professional persons.
   d. Recognizes revenues when cash is received and recognizes expenses when incurred.
2. The accrual basis of accounting:
   a. Recognizes revenues only when cash is received.
   b. Is used by almost all companies.
   c. Recognizes expenses only when cash is paid out.
   d. Recognizes revenues when sales are made or services are performed and recognizes expenses only when cash is paid out.

Exercise 3-2
Answer multiple-
choice questions
(L.O. 2)

Select the correct response for each of the following multiple-choice questions:

1. The least common accounting period among the following is:
   a. One month.
   b. Two months.
   c. Three months.
   d. Twelve months.
2. The need for adjusting entries is based on:
   a. The matching principle.
   b. Source documents.
   c. The cash basis of accounting.
   d. Activity that has already been recorded in the proper accounts.

Exercise 3-3
Answer multiple-choice
questions (L.O. 3)

Select the correct response for each of the following multiple-choice questions:

1. Which of the following types of adjustments belongs to the deferred items class?
   a. Asset/revenue adjustments.
   b. Liability/expense adjustments.
   c. Asset/expense adjustments.
   d. Asset/liability adjustments.
2. Which of the following types of adjustments belongs to the accrued items class?
   a. Asset/expense adjustments.
   b. Liability/revenue adjustments.
   c. Asset/liability adjustments.
   d. Liability/expense adjustments.

Exercise 3-4
Prepare and post
adjusting entry for
insurance (L.O. 4)

a. A one-year insurance policy was purchased on August 1 for $2,400, and the following entry was made at that time:

| Prepaid Insurance | 2,400 | |
| Cash | | 2,400 |

What adjusting entry is necessary at December 31, the end of the accounting year?

b. Show how the T-accounts for Prepaid Insurance and Insurance Expense would appear after the entries are posted.

Assume that rent of $12,000 was paid on September 1, 2012, to cover a one-year period from that date. Prepaid Rent was debited. If financial statements are prepared only on December 31 of each year, what adjusting entry is necessary on December 31, 2012, to bring the accounts involved to their proper balances?

Exercise 3-5
Prepare adjusting entry
for rent (L.O. 4)

At December 31, 2012, an adjusting entry was made as follows:

| Rent Expense | 1,500 | |
| Prepaid Rent | | 1,500 |

Exercise 3-6
Determine date and
entry for rent paid
(L.O. 4)

You know that the gross amount of rent paid was $4,500, which was to cover a one-year period. Determine:

a. The opening date of the year to which the $4,500 of rent applies.
b. The entry that was made on the date the rent was paid.

Supplies were purchased for cash on May 2, 2012, for $8,000. Show how this purchase would be recorded. Then show the adjusting entry that would be necessary, assuming that $2,500 of the supplies remained at the end of the year.

Exercise 3-7
Prepare entries for
purchase of supplies
and adjustment at
year-end (L.O. 4)

Assume that a company acquired a building on January 1, 2012, at a cost of $1,000,000. The building has an estimated useful life of 40 years and an estimated salvage value of $200,000. What adjusting entry is needed on December 31, 2012, to record the depreciation for the entire year 2012?

Exercise 3-8
Prepare adjusting
entry for depreciation
(L.O. 4)

On September 1, 2012, Professional Golfer Journal, Inc., received a total of $120,000 as payment in advance for one-year subscriptions to a monthly magazine. A liability account was credited to record this cash receipt. By the end of the year, one-third of the magazines paid for in advance had been delivered. Give the entries to record the receipt of the subscription fees and to adjust the accounts at December 31, assuming annual financial statements are prepared at year-end.

Exercise 3-9
Prepare entries for
receipt of subscription
fees and adjustment
at year-end
(L.O. 4)

On April 15, 2012, Rialto Theater sold $90,000 in tickets for the summer musicals to be performed (one per month) during June, July, and August. On July 15, 2012, Rialto Theater discovered that the group that was to perform the July and August musicals could not do so. It was too late to find another group qualified to perform the musicals. A decision was made to refund the remaining unearned ticket revenue to its ticket holders, and this was done on July 20. Show the appropriate journal entries to be made on April 15, June 30, and July 20. Rialto has a June 30th year-end.

Exercise 3-10
Prepare entries for
receipt of ticket fees,
adjustment for earning
revenue, and refund
of fees(L.O. 4)

Guilty & Innocent, a law firm, performed legal services in late December 2012 for clients. The $30,000 of services would be billed to the clients in January 2013. Give the adjusting entry that is necessary on December 31, 2012, if financial statements are prepared at the end of each month.

Exercise 3-11
Prepare adjusting
entry for accrued legal
services(L.O.4)

A firm borrowed $30,000 on November 1. By December 31, $300 of interest had been incurred. Prepare the adjusting entry required on December 31.

Exercise 3-12
Prepare adjusting
entry for accrued
interest(L.O. 4)

Convenient Mailing Services, Inc., incurs salaries at the rate of $3,000 per day. The last payday in January is Friday, January 27. Salaries for Monday and Tuesday of the next week have not been recorded or paid as of January 31. Financial statements are prepared monthly. Give the necessary adjusting entry on January 31.

Exercise 3-13
Prepare adjusting entry
for accrued salaries
(L.O. 4)

Exercise 3-14
Determine effect on net income from failing to record adjusting entries
(L.O. 5)

State the effect that each of the following independent situations would have on the amount of annual net income reported for 2012 and 2013.

a. No adjustment was made for accrued salaries of $8,000 as of December 31, 2012.

b. The collection of $5,000 for services yet unperformed as of December 31, 2012, was credited to a revenue account and not adjusted. The services are performed in 2013.

Exercise 3-15
Show the effects of failing to recognize indicated adjustments(L.O. 5)

In the following table, indicate the effects of failing to recognize each of the indicated adjustments by writing "O" for overstated and "U" for understated.

| | | | Effect on Balance Sheet Items | | |
	Failure to Recognize	**Effect on Net Income**	**Assets**	**Liabilities**	**Stockholders' Equity**
1.	Depreciation on a building				
2.	Consumption of supplies on hand				
3.	The earning of ticket revenue received in advance				
4.	The earning of interest on a bank account				
5.	Salaries incurred by unpaid				

Exercise 3-16
Calculate the trend percentages for net income (loss) for Ford Motor Company and comment (L.O. 6)

The following data regarding net income (loss) are for the Ford Motor Company for the period 1999–2010. Ford is one of the world's largest auto manufacturers.

	Net Income (Loss) ($ millions)		Net Income (Loss) ($ millions)
1999	$7,237	2005	$1,440
2000	3,467	2006	(12,613)
2001	5,453	2007	(2,723)
2002	(980)	2008	(14,766)
2003	495	2009	2,717
2004	3,038	2010	6,561

Using 1999 as the base year, calculate the trend percentages, and comment on the results.

Problems

Problem 3-1
Prepare adjusting entries(L.O. 4)

Among other items, the trial balance of Filmblaster, Inc., a movie rental company, at December 31 of the current year includes the following account balances:

	Debits
Prepaid Insurance	$10,000
Prepaid Rent	14,400
Supplies on Hand	2,800

Examination of the records shows that adjustments should be made for the following items:

a. Of the prepaid insurance in the trial balance, $4,000 is for coverage during the months after December 31 of the current year.

b. The balance in the Prepaid Rent account is for a 12-month period that started October 1 of the current year.

c. $300 of interest has been earned but not received.

d. Supplies used during the year amount to $1,800.

Required ➲ Prepare the annual year-end adjusting journal entries at December 31.

Problem 3-2
Prepare adjusting entries and post to ledger accounts
(L.O. 4)

Marathon Magazine, Inc., has the following account balances, among others, in its trial balance at December 31 of the current year:

	Debits	**Credits**
Supplies on Hand	$3,720	
Prepaid Rent	7,200	
Unearned Subscription Fees		$15,000
Subscriptions Revenue		261,000
Salaries Expense		123,000

1. The inventory of supplies on hand at December 31 amounts to $720.
2. The balance in the Prepaid Rent account is for a one-year period starting October 1 of the current year.
3. One-third of the $15,000 balance in Unearned Subscription Fees has been earned.
4. Since the last payday, the employees of the company have earned additional salaries in the amount of $5,430.

⮚ *Additional data*

  a. Prepare the year-end adjusting journal entries at December 31. Assume you used page 22 of the general journal to record the journal entries.
  b. Open ledger accounts for each of the accounts involved, enter the balances as shown in the trial balance, post the adjusting journal entries, and calculate year-end balances.

⮚ *Required*

Hillside Apartments, Inc., adjusts and closes its books each December 31. Assume the accounts for all prior years have been properly adjusted and closed. Following are some of the company's account balances prior to adjustment on December 31, 2012:

Problem 3-3
Prepare adjusting
entries (L.O. 4)

HILLSIDE APARTMENTS, INC.
Partial Trial Balance
December 31, 2012

	Debits	Credits
Prepaid Insurance	$7,500	
Supplies on Hand	7,000	
Buildings	255,000	
Accumulated Depreciation—Buildings	$96,000	
Unearned Rent		2,700
Salaries Expense	69,000	
Rental Revenue		277,500

1. The Prepaid Insurance account balance represents the remaining cost of a four-year insurance policy dated June 30, 2010, having a total premium of $12,000.
2. The physical inventory of the office supply stockroom indicates that the supplies on hand cost $3,000.
3. The building was originally acquired on January 1, 1996, at which time management estimated that the building would last 40 years and have a salvage value of $15,000.
4. Salaries earned since the last payday but unpaid at December 31 amount to $5,000.
5. Interest earned but not collected on a savings account during the year amounts to $400.
6. The Unearned Rent account arose through the prepayment of rent by a tenant in the building for 12 months beginning October 1, 2012.

Prepare the annual year-end adjusting entries indicated by the additional data.

⮚ *Required*

The reported net income amounts for Gulf Coast Magazine, Inc., for calendar years 2012 and 2013 were $200,000 and $222,000, respectively. No annual adjusting entries were made at either year-end for any of the following transactions:

Problem 3-4
Calculate correct net
income (L.O.5)

1. A fire insurance policy to cover a three-year period from the date of payment was purchased on March 1, 2012 for $3,600. The Prepaid Insurance account was debited at the date of purchase.
2. Subscriptions for magazines in the amount of $72,000 to cover an 18-month period from May 1, 2012, were received on April 15, 2012. The Unearned Subscription Fees account was credited when the payments were received.
3. A building costing $180,000 and having an estimated useful life of 50 years and a salvage value of $30,000 was purchased and put into service on January 1, 2012.
4. On January 12, 2013, salaries of $9,600 were paid to employees. The account debited was Salaries Expense. One-third of the amount paid was earned by employees in December of 2012.

Calculate the correct net income for 2012 and 2013. In your answer, start with the reported net income. Then show the effects of each correction (adjustment), using a plus or a minus

⮚ *Required*

to indicate whether reported income should be increased or decreased as a result of the correction. When the corrections are added to or deducted from the reported net income amounts, the result should be the correct net income amounts. The answer format should appear as follows:

Explanation of Corrections	2012	2013
Reported net income	$200,000	$222,000
To correct error in accounting for:		
a. Fire insurance policy premium:		
Correct expense in 2012	−1,000	
Correct expense in 2013		−1,200

Problem 3-5
Prepare journal
entries under cash
basis and accrual
basis (L.O. 1, 4)

Jupiter Publishing Company began operations on December 1, 2012. The company's bookkeeper intended to use the cash basis of accounting. Consequently, the bookkeeper recorded all cash receipts and disbursements for items relating to operations in revenue and expense accounts. No adjusting entries were made prior to preparing the financial statements for December.

Transactions ➥

Dec.   1 Issued capital stock for $300,000 cash.
         3 Received $144,000 for magazine subscriptions to run for two years from this date. The magazine is published monthly on the 23rd.
         4 Paid for advertising to be run in a national periodical for six months (starting this month). The cost was $36,000.
         7 Purchased for cash an insurance policy to cover a two-year period beginning December 15, $24,000.
        12 Paid the annual rent on the building, $36,000, effective through November 30, 2013.
        15 Received $216,000 cash for two-year subscriptions starting with the December issue.
        15 Salaries for the period December 1–15 amounted to $48,000. Beginning as of this date, salaries will be paid on the 5th and 20th of each month for the preceding two-week period.
        20 Salaries for the period December 1–15 were paid.
        23 Supplies purchased for cash, $21,600. (Only $1,800 of these were subsequently used in 2012.)
        27 Printing costs applicable equally to the next six issues beginning with the December issue were paid in cash, $144,000.
        31 Cash sales of the December issue, $84,000.
        31 Unpaid salaries for the period December 16–31 amounted to $22,000.
        31 Sales on account of December issue, $14,000.

Required ➥

a. Prepare journal entries for the transactions as the bookkeeper prepared them.
b. Prepare journal entries as they would have been prepared under the accrual basis.
     Where the entry is the same as under the cash basis, merely indicate "same."
Where possible, record the original transaction so that no adjusting entry would be necessary at the end of the month. Ignore explanations.

Alternate Problems

Problem 3-1A
Prepare adjusting
entries (L.O. 4)

The trial balance of Caribbean Vacation Tours, Inc., at December 31 of the current year includes, among other items, the following account balances:

	Debits	Credits
Prepaid Insurance	$24,000	
Prepaid Rent	24,000	
Buildings		188,000
Accumulated Depreciation—Buildings		$31,600
Salaries Expense		200,000

1. The balance in the Prepaid Insurance account is the advance premium for one year from September 1 of the current year.
2. The buildings are expected to last 25 years, with an expected salvage value of $30,000.
3. Salaries incurred but not paid as of December 31 amount to $8,400.
4. The balance in Prepaid Rent is for a one-year period that started March 1 of the current year.

Additional data

Prepare the annual year-end adjusting journal entries at December 31.

Required

Among the account balances shown in the trial balance of Dunwoody Mail Station, Inc., at December 31 of the current year are the following:

Problem 3-2A
Prepare adjusting
entries and post to
ledger accounts
(L.O. 4)

	Debits	Credits
Supplies on Hand	$10,000	
Prepaid Insurance	6,000	
Buildings	168,000	
Accumulated Depreciation—Buildings		$39,000

1. The inventory of supplies on hand at December 31 amounts to $3,000.
2. The balance in the Prepaid Insurance account is for a two-year policy taken out June 1 of the current year.
3. Depreciation for the buildings is based on the cost shown in the Buildings account, less salvage value estimated at $18,000. When acquired, the lives of the buildings were estimated at 50 years each.
   a. Prepare the year-end adjusting journal entries at December 31.
   b. Open ledger accounts for each of the accounts involved, enter the balances as shown in the trial balance, post the adjusting journal entries, and calculate year-end balances.

Additional data

Required

Nevada Camping Equipment Rental Company occupies rented quarters on the main street of Las Vegas. To get this location, the company rented a store larger than needed and subleased (rented) a portion of the area to Max's Restaurant. The partial trial balance of Nevada Camping Equipment Rental Company as of December 31, 2012, is as follows:

Problem 3-3A
Prepare adjusting
entries(L.O. 4)

NEVADA CAMPING EQUIPMENT RENTAL COMPANY
Trial Balance
December 31, 2012

	Debits	Credits
Cash	$100,000	
Prepaid Insurance	11,400	
Supplies on Hand	20,000	
Camping Equipment	176,000	
Accumulated Depreciation—Camping Equipment		$ 19,200
Notes Payable		40,000
Equipment Rental Revenue		1,500,000
Sublease Rental Revenue		8,800
Building Rent Expense	14,400	
Salaries Expense	196,000	

a. Salaries of employees amount to $300 per day and were last paid through Wednesday,

Additional data

Balance, January 1, 2012	$128,000
Addition, July 1, 2012	48,000
Balance, December 31, 2012, per trial balance	$176,000

December 27. December 31 is a Sunday. The store is closed Sundays.
b. An analysis of the Camping Equipment account disclosed:
The company estimates that all equipment will last 20 years from the date they were acquired and that the salvage value will be zero.
c. The store carries one combined insurance policy, which is taken out once a year effective August 1. The premium on the policy now in force amounts to $7,200 per year.

d. Unused supplies on hand at December 31, 2012, have a cost of $9,200.

e. December's rent from Max's Restaurant has not yet been received, $800.

f. Interest accrued on the note payable is $700.

Required ➲   Prepare the annual year-end entries required by the preceding statement of facts.

Problem 3-4A
Calculate correct net income(L.O. 5)

The reported net income amounts for Safety Waste Control Company were 2012, $200,000; and 2013, $230,000. *No* annual adjusting entries were made at either year-end for any of these transactions:

a. A building was rented on April 1, 2012. Cash of $14,400 was paid on that date to cover a two-year period. Prepaid Rent was debited.

b. The balance in the Office Supplies on Hand account on December 31, 2012, was $6,000. An inventory of the supplies on December 31, 2012, revealed that only $3,500 were actually on hand at that date. No new supplies were purchased during 2013. At December 31, 2013, an inventory of the supplies revealed that $800 were on hand.

c. A building costing $1,200,000 and having an estimated useful life of 40 years and a salvage value of $240,000 was put into service on January 1, 2012.

d. Services were performed for customers in December 2012. The $24,000 bill for these services was not sent until January 2013. The only transaction that was recorded was a debit to Cash and a credit to Service Revenue when payment was received in January.

Required ➲   Calculate the correct net income for 2012 and 2013. In your answer, start with the reported net income amounts. Then show the effects of each correction (adjustment) using a plus or a minus to indicate whether reported income should be increased or decreased as a result of the correction. When the corrections are added to or deducted from the reported net income amounts, the result should be the correct net income amounts. The answer format should be as follows:

Explanation of Corrections	2012	2013
Reported net income	$200,000	$230,000
To correct error in accounting for:		
a. Prepaid rent:		
Correct expense in 2012	−5,400	
Correct expense in 2013		−7,200

Problem 3-5A
Prepare journal entries under cash basis and accrual basis(L.O. 1, 4)

On June 1, 2012, Richard Cross opened a swimming pool cleaning and maintenance service, Cross Pool Company. He vaguely recalled the process of making journal entries and establishing ledger accounts from a high school bookkeeping course he had taken some years ago. At the end of June, he prepared an income statement for the month of June, but he had the feeling that he had not proceeded correctly. He contacted his brother, John, a recent college graduate with a major in accounting, for assistance. John immediately noted that his brother had kept his records on a cash basis.

Transactions ➲   June   1   Received cash of $28,000 from various customers in exchange for service agreements to clean and maintain their pools for June, July, August, and September.

5   Paid rent for automotive and cleaning equipment to be used during the period June through September, $8,000. The payment covered the entire period.

8   Purchased a two-year liability insurance policy effective June 1 for $12,000 cash.

10   Received an advance of $9,000 from a Florida building contractor in exchange for an agreement to help service pools in his housing development during October through May.

16   Paid salaries for the first half of June, $8,400.

17   Paid $900 for advertising to be run in a local newspaper for two weeks in June and four weeks in July.

19   Paid the rent of $24,000 under a four-month lease on a building rented and occupied on June 1.

June   26   Purchased $5,400 of supplies for cash. (Only $900 of these supplies were used in June.)

29   Billed various customers for services rendered, $16,000.

30   Unpaid employee services received in the last half of June amounted to $12,600.

30   Received a bill for $600 for gas and oil used in June.

a. Prepare the entries for the transactions as Richard must have recorded them under the cash basis of accounting.

b. Prepare journal entries as they would have been prepared under the accrual basis. Where the entry is the same as under the cash basis, merely indicate "same." Where possible, record the original transaction so that no adjusting entry would be necessary at the end of the month. Ignore explanations.

Required

Beyond the Numbers—Critical Thinking

You have just been hired by Top Executive Employment Agency, Inc., to help prepare adjusting entries at the end of an accounting period. It becomes obvious to you that management does not seem to have much of an understanding about the necessity or adjusting entries or which accounts might possibly need adjustment. The first step you take is to prepare the following unadjusted trial balance from the general ledger. Only those ledger accounts that had end-of-year balances are included in the trial balance.

Business Decision Case 3-1
Explain why adjusting entries are made and which accounts need adjustment (L.O. 2, 4)

	Debits	Credits
Cash	$ 80,000	
Accounts Receivable	28,000	
Supplies on Hand	3,000	
Prepaid Insurance	2,700	
Office Equipment	120,000	
Accumulated Depreciation—Office Equipment		$ 45,000
Buildings	360,000	
Accumulated Depreciation—Buildings		105,000
Accounts Payable		9,000
Loan Payable (Bank)		15,000
Unearned Commission Fees		30,000
Capital Stock		160,000
Retained Earnings		89,300
Commissions Revenue		270,000
Advertising Expense	6,000	
Salaries Expense	112,500	
Utilities Expense	7,500	
Miscellaneous Expense	3,600	
	$723,300	$723,300

a. Explain to management why adjusting entries in general are made.

b. Explain to management why some of the specific accounts appearing in the trial balance may need adjustment and what the nature of each adjustment might be (do not worry about specific dollar amounts).

Required

A friend of yours, Jack Andrews, is quite excited over the opportunity he has to purchase the land and several miscellaneous assets of Drake Bowling Lanes Company for $400,000. Andrews tells you that Mr. and Mrs. Drake (the sole stockholders in the company) are moving due to Mr. Drake's ill health. The annual rent on the building and equipment is $54,000.

Drake reports that the business earned a profit of $100,000 in 2012 (last year). Andrews believes an annual profit of $100,000 on an investment of $400,000 is a really good deal. But, before completing the deal, he asks you to look it over. You agree and discover the following:

Business Decision Case 3-2
Prepare an appraisal and an approximate income statement (L.O. 1, 4)

1. Drake has computed his annual profit for 2012 as the sum of his cash dividends plus the increase in the Cash account: Dividends of $60,000 + Increase in Cash account of $40,000 = $100,000 profit.

2. As buyer of the business, Andrews will take over responsibility for repayment of a $300,000 loan (plus interest) on the land. The land was acquired at a cost of $624,000 seven years ago.

3. An analysis of the Cash account shows the following for 2012:

Rental revenues received		$465,000
Cash paid out in 2012 for—		
Salaries paid to employees	$260,000	
Utilities paid	18,000	
Advertising expenses paid	15,000	
Supplies purchased and used	24,000	
Interest paid on loan	18,000	
Loan principal paid	30,000	
Cash dividends	60,000	425,000
Increase in cash balance for the year		$ 40,000

4. You also find that the annual rent of $54,000, a December utility bill of $4,000, and an advertising bill of $6,000 have not been paid.

Required ➡

    a. Prepare a written report for Andrews giving your appraisal of Drake Bowling Lanes Company as an investment. Comment on Drake's method of computing the annual profit of the business.

    b. Include in your report an approximate income statement for 2012.

Group Project 3-3
Undertake internet project concerning annual reports (L.O. 6)

In teams of two or three students, go to the library to locate one company's annual report for the most recent year. Identify the name of the company and the major products or services offered, as well as gross revenues, major expenses, and the trend of profits over the last three years. Calculate trend percentages for revenues, expenses, and profits using the oldest year as the base year. Each team should write a memorandum to management summarizing the data and commenting on the trend percentages. The heading of the memorandum should contain the date, to whom it is written, from whom, and the subject matter.

Group Project 3-4
Perform library research

With one or two other students and using library and internet sources, write a paper on Statement of Accounting Standards No. 106, "Accounting for Postretirement Benefits Other Than Pensions" (now codified in ASC 715, "Benefits – Retirement Benefits"). This standard resulted in some of the largest adjusting entries ever made. Companies had to record an expense and a liability to account for these costs on an accrual basis. In the past they typically had recorded this expense on a cash basis, recognizing the expense only when cash was paid to retirees. Be sure to cite your sources and treat direct quotes properly.

Group Project 3-5
Perform library research

With one or two other students and using library sources, write a paper on human resource accounting. Generally accepted accounting principles do not allow "human assets" to be included among assets on the balance sheet. Why is this? Be sure to cite your sources and to treat direct quotes properly.

Using the Internet—A View of the Real World

Visit the website:

http://www.pwc.com

Click on the "Our Services" and then the "IFRS" tab. Read the most recent news story and write a brief report to your instructor summarizing your findings.

Internet Project 3-6
Check out
PricewaterhouseCoopers
and IFRS news

Visit the website:

http://www.accounting.smartpros.com

Then click on Students. Look for news items and you will find a list of articles and surveys related to accounting and finance. Pick a topic and write a report to your instructor summarizing the article.

Internet Project 3-7
Check out Smartpros.
com

Answers to Self-Test

True-False

1. **True.** Every adjusting entry involves either moving previously recorded data from an asset account to an expense account or from a liability account to a revenue account (or in the opposite direction) or simultaneously entering new data in an asset account and a revenue account or in a liability account and an expense account.
2. **True.** A fiscal year is any 12 consecutive months, so all calendar years are also fiscal years. A calendar year, however, must end on December 31, so it does not include fiscal years that end on any date other than December 31 (such as June 30).
3. **False.** The accumulated depreciation account is a *contra asset* that shows the total of all depreciation recorded on an asset from its acquisition date up through the balance sheet date.
4. **False.** The Unearned Delivery Fees account is a liability. As the fees are earned, the amount in that account is transferred to a revenue account.
5. **True.** If an adjusting entry is overlooked and not made, at least one income statement account and one balance sheet account will be incorrect.

Multiple-Choice

1. **d.** One-third of the benefits have expired. Therefore, $400 must be moved from the asset (credit) to an expense (debit).
2. **a.** $1,100 of the supplies have been used, so that amount must be moved from the asset (credit) to an expense (debit).
3. **c.** The amount of annual depreciation is determined as ($20,000 – $5,000) divided by 5 = $3,000. The debit is to Depreciation Expense—Trucks, and the credit is to Accumulated Depreciation—Trucks, a contra asset account.
4. **b.** Each month $2,000 would be transferred from the liability account (debit), Unearned Subscription Fees, to a revenue account (credit).
5. **b.** An asset, Interest Receivable, is debited, and Interest Revenue is credited.
6. **a.** The debit would be to Salaries Expense, and the credit would be to Salaries Payable.

Careers in Accounting

A Career in Information Technology

Have you ever heard the sayings "knowledge is power" or "information is money"? When people talk about accounting, what they are really talking about is information. The information used by businesses, as well as the technology that supports that information, represents some of the most valuable assets for organizations around the world. Very often, the success of a business depends on effective creation, management, and use of information.

As companies become ever more reliant on technology, the need for well-educated Information Technology (IT) auditors and control professionals increases. Improved technology has the potential to dramatically improve business organizations and practices, reduce costs and exploit new business and investment opportunities. At the same time, companies face constant challenges in selecting and implementing these new technologies. Because of their high value and inherent complexity, the development, support, and auditing of information systems has become one of the fastest growing specialties in accounting.

Graduates with special interests and skills in computing and technology have expansive opportunities. In addition to traditional accounting and auditing functions, IT professionals perform evaluations of technologies and communications protocols involving electronic data interchange, client servers, local and wide area networks, data communications, telecommunications, and integrated voice/data/video systems. In public accounting, technology has impacted the auditing profession by extending the knowledge required to draw conclusions and the skills required to audit advanced accounting and information systems.

With management consulting practices growing and information systems becoming a larger percentage of public accounting revenue, IT professionals are in high demand. If you are considering a degree in computer or information systems, you should consider the advantages that an accounting major or minor can give you in working closely with businesses and consulting firms. A dual major in accounting and IT is one of the most desirable undergraduate degree combinations in the workforce.

4

Completing the Accounting Cycle

This chapter explains two new steps in the **accounting cycle**—the preparation of the work sheet and closing entries. In addition, we briefly discuss the evolution of accounting systems and present a classified balance sheet. This balance sheet format more closely resembles actual company balance sheets. After completing this chapter, you will understand how accounting begins with source documents that are evidence of a business entity's transactions and ends with financial statements that show the solvency and profitability of the entity.

The Accounting Cycle Summarized

In Chapter 1, you learned that when an event is a measureable business transaction, you need adequate proof of this transaction. Then, you analyze the transaction's effects on the accounting equation, Assets = Liabilities + Stockholders' equity. In Chapters 2 and 3, you performed other steps in the accounting cycle. Chapter 2 presented the eight steps in the accounting cycle as a preview of the content of Chapters 2 through 4. As a review, study the diagram of the eight steps in the accounting cycle in Illustration 4.1 (page 135). Remember that the first three steps occur during the accounting period and the last five occur at the end. The next section explains how to use the work sheet to facilitate the completion of the accounting cycle.

The Work Sheet

The **work sheet** is a columnar sheet of paper or a computer spreadsheet on which accountants summarize information needed to make the adjusting and closing entries

Learning Objectives

After studying this chapter, you should be able to:

1. Summarize the steps in the accounting cycle.

2. Prepare a work sheet for a service company.

3. Prepare an income statement, statement of retained earnings, and balance sheet using information contained in the work sheet.

4. Prepare adjusting and closing entries using information contained in the work sheet.

5. Prepare a post-closing trial balance.

6. Describe the evolution of accounting systems.

(continued)

Objectives

7. Prepare a classified balance sheet.

8. Analyze and use the financial results—the current ratio.

Objective 1
Summarize the steps in the accounting cycle.

Objective 2
Prepare a work sheet for a service company.

The Trial Balance Columns

Note to the Student
1. The work sheet is not a formal financial statement; usually only the accountant sees it.
2. Its major purpose is to organize data into a convenient form prior to preparing the financial statements.
3. Some accountants do not prepare a work sheet; however, many believe it makes the end-of-period work easier.

The Trial Balance Columns

Reinforcing Problem
E4-1 Identify the steps in the accounting cycle.

and to prepare the financial statements. Usually, they save these work sheets to document the end-of-period entries. A work sheet is only an accounting tool and not part of the formal accounting records. Therefore, work sheets may vary in format; some are prepared in pencil so that errors can be corrected easily. Other work sheets are prepared on personal computers with spreadsheet software. Accountants prepare work sheets each time financial statements are needed—monthly, quarterly, or at the end of the accounting year.

This chapter illustrates a 12-column work sheet that includes sets of columns for an unadjusted trial balance, adjustments, adjusted trial balance, income statement, statement of retained earnings, and balance sheet. Each set has a debit and a credit column. (See Illustration 4.2 on page 136.)

Accountants use these initial steps in preparing the work sheet. The following sections describe the detailed steps for completing the work sheet.

1. Enter the titles and balances of ledger accounts in the Trial Balance columns.
2. Enter adjustments in the Adjustments columns.
3. Enter adjusted account balances in the Adjusted Trial Balance columns.
4. Extend adjusted balances of revenue and expense accounts from the Adjusted Trial Balance columns to the Income Statement columns.
5. Extend any balances in the Retained Earnings and Dividends accounts to the Statement of Retained Earnings columns.
6. Extend adjusted balances of asset, liability, and capital stock accounts from the Adjusted Trial Balance columns to the Balance Sheet columns.

Instead of preparing a separate trial balance as we did in Chapter 2, accountants use the Trial Balance columns on a work sheet. Look at Illustration 4.2 and note that the numbers and titles of the ledger accounts of MicroTrain Company are on the left portion of the work sheet. Usually, only those accounts with balances as of the end of the accounting period are listed. (Some accountants do list the entire chart of accounts, even those with zero balances.) Assume you are MicroTrain's accountant. You list the Retained Earnings account in the trial balance even though it has a zero balance to (1) show its relative position among the accounts and (2) indicate that December 2012 is the first month of operations for this company. Next, you enter the balances of the ledger accounts in the Trial Balance columns. The accounts are in the order in which they appear in the general ledger: assets, liabilities, stockholders' equity, dividends, revenues, and expenses. Then, total the columns. If the debit and credit column totals are not equal, an error exists that must be corrected before you proceed with the work sheet.

As you learned in Chapter 3, adjustments bring the accounts to their proper balances before accountants prepare the income statement, statement of retained earnings, and balance sheet. You enter these adjustments in the Adjustments columns of the work sheet. Also, you cross-reference the debits and credits of the entries by placing a key number or letter to the left of the amounts. This key number facilitates the actual journalizing of the adjusting entries later because you do not have to rethink the adjustments to record them. For example, the number *(1)* identifies the adjustment debiting Insurance Expense and crediting Prepaid Insurance. Note in the Account Titles column that the Insurance Expense account title is below the trial balance totals because the Insurance Expense account did not have a balance before the adjustment and, therefore, did not appear in the trial balance.

Work sheet preparers often provide brief explanations at the bottom for the keyed entries as in Illustration 4.2. Although these explanations are optional, they provide valuable information for those who review the work sheet later.

The adjustments (which were discussed and illustrated in Chapter 3) for MicroTrain Company are:

Illustration 4.1   Steps in the Accounting Cycle

- Entry *(1)* records the expiration of $200 of prepaid insurance in December.
- Entry *(2)* records the expiration of $400 of prepaid rent in December.
- Entry *(3)* records the using up of $500 of supplies during the month.
- Entry *(4)* records $750 depreciation expense on the trucks for the month. MicroTrain acquired the trucks at the beginning of December.
- Entry *(5)* records the earning of $1,500 of the $4,500 in the Unearned Service Fees account.
- Entry *(6)* records $600 of interest earned in December.
- Entry *(7)* records $1,000 of unbilled training services performed in December.
- Entry *(8)* records the $180 accrual of salaries expense at the end of the month.

Reinforcing Problems
E4-2 Determine where items would appear in the work sheet.
E4-3 Determine where items would appear in the work sheet.
E4-4 Determine where items would appear in the work sheet.

Often it is difficult to discover all the adjusting entries that should be made. The following steps are helpful:

1. Examine adjusting entries made at the end of the preceding accounting period. The same types of entries often are necessary period after period.
2. Examine the account titles in the trial balance. For example, if the company has an account titled Trucks, an entry must be made for depreciation.
3. Examine various business documents (such as bills for services received or rendered) to discover other assets, liabilities, revenues, and expenses that have not yet been recorded.
4. Ask the manager or other personnel specific questions regarding adjustments that may be necessary. For example, "Were any services performed during the month that have not yet been billed?"

Illustration 4.2   Completed Work Sheet

MICROTRAIN COMPANY
Work Sheet
For the Month Ended December 31, 2012

Acct. No.	Account Titles	Trial Balance Debit	Trial Balance Credit	Adjustments Debit	Adjustments Credit	Adjusted Trial Balance Debit	Adjusted Trial Balance Credit	Income Statement Debit	Income Statement Credit	Statement of Retained Earnings Debit	Statement of Retained Earnings Credit	Balance Sheet Debit	Balance Sheet Credit
100	Cash	8,250				8,250						8,250	
103	Accounts Receivable	5,200		(7) 1,000		6,200						6,200	
107	Supplies on Hand	1,400			(3) 500	900						900	
108	Prepaid Insurance	2,400			(1) 200	2,200						2,200	
112	Prepaid Rent	1,200			(2) 400	800						800	
150	Trucks	40,000				40,000						40,000	
200	Accounts Payable		730				730						730
216	Unearned Service Fees		4,500	(5) 1,500			3,000						3,000
300	Capital Stock		50,000				50,000						50,000
310	Retained Earnings, 12/1/12		—0—				—0—				—0—		
320	Dividends	3,000				3,000				3,000			
400	Service Revenue		10,700		(5) 1,500 (7) 1,000		13,200		13,200				
505	Advertising Expense	50				50		50					
506	Gas and Oil Expense	680				680		680					
507	Salaries Expense	3,600		(8) 180		3,780		3,780					
511	Utilities Expense	150				150		150					
		65,930	65,930										
512	Insurance Expense			(1) 200		200		200					
515	Rent Expense			(2) 400		400		400					
518	Supplies Expense			(3) 500		500		500					
521	Depreciation Expense— Trucks			(4) 750		750		750					
151	Accumulated Depreciation— Trucks				(4) 750		750						750
121	Interest Receivable			(6) 600		600						600	
418	Interest Revenue				(6) 600		600		600				
206	Salaries Payable				(8) 180		180						180
				5,130	5,130	68,460	68,460	6,510	13,800				
	Net Income							7,290			7,290		
								13,800	13,800	3,000	7,290		
	Retained Earnings, 12/31/12									4,290			4,290
										7,290	7,290	58,950	58,950

Adjustment Explanations:
(1) To record insurance expenses for December.
(2) To record rent expenses for December.
(3) To record supplies expenses for December.
(4) To record depreciation expenses for December.
(5) To transfer fees for service provided in December from the liability account to the revenue account.
(6) To record one month's interest revenue.
(7) To record unbilled training services performed in December.
(8) To accrue one day's salaries that were earned but are unpaid.

After all the adjusting entries are entered in the Adjustments columns, total the two columns. The totals of these two columns should be equal when all debits and credits are entered properly.

The Adjusted Trial Balance Columns

After MicroTrain's adjustments, compute the adjusted balance of each account and enter these in the Adjusted Trial Balance columns. For example, Supplies on Hand (Account No. 107) had an unadjusted balance of $1,400. Adjusting entry (3) credited the account for $500, leaving a debit balance of $900. This amount is a debit in the Adjusted Trial Balance columns.

Next, extend all accounts having balances to the Adjusted Trial Balance columns. Note carefully how the rules of debit and credit apply in determining whether an adjustment increases or decreases the account balance. For example, Salaries Expense

(Account No. 507) has a $3,600 debit balance in the Trial Balance columns. A $180 debit adjustment increases this account, which has a $3,780 debit balance in the Adjusted Trial Balance columns.

Some account balances remain the same because no adjustments have affected them. For example, the balance in Accounts Payable (Account No. 200) does not change and is simply extended to the Adjusted Trial Balance columns.

Now, total the Adjusted Trial Balance debit and credit columns. The totals must be equal before taking the next step in completing the work sheet. When the Trial Balance and Adjustments columns both balance but the Adjusted Trial Balance columns do not, the most probable cause is a math error or an error in extension. The Adjusted Trial Balance columns make the next step of sorting the amounts to the Income Statement, the Statement of Retained Earnings, and the Balance Sheet columns much easier.

Note to the Student
In computing the Adjusted Trial Balance column amounts, the process is to add debits plus debits and credits plus credits in the Trial Balance and Adjustments columns, and to subtract debits and credits.

The Income Statement Columns

Begin by extending all of MicroTrain's revenue and expense account balances in the Adjusted Trial Balance columns to the Income Statement columns. Since revenues carry credit balances, extend them to the credit column. After extending expenses to the debit column, subtotal each column. MicroTrain's total expenses are $6,510 and total revenues are $13,800. Thus, net income for the period is $7,290 ($13,800 – $6,510). Enter this $7,290 income in the debit column to make the two column totals balance. You would record a net loss in the opposite manner; expenses (debits) would have been larger than revenues (credits) so a net loss would be entered in the credit column to make the columns balance.

The Statement of Retained Earnings Columns

Next, complete the Statement of Retained Earnings columns. Enter the $7,290 net income amount for December in the credit Statement of Retained Earnings column. Thus, this net income amount is the balancing figure for the Income Statement columns and is also in the credit Statement of Retained Earnings column. Net income appears in the Statement of Retained Earnings credit column because it causes an increase in retained earnings. Add the $7,290 net income to the beginning retained earnings balance of $–0–, and deduct the dividends of $3,000. As a result, the ending balance of the Retained Earnings account is $4,290.

The Balance Sheet Columns

Now extend the assets, liabilities, and capital stock accounts in the Adjusted Trial Balance columns to the Balance Sheet columns. Extend asset amounts as debits and liability and capital stock amounts as credits.

Note that the ending retained earnings amount determined in the Statement of Retained Earnings columns appears again as a credit in the Balance Sheet columns. The ending retained earnings amount is a debit in the Statement of Retained Earnings columns to balance the Statement of Retained Earnings columns. The ending retained earnings is a credit in the Balance Sheet columns because it increases stockholders' equity, and increases in stockholders' equity are credits. (Retained earnings would have a debit ending balance only if cumulative losses and dividends exceed cumulative earnings.) With the inclusion of the ending retained earnings amount, the Balance Sheet columns balance.

Reinforcing Problems
E4-6 Prepare a work sheet.
P4-4 Prepare a work sheet and closing entries.

Locating Errors

When the Balance Sheet column totals do not agree on the first attempt, work backward through the process used in preparing the work sheet. Specifically, take the following steps until you discover the error:

1. Retotal the two Balance Sheet columns to see if you made an error in addition. If the column totals do not agree, check to see if you did not extend a balance sheet item or if you made an incorrect extension from the Adjusted Trial Balance columns.

Reinforcing Problem
E4-5 Find the causes of Balance Sheet columns not in balance.

Illustration 4.3   Income Statement

MICROTRAIN COMPANY
Income Statement
For the Month Ended December 31, 2012

Revenues:		
Service Revenue		$13,200
Interest Revenue		600
Total Revenue		$13,800
Expenses:		
Advertising Expense	$ 50	
Gas and Oil Expense	680	
Salaries Expense	3,780	
Utilities Expense	150	
Insurance Expense	200	
Rent Expense	400	
Supplies Expense	500	
Depreciation Expense—Trucks	750	
Total Expense		6,510
Net Income		$ 7,290

2. Retotal the Statement of Retained Earnings columns and determine whether you entered the correct amount of retained earnings in the appropriate Statement of Retained Earnings and Balance Sheet columns.

3. Retotal the Income Statement columns and determine whether you entered the correct amount of net income or net loss for the period in the appropriate Income Statement and Statement of Retained Earnings columns.

An Accounting Perspective

USES OF TECHNOLOGY Electronic spreadsheets have numerous applications in accounting. An electronic spreadsheet is simply a large blank page that contains rows and columns on the computer screen. The blocks created by the intersection of the rows and columns are cells; each cell can hold one or more words, a number, or the product of a mathematical formula. Spreadsheets are ideal for creating large work sheets, trial balances, and other schedules, and for performing large volumes of calculations such as depreciation calculations.

Objective 3
Prepare an income statement, statement of retained earnings, and balance sheet using information contained in the work sheet.

Income Statement

Statement of Retained Earnings

Reinforcing Problem
E4-7 Prepare a statement of retained earnings.

Preparing Financial Statements from the Work Sheet

When the work sheet is completed, all the necessary information to prepare the income statement, statement of retained earnings, and balance sheet is readily available. Now, you need only recast the information into the appropriate financial statement format.

The information you need to prepare the income statement in Illustration 4.3 is in the work sheet's Income Statement columns in Illustration 4.2.

The information you need to prepare the statement of retained earnings is taken from the Statement of Retained Earnings columns in the work sheet. Look at Illustration 4.4, MicroTrain Company's statement of retained earnings for the month ended December 31, 2012. To prepare this statement, use the beginning Retained Earnings account balance (Account No. 310), add the net income (or deduct the net loss), and then subtract the Dividends (Account No. 320). Carry the ending Retained Earnings balance

Illustration 4.4   Statement of Retained Earnings

MICROTRAIN COMPANY
Statement of Retained Earnings
For the Month Ended December 31, 2012

Retained earnings, December 1, 2012	$ —0—
Net income for the December	7,290
Total	$ 7,290
Less: Dividends	3,000
Retained earnings, December 31, 2012	$ 4,290

Illustration 4.5   Balance Sheet

MICROTRAIN COMPANY
Balance Sheet
December 31, 2012

Assets

Cash		$ 8,250
Accounts receivable		6,200
Supplies on hand		900
Prepaid insurance		2,200
Prepaid rent		800
Interest receivable		600
Trucks	$ 40,000	
Less: Accumulated depreciation	750	39,250
Total assets		$ 58,200

Liabilities and Stockholders' Equity

Liabilities:		
Accounts payable	$ 730	
Unearned service fees	3,000	
Salaries payable	180	
Total liabilities		$ 3,910
Stockholders' equity:		
Capital stock	$ 50,000	
Retained earnings	4,290	
Total stockholders' equity		54,290
Total liabilities and stockholders' equity		$ 58,200

Real World Example
On May 26, 2011, aircraft maker Lockheed Martin announced that it was eliminating 300 jobs at a factory in South Carolina. The company made the announcement shortly after learning that it did not receive a $104 million contract with the U.S. Navy related to the P-3 Orion aircraft. Consider how these two events, the elimination of jobs and the failure to win the contract, affect the financial statements.

forward to the balance sheet. Remember that the statement of retained earnings helps to relate income statement information to balance sheet information. It does this by indicating how net income on the income statement relates to retained earnings on the balance sheet.

The information needed to prepare a balance sheet comes from the Balance Sheet columns of MicroTrain's work sheet (Illustration 4.2). As stated earlier, the correct amount for the ending retained earnings appears on the statement of retained earnings. See the completed balance sheet for MicroTrain in Illustration 4.5.

Balance Sheet

Journalizing Adjusting Entries

After completing MicroTrain's financial statements from the work sheet, you should enter the adjusting entries in the general journal and post them to the appropriate ledger accounts. You would prepare these adjusting entries as you learned in Chapter 3, except that the work sheet is now your source for making the entries. The preparation of a work sheet does not eliminate the need to prepare and post adjusting entries because the work sheet is only an informal accounting tool and is not part of the formal accounting records.

Reinforcing Problem
E4-8 Prepare adjusting entries and determine the correct net income.

The numerical notations in the Adjustments columns and the adjustments explanations at the bottom of the work sheet identify each adjusting entry. The Adjustments columns show each entry with its appropriate debit and credit. MicroTrain's adjusting entries as they would appear in the general journal after posting are:

MICROTRAIN COMPANY
General Journal

Page 3

Date		Account Titles and Explanation	Post. Ref.	Debit	Credit
2012		**Adjusting Entries**			
Dec.	31	Insurance Expense	512	2 0 0	
		Prepaid Insurance	108		2 0 0
		To record insurance expense for December.			
	31	Rent Expense	515	4 0 0	
		Prepaid Rent	112		4 0 0
		To record rent expense for December.			
	31	Supplies Expense	518	5 0 0	
		Supplies on Hand	107		5 0 0
		To record supplies used during December.			
	31	Depreciation Expense—Trucks	521	7 5 0	
		Accumulated Depreciation—Trucks	151		7 5 0
		To record depreciation expense for December.			
	31	Unearned Service Fees	216	1 5 0 0	
		Service Revenue	400		1 5 0 0
		To transfer a portion of training fees from the liability account to the revenue account.			
	31	Interest Receivable	121	6 0 0	
		Interest Revenue	418		6 0 0
		To record one month's interest revenue.			
	31	Accounts Receivable	103	1 0 0 0	
		Service Revenue	400		1 0 0 0
		To record unbilled training services performed in December.			
	31	Salaries Expense	507	1 8 0	
		Salaries Payable	206		1 8 0
		To accrue one day's salaries that were earned but are unpaid.			

The Closing Process

In Chapter 2, you learned that revenue, expense, and dividends accounts are nominal (temporary) accounts that are merely subclassifications of a real (permanent) account, Retained Earnings. You also learned that we prepare financial statements for certain accounting periods. The **closing process** transfers (1) the balances in the revenue and expense accounts to a clearing account called *Income Summary* and then to Retained Earnings and (2) the balance in the Dividends account to the Retained Earnings account. The closing process reduces revenue, expense, and Dividends account balances to zero so they are ready to receive data for the next accounting period. Accountants may perform the closing process monthly or annually.

The **Income Summary account** is a clearing account used only at the end of an accounting period to summarize revenues and expenses for the period. After transferring all revenue and expense account balances to Income Summary, the balance in the Income Summary account represents the net income or net loss for the period. Closing or transferring the balance in the Income Summary account to the Retained Earnings account results in a zero balance in Income Summary.

Also closed at the end of the accounting period is the Dividends account containing the dividends declared by the board of directors to the stockholders. We close the Dividends account directly to the Retained Earnings account and not to Income Summary because dividends have no effect on income or loss for the period.

In accounting, we often refer to the process of closing as closing the books. Remember that only revenue, expense, and Dividend accounts are closed—not asset, liability, Capital Stock, or Retained Earnings accounts. The four basic steps in the closing process are:

1. **Closing the revenue accounts**—transferring the balances in the revenue accounts to a clearing account called Income Summary.
2. **Closing the expense accounts**—transferring the balances in the expense accounts to a clearing account called Income Summary.
3. **Closing the Income Summary account**—transferring the balance of the Income Summary account to the Retained Earnings account.
4. **Closing the Dividends account**—transferring the balance of the Dividends account to the Retained Earnings account.

Notes to the Student
Review the previous steps in the accounting cycle. Describe the purpose of each step as the cycle is completed.
    Identify which accounts on a trial balance are permanent (real) or temporary (nominal).

Revenues appear in the Income Statement credit column of the work sheet. The two revenue accounts in the Income Statement credit column for MicroTrain Company are service revenue of $13,200 and interest revenue of $600 (Illustration 4.2). Because revenue accounts have credit balances, you must debit them for an amount equal to their balance to bring them to a zero balance. When you debit Service Revenue and Interest Revenue, credit Income Summary (Account No. 600). Enter the account numbers in the Posting Reference column when the journal entry has been posted to the ledger. Do this for all other closing journal entries.

Step 1: Closing the Revenue Accounts

MICROTRAIN COMPANY
General Journal

Page 4

Date		Account Titles and Explanation	Post. Ref.	Debit	Credit
2012		**Closing Entries**			
Dec.	31	Service Revenue	400	1 3 2 0 0	
		Interest Revenue	418	6 0 0	
		Income Summary	600		1 3 8 0 0
		To close the revenue accounts in the Income Statement credit column to Income Summary.			

After the closing entries have been posted, the Service Revenue and Interest Revenue accounts (in T-account format) of MicroTrain appear as follows. Note that the accounts now have zero balances.

As a result of the previous entry, you would credit the Income Summary account for $13,800. We show the Income Summary account in Step 3.

Step 2: Closing the Expense Accounts

Expenses appear in the Income Statement debit column of the work sheet. MicroTrain Company has eight expenses in the Income Statement debit column. As shown by the column subtotal, these expenses add up to $6,510. Since expense accounts have debit balances, credit each account to bring it to a zero balance. Then, make the debit in the closing entry to the Income Summary account for $6,510. Thus, to close the expense accounts, MicroTrain makes the following entry:

MICROTRAIN COMPANY
General Journal

Page 4

Date		Account Titles and Explanation	Post. Ref.	Debit	Credit
2012					
Dec.	31	Income Summary	600	6 5 1 0	
		Advertising Expense	505		5 0
		Gas and Oil Expense	506		6 8 0
		Salaries Expense	507		3 7 8 0
		Utilities Expense	511		1 5 0
		Insurance Expense	512		2 0 0
		Rent Expense	515		4 0 0
		Supplies Expense	518		5 0 0
		Depreciation Expense—Trucks	521		7 5 0
		To close the expense accounts appearing in the Income			
		Statement debit column to Income Summary.			

The debit of $6,510 to the Income Summary account agrees with the Income Statement debit column subtotal in the work sheet. This comparison with the work sheet serves as a check that all revenue and expense items have been listed and closed. If the debit in the preceding entry was made for a different amount than the column subtotal, the company would have an error in the closing entry for expenses.

After they have been closed, MicroTrain's expense accounts appear as follows. Note that each account has a zero balance after closing.

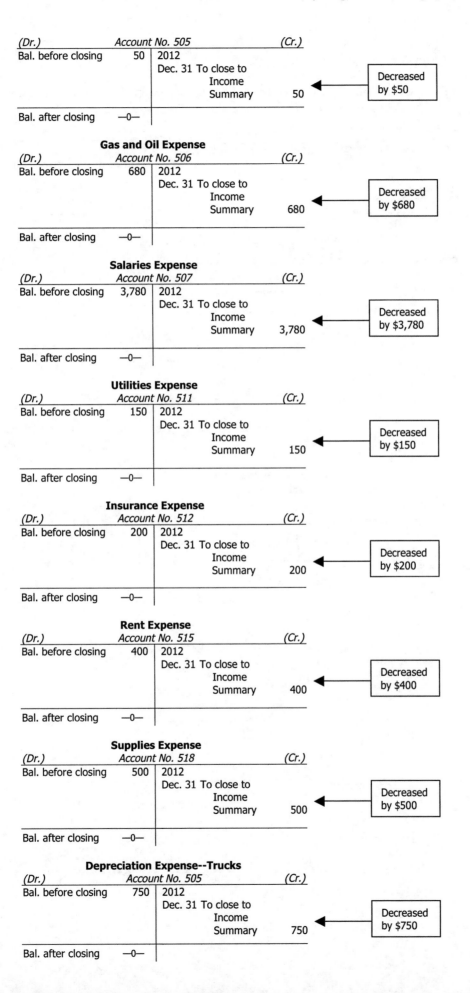

(Dr.)		Account No. 505		(Cr.)
Bal. before closing	50	2012		
		Dec. 31 To close to		
		Income		
		Summary	50	
Bal. after closing	—0—			

Decreased by $50

Gas and Oil Expense

(Dr.)		Account No. 506		(Cr.)
Bal. before closing	680	2012		
		Dec. 31 To close to		
		Income		
		Summary	680	
Bal. after closing	—0—			

Decreased by $680

Salaries Expense

(Dr.)		Account No. 507		(Cr.)
Bal. before closing	3,780	2012		
		Dec. 31 To close to		
		Income		
		Summary	3,780	
Bal. after closing	—0—			

Decreased by $3,780

Utilities Expense

(Dr.)		Account No. 511		(Cr.)
Bal. before closing	150	2012		
		Dec. 31 To close to		
		Income		
		Summary	150	
Bal. after closing	—0—			

Decreased by $150

Insurance Expense

(Dr.)		Account No. 512		(Cr.)
Bal. before closing	200	2012		
		Dec. 31 To close to		
		Income		
		Summary	200	
Bal. after closing	—0—			

Decreased by $200

Rent Expense

(Dr.)		Account No. 515		(Cr.)
Bal. before closing	400	2012		
		Dec. 31 To close to		
		Income		
		Summary	400	
Bal. after closing	—0—			

Decreased by $400

Supplies Expense

(Dr.)		Account No. 518		(Cr.)
Bal. before closing	500	2012		
		Dec. 31 To close to		
		Income		
		Summary	500	
Bal. after closing	—0—			

Decreased by $500

Depreciation Expense--Trucks

(Dr.)		Account No. 505		(Cr.)
Bal. before closing	750	2012		
		Dec. 31 To close to		
		Income		
		Summary	750	
Bal. after closing	—0—			

Decreased by $750

Reinforcing Problems

E4-9 Prepare adjusting and closing entries.

E4-11 Show how closing entries would be posted to T-accounts.

E4-12 Prepare closing entries.

The expense accounts could be closed before the revenue accounts; the end result is the same.

Step 3: Closing the Income Summary Account

As the result of closing the revenues and expenses of MicroTrain, the total revenues and expenses have been transferred to the Income Summary account.

Income Summary

| If total expenses exceed total revenues, the account has a debit balance, which is the net loss for the period | **Total expenses** | **Total revenues** | If total revenues exceed total expenses, the account has a credit balance, which is the net income for the period. |

MicroTrain's Income Summary account now has a credit balance of $7,290, the company's net income for December.

Reinforcing Problem
E4-10 Post to Income Summary account from Income Statement column totals.

Income Summary

(Dr.)			(Cr.)
2012		2012	
Dec. 31 From closing the expense accounts	6,510	Dec. 31 From closing the revenue accounts	13,800
		Bal. before closing this account (net income)	7,290

Next, close MicroTrain's Income Summary account to its Retained Earnings account. The journal entry to do this is:

MICROTRAIN COMPANY
General Journal

Page 4

Date		Account Titles and Explanation	Post. Ref.	Debit	Credit
2012					
Dec.	31	Income Summary	600	7 2 9 0	
		Retained Earnings	310		7 2 9 0
		To close the Income Summary account to the Retained			
		Earnings account.			

Note to the Student
Points to remember:
1. The Income Summary account is a temporary account. It is opened and closed during the closing process.
2. The Income Summary account does not have a normal balance. It is used to close and clear the balances of the revenue and expense accounts.
3. An important function of the Income Summary account is to avoid unnecessary detail in the Retained Earnings account when closing the revenue and expense accounts.

After its Income Summary account is closed, the company's Income Summary and Retained Earnings accounts appear as follows:

Income Summary
Account No. 600

(Dr.)			(Cr.)
2012		2012	
Dec. 31 From closing the expense accounts	6,510	Dec. 31 From closing The revenue accounts	13,800
		Bal. before closing this account (net income)	7,290
Dec. 31 To close this account to Retained Earnings	7,290		
		Bal. after closing	—0—

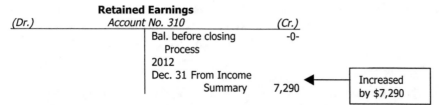

The last closing entry closes MicroTrain's Dividends account. This account has a debit balance before closing. To close the account, credit the Dividends account and debit the Retained Earnings account. The Dividends account is not closed to the Income Summary because it is not an expense and does not enter into income determination. The journal entry to close MicroTrain's Dividends account is:

Step 4: Closing the Dividends Account

MICROTRAIN COMPANY
General Journal

Page 4

Date		Account Titles and Explanation	Post. Ref.	Debit	Credit
2012 Dec.	31	Retained Earnings	310	3 0 0 0	
		Dividends	320		3 0 0 0
		To close the Dividends account to the Retained Earnings			
		account.			

After this closing entry is posted, the company's Dividends and Retained Earnings accounts appear as follows:

Note to the Student
Retained Earnings contains single closing entries for each year presenting a historical summary of annual dividends paid and annual income or loss. For many years, the only increases or decreases in stockholders' equity take place through changes in retained earnings. Consider why this is usually the case.

After you have completed the closing process, the only accounts in the general ledger that have not been closed are the permanent balance sheet accounts. Because these accounts contain the opening balances for the coming accounting period, debit balance totals must equal credit balance totals. The preparation of a post-closing trial balance serves as a check on the accuracy of the closing process and ensures that the books are in balance at the start of the new accounting period. The post-closing trial balance differs from the adjusted trial balance in only two important respects: (1) it excludes all temporary accounts since they have been closed; and (2) it updates the Retained Earnings account to its proper ending balance.

A **post-closing trial balance** is a trial balance taken after the closing entries have been posted. The only accounts that should be open are assets, liabilities, capital

Post-Closing Trial Balance

Objective 5
Prepare a post-closing trial balance.

Reinforcing Problem
E4-13 Identify accounts in the post-closing trial balance.

stock, and Retained Earnings accounts. List all the account balances in the debit and credit columns and total them to make sure debits and credits are equal.

Look at Illustration 4.6, a post-closing trial balance for MicroTrain Company as of December 31, 2012. The amounts in the post-closing trial balance are from the ledger after the closing entries have been posted.

The next section briefly describes the evolution of accounting systems from the one-journal, one-ledger manual system you have been studying to computerized systems. Then, we discuss the role of an accounting system.

An Accounting Perspective

USES OF TECHNOLOGY You may want to visit the American Institute of Certified Public Accountants website at:

http://www.aicpa.org

You will find information about the CPA exam, about becoming a CPA, hot accounting topics, and various other topics, such as the states that have passed a 150-hour requirement to sit for the CPA exam. You can also find the phone numbers and mailing addresses of state boards of accountancy and state societies of CPAs. Browse around this site to investigate anything else that is of interest.

Accounting Systems: From Manual to Computerized

Objective 6
Describe the evolution of accounting systems.

The manual accounting system with only one general journal and one general ledger has been in use for hundreds of years and is still used by some very small companies. Gradually, some manual systems evolved to include multiple journals and ledgers for increased efficiency. For instance, a manual system with multiple journals and ledgers often includes (1) a sales journal to record all credit sales, (2) a purchases journal to record all credit purchases, (3) a cash receipts journal to record all cash receipts, and (4) a cash disbursements journal to record all cash payments. Still recorded in the general journal are adjusting and closing entries and any other entries that do not fit in one of the special journals. Besides the general ledger, such a system normally has subsidiary ledgers for accounts receivable and accounts payable showing how much each customer owes and how much is owed to each supplier. The general ledger shows the total amount of accounts receivable and accounts payable, but the details in the subsidiary ledgers allow companies to send bills to customers and pay bills to suppliers.

Another innovation in manual systems was the "one write" or pegboard system. By creating one document and aligning other records under it on a pegboard, companies could record transactions more efficiently. These systems permit the writing of a check and the simultaneous recording of the check in the cash disbursements journal. Even though some of these systems are still in use today, computers make them obsolete.

During the 1950s, companies also used bookkeeping machines to supplement manual systems. These machines recorded recurring transactions such as sales on account. They posted transactions to the general ledger and subsidiary ledger accounts and computed new balances. With the development of computers, bookkeeping machines became obsolete. They were quite expensive, and computers easily outperformed them. In the mid-1950s, large companies began using mainframe computers. Early accounting applications were in payroll, accounts receivable, accounts payable, and inventory. Within a few years, programs existed for all phases of accounting, including manufacturing operations and the total integration of other accounting programs with the general ledger. Until the 1980s, small and medium-sized companies either continued

Illustration 4.6   Post Closing Trial Balance

MICROTRAIN COMPANY
Trial Balance
December 31, 2012

Acct. No.	Account Title	Debits	Credits
100	Cash	$ 8,250	
103	Accounts Receivable	6,200	
107	Supplies on Hand	900	
108	Prepaid Insurance	2,200	
112	Prepaid Rent	800	
121	Interest Receivable	600	
150	Trucks	40,000	
151	Accumulated Depreciation—Trucks		$ 750
200	Accounts Payable		730
206	Salaries Payable		180
216	Unearned Service Fees		3,000
300	Capital Stock		50,000
310	Retained Earnings		4,290
		$ 58,950	$ 58,950

with a manual system, rented time on another company's computer, or hired a service bureau to perform at least some accounting functions.

BUSINESS INSIGHT Imagine a company with an Accounts Receivable account and an Accounts Payable account in its general ledger and no Accounts Receivable Subsidiary Ledger or Accounts Payable Subsidiary Ledger. How would this company know to whom to send bills and in what amounts? Also, how would employees know for which suppliers to write checks and in what amounts? Such subsidiary records are necessary either on paper or in a computer file.

Here is how the general ledger and subsidiary ledgers might look:

An Accounting Perspective

Subsidiary Accounts Receivable Ledger	General Ledger	Subsidiary Accounts Payable Ledger
JOHN JONES	ACCOUNTS RECEIVABLE	BELL CORPORATION
200	900	100
SYLVIA SMITH		GRANGER CORPORATION
300	ACCOUNTS PAYABLE	600
	1,000	
JAMES WELLS		WONG CORPORATION
400		300

When a sale on account is made to John Jones, the debit is posted to both the control account, Accounts Receivable, in the General Ledger and the subsidiary account, John Jones, in the Subsidiary Accounts Receivable Ledger. Likewise, when a purchase on account is made from Bell Corporation, the credit is posted to both the control account, Accounts Payable, in the General Ledger and to the subsidiary account, Bell Corporation, in the Subsidiary Accounts Payable Ledger. At the end of the accounting period, the balances in each of the control accounts in the General Ledger must agree with the totals of the accounts in their respective subsidiary ledgers as shown above. A given company could have hundreds or even thousands of accounts in their subsidiary ledgers that show the detail not supplied by the totals in the control accounts.

A Broader Perspective

Skills for the Long Haul

The decision has been made: You [Tracy] have opted to start your career by joining an international accounting firm. But you can't help wondering if you have the right skills both for short and long-term success in public accounting.

Most students understand that accounting knowledge, organizational ability and interpersonal skills are critical to success in public accounting. But it is important for the beginner to realize that different skills are emphasized at different points in a public accountant's career.

Let's examine the duties and skills needed at each level—Staff Accountant (years 1–2), Senior Accountant (years 3–4), Manager/Senior Manager (years 5–11) and Partner (years 11+).

Staff accountant—Enthusiastic learner

Let's travel with Tracy as she begins her career at the staff level. At the outset, she works directly under a senior accountant on each of her audits and is responsible for completing audits and administrative tasks assigned to her. Her duties include documenting workpapers, interacting with client accounting staff, clerical tasks and discussing questions that arise with her senior. Tracy will work on different audit engagements during her first year and learn the firm's audit approach. She will be introduced to various industries and accounting systems.

The two most important traits to be demonstrated at the staff level are (1) a positive attitude and (2) the ability to learn quickly while adapting to unfamiliar situations.

Senior accountant—Organizer and teacher

As a senior accountant, Tracy will be responsible for the day-to-day management of several audit engagements during the year. She will plan the audits, oversee the performance of interim audit testing and direct year-end field work. She will also perform much of the final wrap-up work, such as preparing checklists, writing the management letter and reviewing or drafting the financial statements. Throughout this process, Tracy will spend a substantial amount of time instructing and supervising staff accountants.

The two most critical skills needed at the senior level are (1) the ability to organize and control an audit and (2) the ability to teach staff accountants how to audit.

Manager/senior manager—General manager and salesperson

Upon promotion to manager, Tracy will begin the transformation from auditor to executive. She will manage several audits at one time and become active in billing clients as well as negotiating audit fees. She will handle many important client meetings and closing conferences. Tracy will also become more involved in the firm's administrative tasks. Finally, outside of her client service and administrative duties, Tracy will be evaluated to a large extent on her community involvement and ability to assist the partners in generating new business for the firm.

The two skills most emphasized at the manager level are (1) general management ability and (2) sales and communication skills.

Partner—Leader and expert

As a partner in the firm, Tracy will have many broad responsibilities. She will engage in high-level client service activities, business development, recruiting, strategic planning, office administration and counseling. Besides serving as the engagement partner on several audits, she will have ultimate responsibility for the quality of service provided to each of her clients. Although a certain industry or administrative function will become her specialty, she will often be called upon to perform a wide variety of audit and administrative duties when other partners have scheduling conflicts. She will be expected to serve as a positive example to those who work for her and will train others in her areas of expertise.

At the partnership level, what's looked for is leadership ability plus the ability to become an expert in a specific industry or administrative function.

In the meantime

Those planning on a public accounting career should do more than just learn accounting. To develop the needed skills, a broad education background in business and nonbusiness courses is required plus participation in extracurricular activities that promote leadership and communication skills. It is never too early to start building the skills for long-term success.

Source: Dana R. Hermanson and Heather M. Hermanson, *New Accountant*, January 1990, pp. 24–26, © 1990, New DuBois Corporation.

The development of the microcomputer in 1975 and its widespread use a decade later drastically changed the accounting systems of small and medium-sized businesses. The number and quality of accounting software packages for these computers and the power of the microcomputers quickly increased. Soon small and medium-sized businesses could maintain all accounting functions on a microcomputer. By the 1990s, the cost of microcomputers and accounting software packages had decreased significantly, accounting software packages had become more user-friendly, and computer literacy had increased so much that many very small businesses converted from manual to computerized systems. However, some small business owners still use manual systems because they are familiar and meet their needs, and the persons keeping the records may not be computer literate.

Your knowledge of the basic manual accounting system described in these first four chapters enables you to better understand a computerized accounting system. The computer automatically performs some of the steps in the accounting cycle, such as posting journal entries to the ledger accounts, closing the books, and preparing the financial statements. However, if you understand all of the steps in the accounting cycle, you will better understand how to use the resulting data in decision making.

THE IMPACT OF TECHNOLOGY Results from a recent survey of 1,400 chief financial officers (CFOs) indicate that tomorrow's accounting professionals will be called upon to bridge the gap between technology and business. With the rise of integrated accounting and information systems, technical expertise will go hand in hand with general business knowledge.

An Accounting Perspective

The Role of an Accounting System

As we show in Illustration 4.7, an **accounting system** is a set of records and the procedures and equipment used to perform the accounting functions. Manual systems consist of journals and ledgers on paper. Computerized accounting systems consist of accounting software, computer files, computers, and related peripheral equipment such as printers.

Regardless of the system, the functions of accountants include: (1) observing, identifying, and measuring economic events; (2) recording, classifying, and summarizing measurements; and (3) reporting economic events and interpreting financial statements. Both internal and external users tell accountants their information needs. The accounting system enables a company's accounting staff to supply relevant accounting information to meet those needs. As internal and external users make decisions that become economic events, the cycle of information, decisions, and economic events begins again.

The primary focus of the first four chapters has been on how you can use an accounting system to prepare financial statements. However, we also discussed how to use that information in making decisions. Later chapters also show how to prepare information and how that information helps users to make informed decisions. *We have not eliminated the preparation aspects because we believe that the most informed users are ones who also understand how the information was prepared.* These users understand not only the limitations of the information but also its relevance for decision making.

The next section discusses and illustrates the classified balance sheet, which aids in the analysis of the financial position of companies. One example of this analysis is the current ratio and its use in analyzing the short-term debt-paying ability of a company.

Illustration 4.7 The Role of an Accounting System

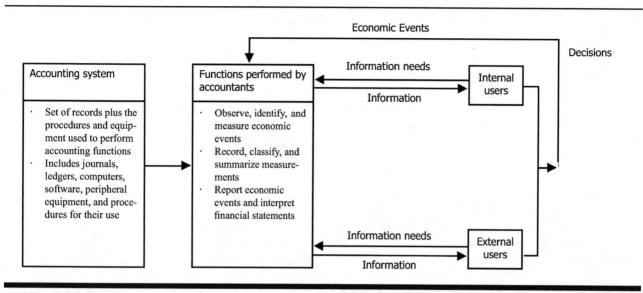

An Accounting Perspective	**USES OF TECHNOLOGY** Accounting software packages are typically menu driven and organized into modules such as general ledger, accounts payable, accounts receivable, invoicing, inventory, payroll, fixed assets, job cost, and purchase order. For instance, general journal entries are made in the general ledger module, and this module contains all of the company's accounts. The accounts payable module records all transactions involving credit purchases from suppliers and payments made to those suppliers. The accounts receivable module records all sales on credit to various customers and amounts received from customers.

A Classified Balance Sheet

Objective 7
Prepare a classified balance sheet.

The balance sheets we presented so far have been unclassified balance sheets. As shown in Illustration 4.5, an **unclassified balance sheet** has three major categories: assets, liabilities, and stockholders' equity. A **classified balance sheet** contains the same three major categories and subdivides them to provide useful information for interpretation and analysis by users of financial statements.

Illustration 4.8 on page 151, shows a slightly revised classified balance sheet for The Home Depot, Inc., and subsidiaries.[1] Note that The Home Depot classified balance sheet is in a vertical format (assets appearing above liabilities and stockholders' equity) rather than the horizontal format (assets on the left and liabilities and stockholders' equity on the right). The two formats are equally acceptable.

The Home Depot classified balance sheet subdivides two of its three major categories. The Home Depot subdivides its assets into current assets, property and equipment, long-term investments, long-term notes receivable, intangible assets (cost in excess of the fair value of net assets acquired), and other assets. The company subdivides its liabilities into current liabilities and long-term liabilities (including deferred income taxes). A later chapter describes minority interest. Stockholders' equity is the same in a classified balance sheet as in an unclassified balance sheet. Later chapters describe further subdivisions of the stockholders' equity section.

Reinforcing Problem
E4-14 Categorize items for classified balance sheet.

We discuss the individual items in the classified balance sheet later in the text. Our only purpose here is to briefly describe the items that can be listed under each category. Some of these items are not in The Home Depot's balance sheet.

[1]Founded in 1978, The Home Depot is America's largest home improvement retailer and ranks among the nation's 30 largest retailers. The company has more than 2,200 full-service warehouse stores. Their primary customers are "do-it-yourselfers".

Illustration 4.8   A Classified Balance Sheet

THE HOME DEPOT, INC. AND SUBSIDIARIES
Consolidated Balance Sheet
January 30, 2011
(amounts in millions, except share data)

	January 30, 2011	
Assets		
Current Assets:		
Cash and Cash Equivalents	$ 545	
Receivables, net	1,085	
Merchandise Inventories	10,625	
Other Current Assets	1,224	
Total Current Assets		$ 13,479
Property and Equipment, at cost:		
Land	$ 8,497	
Buildings	17,606	
Furniture, Fixtures and Equipment	9,687	
Leasehold Improvements	1,373	
Construction in Progress	654	
Capital Leases	568	
	$ 38,385	
Less: Accumulated Depreciation and Amortization	13,325	
Net Property and Equipment	$ 25,060	
Notes Receivable	139	
Goodwill	1,187	
Other Assets	260	26,646
Total assets		$ 40,125
Liabilities and Stockholders' Equity		
Current Liabilities:		
Accounts Payable	$ 4,717	
Accrued Salaries and Related Expenses	1,290	
Sales Taxes Payable	368	
Other Accrued Expenses	2,692	
Income Taxes Payable	13	
Current Installments of Long-Term Debt	1,042	
Total Current Liabilities		$ 10,122
Long-Term Debt, excluding current installments	$ 8,707	
Other Long-Term Liabilities	2,135	
Deferred Income Taxes	272	11,114
Total Liabilities		$ 21,236
Stockholders' equity:		
Common Stock, par value $0.05. Authorized: 10 billion shares; issued: 1.722 billion shares; outstanding: 1.623 billion shares	$ 86	
Paid-In Capital	6,556	
Retained Earnings	14,995	
Accumulated Other Comprehensive Income	445	
	$ 22,082	
Less: Treasury Stock	3,193	
Total Stockholders' Equity		18,889
Total Liabilities and Stockholders' Equity		$ 40,125

Current Assets

Current assets are cash and other assets that a business can convert to cash or uses up in a relatively short period—one year or one operating cycle, whichever is longer. An **operating cycle** is the time it takes to start with cash, buy necessary items to produce revenues (such as materials, supplies, labor, and/or finished goods), sell services or goods, and receive cash by collecting the resulting receivables. Companies in service industries and merchandising industries generally have operating cycles shorter than one year. Companies in some manufacturing industries, such as distilling and lumber, have operating cycles longer than one year. However, since most operating cycles are

Notes to the Student
During the operating cycle, management needs to monitor the company's liquidity and solvency. Much of the monitoring is performed by various levels of management using a variety of information besides the general ledger account balances including ratios, unfilled orders, sales backlog, and customer counts.

It's important to remember that current assets are listed on the balance sheet according to liquidity—how quickly they can be turned back to cash or how quickly they can be consumed or expire.

shorter than one year, the one-year period is usually used in identifying current assets and current liabilities. Common current assets in a service business include cash, marketable securities, accounts receivable, notes receivable, interest receivable, and prepaid expenses. Note that on a balance sheet, current assets are in order of how easily they are convertible to cash, from most liquid to least liquid.

Cash includes deposits in banks available for current operations at the balance sheet date plus cash on hand consisting of currency, undeposited checks, drafts, and money orders. Cash is the first current asset to appear on a balance sheet. The term *cash* normally includes cash equivalents.

Cash equivalents are highly liquid, short-term investments acquired with temporarily idle cash and easily convertible into a known cash amount. Examples are Treasury bills, short-term notes maturing within 90 days, certificates of deposit, and money market funds.

Marketable securities are temporary investments such as short-term ownership of stocks and bonds of other companies. Such investments do not qualify as cash equivalents. These investments earn additional money on cash that the business does not need at present but will probably need within one year.

Accounts receivable (also called *trade accounts receivable*) are amounts owed to a business by customers. An account receivable arises when a company performs a service or sells merchandise on credit. Customers normally provide no written evidence of indebtedness on sales invoices or delivery tickets except their signatures. Notice the term "*net*" in the balance sheet of The Home Depot (Illustration 4.8). This term indicates the possibility that the company may not collect some of its accounts receivable. In the balance sheet, the accounts receivable amount is the sum of the individual accounts receivable from customers shown in a subsidiary ledger or file.

Merchandise inventories are goods held for sale. Chapter 6 begins our discussion of merchandise inventories.

A **note** is an unconditional written promise to pay another party the amount owed either when demanded or at a certain specified date, usually with interest (a charge made for use of the money) at a specified rate. A *note receivable* appears on the balance sheet of the company to which the note is given. A note receivable arises (1) when a company makes a sale and receives a note from the customer, (2) when a customer gives a note for an amount due on an account receivable, or (3) when a company loans money and receives a note in return. Chapter 9 discusses notes at length.

Other current assets might include interest receivable and prepaid expenses. **Interest receivable** arises when a company has earned but not collected interest by the balance sheet date. Usually, the amount is not due until later. **Prepaid expenses** include rent, insurance, and supplies that have been paid for but from which all the benefits have not yet been realized (or consumed). If prepaid expenses had not been paid for in advance, they would require the future disbursement of cash. Furthermore, prepaid expenses are considered assets because they have service potential.

Long-Term Assets

Long-term assets are assets that a business has on hand or uses for a relatively long time. Examples include property, plant, and equipment; long-term investments; and intangible assets.

Property, Plant, and Equipment   **Property, plant, and equipment** are assets with useful lives of more than one year; a company acquires them for use in the business rather than for resale. (These assets are called property and equipment in The Home Depot's balance sheet.) The terms *plant assets* or *fixed assets* are also used for property, plant, and equipment. To agree with the order in the heading, balance sheets generally list property first, plant next, and equipment last. These items are *fixed assets* because the company uses them for long-term purposes. We describe several types of property, plant, and equipment next.

Land is ground the company uses for business operations; this includes ground on which the company locates its business buildings and that is used for outside storage space or parking. Land owned for investment is not a plant asset because it is a long-term investment.

Buildings are structures the company uses to carry on its business. Again, the buildings that a company owns as investments are not plant assets.

Office furniture includes file cabinets, desks, chairs, and shelves.

Office equipment includes computers, copiers, printers, and phone systems.

Leasehold improvements are any physical alterations made by the lessee to the leased property when these benefits are expected to last beyond the current accounting period. An example is when the lessee builds room partitions in a leased building. (The lessee is the one obtaining the rights to possess and use the property.)

Construction in progress represents the partially completed stores or other buildings that a company such as The Home Depot plans to occupy when completed.

Accumulated depreciation is a contra asset account to depreciable assets such as buildings, machinery, and equipment. This account shows the total depreciation taken for the depreciable assets. On the balance sheet, companies deduct the accumulated depreciation (as a contra asset) from its related asset.

Long-Term Investments   A **long-term investment** usually consists of securities of another company held with the intention of (1) obtaining control of another company, (2) securing a permanent source of income for the investor, or (3) establishing friendly business relations. The long-term investment classification in the balance sheet does not include those securities purchased for short-term purposes. For most businesses, long-term investments may be stocks or bonds of other corporations. Occasionally, long-term investments include funds accumulated for specific purposes, rental properties, and plant sites for future use.

Intangible Assets   **Intangible assets** consist of the noncurrent, nonmonetary, non-physical assets of a business. Companies must charge the costs of intangible assets to expense over the period benefited. Among the intangible assets are rights granted by governmental bodies, such as patents and copyrights. Other intangible assets include leaseholds and goodwill.

A **patent** is a right granted by the federal government; it gives the owner of an invention the authority to manufacture a product or to use a process for a specified time.

A **copyright** granted by the federal government gives the owner the exclusive privilege of publishing written material for a specified time.

Leaseholds are rights to use rented properties, usually for several years.

Goodwill is an intangible value attached to a business, evidenced by the ability to earn larger net income per dollar of investment than that earned by competitors in the same industry. The ability to produce superior profits is a valuable resource of a business. Normally, companies record goodwill only at the time of purchase and then only at the price paid for it. The Home Depot has labeled its goodwill "cost in excess of the fair value of net assets acquired."

Accumulated amortization is a contra asset account to intangible assets. This account shows the total amortization taken on the intangible assets.

Current liabilities are debts due within one year or one operating cycle, whichever is longer. The payment of current liabilities normally requires the use of current assets. Balance sheets list current liabilities in the order they must be paid; the sooner a liability must be paid, the earlier it is listed. Examples of current liabilities follow.

Current Liabilities

Accounts payable are amounts owed to suppliers for goods or services purchased on credit. Accounts payable are generally due in 30 or 60 days and do not bear interest. In the balance sheet, the accounts payable amount is the sum of the individual accounts payable to suppliers shown in a subsidiary ledger or file.

Notes payable are unconditional written promises by the company to pay a specific sum of money at a certain future date. The notes may arise from borrowing money from a bank, from the purchase of assets, or from the giving of a note in settlement of an account payable. Generally, only notes payable due in one year or less are included as current liabilities.

Salaries payable are amounts owed to employees for services rendered. The company has not paid these salaries by the balance sheet date because they are not due until later.

Sales taxes payable are the taxes a company has collected from customers but not yet remitted to the taxing authority, usually the state.

Other accrued expenses might include taxes withheld from employees, income taxes payable, and interest payable. **Taxes withheld from employees** include federal income taxes, state income taxes, and social security taxes withheld from employees' paychecks. The company plans to pay these amounts to the proper governmental agencies within a short period. **Income taxes payable** are the taxes paid to the state and federal governments by a corporation on its income. **Interest payable** is interest that the company has accumulated on notes or bonds but has not paid by the balance sheet date because it is not due until later.

Dividends payable, or amounts the company has declared payable to stockholders, represent a distribution of income. Since the corporation has not paid these declared dividends by the balance sheet date, they are a liability.

Unearned revenues (revenues received in advance) result when a company receives payment for goods or services before earning the revenue, such as payments for subscriptions to a magazine. These unearned revenues represent a liability to perform the agreed services or other contractual requirements or to return the assets received.

Companies report any current installment on long-term debt due within one year under current liabilities. The remaining portion continues to be reported as a long-term liability.

Long-Term Liabilities

Long-term liabilities are debts such as a mortgage payable and bonds payable that are not due for more than one year. Companies should show maturity dates in the balance sheet for all long-term liabilities. Normally, the liabilities with the earliest due dates are listed first.

Notes payable with maturity dates at least one year beyond the balance sheet date are long-term liabilities.

Bonds payable are long-term liabilities and are evidenced by formal printed certificates sometimes secured by liens (claims) on property, such as mortgages. Maturity dates should appear on the balance sheet for all major long-term liabilities.

The deferred income taxes on The Home Depot's balance sheet result from a difference between income tax expense in the accounting records and the income tax payable on the company's tax return.

Stockholders' Equity

Stockholders' equity shows the owners' interest in the business. This interest is equal to the amount contributed plus the income left in the business.

The items under stockholders' equity in The Home Depot's balance sheet are paid-in capital (including common stock) and retained earnings. **Paid-in capital** shows the capital paid into the company as the owners' investment. **Retained earnings** shows the cumulative income of the company less the amounts distributed to the owners in the form of dividends. **Accumulated other comprehensive income** results from translating foreign currencies into U.S. dollars and other transactions that are discussed in advanced accounting courses. **Treasury stock** represents shares of its own stock that The Home Depot has purchased to hold for future use. Treasury stock is discussed in Chapter 13.

The next section shows how two categories on the classified balance sheet relate to each other. Together they help reveal a company's short-term debt-paying ability.

Analyzing and Using the Financial Results— The Current Ratio

The current ratio indicates the short-term debt-paying ability of a company. To find the **current ratio**, we divide current assets by current liabilities. For instance, Illustration 4.8 shows that The Home Depot's current assets as of January 30, 2011, were $13,479,000,000 and its current liabilities were $10,122,000,000. Thus, its curent ratio was:

$$\text{Current Ratio} = \frac{\text{Current Assets}}{\text{Current Liabilities}} = \frac{\$13,479,000,000}{\$10,122,000,000} = 1.33:1$$

The current ratio of 1.33:1 for The Home Depot means that it has about one-third more invested in current assets than it owes in current liabilities. Because current liabilities are normally paid with current assets, the company appears to be able to pay its short-term obligations.

In evaluating a company's short-term debt-paying ability, you should also examine the quality of the current assets. If they include large amounts of uncollectable accounts receivable and/or obsolete and unsalable inventory, even a 2:1 current ratio may be inadequate to allow the company to pay its current liabilities. The Home Depot undoubtedly does not have such a problem.

The current assets, current liabilities, and current ratios of some other companies as of the 1st quarter of 2011 were:

Company	Current Assets	Current Liabilities	Ratio
Hewlett-Packard Company	56,075,000,000	51,370,000,000	1.09:1
3M Corporation	12,645,000,000	5,900,000,000	2.14:1
General Electric Company	468,146,000,000	221,810,000,000	2.11:1
Johnson & Johnson	49,221,000,000	24,011,000,000	2.05:1

We described each of these companies earlier in the text.

As you can see from these comparisons, the current ratios vary a great deal. An old rule of thumb is that the current ratio should be at least 2:1. However, what constitutes an adequate current ratio depends on available lines of credit, the cash-generating ability of the company, and the nature of the industry in which the company operates. For instance, companies in the airline industry are able to generate huge amounts of cash on a daily basis and may be able to pay their current liabilities even if their current ratio is less than 1:1. Comparing a company's current ratio with other companies in the same industry makes sense because all of these companies face about the same economic conditions. A company with the lowest current ratio in its industry may be unable to pay its short-term obligations on a timely basis, unless it can borrow funds from a bank on a line of credit. A company with the highest current ratio in its industry may have on hand too many current assets, such as cash and marketable securities, which could be invested in more productive assets.

Objective 8
Analyze and use the financial results—the current ratio.

Reinforcing Problem
E4-15 Calculate current ratios for The Procter & Gamble Company and subsidiaries and comment.

The next chapter describes the assumptions, concepts, and principles that constitute the accounting theory underlying financial accounting. Thus, accounting theory dictates the standards and procedures applied to the reporting of financial information in the financial statements.

Understanding the Learning Objectives

Objective 1
Summarize the steps in the accounting cycle.

- Analyze transactions by examining source documents.
- Journalize transactions in the journal.
- Post journal entries to the accounts in the ledger.
- Prepare a trial balance of the accounts and complete the work sheet.
- Prepare financial statements.
- Journalize and post adjusting entries.
- Journalize and post closing entries.
- Prepare a post-closing trial balance.
- The work sheet is a columnar sheet of paper on which accountants summarize information needed to make the adjusting and closing entries and to prepare the financial statements.

Objective 2
Prepare a work sheet for a service company.

- Work sheets may vary in format. The work sheet illustrated in the chapter has 12 columns—two each for trial balance, adjustments, adjusted trial balance, income statement, statement of retained earnings, and balance sheet.
- The information needed to prepare the income statement is in the Income Statement columns of the work sheet. Net income for the period is the amount needed to balance the two Income Statement columns in the work sheet.

Objective 3
Prepare an income statement, statement of retained earnings, and balance sheet using information contained in the work sheet.

- The information needed to prepare the statement of retained earnings is in the Statement of Retained Earnings columns of the work sheet. The ending Retained Earnings balance is carried forward to the balance sheet.
- The information needed to prepare the balance sheet is in the Balance Sheet columns of the work sheet.

Objective 4
Prepare adjusting and closing entries using information contained in the work sheet.

- As explained in Chapter 3, adjusting entries are necessary to bring the accounts to their proper balances before preparing the financial statements.
- Closing entries are necessary to reduce the balances of revenue, expense, and Dividends accounts to zero so they are ready to receive data for the next accounting period.
- Revenue accounts are closed by debiting them and crediting the Income Summary account.
- Expense accounts are closed by crediting them and debiting the Income Summary account.
- The balance in the Income Summary account represents the net income or net loss for the period.
- To close the Income Summary account, the balance is transferred to the Retained Earnings account.
- To close the Dividends account, the balance is transferred to the Retained Earnings account.

- Only the balance sheet accounts have balances and appear on the post-closing trial balance.
- All revenue, expense, and Dividends accounts have zero balances and are not included in the post-closing trial balance.

- Manual systems and computerized systems perform the same accounting functions.
- The ease of accounting with a microcomputer has encouraged even small companies to convert to computerized systems.

- A classified balance sheet subdivides the major categories on the balance sheet. For instance, a classified balance sheet subdivides assets into current assets; long-term investments; property, plant, and equipment; and intangible assets. It subdivides liabilities into current liabilities and long-term liabilities. Later chapters show more accounts in the stockholders' equity section, but the subdivisions remain basically the same.

- The current ratio gives some indication of the short-term debt-paying ability of a company.
- To find the current ratio, divide current assets by current liabilities.

Objective 5
Prepare a post-closing trial balance.

Objective 6
Describe the evolution of accounting systems.

Objective 7
Prepare a classified balance sheet.

Objective 8
Analyze and use the financial results—the current ratio.

Demonstration Problem

This problem involves using a work sheet for Green Hills Riding Stable, Incorporated, for the month ended July 31, 2012, and performing the closing process. The trial balance for Green Hills Riding Stable, Incorporated, as of July 31, 2012, was as follows:

GREEN HILLS RIDING STABLE, INCORPORATED
Trial Balance
July 31, 2012

Acct. No.	Account Title	Debits	Credits
100	Cash	$ 10,700	
103	Accounts Receivable	8,100	
130	Land	40,000	
140	Buildings	24,000	
200	Accounts Payable		$ 1,100
201	Notes Payable		40,000
300	Capital Stock		35,000
310	Retained Earnings, July 1, 2012		3,100
320	Dividends	1,000	
402	Horse Boarding Fees Revenue		4,500
404	Riding Lesson Fees Revenue		3,600
507	Salaries Expense	1,400	
513	Feed Expense	1,100	
540	Interest Expense	200	
568	Miscellaneous Expense	800	
		$ 87,300	$ 87,300

Depreciation expense for the month is $200. Accrued salaries on July 31 are $300.

 Additional data

a. Prepare a 12-column work sheet for the month ended July 31, 2012.
b. Journalize the adjusting entries.
c. Journalize the closing entries.

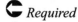 *Required*

Solution to Demonstration Problem

a. See the work sheet below.

GREEN HILLS RIDING STABLE, INCORPORATED
Work Sheet
For the Month Ended July 31, 2012

Acct. No.	Account Titles	Trial Balance Debit	Trial Balance Credit	Adjustments Debit	Adjustments Credit	Adjusted Trial Balance Debit	Adjusted Trial Balance Credit	Income Statement Debit	Income Statement Credit	Statement of Retained Earnings Debit	Statement of Retained Earnings Credit	Balance Sheet Debit	Balance Sheet Credit
100	Cash	10,700				10,700						10,700	
103	Accounts Receivable	8,100				8,100						8,100	
130	Land	40,000				40,000						40,000	
140	Buildings	24,000				24,000						24,000	
200	Accounts Payable		1,100				1,100						1,100
201	Notes Payable		40,000				40,000						40,000
300	Capital Stock		35,000				35,000						35,000
310	Retained Earnings, July 1, 2012		3,100				3,100				3,100		
320	Dividends	1,000				1,000				1,000			
402	Horse Boarding Fees Revenue		4,500				4,500		4,500				
404	Riding and Lesson Fees Revenue		3,600				3,600		3,600				
507	Salaries Expense	1,400		(2) 300		1,700		1,700					
513	Feed Expense	1,100				1,100		1,100					
540	Interest Expense	200				200		200					
568	Miscellaneous Expense	800				800		800					
		87,300	87,300										
520	Depreciation Expense—Buildings			(1) 200		200		200					
141	Accumulated Depreciation—Buildings				(1) 200		200						200
206	Salaries Payable				(2) 300		300						300
				500	500	87,800	87,800						
								4,000	8,100				
	Net Income							4,100			4,100		
								8,100	8,100	1,000	7,200	82,800	76,600
	Retained Earnings, July 31, 2012									6,200			6,200
										7,200	7,200	82,800	82,800

Adjustments:
(1) To record depreciation of building for July.
(2) To record accrued salaries of $300.

b.

GREEN HILLS RIDING STABLE, INCORPORATED
General Journal

Page 4

Date		Account Titles and Explanation	Post. Ref.	Debit	Credit
2012		**Adjusting Entries**			
July	31	Depreciation Expense—Buildings	520	200	
		Accumulated Depreciation—Buildings	141		200
		To record depreciation expense.			
	31	Salaries Expense	507	300	
		Salaries Payable	206		300
		To record accrued salaries.			

c.

GREEN HILLS RIDING STABLE, INCORPORATED
General Journal

Page 4

Date		Account Titles and Explanation	Post. Ref.	Debit	Credit
2012		**Closing Entries**			
July	31	Horse Boarding Fees Revenue	402	4 5 0 0	
		Riding Lesson Fees Revenue	404	3 6 0 0	
		Income Summary	600		8 1 0 0
		To close revenue accounts.			
	31	Income Summary	600	4 0 0 0	
		Salaries Expense	507		1 7 0 0
		Feed Expense	513		1 1 0 0
		Interest Expense	540		2 0 0
		Miscellaneous Expense	568		8 0 0
		Depreciation Expense—Buildings	520		2 0 0
		To close expense accounts.			
	31	Income Summary	600	4 1 0 0	
		Retained Earnings	310		4 1 0 0
		To close Income Summary account.			
	31	Retained Earnings	310	1 0 0 0	
		Dividends	320		1 0 0 0
		To close dividends account.			

New Terms*

Accounting cycle   Series of steps performed during the accounting period to analyze, record, classify, summarize, and report useful financial information for the purpose of preparing financial statements. The steps include analyzing transactions, journalizing transactions, posting journal entries, taking a trial balance and completing the work sheet, preparing financial statements, journalizing and posting adjusting entries, journalizing and posting closing entries, and taking a post-closing trial balance. *133*

Accounting system   A set of records and the procedures and equipment used to perform accounting functions. *149*

Accounts payable   Amounts owed to suppliers for goods or services purchased on credit. *154*

Accounts receivable   Amounts due from customers for services performed or merchandise sold on credit. *152*

Accumulated amortization   A contra account to intangible assets. *153*

Accumulated depreciation   A contra account to depreciable assets such as buildings, machinery, and equipment. *153*

Bonds payable   Written promises to pay a definite sum at a certain date as evidenced by formal printed certificates that are sometimes secured by liens on property, such as mortgages. *154*

Buildings   Structures used to carry on the business. *153*

Cash   Includes deposits in banks available for current operations at the balance sheet date plus cash on hand consisting of currency, undeposited checks, drafts, and money orders. *152*

Cash equivalents   Highly liquid, short-term investments acquired with temporarily idle cash. *152*

Classified balance sheet   Subdivides the three major balance sheet categories (assets, liabilities, and stockholders' equity) to provide more information for users of financial statements. Assets may be divided into current assets; long-term investments; property, plant, and equipment; and intangible assets. Liabilities may be divided into current liabilities and long-term liabilities. *150*

Closing process   The act of transferring the balances in the revenue and expense accounts to a clearing account called *Income Summary* and then to the Retained Earnings account. The balance in the

*Some of these terms have been defined in earlier chapters but are included here for your convenience.

Dividends account is also transferred to the Retained Earnings account. *141*

Construction in progress   Represents the partially completed stores or other buildings that a company plans to occupy when completed. *153*

Copyright   Grants the owner the exclusive privilege of publication of written material for a specific time. *153*

Current assets   Cash and other assets that a business can convert into cash or use up in one year or one operating cycle, whichever is longer. *151*

Current liabilities   Debts due within one year or one operating cycle, whichever is longer. The payment of current liabilities normally requires the use of current assets. *153*

Current ratio   Calculated by dividing current assets by current liabilities. *155*

Dividends payable   Amounts declared payable to stockholders and that represent a distribution of income. *154*

Goodwill   An intangible value attached to a business, evidenced by the ability to earn larger net income per dollar of investment than that earned by competitors in the same industry. *153*

Income Summary account   A clearing account used only at the end of an accounting period to summarize revenues and expenses for the period. *141*

Income taxes payable   Are the taxes payable to the state and federal governments by a corporation based on its income. *154*

Intangible assets   Noncurrent, nonmonetary, nonphysical assets of a business. *153*

Interest payable   Interest that has accumulated on debts, such as notes or bonds. This accrued interest has not been paid at the balance sheet date because it is not due until later. *154*

Interest receivable   Arises when interest has been earned but not collected at the balance sheet date. *152*

Land   Ground the company uses for business operations. Land could include ground on which the company locates its business buildings and that used for outside storage space or a parking lot. *153*

Leasehold improvements   Are any physical alterations made by the lessee to the leased property when these benefits are expected to last beyond the current accounting period. *153*

Leaseholds   Rights to use rented properties. *153*

Long-term assets   Assets that are on hand or used by a business for a relatively long time. Examples include long-term investments; property, plant, and equipment; and intangible assets. *152*

Long-term investment   Usually securities of another company held with the intention of *(1)* obtaining control of another company, *(2)* securing a permanent source

of income for the investor, or *(3)* establishing friendly business relations. *153*

Long-term liabilities   Debts such as a mortgage payable and bonds payable that are not due for more than one year. *154*

Marketable securities   Temporary investments that a company makes to earn a return on idle cash. *152*

Merchandise inventory   Goods held for sale. *152*

Note   An unconditional written promise to pay to another party the amount owed either when demanded or at a certain date. *152*

Notes payable   Unconditional written promises by a company to pay a specific sum of money at a certain future date. *154*

Office equipment   Includes computers, copiers, FAX machines, and phone answering machines. *153*

Office furniture   Includes file cabinets, desks, chairs, and shelves. *153*

Operating cycle   The time it takes to start with cash, buy necessary items to produce revenues (such as materials, supplies, labor, and/or inventories), sell services or goods, and receive cash by collecting the resulting receivables. *151*

Paid-in capital   Shows the capital paid into the company as the owners' investment. *154*

Patent   A right granted by the federal government authorizing the owner of an invention to manufacture a product or to use a process for a specific time. *153*

Post-closing trial balance   A trial balance taken after the closing entries have been posted. *145*

Prepaid expenses   Assets awaiting assignment to expense. Items such as rent, insurance, and supplies that have been paid for but from which all of the benefits have not yet been realized (or consumed). Prepaid expenses are classified as current assets. *152*

Property, plant, and equipment   Assets with useful lives of more than one year that a company acquired for use in a business rather than for resale; also called *plant assets* or *fixed assets*. *152*

Retained earnings   Shows the cumulative income of the company less the amounts distributed to the owners in the form of dividends. *154*

Salaries payable   Amounts owed to employees for services rendered. *154*

Sales taxes payable   Are taxes a company has collected from customers but has not remitted to the taxing authority, usually the state. *154*

Stockholders' equity   Shows the owners' interest (equity) in the business. *154*

Taxes withheld from employees   Items such as federal income taxes, state income taxes, and social security taxes withheld from employees' paychecks. *154*

Unclassified balance sheet   A balance sheet showing only three major categories: assets, liabilities, and stockholders' equity. *150*

Unearned revenues (revenues received in advance)   Result when payment is received for goods or services before revenue has been earned. *154*

Work sheet   A columnar sheet of paper on which accountants have summarized information needed to make the adjusting and closing entries and to prepare the financial statements. *133*

Self-Test

True-False

Indicate whether each of the following statements is true or false.

1. At the end of the accounting period, three trial balances are prepared.
2. The amounts in the Adjustments columns are always added to the amounts in the Trial Balance columns to determine the amounts in the Adjusted Trial Balance columns.
3. If a net loss occurs, it appears in the Income Statement credit column and Statement of Retained Earnings debit column.
4. After the closing process is complete, no balance can exist in any revenue, expense, Dividends, or Income Summary account.
5. The post-closing trial balance may contain revenue and expense accounts.
6. All accounting systems currently in use are computerized.

Multiple-Choice

Select the best answer for each of the following questions.

1. Which of the following accounts is *least* likely to be adjusted on the work sheet?
   a. Supplies on Hand.
   b. Land.
   c. Prepaid Rent.
   d. Unearned Delivery Fees.
2. f the Balance Sheet columns do not balance, the error is most likely to exist in the:
   a. General journal.
   b. General ledger.
   c. Last six columns of the work sheet.
   d. First six columns of the work sheet.
3. Net income for a period appears in all but which one of the following?
   a. Income Statement debit column of the work sheet.
   b. Statement of Retained Earnings credit column of the work sheet.
   c. Statement of retained earnings.
   d. Balance sheet.

4. Which of the following statements is *false* regarding the closing process?
   a. The Dividends account is closed to Income Summary.
   b. The closing of expense accounts results in a debit to Income Summary.
   c. The closing of revenues results in a credit to Income Summary.
   d. The Income Summary account is closed to the Retained Earnings account.
5. Which of the following statements is *true* regarding the classified balance sheet?
   a. Current assets include cash, accounts receivable, and equipment.
   b. Plant, property, and equipment is one category of long-term assets.
   c. Current liabilities include accounts payable, salaries payable, and notes receivable.
   d. Stockholders' equity is subdivided into current and long-term categories.

Now turn to page 173 to check your answers.

Questions

1. At which stage of the accounting cycle is a work sheet usually prepared?
2. Why are the financial statements prepared before the adjusting and closing entries are journalized and posted?
3. Describe the purposes for which the work sheet is prepared.
4. You have taken over a set of accounting books for a small business as a part-time job. At the end of the first accounting period, you have partially completed the work sheet by entering the proper ledger accounts and balances in the Trial Balance columns. You turn to the manager and ask, "Where is the list of additional information I can use in entering the adjusting entries?" The manager indicates there is no such list. (In all the text problems you have done, you have always been given this information.) How would you obtain the information for this real-life situation? What are the consequences of not making all of the required adjustments at the end of the accounting period?
5. How are the amounts in the Adjusted Trial Balance columns of a work sheet determined?
6. The work sheet for Bridges Company shows net income of $40,000. The following four adjustments were ignored:
   1. Subscriptions Fees earned, $1,200.
   2. Depreciation of equipment, $4,000.
   3. Depreciation of building, $10,000.
   4. Salaries accrued, $3,000.
   What is the correct net income?
7. After the Adjusted Trial Balance columns of a work sheet have been totaled, which account balances are extended to the Income Statement columns, which account balances are extended to the Statement of Retained Earnings columns, and which account balances are extended to the Balance Sheet columns?
8. How is the statement of retained earnings prepared?
9. What is the purpose of closing entries? What accounts are not affected by closing entries?

10. A company has net income of $50,000 for the year. In which columns of the work sheet would net income appear?
11. Is it possible to prepare monthly financial statements without journalizing and posting adjusting and closing entries? How?
12. What is the purpose of a post-closing trial balance?
13. Describe some of the ways in which the manual accounting system has evolved.
14. When did computerized accounting systems come into use?
15. Define an accounting system.
16. How is a classified balance sheet different than an unclassified balance sheet?

17. **Real World Question**
    Refer to "A Broader Perspective" on page 148 to answer the following true-false questions:
    a. The same skills are needed at each level in a CPA firm.
    b. The two most important traits at the staff accountant level are a positive attitude and the ability to learn quickly while adapting to unfamiliar situations.
    c. The senior accountant needs management skills in addition to technical skills.
    d. Partners become increasingly involved in technical matters and have less and less interaction with people.

18. **Real World Question**
    Referring to the Annual Report Appendix in your text, identify the classifications (or categories) of assets used by Wal-Mart Stores, Inc., in its balance sheet.

19. **Real World Question**
    Referring to the Annual Report Appendix in your text, identify the classifications (or categories) of liabilities used by Wal-Mart Stores, Inc., in its balance sheet.

Exercises

Exercise 4–1
Identify the steps in the accounting cycle
(L.O. 1)

List the steps in the accounting cycle. Would the system still work if any of the steps were performed out of order?

Three of the major column headings on a work sheet are Trial Balance, Income Statement, and Balance Sheet. Determine under which major column headings each of the following items would appear and whether it would be a debit or credit. (For example, Cash would appear on the debit side of the Trial Balance and Balance Sheet columns.)

Exercise 4-2
Determine where items would appear in the work sheet (L.O. 2)

	Account Titles	Trial Balance		Income Statement		Statement of Retained Earnings		Balance Sheet	
		Debit	Credit	Debit	Credit	Debit	Credit	Debit	Credit
a.	Accounts Receivable								
b.	Accounts Payable								
c.	Interest Revenue								
d.	Advertising Expense								
e.	Capital Stock								
f.	Retained Earnings (Beg.)								
g.	Net income for the month								
h.	Retained Earnings (Endg.)								

Assume a beginning balance in Retained Earnings of $84,000 and net income for the year of $36,000. Illustrate how these would appear in the Statement of Retained Earnings columns and Balance Sheet columns in the work sheet.

Exercise 4-3
Determine where items would appear in the work sheet (L.O. 2)

In Exercise 4–3, if there was a debit balance of $216,000 in the Retained Earnings account as of the beginning of the year and a net loss of $192,000 for the year, show how these would be treated in the work sheet.

Exercise 4-4
Determine where items would appear in the work sheet (L.O. 2)

Damon Davis was preparing the work sheet for Drano Plumbing Company. He calculated the net income to be $50,000. When he totaled the Balance Sheet columns, the column totals were debit, $400,000; and credit, $300,000. What was the probable cause of this difference? If this was not the cause, what should he do to find the error?

Exercise 4-5
Find cause of Balance Sheet columns not in balance (L.O. 2)

The Trial Balance of the Printer Repair Company at December 31, 2012, contains the following account balances listed in alphabetical order to increase your skill in sorting amounts to the proper work sheet columns.

Exercise 4-6
Prepare a work sheet (L.O. 2)

PRINTER REPAIR COMPANY
Trial Balance Account Balances
December 31, 2012

Accounts Payable	$ 41,000
Accounts Receivable	92,000
Accumulated Depreciation—Buildings	25,000
Accumulated Depreciation—Equipment	9,000
Buildings	140,000
Capital Stock	65,000
Cash	60,000
Equipment	36,000
Prepaid Insurance	3,600
Retained Earnings, January 1, 2012	4,800
Salaries Expense	96,000
Service Revenue	290,000
Supplies on Hand	4,000
Utilities Expense	3,200

Using these account balances and the following additional information, prepare a work sheet for Printer Repair Company. Arrange the accounts in their approximate usual order.

1. Supplies on hand at December 31, 2012, have a cost of $2,400.
2. The balance in the Prepaid Insurance account represents the cost of a two-year insurance policy covering the period from January 1, 2012, through December 31, 2013.

 Additional data

3. The estimated lives of depreciable assets are buildings, 40 years, and equipment, 20 years. No salvage values are anticipated.

Exercise 4-7
Prepare statement
of retained earnings
(L.O. 3)

Texban Corporation had a January 1, 2012, balance in its Retained Earnings account of $90,000. For the year 2012, net income was $50,000 and dividends declared and paid were $24,000. Prepare a statement of retained earnings for the year ended December 31, 2012.

Exercise 4-8
Prepare adjusting
entries and determine
correct net income
(L.O. 4)

Rubino Company reported net income of $100,000 for the current year. Examination of the work sheet and supporting data indicates that the following items were ignored:

1. Accrued salaries were $6,000 at December 31.
2. Depreciation on equipment acquired on July 1 amounted to $4,000.

Based on this information, *(a)* what adjusting journal entries should have been made at December 31, and *(b)* what is the correct net income?

Exercise 4-9
Prepare adjusting and
closing entries (L.O. 4)

Refer to the work sheet prepared in Exercise 4–6. Prepare the adjusting and closing journal entries.

Exercise 4-10
Post to Income
Summary account from
Income Statement
column totals (L.O. 4)

The Income Statement column totals on a work sheet prepared at December 31, 2012, are debit, $500,000; and credit, $900,000. In T-account format, show how the postings to the Income Summary account would appear as a result of the closing process. Identify what each posting represents.

	Debits	Credits
Retained Earnings		$540,000
Rental Revenue		960,000
Salaries Expense	$336,000	
Depreciated Expense—Buildings	64,000	
Utilities Expense	208,000	
Dividends	32,000	

After adjustment, these selected account balances of Cold Stream Campground are:

Exercise 4-11
Show how closing
entries would be posted
to T-accounts (L.O. 4)

In T-account format, show how journal entries to close the books for the period would be posted. (You do not need to show the closing journal entries.) Enter these balances in the accounts before doing so. Key the postings from the first closing entry with the number (1), the second with the number (2), and so on.

Exercise 4-12
Prepare closing
entries (L.O. 4)

The following account balances appeared in the Income Statement columns of the work sheet prepared for Liu Company for the year ended December 31, 2012:

	Income Statement	
Account Titles	**Debit**	**Credit**
Service Revenue		330,000
Advertising Expense	1,350	
Salaries Expense	130,000	
Utilities Expense	2,250	
Insurance Expense	900	
Rent Expense	6,750	
Supplies Expense	2,250	
Depreciation Expense—Equipment	4,500	
Interest Expense	562	
Interest Revenue		1,125
	148,562	331,125
Net Income	182,563	
	331,125	331,125

Prepare the closing journal entries.

Which of the following accounts are likely to appear in the post-closing trial balance for the Blake Company?

Exercise 4-13
Identify accounts in the post-closing trial balance (L.O. 5)

1. Accounts Receivable
2. Cash
3. Service Revenue
4. Buildings
5. Salaries Expense
6. Capital Stock
7. Dividends
8. Accounts Payable
9. Income Summary
10. Unearned Subscription Fees

Using the legend at the right, determine the category (number) into which you would place each of these items.

Exercise 4-14
Categorize items for classified balance sheet (L.O. 7)

Item	**Legend**
____ a. Land.	1. Current assets.
____ b. Marketable securities.	2. Long-term investments.
____ c. Notes payable, due in three years.	3. Property, plant, and equipment.
____ d. Taxes withheld from employees.	4. Intangible assets.
____ e. Patents.	5. Current liabilities.
____ f. Retained earnings.	6. Long-term liabilities.
____ g. Unearned subscription fees.	7. Stockholders' equity.
____ h. Bonds of another corporation (a 20-year investment).	
____ i. Notes payable, due in six months.	
____ j. Accumulated depreciation.	

The following data are from the 2010 annual report of The Procter & Gamble Company and its subsidiaries. This company markets a broad range of laundry, cleaning, paper, beauty care, and health care products in roughly 180 countries around the world. Leading brands include Tide, Crest, Pampers, Pantene, Gillette, Vicks, and Bounty. The dollar amounts are in millions.

Exercise 4-15
Calculate current ratios for The Procter & Gamble Company and subsidiaries and comment (L.O. 8)

	June 30	
	2010	**2009**
Current assets	$18,782	$21,905
Current liabilities	24,282	30,901

Calculate the current ratios for the two years. Comment on whether the trend is favorable or unfavorable.

Problems

Problem 4-1
Prepare closing
entries (L.O. 4)

The following adjusted trial balance is for Jasper Appliance Repair Company:

JASPER APPLIANCE REPAIR COMPANY
Adjusted Trial Balance
June 30, 2012

	Debits	Credits
Cash	$ 63,000	
Accounts Receivable	42,000	
Trucks	110,000	
Accumulated Depreciation—Trucks		$ 30,000
Accounts Payable		10,800
Notes Payable		20,000
Capital Stock		50,000
Retained Earnings, July 1, 2011		5,500
Dividends	10,000	
Service Revenue		230,000
Rent Expense	12,000	
Advertising Expense	5,000	
Salaries Expense	90,000	
Supplies Expense	1,500	
Insurance Expense	1,200	
Depreciation Expense—Trucks	10,000	
Interest Expense	1,000	
Miscellaneous Expense	600	
	$346,300	$346,300

Required Prepare the closing journal entries at the end of the fiscal year, June 30, 2012.

Problem 4-2
Prepare income
statement, statement
of retained earnings,
classified balance
sheet, closing entries,
and post-closing trial
balance (L.O. 3-5, 7)

The adjusted trial balance for Denver Architects, Inc., follows.

DENVER ARCHITECTS, INC.
Adjusted Trial Balance
December 31, 2012

	Debits	Credits
Cash	$ 90,000	
Accounts Receivable	20,000	
Interest Receivable	200	
Notes Receivable	4,000	
Prepaid Insurance	960	
Prepaid Rent	2,400	
Supplies on Hand	600	
Equipment	60,000	
Accumulated Depreciation—Equipment		$ 12,500
Buildings	140,000	
Accumulated Depreciation—Buildings		15,000
Land	56,240	
Accounts Payable		60,000
Notes Payable		10,000
Interest Payable		750
Salaries Payable		7,000
Capital Stock		100,000
Retained Earnings, January 1, 2012		20,200
Dividends	40,000	
Service Revenue		360,000
Insurance Expense	1,920	
Rent Expense	9,600	
Advertising Expense	1,200	
Depreciation Expense—Equipment	2,500	
Depreciation Expense—Buildings	3,000	
Supplies Expense	2,280	
Salaries Expense	150,000	
Interest Expense	750	
Interest Revenue		200
	$ 585,650	$ 585,650

a. Prepare an income statement.
b. Prepare a statement of retained earnings.
c. Prepare a classified balance sheet.
d. Prepare the closing journal entries.
e. Show the post-closing trial balance assuming you had posted the closing entries to the general ledger.

The following trial balance and additional data are for Sure Sale Realty Company:

Problem 4-3
Prepare work sheet,
adjusting entries, and
closing entries
(L.O. 2, 4)

SURE SALE REALTY COMPANY
Trial Balance
December 31, 2012

	Debits	Credits
Cash	$ 62,800	
Accounts Receivable	117,120	
Prepaid Rent	46,080	
Equipment	173,760	
Accumulated Depreciation—Equipment		$ 21,120
Accounts Payable		62,400
Capital Stock		96,000
Retained Earnings, January 1, 2012		49,920
Dividends	46,080	
Commissions Revenue		653,200
Salaries Expense	321,600	
Travel Expense	96,480	
Miscellaneous Expense	18,720	
	$ 882,640	$ 882,640

1. The prepaid rent is for the period July 1, 2012, to June 30, 2013.
2. The equipment has an expected life of 10 years with no salvage value.
3. Accrued salaries are $11,520.
4. Travel expenses accrued but unreimbursed to sales staff at December 31 were $17,280.

➔ *Additional data*

a. Prepare a 12-column work sheet for the year ended December 31, 2012. You need not include account numbers or explanations of adjustments.
b. Prepare adjusting journal entries.
c. Prepare closing journal entries.

➔ *Required*

The following trial balance and additional data are for South Sea Tours, Inc.:

Problem 4-4
Prepare work sheet
and closing entries
(L.O. 2, 4)

SOUTH SEA TOURS, INC.
Trial Balance
December 31, 2012

	Debits	Credits
Cash	$ 109,050	
Accounts Receivable	133,750	
Prepaid Insurance	4,350	
Prepaid Advertising	18,000	
Notes Receivable	11,250	
Land	90,000	
Buildings	165,000	
Accumulated Depreciation—Buildings		$ 49,500
Office Equipment	83,400	
Accumulated Depreciation—Office Equipment		16,680
Accounts Payable		56,850
Notes Payable		75,000
Capital Stock		240,000
Retained Earnings, January 1, 2012		47,820
Dividends	30,000	
Service Revenue		368,350
Salaries Expense	96,000	
Travel Expense	111,000	
Interest Revenue		600
Interest Expense	3,000	
	$ 854,800	$ 854,800

The company consistently followed the policy of initially debiting all prepaid items to asset accounts.

Additional data   1. The buildings have an expected life of 50 years with no salvage value.
2. The office equipment has an expected life of 10 years with no salvage value.
3. Accrued interest on notes receivable is $450.
4. Accrued interest on the notes payable is $1,000.
5. Accrued salaries are $2,100.
6. Expired prepaid insurance is $3,750.
7. Expired prepaid advertising is $16,500.

Required   a. Prepare a 12-column work sheet for the year ended December 31, 2012. You need not include account numbers. Briefly explain the entries in the Adjustments columns at the bottom of the work sheet, as was done in Illustration 4.2.
b. Prepare the required closing entries.

Problem 4-5
Prepare work sheet, income statement, statement of retained earnings, classified balance sheet, and adjusting and closing entries (L.O. 2-5, 7)

The following trial balance and additional data are for Florida Time-Share Property Management Company:

FLORIDA TIME-SHARE PROPERTY MANAGEMENT COMPANY
Trial Balance
December 31, 2012

	Debits	Credits
Cash	$ 424,000	
Prepaid Rent	28,800	
Prepaid Insurance	7,680	
Supplies on Hand	2,400	
Office Equipment	24,000	
Accumulated Depreciation—Office Equipment		$ 5,760
Automobiles	64,000	
Accumulated Depreciation—Automobiles		16,000
Accounts Payable		2,880
Unearned Management Fees		12,480
Capital Stock		360,000
Retained Earnings, January 1, 2012		120,640
Dividends	28,000	
Commissions Revenue		260,000
Management Fee Revenue		19,200
Salaries Expense	199,840	
Advertising Expense	2,400	
Gas and Oil Expense	14,240	
Miscellaneous Expense	1,600	
	$ 796,960	$ 796,960

Additional data   1. Insurance expense for the year, $3,840.
2. Rent expense for the year, $19,200.
3. Depreciation expense: office equipment, $2,880; and automobiles, $12,800.
4. Salaries earned but unpaid at December 31, $26,640.
5. Supplies on hand at December 31, $1,000.
6. The unearned management fees were received and recorded on November 1, 2012. The advance payment covered six months' management of an apartment building.

Required   a. Prepare a 12-column work sheet for the year ended December 31, 2012. You need not include account numbers or explanations of adjustments.
b. Prepare an income statement.
c. Prepare a statement of retained earnings.
d. Prepare a classified balance sheet.
e. Prepare adjusting and closing entries.

Alternate Problems

The following adjusted trial balance is for Dream Home Realty Company:

Problem 4-1A
Prepare closing entries
(L.O. 4)

DREAM HOME REALTY COMPANY
Adjusted Trial Balance
June 30, 2012

	Debits	Credits
Cash	$ 98,000	
Accounts Receivable	40,000	
Office Equipment	35,000	
Accumulated Depreciation—Office Equipment		$ 14,000
Automobiles	40,000	
Accumulated Depreciation—Automobiles		20,000
Accounts Payable		63,000
Capital Stock		75,000
Retained Earnings, July 1, 2011		54,700
Dividends	5,000	
Commissions Revenue		170,000
Salaries Expense	25,000	
Commissions Expense	120,000	
Gas and Oil Expense	4,000	
Rent Expense	14,800	
Supplies Expense	1,400	
Utilities Expense	2,000	
Depreciation Expense—Office Equipment	3,500	
Depreciation Expense—Automobiles	8,000	
	$ 396,700	$ 396,700

Prepare the closing journal entries at the end of the fiscal year, June 30, 2012.

☛ *Required*

The adjusted trial balance for Penrod Insurance Consultants, Inc., follows:

Problem 4-2A
Prepare income statement, statement of retained earnings, classified balance sheet, closing entries, and post-closing trial balance(L.O. 3-5, 7)

Penrod Insurance Consultants, Inc.
Adjusted Trial Balance
December 31, 2012

	Debits	Credits
Cash	$ 107,200	
Accounts Receivable	68,000	
Interest Receivable	400	
Notes Receivable	20,000	
Prepaid Insurance	2,400	
Supplies on Hand	1,800	
Land	32,000	
Buildings	190,000	
Accumulated Depreciation—Buildings		$ 40,000
Office Equipment	28,000	
Accumulated Depreciation—Office Equipment		8,000
Accounts Payable		48,000
Salaries Payable		8,500
Interest Payable		900
Notes Payable (due 2013)		64,000
Capital Stock		120,000
Retained Earnings, January 1, 2012		42,800
Dividends	40,000	
Commissions Revenue		392,520
Advertising Expense	24,000	
Commissions Expense	75,440	
Travel Expense	12,880	
Depreciation Expense—Buildings	8,500	
Salaries Expense	98,400	
Depreciation Expense—Office Equipment	2,800	
Supplies Expense	3,800	
Insurance Expense	3,600	
Repairs Expense	1,900	
Utilities Expense	3,400	
Interest Expense	1,800	
Interest Revenue		1,600
	$ 726,320	$ 726,320

Required ➡

a. Prepare an income statement for the year ended December 31, 2012.
b. Prepare a statement of retained earnings.
c. Prepare a classified balance sheet.
d. Prepare the closing journal entries.
e. Show the post-closing trial balance assuming you had posted the closing entries to the general ledger.

Problem 4-3A
Prepare work sheet,
adjusting entries, and
closing entries
(L.O. 2, 4)

The following trial balance and additional data are for Ramon Data Processing Company:

RAMON DATA PROCESSING COMPANY
Trial Balance
December 31, 2012

	Debits	Credits
Cash	$ 76,000	
Accounts Receivable	98,000	
Prepaid Rent	7,200	
Prepaid Insurance	2,400	
Equipment	80,000	
Accumulated Depreciation—Equipment		$ 40,000
Accounts Payable		30,000
Capital Stock		100,000
Retained Earnings, January 1, 2012		65,600
Dividends	24,000	
Service Revenue		370,000
Commissions Expense	270,000	
Travel Expense	36,000	
Miscellaneous Expense	12,000	
	$ 605,600	$ 605,600

Additional data ➡

1. The prepaid rent is for the period January 1, 2012, to December 31, 2013.
2. The equipment is expected to last 10 years with no salvage value.
3. The prepaid insurance was for the period April 1, 2012, to March 31, 2013.
4. Accrued commissions payable total $3,000 at December 31.

Required ➡

a. Prepare a 12-column work sheet for the year ended December 31, 2012. You need not include account numbers or explanations of adjustments.
b. Prepare the adjusting journal entries.
c. Prepare the closing journal entries.

Problem 4-4A
Prepare work sheet
and closing entries
(L.O. 2, 4)

The following trial balance and additional data are for Best-Friend Pet Hospital, Inc.:

BEST-FRIEND PET HOSPITAL, INC.
Trial Balance
December 31, 2012

	Debits	Credits
Cash	$ 16,490	
Accounts Receivable	54,390	
Supplies on Hand	900	
Prepaid Fire Insurance	1,800	
Prepaid Rent	21,600	
Equipment	125,000	
Accumulated Depreciation—Equipment		$ 25,000
Accounts Payable		29,550
Notes Payable		9,000
Capital Stock		150,000
Retained Earnings, January 1, 2012		20,685
Service Revenue		179,010
Interest Expense	225	
Salaries Expense	142,200	
Advertising Expense	29,250	
Supplies Expense	2,135	
Miscellaneous Expense	3,705	
Legal and Accounting Expense	13,750	
Utilities Expense	1,800	
	$ 413,245	$ 413,245

The company consistently followed the policy of initially debiting all prepaid items to asset accounts.

Additional data

1. Prepaid fire insurance is $600 as of the end of the year.
2. Supplies on hand are $638 as of the end of the year.
3. Prepaid rent is $2,625 as of the end of the year.
4. The equipment is expected to last 10 years with no salvage value.
5. Accrued salaries are $2,625.

Required

a. Prepare a 12-column work sheet for the year ended December 31, 2012. You need not include account numbers. Briefly explain the entries in the Adjustments columns at the bottom of the work sheet, as was done in Illustration 4.2.
b. Prepare the December 31, 2012, closing entries.

The following trial balance and additional data are for Roswell Interior Decorators, Inc.:

Problem 4-5A
Prepare work sheet, income statement, statement of retained earnings, classified balance sheet, and adjusting and closing entries (L.O. 2-5, 7)

ROSWELL INTERIOR DECORATORS, INC
Trial Balance
December 31, 2012

	Debits	Credits
Cash	$ 85,400	
Accounts Receivable	81,600	
Supplies on Hand	4,000	
Prepaid Rent	12,240	
Prepaid Advertising	2,880	
Prepaid Insurance	4,400	
Office Equipment	7,600	
Accumulated Depreciation—Office Equipment		$ 2,760
Office Furniture	29,200	
Accumulated Depreciation—Office Furniture		8,280
Accounts Payable		25,200
Notes Payable (due 2013)		4,000
Capital Stock		100,000
Retained Earnings, January 1, 2012		22,400
Dividends	45,520	
Service Revenue		250,000
Salaries Expense	98,800	
Utilities Expense	20,000	
Miscellaneous Expense	24,000	
	$ 412,640	$ 412,640

1. Supplies on hand at December 31, 2012, are $1,000.
2. Rent expense for 2012 is $10,000.
3. Advertising expense for 2012 is $2,304.
4. Insurance expense for 2012 is $2,400.
5. Depreciation expense is office equipment, $912, and office furniture, $3,000.
6. Accrued interest on notes payable is $150.
7. Accrued salaries are $4,200.

Additional data

a. Prepare a 12-column work sheet for the year ended December 31, 2012. You need not include account numbers or explanations of adjustments.
b. Prepare an income statement.
c. Prepare a statement of retained earnings.
d. Prepare a classified balance sheet.
e. Prepare adjusting and closing entries.

Required

Beyond the Numbers—Critical Thinking

**Business Decision
Case 4-1**
Prepare report
on profitability of
business (L.O. 3)

Heather and Dan Holt met while both were employed in the interior trim and upholstery department of an auto manufacturer. After their marriage, they decided to earn some extra income by doing small jobs involving canvas, vinyl, and upholstered products. Their work was considered excellent, and at the urging of their customers, they decided to go into business for themselves, operating out of the basement of the house they owned. To do this, they invested $120,000 cash in their business. They spent $10,500 for a sewing machine (expected life, 10 years) and $12,000 for other miscellaneous tools and equipment (expected life, 5 years). They undertook only custom work, with the customers purchasing the required materials, to avoid stocking any inventory other than supplies. Generally, they required an advance deposit on all jobs.

The business seemed successful from the start, as the Holts received orders from many customers. But they felt something was wrong. They worked hard and charged competitive prices. Yet there seemed to be barely enough cash available from the business to cover immediate personal needs. Summarized, the checkbook of the business for 2012, their second year of operations, showed:

Balance, January 1, 2012		$ 99,200
Cash received from customers:		
For work done in 2011	$ 36,000	
For work done in 2012	200,000	
For work to be done in 2013	48,000	284,000
		$ 383,200
Cash paid out:		
Two-year insurance policy dated January 1, 2012	$ 19,200	
Utilities	48,000	
Supplies	104,000	
Other Expenses	72,000	
Taxes, including sales taxes	26,400	
Dividends	40,000	309,600
Balance, December 31, 2012		$ 73,600

Considering how much they worked, the Holts were concerned that the cash balance decreased by $25,600 even though they only received dividends of $40,000. Their combined income from the auto manufacturer had been $45,000. They were seriously considering giving up their business and going back to work for the auto manufacturer. They turned to you for advice. You discovered the following:

1. Of the supplies purchased in 2012, $24,000 were used on jobs billed to customers in 2012; no supplies were used for any other work.
2. Work completed in 2012 and billed to customers for which cash had not yet been received by year-end amounted to $40,000.

Required ➲ Prepare a written report for the Holts, responding to their belief that their business is not sufficiently profitable. (Hint: Prepare an income statement for 2012 and include it in your report.)

**Annual Report
Analysis 4-2**
Calculate current
ratios for a real
company (L.O. 8)

Using the Annual Report Appendix, calculate the current ratios for the two years shown for Wal-Mart Stores, Inc. Write a summary of the results of your calculations. Also, look at some of the other data provided by the company in preparing your comments. For instance, look at the net income for the last three years.

Read the "A Broader Perspective" on page 148. Write a description of a career in public accounting at each level within the firm. Discuss the skills needed and how you could develop these skills.

**Broader Perspective–
Writing Experience
4-3**

In teams of two or three students, interview a management accountant. Management accountants may have the title of chief financial officer (CFO), controller, or some other accounting title within a company. Seek information on the advantages and disadvantages of working as a management accountant. Also inquire about the nature of the work and any training programs offered by the company. As a team, write a memorandum to the instructor summarizing the results of the interview. The heading of the memorandum should contain the date, to whom it is written, from whom, and the subject matter.

Group Project 4-4
Interview a
management
accountant

With a small group of students, obtain an annual report of a company in which you have some interest. You may obtain the annual report from your instructor, the library, the Internet, or the company. Describe the nature of each item on the classified balance sheet. You may have to do library research on some of the items. Also, calculate the current ratio for the most recent two years and comment. Write a report to your instructor summarizing the results of the project.

Group Project 4-5
Perform annual
report analysis

With a small group of students and using library sources, write a paper comparing the features of three different accounting software packages (such as Sage Peachtree Complete, QuickBooks Pro 3, Sage MAS 90, Microsoft Dynamics GP, TRAVERSE by Open Systems Accounting Software, and SAP Business One). Give the strengths and weaknesses of each. Cite sources for the information and treat direct quotes properly.

Group Project 4-6
Evaluate accounting
software packages

Using the Internet—A View of the Real World

Visit the following Internet site:
   http://www.merck.com
Pursue choices you are offered on the screen under "Investors" until you locate the consolidated balance sheet in the most recent annual report. In a short report to your instructor, describe how you got to the balance sheet and identify the major headings used in the balance sheet. For instance, the first such heading is Assets. Also, calculate the current ratio.

Internet Project 4-7
Investigate a
consolidated balance
sheet

Visit the following Internet site:
   http://www.kodak.com
Go to "About Kodak" to access the corporate home page. Click on "Investor Center" to locate the most recent annual report, and then find the consolidated statement of financial position. Identify the major headings within the balance sheet and calculate the current ratio for the most recent year. Write a memo to your instructor summarizing your findings.

Internet Project 4-8
Investigate a
consolidated balance
sheet

Answers to Self-Test

True-False

1. **True.** The three trial balances are the unadjusted trial balance, the adjusted trial balance, and the post-closing trial balance. The first two trial balances appear on the work sheet.
2. **False.** If a debit-balance account (such as Prepaid Rent) is credited in the adjustment, the amount in the Adjustments columns is deducted from the amount in the Trial Balance columns to determine the amount for that item in the Adjusted Trial Balance columns.

3. **True.** The net loss appears in the Income Statement credit column to balance the Income Statement columns. Then the loss appears in the Statement of Retained Earnings debit column because it reduces Retained Earnings.
4. **True.** All of these accounts are closed, or reduced to zero balances, as a result of the closing process.
5. **False.** All revenue and expense accounts have zero balances after closing.
6. **False.** Some manual accounting systems are still in use.

Multiple-Choice

1. **b.** The other accounts are very likely to be adjusted. The Land account would be adjusted only if an error has been made involving that account.

2. **c.** The Adjusted Trial Balance columns should balance before items are spread to the Income Statement, Statement of Retained Earnings, and Balance Sheet columns. Therefore, if the Balance Sheet columns do not balance, the error is likely to exist in the last six columns of the work sheet.

3. **d.** The net income for the period does not appear in the balance sheet. It does appear in all of the other places listed.

4. **a.** The Dividends account is closed to the Retained Earnings account rather than to the Income Summary account.

5. **b.** Plant, property, and equipment is one of the long-term asset categories. Response **a** should not include equipment. Response **c** should not include notes receivable. Stockholders' equity is not subdivided into current and long-term categories.

Careers in Accounting

A Career as an Accounting Professor

Do you enjoy college life? Do you enjoy teaching others? If so, you might want to consider a career as a college professor. Although a position as a college professor may pay less than some other career alternatives, the intangible benefits are beyond measure. A college professor can make a real difference in the lives of hundreds, even thousands, of students over a career. Students come to college with great potential, but are in need of some additional training and guidance. The work of a college professor is a valuable investment in our nation's most valuable resource – people.

College faculty generally teach fewer hours each week than elementary and secondary school teachers. This is because most college faculty have at least two additional important responsibilities: research and service. The research component represents far more than just summarizing what others have already learned. It represents arriving at new knowledge by discovering things that previously were unknown. For instance, accounting research has demonstrated the ways in which accounting numbers such as earnings and stockholder's equity are related to stock prices. This illustrates the importance of accounting numbers and has resulted in a large stream of discovery called Capital Markets research. Besides teaching and research, most faculty have significant service responsibilities as well. Accounting faculty are involved in service to the university, the accounting profession, and to the general public. Many college faculty dedicate 10-20 hours or more each week to the service component of their jobs.

The demand for college professors varies greatly by discipline. In fields such as psychology, history, and sociology there is a large supply of candidates with advanced degrees and, thus, the competition for positions as college professors in these areas is intense. However, in applied fields such as accounting and engineering, there is a shortage of candidates with advanced degrees. The opportunities for professors in these applied fields are excellent, and the chance to make a real difference in the lives of others is exciting.

Accounting Theory

Chapter 1 briefly introduced the body of theory underlying accounting procedures. In this chapter, we discuss accounting theory in greater depth. Now that you have learned some accounting procedures, you are better able to relate these theoretical concepts to accounting practice. Accounting theory is "a set of basic concepts and assumptions and related principles that explain and guide the accountant's actions in identifying, measuring, and communicating economic information."[1]

To some people, the word *theory* implies something abstract and out of reach. Understanding the theory behind the accounting process, however, helps one make decisions in diverse accounting situations. Accounting theory provides a logical framework for accounting practice.

The first part of the chapter describes underlying accounting assumptions or concepts, the measurement process, the major principles, and modifying conventions or constraints. Accounting theory has developed over the years and is contained in authoritative accounting literature and textbooks. The next part of the chapter describes the development of the Financial Accounting Standards Board's (FASB) conceptual framework for accounting. This framework builds on accounting theory developed over time and serves as a basis for formulating accounting standards in the future. Presenting the traditional body of theory first and the conceptual framework second gives you a sense of the historical development of accounting theory. Despite some overlap between the two parts of the chapter, remember that FASB's conceptual framework builds on traditional theory rather than replaces it. The final part of the chapter discusses significant accounting policies contained in annual reports issued by companies and illustrates them with an actual example from an annual report of the Walt Disney Company.

Learning Objectives

After studying this chapter, you should be able to:

1. Identify and discuss the underlying assumptions or concepts of accounting.

2. Identify and discuss the major principles of accounting.

3. Identify and discuss the modifying conventions (or constraints) of accounting.

4. Describe the conceptual framework project of the Financial Accounting Standards Board.

5. Discuss the nature and content of a company's summary of significant accounting policies in its annual report.

[1]American Accounting Association, *A Statement of Basic Accounting Theory* (Sarasota, Fla., 1966), pp. 1–2.

Traditional Accounting Theory

Traditional accounting theory consists of underlying assumptions, rules of measurement, major principles, and modifying conventions (or constraints). The following sections describe these aspects of accounting theory that greatly influence accounting practice.

Underlying Assumptions or Concepts

The major underlying assumptions or concepts of accounting are (1) business entity, (2) going concern (continuity), (3) money measurement, (4) stable dollar, and (5) periodicity. This section discusses the effects of these assumptions on the accounting process.

Business Entity

Objective 1
Identify and discuss the underlying assumptions or concepts of accounting.

Data gathered in an accounting system must relate to a specific business unit or entity. The business entity concept assumes that each business has an existence separate from its owners, creditors, employees, customers, interested parties, and other businesses. For each business (such as a horse stable or a fitness center), the business, not the business owner, is the accounting entity. Therefore, financial statements are identified as belonging to a particular business entity. The content of these financial statements reports only on the activities, resources, and obligations of that entity.

A business entity may be made up of several different legal entities. For instance, a large business (such as General Electric Corporation) may consist of several separate corporations, each of which is a separate legal entity. For reporting purposes, however, the corporations may be considered as one business entity because they have a common ownership. Chapter 14 illustrates this concept.

Going Concern (Continuity)

Note to the Student
The going-concern concept is linked to depreciation by the assumption that a business will continue at least as long as its longest lived plant asset.

When accountants record business transactions for an entity, they assume it is a going concern. The going-concern (continuity) assumption states that an entity will continue to operate indefinitely unless strong evidence exists that the entity will terminate. The termination of an entity occurs when a company ceases business operations and sells its assets. The process of termination is called liquidation. If liquidation appears likely, the going-concern assumption is no longer valid.

Accountants often cite the going-concern assumption to justify using historical costs rather than market values in measuring assets. Market values are of less significance to an entity that is using its assets for operations rather than selling them. On the other hand, if an entity is liquidating, it should use liquidation values to report assets.

Money Measurement

The economic activity of a business is normally recorded and reported in money terms. Money measurement is the use of a monetary unit such as the dollar instead of physical or other units of measurement. Using a particular monetary unit provides accountants with a common unit of measurement to report economic activity. Without a monetary unit, it would be impossible to add such items as buildings, equipment, and inventory on a balance sheet.

Financial statements identify their unit of measure (such as the dollar in the United States) so the statement user can make valid comparisons of amounts. For example, it would be difficult to compare relative asset amounts or profitability of a company reporting in U.S. dollars with a company reporting in Japanese yen.

Stable Dollar

In the United States, accountants make another assumption regarding money measurement—the stable dollar assumption. Under the stable dollar assumption, the dollar is accepted as a reasonably stable unit of measurement. Thus, accountants make no adjustments for the changing value of the dollar in the primary financial statements.

Using the stable dollar assumption creates a difficulty in depreciation accounting. Assume, for example, that a company acquired a building in 1985 and computed the 30-year straight-line depreciation on the building without adjusting for any changes in the value of the dollar. Thus, the depreciation deducted in 2015 is the same as the depreciation deducted in 1985. The company makes no adjustments for the difference between the values of the 1985 dollar and the 2015 dollar. Both dollars are treated as equal monetary units of measurement despite substantial price inflation over the 30-year period. Accountants and business executives have expressed concern over this inflation problem, especially during periods of high inflation.

According to the periodicity (time periods) assumption, accountants divide an entity's life into months or years to report its economic activities. Then, accountants attempt to prepare accurate reports on the entity's activities for these periods. Although these time-period reports provide useful and timely financial information for investors and creditors, they may be inaccurate for some of these time periods because accountants must estimate depreciation expense and certain other adjusting entries.

Periodicity (Time Periods)

Accounting reports cover relatively short periods. These time periods are usually of equal length so that statement users can make valid comparisons of a company's performance from period to period. The length of the accounting period must be stated in the financial statements. For instance, so far, the income statements in this text were for either one month or one year. Companies that must publish their financial statements, such as publicly held corporations, generally prepare monthly statements for internal management and publish financial statements quarterly and annually for external statement users.

Accrual Basis and Periodicity   Chapter 3 demonstrated that financial statements more accurately reflect the financial status and operations of a company when prepared under the accrual basis rather than the cash basis of accounting. Under the cash basis, we record revenues when cash is received and expenses when cash is paid. Under the accrual basis, however, we record revenues when services are rendered or products are sold and expenses when incurred.

The periodicity assumption requires preparing adjusting entries under the accrual basis. Without the periodicity assumption, a business would have only one time period running from its inception to its termination. Then, the concepts of cash basis and accrual basis accounting would be irrelevant because all revenues and all expenses would be recorded in that one time period and would not have to be assigned to artificially short periods of one year or less.

Approximation and Judgment because of Periodicity   To provide periodic financial information, accountants must often estimate expected uncollectible accounts (see Chapter 9) and the useful lives of depreciable assets. Uncertainty about future events prevents precise measurement and makes estimates necessary in accounting. Fortunately, these estimates are often reasonably accurate.

Other Basic Concepts

Other basic accounting concepts that affect accounting for entities are (1) general-purpose financial statements, (2) substance over form, (3) consistency, (4) double entry, and (5) articulation. We discuss these basic accounting concepts next.

Accountants prepare general-purpose financial statements at regular intervals to meet many of the information needs of external parties and top-level internal managers. In contrast, accountants can gather special-purpose financial information for a specific decision, usually on a one-time basis. For example, management may need specific

General-Purpose Financial Statements

information to decide whether to purchase a new computer system. Since special-purpose financial information must be specific, this information is best obtained from the detailed accounting records rather than from the financial statements.

Substance over Form

In some business transactions, the economic substance of the transaction conflicts with its legal form. For example, a contract that is legally a lease may, in fact, be equivalent to a purchase. A company may have a three-year contract to lease (rent) an automobile at a stated monthly rental fee. At the end of the lease period, the company receives title to the auto after paying a nominal sum (say, $1). The economic substance of this transaction is a purchase rather than a lease of the auto. Thus, under the substance-over-form concept, the auto is an asset on the balance sheet and is depreciated instead simply showing the monthly payments as rent expense on the income statement. Accountants record a transaction's *economic substance* rather than its *legal form.*

Consistency

Consistency generally requires that a company use the same accounting principles and reporting practices through time. This concept prohibits indiscriminate switching of accounting principles or methods, such as changing inventory methods every year. However, consistency does not prohibit a change in accounting principles if the information needs of financial statement users are better served by the change. When a company makes a change in accounting principles, it must make the following disclosures in the financial statements: (1) nature of the change; (2) reasons for the change; (3) effect of the change on current net income, if significant; and (4) cumulative effect of the change on past income.

Double Entry

Chapter 2 introduced the basic accounting concept of the double-entry method of recording transactions. Under the double-entry approach, every transaction has a two-sided effect on each party engaging in the transaction. Thus, to record a transaction, each party debits at least one account and credits at least one account. The total debits equal the total credits in each journal entry.

Articulation

When learning how to prepare work sheets in Chapter 4, you learned that financial statements are fundamentally related and articulate (interact) with each other. For example, we carry the amount of net income from the income statement to the statement of retained earnings. Then we carry the ending balance on the statement of retained earnings to the balance sheet to bring total assets and total equities into balance.

In Illustration 5.1 we summarize the underlying assumptions or concepts. The next section discusses the measurement process used in accounting.

The Measurement Process in Accounting

Earlier, we defined accounting as "the process of identifying, measuring, and communicating economic information to permit informed judgments and decisions by the users of the information."[2] In this section, we focus on the *measurement process* of accounting

Accountants measure a business entity's assets, liabilities, and stockholders' equity and any changes that occur in them. By assigning the effects of these changes to particular time periods (periodicity), they can find the net income or net loss of the accounting entity for those periods.

Measuring Assets and Liabilities

Accountants measure the various assets of a business in different ways. They measure cash at its specified amount. Chapter 9 explains how they measure claims to cash, such as accounts receivable, at their expected cash inflows, taking into consideration possible uncollectibles. They measure inventories, prepaid expenses, plant assets, and intangibles at their historical costs (actual amounts paid). After the acquisition

---

[2]Ibid., p. 1.

Illustration 5.1   The Underlying Assumptions or Concepts

Assumption or Concept	Description	Importance
Business entity	Each business has an existence separate from its owners, creditors, employees, customers, other interested parties, and other businesses.	Defines the scope of the business such as a horse stable or physical fitness center. Identifies which transactions should be recorded on the company's books.
Going concern (continuity)	An entity will continue to operate indefinitely unless strong evidence exists that the entity will terminate.	Allows a company to continue carrying plant assets at their historical costs in spite of a change in their market values.
Money measurement	Each business uses a monetary unit of measurement, such as the dollar, instead of physical or other units of measurement.	Provides accountants with a common unit of measure to report economic activity. This concept permits us to add and subtract items on the financial statements.
Stable dollar	The dollar is accepted as a reasonably stable unit of measure.	Permits us to make no adjustments in the financial statements for the changing value of the dollar. This assumption works fairly well in the United States because of our relatively low rate of inflation.
Periodicity (time periods)	An entity's life can be subdivided into months or years to report its economic activities.	Permits us to prepare financial statements that cover periods shorter than the entire life of a business. Thus, we know how well a business is performing before it terminates its operations. The need for adjusting entries arises because of this concept and the use of accrual accounting.
General-purpose financial statements	One set of financial statements serves the needs of all users.	Allows companies to prepare only one set of financial statements instead of a separate set for each potential type of user of those statements. The financial statements should be free of bias so they do not favor the interests of any one type of user.
Substance over form	Accountants should record the economic substance of a transaction rather than its legal form.	Encourages the accountant to record the true nature of a transaction rather than its apparent nature. This approach is the accounting equivalent of "tell it like it is." An apparent lease transaction that has all the characteristics of a purchase should be recorded as a purchase.
Consistency	Generally requires that a company use the same accounting principles and reporting practices every accounting period.	Prevents a company from changing accounting methods whenever it likes to present a better picture or to manipulate income. The inventory and depreciation chapters (Chapters 7 and 10) both mention the importance of this concept.
Double entry	Every transaction has a two-sided effect on each company or party engaging in the transaction.	Uses a system of checks and balances to help identify whether or not errors have been made in recording transactions. When the debits do not equal the credits, this inequality immediately signals us to stop and find the error.
Articulation	Financial statements are fundamentally related and articulate (interact) with each other.	Changes in account balances during an accounting period are reflected in financial statements that are related to one another. For instance, earning revenue increases net income on the income statement, retained earnings on the statement of retained earnings, and assets and retained earnings on the balance sheet. The statement of retained earnings ties the income statement and balance sheet together.

date, they carry some items, such as inventory, at the lower-of-cost-or-market value. After the acquisition date, they carry plant assets and intangibles at original cost less accumulated depreciation or amortization. They measure liabilities at the amount of cash that will be paid or the value of services that will be performed to satisfy the liabilities.

Measuring Changes in Assets and Liabilities

Accountants can easily measure some changes in assets and liabilities, such as the acquisition of an asset on credit and the payment of a liability. Other changes in assets and liabilities, such as those recorded in adjusting entries, are more difficult to measure because they often involve estimates and/or calculations. The accountant must determine when a change has taken place and the amount of the change. These decisions involve matching revenues and expenses and are guided by the principles discussed next.

The Major Principles

Objective 2
Identify and discuss the major principles of accounting.

Generally accepted accounting principles (GAAP) set forth standards or methods for presenting financial accounting information. A standardized presentation format enables users to compare the financial information of different companies more easily. Generally accepted accounting principles have been either developed through accounting practice or established by authoritative organizations. Organizations that have contributed to the development of the principles are the American Institute of Certified Public Accountants (AICPA), the Financial Accounting Standards Board (FASB), the Securities and Exchange Commission (SEC), the American Accounting Association (AAA), the Financial Executives Institute (FEI), and the Institute of Management Accounting (IMA). This section explains the following major principles:

Reinforcing Problem
E5-1 Match theory terms with definitions.

1. Exchange-price (or cost) principle.
2. Revenue recognition principle.
3. Matching principle.
4. Gain and loss recognition principle.
5. Full disclosure principle.

Exchange-Price (or Cost) Principle

Whenever resources are transferred between two parties, such as buying merchandise on account, the accountant must follow the *exchange-price (or cost) principle* in presenting that information. The **exchange-price (or cost) principle** requires an accountant to record transfers of resources at prices agreed on by the parties to the exchange at the time of exchange. This principle sets forth (1) what goes into the accounting system—transaction data; (2) when it is recorded—at the time of exchange; and (3) the amounts—exchange prices—at which assets, liabilities, stockholders' equity, revenues, and expenses are recorded.

As applied to most assets, this principle is often called the **cost principle**. It dictates that purchased or self-constructed assets are initially recorded at historical cost. **Historical cost** is the amount paid, or the fair market value of the liability incurred or other resources surrendered, to acquire an asset and place it in a condition and position for its intended use. For instance, when the cost of a plant asset (such as a machine) is recorded, its cost includes the net purchase price plus any costs of reconditioning, testing, transporting, and placing the asset in the location for its intended use. Accountants prefer the term *exchange-price principle* to cost principle because it seems inappropriate to refer to liabilities, stockholders' equity, and such assets as cash and accounts receivable as being measured in terms of cost.

> **Business Insight** In some European countries, the financial statements contain secret reserves. These secret reserves arise from a company not reporting all of its profits when it has a very good year. The justification is that the stockholders in those countries vote on the amount of dividends they receive each year; if all profits were reported, the stockholders might vote to pay the entire amount out as dividends. By holding back some profits, not only are the creditors more protected but the company is also more solvent and has more resources to invest in productive assets.

An Accounting Perspective

Revenue is not difficult to define or measure; it is the inflow of assets from the sale of goods and services to customers, measured by the cash expected to be received from customers. However, the crucial question for the accountant is when to record an item of revenue. Under the revenue recognition principle, revenues should be earned and realized before they are recognized (recorded).

Revenue Recognition Principle

Earning of Revenue   All economic activities undertaken by a company to create revenues are part of the earning process. Many activities may have preceded the actual receipt of cash from a customer, including (1) placing advertisements, (2) calling on the customer several times, (3) submitting samples, (4) acquiring or manufacturing goods, and (5) selling and delivering goods. For these activities, the company incurs costs. Although revenue was actually being earned by these activities, accountants do not recognize revenue until the time of sale because of the requirement that revenue be *substantially* earned before it is recognized (recorded). This requirement is the earning principle.

Realization of Revenue   Under the realization principle, the accountant does not recognize (record) revenue until the seller acquires the right to receive payment from the buyer. The seller acquires this right from the buyer at the time of sale for merchandise transactions or when services have been performed in service transactions. Legally, a sale of merchandise occurs when title to the goods passes to the buyer. The time at which title passes normally depends on the shipping terms—FOB shipping point or FOB destination (as we discuss in Chapter 6). As a practical matter, accountants generally record revenue when goods are delivered.

The advantages of recognizing revenue at the time of sale are (1) the actual transaction—delivery of goods—is an observable event; (2) revenue is easily measured; (3) risk of loss due to price decline or destruction of the goods has passed to the buyer; (4) revenue has been earned, or substantially so; and (5) because the revenue has been earned, expenses and net income can be determined. As discussed later, the disadvantage of recognizing revenue at the time of sale is that the revenue might not be recorded in the period during which most of the activity creating it occurred.

Exceptions to the Realization Principle   The following three examples are instances when practical considerations may cause accountants to vary the point of revenue recognition from the time of sale. These examples illustrate the effect that the business environment has on the development of accounting principles and standards.

• **Cash Collection as Point of Revenue Recognition**   Some small companies record revenues and expenses at the time of cash collection and payment, which may not occur at the time of sale. This procedure is the cash basis of accounting. The cash basis is acceptable primarily in service enterprises that do not have substantial credit transactions or inventories, such as business entities of doctors or dentists.

• **Installment Basis of Revenue Recognition**   When collecting the selling price of goods sold in monthly or annual installments and considerable doubt exists as to collectibility, the company may use the installment basis of accounting. Companies make these sales in spite of the doubtful collectibility of the account because their margin of profit is high and the goods can be repossessed if the payments are not received. Under the installment basis, the percentage of total gross margin (selling price of a good minus its cost) recognized in a period is equal to the percentage of total cash from a sale that is received in that period. Thus, the gross margin recognized in a period is equal to the cash received times the gross margin percentage (gross margin divided by selling price). The formula to recognize gross profit on cash collections made on installment sales of a certain year is:

$$\text{Cash collections} \times \text{Gross margin percentage} = \text{Gross margin recognized}$$

To be more precise, we expand the descriptions in the formula as follows:

$$\begin{array}{c}\text{Cash collections this year resulting from installment sales made in a certain year}\end{array} \times \begin{array}{c}\text{Gross margin percentage for the year of sale}\end{array} = \begin{array}{c}\text{Gross margin recognized this year on cash collections this year from installment sales made in a certain year}\end{array}$$

Reinforcing Problems
E5-2 Compute net income under accrual basis and under installment basis.
P5-2 Compute net income assuming revenues are recognized at time of sale and then assuming installment basis is used.

To illustrate, assume a company sold a stereo set. The facts of the sale are:

Date of Sale	Selling Price	Cost	Gross Margin (Selling price – Cost)	Gross Margin Percentage (Gross margin ÷ Selling price)
Oct. 1, 2012	$500	$300	($500 – $300) = $200	($200 ÷ $500) = 40%

The buyer makes 10 equal monthly installment payments of $50 to pay for the set (10 × $50 = $500). If the company receives three monthly payments in 2012, the total amount of cash received in 2012 is $150 (3 × $50). The gross margin to recognize in 2012 is:

$$\begin{array}{c}\text{2012 cash collections from 2012 installment sales}\end{array} \times \begin{array}{c}\text{Gross margin percentage on 2012 installment sales}\end{array} = \begin{array}{c}\text{2012 gross margin recognized on 2012 cash collections from 2012 installment sales}\end{array}$$

$$\$150 \times 40\% = \$60$$

The company collects the other installments when due so it receives a total of $350 in 2013 from 2012 installment sales. The gross margin to recognize in 2013 on these cash collections is as follows:

$$\begin{array}{c}\text{2013 cash collections from 2012 installment sales}\end{array} \times \begin{array}{c}\text{Gross margin percentage on 2012 installment sales}\end{array} = \begin{array}{c}\text{2013 gross margin recognized on 2013 cash collections from 2012 installment sales}\end{array}$$

$$\$350 \times 40\% = \$140$$

Note to the Student
The installment basis of revenue recognition is acceptable only when considerable doubt exists about the collectibility of the installment. The installment basis delays some revenue recognition beyond the time of sale.

In summary, the total receipts and gross margin recognized in the two years are as follows:

Year	Total Amount of Cash Recognized		Gross Margin Recognized	
2012	$150	30%	$60	30%
2013	350	70%	140	70%
	$500	100%	$200	100%

Because the installment basis delays some revenue recognition beyond the time of sale, it is acceptable for accounting purposes only when considerable doubt exists as to collectibility of the installments.

Revenue Recognition on Long-Term Construction Projects   Companies recognize revenue from a long-term construction project under two different methods: (1) the completed-contract method or (2) the percentage-of-completion method. The completed-contract method does not recognize any revenue until the project is completed. In that period, they recognize all revenue even though the contract may have required three years to complete. Thus, the completed-contract method recognizes revenues at the time of sale, as is true for most sales transactions. Companies carry costs incurred on the project forward in an inventory account (Construction in Process) and charge them to expense in the period in which the revenue is recognized.

Some accountants argue that waiting so long to recognize any revenue is unreasonable. They believe that because revenue-producing activities have been performed during each year of construction, revenue should be recognized in each year of construction even if estimates are needed. The **percentage-of-completion method** recognizes revenue based on the estimated stage of completion of a long-term project. To measure the stage of completion, firms compare actual costs incurred in a period with the total estimated costs to be incurred on the project.

To illustrate, assume that a company has a contract to build a dam for $44 million. The estimated construction cost is $40 million. You calculate the estimated gross margin as follows:

Sales Price of Dam	Estimated Costs to Construct Dam	Estimated Gross Margin (Sales price – Estimated costs)
$44 million	$40 million	($44 million – $40 million) = $4 million

The firm recognizes the $4 million gross margin in the financial statements by recording the assigned revenue for the year and then deducting actual costs incurred that year. The formula to recognize revenue is:

Actual construction costs incurred during the period	÷	Total estimated construction costs for the entire project	×	Total sales price	=	Revenue recognized for period

Suppose that by the end of the first year (2012), the company had incurred actual construction costs of $30 million. These costs are 75% of the total estimated construction costs ($30 million ÷ $40 million = 75%). Under the percentage-of-completion method, the firm would use the 75% figure to assign revenue to the first year. In 2013, it incurs another $6 million of construction costs. In 2014, it incurs the final $4 million of construction costs. The amount of revenue to assign to each year is as follows:

Year	Ratio of Actual Construction Costs to Total Estimated Construction Costs	X	Agreed Price of Dam	=	Amount of Revenue to Recognize (Assign)
2012	($30 million ÷ $40 million = 75%) 75%	X	$44 million	=	$33 million
2013	($6 million ÷ $40 million = 15%) 15%	X	$44 million	=	$6.6 million
2014	($4 million ÷ $40 million = 10%) 10%	X	$44 million	=	$4.4 million
					$44 million

The amount of gross margin to recognize in each year is as follows:

Year	Assigned Revenues	-	Actual Construction Costs	=	Recognized Gross Margin
2012	$33.0 million	-	$30.0 million	=	$3.0 million
2013	6.6	-	6.0	=	0.6
2014	4.4	-	4.0	=	0.4
	$44.0 million		$40.0 million		$4.0 million

Reinforcing Problems
E5-3 Recognize revenue under percentage-of-completion method.
P5-3 Compute income under completed-contract and percentage-of-completion methods.

Real World Example
Only small contractors are allowed to use the completed-contract method for tax purposes. Large contractors must use one of two variations of the percentage-of-completion method.

Illustration 5.2   Methods of Accounting for Long-Term Contracts

	Number of Companies			
	2009	2008	2007	2006
Percentage of completion: Input based	63	56	76	81
Percentage of completion: Output based	41	40	43	55
Completed contract	20	17	24	9

Source: American Institute of Certified Public Accountants, *Accounting Trends & Techniques* (New York: AICPA, 2004), p. 432

This company would deduct other costs incurred in the accounting period, such as general and administrative expenses, from gross margin to determine net income. For instance, assuming general and administrative expenses were $100,000 in 2012, net income would be ($3,000,000 – $100,000) = $2,900,000.

Matching Principle

Reinforcing Problem
E5-4 Compute the effect on financial statements of incorrectly expensing an asset.

Expense recognition is closely related to, and sometimes discussed as part of, the revenue recognition principle. The **matching principle** states that expenses should be recognized (recorded) as they are incurred to produce revenues. An expense is the outflow or using up of assets in the generation of revenue. Firms voluntarily incur expense to produce revenue. For instance, a television set delivered by a dealer to a customer in exchange for cash is an asset consumed to produce revenue; its cost becomes an expense. Similarly, the cost of services such as labor are voluntarily incurred to produce revenue.

The Measurement of Expense   Accountants measure most assets used in operating a business by their historical costs. Therefore, they measure a depreciation expense resulting from the consumption of those assets by the historical costs of those assets. They measure other expenses, such as wages that are paid for currently, at their current costs.

The Timing of Expense Recognition   The matching principle implies that a relationship exists between expenses and revenues. For certain expenses, such as costs of acquiring or producing the products sold, you can easily see this relationship. However, when a direct relationship cannot be seen, we charge the costs of assets with limited lives to expense in the periods benefited on a systematic and rational allocation basis. Depreciation of plant assets is an example.

Product costs are costs incurred in the acquisition or manufacture of goods. As you will see in the next chapter, included as product costs for purchased goods are invoice, freight, and insurance-in-transit costs. For manufacturing companies, product costs include all costs of materials, labor, and factory operations necessary to produce the goods. Product costs attach to the goods purchased or produced and remain in inventory accounts as long as the goods are on hand. We charge product costs to expense when the goods are sold. The result is a precise matching of cost of goods sold expense to its related revenue.

Period costs are costs not traceable to specific products and are expensed in the period incurred. Selling and administrative costs are period costs.

Gain and Loss Recognition Principle

The **gain and loss recognition principle** states that we record gains only when realized, but losses when they first become evident. Thus, we recognize losses at an earlier point than gains. This principle is related to the conservatism concept.

Gains typically result from the sale of long-term assets for more than their book value. Firms should not recognize gains until they are realized through sale or exchange. Recognizing potential gains before they are actually realized is not allowed.

Losses consume assets, as do expenses. However, unlike expenses, they do not produce revenues. Losses are usually *involuntary,* such as the loss suffered from destruction by fire on an uninsured building. A loss on the sale of a building may be voluntary when management decides to sell the building even though incurring a loss.

Real World Example
The involuntary losses due to the terrorist attacks on September 11, 2001, resulted in insurance claims of more than $40 billion.

The **full disclosure principle** states that information important enough to influence the decisions of an informed user of the financial statements should be disclosed. Depending on its nature, companies should disclose this information either in the financial statements, in notes to the financial statements, or in supplemental statements. In judging whether or not to disclose information, it is better to err on the side of too much disclosure rather than too little. Many lawsuits against CPAs and their clients have resulted from inadequate or misleading disclosure of the underlying facts.

Full Disclosure Principle

We summarize the major principles and describe the importance of each in Illustration 5.3.

Business Insight The accounting model involves reporting revenues earned and expenses incurred by the company. Some have argued that social benefits and social costs created by the company should also be reported. Suppose, for instance, that a company is dumping toxic waste into a river and this action causes cancer among the citizens downstream. Should this cost be reported when preparing financial statements showing the performance of the company? What do you think?

An Accounting Perspective

Modifying Conventions (or Constraints)

In certain instances, companies do not strictly apply accounting principles because of modifying conventions (or constraints). **Modifying conventions** are customs emerging from accounting practice that alter the results obtained from a strict application of accounting principles. Three modifying conventions are cost-benefit, materiality, and conservatism.

Objective 3
Identify and discuss the modifying conventions (or constraints) of accounting.

Cost-Benefit   The **cost-benefit consideration** involves deciding whether the benefits of including optional information in financial statements exceed the costs of providing the information. Users tend to think information is cost free since they incur none of the costs of providing the information. Preparers realize that providing information is costly. The benefits of using information should exceed the costs of providing it. The measurement of benefits is inexact, which makes application of this modifying convention difficult in practice.

Materiality   **Materiality** is a modifying convention that allows accountants to deal with immaterial (unimportant) items in an expedient but theoretically incorrect manner. The fundamental question accountants must ask in judging the materiality of an item is whether a knowledgeable user's decisions would be different if the information were presented in the theoretically correct manner. If not, the item is immaterial and may be reported in a theoretically incorrect but expedient manner. For instance, because inexpensive items such as calculators often do not make a difference in a statement user's decision to invest in the company, they are *immaterial* (unimportant) and may be expensed when purchased. However, because expensive items such as mainframe computers usually do make a difference in such a decision, they are *material* (important) and should be recorded as assets and depreciated. Accountants should record all material items in a theoretically correct manner. They may record immaterial items in a theoretically incorrect manner simply because it is more convenient and less expensive to do so. For example, they may debit the cost of a wastebasket to an expense account

Illustration 5.3   The Major Principles

Principle	Description	Importance
Exchange-price (or cost)	Requires transfers of resources to be recorded at prices agreed on by the parties to the exchange at the time of the exchange.	Tells the accountant to record a transfer of resources at an objectively determinable amount at the time of the exchange. Also, self-constructed assets are recorded at their actual cost rather than at some estimate of what they would have cost if they had been purchased.
Revenue recognition	Revenues should be earned and realized before they are recognized (recorded).	Informs accountant that revenues generally should be recognized when services are performed or goods are sold. Exceptions are made for items such as installment sales and long-term construction projects.
Matching	Expenses should be recognized (recorded) as they are incurred to produce revenues.	Indicates that expenses are to be recorded as soon as they are incurred rather than waiting until some future time.
Gain and loss recognition	Gains may be recorded only when realized, but losses should be recorded when they first become evident.	Tells the accountant to be conservative when recognizing gains and losses. Gains can only be recognized when they have been realized through sale or exchange. Losses should be recognized as soon as they become evident. Thus, potential losses can be recorded, but only gains that have actually been realized can be recorded.
Full disclosure	Information important enough to influence the decisions of an informed user of the financial statements should be disclosed.	Requires the accountant to disclose everything that is important. A good rule to follow is—if in doubt, disclose. Another good rule is—if you are not consistent, disclose all the facts and the effect on income.

rather than an asset account even though the wastebasket has an expected useful life of 30 years. It simply is not worth the cost of recording depreciation expense on such a small item over its life.

The FASB defines materiality as "the magnitude of an omission or misstatement of accounting information that, in the light of surrounding circumstances, makes it probable that the judgment of a reasonable person relying on the information would have been changed or influenced by the omission or misstatement."[3] The term *magnitude* in this definition suggests that the materiality of an item may be assessed by looking at its relative size. A $10,000 error in an expense in a company with earnings of $30,000 is material. The same error in a company earning $30,000,000 may not be material.

Materiality involves more than the relative dollar amounts. Often the nature of the item makes it material. For example, it may be quite significant to know that a company is paying bribes or making illegal political contributions, even if the dollar amounts of such items are relatively small.

Conservatism   **Conservatism** means being cautious or prudent and making sure that assets and net income are not overstated. Such overstatements can mislead potential investors in the company and creditors making loans to the company. We apply conservatism when the lower-of-cost-or-market rule is used for inventory (see Chapter 7). Accountants must realize a fine line exists between conservative and incorrect accounting.

See Illustration 5.4 for a summary of the modifying conventions and their importance.

The next section of this chapter discusses the conceptual framework project of the Financial Accounting Standards Board. The FASB designed the conceptual

---

[3]FASB, *Statement of Financial Accounting Concepts No. 2*, "Qualitative Characteristics of Accounting Information" (Stamford, Conn., 1980), p. xv. Copyright © by the Financial Accounting Standards Board, High Ridge Park, Stamford, Connecticut 06905, U.S.A. Quoted (or excerpted) with permission. Copies of the complete documents are available from the FASB.

Illustration 5. 4   Modifying Conventions

Modifying Convention	Description	Importance
Cost-benefit	Optional information should be included in financial statements only if the benefits of providing it exceed its costs.	Lets the accountant know that information that is not required should be made available only if its benefits exceed its costs. An example may be companies incurring the expense of providing information on the effects of inflation when the inflation rate is low and/or users do not seem to benefit significantly from the information.
Materiality	Only items that would affect a knowledgeable user's decision are material (important) and must be reported in a theoretically correct way.	Allows accountants to treat immaterial (relatively small dollar amount) information in a theoretically incorrect but expedient manner. For instance, a wastebasket can be expensed rather than capitalized and depreciated even though it may last for 30 years.
Conservatism	Transactions should be recorded so that assets and net income are not overstated.	Warns accountants that assets and net income are not to be overstated. "Anticipate (and record) all possible losses and do not anticipate (or record) any possible gains" is common advice under this constraint. Also, conservative application of the matching principle involves making sure that adjustments for expenses for such items as uncollectible accounts, warranties, and depreciation are adequate.

framework project to resolve some disagreements about the proper theoretical foundation for accounting. We present only the portions of the project relevant to this text.

The Financial Accounting Standards Board's Conceptual Framework Project

Experts have debated the exact nature of the basic concepts and related principles composing accounting theory for years. The debate continues today despite numerous references to generally accepted accounting principles (GAAP). To date, all attempts to present a concise statement of GAAP have received only limited acceptance.

Due to this limited success, many accountants suggest that the starting point in reaching a concise statement of GAAP is to seek agreement on the objectives of financial accounting and reporting. The belief is that if a person (1) carefully studies the environment, (2) knows what objectives are sought, (3) can identify certain qualitative traits of accounting information, and (4) can define the basic elements of financial statements, that person can discover the principles and standards leading to the stated objectives. The FASB completed the first three goals by publishing "Objectives of Financial Reporting by Business Enterprises" and "Qualitative Characteristics of Accounting Information."[4] Addressing the fourth goal are concepts statements entitled "Elements of Financial Statements of Business Enterprises" and "Elements of Financial Statements."[5]

> **Objective 4**
> Describe the conceptual framework project of the Financial Accounting Standards Board.

---

[4]FASB, *Statement of Financial Accounting Concepts No. 1,* "Objectives of Financial Reporting by Business Enterprises" (Stamford, Conn., 1978); and *Statement of Financial Accounting Concepts No. 2,* "Qualitative Characteristics of Accounting Information" (Stamford, Conn., 1980). Copyright © by the Financial Accounting Standards Board, High Ridge Park, Stamford, Connecticut 06905, U.S.A. Quoted (or excerpted) with permission. Copies of the complete documents are available from the FASB.
[5]FASB, *Statement of Financial Accounting Concepts No. 3,* "Elements of Financial Statements of Business Enterprises" (Stamford, Conn., 1980); and *Statement of Financial Accounting Concepts No. 6,* "Elements of Financial Statements" (Stamford, Conn., 1985). Copyright © by the Financial Accounting Standards Board, High Ridge Park, Stamford, Connecticut 06905, U.S.A. Quoted (or excerpted) with permission. Copies of the complete documents are available from the FASB.

Objectives of Financial Reporting

Financial reporting objectives are the broad overriding goals sought by accountants engaging in financial reporting. According to the FASB, the first objective of financial reporting is to:

provide information that is useful to present and potential investors and creditors and other users in making rational investment, credit, and similar decisions. The information should be comprehensible to those who have a reasonable understanding of business and economic activities and are willing to study the information with reasonable diligence.[6]

Interpreted broadly, the term *other users* includes employees, security analysts, brokers, and lawyers. Financial reporting should provide information to all who are willing to learn to use it properly.

The second objective of financial reporting is to:

provide information to help present and potential investors and creditors and other users in assessing the amounts, timing, and uncertainty of prospective cash receipts from dividends [owner withdrawals] or interest and the proceeds from the sale, redemption, or maturity of securities or loans. Since investors' and creditors' cash flows are related to enterprise cash flows, financial reporting should provide information to help investors, creditors, and others assess the amounts, timing, and uncertainty of prospective net cash inflows to the related enterprise.[7]

This objective ties the cash flows of investors (owners) and creditors to the cash flows of the enterprise, a tie-in that appears entirely logical. Enterprise cash inflows are the source of cash for dividends, interest, and the redemption of maturing debt.

Third, financial reporting should:

provide information about the economic resources of an enterprise, the claims to those resources (obligations of the enterprise to transfer resources to other entities and owners' equity), and the effects of transactions, events, and circumstances that change its resources and claims to those resources.[8]

We can draw some conclusions from these three objectives and from a study of the environment in which financial reporting is carried out. For example, financial reporting should:

1. Provide information about an enterprise's past performance because such information is a basis for predicting future enterprise performance.
2. Focus on earnings and its components, despite the emphasis in the objectives on cash flows. (Earnings computed under the accrual basis generally provide a better indicator of ability to generate favorable cash flows than do statements prepared under the cash basis.)

On the other hand, financial reporting does not seek to:

1. Measure the value of an enterprise but to provide information useful in determining its value.
2. Evaluate management's performance, predict earnings, assess risk, or estimate earning power but to provide information to persons who wish to make these evaluations.

These conclusions are some of those reached in *Statement of Financial Accounting Concepts No. 1*. As the Board stated, these statements "are intended to establish the objectives and concepts that the Financial Accounting Standards Board will use in

---

[6]FASB, *Statement of Financial Accounting Concepts No. 1*, p. viii.
[7]Ibid.
[8]Ibid.

developing standards of financial accounting and reporting."[9] How successful the Board will be in the approach adopted remains to be seen.

Qualitative Characteristics

Accounting information should possess **qualitative characteristics** to be useful in decision making. This criterion is difficult to apply. The usefulness of accounting information in a given instance depends not only on information characteristics but also on the capabilities of the decision makers and their professional advisers. Accountants cannot specify who the decision makers are, their characteristics, the decisions to be made, or the methods chosen to make the decisions. Therefore, they direct their attention to the characteristics of accounting information. Note the FASB's graphic summarization of the qualities accountants consider in Illustration 5.5.[10]

To have **relevance**, information must be pertinent to or affect a decision. The information must make a difference to someone who does not already have it. Relevant information makes a difference in a decision either by affecting users' predictions of outcomes of past, present, or future events or by confirming or correcting expectations. Note that information need not be a prediction to be useful in developing, confirming, or altering expectations. Expectations are commonly based on the present or past. For example, any attempt to predict future earnings of a company would quite likely start with a review of present and past earnings. Although information that merely confirms prior expectations may be less useful, it is still relevant because it reduces uncertainty.

> **Relevance**

    Critics have alleged that certain types of accounting information lack relevance. For example, some argue that a cost of $1 million paid for a tract of land 40 years ago and reported in the current balance sheet at that amount is irrelevant (except for possible tax implications) to users for decision making today. Such criticism has encouraged research into the types of information relevant to users. Some suggest using a different valuation basis, such as current cost, in reporting such assets.

Predictive Value and Feedback Value   Since actions taken now can affect only future events, information is obviously relevant when it possesses **predictive value**, or improves users' abilities to predict outcomes of events. Information that reveals the relative success of users in predicting outcomes possesses **feedback value**. Feedback reports on past activities and can make a difference in decision making by (1) reducing uncertainty in a situation, (2) refuting or confirming prior expectations, and (3) providing a basis for further predictions. For example, a report on the first quarter's earnings of a company reduces the uncertainty surrounding the amount of such earnings, confirms or refutes the predicted amount of such earnings, and provides a possible basis on which to predict earnings for the full year. Remember that although accounting information may possess predictive value, it does not consist of predictions. Making predictions is a function performed by the decision maker.

Timeliness   **Timeliness** requires accountants to provide accounting information at a time when it may be considered in reaching a decision. Utility of information decreases with age—to know what the net income for 2012 was in early 2013 is much more useful than receiving this information a year later. If information is to be of any value in decision making, it must be available before the decision is made. If not, the information is of little value. In determining what constitutes timely information, accountants consider the other qualitative characteristics and the cost of gathering information. For example, a timely estimate for uncollectible accounts may be more valuable than a later, verified actual amount. Timeliness alone cannot make information relevant, but potentially relevant information can be rendered irrelevant by a lack of timeliness.

---

[9]Ibid., p. i.
[10]FASB, *Statement of Financial Accounting Concepts No. 2*, p. 15.

Illustration 5.5   A Hierarchy of Accounting Qualities

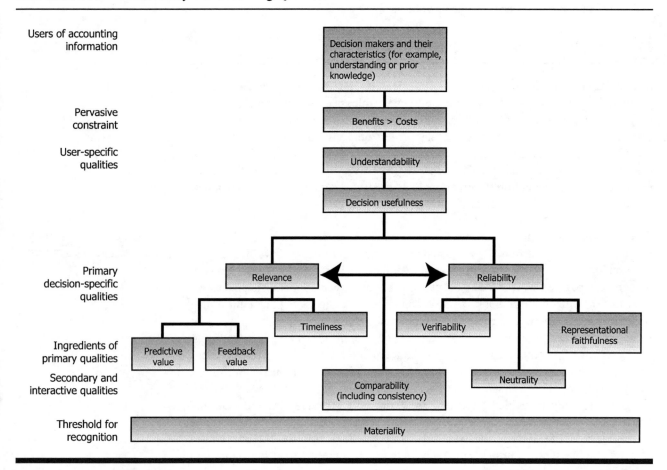

Users of accounting information	Decision makers and their characteristics (for example, understanding or prior knowledge)
Pervasive constraint	Benefits > Costs
User-specific qualities	Understandability
	Decision usefulness
Primary decision-specific qualities	Relevance ←→ Reliability
	Timeliness / Verifiability / Representational faithfulness
Ingredients of primary qualities	Predictive value / Feedback value
Secondary and interactive qualities	Comparability (including consistency) / Neutrality
Threshold for recognition	Materiality

Reliability

In addition to being relevant, information must be reliable to be useful. Information has **reliability** when it faithfully depicts for users what it purports to represent. Thus, accounting information is reliable if users can depend on it to reflect the underlying economic activities of the organization. The reliability of information depends on its representational faithfulness, verifiability, and neutrality. The information must also be complete and free of bias.

Representational Faithfulness   To gain insight into this quality, consider a map. When it shows roads and bridges where roads and bridges actually exist, a map possesses **representational faithfulness**. A correspondence exists between what is on the map and what is present physically. Similarly, representational faithfulness exists when accounting statements on economic activity correspond to the actual underlying activity. Where there is no correspondence, the cause may be (1) bias or (2) lack of completeness.

1. **Effects of bias.** Accounting measurements contain bias if they are consistently too high or too low. Accountants create bias in accounting measurements by choosing the wrong measurement method or introducing bias either deliberately or through lack of skill.
2. **Completeness.** To be free from bias, information must be sufficiently complete to ensure that it validly represents underlying events and conditions. Completeness means disclosing all significant information in a way that aids understanding and does not mislead. Firms can reduce the relevance of information by omitting information that would make a difference to users. Currently, full disclosure requires

presentation of a balance sheet, an income statement, a statement of cash flows, and necessary notes to the financial statements and supporting schedules. Also required in annual reports of corporations are statements of changes in stockholders' equity which contain information included in a statement of retained earnings. Such statements must be complete, with items properly classified and segregated (such as reporting sales revenue separately from other revenues). Required disclosures may be made in (1) the body of the financial statements, (2) the notes to such statements, (3) special communications, and/or (4) the president's letter or other management reports in the annual report.

Another aspect of completeness is fully disclosing all changes in accounting principles and their effects.[11] Disclosure should include unusual activities (loans to officers), changes in expectations (losses on inventory), depreciation expense for the period, long-term obligations entered into that are not recorded by the accountant (a 20-year lease on a building), new arrangements with certain groups (pension and profit-sharing plans for employees), and significant events that occur after the date of the statements (loss of a major customer). Firms must also disclose accounting policies (major principles and their manner of application) followed in preparing the financial statements.[12] Because of its emphasis on disclosure, we often call this aspect of reliability the *full disclosure principle.*

Verifiability   Financial information has **verifiability** when independent measurers can substantially duplicate it by using the same measurement methods. Verifiability eliminates measurer bias. The requirement that financial information be based on objective evidence arises from the demonstrated needs of users for reliable, unbiased financial information. Unbiased information is especially necessary when parties with opposing interests (credit seekers and credit grantors) rely on the same information. If the information is verifiable, this enhances the reliability of information.

Financial information is never completely free of subjective opinion and judgment; it always possesses varying degrees of verifiability. Canceled checks and invoices support some measurements. Accountants can never verify other measurements, such as periodic depreciation charges, because of their very nature. Thus, financial information in many instances is verifiable only in that it represents a consensus of what other accountants would report if they followed the same procedures.

Neutrality   **Neutrality** means that the accounting information should be free of measurement method bias. The primary concern should be relevance and reliability of the information that results from application of the principle, not the effect that the principle may have on a particular interest. Nonneutral accounting information favors one set of interested parties over others. For example, a particular form of measurement might favor stockholders over creditors, or vice versa. "To be neutral, accounting information must report economic activity as faithfully as possible, without coloring the image it communicates for the purpose of influencing behavior in *some particular direction.*"[13] Accounting standards are not like tax regulations that deliberately foster or restrain certain types of activity. Verifiability seeks to eliminate measurer bias; neutrality seeks to eliminate measurement method bias.

Reinforcing Problems
E5-5 Match accounting qualities with proper descriptions.
P5-5 Answer questions regarding the conceptual framework project.

When **comparability** exists, reported differences and similarities in financial information are real and not the result of differing accounting treatments. Comparable information reveals relative strengths and weaknesses in a single company through time and between two or more companies at the same time.

Consistency requires that a company use the same accounting principles and reporting practices through time. Consistency leads to comparability of financial information for a single company through time. Comparability between companies

Comparability (and Consistency)

[11]APB, *APB Opinion No. 20,* "Accounting Changes" (New York: AICPA, July 1971).
[12]APB, *APB Opinion No. 22,* "Disclosure of Accounting Policies" (New York: AICPA, April 1972).
[13]FASB, *Statement of Financial Accounting Concepts No. 2,* par. 100.

is more difficult because they may account for the same activities in different ways. For example, Company B may use one method of depreciation, while Company C accounts for an identical asset in similar circumstances using another method. A high degree of intercompany comparability in accounting information does not exist unless accountants are required to account for the same activities in the same manner across companies and through time.

Functions and Advantages of a Journal	As we show in Illustration 5.5, accountants must consider one pervasive constraint and one threshold for recognition in providing useful information. First, the benefits secured from the information must be greater than the costs of providing that information. Second, only material items need be disclosed and accounted for strictly in accordance with generally accepted accounting principles (GAAP). We discussed cost-benefit and materiality earlier in the chapter.

An Accounting Perspective	USES OF TECHNOLOGY You may want to visit the home page of the Financial Accounting Standards Board at: **http://www.fasb.org** You can check out the latest developments at the FASB to see how the rules of accounting might be changing. You can investigate facts about the FASB, press releases, exposure drafts, publications, emerging issues, board actions, forthcoming meetings, and many other topics.

The Basic Elements of Financial Statements

Thus far we have discussed objectives of financial reporting and qualitative characteristics of accounting information. A third important task in developing a conceptual framework for any discipline is identifying and defining its basic elements. The FASB identified and defined the basic elements of financial statements in *Concepts Statement No. 3*. Later, *Concepts Statement No. 6* revised some of the definitions. We defined most of the terms earlier in this text in a less technical way; the more technical definitions follow. (These items are not repeated in this chapter's New Terms.)

Note to the Student
Review the definitions of all the terms listed.

Assets are probable future economic benefits obtained or controlled by a particular entity as a result of past transactions or events.

Liabilities are probable future sacrifices of economic benefits arising from present obligations of a particular entity to transfer assets or provide services to other entities in the future as a result of past transactions or events.

Equity or net assets is the residual interest in the assets of an entity that remains after deducting its liabilities. In a business enterprise, the equity is the ownership interest. In a not-for-profit organization, which has no ownership interest in the same sense as a business enterprise, net assets is divided into three classes based on the presence or absence of donor-imposed restrictions—permanently restricted, temporarily restricted, and unrestricted net assets.

Comprehensive income is the change in equity of a business enterprise during a period from transactions and other events and circumstances from nonowner sources. It includes all changes in equity during a period except those resulting from investments by owners and distributions to owners.

Revenues are inflows or other enhancements of assets of any entity or settlements of its liabilities (or a combination of both) from delivering or producing goods, rendering services, or other activities that constitute the entity's ongoing major or central operations.

Expenses are outflows or other using up of assets or incurrences of liabilities (or a combination of both) from delivering or producing goods, rendering services, or carrying out other activities that constitute the entity's ongoing major or central operations.

Gains are increases in equity (net assets) from peripheral or incidental transactions of an entity and from all other transactions and other events and circumstances affecting the entity except those that result from revenues or investments by owners.

Losses are decreases in equity (net assets) from peripheral or incidental transactions of an entity and from all other transactions and other events and circumstances affecting the entity except those that result from expenses or distributions to owners.

Investments by owners are increases in equity of a particular business enterprise resulting from transfers to it from other entities of something valuable to obtain or increase ownership interests (or equity) in it. Assets are most commonly received as investments by owners, but that which is received may also include services or satisfaction or conversion of liabilities of the enterprise.

Distributions to owners are decreases in equity of a particular business enterprise resulting from transferring assets, rendering services, or incurring liabilities by the enterprise to owners. Distributions to owners decrease ownership interest (or equity) in an enterprise.[14]

Business Insight Accountants record expenditures on physical resources such as land, buildings, and equipment that benefit future periods as assets. However, they expense expenditures on human resources for hiring and training that benefit future periods. Also, when a computer is dropped and destroyed, accountants record a loss. However, when the president of the company dies, they record no loss. Should the accounting model be changed regarding the accounting for human resources?

An Accounting Perspective

Recognition and Measurement in Financial Statements

In December 1984, the FASB issued *Statement of Financial Accounting Concepts No. 5*, "Recognition and Measurement in Financial Statements of Business Enterprises," describing recognition criteria and providing guidance for the timing and nature of information included in financial statements.[15] The recognition criteria established in the *Statement* are fairly consistent with those used in current practice. The *Statement* indicates, however, that when information more useful than currently reported information is available at a reasonable cost, it should be included in financial statements.

Summary of Significant Accounting Policies

As part of their annual reports, companies include summaries of significant accounting policies. These policies assist users in interpreting the financial statements. To a large extent, accounting theory determines the nature of these policies. Companies must follow generally accepted accounting principles in preparing their financial statements.

The accounting policies of The Walt Disney Company, one of the world's leading entertainment companies, as contained in a recent annual report follow. After each, the

Objective 5
Discuss the nature and content of a company's summary of significant accounting policies in its annual report.

---

[14]FASB, *Statement of Financial Accounting Concepts No. 6.*
[15]FASB, *Statement of Financial Accounting Concepts No. 5*, "Recognition and Measurement in Financial Statements of Business Enterprises" (Stamford, Conn., 1984). Copyright © by the Financial Accounting Standards Board, High Ridge Park, Stamford, Connecticut 06905, U.S.A. Copies of the complete document are available from the FASB. (In case you are wondering why we do not mention *Statement of Financial Accounting Concepts No. 4,* it pertains to accounting for not-for-profit organizations and is, therefore, not relevant to this text.)

An Ethical Perspective **Maplehurst Company**	Maplehurst Company manufactures large spinning machines for the textile industry. The company had purchased $100,000 of small hand tools to use in its business. The company's accountant recorded the tools in an asset account and was going to write them off over 20 years. Management wanted to write these tools off as an expense of this year because revenues this year had been abnormally high and were expected to be lower in the future. Management's goal was to smooth out income rather than showing sharp increases and decreases. When	told by the accountant that $100,000 was a material item that must be accounted for in a theoretically correct manner, management decided to consider the tools as consisting of 10 groups, each having a cost of $10,000. Since amounts under $20,000 are considered immaterial for this company, all of the tools could then be charged to expense this year. The accountant is concerned about this treatment. She doubts that she could successfully defend management's position if the auditors challenge the expensing of these items.

chapter of this text where we discuss that particular policy is in parentheses. While a few of the items have already been covered, the remainder offer a preview of the concepts explained in later chapters.

Summary of Significant Accounting Policies

Principles of Consolidation

The consolidated financial statements of the Company include the accounts of The Walt Disney Company and its majority-owned and controlled subsidiaries. Intercompany accounts and transactions have been eliminated in consolidation. (Chapter 14)

Revenue Recognition

Broadcast advertising revenues are recognized when commercials are aired. Revenues from advance theme park ticket sales are recognized when the tickets are used. Revenues from the theatrical distribution of motion pictures are recognized when motion pictures are exhibited. Revenues from DVD and video game sales, net of anticipated returns and customer incentives, are recognized on the date that video units are made available for sale by retailers. Revenues from the licensing of feature films and television programming are recorded when the content is available for telecast by the licensee and when certain other conditions are met. (Chapter 5)

Allowance for doubtful accounts

The Company maintains an allowance for doubtful accounts to reserve for potentially uncollectible receivables. The allowance for doubtful accounts is estimated based on our analysis of trends in overall receivables aging, specific identification of certain receivables that are at risk of not being paid, past collection experience and current economic trends. (Chapter 9)

Cash and Cash Equivalents

Cash and cash equivalents consist of cash on hand and marketable securities with original maturities of three months or less. (Chapter 8)

Investments

Debt securities that the Company has the positive intent and ability to hold to maturity are classified as "held-to-maturity" and reported at amortized cost. Debt securities not classified as held-to-maturity and marketable equity securities are classified as either "trading" or "available-for-sale". Trading and available-for-sale securities are recorded at fair value with unrealized gains and losses included in earnings or accumulated other comprehensive income/(loss), respectively. All other equity securities are accounted for using either the cost method or the equity method. (Chapter 14)

Inventories

Carrying amounts of merchandise, materials, and supplies inventories are generally determined on a moving average cost basis and are recorded at the lower of cost or market. (Chapter 7)

Film and Television Costs

Film and television costs include capitalizable production costs, production overhead, interest, development costs, and acquired production costs are stated at the lower of cost, less accumulated amortization, or fair value.

The costs of television broadcast rights for acquired movies, series and other programs are expensed based on the number of times the program is expected to be aired or on a straight-line basis over the useful life, as appropriate. (Chapter 11)

Parks, Resorts and Other Property

Parks, resorts, and other property are carried at cost. Depreciation is computed on the straight-line method over estimated useful lives. (Chapter 10)

Goodwill, Other Intangible Assets and Long-Lived Assets

The Company is required to test goodwill and other indefinite-lived intangible assets for impairment on an annual basis and if current events or circumstances require, on an interim basis. The Company is required to compare the fair values of other indefinite-lived intangible assets to their carrying amounts. If the carrying amount of an indefinite-lived intangible asset exceeds its fair value, an impairment loss is recognized. Amortizable intangible assets are generally amortized on a straight-line basis over period up to 40 years. (Chapter 11)

Risk Management Contracts

In the normal course of business, the Company employs a variety of financial instruments to manage its exposure to fluctuations in interest rates, foreign currency exchange rates, and investments in equity and debt securities, including interest rate and cross-currency swap agreements; forward, option, and "swaption" contracts, and interest rate caps. The Company designates and assigns the financial instruments as hedges of forecasted transactions, specific assets or specific liabilities. When hedged assets or liabilities are sold or extinguished or the forecasted transactions being hedged are no longer expected to occur, the Company recognizes the gain or loss on the designated hedging instruments. Realized gains and losses from hedges are classified in the income statement consistent with the accounting treatment of the items being hedged. Gains and losses on the termination of effective swap agreements, prior to the original maturity, are deferred and amortized to interest expense over the remaining term of the underlying hedged transactions. (Chapter 14)

Cash flows from hedging activities are classified in the same category as the cash flows from the related assets, liabilities or forecasted transactions. (Chapter 16)

Earnings Per Share

The Company presents both basic and diluted earnings per share (EPS) amounts. Basic EPS is calculated by dividing net income by the weighted average number of common shares outstanding during the year. Common equivalent shares are excluded from the computation of diluted EPS in periods for which they have an anti-dilutive effect. (Chapter 13)

As you proceed through the remaining chapters, you can see the accounting theories introduced in this chapter being applied. In Chapter 6, for instance, we discuss why sales revenue is recognized and recorded only after goods have been delivered to the customer. So far, we have used service companies to illustrate accounting techniques. Chapter 6 introduces merchandising operations. Merchandising companies, such as clothing stores, buy goods in their finished form and sell them to customers.

Understanding the Learning Objectives

- The major underlying assumptions or concepts of accounting are (1) business entity, (2) going concern (continuity), (3) money measurement, (4) stable dollar, (5) periodicity, and (6) accrual basis and periodicity.
- Other basic accounting concepts that affect the accounting for entities are (1) general-purpose financial statements, (2) substance over form, (3) consistency, (4) double entry, and (5) articulation.
- The major principles include exchange-price (or cost), revenue recognition, matching, gain and loss recognition, and full disclosure. Major exceptions to the realization principle include cash collection as point of revenue recognition, installment basis of revenue recognition, and the percentage-of-completion method of recognizing revenue on long-term construction projects.

> **Objective 1**
> Identify and discuss the underlying assumptions or concepts of accounting.

> **Objective 2**
> Identify and discuss the major principles of accounting.

- Modifying conventions include cost-benefit, materiality, and conservatism.

- The FASB has defined the objectives of financial reporting, qualitative characteristics of accounting information, and elements of financial statements.
- Financial reporting objectives are the broad overriding goals sought by accountants engaging in financial reporting.
- Qualitative characteristics are those that accounting information should possess to be useful in decision making. The two primary qualitative characteristics are relevance and reliability. Another qualitative characteristic is comparability.
- Pervasive constraints include cost-benefit analysis and materiality.
- The FASB has identified and defined the basic elements of financial statements.
- The FASB has also described revenue recognition criteria and provided guidance as to the timing and nature of information to be included in financial statements.
- The summary of significant accounting policies aid users in interpreting the financial statements.
- To a large extent, accounting theory determines the nature of those policies.

Demonstration Problem

For each of the following transactions or circumstances and the entries made, state which, if any, of the assumptions, concepts, principles, or modifying conventions of accounting have been violated. For each violation, give the entry to correct the improper accounting assuming the books have not been closed.

During the year, Dorsey Company did the following:

1. Had its buildings appraised. They were found to have a market value of $410,000, although their book value was only $380,000. The accountant debited the Buildings and Accumulated Depreciation—Buildings accounts for $15,000 each and credited Paid-in Capital—From Appreciation. No separate mention was made of this action in the financial statements.
2. Purchased new electric pencil sharpeners for its offices at a total cost of $60. These pencil sharpeners were recorded as assets and are being depreciated over five years.

Solution to Demonstration Problem

1. The cost principle and the modifying convention of conservatism may have been violated. Such write-ups simply are not looked on with favor in accounting. To correct the situation, the entry made needs to be reversed:

Paid-in Capital	30,000	
Building		15,000
Accumulated Depreciation—Building		15,000

2. Theoretically, no violations occurred, but the cost of compiling insignificant information could be considered a violation of acceptable accounting practice. As a practical matter, the $60 could have been expensed on materiality grounds.

New Terms

Accounting theory   "A set of basic concepts and assumptions and related principles that explain and guide the accountant's actions in identifying, measuring, and communicating economic information." *177*

Bias   Exists when accounting measurements are consistently too high or too low. *192*

Business entity concept   The specific unit for which accounting information is gathered. Business entities have a separate existence from owners, creditors, employees, customers, other interested parties, and other businesses. *178*

Comparability   A qualitative characteristic of accounting information; when information is comparable, it reveals differences and similarities that are real and are not the result of differing accounting treatments. *193*

Completed-contract method   A method of recognizing revenue on long-term projects under which no revenue is recognized until the period in which the project is completed; similar to recognizing revenue upon the completion of a sale. *185*

Completeness   A qualitative characteristic of accounting information; requires disclosure of all significant information in a way that aids understanding and does not mislead; sometimes called the *full disclosure principle. 192*

Conservatism   Being cautious or prudent and making sure that net assets and net income are not overstated. *188*

Consistency   Requires a company to use the same accounting principles and reporting practices through time. *180, 193*

Cost-benefit consideration   Determining whether benefits of including information in financial statements exceed costs. *187*

Cost principle   See Exchange-price principle.

Earning principle   The requirement that revenue be substantially earned before it is recognized (recorded). *183*

Exchange-price (or cost) principle   Transfers of resources are recorded at prices agreed on by the parties at the time of the exchange. *182*

Feedback value   A qualitative characteristic that information has when it reveals the relative success of users in predicting outcomes. *191*

Financial reporting objectives   The broad overriding goals sought by accountants engaging in financial reporting. *190*

Full disclosure principle   Information important enough to influence the decisions of an informed user of the financial statements should be disclosed. *187*

Gain and loss recognition principle   Gains may be recorded only when realized, but losses should be recorded when they first become evident. *186*

Gains   Typically result from the sale of long-term assets for more than their book value. *186*

Going-concern (continuity) assumption   The assumption that an entity will continue to operate indefinitely unless strong evidence exists that the entity will terminate. *178*

Historical cost   The amount paid, or the fair market value of a liability incurred or other resources surrendered, to acquire an asset and place it in a condition and position for its intended use. *182*

Installment basis   A revenue recognition procedure in which the percentage of total gross margin recognized in a period on an installment sale is equal to the percentage of total cash from the sale that is received in that period. *184*

Liquidation   Terminating a business by ceasing business operations and selling off its assets. *178*

Losses   Asset expirations that are usually involuntary and do not create revenues. *187*

Matching principle   Expenses should be recognized as they are incurred to produce revenues. *186*

Materiality   A modifying convention that allows the accountant to deal with immaterial (unimportant) items in an expedient but theoretically incorrect manner; also a qualitative characteristic specifying that financial accounting report only information significant enough to influence decisions or evaluations. *187*

Modifying conventions   Customs emerging from accounting practice that alter the results obtained from a strict application of accounting principles; conservatism is an example. *187*

Money measurement   Use of a monetary unit of measurement, such as the dollar, instead of physical or other units of measurement—feet, inches, grams, and so on. *178*

Neutrality   A qualitative characteristic that requires accounting information to be free of measurement method bias. *193*

Percentage-of-completion method   A method of recognizing revenue based on the estimated stage of completion of a long-term project. The stage of completion is measured by comparing actual costs incurred in a period with total estimated costs to be incurred in all periods. *185*

Period costs   Costs that cannot be traced to specific products and are expensed in the period incurred. *186*

Periodicity (time periods) assumption An assumption of the accountant that an entity's life can be divided into time periods for reporting its economic activities. *179*

Predictive value A qualitative characteristic that information has when it improves users' abilities to predict outcomes of events. *191*

Product costs Costs incurred in the acquisition or manufacture of goods. Product costs are accounted for as if they were attached to the goods, with the result that they are charged to expense when the goods are sold. *186*

Qualitative characteristics Characteristics that accounting information should possess to be useful in decision making. *191*

Realization principle A principle that directs that revenue is recognized only after the seller acquires the right to receive payment from the buyer. *183*

Relevance A qualitative characteristic requiring that information be pertinent to or affect a decision. *191*

Reliability A qualitative characteristic requiring that information faithfully depict for users what it purports to represent. *192*

Representational faithfulness A qualitative characteristic requiring that accounting statements on economic activity correspond to the actual underlying activity. *192*

Revenue recognition principle The principle that revenues should be earned and realized before they are recognized (recorded). *183*

Stable dollar assumption An assumption that the dollar is a reasonably stable unit of measurement. *178*

Timeliness A qualitative characteristic requiring that accounting information be provided at a time when it may be considered before making a decision. *191*

Verifiability A qualitative characteristic of accounting information; information is verifiable when it can be substantially duplicated by independent measurers using the same measurement methods. *193*

Self-Test

True-False

Indicate whether each of the following statements is true or false.

1. The business entity concept assumes that each business has an existence separate from all parties except its owners.
2. When the substance of a transaction differs from its legal form, the accountant should record the economic substance.
3. The matching principle is fundamental to the accrual basis of accounting.
4. Exceptions to the realization principle include the installment basis of revenue recognition for sales revenue and the completed-contract method for long-term construction projects.
5. Immaterial items do not have to be recorded at all.
6. The conceptual framework project resulted in identifying two primary qualitative characteristics that accounting information should possess— relevance and reliability.

Multiple-Choice

Select the best answer for each of the following questions.

1. The underlying assumptions of accounting include all the following except:
   a. Business entity.
   b. Going concern.
   c. Matching.
   d. Money measurement and periodicity.
2. The concept that requires companies to use the same accounting practices and reporting practices through time is:
   a. Substance over form.
   b. Consistency.
   c. Articulation.
   d. None of the above.
3. Which of the following statements is false regarding the revenue recognition principle?
   a. Revenue must be substantially earned before it is recognized.
   b. The accountant usually recognizes revenue before the seller acquires the right to receive payment from the buyer.
   c. Some small companies use the cash basis of accounting.
   d. Under the installment basis, the gross margin recognized in a period is equal to the amount of cash received from installment sales times the gross margin percentage for the year of sale.

4. Assume the following facts regarding the construction of a bridge:

Construction costs this period......	$3,000,000
Total estimated construction costs...	10,000,000
Total sales price................	15,000,000

The revenue that should be recognized this period is:
  a. $3,000,000.
  b. $4,500,000.
  c. $5,000,000.
  d. $6,500,000.

5. Modifying conventions include all of the following except:
  a. Periodicity.
  b. Cost-benefit.
  c. Materiality.
  d. Conservatism.

6. Which of the following is not part of the conceptual framework project?
  a. Objectives of financial reporting.
  b. Quantitative characteristics.
  c. Qualitative characteristics.
  d. Basic elements of financial statements.

Now turn to page 211 to check your answers.

Questions

1. Name the assumptions underlying generally accepted accounting principles. Comment on the validity of the stable unit of measurement assumption during periods of high inflation.

2. Why does the accountant use the business entity concept?

3. When is the going-concern assumption not to be used?

4. What is meant by the term *accrual basis of accounting?* What is its alternative?

5. What does it mean to say that accountants record substance rather than form?

6. If a company changes an accounting principle because the change better meets the information needs of users, what disclosures must be made?

7. What is the exchange-price (or cost) principle? What is the significance of adhering to this principle?

8. What two requirements generally must be met before recognizing revenue in a period?

9. Under what circumstances, if any, is the receipt of cash an acceptable time to recognize revenue?

10. What two methods may be used in recognizing revenues on long-term construction contracts?

11. Define expense. What principles guide the recognition of expense?

12. How does an expense differ from a loss?

13. What is the full disclosure principle?

14. What role does cost-benefit play in financial reporting?

15. What is meant by the accounting term *conservatism?* How does it affect the amounts reported in the financial statements?

16. Does materiality relate only to the relative size of dollar amounts?

17. Identify the three major parts of the conceptual framework project.

18. What are the two primary qualitative characteristics?

19. **Real World Question** A recent annual report of the RPM International Inc. stated:
Certain long-term construction contracts are accounted for under the percentage-of-completion method, and therefore we record contract revenues and related costs as our contracts progress... When reasonable dependable estimates cannot be made (of progress toward completion), or if other factors make estimates doubtful, the completed contract method is applied. Under the completed contract method, billings and costs are accumulated on the balance sheet as the contract progresses, but no revenue is recognized until the contract is complete or substantially complete.

How does the company's accounting policy comply with the realization principle?

20. **Real World Question** A recent annual report of Chevron Corporation stated:
Environmental expenditures that relate to ongoing operations or to conditions caused by past operations are expensed. Expenditures that create future benefits or contribute to future revenue generation are capitalized.
Which principle of accounting is being followed by this policy?

21. What is the purpose of including a "Summary of Significant Accounting Policies" in the company's annual report?

Exercises

Match the items in Column A with the proper descriptions in Column B.

Exercise 5-1
Match theory terms with
definitions (L.O. 1-3)

Column A	**Column B**
1. Going concern (continuity).	**a.** An assumption relied on in the preparation of the primary financial statements that would be unreasonable when the inflation rate is high.
2. Consistency.	
3. Disclosure.	
4. Periodicity.	**b.** Concerned with relative dollar amounts.
5. Conservatism.	**c.** The usual basis for the recording of assets.
6. Stable dollar.	**d.** Required if the accounting treatment differs from that previously used for a particular item.
7. Matching.	
8. Materiality.	**e.** An assumption that would be unreasonable to use in reporting on a firm that had become insolvent.
9. Exchange-price (cost).	
10. Business entity.	**f.** None of these.
	g. Requires a company to use the same accounting procedures and practices through time.
	h. An assumption that the life of an entity can be subdivided into time periods for reporting purposes.
	i. Discourages undue optimism in measuring and reporting net assets and net income.
	j. Requires separation of personal from business activities in the recording and reporting processes.

Parker Clothing Company sells its products on an installment sales basis. Data for 2012 and 2013 follow:

Exercise 5-2
Compute net income
under accrual basis and
under installment basis
(L.O. 2)

	2012	**2013**
Installment sales.	$800,000	$960,000
Cost of goods sold on installment sales	560,000	720,000
Other expenses.	120,000	160,000
Cash collected from 2012 sales.	480,000	240,000
Cash collected from 2013 sales.		640,000

a. Compute the net income for 2013, assuming use of the accrual (sales) basis of revenue recognition.

b. Compute the net income for 2013, assuming use of the installment basis of recognizinggross margin.

A company has a contract to build a ship at a price of $500 million and an estimated cost of $400 million. Costs of $100 million were incurred. Under the percentage-of-completion method, how much revenue would be recognized?

Exercise 5-3
Recognize revenue
under percentage-of-
completion method
(L.O. 2)

A company follows a practice of expensing the premium on its fire insurance policy when the policy is paid. In 2012, the company charged to expense the $6,000 premium paid on a three-year policy covering the period July 1, 2012, to June 30, 2015. In 2005, a premium of $5,400 was charged to expense on the same policy for the period July 1, 2009, to June 30, 2012.

Exercise 5-4
Compute the effect on
financial statements of
incorrectly expensing an
asset (L.O. 2)

a. State the principle of accounting that was violated by this practice.

b. Compute the effects of this violation on the financial statements for the calendar year 2012.

c. State the basis on which the company's practice might be justified.

Exercise 5-5
Match accounting
qualities with proper
descriptions (L.O. 4)

Match the descriptions in Column B with the accounting qualities in Column A. Use some descriptions more than once.

Column A: Accounting Qualities
1. Relevance.
2. Feedback value.
3. Decision makers.
4. Representational faithfulness.
5. Reliability.
6. Comparability.
7. Benefits exceed costs.
8. Predictive value.
9. Timeliness.
10. Decision usefulness.
11. Verifiability.
12. Understandability.
13. Neutrality.
14. Materiality.

Column B: Descriptions
a. Users of accounting information.
b. Pervasive constraint.
c. User-specific qualities.
d. Primary decision-specific qualities.
e. Ingredients of primary qualities.
f. Secondary and interactive qualities.
g. Threshold for recognition.

Problems

Problem 5-1
Answer multiple-choice
questions regarding
accounting theory
(L.O. 1-3)

Select the best answer to each of the following questions:

1. The assumption that each business has an existence separate from its owners, creditors, employees, customers, other interested parties, and other businesses is the:
   a. Going-concern assumption.
   b. Business entity concept.
   c. Separate entity concept.
   d. Corporation concept.

2. Companies should use liquidation values to report assets if which of the following conditions exists?
   a. There are changes in the value of the dollar.
   b. The periodicity assumption is applied.
   c. The company is not a going concern and will be dissolved.
   d. The accrual basis of accounting is not used.

3. Assume that a company has paid for advertising and that the ad has already appeared. The company chose to report the item as prepaid advertising and includes it among the assets on the balance sheet. Previously, the company had always expensed expenditures such as this. This practice is a violation of:
   a. Generally accepted accounting principles.
   b. The matching concept.
   c. The consistency concept.
   d. All of the above.

4. Recording revenue only after the seller has obtained the right to receive payment from the buyer for merchandise sold or services performed is called the:
   a. Earning principle.
   b. Installment basis.
   c. Realization principle.
   d. Completed-contract method.

Ramirez Video, Inc., sells video production equipment under terms calling for a small down payment and monthly payments spread over three years. Following are data for the first three years of the company's operations:

	2010	2011	2012
Gross margin rate	30%	40%	50%
Cash collected in 2012:			
From sales in	$216,000		
From sales in		$288,000	
From sales in			$480,000

Total sales for 2012 were $1,600,000, while general and selling expenses amounted to $400,000.

a. Compute net income for 2012, assuming revenues are recognized at the time of sale.
b. Compute net income for 2012, using the installment method of accounting for sales and gross margin.

Required

The following data relate to Merit Construction Company's long-term construction projects for the year 2012:

	Completed Projects	Incomplete Projects
Contract price	$20,000,000	$100,000,000
Costs incurred prior to 2012	3,700,000	16,000,000
Costs incurred in 2012	11,100,000	32,000,000
Estimated costs to be incurred in future years	- 0-	32,000,000

General and administrative expenses incurred in 2012 amounted to $2 million, none of which is to be considered a construction cost.

a. Compute net income for 2012 under the completed-contract method.
b. Compute net income for 2012 under the percentage-of-completion method.

Required

For each of the following numbered items, state the letter or letters of the principle(s), assumption(s), or concept(s) used to justify the accounting procedure followed. The accounting procedures are all correct.

a. Business entity.
b. Conservatism.
c. Earning principle of revenue recognition.
d. Going concern (continuity).
e. Exchange-price (cost) principle.
f. Matching principle.
g. Period cost (or principle of immediate recognition of expense).
h. Realization principle.
i. Stable dollar assumption.

1. Inventory is recorded at the lower of cost or market value.
2. A truck purchased in January was reported at 80% of its cost even though its market value at year-end was only 70% of its cost.
3. The collection of $40,000 of cash for services to be performed next year was reported as a current liability.
4. The president's salary was treated as an expense of the year even though he spent most of his time planning the next two years' activities.

5. No entry was made to record the company's receipt of an offer of $800,000 for land carried in its accounts at $435,000.

6. A supply of printed stationery, checks, and invoices with a cost of $8,500 was treated as a current asset at year-end even though it had no value to others.

7. A tract of land acquired for $180,000 was recorded at that price even though it was appraised at $230,000, and the company would have been willing to pay that amount.

8. The company paid and charged to expense the $4,200 paid to Craig Nelson for rent of a truck owned by him. Craig Nelson is the sole stockholder of the company.

Problem 5-5
Answer matching question regarding the conceptual framework project (L.O. 4)

Match the descriptions in Column B with the proper terms in Column A.

Column A
1. Financial reporting objectives.
2. Qualitative characteristics.
3. Relevance.
4. Predictive value.
5. Feedback value.
6. Timeliness.
7. Reliability.
8. Representational faithfulness.
9. Verifiability.
10. Neutrality.
11. Comparability.
12. Consistency.
13. Cost-benefit.
14. Materiality.

Column B
a. Information is free of measurement method bias.
b. The benefits exceed the costs.
c. Relatively large items must be accounted for in a theoretically correct way.
d. The information can be substantially duplicated by independent measurers using the same measurement methods.
e. When information improves users' ability to predict outcomes of events.
f. Broad overriding goals sought by accountants engaging in financial reporting.
g. When information is pertinent or bears on a decision.
h. The characteristics that accounting information should possess to be useful in decision making.
i. Information that reveals the relative success of users in predicting outcomes.
j. When accounting statements on economic activity correspond to the actual underlying activity.
k. When information is provided soon enough that it may be considered in decision making.
l. When information faithfully depicts for users what it purports to represent.
m. Requires a company to use the same accounting principles and reporting practices through time.
n. When reported differences and similarities in information are real and not the result of differing accounting treatments.

Alternate Problems

Problem 5-1A
Answer multiple-choice questions regarding accounting theory (L.O. 1-3)

Select the best answer to each of the following questions:

1. A set of basic concepts and assumptions and related principles that explain and guide the accountant's actions in identifying, measuring, and communicating economic information is called:

   a. Accounting theory.
   b. Accounting rules.
   c. Accrual basis.
   d. Matching concept.

2. Which of the following statements is false?

   a. Several separate legal entities properly may be considered to be one accounting entity.
   b. The stable dollar assumption is used only when the dollar is absolutely stable.
   c. Publicly held corporations generally prepare monthly financial statements for internal management and publish quarterly and annual financial statements for users outside the company.
   d. Without the periodicity assumption, a business would have only one time period running from the inception of the business to its termination.

3. Which of the following statements is true?

   a. When the substance of a transaction conflicts with the legal form of the transaction, the accountant should be guided by the legal form in recording the transaction.
   b. The consistency concept prohibits a change in accounting principle even when such a change would better meet the information needs of financial statement users.
   c. Under the double-entry approach, each transaction must be recorded with one debit and one credit of equal dollar amounts.
   d. Special-purpose financial information for a specific decision, such as whether or not to purchase a new machine, is best obtained from the detailed accounting records rather than from the financial statements.

4. Which of the following statements is true?

   a. All assets are carried indefinitely at their original costs in the financial statements.
   b. Liabilities are measured in the cash to be paid or the value of services to be performed to satisfy the liabilities.
   c. Accounting principles are derived by merely summarizing accounting practices used to date.
   d. Accountants can easily measure all changes in assets and liabilities since they never involve estimates or calculations.

5. Which of the following statements is false?

   a. The exchange-price principle is also called the cost principle.
   b. The matching principle is closely related to the revenue recognition principle.
   c. The installment sales method recognizes revenue sooner than it would normally be recognized.
   d. The percentage-of-completion method recognizes revenue sooner than the completed-contract method.

Problem 5-2A
Compute net income assuming revenues are recognized at time of sale and then assuming the installment basis is used (L.O. 2)

Nevada Real Estate Sales Company sells lots in its development in Dry Creek Canyon under terms calling for small cash down payments with monthly installment payments spread over a few years. Following are data on the company's operations for its first three years:

	2010	2011	2012
Gross margin rate	45%	48%	50%
Cash collected in 2012 from sales of lots made in	$640,000	$800,000	$900,000

The total selling price of the lots sold in 2012 was $3,000,000, while general and administrative expenses (which are not included in the costs used to determine gross margin) were $800,000.

Required

a. Compute net income for 2012 assuming revenue is recognized on the sale of a lot.
b. Compute net income for 2012 assuming use of the installment basis of accounting for sales and gross margin.

Problem 5-3A
Compute net income under completed-contract and percentage-of-completion methods (L.O. 2)

The following contract prices and costs relate to all of Orlando Construction Company's long-term construction projects (in millions of dollars):

		Costs Incurred		
	Contract Price	Prior to 2012	In 2012	Cost to Be Incurred in Future Years
On projects completed in 2012	$46	$4	$36	$0
On incomplete projects	144	24	48	48

General and administrative expenses for 2012 amounted to $1,200,000. Assume that the general and administrative expenses are not to be treated as a part of the construction cost.

Required ➲   **a.** Compute net income for 2012 using the completed-contract method.
b. Compute net income for 2012 using the percentage-of-completion method.

Problem 5-4A
Indicate agreement or disagreement with accounting practices followed and comment (L.O. 1-3)

In each of these circumstances, the accounting practices may be questioned. Indicate whether you agree or disagree with the accounting practice employed and state the assumptions, concepts, or principles that justify your position.

1. The salaries paid to the top officers of the company were charged to expense in the period in which they were incurred even though the officers spent over half of their time planning next year's activities.
2. No entry was made to record the belief that the market value of the land owned (carried in the accounts at $800,000) had increased.
3. The acquisition of a tract of land was recorded at the price paid for it of $400,000, even though the company would have been willing to pay $600,000.
4. A truck acquired at the beginning of the year was reported at year-end at 80% of its acquisition price even though its market value then was only 65% of its original acquisition price.

Problem 5-5A
Answer multiple-choice questions regarding the conceptual framework project (L.O. 4)

Select the best answer to each of the following questions:

1. In the conceptual framework project, how many financial reporting objectives were identified by the FASB?
   a. One.
   b. Two.
   c. Three.
   d. Four.

2. The two primary qualitative characteristics are:
   a. Predictive value and feedback value.
   b. Timeliness and verifiability.
   c. Comparability and neutrality.
   d. Relevance and reliability.

3. A pervasive constraint of accounting information is that:
   a. Benefits must exceed costs.
   b. The information must be timely.
   c. The information must be neutral.
   d. The information must be verifiable.

4. To be reliable, information must (identify the *incorrect* quality):
   a. Be verifiable.
   b. Be timely.
   c. Have representational faithfulness.
   d. Be neutral.

5. The *basic elements* of financial statements consist of:
   a. Terms and their definitions.
   b. The objectives of financial reporting.
   c. The qualitative characteristics.
   d. The new income statement format.

Beyond the Numbers—Critical Thinking

Jim Casey recently received his accounting degree from State University and went to work for a Big-Four CPA firm. After he had been with the firm for about six months, he was sent to the Ling Clothing Company to work on the audit. He was not very confident of his knowledge at this early point in his career. He noticed, however, that some of the company's transactions and events were recorded in a way that might be in violation of accounting theory and generally accepted accounting principles.

**Business Decision
Case 5-1**
Evaluate correctness
of accounting practices
and give reasons for
conclusions (L.O. 1-3)

Study each of the following facts to see if the auditors should challenge the financial accounting practices used or the intentions of management. Write your decisions and the reasoning behind your conclusions.

 Required

This problem can serve as an opportunity to apply accounting theory to situations with which you are not yet familiar and as a preview of future chapters. Some of the following situations relate to material you have already covered, and some situations relate to material to be covered in future chapters. After each item, we have given an indication of the chapter in which that item is discussed. You may research future chapters to find the correct answer. Alternatively, you could use your present knowledge of accounting theory to determine whether or not Casey should challenge each of the financial accounting practices used. Realize, however, that some generally accepted accounting practices were based on compromise and seem to differ with accounting theory as described in this chapter.

1. One of the senior members of management stated the company planned to replace all of the furniture next year. He said that the cash in the Accumulated Depreciation account would be used to pay for the furniture. (Ch. 3)
2. The company held the books open at the end of 2012 so they could record some early 2013 sales as 2012 revenue. The justification for this practice was that 2012 was not a good year for profits. (Ch. 3, 5, 6)
3. The company's buildings were appraised for insurance purposes. The appraised values were $10,000,000 higher than the book value. The accountant debited Buildings and credited Paid-in Capital from Appreciation for the difference. (Ch. 5)
4. The company recorded purchases of merchandise at the list price rather than the gross selling (invoice) price. (Ch. 6)
5. Goods shipped to the company from a supplier, FOB destination, were debited to Purchases. The goods were not included in ending inventory because the goods had not yet arrived. (Ch. 5, 6)
6. The company counted some items twice in taking the physical inventory at the end of the year. The person taking the inventory said he had forgotten to include some items in last year's physical inventory, and counting some items twice would make up for the items missed last year so that net income this year would be about correct. (Ch. 7)
7. The company switched from FIFO to LIFO in accounting for inventories. The preceding year it had switched from the weighted-average method to FIFO. The reason given for the most recent change was that federal income taxes would be lower. No indication of this switch was to appear in the financial statements. (Ch. 5, 7)
8. Since things were pretty hectic at year-end, the accountant made no effort to reconcile the bank account. His reason was that the bank probably had not made any errors. The bank balance was lower than the book balance, so the accountant debited Miscellaneous Expense and credited Cash for the difference. (Ch. 8)
9. When a customer failed to pay the amount due, the accountant debited Allowance for Uncollectible Accounts and credited Accounts Receivable. The amount of accounts written off in this manner was huge. (Ch. 9)

10. A completely depreciated machine was still being used. The accountant left the asset and its related accumulated depreciation on the books, stopped recording depreciation on the machine, and did not go back and correct earlier years' net income and reduce accumulated depreciation. (Ch. 10)

11. The accountant stated that even though research and development costs incurred to develop a new product would benefit future periods, these costs must be expensed as incurred. This year $200,000 of these costs were charged to expense. (Ch. 11)

12. An old truck was traded for a new truck. Since the trade-in value of the old truck was higher than its book value, a gain was recorded on the transaction. (Ch. 11)

13. The company paid for a franchise giving it the exclusive right to operate in a given geographical area for 60 years. The accountant is amortizing the asset over 60 years. (Ch. 11)

14. The company leases a building and has a nonrenewable lease that expires in 15 years. The company made some improvements to the building. Since the improvements will last 30 years, they are being written off over 30 years. (Ch. 11)

Annual Report Analysis 5-2
List 'Summary of Significant Accounting Policies' for a real company (L.O. 5)

Refer to the "Summary of Significant Accounting Policies" in the annual report of Wal-Mart Stores, Inc. List the policies discussed. For each of the policies, explain in writing what the company is trying to communicate.

Ethics–A Writing Experience 5-3
Answer questions regarding ethics case

Refer to the item "An Ethical Perspective" on page 196. Write out the answers to the following questions:

Is management being ethical in this situation? Explain.

Is the accountant correct in believing that management's position could not be successfully defended? Explain.

What would you do if you were the accountant? Describe in detail.

Group Project 5-4
Undertake research project concerning annual reports

In teams of two or three students, go to the library to locate one company's annual report for the most recent year. (As an alternative, annual reports can be downloaded from the SEC's EDGAR site at www.sec.gov/edgar.shtml) Examine the "Summary of Accounting Policies," which is part of the "Notes to Financial Statements" section immediately following the financial statements. As a team, write a memorandum to the instructor detailing the significant accounting policies of the company. The heading of the memorandum should contain the date, to whom it is written, from whom, and the subject matter.

Group Project 5-5
Perform library research

With one or two other students and using library sources, write a paper on the history and achievements of the Financial Accounting Standards Board. This board is responsible for establishing the accounting standards and principles for financial accounting in the private sector. It was formed in 1973 and took over the rule setting function from the Accounting Principles Board of the American Institute of Certified Public Accountants at that time. Be sure to cite sources used and to treat direct quotes properly.

Using the Internet—A View of the Real World

Visit the following Internet site for General Electric:

http://www.ge.com

Click on "Investor Relations" and then "Financial Reporting". Find the annual report listed under Financial Reporting and then Notes to Consolidated Financial Statements. Print a copy of the summary of Significant Accounting Policies. Write a short report to your instructor summarizing your findings.

Internet Project 5-6
Check out significant accounting policies

Visit the following Internet site for Tootsie Roll Industries, Inc:

http://www.tootsie.com

Click on "Company Information" and then "Financial Information". Open the most current annual report listed, and locate the notes to the consolidated financial statements. Print a copy of the Significant Accounting Policies. Write a short report to your instructor summarizing your findings.

Internet Project 5-7
Check on company notes to financial statements

Answers to Self-Test

True-False

1. **False.** The business entity concept assumes that each business has an existence separate from its owners, creditors, employees, customers, other interested parties, and other businesses.
2. **True.** Accountants should be guided by the economic substance of a transaction rather than its legal form.
3. **True.** The accrual basis of accounting seeks to match effort and accomplishment by matching expenses against the revenues they created.
4. **False.** Exceptions include the installment basis of revenue recognition for sales and the percentage-of-completion method for long-term construction projects.
5. **False.** Immaterial items do have to be recorded, but they can be recorded in a theoretically incorrect way (e.g., expensing a wastebasket that will last many years).
6. **True.** Relevance and reliability are the two primary characteristics.

Multiple-Choice

1. **c.** The matching concept is one of the major principles of accounting rather than an assumption.
2. **b.** The consistency concept requires that a company use the same accounting principles and reporting practices through time.
3. **b.** Usually, the accountant does not recognize revenue until the seller acquires the right to receive payment from the buyer.
4. **b.** $\$3,000,000/\$10,000,000 \times \$15,000,000 = \$4,500,000$.
5. **a.** Periodicity is an underlying assumption rather than a modifying convention.
6. **b.** The category, quantitative characteristics, is not part of the conceptual framework project.

Careers in Accounting

A Career as a CEO

Are you a leader? Would you enjoy someday becoming the president or chief executive officer (CEO) of the company you work for? Then you should consider a degree in accounting. The accounting field greatly values individuals with leadership potential. Accounting students with the most job offers and the highest starting salaries are also likely to be the ones who best demonstrate an ability to lead others. Recruiters in public accounting (i.e., auditing, tax, consulting) and private accounting (i.e., financial reporting, cost accounting, financial analysis, internal auditing) alike demonstrate a strong preference for students with leadership potential.

Fortunately, you do not have to run a company to demonstrate leadership abilities to college recruiters. Some examples of leadership potential that would look good on a resumé include organizing a successful fund-raiser, participating effectively as an officer in a student club, or taking the lead in a group project. If you do not have a resumé yet, stop by the career placement center at your college and ask them to assist you in preparing one. Many students at your level already have a resumé, and it takes time to refine and develop an effective one. A well-prepared resumé will be important for securing internship opportunities and part-time work in the business field, as well as for landing that first job upon graduation.

Did you know that the current and former chief executive officers of many of the largest manufacturing, merchandising, and service organizations in the United States hold degrees in accounting? Phil Knight at Nike, Doug Ivestor of Coca-Cola, Lynn Townsend at Chrysler, Thomas J. Falk of Kimberly-Clark (Kleenex), Duane McDougall of Williamette Industries (Building Products), Al Reser of Reser Fine Foods (Potato Salad), as well as current or former presidents of Home Depot, McDonalds, and John H. Harland all have degrees in accounting. It is really not that surprising that accounting majors are so successful, as accounting provides an excellent foundation in business. With a strong accounting foundation and the continued development of leadership abilities over your career, you might become a CEO yourself someday.

6

Merchandising Transactions
Introduction to Inventories and the Classified Income Statement

Your study of accounting began with service companies as examples because they are the least complicated type of business. You are now ready to apply the accounting process to a more complex business—a merchandising company. Although the fundamental accounting concepts for service businesses apply to merchandising businesses, merchandise accounting requires some additional accounts and techniques to record sales and purchases.

The normal flow of goods from manufacturer to final customer is as follows:

Merchandising Companies

Manufacturers produce goods from raw materials and normally sell them to wholesalers. After performing certain functions, such as packaging or labeling, **wholesalers** sell the goods to retailers. **Retailers** sell the goods to final customers. The two middle boxes in the diagram represent merchandising companies. These companies buy goods in finished form for resale.

This chapter begins by comparing the income statement of a service company with that of a merchandising company. Then, we describe (1) how to record merchandise-related transactions (2) a classified income statement and (3) the gross margin percentage. Finally, in the appendix we explain the work sheet and the closing process for a merchandising company.

Learning Objectives

After studying this chapter, you should be able to:

1. Record journal entries for sales transactions involving merchandise.

2. Describe briefly cost of goods sold and the distinction between perpetual and periodic inventory procedures.

3. Record journal entries for purchase transactions involving merchandise.

4. Describe the freight terms and record transportation costs.

5. Determine cost of goods sold.

6. Prepare a classified income statement.

(continued)

Illustration 6.1 Condensed Income Statements of a Service Company and a Merchandising Company Compared

SERVICE COMPANY Income Statement For the Year Ended December 31, 2012		MERCHANDISING COMPANY Income Statement For the Year Ended December 31, 2012	
Service revenues	$13,200	Sales revenues	$262,000
		Cost of goods sold	159,000
		Gross Margin	$103,000
Expenses	6,510	Expenses	74,900
Net income	$ 6,690	Net income	$ 28,100

Two Income Statements Compared— Service Company and Merchandising Company

In Illustration 6.1 we compare the main divisions of an income statement for a service company with those for a merchandising company. To determine profitability or net income, a service company deducts total expenses incurred from revenues earned. A merchandising company is a more complex business and, therefore, has a more complex income statement.

As shown in Illustration 6.1, merchandising companies must deduct from revenues the cost of the goods they sell to customers to arrive at gross margin. Then, they deduct other expenses. The income statement of a merchandising company has three main divisions: (1) sales revenues, which result from the sale of goods by the company; (2) cost of goods sold, which is an expense that indicates how much the company paid for the goods sold; and (3) expenses, which are the company's other expenses in running the business.

In the next two sections we discuss the first two main divisions of the income statement of a merchandising company. The third division (expenses) is similar to expenses for a service company, which we illustrated in preceding chapters. As you study these sections, keep in mind how the divisions of the merchandising income statement are related to each other and produce the final figure—net income or net loss—which indicates the profitability of the company.

Sales Revenues

Objective 1
Record journal entries for sales transactions involving merchandise.

The sale of goods occurs between two parties. The seller of the goods transfers them to the buyer in exchange for cash or a promise to pay at a later date. This exchange is a relatively simple business transaction. Sellers make sales to create revenues; this inflow of assets in the form of cash or accounts receivable results from selling goods to customers.

In Illustration 6.1, we show a condensed income statement to emphasize its major divisions. Next, we describe the more complete income statement actually prepared by accountants. The merchandising company that we use to illustrate the income statement is Hanlon Retail Food Store. This section explains how to record sales revenues, including the effect of trade discounts. Then, we explain how to record two deductions from sales revenues—sales discounts and sales returns and allowances (Illustration 6.2). The amount that remains is **net sales**. The formula for determining net sales is:

Net sales = Gross sales – (Sales discounts + Sales returns and allowances)

Illustration 6.2   Partial Income Statement of Merchandising Company

HANLON RETAIL FOOD STORE
Partial income Statement
For the Year Ended December 31, 2012

Operating revenues:		
Gross sales		$282,000
Less: Sales discounts	$ 5,000	
Sales returns and allowances	15,000	20,000
Net sales		$262,000

Illustration 6.3   Invoice

BRYAN WHOLESALE CO. **476 Mason Street** **Detroit, Michigan 48823**	**Invoice No.:** 1258 **Date:** Dec. 19, 2012

Customer's Order No.: 218
Sold to: Baier Company
 ddress: 2255 Hannon Street
          Big Rapids, Michigan 48106   **Date Shipped:**   Dec. 19, 2012
 erms: Net 30, FOB Destination   **Shipped by:** Nagel Trucking Co.

Description	Item Number	Quantity	Price per Unit	Total Amount
rue-tone stereo radio	Model No. 5868-24393	200	$100	$20,000
		Total		$20,000

In a sales transaction, the seller transfers the legal ownership (title) of the goods to the buyer. Usually, the physical delivery of the goods occurs at the same time as the sale of the goods. A business document called an *invoice* (a *sales invoice* for the seller and a *purchase invoice* for the buyer) becomes the basis for recording the sale.

An **invoice** is a document prepared by the seller of merchandise and sent to the buyer. The invoice contains the details of a sale, such as the number of units sold, unit price, total price billed, terms of sale, and manner of shipment. A retail company prepares the invoice at the point of sale. A wholesale company, which supplies goods to retailers, prepares the invoice after the shipping department notifies the accounting department that it has shipped the goods to the retailer. Illustration 6.3 is an example of an invoice prepared by a wholesale company for goods sold to a retail company.

Using the invoice as the source document, a wholesale company records the revenue from the sale at the time of the sale for the following reasons:

1. The seller has passed *legal title* of the goods to the buyer, and the goods are now the responsibility and property of the buyer.
2. The seller has established the selling price of the goods.
3. The seller has completed its obligation.
4. The seller has exchanged the goods for another asset, such as cash or accounts receivable.
5. The seller can determine the costs incurred in selling the goods.

Recording Gross Sales

Note to the Student
A common example of an invoice is a sales ticket. It serves as the merchant's sales invoice and the customer's purchase invoice.

Each time a company makes a sale, the company earns revenue. This revenue increases a revenue account called *Sales*. Recall from Chapter 2 that credits increase revenues. Therefore, the firm credits the Sales account for the amount of the sale.

Usually sales are for cash or on account. When a sale is for cash, the company credits the Sales account and debits Cash. For example, it records a $20,000 sale for cash as follows:

Cash	20,000	
Sales		20,000
To record the sales of merchandise for cash.		

When a sale is on account, it credits the Sales account and debits Accounts Receivable. The following entry records a $20,000 sale on account:

Accounts Receivable	20,000	
Sales		20,000
To record the sales of merchandise on account.		

Usually, a seller quotes the gross selling price, also called the invoice price, of goods to the buyer. However, sometimes a seller quotes a list price of goods along with available trade discounts. In this latter situation, the buyer must calculate the gross selling price. The list price less all trade discounts is the **gross selling price**. Merchandising companies that sell goods use the gross selling price as the credit to sales.

An Accounting Perspective

USES OF TECHNOLOGY A database management system stores related data—such as monthly sales data (salespersons, customers, products, and sales amounts)—independent of the application. Once you have defined this information to the database management system, you can use commands to answer such questions as: Which products have been sold to which customers? What are the amounts of sales by individual salespersons? You could also print a customer list sorted by ZIP code, the alphabet, or salesperson.

Determining Gross Selling Price when Companies Offer Trade Discounts

Note to the Student
Have you ever noticed at a paint store or a plumbing supplies shop that professional painters and plumbers generally pay less for the paint and plumbing supplies they use in their businesses than you have to pay? Painters and plumbers have to make a profit on items they must use in their businesses. A portion of this profit arises from trade discounts received on their purchases.

A **trade discount** is a percentage deduction, or discount, from the specified list price or catalog price of merchandise. Companies use trade discounts to:

1. Reduce the cost of catalog publication. A seller can use a catalog for a longer time by printing list prices in the catalog and giving separate discount sheets to salespersons whenever prices change.
2. Grant quantity discounts.
3. Allow quotation of different prices to various customers, such as retailers and wholesalers.

The seller's invoice may show trade discounts. However, sellers do not record trade discounts in their accounting records because the discounts are used only to calculate the gross selling price. Nor do trade discounts appear on the books of the purchaser. To illustrate, assume an invoice contains the following data:

List price, 200 swimsuits at $24	$4,800
Less: Trade discount, 30%	1,440
Gross selling price (invoice price)	$3,360

The seller records a sale of $3,360. The purchaser records a purchase of $3,360. Thus, neither the seller nor the purchaser enters list prices and trade discounts on their books.

Sometimes the list price of a product is subject to several trade discounts; this series of discounts is a **chain discount**. Chain discounts exist, for example, when a wholesaler receives two trade discounts for services performed, such as packaging and distributing. When more than one discount is given, the buyer applies each discount to the declining balance successively. If a product has a list price of $100 and is subject to trade discounts of 20% and 10%, the gross selling price (invoice price) would be $100 − 0.2($100) = $80; $80 − 0.1($80) = $72, computed as follows:

Note to the Student
The order in which the discounts are applied does not matter because the result is the same. Here is proof: Example: A $100 sale with a chain trade discount of 5%, 3%, and 1%.
Solution:
$100 × 95% × 97% × 99% = $91.23
$100 × 99% × 95% × 97% = $91.23

List price	$100
Less 20%	- 20
	$ 80
Less 10%	- 8
Gross selling price (invoice price)	$ 72

You could obtain the same results by multiplying the list price by the complements of the trade discounts allowed. The complement of 20% is 80% because 20% + 80% = 100%. The complement of 10% is 90% because 10% + 90% = 100%. Thus, the gross selling price is $100 × 0.8 × 0.9 = $72.

Two common deductions from gross sales are (1) sales discounts and (2) sales returns and allowances. Sellers record these deductions in contra revenue accounts to the Sales account. Contra accounts have normal balances that are opposite to the balance of the account they reduce. For example, since the Sales account normally has a credit balance, the Sales Discounts account and Sales Returns and Allowances account have debit balances. We explain the methods of recording these contra revenue accounts next.

Recording Deductions from Gross Sales

Sales Discounts   Whenever a company sells goods on account, it clearly specifies terms of payment on the invoice. For example, the invoice in Illustration 6.3 states the terms of payment as "net 30."

Net 30 is sometimes written as "n/30." Either way, this term means that the buyer may not take a discount and must pay the entire amount of the invoice ($20,000) on or before 30 days after December 19, 2012 (invoice date)—or January 18, 2013. In Illustration 6.3, if the terms had read "n/10/EOM" (EOM means end of month), the buyer could not take a discount, and the invoice would be due on the 10th day of the month following the month of sale—or January 10, 2013. Credit terms vary from industry to industry.

In some industries, credit terms include a *cash discount* of 1% to 3% to induce early payment of an amount due. A **cash discount** is a deduction from the invoice price that can be taken only if the invoice is paid within a specified time. A cash discount differs from a trade discount in that a cash discount is a deduction from the gross selling price for the prompt payment of an invoice. In contrast, a trade discount is a deduction from the list price to determine the gross selling price (or invoice price). Sellers call a cash discount a **sales discount** and buyers call it a **purchase discount**.

Companies often state cash discount terms as follows:

Note to the Student
A company offers sales discounts to encourage early payment. The longer a company has to wait for payment from a customer, the more likely the customer is to not pay at all.

Reinforcing Problem
E6 5 Calculate gross selling price and final payment.

- **2/10, n/30**—means a buyer who pays within 10 days following the invoice date may deduct a discount of 2% of the invoice price. If payment is not made within the discount period, the entire invoice price is due 30 days from the invoice date.

- **2/EOM, n/60**—means a buyer who pays by the end of the month of purchase may deduct a 2% discount from the invoice price. If payment is not made within the discount period, the entire invoice price is due 60 days from the invoice date.
- **2/10/EOM, n/60**—means a buyer who pays by the 10th of the month following the month of purchase may deduct a 2% discount from the invoice price. If payment is not made within the discount period, the entire invoice price is due 60 days from the invoice date.

Sellers cannot record the sales discount before they receive the payment since they do not know when the buyer will pay the invoice. A cash discount taken by the buyer reduces the cash that the seller actually collects from the sale of the goods, so the seller must indicate this fact in its accounting records. The following entries show how to record a sale and a subsequent sales discount.

Assume that on July 12, a business sold merchandise for $2,000 on account; terms are 2/10, n/30. On July 21 (nine days after invoice date), the business received a $1,960 check in payment of the account. The required journal entries for the seller are:

July	12	Accounts Receivable	2,000	
		Sales		2,000
		To record sale on account; terms 2/10, n/30		
	21	Cash	1,960	
		Sales Discounts	40	
		Accounts Receivable		2,000
		To record collection on account, less a discount.		

The **Sales Discounts account** is a contra revenue account to the Sales account. In the income statement, the seller deducts this contra revenue account from gross sales. Sellers use the Sales Discounts account (rather than directly reducing the Sales account) so management can examine the sales discounts figure to evaluate the company's sales discount policy. Note that the Sales Discounts account is not an expense incurred in generating revenue. Rather, the purpose of the account is to reduce recorded revenue to the amount actually realized from the sale.

Sales Returns and Allowances   Merchandising companies usually allow customers to return goods that are defective or unsatisfactory for a variety of reasons, such as wrong color, wrong size, wrong style, wrong amounts, or inferior quality. In fact, when their policy is satisfaction guaranteed, some companies allow customers to return goods simply because they do not like the merchandise. A sales return is merchandise returned by a buyer. Sellers and buyers regard a sales return as a cancellation of a sale. Alternatively, some customers keep unsatisfactory goods, and the seller gives them an allowance off the original price. A sales allowance is a deduction from the original invoiced sales price granted when the customer keeps the merchandise but is dissatisfied for any of a number of reasons, including inferior quality, damage, or deterioration in transit. When a seller agrees to the sales return or sales allowance, the seller sends the buyer a credit memorandum indicating a reduction (crediting) of the buyer's account receivable. A credit memorandum is a document that provides space for the name and address of the concerned parties, followed by a space for the reason for the credit and the amount to be credited. A credit memorandum becomes the basis for recording a sales return or a sales allowance.

In theory, sellers could record both sales returns and sales allowances as debits to the Sales account because they cancel part of the recorded selling price.

However, because the amount of sales returns and sales allowances is useful information to management, it should be shown separately. The amount of returns and allowances in relation to goods sold can indicate the quality of the goods (high-return percentage, equals low quality) or of pressure applied by salespersons (high-return percentage, equals high-pressure sales). Thus, sellers record sales returns and sales allowances in a separate *Sales Returns and Allowances account.* The **Sales Returns and Allowances account** is a contra revenue account (to Sales) that records the selling price of merchandise returned by buyers or reductions in selling prices granted. (Some companies use separate accounts for sales returns and for sales allowances, but this text does not.)

Following are two examples illustrating the recording of sales returns in the Sales Returns and Allowances account:

1. Assume that a customer returns $300 of goods sold on account. If payment has not yet been received, the required entry is:

Sales Returns and Allowances	300	
Accounts Receivable		300
To record a sales return from a customer.		

2. Assume that the customer has already paid the account and the seller gives the customer a cash refund. Now, the credit is to Cash rather than to Accounts Receivable. If the customer has taken a 2% discount when paying the account, the company would return to the customer the sales price less the sales discount amount. For example, if a customer returns goods that sold for $300, on which a 2% discount was taken, the following entry would be made:

Sales Returns and Allowances	300	
Cash		294
Sales Discount		6
To record a sales return from a customer who had taken a discount and was sent a cash refund.		

The debit to the Sales Returns and Allowances account is for the full selling price of the purchase. The credit of $6 reduces the balance of the Sales Discounts account.

Next, we illustrate the recording of a sales allowance in the Sales Returns and Allowances account. Assume that a company grants a $400 allowance to a customer for damage resulting from improperly packed merchandise. If the customer has not yet paid the account, the required entry would be:

Sales Returns and Allowances	400	
Accounts Receivable		400
To record a sales allowance granted for damaged merchandise.		

If the customer has already paid the account, the credit is to Cash instead of Accounts Receivable. If the customer took a 2% discount when paying the account, the company would refund only the net amount ($392). Sales Discounts would be credited for $8. The entry would be:

Sales Returns and Allowances	400	
Cash		392
Sales Discount		8
To record a sales allowance when a customer has paid and taken a 2% discount.		

Illustration 6.4   Partial Income Statement*

HANLON RETAIL FOOD STORE
Partial income Statement
For the Year Ended December 31, 2012

Operating revenues:

Gross sales		$282,000
Less: Sales discounts	$ 5,000	
Sales returns and allowances	15,000	20,000
Net sales		$262,000

*This illustration is the same as Illustration 6.2, repeated here for your convenience.

Reporting Net Sales in the Income Statement

Illustration 6.4 shows how a company could report sales, sales discounts, and sales returns and allowances in the income statement. More often, the income statement in a company's annual report begins with "Net sales" because sales details are not important to external financial statement users.

An Accounting Perspective

BUSINESS INSIGHT When examining a company's sales cycle, management and users of financial data should be aware of any seasonal changes that may affect its reported sales. Systemax Inc. is a national retailer of personal computers and related products and services. Systemax includes the following disclosure in its Annual Report regarding seasonality.

Our earnings and cash flows are seasonal in nature, with the fourth quarter of the fiscal year generating higher earnings and cash flows that the other quarters.

An Accounting Perspective

BUSINESS INSIGHT For many retailers a large percentage of their annual sales occurs during the period from Thanksgiving to Christmas. They attempt to stock just the right amount of goods to meet demand. Since this is a difficult estimate to make accurately, many retailers end up with a large amount of unsold goods at the end of this season. The only way they can unload these goods is to offer huge discounts during the following period.

Cost of Goods Sold

Objective 2
Describe briefly cost of goods sold and the distinction between perpetual and periodic inventory procedures.

The second main division of an income statement for a merchandising business is cost of goods sold. **Cost of goods sold** is the cost to the seller of the goods sold to customers. For a merchandising company, the cost of goods sold can be relatively large. All merchandising companies have a quantity of goods on hand called *merchandise inventory* to sell to customers. **Merchandise inventory** (or *inventory*) is the quantity of goods available for sale at any given time. Cost of goods sold is determined by computing the cost of (1) the beginning inventory, (2) the net cost of goods purchased, and (3) the ending inventory.

Real World Example
Abercrombie & Fitch recently reported Net Sales of $3.469 billion and Cost of goods sold of $1.257 billion. The cost of goods sold was about 36% of sales.

Look at the cost of goods sold section of Hanlon Retail Food Store's income statement in Illustration 6.5. The merchandise inventory on January 1, 2012, was $24,000. The net cost of purchases for the year was $166,000. Thus, Hanlon had $190,000 of merchandise available for sale during 2012. On December 31, 2012,

Illustration 6.5   Determination of Cost of Goods Sold for Hanlon Retail Food Store

Cost of goods sold:			
Merchandise inventory, January 1, 2012			$ 24,000
Purchases		$167,000	
Less: Purchase discounts	$3,000		
Purchase returns and allowances	8,000	11,000	
Net Purchases		$156,000	
Add: Transportation-in		10,000	
Net cost of purchases			166,000
Cost of goods available for sale			$190,000
Less: Merchandise inventory, December 31, 2012			31,000
Cost of goods sold			$159,000

the merchandise inventory was $31,000, meaning that this amount was left unsold. Subtracting the unsold inventory (the ending inventory), $31,000, from the amount Hanlon had available for sale during the year, $190,000, gives the cost of goods sold for the year of $159,000. Understanding this relationship shown on Hanlon Retail Food Store's partial income statement gives you the necessary background to determine the cost of goods sold as presented in this section.

To determine the cost of goods sold, accountants must have accurate merchandise inventory figures. Accountants use two basic methods for determining the amount of merchandise inventory—perpetual inventory procedure and periodic inventory procedure. We mention perpetual inventory procedure only briefly here. In the next chapter, we emphasize perpetual inventory procedure and further compare it with periodic inventory procedure.

Two Procedures for Accounting for Inventories

When discussing inventory, we need to clarify whether we are referring to the physical goods on hand or the Merchandise Inventory account, which is the financial representation of the physical goods on hand. The difference between perpetual and periodic inventory procedures is the frequency with which the Merchandise Inventory account is updated to reflect what is physically on hand. Under **perpetual inventory procedure**, the Merchandise Inventory account is continuously updated to reflect items on hand. For example, your supermarket uses a scanner to ring up your purchases. When your box of Rice Krispies crosses the scanner, the Merchandise Inventory account shows that one less box of Rice Krispies is on hand.

Under **periodic inventory procedure**, the Merchandise Inventory account is updated periodically after a physical count has been made. Usually, the physical count takes place immediately before the preparation of financial statements.

Perpetual Inventory Procedure   Companies use perpetual inventory procedure in a variety of business settings. Historically, companies that sold merchandise with a high individual unit value, such as automobiles, furniture, and appliances, used perpetual inventory procedure. Today, computerized cash registers, scanners, and accounting software programs automatically keep track of inflows and outflows of each inventory item. Computerization makes it economical for many retail stores to use perpetual inventory procedure even for goods of low unit value, such as groceries.

Under perpetual inventory procedure, the Merchandise Inventory account provides close control by showing the cost of the goods that are supposed to be on hand at any particular time. Companies debit the Merchandise Inventory account for each purchase and credit it for the cost of each sale so that the current balance is shown in the account at all times. Usually, firms also maintain detailed unit records showing the quantities of each type of goods that should be on hand. Company personnel also take a physical inventory by actually counting the units of inventory on hand. Then they compare this physical count with the records showing the units that should be on hand. Chapter 7 describes perpetual inventory procedure in more detail.

Periodic Inventory Procedure   Merchandising companies selling low unit value merchandise (such as nuts and bolts, nails, Christmas cards, or pencils) that have not computerized their inventory systems often find that the extra costs of record-keeping under perpetual inventory procedure more than outweigh the benefits. These merchandising companies often use periodic inventory procedure.

Under periodic inventory procedure, companies do not use the Merchandise Inventory account to record each purchase and cost of sale of merchandise. Instead, a company corrects the balance in the Merchandise Inventory account as the result of a physical inventory count at the end of the accounting period. Also, the company usually does not maintain other records showing the exact number of units that should be on hand. Although periodic inventory procedure reduces record-keeping, it also reduces control over inventory items.

Companies using periodic inventory procedure make no entries to the Merchandise Inventory account nor do they maintain unit records during the accounting period. Thus, these companies have no up-to-date balance against which to compare the physical inventory count at the end of the period. Also, these companies make no attempt to determine the cost of goods sold at the time of each sale. Instead, they calculate the cost of all the goods sold during the accounting period at the *end* of the period. To determine the cost of goods sold, a company must know:

1. Beginning inventory (cost of goods on hand at the beginning of the period).
2. Net cost of purchases during the period.
3. Ending inventory (cost of unsold goods at the end of the period).

The company would show this information as follows:

Beginning inventory	$ 34,000
Add: Net cost of purchases during the period	140,000
Cost of goods available for sale during the period	$174,000
Deduct: Ending inventory	20,000
Cost of goods sold during the period	$154,000

In this schedule, notice that the company began the accounting period with $34,000 of merchandise and purchased an additional $140,000, making a total of $174,000 of goods that could have been sold during the period. Then, a physical inventory showed that $20,000 remained unsold, which implies that $154,000 was the cost of goods sold during the period. Of course, the $154,000 is not necessarily the precise amount of goods sold because no actual record was made of the dollar cost of the goods sold. Periodic inventory procedure basically assumes that everything not on hand at the end of the period has been sold. This method disregards problems such as theft or breakage because the Merchandise Inventory account contains no up-to-date balance at the end of the accounting period against which to compare the physical count.

Purchases of Merchandise

Under periodic inventory procedure, a merchandising company uses the **Purchases account** to record the cost of merchandise bought for resale during the current accounting period. The Purchases account, which is increased by debits, appears with the income statement accounts in the chart of accounts.

To illustrate entries affecting the Purchases account, assume that Hanlon Retail Food Store made two purchases of merchandise from Smith Wholesale Company. Hanlon purchased $30,000 of merchandise on credit (on account) on May 4, and on May 21 purchased $20,000 of merchandise for cash. The required journal entries for Hanlon are:

Objective 3
Record journal entries for purchase transactions involving merchandise.

May	4	Purchases	30,000	
		Accounts Payable		30,000
		To record purchases of merchandise on account.		
	21	Purchases	20,000	
		Cash		20,000
		To record purchase of merchandise for cash.		

Reinforcing Problem
E6-1 Apply rules of debit and credit for merchandise-related accounts

The buyer deducts purchase discounts and purchase returns and allowances from purchases to arrive at net purchases. The accountant records these items in contra accounts to the Purchases account.

Deductions from Purchases

Purchase Discounts   Often companies purchase merchandise under credit terms that permit them to deduct a stated cash discount if they pay invoices within a specified time. Assume that credit terms for Hanlon's May 4 purchase are 2/10, n/30. If Hanlon pays for the merchandise by May 14, the store may take a 2% discount. Thus, Hanlon must pay only $29,400 to settle the $30,000 account payable. The entry to record the payment of the invoice on May 14 is:

Reinforcing Problems
E6-2 Prepare entries for merchandise purchase/ sale, return, and allowance on both buyer's and seller's books.
E6-3 Determine end of the discount period and prepare an entry to record payment.
E6-4 Calculate the effect of trade and cash discounts on payment.

May	14	Accounts Payable	30,000	
		Cash		29,400
		Purchase Discount		600
		To record payment on account within the discount period.		

The buyer records the purchase discount only when the invoice is paid within the discount period and the discount is taken. The **Purchase Discounts account** is a contra account to Purchases that reduces the recorded invoice price of the goods purchased to the price actually paid. Hanlon reports purchase discounts in the income statement as a deduction from purchases.

Companies base purchase discounts on the invoice price of goods. If an invoice shows purchase returns or allowances, they must be deducted from the invoice price before calculating purchase discounts. For example, in the previous transaction, the invoice price of goods purchased was $30,000. If Hanlon returned $2,000 of the goods, the seller calculates the 2% purchase discount on $28,000.

Interest Rate Implied in Cash Discounts   To decide whether you should take advantage of discounts by using your cash or borrowing, make this simple analysis. Assume that you must pay $10,000 within 30 days or $9,800 within 10 days to settle a $10,000 invoice with terms of 2/10, n/30. By advancing payment 20 days from the final due date, you can secure a discount of $200. The interest expense incurred to borrow $9,800 at 12% per year for 20 days is $65.33, calculated as ($9,800 × .12 × 20/360). You would save $134.67 ($200 – $65.33) by borrowing the money and paying the invoice within the discount period.

In terms of an annual rate of interest, the 2% rate of discount for 20 days is equivalent to a 36% annual rate: (360 ÷ 20) × 2%. The formula is:

$$\text{Equivalent annual rate of interest} = \frac{\text{The number of days in a year (assumed to be 360)}}{\text{The number of days from the end of the discount period until the final due date}} \times \text{The percentage rate of discount}$$

You can convert all cash discount terms to their approximate annual interest rate equivalents by use of this formula. Thus, a company could afford to pay up to 36% [(360 ÷ 20) × 2%] on borrowed funds to take advantage of discount terms of 2/10, n/30. The company could pay 18% on terms of 1/10, n/30.

Purchase Returns and Allowances   A purchase return occurs when a buyer returns merchandise to a seller. When a buyer receives a reduction in the price of goods shipped, a purchase allowance results. Then, the buyer commonly uses a debit memorandum to notify the seller that the account payable with the seller is being reduced (Accounts Payable is debited). The buyer may use a copy of a debit memorandum to record the returns or allowances or may wait for confirmation, usually a credit memorandum, from the seller.

Both returns and allowances reduce the buyer's debt to the seller and decrease the cost of the goods purchased. The buyer may want to know the amount of returns and allowances as the first step in controlling the costs incurred in returning unsatisfactory merchandise or negotiating purchase allowances. For this reason, buyers record purchase returns and allowances in a separate **Purchase Returns and Allowances account**. If Hanlon returned $350 of merchandise to Smith Wholesale before paying for the goods, it would make this journal entry:

Accounts Payable	350	
Purchase Returns and Allowances		350
To record return of damaged merchandise to supplier		

The entry would have been the same to record a $350 allowance. Only the explanation would change.

If Hanlon had already paid the account, the debit would be to Cash instead of Accounts Payable, since Hanlon would receive a refund of cash. If the company took a discount at the time it paid the account, only the net amount would be refunded. For instance, if a 2% discount had been taken, Hanlon's journal entry for the return would be:

Cash	343	
Purchase Discounts	7	
Purchase Returns and Allowances		350
To record return of damaged merchandise to supplier and record receipt of cash.		

Purchase Returns and Allowances is a contra account to the Purchases account, and the income statement shows it as a deduction from purchases. When both purchase discounts and purchase returns and allowances are deducted from purchases, the result is **net purchases**.

Transportation Costs

Transportation costs are an important part of cost of goods sold. To understand how to account for transportation costs, you must know the meaning of the following terms:

Objective 4
Describe the freight terms and record transportation costs.

- **FOB shipping point** means "free on board at shipping point." The buyer incurs all transportation costs after the merchandise has been loaded on a railroad car or truck at the point of shipment. Thus, the buyer is responsible for *ultimately* paying the freight charges.
- **FOB destination** means "free on board at destination." The seller ships the goods to their destination without charge to the buyer. Thus, the seller is *ultimately* responsible for paying the freight charges.
- **Passage of title** is a term that indicates the transfer of the legal ownership of goods. Title to the goods normally passes from seller to buyer at the FOB point. Thus, when goods are shipped FOB shipping point, title usually passes to the buyer at the shipping point. When goods are shipped FOB destination, title usually passes at the destination.
- **Freight prepaid** means the *seller* must *initially* pay the freight at the time of shipment.
- **Freight collect** indicates the *buyer* must *initially* pay the freight bill on the arrival of the goods.

To illustrate the use of these terms, assume that a company ships goods FOB shipping point, freight collect. Title passes at the shipping point. The buyer is responsible for paying the $100 freight costs and does so. The seller makes no entry for freight charges; the entry on the *buyer's books* is:

Transportation-In (or Freight-In)	100	
Cash		100
To record payment of freight bill on goods purchased.		

The **Transportation-In account** records the inward freight costs of acquiring merchandise. Transportation-In is an adjunct account in that it is added to net purchases to arrive at **net cost of purchases**. An **adjunct account** is closely related to another account (Purchases, in this instance), and its balance is added to the balance of the related account in the financial statements. Recall that a contra account is just the opposite of an adjunct account. Buyers deduct a contra account, such as accumulated depreciation, from the related fixed asset account in the financial statements.

When shipping goods FOB destination, freight prepaid, the seller is responsible for and pays the freight bill. Because the seller cannot bill a separate freight cost to the buyer, the buyer shows no entry for freight on its books. The seller, however, has undoubtedly considered the freight cost in setting selling prices. The following entry is required on the *seller's books:*

Delivery Expense (or Transportation-Out Expense)	100	
Cash		100
To record freight cost on goods sold.		

When the terms are FOB destination, the seller records the freight costs as **delivery expense**; this selling expense appears on the income statement with other selling expenses.

FOB terms are especially important at the end of an accounting period. Goods in transit then belong to either the seller or the buyer, and one of these parties must include these goods in its ending inventory. Goods shipped FOB destination belong to the seller while in transit, and the seller includes these goods in its ending inventory. Goods shipped FOB shipping point belong to the buyer while in transit, and the buyer records these goods as a purchase and includes them in its ending inventory. For

Reinforcing Problem
E6-6 Determine cash discount available and amount of cash paid.

Note to the Student
An easy way to interpret FOB terms is to identify either the destination or shipping point as the location where the goods change ownership.

example, assume that a seller ships goods on December 30, 2011, and they arrive at their destination on January 5, 2012. If terms are FOB destination, the seller includes the goods in its December 31, 2011, inventory, and neither seller nor buyer records the exchange transaction until January 5, 2012. If terms are FOB shipping point, the buyer includes the goods in its December 31, 2011, inventory, and both parties record the exchange transaction as of December 30, 2011.

Sometimes the seller prepays the freight as a convenience to the buyer, even though the buyer is ultimately responsible for it. The buyer merely reimburses the seller for the freight paid. For example, assume that Wood Company sold merchandise to Loud Company with terms of FOB shipping point, freight prepaid. The freight charges were $100. The following entries are necessary on the books of the buyer and the seller:

Buyer—Loud Company			Seller—Wood Company		
Transportation-In	100		Accounts Receivable	100	
Accounts Payable		100	Cash		100

Reinforcing Problems
E6-7 Prepare entries for purchase, transportation-in, purchase discounts, and payment.
P6-1 Journalize merchandise transactions for two different companies.
P6-2 Journalize merchandise transactions on both the buyer's and seller's books.

Such entries are necessary because Wood initially paid the freight charges when not required to do so. Therefore, Loud Company must reimburse Wood for the charges. If the buyer pays freight for the seller (e.g., FOB destination, freight collect), the buyer merely deducts the freight paid from the amount owed to the seller. The following entries are necessary on the books of the buyer and the seller:

Buyer—Loud Company			Seller—Wood Company		
Accounts Payable	100		Delivery Expense	100	
Cash		100	Accounts Receivable		100

Purchase discounts may be taken only on the purchase price of goods. Therefore, a buyer who owes the seller for freight charges cannot take a discount on the freight charges owed, even if the buyer makes payment within the discount period. We summarize our discussion of freight terms and the resulting journal entries to record the freight charges in Illustration 6.6.

Merchandise Inventory

Merchandise inventory is the cost of goods on hand and available for sale at any given time. To determine the cost of goods sold in any accounting period, management needs inventory information. Management must know its cost of goods on hand at the start of the period (beginning inventory), the net cost of purchases during the period, and the cost of goods on hand at the close of the period (ending inventory). Since the ending inventory of the preceding period is the beginning inventory for the current period, management already knows the cost of the beginning inventory. Companies record purchases, purchase discounts, purchase returns and allowances, and transportation-in throughout the period. Therefore, management needs to determine only the cost of the ending inventory at the end of the period in order to calculate cost of goods sold.

Note to the Student
A physical inventory is required whether the inventory system is periodic or perpetual. A complicating factor is placing a value on the unsold inventory that has been counted. We discuss several approaches to pricing the unsold items in the next chapter.

Taking a Physical Inventory   Under periodic inventory procedure, company personnel determine ending inventory cost by taking a *physical inventory*. Taking a physical inventory consists of counting physical units of each type of merchandise on hand. To calculate inventory cost, they multiply the number of each kind of merchandise by its unit cost. Then, they combine the total costs of the various kinds of merchandise to provide the total ending inventory cost.

In taking a physical inventory, company personnel must be careful to count all goods owned, regardless of where they are located, and include them in the inventory.

Illustration 6.6   Summary of Shipping Terms

Shipping point: Detroit ————————————————→ Destination: San Diego

Goods travel from shipping point to destination

If shipping terms are:

FOB shipping point—Buyer incurs the freight charges

FOB destination—Seller incurs the freight charge

Freight prepaid—Seller initially pays the freight charges

Freight collect—Buyer initially pays the freight charges

If the freight terms are combined as follows:

Terms	Party that Initially Pays	Party that Ultimately Bears Expense
(1) FOB shipping point, freight collect	Buyer	Buyer
(2) FOB destination, freight prepaid	Seller	Seller
(3) FOB shipping point, freight prepaid	Seller	Buyer
(4) FOB destination, freight collect	Buyer	Seller

Explanations:

FOB shipping point, freight collect—Buyer both incurs and initially pays the freight charges. The proper party (buyer) paid the freight. The buyer debits Transportation-In and credits Cash.

FOB destination, freight prepaid—Seller both incurs and initially pays the freight charges. The proper party (seller) paid the freight. The seller debits Delivery Expense and credits Cash.

FOB shipping point, freight prepaid—Buyer incurs the freight charges, and seller initially pays the freight charges. Buyer must reimburse seller for freight charges. The seller debits Accounts Receivable and credits Cash upon paying the freight. The buyer debits Transportation-In and credits Accounts Payable when informed of the freight charges.

FOB destination, freight collect—Seller incurs freight charges, and buyer initially pays freight charges. Buyer deducts freight charges from amount owed to seller. The buyer debits Accounts Payable and credits Cash when paying the freight. The seller debits Delivery Expense and credits Accounts Receivable when informed of the freight charges.

Thus, companies should include goods shipped to potential customers on approval in their inventories. Similarly, companies should not record **consigned goods** (goods delivered to another party who attempts to sell them for a commission) as sold goods. These goods remain the property of the owner (consignor) until sold by the consignee and must be included in the owner's inventory.

Merchandise in transit is merchandise in the hands of a freight company on the date of a physical inventory. As stated above, buyers must record merchandise in transit at the end of the accounting period as a purchase if the goods were shipped FOB shipping point and they have received title to the merchandise. In general, the goods belong to the party who ultimately bears the transportation charges.

When accounting personnel know the beginning and ending inventories and the various items making up the net cost of purchases, they can determine the cost of goods sold. To illustrate, assume the following account balances for Hanlon Retail Food Store as of December 31, 2012:

Merchandise Inventory, January 1, 2012	$ 24,000	Dr.
Purchases	167,000	Dr.
Purchase Discounts	3,000	Cr.
Purchase Returns and Allowances	8,000	Cr.
Transportation-In	10,000	Dr.

By taking a physical inventory, Hanlon determined the December 31, 2012, merchandise inventory to be $31,000. Hanlon then calculated its cost of goods sold as shown in

Determining Cost of Goods Sold

Objective 5
Determine cost of goods sold.

Reinforcing Problem
E6-8 Determine cost of goods sold.

Illustration 6.7   Determination of Cost of Goods Sold for Hanlon Retail Food Store*

Cost of goods sold:			
Merchandise inventory, January 1, 2012			$ 24,000
Purchases		$167,000	
Less: Purchase discounts	$3,000		
Purchase returns and allowances	8,000	11,000	
Net Purchases		$156,000	
Add: Transportation-in		10,000	
Net cost of purchases			166,000
Cost of goods available for sale			$190,000
Less: Merchandise inventory, December 31, 2012			31,000
Cost of goods sold			$159,000

*This illustration is the same as Illustration 6.5, repeated here for your convenience.

Illustration 6.7. This computation appears in a section of the income statement directly below the calculation of net sales.

In Illustration 6.7, Hanlon's beginning inventory ($24,000) plus net cost of purchases ($166,000) is equal to **cost of goods available for sale** ($190,000). The firm deducts the ending inventory cost ($31,000) from cost of goods available for sale to arrive at cost of goods sold ($159,000).

Another way of looking at this relationship is the following diagram:

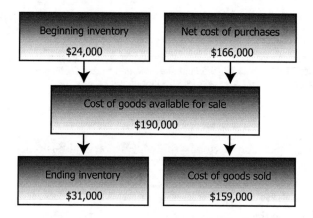

Note to the Student
The word stolen often implies a burglar entering and taking a company's assets. However stolen also includes goods taken by employees or by shoplifting customers. An executive of a Midwest department store chain remarked that stealing by employees was much more frequent than shoplifting by customers.

Beginning inventory and net cost of purchases combine to form cost of goods available for sale. Hanlon divides the cost of goods available for sale into ending inventory (which is the cost of goods not sold) and cost of goods sold.

To continue the calculation appearing in Illustration 6.7, net cost of purchases ($166,000) is equal to purchases ($167,000), *less* purchase discounts ($3,000) and purchase returns and allowances ($8,000), *plus* transportation-in ($10,000).

As shown in Illustration 6.7, ending inventory cost (merchandise inventory) appears in the income statement as a deduction from cost of goods available for sale to compute cost of goods sold. Ending inventory cost (merchandise inventory) is also a current asset in the end-of-period balance sheet.

Lack of Control under Periodic Inventory Procedure

Companies use periodic inventory procedure because of its simplicity and relatively low cost. However, periodic inventory procedure provides little control over inventory. Firms assume any items not included in the physical count of inventory at the end of the period have been sold. Thus, they mistakenly assume items that have been stolen have been sold and include their cost in cost of goods sold.

To illustrate, suppose that the cost of goods available for sale was $200,000 and ending inventory was $60,000. These figures suggest that the cost of goods sold was

$140,000. Now suppose that $2,000 of goods were actually shoplifted during the year. If such goods had not been stolen, the ending inventory would have been $62,000 and the cost of goods sold only $138,000. Thus, the $140,000 cost of goods sold calculated under periodic inventory procedure includes both the cost of the merchandise delivered to customers and the cost of merchandise stolen.

> **USES OF TECHNOLOGY** Many companies are building private networks to link their employees, customers, and suppliers together. These networks within the Internet are referred to as companies' *intranets*. The Internet can be likened to the entire universe, while an intranet can be likened to a solar system within the universe. A company's intranet is built to be secure from outside users. For instance, these networks are designed to be secure against "hackers" and other unauthorized persons. The intranet software typically encrypts data sent over the Internet to safeguard financial transactions.

An Accounting Perspective

Classified Income Statement

In preceding chapters, we illustrated the unclassified (or single-step) income statement. An **unclassified income statement** has only two categories—revenues and expenses. In contrast, a **classified income statement** divides both revenues and expenses into operating and nonoperating items. The statement also separates operating expenses into selling and administrative expenses. A classified income statement is also called a multiple-step income statement.

In Illustration 6.8, we present a classified income statement for Hanlon Retail Food tore. This statement uses the previously presented data on sales (Illustration 6.4) and cost of goods sold (Illustration 6.7), together with additional assumed data on operating expenses and other expenses and revenues. Note in Illustration 6.8 that a classified income statement has the following four major sections:

> **Objective 6**
> Prepare a classified income statement.

1. Operating revenues.
2. Cost of goods sold.
3. Operating expenses.
4. Nonoperating revenues and expenses (other revenues and other expenses).

The classified income statement shows important relationships that help in analyzing how well the company is performing. For example, by deducting cost of goods sold from operating revenues, you can determine by what amount sales revenues exceed the cost of items being sold. If this margin, called gross margin, is lower than desired, a company may need to increase its selling prices and/or decrease its cost of goods sold. The classified income statement subdivides operating expenses into selling and administrative expenses. Thus, statement users can see how much expense is incurred in selling the product and how much in administering the business. Statement users can also make comparisons with other years' data for the same business and with other businesses. Nonoperating revenues and expenses appear at the bottom of the income statement because they are less significant in assessing the profitability of the business.

> **Reinforcing Problems**
> P6-3 Prepare and post journal entries, and prepare a trial balance and classified income statement.
> Annual Report Analysis 6-3 Classify income statement items and calculate gross margin percentages.

> **BUSINESS INSIGHT** Management chooses whether to use a classified or unclassified income statement to present a company's financial data. This choice may be based either on how their competitors present their data or on the costs associated with assembling the data.

An Accounting Perspective

Illustration 6.8 Classified Income Statement for a Merchandising Company

HANLON RETAIL FOOD STORE
Income Statement
For the Year Ended December 31, 2012

Operating revenues:

Gross sales			$282,000
Less: Sales discounts		$ 5,000	
Sales return and allowances		15,000	20,000
Net sales			$262,000

Cost of goods sold:

Merchandise inventory, January 1, 2012			$24,000	
Purchases		$167,000		
Less: Purchase discount	$3,000			
Purchase returns and allowances	8,000	11,000		
Net purchases		$156,000		
Add: Transportation-in		10,000		
Net cost of purchases			166,000	
Cost of goods available for sale			$190,000	
Less: Merchandise inventory, December 31, 2012			31,000	
Cost of goods sold				159,000
Gross Margin				$103,000

Operating expenses:

Selling expenses:

Salaries and commissions expense	$ 26,000	
Salespersons' travel expense	3,000	
Delivery expense	2,000	
Advertising expense	4,000	
Rent expense—store building	2,500	
Supplies expense	1,000	
Utilities expense	1,800	
Depreciation expense—store equipment	700	
Other selling expense	400	$41,400

Administrative expenses:

Salaries expense, executive	$29,000		
Rent expense—administrative building	1,600		
Insurance expense	1,500		
Supplies expense	800		
Depreciation expense—office equipment	1,100		
Other administrative expenses	300	34,300	
Total operating expenses			75,700
Income from operations			$ 27,300

Nonoperating revenues and expenses:

Nonoperating revenues:

Interest revenue	1,400
	$ 28,700

Nonoperating expenses:

Interest expense	600
Net income	$ 28,100

Note to the Student
What do you think the gross margin rates for different types of retail stores in your area, such as jewelry versus groceries, would be? Would you rather purchase goods from a store with a high or low gross margin rate?

Next, we explain the major headings of the classified income statement in Illustration 6.8. The terms in some of these headings are already familiar to you. Although future illustrations of classified income statements may vary somewhat in form, we retain the basic organization.

1. **Operating revenues** are the revenues generated by the major activities of the business—usually the sale of products or services or both.
2. **Cost of goods sold** is the major expense in merchandising companies. Note the cost of goods sold section of the classified income statement in Illustration 6.8. This chapter has already discussed the items used in calculating cost of goods

sold. Merchandisers usually highlight the amount by which sales revenues exceed the cost of goods sold in the top part of the income statement. The excess of net sales over cost of goods sold is the **gross margin or gross profit**. To express gross margin as a percentage rate, we divide gross margin by net sales. In Illustration 6.8, the gross margin rate is approximately 39.3% ($103,000/$262,000). The gross margin rate indicates that out of each sales dollar, approximately 39 cents is available to cover other expenses and produce income. Business owners watch the gross margin rate closely since a small percentage fluctuation can cause a large dollar change in net income. Also, a downward trend in the gross margin rate may indicate a problem, such as theft of merchandise. For instance, one Southeastern sporting goods company, SportsTown, Inc., suffered significant gross margin deterioration from increased shoplifting and employee theft.

3. **Operating expenses** for a merchandising company are those expenses, other than cost of goods sold, incurred in the normal business functions of a company. Usually, operating expenses are either selling expenses or administrative expenses. **Selling expenses** are expenses a company incurs in selling and marketing efforts. Examples include salaries and commissions of salespersons, expenses for salespersons' travel, delivery, advertising, rent (or depreciation, if owned) and utilities on a sales building, sales supplies used, and depreciation on delivery trucks used in sales. **Administrative expenses** are expenses a company incurs in the overall management of a business. Examples include administrative salaries, rent (or depreciation, if owned) and utilities on an administrative building, insurance expense, administrative supplies used, and depreciation on office equipment. Certain operating expenses may be shared by the selling and administrative functions. For example, a company might incur rent, taxes, and insurance on a building for both sales and administrative purposes. Expenses covering both the selling and administrative functions must be analyzed and prorated between the two functions on the income statement. For instance, if $1,000 of depreciation expense relates 60% to selling and 40% to administrative based on the square footage or number of employees, the income statement would show $600 as a selling expense and $400 as an administrative expense.

4. **Nonoperating revenues (other revenues) and nonoperating expenses (other expenses)** are revenues and expenses not related to the sale of products or services regularly offered for sale by a business. An example of a nonoperating revenue is interest that a business earns on notes receivable. An example of a nonoperating expense is interest incurred on money borrowed by the company.

Real World Example
Abercrombie & Fitch had operating expenses of $1,980 million on a gross margin of $2,212 million for income from operations in 2010 of $232 million.

To summarize the more important relationships in the income statement of a merchandising firm in equation form:

Important Relationships in the Income Statement

1. **Net sales** = Gross sales – (Sales discounts + Sales returns and allowances).
2. **Net purchases** = Purchases – (Purchase discounts + Purchase returns and allowances).
3. **Net cost of purchases** = Net purchases + Transportation-in.
4. **Cost of goods sold** = Beginning inventory + Net cost of purchases – Ending inventory.
5. **Gross margin** = Net sales – Cost of goods sold.
6. **Income from operations** = Gross margin – Operating (selling and administrative) expenses.
7. **Net income** = Income from operations + Nonoperating revenues – Nonoperating expenses.

Reinforcing Problems
E6-9 Supply missing amounts in the income statement.
E6-10 Supply missing terms in formulas showing income statement relationships.

Each of these relationships is important because of the way it relates to an overall measure of business profitability. For example, a company may produce a high gross

| An Ethical Perspective

World Auto Parts Corporation | John Bentley is the chief financial officer for World Auto Parts Corporation. The company buys approximately $500 million of auto parts each year from small suppliers all over the world and resells them to auto repair shops in the United States.

Most of the suppliers have cash discount terms of 2/10, n/30. John has instructed his personnel to pay invoices on the 30th day after the invoice date but to take the 2% discount even though they are not entitled to do so. Whenever a supplier complains, John instructs his purchasing agent to find another supplier who will go along with this practice. When some of his own employees questioned the practice, John responded as follows: | This practice really does no harm. These small suppliers are much better off to go along and have our business than to not go along and lose it. For most of them, we are their largest customer. Besides, if they are willing to sell to others at a 2% discount, why should they not be willing to sell to us at that same discount even though we pay a little later? The benefit to our company is very significant. Last year our profits were $100 million. A total of $10 million of the profits was attributable to this practice. Do you really want me to change this practice and give up $10 million of our profits? |

margin on sales. However, because of large sales commissions and delivery expenses, the owner may realize only a very small percentage of the gross margin as profit. The classifications in the income statement allow a user to focus on the whole picture as well as on how net income was derived (statement relationships).

Analyzing and Using the Financial Results— Gross Margin Percentage

Objective 7
Analyze and use the financial results—gross margin percentage.

As discussed earlier, you can calculate the **gross margin percentage** by using the following formula:

$$\text{Gross margin percentage} = \frac{\text{Gross margin}}{\text{Net sales}}$$

To demonstrate the use of this ratio, consider the following information from the 2010 Annual Report of Abercrombie & Fitch.

($ millions)	2010	2009	2008
Revenues	$3,468.8	$2,928.6	$3,484.1
Gross profit	2,212.2	1,883.6	2,331.4
Gross profit (margin) percentage	$\frac{\$2,212.0}{\$3,468.8} = 63.77\%$	$\frac{\$1,883.6}{\$2,928.6} = 64.32\%$	$\frac{\$2,331.4}{\$3,484.1} = 66.91\%$

Abercrombie's gross margin held at a rather high 63–67% over those three years.

You should now understand the distinction between accounting for a service company and a merchandising company. The next chapter continues the discussion of merchandise inventory carried by merchandising companies.

Understanding the Learning Objectives

- In a sales transaction, the seller transfers the legal ownership (title) of the goods to the buyer.
- An invoice is a document, prepared by the seller of merchandise and sent to the buyer, that contains the details of a sale, such as the number of units sold, unit price, total price, terms of sale, and manner of shipment.
- Usually sales are for cash or on account. When a sale is for cash, the debit is to   Cash and the credit is to Sales. When a sale is on account, the debit is to Accounts Receivable and the credit is to Sales.
- When companies offer trade discounts, the gross selling price (gross invoice price) at which the sale is recorded is equal to the list price minus any trade discounts.
- Two common deductions from gross sales are (1) sales discounts and (2) sales returns and allowances. These deductions are recorded in contra revenue accounts to the Sales account. Both the Sales Discounts account and the Sales Returns and Allowances account normally have debit balances. Net sales = Sales – (Sales discounts + Sales returns and allowances).
- Sales discounts arise when the seller offers the buyer a cash discount of 1% to 3% to induce early payment of an amount due.
- Sales returns result from merchandise being returned by a buyer because the goods are considered unsatisfactory or have been damaged. A sales allowance is a deduction from the original invoiced sales price granted to a customer when the customer keeps the merchandise but is dissatisfied.

> **Objective 1**
> Record journal entries for sales transactions involving merchandise.

- Cost of goods sold = Beginning inventory + Net cost of purchases – Ending inventory. Net cost of purchases = Purchases – (Purchase discounts + Purchase returns and allowances) + Transportation-in.
- Two methods of accounting for inventory are perpetual inventory procedure and periodic inventory procedure. Under perpetual inventory procedure, the inventory account is continuously updated during the accounting period. Under periodic inventory procedure, the inventory account is updated only periodically—after a physical count has been made.

> **Objective 2**
> Describe briefly cost of goods sold and the distinction between perpetual and periodic inventory procedures.

- Purchases of merchandise are recorded by debiting Purchases and crediting Cash (for cash purchases) or crediting Accounts Payable (for purchases on account).
- Two common deductions from purchases are (1) purchase discounts and (2) purchase returns and allowances. In the general ledger, both of these items normally carry credit balances. From the buyer's side of the transactions, cash discounts are purchase discounts, and merchandise returns and allowances are purchase returns and allowances.

> **Objective 3**
> Record journal entries for purchase transactions involving merchandise.

- FOB shipping point means free on board at shipping point—the buyer incurs the freight.
- FOB destination means free on board at destination—the seller incurs the freight.
- Passage of title is a term indicating the transfer of the legal ownership of goods.
- Freight prepaid is when the seller must initially pay the freight at the time of shipment.

> **Objective 4**
> Describe the freight terms and record transportation costs.

- Freight collect is when the buyer must initially pay the freight on the arrival of the goods.

Objective 5
Determine cost of goods sold.

- Expansion and application of the relationship introduced in Learning Objective 2. Beginning inventory + Net cost of purchases = Cost of goods available for sale. Cost of goods available for sale − Ending inventory = Cost of goods sold.

Objective 6
Prepare a classified income statement.

- A classified income statement has four major sections—operating revenues, cost of goods sold, operating expenses, and nonoperating revenues and expenses.
- Operating revenues are the revenues generated by the major activities of the business—usually the sale of products or services or both.
- Cost of goods sold is the major expense in merchandising companies.
- Operating expenses for a merchandising company are those expenses other than cost of goods sold incurred in the normal business functions of a company. Usually, operating expenses are classified as either selling expenses or administrative expenses.
- Nonoperating revenues and expenses are revenues and expenses not related to the sale of products or services regularly offered for sale by a business.

Objective 7
Analyze and use the financial results—gross margin percentage.

- Gross margin percentage = Gross margin/Net sales.
- The gross margin rate indicates the amount of sales dollars available to cover expenses and produce income.

Objective 8
Prepare a work sheet and closing entries for a merchandising company (Appendix).

- Except for the merchandise-related accounts, the work sheet for a merchandising company is the same as for a service company.
- Any revenue accounts and contra purchases accounts in the Adjusted Trial Balance credit column of the work sheet are carried to the Income Statement credit column.
- Beginning inventory, contra revenue accounts, Purchases, Transportation-In, and expense accounts in the Adjusted Trial Balance debit column are carried to the Income Statement debit column.
- Ending merchandise inventory is entered in the Income Statement credit column and in the Balance Sheet debit column.
- Closing entries may be prepared directly from the work sheet. The first journal entry debits all items appearing in the Income Statement credit column and credits Income Summary. The second entry credits all items appearing in the Income Statement debit column and debits Income Summary. The third entry debits Income Summary and credits the Retained Earnings account (assuming positive net income). The fourth entry debits the Retained Earnings account and credits the Dividends account.

The Work Sheet for a Merchandising Company   APPENDIX

Illustration 6.9 shows a work sheet for a merchandising company. Lyons Company is a small sporting goods firm. The illustration for Lyons Company focuses on merchandise-related accounts. Thus, we do not show the fixed assets (land, building, and equipment). Except for the merchandise-related accounts, the work sheet for a merchandising company is the same as for a service company. Recall that use of a work sheet assists in the preparation of the adjusting and closing entries. The work sheet also contains all the information needed for the preparation of the financial statements.

To further simplify this illustration, assume Lyons needs no adjusting entries at month-end. The trial balance is from the ledger accounts at December 31, 2012. The $7,000 merchandise inventory in the trial balance is the beginning inventory. The sales and sales-related accounts and the purchases and purchases-related accounts summarize the merchandising activity for December 2012.

Lyons carries any revenue accounts (Sales) and contra purchases accounts (Purchase Discounts, Purchase Returns and Allowances) in the Adjusted Trial Balance credit columns of the work sheet to the Income Statement credit column. It carries beginning inventory, contra revenue accounts (Sales Discounts, Sales Returns and Allowances), Purchases, Transportation-In, and expense accounts (Selling Expenses, Administrative Expenses) in the Adjusted Trial Balance debit column to the Income Statement debit column.

Assume that ending inventory is $8,000. Lyons enters this amount in the Income Statement credit column because it is deducted from cost of goods available for sale (beginning inventory plus net cost of purchases) in determining cost of goods sold. It also enters the ending inventory in the Balance Sheet debit column to establish the proper balance in the Merchandise Inventory account. The beginning and ending inventories are on the Income Statement because Lyons uses both to calculate cost of goods sold in the income statement. Net income of $5,843 for the period balances the Income Statement columns. The firm carries the net income to the Statement of Retained Earnings credit column. Retained earnings of $18,843 balances the Statement of Retained Earnings columns. Lyons Company carries the retained earnings to the Balance Sheet credit column.

Lyons carries all other asset account balances (Cash, Accounts Receivable, and ending Merchandise Inventory) to the Balance Sheet debit column. It also carries the liability (Accounts Payable) and Capital Stock account balances to the Balance Sheet credit column. The balance sheet columns total to $29,543.

Once the work sheet has been completed, Lyons prepares the financial statements. After entering any adjusting and closing entries in the journal, the firm posts them to the ledger. This process clears the records for the next accounting period. Finally, it prepares a post-closing trial balance.

Income Statement   Illustration 6.10 shows the income statement Lyons prepared from its work sheet in Illustration 6.9. The focus in this income statement is on determining the cost of goods sold.

Statement of Retained Earnings   The statement of retained earnings, as you recall, is a financial statement that summarizes the transactions affecting the Retained Earnings account balance. In Illustration 6.11, the statement of retained earnings shows an increase in equity resulting from net income and a decrease in equity resulting from dividends.

Objective 8
Prepare a work sheet and closing entries for a merchandising company (Appendix).

Reinforcing Problem
E6-11 Prepare a partial work sheet using merchandise-related accounts.

Completing the Work Sheet

Note to the Student
Illustrate the placement of the beginning and ending inventory amounts in the work sheet using the BEE approach, where B stands for beginning and E stands for ending. Place the beginning inventory in the Income Statement debit column. Place the ending inventory in the Income Statement credit column. Place the ending inventory in the Balance Sheet debit column. The word BEE is spelled out on the work sheet.

Financial Statements for a Merchandising Company

Reinforcing Problems
P6-5 and P6-5A Prepare a work sheet, classified income statement, statement of retained earnings, classified balance sheet, and closing entries.

Illustration 6.9 Work Sheet for a Merchandising Company

LYONS COMPANY
Worksheet
For the Month Ended December 31, 2012

Acct. No.	Account Titles	Trial Balance		Adjustments		Adjusted Trial Balance		Income Statement		Statement of Retained Earnings		Balance Sheet	
		Debit	Credit	Debit	Credit	Debit	Credit	Debit	Credit	Debit	Credit	Debit	Credit
100	Cash	19,663				19,663						19,663	
103	Accounts Receivable	1,880				1,880						1,880	
105	Merchandise Inventory, December 1	7,000				7,000		7,000	8,000			8,000	
200	Accounts Payable		700				700						700
300	Capital Stock		10,000				10,000						10,000
310	Retained Earnings, December 1		15,000				15,000				15,000		
320	Dividends	2,000				2,000				2,000			
410	Sales		14,600				14,600		14,600				
411	Sales Discounts	44				44		44					
412	Sales Returns and Allowances	20				20		20					
500	Purchases	6,000				6,000		6,000					
501	Purchases Discounts		82				82		82				
502	Purchase Returns and Allowances		100				100		100				
503	Transportation-In	75				75		75					
557	Miscellaneous Selling Expenses	2,650				2,650		2,650					
567	Miscellaneous Administrative Expenses	1,150				1,150		1,150					
		40,482	40,482			40,482	40,482	16,939	22,782				
	Net Income							5,843			5,843		
								22,782	22,782	2,000	20,843	29,543	10,700
	Retained Earnings, December 31									18,843			18,843
										20,843	20,843	29,543	29,543

Illustration 6.10 Income Statement for a Merchandising Company

LYONS COMPANY
Income Statement
For the Month Ended December 31, 2012

Operating revenues:
Gross sales			$14,600
Less: Sales discounts		$ 44	
Sales return and allowances		20	64
Net sales			$14,536

Cost of goods sold:
Merchandise inventory, January 1, 2012			$ 7,000
Purchases		$ 6,000	
Less: Purchase discount	$ 82		
Purchase returns and allowances	100	182	
Net purchases		$5,818	
Add: Transportation-in		75	
Net cost of purchases			5,893
Cost of goods available for sale			$12,893
Less: Merchandise inventory, December 31, 2012			8,000
Cost of goods sold			4,893
Gross Margin			$ 9,643

Operating expenses:
Miscellaneous selling expense			$2,650
Miscellaneous administrative expense			1,150
Total operating expenses			3,800
Net income			$ 5,843

Illustration 6.11   Statement of Retained Earnings

LYONS COMPANY
Statement of Retained Earnings
For the Month Ended December 31, 2012

Retained earnings, December 1, 2012	$15,000
Add: Net income for the month	5,843
Total	$20,843
Deduct: Dividends	2,000
Retained earnings, December 31, 2012	$18,843

Illustration 6.12   Balance Sheet for a Merchandising Company

LYONS COMPANY
Balance Sheet
December 31, 2012

Assets

Cash	$19,663
Accounts receivable	1,880
Merchandise inventory	8,000
Total assets	$29,543

Liabilities and Stockholders' Equity

Liabilities:		
Accounts payable		$ 700
Stockholders' equity:		
Capital stock	$ 10,000	
Retained earnings	18,843	
Total stockholders' equity		28,843
Total liabilities and stockholders' equity		$29,543

Balance Sheet   The balance sheet, Illustration 6.12, contains the assets, liabilities, and stockholders' equity items taken from the work sheet. Note the $8,000 ending inventory is a current asset. The Retained Earnings account balance comes from the statement of retained earnings.

Recall from Chapter 4 that the closing process normally takes place after the accountant has prepared the financial statements for the period. The closing process closes revenue and expense accounts by transferring their balances to a clearing account called Income Summary and then to Retained Earnings. The closing process reduces the revenue and expense account balances to zero so that information for each accounting period may be accumulated separately.

Closing Entries

Lyons's accountant would prepare closing entries directly from the work sheet in Illustration 6.9 using the same procedure presented in Chapter 4. The closing entries for Lyons Company follow.

The first journal entry *debits* all items appearing in the Income Statement credit column of the work sheet and *credits* Income Summary for the total of the column, $22,782.

Reinforcing Problem
E6-12 Prepare and post closing entries using T-accounts.

	2012			
	Dec.	31 Merchandise Inventory (ending)	8,000	
		Sales	14,600	
		Purchase Discounts	82	
•1st entry		Purchase Returns and Allowances	100	
		Income Summary		22,782
		To close accounts with a credit balance in the		
		Income Statement columns and to establish ending		
		merchandise inventory.		

The second entry *credits* all items appearing in the Income Statement debit column and *debits* Income Summary for the total of that column, $16,939.

	2012			
	Dec.	31 Income Summary	16,939	
		Merchandise Inventory (beginning)		7,000
		Sales Discounts		44
		Sales Returns and Allowance		20
		Purchases		6,000
•2nd entry		Transportation-In		75
		Miscellaneous Selling Expenses		2,650
		Miscellaneous Administrative Expenses		1,150
		To close accounts with a debit balance in the Income		
		Statement columns.		

Note to the Student
How would this closing entry be different if the company had a net loss?

The third entry closes the credit balance in the Income Summary account of $5,843 to the Retained Earnings account.

	2012			
	Dec.	31 Income Summary	5,843	
		Retained Earnings		5,843
		To close the Income Summary account to the		
•3rd entry		Retained Earnings account.		

The fourth entry closes the Dividends account balance of $2,000 to the Retained Earnings account by debiting Retained Earnings and crediting Dividends.

	2012			
	Dec.	31 Retained Earnings	2,000	
		Dividends		2,000
		To close the Dividends account to the Retained		
•4th entry		Earnings account.		

Note how the first three closing entries tie into the totals in the Income Statement columns of the work sheet in Illustration 6.9. In the first closing journal entry, the credit to the Income Summary account is equal to the total of the Income Statement credit column. In the second entry, the debit to the Income Summary account is equal to the subtotal of the Income Statement debit column. The difference between the totals of the two Income Statement columns ($5,843) represents net income and is the amount of the third closing entry.

Demonstration Problem

The following transactions occurred between Companies C and D in June of 2012:

June 10 Company C purchased merchandise from Company D for $80,000; terms 2/10/EOM, n/60, FOB destination, freight prepaid.
11 Company D paid freight of $1,200.
14 Company C received an allowance of $4,000 from the gross selling price because of damaged goods.
23 Company C returned $8,000 of goods purchased because they were not the quality ordered.
30 Company D received payment in full from Company C.

a. Journalize the transactions for Company C.
b. Journalize the transactions for Company D.

 Required

Solution to Demonstration Problem

a.

General Journal

Date	Account Titles and Explanation	Post. Ref.	Debit	Credit
2012	**Company C**			
June 10	Purchases		80000	
	Accounts Payable			80000
	Purchased merchandise from Company D; terms 2/10/EOM, n/60			
14	Accounts Payable		4000	
	Purchase Return and Allowances			4000
	Received an allowance from Company D for damaged goods.			
23	Accounts Payable		8000	
	Purchase Returns and Allowances			8000
	Returned merchandise to Company D because of improper quality			
30	Accounts Payable ($80,000 - $4,000 - $8,000)		68000	
	Purchase Discounts ($68,000 x 0.02)			1360
	Cash ($68,000 - $1,360)			66640
	Paid the amount due to Company D.			

b.

General Journal

Date		Account Titles and Explanation	Post. Ref.	Debit	Credit
2012 June		**Company D**			
	10	Accounts Receivable		8 0 0 0 0	
		Sales			8 0 0 0 0
		Sold merchandise to Company C; terms 2/10/EOM, n/60			
	11	Delivery Expense		1 2 0 0	
		Cash			1 2 0 0
		Paid freight on sale of merchandise shipped FOB destination,			
		freight prepaid.			
	14	Sales Returns and Allowances		4 0 0 0	
		Accounts Receivable			4 0 0 0
		Granted an allowance to Company C for damaged goods.			
	23	Sales Returns and Allowances		8 0 0 0	
		Accounts Receivable			8 0 0 0
		Merchandise returned from Company C due to improper quality.			
	30	Cash ($68,000 - $1,360)		6 6 6 4 0	
		Sales Discounts ($68,000 x 0.02)		1 3 6 0	
		Accounts Receivable ($80,000 - $4,000 - $8,000)			6 8 0 0 0
		Received the amount due from Company C.			

New Terms

Adjunct account   Closely related to another account; its balance is added to the balance of the related account in the financial statements. *225*

Administrative expenses   Expenses a company incurs in the overall management of a business. *231*

Cash discount   A deduction from the invoice price that can be taken only if the invoice is paid within a specified time. To the seller, it is a sales discount; to the buyer, it is a purchase discount. *217*

Chain discount   Occurs when the list price of a product is subject to a series of trade discounts. *217*

Classified income statement   Divides both revenues and expenses into operating and nonoperating items. The statement also separates operating expenses into selling and administrative expenses. Also called the multiple-step income statement. *229*

Consigned goods   Goods delivered to another party who attempts to sell the goods for the owner at a commission. *227*

Cost of goods available for sale   Equal to beginning inventory plus net cost of purchases. *228*

Cost of goods sold   Shows the cost to the seller of the goods sold to customers; under periodic inventory procedure, cost of goods sold is computed as Beginning inventory + Net cost of purchases − Ending inventory. *220, 231*

Delivery expense   A selling expense recorded by the seller for freight costs incurred when terms are FOB destination. *225*

FOB destination   Means free on board at destination; goods are shipped to their destination without charge to the buyer; the seller is responsible for paying the freight charges. *225*

FOB shipping point   Means free on board at shipping point; buyer incurs all transportation costs after the merchandise is loaded on a railroad car or truck at the point of shipment. *225*

Freight collect   Terms that require the buyer to pay the freight bill on arrival of the goods. *225*

Freight prepaid   Terms that indicate the seller has paid the freight bill at the time of shipment. *225*

Gross margin or gross profit   Net sales − Cost of goods sold; identifies the number of dollars available to cover expenses other than cost of goods sold. *231*

Gross margin percentage   Gross margin divided by net sales. *232*

Gross selling price   (also called the invoice price) The list price less all trade discounts. *216*

Income from operations   Gross margin − Operating (selling and administrative) expenses. *231*

Invoice   A document prepared by the seller of merchandise and sent to the buyer. It contains the details of a sale, such as the number of units sold, unit price, total price billed, terms of sale, and manner of shipment. It is a purchase invoice from the buyer's point of view and a sales invoice from the seller's point of view. *215*

Manufacturers   Companies that produce goods from raw materials and normally sell them to wholesalers. 213

Merchandise in transit   Merchandise in the hands of a freight company on the date of a physical inventory. 227

Merchandise inventory   The quantity of goods available for sale at any given time. 220, 226

Net cost of purchases   Net purchases + Transportation-in. 225, 231

Net income   Income from operations + Nonoperating revenues − Nonoperating expenses. 231

Net purchases   Purchases − (Purchase discounts + Purchase returns and allowances). 224, 231

Net sales   Gross sales − (Sales discounts + Sales returns and allowances). 214, 231

Nonoperating expenses (other expenses)   Expenses incurred by a business that are not related to the acquisition and sale of the products or services regularly offered for sale. 231

Nonoperating revenues (other revenues)   Revenues not related to the sale of products or services regularly offered for sale by a business. 231

Operating expenses   Those expenses other than cost of goods sold incurred in the normal business functions of a company. 231

Operating revenues   Those revenues generated by the major activities of a business. 230

Passage of title   A legal term used to indicate transfer of legal ownership of goods. 225

Periodic inventory procedure   A method of accounting for merchandise acquired for sale to customers wherein the cost of merchandise sold and the cost of merchandise on hand are determined only at the end of the accounting period by taking a physical inventory. 221

Perpetual inventory procedure   A method of accounting for merchandise acquired for sale to customers wherein the Merchandise Inventory account is continuously updated to reflect items on hand; this account is debited for each purchase and credited for each sale so that the current balance is shown in the account at all times. 221

Physical inventory   Consists of counting physical units of each type of merchandise on hand. 226

Purchase discount   See Cash discount.

Purchase Discounts account   A contra account to Purchases that reduces the recorded gross invoice cost of the purchase to the price actually paid. 223

Purchase Returns and Allowances account   An account used under periodic inventory procedure to record the cost of merchandise returned to a seller and to record reductions in selling prices granted by a seller because merchandise was not satisfactory to a buyer; viewed as a reduction in the recorded cost of purchases. 224

Purchases account   An account used under periodic inventory procedure to record the cost of goods or merchandise bought for resale during the current accounting period. 222

Retailers   Companies that sell goods to final consumers. 213

Sales allowance   A deduction from original invoiced sales price granted to a customer when the customer keeps the merchandise but is dissatisfied for any of a number of reasons, including inferior quality, damage, or deterioration in transit. 218

Sales discount   See Cash discount.

Sales Discounts account   A contra revenue account to Sales; it is shown as a deduction from gross sales in the income statement. 218

Sales return   From the seller's point of view, merchandise returned by a buyer for any of a variety of reasons; to the buyer, a purchase return. 218

Sales Returns and Allowances account   A contra revenue account to Sales used to record the selling price of merchandise returned by buyers or reductions in selling prices granted. 219

Selling expenses   Expenses a company incurs in selling and marketing efforts. 231

Trade discount   A percentage deduction, or discount, from the specified list price or catalog price of merchandise to arrive at the gross invoice price; granted to particular categories of customers (e.g., retailers and wholesalers). Also see Chain discount. 216

Transportation-In account   An account used under periodic inventory procedure to record inward freight costs incurred in the acquisition of merchandise; a part of cost of goods sold. 225

Unclassified income statement   Shows only major categories for revenues and expenses. Also called the single-step income statement. 229

Wholesalers   Companies that normally sell goods to other companies (retailers) for resale. *213*

Self-Test

True-False

Indicate whether each of the following statements is true or false.

1. To compute net sales, sales discounts are added to, and sales returns and allowances are deducted from, gross sales.
2. Under perpetual inventory procedure, the Merchandise Inventory account is debited for each purchase and credited for each sale.
3. Purchase discounts and purchase returns and allowances are recorded in contra accounts to the Purchases account.
4. In taking a physical inventory, consigned goods delivered to another party who attempts to sell the goods are not included in the ending inventory of the company that sent the goods.
5. A classified income statement consists of only two categories of items, revenues and expenses.

Multiple-Choice

Select the best answer for each of the following questions.

1. A seller sold merchandise which has a list price of $4,000 on account, giving a trade discount of 20%. The entry on the books of the seller is:

a.	Accounts Receivable	3,200	
	Trade Discounts	800	
	Sales		4,000
b.	Accounts Receivable	4,000	
	Sales		4,000
c.	Accounts Receivable	3,200	
	Trade Discounts	800	
	Sales		4,000
d.	Accounts Receivable	3,200	
	Sales		3,200

2. X Company began the accounting period with $60,000 of merchandise, and net cost of purchases was $240,000. A physical inventory showed $72,000 of merchandise unsold at the end of the period. The cost of goods sold of Y Company for the period is:
   a. $300,000.
   b. $228,000.
   c. $252,000.
   d. $168,000.
   e. None of the above.

3. A business purchased merchandise for $12,000 on account; terms are 2/10, n/30. If $2,000 of the merchandise was returned and the remaining amount due was paid within the discount period, the purchase discount would be:
   a. $240.
   b. $200.
   c. $1,200.
   d. $1,000.
   e. $3,600.

4. A classified income statement consists of all of the following major sections except for:
   a. Operating revenues.
   b. Cost of goods sold.
   c. Operating expenses.
   d. Nonoperating revenues and expenses.
   e. Current assets.

5. (Appendix) Closing entries for merchandise-related accounts include all of the following except for:
   a. A credit to Sales Discounts.
   b. A credit to Merchandise Inventory for the cost of ending inventory.
   c. A debit to Purchase Discounts.
   d. A credit to Transportation-In.
   e. A debit to Sales.

Now turn to page 254 to check your answers.

Questions

1. Which account titles are likely to appear in a merchandising company's ledger that do not appear in the ledger of a service enterprise?
2. What entry is made to record a sale of merchandise on account under periodic inventory procedure?
3. Describe trade discounts and chain discounts.
4. Sales discounts and sales returns and allowances are deducted from sales on the income statement to arrive at net sales. Why not deduct these directly from the Sales account by debiting Sales each time a sales discount, return, or allowance occurs?
5. What are the two basic procedures for accounting for inventory? How do these two procedures differ?
6. What useful purpose does the Purchases account serve?
7. What do the letters FOB stand for? When terms are *FOB destination,* who incurs the cost of freight?
8. What type of an expense is delivery expense? Where is this expense reported in the income statement?
9. Periodic inventory procedure is said to afford little control over inventory. Explain why.
10. How does the accountant arrive at the total dollar amount of the inventory after taking a physical inventory?
11. How is cost of goods sold determined under periodic inventory procedure?
12. If the cost of goods available for sale and the cost of the ending inventory are known, what other amount appearing on the income statement can be calculated?
13. What are the major sections in a classified income statement for a merchandising company, and in what order do these sections appear?

14. What is gross margin? Why might management be interested in the percentage of gross margin to net sales?

15. (Appendix) After closing entries are posted to the ledger, which types of accounts have balances? Why?

16. Wal-Mart Based on the financial statements of Wal-Mart Stores, Inc., in the Annual Report Appendix, what were the 2011 operating, selling, general and administrative expenses? For each of the three years shown, what percentage of net sales were these expenses? Is the trend favorable or unfavorable?

17. Wal-Mart Based on the financial statements of Wal-Mart Stores, Inc., in the Annual Report Appendix, what was the 2011 cost of goods sold? For each of the three years shown, what percentage of net sales were these expenses? Is the trend favorable or unfavorable?

Exercises

Exercise 6-1
Apply rules of debit and credit for merchandise-related accounts
(L.O. 1, 3)

In the following table, indicate how to increase or decrease (debit or credit) each account, and indicate its normal balance (debit or credit).

Title of Account	Increased by (debit or credit)	Decreased by (debit or credit)	Normal Balance (debit or credit)
Merchandise Inventory			
Sales			
Sales Returns and Allowances			
Sales Discounts			
Accounts Receivable			
Purchases			
Purchase Returns and Allowances			
Purchase Discounts			
Accounts Payable			
Transportation-In			

Exercise 6-2
Prepare entries for merchandise purchase/ sale, return, and allowance on both buyer's and seller's books
L.O. 1, 3)

a. Silver Company purchased $56,000 of merchandise from Milton Company on account. Before paying its account, Silver Company returned damaged merchandise with an invoice price of $11,680. Assuming use of periodic inventory procedure, prepare entries on both companies' books to record both the purchase/sale and the return.

b. Show how any of the required entries would change assuming that Milton Company granted an allowance of $3,360 on the damaged goods instead of giving permission to return the merchandise.

Exercise 6-3
Determine end of discount period and prepare an entry to record payment
(L.O. 1, 3)

What is the last payment date on which the cash discount can be taken on goods sold on March 5 for $51,200; terms 3/10/EOM, n/60? Assume that the bill is paid on this date and prepare the correct entries on both the buyer's and seller's books to record the payment.

You have purchased merchandise with a list price of $36,000. Because you are a wholesaler, you are granted a trade discount of 49.6%. The cash discount terms are 2/EOM, n/60. How much will you remit if you pay the invoice by the end of the month of purchase? How much will you remit if you do not pay the invoice until the following month?

Exercise 6-4
Calculate effect of trade and cash discounts on payment (L.O. 1, 3)

Lasky Company sold merchandise with a list price of $60,000 on July 1. For each of the following independent assumptions, calculate (1) the gross selling price used to record the sale and (2) the amount that the buyer would have to remit when paying the invoice.

Exercise 6-5
Calculate gross selling price and final payment (L.O. 1, 3)

Trade Discount Granted	Credit Terms	Date Paid
a. 30%, 20%	2/10, n/30	July 10
b. 40%, 10%	2/EOM, n/60	August 10
c. 30%, 10%, 5%	3/10/EOM, n/60	August 10
d. 40%	1/10, n/30	July 12

Raiser Company purchased goods at a gross selling price of $2,400 on August 1. Discount terms of 2/10, n/30 were available. For each of the following independent situations, determine (1) the cash discount available on the final payment and (2) the amount paid if payment is made within the discount period.

Exercise 6-6
Determine cash discount available and amount of cash paid (L.O. 1, 3, 4)

Transportation Terms	Freight Paid (by)	Purchase Allowance Granted
a. FOB shipping point	$240 (buyer)	$480
b. FOB destination	120 (seller)	240
c. FOB shipping point	180 (seller)	720
d. FOB destination	192 (buyer)	120

Stuart Company purchased goods for $84,000 on June 14, under the following terms: 3/10, n/30; FOB shipping point, freight collect. The bill for the freight was paid on June 15, $1,200.

Exercise 6-7
Prepare entries for purchase, transportation-in, purchase discounts, and payment (LO. 3, 4)

a. Assume that the invoice was paid on June 24, and prepare all entries required on Stuart Company's books.

b. Assume that the invoice was paid on July 11. Prepare the entry to record the payment made on that date.

Cramer Company uses periodic inventory procedure. Determine the cost of goods sold for the company assuming purchases during the period were $40,000, transportation-in was $300, purchase returns and allowances were $1,000, beginning inventory was $25,000, purchase discounts were $2,000, and ending inventory was $13,000.

Exercise 6-8
Determine cost of goods sold (LO. 2, 3, 5)

In each case, use the following information to calculate the missing information:

Exercise 6-9
Supply missing amounts in the income statement (LO. 1-4, 6)

	Case 1	Case 2	Case 3
Gross sales	$ 640,000	$?	$?
Sales discounts	?	25,600	19,200
Sales returns and allowances	19,200	44,800	32,000
Net sales	608,000	1,209,600	?
Merchandise inventory, January 1	256,000	?	384,000
Purchases	384,000	768,000	?
Purchase discounts	7,680	13,440	12,800
Purchase returns and allowances	24,320	31,360	32,000
Net purchases	352,000	?	672,000
Transportation-in	25,600	38,400	32,000
Net cost of purchases	377,600	761,600	?
Cost of goods available for sale	?	1,081,600	1,088,000
Merchandise inventory, December 31	?	384,000	448,000
Cost of goods sold	320,000	?	640,000
Gross margin	?	512,000	320,000

Exercise 6-10
Supply missing terms in formulas showing income statement relationships (L.O. 6)

In each of the following equations supply the missing term(s):

a. Net sales = Gross sales − (_____ _____ + Sales returns and allowances).

b. Cost of goods sold = Beginning inventory + Net cost of purchases −
_____ _____ .

c. Gross margin = _____ _____ − Cost of goods sold.

d. Income from operations = _____ _____ − Operating expenses.

e. Net income = Income from operations + _____ _____ −
_____ _____ .

Exercise 6-11
Prepare a partial work sheet using merchandise-related accounts (based on Appendix) (L.O. 8)

Given the balances in this partial trial balance, indicate how the balances would be treated in the work sheet. The ending inventory is $96. (The amounts are unusually small for ease in rewriting the numbers. We purposely left out the Statement of Retained Earnings columns since they are not used.)

Accounts Titles	Trial Balance		Adjustments		Adjusted Trial Balance		Income Statement		Balance Sheet	
	Debit	Credit	Debit	Credit	Debit	Credit	Debit	Credit	Debit	Credit
Merchandise Inventory	120									
Sales		840								
Sales Discounts	18									
Sales Returns and Allowances	48									
Purchases	600									
Purchase Discounts		12								
Purchase Returns and Allowances		24								
Transportation-In	36									

Exercise 6-12
Prepare and post closing entries using T-accounts (based on Appendix) (L.O. 8)

Using the data in Exercise 6–11 prepare closing entries for the preceding accounts. Do not close the Income Summary account.

Problems

Problem 6-1
Journalize merchandise transactions for two different companies (L.O. 1, 3, 4)

a. Spencer Sporting Goods Company engaged in the following transactions in April 2012:

Apr.   1 Sold merchandise on account for $288,000; terms 2/10, n/30, FOB shipping point, freight collect.
         5 $43,200 of the goods sold on account on April 1 were returned for a full credit. Payment for these goods had not yet been received.
         8 A sales allowance of $5,760 was granted on the merchandise sold on April 1 because the merchandise was damaged in shipment.
        10 Payment was received for the net amount due from the sale of April 1.

b. High Stereo Company engaged in the following transactions in July 2012:

July   2   Purchased stereo merchandise on account at a cost of $43,200; terms 2/10, n/30, FOB destination, freight prepaid.

15   Sold merchandise for $64,800, terms 2/10, n/30, FOB destination, freight prepaid.

16   Paid freight costs on the merchandise sold, $2,160.

20   High Stereo Company was granted an allowance of $2,880 on the purchase of July 2 because of damaged merchandise.

31   Paid the amount due on the purchase of July 2.

Prepare journal entries to record the transactions.

 Required

Mars Musical Instrument Company and Tiger Company engaged in the following transactions with each other during July 2012:

Problem 6-2
Journalize merchandise transactions on both buyer's and seller's books (L.O. 1, 3, 4)

July   2   Mars Musical Instrument Company purchased merchandise on account with a list price of $48,000 from Tiger Company. The terms were 3/EOM, n/60, FOB shipping point, freight collect. Trade discounts of 15%, 10%, and 5% were granted by Tiger Company.

5   The buyer paid the freight bill on the purchase of July 2, $1,104.

6   The buyer returned damaged merchandise with an invoice price of $2,790 to the seller and received full credit.

On the last day of the discount period, the buyer paid the seller for the merchandise.

Prepare all the necessary journal entries for the buyer and the seller.

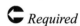 *Required*

The following data for June 2012 are for Rusk Company's first month of operations:

Problem 6-3
Prepare and post journal entries, and prepare a trial balance and classified income statement (L.O. 1-6)

June   1   Rusk Company was organized, and the stockholders invested $1,008,000 cash, $336,000 of merchandise inventory, and a $288,000 plot of land in exchange for capital stock.

4   Merchandise was purchased for cash, $432,000; FOB shipping point, freight collect.

9   Cash of $10,080 was paid to a trucking company for delivery of the merchandise purchased June 4.

13   The company sold merchandise on account, $288,000; terms 2/10, n/30.

15   The company sold merchandise on account, $230,400; terms 2/10, n/30.

16   Of the merchandise sold June 13, $31,680 was returned for credit.

20   Salaries for services received were paid as follows: to office employees, $31,680; to salespersons, $83,520.

22   The company collected the amount due on the remaining $256,320 of accounts receivable arising from the sale of June 13.

24   The company purchased merchandise on account at a cost of $345,600; terms 2/10, n/30, FOB shipping point, freight collect.

26   The company returned $57,600 of the merchandise purchased June 24 to the vendor for credit.

27   A trucking company was paid $7,200 for delivery to Rusk Company of the goods purchased June 24.

29   The company sold merchandise on account, $384,000; terms 2/10, n/30.

30   Sold merchandise for cash, $172,800.

30   Payment was received for the sale of June 15.

30   Paid store rent for June, $43,200.

30   Paid the amount due on the purchase of June 24.

The inventory on hand at the close of business June 30 was $672,000 at cost.

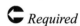 *Additional data*

Required ➲ **a.** Prepare journal entries for the transactions.

b. Post the journal entries to the proper ledger accounts. Use the account numbers in the chart of accounts shown in a separate file at the end of the text. Assume that all postings are from page 20 of the general journal.

c. Prepare a trial balance as of June 30, 2012.

d. Prepare a classified income statement for the month ended June 30, 2012. No adjusting entries are needed.

Problem 6-4
Prepare and post journal entries, prepare trial balance, classified income statement, and classified balance sheet (L.O. 1-6)

The Western Wear Company, a wholesaler of western wear clothing, sells to retailers. The company entered into the following transactions in May 2012:

May | 1 | The Western Wear Company was organized as a corporation. The stockholders purchased stock at par for the following assets in the business: $462,000 cash, $168,000 merchandise, and $105,000 land.
| 1 | Paid rent on administrative offices for May, $25,200.
| 5 | The company purchased merchandise from Carl Company on account, $189,000; terms 2/10, n/30. Freight terms were FOB shipping point, freight collect.
| 8 | Cash of $8,400 was paid to a trucking company for delivery of the merchandise purchased May 5.
| 14 | The company sold merchandise on account, $315,000; terms 2/10, n/30.
| 15 | Paid Carl Company the amount due on the purchase of May 5.
| 16 | Of the merchandise sold May 14, $13,860 was returned for credit.
| 19 | Salaries for services received were paid for May as follows: office employees, $16,800; salespersons, $33,600.
| 24 | The company collected the amount due on $126,000 of the accounts receivable arising from the sale of May 14.
| 25 | The company purchased merchandise on account from Bond Company, $151,200; terms 2/10, n/30. Freight terms were FOB shipping point, freight collect.
| 27 | Of the merchandise purchased May 25, $25,200 was returned to the vendor.
| 28 | A trucking company was paid $2,100 for delivery to The Western Wear Company of the goods purchased May 25.
| 29 | The company sold merchandise on open account, $15,120; terms 2/10, n/30.
| 30 | Cash sales were $74,088.
| 30 | Cash of $100,800 was received from the sale of May 14.
| 31 | Paid Bond Company for the merchandise purchased on May 25, taking into consideration the merchandise returned on May 27.

Additional data ➲ The inventory on hand at the close of business on May 31 is $299,040.

Required ➲ From the data given for The Western Wear Company:

a. Prepare journal entries for the transactions.

b. Post the journal entries to the proper ledger accounts. Use the account numbers in the chart of accounts shown in a separate file at the end of the text. Assume that all postings are from page 15 of the general journal.
(There were no adjusting journal entries.)

c. Prepare a trial balance.

d. Prepare a classified income statement for the month ended May 31, 2012.

e. Prepare a classified balance sheet as of May 31, 2012.

The following data are for Leone Lumber Company:

Problem 6-5
Prepare work sheet, classified income statement, statement of retained earnings, classified balance sheet, and closing entries (based on Appendix) (L.O. 5-8)

LEONE LUMBER COMPANY
Trial Balance
December 31. 2012

Acct. No.	Account Title	Debits	Credits
100	Cash	$ 70,640	
103	Accounts Receivable	159,520	
105	Merchandise Inventory, January 1, 2012	285,200	
107	Supplies on Hand	5,360	
108	Prepaid Insurance	4,800	
112	Prepaid Rent	57,600	
170	Equipment	88,000	
171	Accumulated Depreciation—Equipment		$ 17,600
200	Accounts Payable		102,800
300	Capital Stock		200,000
310	Retained Earnings, 1/1/12		219,640
410	Sales		1,122,360
412	Sales Returns and Allowances	5,160	
418	Interest Revenue		1,000
500	Purchases	500,840	
502	Purchases Returns and Allowances		4,040
503	Transportation-In	7,840	
505	Advertising Expense	78,000	
508	Sales Salaries Expense	138,400	
509	Office Salaries Expense	80,800	
510	Officers' Salaries Expense	160,000	
511	Utilities Expense	4,800	
536	Legal and Accounting Expense	10,000	
540	Interest Expense	600	
567	Miscellaneous Administrative Expense	9,880	
		$1,667,440	$1,667,440

Additional data

1. A total of $3,400 of the prepaid insurance has expired.
2. An inventory of supplies showed that $1,700 are still on hand.
3. Prepaid rent expired during the year is $50,600.
4. Depreciation expense on store equipment is $8,800.
5. Accrued sales salaries are $4,000.
6. Accrued office salaries are $3,000.
7. Merchandise inventory on hand is $350,000.

Prepare the following:

Required

a. A work sheet for the year ended December 31, 2012. Refer to the chart of accounts shown in a separate file at the end of the text for any other account numbers you need.
b. A classified income statement. The only selling expenses are sales salaries, advertising, supplies, and depreciation expense—equipment.
c. A statement of retained earnings.
d. A classified balance sheet.
e. Required closing entries.

Alternate Problems

Problem 6-1A
Journalize merchandise transactions for two different companies (L.O. 1, 3, 4)

a. Candle Carpet Company engaged in the following transactions in August 2012:

Aug.   2   Sold merchandise on account for $300,000; terms 2/10, n/30, FOB shipping point, freight collect.
        18   Received payment for the sale of August 2.
        20   A total of $10,000 of the merchandise sold on August 2 was returned, and a full refund was made because it was the wrong merchandise.
        28   An allowance of $16,000 was granted on the sale of August 2 because some merchandise was found to be damaged; $16,000 cash was returned to the customer.

b. Lee Furniture Company engaged in the following transactions in August 2012:

Aug.   4   Purchased merchandise on account at a cost of $140,000; terms 2/10, n/30, FOB shipping point, freight collect.
         6   Paid freight of $2,000 on the purchase of August 4.
        10   Sold goods for $100,000; terms 2/10, n/30.
        12   Returned $24,000 of the merchandise purchased on August 4.
        14   Paid the amount due on the purchase of August 4.

Required ➡ Prepare journal entries for the transactions.

Problem 6-2A
Journalize merchandise transactions on both buyer's and seller's books (L.O. 1, 3, 4)

Edwardo Auto Parts Company and Spoon Company engaged in the following transactions with each other during August 2012:

Aug.   15   Edwardo Auto Parts Company purchased merchandise on account with a list price of $192,000 from Spoon Company. Trade discounts of 20% and 10% were allowed. Terms were 2/10, n/30, FOB destination, freight prepaid.
        16   The seller paid the freight charges, $2,400.
        17   The buyer requested an allowance of $4,512 against the amount due because the goods were damaged in transit.
        20   The seller granted the allowance requested on August 17.

The buyer paid the amount due on the last day of the discount period.

Required ➡ Record all of the entries required on the books of both the buyer and the seller.

Problem 6-3A
Prepare and post journal entries, and prepare trial balance and classified income statement (L.O. 1-6)

Gardner Company engaged in the following transactions in June 2012, the company's first month of operations:

June   1   Stockholders invested $384,000 cash and $144,000 of merchandise inventory in the business in exchange for capital stock.
         3   Merchandise was purchased on account, $192,000; terms 2/10, n/30, FOB shipping point, freight collect.
         4   Paid freight on the June 3 purchase, $5,280.
         7   Merchandise was purchased on account, $96,000; terms 2/10, n/30, FOB destination, freight prepaid.
        10   Sold merchandise on account, $230,400; terms 2/10, n/30, FOB shipping point, freight collect.
        11   Returned $28,800 of the merchandise purchased on June 3.
        12   Paid the amount due on the purchase of June 3.
        13   Sold merchandise on account, $240,000; terms 2/10, n/30, FOB destination, freight prepaid.
        14   Paid freight on sale of June 13, $14,400.
        20   Paid the amount due on the purchase of June 7.
        21   $48,000 of the goods sold on June 13 were returned for credit.

22   Received the amount due on sale of June 13.

25   Received the amount due on sale of June 10.

29   Paid rent for the administration building for June, $19,200.

30   Paid sales salaries of $57,600 for June.

30   Purchased merchandise on account, $48,000; terms 2/10, n/30, FOB destination, freight prepaid.

The inventory on hand on June 30 was $288,000.

◖ *Additional data*

a. Prepare journal entries for the transactions.

◖ *Required*

b. Post the journal entries to the proper ledger accounts. Use the account numbers in the chart of accounts shown in a separate file at the end of the text. Assume that all postings are from page 10 of the general journal.

c. Prepare a trial balance as of June 30, 2012.

d. Prepare a classified income statement for the month ended June 30, 2012. No adjusting entries are needed.

Organized on May 1, 2012, Noah Cabinet Company engaged in the following transactions:

Problem 6-4A
Prepare and post
journal entries;
prepare trial balance
and classified income
statement (L.O. 1-6)

May   1   The stockholders invested $900,000 in this new business by purchasing capital stock.

1   Purchased merchandise on account from String Company, $46,800; terms n/60, FOB shipping point, freight collect.

3   Sold merchandise for cash, $28,800.

6   Paid transportation charges on May 1 purchase, $1,440 cash.

7   Returned $3,600 of merchandise to String Company due to improper size.

10   Requested and received an allowance of $1,800 from String Company for improper quality of certain items.

14   Sold merchandise on account to Texas Company, $18,000; terms 2/20, n/30, FOB shipping point, freight collect.

16   Issued cash refund for return of merchandise relating to sale made on May 3, $180.

18   Purchased merchandise on account from Tan Company invoiced at $28,800; terms 2/15, n/30, FOB shipping point, freight collect.

18   Received a bill for freight charges of $900 from Ball Trucking Company on the purchase from Tan Company.

19   Texas Company returned $360 of merchandise purchased on May 14.

24   Returned $2,880 of defective merchandise to Tan Company. Received full credit.

28   Texas Company remitted balance due on sale of May 14.

31   Paid Tan Company for the purchase of May 18 after adjusting for transaction of May 24.

31   Paid miscellaneous selling expenses of $7,200.

31   Paid miscellaneous administrative expenses of $10,800.

The May 31st inventory is $57,600.

◖ *Additional data*

From the data for Noah Cabinet Company:

◖ *Required*

a. Journalize the transactions. Round all amounts to the nearest dollar.

b. Post the entries to the proper ledger accounts. Use the account numbers appearing in the chart of account shown in a separate file at the end of the text. Assume all postings are from page 5 of the general journal. (There were no adjusting journal entries.)

c. Prepare a trial balance.

d. Prepare a classified income statement for the month ended May 31, 2012.

Problem 6-5A
Prepare a work sheet,
classified income
statement, statement
of retained earnings,
classified balance
sheet, and closing
entries (based on
Appendix) (L.O. 5-8)

The following data are for Bayer Lamp Company:

BAYER LAMP COMPANY
Trial Balance
December 31, 2012

Acct. No.	Account Title	Debits	Credits
100	Cash	$ 228,800	
103	Accounts Receivable	193,200	
105	Merchandise Inventory, January 1, 2012	166,400	
108	Prepaid Insurance	11,600	
130	Land	240,000	
140	Building	440,000	
141	Accumulated Depreciation—Building		$ 132,000
174	Store Fixtures	222,400	
175	Accumulated Depreciation—Store Fixtures		44,480
200	Accounts Payable		151,600
300	Capital Stock		400,000
310	Retained Earnings, 1/1/12		480,720
410	Sales		2,206,000
411	Sales Discounts	14,800	
412	Sales Returns and Allowances	8,000	
418	Interest Revenue		1,600
500	Purchases	1,251,600	
501	Purchases Discounts		10,400
502	Purchases Returns and Allowances		5,600
503	Transportation-In	29,200	
505	Advertising Expense	48,000	
508	Sales Salaries Expense	256,000	
509	Office Salaries Expense	296,000	
519	Delivery Expense	18,400	
540	Interest Expense	8,000	
		$3,432,400	$3,432,400

Additional data
1. Depreciation expense on the store building is $8,800.
2. Depreciation expense on the store fixtures is $22,240.
3. Accrued sales salaries are $5,600.
4. Insurance expired in 2012 is $10,000.
5. Cost of merchandise inventory on hand December 31, 2012, is $222,000.

Required Prepare the following:

a. A work sheet for the year ended December 31, 2012. Refer to the chart of accounts shown in a separate file at the end of the text for any other account numbers you need.
b. A classified income statement. The only administrative expenses are office salaries and insurance. The building depreciation is on the store building.
c. A statement of retained earnings.
d. A classified balance sheet.
e. The required closing entries.

Beyond the Numbers—Critical Thinking

Business Decision Case 6-1
Prepare income statements and evaluate feasibility
(L.O. 5, 6)

Candy's Shirts, Inc., has an opportunity to purchase 40,000 shirts with the logo of her favorite school in January 2011. Candy, who is not currently in business, is considering buying these shirts and then renting a display cart from which to sell these shirts (called a kiosk) in a shopping mall. Based on the following information and estimates, Candy needs to decide if the business would be profitable:

1. Cost of the 40,000 shirts, all of which must be purchased in January 2011, is $440,000.
2. Candy thinks it would take two years to sell all of the shirts. She estimates her sales at 25,000 shirts in 2011 and 15,000 shirts in 2012.
3. Rent of the kiosk would be $1,500 per month in 2011 and $1,600 per month in 2012.
4. Candy can buy some counters on which to display the merchandise for $4,000. She could sell the counters for $500 at the end of the second year.
5. Candy estimates the cost to decorate her kiosk would be $2,500.
6. Candy would hire employees and pay them $1 per shirt sold.
7. Candy plans to sell the shirts for $17 each.
8. Candy and her husband purchased $100,000 of capital stock in the business. Therefore, she plans to borrow $400,000 from their family banker. Interest expense on this loan will be $52,000 in 2011 and $6,500 in 2012. Candy plans to repay $300,000 on January 2, 2012, and the remaining $100,000 on July 1, 2012.
9. Candy needs to rent some storage space because all 40,000 shirts cannot be stored at the kiosk. Storage space costs $2,500 per year.

a. Prepare estimated income statements for 2011 and 2012 for Candy's business. Does it appear that the business will be profitable?

 Required

b. Will Candy have the cash available to pay the bank loan as she planned?

In the Annual Report Appendix, refer to the consolidated statements of income for Wal-Mart Stores, Inc. Calculate the gross margin percentage and write an explanation of what the results mean for each of the three years presented.

Business Decision Case 6-2
Analyze the importance of the gross margin percentage (L.O. 7)

Refer to the consolidated statements of income of Wal-Mart Stores, Inc., in the Annual Report Appendix. Identify the 2011, 2010, and 2009 net sales; cost of goods sold; operating, selling, general and administrative expenses; and operating income. Do the results present a favorable trend? Comment on the results.

Annual Report Analysis 6-3
Classify income statement items and calculate gross margin percentages (L.O. 6, 7)

Based on the ethics case related to World Auto Parts Corporation on page 232, respond in writing to the following questions:

Ethics Case—Writing Experience 6-4
Respond to questions regarding ethics case

a. Do you agree that the total impact of this practice could be as much as $10 million?
b. Are the small suppliers probably better off going along with the practice?
c. Is this practice ethical?

In teams of two or three students, go to the library (or find an annual report at www.sec.gov/edgar.shtml) to locate one merchandising company's annual report for the most recent year. Calculate the company's gross margin percentage for each of the most recent three years. As a team, write a memorandum to the instructor showing your calculations and commenting on the results. The heading of the memorandum should contain the date, to whom it is written, from whom, and the subject matter.

Group Project 6-5
Undertake library project concerning annual reports—gross margin percentages (L.O. 7)

In a team of two or three students, contact a variety of businesses in your area and inquire as to the types of sales discount terms they offer to credit customers and the types of purchase discount terms they are offered by their suppliers. Calculate the approximate annual rate of interest implied in several of the more common discount terms. For instance, the book states that the implied annual rate of interest on terms of 2/10, n/30 is 36%, assuming we use a 360-day year. Present your findings in a written report to your instructor.

Group Project 6-6
Investigate sales and purchase discounts offered

In a team of two or three students, obtain access to several annual reports of companies in different industries (see www.sec.gov/edgar.shtml.) Examine their income statements and identify differences in their formats. Discuss these differences within your group and then present your findings in a report to your instructor.

Group Project 6-7
Study income statements in annual reports

Using the Internet—A View of the Real World

Internet Project 6-8
Investigate the Hasbro website

Internet Project 6–8 Visit the Hasbro, Inc. website at:

http://www.hasbro.com

Browse around the site for interesting information. What products do they sell? What journal entries would they make to record sales of these products? Write a report to your instructor summarizing your experience at this site.

Answers to Self-Test

True-False

1. **False**. Sales discounts, as well as sales returns and allowances, are deducted from gross sales.
2. **True**. Under perpetual inventory procedure, the Merchandise Inventory account is debited for each purchase and credited for each sale.
3. **True**. Purchase Discounts and Purchase Returns and Allowances are contra accounts to the Purchases account. The balances of those accounts are deducted from purchases to arrive at net purchases.

4. **False**. Consigned goods delivered to another party for attempted sale are included in the ending inventory of the company that sent the goods.
5. **False**. An unclassified income statement, not a classified income statement, has only two categories of items.

Multiple-Choice

1. **d.** Trade discounts are not recorded on the books of either a buyer or a seller. In other words, the invoice price of sales (purchases) is recorded: $4,000 \times 0.8 = \$3,200$
2. **b.** The cost of goods sold is computed as follows:

Beginning inventory	$ 60,000
Net cost of purchases	240,000
Cost of goods available for sale	$300,000
Ending inventory	72,000
Cost of goods sold	$228,000

3. **b.** Purchase discounts are based on invoice prices less purchase returns and allowances, if any.

Purchase
discount = ($12,000 − $2,000) × 0.02 = $200

4. **e.** All of the sections mentioned in (a–d) appear in a classified income statement. Current assets appear on a classified balance sheet.
5. **b.** Merchandise Inventory is debited for the cost of ending inventory.

[1]You may close debit balanced accounts (in the income statement) before credit balanced accounts. This practice does not affect the balance of the Income Summary account or the amount of net income.

Careers in Accounting

Choosing an Accounting Career

Chapter 7 discusses how companies have a choice in inventory cost methods between specific identification, FIFO, LIFO, and weighted-average. Similarly, one of the greatest benefits of obtaining an accounting degree is the broad range of career choices available. There are over 40 different types of accounting jobs available in public accounting, private industry, and governmental accounting. For example, check out the list of accounting jobs at www.uncw.edu/career/accountancy.html#careers.

One of the primary reasons many students go into accounting is successful job placement. Accounting majors have been better able to find positions than majors in any of the other business options, with the possible exception of management information systems (MIS). Even the relative demand for MIS majors has diminished recently, while the demand for accounting majors remains strong. We are currently experiencing a shortage of accounting majors across the nation. Another important factor to keep in mind regarding job placement is where you would like to be three to five years from now. Accounting offers an excellent foundation with opportunities for advancement, whereby many accounting graduates make double their entry-level salary in only five years.

Many students pursue an accounting degree because it does not restrict their career opportunities as much as having a different business degree. For example, with an accounting degree, a student can apply for positions in management, marketing, and finance, as well as accounting. In fact, many recruiters in business favor accounting graduates because they recognize an accounting degree as a more difficult business degree to obtain. However, management, marketing, and finance students cannot apply for accounting positions because they lack necessary accounting coursework. In fact, with some additional courses in systems, an accounting major is well equipped to pursue a career in any business field including information systems.

7

Measuring and Reporting Inventories

Have you ever taken advantage of a pre-inventory sale at your favorite retail store? Many stores offer bargain prices to reduce the merchandise on hand and to minimize the time and expense of taking the inventory. A smaller inventory also enhances the probability of taking an accurate inventory since the store has less merchandise to count. From Chapter 6 you know that companies use inventory amounts to determine the cost of goods sold; this major expense affects a merchandising company's net income. In this chapter, you learn how important inventories are in preparing an accurate income statement, statement of retained earnings, and balance sheet.

This chapter discusses merchandise inventory carried by merchandising retailers and wholesalers. **Merchandise inventory** is the quantity of goods held by a merchandising company for resale to customers. Merchandising companies determine the quantity of inventory items by a physical count.

The merchandise inventory figure used by accountants depends on the quantity of inventory items and the cost of the items. This chapter discusses four accepted methods of costing the items: (1) specific identification; (2) first-in, first-out (FIFO); (3) last-in, first-out (LIFO); and (4) weighted-average. Each method has advantages and disadvantages.

This chapter stresses the importance of having accurate inventory figures and the serious consequences of using inaccurate inventory figures. When you finish this chapter, you should understand how taking inventory connects with the cost of goods sold figure on the store's income statement, the retained earnings amount on the statement of retained earnings, and both the inventory figure and the retained earnings amount on the store's balance sheet.

(continued)

Inventories and Cost of Goods Sold

Inventory is often the largest and most important asset owned by a merchandising business. The inventory of some companies, like car dealerships or jewelry stores, may cost several times more than any other asset the company owns. As an asset, the inventory figure has a direct impact on reporting the solvency of the company in the balance sheet. As a factor in determining cost of goods sold, the inventory figure has a direct impact on the profitability of the company's operations as reported in the income statement. Thus, the importance of the inventory figure should not be underestimated.

Importance of Proper Inventory Valuation

A merchandising company can prepare accurate income statements, statements of retained earnings, and balance sheets only if its inventory is correctly valued. On the income statement, a company using the periodic inventory procedure takes a physical inventory to determine the cost of goods sold. Since the cost of goods sold figure affects the company's net income, it also affects the balance of retained earnings on the statement of retained earnings. On the balance sheet, incorrect inventory amounts affect both the reported ending inventory and retained earnings. Inventories appear on the balance sheet under the heading "Current Assets," which reports current assets in a descending order of liquidity. Because inventories are consumed or converted into cash within a year or one operating cycle, whichever is longer, inventories usually follow cash and receivables on the balance sheet.

Recall that under the periodic inventory procedure we determine the cost of goods sold figure by adding the beginning inventory to the net cost of purchases and deducting the ending inventory. In each accounting period, the appropriate expenses must be matched with the revenues of that period to determine the net income. Applied to inventory, matching involves determining (1) how much of the cost of goods available for sale during the period should be deducted from current revenues and (2) how much should be allocated to goods on hand and thus carried forward as an asset (merchandise inventory) in the balance sheet to be matched against future revenues. Because we determine the cost of goods sold by deducting the ending inventory from the cost of goods available for sale, a highly significant relationship exists: *Net income for an accounting period depends directly on the valuation of ending inventory.* This relationship involves three items:

First, a merchandising company must be sure that it has properly valued its ending inventory. If the ending inventory is overstated, cost of goods sold is understated, resulting in an overstatement of gross margin and net income. Also, overstatement of ending inventory causes current assets, total assets, and retained earnings to be overstated. Thus, any change in the calculation of ending inventory is reflected, dollar for dollar (ignoring any income tax effects), in net income, current assets, total assets, and retained earnings.

Second, when a company misstates its ending inventory in the current year, the company carries forward that misstatement into the next year. This misstatement occurs because the ending inventory amount of the current year is the beginning inventory amount for the next year.

Third, an error in one period's ending inventory automatically causes an error in net income in the opposite direction in the next period. After two years, however, the error washes out, and assets and retained earnings are properly stated.

Illustrations 7.1 and 7.2 prove that net income for an accounting period depends directly on the valuation of the inventory. Allen Company's income statements and the statments of retained earnings for years 2011 and 2012 show this relationship.

Illustration 7.1   Effects of an Overstated Ending Inventory

ALLEN COMPANY

For Year Ended December 31, 2011

Income Statement	Ending Inventory Correctly Stated		Ending Inventory Overstated By $5,000	
Sales		$400,000		$400,000
Cost of goods available for sale	$300,000		$300,000	
Ending inventory	35,000		40,000	
Cost of goods sold		265,000		260,000
Gross margin		$135,000		$140,000
Other expenses		$85,000		85,000
Net income		$ 50,000		$55,000
Statement of Retained Earnings				
Beginning retained earnings		$120,000		$120,000
Net income		50,000		55,000
Ending retained earnings		$170,000		$175,000

Note to the Student
The concept of cost of goods sold versus ending inventory is sometimes difficult to understand. Refer to the text illustration showing that Goods Available for Sale is divided between cost of goods sold and ending inventory. This means that everything available for sale is either sold or not sold. If it is sold, it is a part of cost of goods sold. If it is not sold, it is part of ending inventory.

Illustration 7.2   Effects of an Overstated Beginning Inventory

ALLEN COMPANY

For Year Ended December 31, 2012

Income Statement	Beginning Inventory Correctly Stated		Beginning Inventory Overstated By $5,000	
Sales		$425,000		$425,000
Beginning inventory	$ 35,000		$40,000	
Purchases	290,000		290,000	
Cost of goods available for sale	$325,000		$330,000	
Ending inventory	45,000		45,000	
Cost of goods sold		280,000		285,000
Gross margin		$145,000		$140,000
Other expenses		53,500		53,500
Net income		$ 91,500		$ 86,500
Statement of Retained Earnings				
Beginning retained earnings		$170,000		$175,000
Net income		91,500		86,500
Ending retained earnings		$261,500		$261,500

In Illustration 7.1, the correctly stated ending inventory for the year 2011 is $35,000. As a result, Allen has a gross margin of $135,000 and net income of $50,000. The statement of retained earnings shows a beginning retained earnings of $120,000 and an ending retained earnings of $170,000. When the ending inventory is overstated by $5,000, as shown on the right in Illustration 7.1, the gross margin is $140,000, and net income is $55,000. The statement of retained earnings then has an ending retained earnings of $175,000. The ending inventory overstatement of $5,000 causes a $5,000 overstatement of net income and a $5,000 overstatement of retained earnings. The balance sheet would show both an overstated inventory and an overstated retained earnings. Due to the error in ending inventory, both the stockholders and creditors may overestimate the profitability of the business.

Illustration 7.2 is a continuation of Illustration 7.1 and contains Allen's operating results for the year ended December 31, 2012. Note that the ending inventory in Illustration 7.1 now becomes the beginning inventory of Illustration 7.2. However, Allen's inventory at December 31, 2012, is now an accurate inventory of $45,000. As a result, the gross margin in the income statement with the beginning inventory correctly stated is $145,000, and Allen Company has net income of $91,500 and an ending retained earnings of $261,500. In the income statement columns at the right, in which the beginning inventory is overstated by $5,000, the gross margin is $140,000 and net income is $86,500, with the ending retained earnings also at $261,500.

Thus, in contrast to an overstated ending inventory, resulting in an overstatement of net income, an overstated beginning inventory results in an understatement of net income. If the beginning inventory is overstated, then cost of goods available for sale and cost of goods sold also are overstated. Consequently, gross margin and net income are understated. Note, however, that when net income in the second year is closed to retained earnings, the retained earnings account is stated at its proper amount. The overstatement of net income in the first year is offset by the understatement of net income in the second year. For the two years combined the net income is correct. At the end of the second year, the balance sheet contains the correct amounts for both inventory and retained earnings. Illustration 7.3 summarizes the effects of errors of inventory valuation:

Illustration 7.3   Inventory Errors

	Ending Inventory		Beginning Inventory	
	Understated	**Overstated**	**Understated**	**Overstated**
Cost of good sold	Overstated	Understated	Understated	Overstated
Net income	Understated	Overstated	Overstated	Understated

Determining Inventory Cost

To place the proper valuation on inventory, a business must answer the question: Which costs should be included in inventory cost? Then, when the business purchases identical goods at different costs, it must answer the question: Which cost should be assigned to the items sold? In this section, you learn how accountants answer these questions.

The costs included in inventory depend on two variables: quantity and price. To arrive at a current inventory figure, companies must begin with an accurate physical count of inventory items. They multiply the quantity of inventory by the unit cost to compute the cost of ending inventory. This section discusses the taking of a physical inventory and the methods of costing the physical inventory under both perpetual and periodic inventory procedures. The remainder of the chapter discusses departures from the cost basis of inventory measurement.

Taking a Physical Inventory

As briefly described in Chapter 6, to take a physical inventory, a company must count, weigh, measure, or estimate the physical quantities of the goods on hand. For example, a clothing store may count its suits; a hardware store may weigh bolts, washers, and nails; a gasoline company may measure gasoline in storage tanks; and a lumberyard may estimate quantities of lumber, coal, or other bulky materials. Throughout the taking of a physical inventory, the goal should be accuracy.

Taking a physical inventory may disrupt the normal operations of a business. Thus, the count should be administered as quickly and as efficiently as possible. The actual taking of the inventory is not an accounting function; however, accountants

Illustration 7.4   Inventory Tag

**Inventory Tag
JMA Corp.**

Inventory Tag No. _281_   Date _____

Description _____

_____

Location _____

Quantity Counted _____

Counted by _____

Checked by _____

- -

Duplicate Inventory Tag

Inventory Tag No. _281_   Date _____

Description _____

_____

Location _____

Quantity Counted _____

Counted by _____

Checked by _____

---

often plan and coordinate the count. Proper forms are required to record accurate counts and determine totals. Identification names or symbols must be chosen, and those persons who count, weigh, or measure the inventory items must know these symbols.

Taking a physical inventory often involves using inventory tags, such as that in Illustration 7.4. These tags are consecutively numbered for control purposes. A tag usually consists of a stub and a detachable duplicate section. The duplicate section facilitates checking discrepancies. The format of the tags can vary. However, the tag usually provides space for (1) a detailed description and identification of inventory items by product, class, and model; (2) location of items; (3) quantity of items on hand; and (4) initials of the counters and checkers.

The descriptive information and count may be entered on one copy of the tag by one team of counters. Another team of counters may record its count on the duplicate copy of the tag. Discrepancies between counts of the same items by different teams are reconciled by supervisors, and the correct counts are assembled on intermediate inventory sheets. Only when the inventory counts are completed and checked does management send the final sheets to the accounting department for pricing and extensions (quantity × price). The tabulated result is the dollar amount of the physical inventory. Later in the chapter we explain the different methods accountants use to cost inventory.

Usually, inventory cost includes all the necessary outlays to obtain the goods, get the goods ready to sell, and have the goods in the desired location for sale to customers. Thus, inventory cost includes:

Costs Included in Inventory Cost

1. Seller's invoice price less any purchase discount.
2. Cost of the buyer's insurance to cover the goods while in transit.
3. Transportation charges when borne by the buyer.
4. Handling costs, such as the cost of pressing clothes wrinkled during shipment.

In theory, the cost of each unit of inventory should include its net invoice price plus its share of other costs incurred in shipment. The 1986 Tax Reform Act required companies to assign these costs to inventory for tax purposes. For accounting purposes, these cost assignments are recommended but not required.

Practical difficulties arise in allocating some of these costs to inventory items. Assume, for example, that the freight bill on a shipment of clothes does not separate out the cost of shipping one shirt. Also, assume that the company wants to include the freight cost as part of the inventory cost of the shirt. Then, the freight cost would have to be *allocated* to each unit because it cannot be measured directly. In practice, allocations of freight, insurance, and handling costs to the individual units of inventory purchased are often not worth the additional cost. Consequently, in the past many companies have not assigned the costs of freight, insurance, and handling to inventory. Instead, they have expensed these costs as incurred. When companies omit these costs from both beginning and ending inventories, they minimize the effect of expensing these costs on net income. The required allocation for tax purposes has probably resulted in many companies using the same inventory amounts in their financial statements.

Even if a company derives a cost for each unit in inventory, the inventory valuation problem is not solved. Management must consider two other aspects of the problem:

Note to the Student
Hi-Fi Buys, Inc.
Hi-Fi Buys is a well-known retailer of electronic products, including home stereo systems, televisions, VCRs, DVDs, and cameras.

1. If goods were purchased at varying unit costs, how should the cost of goods available for sale be allocated between the units sold and those that remain in inventory? For example, assume Hi-Fi Buys, Inc., purchased two identical DVD players for resale. One cost $250 and the other, $200. If one was sold during the period, should Hi-Fi Buys assign it a cost of $250, $200, or an average cost of $225?
2. Does the fact that current replacement costs are less than the costs of some units in inventory have any bearing on the amount at which inventory should be carried? Using the same example, if Hi-Fi Buys can currently buy all DVD players for $200, is it reasonable to carry some units in inventory at $250 rather than $200?

We answer these questions in the next section.

Inventory Valuation under Changing Prices

Generally, companies should account for inventories at historical cost; that is, the cost at which the items were purchased. However, this rule does not indicate how to assign costs to ending inventory and to cost of goods sold when the goods have been purchased at different unit costs. For example, suppose a retailer has three shirts on hand. One costs $20; another, $22; and a third, $24. If the retailer sells two shirts for $30 each, what is the cost of the two shirts sold?

Methods of Determining Inventory Cost

Accountants developed these four inventory costing methods to solve costing problems: (1) specific identification; (2) first-in, first-out (FIFO); (3) last-in, first-out (LIFO); and (4) weighted-average. Before explaining the inventory costing methods, we briefly introduce the perpetual inventory procedure and compare periodic and perpetual inventory procedures.

Perpetual Inventory Procedure

In Chapter 6, the emphasis was on the periodic inventory procedure. Under the periodic inventory procedure, firms debit the Purchases account when goods are acquired; they use other accounts, such as Purchase Discounts, Purchase Returns and Allowances, and Transportation-In, for purchase-related transactions. Companies determine cost of goods sold only at the end of the period as the difference between cost of goods available for sale and ending inventory. They keep no records of the cost of items as they are sold, and they have no information on possible inventory shortages. They assume any goods not in ending inventory have been sold.

The availability of inventory management software packages is causing more and more businesses to change from periodic to perpetual inventory procedures. Under

Illustration 7.5   Perpetual Inventory Record (FIFO menthod)

| | | | | Item TV-96874 | | | Maximum 26 | | | | |
| | | | | Location | | | Minimum 6 | | | | |

| 2010 Date | Purchased | | | Sold | | | Balance | | |
	Units	Unit Cost	Total Cost	Units	Unit Cost	Total Cost	Units	Unit Cost	Total Cost
Beg. inv.							8	$300	$2,400
July 5	10	$300	$3,000				18	300	5,400
7				12	$300	$3,600	6	300	1,800
12	10	315	3,150				{ 6	300	1,800
22				{ 6	300	1,800	{ 10	315	3,150
				{ 2	315	630			
24	8	320	2,560				8	315	2,520
							{ 8	315	2,520
							{ 8	320	2,560

the perpetual inventory procedure, companies have no Purchases and purchase-related accounts. Instead, they make all entries involving merchandise purchased for sale to customers directly in the Merchandise Inventory account. Thus, they debit or credit Merchandise Inventory in place of debiting or crediting Purchases, Purchase Discounts, Purchase Returns and Allowances, and Transportation-In. At the time of each sale, firms make two entries: the first debits Accounts Receivable or Cash and credits Sales at the retail selling price. The second debits Cost of Goods Sold and credits Merchandise Inventory at cost. Therefore, at the end of the period the Merchandise Inventory account shows the cost of the inventory that should be on hand. Comparison of this amount with the cost obtained by taking and pricing a physical inventory may reveal inventory shortages. Thus, the perpetual inventory procedure is an important element in providing internal control over goods in inventory.

Note to the Student
The first of the two entries can be described as the revenue phase (sales are recorded) and the other as the expense phase (cost of goods sold is recorded).

Perpetual Inventory Records   Even though companies could apply the perpetual inventory procedure manually, tracking units and dollars in and out of inventory is much easier using a computer. Both manual and computer processing maintain a record for each item in inventory. Look at Illustration 7.5, an inventory record for Entertainment World, a firm that sells many different brands of television sets. This inventory record shows the information on one particular brand and model of television set carried in inventory. Other information on the record includes (1) the maximum and minimum number of units the company wishes to stock at any time, (2) when and how many units were acquired and at what cost, and (3) when and how many units were sold and what cost was assigned to cost of goods sold. The number of units on hand and their cost are readily available also. Entertainment World assumes that the first units acquired are the first units sold. This assumption is the first-in, first-out (FIFO) method of inventory costing; we will discuss it later.

USES OF TECHNOLOGY Keeping track of inventories under a perpetual inventory system is much more cost-effective with computers. Under a manual system, the cost of an up-to-date inventory for stores with high turnover would outweigh the benefit. Most retail stores use scanning devices to read the inventory numbers of products purchased at the cash register. These scanning tags not only provide accurate sales prices but also record the merchandise sold so that the total cost of the store's inventory is up to date.

An Accounting Perspective

Comparing Journal Entries under the Periodic and Perpetual Inventory Procedures

The following comparison reveals several differences between accounting for inventories under the periodic and perpetual procedures. We explain these differences by using data from Illustration 7.5 and making additional assumptions. Later, we discuss other journal entries under the perpetual inventory procedure.

These entries record the purchase on July 5 under each of the methods:

Periodic Procedure			Perpetual Procedure		
Purchases	3,000		Merchandise Inventory	3,000	
Accounts Payable		3,000	Accounts Payable		3,000

Assuming the merchandise sold on July 7 was priced at $4,800, these entries record the sale:

Periodic Procedure			Perpetual Procedure		
Accounts Receivable	4,800		Accounts Receivable	4,800	
Sales		4,800	Sales		4,800
			Cost of Goods Sold	3,600	
			Merchandise Inventory		3,600

Several other transactions not included in Illustration 7.5 could occur:

1. Assume that two of the units purchased on July 5 were returned to the supplier because they were defective. The entries would be:

Periodic Procedure			Perpetual Procedure		
Accounts Payable	600		Accounts Payable	600	
Purchase Returns and Allowances		600	Merchandise Inventory		600

2. Assume that the supplier instead granted an allowance of $600 to the company because of the defective merchandise. The entries would be:

Periodic Procedure			Perpetual Procedure		
Accounts Payable	600		Accounts Payable	600	
Purchase Returns and Allowances		600	Merchandise Inventory		600

3. Assume that the company incurred and paid freight charges of $100 on the purchase of July 5. The entries would be:

Periodic Procedure			Perpetual Procedure		
Transportation-In	100		Merchandise Inventory	100	
Cash		100	Cash		100

Note to the Student
If Purchase Discounts and Purchase Returns and Allowances accounts are used, they appear as deductions from Purchases on the income statement. Since we have no Purchases account under the perpetual inventory procudure, we cannot deduct any amounts from it, so these accounts cannot exist.

In these entries, notice that under the perpetual inventory procedure, the Merchandise Inventory account records purchases, purchase returns and allowances, purchase discounts, and transportation-in. Also, when goods are sold, the seller debits (increases) Cost of Goods Sold and credits or reduces Merchandise Inventory.

At the end of the accounting period, under the perpetual inventory procedure, the only merchandise-related expense account to be closed is Cost of Goods Sold. The Purchases, Purchase Returns and Allowances, Purchase Discounts, and Transportation-In accounts do not even exist.

Illustration 7.6   Beginning Inventory, Purchases and Sales

Beginning Inventory and Purchases				Sales			
Date	Units	Unit Cost	Total Cost	Date	Units	Price	Total
Beginning inventory	10	$8.00	$ 80	March 10	10	$12.00	$120
March 2	10	8.50	85	July 14	20	12.00	240
May 28	20	8.40	168	September 7	10	14.00	140
August 12	10	9.00	90	November 22	20	14.00	280
October 12	20	8.80	176				
December 21	10	9.10	91				
	80		$690		60		$780

Ending inventory = 20 units, determined by taking a physical inventory.

BUSINESS INSIGHT When you buy a box of breakfast cereal at the supermarket, the cashier scans the bar code on the box. The name of the item and the price appear on a video display that you can see. The information is also printed on the sales slip so that you can later compare the items paid for with the items received. But this is not the end of the story. The information is also fed to the store's computer to update the inventory records. The information is included with other information and is used to order more merchandise from the warehouse so the items can be replenished in the store. At a certain point, the company also uses the reduced inventory levels to order more merchandise from suppliers, such as wholesalers that supply the region with breakfast cereals and other goods. The paperwork for the purchase and payment are often handled electronically through a process called *electronic data interchange (EDI)* and *electronic funds transfer (EFT)*.

An Accounting Perspective

An Illustration of Four Inventory Methods under the Periodic and Perpetual Inventory Procedures

Using the data for purchases, sales, and beginning inventory in Illustration 7.6, next we explain the four inventory costing methods. Except for the specific identification method, we first present all of the methods using the periodic inventory procedure and then present all of the methods using the perpetual inventory procedure. Total goods available for sale consist of 80 units with a total cost of $690. A physical inventory determined that 20 units are on hand at the end of the period. Sales revenue for the 60 units sold was $780. The questions to be answered are: What is the cost of the 20 units in inventory? What is the cost of the 60 units sold?

Specific Identification   The **specific identification method** of inventory costing attaches the actual cost to an identifiable unit of product. Firms find this method easy to apply when purchasing and selling large inventory items such as autos. Under the specific identification method, the firm must identify each unit in inventory, unless it is unique, with a serial number or identification tag.

Objective 3
Calculate cost of ending inventory and cost of goods sold under the four major inventory costing methods using periodic and perpetual inventory procedures.

To illustrate, assume that the company in Illustration 7.6 can identify the 20 units on hand at year-end as 10 units from the August 12 purchase and 10 units from the December 21 purchase. The company computes the ending inventory as shown in Illustration 7.7; it subtracts the $181 ending inventory cost from the $690 cost of goods available for sale to obtain the $509 cost of goods sold. Note that you can also determine the cost of goods sold for the year by recording the cost of each unit sold. The $509 cost of goods sold is an expense on the income statement, and the $181 ending inventory is a current asset on the balance sheet.

The specific identification costing method attaches cost to an identifiable unit of inventory. The method does not involve any assumptions about the flow of the costs as in the other inventory costing methods. Conceptually, the method matches

Reinforcing Problems
E7-2 Compute the impact on net income under specific identification.
P7-3 Maximize and minimize gross margin using specific identification.

Illustration 7.7   Determining Ending Inventory under Specific Identificaiton

	Units	Unit Cost	Total Cost
Ending inventory composed of purchases made on:			
August 12	10	$ 9.00	$ 90
December 21	10	9.10	91
Ending inventory	20		$181
Cost of goods sold composed of:			
Beginning inventory	10	8.00	$ 80
Purchases made on:			
March 2	10	8.50	85
May 28	20	8.40	168
October 12	20	8.80	176
			$509
Cost of goods available for sale			$690
Ending inventory			181
Cost of goods sold			$509

the cost to the physical flow of the inventory and eliminates the emphasis on the timing of the cost determination. Therefore, periodic and perpetual inventory procedures produce the same results for the specific identification method.

FIFO (First-In, First-Out) Under the Periodic Inventory Procedure   The FIFO (first-in, first-out) method of inventory costing assumes that the costs of the first goods purchased are those charged to cost of goods sold when the company actually sells goods. This method assumes the first goods purchased are the first goods sold. In some companies, the first units in (bought) must be the first units out (sold) to avoid large losses from spoilage. Such items as fresh dairy products, fruits, and vegetables should be sold on a FIFO basis. In these cases, an assumed first-in, first-out flow corresponds with the actual physical flow of goods.

Note to the Student
When determining the ending inventory using the FIFO, you can also use the acronym, LISH, which stands for last in, still here.

Because a company using the FIFO assumes the older units are sold first and the newer units are still on hand, the ending inventory consists of the most recent purchases. When using the periodic inventory procedure, to determine the cost of the ending inventory at the end of the period under FIFO, you would begin by listing the cost of the most recent purchase. If the ending inventory contains more units than acquired in the most recent purchase, it also includes units from the next-to-the-latest purchase at the unit cost incurred, and so on. You would list these units from the latest purchases until that number agrees with the units in the ending inventory.

In Illustration 7.8, you can see how to determine the cost of ending inventory under FIFO using periodic inventory procedure. The company assumes that the 20 units in inventory consist of 10 units purchased December 21 and 10 units purchased October 12. The total cost of ending inventory is $179, and the cost of goods sold is $511.

We show the relationship between the cost of goods sold and the cost of ending inventory under FIFO using the periodic inventory procedure in Illustration 7.9. The 80 units in cost of goods available for sale consists of the beginning inventory and all of the purchases during the period. Under FIFO, the ending inventory of 20 units consists of the most recent purchases—10 units of the December 21 purchase and 10 units of the October 12 purchase—costing $179. We assume the beginning inventory and other earlier purchases have been sold during the period, representing the cost of goods sold of $511.

Illustration 7.8   Determining FIFO Cost of Ending Inventory under the Periodic Inventory Procedure

	Units	Unit Cost	Total Cost
Ending inventory composed of purchases made on:			
December 21	10	$9.10	$ 91
October 12	10	8.80	88
Ending inventory	20		$179
Cost of goods sold composed of:			
Beginning inventory	10	8.00	$ 80
Purchases made on:			
March 2	10	8.50	85
May 28	20	8.40	168
August 12	10	9.00	90
October 12	10	8.80	88
			$511
Cost of goods available for sale			$690
Ending inventory			179
Cost of goods sold			$511

Used to establish the ending balance in the Merchandise Inventory account.

Illustration 7.9   FIFO Flow of Costs

LIFO (Last-In, First-Out) under the Periodic Inventory Procedure   The **LIFO (last-in, first-out)** method of inventory costing assumes that the costs of the most recent purchases are the first costs charged to cost of goods sold when the company actually sells the goods.

In Illustration 7.10, we show the use of LIFO under the periodic inventory procedure. Since the company charges the latest costs to cost of goods sold under the periodic inventory procedure, the ending inventory always consists of the oldest costs. Therefore, when determining the cost of inventory under the periodic inventory procedure, the company lists the oldest units and their costs. The first units listed are those in beginning inventory, then the first purchase, and so on, until the number listed agrees with the units in ending inventory. Thus, ending inventory in Illustration 7.10 consists of the 10 units from beginning inventory and the 10 units purchased on March 2. The total cost of these 20 units, $165, is the ending inventory cost; the cost of goods sold is $525. Illustration 7.11 is a graphic representation of the LIFO flow of costs under the periodic inventory procedure.

Note to the Student
When determining the ending inventory using the LIFO, you can also use the acronym, FISH, which stands for first in, still here.

Illustration 7.10   Determining LIFO Cost of Ending Inventory under the Periodic Inventory Procedure

	Units	Unit Cost	Total Cost
Ending inventory composed of:			
Beginning inventory	10	$8.00	$ 80
March 2 purchase	10	8.50	85
Ending inventory	20		$165
Cost of goods sold composed of purchases made on:			
December 21	10	9.10	$ 91
October 12	20	8.80	176
August 12	10	9.00	90
May 28	20	8.40	168
			$525
Cost of goods available for sale			$690
Ending inventory			165
Cost of goods sold			$525

Illustration 7.11   LIFO Flow of Costs under the Periodic Inventory Procedure

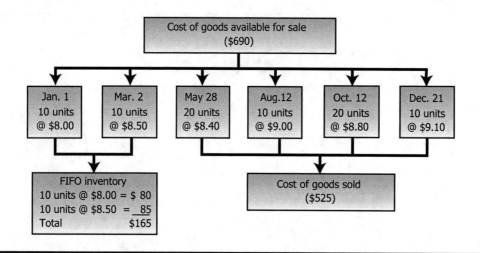

Reinforcing Problem
E7-10 Prepare journal entries affecting inventory using weighted-average periodic inventory procedure.

Weighted-Average under the Periodic Inventory Procedure   The **weighted-average method** of inventory costing is a means of costing ending inventory using a weighted-average unit cost. Companies most often use the weighted-average method to determine a cost for units that are basically the same, such as identical games in a toy store or identical electrical tools in a hardware store. Since the units are alike, firms can assign the same unit cost to them.

Under the periodic inventory procedure, a company determines the average cost at the end of the accounting period by dividing the total units purchased plus those in beginning inventory into total cost of goods available for sale. The ending inventory is carried at this per unit cost. To see how a company uses the weighted-average method to determine inventory costs using the periodic inventory procedure, look at Illustration 7.12. Note that we compute weighted-average cost per unit by dividing the cost of units available for sale, $690, by the total number of units available for sale, 80. Thus, the weighted-average cost per unit is $8.625, meaning that each unit sold or remaining in inventory is valued at $8.625.

Illustration 7.12 Determining Ending Inventory under Weighted-Average Method Using the Periodic Inventory Procedure

	Units	Unit Cost	Total Cost
Beginning inventory	10	$8.00	$ 80.00
Purchases			
March 2	10	8.50	85.00
May 28	20	8.40	168.00
August 12	10	9.00	90.00
October 12	20	8.80	176.00
December 21	10	9.10	91.00
Total	80		$690.00

Weighted-average unit cost is
$690 ÷ 80, or $8.625
Ending inventory then is $8.625 x 20 .... 172.50

Cost of goods sold:
$8.625 x 60 .... $517.50

Illustration 7.13 Determining FIFO cost of Ending Inventory under the Perpetual Inventory Procedure

	Purchased			Sold			Balance		
Date	Units	Unit Cost	Total Cost	Units	Unit Cost	Total Cost	Units	Unit Cost	Total Cost
Beg. inv.							10	$8.00	80
Mar. 2	10	$8.50	$85				10	8.00	80
							10	8.50	85
Mar. 10				10	$8.00	$80	10	8.50	85
May 28	20	8.40	168				10	8.50	85
							20	8.40	168
July 14				10	8.50	85			
				10	8.40	85	10	8.40	84
Aug. 12	10	9.00	90				10	8.40	84
							10	9.00	90
Sept. 7				10	8.40	84	10	9.00	90
Oct. 12	20	8.80	176				10	9.00	90
							20	8.80	176
Nov. 22				10	9.00	90			
				10	8.80	88	10	8.80	88
Dec 21	10	9.10	91				10	8.80	88
							10	9.10	91

Sales are assumed to be from the oldest units on hand.

Total of $179 would agree with balance already existing in Merchandise Inventory account.

Total cost of ending inventory = $179

FIFO under the Perpetual Inventory Procedure Under the perpetual inventory procedure, the ending balance in the Merchandise Inventory account reflects the most recent purchases as a result of making the required entries during the period. Also, the firm has already recorded the cost of goods sold in the Cost of Goods Sold account. Illustration 7.13 shows how to determine the cost of ending inventory under FIFO using perpetual inventory procedure. This illustration uses the same format as the earlier perpetual inventory record in Illustration 7.5. The company keeps a record of the balance in the inventory account as it makes purchases and sells items from inventory.

Perpetual Inventory Procedure

Illustration 7.14   Determining LIFO Cost of Ending Inventory under the Perpetual Inventory Procedure

	Purchased			Sold			Balance		
Date	Units	Unit Cost	Total Cost	Units	Unit Cost	Total Cost	Units	Unit Cost	Total Cost
Beg. inv.							10	$8.00	80
Mar. 2	10	$8.50	$85				10	8.00	80
							10	8.50	85
Mar. 10				10	$8.50	$85 ←	10	8.00	80
May 28	20	8.40	168				10	8.00	80
							20	8.40	168
July 14				20	8.40	168 ←	10	8.00	80
Aug. 12	10	9.00	90				10	8.00	80
							10	9.00	90
Sept. 7				10	9.00	90 ←	10	8.00	80
Oct. 12	20	8.80	176				10	8.00	80
							20	8.80	176
Nov. 22				20	8.80	176 ←	10	8.00	80
Dec. 21	10	9.10	91				10	8.00	80
							10	9.10	91

Sales are assumed to be from the most recent purchases.

Total of $171 would agree with balance already existing in Merchandise Inventory account.

Total cost of ending inventory = $171

Reinforcing Problems
E7-3 Compute ending inventory using the FIFO perpetual inventory procedure.
P7-4 Compute cost of goods sold using the FIFO for both perpetual and periodic inventory procedures.

Notice in Illustration 7.13 that each time a sale occurs, the company assumes the items sold are the oldest on hand. Thus, after each transaction, it can readily determine the balance in the Merchandise Inventory account from the perpetual inventory record. The balance after the December 21 purchase represents the 20 units from the most recent purchases. The total cost of ending inventory is $179, which the company reports as a current asset on the balance sheet. During the accounting period, as sales occurred the firm would have debited a total of $511 to Cost of Goods Sold. Adding this $511 to the ending inventory of $179 accounts for the $690 cost of goods available for sale. *Under FIFO, using either perpetual or periodic inventory procedures results in the same total amounts for ending inventory and for cost of goods sold.*

Reinforcing Problem
E7-4 Compute ending inventory under LIFO perpetual inventory procedure.

LIFO under the Perpetual Inventory Procedure   Look at Illustration 7.14 to see the LIFO method using the perpetual inventory procedure. Under this procedure, the inventory composition and balance are updated with each purchase and sale. Notice in Illustration 7.14 that each time a sale occurs, the items sold are assumed to be the most recent ones acquired. Despite numerous purchases and sales during the year, the ending inventory still includes the 10 units from beginning inventory in our example. The remainder of the ending inventory consists of the last purchase because no sale occurred after the December 21 purchase. The total cost of the 20 units in ending inventory is $171; the cost of goods sold is $519. Illustration 7.15 shows graphically the LIFO flow of costs under the perpetual inventory procedure.

Applying LIFO on a perpetual basis during the accounting period, as shown in Illustration 7.14, results in different ending inventory and cost of goods sold figures than applying LIFO only at year-end using periodic inventory procedures. (Compare Illustrations 7.14 and 7.10 to verify that ending inventory and cost of goods sold are different under the two procedures.) For this reason, if LIFO is applied on a perpetual basis during the period, special adjustments are sometimes necessary at year-end to

Illustration 7.15   LIFO Flow of Costs under the Perpetual Inventory Procedure

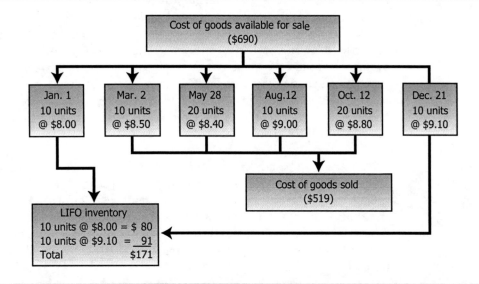

Illustration 7.16   Determining Ending Inventory under Weighted-Average Method Using the Perpetual Inventory Procedure

Date	Purchased Units	Purchased Unit Cost	Purchased Total Cost	Sold Units	Sold Unit Cost	Sold Total Cost	Balance Units	Balance Unit Cost	Balance Total Cost	
Beg. inv.							10	$8.00	80.00	A new unit cost is calculated after each purchase.
Mar. 2	10	$8.50	$85				20	8.25[a]	165.00	
Mar. 10				10	$8.25	$82.50	10	8.25	82.50	The unit cost of sales is the most recently calculated unit cost.
May 28	20	8.40	168				30	8.35[b]	250.50	
July 14				20	8.35	167.00	10	8.35	83.50	
Aug. 12	10	9.00	90				20	8.675[c]	173.50	Balance of $178.58 would agree with balance already existing in the Merchandise Inventory account.
Sept. 7				10	8.675	86.75	10	8.675	86.75	
Oct. 12	20	8.80	176				30	8.758[c]	262.75	
Nov. 22					8.758	175.17	10	8.758	87.58	
Dec 21	10	9.10	91				20	$8.929[e]	$178.58	

[a]$165.00/20 = $8.25. [b]$250.50/30 = $8.35. [c]$173.50/20 = $8.675. [d]$262.75/30 = $8.758.
[e]$175.58/20 = $8.929 * rounding difference.

take full advantage of using the LIFO for tax purposes. Complicated applications of LIFO perpetual inventory procedures that require such adjustments are beyond the scope of this text.

Look at Illustrations 7.15 and 7.11, the flow of inventory costs under LIFO using both the perpetual and periodic inventory procedures. Note that ending inventory and cost of goods sold are different under the two procedures.

Reinforcing Problem
E7-5 Compute ending inventory under weighted-average perpetual inventory procedure.

Weighted-Average under the Perpetual Inventory Procedure   Under the perpetual inventory procedure, firms compute a new weighted-average unit cost after each purchase by dividing total cost of goods available for sale by total units available for sale. The unit cost is a moving weighted-average because it changes after each purchase. In Illustration 7.16, you can see how to compute the moving weighted-average using the perpetual inventory procedure. The new weighted-average unit cost computed after each purchase is the unit cost for inventory items sold until a new purchase is made. The unit cost of the 20 units in ending inventory is $8.929 for a total inventory cost of $178.58. Cost of goods sold under this procedure is $690 minus the $178.58, or $511.42.

Advantages and Disadvantages of Inventory Methods

Objective 4
Explain the advantages and disadvantages of the four major inventory costing methods.

Advantages and Disadvantages of Specific Identification   Companies that use the specific identification method of inventory costing state their cost of goods sold and ending inventory at the actual cost of specific units sold and on hand. Some accountants argue that this method provides the most precise matching of costs and revenues and is, therefore, the most theoretically sound method. This statement is true for some one-of-a-kind items, such as autos or real estate. For these items, use of any other method would seem illogical.

One disadvantage of the specific identification method is that it permits the manipulation of income. For example, assume that a company bought three identical units of a given product at different prices. One unit cost $2,000, the second cost $2,100, and the third cost $2,200. The company sold one unit for $2,800. The units are alike, so the customer does not care which of the identical units the company ships. However, the gross margin on the sale could be either $800, $700, or $600, depending on which unit the company ships.

Advantages and Disadvantages of FIFO   The FIFO method has four major advantages: (1) it is easy to apply, (2) the assumed flow of costs corresponds with the normal physical flow of goods, (3) no manipulation of income is possible, and (4) the balance sheet amount for inventory is likely to approximate the current market value. All the advantages of FIFO occur because when a company sells goods, the first costs it removes from inventory are the oldest unit costs. A company cannot manipulate income by choosing which unit to ship because the cost of a unit sold is not determined by a serial number. Instead, the cost attached to the unit sold is always the oldest cost. Under FIFO, purchases at the end of the period have no effect on cost of goods sold or net income.

The disadvantages of FIFO include (1) the recognition of paper profits and (2) a heavier tax burden if used for tax purposes in periods of inflation. We discuss these disadvantages later as advantages of LIFO.

Advantages and Disadvantages of LIFO   The advantages of the LIFO method are based on the fact that prices have risen almost constantly for decades. LIFO supporters claim this upward trend in prices leads to *inventory, or paper, profits* if the FIFO method is used. **Inventory, or paper, profits** are equal to the current replacement cost of a unit of inventory at the time of sale minus the unit's historical cost.

For example, assume a company has three units of a product on hand, each purchased at a different cost: $12, $15, and $20 (the most recent cost). The sales price of the unit normally rises because the unit's replacement cost is rising. Assume that the company sells one unit for $30. FIFO gross margin would be $18 ($30 − $12), while LIFO would show a gross margin of $10 ($30 − $20). LIFO supporters would say that the extra $8 gross margin shown under FIFO represents inventory (paper) profit; it is merely the additional amount that the company must spend over cost of goods sold to purchase another unit of inventory ($8 + $12 = $20). Thus, the profit is not real; it exists only on paper. The company cannot distribute the $8 to owners, but must retain it to continue handling that particular product. LIFO shows the actual profits that the company can distribute to the owners while still replenishing inventory.

During periods of inflation, LIFO shows the largest cost of goods sold of any of the costing methods because the newest costs charged to cost of goods sold are also the highest costs. The larger the cost of goods sold, the smaller the net income.

Those who favor LIFO argue that its use leads to a better matching of costs and revenues than the other methods. When a company uses LIFO, the income statement reports both sales revenue and cost of goods sold in current dollars. The resulting gross margin is a better indicator of management's ability to generate income than gross margin computed using the FIFO, which may include substantial inventory (paper) profits.

Supporters of FIFO argue that LIFO (1) matches the cost of goods not sold against revenues, (2) grossly understates inventory, and (3) permits income manipulation.

The first criticism—that LIFO matches the cost of goods not sold against revenues—is an extension of the debate over whether the assumed flow of costs should agree with the physical flow of goods. LIFO supporters contend that it makes more sense to match current costs against current revenues than to worry about matching costs for the physical flow of goods.

The second criticism—that LIFO grossly understates inventory—is valid. A company may report LIFO inventory at a fraction of its current replacement cost, especially if the historical costs are from several decades ago. LIFO supporters contend that the increased usefulness of the income statement more than offsets the negative effect of this undervaluation of inventory on the balance sheet.

The third criticism—that LIFO permits income manipulation—is also valid. Income manipulation is possible under LIFO. For example, assume that management wishes to reduce income. The company could purchase an abnormal amount of goods at current high prices near the end of the current period, with the purpose of selling the goods in the next period. Under LIFO, these higher costs are charged to cost of goods sold in the current period, resulting in a substantial decline in reported net income. To obtain higher income, management could delay making the normal amount of purchases until the next period and thus include some of the older, lower costs in cost of goods sold.

Tax Benefit of LIFO   The LIFO method results in the lowest taxable income, and thus the lowest income taxes, when prices are rising. The Internal Revenue Service allows companies to use LIFO for tax purposes only if they use LIFO for financial reporting purposes. Companies may also report an alternative inventory amount in the notes to their financial statements for comparison purposes. Because of high inflation during the 1970s, many companies switched from FIFO to LIFO for tax advantages.

Advantages and Disadvantages of Weighted-Average   When a company uses the weighted-average method and prices are rising, its cost of goods sold is less than that obtained under LIFO, but more than that obtained under FIFO. Inventory is not as badly understated as under LIFO, but it is not as up to date as under FIFO. Weighted-average costing takes a middle-of-the-road approach. A company can manipulate income under the weighted-average costing method by buying or failing to buy goods near year-end. However, the averaging process reduces the effects of buying or not buying.

The four inventory costing methods—specific identification, FIFO, LIFO, and weighted-average—involve assumptions about how costs flow through a business. In some instances, assumed cost flows may correspond with the actual physical flow of goods. For example, fresh meats and dairy products must flow in a FIFO manner to avoid

International Insight
The United States is one of the few countries that permits LIFO. LIFO is not allowed in many countries as it is not consistent with the normal physical flow of goods.

Differences in Costing Methods Summarized

Reinforcing Problems
P7-5 Compute ending inventory under FIFO, LIFO, and weighted-average using perpetual and periodic inventory procedures.
P7-7 Compute ending inventory and cost of goods sold under FIFO, LIFO, and weighted-average using perpetual and periodic inventory procedures.
P7-8 Compute gross margin using the FIFO and LIFO illustrating effects of end-of-year purchases.
E7-6 Compute cost of ending inventory using the FIFO, LIFO, and weighted-average under the periodic inventory procedure.

spoilage losses. In contrast, firms use coal stacked in a pile in a LIFO manner because the newest units purchased are unloaded on top of the pile and sold first. Gasoline held in a tank is a good example of an inventory that has an average physical flow. As the tank is refilled, the new gasoline mixes with the old. Thus, any amount used is a blend of the old gas with the new.

Although physical flows are sometimes cited as support for an inventory method, accountants now recognize that an inventory method's assumed cost flows need not necessarily correspond with the actual physical flow of the goods. In fact, good reasons exist for simply ignoring physical flows and choosing an inventory method based on other criteria.

In Illustrations 7.17 and 7.18, we use data from Illustration 7.6 to show the cost of goods sold, inventory cost, and gross margin for each of the four basic costing methods using perpetual and periodic inventory procedures. The differences for the four methods occur because the company paid different prices for goods purchased. No differences would occur if purchase prices were constant. Since a company's purchase prices are seldom constant, inventory costing method affects cost of goods sold, inventory cost, gross margin, and net income. Therefore, companies must disclose on their financial statements which inventory costing methods were used.

Which Is The Correct Method?   All four methods of inventory costing are acceptable; no single method is the only correct method. Different methods are attractive under different conditions.

If a company wants to match sales revenue with current cost of goods sold, it would use LIFO. If a company seeks to reduce its income taxes in a period of rising prices, it would also use LIFO. On the other hand, LIFO often charges against revenues the cost of goods not actually sold. Also, LIFO may allow the company to manipulate net income by changing the timing of additional purchases.

The FIFO and specific identification methods result in a more precise matching of historical cost with revenue. However, FIFO can give rise to paper profits, while specific identification can give rise to income manipulation. The weighted-average method also allows manipulation of income. Only under FIFO is the manipulation of net income not possible.

An Accounting Perspective

BUSINESS INSIGHT Management decides which inventory costing method or methods (LIFO, FIFO, etc.) to use. Also, management must determine which method is the most meaningful and useful in representing economic results. Then, it must use the selected method consistently.

The principal business of Kellwood Company is the marketing, merchandising, and manufacturing of apparel, primarily for women. Note in the following footnote from Kellwood's financial statements that it, like other companies, uses several costing methods within the same enterprise:

Summary of Significant Accounting Policies
3. Inventories and Revenue Recognition
Inventories are stated at the lower of cost or market. The first-in, first-out (FIFO) method is used to determine the value of 46% of the domestic inventories, and the last-in, first-out (LIFO) method is used to value the remaining domestic inventories. Inventories of foreign subsidiaries are valued using the specific identification method. Sales are recognized when goods are shipped.

Changing Inventory Methods

Generally, companies use the inventory method that best fits their individual circumstances. However, this freedom of choice does not include changing inventory methods every year or so, especially if the goal is to report higher income. Continuous switching of methods violates the accounting principle of *consistency,* which requires

Illustration 7.17   Effects of Different Inventory Costing Methods Using Perpetual Inventory Procedure

	Specific Identification	FIFO	LIFO	Weighted-Average
Sales	$780.00	$780.00	$780.00	$780.00
Cost of goods sold:				
Beginning inventory	$ 80.00	$ 80.00	$ 80.00	$ 80.00
Purchases	610.00	610.00	610.00	610.00
Cost of goods available for sale	$690.00	$690.00	$690.00	$690.00
Ending inventory	181.00	179.00	171.00	178.58
Cost of goods sold	$509.00	$511.00	$519.00	$511.42
Gross Margin	$271.00	$269.00	$261.00	$268.58

Illustration 7.18   Effects of Different Inventory Costing Methods Using Periodic Inventory Procedure

	Specific Identification	FIFO	LIFO	Weighted-Average
Sales	$780.00	$780.00	$780.00	$780.00
Cost of goods sold:				
Beginning inventory	$ 80.00	$ 80.00	$ 80.00	$ 80.00
Purchases	610.00	610.00	610.00	610.00
Cost of goods available for sale	$690.00	$690.00	$690.00	$690.00
Ending inventory	181.00	179.00	165.00	172.50
Cost of goods sold	$509.00	$511.00	$525.00	$517.50
Gross Margin	$271.00	$269.00	$255.00	$262.50

using the same accounting methods from period to period in preparing financial statements. Consistency of methods in preparing financial statements enables financial statement users to compare statements of a company from period to period and determine trends.

An Accounting Perspective

BUSINESS INSIGHT Sometimes, companies change inventory methods in spite of the principle of consistency. Improved financial reporting is the only justification for a change in inventory method. A company that changes its inventory method must make a full disclosure of the change. Usually, the company makes a full disclosure in a footnote to the financial statements. The footnote consists of a complete description of the change, the reasons why the change was made, and, if possible, the effect of the change on net income.

J. M. Tull Industries, Inc., sells a diverse range of metals (aluminum, brass, copper, steel, stainless steel, and nickel alloys) for severe corrosion conditions and high-temperature applications. When J. M. Tull changed from lower of average cost or market to LIFO, the following footnote appeared in its annual report:

Note B. Change in accounting method for inventory
The company changed its method of determining inventory cost from the lower of average cost or market method to the last-in, first-out (LIFO) method for substantially all inventory. This change was made because management believes LIFO more clearly reflects income by providing a closer matching of current cost against current revenue.

Now we illustrate in more detail the journal entries made when using perpetual inventory procedure. Data from Illustration 7.13 serve as the basis for some of the entries.

You would debit the Merchandise Inventory account to record the increases in the asset due to purchase costs and transportation-in costs. And you would credit Merchandise Inventory to record the decreases in the asset brought about by purchase returns and allowances, purchase discounts, and cost of goods sold to customers. The balance in the account is the cost of the inventory that should be on hand at any date. This entry records the purchase of 10 units on March 2 in Illustration 7.13:

Mar.	2	Merchandise Inventory	85	
		Accounts Payable		85
		To record purchases of 10 units at $8.50 on account.		

You would also record the 10 units sold on the perpetual inventory record in Illustration 7.13. Perpetual inventory procedure requires two journal entries for each sale. One entry is at selling price—a debit to Accounts Receivable (or Cash) and a credit to Sales. The other entry is at cost—a debit to Cost of Goods Sold and a credit to Merchandise Inventory. Assuming that the 10 units sold on March 10 in Illustration 7.13 had a retail price of $12 each, you would record the following entries:

Mar.	10	Accounts Receivable	120	
		Sales		120
		To record 10 units sold at $12 each on account.		
	10	Cost of Goods Sold	80	
		Merchandise Inventory		80
		To record cost of $8 on each of the 10 units sold.		

When a company sells merchandise to customers, it transfers the cost of the merchandise from an asset account (Merchandise Inventory) to an expense account (Cost of Goods Sold). The company makes this transfer because the sale reduces the asset, and the cost of the goods sold is one of the expenses of making the sale. Thus, the Cost of Goods Sold account accumulates the cost of all the merchandise that the company sells during a period.

A sales return also requires two entries, one at selling price and one at cost. Assume that a customer returned merchandise that cost $20 and originally sold for $32. The entry to reduce the accounts receivable and to record the sales return of $32 is:

Mar.	17	Sales Return and Allowances	32	
		Accounts Receivable		32
		To record the reduction in amount owed by a customer upon return of goods.		

The entry that increases the Merchandise Inventory account and decreases the Cost of Goods Sold account by $20 is as follows:

Mar.	17	Merchandise Inventory	20	
		Cost of Goods Sold		20
		To record replacement of goods returned to inventory.		

Sales returns affect both revenues and cost of goods sold because the goods charged to cost of goods sold are actually returned to the seller. In contrast, sales allowances granted to customers affect only revenues because the customers do not have to return goods. Thus, if the company had granted a sales allowance of $32 on March 17, only the first entry would be required.

The balance of the Merchandise Inventory account is the cost of the inventory that should be on hand. This fact is a major reason some companies choose to use perpetual inventory procedure. The cost of inventory that should be on hand is readily available. A physical inventory determines the accuracy of the account balance. Management may investigate any major discrepancies between the balance in the account and the cost based on the physical count. It thereby achieves greater control over inventory. When a shortage is discovered, an adjusting entry is required. Assuming a $15 shortage (at cost) is discovered, the entry is:

Dec.	31	Loss from Inventory Shortage	15	
		Merchandise Inventory		15
		To record inventory shortage		

Assume that the Cost of Goods Sold account had a balance of $200,000 by year-end when it is closed to Income Summary. There are no other purchase-related accounts to be closed. The entry to close the Cost of Goods Sold account is:

Dec.	31	Income Summary	200,000	
		Cost of Goods Sold		200,000
		To close Cost of Goods Sold account to Income Summary at the end of the year.		

Departures from Cost Basis of Inventory Measurement

Generally, companies should use historical cost to value inventories and cost of goods sold. However, some circumstances justify departures from historical cost. One of these circumstances is when the utility or value of inventory items is less than their cost. A decline in the selling price of the goods or their replacement cost may indicate such a loss of utility. This section explains how accountants handle some of these departures from the cost basis of inventory measurement.

Companies should not carry goods in inventory at more than their net realizable value. **Net realizable value** is the estimated selling price of an item less the estimated costs that the company incurs in preparing the item for sale and selling it. Damaged, obsolete, or shopworn goods often have a net realizable value lower than their historical cost and must be written down to their net realizable value. However, goods do not have to be damaged, obsolete, or shopworn for this situation to occur. Technological changes and increased competition have caused significant reductions in selling prices for such products as computers, DVD players, and microwave ovens.

To illustrate a necessary write-down in the cost of inventory, assume that an automobile dealer has a demonstrator on hand. The dealer acquired the auto at a cost of $18,000. The auto had an original selling price of $19,600. Since the dealer used the auto as a demonstrator and the new models are coming in, the auto now has an estimated selling price of only $18,100. However, the dealer can get the $18,100 only if the demonstrator receives some scheduled maintenance, including a tune-up and some paint damage repairs. This work and the sales commission cost $300. The net realizable value of the demonstrator, then, is $17,800 (selling price of $18,100 less costs of $300). For inventory purposes, the required journal entry is:

Net Realizable Value

Objective 6
Apply net realizable value and the lower-of-cost-or-market method to inventory.

Reinforcing Problems
E7-13 Using net realizable value, compute carrying cost of inventory item.
E7-14 Determine the proper carrying value of damaged goods.

Loss Due to the Decline in Market Value of Inventory	200	
Merchandise Inventory		200
To write down inventory to net realizable value		
($18,000 - $17,800)		

This entry treats the $200 inventory decline as a loss in the period in which the decline in utility occurred. Such an entry is necessary only when the net realizable value is less than cost. If net realizable value declines but still exceeds cost, the dealer would continue to carry the item at cost.

The lower-of-cost-or-market (LCM) method is an inventory costing method that values inventory at the lower of its historical cost or its current market (replacement) cost. The term *cost* refers to historical cost of inventory as determined under the specific identification, FIFO, LIFO, or weighted-average inventory method. *Market* generally refers to a merchandise item's replacement cost in the quantity usually purchased. The basic assumption of the LCM method is that if the purchase price of an item has fallen, its selling price also has fallen or will fall. The LCM method has long been accepted in accounting.

Real World Example
Merck & Co. reported the following concerning its inventories in the notes to its financial statements: The majority of domestic inventories are valued at the lower of last-in, first-out (LIFO) cost or market. Remaining inventories are valued at the lower of first-in (FIFO) cost or market.

Under LCM, inventory items are written down to market value when the market value is less than the cost of the items. For example, assume that the market value of the inventory is $39,600 and its cost is $40,000. Then, the company would record a $400 loss because the inventory has lost some of its revenue-generating ability. The company must recognize the loss in the period the loss occurred. On the other hand, if ending inventory has a market value of $45,000 and a cost of $40,000, the company would not recognize this increase in value. To do so would recognize revenue before the time of sale.

LCM Applied   A company may apply LCM to each inventory item (such as Trivial Pursuit), each inventory class (such as games), or total inventory. To see how the company would apply the method to individual items and total inventory, look at Illustration 7.19.

Reinforcing Problems
E7-15 Compute value of ending inventory using LCM applied on item-by-item basis.
E7-16 Compute value of total inventory using LCM.
P7-9A Compute ending inventory using LCM.

If LCM is applied on an item-by-item basis, ending inventory would be $5,000. The company would deduct the $5,000 ending inventory from cost of goods available for sale on the income statement and report this inventory in the current assets section of the balance sheet. Under the class method, a company applies LCM to the total cost and total market for each class of items compared. One class might be games; another might be toys. Then, the company values each class at the lower of its cost or market amount. If LCM is applied on a total inventory basis, ending inventory would be $5,100, since total cost of $5,100 is lower than total market of $5,150.

An annual report of Du Pont contains an actual example of applying LCM. The report states that "substantially all inventories are valued at cost as determined by the last-in, first-out (LIFO) method; in the aggregate, such valuations are not in excess of market." The term *in the aggregate* means that Du Pont applied LCM to total inventory.

An Accounting Perspective

BUSINESS INSIGHT Procter & Gamble markets a broad range of laundry, cleaning, paper, beauty care, health care, food, and beverage products around the world. Procter & Gamble's footnote in its Notes to Consolidated Financial Statements in its annual report illustrates that companies often disclose LCM in their notes to financial statements.

Inventories are valued at cost, which is not in excess of current market price. Cost is primarily determined by either the average cost or the last-in, first-out method. The replacement cost of last-in, first-out inventories exceeds carrying value by approximately $169 [million].

Illustration 7.19   Application of Lower-of-Cost-or-Market Method

Item	Quantity	Unit Cost	Unit Market	Total Cost	Total Market	LCM on Item-by-Item Basis
1	100 units	$10	$9.00	$1,000	$ 900	$ 900
2	200 units	8	8.75	1,600	1,750	1,600
3	500 units	5	5.00	2,500	2,500	2,500
				$5,100	$5,150	$5,000

Illustration 7.20   Inventory Estimation Using Gross Margin Method

Merchandise inventory, January 1, 2012		$ 40,000
Net cost of purchases		480,000
Cost of goods available for sale		$520,000
Less estimated cost of goods sold:		
Net sales	$700,000	
Gross margin (30% of $700,000)	210,000	
Estimated cost of goods sold		490,000
Estimated inventory, December 31, 2012		$ 30,000

A company using periodic inventory procedure may estimate its inventory for any of the following reasons:

1. To obtain an inventory cost for use in monthly or quarterly financial statements without taking a physical inventory. The effort of taking a physical inventory can be very expensive and disrupts normal business operations; once a year is often enough.
2. To compare with physical inventories to determine whether shortages exist.
3. To determine the amount recoverable from an insurance company when fire has destroyed inventory or the inventory has been stolen.

Next, we introduce two recognized methods of estimating the cost of ending inventory when a company has not taken a physical inventory—the gross margin method and the retail inventory method.

Gross Margin Method   The steps in calculating ending inventory under the gross margin method are:

1. Estimate gross margin (based on net sales) using the same gross margin rate experienced in prior accounting periods.
2. Determine estimated cost of goods sold by deducting estimated gross margin from net sales.
3. Determine estimated ending inventory by deducting estimated cost of goods sold from cost of goods available for sale.

Thus, the **gross margin method** estimates ending inventory by deducting estimated cost of goods sold from cost of goods available for sale.

The gross margin method assumes that a fairly stable relationship exists between gross margin and net sales. In other words, gross margin has been a fairly constant percentage of net sales, and this relationship has continued into the current period. If this percentage relationship has changed, the gross margin method does not yield satisfactory results.

Estimating Inventory

Objective 7
Estimate cost of ending inventory using the gross margin and retail inventory methods.

Note to the Student
Auditors sometimes use the gross margin method of estimating inventory to check that the amount reported by the company as ending inventory is reasonable.

Reinforcing Problems
E7-17 Estimate ending inventory using gross margin method.
E7-18 Estimate ending inventory using gross margin method.
P7-10 Estimate inventory using gross margin method.

To illustrate the gross margin method of computing inventory, assume that for several years Field Company has maintained a 30% gross margin on net sales. The following data for 2012 are available: The January 1 inventory was $40,000; net cost of purchases of merchandise was $480,000; and net sales of merchandise were $700,000. As shown in Illustration 7.20, Field can estimate the inventory for December 31, 2012, by deducting the estimated cost of goods sold from the actual cost of goods available for sale.

An alternative format for calculating estimated ending inventory uses the standard income statement format and solves for the one unknown (ending inventory):

Net sales		$700,000
Less cost of goods sold:		
Merchandise inventory, January 1, 2012	$ 40,000	
Net cost of purchases	480,000	
Cost of goods available for sale	$520,000	
Less estimated inventory, December 31, 2012	?	
Estimated cost of goods sold		490,000 (70% of net sales
Estimated gross margin		$210,000 (30% of net sales)

We know that:

$$\begin{array}{ccccc} \text{Cost of goods} & & \text{Ending} & & \text{Cost of} \\ \text{available for sale} & - & \text{inventory} & = & \text{goods sold} \end{array}$$

Therefore (let X = Ending inventory):

$$\$520,000 - X = \$490,000$$
$$X = \$30,000$$

The gross margin method is not precise enough to be used for year-end financial statements. At year-end, a physical inventory must be taken and valued by either the specific identification, FIFO, LIFO, or weighted-average methods.

Retail Inventory Method   Retail stores frequently use the retail inventory method to estimate ending inventory at times other than year-end. Taking a physical inventory during an accounting period (such as monthly or quarterly) is too time consuming and significantly interferes with business operations. The **retail inventory method** estimates the cost of the ending inventory by applying a cost/retail price ratio to ending inventory stated at retail prices. The advantage of this method is that companies can estimate ending inventory (at cost) without taking a physical inventory. Thus, the use of this estimate permits the preparation of interim financial statements (monthly or quarterly) without taking a physical inventory. The steps for finding the ending inventory by the retail inventory method are:

1. Total the beginning inventory and the net amount of goods purchased during the period at both cost and retail prices.
2. Divide the cost of goods available for sale by the retail price of the goods available for sale to find the cost/retail price ratio.
3. Deduct the retail sales from the retail price of the goods available for sale to determine ending inventory at retail.
4. Multiply the cost/retail price ratio or percentage by the ending inventory at retail prices to reduce it to the ending inventory at cost.

In Illustration 7.21, we show the retail inventory method. In the illustration, the cost ($22,000) and retail ($40,000) amounts for beginning inventory are available

Note to the Student
It seems that it would be just as easy to physically count and determine the actual inventory instead of keeping retail records and calculating an estimate. However, a physical inventory involves applying a cost flow method and takes longer than keeping retail records as goods are purchased.

Illustration 7.21   Inventory Estimation

	Cost	Retail
Merchandise inventory, January 1, 2012	$ 22,000	$ 40,000
Purchases	182,000	303,000
Purchase returns	(2,000)	(3,000)
Purchase allowances	(3,000)	
Transportation-in	5,000	
Goods available for sale	$204,000	$340,000
Cost/retail price ratio:		
$204,000/$340,000=60%		
Sales		280,000
Ending inventory at retail prices		$ 60,000
Times cost/retail price ratio		x 60%
Ending inventory at cost, March 31, 2012		$ 36,000

from the preceding period's computation. The amounts for the first quarter purchases, purchase returns, purchase allowances, and transportation-in came from the accounting records. The amounts for purchase allowances and transportation-in appear only in the cost column. The first quarter sales amount ($280,000) is from the Sales account and stated at retail (sales) prices. The difference between what was available for sale at retail prices and what was sold at retail prices (which is sales) equals what should be on hand (March 31 inventory of $60,000) expressed in retail prices. The retail price of the March 31 inventory needs to be converted into cost for use in the financial statements. We do this by multiplying it times the cost/retail price ratio. In the example, the cost/retail price ratio is 60%, which means that on the average, 60 cents of each sales dollar is cost of goods sold. To find the March 31, 2012, inventory at cost ($36,000), we multiplied the ending inventory at retail ($60,000) by 60%.

Once the March 31 inventory has been estimated at cost ($36,000), we deduct the cost of the inventory from cost of goods available for sale ($204,000) to determine cost of goods sold ($168,000). We can also find the cost of goods sold by multiplying the cost/retail price ratio of 60% by sales of $280,000.

For the next quarterly period, the $36,000 and $60,000 amounts would appear on the schedule as beginning inventory at cost and retail, respectively. We would include other quarterly data regarding purchases, purchase returns, purchase allowances, and transportation-in to determine goods available for sale at cost and at retail. From these amounts, we could compute a new cost/retail price ratio for the second quarter.

At the end of each year, merchandisers usually take a physical inventory at retail prices. Since the retail prices are on the individual items (while the cost is not), taking an inventory at retail prices is more convenient than taking an inventory at cost. Accountants can then compare the results of the physical inventory to the calculation of inventory at retail under the retail inventory method for the fourth quarter to determine whether a shortage exists.

Both the gross margin and the retail inventory methods can help you detect inventory shortages. To illustrate how you can determine inventory shortages using the retail method, assume that a physical inventory taken at year end showed only $62,000 of retail-priced goods in the store. Assume that use of the retail method for the fourth quarter showed that $66,000 of goods should be on hand, thus indicating a $4,000 inventory shortage at retail. After converting the $4,000 to $2,400 of cost ($4,000 × 0.60), you would report this as a "Loss from inventory shortage" in the income statement. Knowledge of such shortages may lead management to reduce or prevent them, by increasing security or improving the training of employees.

Reinforcing Problem
E7-19 Estimate ending inventory using retail inventory method.

Reinforcing Problem
P7-11A Estimate ending inventory using retail inventory method.

Terry Dorsey started Dorsey Hardware, a small hardware store, two years ago and has struggled to make it successful. The first year of operations resulted in a substantial loss; in the second year, there was a small net income. His initial cash investment was almost depleted because he had to withdraw money for living expenses. The current year of operations looked much better. His customer base was growing and seemed to be loyal. To increase sales, however, Terry had to invest his remaining funds and the proceeds of a $40,000 bank loan into doubling the size of his inventory and purchasing some new display shelves and a new truck.

At the end of the third year, Terry's accountant asked him for his ending inventory figure and later told him that initial estimates indicated that net income (and taxable income) for the year would be approximately $80,000. Terry was delighted until he learned that the federal income taxes on that income would be about $17,250. He told the accountant that he did not have enough cash to pay the taxes and could not even borrow it, since he already had an outstanding loan at the bank.

Terry asked the accountant for a copy of the income statement figures so he could see if any items had been overlooked that might reduce his net income. He noticed that ending inventory of $160,000 had been deducted from cost of goods available for sale of $640,000 to arrive at cost of goods sold of $480,000. Net sales of $720,000 and expenses of $160,000 could not be changed. But Terry hit on a scheme to reduce his net income. The next day he told his accountant that he had made an error in determining ending inventory and that its correct amount was $120,000. This lower inventory amount would increase cost of goods sold by $40,000 and reduce net income by that same amount. The resulting income taxes would be about $6,000, which was just about what Terry had paid in estimated taxes.

To justify his action in his own mind, Terry used the following arguments: (1) federal taxes are too high, and the federal government seems to be taxing the little guy out of existence; (2) no harm is really done because, when the business becomes more profitable, I will use correct inventory amounts, and this loan from the government will be paid back; (3) since I am the only one who knows the correct ending inventory I will not get caught; and (4) I'll bet a lot of other people do this same thing.

Analyzing and Using Financial Results— Inventory Turnover Ratio

An important ratio for managers, investors, and creditors to consider when analyzing a company's inventory is the inventory turnover ratio. This ratio tests whether a company is generating a sufficient volume of business based on its inventory. To calculate the **inventory turnover ratio:**

$$\text{Inventory turnover ratio} = \frac{\text{Cost of goods sold}}{\text{Average inventory}}$$

Inventory turnover measures the efficiency of the firm in managing and selling inventory; thus, it gauges the liquidity of the firm's inventory. A high inventory turnover is generally a sign of efficient inventory management and profit for the firm; the faster inventory sells, the less time funds are tied up in inventory. A relatively low turnover could be the result of a company carrying too much inventory or stocking inventory that is obsolete, slow-moving, or inferior.

In assessing inventory turnover, analysts also consider the type of industry. When making comparisons among firms, they check the cost-flow assumption used to value inventory and cost of products sold.

Abercrombie & Fitch reported the following financial data for 2011 (in thousands):

Cost of goods sold	$1,639,188
Beginning inventory	385,857
Ending inventory	569,818

Their inventory turnover is:

$$\$1,639,188/[(\$385,857 + \$569,818)/2] = 3.4 \text{ times}$$

You should now understand the importance of taking an accurate physical inventory and knowing how to value this inventory. In the next chapter, you will learn the general principles of internal control and how to control cash. Cash is one of a company's most important and mobile assets.

Understanding the Learning Objectives

- Net income for an accounting period depends directly on the valuation of ending inventory.
- If ending inventory is overstated, cost of goods sold is understated, resulting in an overstatement of gross margin, net income, and retained earnings.
- When ending inventory is misstated in the current year, companies carry that misstatement forward into the next year.
- An error in the net income of one year caused by misstated ending inventory automatically causes an error in net income in the opposite direction in the next period because of the misstated beginning inventory.

> **Objective 1**
> Explain and calculate the effects of inventory errors on certain financial statement items.

- Inventory cost includes all necessary outlays to obtain the goods, get the goods ready to sell, and have the goods in the desired location for sale to customers.
- Inventory cost includes:
  - **a.** Seller's gross selling price less purchase discount.
  - **b.** Cost of insurance on the goods while in transit.
  - **c.** Transportation charges when borne by the buyer.
  - **d.** Handling costs, such as the cost of pressing clothes wrinkled during shipment.

> **Objective 2**
> Indicate which costs are properly included in inventory.

- **Specific identification:** Attaches actual cost of each unit of product to units in ending inventory and cost of goods sold. Specific identification creates precise matching in determining net income.
- **FIFO (first-in, first-out):** Ending inventory consists of the most recent purchases. FIFO assumes that the costs of the first goods purchased are those charged to cost of goods sold when goods are sold. During periods of rising prices, FIFO creates higher net income since the costs charged to cost of goods sold are lower.
- **LIFO (last-in, first-out):** Ending inventory consists of the oldest costs. LIFO assumes that the costs of the most recent purchases are the first costs charged to cost of goods sold. Net income is usually lower under LIFO since the costs charged to cost of goods sold are higher due to inflation. The ending inventory may differ between perpetual and periodic inventory procedures.
- **Weighted-average:** Ending inventory is priced using a weighted-average unit cost. Under the perpetual inventory procedure, a new weighted-average is determined after each purchase. Under the periodic procedure, the average is determined at the end of the accounting period by dividing the total number

> **Objective 3**
> Calculate cost of ending inventory and cost of goods sold under the four major inventory costing methods using periodic and perpetual inventory procedures.

of units purchased plus those in beginning inventory into total cost of goods available for sale. In determining cost of goods sold, this average unit cost is applied to each item. Under the weighted-average method, in a period of rising prices net income is usually higher than income under LIFO and lower than income under FIFO.

- **Specific identification:** *Advantages:* (1) States cost of goods sold and ending inventory at the actual cost of specific units sold and on hand, and (2) provides the most precise matching of costs and revenues. *Disadvantage:* Income manipulation is possible.
- **FIFO:** *Advantages:* (1) FIFO is easy to apply, (2) the assumed flow of costs often corresponds with the normal physical flow of goods, (3) no manipulation of income is possible, and (4) the balance sheet amount for inventory is likely to approximate the current market value. *Disadvantages:* (1) Recognizes paper profits, and (2) tax burden is heavier if used for tax purposes when prices are rising.
- **LIFO:** *Advantages:* (1) LIFO reports both sales revenue and cost of goods sold in current dollars, and (2) lower income taxes result if used for tax purposes when prices are rising. *Disadvantages:* (1) Often matches the cost of goods *not* sold against revenues, (2) grossly understates inventory, and (3) permits income manipulation.
- **Weighted-average:** *Advantages:* Due to the averaging process, the effects of year-end buying or not buying are lessened. *Disadvantage:* Manipulation of income is possible.

- Perpetual inventory procedure requires an entry to Merchandise Inventory whenever goods are purchased, returned, sold, or otherwise adjusted, so that inventory records reflect actual units on hand at all times. Thus, an entry is required to record cost of goods sold for each sale.

- Companies should not carry goods in inventory at more than their net realizable value. Net realizable value is the estimated selling price of an item less the estimated costs incurred in preparing the item for sale and selling it.
- Inventory items are written down to market value when the market value is less than the cost of the items. If market value is greater than cost, the increase in value is not recognized. LCM may be applied to each inventory item, each inventory class, or total inventory.

- The steps in calculating ending inventory under the gross margin method are:
  a. Estimate gross margin (based on net sales) using the same gross margin rate experienced in prior accounting periods.
  b. Determine estimated cost of goods sold by deducting estimated gross margin from net sales.
  c. Determine estimated ending inventory by deducting estimated cost of goods sold from cost of goods available for sale.
- The retail inventory method estimates the cost of the ending inventory by applying a cost/retail price ratio to ending inventory stated at retail prices. To find the cost/retail price ratio, divide the cost of goods available for sale by the retail price of the goods available for sale.

- Inventory turnover ratio = $\dfrac{\text{Cost of goods sold}}{\text{Average inventory}}$
- Inventory turnover measures the efficiency of the firm in managing and selling inventory. It gauges the liquidity of the firm's inventory.

Demonstration Problem 7–A

Following are data related to Adler Company's beginning inventory, purchases, and sales:

	Beginning Inventory and Purchases			Sales	
	Units		**Unit Cost**		**Units**
Beginning inventory	6,250	@	$3.00	February 3	5,250
March 15	5,000	@	3.12	May 4	4,500
May 10	8,750	@	3.30	September 16	8,000
August 12	6,250	@	3.48	October 9	7,250
November 20	3,750	@	3.72		
	30,000				25,000

● *Required*

a. Compute the ending inventory under each of the following methods:
   1. Specific identification (assume ending inventory is taken equally from the August 12 and November 20 purchases).
   2. FIFO: (a) Assume use of perpetual inventory procedure.
            (b) Assume use of periodic inventory procedure.
   3. LIFO: (a) Assume use of perpetual inventory procedure.
            (b) Assume use of periodic inventory procedure.
   4. Weighted-average:
            (a) Assume use of perpetual inventory procedure.
            (b) Assume use of periodic inventory procedure.
   (Carry unit cost to four decimal places and round total cost to nearest dollar.)
b. Give the journal entries to record the individual purchases and sales (Cost of Goods Sold entry only) under the LIFO method and perpetual procedure.

Solution to Demonstration Problem 7–A

a. The ending inventory is 5,000 units, calcuated as follows:

	Units
Beginning inventory	6,250
Purchases	23,750
Goods available	30,000
Sales	25,000
Ending inventory	5,000

   1. Ending inventory under specific identification:

Purchased	**Units**	**Unit Cost**	**Total Cost**
November 20	2,500	$3.72	$ 9,300
August 12	2,500	3.48	8,700
			$ 18,000

2. Ending inventory under FIFO:
  (a) Perpetual:

Date	Purchased Units	Unit Cost	Total Cost	Sold Units	Unit Cost	Total Cost	Balance Units	Unit Cost	Total Cost
Beg. inv.							6,250	$3.00	$18,750
Feb. 3				5,250	$3.00	$15,750	1,000	3.00	3,000
Mar. 15	5,000	$3.12	$15,600				1,000	3.00	3,000
							5,000	3.12	15,600
May 4				1,000	3.00	3,000			
				3,500	3.12	10,920	1,500	3.12	4,680
May 10	8,750	3.30	28,875				1,500	3.12	4,680
							8,750	3.30	28,875
Aug. 12	6,250	3.48	21,750				1,500	3.12	4,680
							8,750	3.30	28,875
							6,250	3.48	21,750
Sept. 16				1,500	3.12	4,680			
				6,500	3.30	21,450	2,250	3.30	7,425
							6,250	3.48	21,750
Oct. 9				2,250	3.30	7,425			
				5,000	3.48	17,400	1,250	3.48	4,350
Nov. 20	3,750	3.72	13,950				1,250	3.48	4,350
							3,750	3.72	13,950

Ending inventory = (1,250 X $3.48) + (3,750 X $3.72) = $18,300

  (b) Periodic:

Purchased	Units	Unit Cost	Total Cost
November 20	3,750	$3.72	$ 13,950
August 12	1,250	3.48	4,350
	5,000		$ 18,300 *

* Note that the cost of ending inventory is the same as under perpetual.

3. Ending inventory under LIFO:
  (a)   Perpetual:

Date	Purchased Units	Unit Cost	Total Cost	Sold Units	Unit Cost	Total Cost	Balance Units	Unit Cost	Total Cost
Beg. inv.							6,250	$3.00	$18,750
Feb. 3				5,250	$3.00	$15,750	1,000	3.00	3,000
Mar. 15	5,000	$3.12	$15,600				1,000	3.00	3,000
							5,000	3.12	15,600
May 4				4,500	3.12	14,040	1,000	3.00	3,000
							500	3.12	1,560
May 10	8,750	3.30	28,875				1,000	3.00	3,000
							500	3.12	1,560
							8,750	3.30	28,875
Aug. 12	6,250	3.48	21,750				1,000	3.00	3,000
							500	3.12	1,560
							8,750	3.30	28,875
							6,250	3.48	21,750
Sept. 16				6,250	3.48	21,750			
				1,750	3.30	5,775	1,000	3.00	3,000
							500	3.12	1,560
							7,000	3.30	23,100
Oct. 9				7,000	3.30	23,100			
				250	3.12	780	1,000	3.00	3,000
							250	3.12	780
Nov. 20	3,750	3.72	13,950				1,000	3.00	3,000
							250	3.12	780
							3,750	3.72	13,950

Ending inventory = (1,000 X $3.00) + (250 X $3.12) + (3,750 X $3.72) = $17,730 *(b)* Periodic:

	Units	Unit Cost	Total Cost
Merchandise Inventory, January 1	5,000	$3.00	$ 15,000

4. Ending inventory under weighted-average:

(a) Perpetual:

Date	Purchased Units	Unit Cost	Total Cost	Sold Units	Unit Cost	Total Cost	Balance Units	Unit Cost	Total Cost
Beg. inv.							6,250	$3.0000	$18,750
Feb. 3				5,250	$3.00	$15,750	1,000	3.0000	3,000
Mar. 15	5,000	$3.12	$15,600				6,000	3.1000 [a]	18,600
May 4				4,500	3.10	13,950	1,500	3.1000	4,650
May 10	8,750	3.30	28,875				10,250	3.2707 [b]	33,525
Aug. 12	6,250	3.48	21,750				16,500	3.3500 [c]	55,275
Sept. 16				8,000	3.35	26,800	8,500	3.3500	28,475
Oct. 9				7,250	3.35	24,288	1,250	3.3500	4,187 *
Nov. 20	3,750	3.72	13,950				5,000	3.6274 [d]	18,137

Ending inventory = (5,000 X $3.6274) = $18,137

[a] $\dfrac{\$18,600}{6,000} = \$3.100$ [b] $\dfrac{\$33,525}{10,250} = \$3.2707$ [c] $\dfrac{\$55,275}{16,500} = \$3.3500$ [d] $\dfrac{\$18,137}{5,000} = \$3.6274$

* Rounding difference.

(b) Periodic

Purchased	Units	Unit Cost	Total Cost
Merchandise Inventory, January 1	6,250	$3.00	$ 18,750
March 15	5,000	3.12	15,600
May 10	8,750	3.30	28,875
August 12	6,250	3.48	21,750
November 20	3,750	3.72	13,950
	30,000		$ 98,925

Weighted-average unit cost = $98,925/30,000 = $3.2975
Ending inventory cost = $3.2975 x 5,000 = $16,488*
*Rounding difference.

b. Journal entries under LIFO perpetual:

Feb.	3	Cost of Goods Sold	15,750	
		Merchandise Inventory		15,750
		To record cost of $3 on 5,200 units sold		
Mar.	15	Merchandise Inventory	15,600	
		Accounts Payable		15,600
		To record purchase of 5,000 units at $3.12 on Account.		
May	4	Cost of Goods Sold	14,040	
		Merchandise Inventory		14,040
		To record cost of $3.12 on 4,500 units sold.		
	10	Merchandise Inventory	28,875	
		Accounts Payable		28,875
		To record purchase of 8,750 units at $3.30 on account.		
Aug.	12	Merchandise Inventory	21,750	
		Accounts Payable		21,750
		To record purchase of 6,250 units at $3.48 on account		
Sept.	16	Cost of Goods Sold	27,525	
		Merchandise Inventory		27,525
		To record costs of $3.48 and $3.30 on 6,250 units at 1,750 units sold, respectively.		
Oct.	9	Cost of Goods Sold	23,880	
		Merchandise Inventory		23,880
		To record costs of $3.30 and $3.12 on 7,000 units and 250 units sold, respectively.		
Nov.	20	Merchandise Inventory	13,950	
		Accounts Payable		13,950
		To record purchase of 3,750 units at $3.72 on account.		

Demonstration Problem 7-B

a. Joel Company reported annual net income as follows:

2009	$27,200
2010	28,400
2011	24,000

Analysis of the inventories shows that certain clerical errors were made with the following results:

	Incorrect Inventory Amount	Correct Inventory Amount
December 31, 2009	$4,800	$5,680
December 31, 2010	5,600	4,680

Required What is the corrected net income for 2009, 2010, and 2011?

b. The records of Little Corporation show the following account balances on the day a fire destroyed the company's inventory:

Merchandise inventory, January 1	$ 40,000
Net cost of purchases (to date)	200,000
Sales (to date)	300,000
Average rate of gross margin for the past five years	30% of net sales

Compute an estimated value of the ending inventory using the gross margin method.   **Required**

c. The records of Draper Company show the following account balances at year-end:

	Cost	Retail
Merchandise inventory, January 1	$17,600	$25,000
Purchases	68,000	100,000
Transportation-in	1,900	
Sales		101,000

Compute the estimated ending inventory at cost using the retail inventory method.   **Required**

Solution to Demonstration Problem 7–B

a.   Corrected net income:

	2009	2010	2011	Total
Net income as reported	$27,200	$28,400	$24,000	$79,600
Adjustments				
(1)	880			
(2)		(880)		
		(920)		
(3)			920	
Corrected net income	$28,080	$26,600	$24,920	$79,600

(1) Ending inventory understated ($5,680 - $4,800 = $880).
(2) Beginning inventory understated ($5,680 - $4,800) = $880).
    Ending inventory overstated ($5,600 - $4,680 = $920).
(3) Beginning inventory overstated ($5,600 - $4,680 = $920).

b.   Computation of inventory:

Merchandise Inventory, January 1		$ 40,000
Net cost of purchases		200,000
Cost of goods available for sale		$ 240,000
Less estimated cost of goods sold:		
Net Sales	$ 300,000	
Gross margin ($300,000 X 0.30)	90,000	
Estimated cost of goods sold		210,000
Inventory at cost, estimated by gross margin method.		$ 30,000

c.   Computation of inventory:

	Cost	Retail
Merchandise Inventory, January 1	$ 17,600	$ 25,000
Purchases	68,000	100,000
Transportation-in	1,900	—
Goods available for sale	$ 87,500	$ 125,000
Cost/retail price ratio:		
$87,500/$125,000 = 70%		
Sales		101,000
Ending inventory at retail price		$ 24,000
Times cost/retail price ratio		X 70%
Ending inventory at cost, December 31.		$ 16,800

New Terms

FIFO (first-in, first-out)   A method of costing inventory that assumes the costs of the first goods purchased are those charged to cost of goods sold when the company actually sells goods. *266*

Gross margin method   A procedure for estimating inventory cost in which estimated cost of goods sold (determined using an estimated gross margin) is deducted from the cost of goods available for sale to determine estimated ending inventory. The estimated gross margin is calculated using gross margin rates (in relation to net sales) of prior periods. *279*

Inventory, or paper, profits   Equal to the current replacement cost to purchase a unit of inventory at time of sale minus the unit's historical cost. *272*

Inventory turnover ratio   Cost of goods sold ÷ Average inventory. *282*

LIFO (last-in, first-out)   A method of costing inventory that assumes the costs of the most recent purchases are the first costs charged to cost of goods sold when the company actually sells the goods. *267*

Lower-of-cost-or-market (LCM) method   An inventory costing method that values inventory at the lower of its historical cost or its current market (replacement) cost. *278*

Merchandise inventory   The quantity of goods held by a merchandising company for resale to customers. *257*

Net realizable value   Estimated selling price of an item less the estimated costs incurred in preparing the item for sale and selling it. *277*

Retail inventory method   A procedure for estimating the cost of the ending inventory by applying a cost/ retail price ratio to ending inventory stated at retail prices. *280*

Specific identification method   An inventory costing method that attaches the actual cost to an identifiable unit of product. *265*

Weighted-average method   A method of costing ending inventory using a weighted-average unit cost. Under the perpetual inventory procedure, a new weighted-average is calculated after each purchase. Under the periodic procedure, the weighted-average is determined by dividing the total number of units purchased plus those in beginning inventory into total cost of goods available for sale. Units in the ending inventory are carried at this per unit cost. *268*

Self-Test

True-False

Indicate whether each of the following statements is true or false.

1. Overstated ending inventory results in an overstatement of cost of goods sold and an understatement of gross margin and net income.
2. In a period of rising prices, FIFO results in the lowest cost of goods sold.
3. Under LCM, inventory is written down to market value when the market value is less than the cost, and inventory is written up to market value when the market value is greater than the cost.

4. Under the gross margin method, an estimate must be made of gross margin to determine estimated cost of goods sold and estimated ending inventory.
5. To use the retail inventory method, both cost and retail prices must be known for the goods available for sale.
6. Under the perpetual procedure, cost of goods sold is determined as a result of the closing entries made at the end of the period.

Multiple-Choice

Select the best answer for each of the following questions.

Jack Company began the accounting period with inventory of 3,000 units at $30 each. During the period, the company purchased an additional 5,000 units at $36 each and sold 4,600 units. Assume the use of the periodic inventory procedure for Questions 1–6.

1. Cost of ending inventory using the FIFO is:
   a. $104,400.
   b. $122,400.
   c. $120,000.
   d. $147,600.
   e. None of the above.
2. Cost of goods sold using the FIFO is:
   a. $165,600.
   b. $150,000.
   c. $147,600.
   d. $122,400.
   e. None of the above.

3. Cost of ending inventory using the LIFO is:
   a. $104,400.
   b. $114,750.
   c. $156,000.
   d. $122,400.
   e. None of the above.
4. Cost of goods sold using the LIFO is:
   a. $155,250.
   b. $114,000.
   c. $147,600.
   d. $165,600.
   e. None of the above.
5. Cost of ending inventory using weighted-average is:
   a. $114,750.
   b. $157,600.
   c. $122,400.
   d. $109,650.
   e. None of the above.

6. Cost of goods sold using weighted-average is:
   a. $147,200.
   b. $160,350.
   c. $155,250.
   d. $114,000.
   e. None of the above.
7. During a period of rising prices, which inventory method might be expected to give the highest net income?
   a. Weighted-average.
   b. FIFO.
   c. LIFO.
   d. Specific identification.
   e. Cannot determine.

Now turn to page 304 to check your answers.

Questions

1. Why is proper inventory valuation so important?
2. Why does an understated ending inventory understate net income for the period by the same amount?
3. Why does an error in ending inventory affect two accounting periods?
4. What is the meaning of taking a physical inventory?
5. What is the accountant's responsibility regarding taking a physical inventory?
6. Which cost elements are included in inventory? What practical problems arise by including the costs of such elements?
7. Which accounts that are used under the periodic inventory procedure are not used under the perpetual inventory procedure?
8. What entries are necessary under the perpetual inventory procedure when goods are sold?
9. Why is there closer control over inventory under the perpetual inventory procedure than under the periodic inventory procedure?
10. Why is the perpetual inventory procedure being used increasingly in business?
11. What is the cost flow assumption? What is meant by the physical flow of goods? Does a relationship between cost flows and the physical flow of goods exist, or should such a relationship exist?
12. Indicate how a company can manipulate its net income if it uses LIFO. Is the same opportunity available under FIFO? Why or why not?
13. What are the main advantages of using the FIFO and LIFO?

14. Which inventory method is the correct one? Can a company change inventory methods?
15. Why are ending inventory and cost of goods sold the same under FIFO perpetual and FIFO periodic?
16. Would you agree with the following statement? Reducing the amount of taxes payable currently is a valid objective of business management and, since LIFO results in such a reduction, all businesses should use LIFO.
17. What is net realizable value, and how is it used?
18. Why is it acceptable accounting practice to recognize a loss by writing down an item in inventory to market, but unacceptable to recognize a gain by writing up an inventory item?
19. Under what conditions would the gross margin method of computing an estimated inventory yield approximately correct amounts?
20. What are the main reasons for estimating ending inventory?
21. Should a company rely exclusively on the gross margin method to determine the ending inventory and cost of goods sold for the end-of-year financial statements?
22. How can the retail method be used to estimate inventory?

23. **Wal-Mart** Based on the notes to the financial statements of Wal-Mart Stores, Inc. contained in the Annual Report Appendix, what inventory methods were used?

Exercises

Exercise 7-1
Determine effects of inventory errors
(L.O. 1)

Crocker Company reported annual net income as follows:

2010	$484,480
2011	487,680
2012	409,984

Analysis of its inventories revealed the following incorrect inventory amounts and these correct amounts:

	Incorrect Inventory Amount	Correct Inventory Amount
December 31, 2010	$ 76,800	$89,600
December 31, 2011	86,400	77,600

Compute the annual net income for each of the three years assuming the correct inventories had been used.

Exercise 7-2
Compute the impact on net income under specific identification
(L.O. 3, 4)

Slate Truck Company manufactures trucks and identifies each truck with a unique serial plate. On December 31, a customer ordered 5 trucks from the company, which currently has 20 trucks in its inventory. Ten of these trucks cost $20,000 each, and the other 10 cost $25,000 each. If Slate wished to minimize its net income, which trucks would it ship? By how much could Slate reduce net income by selecting units from one group versus the other group?

Exercise 7-3
Compute ending inventory using the FIFO perpetual inventory procedure
(L.O. 3)

Miami Discount Company inventory records show:

	Units	Unit Cost	Total Cost
Beginning inventory	3,000	$38.00	$114,000
Purchases:			
February 14	900	39.00	35,100
March 18	2,400	40.00	96,000
July 21	1,800	40.30	72,540
September 27	1,800	40.60	73,080
November 27	600	41.00	24,600
Sales:			
April 15	2,800		
August 20	2,000		
October 3	1,500		

The December 31 inventory was 4,200 units. Miami Discount Company uses the perpetual inventory procedure. Present a schedule showing the measurement of the ending inventory using the FIFO perpetual inventory procedure.

Using the data in Exercise 7–3 for Miami Discount Company, present a schedule showing the measurement of the ending inventory using the LIFO perpetual inventory procedure.

Exercise 7-4
Compute ending inventory under LIFO perpetual inventory procedure (L.O. 3)

London Company had a beginning inventory of 160 units at $24 (total = $3,840) and the following inventory transactions during the year:
1. January 8, sold 40 units.
2. January 11, purchased 80 units at $30.00.
3. January 15, purchased 80 units at $32.00.
4. January 22, sold 80 units.

Using the preceding information, price the ending inventory at its weighted-average cost, assuming the perpetual inventory procedure.

Exercise 7-5
Compute ending inventory under weighted-average perpetual inventory procedure (L.O. 3)

Kettle Company made the following purchases of Product A in its first year of operations:

	Units		Units Cost
January 2	1,400	@	$7.40
March 31	1,200	@	7.00
July 5	2,400	@	7.60
November 1	1,800	@	8.00

The ending inventory that year consisted of 2,400 units. Kettle uses periodic inventory procedure.

a. Compute the cost of the ending inventory using each of the following methods: (1) FIFO, (2) LIFO, and (3) weighted-average.
b. Which method would yield the highest amount of gross margin? Explain why it does.

Exercise 7-6
Compute cost of ending inventory using the FIFO, LIFO, and weighted-average under the periodic inventory procedure (L.O. 3)

The following are selected transactions and other data of the Custer Company:
1. Purchased 20 units @ $360 per unit on account on September 18, 2012.
2. Sold 6 units on account for $576 per unit on September 20, 2012.
3. Discovered a shortage of $2,640 at year-end after a physical inventory.

Prepare journal entries for these transactions using the FIFO perpetual inventory procedure. Assume the beginning inventory consists of 20 units @ $336 per unit.

Exercise 7-7
Prepare journal entries for inventory under FIFO perpetual inventory procedure (L.O. 3, 5)

Following are selected transactions of Gamble Company:
1. Purchased 100 units of merchandise at $240 each; terms 2/10, n/30.
2. Paid the invoice in transaction 1 within the discount period.
3. Sold 80 units at $384 each for cash.
4. Purchased 100 units at $360; terms 2/10, n/30.
5. Paid the invoice in transaction 4 within the discount period.
6. Sold 60 units at $552 each for cash.

Prepare journal entries for the six preceding items. Assume Gamble uses the FIFO perpetual inventory procedure.

Exercise 7-8
Prepare journal entries under FIFO perpetual inventory procedure (L.O. 3, 5)

Wells Company had the following transactions during February:
1. Purchased 135 units at $65 on account.
2. Sold 108 units at $90 on account.
3. Purchased 170 units at $75 on account.
4. Sold 122 units at $95 on account.
5. Sold 67 units at $100 on account.

The beginning inventory consisted of 67 units purchased at a cost of $55.

Prepare the journal entries relating to inventory for these five transactions, assuming Wells accounts for inventory using the perpetual inventory procedure and the LIFO inventory method. Do not record the entries for sales.

Exercise 7-9
Prepare journal entries affecting inventory using the LIFO perpetual inventory procedure (L.O. 3, 5)

Exercise 7-10
Prepare journal entries affecting inventory using weighted-average periodic inventory procedure (L.O. 3)

Following are inventory data for Kintech Company:

1. January 1 inventory on hand, 400 units @ $28.80.
2. January sales were 80 units.
3. February sales totaled 120 units.
4. March 1, purchased 200 units @ $30.24.
5. Sales for March through August were 160 units.
6. September 1, purchased 40 units @ $33.12.
7. September through December sales were 180 units.

A physical inventory on December 31, showed 100 units on hand. Determine the cost of the ending inventory using the weighted-average method under the periodic inventory procedure.

Exercise 7-11
Compute inventory (paper) profit under FIFO (L.O. 3, 4)

A company purchased 1,000 units of a product at $12.00 and 2,000 units at $13.20. It sold all of these units at $18.00 each at a time when the current cost to replace the units sold was $13.80. Compute the amount of gross margin under FIFO that LIFO supporters would call inventory, or paper, profits.

Exercise 7-12
Indicate whether FIFO or LIFO would yield the higher net income (L.O. 3, 4)

Clayton Company's inventory was 12,000 units with a cost of $160 each on January 1, 2012. During 2012, numerous units were purchased and sold. Also during 2012, the purchase price of this product fell steadily until at year-end it was $120. The inventory at year-end was 18,000 units. State which method of inventory measurement, LIFO or FIFO, would have resulted in higher reported net income, and explain briefly.

Exercise 7-13
Using net realizable value, compute carrying cost of inventory item (L.O. 6)

Levi Motor Company owns a luxury automobile that it has used as a demonstrator for eight months. The auto has a list or sticker price of $85,000 and cost Levi $75,000. At the end of the fiscal year, the auto is on hand and has an expected selling price of $80,000. Costs expected to be incurred to sell the auto include tune-up and maintenance costs of $3,000, advertising of $1,000, and a commission of 5% of the selling price to the employee selling the auto. Compute the amount at which the auto should be carried in inventory.

Exercise 7-14
Determine the proper carrying value of damaged goods (L.O. 6)

Pure Sound Systems used one sound system as a floor model. It cost $3,600 and had an original selling price of $4,800. After six months, the sound system was damaged and replaced by a newer model. The sound system had an estimated selling price of $2,880, but when the company performed $480 in repairs, it could be sold for $3,840. Prepare the journal entry, if any, that must be made on Pure Sound's books to record the decline in market value.

Exercise 7-15
Compute value of ending inventory using LCM applied on an item-by-item basis (L.O. 6)

Your assistant has compiled the following data:

Item	Quantity (units)	Unit Cost	Unit Market	Total Cost	Total Market
A	300	$ 57.60	$ 55.20	$17,280	$16,560
B	300	28.80	33.60	8,640	10,080
C	900	21.60	21.60	19,440	19,440
D	500	12.00	13.20	6,000	6,600

Calculate the dollar amount of the ending inventory using the LCM method, applied on an item-by-item basis, and the amount of the decline from cost to lower-of-cost-or-market.

Exercise 7-16
Compute value of total inventory using LCM (L.O. 6)

Use the data in Exercise 7–15 to compute the cost of the ending inventory using the LCM method applied to the total inventory.

Tilley-Mill Company takes a physical inventory at the end of each calendar-year accounting period to establish the ending inventory amount for financial statement purposes. Its financial statements for the past few years indicate an average gross margin on net sales of 25%. On July 18, a fire destroyed the entire store building and its contents. The records in a fireproof vault were intact. Through July 17, these records show:

Merchandise inventory, January 1	$ 672,000
Merchandise purchases	9,408,000
Purchase returns	134,400
Transportation-in	504,000
Sales	14,336,000
Sales returns	672,000

The company was fully covered by insurance and asks you to determine the amount of its claim for loss of merchandise.

Ryan Company takes a physical inventory at the end of each calendar-year accounting period. Its financial statements for the past few years indicate an average gross margin on net sales of 30%.

On June 12, a fire destroyed the entire store building and the inventory. The records in a fireproof vault were intact. Through June 11, these records show:

Merchandise inventory, January 1	$120,000
Merchandise purchases	3,000,000
Purchase returns	36,000
Transportation-in	204,000
Sales	3,720,000

The company was fully covered by insurance and asks you to determine the amount of its claim for loss of merchandise.

Victoria Falls Company, Inc., records show the following account balances for the year ending December 31, 2012:

	Cost	Retail
Beginning inventory	$42,000	$57,500
Purchases	25,000	37,500
Transportation-in	500	
Sales		52,500

Using these data, compute the estimated cost of ending inventory using the retail method of inventory valuation.

Problems

Kelley Company reported net income of $358,050 for 2011, $371,400 for 2012, and $325,800 for 2013, using the incorrect inventory amounts shown for December 31, 2011, and 2012. Recently, Kelley corrected the inventory amounts for those dates. Kelley used the correct December 31, 2013, inventory amount in calculating 2013 net income.

	Incorrect	Correct
December 31, 2011	$72,600	$85,200
December 31, 2012	84,000	70,200

Prepare a schedule that shows: *(a)* the reported net income for each year, *(b)* the amount of correction needed for each year, and *(c)* the correct net income for each year.

Required

An examination of the financial records of Lanal Company on December 31, 2011, disclosed the following with regard to merchandise inventory for 2011 and prior years:

1. December 31, 2007, inventory was correct.
2. December 31, 2008, inventory was overstated $200,000.
3. December 31, 2009, inventory was overstated $100,000.
4. December 31, 2010, inventory was understated $220,000.
5. December 31, 2011, inventory was correct.

The reported net income for each year was:

2008	$384,000
2009	544,000
2010	670,000
2011	846,000

Required ➲

a. Prepare a schedule of corrected net income for each of the four years—2008–2011.
b. What error(s) would have been included in each December 31 balance sheet? Assume each year's error is independent of the other years' errors.
c. Comment on the implications of your corrected net income as contrasted with reported net income.

Problem 7-3
Maximize and minimize gross margin using specific identification (L.O. 3, 4)

Brett Company sells computers and uses the specific identification method to account for its inventory. On November 30, 2012, the company had 46 Orange III computers on hand that were acquired on the following dates and at these stated costs:

	Units		Unit Cost
July 3	10	@	$10,080
September 10	20	@	9,600
November 29	16	@	10,700

Brett sold 36 Orange III computers at $12,720 each in December. There were no purchases of this model in December.

Required ➲

a. Compute the gross margin on December sales of Orange III computers assuming the company shipped those units that would maximize reported gross margin.
b. Repeat part a assuming the company shipped those units that would minimize reported gross margin for December.
c. In view of your answers to parts **a** and **b**, what would be your reaction to an assertion that the specific identification method should not be considered an acceptable method for costing inventory?

Problem 7-4
Prepare journal entries for purchases and sales using the FIFO perpetual inventory procedures (L.O. 3, 5)

The inventory records of Thimble Company show the following:

Mar. 1 Beginning inventory consists of 10 units costing $40 per unit.
  3 Sold 5 units at $94 per unit.
  10 Purchased 16 units at $48 per unit.
  12 Sold 8 units at $96 per unit.
  20 Sold 7 units at $96 per unit.
  25 Purchased 16 units at $50 per unit.
  31 Sold 8 units at $96 per unit.

Assume all purchases and sales are made on credit.

Required ➲

Using the FIFO perpetual inventory procedure, prepare the appropriate journal entries for March.

Problem 7-5
Compute ending inventory under FIFO, LIFO, and weighted-average using perpetual and periodic inventory procedures (L.O. 3)

The following purchases and sales for Ripple Company are for April 2012. There was no inventory on April 1.

Purchases				Sales	
	Units		Unit Cost		Units
April 3	3,200	@	$33.00	April 6	1,500
April 10	1,600	@	34.00	April 12	1,400
April 22	2,000	@	35.00	April 25	2,300
April 28	1,800	@	36.00		

a. Compute the ending inventory as of April 30, 2012, using the perpetual inventory procedure, under each of the following methods: (1) FIFO, (2) LIFO, and (3) weighted-average (carry unit cost to four decimal places and round total cost to nearest dollar).

b. Repeat **a** using the periodic inventory procedure.

⬤ *Required*

Refer to the data in Problem 7–5.

a. Using the LIFO perpetual inventory procedure, prepare the journal entries for the purchases and sales (Cost of Goods Sold entry only).

b. Repeat **a** using the LIFO periodic inventory procedure, including closing entries. (Note: You may want to refer to the Appendix in Chapter 6 for this part.)

Problem 7-6
Record journal entries for purchases and sales under FIFO perpetual and periodic inventory procedures (L.O. 5)

⬤ *Required*

The following data relate to the beginning inventory, purchases, and sales of Braxton Company for the year 2012:

Problem 7-7
Compute ending inventory and cost of goods sold under FIFO, LIFO, and weighted-average using perpetual and periodic inventory procedures (L.O.3)

	Units	Unit Cost
Merchandise Inventory, January 1	1,400 @	$5.04
Purchases:		
February 2	1,000 @	4.80
April 5	2,000 @	3.60
June 15	1,200 @	3.00
September 30	1,400 @	2.88
November 28	1,800 @	4.20
Sales:		
March 10	900	
May 15	1,800	
July 6	800	
August 23	600	
December 22	2,500	

a. Assuming use of the perpetual inventory procedure, compute the ending inventory and cost of goods sold under each of the following methods: (1) FIFO, (2) LIFO, and (3) weighted-average (carry unit cost to four decimal places and round total cost to nearest dollar).

b. Repeat **a** assuming use of the periodic inventory procedure.

⬤ *Required*

Welch Company accounts for a product it sells using the LIFO periodic inventory procedure. Product data for the year ended December 31, 2011, are shown below. Merchandise inventory on January 1 was 3,000 units at $14.40 each.

Problem 7-8
Compute gross margin using the FIFO and LIFO illustrating effects of end-of- year purchases (L.O. 3, 4)

Purchases			Sales		
	Units	Unit Cost		Units	Unit Cost
January 5	6,000 @	$18.00	January 10	4,000 @	$28.80
March 31	18,000 @	21.60	April 2	15,000 @	32.40
August 12	12,000 @	27.00	August 22	16,000 @	36.00
December 26	6,000 @	28.80	December 24	3,000 @	39.60

a. Compute the gross margin earned on sales of this product for 2011.

b. Repeat part **a** assuming that the December 26 purchase was made in January of 2012.

c. Recompute the gross margin assuming that 10,000 rather than 6,000 units were purchased on December 26 at the same cost per unit.

d. Solve parts **a, b,** and **c** using the FIFO method.

⬤ *Required*

Problem 7-9
Compute ending
inventory using LCM
(L.O. 6)

The accountant for Gentry Company prepared the following schedule of the company's inventory at December 31, 2011, and used the LCM method applied to total inventory in determining cost of goods sold:

Item	Quantity	Unit Cost	Unit Market
Q	4,200	$7.20	$7.20
R	2,400	6.00	5.76
S	5,400	4.80	4.56
T	4,800	4.20	4.32

Required

a. State whether this approach is an acceptable method of inventory measurement and show the calculations used to determine the amounts.
b. Compute the amount of the ending inventory using the LCM method on an item-by-item basis.
c. State the effect on net income in 2011 if the method in **b** was used rather than the method referred to in **a**.

Problem 7-10
Prepare quarterly and
six-month income
statements using the
gross margin method
(L.O. 7)

As part of a loan agreement with a local bank, Brazos Company must present quarterly and cumulative income statements for the year 2011. The company uses periodic inventory procedure and marks its merchandise to sell at a price yielding a gross margin of 30%. Selected data for the first six months of 2011 are as follows:

	First Quarter	Second Quarter
Sales	$248,000	$256,000
Purchases	160,000	184,000
Purchase returns and allowances	9,600	11,200
Purchase discounts	3,200	3,520
Sales returns and allowances	8,000	4,800
Transportation-in	8,000	8,320
Miscellaneous selling expenses	25,600	24,000
Miscellaneous administrative expenses	9,600	8,000

The cost of the physical inventory taken December 31, 2010, was $30,400.

Required

a. Indicate how income statements can be prepared without taking a physical inventory at the end of each of the first two quarters of 2011.
b. Prepare income statements for the first quarter, the second quarter, and the first six months of 2011.

Problem 7-11
Estimate ending
inventory using retail
inventory method
(L.O. 7)

Cobb Company records show the following information for 2012:

	Cost	Retail
Sales	—	$350,400
Purchases	$270,000	420,000
Transportation-in	26,280	—
Merchandise inventory,		
January 1	12,000	17,400
Purchase returns	15,120	18,600

Required

Compute the estimated year-end inventory balance at cost using the retail method of estimating inventory.

Alternate Problems

Problem 7-1A
Compute corrected net
income given inventory
errors (L.O. 1)

Harris Company reported net income of $312,000 for 2011, $324,000 for 2012, and $348,000 for 2013, using the incorrect inventory amounts shown for December 31, 2011, and 2012. Recently Harris corrected these inventory amounts. Harris used the correct December 31, 2013, inventory amount in calculating 2013 net income.

	Incorrect	Correct
December 31, 2011	$96,000	$108,000
December 31, 2012	91,200	84,000

Prepare a schedule that shows: *(a)* the reported net income for each year, *(b)* the amount of correction needed for each year, and *(c)* the correct net income for each year. **⊂** *Required*

An examination of the financial records of Jersey Company on December 31, 2011, disclosed the following with regard to merchandise inventory for 2011 and prior years:

Problem 7-2A
Compute corrected net income given inventory errors; indicate balance sheet errors and comment (L.O. 1)

1. December 31, 2007, inventory was correct.
2. December 31, 2008, inventory was understated $50,000.
3. December 31, 2009, inventory was overstated $35,000.
4. December 31, 2010, inventory was understated $30,000.
5. December 31, 2011, inventory was correct.

The reported net income for each year was:

2008	$292,500
2009	355,000
2010	382,500
2011	350,000

a. Prepare a schedule of corrected net income for each of the four years—2008–2011. **⊂** *Required*
b. What errors would have been included in each December 31 balance sheet? Assume each year's error is independent of the other years' errors.
c. Comment on the implications of the corrected net income as contrasted with reported net income.

High Surf Company sells the Ultra-Light model wind surfer and uses the specific identification method to account for its inventory. The Ultra-Lights are identical except for identifying serial numbers. On August 1, 2011, the company had three Ultra-Lights that cost $14,000 each in its inventory. During the month, the company purchased the following:

Problem 7-3A
Maximize and minimize gross margin using specific identification (L.O. 3, 4)

	Units		Unit Cost
August 3	5	@	$13,000
August 17	6	@	14,500
August 28	6	@	15,000

High Surf Company sold 13 Ultra-Lights in August at $20,000 each.

a. Compute the gross margin earned by the company in August if it shipped the units that would maximize gross margin. **⊂** *Required*
b. Repeat part a assuming the company shipped the units that would minimize gross margin.
c. Do you think High Surf Company should be permitted to use the specific identification method of accounting for Ultra-Lights in view of the manipulation possible as shown by your calculations in a and b?

The inventory records of Coral Company show the following:

Problem 7-4A
Compute cost of goods sold using the FIFO for both perpetual and periodic inventory procedures (L.O. 3, 5)

Jan.	1	Beginning inventory consists of 12 units costing $48 per unit.
	5	Purchased 15 units @ $49.92 per unit.
	10	Sold 9 units @ $108 per unit.
	12	Sold 7 units @ $108 per unit.
	20	Purchased 20 units @ $50.16 per unit.
	22	Purchased 5 units @ $48 per unit.
	30	Sold 20 units @ $110.40 per unit.

Assume all purchases and sales are made on account.

Required ➡

a. Using the FIFO perpetual inventory procedure, compute cost of goods sold for January.
b. Using the FIFO perpetual inventory procedure, prepare the journal entries for January.
c. Compute the cost of goods sold under the FIFO periodic inventory procedure. Is there a difference between the amount computed using the two different procedures?

Problem 7-5A
Compute ending inventory under FIFO, LIFO, and weighted-average using perpetual and periodic inventory procedures (L.O. 3)

Following are data for Dandy Company for the year 2012:

	Units	Unit Cost
Merchandise Inventory, January 1	700 @	$20.40
Purchases:		
February 2	500 @	21.00
April 5	1,000 @	24.00
June 15	600 @	27.00
September 30	700 @	30.00
November 28	900 @	31.20
	4,400	
Sales:		
March 5	400	
July 18	1,200	
August 12	800	
October 15	900	
	3,300	

Required ➡

a. Compute the ending inventory as of December 31, 2012, assuming use of the perpetual inventory procedure, under each of the following methods: (1) FIFO, (2) LIFO, and (3) weighted-average (carry unit cost to four decimal places and round total cost to nearest dollar).
b. Compute the ending inventory as of December 31, 2012, assuming use of the periodic inventory procedure, under each of the following methods: (1) FIFO, (2) LIFO, and (3) weighted-average.

Problem 7-6A
Prepare journal entries for purchases and sales using the LIFO perpetual and periodic inventory procedures (L.O. 5)

Refer to the data in Problem 7–5A.

a. Give the journal entries to record the purchases and sales (Cost of Goods Sold entry only) for the year under FIFO perpetual.
b. Give the journal entries to record the purchases for the year and necessary year-end entries to charge Income Summary with the cost of goods sold for the year under FIFO periodic. (Note: You may want to refer to the Appendix in Chapter 6 for this part.)

Required ➡

Problem 7-7A
Compute ending inventory and cost of goods sold under FIFO, LIFO, and weighted-average using perpetual and periodic inventory procedures (L.O. 3)

Following are data related to a product of Coen Company for the year 2012:

	Units	Unit Cost
Merchandise Inventory, January 1	2,100 @	$12.60
Purchases:		
March 10	1,500 @	12.00
May 24	3,000 @	11.20
July 15	1,800 @	10.50
September 20	2,100 @	9.00
December 1	2,700 @	10.00
Sales:		
April 15	1,400	
June 13	2,900	
October 9	2,300	
November 21	1,700	

a. Assuming use of perpetual inventory procedure, compute the ending inventory and cost of goods sold under each of the following methods: (1) FIFO, (2) LIFO, and (3) weighted-average (carry unit cost to four decimal places and round total cost to nearest dollar).   ◖ *Required*

b. Assuming use of periodic inventory procedure, compute the ending inventory and cost of goods sold under each of the following methods: (1) FIFO, (2) LIFO, and (3) weighted-average (carry unit cost to four decimal places and round total cost to nearest dollar).

Star Company accounts for its inventory using the LIFO method under the periodic inventory procedure. Data on purchases, sales, and inventory for the year ended December 31, 2011, are:

Problem 7-8A
Compute gross margin using the LIFO and FIFO illustrating effects of the end-of-year purchases (L.O. 3, 4)

	Units		Unit Cost
Merchandise inventory,			
January 1	2,000	@	$20
Purchases:			
January 7	5,000	@	24
July 7	10,000	@	28
December 21	6,000	@	32

During 2011, 16,000 units were sold for $1,280,000, leaving an inventory on December 31, 2011, of 7,000 units.

◖ *Required*

a. Compute the gross margin earned on sales during 2011.

b. Compute the change in gross margin that would have resulted if the purchase of December 21 had been delayed until January 6, 2012.

c. Recompute the gross margin assuming that 9,000 units rather than 6,000 units were purchased on December 21 at the same cost per unit.

d. Solve parts **a, b,** and **c** using the FIFO method.

Data on the ending inventory of Jannis Company on December 31, 2011, are:

Problem 7-9A
Compute ending inventory using LCM (L.O. 6)

Item	Quantity	Unit Cost	Unit Market
1	8,400	$3.20	$3.12
2	16,800	2.88	3.04
3	5,600	2.80	2.88
4	14,000	3.84	3.60
5	11,200	3.60	3.68
6	2,800	3.04	2.88

◖ *Required*

a. Compute the ending inventory applying the LCM method to the total inventory.

b. Determine the ending inventory by applying the LCM method on an item-by-item basis.

The sales and cost of goods sold for Lively Company for the past five years were as follows:

Problem 7-10A
Estimate inventory using gross margin method (L.O. 7)

Year	Sales (net)	Cost of Goods Sold
2006	$9,984,960	$6,240,600
2007	10,794,240	6,746,400
2008	12,346,560	7,716,600
2009	11,926,080	7,272,000
2010	12,747,840	7,920,000

The following information is for the seven months ended July 31, 2011:

Sales	$7,748,000
Purchases	4,588,800
Purchase returns	28,800
Sales returns	173,760
Merchandise inventory,	
January 1, 2011	948,000

To secure a loan, Lively Company has been asked to present current financial state-ments. However, the company does not wish to take a complete physical inventory as of July 31, 2011.

Required
a. Indicate how financial statements can be prepared without taking a complete physical inventory.
b. From the data given, compute the estimated inventory as of July 31, 2011.

Problem 7-11A
Estimate ending
inventory using retail
inventory method
(L.O. 7)

Apple Company's records contained the following inventory information:

	Cost	Retail
Sales	—	$420,000
Purchases	$396,000	582,000
Purchase returns	8,400	12,000
Transportation-in	10,800	—
Merchandise inventory,		
January 1	21,600	30,000

Required
Compute the estimated year-end inventory balance at cost using the retail method of inventory valuation.

Beyond the Numbers—Critical Thinking

**Business Decision
Case 7-1**
Prepare income
statement using
the LIFO and FIFO.
Determine inventory
turnover (L.O. 3, 4, 8)

Susan Green and Carol Lewis, were interested in starting part-time business activities to supplement their family incomes. Both heard a presentation by the manufacturer of an exercise device and decided to become a distributor of this exerciser. Green's sales territory is Cobb County, and Lewis's sales territory is Gwinett County. Each owns her own business.

To induce Green and Lewis to become distributors, the manufacturer made price conces-sions on the first 1,000 units purchased. The manufacturer sold the first 200 units at $15 each, the next 300 at $18 per unit, and the next 500 at $19 per unit. After that, Green and Lewis had to pay $20 per unit.

During the first year, each bought 1,200 units; coincidentally, both sold exactly 950 units for $27 each. Green had $2,600 of selling expenses; Lewis incurred $1,700 of selling expenses. (Green's expenses were considerably higher because on December 28 she distributed 4,000 sales brochures to households in her territory at a cost of $800. The brochures stressed that people would want to take off the extra pounds gained during the holiday season; also, these exercisers were inexpensive and could be used at home.)

At the end of the year, both had to determine their net incomes. Green received a B in the accounting course she took at State University. She remembered the FIFO inven-tory method and plans to use it. Lewis knows nothing about inventory costing methods. However, her husband is acquainted with the LIFO inventory method used at the company where he works. He will help her compute the cost of the ending inventory and the cost of goods using the LIFO.

Required
a. Prepare income statements for Green and Lewis.
b. Which business has performed better? Explain why.
c. Determine the inventory turnovers for Green and Lewis.

**Business Decision
Case 7-2**
Determine insurance
settlement using gross
margin method
(L.O. 7)

Connie Dalton owns and operates a sporting goods store. On February 2 the store suffered extensive fire damage, and all of the inventory was destroyed. Dalton uses periodic inventory procedure and has the following information in her accounting records, which were undamaged:

Merchandise inventory, January 1	$80,0000
Purchases:	
January 8	32,000
January 20	48,000
January 30	64,000
Net Sales:	
During January	240,000
February 1 and 2	16,000

Dalton's gross margin rate on net sales has been 40% for the past three years. Her insurance company offered to pay $56,000 to settle this inventory loss unless Dalton can show that she suffered a greater loss. She has asked you, her CPA, to help her in determining her loss.

Answer these questions: Based on your analysis, should Dalton settle for $56,000? If not, how can she show that she suffered a greater loss? What is your estimate of her loss?

 Required

Refer to the financial statements of Wal-Mart Stores, Inc. in the Annual Report Appendix. Describe how inventory values are determined (see Footnote 1). Also, determine the inventory turnover ratio for fiscal year 2011.

Annual Report Analysis 7-3
Determine inventory method and inventory turnover rate (L.O. 6)

Respond in writing to the following questions based on the ethics case concerning Terry Dorsey on page 282:

Ethics CaseÑ Writing Experience 7-4

a. Do you believe that Terry's scheme will work?
b. What would you do if you were Terry's accountant?
c. Comment on each of Terry's points of justification.

In teams of two or three students, interview the manager of a merchandising company. Inquire about inventory control methods, inventory costing methods, and any other information about the company's inventory procedures. As a team, write a memorandum to your instructor summarizing the results of the interview. The heading of the memorandum should include the date, to whom it is written, from whom, and the subject matter.

Group Project 7-5
Inventory control and measurementÑinterview with manager of merchandising company

In a team of two or three students, locate and visit a nearby retail store that uses perpetual inventory procedure and a computerized inventory management system. Investigate how the system works by interviewing a knowledgeable person in the company. Write a report to your instructor and make a short presentation to the class on your findings.

Group Project 7-6
Examine use of computer in inventory management

With a small group of students, identify and visit a retail store that uses periodic inventory procedure and uses the retail inventory method for preparing interim (monthly or quarterly) financial reports. Discover how the retail inventory method is applied and how the end-of-year inventory amount is calculated. Write a report to your instructor summarizing your findings.

Group Project 7-7
Examine use of the retail inventory method

Using the Internet—A View of the Real World

Visit the National Association of State Boards of Accountancy website at:
    http://www.nasba.org
Find the address of the state board of accountancy in your state. Also check out some of the information provided at websites of other state boards by clicking on any sites that appear at the end of a listing for a particular state. In a report to your instructor, summarize what you learned about state boards at some of these sites.

Internet Project 7-8
Locate state boards of accountancy

**Internet Project
7-9**
Investigate the Lexis-
Nexis website
Visit the Lexis-Nexis website at:

http://www.lexis-nexis.com

Determine the kinds of information that can be obtained at this site. Specifically, what kinds of products and services are available? What is the background of Lexis-Nexis? What pricing information is available for using its services? Write a report to your instructor summarizing your findings.

Answers to Self-Test

True-False

1. **False.** Overstated ending inventory results in an understatement of cost of goods sold and an overstatement of gross margin and net income.
2. **True.** The cost of goods sold consists of the earliest purchases at the lowest costs in a period of rising prices.
3. **False.** Under LCM, inventory is adjusted to market value only when the market (replacement) value is less than the cost.
4. **True.** The first step in the gross margin method is to estimate gross margin using the gross margin rate experienced in the past.
5. **True.** The cost/retail ratio is computed by dividing the cost of goods available for sale by the retail price of the goods available for sale.
6. **False.** Under the perpetual procedure, the Cost of Goods Sold account is updated as sales occur.

Multiple-Choice

1. **b.** The cost of ending inventory using the FIFO consists of the most recent purchase:

   Cost of ending inventory = 3,400 × $36= $122,400

2. **c.** The cost of goods sold using the FIFO is:

   Cost of goods
   available for sale = (3,000 × $30) + (5,000 × $36)

                       = $270,000

   Cost of
   goods sold = $270,000 – $122,400
              = $147,600

3. **a.** The cost of ending inventory using the LIFO is:

   (3,000 × $30) + (400 × $36) = $104,400

4. **d.** The cost of goods sold using LIFO is:

   $270,000 – $104,400 = $165,600

5. **a.** The cost of ending inventory using weighted-average cost is computed:

   Unit cost = $270,000 ÷ 8,000 = $33.75

   Cost of ending inventory = 3,400 × $33.75
                             = $114,750

6. **c.** The cost of goods sold using weighted-average cost is:

   $270,000 – $114,750 = $155,250

7. **b.** During a period of rising prices, FIFO results in the lowest cost of goods sold, thus the highest net income.

Careers in Accounting

A Career in Forensic Accounting

This chapter emphasizes the importance of having effective internal controls in every business. Unfortunately, many smaller companies do not heed this advice. Failure to implement adequate internal controls can result in financial statement fraud (purposely misstated financial statements) or embezzlement (theft). This is when the services of a forensic accountant may be necessary. Forensic accounting is the application of accounting methodology to legal issues. It is frequently associated with the investigation of civil or criminal white-collar crime such as fraud, embezzlement, and general abuse of funds issues. Typical tools used in forensic accounting are bank records, personal financial statements, interviews, and credit reports. The forensic accountant's responsibility is to gather and analyze the evidence and deliver clear, accurate, and unbiased reports reflecting the results of the investigation. Forensic accounting is commonly performed by Certified Fraud Examiners (CFEs). CFEs are members of the Association of Certified Fraud Examiners and have extensive training and possess special expertise in investigation and interview techniques specifically designed to detect or prevent fraud. Also, the American Institute of Certified Public Accountants has created a certification in financial forensics (CFF).

A well-known agency performing forensic accounting in the United States is in the Federal Bureau of Investigation (FBI). You can learn more about the FBI from their homepage at **www.fbi.gov**. Click on employment in the 'Jobs' section and then click on special agent employment to learn more about what it takes to be an FBI special agent. Did you know that one of the fastest tracks to becoming an FBI agent is with an accounting degree? There are five entry programs for becoming an FBI special agent: accounting, computer science/information technology, law, language, and diversified. Why is accounting one of those tracks? Because an ever-increasing portion of crimes investigated by the FBI are white-collar crimes where accounting knowledge is essential.

8

Control of Cash

In a small corporation the president might make all the important decisions and will usually maintain a close watch over the affairs of the business. However, as the business grows and the need arises for additional employees, officers, and managers, the president begins to lose absolute control. Realizing that precautions are necessary to protect the company's interests, the company establishes an internal control structure at this point.

The **internal control structure** of a company consists of "the policies and procedures established to provide reasonable assurance that specific entity objectives will be achieved."[1] The three elements of an internal control structure are the control environment, the accounting system, and the control procedures.

The **control environment** reflects the overall attitude, awareness, and actions of the board of directors, management, and stockholders. The **accounting system** consists of the methods and records that identify, assemble, analyze, classify, record, and report an entity's transactions to provide complete, accurate, and timely financial information. The **control procedures** of a company are additional policies and procedures that management establishes to provide reasonable assurance that the company achieves its specific objectives. These control procedures may pertain to proper authorization, segregation of duties, design and use of adequate documents and records, adequate safeguards over access to assets, and independent checks on performance.

Internal control not only prevents theft and fraud but also serves many purposes: (1) Companies must implement policies requiring compliance with federal law; (2) personnel must perform their assigned duties to promote efficiency of operations; and (3) correct accounting records must supply accurate and reliable information in the accounting reports.

This chapter discusses the internal control structure that a company establishes to protect its assets and promote the accuracy of its accounting records.

[1]AICPA, *Statement on Auditing Standards No. 55,* "Consideration of the Internal Control Structure in a Financial Statement Audit" (New York, 1988), p. 4."

Learning Objectives

After studying this chapter, you should be able to:

1. Describe the necessity for and features of internal control.

2. Define cash and list the objectives sought by management in handling a company's cash.

3. Identify procedures for controlling cash receipts and disbursements.

4. Prepare a bank reconciliation and make necessary journal entries based on that schedule.

5. Explain why a company uses a petty cash fund, describe its operations, and make the necessary journal entries.

6. Analyze and use the financial results—quick ratio.

You will learn how to establish internal control through control of cash receipts and cash disbursements, proper use of the bank checking account, preparation of the bank reconciliation, and protection of petty cash funds. The internal control structure is enhanced by hiring competent and trustworthy employees, a fact you will appreciate if you become a business owner.

Internal Control

An effective **internal control structure** includes a company's plan of organization and all the procedures and actions it takes to:

1. Protect its assets against theft and waste.
2. Ensure compliance with company policies and federal law.
3. Evaluate the performance of all personnel to promote efficient operations.
4. Ensure accurate and reliable operating data and accounting reports.

As you study the basic procedures and actions of an effective internal control structure, remember that even small companies can benefit from using some internal control measures. Preventing theft and waste is only a part of internal control.

In general terms, the purpose of internal control is to ensure the efficient operations of a business, thus enabling the business to effectively reach its goals. Since additional control procedures are necessary in a computer environment, a discussion of these controls concludes this section on internal control.

An Accounting Perspective

BUSINESS INSIGHT When performing an audit, one of an outside auditor's first duties is to examine the internal control structure of the corporation. To understand the internal control structure, an auditor focuses mainly on management's attitude and awareness concerning controls and the accounting system's processing of transactions. To increase understanding, the auditor inspects documents in the accounting system, discusses external influences on the company with management, reads accounting manuals, and observes the happenings in the company. This understanding of the company's control environment helps the auditor to plan the audit and to determine the nature, timing, and extent of tests.

Protection of Assets

Companies protect their assets by (1) segregating employee duties, (2) assigning specific duties to each employee, (3) rotating employee job assignments, and (4) using mechanical devices.

Real World Example
Even a small business should have separation of duties. If the accountant writes the checks and keeps the ledger, the owner should sign the checks and reconcile the bank statements.

Segregation of Employee Duties   **Segregation of duties** requires that someone other than the employee responsible for safeguarding an asset must maintain the accounting records for that asset. Also, employees share responsibility for related transactions so that one employee's work serves as a check on the work of other employees.

When a company segregates the duties of employees, it minimizes the probability of an employee being able to steal assets and cover up the theft. For example, an employee could not steal cash from a company and have the theft go undetected unless someone changes the cash records to cover the shortage. To change the records, the employee stealing the cash must also maintain the cash records or be in collusion with the employee who maintains the cash records.

Assignment of Specific Duties to Each Employee   When the responsibility for a particular work function is assigned to one employee, that employee is accountable for specific tasks. Should a problem occur, the company can quickly identify the responsible employee.

When a company gives each employee specific duties, it can trace lost documents or determine how a particular transaction was recorded. Also, the employee responsible for a given task can provide information about that task. Being responsible for specific duties gives people a sense of pride and importance that usually makes them want to perform to the best of their ability.

Rotation of Employee Job Assignments   Some companies rotate job assignments to discourage employees from engaging in long-term schemes to steal from them. Employees realize that if they steal from the company, the next employees assigned to their positions may discover the theft.

Frequently, companies have the policy that all employees must take an annual vacation. This policy also discourages theft because many dishonest schemes collapse when the employee does not attend to the scheme on a daily basis.

Use of Mechanical Devices   Companies use several mechanical devices to help protect their assets. Check protectors (machines that perforate the check amount into the check), cash registers, and time clocks make it difficult for employees to alter certain company documents and records.

Internal control policies are effective only when employees follow them. To ensure that they carry out its internal control policies, a company must hire competent and trustworthy employees. Thus, the execution of effective internal control begins with the time and effort a company expends in hiring employees. Once the company hires the employees, it must train those employees and clearly communicate to them company policies, such as obtaining proper authorization before making a cash disbursement. Frequently, written job descriptions establish the responsibilities and duties of employees. The initial training of employees should include a clear explanation of their duties and how to perform them.

In publicly held corporations, the company's internal control structure must satisfy the requirements of federal law. In December 1977, Congress enacted the Foreign Corrupt Practices Act (FCPA). This law requires a publicly held corporation to devise and maintain an effective internal control structure and to keep accurate accounting records. This law came about partly because company accounting records covered up bribes and kickbacks made to foreign governments or government officials. The FCPA made this specific type of bribery illegal.

Also, the Sarbanes-Oxley Act (SOX), which was passed in 2002 after the Enron accounting scandal, added additional requirements in the area of internal control for publicly held corporations. SOX requires the top officers of such corporations to certify that the corporation is responsible to establish and maintain an effective system of internal controls. Under SOX, the external auditors of such a corporation are required to test the internal control system of the corporation and issue a report as to the effectiveness of the system as it applies to financial reporting.

To evaluate how well employees are doing their jobs, many companies use an internal auditing staff. **Internal auditing** consists of investigating and evaluating employees' compliance with the company's policies and procedures. Companies employ **internal auditors** to perform these audits. Trained in company policies and internal auditing duties, internal auditors periodically test the effectiveness of controls and procedures throughout the company.

Internal auditors encourage operating efficiency throughout the company and are alert for breakdowns in the company's internal control structure. In addition, internal auditors make recommendations for the improvement of the company's internal control structure. All companies and nonprofit organizations can benefit from internal auditing. However, internal auditing is especially necessary in large organizations because the owners (stockholders) cannot be involved personally with all aspects of the business.

Companies should maintain complete and accurate accounting records. The best method to ensure such accounting records is to hire and train competent and honest individuals. Periodically, supervisors evaluate an employee's performance to make sure the employee

Real World Example
Many companies have a mandatory vacation policy for employees. Most require a minimum of one week, many require two weeks.

Compliance with Company Policies and Federal Law

Evaluation of Personnel Performance

Accuracy of Accounting Records

Illustration 8.1   Purchase Requisition

PURCHASE REQUISITION		No. _2416_	
BRYAN WHOLESALE COMPANY			

From: Automotive Supplies Department

To: Purchasing Department

Date: *November 20, 2012*

Suggested supplier: *Wilkes Radio Company*

Please purchase the following items:

Description	Item Number	Quantity	Estimated Price
	Model No. 5868-24393	200	$50 per unit

Reason for request:

Customer order

Baier Company

To be filled in by purchasing department:

Dated ordered *11/29/2012*

Purchase order number   *N-145*

Approved *R.S.T.*

is following company policies. Inaccurate or inadequate accounting records serve as an invitation to theft by dishonest employees because theft can be concealed more easily.

One or more business documents support most accounting transactions. These source documents are an integral part of the internal control structure. For optimal control, source documents should be serially numbered. (Transaction documentation and related aspects of internal control are presented throughout the text.)

Since source documents serve as documentation of business transactions, from time to time firms check the validity of these documents. For example, to review a purchase transaction, they check the documents used to record the transaction against the proper accounting records. When the accounting department records a purchase transaction, it should receive copies of the following four documents:

1. A **purchase requisition** (Illustration 8.1) is a written request from an employee inside the company to the purchasing department to purchase certain items.
2. A **purchase order** (Illustration 8.2) is a document sent from the purchasing department to a supplier requesting that merchandise or other items be shipped to the purchaser.
3. An **invoice** (Illustration 8.3) is the statement sent by the supplier to the purchaser requesting payment for the merchandise shipped.
4. A **receiving report** is a document prepared by the receiving department showing the descriptions and quantities of all items received from a supplier in a particular shipment. A copy of the purchase order can serve as a receiving report if the quantity ordered is omitted. Then, because receiving department personnel do not know what quantity to expect, they will count the quantity received more accurately.

Real World Example
Prenumbering of documents is not an effective control unless unused documents are safeguarded and all numbered documents are accounted for—never destroyed. Examples: voided checks, voided purchase orders, or canceled sales invoices.

These four documents together serve as authorization to pay for merchandise and should be checked against the accounting records. Without these documents, a company might fail to pay a legitimate invoice, pay fictitious invoices, or pay an invoice more than once. Companies can accomplish proper internal control only by periodically checking the source documents of business transactions with the accounting records of those transactions. In a "paperless" environment, these documents would exist in electronic form. In Illustration 8.4 we show the flow of documents and goods in a merchandise transaction.

Illustration 8.2   Purchase Order

PURCHASE ORDER			No.	N-145

BRYAN WHOLESALE COMPANY
476 Mason Street
Detroit, Michigan 48823

To: Wilkes Radio Company
2515 West Peachtree Street   **Date:**   November 21, 2012
Atlanta, Georgia 30303   **Ship by:** December 20, 2012
Ship to: Above address   **FOB terms requested:**   Destination
                                    Discount terms requested: 2/10, n/30

Please send the following item:

Description	Item Number	Quantity	Price Per Unit	Total Amount
True-tone stereo radios	Model No. 5868-24393	200	$50	$10,000

Ordered by: _Jane Knight_   Please include order number on all
                                                invoice and shipments.

Unfortunately, even though a company implements all of these features in its internal control structure, theft may still occur. If employees are dishonest, they can usually figure out a way to steal from a company, thus circumventing even the most effective internal control structure. Therefore, companies should carry adequate casualty insurance on assets. This insurance reimburses the company for loss of a nonmonetary asset such as specialized equipment. Companies should also have **fidelity bonds** on employees handling cash and other negotiable instruments. These bonds ensure that a company is reimbursed for losses due to theft of cash and other monetary assets. With both casualty insurance on assets and fidelity bonds on employees, a company can recover at least a portion of any loss that occurs.

According to the Committee of Sponsoring Organizations of the Treadway Commission, there are five components of an internal control structure. When these components are linked to the organization's operations, they can quickly respond to shifting conditions. The components are:

Components of Internal Control

1. **Control environment.** The control environment is the basis for all other elements of the internal control structure. The control environment includes many factors such as ethical values, management's philosophy, the integrity of the employees of the corporation, and the guidance provided by management or the board of directors.
2. **Risk assessment.** After the entity sets objectives, the risks (such as theft and waste of assets) from external and internal sources must be assessed. Examining the risks associated with each objective allows management to develop the means to control these risks.
3. **Control activities.** To address the risks associated with each objective, management establishes control activities. These activities include procedures that employees must follow. Examples include procedures to protect the assets through segregation of employee duties and the other means we discussed earlier.
4. **Information and communication.** Information relevant to decision making must be collected and reported in a timely manner. The events that yield these data may

Illustration 8.3   Invoice

INVOICE			**Invoice No.** ___1574___	
			Date: Dec. 15, 2012	

WILKES RADIO COMPANY
2515 West Peachtree Street
Atlanta, Georgia 30303

Customer's Orders No.: N-145

Sold to: Bryan Wholesale Co.
Address: 476 Mason Street
              Detroit, Michigan 48823
Terms: 2/10, n/30, FOB destination

Date shipped: *December 15, 2012*
Shipped by: *Nagel Trucking Co.*

Description	Item Number	Quantity	Price Per Unit	Total Amount
	Model No. 5868-24393	200	$50	$10,000
		Total		$10,000

come from internal or external sources. Communication throughout the entity is important to achieve management's goals. Employees must understand what is expected of them and how their responsibilities relate to the work of others. Communication with external parties such as suppliers and shareholders is also important.

5. Monitoring. After the internal control structure is in place, the firm should monitor its effectiveness so that it can make changes before serious problems arise. In testing components of the internal control structure, companies base their thoroughness on the risk assigned to those components.

Responsibility for Internal Control

Internal control is the general responsibility of all members in an organization. However, the following three groups have specific responsibilities regarding the internal control structure.

Management holds ultimate responsibility for establishing and maintaining an effective internal control structure. Through leadership and example, management demonstrates ethical behavior and integrity within the company.

The *board of directors* provides guidance to management. Because board members have a working knowledge of the functions of the company, they help shield the company from managers who try to override some control procedures for dishonest purposes. Often, an efficient board that has access to the company's internal auditors can discover such fraud. Also, under the provisions of the Sarbanes-Oxley Act (SOX), publicly held corporations must create an audit committee of board members other than members of the management team. The corporation's external auditors will communicate to the audit committee any concerns about internal control that arise during the audit of the financial statements.

Auditors within the organization evaluate the effectiveness of the internal control structure and determine whether company policies and procedures are being followed. All employees are part of a communications network that enables an internal control structure to work effectively.

Internal Control in a Computer Environment

Computerized financial records require the same internal control principles of separation of duties and control over access as a manual accounting system. The exact control steps depend on whether a company is using mainframe computers and minicomputers or microcomputers.

Large corporations might use all three types of computers in their accounting environments. The size and complexity of mainframe computers and minicomputers require

Illustration 8.4   Flow of Documents and Goods in a Merchandising Transaction

Steps

1. Requesting department sends purchase requisition to purchasing department.
2. Purchasing department sends purchase order to supplier, with copies going to the receiving department (without quantities ordered) and the accounting department.
3. Supplier sends goods to receiving department, where goods received are checked against purchase order, and sends invoice to accounting department.
4. Receiving department sends goods to requesting department and sends receiving report to accounting department.
5. Accounting department checks receiving report against purchase order and invoice and sends check in payment of invoice to the supplier.

specially trained persons to keep these systems operating. While systems specialists operate the computer system itself, programmers develop the programs that direct the computer to perform specific tasks. In a mainframe or minicomputer environment, internal control should include the following:

- Control computer access by placing the computer in an easily secured room, and allow only persons authorized to operate the computer to enter the room.
- Restrict the access of systems specialists (who operate the computer) to software programs and the access of programmers to the computer. This policy prevents the running of unauthorized, altered programs.
- Require the use of passwords to access sensitive company data and confidential personal data. Change the passwords as necessary.

Many smaller companies use microcomputers instead of a mainframe or a mini-computer. Also, large companies often supply certain employees with microcomputers.

Reinforcing Problems
E8-1 Answer true-false questions about internal control.
E8-2 Answer multiple-choice question about internal control.

The use of microcomputers changes the control environment somewhat. Small companies generally do not employ systems specialists and programmers. Instead, these companies use off-the-shelf programs such as accounting, spreadsheet, database management, and word processing packages. The data created by use of these programs are valuable (e.g., the company's accounting records) and often sensitive. Thus, controls are also important. In a microcomputer environment, the following controls can be useful:

- Require computer users to have tight control over storage of programs and data. Just as one person maintains custody over a certain set of records in a manual system, in a computer system one person maintains custody over certain information (such as the accounts receivable subsidiary ledger). Make backup copies that are retained in a different secured location.
- Require passwords (kept secret) to gain entry into data files maintained on the hard disk.
- In situations where a local area network (LAN) links the microcomputers into one system, permit only certain computers and persons in the network to have access to some data files (the accounting records, for example).

Computerized accounting systems do not lessen the need for internal control. In fact, access to a computer by an unauthorized person could result in significant theft in less time than with a manual system.

Controlling Cash

Objective 2
Define cash and list the objectives sought by management in handling a company's cash.

Since cash is the most liquid of all assets, a business cannot survive and prosper if it does not have adequate control over its cash. In accounting, **cash** includes coins; currency; undeposited negotiable instruments such as checks, bank drafts, and money orders; amounts in checking and savings accounts; and demand certificates of deposit. A **certificate of deposit (CD)** is an interest-bearing deposit that can be withdrawn from a bank at will (demand CD) or at a fixed maturity date (time CD). Only demand CDs that may be withdrawn at any time without prior notice or penalty are included in cash. Cash does not include postage stamps, IOUs, time CDs, or notes receivable.

In its general ledger, a company usually maintains two cash accounts—Cash and Petty Cash. On the company's balance sheet, it combines the balances of these two accounts into one amount reported as Cash.

An Accounting Perspective	**Business Insight** Users of financial data must look to see the real meaning behind the numbers. Reader's Digest publishes the world's most widely read magazine as well as various other books, home entertainment products, and special interest magazines. In Reader's Digest's annual report, for example, the company defines cash and cash equivalents in this footnote: The company considers all highly liquid debt instruments with original maturities of three months or less to be cash equivalents.

Since many business transactions involve cash, it is a vital factor in the operation of a business. Of all the company's assets, cash is the most easily mishandled either through theft or carelessness. To control and manage its cash, a company should:

1. Account for all cash transactions accurately so that correct information is available regarding cash flows and balances.
2. Make certain that enough cash is available to pay bills as they come due.
3. Avoid holding too much idle cash because excess cash could be invested to generate income, such as interest.
4. Prevent loss of cash due to theft or fraud.

The need to control cash is clearly evident and has many aspects. Without the proper timing of cash flows and the protection of idle cash, a business cannot survive. This section discusses cash receipts and cash disbursements. Later in the chapter, we explain the importance of preparing a bank reconciliation for each bank checking account and controlling the petty cash fund.

When a merchandising company sells its merchandise inventory, it may receive cash immediately or several days or weeks later. A clerk receives the cash immediately *over the counter,* records it, and places it in a cash register. The presence of the customer as the sale is *rung up* usually ensures that the cashier enters the correct amount of the sale in the cash register. At the end of each day, stores reconcile the cash in each cash register with the cash register tape or computer printout for that register. Payments received later are almost always in the form of checks. Stores prepare a record of the checks received as soon as they are received. Some merchandising companies receive all their cash receipts on a delayed basis as payments on accounts receivable. (See the cash receipts cycle for merchandise transactions in Illustration 8.5.)

Although businesses vary their specific procedures for controlling cash receipts, they usually observe the following principles:

1. Prepare a record of all cash receipts as soon as cash is received. Most thefts of cash occur before a record is made of the receipt. Once a record is made, it is easier to trace a theft.
2. Deposit all cash receipts intact as soon as feasible, preferably on the day they are received or on the next business day. Undeposited cash is more susceptible to misappropriation.
3. Arrange duties so that the employee who handles cash receipts does not record the receipts in the accounting records. This control feature follows the general principle of *segregation of duties* given earlier in the chapter, as does item 4.
4. Arrange duties so that the employee who receives the cash does not disburse the cash. This control measure is possible in all but the smallest companies.

Companies also need controls over cash disbursements. Since a company spends most of its cash by check, many of the internal controls for cash disbursements deal with checks and authorizations for cash payments. The basic principle of segregation of duties also applies in controlling cash disbursements. Following are some basic control procedures for cash disbursements:

- Make all disbursements by check or from petty cash. Obtain proper approval for all disbursements and create a permanent record of each disbursement. Many retail stores make refunds for returned merchandise from the cash register. When this practice is followed, clerks should have refund tickets approved by a supervisor before refunding cash.
- Require all checks to be serially numbered and limit access to checks to employees authorized to write checks.
- Require two signatures on each check over a material amount so that one person cannot withdraw funds from the bank account.

Illustration 8.5 Cash Receipts Cycle for Merchandise Transactions

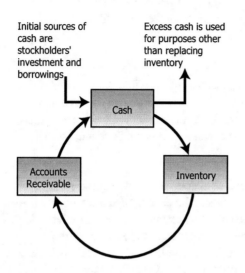

Initial sources of cash are stockholders' investment and borrowings.

Excess cash is used for purposes other than replacing inventory

Cash

Accounts Receivable

Inventory

Cash initially comes into the business from stockholders' investment and borrowing. Cash is then invested in inventory and other assets. When inventory is sold, cash may be received immediately, or receipt may be delayed and involve accounts receivable. The inventory generally is sold at more than cost so the company can make a profit. Each time the cycle is completed, the amount of cash grows and may be used for purposes other than replacing inventory.

- Arrange duties so that the employee who authorizes payment of a bill does not sign checks. Otherwise, the checks could be written to friends in payment of fictitious invoices.
- Require approved documents to support all checks issued.
- Instruct the employee authorizing cash disbursements to make certain that payment is for a legitimate purpose and is made out for the exact amount and to the proper party.
- Stamp the supporting documents *paid* when liabilities are paid and indicate the date and number of the check issued. These procedures lessen the chance of paying the same debt more than once.
- Arrange duties so that those employees who sign checks neither have access to canceled checks nor prepare the bank reconciliation. This policy makes it more difficult for an employee to conceal a theft.
- Have an employee who has no other cash duties prepare the bank reconciliation each month, so that errors and shortages can be discovered quickly.
- Void all checks incorrectly prepared. Mark these checks void and retain them to prevent unauthorized use.

Real World Example
Texas Instruments requires all of its vendors to be Electronic Data Interchange (EDI) capable. EDI systems enable trading partners to conduct business such as ordering, shipping, billing, and payment transactions over computer networks rather than sending paper copies of documents. 'A Guide to Electronic Commerce,' *Management Accounting*, September 1996, p. 43.

Illustration 8.6 shows an overview of some of the internal control considerations relating to cash.

Most companies use checking accounts to handle their cash transactions. The company deposits its cash receipts in a bank checking account and writes checks to pay its bills. The bank sends the company a statement each month. The company checks this statement against its records to determine if it must make any corrections or adjustments in either the company's balance or the bank's balance. You learn how to do bank reconciliations later in this chapter. In the next section, we discuss the bank checking account. If you have a personal checking account, some of this information will be familiar to you.

Illustration 8.6 Internal Control Considerations Regarding Cash

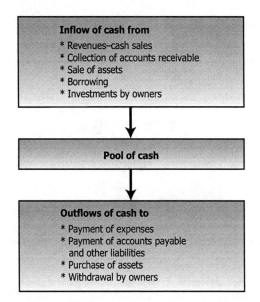

Inflow of cash from

* Revenues–cash sales
* Collection of accounts receivable
* Sale of assets
* Borrowing
* Investments by owners

Pool of cash

Outflows of cash to

* Payment of expenses
* Payment of accounts payable
  and other liabilities
* Purchase of assets
* Withdrawal by owners

Internal control considerations

1. Are all cash receipts being properly recorded and actually going into the company's pool of cash, or are individuals siphoning off some of these receipts for their own use?
2. Is the pool of cash protected from theft? Is the cash on hand managed so as to produce income for the company and yet available when needed to make legitimate disbursements?
3. Is there close control over cashdisbursements to ensure that only legitimate disbursements are made in the proper amounts and on a timely basis?

An Accounting Perspective

USES OF TECHNOLOGY Many companies are using Electronic Data Interchange (EDI) to transmit business documents such as purchase orders, invoices, and even payments for goods and services. Instead of mailing paper copies of these documents, the entire transaction is done electronically. This procedure speeds up the transaction and eliminates the expense of sending paper copies. One concern of such procedures is the security of the transaction. Since this issue is being successfully addressed by various methods, including encrypting the data, we can expect the use of EDI to continue to increase in the future, even among relatively small companies.

The Bank Checking Account

Banks earn income by providing a variety of services to individuals, businesses, and other entities such as churches or libraries. One of these services is the checking account. A **checking account** is a money balance maintained in the bank; it is subject to withdrawal by the depositor, or owner of the money, on demand. To provide depositors with an accurate record of depositor funds received and disbursed, a bank uses the business documents discussed in this section.[2]

A bank requires a new depositor to complete a **signature card**, which provides the signatures of persons authorized to sign checks drawn on an account. The bank retains the card and uses it to identify signatures on checks it pays. The bank does not compare every check with this signature card. Usually, it makes a comparison only when the depositor disputes the validity of a check paid by the bank or when someone presents a check for an unusually large sum for payment.

When depositors make a bank deposit, they prepare a deposit ticket or slip. A **deposit ticket** is a form that shows the date and the items that make up the deposit (Illustration 8.7). Often, the ticket is preprinted to show the depositor's name, address,

Note to the Student
The bank has the responsibility of verifying the signature on checks. Since this is not always feasible with the high volume of checks, the bank sometimes incurs a loss.

Signature Card

Deposit Ticket

---

[2]Due to relaxed federal regulations, institutions other than banks—such as brokerage firms and credit unions—also now offer checking account services. All of these institutions function somewhat similarly; but, for simplicity's sake, we discuss only banks here.

Illustration 8.7   Deposit Ticket

NAME M. MILLER COMPANY		CURRENCY	150	–
ACCT. NO. 326-587-90		COIN	45	50
		Williams	100	–
DATE July 7, 2012		Sloans	200	–

45-123/321

DEPOSIT TICKET
PLEASE ITEMIZE ADDITIONAL CHECKS ON REVERSE SIDE

| SUB-TOTAL | 495 | 50 |
| | 495 | 50 |

USA BANK
Corvallis, OR 97330

⑆0123456781⑆

Illustration 8.8   Check with Attached Remittance Advice

JOSIAH C. SCOTT
1234 Dawson Road
Corvallis, OR 97330

1428

96-678/1232 61

DATE July 6, 2012

PAY TO THE ORDER OF   John Doe's Company $ 560.00

Five hundred sixty and no/100------------------------------DOLLARS

USA BANK

FOR   Invoice #4501

Josiah C. Scott

⑈001428⑈ ⑆123456789⑆ 361 3739⑈

DETACH AND RETAIN THIS STATEMENT
THE ATTACHED CHECK IS IN PAYMENT OF ITEMS DESCRIBED ABOVE
IF NOT CORRECT PLEASE NOTIFY US PROMPTLY. NO RECEIPT DESIRED.

USA BANK

DATE	DESCRIPTION	AMOUNT
07/06/12	P.O. No. R1230 – Payment of invoice #4501	$560.00

and account number. A depositor enters the items constituting the deposit—cash and a list of checks—on the ticket when making the deposit. The depositor receives a receipt showing the date of deposit and the amount deposited.

Check

A **check** is a written order to a bank to pay a specific sum of money to the party designated as the payee by the party issuing the check. Thus, every check transaction involves three parties: the *bank,* the **payee** (party to whom the check is made payable), and the **drawer** (depositor). Most depositors use serially numbered checks preprinted with information about the depositor, such as name, address, and telephone number. Often a business check has an attached remittance advice. A **remittance advice** informs the payee why the **drawer** (or maker) of the check is making this payment. Before cashing or depositing it, the payee detaches the remittance advice from the check (Illustration 8.8).

Note to the Student
A bank statement balance does not usually represent the amount that appears in the ledger account; deposits in transit and outstanding checks have not been recorded by the bank as of the statement date.

Illustration 8.9   Bank Statement

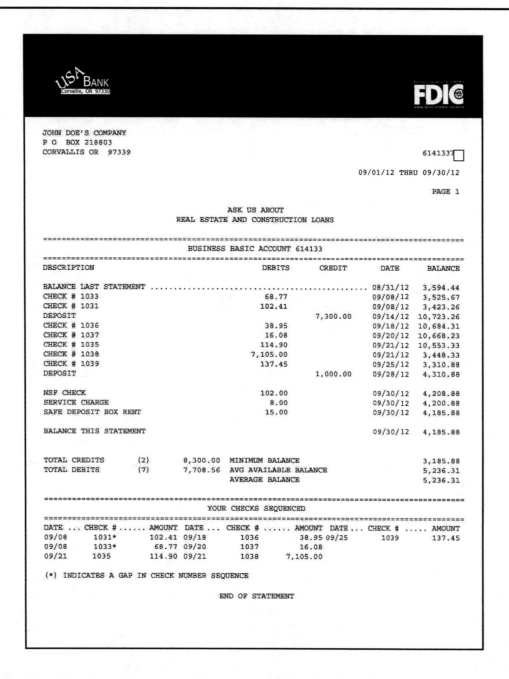

A **bank statement** is a statement issued (usually monthly) by a bank describing the activities in a depositor's checking account during the period. Illustration 8.9 shows a bank statement that includes the following data:

1. Deposits made to the checking account during the period.
2. Checks paid out of the depositor's checking account by the bank during the period. These checks have *cleared* the bank and are *canceled.*
3. Other deductions from the checking account for service charges, NSF (not sufficient funds) checks, safe-deposit box rent, and check printing fees. Banks assess **service charges** on the depositor to cover the cost of handling the checking account, such as check clearing charges. An **NSF (not sufficient funds)** check

Reinforcing Problem
E8-3 Determine available cash balance from bank statement and Cash account data.

Illustration 8.10 Debit Memorandum (top) and Credit Memorandum (bottom)

Debit USA BANK	Account Title	Josiah C. Scott		Account Number	43613739
	Requested by	Ryan		DATE	7/6/12
	Phone Number	567-1234			

DESCRIPTION	AMOUNT
Safe Deposit Box Rental	$ 15.00
TOTAL	$ 15.00

DRAWN BY __AJC__   APPROVED BY __JIC__

⑇ 123456789 ⑈

Credit USA BANK	Account Title	Josiah C. Scott		Account Number	43613739
	Requested by	Ryan		DATE	7/6/12
	Phone Number	567-1234			

DESCRIPTION	AMOUNT
Collection of John Doe Co. note from X Co.	$ 1,225.00
TOTAL	$ 1,225.00

DRAWN BY __AJC__   APPROVED BY __JIC__

⑇ 123456789 ⑈

is a customer's check returned from the customer's bank to the depositor's bank because the funds in the customer's checking account balance were insufficient to cover the check. The depositor's bank deducts the amount of the returned check from the depositor's checking account. Since the customer still owes the depositor money, the depositor restores the amount of the NSF check to the account receivable for that customer in the company's books.

4. Other additions to the checking account from proceeds of a note collected by the bank for the depositor and interest earned on the account.

In addition to the data in the bank statement in Illustration 8.9, bank statements also can show nonroutine deposits made to the depositor's checking account. Such deposits are made by a third party. For example, the bank may have received a wire transfer of funds for the depositor.

A **wire transfer** of funds is an interbank transfer of funds by telephone. Companies that operate in many widely scattered locations and have checking accounts with several different local banks often use interbank transfers of funds. These companies may set up special procedures to avoid accumulating too much idle cash in local bank accounts. One such procedure involves the use of special-instruction bank accounts. For example, a company may set up **transfer bank accounts** so local banks automatically transfer to a central bank (by wire or bank draft) all amounts on deposit in excess of a stated amount. In this way, transfers move funds not needed for local operations quickly to headquarters, where the company can use the funds or invest them.

Real World Example
A business must keep a separate cash account in the general ledger for each bank account or a subsidiary ledger of accounts. Otherwise, reconciliation of individual bank accounts would not be possible.

Frequently, the bank returns canceled checks and original deposit tickets with the bank statement. Since it is expensive to sort, handle, and mail these items, some banks no longer return them to depositors. These banks usually store the documents digitally, with photocopies available if needed. Most depositors need only a detailed bank statement, as shown in Illustration 8.9, and not the original documents to show what transactions occurred during a given period.

When banks debit or credit a depositor's checking account, they prepare debit and credit memoranda (memos). Banks may also return these memos with the bank statement. A **debit memo** is a form used by a bank to explain a deduction from the depositor's account; a **credit memo** explains an addition to the depositor's account. The terms *debit memo* and *credit memo* may seem reversed, but remember that the depositor's checking account is a liability—an account payable—of the bank. So, when the bank seeks to reduce a depositor's balance, it prepares a debit memo. To increase the balance, it prepares a credit memo. Illustration 8.10 contains examples of debit and credit memos. Some banks no longer mail these documents to the depositor and rely instead on explanations in the bank statements.

Information that the depositor did not know before receiving the bank statement (items 3 and 4 on pages 319–320) requires new journal entries on the company's books. After the entries have been made to record the new information, the balance in the Cash account is the actual cash available to the company. When the depositor has already received notice of NSF checks and other bank charges or credits, the needed journal entries may have been made earlier. In this chapter, we assume no entries have been made for these items unless stated otherwise.

When a company receives its bank statement, it must reconcile the balance shown by the bank with the cash balance in the company's books. If you have a personal checking account, you also should reconcile your bank statement with your checkbook. You can use the reconciliation form on the back of the bank statement to list your checks that have not yet been paid by the bank and your deposits not yet shown on the bank statement. Some small businesses use this form. Others prepare a separate bank reconciliation, which we discuss in the next section.

Bank Reconciliation

A **bank reconciliation** is a schedule the company (depositor) prepares to reconcile, or explain, the difference between the cash balance on the bank statement and the cash balance on the company's books. The company prepares a bank reconciliation to determine its actual cash balance and prepare the entry(ies) to correct the cash balance in the ledger.

Objective 4
Prepare a bank reconciliation and make necessary journal entries based on that schedule.

BUSINESS INSIGHT Within the internal control structure, segregation of duties is an important way to prevent fraud. One place to segregate duties is between the cash disbursement cycle and bank reconciliations. To prevent collusion among employees, the person who reconciles the bank account should not be involved in the cash disbursement cycle. Also, the bank should mail the statement directly to the person who reconciles the bank account each month. Sending the statement directly limits the number of employees who would have an opportunity to tamper with the statement.

An Accounting Perspective

Look at Illustration 8.11; the bank reconciliation has two main sections. The top section begins with the balance on the bank statement. The bottom section begins with the balance on the company's books. After the company makes adjustments to both the *bank* and *book* balances, both adjusted balances should be the same. The steps in preparing a bank reconciliation are as follows:

Deposits. Compare the deposits listed on the bank statement with the deposits on the company's books. To make this comparison, place check marks in the bank statement and in the company's books by the deposits that agree. Then determine the deposits in transit. A **deposit in transit** is typically a day's cash receipts recorded in the depositor's books in one period but recorded as a deposit by the bank in the succeeding period. The most common deposit in transit is the cash receipts deposited on the last business day of the month. Normally, deposits in transit occur only near the end of the period covered by the bank statement. For example, a deposit made in a bank's night depository on May 31 would be recorded by the company on May 31 and by the bank on June 1. Thus, the deposit does not appear on a bank statement for the month ended May 31. Also check the deposits in transit listed in last month's bank reconciliation against the bank statement. Immediately investigate any deposit made during the month but missing from the bank statement (unless it involves a deposit made at the end of the period).

Paid checks. If canceled checks are returned with the bank statement, compare them to the statement to be sure both amounts agree. Then, sort the checks in numerical order. Next, determine which checks are outstanding. **Outstanding checks** are those issued by a depositor but not paid by the bank on which they are drawn. The party receiving the check may not have deposited it immediately. Once deposited, checks may take several days to clear the banking system. Determine the outstanding checks by comparing the check numbers that have cleared the bank with the check numbers issued by the company. Use check marks in the company's record of checks issued to identify those checks returned by the bank. Checks issued that have not yet been returned by the bank are the outstanding checks. If the bank does not return checks but only lists the cleared checks on the bank statement, determine the outstanding checks by comparing this list with the company's record of checks issued. Sometimes checks written long ago are still outstanding. Checks outstanding as of the beginning of the month appear on the prior month's bank reconciliation. Most of these have cleared during the current month; list those that have not cleared as still outstanding on the current month's reconciliation.

Bank debit and credit memos. Verify all debit and credit memos on the bank statement. Debit memos reflect deductions for such items as service charges, NSF checks, safe-deposit box rent, and notes paid by the bank for the depositor. Credit memos reflect additions for such items as notes collected for the depositor by the bank and wire transfers of funds from another bank in which the company sends funds to the home office bank. Check the bank debit and credit memos with the depositor's books to see if they have already been recorded. Make journal entries for any items not already recorded in the company's books.

Errors. List any errors. A common error by depositors is recording a check in the accounting records at an amount that differs from the actual amount. For example, a $47 check may be recorded as $74. Although the check clears the bank at the amount written on the check ($47), the depositor frequently does not catch the error until reviewing the bank statement or canceled checks.

Deposits in transit, outstanding checks, and bank service charges usually account for the difference between the company's Cash account balance and the bank balance. (These same items can cause a difference between your personal checkbook balance and the balance on your bank statement.) Remember that all items shown on the bank reconciliation as adjustments of the book (ledger) balance require journal entries to adjust the Cash account (items 4, 5, and 6 in Illustration 8.11 and in the following example). Items appearing as adjustments to the balance per bank statement do not require entries by the depositor (items 2 and 3). Of course, you should call any bank errors to the bank's attention.

Illustration 8.11   Bank Reconciliation

R.L. LEE COMPANY
Bank Reconciliation
May 31, 2012

①	Balance per bank statement, May 31, 2012		$3,252
②	Add: Deposit in transit		452
			$3,704
③	Less: Outstanding checks:		
	No. 9544	$322	
	No. 9545	168	
	No. 9546	223	713
	Adjusted balance, May 31, 2012		$2,991
①	Balance per ledger, May 31, 2012		$1,891
④	Add: Note collected (including interest of $25)		1,225
			$3,116
⑤	Less: NSF check (R. Johnson)	$102	
⑥	Safe-deposit box rent	15	
⑥	Service charges	8	125
	Adjusted balance, May 31, 2012		$2,991

To illustrate the preparation of the bank reconciliation in Illustration 8.11, assume the following (these items are keyed to numbers in that illustration):

1. On May 31, R. L. Lee Company showed a balance in its Cash account of $1,891. On June 2, Lee received its bank statement for the month ended May 31, which showed an ending balance of $3,252.
2. A matching of debits to the Cash account on the books with deposits on the bank statement showed that the $452 receipts of May 31 were included in Cash but not included as a deposit on the bank statement. This deposit was in the bank's night deposit chute on May 31.
3. A comparison of checks issued with checks that had cleared the bank showed three checks outstanding:

No. 9544	$322
No. 9545	168
No. 9546	223
Total	$713

4. Included with the bank statement was a credit memo for $1,225 (principal of $1,200 + interest of $25) for collection of a note owed to Lee by Shipley Company.
5. Included with the bank statement was a $102 debit memo for an NSF check written by R. Johnson and deposited by Lee.
6. Charges made to Lee's account include $15 for safe-deposit box rent and $8 for service charges.

After reconciling the book and bank balances as shown in Illustration 8.11, Lee Company finds that its actual cash balance is $2,991. The following entries record information from the bank reconciliation:

Reinforcing Problem
E8-7 Determine deposits in transit.

Reinforcing Problem
E8-6 Determine checks outstanding.

④	Cash	1,225	
	Notes Receivable—Shipley Company		1,200
	Interest Revenue		25
	To record note collected from Shipley Company.		
⑤	Accounts Receivable—R. Johnson*	102	
	Cash		102
	To charge NSF check back to customer, R. Johnson.		
⑥	Bank Service Charge Expense	23	
	Cash		23
	To record bank service charges.		

*This debit would be posted to the Accounts Receivable control account in the general ledger and to R. Johnson's account in the Accounts Receivable subsidiary ledger.

The income statement would include the $23 bank service charge as an expense and the $25 interest as revenue. The May 31 balance sheet would show $2,991 cash, the actual cash balance. You could combine the preceding three entries into one compound entry as follows:

Cash	1,100	
Bank Service Charge Expense	23	
Account Receivable—R. Johnson	102	
Note Receivable		1,200
Interest Revenue		25
To correct the accounts for needed changes identified in the bank reconciliation.		

Reinforcing Problems
E8-4 Prepare a bank reconciliation and specify cash available.
E8-5 Record necessary journal entry or entries to correct cash balance.
E8-8 Prepare a bank reconciliation and necessary journal entry or entries.

The bank routinely handles the deposit in transit and any outstanding checks already recorded in the depositor's books. Since these items appear on the bank balance side of the reconciliation, they require no entry in the company's books. The bank processes these items in the subsequent period.

When a company maintains more than one checking account, it must reconcile each account separately with the balance on the bank statement for that account. The depositor should also check carefully to see that the bank did not combine the transactions of the two accounts.

Certified and Cashier's Checks

To make sure a check cannot *bounce* and become an NSF check, a payee may demand a certified or cashier's check from the maker. Both certified checks and cashier's checks are liabilities of the issuing bank rather than the depositor. As a result, payees usually accept these checks without question.

• A **certified check** is a check written, or drawn, by a depositor and taken to the depositor's bank for certification. The bank stamps certified across the face of the check and inserts the name of the bank and the date; a bank official signs the certification. The bank certifies a check only when the depositor's balance is large enough to cover the check. The bank deducts the amount of the check from the depositor's account at the time it certifies the check.

• A **cashier's check** is a check made out to either the depositor or a third party and written, or drawn, by a bank after deducting that amount from the depositor's account or receiving cash from the depositor.

In this section, you learned that all cash receipts should be deposited in the bank and all cash disbursements should be made by check. However, the next section explains the convenience of having small amounts of cash (petty cash) available for minor expenditures.

Uses of Technology Most companies now offer to deposit employees' paychecks directly into their bank accounts. This process of transferring money by telephone, computer, or wire is called electronic fund transferring. Often companies prefer this method because it limits the number of employees involved in the payroll process. Manipulation and fraud can still occur whenever firms do not separate duties; however, limiting access to the payroll function may eliminate some of the risk associated with internal control weaknesses.

An Accounting Perspective

Petty Cash Funds

At times, every business finds it convenient to have small amounts of cash available for immediate payment of items such as delivery charges, postage stamps, taxi fares, supper money for employees working overtime, and other small items. To permit these cash disbursements and still maintain adequate control over cash, companies frequently establish a **petty cash fund** of a round figure such as $100 or $500.

Objective 5
Explain why a company uses a petty cash fund, describe its operations, and make the necessary journal entries.

Usually one individual, called the *petty cash custodian* or *cashier,* is responsible for the control of the petty cash fund and documenting the disbursements made from the fund. By assigning the responsibility for the fund to one individual, the company has internal control over the cash in the fund.

A business establishes a petty cash fund by writing a check for, say, $100. It is payable to the petty cash custodian. The petty cash fund should be large enough to make disbursements for a reasonable period, such as a month. The following entry records this transaction as follows:

Establishing the Fund

Petty Cash	100	
Cash		100
To establish a petty cash fund.		

After the check is cashed, the petty cash custodian normally places the money in a small box that can be locked. The fund is now ready to be disbursed as needed.

One of the conveniences of the petty cash fund is that payments from the fund require no journal entries at the time of payment. Thus, using a petty cash fund avoids the need for making many entries for small amounts. Only when the fund is reimbursed, or when the end of the accounting period arrives, does the firm make an entry in the journal.

Operating the Fund

When disbursing cash from the fund, the petty cash custodian prepares a petty cash voucher, which should be signed by the person receiving the funds. A **petty cash voucher** (Illustration 8.12) is a document or form that shows the amount of and reason for a petty cash disbursement. The custodian should prepare a voucher for each disbursement and staple any invoices for expenditures to the petty cash voucher. At all times, the employee responsible for petty cash is accountable for having cash and petty cash vouchers equal to the total amount of the fund.

Companies replenish the petty cash fund at the end of the accounting period, or sooner if it becomes low. The reason for replenishing the fund at the end of the accounting period is that no record of the fund expenditures is in the accounts until the check is written and a journal entry is made. (Sometimes we refer to this fund as an *imprest* fund since it is replenished when it becomes low.) The petty cash custodian presents the vouchers to the employee having authority to order that the fund be reimbursed. After the vouchers are examined, if all is in order, that employee draws a check to restore the fund to its original amount.

Replenishing the Fund

Illustration 8.12   Petty Cash Voucher

```
┌─────────────────────────────────────────────────┐
│           PETTY CASH VOUCHERS NO. 359             │
│                                                   │
│   To  Local Cartage, Inc.        Date  June 29, 2012 │
│                                                   │
│  ┌──────────────────┬──────────┬─────────────┐   │
│  │   EXPLANATION     │ ACCT NO. │   AMOUNT     │   │
│  ├──────────────────┼──────────┼─────────────┤   │
│  │ Freight on parts  │    27    │  12 │  57    │   │
│  │                   │          │     │        │   │
│  │                   │          │     │        │   │
│  └──────────────────┴──────────┴─────────────┘   │
│                                                   │
│   APPROVED BY  A.E.C.     RECEIVED BY  Ken Black  │
└─────────────────────────────────────────────────┘
```

Note to the Student
When the petty cash fund is replenished, the Petty Cash account is neither debited nor credited.

To determine which accounts to debit, an employee summarizes the petty cash vouchers according to the reasons for expenditure. Next, that person stamps or defaces the petty cash vouchers to prevent reuse. The journal entry to record replenishing the fund would debit the various accounts indicated by the summary and credit Cash.

For example, assume the $100 petty cash fund currently has a money balance of $7.40. A summary of the vouchers shows payments of $22.75 for shipping, $50.80 for stamps, and $19.05 for an advance to an employee; these payments total $92.60. After the vouchers have been examined and approved, an employee draws a check for $92.60 which, when cashed, restores the cash in the fund to its $100 balance. The journal entry to record replenishment is:

Delivery Expense	22.75	
Postage Expense	50.80	
Receivable from Employees (or Advances to Employees)	19.05	
Cash		92.60
To replenish a petty cash fund.		

Note that the entry to record replenishing the fund does not credit the Petty Cash account. We make entries to the Petty Cash account only when the fund is established, when the end of the accounting period arrives and the fund is not replenished, or when the size of the fund is changed.

At the end of an accounting period, the firm records any petty cash disbursements for which the fund has not yet been replenished. Since the fund has not been replenished, the credit would be to Petty Cash rather than Cash. Failure to make an entry at the end of an accounting period would cause errors in both the income statement and balance sheet. The easiest way to record these disbursements is to replenish the fund.

After a time, if the petty cash custodian finds that the petty cash fund is larger than needed, the excess petty cash should be deposited in the company's checking account. The required entry to record a decrease in the fund debits Cash and credits Petty Cash for the amount returned and deposited. On the other hand, a petty cash fund may be too small, requiring replenishment every few days. The entry to record an increase in the fund debits Petty Cash and credits Cash for the amount of the increase.

To illustrate, the entry to *decrease* the petty cash fund by $50 would be:

Cash	50	
Petty Cash		50
To decrease the size of the petty cash fund by $50.		

The entry to *increase* the petty cash fund by $600 would be:

Petty Cash	600	
Cash		600
To increase the size of the petty cash fund by $600.		

The following rules summarize how the Petty Cash account is debited and credited:

Debited to establish

Debited to increase

Credited to decrease

Credited to terminate

Sometimes, the petty cash custodian makes errors in making change from the fund. These errors cause the cash in the fund to be more or less than the amount of the fund less the total vouchers. When the fund is restored to its original amount, the credit to Cash is for the difference between the established amount and the actual cash in the fund. We would debit all vouchered items. Any discrepancy should be debited or credited to an account called *Cash Short and Over.* The Cash Short and Over account is an expense or a revenue, depending on whether it has a debit or credit balance.

To illustrate, assume in the preceding example that the balance in the fund was only $6.10 instead of $7.40. Restoring the fund to $100 requires a check for $93.90. Since the petty cash vouchers total only $92.60, the fund is short $1.30. The entry for replenishment is:

Reinforcing Problems
E8-9 and E8-10 Record the reimbursement of petty cash fund.
E8-11 Prepare journal entries regarding petty cash.

Delivery Expense	22.75	
Postage Expense	50.80	
Receivable from Employees	19.05	
Cash Short and Over	1.30	
Cash		93.90
To replenish a petty cash fund.		

Entries in the Cash Short and Over account also result from other change-making activities. For example, assume that a clerk accidentally shortchanges a customer $1 and that total cash sales for the day are $740.50. At the end of the day, actual cash is $1 over the sum of the sales tickets or the total of the cash register tape. The journal entry to record the day's cash sales is:

Cash	741.50	
Sales		740.50
Cash Short and Over		1.00
To record cash sales for the day.		

Analyzing and Using the Financial Results— The Quick Ratio

The **quick ratio** measures a company's short-term debt-paying ability. It is the ratio of quick assets (cash, marketable securities, and net receivables) to current liabilities. When computing quick assets, we do not include inventories and prepaid expenses because they might not be readily convertible into cash. A rule of thumb is that the ratio of quick assets to current liabilities should be 1:1 or higher. However, a lower quick ratio is satisfactory in companies that generate a steady flow of cash in their operations. Short-term creditors are interested in this ratio since it relates the pool of cash and immediate cash inflows to immediate cash outflows. The formula for the quick ratio is:

Objective 6
Analyze and use the financial results—quick ratio.

An Ethical Perspective City Club Restaurant	The City Club Restaurant is a member-owned entity in Carson City. For 20 years, John Blue has managed the restaurant and received only minimal salary increases. He believes he is grossly underpaid in view of the significant inflation that has occurred. A few years ago he began supplementing his income by placing phony invoices in the petty cash box, writing a petty cash voucher for the amount of each invoice, withdrawing	cash equal to the amount of each invoice for his personal use, and later approving the vouchers for reimbursement. Through this mechanism, John increased his income by about $12,000 per year, an amount that he considered fair. No one else knows what is happening, and the manager feels fully justified in supplementing his income in this way.

$$\text{Quick ratio} = \frac{\text{Quick assets}}{\text{Current liabilities}}$$

Based on the following information, we can determine that the 2012 and 2011 quick ratios are 6.85 and 6.84, respectively:

	2012	2011
Cash	$315,064	$283,913
Short-term investments	119,093	314,872
Net receivables	320,892	177,300
Total quick assets	$755,049	$776,085
Current liabilities	$110,147	$113,430

$$\frac{\text{Total quick assets}}{\text{Current liabilities}} \qquad \frac{\$755,049}{\$110,147} = 6.85 \qquad \frac{\$776,085}{\$113,430} = 6.84$$

Now that you have learned how to control a company's most liquid asset, cash, in the next chapter you are ready to study receivables and payables. As you realize, the backbone of our economy is credit. In all probability, the next automobile you plan to buy will be financed. Companies are anxious to offer credit to worthy customers and prospective customers. The many offers of credit we receive from various businesses are evidence of the importance companies place on credit as a method of stimulating sales and expanding their business.

Understanding the Learning Objectives

Objective 1 Describe the necessity for and features of internal control.

- The internal control structure of a company includes its plan of organization and all the procedures and actions taken by the company to protect its assets against theft and waste, ensure compliance with company policies and federal law, evaluate the performance of all personnel in the company to promote efficiency of operations, and ensure accurate and reliable operating data and accounting records.
- The purpose of internal control is to ensure the efficient operation of a business.
- Cash includes coins; currency; undeposited negotiable instruments such as checks, bank drafts, and money orders; amounts in checking and saving accounts; and demand certificates of deposit.

Objective 2 Define cash and list the objectives sought by management in handling a company's cash.

- To protect their cash, companies should account for all cash transactions accurately, make certain enough cash is available to pay bills as they come due, avoid holding too much idle cash, and prevent loss of cash due to theft or fraud.

- Procedures for controlling cash receipts include such basic principles as recording all cash receipts as soon as cash is received; depositing all cash receipts on the day they are received or on the next business day; and preventing the employee who handles cash receipts from also recording the receipts in the accounting records or from disbursing cash.

- Procedures for controlling cash disbursements include, among others, making all disbursements by check or from petty cash, using checks that are serially numbered, requiring two signatures on each check, and having a different person authorize payment of a bill than the persons allowed to sign checks.

- A bank reconciliation is prepared to *reconcile,* or explain, the difference between the cash balance on the bank statement and the cash balance on the company's books and to make the required entry(ies) to correct the cash balance in the ledger.

- A bank reconciliation is shown in Illustration 8.11.

- Journal entries are needed for all items that appear in the bank reconciliation as adjustments to the balance per ledger to arrive at the adjusted cash balance.

- Companies establish a petty cash fund to permit minor cash disbursements and still maintain adequate control over cash.

- When the cash in the petty cash fund becomes low, the fund should be replenished. A journal entry is necessary to record the replenishment.

- Quick ratio equals cash, marketable securities, and net receivables divided by current liabilities.

- The quick ratio measures a company's short-term debt-paying ability.

> **Objective 3**
> Identify procedures for controlling cash receipts and disbursements.

> **Objective 4**
> Prepare a bank reconciliation and make necessary journal entries based on that schedule.

> **Objective 5**
> Explain why a company uses a petty cash fund, describe its operations, and make the necessary journal entries.

> **Objective 6**
> Analyze and use the financial results—quick ratio.

Demonstration Problem 8–A

You are the manager of a restaurant that has an ice cream parlor as a separate unit. Your accountant comes in once a year to prepare financial statements and the tax return. In the current year, you have a feeling that even though business seems good, net income is going to be lower. You ask the accountant to prepare condensed statements on a monthly basis. All sales are priced to yield an estimated gross margin of 40%. You, your accountant, and several of the accountant's assistants take physical inventories at the end of each of the following four months. The resulting sales, cost of goods sold, and gross margins are:

	March		April		May		June	
	Restaurant	**Ice Cream Parlor**	**Restaurant**	**Ice Cream Parlor**	**Restaurant**	**Ice Cream Parlor**	**Restaurant**	**Ice Cream Parlor**
Sales	$36,300	$53.000	$39,050	$42,750	$38,100	$39,000	$41,250	$35,500
Cost of goods sold	23,275	31,500	23,800	31,000	22,975	30,750	25,500	31,125
Gross Margin	$13,025	$21,500	$15,250	$11,750	$15,125	$8,250	$15,750	$4,375

What would you suspect after analyzing these reports? What sales control procedures would you recommend to correct the situation? All of the points in this problem were not specifically covered in the chapter, although the principles were. Use logic, common sense, and knowledge gained elsewhere in coming up with some of the control procedures.

 Required

Solution to Demonstration Problem 8–A

The gross margin percentages are as follows:

	March	April	May	June
Restaurant	35.88%	39.05%	39.70%	38.18%
Ice cream parlor	40.57	27.49	21.15	12.32

Either cash or inventory is being stolen or given away in the ice cream parlor. Employees or outsiders may be pocketing cash. Or the employees may be giving extra-large ice cream cones to friends, or eating the ice cream themselves. Several things could be done to improve the sales control procedures:

1. The manager could hire an investigator to come in and watch the employees in action. If cash is being pocketed, the employees could be fired.
2. The prices of ice cream cones could be changed to odd amounts so that employees would not be as able to make change without going to the cash register. Also, the No Sale lever could be removed from the cash register.
3. The customers could be encouraged to ask for their cash register receipts by having a monthly drawing (for some prize) by cash register receipt number.
4. The cash register should be placed in a prominent position so that each customer could see the amount recorded for each sale. No customer is going to be willing to pay $1.75 when the employee rings up $1.00.
5. The cash register tapes should be inaccessible to the employees. The manager (and possibly assistant manager) should have the only keys to the cash registers.
6. Pay the employees a competitive wage.
7. Require that all sales be rung up immediately after the sale.
8. The manager or assistant manager should reconcile the cash register tapes at the end of each day.

Demonstration Problem 8–B

The following data pertain to Carr Company:

1. Balance per bank statement, dated March 31, 2012, is $4,450.
2. Balance of the Cash account on the company's books as of March 31, 2012, is $4,459.
3. The $1,300 deposit of March 31 was not on the bank statement.
4. Of the checks recorded as cash disbursements in March, some checks, totaling $1,050, have not yet cleared the bank.
5. Service and collection charges for the month were $10.
6. The bank erroneously charged the Carr Company account for the $200 check of another company. The check was included with the canceled checks returned with the bank statement.
7. The bank credited the company's account with the $1,000 proceeds of a noninterest-bearing note that it collected for the company.
8. A customer's $75 check marked NSF was returned with the bank statement.
9. As directed, the bank paid and charged to the company's account a $507.50 noninterest-bearing note of Carr Company. This payment has not been recorded by the company.
10. An examination of the cash receipts and the deposit tickets revealed that the bookkeeper erroneously recorded a customer's check of $148.50 as $135.00.
11. The bank credited the company's checking account for $20 interest earned.
    a. Prepare a bank reconciliation as of March 31, 2012.
    b. Prepare the necessary journal entry or entries to adjust the Cash account.

Required

Solution to Demonstration Problem 8–B

a.

CARR COMPANY
Bank Reconciliation
March 31, 2012

Balance per bank statement, March 31, 2012		$4,450.00
Add: Deposit in transit	$1,300.00	
Check charged in error	200.00	1,500.00
		$5,950.00
Less: Outstanding checks		1,050.00
Adjusted balance, March 31, 2012		$4,900.00
Balance per ledger, March 31, 2012		$4,459.00
Add: Note collected	$1,000.00	
Interest earned on checking account	20.00	
Error in recording customer's check	13.50	1,033.50
		$5,492.50
Less: Service and collection charges	$10.00	
NSF check	75.00	
Carr Company noted charged against account	507.50	592.50
Adjusted balance, March 31, 2012		$4,900.00

Mar.	31	Cash	441.00	
		Bank Service Charge Expense	10.00	
		Accounts Receivable	75.00	
		Notes Payable	507.50	
		Notes Receivable		1,000.00
		Interest Revenue		20.00
		Accounts Receivable		13.50
		To record adjustments to Cash account		

b.

Alternatively:

Mar.	31	Cash	1,033.50	
		Notes Receivable		1,000.00
		Interest Revenue		20.00
		Accounts Receivable		13.50
		To record additions to Cash account.		
		Bank Service Charge Expense	10.00	
		Accounts Receivable	75.00	
		Notes Payable	507.50	
		Cash		592.50
		To record deductions from Cash account.		

New Terms

Accounting system   Methods and records established to identify, assemble, analyze, classify, record, and report an entity's transactions to provide complete, accurate, and timely financial information. *307*

Bank reconciliation   A schedule the company (depositor) prepares to *reconcile,* or explain, the difference between the cash balance on the bank statement and the cash balance on the company's books; often called a *bank reconciliation statement* or *schedule. 321*

Bank statement   A statement issued (usually monthly) by a bank describing the activities in a depositor's checking account during the period. *319*

Cash   Includes coins; currency; certain undeposited negotiable instruments such as checks, bank drafts, and money orders; amounts in checking and savings accounts; and demand certificates of deposit. *314*

Cashier's check   A check made out to either the depositor or a third party and written, or drawn, by a bank after deducting the amount of the check from the depositor's account or receiving cash from the depositor. *324*

Certificate of deposit (CD)   An interest-bearing deposit that can be withdrawn from a bank at will (demand CD) or at a fixed maturity date (time CD).*314*

Certified check   A check written, or drawn, by a depositor and taken to the depositor's bank for certification. The check is deducted from the depositor's balance immediately and becomes a liability of the bank. Thus, it usually is accepted without question. *324*

Check   A written order to a bank to pay a specific sum of money to the party designated as the payee by the party issuing the check. *318*

Checking account   A money balance maintained in a bank that is subject to withdrawal by the depositor, or owner of the money, on demand. *317*

Control environment   Reflects the overall attitude, awareness, and actions of the board of directors, management, and stockholders. *307*

Control procedures   Policies and procedures in addition to the control environment and the accounting system that management has established to provide reasonable assurance that the company will achieve its specific objectives. 307

Credit memo   A form used by a bank to explain an addition to the depositor's account. *321*

Debit memo   A form used by a bank to explain a deduction from the depositor's account. *321*

Deposit in transit   Typically, a day's cash receipts recorded in the depositor's books in one period but recorded as a deposit by the bank in the succeeding period. *322*

Deposit ticket   A form that shows the date and the items that make up the deposit. *317*

Drawer   The party (depositor) writing a check. *318*

Fidelity bonds   Ensure that a company is reimbursed for losses due to theft of cash and other monetary assets. *311*

Internal auditing   Consists of investigating and evaluating employees' compliance with the company's policies and procedures. Internal auditing is performed by company personnel. *309*

Internal auditors   Auditors employed by the company to perform internal audits. These auditors are trained in company policies and in internal auditing duties such as testing effectiveness of controls and procedures involving cash receipts and cash disbursements. *309*

Internal control structure   Policies and procedures established to provide reasonable assurance that specific entity objectives will be achieved. *307, 308*

Invoice   Statement sent by the supplier to the purchaser requesting payment for the merchandise shipped. *310*

NSF (not sufficient funds) check   A customer's check returned from the customer's bank to the depositor's bank because the funds in the customer's checking account balance were insufficient to cover the check. *319*

Outstanding checks   Checks issued by a depositor that have not yet been paid by the bank on which they are drawn. *322*

Payee   The party to whom a check is made payable. *318*

Petty cash fund   A nominal sum of money established as a separate fund from which minor cash disbursements for valid business purposes are made. The cash in the fund plus the vouchers covering disbursements should always equal the balance at which the fund was established and at which it is carried in the Petty Cash account. *325*

Petty cash voucher   A document or form that shows the amount of, and reason for, a petty cash disbursement. *325*

Purchase order   A document sent from the purchasing department to a supplier requesting that merchandise or other items be shipped to the purchaser. *310*

Purchase requisition   A written request from an employee inside the company to the purchasing department to purchase certain items. *310*

Quick ratio The ratio of quick assets (cash, marketable securities, and net receivables) to current liabilities. The quick ratio measures a company's short-term debt-paying ability. *327*

Receiving report A document prepared by the receiving department showing the descriptions and quantities of all items received from a supplier in a particular shipment. *310*

Remittance advice Informs the payee why the drawer (or maker) of the check is making this payment. *318*

Segregation of duties Having one employee responsible for safeguarding an asset and a second employee responsible for maintaining the accounting records for that asset. *308*

Service charges Charges assessed by the bank on the depositor to cover the cost of handling the checking account. *319*

Signature card Provides the signatures of persons authorized to sign checks drawn on an account. *317*

Transfer bank accounts Bank accounts set up so that local banks automatically transfer to a central bank (by wire or written bank draft) all amounts on deposit in excess of a stated amount. *320*

Wire transfer of funds Interbank transfer of funds by telephone. *320*

Self-Test

True-False
Indicate whether each of the following statements is true or false.
1. Cash includes coin, currency, postdated checks, money orders, and money on deposit with banks.
2. To effectively manage its cash, a company should make certain that enough cash is available to pay bills as they come due.
3. The cash balance on the bank statement is usually equal to the cash balance in the depositor's books.
4. A deposit in transit requires an entry in the depositor's books after the bank reconciliation is prepared.
5. For control purposes, a company should issue checks for every payment, regardless of its amount.

Multiple-Choice
Select the best answer for each of the following questions.
1. The objectives of the internal control structure of a company include all of the following except:
   a. Compliance with company policies and federal law.
   b. Protection of its assets.
   c. Increase in accuracy and reliability of accounting data.
   d. Guarantee of a certain level of profit.
   e. Evaluation of personnel performance to promote efficiency of operations.

Use the following information to answer Questions 2–4:

Balance per bank statement	$1,951.20
Balance per ledger	1,869.60
Deposits in transit	271.20
Outstanding checks	427.80
NSF check	61.20
Service charges	13.80

2. The adjusted cash balance is:
   a. $1,794.60.
   b. $1,719.60.
   c. $1,638.00.
   d. $1,713.00.
   e. $1,876.20.
3. In a bank reconciliation, deposits in transit should be:
   a. Deducted from the balance per books.
   b. Deducted from the balance per bank statement.
   c. Added to the balance per ledger.
   d. Added to the balance per bank statement.
   e. Disregarded in the bank reconciliation.
4. After the bank reconciliation is prepared, the entry to record bank service charges would have a credit to:
   a. Bank Service Charge Expense.
   b. Cash.
   c. Petty Cash.
   d. Cash Short and Over.
   e. None of the above.
5. The entry to replenish the petty cash fund for disbursements made for stamps includes:
   a. A credit to Petty Cash.
   b. A credit to Postage Expense.
   c. A debit to Accounts Payable.
   d. A credit to Cash.
   e. None of the above.

Now turn to page 343 to check your answers.

Questions

1. Why should a company establish an internal control structure?
2. Why are mechanical devices used in an internal control structure?
3. Identify some features that could strengthen an internal control structure.
4. Name several control documents used in merchandise transactions.
5. What are the four objectives sought in effective cash management?
6. List four essential features of internal control over cash receipts.
7. The bookkeeper of a given company was stealing cash received from customers in payment of their accounts. To conceal the theft, the bookkeeper made out false credit memos indicating returns and allowances made by or granted to customers. What feature of internal control would have prevented the thefts?
8. List six essential features of internal control over cash disbursements.
9. What types of items cause the balance per ledger and the balance per bank statement to disagree?
10. "The difference between a company's Cash account balance and the balance on its bank statement is usually a matter of timing." Do you agree or disagree? Why?
11. Explain how transfer bank accounts can help bring about effective cash management.
12. Describe the operation of a petty cash fund and its advantages. Indicate how control is maintained over petty cash transactions.
13. When are entries made to the Petty Cash account?
14. **Wal-Mart**   Based on the financial statements of Wal-mart, Inc., in the Annual Report Appendix, what was the quick ratio for each of the two years shown?
15. **Wal-Mart**   Based on the financial statements of Wal-mart, Inc., in the Annual Report Appendix, what was the ending cash and equivalents balance? What percentage of current assets does the amount of cash and equivalents represent for each of the two years shown?

Exercises

Exercise 8-1
Answer true-false questions about internal control
(L.O. 1)

State whether each of the following statements about internal control is *true* or *false*:

a. Those employees responsible for safeguarding an asset should maintain the accounting records for that asset.
b. Complete, accurate, and up-to-date accounting records should be maintained.
c. Whenever possible, responsibilities should be assigned and duties subdivided in such a way that only one employee is responsible for a given function.
d. Employees should be assigned to one job and should remain in that job so that skill levels will be as high as possible.
e. The use of check protectors, cash registers, and time clocks is recommended.
f. An internal auditing function should not be implemented because it leads the employees to believe that management does not trust them.
g. One of the best protections against theft is to hire honest, competent employees.
h. A foolproof internal control structure can be devised if management puts forth the effort.

Concerning internal control, which one of the following statements is correct? Explain.

a. Broadly speaking, an internal control structure is only necessary in large organizations.
b. The purposes of internal control are to check the accuracy of accounting data, safeguard assets against theft, promote efficiency of operations, and ensure that management's policies are being followed.
c. Once an internal control structure has been established, it should be effective as long as the formal organization remains unchanged.
d. An example of internal control is having one employee count the day's cash receipts and compare the total with the total of the cash register tapes.

Exercise 8-2
Answer multiple-choice question about internal control (L.O. 1)

The bank statement for Yarley Company at the end of August showed a balance of $12,862. Checks outstanding totaled $3,937, and deposits in transit were $5,990. If these amounts are the only pertinent data available to you, what was the adjusted balance of cash at the end of August?

Exercise 8-3
Determine available cash balance from bank statement and Cash account data (L.O. 4)

From the following data, prepare a bank reconciliation and determine the correct available cash balance for Reed Company as of October 31, 2012.

Exercise 8-4
Prepare a bank reconciliation and specify cash available (L.O. 4)

Balance per bank statement, October 31, 2012	$13,974
Ledger account balance. October 31, 2012	8,088
Proceeds of a note collected by bank not yet entered in ledger (includes $500 of interest)	6,000
Bank service charges not yet entered by Reed Company	18
Deposit in transit	1,680
Outstanding checks:	
No. 327	654
No. 328	288
No. 329	390
No. 331	252

The following is a bank reconciliation for Brian Company as of August 31.

Exercise 8-5
Record necessary journal entry or entries to correct cash balance (L.O. 4)

Balance per bank statement, August 31		$ 7,470
Add: Deposit in transit		5,676
		$13,146
Less: Outstanding checks		6,024
Adjusted balance, August 31		$ 7,122
Balance per ledger, August 31		$ 7,248
Add: Error correction*		54
		$ 7,302
Less: NSF check	$150	
Service and collection charges	30	180
Adjusted balance, August 31		$ 7,122

* The error occurred when the bookkeeper debited Accounts Payable and credited Cash for $93.00, instead of the correct amount, $39.00

Prepare the journal entry or entries needed to adjust or correct the Cash account.

On March 1 of the current year, Shelbey Company had outstanding checks of $15,000. During March, the company issued an additional $57,000 of checks. As of March 31, the bank statement showed $48,000 of checks had cleared the bank during the month. What is the amount of outstanding checks on March 31?

Exercise 8-6
Determine checks outstanding (L.O. 4)

Matson Company's bank statement as of August 31, shows total deposits into the company's account of $15,000 and a total of 14 separate deposits. On July 31, deposits of $410 and $330 were in transit. The total cash receipts for August were $19,000, and the company's records show 13 deposits made in August. What is the amount of deposits in transit at August 31?

Exercise 8-7
Determine deposits in transit (L.O. 4)

<table>
<tr><td>**Exercise 8-8**
Prepare a bank reconciliation and necessary journal entry or entries
(L.O. 4)</td><td>Holder Company deposits all cash receipts intact each day and makes all payments by check. On October 31, after all posting was completed, its Cash account had a debit balance of $4,325. The bank statement for the month ended on October 31 showed a balance of $3,988. Other data are:

1. Outstanding checks total $425.
2. October 31 cash receipts of $838 were placed in the bank's night depository and do not appear on the bank statement.
3. Bank service charges for October are $14.
4. Check No. 772 for store supplies on hand was entered at $405, but paid by the bank at its actual amount of $315.

Prepare a bank reconciliation for Holder Company as of October 31. Also prepare any necessary journal entry or entries.</td></tr>
<tr><td>**Exercise 8-9**
Record the reimbursement of petty cash fund (L.O. 5)</td><td>On August 31, Brighton Company's petty cash fund contained coins and currency of $260, an IOU from an employee of $30, and vouchers showing expenditures of $120 for postage, $52 for taxi fare, and $138 to entertain a customer. The Petty Cash account shows a balance of $600. The fund is replenished on August 31 because financial statements are to be prepared. What journal entry is required on August 31?</td></tr>
<tr><td>**Exercise 8-10**
Record the reimbursement of petty cash fund (L.O. 5)</td><td>Use the data in Exercise 8–9. What entry would have been required if the amount of coin and currency had been $247.20? Which of the accounts debited would not appear in the income statement?</td></tr>
<tr><td>**Exercise 8-11**
Prepare journal entries regarding petty cash (L.O. 5)</td><td>Rock Company has a $450 petty cash fund. The following transactions occurred in December:

Dec. 2 The petty cash fund was increased to $1,350.
      8 Petty Cash Voucher No. 318 for $14.20 delivery expense was prepared and paid. The fund was not replenished at this time.
     20 The company decided that the fund was too large and reduced it to $1,120.

Prepare any necessary journal entries for these transactions.</td></tr>
</table>

Problems

Problem 8-1
Prepare bank reconciliation with necessary journal entry or entries
(L.O. 4)

The following June 30, 2012, bank reconciliation pertains to Tiffany Company:

		Cash Amount	Bank Statement
Balance , June 30		$29,143.36	$28,644.31
Add: Deposit not credited by bank			942.60
Total			$29,586.91
Less: Outstanding checks:			
No. 724	$18.45		
No. 886	15.00		
No. 896	143.55		
No. 897	187.65		
No. 898	78.90		443.55
Adjusted cash balance, June 30		$29,143.36	$29,143.36

Tiffany's July bank statement follows:

Balance, July 1		$28,644.31	
Deposits during July		5,441.94	$34,086.25
Canceled checks returned:			
No. 724	$ 18.45		
No. 896	143.55		
No. 897	187.65		
No. 898	78.90		
No. 899	18.86		
No. 900	1,349.55		
No. 902	946.92		
No. 904	44.01	$2,787.89	
NSF Check of Starr Company		139.98	2,927.87
Bank statement balance, July 31			$31,158.38

The cash receipts deposited in July, including receipts of July 31, amounted to $5,178.30. Tiffany wrote these checks in July:

No. 899	$ 18.86
No. 900	1,349.55
No. 901	27.75
No. 902	946.92
No. 903	59.70
No. 904	44.01
No. 905	1,093.50
No. 906	15.00

The cash balance per the ledger on July 31, 2012, was $30,766.37.

Prepare a bank reconciliation as of July 31, 2012, and any necessary journal entry or entries to correct the accounts. ◖ *Required*

The following information pertains to Hughes Company as of May 31, 2012:

Problem 8-2
Prepare bank reconciliation with necessary journal entry or entries (L.O. 4)

1. Balance per bank statement as of May 31, 2012, was $59,410.
2. Balance per Hughes Company's Cash account at May 31, 2012, was $60,904.
3. A late deposit on May 31 did not appear on the bank statement, $4,275.
4. Outstanding checks as of May 31 totaled $7,614.
5. During May, the bank credited Hughes Company with the proceeds, $6,795, of a note which it had collected for the company. Interest revenue was $45 of the total.
6. Bank service and collection charges for May amounted to $18.
7. Comparison of the canceled checks with the check register revealed that one check in the amount as $1,458 had been recorded in the books as $1,539. The check had been issued in payment of an account payable.
8. A review of the deposit slips with the bank statement showed that a deposit for $2,250 of a company with a similar account number had been credited to the Hughes Company account in error.
9. A $270 check received from a customer, R. Petty, was returned with the bank statement marked NSF.
10. During May, the bank paid a $13,500 note of Hughes Company plus interest of $135 and charged it to the company's account per instructions received. Hughes Company had not recorded the payment of this note.
11. An examination of the cash receipts and the deposit tickets revealed that the bookkeeper erroneously recorded a check from a customer, C. Parker, of $1,458 as $1,944.
12. The bank statement showed a credit to the company's account for interest earned on the account balance in May of $450.
    a. Prepare a bank reconciliation as of May 31, 2012.
    b. Prepare the journal entry or entries necessary to adjust the accounts as of May 31, 2012.

 Required

PART III   Management's Perspectives in Accounting for Resources

Problem 8-3
Prepare journal entries
to record establishment
and reimbursement of
petty cash fund
(L.O. 5)

The following transactions pertain to the petty cash fund of Carrington Company:

Nov.   2   A $450 check is drawn, cashed, and the cash placed in the care of the assistant
            office manager to be used as a petty cash fund.

Dec.   17   The fund is replenished. An analysis of the fund shows:

Coins and currency	$147.40
Petty cash vouchers for:	
Delivery expenses	173.48
Transportation-in	111.12
Postage stamps purchased	15.00

       31   The end of the accounting period falls on this date. The fund was not
            replenished. The fund's contents on this date consist of:

Coins and currency	$352.05
Petty cash vouchers for:	
Delivery expenses	31.65
Postage stamps purchased	36.30
Employee's IOU	30.00

Required ➧   Present journal entries to record these transactions. Use the Cash Short and Over account for
any shortage or overage in the fund.

Problem 8-4
Prepare journal
entries to record
establishment,
reimbursement, and
increase of petty cash
fund (L.O. 5)

The following transactions relate to the petty cash fund of Jarvis Wrecking Company

Apr.   1   The petty cash fund is set up with a $350 cash balance.
       19   Because the money in the fund is down to $70.20, the fund is replenished. Petty
            cash vouchers are as follows:

Flowers for hospitalized employee	
(miscellaneous expense)	$84.38
Postage stamps	135.00
Office supplies	46.71

       30   The cash in the fund is $193.07. The fund is replenished to include petty cash
            payments in this period's financial statements. The petty cash vouchers are for
            the following:

Transportation-in	$64.12
Office supplies	92.81

May   1   The petty cash fund balance is increased to $400.

Required ➧   Prepare the journal entries to record these transactions.

Alternate Problems

Problem 8-1A
Prepare bank
reconciliation with
necessary journal entry
or entries
(L.O. 4)

The following data pertain to England Company:

1. Balance per the bank statement dated June 30, 2012, is $30,000.
2. Balance of the Cash in Bank account on the company books as of June 30, 2012,
   is $8,795.
3. Outstanding checks as of June 30, 2012, total $14,300.
4. Bank deposit of June 30 for $2,735 was not included in the deposits per the bank statement.
5. The bank had collected proceeds of a note, $22,612 (of which $112 was interest), that it
   credited to the England Company account. The bank charged the company a collection
   fee of $15 on the note.
6. The bank erroneously charged the England Company account for a $10,500 debit memo
   of another company that has a similar name.
7. Bank service charges for June, exclusive of the collection fee, amounted to $95.

8. Among the canceled checks was one for $700 given in payment of an account. The bookkeeper had recorded the check at $920 in the company records.
9. A check of Crosby, a customer, for $2,447, deposited on June 20, was returned by the bank marked NSF. No entry has been made to reflect the returned check on the company records.
10. A check for $1,435 of Malcolm, a customer, which had been deposited in the bank, was erroneously recorded by the bookkeeper as $1,570. The check had been received as a payment on the customer's account receivable.

Prepare a bank reconciliation as of June 30, 2012, and any necessary journal entry or entries to correct the accounts. ☞ *Required*

The bank statement of Irish Company's checking account with the 2nd National Bank shows:

Balance, June 30, 2012		$166,118
Deposits		245,700
		411,818
Less: Checks deducted	$243,001	
Service charges	67	243,068
Balance, July 31, 2012		$168,750

Problem 8-2A
Prepare bank reconciliation with necessary journal entry or entries
(L.O. 4)

The following additional data are available:

1. Balance per ledger account as of July 31 was $128,209.
2. A credit memo included with the bank statement indicated the collection of a note by the bank for Irish Company. Proceeds were $13,500, of which $375 was interest.
3. An NSF check in the amount of $6,210 was returned by the bank and included in the total of checks deducted on the bank statement.
4. Deposits in transit as of July 31 totaled $33,750.
5. Checks outstanding as of July 31 were $55,350.
6. The bank added the $29,025 deposit of another company to Irish's account in error.
7. The bank deducted one of Irish's checks as $20,250 instead of the correct amount of $2,025.
8. Deposit of July 21 was recorded by the company as $4,299.75 and by the bank at the actual amount of $4,542.75. The receipts for the day were from collections on account.
9. The deposits amount shown on the bank statement includes $675 of interest earned by Irish on its checking account with the bank.
   a. Prepare a bank reconciliation as of July 31, 2012, for Irish Company.
   b. Prepare any journal entry or entries needed at July 31, 2012. ☞ *Required*

Transactions involving the petty cash fund of Sonar Company are as follows:

Problem 8-3A
Prepare journal entries to record establishment and reimbursement of petty cash fund
(L.O. 5)

Mar. 1 Established a petty cash fund of $750, which will be under the control of the assistant office manager.
   31 Fund was replenished on this date. Prior to replenishment, the fund consisted of the following:

Coins and currency	$491.50
Petty cash voucher indicating disbursements for:	
Postage stamps	82.00
Suppliers money for office employees working overtime	36.00
Office supplies	32.70
Window washing service	60.00
Flowers for wedding of employee	15.00
Flower for hospitalized employee	15.00
Employee's IOU	15.00

Required   Present journal entries for these transactions. Use the Cash Short and Over account for any shortage or overage in the fund.

Problem 8-4A
Prepare journal entries to record establishment, reimbursement, and increase of petty cash fund (L.O. 5)

Sun Company has decided to use a petty cash fund. Transactions involving this fund follow:

June   4   Set up a petty cash fund of $225.
         22   When the fund had a cash amount of $31.35, the custodian of the fund was reimbursed for expenditures made, including:

Transportation-in	$82.50
Postage 27.00	
Office supplies	81.75

         30   The fund was reimbursed to include petty cash items in the financial statements prepared for the fiscal year ending on this date. The fund had the following cash and vouchers before reimbursement:

Coins and currency	$174.00
Petty cash vouchers for:	
Employee's IOU	15.00
Postage 27.00	
Office supplies	11.10

July   1   The petty cash fund balance is increased to $300.

Required   Prepare journal entries for all of these transactions.

Beyond the Numbers—Critical Thinking

Business Decision Case 8-1
Discuss steps to prevent theft (L.O. 1, 3)

During a national emergency, a managerial accountant was called back to active duty with the U.S. Army. An acquaintance of the accountant forged papers and assumed the identity of the accountant. He obtained a position in a small company as the only accountant. Eventually he took over from the manager the functions of approving bills for payment, preparing and signing checks, and almost all other financial duties. On one weekend, he traveled to some neighboring cities and mailed invoices made out to the company for which he worked. On Monday morning, he returned to work and began receiving, approving, and paying the invoices he had prepared. The following weekend he returned to the neighboring cities and cashed and deposited the checks in bank accounts under his own name. After continuing this practice for several months, he withdrew all of the funds and never was heard from again.

Required   Prepare a written list of the steps you would have taken to prevent this theft. Remember that this small company had limited financial resources.

Business Decision Case 8-2
List procedures that would have prevented theft of cash (L.O. 1, 3)

John Billings was set up in business by his father, who purchased the business of an elderly acquaintance wishing to retire. One of the few changes in personnel made by Billings was to install a college classmate as the office manager-bookkeeper-cashier-sales manager. During the course of the year, Billings borrowed money from the bank with his father as cosigner. Although his business seemed profitable, there was a shortage of cash. The company's investments in inventories and receivables grew substantially. Finally, after a year had elapsed, Billings's father employed you, a certified public accountant, to audit the records of his business. You reported that the office manager-bookkeeper-cashier-sales manager had been misappropriating funds and had been using a variety of schemes to cover his actions. More specifically, he had:

1. Pocketed cash receipts from sales and understated the cash register readings at the end of the day or altered the copies of the sales tickets retained.
2. Stolen checks mailed to the company in payment of accounts receivable, credited the proper accounts, and then debited fictitious receivables to keep the records in balance.

3. Issued checks to fictitious suppliers and deposited them in accounts bearing these names with himself as signer of checks drawn on these accounts; the books were kept in balance by debiting the Purchases account.
4. Stolen petty cash funds by drawing false vouchers purporting to cover a variety of expenses incurred.
5. Prepared false sales returns vouchers indicating the return of cash sales to cover further thefts of cash receipts.

For each item in the preceding list, describe in writing at least one feature of good internal ◗ *Required*
control that would have prevented the losses due to dishonesty.

The outstanding checks of Brothers Company at November 30, 2012, were:

**Business Decision
Case 8-3***
Describe method
used to steal cash;
determine amount
stolen; prepare correct
bank reconciliation; and
describe internal control
procedures that would
have prevented such
theft (L.O. 1, 3, 4)

No. 229	$1,000
No. 263	1,089
No. 3678	679
No. 3679	804
No. 3680	1,400

During December, Brothers issued checks numbered 3681–3720; and all of these checks cleared the bank except 3719 and 3720 for $963 and $726, respectively. Checks 3678, 3679, and 3680 also cleared the bank.

The bank statement on December 31 showed a balance of $23,944. Service charges amounted to $20, and two checks were returned by the bank, one marked NSF in the amount of $114 and the other marked "No account" in the amount of $2,000.

Brian Askew recently retired as the office manager-cashier-bookkeeper for Brothers Company and was replaced by Fred Hannah. Hannah noted the absence of an internal control structure but was momentarily deterred from embezzling for lack of a scheme of concealment. Finally, he hit upon several schemes. The $2,000 check marked "No account" by the bank is the product of one scheme. Hannah took cash receipts and replaced them with a check drawn on a nonexistent account to make it appear that a customer had given the company a worthless check.

The other scheme was more subtle. Hannah pocketed cash receipts in an amount equal to two unlisted outstanding checks and prepared the following bank reconciliation:

Balance per bank statement, December 31, 2012		$23,944.00
Add: Deposit in transit		2,837.80
		$26,781.80
Less: Outstanding checks		
No. 3719	$ 963.00	
No. 3720	726.00	1,689.00
Adjusted balance, December 31, 2012		$25,092.80
Balance per ledger, December 31, 2012		$27,226.80
Add: Worthless check	$2,000.00	
NSF check	114.00	
Service charges	20.00	2,134.00
Adjusted balance, December 31, 2012		$25,092.80

a. State the nature of the second scheme hit on by Hannah. How much in total does it ◗ *Required*
appear he has stolen by use of the two schemes together?
b. Prepare a correct bank reconciliation as of December 31, 2012.
c. After your analysis in (a) and (b), describe several procedures that would have defeated Fred Hannah's attempts to misappropriate funds and conceal these actions.

---

*Note: This challenging problem was not specifically illustrated in the chapter, but it can be worked by applying the principles discussed in the chapter.

**Annual Report
Analysis 8-4**
Discuss internal control
elements (L.O. 1)

In Reader's Digest's Annual Report, under Report of Management, the chairman and chief executive officer and the executive vice president and chief financial officer stated:

The company maintains a system of internal accounting controls designed to provide reasonable assurance, at reasonable cost, that transactions and events are recorded properly and that assets are safeguarded. The internal control system is supported by written policies and procedures and by the careful selection, training, and supervision of qualified personnel, and is monitored by an internal audit function.

Required ➲

What is the purpose of this statement? To which basic elements of the internal control structure does the statement refer?

**Annual Report
Analysis 8-5**
Calculate the quick ratio
(L.O. 6)

Obtain an annual report for a company (your library may have some annual reports, or you can often download them from company websites). Determine the quick ratios for the two most recent years for the company. Comment on the results

**Ethics Case—
Writing Experience
8-6**
Respond regarding the
ethics case

After reading the ethics case on page 328, discuss the ethical situation at the City Club Restaurant. Describe the steps the owners could take to end John Blue's wage supplement scheme.

Group Project 8-7
Evaluate internal
controls

With a small group of students, visit a large local company to inquire about its internal control structure. Specifically, discover how it protects its assets against theft and waste, ensures compliance with company policies and federal laws, evaluates performance of its personnel, and ensures accurate and reliable operating data and accounting reports. If an internal audit staff exists, inquire about some of its activities. Write a report to your instructor summarizing your findings and be prepared to make a short presentation to the class.

Group Project 8-8
Evaluate controls over
petty cash

With one or two other students, locate and visit two companies that maintain petty cash funds. Interview the custodians of those funds to identify the controls that are used to manage those funds. Write a report to your instructor comparing the controls used, pointing out any differences between the control systems and any deficiencies in the systems. Be prepared to make a short presentation to the class.

Group Project 8-9
Perform library
research

"Kiting" of bank accounts has been used to conceal shortages in bank accounts. With one or two other students, research this topic in the library. Write a paper to your instructor describing how this technique works and the steps that can be taken to detect it once it occurs and to prevent it in the future.

Using the Internet—A View of the Real World

**Internet Project
8-10**
Learn about internal
control department

Visit the following site:
        http://www.vfauditmall.com/
This is the internet site for the Vanity Fair Audit Mall. Click on the visitors center, CCA Studio, Tool Box, Job Shop, Tek Shak, Risk Depot, Contact Plaza, and Arcade. After browsing the site write a one page memo as to what you learned about internal audit.

**Internet Project
8-11**
Investigate EDGAR

Visit the Securities and Exchange website and find the EDGAR database at:
        http://www.sec.gov/edgar.shtml
EDGAR stands for the Electronic Data Gathering, Analysis, and Retrieval system. What is its purpose? What kinds of information can be found at this site? Select a company of your choice and search the EDGAR database for information on that company. Write a report to your instructor summarizing your findings.

Answers to Self-Test

True-False

1. **False.** Postdated checks are not included as cash.
2. **True.** A company should make sure that enough cash is available to pay bills as they come due.
3. **False.** The cash balance on a bank statement is not usually the same as the cash balance in the depositor's books because of deposits in transit, outstanding checks, and bank service charges.

4. **False.** A deposit in transit is one of the items that has been correctly recorded as a debit to the Cash account of the depositor and will be recorded as a deposit by the bank after the bank employees open the night deposit chute.
5. **False.** For convenience, a company may use a petty cash fund for small amounts of cash payments such as delivery charges or postage stamps.

Multiple-Choice

1. **d.** An effective internal control structure does not necessarily guarantee a certain level of profits.
2. **a.**

Balance per bank statement	$1,951.20
Add: Deposit in transit	271.20
Less: Outstanding checks	(427.80)
Adjusted balance	$1,794.60
Balance per ledger	$1,869.60
Less: NSF check	(61.20)
Service charges	(13.80)
Adjusted balance	$1,794.60

3. **d.** Deposits in transit have been recorded in the company's accounting records but have not yet been recorded in the bank's records.

4. **b.** The entry to record bank service charges on the books is:

Bank Service Charge Expense	13.80	
Cash		13.80

5. **d.** The entry to replenish the petty cash fund has a credit to Cash, not Petty Cash.

Postage Expense	xxx	
Cash		xxx

Careers in Accounting

A Career In Litigation Support

What is litigation support? It does not mean working in an attorney's office. It involves assisting legal counsel in attempting to gain favorable verdicts in a court of law. Persons involved in litigation support generally work for a public accounting firm, a consulting firm, or as a sole proprietor or in partnership with others. An experienced litigation support person can expect to earn an income well into six figures.

Litigation support in a broad sense encompasses fraud auditing, valuation analysis, investigative accounting, and forensic accounting. The practice of litigation support involves assisting legal counsel in such things as product liability disputes, shareholder disputes, contract breaches, and major losses reported by entities. These investigations require the accountant to gather and evaluate evidence to assess the integrity and dollar amounts surrounding the aforementioned situations.

The accountant can be, and often is, requested to serve as an expert witness in a court of law. This experience requires knowledge of accounting and auditing in addition to possessing good communication skills, appropriate credentials, relevant experience, and critical information that could result in successful resolution of the issue.

What kind of person pursues litigation support as a career? It takes a very special individual. The person must be part accountant, part auditor, part lawyer, and part skilled businessperson. An undergraduate accounting degree, an MBA, and a law degree would be the perfect educational background needed for such a career. Many universities offer a combined MBA/JD program. Such a program fulfills the graduate needs of the litigation support person.

In addition to the degree, work experience in the business sector is essential. A career in public accounting, industry, or with a government agency would serve as valuable experience in pursuing a career in litigation support.

9

Receivables and Payables

Much of the growth of business in recent years is due to the immense expansion of credit. Managers of companies have learned that by granting customers the privilege of *charging* their purchases, sales and profits increase. Using credit is not only a convenient way to make purchases but also the only way many people can own high-priced items such as automobiles.

This chapter discusses receivables and payables. For a company, a **receivable** is any sum of money due to be paid to that company from any party for any reason. Similarly, a **payable** describes any sum of money to be paid by that company to any party for any reason.

Primarily, receivables arise from the sale of goods and services. The two types of receivables are accounts receivable, which companies offer for short-term credit with no interest charge; and notes receivable, which companies sometimes extend for both short- and long-term credit with an interest charge. We pay particular attention to accounting for uncollectible accounts receivable.

Like their customers, companies use credit, which they show as accounts payable or notes payable. Accounts payable normally result from the purchase of goods or services and do not carry an interest charge. Short-term notes payable carry an interest charge and may arise from the same transactions as accounts payable, but they can also result from borrowing money from a bank or other institution. Chapter 4 identified accounts payable and short-term notes payable as current liabilities. A company also incurs other current liabilities, including payables such as sales tax payable, estimated product warranty payable, and certain liabilities that are contingent on the occurrence of future events. Long-term notes payable usually result from borrowing money from a bank or other institution to finance the acquisition of plant assets. As you study this chapter and learn how important credit is to our economy, you will realize that credit in some form will probably always be with us.

Learning Objectives

After studying this chapter, you should be able to:

1. Account for uncollectible accounts receivable under the allowance method.

2. Record credit card sales and collections.

3. Define liabilities, current liabilities, and long-term liabilities.

4. Define and account for clearly determinable, estimated, and contingent liabilities.

5. Account for notes receivable and payable, including calculation of interest.

(continued)

Objectives

6. Account for borrowing money using an interest-bearing note versus a noninterest-bearing note.

7. Analyze and use the financial results—accounts receivable turnover and the number of days' sales in accounts receivable.

Note to the Student
How many credit cards do you use? Which type? What form of credit do you use to purchase a car? What form of credit would you use to purchase a CD player?

Accounts Receivable

In Chapter 3, you learned that most companies use the accrual basis of accounting since it better reflects the actual results of the operations of a business. Under the accrual basis, a merchandising company that extends credit records revenue when it makes a sale because at this time it has earned and realized the revenue. The company has earned the revenue because it has completed the seller's part of the sales contract by delivering the goods. The company has realized the revenue because it has received the customer's promise to pay in exchange for the goods. This promise to pay by the customer is an account receivable to the seller. Accounts receivable are amounts that customers owe a company for goods sold and services rendered on account. Frequently, these receivables resulting from credit sales of goods and services are called **trade receivables**.

When a company sells goods on account, customers do not sign formal, written promises to pay, but they agree to abide by the company's customary credit terms. However, customers may sign a sales invoice to acknowledge purchase of goods. Payment terms for sales on account typically run from 30 to 60 days. Companies usually do not charge interest on amounts owed, except on some past-due amounts.

Because customers do not always keep their promises to pay, companies must provide for these uncollectible accounts in their records. Companies use two methods for handling uncollectible accounts. The *allowance method* provides in advance for uncollectible accounts. The *direct write-off method* recognizes bad accounts as an expense at the point when judged to be uncollectible and is the required method for federal income tax purposes. However, since the allowance method represents the accrual basis of accounting and is the accepted method to record uncollectible accounts for financial accounting purposes, we only discuss and illustrate the allowance method in this text.

The Allowance Method for Recording Uncollectible Accounts

Objective 1
Account for uncollectible accounts receivable under the allowance method.

Note to the Student
Why would a company sell for credit and risk uncollectible expenses? Answer: The profit from additional sales a company makes by granting credit is greater than the cost of granting credit—uncollectible accounts expense.

Even though companies carefully screen credit customers, they cannot eliminate all uncollectible accounts. Companies expect some of their accounts to become uncollectible, but they do not know which ones. The matching principle requires deducting expenses incurred in producing revenues from those revenues during the accounting period. The allowance method of recording uncollectible accounts adheres to this principle by recognizing the uncollectible accounts expense in advance of identifying *specific accounts* as being uncollectible. The required entry has some similarity to the depreciation entry in Chapter 3 because it debits an expense and credits an allowance (contra asset). The purpose of the entry is to make the income statement fairly present the proper expense and the balance sheet fairly present the asset. **Uncollectible accounts expense** (also called *doubtful accounts expense* or **bad debts expense**) is an operating expense that a business incurs when it sells on credit. We classify uncollectible accounts expense as a selling expense because it results from credit sales. Other accountants might classify it as an administrative expense because the credit department has an important role in setting credit terms.

To adhere to the matching principle, companies must match the uncollectible accounts expense against the revenues it generates. Thus, an uncollectible account arising from a sale made in 2012 is a 2012 expense even though this treatment requires the use of estimates. Estimates are necessary because the company sometimes cannot determine until 2013 or later which 2012 customer accounts will become uncollectible.

Recording the Uncollectible Accounts Adjustment   A company that estimates uncollectible accounts makes an adjusting entry at the end of each accounting period.

It debits Uncollectible Accounts Expense, thus recording the operating expense in the proper period. The credit is to an account called *Allowance for Uncollectible Accounts.*

As a contra account to the Accounts Receivable account, the **Allowance for Uncollectible Accounts** (also called *Allowance for Doubtful Accounts* or *Allowance for Bad Debts*) reduces accounts receivable to their net realizable value. **Net realizable value** is the amount the company expects to collect from accounts receivable. When the firm makes the uncollectible accounts adjusting entry, it does not know which specific accounts will become uncollectible. Thus, the company cannot enter credits in either the Accounts Receivable control account or the customers' accounts receivable subsidiary ledger accounts. If only one or the other were credited, the Accounts Receivable control account balance would not agree with the total of the balances in the accounts receivable subsidiary ledger. Without crediting the Accounts Receivable control account, the allowance account lets the company show that some of its accounts receivable are probably uncollectible.

To illustrate the adjusting entry for uncollectible accounts, assume a company has $100,000 of accounts receivable and estimates its uncollectible accounts expense for a given year at $4,000. The required year-end adjusting entry is:

Dec.	31	Uncollectible Accounts Expense	4,000	
		Allowance for Uncollectible Accounts		4,000
		To record estimated uncollectible accounts.		

Note to the Student
Accounts receivable - Allowance for uncollectible accounts = Net realizable value. This formula reflects what management expects to collect on its total accounts receivable.

The debit to Uncollectible Accounts Expense brings about a matching of expenses and revenues on the income statement; uncollectible accounts expense is matched against the revenues of the accounting period. The credit to Allowance for Uncollectible Accounts reduces accounts receivable to their net realizable value on the balance sheet. When the books are closed, the firm closes Uncollectible Accounts Expense to Income Summary. It reports the allowance on the balance sheet as a deduction from accounts receivable as follows:

BRICE COMPANY
Balance Sheet
December 31, 2012

Current Assets		
Cash		$ 21,200
Accounts receivable	$ 100,000	
Less: Allowance for Uncollectible accounts	4,000	96,000

Estimating Uncollectible Accounts   Accountants use two basic methods to estimate uncollectible accounts for a period. The first method—percentage-of-sales method—focuses on the income statement and the relationship of uncollectible accounts to sales. The second method—percentage-of-receivables method—focuses on the balance sheet and the relationship of the allowance for uncollectible accounts to accounts receivable.

Percentage-of-Sales Method   The percentage-of-sales method estimates uncollectible accounts from the credit sales of a given period. In theory, the method is based on a percentage of prior years' actual uncollectible accounts to prior years' *credit sales.* When cash sales are small or make up a fairly constant percentage of total sales, firms base the calculation on *total net sales.* Since at least one of these conditions is usually met, companies commonly use total net sales rather than credit sales. The formula to determine the amount of the entry is:

$$\text{Amount of journal entry for uncollectible accounts} = \text{Net sales (total or credit)} \times \text{Percentage estimated as uncollectible}$$

To illustrate, assume that Rankin Company's uncollectible accounts from 2010 sales were 1.1% of total net sales. A similar calculation for 2011 showed an uncollectible account percentage of 0.9%. The average for the two years is 1% $[(1.1 + 0.9) \div 2]$. Rankin does not expect 2012 to differ from the previous two years. Total net sales for 2012 were $500,000; receivables at year-end were $100,000; and the Allowance for Uncollectible Accounts had a zero balance. Rankin would make the following adjusting entry for 2012:

Dec.	31	Uncollectible Accounts Expense	5,000	
		Allowance for Uncollectible Accounts		5,000
		To record estimated uncollectible accounts		
		($500,000 X 0.01).		

Using T-accounts, Rankin would show:

Note to the Student
Under the percentage-of-sales method, we focus on matching revenues (Sales) and expenses (Uncollectible Accounts Expense), ignoring the balance in the allowance account.

Uncollectible Accounts Expense		Allowance for Uncollectible Accounts	
Dec. 31		Bal. before	
Adjustment 5,000		adjustment -0-	
		Dec. 31	
		Adjustment 5,000	
		Bal. after	
		adjustment 5,000	

Rankin reports Uncollectible Accounts Expense on the income statement. It reports the accounts receivable less the allowance among current assets in the balance sheet as follows:

Accounts receivable	$ 100,000	
Less: Allowance for uncollectible accounts	5,000	$ 95,000

Or Rankin's balance sheet could show:

Accounts receivable (less estimated		
uncollectible accounts, $5,000)	$95,000	

On the income statement, Rankin would match the uncollectible accounts expense against sales revenues in the period. We would classify this expense as a selling expense since it is a normal consequence of selling on credit.

The Allowance for Uncollectible Accounts account may have either a debit or credit balance *before* the year-end adjustment. Under the percentage-of-sales method, the company ignores any existing balance in the allowance when calculating the amount of the year-end adjustment (except that the allowance account must have a credit balance after adjustment).

For example, assume Rankin's allowance account had a $300 credit balance before adjustment. The adjusting entry would still be for $5,000. However, the balance sheet would show $100,000 accounts receivable less a $5,300 allowance for uncollectible accounts, resulting in net receivables of $94,700. On the income statement, Uncollectible Accounts Expense would still be 1% of total net sales, or $5,000.

In applying the percentage-of-sales method, companies annually review the percentage of uncollectible accounts that resulted from the previous year's sales. If the percentage rate is still valid, the company makes no change. However, if the situation has changed significantly, the company increases or decreases the percentage rate to reflect the changed condition. For example, in periods of recession and high unemployment, a firm may increase the percentage rate to reflect the customers' decreased ability to pay. However, if the company adopts a more stringent credit policy, it may have to decrease the percentage rate because the company would expect fewer uncollectible accounts.

Percentage-of-Receivables Method   The **percentage-of-receivables method** estimates uncollectible accounts by determining the desired size of the Allowance for Uncollectible Accounts. Rankin Company would multiply the ending balance in Accounts Receivable by a rate (or rates) based on its uncollectible accounts experience. In the percentage-of-receivables method, the company may use either an overall rate or a different rate for each age category of receivables.

To calculate the amount of the entry for uncollectible accounts under the percentage-of-receivables method using an overall rate, Rankin would use:

Note to the Student
Under the percentage-of-receivables method, we focus on the valuation of the receivables on the balance sheet. Our goal is to accurately reflect the net realizable value of receivables.

$$\begin{matrix} \text{Amount of} \\ \text{entry for} \\ \text{uncollectible} \\ \text{accounts} \end{matrix} = \begin{pmatrix} \text{Accounts} & \text{Percentage} \\ \text{Receivable} \times \text{estimated as} \\ \text{ending} & \text{uncollectible} \\ \text{balance} \end{pmatrix} - \begin{matrix} \text{Existing credit} \\ \text{balance in} \\ \text{Allowance for} \\ \text{Uncollectible} \\ \text{Accounts or} \end{matrix} + \begin{matrix} \text{Existing debit} \\ \text{balance in} \\ \text{Allowance for} \\ \text{Uncollectible} \\ \text{Accounts} \end{matrix}$$

Using the same information as before, Rankin makes an estimate of uncollectible accounts at the end of 2012. The balance of accounts receivable is $100,000, and the allowance account has no balance. If Rankin estimates that 6% of the receivables will be uncollectible, the adjusting entry would be:

Dec.	31	Uncollectible Accounts Expense	6,000	
		Allowance for Uncollectible Accounts		6,000
		To record estimated uncollectible accounts		
		($100,000 X 0.06).		

Using T-accounts, Rankin would show:

Uncollectible Accounts Expense		**Allowance for Uncollectible Accounts**	
Dec. 31		Bal. before	
Adjustment 6,000		Adjustment -0-	
		Dec. 31	
		Adjustment 6,000	
		Bal. after	
		Adjustment 6,000	

If Rankin had a $300 credit balance in the allowance account before adjustment, the entry would be the same, except that the amount of the entry would be $5,700. The difference in amounts arises because management wants the allowance account to contain a credit balance equal to 6% of the outstanding receivables when presenting the two accounts on the balance sheet. The calculation of the necessary adjustment is [($100,000 × 0.06) − $300] = $5,700. Thus, under the percentage-of-receivables method, firms consider any existing balance in the allowance account when adjusting for uncollectible accounts. Using T-accounts, Rankin would show:

Uncollectible Accounts Expense		**Allowance for Uncollectible Accounts**	
Dec. 31		Bal. before	
Adjustment 5,700		Adjustment 300	
		Dec. 31	
		Adjustment 5,700	
		Bal. after	
		Adjustment 6,000	

Illustration 9.1   Accounts Receivable Aging Schedule

			Days Past Due			
Customer	**Accounts Receivable Balance**	**Not Yet Due**	**1-30**	**31-60**	**61-90**	**Over 90**
X	$ 5,000					$ 5,000
Y	14,000		$ 12,000	$2,000		
Z	400				$200	200
All others	808,600	$ 560,000	240,000	2,000	600	6,000
	$ 828,000	$ 560,000	$252,000	$4,000	$800	$11,200
Percentage estimated as uncollectible		1%	5%	10%	25%	50%
Estimated amount uncollectible	$ 24,400	$ 5,600	$ 12,600	$ 400	$200	$ 5,600

ALLEN COMPANY — Accounts Receivable Aging Schedule — December 31, 2012

As another example, suppose that Rankin Company had a $300 *debit* balance in the allowance account before adjustment. Then, a credit of $6,300 would be necessary to get the balance to the required $6,000 credit balance. The calculation of the necessary adjustment is [($100,000 × 0.06) + $300] = $6,300. Using T-accounts, Rankin would show:

Reinforcing Problem E9-1 Prepare journal entries to record uncollectible accounts expense.

Uncollectible Accounts Expense

Dec. 31 Adjustment   6,300

Allowance for Uncollectible Accounts

Bal. before Adjustment   300 | Dec. 31 Adjustment   6,300

Bal. after Adjustment   6,000

No matter what the preadjustment allowance account balance is, when using the percentage-of-receivables method, Rankin adjusts the Allowance for Uncollectible Accounts so that it has a credit balance of $6,000—equal to 6% of its $100,000 in Accounts Receivable. The desired $6,000 ending credit balance in the Allowance for Uncollectible Accounts serves as a "target" in making the adjustment.

So far, we have used one uncollectibility rate for all accounts receivable, regardless of their age. However, some companies use a different percentage for each age category of accounts receivable. When accountants decide to use a different rate for each age category of receivables, they prepare an aging schedule. An **aging schedule** classifies accounts receivable according to how long they have been outstanding and uses a different uncollectibility percentage rate for each age category. Companies base these percentages on experience. In Illustration 9.1, the aging schedule shows that the older the receivable, the less likely the company is to collect it.

Classifying accounts receivable according to age often gives the company a better basis for estimating the total amount of uncollectible accounts. For example, based on experience, a company can expect only 1% of the accounts not yet due (sales made less than 30 days before the end of the accounting period) to be uncollectible. At the other extreme, a company can expect 50% of all accounts over 90 days past due to be uncollectible. For each age category, the firm multiplies the accounts receivable by the percentage estimated as uncollectible to find the estimated amount uncollectible.

Note to the Student An accounts receivable aging schedule emphasizes valuing the uncollectibles based on the age of the accounts. Many consider this to be the best of the methods presented.

Note to the Student The longer an account receivable is outstanding, the less likely is the seller's chance of collection. Even if it is collected in full later, the seller has not had the cash to use in the business. This increases the seller's cost of doing business.

The sum of the estimated amounts for all categories yields the total estimated amount uncollectible and is the desired credit balance (the target) in the Allowance for Uncollectible Accounts.

Since the aging schedule approach is an alternative under the percentage-of-receivables method, the balance in the allowance account before adjustment affects the year-end adjusting entry amount recorded for uncollectible accounts. For example, the schedule in Illustration 9.1 shows that $24,400 is needed as the ending credit balance in the allowance account. If the allowance account has a $5,000 credit balance before adjustment, the adjustment would be for $19,400.

The information in an aging schedule also is useful to management for other purposes. Analysis of collection patterns of accounts receivable may suggest the need for changes in credit policies or for added financing. For example, if the age of many customer balances has increased to 61–90 days past due, collection efforts may have to be strengthened. Or, the company may have to find other sources of cash to pay its debts within the discount period. Preparation of an aging schedule may also help identify certain accounts that should be written off as uncollectible.

Reinforcing Problem
E9-2 Use aging schedule to estimate allowance for uncollectible accounts

> **Business Insight** According to the Fair Debt Collection Practices Act, collection agencies can call persons only between 8 a.m. and 9 p.m., and cannot use foul language. Agencies can call employers only if the employers allow such calls. They can threaten to sue only if they really intend to do so. At present, agencies cannot contact a debtor via e-mail, text messaging, or via the debtor's cell phone without having been provided that contact information by the debtor.

An Accounting Perspective

Write-Off of Receivables As time passes and a firm considers a specific customer's account to be uncollectible, it writes that account off. It debits the Allowance for Uncollectible Accounts. The credit is to the Accounts Receivable control account in the general ledger and to the customer's individual account in the accounts receivable subsidiary ledger. For example, assume Smith's $750 account has been determined to be uncollectible. The entry to write off this account is:

Allowance for Uncollectible Accounts	750	
Accounts Receivable—Smith		750
To write off Smith's account as uncollectible.		

Reinforcing Problem
E9-3 Record write-off and subsequent collection of account.

The credit balance in Allowance for Uncollectible Accounts before making this entry represented potential uncollectible accounts not yet specifically identified. Debiting the allowance account and crediting Accounts Receivable shows that the firm has identified Smith's account as uncollectible. *Notice that the debit in the entry to write off an account receivable does not involve recording an expense.* The company recognized the uncollectible accounts expense in the same accounting period as the sale. If Smith's $750 uncollectible account were recorded in Uncollectible Accounts Expense again, it would be counted as an expense twice.

Notice also that a write-off does not affect the net realizable value of accounts receivable. For example, suppose that Amos Company has total accounts receivable of $50,000 and an allowance of $3,000 before the previous entry; the net realizable value of the accounts receivable is $47,000. After posting that entry, accounts receivable are $49,250, and the allowance is $2,250; net realizable value is still $47,000, as shown here:

	Before Write-Off	Entry for Write-Off	After Write-Off
Accounts receivable	$ 50,000 Dr.	$750 Cr.	$ 49,250 Dr.
Allowance for uncollectible accounts	3,000 Cr.	750 Dr.	2,250 Cr.
Net realizable value	$47,000		$ 47,000

You might wonder how the allowance account can develop a debit balance before adjustment. To explain this, assume that Jenkins Company began business on January 1, 2011, and decided to use the allowance method and make the adjusting entry for uncollectible accounts only at year-end. Thus, the allowance account would not have any balance at the beginning of 2011. If the company wrote off any uncollectible accounts during 2011, it would debit Allowance for Uncollectible Accounts and cause a debit balance in that account. At the end of 2011, the company would debit Uncollectible Accounts Expense and credit Allowance for Uncollectible Accounts. This adjusting entry would cause the allowance account to have a credit balance. During 2012, the company would again begin debiting the allowance account for any write-offs of uncollectible accounts. Even if the adjustment at the end of 2011 was adequate to cover all accounts receivable existing at that time that would later become uncollectible, some accounts receivable from 2012 sales may be written off before the end of 2012. If so, the allowance account would again develop a debit balance before the end-of-year 2012 adjustment.

Uncollectible Accounts Recovered   Sometimes companies collect accounts previously considered to be uncollectible after the accounts have been written off. A company usually learns that an account has been written off erroneously when it receives payment. Then the company reverses the original write-off entry and reinstates the account by debiting Accounts Receivable and crediting Allowance for Uncollectible Accounts for the amount received. It posts the debit to both the general ledger account and to the customer's accounts receivable subsidiary ledger account. The firm also records the amount received as a debit to Cash and a credit to Accounts Receivable. And it posts the credit to both the general ledger and to the customer's accounts receivable subsidiary ledger account.

To illustrate, assume that on May 17 a company received a $750 check from Smith in payment of the account previously written off. The two required journal entries are:

May	17	Accounts Receivable—Smith	750	
		Allowance for Uncollectible Accounts		750
		To reverse original write-off of Smith account.		
May	17	Cash	750	
		Accounts Receivable—Smith		750
		To record collection of account.		

The debit and credit to Accounts Receivable—Smith on the same date is to show in Smith's subsidiary ledger account that he did eventually pay the amount due. As a result, the company may decide to sell to him in the future.

When a company collects part of a previously written off account, the usual procedure is to reinstate only that portion actually collected, unless evidence indicates the amount will be collected in full. If a company expects full payment, it reinstates the entire amount of the account.

Because of the problems companies have with uncollectible accounts when they offer customers credit, many now allow customers to use bank or external credit cards. This policy relieves the company of the headaches of collecting overdue accounts.

Recognition of losses on financing receivables. GECS financing receivables include both loans and financing leases. Loans represent transactions in a variety of forms, including revolving charge and credit, mortgages, installment loans, intermediate-term loans and revolving loans secured by business assets.

Investment in financing leases consists of direct financing and leveraged leases of aircraft, railroad rolling stock, autos, other transportation equipment, data processing equipment, medical equipment, commercial real estate and other manufacturing, power generation, and commercial equipment and facilities.

Substantially all of our commercial financing receivables portfolio is secured lending and we assess the overall quality of the portfolio based on the potential risk of loss measure. The metric incorporates both the borrower's credit quality along with any related collateral protection.

Our internal risk ratings process is an important source of information in determining our allowance for losses and represents a comprehensive, statistically validated approach to evaluate risk in our financing receivable portfolios. Our internal risk ratings process and the models we use are subject to regular monitoring and validation controls. The frequency of rating updates is set by our credit risk policy, which requires annual Audit Committee approval.

	(In millions)
Balance at January 1, 2010	$9,556
Provisions charged to operations	7,191
Effects of currency exchanges	(222)
Amounts written off–net	(8,453)
Balance at December 31, 2010	$8,072

Source: General Electric Company, 2010 Annual Report.

**An Accounting
Perspective**

Uses of Technology Auditors use expert systems to review a client's internal control structure and to test the reasonableness of a client's Allowance for Uncollectible Accounts balance. The expert system reaches conclusions based on rules and information programmed into the expert system software. The rules are modeled on the mental processes that a human expert would use in addressing the situation. In the medical field, for instance, the rules constituting the expert system are derived from modeling the diagnostic decision processes of the foremost experts in a given area of medicine. A physician can input information from a remote location regarding the symptoms of a certain patient, and the expert system will provide a probable diagnosis based on the expert model. In a similar fashion, an accountant can feed client information into the expert system and receive an evaluation as to the appropriateness of the account balance or internal control structure.

Credit Cards

Objective 2
Record credit card sales and collections.

Credit cards are either nonbank (American Express and Diners Club) or bank (VISA and MasterCard) charge cards that customers use to purchase goods and services. For some businesses, uncollectible account losses and other costs of extending credit are a burden. By paying a service charge of 2% to 6%, businesses pass these costs on to banks and agencies issuing national credit cards. The banks and credit card agencies then absorb the uncollectible accounts and costs of extending credit and maintaining records.

Usually, banks and agencies issue credit cards to approved credit applicants for an annual fee. When a business agrees to honor these credit cards, it also agrees to pay the percentage fee charged by the bank or credit agency.

When making a credit card sale, the seller checks to see if the customer's card has been canceled and requests approval if the sale exceeds a prescribed amount, such as $50. This procedure allows the seller to avoid accepting lost, stolen, or canceled cards. Also, this policy protects the credit agency from sales causing customers to exceed their established credit limits.

The seller's accounting procedures for credit card sales differ depending on whether the business accepts a nonbank or a bank credit card. To illustrate the entries for the use of *nonbank* credit cards (such as American Express or Diners Club), assume that a restaurant has Diners Club invoices amounting to $1,400 at the end of a day. The Diners Club charges the restaurant a 5% service charge. The restaurant uses the **Credit Card Expense account** to record the credit card agency's service charge and makes the following entry:

Reinforcing Problem
E9-4 Record use of nonbank and bank credit cards.

Accounts Receivable—Diners Club	1,330	
Credit Card Expense	70	
Sales		1,400
To record credit card sales.		

The restaurant mails the invoices to Diners Club. Sometime later, the restaurant receives payment from Diners Club and makes the following entry:

Note to the Student
Why would a company accept credit cards as a means of payment if it costs the company 2% to 6% of the sales revenue?
Answer: To encourage more immediate purchases from buyers and to ensure payment from the sales. Also, a company can avoid bad debts and collection costs.

Cash	1,330	
Accounts Receivable—Diners Club		1,330
To record remittance from Diners Club.		

To illustrate the accounting entries for the use of *bank* credit cards (such as VISA or MasterCard), assume that a retailer has made sales of $1,000 for which VISA cards were accepted and the service charge is $30 (which is 3% of sales). VISA sales are treated as cash sales because the receipt of cash is certain. The retailer deposits the credit card sales invoices in its VISA checking account at a bank just as it deposits checks in its regular checking account. The entry to record this deposit is:

Cash	970	
Credit Card Expense	30	
Sales		1,000
To record credit Visa card sales.		

An Accounting Perspective

Business Insight Recent innovations in credit cards include picture IDs on cards to reduce theft, credits toward purchases of new automobiles (Ford Citibank and General Motors cards), credit toward free trips on airlines, and cash rebates on all purchases. Discover Card remits 1% of all charges back to credit card holders at the end of the year. Also some credit card companies have reduced interest rates on unpaid balances and have eliminated the annual fee.

Just as every company must have current assets such as cash and accounts receivable to operate, every company incurs current liabilities in conducting its operations. Corporations (IBM and General Motors), partnerships (CPA firms), and single proprietorships (corner grocery stores) all have one thing in common—they have liabilities. The next section discusses some of the current liabilities companies incur.

Current Liabilities

Liabilities result from some past transaction and are obligations to pay cash, provide services, or deliver goods at some future time. This definition includes each of the liabilities discussed in previous chapters and the new liabilities presented in this chapter. The balance sheet divides liabilities into current liabilities and long-term liabilities. **Current liabilities** are obligations that (1) are payable within one year or one operating cycle, whichever is longer, or (2) will be paid out of current assets or create other current liabilities. **Long-term liabilities** are obligations that do not qualify as current liabilities. This chapter focuses on current liabilities and Chapter 15 describes long-term liabilities.

Note the definition of a current liability uses the term *operating cycle*. An **operating cycle** (or cash cycle) is the time it takes to begin with cash, buy necessary items to produce revenues (such as materials, supplies, labor, and/or finished goods), sell goods or services, and receive cash by collecting the resulting receivables. For most companies, this period is no longer than a few months. Service companies generally have the shortest operating cycle, since they have no cash tied up in inventory. Manufacturing companies generally have the longest cycle because their cash is tied up in inventory accounts and in accounts receivable before coming back. Even for manufacturing companies, the cycle is generally less than one year. Thus, as a practical matter, current liabilities are due in one year or less, and long-term liabilities are due after one year from the balance sheet date.

The operating cycles for various businesses follow:

Type of Business	Operating Cycle
Service company selling for cash only	Instantaneous
Service company selling on credit	Cash → Accounts Receivable → Cash
Merchandising company selling for cash	Cash → Inventory → Cash
Merchandising company selling on credit	Cash → Inventory → Accounts receivable → Cash
Manufacturing company selling on credit	Cash → Materials inventory → Work in process inventory → Finished goods inventory → Accounts Receivable → Cash

Current liabilities fall into these three groups:

1. **Clearly determinable liabilities.** The existence of the liability and its amount are certain. Examples include most of the liabilities discussed previously, such as accounts payable, notes payable, interest payable, unearned delivery fees, and wages payable. Sales tax payable, federal excise tax payable, current portions of long-term debt, and payroll liabilities are other examples.
2. **Estimated liabilities.** The existence of the liability is certain, but its amount only can be *estimated*. An example is estimated product warranty payable.
3. **Contingent liabilities.** The existence of the liability is uncertain and usually the amount is uncertain because contingent liabilities depend (or are *contingent*) on some future event occurring or not occurring. Examples include liabilities arising from lawsuits, discounted notes receivable, income tax disputes, penalties that may be assessed because of some past action, and failure of another party to pay a debt that a company has guaranteed.

The following table summarizes the characteristics of current liabilities:

Type of Liability	Is the Existence Certain?	Is the Amount Certain?
Clearly determinable liabilities	Yes	Yes
Estimated liabilities	Yes	No
Contingent liabilities	No	No

Objective 3
Define liabilities, current liabilities, and long-term liabilities.

Objective 4
Define and account for clearly determinable, estimated, and contingent liabilities.

Clearly determinable liabilities have clearly determinable amounts. In this section, we describe liabilities not previously discussed that are clearly determinable—sales tax payable, federal excise tax payable, current portions of long-term debt, and payroll liabilities. Later in this chapter, we discuss clearly determinable liabilities such as notes payable.

Sales Tax Payable   Many states have a state sales tax on items purchased by consumers. The company selling the product is responsible for collecting the sales tax from customers. When the company collects the taxes, the debit is to Cash and the credit is to Sales Tax Payable. Periodically, the company pays the sales taxes collected to the state. At that time, the debit is to Sales Tax Payable and the credit is to Cash.

To illustrate, assume that a company sells merchandise in a state that has a 6% sales tax. If it sells goods with a sales price of $1,000 on credit, the company makes this entry:

Accounts Receivable	1,060	
Sales		1,000
Sales Tax Payable		60
To record sales and sales tax payable.		

Real World Example
Comingling of sales taxes collected with sales revenue can lead to serious problems. When cash inflow is lean, often companies use sales taxes collected to pay business expenses, making sales taxes collected unavailable on the tax payment date. Taxing authorities take vigorous enforcement and collection action against this practice.

Now assume that sales for the entire period are $100,000 and that $6,000 is in the Sales Tax Payable account when the company remits the funds to the state taxing agency. The following entry shows the payment to the state:

Sales Tax Payable	6,000	
Cash		6,000
To record the payment to the state for sales taxes collected		
from customers.		

An alternative method of recording sales taxes payable is to include these taxes in the credit to Sales. For instance, the previous company could record sales as follows:

Reinforcing Problem
E9-5 Determine sales revenue and sales tax payable.

Accounts Receivable	1,060	
Sales		1,060

When recording sales taxes in the same account as sales revenue, the firm must separate the sales tax from sales revenue at the end of the accounting period. To make this separation, it adds the sales tax rate to 100% and divides this percentage into recorded sales revenue. For instance, assume that total recorded sales revenues for an accounting period are $10,600, and the sales tax rate is 6%. To find the sales revenue, use the following formula:

$$\text{Sales} = \frac{\text{Amount recorded in Sales account}}{100\% + \text{Sales tax rate}}$$

$$= \frac{\$10,600}{106\%} = \$10,000$$

The sales revenue is $10,000 for the period. Sales tax is equal to the recorded sales revenue of $10,600 less actual sales revenue of $10,000, or $600.

Federal Excise Tax Payable   Consumers pay federal excise tax on some goods, such as alcoholic beverages, tobacco, gasoline, cosmetics, tires, and luxury automobiles. The types and amounts of such taxes change from time to time as a result of Congressional legislation. The entries a company makes when selling goods subject to the federal excise tax are similar to those made for sales taxes payable. For example, assume that the Dixon Jewelry Store sells a diamond ring to a young couple for $2,000. The sale is subject to a 6% sales tax and a 10% federal excise tax. The entry to record the sale is:

Accounts Receivable	2,320	
Sales		2,000
Sales Tax Payable		120
Federal Excise Tax Payable		200
To record the sale of a diamond ring.		

The company records the remittance of the taxes to the federal taxing agency by debiting Federal Excise Tax Payable and crediting Cash.

States often also subject gasoline and other products to excise taxes. Thus, companies will also report State Excise Tax Payable.

Current Portions of Long-Term Debt   Accountants move any portion of long-term debt that becomes due within the next year to the current liability section of the balance sheet. For instance, assume a company signed a series of 10 individual notes payable for $10,000 each; beginning in the 6th year, one comes due each year through the 15th year. Beginning in the 5th year, an accountant would move a $10,000 note from the long-term liability category to the current liability category on the balance sheet. The current portion would then be paid within one year.

> **Uses of Technology** Many companies use service bureaus to process their payrolls because these bureaus keep up to date on rates, bases, and changes in the laws affecting payroll. Companies can either send their data by modem or have the service bureaus pick up time sheets and other data. Managers instruct service bureaus either to print the payroll checks, to have the funds transferred electronically directly into employees' bank accounts, or to transfer data back to the company, so it can print the checks.

An Accounting Perspective

Payroll Liabilities   In most business organizations, accounting for payroll is particularly important because (1) payrolls often are the largest expense that a company incurs, (2) both federal and state governments require maintaining detailed payroll records, and (3) companies must file regular payroll reports with state and federal governments and remit amounts withheld or otherwise due. Payroll liabilities include taxes and other amounts withheld from employees' paychecks and taxes paid by employers.

Employers normally withhold amounts from employees' paychecks for federal income taxes; state income taxes; FICA (social security and Medicare) taxes; and other items such as union dues, medical insurance premiums, life insurance premiums, pension plans, and pledges to charities. Assume that a company had a payroll of $35,000 for the month of April 2012. The company withheld the following amounts from the employees' pay: federal income taxes, $4,100; state income taxes, $360; FICA taxes, $2,678; and medical insurance premiums, $940. This entry records the payroll:

2012				
April	30	Salaries Expense	35,000	
		Employees' Federal Income Taxes Payable		4,100
		Employees' State Income Taxes Payable		360
		FICA Taxes Payable		2,678
		Employees' Medical Insurance Premiums Payable		940
		Salaries Payable		26,922
		To record the payroll for the month ending April 30.		

All accounts credited in the entry are current liabilities and will be reported on the balance sheet if not paid prior to the preparation of financial statements. When these liabilities are paid, the employer debits each one and credits Cash.

Employers are also required to pay certain payroll taxes on the salaries and wages paid to employees. These include federal unemployment taxes, state unemployment taxes, and the employer's portion of FICA taxes. Employers normally record payroll taxes at the same time as the payroll to which they relate. Assume the payroll taxes an employer pays for April are FICA taxes, $2,678; state unemployment taxes, $1,890; and federal unemployment taxes, $280. The entry to record these payroll taxes would be:

2012				
April	30	Payroll Taxes Expense	4,848	
		FICA Taxes Payable		2,678
		State Unemployment Taxes Payable		1,890
		Federal Unemployment Taxes Payable		280
		To record employer's payroll taxes.		

These amounts are in addition to the amounts withheld from employees' paychecks. The credit to FICA Taxes Payable is equal to the amount withheld from the employees' paychecks. The company can credit both its own and the employees' FICA taxes to the same liability account, since both are payable at the same time to the same agency. When these liabilities are paid, the employer debits each of the liability accounts and credits Cash.

An Accounting Perspective	**Uses of Technology** One of the basic components in accounting software packages is the payroll module. As long as companies update this module each time rates, bases, or laws change, they can calculate withholdings, print payroll checks, and complete reporting forms for taxing agencies. In addition to calculating the employer's payroll taxes, this software maintains all accounting payroll records.

Estimated Liabilities

Managers of companies that have estimated liabilities know these liabilities exist but can only estimate the amount. The primary accounting problem is to estimate a reasonable liability as of the balance sheet date. An example of an estimated liability is product warranty payable. One of the largest estimated liabilities that many companies face is for pension costs for current and future retirees. This topic is covered thoroughly in intermediate accounting and will not be dealt with here.

Estimated Product Warranty Payable   When companies sell products such as computers, often they must guarantee against defects by placing a warranty on their products. When defects occur, the company is obligated to reimburse the customer or repair the product. For many products, companies can predict the number of defects based on experience. To provide for a proper matching of revenues and expenses, the accountant estimates the warranty expense resulting from an accounting period's sales. The debit is to Product Warranty Expense and the credit to Estimated Product Warranty Payable.

To illustrate, assume that a company sells personal computers and warrants all parts for one year. The average price per computer is $1,500, and the company sells 1,000 computers in 2012. The company expects 10% of the computers to develop defective parts within one year. By the end of 2012, customers have returned 40 computers sold that year for repairs, and the repairs on those 40 computers have been recorded. The estimated average cost of warranty repairs per defective computer is $150. To arrive at a reasonable estimate of product warranty expense, the accountant makes the following calculation:

Number of computers sold	1,000
Percent estimated to develop defects	X 10%
Total estimated defective computers	100
Deduct computers returned as defective to date	40
Estimated additional number to become defective during warranty period	60
Estimated average warranty repair cost per computer	X $ 150
Estimated product warranty payable	$9,000

The entry made at the end of the accounting period is:

Product Warranty Expense	9,000	
Estimated Product Warranty Payable		9,000
To record estimated product warranty expense.		

When a customer returns one of the computers purchased in 2012 for repair work in 2013 (during the warranty period), the company debits the cost of the repairs to Estimated Product Warranty Payable. For instance, assume that Evan Holman returns his computer for repairs within the warranty period. The repair cost includes parts, $40, and labor, $160. The company makes the following entry:

Estimated Product Warranty Payable	200	
Repair Parts Inventory		40
Wages Payable		160
To record replacement of parts under warranty.		

> **Business Insight** Another estimated liability that is quite common relates to clean-up costs for industrial pollution. One company had the following note in its recent financial statements:
>
> *In the past, the Company treated hazardous waste at its chemical facilities. Testing of the ground waters in the areas of the treatment impoundments at these facilities disclosed the presence of certain contaminants. In compliance with environmental regulations, the Company developed a plan that will prevent further contamination, provide for remedial action to remove the present contaminants, and establish a monitoring program to monitor ground water conditions in the future. A similar plan has been developed for a site previously used as a metal pickling facility. Estimated future costs of $2,860,000 have been accrued in the accompanying financial statements . . . to complete the procedures required under these plans.*

An Accounting Perspective

Contingent Liabilities

When liabilities are contingent, the company usually is not sure that the liability exists and is uncertain about the amount. *FASB Statement No. 5* defines a contingency as "an existing condition, situation, or set of circumstances involving uncertainty as to possible gain or loss to an enterprise that will ultimately be resolved when one or more future events occur or fail to occur."[1]

According to *FASB Statement No. 5,* if the liability is probable and the amount can be reasonably estimated, companies should record contingent liabilities in the accounts. However, since most contingent liabilities may not occur and the amount often cannot be reasonably estimated, the accountant usually does not record them in the accounts. Instead, firms typically disclose these contingent liabilities in notes to their financial statements.

Many contingent liabilities arise as the result of lawsuits. In fact, 379 of the 500 companies contacted in the AICPA's annual survey of accounting practices reported contingent liabilities resulting from litigation.[2]

Reinforcing Problem
E9-6 Answer questions regarding note in financial statements.

---

[1]FASB, *Statement of Financial Accounting Standards No. 5,* "Accounting for Contingencies" (Stamford, Conn., 1975). Copyright © by Financial Accounting Standards Board, High Ridge Park, Stamford, Connecticut 06905, USA.
[2]AICPA, *Accounting Trends & Techniques* (New York, 2010), p. 86.

The following two examples from annual reports are typical of the disclosures made in notes to the financial statements. Be aware that just because a suit is brought, the company being sued is not necessarily guilty. One company included the following note in its annual report to describe its contingent liability regarding various lawsuits against the company:

Contingent Liabilities:

Various lawsuits and claims, including those involving ordinary routine litigation incidental to its business, to which the Company is a party, are pending, or have been asserted, against the Company. In addition, the Company was advised . . . that the United States Environmental Protection Agency had determined the existence of PCBs in a river and harbor near Sheboygan, Wisconsin, and that the Company, as well as others, allegedly contributed to that contamination. It is not presently possible to determine with certainty what corrective action, if any, will be required, what portion of any costs thereof will be attributable to the Company, or whether all or any portion of such costs will be covered by insurance or will be recoverable from others. Although the outcome of these matters cannot be predicted with certainty, and some of them may be disposed of unfavorably to the Company, management has no reason to believe that their disposition will have a materially adverse effect on the consolidated financial position of the Company.

Another company dismissed an employee and included the following note to disclose the contingent liability resulting from the ensuing litigation:

Contingencies:

. . . A jury awarded $5.2 million to a former employee of the Company for an alleged breach of contract and wrongful termination of employment. The Company has appealed the judgment on the basis of errors in the judge's instructions to the jury and insufficiency of evidence to support the amount of the jury's award. The Company is vigorously pursuing the appeal.

The Company and its subsidiaries are also involved in various other litigation arising in the ordinary course of business.

Since it presently is not possible to determine the outcome of these matters, no provision has been made in the financial statements for their ultimate resolution. The resolution of the appeal of the jury award could have a significant effect on the Company's earnings in the year that a determination is made; however, in management's opinion, the final resolution of all legal matters will not have a material adverse effect on the Company's financial position.

Contingent liabilities may also arise from discounted notes receivable, income tax disputes, penalties that may be assessed because of some past action, and failure of another party to pay a debt that a company has guaranteed.

The remainder of this chapter discusses notes receivable and notes payable. Business transactions often involve one party giving another party a note.

Notes Receivable and Notes Payable

Objective 5
Account for notes receivable and payable, including calculation of interest.

A note (also called a **promissory note**) is an unconditional written promise by a borrower (**maker**) to pay a definite sum of money to the lender (**payee**) on demand or on a specific date. On the balance sheet of the lender (payee), a note is a receivable; on the balance sheet of the borrower (maker), a note is a payable. Since the note is usually negotiable, the payee may transfer it to another party, who then receives payment from the maker. Look at the promissory note in Illustration 9.2.

A customer may give a note to a business for an amount due on an account receivable or for the sale of a large item such as a refrigerator. Also, a business may give a note to a supplier in exchange for merchandise to sell or to a bank or an individual

Illustration 9.2   Promissory Note

Principal ——————

Payee ——————

Interest rate ——————

Maker ——————

$ 2,400.00 _____   July 1 , ____ 2012 ___

Sixty days -------------------------- AFTER DATE __We__ PROMISE TO PAY TO

THE ORDER OF   **SAXON CORPORATION**

Twenty-four hundred and no/100 --------------------------- DOLLARS

AT _Saxon Corporation, Lansing, Michigan_

FOR VALUE RECEIVED WITH INTEREST AT THE RATE OF __10%__ PER ANNUM FROM _July 1,2012_

This note is one of a series of _____ notes of even date herewith, numbered __487__ to __--__ inclusive, and all of said notes shall become immediately due and payable at the option of the holder hereof on default being made in the payment of any one at maturity.

NO.___487___ DUE _August 31, 2012_   MOTOR WHEEL COMPANY   (SEAL)

Michael D. Smith, Treasurer   (SEAL)

---

for a loan. Thus, a company may have notes receivable or notes payable arising from transactions with customers, suppliers, banks, or individuals.

Companies usually do not establish a subsidiary ledger for notes. Instead, they maintain a file of the actual notes receivable and copies of notes payable.

Interest Calculation

Most promissory notes have an explicit interest charge. **Interest** is the fee charged for use of money over a period. To the maker of the note, or borrower, interest is an expense; to the payee of the note, or lender, interest is a revenue. A borrower incurs interest expense; a lender earns interest revenue. For convenience, bankers sometimes calculate interest on a 360-day year; we calculate it on that basis in this text. (Some companies use a 365-day year.)

The basic formula for computing interest is:

$$\text{Interest} = \text{Principal} \times \text{Rate} \times \text{Time, or I} = P \times R \times T$$

Principal is the face value of the note. The **rate** is the stated interest rate on the note; interest rates are generally stated on an annual basis. **Time**, which is the amount of time the note is to run, can be either days or months.

To show how to calculate interest, assume a company borrowed $20,000 from a bank. The note has a principal (face value) of $20,000, an annual interest rate of 10%, and a life of 90 days. The interest calculation is:

$$\text{Interest} = \$20,000 \times 0.10 \times {}^{90}/_{360}$$
$$\text{Interest} = \$500$$

Note that in this calculation we expressed the time period as a fraction of a 360-day year because the interest rate is an annual rate.

Determination of Maturity Date

The **maturity date** is the date on which a note becomes due and must be paid. Sometimes notes require monthly installments (or payments) but usually all of the principal and interest must be paid at the same time as in Illustration 9.2. The wording in the note expresses the maturity date and determines when the note is to be paid. A note falling due on a Sunday or a holiday is due on the next business day. Examples of the maturity date wording are:

1. *On demand.* "On demand, I promise to pay . . ." When the maturity date is on demand, it is at the option of the holder and cannot be computed. The holder is the payee, or another person who legally acquired the note from the payee.
2. *On a stated date.* "On July 18, 2012, I promise to pay . . ." When the maturity date is designated, computing the maturity date is not necessary.
3. *At the end of a stated period.*
   a. "One year after date, I promise to pay . . ." When the maturity is expressed in years, the note matures on the same day of the same month as the date of the note in the year of maturity.
   b. "Four months after date, I promise to pay . . ." When the maturity is expressed in months, the note matures on the same date in the month of maturity. For example, one month from July 18, 2012, is August 18, 2012, and two months from July 18, 2012, is September 18, 2012. If a note is issued on the last day of a month and the month of maturity has fewer days than the month of issuance, the note matures on the last day of the month of maturity. A one-month note dated January 31, 2012, matures on February 28, 2012.
   c. "Ninety days after date, I promise to pay . . ." When the maturity is expressed in days, the exact number of days must be counted. The first day (date of origin) is omitted, and the last day (maturity date) is included in the count. For example, a 90-day note dated October 19, 2012, matures on January 17, 2013, as shown here:

Life of note (days)		90 days
Days remaining in October not counting date of origin of note:		
Days to count in October (31 − 19)	12	
Total days in November	30	
Total Days in December	31	73
Maturity date in January		17 days

Accounting for Notes in Normal Business Transactions

Sometimes a company receives a note when it sells high-priced merchandise; more often, a note results from the conversion of an overdue account receivable. When a customer does not pay an account receivable that is due, the company (creditor) may insist that the customer (debtor) give a note in place of the account receivable. This action allows the customer more time to pay the balance due, and the company earns interest on the balance until paid. Also, the company may be able to sell the note to a bank or other financial institution.

To illustrate the conversion of an account receivable to a note, assume that Price Company (maker) had purchased $18,000 of merchandise on August 1 from Cooper Company (payee) on account. The normal credit period has elapsed, and Price cannot pay the invoice. Cooper agrees to accept Price's $18,000, 15%, 90-day note dated September 1 to settle Price's open account. Assuming Price paid the note at maturity and both Cooper and Price have a December 31 year-end, the entries on the books of the payee and the maker are:

Cooper Company, Payee

Aug.	1	Accounts Receivable—Price Company	18,000	
		Sales		18,000
		To record sale of merchandise on account.		
Sept.	1	Notes Receivable	18,000	
		Accounts Receivable—Price Company		18,000
		To record exchange of a note from Price Company for open account.		
Nov.	30	Cash	18,675	
		Notes Receivable		18,000
		Interest Revenue ($18,000 × 0.15 × $90/360$).		675
		To record receipt of Price Company note principal and interest.		

Price Company, Maker

Aug.	1	Purchase	18,000	
		Accounts Payable—Cooper Company		18,000
		To record purchase of merchandise on account.		
Sept.	1	Accounts Payable—Cooper Company	18,000	
		Notes Payable		18,000
		To record exchange of a note to Cooper Company for open account.		
Nov.	30	Notes Payable	18,000	
		Interest Expense ($18,000 × 0.15 × $90/360$).	675	
		Cash		18,675
		To record payment of note principal and interest.		

The $18,675 paid by Price to Cooper is called the *maturity value of the note.* **Maturity value** is the amount that the maker must pay on a note on its maturity date; typically, it includes principal and accrued interest, if any.

Sometimes the maker of a note does not pay the note when it becomes due. The next section describes how to record a note not paid at maturity.

A **dishonored note** is a note that the maker failed to pay at maturity. Since the note has matured, the holder or payee removes the note from Notes Receivable and records the amount due in Accounts Receivable (or Dishonored Notes Receivable).

At the maturity date of a note, the maker should pay the principal plus interest. If the interest has not been accrued in the accounting records, the maker of a dishonored note should record interest expense for the life of the note by debiting Interest Expense and crediting Interest Payable. The payee should record the interest earned and remove the note from its Notes Receivable account. Thus, the payee of the note should debit Accounts Receivable for the maturity value of the note and credit Notes Receivable for the note's face value and Interest Revenue for the interest. After these entries have been posted, the full liability on the note—principal plus interest—is included in the records of both parties. Interest continues to accrue on the note until it is paid, replaced by a new note, or written off as uncollectible. To illustrate, assume that Price did not pay the note at maturity. The entries on each party's books are:

Cooper Company, Payee

Nov.	30	Accounts Receivable—Price Company	18,675	
		Notes Receivable		18,000
		Interest Revenue		675
		To record dishonor of Price Company note.		

Reinforcing Problem
E9-8 Prepare entries for a note.

Dishonored Notes

Reinforcing Problem
E9-9 Prepare entries when maker defaults.

Price Company, Maker

Nov.	30	Interest Expense	675	
		Interest Payable		675
		To record interest on note payable.		

When unable to pay a note at maturity, sometimes the maker pays the interest on the original note or includes the interest in the face value of a new note that replaces the old note. Both parties account for the new note in the same manner as the old note. However, if it later becomes clear that the maker of a dishonored note will never pay, the payee writes off the account with a debit to Uncollectible Accounts Expense (or to an account with a title such as Loss on Dishonored Notes) and a credit to Accounts Receivable. The debit should be to the Allowance for Uncollectible Accounts if the payee made an annual provision for uncollectible notes receivable.

Renewal of Notes

Assume that Price Company pays the interest at the maturity date and issues a new 15%, 90-day note for $18,000. The entries on both sets of books would be:

Cooper Company, Payee				Price Company, Maker		
Cash	675			Interest Expense	675	
Interest Revenue		675		Cash		675
To record the				To record the payment		
receipt of interest				of interest on note to		
on Price Company				Cooper Company.		
note.						
(Optional entry)				(Optional entry)		
Notes Receivable	18,000			Notes Payable	18,000	
Notes Receivable		18,000		Notes Payable		18,000
To replace old 15%,				To replace old 15%,		
90-day note from				90-day note to Cooper		
Price Company with				Company with new		
new 15%, 90-day				15%, 90-day note.		
~~note.~~						

Although the second entry on each set of books has no effect on the existing account balances, it indicates that the old note was renewed (or replaced). Both parties substitute the new note, or a copy, for the old note in a file of notes.

Now assume that Price Company does not pay the interest at the maturity date but instead includes the interest in the face value of the new note. The entries on both sets of books would be:

Cooper Company, Payee				Price Company, Maker		
Notes Receivable	18,675			Interest Expense	675	
Interest Revenue		675		Notes Payable	18,000	
Notes Receivable		18,000		Notes Payable		18,675
To record the				To record the		
replacement of the				replacement of the old		
old Price Company				$18,000, 15%, 90-day		
$18,000, 15%, 90-				note to Cooper		
day note with a				Company with a new		
new $18,675, 15%,				$18,675, 15%, 90-day		
90-day note.				note.		

Accruing Interest

On an interest-bearing note, even though interest accrues, or accumulates, on a day-to-day basis, usually both parties record it only at the note's maturity date. If the note is outstanding at the end of an accounting period, however, the time period of the interest overlaps the end of the accounting period and requires an adjusting entry at the end of the accounting period. Both the payee and maker of the note must make an adjusting entry to record the accrued interest and report the proper assets and revenues for the payee and the proper liabilities and expenses for the maker. Failure to record accrued interest understates the payee's assets and revenues by the amount of the interest earned but not collected and understates the maker's expenses and liabilities by the interest expense incurred but not yet paid.

Payee's Books   To illustrate how to record accrued interest on the payee's books, assume that the payee, Cooper Company, has a fiscal year ending on October 31 instead of December 31. On October 31, Cooper would make the following adjusting entry relating to the Price Company note:

Oct.	31	Interest Receivable	450	
		Interest Revenue ($18,000 X 0.15 X 60/360)		450
		To record interest earned on Price Company note		
		for the period September 1 through October 31.		

The **Interest Receivable account** shows the interest earned but not yet collected. Interest receivable is a current asset in the balance sheet because the interest will be collected in 30 days. The interest revenue appears in the income statement. When Price pays the note on November 30, Cooper makes the following entry to record the collection of the note's principal and interest:

Nov.	30	Cash	18,675	
		Notes Receivable		18,000
		Interest Receivable		450
		Interest Revenue		225
		To record collection of Price Company note and		
		interest.		

Note that the entry credits the Interest Receivable account for the $450 interest accrued from September 1 through October 31, which was debited to the account in the previous entry, and credits Interest Revenue for the $225 interest earned in November.

Maker's Books   Assume Price Company's accounting year also ends on October 31 instead of December 31. Price's accounting records would be incomplete unless the company makes an adjusting entry to record the liability owed for the accrued interest on the note it gave to Cooper Company. The required entry is:

Oct.	31	Interest Expense ($18,000 X 0.15 X $^{60}/_{360}$)	450	
		Interest Payable		450
		To record accrued interest on note to Cooper		
		Company for the period September 1 through		
		October 31.		

The **Interest Payable account**, which shows the interest expense incurred but not yet paid, is a current liability in the balance sheet because the interest will be paid in 30 days. Interest expense appears in the income statement. When the note is paid, Price makes the following entry:

Nov.	30	Notes Payable	18,000	
		Interest Payable	450	
		Interest Expense	225	
		Cash		18,675
		To record payment of principal and interest on		
		note to Cooper Company.		

In this illustration, Cooper's financial position made it possible for the company to *carry* the Price note to the maturity date. Alternatively, Cooper could have sold, or discounted, the note to receive the proceeds before the maturity date. This topic is reserved for a more advanced text.

Short-Term Financing through Notes Payable

A company sometimes needs short-term financing. This situation may occur when (1) the company's cash receipts are delayed because of lenient credit terms granted customers, or (2) the company needs cash to finance the buildup of seasonal inventories, such as before Christmas. To secure short-term financing, companies issue interest-bearing or noninterest-bearing notes.

Interest-Bearing Notes   To receive short-term financing, a company may issue an interest-bearing note to a bank. An interest-bearing note specifies the interest rate charged on the principal borrowed. The company receives from the bank the principal borrowed; when the note matures, the company pays the bank the principal plus the interest.

Accounting for an interest-bearing note is simple. For example, assume the company's accounting year ends on December 31. Needham Company issued a $10,000, 90-day, 9% note on December 1, 2011. The following entries would record the loan, the accrual of interest on December 31, 2011, and its payment on March 1, 2012:

2011				
Dec.	1	Cash	10,000	
		Notes Payable		10,000
		To record 90-day bank loan.		
	31	Interest Expense	75	
		Interest Payable		75
		To record accrued interest on a note payable at year-end ($10,000 X 0.09 X $^{30}/_{360}$).		
2012				
Mar.	1	Notes Payable	10,000	
		Interest Expense ($10,000 X 0.09 X $^{60}/_{360}$)	150	
		Interest Payable	75	
		Cash		10,225
		To record principal and interest paid on bank loan.		

Noninterest-Bearing Notes (Discounting Notes Payable)   A company may also issue a noninterest-bearing note to receive short-term financing from a bank. A noninterest-bearing note does not have a stated interest rate applied to the face value of the note. Instead, the note is drawn for a maturity amount less a bank discount; the borrower receives the proceeds. A **bank discount** is the difference between the maturity value of the note and the cash proceeds given to the borrower. The cash proceeds are equal to the maturity amount of a note less the bank discount. This entire process is called discounting a note payable. The purpose of this process is to introduce interest into what appears to be a noninterest-bearing note. The meaning of *discounting* here is to deduct interest in advance.

Because interest is related to time, the bank discount is not interest on the date the loan is made; however, it becomes interest expense to the company and interest revenue to the bank as time passes. To illustrate, assume that on December 1, 2011, Needham Company presented its $10,000, 90-day, noninterest-bearing note to the bank, which discounted the note at 9%. The discount is $225 ($10,000 × 0.09 × 90/360), and the proceeds to Needham are $9,775. The entry required on the date of the note's issue is:

2011					
Dec.	1	Cash	9,775		
		Discount on Notes Payable	225		
		Notes Payable		10,000	
		Issued a 90-day note to bank.			

Needham credits Notes Payable for the face value of the note. **Discount on Notes Payable** is a contra account used to reduce Notes Payable from face value to the net amount of the debt. The balance in the Discount on Notes Payable account appears on the balance sheet as a deduction from the balance in the Notes Payable account.

Over time, the discount becomes interest expense. If Needham paid the note before the end of the fiscal year, it would charge the entire $225 discount to Interest Expense and credit Discount on Notes Payable. However, if Needham's fiscal year ended on December 31, an adjusting entry would be required as follows:

2011				
Dec.	31	Interest Expense	75	
		Discount on Notes Payable		75
		To record accrued interest on note payable at year-end.		

This entry records the interest expense incurred by Needham for the 30 days the note has been outstanding. The expense can be calculated as $10,000 \times 0.09 \times 30/360$, or $30/90 \times \$225$. Notice that for entries involving discounted notes payable, no separate Interest Payable account is needed. The Notes Payable account already contains the total liability that will be paid at maturity, $10,000. From the date the proceeds are given to the borrower to the maturity date, the liability grows by reducing the balance in the Discount on Notes Payable contra account. Thus, the current liability section of the December 31, 2011, balance sheet would show:

Current Liabilities:
Notes payable	$ 10,000	
Less: Discount on notes payable	150	$ 9,850

When the note is paid at maturity, the entry is:

2012					
Mar.	1	Notes Payable	10,000		
		Interest Expense	150		
		Cash		10,000	
		Discount on Notes Payable		150	
		To record note payment and interest expense.			

Reinforcing Problem
E9-11 Prepare entries at maturity date.

The T-accounts for Discount on Notes Payable and for Interest Expense appear as follows:

Discount on Notes Payable					**Interest Expense**			
2011			2012		2011		2011	
Dec. 1		225	Dec. 31	75	Dec. 31	75	Dec. 31 To close 75	
Dec. 31 Balance 150			2012		2012			
			Mar. 1	150	Mar. 1	150		

Reinforcing Problem
E9-10 Prepare entries for noninterest-bearing note and interest-bearing note.

In Illustration 9.3, we compare the journal entries for interest-bearing notes and noninterest-bearing notes used by Needham Company.

Illustration 9.3   Comparison between Interest-Bearing Notes and Noninterest-Bearing Notes

Interest-Bearing Notes							Noninterest-Bearing Notes					
2011							2011					
Dec.	1	Cash	10,000				Dec.	1	Cash	9,775		
		Notes Payable		10,000					Discount on Notes Payable	225		
		To record 90-day bank loan.							Notes Payable		10,000	
									To record 90-day bank loan.			
	31	Interest Expense	75					31	Interest Expense	75		
		Interest Payable		7 5					Discount on Notes Payable		75	
		To record accrued interest on a note payable at year-end.							To record accrued interest on a note payable at year-end.			
2012							2012					
Mar.	1	Notes Payable	10,000				Mar.	1	Notes Payable	10,000		
		Interest Expense	150						Interest Expense	150		
		Interest Payable	75						Cash		10,000	
		Cash		10,225					Discount on Notes Payable		150	
		To record note principal and interest payment.							To record note payment and interest expense.			

Analyzing and Using the Financial Results—Accounts Receivable Turnover and Number of Days' Sales in Accounts Receivable

Accounts receivable turnover is the number of times per year that the average amount of accounts receivable is collected. To calculate this ratio divide net credit sales, or net sales, by the average net accounts receivable (accounts receivable after deducting the allowance for uncollectible accounts):

$$\text{Accounts receivable turnover} = \frac{\text{Net credit sales (or net sales)}}{\text{Average net accounts receivable}}$$

Ideally, average net accounts receivable should represent weekly or monthly averages; often, however, beginning and end-of-year averages are the only amounts available to users outside the company. Although analysts should use net credit sales, frequently net credit sales are not known to those outside the company. Instead, they use net sales in the numerator.

Generally, the faster firms collect accounts receivable, the better. A company with a high accounts receivable turnover ties up a smaller proportion of its funds in accounts receivable than a company with a low turnover. Both the company's credit terms and collection policies affect turnover. For instance, a company with credit terms of 2/10, n/30 would expect a higher turnover than a company with terms of n/60. Also, a company that aggressively pursues overdue accounts receivable has a higher turnover of accounts receivable than one that does not.

Using their recent annual reports, we calculated these accounts receivable turnovers for the following companies:

	Net Sales (millions)	Accounts Receivable	
		Average Net	Turnover
Abercrombie & Fitch	$ 1,238	$ 14	88.43
The Limited, Inc.	10,105	1,012	10.00

We calculate the **number of days' sales in accounts receivable** (also called the *average collection period for accounts receivable*) as follows:

$$\text{Number of days' sales in accounts receivable} = \frac{\text{Number of days in a year (365)}}{\text{Accounts receivable turnover}}$$

This ratio measures the average liquidity of accounts receivable and gives an indication of their quality. The faster a firm collects receivables, the more liquid (the closer to being cash) they are and the higher their quality. The longer accounts receivable remain outstanding, the greater the probability they never will be collected. As the time period increases, so does the probability that customers will declare bankruptcy or go out of business.

Based on 365 days, we calculated the number of days' sales for each of these companies in 2000:

	Accounts Receivable	
Company	Turnover	Number of Day's Sales in
Abercrombie & Fitch	88.43	4.1
The Limited, Inc.	10.00	36.5

These companies have collection periods ranging from 4.1 to 36.5 days. Assuming credit terms of 2/10, n/30, one would expect the average collection period to be under 30 days. If customers do not pay within 10 days and take the discount offered, they incur an annual interest rate of 36.5% on these funds. (They lose a 2% discount and get to use the funds another 20 days, which is equivalent to an annual rate of 36.5%.)

Having studied receivables and payables in this chapter, you will study plant assets in the next chapter. These long-term assets include land and depreciable assets such as buildings, machinery, and equipment.

Understanding the Learning Objectives

- Companies use two methods to account for uncollectible accounts receivable: the allowance method, which provides in advance for uncollectible accounts; and the direct write-off method, which recognizes uncollectible accounts as an expense when judged uncollectible. The allowance method is the preferred method and is the only method discussed and illustrated in this text.

> **Objective 1**
> Account for uncollectible accounts receivable under the allowance method.

- The two basic methods for estimating uncollectible accounts under the allowance method are the percentage-of-sales method and the percentage-of-receivables method.
- The percentage-of-sales method focuses attention on the income statement and the relationship of uncollectible accounts to sales. The debit to Uncollectible Accounts Expense is a certain percent of credit sales or total net sales.
- The percentage-of-receivables method focuses attention on the balance sheet and the relationship of the allowance for uncollectible accounts to accounts receivable. The credit to the Allowance for Uncollectible Accounts is the amount

necessary to bring that account up to a certain percentage of the Accounts Receivable balance. Either one overall percentage or an aging schedule may be used.

Objective 2
Record credit card sales and collections.

- Credit cards are charge cards used by customers to charge purchases of goods and services. These cards are of two types—nonbank credit cards (such as American Express) and bank credit cards (such as VISA).
- The sale is recorded at the gross amount of the sale, and the cash or receivable is recorded at the net amount the company will receive.

Objective 3
Define liabilities, current liabilities, and long-term liabilities.

- Liabilities result from some past transaction and are obligations to pay cash, provide services, or deliver goods at some time in the future.
- Current liabilities are obligations that (1) are payable within one year or one operating cycle, whichever is longer, or (2) will be paid out of current assets or create other current liabilities.
- Long-term liabilities are obligations that do not qualify as current liabilities.

Objective 4
Define and account for clearly determinable, estimated, and contingent liabilities.

- Clearly determinable liabilities are those for which the existence of the liability and its amount are certain. An example is accounts payable.
- Estimated liabilities are those for which the existence of the liability is certain, but its amount can only be estimated. An example is estimated product warranty payable.
- Contingent liabilities are those for which the existence, and usually the amount, are uncertain because these liabilities depend (or are contingent) on some future event occurring or not occurring. An example is a liability arising from a lawsuit.

Objective 5
Account for notes receivable and payable, including calculation of interest.

- A promissory note is an unconditional written promise by a borrower (maker) to pay the lender (payee) or someone else who legally acquired the note a certain sum of money on demand or at a definite time.
- Interest is the fee charged for the use of money through time. Interest = Principal × Rate of interest × Time.

Objective 6
Account for borrowing money using an interest-bearing note versus a noninterest-bearing note.

- Companies sometimes need short-term financing. Short-term financing may be secured by issuing interest-bearing notes or by issuing noninterest-bearing notes.
- An interest-bearing note specifies the interest rate that will be charged on the principal borrowed.
- A noninterest-bearing note does not have a stated interest rate applied to the face value of the note.

Objective 7
Analyze and use the financial results—accounts receivable turnover and the number of days' sales in accounts receivable.

- Calculate accounts receivable turnover by dividing net credit sales, or net sales, by average net accounts receivable.
- Calculate the number of days' sales in accounts receivable (or average collection period) by dividing the number of days in the year by the accounts receivable turnover.
- Together, these ratios show the liquidity of accounts receivable and give some indication of their quality. Generally, the higher the accounts receivable turnover, the better; and the shorter the average collection period, the better.

Demonstration Problem 9–A

a. Prepare the journal entries for the following transactions:
   (1) As of the end of 2012, Post Company estimates its uncollectible accounts expense to be 1% of sales. Sales in 2012 were $1,125,000.
   (2) On January 15, 2013, the company decided that the account for John Nunn in the amount of $750 was uncollectible.
   (3) On February 12, 2013, John Nunn's check for $750 arrived.
b. Prepare the journal entries in the records of Lyle Company for the following:
   (1) On June 15, 2012, Lyle Company received a $22,500, 90-day, 12% note dated June 15, 2012, from Stone Company in payment of its account.
   (2) Assume that Stone Company did not pay the note at maturity. Lyle Company decided that the note was uncollectible.

Solution to Demonstration Problem 9–A

a.

1.	2012					
	Dec.	31	Uncollectible Accounts Expense		11,250	
			Allowance for Uncollectible Accounts			11,250
			To record estimated Uncollectible accounts for the year.			
2.	2013					
	Jan.	15	Allowance for Uncollectible Accounts		750	
			Accounts Receivable—John Nunn			750
			To write off the account of John Nunn as Uncollectible.			
3.	Feb.	12	Accounts Receivable—John Nunn		750	
			Allowance for Uncollectible Accounts			750
			To correct the write-off of John Nunn's account on January 15.			
		12	Cash		750	
			Accounts Receivable—John Nunn			750
			To record the collection of John Nunn's account receivable.			

b.

1.	2012					
	June	15	Notes Receivable		22,500	
			Accounts Receivable—Stone Company			22,500
			To record receipt of a note from Stone Company.			
2.	Sept.	13	Accounts Receivable—Stone Company		23,175	
			Notes Receivable			22,500
			Interest Revenue			675
			To record the default of the Stone Company note of $22,500. Interest revenue was $675.			
		13	Allowance for Uncollectible Accounts*		23,175	
			Accounts Receivable—Stone Company			23,175
			To write off the Stone Company as uncollectible.			

* This debt assumes that Notes Receivable were taken into consideration when an allowance was established. If not, the debit should be to Loss from Dishonored Notes Receivable.

Demonstration Problem 9–B

a. Prepare the entries on the books of Cromwell Company assuming the company borrowed $10,000 at 7% from First National Bank and signed a 60-day noninterest-bearing note payable on December 1, 2011, accrued interest on December 31, 2011, and paid the debt on the maturity date.

b. Prepare the entries on the books of Cromwell Company assuming it purchased equipment from Jones Company for $5,000 and signed a 30-day, 9% interest-bearing note payable on February 24, 2012. Cromwell paid the note on its maturity date.

Solution to Demonstration Problem 9–B

a.

2011					
Dec.	1	Cash		9,883.33	
		Bank Discount ($10,000 X 0.07 X $^{60}/_{360}$)		116.67	
		Notes Payable			10,000.00
	31	Interest Expense		58.33	
		Bank Discount			58.33
		($10,000 X 0.07 X $^{30}/_{360}$)			
2012					
Jan.	30	Notes Payable		10,000.00	
		Interest Expense		58.33	
		Bank Discount			58.33
		Cash			10,000.00

b.

2012					
Feb	24	Equipment		5,000.00	
		Notes Payable			5,000.00
Mar	26	Notes Payable		5,000.00	
		Interest Expense		37.50	
		Cash			5,037.50
		($5,000 X 0.09 X $^{30}/_{360}$) = $37.50			675

New Terms

Accounts receivable turnover   Net credit sales (or net sales) divided by average net accounts receivable. *368*

Aging schedule   A means of classifying accounts receivable according to their age; used to determine the necessary balance in an Allowance for Uncollectible Accounts. A different uncollectibility percentage rate is used for each age category. *350*

Allowance for Uncollectible Accounts   A contra-asset account to the Accounts Receivable account; it reduces accounts receivable to their net realizable value. Also called *Allowance for Doubtful Accounts* or *Allowance for Bad Debts*. *347*

Bad debts expense   See Uncollectible accounts expense.

Bank discount   The difference between the maturity value of a note and the actual amount—the note's proceeds—given to the borrower. *366*

Cash proceeds   The maturity amount of a note less the bank discount. *366*

Clearly determinable liabilities   Liabilities whose existence and amount are certain. Examples include accounts payable, notes payable, interest payable, unearned delivery fees, wages payable, sales tax payable, federal excise tax payable, current portions of long-term debt, and various payroll liabilities. *355*

Contingent liabilities   Liabilities whose existence is uncertain. Their amount is also usually uncertain. Both their existence and amount depend on some future event that may or may not occur. Examples include liabilities arising from lawsuits, discounted notes receivable, income tax disputes, penalties that may be assessed because of some past action, and failure of another party to pay a debt that a company has guaranteed. *355*

Credit Card Expense account   Used to record credit card agency's service charges for services rendered in processing credit card sales. *354*

Credit cards   Nonbank charge cards (American Express and Diners Club) and bank charge cards (VISA and MasterCard) that customers use to charge their purchases of goods and services. *353*

Current liabilities   Obligations that (1) are payable within one year or one operating cycle, whichever is longer, or (2) will be paid out of current assets or result in the creation of other current liabilities. *355*

Discount on Notes Payable   A contra account used to reduce Notes Payable from face value to the net amount of the debt. *367*

Discounting a note payable   The act of borrowing on a noninterest-bearing note drawn for a maturity amount, from which a bank discount is deducted, and the proceeds are given to the borrower. *366*

Dishonored note   A note that the maker failed to pay at maturity. *363*

Estimated liabilities   Liabilities whose existence is certain, but whose amount can only be estimated. An example is estimated product warranty payable. *355*

Interest   The fee charged for use of money over a period of time $(I = P \times R \times T)$. *361*

Interest Payable account   An account showing the interest expense incurred but not yet paid; reported as a current liability in the balance sheet. *365*

Interest Receivable account   An account showing the interest earned but not yet collected; reported as a current asset in the balance sheet. *365*

Liabilities   Obligations that result from some past transaction and are obligations to pay cash, perform services, or deliver goods at some time in the future. *355*

Long-term liabilities   Obligations that do not qualify as current liabilities. *355*

Maker (of a note)   The party who prepares a note and is responsible for paying the note at maturity. *360*

Maturity date   The date on which a note becomes due and must be paid. *361*

Maturity value   The amount that the maker must pay on the note on its maturity date. *363*

Net realizable value   The amount the company expects to collect from accounts receivable. *347*

Number of days' sales in accounts receivable   The number of days in a year (365) divided by the accounts receivable turnover. *369*

Operating cycle   The time it takes to start with cash, buy necessary items to produce revenues (such as materials, supplies, labor, and/or finished goods), sell goods or services, and receive cash by collecting the resulting receivables. *355*

Payable   Any sum of money due to be paid by a company to any party for any reason. *345*

Payee (of a note)   The party who receives a note and will be paid cash at maturity. *360*

Percentage-of-receivables method   A method for determining the desired size of the Allowance for Uncollectible Accounts by basing the calculation on the Accounts Receivable balance at the end of the period. *349*

Percentage-of-sales method   A method of estimating the uncollectible accounts from the sales of a given period's total net credit sales or net sales. *347*

Principal (of a note)   The face value of a note. *361*

Promissory note   An unconditional written promise by a borrower (maker) to pay a definite sum of money to the lender (payee) on demand or at a specific date. *360*

Rate (of a note)   The stated interest rate on the note. *361*

Receivable   Any sum of money due to be paid to a company from any party for any reason. *345*

Time (of a note)   The amount of time the note is to run; can be expressed in days, months, or years. *361*

Trade receivables   Amounts customers owe a company for goods sold or services rendered on account. Also called *accounts receivable* or *trade accounts receivable*. *346*

Uncollectible accounts expense   An operating expense that a business incurs when it sells on credit; also called *doubtful accounts expense* or *bad debts expense*. *346*

Self Test

True-False

Indicate whether each of the following statements is true or false.

1. The percentage-of-sales method estimates the uncollectible accounts from the ending balance in Accounts Receivable.
2. Under the allowance method, uncollectible accounts expense is recognized when a specific customer's account is written off.
3. Bank credit card sales are treated as cash sales because the receipt of cash is certain.
4. Liabilities result from some future transaction.
5. Current liabilities are classified as clearly determinable, estimated, and contingent.
6. A dishonored note is removed from Notes Receivable, and the total amount due is recorded in Accounts Receivable.
7. When an interest-bearing note is given to a bank when taking out a loan, the difference between the cash proceeds and the maturity amount is debited to Discount on Notes Payable.

Multiple-Choice

Select the best answer for each of the following questions.

1. Which of the following statements is false?
   a. Any existing balance in the Allowance for Uncollectible Accounts is ignored in calculating the uncollectible accounts expense under the percentage-of-sales method except that the allowance account must have a credit balance after adjustment.
   b. The percentage-of-receivables method may use either an overall rate or a different rate for each age category.
   c. The Allowance for Uncollectible Accounts reduces accounts receivable to their net realizable value.
   d. A write-off of an account reduces the net amount shown for accounts receivable on the balance sheet.
   e. None of the above.
2. Hunt Company estimates uncollectible accounts using the percentage-of-receivables method and expects that 5% of outstanding receivables will be uncollectible for 2012. The balance in Accounts Receivable is $200,000, and the allowance account has a $3,000 credit balance before adjustment at year-end. The uncollectible accounts expense for 2012 will be:
   a. $7,000.
   b. $10,000.
   c. $13,000.
   d. $9,850.
   e. None of the above.
3. Which type of company typically has the longest operating cycle?
   a. Service company.
   b. Merchandising company.
   c. Manufacturing company.
   d. All equal.
4. Maxwell Company records its sales taxes in the same account as sales revenues. The sales tax rate is 6%. At the end of the current period, the Sales account has a balance of $265,000. The amount of sales tax payable is:
   a. $12,000.
   b. $15,000.
   c. $15,900.
   d. $18,000.

5. Dawson Company sells fax machines. During 2012, the company sold 2,000 fax machines. The company estimates that 5% of the machines require repairs under warranty. To date, 30 machines have been repaired. The estimated average cost of warranty repairs per defective fax machine is $200. The required amount of the adjusting entry to record estimated product warranty payable is:
   a. $400,000.
   b. $6,000.
   c. $14,000.
   d. $–0–.

6. To compute interest on a promissory note, all of the following elements must be known except:
   a. The face value of the note.
   b. The stated interest rate.
   c. The name of the payee.
   d. The life of the note.
   e. None of the above.

7. Keats Company issued its own $10,000, 90-day, noninterest-bearing note to a bank. If the note is discounted at 10%, the proceeds to Keats are:
   a. $10,000.
   b. $9,000.
   c. $9,750.
   d. $10,250.
   e. None of the above.

Now turn to page 382 to check your answers.

Questions

1. In view of the difficulty in estimating future events, would you recommend that accountants wait until collections are made from customers before recording sales revenue? Should they wait until known accounts prove to be uncollectible before charging an expense account?

2. The credit manager of a company has established a policy of seeking to completely eliminate all losses from uncollectible accounts. Is this policy a desirable objective for a company? Explain.

3. What are the two major purposes of establishing an allowance for uncollectible accounts?

4. In view of the fact that it is impossible to estimate the exact amount of uncollectible accounts receivable for any one year in advance, what exactly does the Allowance for Uncollectible Accounts account contain after a number of years?

5. What must be considered before adjusting the allowance for uncollectible accounts under the percentage-of-receivables method?

6. How might information in an aging schedule prove useful to management for purposes other than estimating the size of the required allowance for uncollectible accounts?

7. For a company using the allowance method of accounting for uncollectible accounts, which of the following directly affects its reported net income: (1) the establishment of the allowance, (2) the writing off of a specific account, or (3) the recovery of an account previously written off as uncollectible?

8. Why might a retailer agree to sell by credit card when such a substantial discount is taken by the credit card agency in paying the retailer?

9. Define liabilities, current liabilities, and long-term liabilities.

10. What is an operating cycle? Which type of company is likely to have the shortest operating cycle, and which is likely to have the longest operating cycle? Why?

11. Describe the differences between clearly determinable, estimated, and contingent liabilities. Give one or more examples of each type.

12. In what instances might a company acquire notes receivable?

13. How is the maturity value of a note calculated?

14. What is a dishonored note receivable and how is it reported in the balance sheet?

15. Under what circumstances does the account Discount on Notes Payable arise? How is it reported in the financial statements? Explain why.

16. **Real World Question** Refer to "A Broader Perspective" on page 353. What factors are taken into account by the General Electric Company in determining the adjusting entry to establish the desired balance in the Allowance for Losses?

17. **Real World Question** Refer to "A Broader Perspective" on page 353. Explain how the General Electric Company writes off uncollectible accounts.

Exercises

Exercise 9-1
Prepare journal entries
to record uncollectible
accounts expense
(L.O. 1)

The accounts of Stackhouse Company as of December 31, 2012, show Accounts Receivable, $190,000; Allowance for Uncollectible Accounts, $950 (credit balance); Sales, $920,000; and Sales Returns and Allowances, $12,000. Prepare journal entries to adjust for possible uncollectible accounts under each of the following assumptions:

   a. Uncollectible accounts are estimated at 1% of net sales.
   b. The allowance is to be increased to 3% of accounts receivable.

Exercise 9-2
Use aging schedule to
estimate Allowance for
Uncollectible Accounts
(L.O. 1)

Compute the required balance of the Allowance for Uncollectible Accounts for the following receivables:

Accounts Receivable	Age (months)	Probability of Collection
$180,000	Less than 1	95%
90,000	1–3	85
39,000	3–6	75
12,000	6–9	35
2,250	9–12	10

Exercise 9-3
Record write-off and
subsequent recovery
of account (L.O. 1)

On April 1, 2011, Kelley Company, which uses the allowance method of accounting for uncollectible accounts, wrote off Bob Dyer's $400 account. On December 14, 2011, the company received a check in that amount from Dyer marked "in full payment of account." Prepare the necessary entries.

Exercise 9-4
Record use of nonbank
and bank credit cards
(L.O. 2)

Jamestown Furniture Mart, Inc., sold $80,000 of furniture in May to customers who used their Carte Blanche credit cards. Such sales are subject to a 3% discount by Carte Blanche (a nonbank credit card),

   a. Prepare journal entries to record the sales and the subsequent receipt of cash from the credit card company.
   b. Do the same as requirement a, but assume the credit cards used were VISA cards (a bank credit card).

Exercise 9-5
Determine sales
revenue and sales tax
payable (L.O. 4)

Dunwoody Discount Toys, Inc., sells merchandise in a state that has a 5% sales tax. Rather than record sales taxes collected in a separate account, the company records both the sales revenue and the sales taxes in the Sales account. At the end of the first quarter of operations, when it is time to remit the sales taxes to the state taxing agency, the company has $420,000 in the Sales account. Determine the correct amount of sales revenue and the amount of sales tax payable.

Exercise 9-6
Answer questions
regarding note in
financial statements
(L.O. 3, 4)

Assume the following note appeared in the annual report of a company:

In 2011, two small retail customers filed separate suits against the company alleging misrepresentation, breach of contract, conspiracy to violate federal laws, and state antitrust violations arising out of their purchase of retail grocery stores through the company from a third party. Damages sought range up to $10 million in each suit for actual and treble damages and punitive damages of $2 million in one suit and $10 million in the other. The company is vigorously defending the actions and management believes there will be no adverse financial effect.

What kind of liability is being reported? Why is it classified this way? Do you think it is possible to calculate a dollar amount for this obligation? How much would the company have to pay if it lost the suit and had to pay the full amount?

Determine the maturity date for each of the following notes:

Issue Date	Life
January 13, 2012	30 days
January 31, 2012	90 days
June 4, 2012	1 year
December 2, 2012	1 month

Exercise 9-7
Determine maturity dates on several notes (L.O. 5)

Crawford, Inc., gave a $20,000, 120-day, 12% note to Dunston, Inc., in exchange for merchandise. Crawford uses periodic inventory procedure. Prepare journal entries to record the issuance of the note and the entries needed at maturity for both parties, assuming payment is made.

Exercise 9-8
Prepare entries for a note (L.O. 5)

Based on the facts in the previous exercise, prepare the entries that Crawford, Inc., and Dunston, Inc., would make at the maturity date, assuming Crawford defaults.

Exercise 9-9
Prepare entries when maker defaults (L.O. 5)

John Wood is negotiating a bank loan for his company, Wood, Inc., of $16,000 for 90 days. The bank's current interest rate is 10%. Prepare Wood's entries to record the loan under each of the following assumptions:

a. Wood signs a note for $16,000. Interest is deducted in calculating the proceeds turned over to him.
b. Wood signs a note for $16,000 and receives that amount. Interest is to be paid at maturity.

Exercise 9-10
Prepare entries for noninterest-bearing note and interest-bearing note (L.O. 6)

Based on the previous exercise, prepare the entry or entries that would be made at the maturity date for each alternative, assuming the loan is paid before the end of the accounting period.

Exercise 9-11
Prepare entries at maturity date (L.O. 6)

Pistol Pete provides communication services and products, as well as network equipment and computer systems, to businesses, consumers, communications services providers, and government agencies. The following amounts were included in its 2012 annual report:

Exercise 9-12
Calculate the accounts receivable turnover and the number of days' sales in accounts receivable for Pistol Pete (L.O. 7)

	(Millions)
Net sales	$79,609
Receivables, net, 12/31/12	29,275
Receivables, net, 12/31/11	28,623

Calculate the accounts receivable turnover and the number of days' sales in accounts receivable. Use net sales instead of net credit sales in the calculation. Comment on the results.

Problems

As of December 31, 2011, Fargo Company's accounts prior to adjustment show:
Allowance for uncollectible accounts (credit balance)

Accounts receivable	$40,000
Allowance for uncollectible accounts (credit balance)	750
Sales	250,000

Fargo Company estimates uncollectible accounts at 1% of sales.

Problem 9-1
Write off uncollectible account, record expense under alternative methods of estimation (L.O. 1)

On February 23, 2012, the account of Dan Hall in the amount of $300 was considered uncollectible and written off. On August 12, 2012, Hall remitted $200 and indicated that he intends to pay the balance due as soon as possible. By December 31, 2012, no further remittance had been received from Hall and no further remittance was expected.

 Required

a. Prepare journal entries to record all of these transactions and adjusting entries.

b. Give the entry necessary as of December 31, 2011, if Fargo Company estimated its uncollectible accounts at 8% of outstanding receivables rather than at 1% of sales.

Problem 9-2
Record use of bank and nonbank credit cards (L.O. 2)

At the close of business, Jim's Restaurant had credit card sales of $12,000. Of this amount, $4,000 were VISA (bank credit card) sales invoices, which can be deposited in a bank for immediate credit, less a discount of 3%. The balance of $8,000 consisted of American Express (nonbank credit card) charges, subject to a 5% service charge. These invoices were mailed to American Express. Shortly thereafter, a check was received.

 Required

Prepare journal entries for all these transactions.

Problem 9-3
Prepare journal entries for sales and excise taxes (L.O. 4)

Ruiz Company sells merchandise in a state that has a 5% sales tax. On January 2, 2012, Ruiz sold goods with a sales price of $80,000 on credit. Sales taxes collected are recorded in a separate account. Assume that sales for the entire month were $900,000. On January 31, 2012, the company remitted the sales taxes collected to the state taxing agency.

 Required

a. Prepare the general journal entries to record the January 2 sales revenue. Also prepare the entry to show the remittance of the taxes on January 31.

b. Now assume that the merchandise sold on January 2 also is subject to federal excise taxes of 12%. The federal excise taxes collected are remitted to the proper agency on January 31. Show the entries on January 2 and January 31.

Problem 9-4
Prepare journal entries for product warranty (L.O. 4)

Honest Tim's Auto Company sells used cars and warrants all parts for one year. The average price per car is $10,000, and the company sold 900 in 2011. The company expects 30% of the cars to develop defective parts within one year of sale. The estimated average cost of warranty repairs per defective car is $600. By the end of the year, 80 cars sold that year had been returned and repaired under warranty. On January 4, 2012, a customer returned a car purchased in 2011 for repairs under warranty. The repairs were made on January 8. The cost of the repairs included parts, $400, and labor, $210.

Required

a. Calculate the amount of the estimated product warranty payable.

b. Prepare the entry to record the estimated product warranty payable on December 31, 2011.

c. Prepare the entry to record the repairs made on January 8, 2012.

Problem 9-5
Prepare entries to record a number of note transactions, discounting of a note payable, adjusting entries for interest, and payment of notes (L.O. 5, 6)

Celoron Power Boat Company is in the power boat manufacturing business. As of September 1, 2012, the balance in its Notes Receivable account is $256,000. The balance in Dishonored Notes Receivable is $60,660 (includes the interest of $600 and the protest fee of $60). A schedule of the notes (including the dishonored note) is as follows:

Face Amount	Maker	Date of Note	Life	Interest Rate
$ 100,000	C. Glass Co.	6/01/12	120 days	12%
72,000	A. Lamp Co.	6/15/12	90	8
84,000	C. Wall Co.	7/01/12	90	10
60,000	N. Case Co.	7/01/12	60	6
$316,000				

Following are Celoron Power Boat Company's transactions for September:

Sept.   10   Received $36,660 from N. Case Company as full settlement of the amount due from it. The company does not charge losses on notes to the Allowance for Uncollectible Accounts account.

   ?   The A. Lamp Company note was collected when due.

   ?   The C. Glass Company note was not paid at maturity.

   ?   C. Wall Company paid its note at maturity.

30   Received a new 60-day, 12% note from C. Glass Company for the total balance due on the dishonored note. The note was dated as of the maturity date of the dishonored note. Celoron Power Boat Company accepted the note in good faith.

Prepare dated journal entries for these transactions.   *Required*

Premium Office Equipment, Inc., discounted its own $30,000, noninterest-bearing, 180-day note on November 16, 2011, at Niagara County Bank at a discount rate of 12%.

Problem 9-6
Account for discounted
note payable (L.O. 6)

Prepare dated journal entries for:

a. The original discounting on November 16.   *Required*
b. The adjustment required at the end of the company's calendar-year accounting period.
c. Payment at maturity.

Alternate Problems

The following selected accounts are for Keystone, Inc., a name brand shoe wholesale store, as of December 31, 2011. Prior to closing the accounts and making allowance for uncollectible accounts entries, the $5,000 account of Morgan Company is to be written off (this was a credit sale of February 12, 2011).

Problem 9-1A
Write off uncollectible
account, record
expense under
alternative methods of
estimation (L.O. 1)

Accounts receivable	$360,000
Allowance for uncollectible accounts (credit)	6,000
Sales	1,680,000
Sales returns and allowances	30,000

a. Prepare journal entries to record all of these transactions and the uncollectible accounts expense for the period. Assume the estimated expense is 2% of net sales.
b. Give the entry to record the estimated expense for the period if the allowance account is to be adjusted to 5% of outstanding receivables instead of as in a.

The cash register at Frank's Restaurant at the close of business showed cash sales of $7,500 and credit card sales of $10,000 ($6,000 VISA and $4,000 American Express). The VISA (bank credit card) invoices were discounted 5% when they were deposited. The American Express (nonbank credit card) charges were mailed to the company and were subject to a 5% service charge. A few days later, Frank received a check for the net amount of the American Express credit card charges.

Problem 9-2A
Record use of bank and
nonbank credit cards
(L.O. 2)

Prepare journal entries for all of these transactions.   *Required*

Beacham Hardware, Inc., sells merchandise in a state that has a 6% sales tax. On July 1, 2012, it sold goods with a sales price of $20,000 on credit. Sales taxes collected are recorded in a separate account. Assume that sales for the entire month were $400,000. On July 31, 2012, the company remitted the sales taxes collected to the state taxing agency.

Problem 9-3A
Prepare journal entries
for sales and excise
taxes (L.O. 4)

a. Prepare the general journal entries to record the July 1 sales revenue and sales tax payable. Also prepare the entry to show the remittance of the taxes on July 31.   *Required*
b. Now assume that the merchandise sold also is subject to federal excise taxes of 10% in addition to the 6% sales tax. The company remitted the federal excise taxes collected to the proper agency on July 31. Show the entries on July 1 and July 31.

Quick Wheels, Inc., sells racing bicycles and warrants all parts for one year. The average price per bicycle is $560, and the company sold 4,000 in 2011. The company expects 20% of the bicycles to develop defective parts within one year of sale. The estimated average cost of warranty repairs per defective bicycle is $40. By the end of the year, 500 bicycles sold that year had been returned and repaired under warranty. On January 2, 2012, a customer returned a bicycle purchased in 2011 for repairs under warranty. The repairs were made on January 3. The cost of the repairs included parts, $25, and labor, $15.

Problem 9-4A
Prepare journal entries
for product warranty
(L.O. 4)

Required

a. Calculate the amount of the estimated product warranty payable.
b. Prepare the entry to record the estimated product warranty payable on December 31, 2011.
c. Prepare the entry to record the repairs made on January 3, 2012.

Problem 9-5A
Prepare entries to record a number of note transactions, adjusting entries for interest, and entries for payment of notes
(L.O. 5)

Vance Commercial Properties, Inc., has an accounting period of one year, ending on July 31. On July 1, 2011, the balances of certain ledger accounts are Notes Receivable, $654,000; and Notes Payable, $900,000. A schedule of the notes receivable is as follows:

Face Amount	Maker	Date of Note	Interest Life	Rate
$ 270,000	Parker Co.	5/15/11	60 days	12%
120,000	Dot Co.	5/31/11	60	12
264,000	Fixx Co.	6/15/11	30	10
$654,000				

The note payable is a 60-day bank loan dated May 20, 2011. Notes Payable—Discount was debited for the discount of $6,000. Following are the company's transactions during July:

July 1 Vance Commercial Properties, Inc., discounted its own $90,000, 60-day, noninterest-bearing note at Key Bank. The discount rate is 10%, and the note was dated today.

    3 Received a 20-day, 12% note, dated today, from Sox Company in settlement of an account receivable of $36,000.

    6 Purchased merchandise from Link Company, $288,000, and issued a 60-day, 12% note, dated today, for the purchase.

    8 Sold merchandise to Fan Company, $360,000. A 30-day, 12% note, dated today, is received to cover the sale.

   14 Received payment on the Parker Company note dated June 15, 2011.

   15 Fixx Company sent a $120,000, 30-day, 12% note, dated today, and a check to cover the part of the old note not covered by the new note, *plus* all interest expense incurred on the prior note.

   19 The note payable dated May 20, 2011, was paid in full.

   23 Sox Company dishonored its note of July 3 and sent a check for the interest on the dishonored note and a new 30-day, 12% note dated July 23, 2011.

   30 The Dot Company note dated May 31, 2011, was paid with interest in full.

Required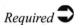

Prepare dated journal entries for these transactions and necessary July 31 adjusting entries.

Problem 9-6A
Account for discounted note payable (L.O. 6)

On November 1, 2012, Grand Strand Property Management, Inc., discounted its own $50,000, 180-day, noninterest-bearing note at its bank at 18%. The note was paid on its maturity date. The company uses a calendar-year accounting period.

Required

Prepare dated journal entries to record *(a)* the discounting of the note, *(b)* the year-end adjustment, and *(c)* the payment of the note.

Beyond the Numbers—Critical Thinking

Business Decision Case 9-1
Compare costs of maintaining own accounts receivable with costs of allowing the use of credit cards; identify other factors to consider (L.O. 1, 3)

Sally Stillwagon owns a hardware store; she sells items for cash and on account. During 2011, which seemed to be a typical year, some of her company's operating data and other data were as follows:

Sales:

For cash	$ 1,200,000
On credit	2,200,000
Cost of obtaining credit reports on customers	3,600
Cost incurred in paying a part-time bookkeeper to keep the accounts receivable subsidiary ledger up to date	12,000
Cost associated with preparing and mailing invoices to customers and other collection activities	18,000
Uncollectible accounts expense	45,000
Average outstanding accounts receivable balance (on which Stillwagon estimates she could have earned 10% if it had been invested in other assets)	180,000

A national credit card agency has tried to convince Stillwagon that instead of carrying her own accounts receivable, she should accept only the agency's credit card for sales on credit. The agency would pay her two days after she submits sales charges, deducting 6% from the amount and paying her 94%.

Required

a. Using the data given, prepare an analysis showing whether or not Stillwagon would benefit from switching to the credit card method of selling on credit.

b. What other factors should she take into consideration?

Jim Perry operates a large fruit and vegetable stand on the outskirts of a city. In a typical year he sells $600,000 of goods to regular customers. His sales are 40% for cash and 60% on credit. He carries all of the credit himself. Only after a customer has a $300 unpaid balance on which no payments have been made for two months does he refuse that customer credit for future purchases. His income before taxes is approximately $95,000. The total of uncollectible accounts for a given year is $48,000.

Business Decision Case 9-2
Evaluate alternative means of making sales (L.O. 3, 4)

You are one of Perry's regular customers. He knows that you are taking a college course in accounting and has asked you to tell him your opinion of several alternatives recommended to him to reduce or eliminate the $48,000 per year uncollectible accounts expense. The alternatives are as follows:

1. Do not sell on credit.
2. Sell on credit by national credit card only.
3. Allow customers to charge only until their account balances reach $50.
4. Allow a bill collector to go after uncollectible accounts and keep half of the amount collected.

Write a report for Perry about the advisability of following any of these alternatives.

Required

Visit the Internet Site:
http://www.cocacola.com
Locate the most recent annual reports of The Coca-Cola Company. Calculate accounts receivable turnover and the number of days' sales in accounts receivable and prepare a written comment on the results.

Annual Report Analysis 9-3
Calculate accounts receivable turnover and the number of days' sales in accounts receivable for The Coca-Cola Company and comment on the results (L.O. 7)

In groups of two or three students, write a two-page, double-spaced paper on one of the following topics:

Group Project 9-4
Write paper on a specific topic

Which is better—the percentage-of-sales method or the percentage-of-receivables method?
Why not eliminate bad debts by selling only for cash?
Why allow customers to use credit cards when credit card expense is so high?
Should banks be required to use 365 days instead of 360 days in interest calculations?

Present your analysis in a convincing manner, without spelling or grammatical errors. Include a cover page with the title and authors' names.

Group Project 9-5
Perform library research

"Lapping" of accounts receivable has been used to conceal the fact that payments received on accounts receivable have been "borrowed" and used by an employee for personal use. With one or two other students, research this topic in the library. Write a paper to your instructor describing how this technique works and the steps that can be taken to detect it once it occurs and to prevent it in the future.

Group Project 9-6
Evaluate management of accounts receivable

In a group of two or three students, visit a fairly large company in your community to investigate the effectiveness of its management of accounts receivable. Inquire about its credit and sales discount policies, collection policies, and how it establishes the amount for the adjusting entry for uncollectible accounts at year-end. Also ask about how it decides to write off accounts as uncollectible. Calculate its accounts receivable turnover and average collection period for each of the last two years. In view of its credit policies, does its collection period seem reasonable?

Using the Internet—A View of the Real World

Internet Project 9-7
Check some mutual funds

Visit one of the following Internet sites:

> **http://www.federatedinvestors.com**
> **http://www.dreyfus.com**
> **http://www.invesco.com**

Follow some of the other options available at the site. Write a report to your instructor on your experience, describing some of the things you learned at this site. You may want to pretend that you invested in one or more of these funds for the duration of the quarter or semester and see how your investment would have fared during that period. Many investors with a limited amount to invest can have a diversified portfolio by investing in mutual funds. Thus, they spread their risk by investing in a mutual fund that, in turn, invests in many different companies.

Internet Project 9-8
Learn about financial highlights

Visit Procter & Gamble's site at:

> **http://www.pg.com**

Procter & Gamble markets more than 250 brands to nearly five billion consumers in over 140 countries. Click on any items that deal with financial news, annual report summary, stock quote, and anything else that looks interesting. Write a memo to your instructor summarizing your findings. Include in your memo some of the financial highlights contained in the annual report summary.

Answers to Self Test

True-False

1. **False.** The percentage-of-sales method estimates the uncollectible accounts from the net credit sales or net sales of a given period.
2. **False.** Uncollectible accounts expense is recognized at the end of the accounting period in an adjusting entry.
3. **True.** The retailer deposits the credit card invoices directly in a special checking account.
4. **False.** Liabilities result from a past transaction.

5. **True.** Current liabilities are classified into those three categories.
6. **True.** The note has passed its maturity date and should be removed from the Notes Receivable account. The maturity value plus any protest fee should be debited to Accounts Receivable.
7. **False.** Discount on Notes Payable is recorded when a noninterest-bearing note is issued.

Multiple-Choice

1. d.   A write-off of an account receivable results in a debit to Allowance for Uncollectible Accounts and a credit to Accounts Receivable for the same amount. The net amount (accounts receivable minus allowance for uncollectible accounts) does not change.

2. a.   The uncollectible accounts expense for 2012 is computed as follows:

Allowance balance after adjustment ($200,000 × 0.05)	$ 10,000
Balance before adjustment	(3,000)
Uncollectible accounts expense	$7,000

3. c.   Manufacturing companies tend to have the longest operating cycle. They must invest cash in raw materials, convert these raw materials into work in process and then finished goods, sell the items on account, and then collect the accounts receivable.

4. b. $265,000 divided by 1.06 = $250,000; $265,000 − $250,000 = $15,000.

5. c.   2,000 × 5% = 100 machines expected to be defective. 100 − 30 already returned = 70 more expected to be returned.
70 × $200 = $14,000 estimated product warranty payable.

6. c.   The name of the payee is not needed to compute interest expense on a promissory note.

7. c.   The proceeds from a bank are computed as follows:
Discount amount = $10,000 × 0.10 × 90/360
                        = $250
Proceeds = $10,000 − $250 = $9,750

Careers in Accounting

A Company Accountant's Role in Managing Plant Assets

Property, plant, and equipment (fixed assets or operating assets) compose more than one-half of total assets in many corporations. These resources are necessary for the companies to operate and ultimately make a profit. It is the efficient use of these resources that in many cases determines the amount of profit corporations will earn.

Accountants employed by a company are deeply involved in nearly all decisions regarding the company's fixed assets, from pre-acquisition planning to the ultimate disposal or sale of those assets. Companies do not view an asset acquisition as merely a purchase, but as an investment. For example, should your company or client purchase an airplane to visit clients? Accountants will investigate all the benefits, both financial and intangible, and compare these benefits to the costs. By determining whether or not the airplane will be a good investment for the company, the accountant can assist the company in making sound strategic business decisions.

Since these assets are so closely related to profits, good management is required. In accounting terms, a good return on operating assets is crucial to the success of the corporation. Many corporations have a staff of accountants whose primary task is to manage operating assets. This task involves making decisions concerning the purchase, use, and disposal of said assets. Once an asset has been acquired, accountants are responsible for determining the original value of the asset, the period over which it will extend benefits to the company, and its current market value while owned by the entity. The accountant must ultimately determine when and how to dispose of such an asset. The decision can range from trading the asset for a new asset to selling the asset to a salvage dealer.

Recently, The Williams Companies, Inc., an energy company based in Tulsa, Oklahoma, had over $20 billion dollars in property, plant, and equipment. In addition, the company also had approximately $226 million in commitments for construction and acquisition of property, plant, and equipment. Managing a portfolio of assets of this magnitude takes both accounting knowledge and analytical skills. Successful management of these assets can be financially rewarding to both the company and the accountant

10

Property, Plant, and Equipment

On a classified balance sheet, the asset section contains: (1) current assets; (2) property, plant, and equipment; and (3) other categories such as intangible assets and long-term investments. Previous chapters discussed current assets. This chapter begins a discussion of property, plant, and equipment that is concluded in Chapter 11. Property, plant, and equipment are often called **plant and equipment** or simply *plant assets*. Plant assets are long-lived assets because they are expected to last for more than one year. Long-lived assets consist of tangible assets and intangible assets. **Tangible assets** have physical characteristics that we can see and touch; they include plant assets such as buildings and furniture, and natural resources such as gas and oil. *Intangible assets* have no physical characteristics that we can see and touch but represent exclusive privileges and rights to their owners.

Nature of Plant Assets

To be classified as a *plant asset,* an asset must: (1) be tangible, that is, capable of being seen and touched; (2) have a useful service life of more than one year; and (3) be used in business operations rather than held for resale. Common plant assets are buildings, machines, tools, and office equipment. On the balance sheet, these assets appear under the heading "Property, plant, and equipment."

Plant assets include all long-lived tangible assets used to generate the principal revenues of the business. Inventory is a tangible asset but not a plant asset because inventory is usually not long-lived and it is held for sale rather than for use. What represents a plant asset to one company may be inventory to another. For example, a business such as a retail appliance store may classify a delivery truck as a plant asset because the truck is used to deliver merchandise. A business such as a truck dealership would classify the same delivery truck as inventory because the truck is held for sale. Also, land held for speculation or not yet put into service is a long-term investment rather than a plant asset because the land

1. List the characteristics of plant assets and identify the costs of acquiring plant assets.

2. List the four major factors affecting depreciation expense.

3. Describe the various methods of calculating depreciation expense.

4. Distinguish between capital and revenue expenditures for plant assets.

5. Describe the subsidiary records used to control plant assets.

6. Analyze and use the financial results—rate of return on operating assets.

is not being used by the business. However, standby equipment used only in peak or emergency periods is a plant asset because it is used in the operations of the business.

Accountants view plant assets as a collection of *service potentials* that are consumed over a long time. For example, over several years, a delivery truck may provide 100,000 miles of delivery services to an appliance business. A new building may provide 40 years of shelter, while a machine may perform a particular operation on 400,000 parts. In each instance, purchase of the plant asset actually represents the advance payment or prepayment for expected services. Plant asset costs are a form of prepaid expense. As with short-term prepayments, the accountant must allocate the cost of these services to the accounting periods benefited.

Accounting for plant assets involves the following four steps:

1. Record the acquisition cost of the asset.
2. Record the allocation of the asset's original cost to periods of its useful life through depreciation.
3. Record subsequent expenditures on the asset.
4. Account for the disposal of the asset.

In Illustration 10.1, note how the asset's life begins with its procurement and the recording of its acquisition cost, which is usually in the form of a dollar purchase. Then, as the asset provides services through time, accountants record the asset's depreciation and any subsequent expenditures related to the asset. Finally, accountants record the disposal of the asset. We discuss the first three steps in this chapter and the disposal of an asset in Chapter 11. The last section in this chapter explains how accountants use subsidiary ledgers to control assets.

Remember that in recording the life history of an asset, accountants match expenses related to the asset with the revenues generated by it. Because measuring the periodic expense of plant assets affects net income, accounting for property, plant, and equipment is important to financial statement users.

Initial Recording of Plant Assets

When a company acquires a plant asset, accountants record the asset at the cost of acquisition (historical cost). This cost is objective, verifiable, and the best measure of an asset's fair market value at the time of purchase. Even if the market value of the asset changes over time, accountants continue to report the acquisition cost in the asset account in subsequent periods.

The **acquisition cost** of a plant asset is the amount of cash or cash equivalents given up to acquire and place the asset in operating condition at its proper location. Thus, cost includes all normal, reasonable, and necessary expenditures to obtain the asset and get it ready for use. Acquisition cost also includes the repair and reconditioning costs for used or damaged assets. Unnecessary costs (such as traffic tickets or fines) that must be paid as a result of hauling machinery to a new plant are not part of the acquisition cost of the asset.

The next sections discuss which costs are capitalized (debited to an asset account) for: (1) land and land improvements; (2) buildings; (3) group purchases of assets; (4) machinery and other equipment; (5) self-constructed assets; (6) noncash acquisitions; and (7) gifts of plant assets.

Land and Land Improvements

The cost of land includes its purchase price and other costs such as option cost, real estate commissions, title search and title transfer fees, and title insurance premiums. Also included are an existing mortgage note or unpaid taxes (back taxes) assumed by the purchaser; costs of surveying, clearing, and grading; and local assessments for

Illustration 10.1   Recording the Life History of a Depreciable Asset

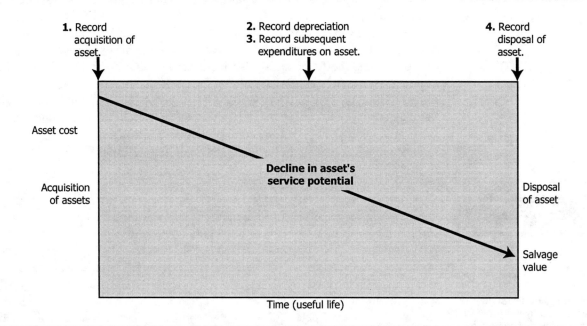

sidewalks, streets, sewers, and water mains. Sometimes land purchased as a building site contains an unusable building that must be removed. Then, the accountant debits the entire purchase price to Land, including the cost of removing the building less any cash received from the sale of salvaged items while the land is being readied for use.

To illustrate, assume that Spivey Company purchased an old farm on the outskirts of San Diego, California, as a factory site. The company paid $225,000 for the property. In addition, the company agreed to pay unpaid property taxes from previous periods (called *back taxes*) of $12,000. Attorneys' fees and other legal costs relating to the purchase of the farm totaled $1,800. Spivey demolished (razed) the farm buildings at a cost of $18,000. The company salvaged some of the structural pieces of the building and sold them for $3,000. Because the firm was constructing a new building at the site, the city assessed Spivey Company $9,000 for water mains, sewers, and street paving. Spivey computed the cost of the land as follows:

Reinforcing Problem
E10-1 Determine cost of land.

	Land
Cost of factory site	$225,000
Back taxes	12,000
Attorneys' fees and other legal costs	1,800
Demolition	18,000
Sale of salvaged parts	(3,000)
City assessment	9,000
	$262,800

Accountants assigned all costs relating to the farm purchase and razing of the old buildings to the Land account because the old buildings purchased with the land were not usable. The real goal was to purchase the land, but the land was not available without the buildings.

Land is considered to have an unlimited life and is therefore not depreciable. However, **land improvements,** including driveways, temporary landscaping, parking lots, fences, lighting systems, and sprinkler systems, are attachments to the land. They have limited lives and therefore are depreciable. Owners record depreciable land improvements in a separate account called Land Improvements. They record the cost of permanent landscaping, including leveling and grading, in the Land account.

Buildings

When a business buys a building, its cost includes the purchase price, repair and remodeling costs, unpaid taxes assumed by the purchaser, legal costs, and real estate commissions paid.

Determining the cost of constructing a new building is often more difficult. Usually this cost includes architect's fees; building permits; payments to contractors; and the cost of digging the foundation. Also included are labor and materials to build the building; salaries of officers supervising the construction; and insurance, taxes, and interest during the construction period. Any miscellaneous amounts earned from the building during construction reduce the cost of the building. For example, an owner who could rent out a small completed portion during construction of the remainder of the building, would credit the rental proceeds to the Buildings account rather than to a revenue account.

Group Purchases of Assets

Reinforcing Problem
E10-2 Determine cost of land and building when acquired together.

Sometimes a company buys land and other assets for a lump sum. When land and buildings purchased together are to be used, the firm divides the total cost and establishes separate ledger accounts for land and for buildings. This division of cost establishes the proper balances in the appropriate accounts. This is especially important later because the depreciation recorded on the buildings affects reported income, while no depreciation is taken on the land.

Returning to our example of Spivey Company, suppose one of the farm buildings was going to be remodeled for use by the company. Then, Spivey would determine what portion of the purchase price of the farm, back taxes, and legal fees ($225,000 + $12,000 + $1,800 = $238,800) it could assign to the buildings and what portion to the land. (The net cost of demolition would not be incurred, and the city assessment would be incurred at a later time.) Spivey would assign the $238,800 to the land and the buildings on the basis of their appraised values. For example, assume that the land was appraised at $162,000 and the buildings at $108,000. Spivey would determine the cost assignable to each of these plant assets as follows:

Asset	Appraised Value	Percent of Total Value	
Land	$162,000	60%	(162/270)
Buildings	108,000	40%	(108/270)
	$270,000	100%	(270/270)

	Percent of Total Value	X	Purchase Price	=	Cost Assigned
Land	60%	X	$238,800*	=	$ 143,280
Buildings	40%	X	$238,800	=	95,520
					$ 238,800

*The purchase price is the sum of the cash price, back taxes, and legal fees.

The journal entry to record the purchase of the land and buildings would be:

Land	143,280	
Buildings	95,520	
Cash		238,800
To record the purchase of land and buildings.		

When the city eventually assessed the charges for the water mains, sewers, and street paving, the company would still debit these costs to the Land account as in the previous example.

Often companies purchase machinery or other equipment such as delivery or office equipment. Its cost includes the seller's *net* invoice price (whether the discount is taken or not), transportation charges incurred, insurance in transit, cost of installation, costs of accessories, and testing and break-in costs. Also included are other costs needed to put the machine or equipment in operating condition in its intended location. The cost of machinery does not include removing and disposing of a replaced, old machine that has been used in operations. Such costs are part of the gain or loss on disposal of the old machine, as discussed in Chapter 11.

Machinery and Other Equipment

Reinforcing Problem
E10-3 Determine cost of a machine.

To illustrate, assume that Clark Company purchased new equipment to replace equipment that it has used for five years. The company paid a net purchase price of $150,000, brokerage fees of $5,000, legal fees of $2,000, and freight and insurance in transit of $3,000. In addition, the company paid $1,500 to remove old equipment and $2,000 to install new equipment. Clark would compute the cost of new equipment as follows:

Net purchase price	$150,000
Brokerage fees	5,000
Legal fees	2,000
Freight and insurance in transit	3,000
Installation costs	2,000
Total cost	$162,000

If a company builds a plant asset for its own use, the cost includes all materials and labor directly traceable to construction of the asset. Also included in the cost of the asset are interest costs related to the asset and amounts paid for utilities (such as heat, light, and power) and for supplies used during construction. To determine how much of these indirect costs to capitalize, the company compares utility and supply costs during the construction period with those costs in a period when no construction occurred. The firm records the increase as part of the asset's cost. For example, assume a company normally incurred a $600 utility bill for June. This year, the company constructed a machine during June, and the utility bill was $975. Thus, it records the $375 increase as part of the machine's cost.

Self-Constructed Assets

To illustrate further, assume that Tanner Company needed a new die-casting machine and received a quote from Smith Company for $23,000, plus $1,000 freight costs. Tanner decided to build the machine rather than buy it. The company incurred the following costs to build the machine: materials, $4,000; labor, $13,000; and indirect services of heat, power, and supplies, $3,000. Tanner would record the machine at its cost of $20,000 ($4,000 + $13,000 + $3,000) rather than $24,000, the purchase price of the machine. The $20,000 is the cost of the resources given up to construct the machine. Also, recording the machine at $24,000 would require Tanner to recognize a gain on construction of the assets. Accountants do not subscribe to the idea that a business can earn revenue (or realize a gain), and therefore net income, by dealing with itself.

You can apply the general guidelines we have just discussed to other plant assets, such as furniture and fixtures. The accounting methods are the same.

When a plant asset is purchased for cash, its acquisition cost is simply the agreed on cash price. However, when a business acquires plant assets in exchange for other noncash assets (shares of stock, a customer's note, or a tract of land) or as gifts, it is more difficult to establish a cash price. This section discusses three possible asset valuation bases.

Noncash Acquisitions

Fair Market Value   **Fair market value** is the price received for an item sold in the normal course of business (not at a forced liquidation sale). Accountants record noncash exchange transactions at fair market value.

Reinforcing Problem
E10-4 Determine cost of machine in noncash acquisition.

The general rule on noncash exchanges is to value the noncash asset received at its fair market value or the fair market value of what was given up, whichever is more clearly evident. The reason for not using the book value of the old asset to value the new asset is that the asset being given up is often carried in the accounting records at historical cost or book value. Neither amount may adequately represent the actual fair market value of either asset. Therefore, if the fair market value of one asset is clearly evident, a firm should record this amount for the new asset at the time of the exchange.

Appraised Value   Sometimes, neither of the items exchanged has a clearly determinable fair market value. Then, accountants record exchanges of items at their appraised values as determined by a professional appraiser. An **appraised value** is an expert's opinion of an item's fair market price if the item were sold. Appraisals are used often to value works of art, rare books, and antiques.

Book Value   The **book value** of an asset is its recorded cost less accumulated depreciation. An old asset's book value is usually not a valid indication of the new asset's fair market value. If a better basis is not available, however, a firm could use the book value of the old asset.

Gifts of Plant Assets

Occasionally, a company receives an asset without giving up anything for it. For example, to attract industry to an area and provide jobs for local residents, a city may give a company a tract of land on which to build a factory. Although such a gift costs the recipient company nothing, it usually records the asset (Land) at its fair market value. Accountants record gifts of plant assets at fair market value to provide information on all assets owned by the company. Omitting some assets may make information provided misleading. They would credit assets received as gifts to a stockholders' equity account titled Paid-in Capital—Donations.

An Accounting Perspective

USE OF TECHNOLOGY How can CPA firms sell services on the Web other than by advertising their services? Ernst & Young has developed a website, Ernst & Young Online, for nonaudit consulting clients in which they charge an annual fixed fee for nonaudit clients to obtain advice from the firm's consultants. The site is secure in that it can only be accessed by those who have paid the fee. The subscribers type in their questions on any business topic and get a response from an expert within two working days. The other large accounting firms undoubtedly have developed or are developing secure websites for providing similar types of services.

Depreciation of Plant Assets

Companies record depreciation on all plant assets except land. Since the amount of depreciation may be relatively large, depreciation expense is often a significant factor in determining net income. For this reason, most financial statement users are interested in the amount of, and the methods used to compute, a company's depreciation expense.

Note to the Student
Depreciation is a device for matching expense against revenue, not a valuation process nor a fund of cash for replacing assets. Once residual (salvage) value and useful life have been estimated, the company selects a method of depreciation.

    Depreciation is the amount of plant asset cost allocated to each accounting period benefiting from the plant asset's use. Depreciation is a *process of allocation,* not valuation. Eventually, all assets except land wear out or become so inadequate or outmoded that they are sold or discarded; therefore, firms must record depreciation on every plant asset except land. They record depreciation even when the market value of a plant asset temporarily rises above its original cost, because eventually the asset is no longer useful to its current owner.

Illustration 10.2   Factors Affecting Depreciation

Major causes of depreciation are (1) physical deterioration, (2) inadequacy for future needs, and (3) obsolescence. **Physical deterioration** results from the use of the asset—wear and tear—and the action of the elements. For example, an automobile may have to be replaced after a time because its body rusted out. The **inadequacy** of a plant asset is its inability to produce enough products or provide enough services to meet current demands. For example, an airline cannot provide air service for 125 passengers using a plane that seats 90. The **obsolescence** of an asset is its decline in usefulness brought about by inventions and technological progress. For example, the development of the xerographic process of reproducing printed matter rendered almost all previous methods of duplication obsolete.

The use of a plant asset in business operations transforms a plant asset cost into an operating expense. Depreciation, then, is an operating expense resulting from the use of a depreciable plant asset. Because depreciation expense does not require a current cash outlay, it is often called a *noncash expense*. The purchaser gave up cash in the period when the asset was acquired, not during the periods when depreciation expense is recorded.

To compute depreciation expense, accountants consider four major factors:

1. Cost of the asset.
2. Estimated salvage value of the asset. **Salvage value** (or *scrap value* or *residual value*) is the amount of money the company expects to recover, less disposal costs, on the date a plant asset is scrapped, sold, or traded in.
3. Estimated useful life of the asset. **Useful life** refers to the time the company owning the asset intends to use it; useful life is not necessarily the same as either economic life or physical life. The economic life of a car may be 7 years and its physical life may be 10 years, but if a company has a policy of trading cars every 3 years, the useful life for depreciation purposes is 3 years. Various firms express useful life in years, months, working hours, or units of production. Obsolescence also affects useful life. For example, a machine capable of producing units for 20 years, may be expected to be obsolete in 6 years. Thus, its estimated useful life is 6 years—not 20. Another example, on TV you may have seen a demolition crew setting off explosives in a huge building (e.g., The Dunes Hotel and Casino in Las Vegas) and wondered why the owners decided to destroy what looked like a perfectly good building. The building was destroyed because it had reached the end of its economic life. The land on which the building stood could be put to use, possibly by constructing a new building.
4. Depreciation method used in depreciating the asset. We describe the four common depreciation methods in the next section.

Factors Affecting Depreciation

Objective 2
List the four major factors affecting depreciation expense.

Illustration 10.3   Depreciation Methods Used

Method	Number of Companies	
	2009	**2008**
Straight-line	488	494
Declining Balance	10	10
Sum of the years' digits	3	3
Accelerated method-not specified	17	21
Units of production	16	14
Other	10	7

Source: Based on American Institute of Certified Public Accountants, *Accounting Trends & Techniques* (New York: AICPA, 2010), p. 389.

In Illustration 10.2, note the relationship among these factors. Assume Ace Company purchased an office building for $100,000. The building has an estimated salvage value of $15,000 and a useful life of 20 years. The *depreciable cost* (or depreciable base) of the building is $85,000 (cost less estimated salvage value). Ace would allocate this depreciable base over the useful life of the building using the proper depreciation method under the circumstances.

Depreciation Methods

Objective 3
Describe the various methods of calculating depreciation expense.

Today, companies can use many different methods to calculate depreciation on assets.[1] This section discusses and illustrates the most common methods—straight-line, units-of-production, and two accelerated depreciation methods (sum-of-the-years' digits and double-declining-balance).

As is true for inventory methods, normally a company is free to adopt the most appropriate depreciation method for its business operations. According to accounting theory, companies should use a depreciation method that reflects most closely their underlying economic circumstances. Thus, companies should adopt the depreciation method that allocates plant asset cost to accounting periods according to the benefits received from the use of the asset. Illustration 10.3 shows the frequency of use of these methods for 500 companies. You can see that most companies use the straight-line method for financial reporting purposes. Note that some companies use one method for certain assets and another method for other assets. In practice, measuring the benefits from the use of a plant asset is impractical and often not possible. As a result, a depreciation method must meet only one standard: the depreciation method must allocate plant asset cost to accounting periods in a systematic and rational manner. The following four methods meet this requirement.

An Accounting Perspective

BUSINESS INSIGHT Regardless of the method or methods of depreciation chosen, companies must disclose their depreciation methods in the footnotes to their financial statements (FASB ACS 360). They often include this information in one of the first footnotes, which summarizes significant accounting policies.

The disclosure is generally straightforward: Sears Holdings Corporation, the parent company of Kmart and Sears, Roebuck, and Co., is the fourth largest broad-line retailer in the United States. Its annual report states simply that depreciation is recorded "using the straight-line method for financial reporting purposes." Companies may use different depreciation methods for different assets. General Electric Company is a highly diversified multinational corporation that develops, manufactures, and markets aerospace products, major appliances, and industrial products, and also provides business and consumer finance services. It uses the sum-of-the-years'-digits method for most of its property, plant, and equipment; however, it depreciates some assets on a straight-line basis.

[1]Because depreciation expense is an estimate, calculations may be rounded to the nearest dollar.

In the illustrations of the four depreciation methods that follow, we assume the following: On January 1, 2012, a company purchased a machine for $54,000 with an estimated useful life of 10 years, or 50,000 units of output, and an estimated salvage value of $4,000.

Straight-Line Method   **Straight-line depreciation** has been the most widely used depreciation method in the United States for many years because, as you saw in Chapter 3, it is easily applied. To apply the straight-line method, a firm charges an equal amount of plant asset cost to each accounting period. The formula for calculating depreciation under the straight-line method is:

$$\text{Depreciation per period} = \frac{\text{Asset cost} - \text{Estimated salvage value}}{\substack{\text{Number of accounting periods in} \\ \text{estimated useful life}}}$$

Using our example of a machine purchased for $54,000, the depreciation is:

$$\frac{\$54,000 - \$4,000}{10 \text{ years}} = \$5,000 \text{ per year}$$

In Illustration 10.4, we present a schedule of annual depreciation entries, cumulative balances in the accumulated depreciation account, and the book (or carrying) values of the $54,000 machine.

Using the straight-line method for assets is appropriate where (1) time rather than obsolescence is the major factor limiting the asset's life and (2) the asset produces relatively constant amounts of periodic services. Assets that possess these features include items such as pipelines, fencing, and storage tanks.

Units-of-Production (Output) Method   The **units-of-production depreciation** method assigns an equal amount of depreciation to each unit of product manufactured or service rendered by an asset. Since this method of depreciation is based on physical output, firms apply it in situations where usage rather than obsolescence leads to the demise of the asset. Under this method, you would compute the depreciation charge per unit of output. Then, multiply this figure by the number of units of goods or services

Reinforcing Problem
E10-5 Record cost of office equipment, depreciation, and repairs expense.

Illustration 10.4   Straight-Line Depreciation Schedule

End of Year	Depreciation Expense Dr.; Accumulated Depreciation Cr.	Total Accumulated Depreciation	Book Value
			$54,000
1	$ 5,000	$ 5,000	49,000
2	5,000	10,000	44,000
3	5,000	15,000	39,000
4	5,000	20,000	34,000
5	5,000	25,000	29,000
6	5,000	30,000	24,000
7	5,000	35,000	19,000
8	5,000	40,000	14,000
9	5,000	45,000	9,000
10	5,000	50,000	4,000*
	$50,000		

* Estimated salvage value.

produced during the accounting period to find the period's depreciation expense. The formula is:

$$\text{Depreciation per unit} = \frac{\text{Asset cost} - \text{Estimated salvage value}}{\substack{\text{Estimated total units of production} \\ \text{(or service) during useful life of asset}}}$$

$$\frac{\text{Depreciation}}{\text{per period}} = \frac{\text{Depreciation}}{\text{per unit}} \times \frac{\text{Number of units of goods or}}{\text{services produced}}$$

You would determine the depreciation charge for the $54,000 machine as:

$$\frac{\$54,000 - \$4,000}{50,000 \text{ units}} = \$1 \text{ per unit}$$

If the machine produced 1,000 units in 2012 and 2,500 units in 2013, depreciation expense for those years would be $1,000 and $2,500, respectively.

Accelerated Depreciation Methods **Accelerated depreciation methods** record higher amounts of depreciation during the early years of an asset's life and lower amounts in the asset's later years. A business might choose an accelerated depreciation method for the following reasons:

1. The value of the benefits received from the asset decline with age (for example, office buildings).
2. The asset is a high-technology asset subject to rapid obsolescence (for example, computers).
3. Repairs increase substantially in the asset's later years; under this method, the depreciation and repairs together remain fairly constant over the asset's life (for example, automobiles).

The two most common accelerated methods of depreciation are the *sum-of-the-years'-digits (SOYD)* method and the *double-declining-balance (DDB)* method.

Illustration 10.5   Sum-of-the-Years'-Digits Depreciation Schedule

End of Year	Depreciation Expense Dr.; Accumulated Depreciation Cr.	Total Accumulated Depreciation	Book Value
			$54,000
1. $50,000* X 10/55	$ 9,091	$ 9,091	44,909
2. $50,000 X 9/55	8,182	17,273	36,727
3. $50,000 X 8/55	7,273	24,546	29,454
4. $50,000 X 7/55	6,364	30,910	23,090
5. $50,000 X 6/55	5,455	36,365	17,635
6. $50,000 X 5/55	4,545	40,910	13,090
7. $50,000 X 4/55	3,636	44,546	9,454
8. $50,000 X 3/55	2,727	47,273	6,727
9. $50,000 X 2/55	1,818	49,091	4,909
10. $50,000 X 1/55	909	50,000	4,000
	$50,000		

* $54,000 cost - $4,000 salvage value.

Sum-of-the-Years'-Digits Method The **sum-of-the-years'-digits (SOYD)** method adds the consecutive digits for each year of an asset's estimated life together and uses that as the denominator of a fraction. The numerator is the years of useful life remaining at the *beginning* of the accounting period. To compute that period's depreciation expense, you would multiply this fraction by the asset cost less the estimated salvage value. The formula is:

$$\text{Depreciation per period} = \frac{\text{Number of years of useful life remaining at beginning of accounting period}}{\text{SOYD}} \left(\text{Asset cost} - \text{Estimated salvage value} \right)$$

The years are totaled to find SOYD. For an asset with a 10-year useful life, SOYD = $10 + 9 + 8 + 7 + 6 + 5 + 4 + 3 + 2 + 1 = 55$. Alternatively, rather than adding the digits for all years together, you can use this formula to find the SOYD for any given number of periods:

$$\text{SOYD} = \frac{n(n+1)}{2}$$

where n is the number of periods in the asset's useful life. Thus, SOYD for an asset with a 10-year useful life is:

$$\text{SOYD} = \frac{10(10+1)}{2} = 55$$

To apply the SOYD method to the $54,000 machine, you would determine that at the beginning of year 1 (2012), the machine has 10 years of useful life remaining. Then, using the formula, compute the first year's depreciation as 10/55 times $50,000 (the $54,000 cost less the $4,000 salvage value). The depreciation for the first year is $9,091 (see Illustration 10.5). Note that the fraction gets smaller every year, resulting in a declining depreciation charge for each successive year.

Double-Declining-Balance Method To apply the **double-declining-balance (DDB)** method of computing periodic depreciation charges you begin by calculating the straight-line depreciation rate. To do this, divide 100% by the number of years of useful life of

Illustration 10.6 Double-Declining-Balance (DDB) Depreciation Schedule

End of Year	Depreciation Expense Dr.; Accumulated Depreciation Cr.	Total Accumulated Depreciation	Book Value
			$54,000
1. (20% of $54,000)	$10,800	$10,800	43,200
2. (20% of $43,200)	8,640	19,440	34,560
3. (20% of $34,560)	6,912	26,352	27,648
4. (20% of $27,648)	5,530	31,882	22,118
5. (20% of $22,118)	4,424	36,306	17,694
6. (20% of $17,694)	3,539	39,845	14,155
7. (20% of $14,155)	2,831	42,676	11,324
8. (20% of $11,324)	2,265	44,941	9,059
9. (20% of $9,059)	1,812	46,753	7,247
10. (20% of $7,247)	1,449*	48,202	5,798

* This amount could be $3,247 to reduce the book value to the estimated salvage value of $4,000. Then, accumulated depreciation would be $50,000.

Illustration 10.7   Summary of Depreciation Methods

Method	Base	Calculation
Straight-line	Asset Cost − Estimated salvage value	Base ⊕ Number of accounting periods in estimated useful life
Units of Production	Asset Cost − Estimated salvage value	Base ⊕ (Estimated total units of production) X Units produced this period
Sum of the years' digits	Asset Cost − Estimated salvage value	Base X Number of years of useful life remaining at beginning of accounting period / SOYD
Double-declining balance	Asset Cost − Accumulated Depreciation	Base X (2 X Straight-line rate)

the asset. Then, multiply this rate by 2. Next, apply the resulting double-declining rate to the *declining book value* of the asset. Ignore salvage value in making the calculations. At the point where book value is equal to the salvage value, no more depreciation is taken. The formula for DDB depreciation is:

$$\frac{\text{Depreciation}}{\text{per period}} = 2 \times \left(\frac{\text{Straight-line}}{\text{rate}}\right) \times \left(\text{Asset cost} - \text{Accumulated depreciation}\right)$$

Look at the calculations for the $54,000 machine using the DDB method in Illustration 10.6. The straight-line rate is 10% ((i.e., 100%/10 years), which, when doubled, yields a DDB rate of 20%. (Expressed as fractions, the straight-line rate is 1/10, and the DDB rate is 2/10.) Since at the beginning of year 1 no accumulated depreciation has been recorded, cost is the basis of the calculation. In each of the following years, book value is the basis of the calculation at the beginning of the year.

In the 10th year, you could increase depreciation to $3,247 if the asset is to be retired and its salvage value is still $4,000. This higher depreciation amount for the last year ($3,247) would reduce the book value of $7,247 down to the salvage value of $4,000. If an asset is continued in service, depreciation should only be recorded until the asset's book value equals its estimated salvage value.

For a summary of the four depreciation methods, see Illustration 10.7.

In Illustration 10.8, we compare three of the depreciation methods just discussed—straight line, sum of the years' digits, and double-declining balance—using the same example of a machine purchased on January 1, 2012, for $54,000. The machine has an estimated useful life of 10 years and an estimated salvage value of $4,000.

An Accounting Perspective	**USES OF TECHNOLOGY** Corporations are subject to corporate income taxes. Also, CPA firms hire many tax professionals to address the tax matters of their clients. If you have an interest in taxes, you may want to visit the following website to learn more about taxes: **http://ey.com** This site was created by the CPA firm, Ernst & Young, and has many interesting features. For instance, you can see highlights of what is new in the world of tax, accounting and legal issues.

Partial-Year Depreciation	So far we have assumed that the assets were put into service at the beginning of an accounting period and ignored the fact that often assets are put into service *during* an accounting period. When assets are acquired during an accounting period, the first recording of depreciation is for a partial year. Normally, firms calculate the depreciation

Illustration 10.8   Comparison of Straight-Line, Sum-of-the-Years'-Digits, and Double-Declining-Balance Depreciation Methods

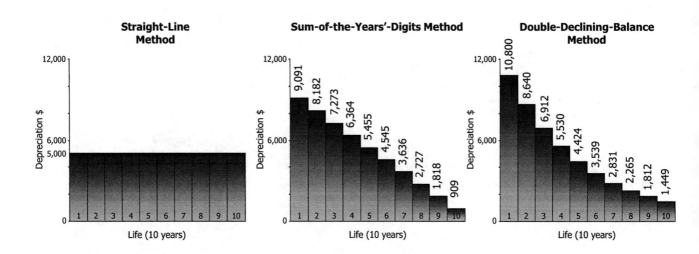

for the partial year to the nearest full month the asset was in service. For example, they treat an asset purchased on or before the 15th day of the month as if it were purchased on the 1st day of the month. And they treat an asset purchased after the 15th of the month as if it were acquired on the 1st day of the following month.

To illustrate how to calculate partial-year depreciation for each of the four depreciation methods, we use a machine purchased for $7,600 on September 1, 2012, with an estimated salvage value of $400, an estimated useful life of five years, and an estimated total units of production of 25,000 units.

Straight-Line Method   Partial-year depreciation calculations for the straight-line depreciation method are relatively easy. Begin by finding the 12-month charge by the normal computation explained earlier. Then, multiply this annual amount by the fraction of the year for which the asset was in use. For example, for the $7,600 machine purchased September 1, 2012 (estimated salvage value, $400; and estimated useful life, five years), the annual straight-line depreciation is [($7,600 – $400)/5 years] = $1,440. The machine would operate for four months prior to the end of the accounting year, December 31, or one-third of a year. The 2012 depreciation is ($1,440 × 1/3) = $480.

Units-of-Production Method   The units-of-production method requires no unusual computations to record depreciation for a partial year. To compute the partial-year depreciation, multiply the depreciation charge per unit by the units produced. The charge for a partial year would be less than for a full year because fewer units of goods or services are produced.

Sum-of-the-Years'-Digits Method   Under the SOYD method, computing partial-year depreciation is more complex. Problems occur because the 12 months for which depreciation is computed using the SOYD fraction do not correspond with the 12 months for which the financial statements are being prepared. For example, the depreciation recorded in 2012 on the $7,600 asset is for the last four months of 2012,

Reinforcing Problems
E10-6 Compute annual depreciation for two years under each of the four different depreciation methods.
E10-7 Determine information concerning machinery.
E10-8 Compute depreciation under SOYD and DDB methods.
E10-9 Compute DDB depreciation.

which is the first one-third of the first year of the asset's life. You would compute the depreciation for the four months of 2012 as ($7,600 – $400) × 5/15 × 1/3; thus, depreciation is $800. In 2013, the depreciation recorded is $2,240, computed as follows:

For the first two-thirds of the year:	($7,200 X 5/15 X 2/3) = $1,600
For the last one-third of the year:	($7,200 X 4/15 X 1/3) = 640
Total depreciation expense for 2013	$2,240

With the SOYD method, you compute annual depreciation charges in this same way throughout the asset's life:

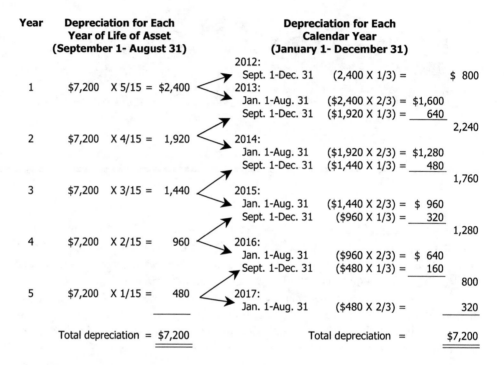

Year	Depreciation for Each Year of Life of Asset (September 1- August 31)	Depreciation for Each Calendar Year (January 1- December 31)		
		2012:		
		Sept. 1-Dec. 31	(2,400 X 1/3) =	$ 800
1	$7,200 X 5/15 = $2,400	**2013:**		
		Jan. 1-Aug. 31	($2,400 X 2/3) =	$1,600
		Sept. 1-Dec. 31	($1,920 X 1/3) =	640
				2,240
2	$7,200 X 4/15 = 1,920	**2014:**		
		Jan. 1-Aug. 31	($1,920 X 2/3) =	$1,280
		Sept. 1-Dec. 31	($1,440 X 1/3) =	480
				1,760
3	$7,200 X 3/15 = 1,440	**2015:**		
		Jan. 1-Aug. 31	($1,440 X 2/3) =	$ 960
		Sept. 1-Dec. 31	($960 X 1/3) =	320
				1,280
4	$7,200 X 2/15 = 960	**2016:**		
		Jan. 1-Aug. 31	($960 X 2/3) =	$ 640
		Sept. 1-Dec. 31	($480 X 1/3) =	160
				800
5	$7,200 X 1/15 = 480	**2017:**		
		Jan. 1-Aug. 31	($480 X 2/3) =	320
	Total depreciation = $7,200	Total depreciation =		$7,200

Double-Declining-Balance Method   Under the double-declining-balance method, it is relatively easy to determine depreciation for a partial year and then for subsequent full years. For the partial year, simply multiply the fixed rate times the cost of the asset times the fraction of the partial year. For example, DDB depreciation on the $7,600 asset for 2012 is ($7,600 × 0.4 × 1/3) = $1,013. For subsequent years, compute the depreciation using the regular procedure of multiplying the book value at the beginning of the period by the fixed rate. The 2013 depreciation would be [($7,600 – $1,013) × 0.4] = $2,635.

An Accounting Perspective

USES OF TECHNOLOGY Most companies report property, plant, and equipment as one amount in the balance sheet in their annual report; however, that account is made up of many items. Computers and accounting software have simplified record-keeping for all of a company's depreciable assets. When depreciable plant assets are purchased, employees enter in the computer the cost, estimated useful life, and estimated salvage value of the assets. In addition, they enter the method of depreciation that the company decides to use on the assets. After processing this information, the computer calculates the company's depreciation expense and accumulates depreciation for each type of asset and each individual asset (e.g., a machine).

After depreciating an asset down to its estimated salvage value, a firm records no more depreciation on the asset even if continuing to use it. At times, a firm finds the estimated useful life of an asset or its estimated salvage value is incorrect before the asset is depreciated down to its estimated salvage value; then, it computes revised depreciation charges for the remaining useful life. These revised charges do not correct past depreciation taken; they merely compensate for past incorrect charges through changed expense amounts in current and future periods. To compute the new depreciation charge per period, divide the book value less the newly estimated salvage value by the newly estimated periods of useful life remaining.

For example, assume that a machine cost $30,000, has an estimated salvage value of $3,000, and originally had an estimated useful life of eight years. At the end of the fourth year of the machine's life, the balance in its accumulated depreciation account (assuming use of the straight-line method) was $(\$30,000 - \$3,000) \times 4/8 = \$13,500$. At the beginning of the fifth year, a manager estimates that the asset will last six more years. The newly estimated salvage value is $2,700. To determine the revised depreciation per period:

Original cost	$ 30,000
Less: Accumulated depreciation at end of 4th year	13,500
Book value at the beginning of 5th year	$ 16,500
Less: Revised salvage value	2,700
Remaining depreciable cost	$ 13,800
Revised depreciation per period: $13,800/6	$ 2,300

Had this company used the units-of-production method, its revision of the life estimate would have been in units. Thus, to determine depreciation expense, compute a new per-unit depreciation charge by dividing book value less revised salvage value by the estimated remaining units of production. Multiply this per unit charge by the periodic production to determine depreciation expense.

Using the double-declining-balance method, the book value at the beginning of year 5 would be $9,492.19 (cost of $30,000 less accumulated depreciation of $20,507.81). Depreciation expense for year 5 would be twice the new straight-line rate times book value. The straight-line rate is $100\%/6 = 16.67\%$. So twice the straight-line rate is 33.33%, or 1/3. Thus, depreciation expense for year $5 = 1/3 \times \$9,492.19 = \$3,164.06$.

Under the sum-of-the-years'-digits method, you must calculate a new fraction. The sum-of-the-years'-digits is now $6 + 5 + 4 + 3 + 2 + 1 = 21$. The fraction for year 5 is 6/21. To compute depreciation under the sum-of-the-years'-digits method:

Book value at the beginning of 5th year	$10,500.00
Revised salvage value	2,700.00
Remaining depreciable base	$ 7,800.00
Depreciation expense for year 5: $7,800 X 6/21	$ 2,228.57

APB Opinion No. 12 requires that companies separately disclose the methods of depreciation they use and the amount of depreciation expense for the period in the body of the income statement or in the notes to the financial statements. Major classes of plant assets and their related accumulated depreciation amounts are reported as shown in Illustration 10.9.

Showing cost less accumulated depreciation in the balance sheet gives statement users a better understanding of the percentages of a company's plant assets that have been used up than simply reporting only the book value (remaining undepreciated cost) of the assets. For example, reporting buildings at $75,000 less $45,000 of accumulated

Illustration 10.9   Partial Balance Sheet

Reed Company
Partial Balance Sheet
June 30, 2012

Property, plant, and equipment		
Land		$ 30,000
Buildings	$ 75,000	
Less: Accumulated depreciation	45,000	30,000
Equipment	$ 9,000	
Less: Accumulated depreciation	1,500	7,500
Total property, plant, and equipment		$ 67,500

depreciation, resulting in a net amount of $30,000, is quite different from merely reporting buildings at $30,000. In the first case, the statement user can see that the assets are about 60% used up. In the latter case, the statement user has no way of knowing whether the assets are new or old.

An Accounting Perspective

BUSINESS INSIGHT In their financial statements, companies often provide one amount for property, plant, and equipment that is net of accumulated depreciation. Nonetheless, notes (footnotes) actually provide the additional information regarding the separate types of assets. Nordstrom, Inc., is one of the nation's leading fashion specialty retailers with more than 200 stores in 28 states. For instance, its Jan. 29, 2011, balance sheet showed land, buildings, and equipment, net, equal to $2.318 million. In a note to the financial statements (slightly modified to clarify), management explained this amount as follows:

(Dollar amounts in thousands)

Land, Buildings and Equipment, Net

	2010	2009
Land and improvements	$ 72	$ 20
Buildings and improvements	2,833	2,659
Store fixtures and improvements	2,745	2,649
Construction in progress	188	180
Total	$5,838	$5,558
Less: accumulated depreciation and amortization	3,530	3,316
Land, buildings and equipment, net	$2,318	$2,242

A Misconception   Some mistaken financial statement users believe that accumulated depreciation represents cash available for replacing old plant assets with new assets. However, the accumulated depreciation account balance does not represent cash; accumulated depreciation simply shows how much of an asset's cost has been charged to expense. Companies use the plant asset and its contra account, accumulated depreciation, so that data on the total original acquisition cost and accumulated depreciation are readily available to meet reporting requirements.

Costs or Market Values in the Balance Sheet   In the balance sheet, firms report plant assets at original cost less accumulated depreciation. One of the justifications for reporting the remaining undepreciated costs of the asset rather than market values is the going-concern concept. As you recall from Chapter 5, the going-concern concept assumes that the company will remain in business indefinitely, which implies the company will use its plant assets rather than sell them. Generally, analysts do not consider market values relevant for plant assets in primary financial statements, although they may be reported in supplemental statements.

(Dollars in Thousands)	2010	2009
Total current assets	$ 580,134	$ 507,681
Property, Plant and Equipment		
Land	826	881
Buildings and improvements	71,724	80,511
Machinery and equipment	129,707	147,197
Software	79,307	74,559
	$281,564	$303,148
Less accumulated depreciation	207,167	229,196
Total plant assets	$ 74,397	$ 73,952
Other Assets		
Goodwill and other intangibles,	$ 55,478	$ 56,198
Cash value of life insurance	36,042	35,405
Deferred income taxes	37,602	35,094
Other	2,922	3,746
Total other assets	$ 132,044	$ 130,443
Total Assets	**$786,575**	**$712,076**

A Broader Perspective

Wolverine World Wide, Inc.

NOTES TO CONSOLIDATED FINANCIAL STATEMENTS

1 (In Part): Summary of Significant Accounting Policies

Property, Plant and Equipment

Property, plant and equipment are stated on the basis of cost and include expenditures for computer hardware and software, store furniture and fixtures, office furniture and machinery and equipment. Normal repairs and maintenance are expensed as incurred.

Depreciation of property, plant and equipment is computed using the straight-line method. The depreciable lives range from five to forty years for buildings and improvements and from three to ten years for machinery and equipment and software. Leasehold improvements are depreciated at the lesser of the estimated useful life or lease term, including reasonably-assured lease renewals as determined at lease inception.

Subsequent Expenditures (Capital and Revenue) on Assets

Companies often spend additional funds on plant assets that have been in use for some time. They debit these expenditures to: (1) an asset account; (2) an accumulated depreciation account; or (3) an expense account.

Expenditures debited to an asset account or to an accumulated depreciation account are **capital expenditures**. Capital expenditures increase the book value of plant assets. **Revenue expenditures**, on the other hand, do not qualify as capital expenditures because they help to generate the current period's revenues rather than future periods' revenues. As a result, companies expense these revenue expenditures immediately and report them in the income statement as expenses.

Objective 4
Distinguish between capital and revenue expenditures for plant assets.

Expenditures Capitalized in Asset Accounts

Betterments or **improvements** to existing plant assets are capital expenditures because they increase the *quality* of services obtained from the asset. Because betterments or improvements add to the service-rendering ability of assets, firms charge them to the asset accounts. For example, installing an air conditioner in an automobile that did not previously have one is a betterment. The debit for such an expenditure is to the asset account, Automobiles.

Expenditures Capitalized as Charges to Accumulated Depreciation

Occasionally, expenditures made on plant assets extend the *quantity* of services *beyond the original estimate* but do not improve the *quality* of the services. Since these expenditures benefit an increased number of future periods, accountants capitalize rather than expense them. However, since there is no visible, tangible addition to, or improvement in, the quality of services, they charge the expenditures to the accumulated depreciation account, thus reducing the credit balance in that account. Such expenditures cancel a part of the existing accumulated depreciation; firms often call them **extraordinary repairs.**

To illustrate, assume that after operating a press for four years, a company spent $5,000 to recondition the press. The reconditioning increased the machine's life to 14 years instead of the original estimate of 10 years. The journal entry to record the extraordinary repair is:

Accumulated Depreciation-Machinery	5,000	
Cash (or Accounts Payable)		5,000
To record the cost of reconditioning a press.		

Assume that the press originally cost $40,000, had an estimated useful life of 10 years, and had no estimated salvage value. At the end of the fourth year, the balance in its accumulated depreciation account under the straight-line method is [($40,000 ÷ 10) × 4] = $16,000. After debiting the $5,000 spent to recondition the press to the accumulated depreciation account, the balances in the asset account and its related accumulated depreciation account are as shown in the last column:

	Before Extraordinary Repair	After Extraordinary Repair
Press	$40,000	$40,000
Accumulated depreciation	16,000	11,000
Book value (end of four years)	$24,000	$29,000

In effect, the expenditure increases the carrying amount (book value) of the asset by reducing its contra account, accumulated depreciation. Under the straight-line method, we would divide the new book value of the press, $29,000, equally among the 10 remaining years in amounts of $2,900 per year (assuming that the estimated salvage value is still zero).

As a practical matter, expenditures for major repairs not extending the asset's life are not expensed in the year they are incurred. Instead, they are charged to accumulated depreciation. This avoids distorting net income by expensing these expenditures in the year incurred. Then, firms calculate a revised depreciation expense, and spread the cost of major repairs over a number of years. This treatment is not theoretically correct.

To illustrate, assume the same facts as in the previous example except that the $5,000 expenditure did not extend the life of the asset. Because of the size of this expenditure, the company still charges it to accumulated depreciation. Now, it would spread the $29,000 remaining book value over the remaining six years of the life of the press. Under the straight-line method, annual depreciation would then be ($29,000 ÷ 6) = $4,833.

Illustration 10.10   Expenditures on Plant Assets after Acquisition

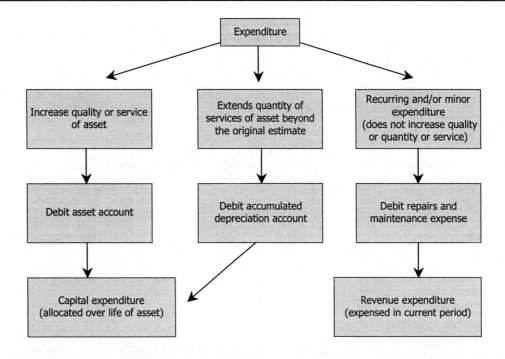

Accountants treat as expenses those recurring and/or minor expenditures that neither add to the asset's service-rendering quality nor extend its quantity of services beyond its original estimated useful life. Thus, firms immediately expense regular maintenance (lubricating a machine) and ordinary repairs (replacing a broken fan belt on an automobile) as revenue expenditures. For example, a company that spends $190 to repair a machine after using it for some time, debits Maintenance Expense or Repairs Expense.

Expenditures Charged to Expense

Low-Cost Items   Most businesses purchase **low-cost items** that provide years of service, such as paperweights, hammers, wrenches, and drills. Because of the small dollar amounts involved, it is impractical to use the ordinary depreciation methods for such assets, and it is often costly to maintain records of individual items. Also, the effect of low-cost items on the financial statements is not significant. Accordingly, it is more efficient to record the items as expenses when they are purchased. For instance, many companies charge any expenditure less than an arbitrary minimum, say, $100, to expense regardless of its impact on the asset's useful life. This practice of accounting for such low unit cost items as expenses is an example of the modifying convention of materiality that was discussed in Chapter 5. In Illustration 10.10, we summarize expenditures on plant assets after acquisition.

In practice, it is difficult to decide whether to debit an expenditure to the asset account or to the accumulated depreciation account. For example, some expenditures seem to affect both the quality and quantity of services. Even if the wrong account were debited for the expenditure, the book value of the plant asset at that point would be the same amount it would have been if the correct account had been debited. However, both the asset and accumulated depreciation accounts would be misstated.

As an example of the effect of misstated asset and accumulated depreciation accounts, assume Watson Company had an asset that had originally cost $15,000 and had been depreciated to a book value of $6,000 at the beginning of 2012. At that time, Watson estimated the equipment had a remaining useful life of two years. The company spent

Errors in Classification

Reinforcing Problems
E10-14 Compute error in net income when installation and freight costs are expensed.
E10-15 Determine the effect of an error in classification.

Illustration 10.11   Expenditure Extending Plant Asset Life

	Jan 1, 2012	After Expenditure Entry Correct	Incorrect
Cost	$15,000	$15,000	$19,000†
Accumulated depreciation	9,000	5,000*	9,000
Book value	$ 6,000	$10,000	$10,000
Remaining life	2 years	6 years	6 years
Depreciation expense per year	$ 3,000	$ 1,667	$1,667

*($9,000 - $4,000)
† ($15,000 + $4,000)

$4,000 in early January 2012 to install a new motor in the equipment. This motor extended the useful life of the asset four years beyond the original estimate. Since the expenditure extended the life, the firm should capitalize it by a debit to the accumulated depreciation account. We show the calculations for depreciation expense if the entry was made correctly and if the expenditure had been improperly charged (debited) to the asset account in Illustration 10.11.

However, if an expenditure that should be expensed is instead capitalized, the effects are more significant. Assume now that $6,000 in repairs expense is incurred for a plant asset that originally cost $40,000 and had a useful life of four years and no estimated salvage value. This asset had been depreciated using the straight-line method for one year and had a book value of $30,000 ($40,000 cost—$10,000 first-year depreciation) at the beginning of 2012. The company capitalized the $6,000 that should have been charged to repairs expense in 2012. The charge for depreciation should have remained at $10,000 for each of the next three years. With the incorrect entry, however, depreciation increases.

Regardless of whether the repair was debited to the asset account or the accumulated depreciation account, the firm would change the depreciation expense amount to $12,000 for each of the next three years [($30,000 book value + $6,000 repairs expense) ÷ 3 more years of useful life]. These errors would cause net income for the year 2012 to be *overstated* $4,000: (1) repairs expense is *understated* by $6,000, causing income to be *overstated* by $6,000; and (2) depreciation expense is *overstated* by $2,000, causing income to be *understated* by $2,000. In 2013, the *overstatement* of depreciation by $2,000 would cause 2013 income to be *understated* by $2,000.

Note that the $6,000 recording error affects more than just the expense accounts and net income. Plant asset and Retained Earnings accounts on the balance sheet also reflect the impact of this error. To see the effect of incorrectly capitalizing the $6,000 to the asset account rather than correctly expensing it, look at Illustration 10.12.

Subsidiary Records Used to Control Plant Assets

Objective 5 Describe the subsidiary records used to control plant assets.

Most companies maintain formal records (ranging from handwritten documents to backup drives) to ensure control over their plant assets. These records include an asset account and a related accumulated depreciation account in the general ledger for *each* major class of depreciable plant assets, such as buildings, factory machinery, office equipment, delivery equipment, and store equipment.

Because the general ledger account has no room for detailed information about each item in a major class of depreciable plant assets, many companies use plant asset subsidiary ledgers. Subsidiary ledgers for Accounts Receivable and Accounts Payable were explained briefly in **An Accounting Perspective** in Chapter 4 on page 147. A company may also use subsidiary ledgers for plant assets. For instance, assume a company

Illustration 10.12   Effect of Revenue Expenditure Treated as Capital Expenditure

	2012	
	Correctly Expensing	**Incorrectly Expensing**
Depreciation expense	$10,000	$12,000
Repair Expense	6,000	-0-
Net in come overstated by $4,000, which affects retained earnings	$16,000	$12,000
Asset cost	$40,000	$46,000
Accumulated depreciation	20,000	22,000
Book value	$20,000	$24,000

	2013	
	Correctly Expensing	**Incorrectly Expensing**
Depreciation expense	$10,000	$12,000
Repair Expense	-0-	-0-
Net in come understated by $2,000, which affects retained earnings	$10,000	$12,000
Asset cost	$40,000	$46,000
Accumulated depreciation	30,000	34,000
Book value	$10,000	$12,000

has a general ledger account for office furniture. The subsidiary ledger for office furniture might contain four separate accounts entitled: Desks, Chairs, File Cabinets and Bookshelves. Alternatively, a company could even have a separate subsidiary account for each piece of furniture. The total of all the subsidiary account balances must equal the total of the general ledger "control" account for Office Furniture at the end of the accounting period. Each general ledger account for each class of depreciable asset, such as Buildings, Delivery Equipment, and so on, could have a subsidiary ledger backing it up and showing information such as the description, cost, and purchase date for each asset. These subsidiary ledgers and detailed records provide more information and allow the company to maintain better control over plant and equipment.

When they are kept for each major class of plant and equipment, a company may have subsidiary ledgers for factory machinery, office equipment, and other classes of depreciable plant assets. Then there may be an additional subsidiary ledger for each type of asset within each category. For example, the subsidiary office equipment ledger may contain accounts for computers, printers, fax machines, copying machines, and so on. Companies also keep a detailed record for each item represented in a subsidiary ledger account. For example, there may be a separate detailed record for each computer represented in the Computer subsidiary ledger account. Each detailed record should include a description of the asset, identification or serial number, location of the asset, date of acquisition, cost, estimated salvage value, estimated useful life, annual depreciation, accumulated depreciation, insurance coverage, repairs, date of disposal, and gain or loss on final disposal of the asset. Note the detailed record for one particular computer as of December 31, 2012, in Illustration 10.13.

To enhance control over plant and equipment, companies stencil on or attach the identification or serial number to each asset. Periodically, firms must take a physical inventory to determine whether all items in the accounting records actually exist, whether they are located where they should be, and whether they are still being used. A company that does not use detailed records and identification numbers or take physical inventories finds it difficult to determine whether assets have been discarded or stolen.

The general ledger control account balance for each major class of plant and equipment should equal the total of the amounts in the subsidiary ledger accounts for that

Illustration 10.13   Detailed Record of a Specific Plant Asset

Item Dell Precision M40	Insurance coverage:
Id. No. Z-43806	United Ins. Co.
Location Rm. 403, Adm. bldg.	Pol. No. 0052-61481-24
Date acquired Jan. 1, 2011	Amt. $3,000
Cost $3,000	Repairs:
Estimated salvage value $200	6/13/12 $140
Estimated useful life 4 yrs.	
Depreciation per year $700	
Accumulated depreciation:	Disposal date _____
12/31/11 $ 700	Gain or loss _____
12/31/12 1,400	
12/31/13 _____	
12/31/14 _____	

class of plant assets. Also, the totals in the detailed records for a specific subsidiary ledger account (such as Computers) should equal the balance of that account. Each time a plant asset is acquired, exchanged, or disposed of, the firm posts an entry to both a general ledger control account and the appropriate subsidiary ledger account. It also updates the detailed record for the items affected.

Illustration 10.14

DEMENT & PEERY, INC.
Consolidated Balance Sheets
December 31, 2012 and 2011
(Dollars in millions)

ASSETS	2012	2011
Current Assets:		
Cash	$ 121	$ 192
Accounts receivable, net of allowance for doubtful accounts of $15 in both 2012 and 2011	379	491
Inventories	247	175
Deposits, prepaid expenses and other	120	58
Total Current Assets	$ 867	$ 916
Investments		
Equity affiliates	170	277
Other assets	87	63
Property and Equipment – Net	4,153	3,919
Deferred Charges	164	154
Total Assets	$ 5,441	$ 5,329
Net Operating Earnings	$ 560	$ 433

Analyzing and Using the Financial Results— Rate of Return on Operating Assets

Objective 6
Analyze and use the financial results—rate of return on operating assets.

Analyzing the ratios of income statement and balance sheet items from one year to the next can reveal important trends. Management uses these ratios to measure performance by establishing targets and evaluating results. As an example, look at Illustration 10.14. Analysts use these figures to calculate the ratios and to explain the importance of this information to management and investors.

To determine the **rate of return on operating assets** for Dement & Peery for 2011 and 2012, use the following formula:

$$\frac{\text{Rate of return on}}{\text{operating assets}} = \frac{\text{Net operating income}}{\text{Operating assets}}$$

2011: $433/$5,329   =   8.13%

2012: $560/$5,441   =   10.29%

Net operating income is also called *net operating earnings* or *income before interest and taxes*. In calculating Dement & Peery's ratio, we have assumed that all assets are operating assets used in producing operating revenues.

This ratio measures the profitability of the company in carrying out its primary business function. For Dement & Peery, these figures indicate a slight increase in the earning power of the company in 2012. Net operating income increased more than proportionately compared to the increase in operating assets. Perhaps this performance justifies the increase in operating assets.

In this chapter, you learned how to account for the acquisition of plant assets and depreciation. The next chapter discusses how to record the disposal of plant assets and how to account for natural resources and intangible assets.

Understanding the Learning Objectives

- To be classified as a plant asset, an asset must: (1) be tangible; (2) have a useful service life of more than one year; and (3) be used in business operations rather than held for resale.

> **Objective 1**
> List the characteristics of plant assets and identify the costs of acquiring plant assets.

- In accounting for plant assets, accountants must:
  1. Record the acquisition cost of the asset.
  2. Record the allocation of the asset's original cost to periods of its useful life through depreciation.
  3. Record subsequent expenditures on the asset.
  4. Account for the disposal of the asset.

> **Objective 2**
> List the four major factors affecting depreciation expense.

- Accountants consider four major factors in computing depreciation: (1) cost of the asset; (2) estimated salvage value of the asset; (3) estimated useful life of the asset; and (4) depreciation method to use in depreciating the asset.
- **Straight-line method:** Assigns an equal amount of depreciation to each period. The formula for calculating straight-line depreciation is:

> **Objective 3**
> Describe the various methods of calculating depreciation expense.

$$\frac{\text{Depreciation}}{\text{per period}} = \frac{\text{Asset cost} - \text{Estimated salvage value}}{\text{Number of accounting periods in estimated useful life}}$$

- **Units-of-production method:** Assigns an equal amount of depreciation to each unit of product manufactured by an asset. The units-of-production depreciation formulas are:

$$\frac{\text{Depreciation}}{\text{per unit}} = \frac{\text{Asset cost} - \text{Estimated salvage value}}{\text{Estimated total units of production (or service) during useful life of asset}}$$

$$\text{Depreciation per period} = \text{Depreciation per unit} \times \text{Number of units of goods or services produced}$$

- **Sum-of-the-years'-digits (SOYD) method:** SOYD is an accelerated depreciation method. The SOYD depreciation formulas are:

$$\text{Depreciation per period} = \frac{\text{Number of years of useful life remaining at beginning of accounting period}}{\text{SOYD}} \left(\text{Asset cost} - \text{Estimated salvage value} \right)$$

$$\text{Sum-of-the-years'-digits (SOYD)} = \frac{n(n+1)}{2}$$

- **Double-declining-balance method:** DDB is an accelerated depreciation method. Salvage value is ignored in making annual calculations. The formula for DDB depreciation is:

$$\text{Depreciation per period} = \left(2 \times \text{Straight-line rate} \right) \times \left(\text{Asset cost} - \text{Accumulated depreciation} \right)$$

Objective 4
Distinguish between capital and revenue expenditures for plant assets.

- Capital expenditures are debited to an asset account or an accumulated depreciation account and increase the book value of plant assets. Expenditures that increase the quality of services or extend the quantity of services beyond the original estimate are capital expenditures.
- Revenue expenditures are expensed immediately and reported in the income statement as expenses. Recurring and or minor expenditures that neither add to the asset's quality of service-rendering abilities nor extend its quantity of services beyond the asset's original estimated useful life are expenses.

Objective 5
Describe the subsidiary records used to control plant assets.

- Plant asset subsidiary ledgers contain detailed information that cannot be maintained in the general ledger account about each item in a major class of depreciable plant assets.
- Control over plant and equipment is enhanced by plant asset subsidiary ledgers and other detailed records. Information in a detailed record may include a description of the asset, identification or serial number, location of the asset, date of acquisition, cost, estimated salvage value, estimated useful life, annual depreciation, accumulated depreciation, insurance coverage, repairs, date of disposal, and gain or loss on final disposal of the asset. A periodic physical inventory should be taken to determine whether items in accounting records actually exist and are still being used at the proper location.

Objective 6
Analyze and use the financial results—rate of return on operating assets.

- To calculate the rate of return on operating assets, divide net operating income by operating assets. This ratio helps management determine how effectively it used assets to produce a profit.

Demonstration Problem 10–A

Cleveland Company purchased a 2-square-mile farm under the following terms: cash paid, $486,000; mortgage note assumed, $240,000; and accrued interest on mortgage note assumed, $6,000. The company paid $55,200 for brokerage and legal services to acquire the property and secure clear title. Cleveland planned to subdivide the property into residential lots and to construct homes on these lots. Clearing and leveling costs of $21,600 were paid. Crops on the land were sold for $14,400. A house on the land, to be moved by the buyer of the house, was sold for $5,040. The other buildings were torn down at a cost of $9,600, and salvaged material was sold for $10,080.

Approximately 6 acres of the land were deeded to the township for roads, and another 10 acres were deeded to the local school district as the site for a future school. After the subdivision was completed, this land would have an approximate value of $7,680 per acre. The company secured a total of 1,200 salable lots from the remaining land.

Present a schedule showing in detail the composition of the cost of the 1,200 salable lots.   ☛ *Required*

Solution to Demonstration Problem 10–A

CLEVELAND COMPANY
Schedule of Cost of 1,200 Residential Lots

Costs incurred:		
Cash paid	$486,000	
Mortgage note assumed	240,000	
Interest accrued on mortgage note		
assumed	6,000	
Broker and legal services	55,200	
Clearing and leveling costs incurred	21,600	
Tearing down costs	9,600	$818,400
Less proceeds from sale of:		
Crops	$ 14,400	
House	5,040	
Salvaged materials	10,080	29,520
Net cost of land to be subdivided into		
1,200 lots		$788,880

Demonstration Problem 10–B

Calvin Company acquired and put into use a machine on January 1, 2012, at a total cost of $45,000. The machine was estimated to have a useful life of 10 years and a salvage value of $5,000. It was also estimated that the machine would produce one million units of product during its life. The machine produced 90,000 units in 2012 and 125,000 units in 2013.

Required ➲ Compute the amounts of depreciation to be recorded in 2012 and 2013 under each of the following:

   a. Straight-line method.
   b. Units-of-production method.
   c. Sum-of-the-years'-digits method.
   d. Double-declining-balance method.
   e. Assume 30,000 units were produced in the first quarter of 2014. Compute depreciation for this quarter under each of the four methods.

Solution to Demonstration Problem 10–B

   a. Straight-line method:
       2012: ($45,000 - $5,000)/10 = $4,000
       2013: ($45,000 - $5,000)10 = $4,000

   b. Units-of-production method:
       2012: [($45,000 - $5,000)/1,000,000] × 90,000 = $3,600
       2013: [($45,000 - $5,000)/1,000,000] × 125,000 = $5,000

   c. Sum-of-the-years'-digits method:
       2012: ($45,000 - $5,000) × (10/55) = $7,272.73
       2013: ($45,000 - $5,000) × (9/55) = $6,545.45

   d. Double-declining-balance method:
       2012: $45,000 × 20% = $9,000
       2013: ($45,000 - $9,000) × 20% = $7,200

   e. Straight-line: ($45,000 - $5,000)/10 × $\frac{1}{4}$ = $1,000

       Units-of-production: (30,000 × $0.04) = $1,200

       Sum-of-the-years'-digits: (($45,000 - $5,000) ×(8/55) × $\frac{1}{4}$) = $1,454.55

       Double-declining-balance: ($45,000 - $9,000 - $7,200) × 0.2 × $\frac{1}{4}$ = $1,440

New Terms

Accelerated depreciation methods Record higher amounts of depreciation during the early years of an asset's life and lower amounts in later years. *394*

Acquisition cost Amount of cash and/or cash equivalents given up to acquire a plant asset and place it in operating condition at its proper location. *386*

Appraised value An expert's opinion as to what an item's market price would be if the item were sold. *390*

Betterments (improvements) Capital expenditures that are properly charged to asset accounts because they add to the service-rendering ability of the assets; they increase the quality of services obtained from an asset. *402*

Book value An asset's recorded cost less its accumulated depreciation. *390*

Capital expenditures Expenditures debited to an asset account or to an accumulated depreciation account. *401*

Depreciation The amount of plant asset cost allocated to each accounting period benefiting from the plant asset's use *(390)*. The **straight-line depreciation** method charges an equal amount of plant asset cost to each period *(393)*. The **units-of-production depreciation** method assigns an equal amount of depreciation for each unit of product manufactured or service rendered by an asset *(393)*. The **sum-of-the-years'-digits (SOYD)** *(395)* and the **double-declining-balance (DDB)** *(395)* methods assign decreasing amounts of depreciation to successive periods of time.

Double-declining-balance (DDB) depreciation See *depreciation.*

Extraordinary repairs Expenditures that cancel a part of the existing accumulated depreciation because they increase the quantity of services expected from an asset. *402*

Fair market value The price that would be received for an item being sold in the normal course of business (not at a forced liquidation sale). *389*

Inadequacy The inability of a plant asset to produce enough products or provide enough services to meet current demands. *391*

Land improvements Attachments to land, such as driveways, landscaping, parking lots, fences, lighting systems, and sprinkler systems, that have limited lives and therefore are depreciable. *387*

Low-cost items Items that provide years of service at a relatively low unit cost, such as hammers, paperweights, and drills. *403*

Obsolescence Decline in usefulness of an asset brought about by inventions and technological progress. *391*

Physical deterioration Results from use of the asset—wear and tear—and the action of the elements. *391*

Plant and equipment A shorter title for property, plant, and equipment; also called *plant assets.* Included are land and manufactured or constructed assets such as buildings, machinery, vehicles, and furniture. *385*

Rate of return on operating assets Net operating income/Operating assets. This ratio helps management determine how effectively it used assets to produce a profit. *406*

Revenue expenditures Expenditures (on a plant asset) that are immediately expensed. *401*

Salvage value The amount of money the company expects to recover, less disposal costs, on the date a plant asset is scrapped, sold, or traded in. Also called *scrap value* or *residual value.* *391*

Straight-line depreciation See *depreciation.*

Sum-of-the-years'-digits (SOYD) depreciation See *depreciation.*

Tangible assets Assets that we can see and touch such as land, buildings, and equipment. *385*

Units-of-production depreciation See *depreciation.*

Useful life Refers to the length of time the company owning the asset intends to use it. *391*

Self-Test

True-False
Indicate whether each of the following statements is true or false.

1. The cost of land includes its purchase price and other related costs, including the cost of removing an old unusable building that is on the land.

2. Depreciation is the process of valuation of an asset to arrive at its market value.

3. The purpose of depreciation accounting is to provide the cash required to replace plant assets.

4. Expenditures made on plant assets that increase the quality of services are debited to the accumulated depreciation account.

5. Plant asset subsidiary ledgers are used to increase control over plant assets.

Multiple-Choice

Select the best answer for each of the following questions.

1. On January 1, 2012, Jackson Company purchased equipment for $400,000, and installation and testing costs totaled $40,000. The equipment has an estimated useful life of 10 years and an estimated salvage value of $40,000. If Jackson uses the straight-line depreciation method, the depreciation expense for 2012 is:
   a. $36,000.
   b. $40,000.
   c. $44,000.
   d. $80,000.
   e. $88,000.

2. In Question 1, if the equipment were purchased on July 1, 2012, and Jackson used the double-declining-balance method, the depreciation expense for 2012 would be:
   a. $88,000.
   b. $72,000.
   c. $36,000.
   d. $44,000.
   e. $40,000.

3. In Question 1, if Jackson acquired the asset on January 1, 2012, and uses the sum-of-the-years'-digits method, the depreciation expense for 2012 is:

   a. $72,727.
   b. $80,000.
   c. $65,454.
   d. $7,272.
   e. $8,000.

4. Hatfield Company purchased a computer on January 2, 2010, for $10,000. The computer had an estimated salvage value of $3,000 and an estimated useful life of five years. At the beginning of 2012, the estimated salvage value changed to $1,000, and the computer is expected to have a remaining useful life of two years. Using the straight-line method, the depreciation expense for 2012 is:
   a. $1,400.
   b. $1,750.
   c. $2,250.
   d. $1,800.
   e. $3,100.

5. The result of recording a capital expenditure as a revenue expenditure is an:
   a. Overstatement of current year's expense.
   b. Understatement of current year's expense.
   c. Understatement of subsequent year's net income.
   d. Overstatement of current year's net income.
   e. None of the above.

Now turn to page 422 to check your answers.

Questions

1. What is the main distinction between inventory and a plant asset?
2. Which of the following items are properly classifiable as plant assets on the balance sheet?
   a. Advertising that will appear in the future to inform the public about new energy-saving programs at a manufacturing plant.
   b. A truck acquired by a manufacturing company to be used to deliver the company's products to wholesalers.
   c. An automobile acquired by an insurance company to be used by one of its salespersons.
   d. Adding machines acquired by an office supply company to be sold to customers.
   e. The cost of constructing and paving a driveway that has an estimated useful life of 10 years.
3. In general terms, what does the cost of a plant asset include?
4. In what way does the purchase of a plant asset resemble the prepayment of an expense?
5. Brown Company purchased an old farm with a vacant building as a factory site for $1,040,000. Brown decided to use the building in its operations. How

should Brown allocate the purchase price between the land and the building? How should this purchase be handled if the building is to be torn down?
6. Describe how a company may determine the cost of a self-constructed asset.
7. In any exchange of noncash assets, the accountant's task is to find the most appropriate valuation for the asset received. What is the general rule for determining the most appropriate valuation in such a situation?
8. Why should periodic depreciation be recorded on all plant assets except land?
9. Define the terms *inadequacy* and *obsolescence* as used in accounting for depreciable plant assets.
10. What four factors must be known to compute depreciation on a plant asset? How *objective* is the calculation of depreciation?
11. A friend, Mindy Jacobs, tells you her car depreciated $5,000 last year. Explain whether her concept of depreciation is the same as the accountant's concept.
12. What does the term *accelerated depreciation* mean? Give an example showing how depreciation is accelerated.

13. Provide a theoretical reason to support using an accelerated depreciation method.

14. If a machine has an estimated useful life of nine years, what will be the total digits to use in calculating depreciation under the sum-of-the-years'-digits method? How is this figure used in the depreciation calculation?

15. Nancy Company purchased a machine that originally had an estimated eight years of useful life. At the end of the third year, Nancy determined that the machine would last only three more years. Does this revision affect past depreciation taken?

16. What does the balance in the accumulated depreciation account represent? Does this balance represent cash that can be used to replace the related plant asset when it is completely depreciated?

17. What is the justification for reporting plant assets on the balance sheet at undepreciated cost (book value) rather than market value?

18. Distinguish between *capital expenditures* and *revenue expenditures.*

19. For each of the following, state whether the expenditure made should be charged to an expense, an asset, or an accumulated depreciation account:
    a. Cost of installing air-conditioning equipment in a building that was not air- conditioned.
    b. Painting of an owned factory building every other year.
    c. Cost of replacing the roof on a 10-year-old building that was purchased new and has an estimated total life of 40 years. The expenditure did not extend the life of the asset beyond the original estimate.
    d. Cost of repairing an electric motor. The expenditure extended the estimated useful life beyond the original estimate.

20. Indicate which type of account (asset, accumulated depreciation, or expense) would be debited for each of the following expenditures:
    a. Painting an office building at a cost of $1,000. The building is painted every year.
    b. Adding on a new plant wing at a cost of $24,000,000.
    c. Expanding a paved parking lot at a cost of $144,000.
    d. Replacing a stairway with an escalator at a cost of $20,000.
    e. Replacing the transmission in an automobile at a cost of $1,600, thus extending its useful life two years beyond the original estimate.
    f. Replacing a broken fan belt at a cost of $600.

21. How do subsidiary records provide control over a company's plant assets?

22. What advantages can accrue to a company that maintains plant asset subsidiary records?

23. **Real World Question**   Based on the financial statements and the notes to those statements of Wal-Mart Stores, Inc., contained in the Annual Report Appendix, what was the 2011 ending net property and equipment balance? Did the company acquire any of these assets in 2011? What depreciation method did the company use?

Exercises

Exercise 10-1
Determine cost of land
(L.O. 1)

Stephon Company paid $640,000 cash for a tract of land on which it plans to erect a new warehouse, and paid $8,000 in legal fees related to the purchase. Stephon also agreed to assume responsibility for $25,600 of unpaid taxes on the property. The company incurred a cost of $28,800 to remove an old apartment building from the land. Prepare a schedule showing the cost of the land acquired.

Exercise 10-2
Determine cost of land
and building when
acquired together
(L.O. 1)

Laural Company paid $840,000 cash for real property consisting of a tract of land and a building. The company intended to remodel and use the old building. To allocate the cost of the property acquired, Laural had the property appraised. The appraised values were as follows: land, $576,000, and office building, $384,000. The cost of clearing the land was $18,000. The building was remodeled at a cost of $76,800. The cost of a new identical office building was estimated to be $432,000. Prepare a schedule showing the cost of the assets acquired.

Exercise 10-3
Determine cost of a
machine (L.O. 1)

Fine Company purchased a heavy machine to be used in its factory for $720,000, less a 2% cash discount. The company paid a fine of $3,600 because an employee hauled the machine over city streets without securing the required permits. The machine was installed at a cost of $21,600, and testing costs of $7,200 were incurred to place the machine in operation. Prepare a schedule showing the recorded cost of the machine.

Exercise 10-4
Determine cost of
machine in noncash
acquisition (L.O. 1)

A machine is acquired in exchange for 50 shares of Marley Corporation capital stock. The stock recently traded at $400 per share. The machine cost $30,000 three years ago. At what amount should the machine be recorded?

Exercise 10-5
Record cost of
office equipment,
depreciation, and
repairs expense
(L.O. 1, 3, 4)

Keely Company purchased some office furniture for $29,760 cash on March 1, 2011. It also paid $480 cash for freight costs incurred. The furniture is being depreciated over four years under the straight-line method, assuming a salvage value of $1,440. The company employs a calendar-year accounting period. On July 1, 2012, it spent $192 to refinish the furniture. Prepare journal entries for the Keely Company to record all of the data, including the annual depreciation adjustments through 2012.

Exercise 10-6
Compute annual
depreciation for two
years under each
of four different
depreciation methods
(L.O. 3)

On January 2, 2011, a new machine was acquired for $900,000. The machine has an estimated salvage value of $100,000 and an estimated useful life of 10 years. The machine is expected to produce a total of 500,000 units of product throughout its useful life. Compute depreciation for 2011 and 2012 using each of the following methods:

a. Straight line.
b. Units of production (assume 30,000 and 60,000 units were produced in 2011 and 2012, respectively).
c. Sum of the years' digits.
d. Double-declining balance.

Exercise 10-7
Determine information
concerning machinery
(L.O. 3)

Terrill Company finds its records are incomplete concerning a piece of machinery used in its plant. According to the company records, the machinery has an estimated useful life of 10 years and an estimated salvage value of $24,000. It has recorded $12,000 in depreciation each year using the straight-line method. If the accumulated depreciation account shows a balance of $72,000, what is the original cost of the machinery and how many years remain to be depreciated?

Exercise 10-8
Compute depreciation
under SOYD and DDB
methods (L.O. 3)

Katherine Company purchased a machine on April 1, 2011, for $72,000. The machine has an estimated useful life of five years with no expected salvage value. The company's accounting year ends on December 31.

Compute the depreciation expense for 2011 and 2012 under (*a*) the sum-of-the-years'-digits method and (*b*) the double-declining-balance method.

Australia Company purchased a machine for $3,200 and incurred installation costs of $800. The estimated salvage value of the machine is $200. The machine has an estimated useful life of four years. Compute the annual depreciation charges for this machine under the double-declining-balance method.

Exercise 10-9
Compute DDB
depreciation (L.O. 3)

Regal Company acquired a delivery truck on January 2, 2011, for $107,200. The truck had an estimated salvage value of $4,800 and an estimated useful life of eight years. At the beginning of 2014, a revised estimate shows that the truck has a remaining useful life of six years. The estimated salvage value changed to $1,600.

   Compute the depreciation charge for 2011 and the revised depreciation charge for 2014 using the straight-line method.

Exercise 10-10
Compute depreciation
before and after revision
of expected life and
salvage value
(L.O. 3)

Assume that the truck described in Exercise 10–10 was used 40% of the time in 2012 to haul materials used in the construction of a building by Regal Company for its own use. (Remember that 2012 is before the revision was made on estimated life.) During the remaining time, Regal used the truck to deliver merchandise to its customers.

   Prepare the journal entry to record straight-line depreciation on the truck for 2012.

Exercise 10-11
Allocate periodic
depreciation to building
and to expense
(L.O. 3)

Vineland Company purchased a computer for $60,000 and placed it in operation on January 2, 2010. Depreciation was recorded for 2010 and 2011 using the straight-line method, a six-year life, and an expected salvage value of $2,400. The introduction of a new model of this computer in 2012 caused the company to revise its estimate of useful life to a total of four years and to reduce the estimated salvage value to zero.

   Compute the depreciation expense on the computer for 2012.

Exercise 10-12
Compute straight-line
depreciation given
changes in estimated life
and salvage value
(L.O. 3)

On January 2, 2011, a company purchased and placed in operation a new machine at a total cost of $60,000. Depreciation was recorded on the machine for 2011 and 2012 under the straight-line method using an estimated useful life of five years and no expected salvage value. Early in 2013, the machine was overhauled at a cost of $20,000. The estimated useful life of the machine was revised upward to a total of seven years.

   Compute the depreciation expense on the machine for 2013.

Exercise 10-13
Compute straight-line
depreciation after major
overhaul (L.O. 3, 4)

Lasky Company purchased a machine on January 3, 2011, at a cost of $50,000. It debited freight and installation charges of $10,000 to Repairs Expense. It recorded straight-line depreciation on the machine in 2011 and 2012 using an estimated life of 10 years and no expected salvage value.

   Compute the amount of the error in net income for 2011 and 2012, and state whether net income is understated or overstated.

Exercise 10-14
Compute error in net
income when installation
and freight costs are
expensed (L.O. 4)

Bragg Company owns a plant asset that originally cost $240,000 in 2008 The asset has been depreciated for three years assuming an eight-year useful life and no salvage value. During 2011, Bragg incorrectly capitalized $120,000 in repairs on the plant asset rather than expensing them. Describe the impact of this error on the asset's cost and Bragg's net income over the next five years.

Exercise 10-15
Determine the effect of
an error in classification
(L.O. 4)

Problems

Problem 10-1
Determine cost of
machine (L.O. 1)

Bolt Company purchased a machine for use in its operations that had an invoice price of $80,000 excluding sales tax. A 4% sales tax was levied on the sale. Terms were net 30. The company estimated the total cost of hauling the machine from the dealer's warehouse to the company's plant at $5,600, which did not include a fine of $1,600 for failure to secure the necessary permits to use city streets in transporting the machine. In delivering the machine to its plant, a Bolt employee damaged the truck used; repairs cost $3,600. The machine was also slightly damaged with repair costs amounting to $1,600.

Bolt incurred installation costs of $32,000 that included the $4,000 cost of shoring up the floor under the machine. Testing costs amounted to $2,400. Safety guards were installed on the machine at a cost of $640, and the machine was placed in operation.

Required ➲ Prepare a schedule showing the amount at which the machine should be recorded in Bolt's accounts.

Problem 10-2
Determine cost of land
and building (L.O. 1)

Pressler Company planned to erect a new factory building and a new office building in Atlanta, Georgia. A report on a suitable site showed an appraised value of $180,000 for land and orchard and $120,000 for a building.

After considerable negotiation, the company and the owner reached the following agreement: Pressler Company was to pay $216,000 in cash, assume a $90,000 mortgage note on the property, assume the interest of $1,920 accrued on the mortgage note, and assume unpaid property taxes of $13,200. Pressler Company paid $18,000 cash for brokerage and legal services in acquiring the property.

Shortly after acquisition of the property, Pressler Company sold the fruit on the trees for $2,640, remodeled the building into an office building at a cost of $38,400, and removed the trees from the land at a cost of $9,000. Construction of the factory building was to begin in a week.

Required ➲ Prepare schedules showing the proper valuation of the assets acquired by Pressler Company.

Problem 10-3
Prepare entry for
acquisition of machine,
for depreciation under
DDB, and for straight-
line depreciation
assuming a change in
estimated life
(L.O. 1, 3)

Timothy Company acquired and placed into use a heavy factory machine on October 1, 2011. The machine had an invoice price of $360,000, but the company received a 3% cash discount by paying the bill on the date of acquisition. An employee of Timothy Company hauled the machine down a city street without a permit. As a result, the company had to pay a $1,500 fine. Installation and testing costs totaled $35,800. The machine is estimated to have a $35,000 salvage value and a seven-year useful life. (A fraction should be used for the DDB calculation rather than a percentage.)

Required ➲
a. Prepare the journal entry to record the acquisition of the machine.
b. Prepare the journal entry to record depreciation for 2011 under the double-declining-balance method.
c. Assume Timothy Company used the straight-line depreciation method. At the beginning of 2014, it estimated the machine will last another six years. Prepare the journal entry to record depreciation for 2014. The estimated salvage value would not change.

Problem 10-4
Compute cost of land,
land improvements,
building, and
machinery; prepare
entry to correct the
accounts
(L.O. 1, 4)

Peach Company has the following entries in its Building account:

Debits

2011			
May	5	Cost of land and building purchased	$200,000
	5	Broker fees incident to purchase of land and building	12,000
2012			
Jan.	3	Contract price of new wing added to south end	84,000
	15	Cost of new machinery, estimated life 10 years	160,000
June	10	Real estate taxes for six months ended 6/30/12	3,600
Aug.	10	Cost of building parking lot for employees in back of building	4,960
Sept.	6	Replacement of windows broken in August	160
Oct.	10	Repairs due to regular usage	2,240

Credits

2011			
May	24	Transfer to Land account, per allocation of purchase cost authorized in minutes of board of directors	32,000
2012			
Jan.	5	Proceeds from leases of second floor for six months ended 12/31/11	8,000

Peach acquired the original property on May 5, 2011. Orange immediately engaged a contractor to construct a new wing on the south end of the building. While the new wing was being constructed, the company leased the second floor as temporary warehouse space to Kellett Company. During this period (July 1 to December 31, 2011), the company installed new machinery costing $160,000 on the first floor of the building. Regular operations began on January 2, 2012.

a. Compute the correct balance for the Buildings account as of December 31, 2012. The company employs a calendar-year accounting period.

b. Prepare the necessary journal entries to correct the records of Peach Company at December 31, 2012. No depreciation entries are required.

Cardine Company acquired and placed into use equipment on January 2, 2011, at a cash cost of $935,000. Transportation charges amounted to $7,500, and installation and testing costs totaled $55,000.

The equipment was estimated to have a useful life of nine years and a salvage value of $37,500 at the end of its life. It was further estimated that the equipment would be used in the production of 1,920,000 units of product during its life. During 2011, 426,000 units of product were produced.

Problem 10-5
Compute depreciation for first year under each of four different depreciation methods (L.O. 3)

Compute the depreciation to the nearest dollar for the year ended December 31, 2011, using:

a. Straight-line method.
b. Units-of-production method.
c. Sum-of-the-years'-digits method.
d. Double-declining-balance method (use a fraction rather than a percentage).

Goodrich Company purchased a machine on October 1, 2011, for $100,000. The machine has an estimated salvage value of $30,000 and an estimated useful life of eight years.

Problem 10-6
Compute depreciation for two years using three depreciation methods; partial-year depreciation used first year (L.O. 3)

Required ➩ Compute to the nearest dollar the amount of depreciation Goodrich should record on the machine for the years ending December 31, 2011, and 2012, under each of the following methods:

    a. Straight-line.
    b. Sum-of-the-years'-digits.
    c. Double-declining-balance.

Alternate Problems

Problem 10-1A
Determine cost of machine (L.O. 1)

Brite Company purchased a machine that had an invoice price of $400,000 excluding sales tax. Terms were net 30. A 4% sales tax was levied on the sale. The company incurred and paid freight costs of $10,000. Special electrical connections were run to the machine at a cost of $14,000, and a special reinforced base for the machine was built at a cost of $18,000. The machine was dropped and damaged while being mounted on this base. Repairs cost $4,000. Raw materials with a cost of $1,000 were consumed in testing the machine. Safety guards were installed on the machine at a cost of $1,400, and the machine was placed in operation. In addition, $500 of costs were incurred in removing an old machine.

Required ➩ Prepare a schedule showing the amount at which the machine should be recorded in Brite Company's account.

Problem 10-2A
Determine cost of land (L.O. 1)

Maxwell Company purchased 2 square miles of farmland under the following terms: $968,000 cash, and liability assumed on mortgage note of $320,000, and interest accrued on the mortgage note assumed of $12,800. The company paid $67,200 of legal and brokerage fees and also paid $3,200 for a title search on the property.

    The company planned to use the land as a site for a new office building and a new fctory. Maxwell paid clearing and leveling costs of $28,800. It sold crops on the land for $7,360 and sold one of the houses on the property for $19,200. The other buildings were torn down at a cost of $14,400; sale of salvaged materials yielded cash proceeds of $13,600. Approximately 1% of the land acquired was deeded to the county for roads. The cost of excavating a basement for the office building amounted to $9,120.

Prepare a schedule showing the amount at which the land should be carried on Maxwell Company's books.

Problem 10-3A
Determine cost of truck; prepare entry for depreciation under DDB and for straight-line depreciation assuming change in estimated life (L.O. 1, 3)

Dawson Towing Company purchased a used panel truck for $28,800 cash. The next day the company's name and business were painted on the truck at a total cost of $1,488. The truck was then given a minor overhaul at a cost of $192, and new "super" tires were mounted on the truck at a cost of $1,920, less a trade-in allowance of $240 for the old tires. The truck was placed in service on April 1, 2011, at which time it had an estimated useful life of five years and a salvage value of $3,360.

Required ➩   **a.** Prepare a schedule showing the cost to be recorded for the truck.
    b. Prepare the journal entry to record depreciation at the end of the calendar-year accounting period, December 31, 2011. Use the double-declining-balance method.
    c. Assume that the straight-line depreciation method has been used. At the beginning of 2014 it is estimated the truck will last another four years. The estimated salvage value changed to $1,920. Prepare the entry to record depreciation for 2014.

You are the new controller for Jayson Company, which began operations on October 1, 2011, after a start-up period that ran from the middle of 2010. While reviewing the accounts, you find an account entitled "Fixed Assets," which contains the following items:

Problem 10-4A
Compute cost of land, land improvements, building, and machinery; prepare entry to correct the accounts
(L.O. 1, 4)

Cash paid to previous owner of land and old buildings	$ 192,000
Cash given to construction company as partial payment for the new building	72,000
Legal and title search fees	2,400
Real estate commission	14,400
Cost of demolishing old building	16,800
Cost of leveling and grading	9,600
Architect's fee (90% of building and 10% improvements)	6,000
Cost of excavating (digging) basement for new building	21,600
Cash paid to construction company for new building	288,000
Repair damage done by vandals	7,200
Sprinkler system for lawn	31,200
Lighting system for parking lot	40,800
Paving of parking lot	60,000
Net invoice price of machinery	1,152,000
Freight cost incurred on machinery	50,400
Installation and testing of machinery	19,200
Medical bill paid for employee injured in installing machinery	3,600
Landscaping (permanent)	38,400
Repair damage to building in installation of machinery	4,800
Special assessment paid to city for water mains and sewer line	45,600
Account balance	$2,106,000

In addition, you discover that cash receipts of $1,200 from selling materials salvaged from the old building were credited to Miscellaneous Revenues in 2011. Digging deeper, you find that the plant manager spent all of his time for the first nine months of 2011 supervising installation of land improvements (10%), building construction (40%), and installation of machinery (50%). The plant manager's nine-month salary of $108,000 was debited to Officers' Salaries Expense.

a. List all items on a form containing columns for Land, Land Improvements, Building, and Machinery. Sort the items into the appropriate columns, omitting those items not properly included as an element of asset cost. Show negative amounts in parentheses. Total your columns.

b. Prepare one compound journal entry to reclassify and adjust the accounts and to eliminate the Fixed Assets account. Do not attempt to record depreciation for the partial year.

☛ *Required*

Land Company acquired and put into use a machine on January 1, 2011, at a cash cost of $120,000 and immediately spent $5,000 to install it. The machine had an estimated useful life of eight years and an estimated salvage value of $15,000 at the end of this time. It was further estimated that the machine would produce 500,000 units of product during its life. In the first year, the machine produced 100,000 units.

Problem 10-5A
Compute depreciation for first year under each of four different depreciation methods
(L.O. 3)

Prepare journal entries to record depreciation to the nearest dollar for 2011, using:

a. Straight-line method.
b. Units-of-production method.
c. Sum-of-the-years'-digits method.
d. Double-declining-balance method.

☛ *Required*

Problem 10-6A
Compute depreciation for two years using three depreciation methods; partial-year depreciation used first year (L.O. 3)

Crawford Company paid $60,000 for a machine on April 1, 2011, and placed it in use on that same date. The machine has an estimated life of 10 years and an estimated salvage value of $10,000.

Required

Compute the amount of depreciation to the nearest dollar the company should record on this asset for the years ending December 31, 2011, and 2012, under each of the following methods:

a. Straight-line.
b. Sum-of-the-years'-digits.
c. Double-declining-balance.

Beyond the Numbers—Critical Thinking

Business Decision Case 10-1
Compute correct cost of land, buildings, and land improvements; compute depreciation; prepare entry to correct the accounts (L.O. 1, 3)

You are a new staff auditor assigned to audit Cray Company's Buildings account. You determine that Cray Company made the following entries in its Buildings account in 2011:

Debits

2011			
Jan.	2	Cost of land and old buildings purchased	$ 720,000
	2	Legal fees incident to purchase	9,600
	2	Fee for title search	1,200
	12	Cost of demolishing old buildings on land	19,200
June	16	Cost of insurance during construction of new building	4,800
July	30	Payment to contractor on completion of new building	1,080,000
Aug.	5	Architect's fees for design of new building	48,000
Sept.	15	City assessment for sewers and sidewalks (considered permanent)	16,800
Oct.	6	Cost of landscaping (considered permanent)	9,600
Nov.	1	Cost of driveways and parking lots	60,000

Credits

Jan.	15	Proceeds received upon sale of salvaged materials from old buildings	4,800

In addition to the entries in the account, you obtained the following information in your interview with the accountant in charge of the Buildings account:

1. The company began using the new building on September 1, 2011. The building is estimated to have a 40-year useful life and no salvage value.
2. The company began using the driveways and parking lots on November 1, 2011. The driveways and parking lots have an estimated 10-year useful life and no salvage value.
3. The company uses the straight-line depreciation method to depreciate all of its plant assets.

Using all of this information, do the following:

a. Prepare a schedule that shows the separate cost of land, buildings, and land improvements.
b. Compute the amount of depreciation expense for 2011.
c. Complete the journal entries required to correct the accounts at December 31, 2011. Assume that closing entries have not been made.
d. Write a brief statement describing to management why depreciation must be recorded and how recording depreciation affects net income.

On October 1, 2012, Besler Company acquired and placed into use new equipment costing $504,000. The equipment has an estimated useful life of five years and an estimated salvage value of $24,000. Besler estimates that the equipment will produce 2 million units of product during its life. In the last quarter of 2012, the equipment produced 120,000 units of product. As the company's accountant, management has asked you to do the following:

a. Compute the depreciation for the last quarter of 2012, using each of the following methods:
   1. Straight-line.
   2. Units-of-production.
   3. Sum-of-the-years'-digits.
   4. Double-declining-balance.

b. Prepare a written report describing the conditions in which each of these four methods would be most appropriate.

Business Decision Case 10-2
Compute partial-year depreciation under each of four different methods; cite circumstances in which each of the different methods seems most appropriate (L.O. 2, 3)

The notes to the financial statements of Wolverine World Wide, Inc., in "A Broader Perspective" on page 401, stated that substantially all fixed assets are depreciated using the straight-line method. Explain why the straight-line method of depreciation may be appropriate for this company.

Business Decision Case 10-3
Discuss why straight-line depreciation method may be appropriate (L.O. 3)

Discuss the meaning of rate of return on operating assets, its elements, and what it means to investors and management.

Calculate the rate of return on operating assets for Wal-Mart Stores, Inc., in the Annual Report Appendix for the two most recent years. Assume all assets are operating assets. Comment on the results.

Business Decision Case 10-4
Discuss the rate of return on operating assets and calculate the ratio for Wal-Mart (L.O. 6)

The following footnote excerpted from a recent annual report of Anadarko Petroleum Corporation describes the company's accounting policies for property, plant, and equipment:

Costs of drilling and equipping successful wells are depreciated using the unit-of-production method. Other properties are stated at historical acquisition cost, net of impairments, and depreciated using the straight-line method.

Annual Report Analysis 10-5
Determine the number of depreciation methods used. Cite the advantages of each method (L.O. 3)

a. How many different depreciation methods are used by Anadarko? Does this practice conform with generally accepted accounting principles?
b. Discuss why management might select each of these methods to depreciate plant assets.

⊖ *Required*

In a group of two or three students, visit a large company in your community and inquire about the subsidiary records it maintains to establish accounting control over its plant assets. Also inquire about physical controls used to protect its equipment that is movable, such as computers, copy machines, and so on. Write a report to your instructor summarizing your findings and be prepared to give a short report to your class.

Group Project 10-6
Describe plant asset records

With a team of two or three students, visit two companies in your community to inquire about why they use certain depreciation methods. Try to locate companies that use several depreciation methods in accounting for various depreciable fixed assets. Interview those who made the decision as to methods to use to find out the reasons for their choices. Write a report to your instructor summarizing your findings.

Group Project 10-7
Determine why certain depreciation methods were used

Group Project 10-8
Determine decision
rules for subsequent
expenditures

In a small group of students, visit a large company in your community to determine how it decides to account for expenditures on fixed assets made after the assets have been in use for some time. In other words, how does it decide whether to debit the asset account, the accumulated depreciation account, or an expense account? What role does materiality play in the decision? Evaluate the reasonableness of the decision model used. Write a report to your instructor summarizing your findings and be prepared to make a short presentation to your class.

Using the Internet—A View of the Real World

**Internet Project
10-9**
Investigate careers
in accounting

Visit the CPA Review site at:
> **http://www.becker.com**

Investigate this site. Identify the major types of professional education services offered. Make note of any interesting information at this site. Write a report to your instructor summarizing your findings. Be prepared to make a short presentation to the class.

**Internet Project
10-10**
Investigate
an accounting
software system

Visit the Sage software website at:
> **http://www.sagenorthamerica.com**

Click on "Accounting Solutions". What types of software does the company sell? Why might a company buy a software package from Sage? Study any other aspect of the information that looks interesting. Write a report to your instructor summarizing your findings.

Answers to Self-Test

True-False

1. **True.** The cost of land includes all normal, reasonable, and necessary expenditures to obtain the land and get it ready for use.
2. **False.** Depreciation is a process of allocation, not valuation, and the book value of an asset has little to do with its market value.
3. **False.** Depreciation accounting does not provide funds required to replace plant assets. Instead, accumulated depreciation simply shows how much of an asset's cost has been charged to expense since the asset was acquired.
4. **False.** Expenditures that improve the quality of services are debited to the asset account.
5. **True.** Plant asset subsidiary ledgers provide detailed information that the general ledger account cannot provide and thus give better control over plant assets.

Multiple-Choice

1. b. The depreciation expense for 2012 using the straight-line method is computed as follows: ($440,000 – $40,000)/10 = $40,000

2. d. Double-declining balance rate
$$= 2 \times (100\%/10)$$
$$= 20\%$$
Depreciation expense for 2012
$$= (20\% \times \$440,000) \times 6/12$$
$$= \$44,000$$

3. a.

$$SOYD = \frac{10\,(10+1)}{2} = 55$$

Depreciation expense
$$= 10/55 \times (\$440,000 - \$40,000)$$
$$= \$72,727$$

4. e. At the beginning of 2012, the balance of accumulated depreciation is $2,800 (annual depreciation of $1,400 × 2) and book value is $7,200, or ($10,000 – $2,800). The revised annual depreciation expense is $3,100, or [($7,200 – $1,000)/2].

5. a. The error in recording a capital expenditure as a revenue expenditure results in an overstatement of current year's expense, as well as an understatement of current year's net income.

Careers in Accounting

A Company Accountant's Role in Measuring Intangibles

Many assets have no physical substance. These assets are referred to as intangible. Even though these assets have no substance, the accountant still must spend time measuring the value of these assets to corporation and how these assets contribute to the cash flow of the entity.

The accountant must first place a value on something that cannot be seen by the naked eye. Then the accountant must determine if the asset is making a contribution toward cash flow of the entity (if so and how long), and finally, the accountant must determine if and when this benefit has indeed expired.

As we move ever more toward an information based economy, the percent of intangible assets to total assets also increases. In many cases, intangible assets compose a significant majority of total assets. Thus, the earning power of such companies is primarily based on the valuation of assets that cannot be seen or touched. Some intangible assets, such as human assets and internally generated intangibles, are not even recorded on the company's books. This makes it even more difficult to value the assets and determine their contribution to earnings.

Investors and analysts often compare book value per share with the market price per share for a corporation. This ratio is referred to as the price-to-book ratio (PB). It measures the market's beliefs about the value of net assets as compared to the recorded amount of net assets. In 2011, Tootsie Roll had a PB ratio of approximately 2.0. The recorded net assets were approximately $669 million, yet the market perceived Tootsie Roll to have net assets worth over $1,390 million. What is the nature of those unrecorded (intangible) assets? Similarly, in 2011, Amazon. com had a PB ratio of approximately 10.4. The real value of Amazon.com's net assets exceeded those reported in the accounting records by a factor of 10.4. It is reasonable to assume that a large portion of the unrecorded assets of Amazon.com must be intangible.How does the accountant value something that has no physical substance and in many cases has not been recorded? It is similar to walking around in a dark closet wearing a blindfold.

This function is closely related to the work of the plant asset accountant. Many of the same questions must be addressed when accounting for intangible assets. The question still remains, how can you measure something you can't see?

Plant Asset Disposals, Natural Resources, and Intangible Assets

Your study of long-term assets—plant assets, natural resources, and intangible assets—began in Chapter 10, which focused on determining plant asset cost, computing depreciation, and distinguishing between capital and revenue expenditures. This chapter begins by discussing the disposal of plant assets. The next topic is accounting for natural resources such as ores, minerals, oil and gas, and timber. The final topic is accounting for intangible assets such as patents, copyrights, franchises, trademarks and trade names, leases, and goodwill.

Note that accounting for all the long-term assets discussed in these chapters is basically the same. A company that purchases a long-term asset records it at cost. As the company receives benefits from the asset and its future service potential decreases, the accountant transfers the cost from an asset account to an expense account. Finally, the asset is sold, retired, or traded in on a new asset. Because the lives of long-term assets can extend for many years, the methods accountants use in reporting such assets can have a dramatic effect on the financial statements of many accounting periods.

Disposal of Plant Assets

All plant assets except land eventually wear out or become inadequate or obsolete and must be sold, retired, or traded for new assets. When disposing of a plant asset, a company must remove both the asset's cost and accumulated depreciation from the accounts. Overall, then, all plant asset disposals have the following steps in common:

1. Bring the asset's depreciation up to date.
2. Record the disposal by:
   a. Writing off the asset's cost.
   b. Writing off the accumulated depreciation.

Learning Objectives

After studying this chapter, you should be able to:

1. Calculate and prepare entries for the sale, retirement, and destruction of plant assets.

2. Describe and record exchanges of nonmonetary assets.

3. Determine the periodic depletion cost of a natural resource and calculate depreciation of plant assets located on extractive industry property.

4. Prepare entries for the acquisition and amortization of intangible assets.

5. Analyze and use the financial results—total assets turnover.

    c. Recording any consideration (usually cash) received or paid or to be received or paid.

    d. Recording the gain or loss, if any.

As you study this section, remember these common procedures accountants use to record the disposal of plant assets. In the paragraphs that follow, we discuss accounting for the (1) sale of plant assets, (2) retirement of plant assets without sale, (3) destruction of plant assets, (4) exchange of plant assets, and (5) cost of dismantling and removing plant assets.

Sale of Plant Assets

Companies frequently dispose of plant assets by selling them. By comparing an asset's book value (cost less accumulated depreciation) with its selling price (or net amount realized if there are selling expenses), the company may show either a gain or loss. If the sales price is greater than the asset's book value, the company shows a gain. If the sales price is less than the asset's book value, the company shows a loss. Of course, when the sales price equals the asset's book value, no gain or loss occurs.

To illustrate accounting for the sale of a plant asset, assume that a company sells equipment costing $45,000 with accumulated depreciation of $14,000 for $35,000. The firm realizes a gain of $4,000:

Equipment cost	$ 45,000
Accumulated depreciation	14,000
Book value	$ 31,000
Sales price	35,000
Gain realized	$ 4,000

The journal entry to record the sale is:

Cash	35,000	
Accumulated Depreciation—Equipment	14,000	
Equipment		45,000
Gain on Disposal of Plant Assets		4,000
To record sale of equipment at a price greater than book value.		

If on the other hand, the company sells the equipment for $28,000, it realizes a loss of $3,000 ($31,000 book value – $28,000 sales price). The journal entry to record the sale is:

Cash	28,000	
Accumulated Depreciation—Equipment	14,000	
Loss from Disposal of Plant Asset	3,000	
Equipment		45,000
To record the sale of equipment at a price less than book value.		

If a firm sells the equipment for $31,000, no gain or loss occurs. The journal entry to record the sale is:

Cash	31,000	
Accumulated Depreciation—Equipment	14,000	
Equipment		45,000
To record sale of equipment at a price equal to book value.		

Accounting for Depreciation to Date of Disposal   When selling or otherwise disposing of a plant asset, a firm must record the depreciation up to the date of sale or disposal. For example, if it sold an asset on April 1 and last recorded depreciation on December 31, the company should record depreciation for three months (January 1–April 1). When depreciation is not recorded for the three months, operating expenses for that period are understated, and the gain on the sale of the asset is understated or the loss overstated.

To illustrate, assume that on August 1, 2013, Ray Company sold a machine for $1,500. When purchased on January 2, 2005, the machine cost $12,000; Ray was depreciating it at the straight-line rate of 10% per year. As of December 31, 2012, after closing entries were made, the machine's accumulated depreciation account had a balance of $9,600. Before determining a gain or loss and before making an entry to record the sale, the firm must make the following entry to record depreciation for the seven months ended July 31, 2013:

July	31	Depreciation Expense—Machinery	700	
		Accumulated Depreciation—Machinery		700
		To record depreciation for seven months		
		[$12,000 X 0.10 X (7/12)]		

An accountant would compute the $200 loss on the sale as follows:

Machine cost	$ 12,000
Accumulated depreciation ($9,600 + $700)	10,300
Book value	$ 1,700
Sales price	1,500
Loss realized	$ 200

The journal entry to record the sale is:

Cash	1,500	
Accumulated Depreciation—Machinery	10,300	
Loss from Disposal of Plant Assets	200	
Machinery		12,000
To record the sale of machinery at a price less than book value.		

When retiring a plant asset from service, a company removes the asset's cost and accumulated depreciation from its plant asset accounts. For example, Hayes Company would make the following journal entry when it retired a fully depreciated machine that cost $15,000 and had no salvage value:

Retirement of Plant Assets without Sale

Accumulated Depreciation—Machinery	15,000	
Machinery		15,000
To record the retirement of a fully depreciated machine.		

Occasionally, a company continues to use a plant asset after it has been fully depreciated. In such a case, the firm should not remove the asset's cost and accumulated depreciation from the accounts until the asset is sold, traded, or retired from service. Of course, the company cannot record more depreciation on a fully depreciated asset, because total depreciation expense taken on an asset may not exceed its cost.

Sometimes a business retires or discards a plant asset before fully depreciating it. When selling the asset as scrap (even if not immediately), the firm removes its cost and accumulated depreciation from the asset and accumulated depreciation accounts. In addition, the accountant records its estimated salvage value in a Salvaged Materials account and recognizes a gain or loss on disposal. To illustrate, assume that a firm retires a machine with a $10,000 original cost and $7,500 of accumulated depreciation. If the machine's estimated salvage value is $500, the following entry is required:

Salvaged materials	500	
Accumulated Depreciation—Machinery	7,500	
Loss from Disposal of Plant Assets	2,000	
Machinery		10,000
To record the retirement of machinery, which will be sold for scrap at a later time.		

An Accounting Perspective

Uses of Technology Think about a small business that you would like to own. Where would you find the financing to be able to start a new business or acquire an existing business? What legal and tax issues would you need to address before making such a large investment? How do you develop a business plan? Where would you go to find answers to these and many other questions? One source of information is the U.S. Small Business Administration. Visit its website at **www.sba.gov** to explore the types of helpful information that the SBA provides to small businesses.

Destruction of Plant Assets

Sometimes accidents, fires, floods, and storms wreck or destroy plant assets, causing companies to incur losses. For example, assume that fire completely destroyed an *uninsured* building costing $40,000 with up-to-date accumulated depreciation of $12,000. The journal entry is:

Fire Loss	28,000	
Accumulated Depreciation—Buildings	12,000	
Buildings		40,000
To record fire loss.		

If the building was *insured,* the company would debit only the amount of the fire loss exceeding the amount to be recovered from the insurance company to the Fire Loss account. To illustrate, assume the company partially insured the building and will recover $22,000 from the insurance company. The journal entry is:

Receivable from Insurance Company	22,000	
Fire Loss	6,000	
Accumulated Depreciation—Buildings	12,000	
Buildings		40,000
To record fire loss and amount recoverable from insurance company.		

Exchanges of Nonmonetary Assets

Exchanges of Nonmonetary Assets   Until late 2009, the rules according to *APB Opinion No. 29* for recording exchanges of nonmonetary assets depended on whether they were exchanges of dissimilar assets such as a truck for a machine or were similar assets such as a truck for a truck.[1] If the exchange classified as an exchange of dissimilar assets, the acquired asset would be recorded at its fair value and any gain or loss would be recognized. In late 2009, the FASB issued a new standard, *Statement of Financial Accounting Standards No. 153*, "Exchanges of Nonoperating Assets: an amendment of APB Opinion No. 29 [2]" (codified as ASC 845). This new standard was issued to bring about greater agreement between U. S. Generally Accepted Accounting Principles and International Financial Reporting Standards.

---

[1]APB, *APB Opinion No. 29*, "Accounting for Nonmonetary Transactions" (New York: AICPA, May 1973).
[2]FASB, *FASB Statement No. 153*, "Exchanges of Nonmonetary Assets: an amendment of APB Opinion No. 29" (Norwalk, CT: FASB Board, December 2009).

The FASB standard does not distinguish between dissimilar and similar asset exchanges. Instead, it differentiates between exchanges that have commercial substance and those that do not have commercial substance. An exchange has **commercial substance** if, as a result of the exchange, future cash flows are expected to change significantly. For instance, if a company exchanges a building for land (a dissimilar exchange), the timing and the future cash flows are likely to be different than if the exchange had not occurred. Most exchanges qualify as having commercial substance. However, if the exchange is not expected to create a significant change in future cash flows, the exchange does not result in commercial substance. For example, if a company exchanges one truck for another truck (a similar exchange) that will perform the same function as the old truck and for the same time period so that the future cash flows are not significantly different, then the exchange does not result in commercial substance. However, if the future cash flows are likely to be significantly different, then the exchange of similar assets has commercial substance.

Exchanges of Nonmonetary Assets Having Commercial Substance   For exchanges of nonmonetary assets that have commercial substance, accountants record the new asset at the fair market value of the asset received or of the asset(s) given up, whichever is more clearly evident. When the cash price of the new asset is stated, they use the cash price to record the new asset. If the cash price is not stated, they assume that the fair market value of the old asset plus any cash paid would equate to the cash price of the new asset and use that value to record the new asset. Thus, accountants would normally record the asset received at either (1) the stated cash price of the new asset or (2) a known fair market value of the asset given up plus any cash paid.

> **Objective 2**
> Describe and record exchanges of nonmonetary assets.

Debiting accumulated depreciation and crediting the old asset removes the book value of the old asset from the accounts. The firm credits the Cash account for any amount paid. If the amount at which the new asset is recorded exceeds the book value of the old asset plus any cash paid, a company records a gain to balance the journal entry. If the situation is reversed, it records a loss to balance the journal entry. To illustrate such an exchange having commercial substance, assume a company exchanges an old machine for a new delivery truck. The future cash flows from the exchange are expected to be significantly different and, therefore, the exchange has commercial substance. The machine cost $45,000 and had an up-to-date accumulated depreciation balance of $38,000. The truck had a $55,000 cash price and was acquired by trading in the machine with a fair value of $3,000 and paying $52,000 cash. The journal entry to record the exchange is:

Trucks	55,000	
Accumulated Depreciation—Machinery	38,000	
Loss from Disposal of Plant Assets	4,000	
Machinery		45,000
Cash		52,000
To record loss on exchange of dissimilar plant assets.		

Another way to compute the $4,000 loss on the exchange is to use the book value of the old asset less the fair market value of the old asset. The calculation is as follows:

Machine cost	$ 45,000
Accumulated depreciation	38,000
Book value	$ 7,000
Fair market value of old asset	
(trade-in allowance)	3,000
Loss realized	$ 4,000

To illustrate the recognition of a gain from such an exchange having commercial substance, assume that the fair market value of the machine was $9,000 instead of $3,000, and that only $46,000 was paid in cash. The journal entry to record the exchange would be:

Trucks	55,000	
Accumulated Depreciation—Machinery	38,000	
Machinery		45,000
Cash		46,000
Gain on Disposal of Plant Assets		2,000
To record gain on exchange of dissimilar assets.		

Another way to compute the gain of $2,000 on the exchange is to use the fair market value of the old asset less the book value of the old asset. The calculation is as follows:

Machine cost	$ 45,000
Accumulated depreciation	38,000
Book value	$ 7,000
Fair market value of old asset	
(trade-in allowance)	9,000
Gain realized	$ 2,000

Remember, when the book value and the market value of the old asset are different, companies always recognize a gain or a loss on an exchange of nonmonetary assets having commercial substance. As discussed earlier, they do not recognize a gain or loss on an exchange of nonmonetary assets not having commercial substance.

Exchanges of Nonmonetary Assets Not Having Commercial Substance   Often firms exchange plant assets such as automobiles, trucks, and office equipment by trading the old asset for a similar new one. Once in a while, such an exchange does not result in an expected change in future cash flows and therefore lacks commercial substance. When such an exchange occurs, the company receives a trade-in allowance for the old asset, and pays the balance in cash.[3] Usually, the cash price of the new asset is stated. If not, accountants assume the cash price of the new asset is the fair market value of the old asset plus the cash paid.

When such assets are exchanged, we must modify the general rule that new assets are recorded at the fair market value of what is given up or received, whichever is clearer. Instead, companies **record the new asset at the book value of the old asset plus the cash paid**. When applying this rule to exchanges of assets where no commercial substance results, firms recognize no losses or gains.

To illustrate the accounting for exchanges of nonmonetary assets that do not have commercial substance, assume that a delivery service exchanged $50,000 cash and truck No. 1—which cost $45,000, had $38,000 of up-to-date accumulated depreciation, and had a $5,000 fair market value—for truck No. 2. The new truck has a cash price (fair market value) of $55,000. The delivery service realized a loss of $2,000 on the exchange, which cannot be recorded. The loss is calculated as follows

The journal entry to record the exchange is:

Cost of trunk No. 1	$ 45,000
Accumulated depreciation	38,000
Book value	$ 7,000
Fair market value of old asset	
(trade-in allowance)	5,000
Loss indicated (but not recorded)	$ 2,000

However, if a loss is indicated and is added to the recorded value of the new asset,

---

[3]Trade-in allowance is sometimes expressed as the difference between *list* price and cash paid, but we choose to define it as the difference between *cash* price and cash paid because this latter definition seems to agree with current practice for exchange transactions.

the asset may later be written down because of rules of impairment (as required by FASB Standard No.144, ASC 360), a topic left to Intermediate Accounting texts.

The journal entry to record the exchange is:

Truck (cost of No. 2)	57,000	
Accumulated Depreciation—Trucks	38,000	
Trucks (cost of No. 1)		45,000
Cash		50,000
To record the exchange of nonmonetary assets with no commercial substance (no loss recorded).		

Accounting for any gain resulting from exchanges of nonmonetary assets having no commercial substance is similar to the case where a loss is present but unrecorded. To illustrate, assume that in the preceding example, the delivery service gave truck No. 1 (now with a fair market value of $9,000) and $46,000 cash in exchange for truck No. 2. The indicated gain on the exchange is $2,000, but would be unrecorded. The calculation of the indicated gain is as follows:

Cost of truck No. 1	$ 45,000
Accumulated depreciation	38,000
Book value	$ 7,000
Fair market value of old asset	9,000
Gain indicated (but not recorded)	$ 2,000

The company would record the new asset at the book value of the old asset ($7,000) plus cash paid ($46,000). Alternatively, the company deducts the indicated gain from the cost of the new asset ($55,000). Thus, the cost basis of the new delivery truck is equal to $55,000 less the $2,000 gain, or $53,000. The delivery service uses this $53,000 cost basis in recording depreciation on the truck and determining any gain or loss on its disposal.

Book value of old truck (No. 1)	$ 7,000
Cash paid	46,000
Cost of new truck (No. 2)	$ 53,000
Fair market value of new truck (No. 2)	$ 55,000
Less: Gain indicated	2,000 (equal)
Cost of new truck (No. 2)	$ 53,000

The journal entry to record the exchange is:

Trucks (cost of No. 2)	53,000	
Accumulated Depreciation—Trucks	38,000	
Trucks (cost of No. 1)		45,000
Cash		46,000
To record exchange of nonmonetary assets with no commercial substance (no gain recorded).		

Firms would realize the gain on an exchange of nonmonetary assets not having commercial substance in future accounting periods as increased net income resulting from smaller depreciation charges on the newly acquired asset. In the preceding example, annual depreciation expense is less if it is based on the truck's $53,000 cost basis than if it is based on the truck's $55,000 cash price. Thus, future net income per year will be larger.

In Illustration 11.1, we summarize the rules for recording nonmonetary asset exchanges.

Note to the Student
Why do accountants not recognize a gain on an exchange of a similar asset? Answer: 1. Accountants substituted one plant asset for another plant asset with a similar production function. 2. By postponing the recognition of the gain, they are applying the conservatism principle.

Reinforcing Problems
E11-4 Record exchange of automobiles.
E11-5 Record variety of cases involving sale, retirement, or exchange of equipment.

Uses of Technology Although sophisticated computer systems automatically compute the gain or loss on the disposal of assets, such programs depend on human input. If an error was made in inputting the type of disposal or exchange, or if the life of the asset was estimated inaccurately, the calculated gain or loss would be incorrect.

An Accounting Perspective

Illustration 11.1   Summary of Rules for Recording Exchanges of Plant Assets

	Exchanges Having Commercial Substance	Exchanges NOT Having Commercial Substance
Recognize Gains?	Yes	No
Recognize Losses?	Yes	No
Record New Asset At:	Fair market value of asset received (new asset) or fair market value of asset given up (old asset), whichever is more clearly evident	Book value of old asset plus cash paid

Removal Costs

Companies incur removal costs when dismantling and removing old plant assets. They deduct these costs from salvage proceeds to determine the asset's net salvage value. (The removal costs could be greater than the salvage proceeds.) Accountants associate removal costs with the old asset, not the new asset acquired as a replacement.

The next section discusses natural resources. Note the underlying accounting principle of matching the expenses with the revenues earned in that same accounting period.

Natural Resources

Real World Example
Weyerhaeuser Company depletes its investment in timber based on the total timber that will be available during the estimated growth cycle.

Resources supplied by nature, such as ore deposits, mineral deposits, oil reserves, gas deposits, and timber stands, are **natural resources** or **wasting assets**. Natural resources represent inventories of raw materials that can be consumed (exhausted) through extraction or removal from their natural setting (e.g., removing oil from the ground).

On the balance sheet, we classify natural resources as a separate group among non-current assets under headings such as "Timber stands" and "Oil reserves." Typically, we record natural resources at their cost of acquisition plus exploration and development costs; on the balance sheet, we report them at total cost less accumulated depletion. (Accumulated depletion is similar to the accumulated depreciation used for plant assets.) When analyzing the financial condition of companies owning natural resources, exercise caution because the historical costs reported for the natural resources may be only a small fraction of their current value.

An Accounting Perspective

Business Insight Anadarko Petroleum Corporation is a global energy and chemical company engaged in oil and gas exploration and production. In notes to its financial statements, Anadarko states that the company complies with disclosure requirements issued by the Securities and Exchange Commission in 2008 regarding the definition of proved oil and gas reserves. The rules require estimates of proved reserves using technologies that have been demonstrated to result in reliable conclusions about reserve volumes.

Depletion is the exhaustion that results from the physical removal of a part of a natural resource. In each accounting period, the depletion recognized is an estimate of the cost of the natural resource that was removed from its natural setting during the period. To record depletion, debit a Depletion account and credit an Accumulated Depletion account, which is a contra account to the natural resource asset account.

By crediting the Accumulated Depletion account instead of the asset account, we continue to report the original cost of the entire natural resource on the financial statements. Thus, statement users can see the percentage of the resource that has been removed. To determine the total cost of the resource available, we combine this depletion cost with other extraction, mining, or removal costs. We can assign this total cost to either the cost of natural resources sold or the inventory of the natural resource still on hand. Thus, we could expense all, some, or none of the depletion and removal costs recognized in an accounting period, depending on the portion sold. If all of the resource is sold, we expense all of the depletion and removal costs. The cost of any portion not yet sold is part of the cost of inventory.

Computing Periodic Depletion Cost To compute depletion charges, companies usually use the units-of-production method. They divide total cost by the estimated number of units—tons, barrels, or board feet—that can be economically extracted from the property. This calculation provides a per-unit depletion cost. For example, assume that in 2012 a company paid $650,000 for a tract of land containing ore deposits. The company spent $100,000 in exploration costs. The results indicated that approximately 900,000 tons of ore can be removed economically from the land, after which the land will be worth $50,000. The company incurred costs of $200,000 to develop the site, including the cost of running power lines and building roads. The total cost subject to depletion is the net cost assignable to the natural resource plus the exploration and development costs.

Objective 3
Determine the periodic depletion cost of a natural resource and calculate depreciation of plant assets located on extractive industry property.

When the property is purchased, a journal entry assigns the purchase price to the two assets purchased—the natural resource and the land. The entry would be:

Land	50,000	
Ore Deposits	600,000	
Cash		650,000
To record purchase of land and mine.		

After the purchase, an entry debits all costs to develop the site (including exploration) to the natural resource account. The entry would be:

Ore Deposits ($100,000 + $200,000)	300,000	
Cash		300,000
To record costs of exploration and development.		

The formula for finding depletion cost per unit is:

$$\text{Depletion cost per unit} = \frac{\text{Cost of site} - \text{Residual value of land (if owned)} + \text{Costs to develop site}}{\text{Estimated number of units that can be economically extracted}}$$

In some instances, companies buy only the right to extract the natural resource from someone else's land. *When the land is not purchased, its residual value is irrelevant and should be ignored.* If there is an obligation to restore the land to a usable condition, the firm adds these estimated restoration costs to the costs to develop the site.

In the example where the land was purchased, the total costs of the mineral deposits equal the cost of the site ($650,000) minus the residual value of land ($50,000) plus costs to develop the site ($300,000), or a total of $900,000. The unit (per ton) depletion charge is $1 (or $900,000/900,000 tons).

The formula to compute the depletion cost of a period is:

$$\text{Depletion cost of a period} = \text{Depletion cost per unit} \quad \text{X} \quad \text{Number of units extracted during period}$$

In this example, if 100,000 tons are mined in 2012, this entry records the depletion cost of $100,000 ($1 × 100,000) for the period:

Depletion	100,000	
Accumulated Depletion—Ore Deposits[4]		100,000
To record depletion for 2012.		

The Depletion account contains the "in the ground" cost of the ore or natural resource mined. Combined with other extractive costs, this cost determines the total cost of the ore mined. To illustrate, assume that in addition to the $100,000 depletion cost, mining labor costs totaled $320,000, and other mining costs, such as depreciation, property taxes, power, and supplies, totaled $60,000. If 80,000 tons were sold and 20,000 remained on hand at the end of the period, the firm would allocate the total cost of $480,000 as follows:

Note to the Student
Notice that the cost per ton is the same for the ore sold and the ore in ending inventory. Remember that depletion costs, labor costs, and other mining costs are included in both computations.

Depletion cost	$100,000
Mining labor costs	320,000
Other mining costs	60,000
Total cost of 100,000 tons mined ($4.80 per ton)	$480,000
Less: Ore inventory (20,000 tons at $4.80)	96,000
Cost of ore sold (80,000 tons at $4.80)	$384,000

Note that the average cost per ton to mine 100,000 tons was $4.80 (or $480,000/100,000). The income statement would show cost of ore sold of $384,000. The mining company does not report depletion separately as an expense because depletion is included in cost of ore sold. The balance sheet would show inventory of ore on hand (a current asset) at $96,000 (or $4.80 × 20,000). Also, it would report the cost less accumulated depletion of the natural resource as follows:

Reinforcing Problems
E11-6 Compute depletion cost per ton.
E11-7 Determine depletion cost and expense.

Ore deposits	$900,000	
Less: Accumulated Depletion	100,000	$800,000

Another method of calculating depletion cost is the percentage of revenue method. Because firms use this method only for income tax purposes and not for financial statements, we do not discuss it in this text.

Depreciation of Plant Assets Located on Extractive Industry Property

Companies depreciate plant assets erected on extractive industry property in the same way as other depreciable assets. If such assets will be abandoned when the natural resource is exhausted, they depreciate these assets over the shorter of the (*a*) physical

---

[4]Instead of crediting the accumulated depletion account, the Ore Deposits account could have been credited directly. But for reasons indicated earlier, the credit is usually to an accumulated depletion account.

life of the asset or (*b*) life of the natural resource. In many cases, firms compute periodic depreciation charges using the units-of-production method. Using this method matches the life of the plant asset with the life of the natural resource. This method is recommended where the *physical* life of the plant asset equals or exceeds the resource's life but its *useful* life is limited to the life of the natural resource.

Assume a mining company acquires mining property with a building it plans to use only in the mining operations. Also assume that the firm uses the units-of-production method for computing building depreciation. Relevant facts are:

Building cost	$310,000
Estimated physical life of building	20 years
Estimated salvage value of building (after mine is exhausted)	$ 10,000
Capacity of mine	1,000,000 tons
Expected life of mine	10 years

Because the life of the mine (10 years or 1,000,000 tons) is shorter than the life of the building (20 years), the building should be depreciated over the life of the mine. The basis of the depreciation charge is tons of ore rather than years because the mine's life could be longer or shorter than 10 years, depending on how rapidly the ore is removed.

Suppose that during the first year of operations, workers extracted 150,000 tons of ore. Building depreciation for the first year is $45,000, computed as follows:

$$\text{Depreciation per unit} = \frac{\text{Asset cost} - \text{Estimated salvage value}}{\text{Total tons of ore in mine that can be economically extracted}}$$

$$= \frac{\$310,000 - \$10,000}{1,000,000 \text{ tons}} = \$0.30 \text{ per ton}$$

$$\text{Depreciation for year} = \text{Depreciation per unit} \quad \text{X} \quad \text{Units extracted}$$

$$= \$0.30 \text{ per ton X } 150,000 \text{ tons} = \$45,000$$

Reinforcing Problem
E11-8 Compute depreciation charge of a plant asset used for mining purposes.

On the income statement, depreciation on the building appears as part of the cost of ore sold and is carried as part of inventory cost for ore not sold during the period. On the balance sheet, accumulated depreciation on the building appears with the related asset account.

Plant assets and natural resources are tangible assets used by a company to produce revenues. A company also may acquire intangible assets to assist in producing revenues.

Intangible Assets

Although they have no physical characteristics, **intangible assets** have value because of the advantages or exclusive privileges and rights they provide to a business. Intangible assets generally arise from two sources: (1) exclusive privileges granted by governmental authority or by legal contract, such as patents, copyrights, franchises, trademarks and trade names, and leases; and (2) superior entrepreneurial capacity or management know-how and customer loyalty, which is called *goodwill.*

All intangible assets are nonphysical, but not all nonphysical assets are intangibles. For example, accounts receivable and prepaid expenses are nonphysical, yet classified as current assets rather than intangible assets. Intangible assets are generally both nonphysical and noncurrent; they appear in a separate long-term section of the balance sheet titled "Intangible assets."

Acquisition of Intangible Assets

Objective 4
Prepare entries for the acquisition and amortization of intangible assets.

Note to the Student
The acquisition cost includes only outright costs such as the legal costs of an intangible asset. The acquisition cost does not include the cost of internal development of self-created assets.

International Reporting
Under IFRS, research expenditures must be expensed as they are incurred. However, in certain circumstances, development costs may be capitalized.

Initially, firms record intangible assets at cost like most other assets. However, computing an intangible asset's acquisition cost differs from computing a plant asset's acquisition cost. Firms may include only outright purchase costs in the acquisition cost of an intangible asset; *the acquisition cost does not include cost of internal development or self-creation of the asset.* If an intangible asset is internally generated in its entirety, none of its costs are capitalized. Therefore, some companies have extremely valuable assets that may not even be recorded in their asset accounts. To explain the reasons for this practice, we discuss the history of accounting for research and development costs next.

Research and development (R&D) costs are costs incurred in a planned search for new knowledge and in translating such knowledge into new products or processes. Prior to 1975, businesses often capitalized research and development costs as intangible assets when future benefits were expected from their incurrence. Due to the difficulty of determining the costs applicable to future benefits, many companies expensed all such costs as incurred. Other companies capitalized those costs that related to proven products and expensed the rest as incurred.

As a result of these varied accounting practices, in 1974 the Financial Accounting Standards Board in *Statement No. 2* (codified as ASC 730) ruled that firms must expense all research and development costs when incurred, unless they were directly reimbursable by government agencies and others. Immediate expensing is justified on the grounds that (1) the amount of costs applicable to the future cannot be measured with any high degree of precision; (2) doubt exists as to whether any future benefits will be received; and (3) even if benefits are expected, they cannot be measured. Thus, research and development costs no longer appear as intangible assets on the balance sheet. The Board applies the same line of reasoning to other costs associated with internally generated intangible assets, such as the internal costs of developing a patent.

Amortization of Intangible Assets

Amortization is the systematic write-off of the cost of an intangible asset to expense. A portion of an intangible asset's cost is allocated to each accounting period in the economic (useful) life of the asset. Not all intangible assets are not subject to amortization. Only recognized intangible assets with finite useful lives are amortized. The **finite useful life** of such an asset is considered to be the length of time it is expected to contribute to the cash flows of the reporting entity. (Pertinent factors that should be considered in estimating useful life include legal, regulatory, or contractual provisions that may limit the useful life.) The method of amortization should be based upon the pattern in which the economic benefits are used up or consumed. If no pattern is apparent, the straight-line method of amortization should be used by the reporting entity.

Recognized intangible assets deemed to have indefinite useful lives are not to be amortized. Amortization will, however, begin when it is determined that the useful life is no longer indefinite. The method of amortization would follow the same rules as intangible assets with finite useful lives.[5]

Straight-line amortization is calculated the same way as straight-line depreciation for plant assets. Generally, we record amortization by debiting Amortization Expense and crediting the intangible asset account. An accumulated amortization account could be used to record amortization. However, the information gained from such accounting would not be significant because normally intangibles do not account for as many total asset dollars as do plant assets.

Patents

A **patent** is a right granted by the federal government. This exclusive right enables the owner to manufacture, sell, lease, or otherwise benefit from an invention for a limited period. The value of a patent lies in its ability to produce revenue. Patents have a legal life of 20 years. Protection for the patent owner begins at the time of patent application and lasts for 20 years from the date the patent is granted.

---

[5]FASB, SFAS No. 142. " Goodwill and Other Intangible Assets" (CT: FASB, June 2006), par. 11 (ASC 350).

When purchasing a patent, a company records it in the Patents account at cost. The firm also debits the Patents account for the cost of the first successful defense of the patent in lawsuits (assuming an outside law firm was hired rather than using internal legal staff). Such a lawsuit establishes the validity of the patent and thereby increases its service potential. In addition, the firm debits the cost of any competing patents purchased to ensure the revenue-generating capability of its own patent to the Patents account.

The firm would amortize the cost of a purchased patent over its finite life which reasonably would not exceed its legal life. If a patent cost $40,000 and has a useful life of 10 years, the journal entries to record the patent and periodic amortization are:

Patents	40,000	
Cash		40,000
To record purchases of patent.		
Patent Amortization Expense	4,000	
Patents		4,000
To record annual patent amortization.		

For a patent that becomes worthless before it is fully amortized, the company expenses the unamortized balance in the Patents account.

As noted earlier, all R&D costs incurred in the internal development of a product, process, or idea that is later patented must be expensed, rather than capitalized. In the previous example, the company amortized the cost of the purchased patent over its useful life of 10 years. If the patent had been the result of an internally generated product or process, the firm would have expensed its cost of $40,000 as incurred, in accordance with *Statement No. 2* of the Financial Accounting Standards Board.

A **copyright** is an exclusive right granted by the federal government giving protection against the illegal reproduction by others of the creator's written works, designs, and literary productions. As a general rule, for works created after January 1, 1978, copyright protection lasts for the life of the creator plus 70 years. Most publications have a limited (finite) life; a creator may amortize the cost of the copyright to expense on a straight-line basis or based upon the pattern in which the economic benefits are used up or consumed.

A **franchise** is a contract between two parties granting the franchisee (the purchaser of the franchise) certain rights and privileges ranging from name identification to complete monopoly of service. In many instances, both parties are private businesses. For example, an individual who wishes to open a hamburger restaurant may purchase a McDonald's franchise; the two parties involved are the individual business owner and McDonald's Corporation. This franchise would allow the business owner to use the McDonald's name and golden arch, and it would provide the owner with advertising and many other benefits. The legal life of a franchise may be limited by contract.

The parties involved in a franchise arrangement are not always private businesses. A government agency may grant a franchise to a private company. A city may give a franchise to a utility company, giving the utility company the exclusive right to provide service to a particular area.

In addition to providing benefits, a franchise usually places certain restrictions on the franchisee. These restrictions generally are related to rates or prices charged; also they may be in regard to product quality or to the particular supplier from whom supplies and inventory items must be purchased.

Reinforcing Problem
E11-9 Determine patent cost and periodic amortization.

Copyrights

Real World Example
Mattel, Inc., holds the copyright for Barbie dolls and has defended this copyright against infringement on several occasions.

Franchises

Reinforcing Problem
E11-10 Record franchise; record accrued franchise fees and franchise amortization.

---

[6]In 1998 Congress changed the period from 50 to 70 years. At this writing, the Supreme Court was reviewing the constitutionality of this change.

If periodic payments to the grantor of the franchise are required, the franchisee debits them to a Franchise Expense account. If a lump-sum payment is made to obtain the franchise, the franchisee records the cost in an asset account titled "Franchise" and amortizes it over the finite useful life of the asset. The legal life (if limited by contract) and the economic life of the franchise may limit the finite useful life.

A **trademark** is a symbol, design, or logo used in conjunction with a particular product or company. A **trade name** is a brand name under which a product is sold or a company does business. Often trademarks and trade names are extremely valuable to a company, but if they have been internally developed, they have no recorded asset cost. However, when a business purchases such items from an external source, it records them at cost and amortizes them over their finite useful life.

A **lease** is a contract to rent property. The property owner is the grantor of the lease and is the *lessor.* The person or company obtaining rights to possess and use the property is the *lessee.* The rights granted under the lease are a **leasehold**. The accounting for a lease depends on whether it is a capital lease or an operating lease.

Capital Leases   A **capital lease** transfers to the lessee virtually all rewards and risks that accompany ownership of property. A lease is a capital lease if, among other provisions, it (1) transfers ownership of the leased property to the lessee at the end of the lease term or (2) contains a bargain purchase option that permits the lessee to buy the property at a price significantly below fair market value at the end of the lease term.

A capital lease is a means of financing property acquisitions; it has the same economic impact as a purchase made on an installment plan. Thus, the lessee in a capital lease must record the leased property as an asset and the lease obligation as a liability. Because a capital lease is an asset, the lessee depreciates the leased property over its useful life. The lessee records part of each lease payment as interest expense and the balance as a payment on the lease liability.

The proper accounting for capital leases for both lessees and lessors has been an extremely difficult problem. We leave further discussion of capital leases for an intermediate accounting text.

Operating Leases   A lease that does not qualify as a capital lease is an **operating lease.** A one-year lease on an apartment and a week's rental of an automobile are examples of operating leases. Such leases make no attempt to transfer any of the rewards and risks of ownership to the lessee. As a result, there may be no recordable transaction when a lease is signed.

In some situations, the lease may call for an immediate cash payment that must be recorded. Assume that a business signed a lease requiring the immediate payment of the annual rent of $15,000 for each of the first and fifth years of a five-year lease. The lessee would record the payment as follows:

Prepaid Rent	15,000	
Leasehold	15,000	
Cash		30,000
To record first and fifth years' rent on a five-year lease.		

Since the Leasehold account is actually a long-term prepaid rent account for the fifth year's annual rent, it is an intangible asset until the beginning of the fifth year. Then the Leasehold account becomes a current asset and may be transferred into a Prepaid Rent

Trademarks; Trade Names

Real World Example
McDonald's and its golden arches are familiar to us all. McDonald's is the company's trade name and the golden arches, its trademark.

Leases

International Reporting
Under IFRS, leases are classified as being either "finance leases" (which are capitalized) or operating leases. The classification of leases under IFRS is more a matter of substance than of form. As a result, IFRS require more leases to be capitalized than under U.S. GAAP.

Reinforcing Problem
E11-11 Record leasehold; record rent accrued and leasehold amortization.

account. Accounting for the balance in the Leasehold account depends on the terms of the lease. In the previous example, the firm would charge the $15,000 in the Leasehold account to expense over the fifth year only. It would charge the balance in Prepaid Rent to expense in the first year. Thus, assuming the lease year and fiscal year coincide, the entry for the first year is:

Rent Expense	15,000	
Prepaid Rent		15,000
To record rent expense.		

The entry in the fifth year is:

Rent Expense	15,000	
Leasehold		15,000
To record rent expense.		

The accounting for the second, third, and fourth years would be the same as for the first year. The lessee records the rent in Prepaid Rent when paid in advance for the year and then expenses it. As stated above, the lessee may transfer the amount in the Leasehold account to Prepaid Rent at the beginning of the fifth year by debiting Prepaid Rent and crediting Leasehold. If that entry had been made at the beginning of the fifth year, the entry at the end of year five would have credited Prepaid Rent.

In some cases, when a lease is signed, the lump-sum payment does not cover a specific year's rent. The lessee debits this payment to the Leasehold account and amortizes it over the life of the lease. The straight-line method is required unless another method can be shown to be superior. Assume the $15,000 rent for the fifth year in the example was, instead, a lump-sum payment on the lease in addition to the annual rent payments. An annual adjusting entry to amortize the $15,000 over five years would read:

Rent Expense	3,000	
Leasehold		3,000
To amortize leasehold.		

In this example, the annual rental expense is $18,000: $15,000 annual cash rent plus $3,000 amortization of leasehold ($15,000/5).

The lessee may base periodic rent on current-year sales or usage rather than being a constant amount. For example, if a lease called for rent equal to 5% of current-year sales and sales were $400,000 in 2012, the rent for 2012 would be $20,000. The rent would either be paid or an adjusting entry would be made at the end of the year.

A **leasehold improvement** is any physical alteration made by the lessee to the leased property in which benefits are expected beyond the current accounting period. Leasehold improvements made by a lessee usually become the property of the lessor after the lease has expired. However, since leasehold improvements are an asset of the lessee during the lease period, the lessee debits them to a Leasehold Improvements account. The lessee then amortizes the leasehold improvements to expense over the period benefited by the improvements. The amortization period for leasehold improvements should be the shorter of the life of the improvements or the life of the lease. If the lease can (and probably will) be renewed at the option of the lessee, the life of the lease should include the option period.

As an illustration, assume that on January 2, 2012, Wolf Company leases a building for 20 years under a nonrenewable lease at an annual rental of $20,000,

Leasehold Improvements

payable on each December 31. Wolf immediately incurs a cost of $80,000 for improvements to the building, such as interior walls for office separation, ceiling fans, and recessed lighting. The improvements have an estimated life of 30 years. The company should amortize the $80,000 over the 20-year lease period, since that period is shorter than the life of the improvements, and Wolf cannot use the improvements beyond the life of the lease. If only annual financial statements are prepared, the following journal entry properly records the rental expense for the year ended December 31, 2012:

Rent Expense (or Leasehold Improvement Expense)	4,000	
Leasehold Improvements		4,000
To record amortization of leasehold improvement.		
Rent Expense	20,000	
Cash		20,000
To record annual rent.		

Thus, the total cost to rent the building each year equals the $20,000 cash rent plus the amortization of the leasehold improvements.

Although leaseholds are intangible assets, leaseholds and leasehold improvements sometimes appear in the property, plant, and equipment section of the balance sheet.

Goodwill

Note to the Student
Goodwill can only be recorded when a business or a part of a business has been purchased. Goodwill cannot be purchased separately nor can it be generated internally.

In accounting, **goodwill** is an intangible value attached to a company resulting mainly from the company's management skill or know-how and a favorable reputation with customers. A company's value may be greater than the total of the fair market value of its tangible and identifiable intangible assets. This greater value means that the company generates an above-average income on each dollar invested in the business. Thus, proof of a company's goodwill is its ability to generate superior earnings or income.

A Goodwill account appears in the accounting records only if goodwill has been purchased. A company cannot purchase goodwill by itself; it must buy an entire business or a part of a business to obtain the accompanying intangible asset, goodwill.

To illustrate, assume that Lenox Company purchased all of Martin Company's assets for $700,000. Lenox also agreed to assume responsibility for a $350,000 mortgage note payable owed by Martin. Goodwill is the difference between the amount paid for the business including the debt assumed ($700,000 + $350,000 = $1,050,000) and the fair market value of the assets purchased. Notice that Lenox would use the fair market value of the assets rather than book value to determine the amount of goodwill. The following computation is for the goodwill purchased by Lenox:

Cash paid		$ 700,000
Mortgage note payable		350,000
Total price paid		$1,050,000
Less fair market values of individually identifiable assets:		
Accounts receivable	$ 95,000	
Merchandise inventory	100,000	
Land	240,000	
Buildings	275,000	
Equipment	200,000	
Patents	65,000	975,000
Goodwill		$ 75,000

Reinforcing Problem
E11-12 Determine the amount of goodwill.

The $75,000 is the goodwill Lenox records as an intangible asset; it records all of the other assets at their fair market values, and the liability at the amount due.

Illustration 11.2   Partial Balance Sheet

ANY COMPANY
Partial Balance Sheet
June 30, 2012

Property, plant, and equipment			
Land		$ 30,000	
Buildings	$ 75,000		
Less: Accumulated depreciation	45,000	30,000	
Equipment	$ 9,000		
Less: Accumulated depreciation	1,500	7,500	
Total property, plant, and equipment			$ 67,500
Natural resources:			
Mineral deposits		$300,000	
Less: Accumulated depletion		100,000	
Total natural resources			$200,000
Intangible assets:			
Patents		$ 10,000	
Goodwill		20,000	
Total intangible assets			$ 30,000

Specific reasons for a company's goodwill include a good reputation, customer loyalty, superior product design, unrecorded intangible assets (because they were developed internally), and superior human resources. Since these positive factors are not individually quantifiable, when grouped together they constitute *goodwill*. The journal entry to record the purchase is:

Accounts Receivable	95,000	
Merchandise Inventory	100,000	
Land	240,000	
Buildings	275,000	
Equipment	200,000	
Patents	65,000	
Goodwill	75,000	
Cash		700,000
Mortgage Note Payable		350,000
To record the purchase of Martin Company's assets and assumption of mortgage note payable.		

The intangible asset goodwill is not amortized. Goodwill is to be tested periodically for impairment. The amount of any goodwill impairment loss is to recognized in the income statement as a separate line before the subtotal income from continuing operations (or similar caption)[6]. The goodwill account would be reduced by the same amount[7].

Look at Illustration 11.2, a partial balance sheet for ANY Company. Unlike plant assets or natural resources, intangible assets usually are a net amount in the balance sheet.

Balance Sheet Presentation

---

[6]Discussion of testing for impairment is beyond the scope of this text. For more information on such testing see SFAS No. 142 (ASC 350)
[7]SFAS No. 142. par. 18.

Analyzing and Using The Financial Results— Total Assets Turnover

Objective 5
Analyze and use the financial results—total assets turnover.

In determining the productivity of assets, management may compare one year's assets turnover ratio to a previous year's. **Total assets turnover** shows the relationship between the dollar volume of sales and the average total assets used in the business. To calculate this ratio:

$$\text{Total assets turnover} = \frac{\text{Net Sales}}{\text{Average total assets}}$$

The Procter & Gamble Company
markets more than 300 brands. Examples include Tide, Ariel, Pantene, Folger's, and Pampers.

This ratio indicates the efficiency with which a company uses its assets to generate sales. When the ratio is low relative to industry standards or the company's ratio in previous years, it could indicate an overinvestment in assets, a slow year in sales, or both. Thus, if the ratio is relatively low and there was no significant decrease in sales during the current year, management should identify and dispose of any inefficient equipment.

The total assets turnover in a recent year for several actual companies was as follows:

Tyco International
manufactures security and fire protection products, valves and controls, and other industrial products worldwide.

Company	Net Sales ($ thousands)	Total Assets ($ thousands)			Turnover
		Beginning of Year	End of Year	Average	
Procter & Gamble	$ 82,559,000	$ 128,172,000	$ 138,354,000	$ 133,263,000	61.95%
Tyco International	17,355,900	27,128,000	26,777,000	26,952,500	64.39%
Kimball International	1,202,597	636,751	626,312	631,531	190.43%

Kimball International, Inc.
manufactures and markets a broad range of diversified consumer durable products including furniture and electronics.

These three companies compete in very different industries. However, they are all manufacturers. To see if each of these companies is performing above standard, management should compare its company's percentage to the industry's standard. In addition, calculating this ratio over approximately five years would help management see any trends indicating problems or confirm successful asset management.

This chapter concludes your study of accounting for long-term assets. In Chapter 12, you learn about classes of capital stock.

Understanding the Learning Objectives

Objective 1
Calculate and prepare entries for the sale, retirement, and destruction of plant assets.

- By comparing an asset's book value (cost less up-to-date accumulated depreciation) with its sales price, the company may show either a gain or a loss. If sales price is greater than book value, the company shows a gain. If sales price is less than book value, the company shows a loss. If sales price equals book value, no gain or loss results.
- When a plant asset is retired from service, the asset's cost and accumulated depreciation must be removed from the plant asset accounts.
- Plant assets are sometimes wrecked in accidents or destroyed by fire, flood, storm, and other causes. If the asset was not insured, the loss is equal to the book value. If the asset was insured, only the amount of the loss exceeding the amount to be recovered from the insurance company would be debited to a loss account.

Objective 2
Describe and record exchanges of nonmonetary assets.

- In exchanges of nonmonetary assets having commercial substance, the firm records the asset received at either (1) the stated cash price of the new asset or (if the cash price is not stated) (2) the known fair market value of the asset given up plus any cash paid.
- In exchanges of nonmonetary assets not having commercial substance, the firm records the new asset at the book value of the old asset plus the cash paid.

A Ethical Perspective

ABC Corporation

In 2007, prior to the tax law change permitting the amortization of goodwill for tax purposes, ABC Corporation acquired XYZ Company for $10,000,000 cash. ABC acquired the following assets:

Accounts receivable		$80,000

	Old Book Value	Fair Market Value
Merchandise inventory	$ 200,000	$ 300,000
Buildings	3,000,000	4,000,000
Land	1,000,000	3,000,000
Equipment	500,000	700,000

An experienced appraiser with an excellent reputation established the fair market value of the assets. ABC also assumed the liability for paying XYZ's $50,000 of accounts payable.

John Gilbert, ABC's accountant, prepared the following journal entry to record the purchase:

Accounts Receivable	80,000	
Merchandise Inventory	300,000	
Buildings	4,000,000	
Land	3,000,000	
Equipment	700,000	
Goodwill	1,970,000	
Accounts Payable		50,000
Cash		10,000,000
To record the purchase of XYZ Company.		

In explaining the entry to ABC's president, Gilbert said that the assets had to be recorded at their fair market values. He also stated that the goodwill could not be amortized for accounting purposes or tax purposes.

The president reacted with, 'It's not fair that we are prohibited from amortizing goodwill when it is a part of the cost of the purchase. Besides, appraisals are very inexact, and maybe some of our other assets are worth more than the one appraiser indicated. I want you to reduce goodwill down to $470,000 and assign the other $1,500,000 to the buildings and equipment. Then, we can benefit from the depreciation on these assets. If I need to find an appraiser who will support the new allocations, I will.'

When Gilbert protested, the president stated, 'If you are going to have a future with us, you need to be a team player. We just can't afford to lose those tax deductions.' Gilbert feared that if he did not go along, he would soon be unemployed.

- Depletion charges usually are computed by the units-of-production method. Total cost is divided by the estimated number of units that are economically extractable from the property. This calculation provides a per unit depletion cost that is multiplied by the units extracted each year to obtain the depletion cost for that year.
- Depreciable assets located on extractive industry property should be depreciated over the shorter of the (1) physical life of the asset or (2) life of the natural resource. The periodic depreciation charges usually are computed using the units-of-production method. Using this method matches the life of the plant asset with the life of the natural resource.

> **Objective 3**
> Determine the periodic depletion cost of a natural resource and calculate depreciation of plant assets located on extractive industry property.

- Only outright purchase costs are included in the acquisition cost of an intangible asset. If an intangible asset is internally generated, its cost is immediately expensed.
- Intangibles should be amortized over their finite useful lives. The method of amortization should be based upon the pattern in which the economic benefits are used up. If no pattern is apparent, straight-line amortization should be used

- $$\text{Total assets turnover} = \frac{\text{Net Sales}}{\text{Average total assets}}$$

- This ratio indicates the efficiency with which a company uses its assets to generate sales.

Demonstration Problem 11–A

On January 2, 2009, Darton Company purchased a machine for $36,000 cash. The machine has an estimated useful life of six years and an estimated salvage value of $1,800. Darton uses the straight-line method of depreciation.

Required

a. Compute the book value of the machine as of July 1, 2012.
b. Assume the machine was disposed of on July 1, 2012. Prepare the journal entries to record the disposal of the machine under each of the following unrelated assumptions:
   (1) The machine was sold for $12,000 cash.
   (2) The machine was sold for $18,000 cash.
   (3) The machine and $24,000 cash were exchanged for a new machine that had a cash price of $39,000. The exchange has commercial substance.
   (4) The machine was completely destroyed by fire. Darton expects to recover cash of $10,800 from the insurance company.

Solution to Demonstration Problem 11–A

a.

DARTON COMPANY
Schedule to Compute Book Value
July 1, 2012

Cost	$ 36,000
Less accumulated depreciation:	
$\frac{\$36,000 - \$1,800}{6 \text{ years}}$ = $5,700 per year	
$5,700 X 3-1/2 years = $19,950	19,950
Book value	$ 16,050

b. (1)

Cash	12,000	
Accumulated Depreciation—Machinery	19,950	
Loss from Disposal of Plant Assets	4,050	
Machinery		36,000
To record the sale of machinery at loss.		

(2)

Cash	18,000	
Accumulated Depreciation—Machinery	19,950	
Machinery		36,000
Gain on Disposal of Plant Assets		1,950
To record sale of machinery at a gain.		

(3)	Machinery (new)	39,000	
	Accumulated Depreciation—Machinery	19,950	
	Loss from Disposal of Plant Asset	1,050	
	Machinery (old)		36,000
	Cash		24,000
	To record exchange of machines.		

The exchange has commercial substance.

(4)	Receivable from Insurance Company	10,800	
	Accumulated Depreciation—Machinery	19,950	
	Fire Loss	5,250	
	Machinery		36,000
	To record loss of machinery.		

Demonstration Problem 11–B

Howard Company acquired on January 1, 2012, a tract of property containing timber at a cost of $8,000,000. After the timber is removed, the land will be worth about $3,200,000 and will be sold to another party. Costs of developing the site were $800,000. A building was erected at a cost of $160,000. The building had an estimated physical life of 20 years and will have an estimated salvage value of $80,000 when the timber is gone. It was expected that 50,000,000 board feet of timber can be economically cut. During the first year, 16,000,000 board feet were cut. Howard uses the units-of-production basis to depreciate the building.

Prepare the entries to record: ☛ *Required*
  a. The acquisition of the property.
  b. The development costs.
  c. Depletion cost for the first year.
  d. Depreciation on the building for the first year.

Solution to Demonstration Problem 11–B

a.	Land	3,200,000	
	Timber Stands	4,800,000	
	Cash		8,000,000
	To record purchase of land and timber.		

b.	Timber Stands	800,000	
	Cash		800,000
	To record costs of development of the site.		

c.	Depletion	1,792,000	
	Accumulated Depletion—Timber Stands		1,792,000
	To record depletion for 2012.		
	($4,800,000 + $800,000/50,000,000 = $0.112 per board foot.		
	$0.112 X 16,000,000 = $1,792,000.)		

d.	Depreciation Expense—Buildings	25,600	
	Accumulated Depreciation—Buildings		25,600
	To record depreciation expense:		

$$\frac{\$160,000 - \$80,000}{50,000,000 \text{ board feet}} = \$0.0016 \text{ per board foot.}$$

$0.0016 X 16,000,000 = $25,600.

Demonstration Problem 11–C

On January 2, 2012, Bedford Company purchased a 10-year sublease on a warehouse for $30,000. Bedford will also pay annual rent of $6,000. Bedford immediately incurred costs of $20,000 for improvements to the warehouse, such as lighting fixtures, replacement of a ceiling, heating system, and loading dock. The improvements have an estimated life of 12 years and no residual value.

Required ➡ Prepare the entries to record:
  a. The payment for the sublease on a warehouse.
  b. The rent payment for the first year.
  c. The payment for the improvements.
  d. Amortization of the leasehold for the first year.
  e. Amortization of the leasehold improvements for the first year.

Solution to Demonstration Problem 11–C

a.	Leasehold	30,000	
	Cash		30,000
	To record purchase of sublease on warehouse.		
b.	Rent Expense	6,000	
	Cash		6,000
	To record annual rent payment.		
c.	Leasehold Improvements	20,000	
	Cash		20,000
	To record payment for leasehold improvements.		
d.	Rent Expense	3,000	
	Leasehold		3,000
	To record leasehold amortization for 2012:		

$$\text{Annual amortization} = \frac{\$30,000}{10 \text{ years}}$$
$$= \$3,000$$

e.	Rent Expense	2,000	
	Leasehold Improvements		2,000
	To amortize leasehold improvements:		

$$\text{Annual amortization} = \frac{\$20,000}{10 \text{ years}}$$
$$= \$2,000$$

New Terms

Amortization   The term used to describe the systematic write-off of the cost of an intangible asset to expense. *436*

Capital lease   A lease that transfers to the lessee virtually all of the rewards and risks that accompany ownership of property. *438*

Commercial substance   The result if an exchange of nonmonetary assets causes future cash flows to differ significantly. *429*

Copyright   An exclusive right granted by the federal government giving protection against the illegal reproduction by others of the creator's written works, designs, and literary productions. *437*

Depletion   The exhaustion of a natural resource; an estimate of the cost of the resource that was removed from its natural setting during the period. *433*

Finite Useful Life   Length of time an intangible asset is expected to contribute to the cash flows of the entity. *436*

Franchise   A contract between two parties granting the franchisee (the purchaser of the franchise) certain rights and privileges ranging from name identification to complete monopoly of service. *437*

Goodwill   An intangible value attached to a company resulting mainly from the company's management skill or know-how and a favorable reputation with customers. Evidenced by the ability to generate an above-average rate of income on each dollar invested in the business. *440*

Intangible assets   Items that have no physical characteristics but are of value because of the advantages or exclusive privileges and rights they provide to a business. *435*

Lease   A contract to rent property. Grantor of the lease is the lessor; the party obtaining the rights to possess and use property is the lessee. *438*

Leasehold   The rights granted under a lease. *438*

Leasehold improvement   Any physical alteration made by the lessee to the leased property in which benefits are expected beyond the current accounting period. *439*

Natural resources   Resources supplied by nature, such as ore deposits, mineral deposits, oil reserves, gas deposits, and timber stands supplied by nature. *432*

Operating lease   A lease that does not qualify as a capital lease. *438*

Patent   A right granted by the federal government giving the owner the exclusive right to manufacture, sell, lease, or otherwise benefit from an invention for a limited period. *436*

Research and development (R&D) costs   Costs incurred in a planned search for new knowledge and in translating such knowledge into a new product or process. *436*

Total assets turnover   Equal to Net sales/Average total assets. This ratio indicates the efficiency with which a company uses its assets to generate sales. *442*

Trademark   A symbol, design, or logo used in conjunction with a particular product or company. *438*

Trade name   A brand name under which a product is sold or a company does business. *438*

Wasting assets   See *Natural resources.*

Self-Test

True-False

Indicate whether each of the following statements is true or false.

1. When a plant asset is still being used after it has been fully depreciated, depreciation can be taken in excess of its cost.

2. In an exchange of nonmonetary assets having commercial substance, the new asset is recorded at the fair market value of the asset received or the fair market value of the asset given up plus cash paid, whichever is more clearly evident.

3. In calculating depletion, the residual value of acquired land containing an ore deposit is included in total costs subject to depletion.

4. All recorded intangible assets are subject to amortization.

Multiple-Choice

Select the best answer for each of the following questions.

1. When a fully depreciated asset is still in use:
   a. Prior years' depreciation should be adjusted.
   b. The cost should be adjusted to market value.
   c. Part of the depreciation should be reversed.
   d. The cost and accumulated depreciation should remain in the ledger and no more depreciation should be taken.
   e. It should be written off the books.

2. A truck costing $45,000 and having an estimated salvage value of $4,500 and an original life of five years is exchanged for a new truck. The cash price of the new truck is $57,000, and a trade-in allowance of $22,500 is received. The old truck has been depreciated for three years using the straight-line method. The exchange does not have commercial substance. The new truck would be recorded at:
   a. $55,200.
   b. $57,000.
   c. $34,500.
   d. $43,200.
   e. None of the above.

3. Land containing a mine having an estimated 1,000,000 tons of economically extractable ore is purchased for $375,000. After the ore deposit is removed, the land will be worth $75,000. If 100,000 tons of ore are mined and sold during the first year, the depletion cost charged to expense for the year is:
   a. $300,000.
   b. $37,500.
   c. $30,000.
   d. $375,000.
   e. None of the above.

4. Bren Company purchased a patent for $36,000. The patent is expected to have a finite life of 10 years even though its legal life is 17 years. The amortization for the first year is:
   a. $36,000.
   b. $3,600.
   c. $2,118.
   d. $3,240.
   e. None of the above.

Questions

Now turn to page 457 to check your answers.

1. When depreciable plant assets are sold for cash, how is the gain or loss measured?

2. A plant asset that cost $27,000 and has a related accumulated depreciation account balance of $27,000 is still being used in business operations. Would it be appropriate to continue recording depreciation on this asset? Explain. When should the asset's cost and accumulated depreciation be removed from the accounting records?

3. A machine and $22,500 cash were exchanged for a delivery truck. The exchange has commercial substance. How should the cost basis of the delivery truck be measured?

4. A plant asset was exchanged for a new asset of a similar type. How is the cost of the new asset determined?

5. When nonmonetary assets not having commercial substance are exchanged, a resulting gain is not recognized. Discuss why this is so.

6. What is the proper accounting treatment for the costs of removing or dismantling a company's old plant assets?

7. a. Distinguish between depreciation, depletion, and amortization. Name two assets that are subject to depreciation, to depletion, and to amortization.
   b. Distinguish between tangible and intangible assets, and classify the assets named in part (a) accordingly.

8. A building with an estimated physical life of 40 years was constructed at the site of a coal mine. The coal mine is expected to be completely exhausted within 20 years. Over what length of time should the building be depreciated, assuming the building will be abandoned after all the coal has been extracted?

9. What are the characteristics of intangible assets? Give an example of an asset that has no physical existence but is not classified as an intangible asset.

10. What reasons justify the immediate expensing of most research and development costs?

11. Over what length of time should intangible assets be amortized?

12. Should costs incurred on internally generated intangible assets be capitalized in asset accounts?

13. Describe the typical accounting for a patent.

14. During 2012, Hardy Company incurred $123,000 of research and development costs in its laboratory to develop a patent that was granted on December 29, 2012. Legal fees (outside counsel) and other costs associated with registration of the patent totaled $22,800. What amount should be recorded as a patent on December 29, 2012?

15. What is a capital lease? What features may characterize a capital lease?

16. What is the difference between a leasehold (under an operating lease contract) and a leasehold improvement? Is there any difference in the accounting procedures applicable to each?

17. Walt Company leased a tract of land for 40 years at an agreed annual rental fee of $18,000. The effective date of the lease was July 1, 2011. During the last six months of 2011, Walt constructed a building on the land at a cost of $450,000. The building was placed in operation on January 2, 2012, at which time it was estimated to have a physical life of 50 years. Over what period should the building be depreciated? Why?

18. You note that a certain store seems to have a steady stream of regular customers, a favorable location, courteous employees, high-quality merchandise, and a reputation for fairness in dealing with customers, employees, and suppliers. Does it follow automatically that this business should have goodwill recorded as an asset? Explain.

Exercises

Plant equipment originally costing $32,400, on which $21,600 of up-to-date depreciation has been accumulated, was sold for $8,100.

a. Prepare the journal entry to record the sale.
b. Prepare the entry to record the sale of the equipment if $90 of removal costs were incurred to allow the equipment to be moved.

Exercise 11-1
Record sale of equipment; account for removal costs (L.O. 1)

On August 31, 2011, Hutch Company sold a truck for $6,900 cash. The truck was acquired on January 1, 2008, at a cost of $17,400. Depreciation of $10,800 on the truck has been recorded through December 31, 2010, using the straight-line method, four-year expected useful life, and an expected salvage value of $3,000.

    Prepare the journal entries to update the depreciation on the truck on August 31, 2011, and to record the sale of the truck.

Exercise 11-2
Update depreciation and record sale of truck (L.O. 1)

A machine costing $120,000, on which $90,000 of up-to-date depreciation has been accumulated, was completely destroyed by fire. What journal entry should record the machine's destruction and the resulting fire loss under each of the following unrelated assumptions?

a. The machine was not insured.
b. The machine was insured, and it is estimated that $22,500 will be recovered from the insurance company.

Exercise 11-3
Record the destruction of machinery by fire—uninsured and insured asset (L.O. 1)

Kale Company owned an automobile acquired on January 1, 2009, at a cash cost of $35,100; at that time, the automobile was estimated to have a useful life of four years and a $2,700 salvage value. Depreciation has been recorded through December 31, 2011, on a straight-line basis. On January 1, 2012, the automobile was traded for a new automobile. The old automobile had a fair market value (trade-in allowance) of $6,750. Cash of $31,050 was paid. The exchange has commercial substance.

    Prepare the journal entry to record the trade-in under generally accepted accounting principles.

Exercise 11-4
Record exchange of automobiles (L.O. 2)

Equipment costing $330,000, on which $225,000 of up-to-date accumulated depreciation has been recorded, was disposed of on January 2, 2011. What journal entries are required to record the equipment's disposal under each of the following unrelated assumptions?

a. The equipment was sold for $120,000 cash.
b. The equipment was sold for $87,000 cash.
c. The equipment was retired from service and hauled to the junkyard. No material was salvaged.
d. The equipment was exchanged for similar equipment having a cash price of $450,000. A trade-in allowance of $150,000 from the cash price was received, and the balance was paid in cash. The exchange has no commercial substance.
e. The equipment was exchanged for similar equipment having a cash price of $450,000. A trade-in allowance of $75,000 was received, and the balance was paid in cash. The exchange has commercial substance.

Exercise 11-5
Record variety of cases involving sale, retirement, or exchange of equipment (L.O. 1, 2)

Nola Mining Company purchased a tract of land containing ore for $630,000. After spending $90,000 in exploration costs, the company determined that 600,000 tons of ore existed on the tract but only 500,000 tons could be economically removed. No other costs were incurred. When the company finishes with the tract, it estimates the land will be worth $180,000. Determine the depletion cost per ton.

Exercise 11-6
Compute depletion cost per ton (L.O. 3)

Exercise 11-7
Determine depletion cost and expense (L.O. 3)

Boyd Company paid $7,200,000 for the right to extract all of the mineral-bearing ore, estimated at 10 million tons, that can be economically extracted from a certain tract of land. During the first year, Boyd Company extracted 1,000,000 tons of the ore and sold 800,000 tons. What part of the $7,200,000 should be charged to expense during the first year?

Exercise 11-8
Compute depreciation charge on plant asset used for mining purposes (L.O. 3)

The Slate Mining Company acquired a tract of land for mining purposes and erected a building on-site at a cost of $675,000 and having no salvage value. Though the building has a useful life of 10 years, the mining operations are expected to last only 6 years. The company has determined that 800,000 tons of ore exist on the tract but only 600,000 tons can be economically removed. If 100,000 tons of ore are extracted in the first year of operations, what is the appropriate depreciation charge using the units-of-production method?

Exercise 11-9
Determine patent cost and periodic amortization (L.O. 4)

Talse Company purchased a patent on January 1, 1997, at a total cost of $61,200. In January 2008, the company hired an outside law firm and successfully defended the patent in a lawsuit. The legal fees amounted to $13,500. What will be the amount of patent cost amortized in 2011? (The finite useful life of the patent is the same as its legal life—17 years.)

Exercise 11-10
Record franchise; record accrued franchise fees and franchise amortization (L.O. 4)

Don Jackson paid Hungry Hannah's Hamburgers $54,000 for the right to operate a fast-food restaurant in Thomasville under the Hungry Hannah's name. Jackson also agreed to pay an operating fee of 0.5% of sales for advertising and other services rendered by Hungry Hannah's. Jackson began operations on January 2, 2011. Sales for 2011 amounted to $540,000. The finite useful life of the franchise is 40 years.

Give the entries to record the payment of the $54,000 and to record expenses incurred relating to the right to use the Hungry Hannah's name.

Exercise 11-11
Record leasehold; record rent accrued and leasehold amortization (L.O. 4)

Lem Company leased the first three floors in a building under an operating lease contract for a 10-year period beginning January 1, 2011. The company paid $240,000 in cash (not representing a specific period's rent) and agreed to make annual payments equal to 1% of the first $1,500,000 of sales and 0.5% of all sales over $1,500,000. Sales for 2011 amounted to $4,500,000. Payment of the annual amount will be made in January 2012.

Prepare journal entries to record the cash payment of January 1, 2011, and the proper expense to be recognized for the use of the space in the leased building for 2011.

Exercise 11-12
Determine the amount of goodwill (L.O. 4)

Rye Company purchased all of the assets of Shef Company for $900,000. Rye Company also agreed to assume responsibility for Shef Company's liabilities of $90,000. The fair market value of the assets acquired was $810,000. How much goodwill should be recorded in this transaction? Give the journal entry to record this transaction.

Problems

Problem 11-1
Record exchange of automobiles (L.O. 2)

Orr Company traded in an automobile that cost $18,000 and on which $15,000 of up-to-date depreciation has been recorded for a new automobile with a cash price of $34,500. The company received a trade-in allowance (its fair value) for the old automobile of $2,100 and paid the balance in cash. The exchange has commercial substance.

Required ➡ Record the exchange of automobiles.

Problem 11-2
Update depreciation and record six cases of asset disposal (L.O. 1, 2)

On January 2, 2009, Blake Company purchased a delivery truck for $78,750 cash. The truck has an estimated useful life of six years and an estimated salvage value of $6,750. The straight-line method of depreciation is being used.

Required ➡ **a.** Prepare a schedule showing the computation of the book value of the truck on December 31, 2011.

b. Assume the truck is to be disposed of on July 1, 2012. Prepare the journal entry to record depreciation for the six months ended June 30, 2012.

c. Prepare the journal entries to record the disposal of the truck on July 1, 2012, under each of the following unrelated assumptions:

   1. The truck was sold for $26,250 cash.

   2. The truck was sold for $48,000 cash.

   3. The truck was retired from service, and it is expected that $20,625 will be received from the sale of salvaged materials.

   4. The truck and $60,000 cash were exchanged for office equipment that had a cash price of $105,000. The exchange has commercial substance.

   5. The truck and $67,500 cash were exchanged for a new delivery truck that had a cash price of $112,500. The exchange has no commercial substance.

   6. The truck was completely destroyed in an accident. Cash of $25,500 is expected to be recovered from the insurance company.

Eagle Moving Company purchased a new moving van on October 1, 2011. The cash price of the new van was $33,750, and the company received a trade-in allowance of $5,600 for a 2009 model. The balance was paid in cash. The 2009 model had been acquired on January 1, 2009, at a cost of $22,500. Depreciation has been recorded through December 31, 2010, on a straight-line basis, with three years of expected useful life and no expected salvage value. The exchange has no commercial substance.

Problem 11-3
Update depreciation and record exchange of plant asset for similar asset (L.O. 2)

Prepare journal entries to update the depreciation and to record the exchange of the moving vans.

◗ *Required*

On January 1, 2011, Moyer Company had the following balances in some of its accounts:

Problem 11-4
Record leasehold amortization; record depreciation and trade-in (L.O. 2, 4)

	Asset	Accumulated Depreciation
Land	$ 624,000	
Leasehold	780,000	
Buildings	3,425,760	$ 286,650
Equipment	2,995,200	1,389,960
Trucks	449,280	218,790

1. The leasehold covers a plot of ground leased on January 1, 2007, for a period of 20 years.

◗ *Additional data*

2. Building No. 1 is on the owned land and was completed on July 1, 2010, at a cost of $1,965,600; its life is set at 40 years with no salvage value. Building No. 2 is on the leased land and was completed on July 1, 2007, at a cost of $1,460,160; its life is also set at 40 years with no expected salvage value.

3. The equipment had an expected useful life of eight years with no estimated salvage value.

4. Truck A, purchased on January 1, 2009, at a cost of $149,760, had an expected useful life of 2-1/2 years and a salvage value of $9,360. Truck B, purchased on July 1, 2009, at a cost of $131,040, had an expected life of two years and an estimated salvage value of $21,840. Truck C, purchased on July 1, 2010, at a cost of $168,480, had an expected life of three years and an estimated salvage value of $21,060.

The following transactions occurred in 2011:

Jan.   2   Rent for 2011 on leased land was paid, $87,360.

April   1   Truck B was traded in for truck D. The cash price of the new truck was $149,760. A trade-in allowance of $28,080 was granted from the cash price. The balance was paid in cash. Truck D has an expected life of 2-1/2 years and an estimated salvage value of $9,360. The exchange has commercial substance.

       1   Truck A was sold for $28,080 cash.

Required ➔ Prepare journal entries to record the 2011 transactions and the necessary December 31, 2011, adjusting entries, assuming a calendar-year accounting period. Use the straight-line depreciation method.

Problem 11-5
Determine depletion for period and depreciation on mining equipment; compute average cost per ton of ore mined (L.O. 3)

On January 2, 2011, York Mining Company acquired land with ore deposits at a cash cost of $1,800,000. Exploration and development costs amounted to $192,000. The residual value of the land is expected to be $360,000. The ore deposits contain an estimated 6 million tons. Present technology will allow the economical extraction of only 85% of the total deposit. Machinery, equipment, and temporary sheds were installed at a cost of $255,000. The assets will have no further value to the company when the ore body is exhausted; they have a physical life of 12 years. In 2011, 200,000 tons of ore were extracted. The company expects the mine to be exhausted in 10 years, with sharp variations in annual production.

Required ➔
a. Compute the depletion charge for 2011. Round to the nearest cent.
b. Compute the depreciation charge for 2011 under the units-of-production method.
c. If all other mining costs, except depletion, amounted to $1,260,000, what was the average cost per ton mined in 2011? (The depreciation calculated in b is included in the $1,260,000.)

Problem 11-6
Record cost and amortization of patent (L.O. 4)

East Company spent $249,900 to purchase a patent on January 2, 2011. Management assumes that the patent's finite useful life is 17 years. In January 2012, the company hired an outside law firm and successfully defended the patent in a lawsuit at a cost of $48,000. Also, in January 2012, the company paid $72,000 to obtain patents that could, if used by competitors, make the earlier East patent useless. The purchased patents will never be used.

Required ➔ Give the entries for 2011 and 2012 to record the information relating to the patents.

Problem 11-7
Record amortization expense for a variety of intangible assets (L.O. 4)

Following are selected transactions and other data relating to Long Company for the year ended December 31, 2011.

a. The company rented the second floor of a building for five years on January 2, 2011, and paid the annual rent of $18,000 for the first and fifth years in advance.
b. In 2010, the company incurred legal fees of $54,000 paid to an outside law firm in applying for a patent and paid a fee of $18,000 to a former employee who conceived a device that substantially reduced the cost of manufacturing one of the company's products. The patent on the device has a market value of $540,000 and is expected to be useful for 10 years.
c. In 2010, the company entered into a 10-year operating lease on several floors of a building, paying $36,000 in cash immediately and agreeing to pay $18,000 at the end of each of the 10 years of life in the lease. The company then incurred costs of $72,000 to install partitions, shelving, and fixtures. These items would normally last 25 years.
d. The company spent $21,600 promoting a trademark in a manner that it believed enhanced the value of the trademark considerably. The trademark has an indefinite life.
e. The company incurred costs amounting to $180,000 in 2010 and $234,000 in 2011 for research and development of new products that are expected to enhance the company's revenues for at least five years.
f. The company paid $180,000 to the author of a book that the company published on July 2, 2011. Sales of the book are expected to be made over a two-year period from that date.

Required ➔ For each of the situations just described, prepare only the journal entries to record the expense applicable to 2011.

Alternate Problems

Ray, Inc., purchased a new 2012 model automobile on December 31, 2012. The cash price of the new automobile was $28,080, from which Ray received a trade-in allowance of $4,320 for a 2010 model traded in. The 2010 model had been acquired on January 1, 2010, at a cost of $20,700. Depreciation has been recorded on the 2010 model through December 31, 2011, using the straight-line method, an expected four-year useful life, and an expected salvage value of $2,700. The exchange has commercial substance.

a. Record depreciation expense for 2012.
b. Prepare the journal entries needed to record the exchange of automobiles.

Problem 11-1A
Update depreciation and record exchange of automobiles (L.O. 2)

☛ *Required*

On January 1, 2009, Wood Company purchased a truck for $43,200 cash. The truck has an estimated useful life of six years and an expected salvage value of $5,400. Depreciation on the truck was computed using the straight-line method.

Problem 11-2A
Update depreciation and record six cases of asset disposal (L.O. 1, 2)

a. Prepare a schedule showing the computation of the book value of the truck on December 31, 2011.
b. Prepare the journal entry to record depreciation for the six months ended June 30, 2012.
c. Prepare journal entries to record the disposal of the truck on June 30, 2012, under each of the following unrelated assumptions:
  (1) The truck was sold for $3,600 cash.
  (2) The truck was sold for $25,200 cash.
  (3) The truck was scrapped. Used parts valued at $6,660 were salvaged.
  (4) The truck (which has a fair market value of $10,800) and $32,400 of cash were exchanged for a used back hoe that did not have a known market value. The transaction has commercial substance.
  (5) The truck and $29,700 cash were exchanged for another truck that had a cash price of $51,300. The exchange has no commercial substance.
  (6) The truck was stolen July 1, and insurance proceeds of $7,560 were expected.

☛ *Required*

Kine Company purchased a new Model II computer October 1, 2011. Cash price of the new computer was $24,960; Jackson received a trade-in allowance of $9,300 from the cash price for a Model I computer. The old computer was acquired on January 1, 2009, at a cost of $23,040. Depreciation has been recorded through December 31, 2010, on a straight-line basis, with an estimated useful life of four years and $3,840 expected salvage value. The exchange has commercial substance.

Prepare the journal entries to record the exchange.

Problem 11-3A
Update depreciation and record exchange of plant asset for similar asset (L.O. 2)

☛ *Required*

On July 1, 2011, Morgan Company had the following balances in some of its accounts:

Problem 11-4A
Record leasehold amortization; record depreciation and trade-in (L.O. 2, 4)

	Asset	Accumulated Depreciation
Land	$ 672,000	
Leasehold	252,000	
Buildings	3,151,680	$434,280
Equipment	1,370,880	436,800
Trucks	238,560	71,652

Additional data   1. The leasehold covers a plot of ground leased on July 1, 2006, for a period of 25 years under an operating lease.

2. The office building is on the leased land and was completed on July 1, 2007, at a cost of $967,680; its physical life is set at 40 years. The factory building is on the owned land and was completed on July 1, 2006, at a cost of $2,184,000; its life is also set at 40 years with no expected salvage value.

3. The equipment has a 15-year useful life with no expected salvage value.

4. The company owns three trucks—A, B, and C. Truck A, purchased on July 1, 2009, at a cost of $53,760, had an expected useful life of three years and a salvage value of $3,360. Truck B, purchased on January 2, 2010, at a cost of $84,000, had an expected life of four years and an estimated salvage value of $6,720. Truck C, purchased on January 2, 2011, at a cost of $100,800, had an expected life of five years and an estimated salvage value of $10,080.

The following transactions occurred in the fiscal year ended June 30, 2012:

2011

July   1   Rent for July 1, 2011, through June 30, 2012, on leased land was paid, $31,920.
Oct.   1   Truck A was traded in on truck D. Cash price of the new truck was $107,520. Cash of $90,720 was paid. Truck D has an expected life of four years and a salvage value of $5,880. The exchange has no commercial substance.

2012

Feb.   2   Truck B was sold for $47,040 cash.
June   1   Truck C was completely demolished in an accident. The truck was not insured.

Required Prepare journal entries to record these transactions and the necessary June 30, 2012, adjusting entries. Use the straight-line depreciation method.

Problem 11-5A
Determine depletion for period and depreciation on building and mining equipment; compute average cost per ton of ore mined (L.O. 3)

In December 2010, Brown Company acquired a mine for $2,700,000. The mine contained an estimated 10 million tons of ore. It was also estimated that the land would have a value of $240,000 when the mine was exhausted and that only 4 million tons of ore could be economically extracted. A building was erected on the property at a cost of $360,000. The building had an estimated useful life of 35 years and no salvage value. Specialized mining equipment was installed at a cost of $495,000. This equipment had an estimated useful life of seven years and an estimated $33,000 salvage value. The company began operating on January 1, 2011, and put all of its assets into use on that date. During the year ended December 31, 2011, 400,000 tons of ore were extracted. The company decided to use the units-of-production method to record depreciation on the building and the straight-line method to record depreciation on the equipment.

Required Prepare journal entries to record the depletion and depreciation charges for the year ended December 31, 2011. Show calculations.

Problem 11-6A
Record cost and amortization of patent (L.O. 4)

Trask Company purchased a patent for $108,000 on January 2, 2011. The patent was estimated to have a finite life of 10 years. The $108,000 cost was properly charged to an asset account and amortized in 2011. On January 1, 2012, the company incurred legal and court costs of $32,400 in a successful defense of the patent in a lawsuit. The legal work was performed by an outside law firm.

Required   a. Compute the patent amortization expense for 2011 and give the entry to record it.
   b. Compute the patent amortization expense for 2012 and give the entry to record it.

Selected transactions and other data for Grant Company:

Problem 11-7A
Record amortization
expense for a variety
of intangible assets
(L.O. 4)

a. The company purchased a patent in early January 2008 for $144,000 and began amortizing it over its finite life of 10 years. In early January 2010, the company hired an outside law firm and successfully defended the patent in an infringement suit at a cost of $38,400.

b. Research and development costs incurred in 2010 of $43,200 were expected to provide benefits over the three succeeding years.

c. On January 2, 2011, the company rented space in a warehouse for five years at an annual fee of $9,600. Rent for the first and last years was paid in advance.

d. A total of $96,000 was spent uniformly throughout 2011 by the company in promoting its lesser known trademark, which is expected to have a finite useful life of 20 years.

e. In January 2009, the company purchased all of the assets and assumed all of the liabilities of another company, paying $192,000 more than the fair market value of all identifiable assets acquired, less the liabilities assumed. The company expects the cash flow benefits for which it paid the $192,000 to last 10 years (finite useful life).

For each of these unrelated transactions, prepare journal entries to record only those entries required for 2011. Note any items that do not require an entry in 2011.

 Required

Beyond the Numbers–Critical Thinking

During your audit examination of the Shirley Company's Plant, Property, and Equipment accounts, the following transaction came to your attention. On January 2, 2011, machine A was exchanged for machine B. Shirley Company acquired machine A for $90,000 on January 2, 2009. Machine A had an estimated useful life of four years and no salvage value, and the machine was depreciated on the straight-line basis. Machine B had a cash price of $108,000. In addition to machine A, cash of $30,000 was given up in the exchange. Machine B has an estimated useful life of five years and no salvage value, and the machine is being depreciated using the straight-line method. The exchange has no commercial substance. Upon further analysis, you discover that the company recorded the transaction as an exchange of nonmonetary assets having commercial substance instead of one not having commercial substance. You must now determine the following:

**Business Decision
Case 11-1**
Record exchange of
similar assets; adjust
accounts for errors
in accounting for
depreciable assets
(L.O. 2)

a. What journal entry did the Shirley Company make when it recorded the exchange of machines? (Show computations.)

b. What journal entry should the Shirley Company have made to record the exchange of machines?

c. Assume the error was discovered on December 31, 2012, before adjusting journal entries have been made. What journal entries should be made to correct the accounting records? (Adjustments of prior years' net income because of errors should be debited or credited to Retained Earnings.) What adjusting journal entry should be made to record depreciation for 2012? (Ignore income taxes.)

d. What effect did the error have on reported net income for 2011? (Ignore income taxes.)

e. How should machine B be reported on the December 31, 2012, balance sheet?

Currently, many corporations are looking for acquisition opportunities. Tyre, Inc., is trying to decide whether to buy Amite Company or Beauman Company. Tyre, Inc., has hired you as a consultant to analyze the two companies' financial information and to determine the more advantageous acquisition. Your review of the companies' books has revealed that both Amite and Beauman have assets with the following book values and fair market values:

**Business Decision
Case 11-2**
Record purchase of
two businesses and
explain differences
between the two;
advise client as to
which company should
be purchased (L.O. 4)

	Book Value	Fair Market Value
Accounts receivable	$150,000	$ 150,000
Inventories	450,000	750,000
Land	375,000	675,000
Buildings	450,000	1,050,000
Equipment	180,000	300,000
Patents	120,000	150,000

Liabilities assumed on the purchase of either company include accounts payable, $300,000, and notes payable, $75,000.

The only difference between the companies is that Amite has net income that is about average for the industry, while Beauman's net income is greatly above average for the industry.

Required ➲ Top-level management at Tyre, Inc., has asked you to respond in writing to the following possible situations:

a. Assume Tyre, Inc., can buy Amite Company for $2,700,000 or Beauman Company for $3,450,000. Prepare the journal entries to record the acquisition of Amite Company and Beauman Company. What accounts for the difference between the purchase price of the two companies?

b. Assume Tyre, Inc, can buy either company for $2,700,000. Write a report for Tyre, Inc., advising which company to buy.

Annual Report Analysis 11-3
Calculate and discuss total assets turnover (L.O. 5)

Created in 1998, Google Incorporated is a multinational internet and software firm that specializes in internet searches, cloud computing, and advertising.

Using the following excerpts from Google's annual reports, calculate the firm's total assets turnover for 2010 and 2009. (Amounts are in $ millions.)

	2010	2009	2008
Net sales	$ 29,321	$ 23,651	$ 21,796
Total assets	57,851	40,497	31,768

In a written report, discuss the meaning of the total assets turnover ratio and what the ratio means to management and investors. Use the total assets turnover ratios you computed for Google as an example in your report.

Ethics Case 11-4
Answer questions regarding ethics case

Based on the situation described in the ethics case on page 443 regarding ABC Corporation, respond in writing to the following questions.

a. Depending on his actions, what are the possible consequences for John Gilbert in this situation?

b. Assuming that the president cannot find another appraiser to support the new allocations, what would you do if you were Gilbert?

c. If the president can find a reputable appraiser to support these new allocations, what would you do if you were Gilbert?

Group Project 11-5
Make intangible assets presentation

In teams of two or three students, find a recent annual report that includes intangible assets on the balance sheet. Select one member of each team to give an informal presentation discussing intangible asset disclosures on the face of the statements and in the notes to the financial statements. All members should be prepared to discuss intangible asset disclosures from their annual report in detail.

Group Project 11-6
Perform library project on accounting for research and development costs

In a group of one or two other students, go to the library and locate *Statement of Financial Accounting Standards No. 2,* "Accounting for Research and Development Costs," published by the Financial Accounting Standards Board (now codified as ASC 730). Write a report to your instructor giving the highlights of the standard. For instance, what alternatives were considered and why did the board conclude that all research and development costs should be expensed when incurred?

In a group of one or two other students, go to the library and locate *Statement of Financial Accounting Standards No. 144*, "Accounting for the Impairment of Long-Lived Assets" (now codified as ASC 360) published by the Financial Accounting Standards Board. Write a report to your instructor giving the highlights of the standard. For instance, what does "impairment" mean and what are its causes? How can one determine that impairment of an asset has possibly occurred? Also review some of the background information as to why this was important enough for the FASB to act.

Group Project 11-7
Perform library project on accounting for the impairment of long-lived assets

Using the Internet—A View of the Real World

Visit the Financial Accounting Standards Board's website:
   http://www.fasb.org
Search window: Accounting Standards Codification
   What free resources are available to students related to the codification process?

Internet Project 11-8
Search the FASB Website

Visit the Small Business Administration site at:
   http://www.sba.gov
Suppose you wanted to start a small business. What helpful information would you find at this site? Would this site provide information on how to finance the business? Browse around this site to see what it offers. Then write a report to your instructor summarizing the types of helpful information this site provides.

Internet Project 11-9
Investigate the Small Business Administration site

Answers to Self-Test

True-False

1. **False.** No more depreciation can be taken on a fully depreciated plant asset.
2. **True.** The new asset is recorded at the fair market value of the asset received or given up, whichever is more clearly evident.

3. **False.** The residual value of land should be deducted from total costs subject to depletion.
4. **False.** Only intangible assets with finite useful lives should be amortized.

Multiple-Choice

1. **d.** The cost and accumulated depreciation should not be removed from the accounts until the disposal of the asset.
2. **a.** On the date of exchange, the book value of the old truck is $20,700 ($45,000 minus accumulated depreciation of $24,300). The trade-in allowance of $22,500 indicates a gain on exchange of $1,800. In an exchange of nonmonetary assets not having commercial substance, a gain is not recognized, but reduces the cost of a new asset. Therefore, the cost of the new truck is $55,200 ($57,000 minus $1,800), and no gain is recognized.

3. **c.** The depletion charge for the first year is:

Depletion charge Per ton = ($375,000 - $75,000)/1,000,000

= $0.30

Depletion charge For the year = $0.30 x 100,000

= $30,000

Since all of the ore that was extracted was sold, all of the $30,000 is expensed as cost of ore sold.

4. **b.** The patent is amortized over 10 years:

Annual amortization expense = $36,000/10
= $3,600

Careers in Accounting

The Accountant As A Corporate Treasurer

Most people think of the stock market as a place to buy and sell stock. However, few people give much thought to the other side of this transaction. The original purpose of the stock market is to allow corporations to raise the money needed to expand into new markets, invent new products, open new stores, and create new jobs. The initial public issuance of stock (i.e., going public) is one of the most significant milestones in the life of a public company.

For most individual investors, trading is done by stockbrokers. Who handles the stock transactions within a company? The treasurer or the person that performs the treasury functions is the person. This role requires someone with a strong background in accounting and finance.

When a company decides to issue bonds or additional shares of stock, the treasurer is the person responsible for executing the transaction at the lowest cost to the entity. The treasurer works closely with investment bankers and lawyers to get the stocks or bonds marketed and issued in accordance with state and federal laws. When a company issues stock for the first time (initial public offering, or IPO), the task requires a thorough review of the financial position of the company and the public disclosure of this information for perhaps the first time. The treasurer/accountant must prepare what is called a prospectus. Among other things, the prospectus includes financial accounting information that is used in setting the price of the IPO.

The treasurer maintains custody of, or has access to, stocks owned by an entity and stock that is under the control of the entity. The treasurer also plays a pivotal role in the distribution of cash and stock dividends. The primary function of this position is controlling the cash inflows and outflows of the entity. A career as a corporate treasurer can involve the oversight of billions of dollars of stock, and the individual can earn a six-figure salary.

Stockholders' Equity
Classes of Capital Stock

In this chapter, you study the corporate form of business organization in greater detail than in preceding chapters. Although corporations are fewer in number than single proprietorships and partnerships, corporations possess the bulk of our business capital and currently supply us with most of our goods and services.

This chapter discusses the advantages and disadvantages of the corporation, how to form and direct a corporation, and some of the unique situations encountered in accounting for and reporting on the different classes of capital stock.

The Corporation

A **corporation** is an entity recognized by law as possessing an existence separate and distinct from its owners; that is, it is a separate legal entity. Endowed with many of the rights and obligations possessed by a person, a corporation can enter into contracts in its own name; buy, sell, or hold property; borrow money; hire and fire employees; and sue and be sued.

Corporations have a remarkable ability to obtain the huge amounts of capital necessary for large-scale business operations. Corporations acquire their capital by issuing **shares of stock**; these are the units into which corporations divide their ownership. Investors buy shares of stock in a corporation for two basic reasons. First, investors expect the value of their shares to increase over time so that the stock may be sold in the future at a profit. Second, while investors hold stock, they expect the corporation to pay them dividends (usually in cash) in return for using their money. Chapter 13 discusses the various kinds of dividends and their accounting treatment.

Learning Objectives

After studying this chapter, you should be able to:

1. State the advantages and disadvantages of the corporate form of business.

2. List the values commonly associated with capital stock and give their definitions.

3. List the various kinds of stock and describe the differences between them.

4. Present in proper form the stockholders' equity section of a balance sheet.

5. Account for the issuances of stock for cash and other assets.

(continued)

Objectives

6. Determine book values of both preferred and common stock.

7. Analyze and use the financial results—return on average common stockholders' equity.

Objective 1
State the advantages and disadvantages of the corporate form of business.

Real World Example
In 2008, there were more than 5.8 million corporations in the United States out of a total of over 31 million enterprises. Corporate total revenues were in excess of $27 trillion. This represented 81% of the total revenues generated in the nation. Source: U.S. Bureau of Census, *Statistical Abstract of the United States: 2012* (Washington, D.C.: U.S. Government Printing Office, 2011), p. 492.

Disadvantages of the Corporate Form of Business

Advantages of the Corporate Form of Business

Corporations have many advantages over single proprietorships and partnerships. The major advantages a corporation has over a single proprietorship are the same advantages a partnership has over a single proprietorship. Although corporations have more owners than partnerships, both have a broader base for investment, risk, responsibilities, and talent than do single proprietorships. Since corporations are more comparable to partnerships than to single proprietorships, the following discussion of advantages contrasts the partnership with the corporation.

1. **Easy transfer of ownership.** In a partnership, a partner cannot transfer ownership in the business to another person if the other partners do not want the new person involved in the partnership. In a publicly held (owned by many stockholders) corporation, shares of stock are traded on a stock exchange between unknown parties; one owner usually cannot dictate to whom another owner can or cannot sell shares.

2. **Limited liability.** Each partner in a partnership is personally responsible for all the debts of the business. In a corporation, the stockholders are not personally responsible for its debts; the maximum amount a stockholder can lose is the amount of his or her investment. However, when a small, closely held corporation (owned by only a few stockholders) borrows money, banks and lending institutions often require an officer of the small corporation to sign the loan agreement. Then, the officer has to repay the loan if the corporation does not.

3. **Continuous existence of the entity.** In a partnership, many circumstances, such as the death of a partner, can terminate the business entity. These same circumstances have no effect on a corporation because it is a legal entity, separate and distinct from its owners.

4. **Easy capital generation.** The easy transfer of ownership and the limited liability of stockholders are attractive features to potential investors. Thus, it is relatively easy for a corporation to raise capital by issuing shares of stock to many investors. Corporations with thousands of stockholders are not uncommon.

5. **Professional management.** Generally, the partners in a partnership are also the managers of that business, regardless of whether they have the necessary expertise to manage a business. In a publicly held corporation, most of the owners (stockholders) do not participate in the day-to-day operations and management of the entity. They hire professionals to run the business on a daily basis.

6. **Separation of owners and entity.** Since the corporation is a separate legal entity, the owners do not have the power to bind the corporation to business contracts. This feature eliminates the potential problem of mutual agency that exists between partners in a partnership. In a corporation, one stockholder cannot jeopardize other stockholders through poor decision making.

The corporate form of business has the following disadvantages:

1. **Double taxation.** Because a corporation is a separate legal entity, its net income is subject to double taxation. The corporation pays a tax on its income, and stockholders pay a tax on corporate income received as dividends.

2. **Government regulation.** Because corporations are created by law, they are subject to greater regulation and control than single proprietorships and partnerships.

3. **Entrenched, inefficient management.** A corporation may be burdened with an inefficient management that remains in control by using corporate funds to solicit the needed stockholder votes to back its positions. Stockholders scattered across the country, who individually own only small portions of a corporation's stock, find it difficult to organize and oppose existing management.

4. **Limited ability to raise creditor capital.** The limited liability of stockholders makes a corporation an attractive means for accumulating stockholder capital. At the same time, this limited liability feature restrains the amount of creditor capital a corporation can amass because creditors cannot look to stockholders to pay the debts of a corporation. Thus, beyond a certain point, creditors do not lend some corporations money without the personal guarantee of a stockholder or officer of the corporation to repay the loan if the corporation does not.

> **Note to the Student**
> How do income tax laws for regular corporations differ from partnership and proprietorship income tax laws?
> Answer: A regular corporation pays income tax on its net income. Then its stockholders pay taxes on dividends received. Partnerships and proprietorships pay no tax on their business income. Their net income becomes the taxable income of the owners.

Incorporating

Corporations are chartered by the state. Each state has a corporation act that permits the formation of corporations by qualified persons. The corporation acts of most states follow the Revised Model Business Corporation Act (RMBCA). **Incorporators** are persons seeking to bring a corporation into existence.

The laws of each state view a corporation organized in that state as a **domestic corporation** and a corporation organized in any other state as a **foreign corporation**. If a corporation intends to conduct business solely within one state, it normally seeks incorporation in that state because most state laws are not as severe for domestic corporations as for foreign corporations. Corporations conducting interstate business usually incorporate in the state that has laws most advantageous to the corporation being formed. Important considerations in choosing a state are the powers granted to the corporation, the taxes levied, the defenses permitted against hostile takeover attempts by others, and the reports required by the state.

Articles of Incorporation

Once incorporators agree on the state in which to incorporate, they apply for a corporate charter. A **corporate charter** is a contract between the state and the incorporators, and their successors, granting the corporation its legal existence. The application for the corporation's charter is called the **articles of incorporation**.

After supplying the information requested in the incorporation application form, incorporators file the articles with the proper office in the state of incorporation. Each state requires different information in the articles of incorporation, but most states ask for the following:

1. Name of corporation.
2. Location of principal offices.
3. Purposes of business.
4. Number of shares of stock authorized, class or classes of shares, and voting and dividend rights of each class of shares.
5. Value of assets paid in by the incorporators (the stockholders who organize the corporation).
6. Limitations on authority of the management and owners of the corporation.

On approving the articles, the state office (frequently the secretary of state's office) grants the charter and creates the corporation.

Bylaws

As soon as the corporation obtains the charter, it is authorized to operate its business. The incorporators call the first meeting of the stockholders. Two of the purposes of this meeting are to elect a board of directors and to adopt the bylaws of the corporation.

The **bylaws** are a set of rules or regulations adopted by the board of directors of a corporation to govern the conduct of corporate affairs. The bylaws must be in agreement with the laws of the state and the policies and purposes in the corporate charter. The bylaws contain, along with other information, provisions for: (1) the place, date, and manner of calling the annual stockholders' meeting; (2) the number of directors and the method for electing them; (3) the duties and powers of the directors; and (4) the method for selecting officers of the corporation.

Organization Costs

Organization costs are the costs of organizing a corporation, such as state incorporation fees and legal fees applicable to incorporation. The firm debits these costs to an account called *Organization Costs*. The Organizational Costs account is an asset because the costs yield benefits over an extended period of the life of the corporation. Theoretically, this asset should not be classified as finite, but sometimes it is classified as finite because of its small immaterial amount. If the asset is classified as a finite intangible asset, it is amortized over its finite useful life. If it is not classified as a finite intangible asset, it is not amortized.

As an illustration, assume that De-Leed Corporation pays state incorporation fees of $10,000 and attorney's fees of $5,000 for services rendered related to the acquisition of a charter with the state. The entry to record these costs is:

Organization Costs	15,000	
Cash		15,000
To record costs incurred in organizing corporation.		

Assuming the corporation amortizes the organization costs over a 10-year period, this entry records amortization at the end of the year:

Amortization Expense—Organization Costs	1,500	
Organization Costs		1,500
To record organization costs amortization expense.		
(15,000/10 years = $1,500).		

Directing the Corporation

Management of the corporation is through the delegation of authority from the stockholders to the directors to the officers, as shown in the organization chart in Illustration 12.1. The stockholders elect the board of directors. The board of directors formulates the broad policies of the company and selects the principal officers, who execute the policies.

Stockholders   Stockholders do not have the right to participate actively in the management of the business unless they serve as directors and/or officers. However, stockholders do have certain basic rights, including the right to (1) dispose of their shares, (2) share in dividends when declared, (3) share in assets in case of liquidation, and (4) participate in management indirectly by voting at the stockholders' meeting.

In some states, shareholders have the right to buy additional newly issued shares in a proportion equal to the percentage of shares they already own (called the **preemptive right**). The preemptive right allows stockholders to maintain their percentage of ownership in a corporation when additional shares are issued. For example, assume Joe Thornton owns 10% of the outstanding shares of Corporation X. When Corporation X decides to issue 1,000 additional shares of stock, Joe Thornton has the right to buy

Illustration 12.1   Typical Corporation's Organization Chart

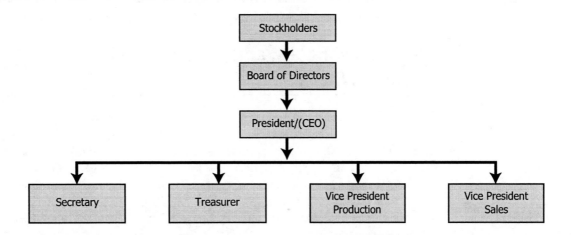

100 (10%) of the new shares. Should he decide to do so, he maintains his 10% interest in the corporation. If he does not wish to exercise his preemptive right, the corporation may sell the shares to others.[1]

Normally, companies hold stockholders' meetings annually. At the annual stockholders' meeting, stockholders indirectly share in management by voting on such issues as changing the charter, increasing the number of authorized shares of stock to be issued, approving pension plans, selecting the independent auditor, and other related matters.

At stockholders' meetings, each stockholder is entitled to one vote for each share of voting stock held. Stockholders who do not personally attend the stockholders' meeting may vote by proxy. A **proxy** is a legal document signed by a stockholder, giving a designated person the authority to vote the stockholder's shares at a stockholders' meeting.

Board of Directors   Elected by the stockholders, the **board of directors** is primarily responsible for formulating policies for the corporation. The board appoints administrative officers and delegates to them the execution of the policies established by the board. The board's more specific duties include: (1) authorizing contracts, (2) declaring dividends, (3) establishing executive salaries, and (4) granting authorization to borrow money. The decisions of the board are recorded in the minutes of its meetings. The minutes are an important source of information to an independent auditor, since they may serve as notice to record transactions (such as a dividend declaration) or to identify certain future transactions (such as a large loan).

Corporate Officers   A corporation's bylaws usually specify the titles and duties of the officers of a corporation. The number of officers and their exact titles vary from corporation to corporation, but most have a president, several vice presidents, a secretary, a treasurer, and a controller.

The president is the chief executive officer (CEO) of the corporation. He or she is empowered by the bylaws to hire all necessary employees except those appointed by the board of directors.

Most corporations have more than one vice president. Each vice president is responsible for one particular corporate operation, such as sales, engineering, or production. The corporate secretary maintains the official records of the company and records the proceedings of meetings of stockholders and directors. The treasurer

---

[1]Some corporations have eliminated the preemptive right because the preemptive right makes it difficult to issue large blocks of stock to the stockholders of another corporation to acquire that corporation. Under the RMBCA, a shareholder does not have preemptive rights unless they are provided for in the articles of incorporation.

is accountable for corporate funds and may supervise the accounting function within the company. A controller carries out the accounting function. The controller usually reports to the treasurer of the corporation.

Documents, Books, and Records Relating to Capital Stock

Capital stock consists of transferable units of ownership in a corporation. Each unit of ownership is called a *share of stock*. Typically, well over a billion shares of stock are sold every business day on the New York Stock Exchange. Millions more shares are sold daily on the American Stock Exchange, the NASDAQ, and on over-the-counter markets. These sales (or *trades*) seldom involve the corporation issuing the stock as a party to the exchange. Existing stockholders sell their shares to other individual or institutional investors. The physical transfer of the stock certificates follows these trades.

A **stock certificate** is a printed or engraved document serving as evidence that the holder owns a certain number of shares of capital stock. When selling shares of stock, the stockholder signs over the stock certificate to the new owner, who presents it to the issuing corporation. When the old certificate arrives, the issuing corporation cancels the certificate and attaches it to its corresponding stub in the stock certificate book. The issuer prepares a new certificate for the new owner. Rather than hold the actual paper stock certificates, many investors prefer to have their brokers keep electronic records of their stock holdings. This is referred to as holding the securities in "street name".

Stockholders' Ledger

Among the more important records maintained by a corporation is the stockholders' ledger. The **stockholders' ledger** contains a group of subsidiary accounts showing the number of shares of stock currently held by *each* stockholder. Since the ledger contains an account for *each* stockholder, in a large corporation this ledger may have more than a million individual accounts. Each stockholder's account shows the number of shares currently or previously owned, their certificate numbers, and the dates on which shares were acquired or sold. Entries are made in the number of shares rather than in dollars.

The stockholders' ledger and the stock certificate book contain the same information, but the stockholders' ledger summarizes it alphabetically by stockholder. Since a stockholder may own a dozen or more certificates, each representing a number of shares, this summary enables a corporation to (1) determine the number of shares a stockholder is entitled to vote at a stockholders' meeting and (2) prepare one dividend check per stockholder rather than one per stock certificate.

Many large corporations with actively traded shares turn the task of maintaining reliable stock records over to an outside *stock-transfer agent* and a *stock registrar*. The **stock-transfer agent,** usually a bank or trust company, transfers stock between buyers and sellers for a corporation. The stock-transfer agent cancels the certificates covering shares sold, issues new stock certificates, and makes appropriate entries in the stockholders' ledger. It sends new certificates to the **stock registrar**, typically another bank, that maintains separate records of the shares outstanding. This control system makes it difficult for a corporate employee to issue stock certificates fraudulently and steal the proceeds.

The Minutes Book

The **minutes book,** kept by the secretary of the corporation, is (1) a record book of the actions taken at stockholders' and board of directors' meetings and (2) the written authorization for many actions taken by corporate officers. Remember that all actions taken by the board of directors and the stockholders must be in accordance with the provisions in the corporate charter and the bylaws. The minutes book contains a variety of data, including:

1. A copy of the corporate charter.
2. A copy of the bylaws.
3. Dividends declared by the board of directors.
4. Authorization for the acquisition of major assets.
5. Authorization for borrowing.
6. Authorization for increases or decreases in capital stock.

Par Value and No-Par Capital Stock

Many times, companies issue par value stock. **Par value** is an arbitrary amount assigned to each share of a given class of stock and printed on the stock certificate. *Par value per share is no indication of the amount for which the stock sells;* it is simply the amount per share credited to the capital stock account for each share issued. Also, the total par value of all issued stock often constitutes the legal capital of the corporation. The concept of legal capital protects creditors from losses. **Legal capital**, or **stated capital**, is an amount prescribed by law (usually the par value or stated value of shares issued) below which a corporation may not reduce stockholders' equity through declaration of dividends or other payments to stockholders. Stated value relates to no-par stock and is explained below. Legal capital does not guarantee that a company can pay its debts, but it does keep a company from compensating owners to the detriment of creditors. The formula for determining legal capital is:

$$\text{Legal Capital} = \text{Shares Issued} \times \text{Par or Stated Value}$$

In 1912, the state of New York first enacted laws permitting the issuance of **no-par stock (stock without par value)**. Many other states have passed similar, but not uniform, legislation.

A corporation might issue no-par stock for two reasons. One reason is to avoid confusion. The use of a par value may confuse some investors because the par value usually does not conform to the market value. Issuing a stock with no par value avoids this source of confusion.

A second reason is related to state laws regarding the original issue price per share. A **discount on capital stock** is the amount by which the shares' par value exceeds their issue price. Thus, if stock with a par value of $100 is issued at $80, the discount is $20. Most states do not permit the original issuance of stock at a discount. Only Maryland, Georgia, and California allow its issuance. The original purchasers of the shares are contingently liable for the discount unless they have transferred (by contract) the discount liability to subsequent holders. If the contingent liability has been transferred, the present stockholders are contingently liable to creditors for the difference between par value and issue price. Although this contingent liability seldom becomes an actual liability, the issuance of no-par stock avoids such a possibility.

The board of directors of a corporation issuing no-par stock may assign a stated value to each share of capital stock. **Stated value** is an arbitrary amount assigned by the board to each share of a given class of no-par stock. The board may set this stated value, like par value, at any amount, although some state statutes specify a minimum amount, such as $5 per share. If not specified by applicable state law, the board may establish stated value either before or after the shares are issued.

Par Value Stock

Objective 2
List the values commonly associated with capital stock and give their definitions.

No-Par Stock

Note to the Student
Companies regard capital stock as the permanent capital of the business. Often we refer to it as the legal capital. In effect, it is an amount for the protection of creditors because it cannot be paid out to shareholders until all creditors' claims have been satisfied.

No-Par Stock with a Stated Value

Other Values Commonly Associated with Capital Stock

Market Value

Market value is the price of shares of capital stock bought and sold by investors in the market; it is the value of greatest interest to investors. Market price is directly affected by (1) all the factors that influence general economic conditions, (2) investors' expectations concerning the corporation, and (3) the corporation's earnings.

Book Value

Book value per share is the amount per share that each stockholder would receive if the corporation were liquidated without incurring any further expenses and if assets were sold and liabilities liquidated at their recorded amounts. A later section discusses book value per share in greater detail.

Liquidation Value

Liquidation value is the amount a stockholder would receive if a corporation discontinued operations and liquidated by selling its assets, paying its liabilities, and distributing the remaining cash among the stockholders. Since the assets might be sold for more or less than the amounts at which they are recorded in the corporation's accounts, liquidation value may be more or less than book value. If only one class of capital stock is outstanding, each stockholder would receive, per share, the amount obtained by dividing the remaining cash by the number of outstanding shares. If two or more classes of stock are outstanding, liquidation value depends on the rights of the various classes.

Redemption Value

A corporation issues certain capital stock with the stipulation that it has the right to redeem it. **Redemption value** is the price per share at which a corporation may call in (or redeem) its capital stock for retirement.

Capital Stock Authorized and Outstanding

Objective 3
List the various kinds of stock and describe the differences between them.

The corporate charter states the number of shares and the par value, if any, per share of each class of stock that the corporation is permitted to issue. **Capital stock authorized** is the number of shares of stock that a corporation is entitled to issue as designated in its charter.

A corporation might not issue all of its authorized stock immediately; it might hold some stock for future issuance when additional funds are needed. If all authorized stock has been issued and more funds are needed, the state of incorporation must consent to an increase in authorized shares.

The authorization to issue stock does not trigger a journal entry. Instead, companies note the authorization in the capital stock account in the ledger (and often in the general journal) as a reminder of the number of shares authorized. **Capital stock issued** is the number of shares of stock sold and issued to stockholders.

Note to the Student
Differentiate between authorized shares and outstanding shares.

Capital stock outstanding is the number of authorized shares of stock issued and currently held by stockholders. The total ownership of a corporation rests with the holders of the capital stock outstanding. For example, when a corporation authorized to issue 10,000 shares of capital stock has issued only 8,000 shares, the holders of the 8,000 shares own 100% of the corporation.

Each outstanding share of stock of a given class carries rights and privileges identical to any other outstanding share of that class. Shares authorized but not yet issued are referred to as **unissued shares** (the previous example had 2,000 unissued shares). No rights or privileges are attached to these shares until they are issued; they are not entitled to dividends, nor can they be voted at stockholders' meetings.

The number of shares issued and the number of shares outstanding may be different. Issued stock has been issued at some time, while outstanding shares are currently held by stockholders. All outstanding stock is issued stock, but the reverse is not necessarily true. The difference is due to shares returned to the corporation by stockholders; it is called *treasury stock*. Chapter 13 discusses treasury stock.

BUSINESS INSIGHT Sanmina-SCI Corporation is a global provider of customized, integrated manufacturing services for a wide variety of industries. The following illustration is adapted from the company's balance sheet. The stockholders' equity section shows the actual number of shares of common stock authorized and outstanding and shows the dollar amounts in thousands:

An Accounting Perspective

	September 30,	
	2011	**2010**
Common Stock, $.01 par value: authorized 166,667,000 common shares, outstanding 80,734,000 shares in 2011 and 79,722,000 shares in 2010.	$807	$797

Classes of Capital Stock

A corporation may issue two basic classes or types of capital stock—common and preferred.

If a corporation issues only one class of stock, this stock is *common stock*. All of the stockholders enjoy equal rights. **Common stock** is usually the *residual equity* in the corporation. This term means that all other claims against the corporation rank ahead of the claims of the common stockholder.

Common Stock

Preferred stock is a class of capital stock that carries certain features or rights not carried by common stock. Within the basic class of preferred stock, a company may have several specific classes of preferred stock, each with different dividend rates or other features.

Preferred Stock

   Companies issue preferred stock to avoid: (1) using bonds with fixed interest charges that must be paid regardless of the amount of net income; (2) issuing so many additional shares of common stock that earnings per share are less in the current year than in prior years; and (3) diluting the common stockholders' control of the corporation, since preferred stockholders usually have no voting rights.

   Unlike common stock, which has no set maximum or minimum dividend, the dividend return on preferred stock is usually stated at an amount per share or as a percentage of par value. Therefore, the firm fixes the dividend per share. Illustration 12.2 shows the various classes and combinations of capital stock outstanding for a sample of public companies.

Illustration 12.2   Capital Structures

	2009	2008	2007	2006
Common stock with:				
No preferred stock	453	452	532	522
One class of preferred stock	39	38	58	70
Two classes of preferred stock	5	8	7	5
Three or more classes of preferred stock	3	2	3	3
Total Companies	**500**	**500**	**600**	**600**
Companies included above with two or more classes of common stock	54	46	57	58

Source: Based on American Institute of Certified Public Accountants, *Accounting Trends & Techniques* (New York: AICPA, 2010), p. 300.

Types of Preferred Stock

When a corporation issues both preferred and common stock, the preferred stock may be:

1. Preferred as to dividends. It may be noncumulative or cumulative.
2. Preferred as to assets in the event of liquidation.
3. Convertible or nonconvertible.
4. Callable.

Stock Preferred as to Dividends

A **dividend** is a distribution of assets (usually cash) that represents a withdrawal of earnings by the owners. Dividends are normally paid in cash.

Stock preferred as to dividends means that the preferred stockholders receive a specified dividend per share before common stockholders receive any dividends. A **dividend on preferred stock** is the amount paid to preferred stockholders as a return for the use of their money. For no-par preferred stock, the dividend is a specific dollar amount per share per year, such as $4.40. For par value preferred stock, the dividend is usually stated as a percentage of the par value, such as 8% of par value; occasionally, it is stated as a specific dollar amount per share. Most preferred stock has a par value.

Usually, stockholders receive dividends on preferred stock quarterly. Such dividends—in full or in part—must be declared by the board of directors before being paid. In some states, corporations can declare preferred stock dividends only if they have retained earnings (income that has been retained in the business) at least equal to the dividend declared.

Reinforcing Problem
E12-1 Determine dividends for common and noncumulative preferred stock.

Noncumulative Preferred Stock **Noncumulative preferred stock** is preferred stock on which the right to receive a dividend expires whenever the dividend is not declared. When noncumulative preferred stock is outstanding, a dividend omitted or not paid in any one year need not be paid in any future year. Because omitted dividends are lost forever, noncumulative preferred stocks are not attractive to investors and are rarely issued.

Note to the Student
The term cumulative means that unpaid dividends in a given year carry over and must be paid to preferred stockholders before common stockholders receive any distributions.

Cumulative Preferred Stock **Cumulative preferred stock** is preferred stock for which the right to receive a basic dividend, usually each quarter, accumulates if the dividend is not paid. Companies must pay unpaid cumulative preferred dividends before paying any dividends on the common stock. For example, assume a company has cumulative, $10 par value, 10% preferred stock outstanding of $100,000, common stock outstanding of $100,000, and retained earnings of $30,000. It has paid no dividends for two years. The company would pay the preferred stockholders dividends of $20,000 ($10,000 per year times two years) before paying any dividends to the common stockholders.

Reinforcing Problem
E12-2 Determine dividends for common and cumulative preferred stock.

Dividends in arrears are cumulative unpaid dividends, including the quarterly dividends not declared for the current year. Dividends in arrears never appear as a liability of the corporation because they are not a legal liability until declared by the board of directors. However, since the amount of dividends in arrears may influence the decisions of users of a corporation's financial statements, firms disclose such dividends in a footnote. An appropriate footnote might read: "Dividends in the amount of $20,000, representing two years' dividends on the company's 10%, cumulative preferred stock, were in arrears as of December 31, 2011."

Note to the Student
Dividends in arrears on cumulative preferred stock are not a liability until declared by the board of directors.

Most preferred stocks are preferred as to assets in the event of liquidation of the corporation. **Stock preferred as to assets** is preferred stock that receives special treatment in liquidation. Preferred stockholders receive the par value (or a larger stipulated liquidation value) per share before any assets are distributed to common stockholders. A corporation's cumulative preferred dividends in arrears at liquidation are payable even if there are not enough accumulated earnings to cover the dividends. Also, the cumulative dividend for the current year is payable. Stock may be preferred as to assets, dividends, or both.

Stock Preferred as to Assets

Convertible preferred stock is preferred stock that is convertible into common stock of the issuing corporation. Many preferred stocks do not carry this special feature; they are nonconvertible. Holders of convertible preferred stock shares may exchange them, at their option, for a certain number of shares of common stock of the same corporation.

Convertible Preferred Stock

Investors find convertible preferred stock attractive for two reasons: First, there is a greater probability that the dividends on the preferred stock will be paid (as compared to dividends on common shares). Second, the conversion privilege may be the source of substantial price appreciation. To illustrate this latter feature, assume that Olsen Company issued 1,000 shares of 6%, $100 par value convertible preferred stock at $100 per share. The stock is convertible at any time into four shares of Olsen $10 par value common stock, which has a current market value of $20 per share. In the next several years, the company reported much higher net income and increased the dividend on the common stock from $1 to $2 per share. Assume that the common stock now sells at $40 per share. The preferred stockholders can: (1) convert each share of preferred stock into four shares of common stock and increase the annual dividend they receive from $6 to $8; (2) sell their preferred stock at a substantial gain, since it sells in the market at approximately $160 per share, the market value of the four shares of common stock into which it is convertible; or (3) continue to hold their preferred shares in the expectation of realizing an even larger gain at a later date.

Note to the Student
Companies record no gain or loss when preferred stock is converted to common stock. The par value plus additional paid-in capital in excess of par or stated value on the preferred stock determines the issue price of the common stock.

If all 1,000 shares of $100 par value Olsen Company preferred stock are converted into 4,000 shares of $10 par value common stock, the entry is:

Preferred Stock	100,000	
Common Stock		40,000
Paid-In Capital in Excess of Par Value—Common		60,000
To record the conversion of preferred stock into		
common stock.		

Business Insight Ford Motor Company has several classes of common stock and cumulative preferred stock outstanding. Due to financial difficulties, Ford eliminated its dividend on the common stock in 2006, and it suspended its dividend on the preferred stock in January 2009. After an impressive turnaround, Ford restored payment of the preferred dividend in July 2010, including $255-million of dividends in arrears. Ford then reinstated the payment of dividends on its Class B common stock in December 2011.

An Accounting Perspective

Most preferred stocks are callable at the option of the issuing corporation. **Callable preferred stock** means that the corporation can inform nonconvertible preferred stockholders that they must surrender their stock to the company. Also, callable convertible preferred stockholders must either surrender their stock or convert it to common shares.

Callable Preferred Stock

Preferred shares are usually callable at par value plus a small premium of 3 or 4% of the par value of the stock. This **call premium** is the difference between the amount at which a corporation calls its preferred stock for redemption and the par value of the stock.

An issuing corporation may force conversion of convertible preferred stock by calling in the preferred stock for redemption. Stockholders who do not want to surrender their stock have to convert it to common shares. When preferred stockholders surrender their stock, the corporation pays these stockholders par value plus the call premium, any dividends in arrears from past years, and a prorated portion of the current period's dividend. If the market value of common shares into which the preferred stock could be converted is higher than the amount the stockholders would receive in redemption, they should convert their preferred shares to common shares. For instance, assume that a stockholder owns 1,000 shares of convertible preferred stock. Each share is callable at $104 per share, convertible to two common shares (currently selling at $62 per share), and entitled to $10 of unpaid dividends. If the issuing corporation calls in its preferred stock, it would give the stockholder either (1) $114,000 [($104 + $10) × 1,000] if the shares are surrendered or (2) common shares worth $124,000 ($62 × 2,000) if the shares are converted. Obviously, the stockholder should convert these preferred shares to common shares.

Why would a corporation call in its preferred stock? Corporations call in preferred stock for many reasons: (1) the outstanding preferred stock may require a 12% annual dividend at a time when the company can secure capital to retire the stock by issuing a new 8% preferred stock; (2) the issuing company may have been sufficiently profitable to retire the preferred stock out of earnings; or (3) the company may wish to force conversion of its convertible preferred stock because the cash dividend on the equivalent common shares is less than the dividend on the preferred shares.

Balance Sheet Presentation of Stock

Objective 4
Present in proper form the stockholders' equity section of a balance sheet.

The stockholders' equity section of a corporation's balance sheet contains two main elements: paid-in capital and retained earnings. **Paid-in capital** is the part of stockholders' equity that normally results from cash or other assets invested by owners. Paid-in capital also results from services performed for the corporation in exchange for capital stock and from certain other transactions discussed in Chapter 13. As stated earlier, **retained earnings** is the part of stockholders' equity resulting from accumulated net income, reduced by dividends and net losses. Net income increases the Retained Earnings account balance and net losses decrease it. In addition, dividends declared to stockholders decrease Retained Earnings. Since Retained Earnings is a stockholders' equity account and represents accumulated net income retained by the company, it normally has a credit balance. We discuss retained earnings in more detail in Chapter 13.

The following illustration shows the proper financial reporting for preferred and common stock. Assume that a corporation is authorized to issue 10,000 shares of $100 par value, 6%, cumulative, convertible preferred stock (five common for one preferred), all of which have been issued and are outstanding; and 200,000 shares of $10 par value common stock, of which 80,000 shares are issued and outstanding. The stockholders' equity section of the balance sheet (assuming $450,000 of retained earnings) is:

Stockholders' equity:
  Paid-in capital:
    Preferred stock—$100 par value, 6%
     cumulative, convertible
     (5 common for 1 preferred); authorized,
     issued, and outstanding, 10,000 shares $1,000,000
    Common stock—$10 par value; authorized,
     200,000 shares; issued and outstanding,
     80,000 shares 800,000
      Total paid-in capital $1,800,000
  Retained earnings 450,000
      Total stockholders' equity $2,250,000

Note to the Student
Note that a corporation's equity consists of two major components: stockholder investments (paid-in capital) and retained earnings.

Notice that the balance sheet lists preferred stock before common stock because the preferred stock is preferred as to dividends, assets, or both. The company discloses the conversion rate in a parenthetical note within the description of preferred stock or in a footnote.

Business Insight Rite Aid Corporation in its 2011 annual report provided the following presentation of preferred stock in the stockholders' equity section of its balance sheet:

An Accounting Perspective

2011

Stockholders' equity:
Preferred stock—Series H, liquidation value
  $100 per share; 2,0000,000 shares authorized
  1,435,000 shares issued $143.5M

Stock Issuances for Cash

Each share of common or preferred capital stock either has a par value or lacks one. The corporation's charter determines the par value printed on the stock certificates issued. Par value may be any amount—1 cent, 10 cents, 16 cents, $1, $5, or $100. Low par values of $10 or less are common in our economy.

Issuance of Par Value Stock for Cash

As previously mentioned, par value gives no clue as to the stock's market value. Shares with a par value of $5 have traded (sold) in the market for more than $600, and many $100 par value preferred stocks have traded for considerably less than par. Par value is not even a reliable indicator of the price at which shares can be issued. New corporations can issue shares at prices well in excess of par value or for less than par value if state laws permit. Par value gives the accountant a constant amount at which to record capital stock issuances in the capital stock accounts. As stated earlier, the total par value of all issued shares is generally the legal capital of the corporation.

Objective 5
Account for the issuances of stock for cash and other assets.

To illustrate the issuance of stock for cash, assume a company issues 10,000 authorized shares of $20 par value common stock at $22 per share. The following entry records the issuance:

Cash	220,000	
Common Stock		200,000
Paid-In Capital in Excess of Par Value—Common		20,000
To record the issuance of 10,000 shares of stock for cash.		

Notice that the credit to the Common Stock account is the par value ($20) times the number of shares issued. The accountant credits the excess over par value ($20,000) to Paid-In Capital in Excess of Par Value; it is part of the paid-in capital contributed by the stockholders. Thus, **paid-in capital in excess of par (or stated) value** represents capital contributed to a corporation in addition to that assigned to the shares issued and recorded in capital stock accounts. The paid-in capital section of the balance sheet appears as follows:

Paid-in capital:	
Common stock—par value, $20; 10,000 shares	
authorized, issued and outstanding	$ 200,000
Paid-in capital in excess of par value—common	20,000
Total paid-in capital	$ 220,000

Issuance of No-Par, Stated Value Stock for Cash

When it issues no-par stock with a stated value, a company carries the shares in the capital stock account at the stated value. Any amounts received in excess of the stated value per share represent a part of the paid-in capital of the corporation and the company credits them to Paid-In Capital in Excess of Stated Value. The legal capital of a corporation issuing no-par shares with a stated value is usually equal to the total stated value of the shares issued.

To illustrate, assume that the DeWitt Corporation, which is authorized to issue 10,000 shares of common stock without par value, assigns a stated value of $20 per share to its stock. DeWitt issues the 10,000 authorized shares for cash at $22 per share. The entry to record this transaction is:

Reinforcing Problems
E12-3 Journalize stock issuance.
E12-4 Prepare entries for stock issuance.

Cash	220,000	
Common Stock		200,000
Paid-In Capital in Excess of Stated Value—Common		20,000
To record the issuance of 10,000 shares of stock for cash.		

The paid-in capital section of the balance sheet appears as follows:

Paid-in capital:	
Common stock—no-par, stated value, $20; 10,000 shares	
authorized, issued and outstanding	$ 200,000
Paid-in capital in excess of stated value—common	20,000
Total paid-in capital	$ 220,000

Note to the Student
Companies do not record paid-in capital received in excess of par as a gain or revenue. Revenues arise from the sale of goods or services. Corporate paid-in capital is part of stockholders' equity.

DeWitt carries the $20,000 received over and above the stated value of $200,000 permanently as paid-in capital because it is a part of the capital originally contributed by the stockholders. However, the legal capital of the DeWitt Corporation is $200,000.

Issuance of No-Par Stock without a Stated Value for Cash

A corporation that issues no-par stock without a stated value credits the entire amount received to the capital stock account. For instance, consider the DeWitt Corporation's issuance of no-par stock. If no stated value had been assigned, the entry would have been as follows:

Cash	220,000	
Common Stock		220,000
To record issuance of 10,000 shares for cash.		

Since the company may issue shares at different times and at differing amounts, its credits to the capital stock account are not uniform amounts per share. This contrasts with issuing par value shares or shares with a stated value.

To continue our example, the paid-in capital section of the company's balance sheet would be as follows:

Paid-in capital:
Common stock—without par or stated value, 10,000 shares
    authorized, issued and outstanding $ 220,000
        Total paid-in capital $ 220,000

Note to the Student
Corporations do not make journal entries when investors buy stock from each other in the marketplace; instead, they register the names of the new holders of the stock.

The actual capital contributed by stockholders is $220,000. In some states, the entire amount received for shares without par or stated value is the amount of legal capital. The legal capital in this example would then be equal to $220,000.

Capital Stock Issued for Property or Services

When issuing capital stock for property or services, companies must determine the dollar amount of the exchange. Accountants generally record the transaction at the fair value of (1) the property or services received or (2) the stock issued, whichever is more clearly evident.

To illustrate, assume that the owners of a tract of land deeded it to a corporation in exchange for 1,000 shares of $12 par value common stock. The firm can only estimate the fair market value of the land. At the time of the exchange, the stock has an established total market value of $14,000. The required entry is:

Land	14,000	
Common Stock		12,000
Paid-In Capital in Excess of Par Value—Common		2,000
To record the receipt of land for capital stock.		

Reinforcing Problems
E12-5 Journalize stock issuance for property.
E12-6 Journalize stock issuance to satisfy liability.
E12-7 Journalize stock issuance for legal services.

As another example, assume a firm issues 100 shares of common stock with a par value of $40 per share in exchange for legal services received in organizing as a corporation. No shares have been traded recently, so there is no established market value. The attorney previously agreed to a price of $5,000 for these legal services but decided to accept stock in lieu of cash. In this example, the correct entry is:

Organization Costs	5,000	
Common Stock		4,000
Paid-In Capital in Excess of Par Value—Common		1,000
To record the receipt of legal services for capital stock.		

The company should value the services at the price previously agreed on since that value is more clearly evident than the market value of the shares. It should debit an intangible asset account because these services benefit the corporation throughout its entire life. The company credits the amount by which the value of the services received exceeds the par value of the shares issued to a Paid-In Capital in Excess of Par Value—Common account.

Note to the Student
Intangible assets are amortized over their finite useful lives.

Balance Sheet Presentation of Paid-In Capital in Excess of Par (or Stated) Value—Common or Preferred

Accountants credit amounts received in excess of the par or stated value of shares to a Paid-In Capital in Excess of Par (or Stated) Value—Common (or Preferred) account. They carry the amounts received in excess of par or stated value in separate accounts for each class of stock issued. Using the following assumed data, the stockholders' equity section of the balance sheet of a company with both preferred and common stock outstanding would appear as follows:

Stockholders' equity:			
Paid-in capital:			
Preferred stock—$100 par value, 6% cumulative; 1,000 shares authorized, issued, and outstanding	$100,000		
Common stock—without par value, stated value, $5; 100,000 shares authorized, 80,000 shares; issued and outstanding	400,000	$ 500,000	
Paid-in capital in excess of par (or stated) value:			
From preferred stock issuances	$ 5,000		
From common stock issuances	20,000	25,000	
Total paid-in capital		$ 525,000	
Retained earnings		200,000	
Total stockholders' equity		$ 725,000	

Book Value

Objective 6
Determine book values of both preferred and common stock.

The total book value of a corporation's outstanding shares is equal to its recorded net asset value—that is, assets minus liabilities. Quite simply, the amount of net assets is equal to stockholders' equity. When only common stock is outstanding, companies compute the **book value per share** by dividing total stockholders' equity by the number of common shares outstanding. In calculating book value, they assume that (1) the corporation could be liquidated without incurring any further expenses, (2) the assets could be sold at their recorded amounts, and (3) the liabilities could be satisfied at their recorded amounts. Assume the stockholders' equity of a corporation is as follows:

Stockholders' equity:		
Paid-in capital:		
Common stock—without par value, stated value, $10; authorized, 20,000 shares; issued and outstanding, 15,000 shares	$ 150,000	
Paid-in capital in excess of stated value	10,000	
Total paid-in capital		$ 160,000
Retained earnings		50,000
Total stockholders' equity		$ 210,000

To determine the book value per share of the stock:

Total stockholders' equity	$210,000
Total shares outstanding	÷15,000
Book value per share	$ 14

Reinforcing Problem
E12-8 Compute the book value and average price of common stock.

When two or more classes of capital stock are outstanding, the computation of book value per share is more complex. The book value for each share of stock depends on the rights of the preferred stockholders. Preferred stockholders typically are entitled to a specified liquidation value per share, plus cumulative dividends in arrears, since most preferred stocks are preferred as to assets and are cumulative. In each case, the specific provisions in the preferred stock contract govern. To illustrate, assume the Celeron Corporation's stockholders' equity is as follows:

Stockholders' equity:		
Paid-in capital:		
Preferred stock—$100 par value, 6% cumulative; 5,000 shares authorized, issued, and outstanding	$ 500,000	
Common stock—$10 par value, 200,000 shares authorized, issued and outstanding	2,000,000	
Paid-in capital in excess of par value—preferred	200,000	
Total paid-in capital		$2,700,000
Retained earnings		400,000
Total stockholders' equity		$3,100,000

The preferred stock is 6%, cumulative. It is preferred as to dividends and as to assets in liquidation to the extent of the liquidation value of $100 per share, plus any cumulative dividends on the preferred stock. Dividends for four years (including the current year) are unpaid. You would calculate the book values of each class of stock as follows:

		Total	Per Share
Total stockholders' equity		$3,100,000	
Book value of preferred stock (5,000 shares)			
Liquidation value (5,000 shares X $100)	$ 500,000		
Dividends (4 years at $30,000)	120,000	620,000	$ 124.00*
Book value of common stock (200,000 shares)		$2,480,000	12.40†

* $620,000 ÷ 5,000 shares.
† $2,480,000 ÷ 200,000 shares.

Notice that Celeron did not assign the paid-in capital in excess of par value—preferred to the preferred stock in determining the book values. Celeron assigned only the liquidation value and cumulative dividends on the preferred stock to the preferred stock.

Assume now that the features attached to the preferred stock are the same except that the preferred stockholders have the right to receive $103 per share in liquidation. The book values of each class of stock would be:

		Total	Per Share
Total stockholders' equity		$3,100,000	
Book value of preferred stock (5,000 shares)			
Liquidation value (5,000 shares X $103)	$ 515,000		
Dividends (4 years at $30,000)	120,000	635,000	$ 127.00
Book value of common stock (200,000 shares)		$2,465,000	12.33

Book value rarely equals market value of a stock because many of the assets have changed in value due to inflation. Thus, the market prices of the shares of many corporations are different from their book values.

Note to the Student
There is not necessarily any direct relationship between book value and the market price of stock.

An Accounting Perspective

Business Insight   *The Wall Street Journal* publishes the New York Stock Exchange (NYSE) Composite Transactions each Monday through Friday except when the exchange is closed. For each stock listed on the NYSE, it lists the following data. We use data for the Kellogg Company, which produces ready-to-eat cereals and other food products, as recently reported in The Wall Street Journal as an example:

52 Weeks										
Ytd % Chg	Hi	Lo	Stock	Sym	Div	Ytd %	PE	Vol 100s	Last	Net Chg
-1.1	57.50	47.28	Kellogg	K	1.72	3.5	15	1978	48.76	-0.06

The first column reflects the stock price percentage change for the calendar year to date, adjusted for stock splits and dividends over 10%. The next two columns show the high and low price over the preceding 52 weeks plus the current week. The next two columns show the company name (Kellogg) and the NYSE's symbol (K) for that company. The Div column is the annual dividend based on the last quarterly, semiannual, or annual declaration. Yield % is calculated as dividends paid divided by the current market price. The PE ratio is the closing market price divided by the total earnings per share for the most recent four quarters. The Vol 100s column shows the unofficial daily total of shares traded, quoted in hundreds. Thus, 1,978,000 shares of Kellogg's were traded that day. The next to last column shows the closing price for that day. The final column shows the change in the closing price as compared to the closing price of the preceding day.

Analyzing and Using the Financial Results— Return on Average Common Stockholders' Equity

Objective 7
Analyze and use the financial results—return on average common stockholders' equity.

Stockholders' equity is particularly important to managers, creditors, and investors in determining the return on equity, which is the return on average common stockholders' equity.

The **return on average common stockholders' equity** measures what a given company earned for its common stockholders from all sources as a percentage of the common stockholders' investment. From the common stockholders' point of view, it is an important measure of the income-producing ability of the company. The ratio's formula is:

$$\text{Return on average common stockholders' equity} = \frac{\text{Net income available to common stockholders}}{\text{Average common stockholders' equity}}$$

If preferred stock is outstanding, the numerator is net income minus the annual dividend on preferred stock, and the denominator is the average total book value of common stock. If no preferred stock is outstanding, the numerator is net income, and the denominator is average stockholders' equity.

Procter & Gamble
Procter & Gamble markets more than 250 brands. Examples include Tide, Ariel, Pantene, Bounty, Always, Pringles, Olay, and Pampers.

The Procter & Gamble Company reported the following information in its 2011 financial statements ($ millions):

	2011
Net earnings	$ 11,797
Stockholders' equity, beginning	61,439
Stockholders' equity, ending	68,001

The return on average common stockholders' equity for Procter & Gamble is 18.2%, or $11,797/[($61,439 + $68,001)/2]. Investors view any increase from year to year as favorable and any decrease as unfavorable.

Since the stock market is frequently referred to as an economic indicator, the knowledge you now have on corporate stock issuances should help you relate to stocks traded in the market. Chapter 13 continues the discussion of paid-in capital and also discusses treasury stock, retained earnings, and dividends.

A Broader Perspective

Belex Corporation

Joe Morrison is the controller for Belex Corporation. He is involved in a discussion with other members of management concerning how to get rid of some potentially harmful toxic waste materials that are a by-product of the company's manufacturing process.

There are two alternative methods of disposing of the materials. The first alternative is to bury the waste in steel drums on a tract of land adjacent to the factory building. There is currently no legal prohibition against doing this. The cost of disposing of the materials in this way is estimated to be $50,000 per year. The best estimate is that the steel drums would not leak for at least 50 years, but probably would begin leaking after that time. The second alternative is to seal the materials in lead drums that would be disposed of at sea by a waste management company. The cost of this alternative is estimated to be $400,000 per year. The federal government has certified this method as the preferred method of disposal. The best estimate is that the lead drums would never rupture or leak.

Belex Corporation has seen some tough economic times. The company suffered losses until last year, when it showed a profit of $750,000 as a result of a new manufacturing project. So far, the waste materials from that project have been accumulating in two large vats on the company's land. However, these vats are almost full, so soon management must decide how to dispose of the materials.

One group of managers is arguing in favor of the first alternative because it is legally permissible and results in annual profits of about $700,000. They point out that using the second alternative would reduce profits to about $350,000 per year and cut managers' bonuses in half. They also claim that some of their competitors are now using the first alternative, and to use the second alternative would place the company at a serious competitive disadvantage.

Another group of managers argues that the second alternative is the only safe alternative to pursue. They claim that when the steel drums start leaking they will contaminate the ground water and could cause serious health problems. When this contamination occurs, the company will lose public support and may even have to pay for the cleanup. The cost of that cleanup could run into the millions.

Understanding the Learning Objectives

- Advantages:
    1. Easy transfer of ownership.
    2. Limited liability.
    3. Continuous existence of the entity.
    4. Easy capital generation.
    5. Professional management.
    6. Separation of owners and entity.

- Disadvantages:
    1. Double taxation.
    2. Government regulation.
    3. Entrenched, inefficient management.
    4. Limited ability to raise creditor capital.

- Par value—an arbitrary amount assigned to each share of a given class of stock and printed on the stock certificate.

- Stated value—an arbitrary amount assigned by the board of directors to each share of a given class of no-par stock.
- Market value—the price at which shares of capital stock are bought and sold in the market.
- Book value—the amount per share that each stockholder would receive if the corporation were liquidated without incurring any further expenses and if assets were sold and liabilities liquidated at their recorded amounts.
- Liquidation value—the amount a stockholder would receive if a corporation discontinues operations, pays its liabilities, and distributes the remaining cash among the stockholders.
- Redemption value—the price per share at which a corporation may call in (redeem) its capital stock for retirement.
- Capital stock authorized—the number of shares of stock that a corporation is entitled to issue as designated in its charter.

- Capital stock issued—the number of shares of stock that have been sold and issued to stockholders.
- Capital stock outstanding—the number of authorized shares of stock that have been issued and that are still currently held by stockholders.
- Two basic classes of capital stock:
  1. Common stock—represents the residual equity.
  2. Preferred stock—may be preferred as to dividends and/or assets. Also may be cumulative and/or callable.

- If the company has paid-in capital in excess of par value, the proper form would be:

Stockholders' equity:			
Paid-in capital:			
Preferred stock—$100 par value, 6% cumulative; 1,000 shares authorized, issued, and outstanding	$ 100,000		
Common stock—without par value, stated value, $5; 100,000 shares authorized, 80,000 shares; issued and outstanding	400,000	$ 500,000	
Paid-in capital in excess of par (or stated) value:			
From preferred stock issuances	$ 5,000		
From common stock issuances	20,000	25,000	
Total paid-in capital			$ 525,000
Retained earnings			200,000
Total stockholders' equity			$ 725,000

The following examples illustrate the issuance for cash of: (1) stock with a par value, (2) no-par value stock with a stated value, and (3) no-par value stock without a stated value.

- Issuance of par value stock for cash—10,000 shares of $20 par value common stock issued for $22 per share.

Cash	220,000	
Common Stock		200,000
Paid-In Capital in Excess of Par Value—Common		20,000

- Issuance of no-par, stated value stock for cash—10,000 shares (no-par value) with $20 per share stated value issued for $22 per share.

Cash	220,000	
Common Stock		200,000
Paid-In Capital in Excess of Stated Value—Common		20,000

- Issuance of no-par stock without a stated value for cash—10,000 shares (no-par value) issued at $22 per share.

Cash	220,000	
Common Stock		220,000

- *Example:* A corporation has 200,000 shares of common stock and 5,000 shares of preferred stock outstanding. Preferred stock is 6% and cumulative. It is preferred as to dividends and as to assets in liquidation to the extent of the liquidation value of $100 per share, plus any cumulative dividends on the preferred stock. Dividends for three years are unpaid. Total stockholders' equity is $4,100,000. Calculations are as follows:

Objective 6
Determine book values of both preferred and common stock.

		Total	Per Share
Total stockholders' equity		$4,100,000	
Book value of preferred stock (5,000 shares)			
Liquidation value (5,000 shares X $100)	$ 500,000		
Dividends (3 years at $30,000)	90,000	590,000	$ 118.00
Book value of common stock (200,000 shares)		$3,510,000	17.55

- The return on average common stockholders' equity equals net income available to common stockholders divided by average common stockholders' equity.
- The return on average common stockholders' equity is an important measure of the income-producing ability of the company.

Objective 7
Analyze and use the financial results—return on average common stockholders' equity.

Demonstration Problem 12–A

Violet Company has paid all required preferred dividends through December 31, 2006. Its outstanding stock consists of 10,000 shares of $125 par value common stock and 4,000 shares of 6%, $125 par value preferred stock. During five successive years, the company's dividend declarations were as follows:

2007	$85,000
2008	52,500
2009	7,500
2010	15,000
2011	67,500

Required Compute the amount of dividends that would have been paid to each class of stock in each of the last five years assuming the preferred stock is:

a. Cumulative.
b. Noncumulative.

Solution to Demonstration Problem 12–A

VIOLET COMPANY

Year	Dividends to	Assumptions	
		a	**b**
2007	Preferred	$30,000*	$30,000
	Common	55,000	55,000
2008	Preferred	30,000	30,000
	Common	22,500	22,500
2009	Preferred	7,500	7,500
	Common	-0-	-0-
2010	Preferred	15,000	15,000
	Common	-0-	-0-
2011	Preferred	67,500†	30,000‡
	Common	-0-	37,500

* 4,000 shares X $125 X 0.06 = $30,000
† $30,000 + $22,500 preferred dividend missed in 2009 + $15,000 preferred dividend missed in 2010.
‡ Only the basic $30,000 dividend is paid because the stock is noncumulative.

Demonstration Problem 12–B

Terrier Company has been authorized to issue 100,000 shares of $6 par value common stock and 1,000 shares of 14%, cumulative, preferred stock with a par value of $12.

Required **a.** Prepare the entries for the following transactions that all took place in June 2011:

    (1) 50,000 shares of common stock are issued for cash at $24 per share.
    (2) 750 shares of preferred stock are issued for cash at $18 per share.
    (3) 1,000 shares of common stock are issued in exchange for legal services received in the incorporation process. The fair market value of the legal services is $9,000.

b. Prepare the paid-in capital section of Terrier's balance sheet as of June 30, 2011.

Solution to Demonstration Problem 12–B

a. (1)

Cash	1,200,000	
Common Stock		300,000
Paid-In Capital in Excess of Par Value—Common Stock		900,000
To record issuance of 50,000 shares at $24 per share.		

(2)	Cash	13,500	
	Preferred Stock		9,000
	Paid-In Capital in Excess of Par Value—Preferred		4,500
	To record the issuance of 750 shares for cash, at $18 per share.		

(3)	Organization Costs	9,000	
	Common Stock		6,000
	Paid-In Capital in Excess of Par Value—Common		3,000
	To record the issuance of 1,000 shares in exchange for legal services.		

b.

TERRIER COMPANY
Partial Balance Sheet
June 30, 2011

Paid-in Capital:
 Preferred stock—$12 par value, 14% cumulative; 1,000 shares authorized; issued and outstanding, 750 shares $ 9,000
 Common stock—$6 par value per share; 100,000 shares authorized; issued and outstanding, 51,000 shares   306,000 $ 315,000

 Paid-in capital in excess of par value:
  From preferred stock issuances $ 4,500
  From common stock issuances   903,000   907,500
   Total paid-in capital $1,222,500

New Terms

Articles of incorporation   The application for the corporation's charter. *461*

Board of directors   Elected by the stockholders to have primary responsibility for formulating policies for the corporation. The board also authorizes contracts, declares dividends, establishes executive salaries, and grants authorization to borrow money. *463*

Book value per share   Stockholders' equity per share; the amount per share each stockholder would receive if the corporation were liquidated without incurring any further expenses and if assets were sold and liabilities liquidated at their recorded amounts. *466, 474*

Bylaws   A set of rules or regulations adopted by the board of directors of a corporation to govern the conduct of corporate affairs. The bylaws must be in agreement with the laws of the state and the policies and purposes in the corporate charter. *462*

Callable preferred stock   If the stock is nonconvertible, it must be surrendered to the company when the holder is requested to do so. If the stock is convertible, it may be either surrendered or converted into common shares when called. *469*

Call premium (on preferred stock)   The difference between the amount at which a corporation calls its preferred stock for redemption and the par value of the stock. *470*

Capital stock   Transferable units of ownership in a corporation. *464*

Capital stock authorized   The number of shares of stock that a corporation is entitled to issue as designated in its charter. *466*

Capital stock issued   The number of shares of stock that have been sold and issued to stockholders. *466*

Capital stock outstanding   The number of shares of authorized stock issued and currently held by stockholders. *466*

Common stock   Shares of stock representing the residual equity in the corporation. If only one class of stock is issued, it is known as *common stock*. All other claims rank ahead of common stockholders' claims. *467*

Convertible preferred stock   Preferred stock that is convertible into common stock of the issuing corporation. *469*

Corporate charter   The contract between the state and the incorporators of a corporation, and their successors, granting the corporation its legal existence. *461*

Corporation   An entity recognized by law as possessing an existence separate and distinct from its owners; that is, it is a separate legal entity. A corporation is granted many of the rights, and placed under many of the obligations, of a natural person. In any given state, all corporations organized under the laws of that state are *domestic corporations* (461); all others are *foreign corporations* (461). *459*

Cumulative preferred stock   Preferred stock for which the right to receive a basic dividend accumulates if any dividends have not been paid; unpaid cumulative preferred dividends must be paid before any dividends can be paid on the common stock. *468*

Discount on capital stock   The amount by which the par value of shares issued exceeds their issue price. The original issuance of shares at a discount is illegal in most states. *465*

Dividend   A distribution of assets (usually cash) that represents a withdrawal of earnings by the owners. *468*

Dividend on preferred stock   The amount paid to preferred stockholders as a return for the use of their money; usually a fixed or stated amount expressed in dollars per share or as a percentage of par value per share. *468*

Dividends in arrears   Cumulative unpaid dividends, including quarterly dividends not declared for the current year. *468*

Domestic corporation   See *corporation.*

Foreign corporation   See *corporation.*

Incorporators   Persons seeking to bring a corporation into existence. *461*

Legal capital (stated capital)   An amount prescribed by law (usually the par value or stated value of shares issued) below which a corporation may not reduce stockholders' equity through the declaration of dividends or other payments to stockholders. *465*

Liquidation value   The amount a stockholder will receive if a corporation discontinues operations and liquidates by selling its assets, paying its liabilities, and distributing the remaining cash among the stockholders. *466*

Market value   The price at which shares of capital stock are bought and sold in the market. *466*

Minutes book   The record book in which actions taken at stockholders' and board of directors' meetings are recorded; the written authorization for many actions taken by corporate officers. *464*

Noncumulative preferred stock   Preferred stock on which the right to receive a dividend expires if the dividend is not declared. *468*

No-par stock   Capital stock without par value, to which a stated value may or may not be assigned. *465*

Organization costs   Costs of organizing a corporation, such as incorporation fees and legal fees applicable to incorporation. *462*

Paid-in capital   Amount of stockholders' equity that normally results from the cash or other assets invested by owners; it may also result from services provided for shares of stock and certain other transactions. *470*

Paid-in capital in excess of par (or stated) value— common or preferred   Capital contributed to a corporation in addition to that assigned to the shares issued and recorded in capital stock accounts. *472*

Par value   An arbitrary amount assigned to each share of a given class of stock and printed on the stock certificate. *465*

Preemptive right   The right of stockholders to buy additional shares in a proportion equal to the percentage of shares already owned. *462*

Preferred stock   Capital stock that carries certain features or rights not carried by common stock. Preferred stock may be preferred as to dividends, as to assets, or as to both dividends and assets. Preferred stock may be callable and/or convertible and may be cumulative or noncumulative. *467*

Proxy   A legal document signed by a stockholder, giving another person the authority to vote the stockholder's shares at a stockholders' meeting. *463*

Redemption value   The price per share at which a corporation may call in (or redeem) its capital stock for retirement. *466*

Retained earnings   The part of stockholders' equity resulting from net income, reduced by dividends and net losses. *470*

Return on average common stockholders' equity A measure of the income-producing ability of the company. It is the ratio of net income available to common stockholders divided by average common stockholders' equity. *476*

Shares of stock   Units of ownership in a corporation. *459*

Stated value   An arbitrary amount assigned by the board of directors to each share of a given class of no-par stock. *465*

Stock certificate   A printed or engraved document serving as evidence that the holder owns a certain number of shares of capital stock. *464*

Stockholders' ledger   Contains a group of subsidiary accounts showing the number of shares of stock currently held by each stockholder. *464*

Stock preferred as to assets   Means that in liquidation, the preferred stockholders are entitled to receive the par value (or a larger stipulated liquidation value) per share before any assets may be distributed to common stockholders. *469*

Stock preferred as to dividends   Means that the preferred stockholders are entitled to receive a specified dividend per share before any dividend on common stock is paid. *468*

Stock registrar   Typically, a bank that maintains records of the shares outstanding for a company. *464*

Stock-transfer agent   Typically, a bank or trust company employed by a corporation to transfer stock between buyers and sellers. *464*

Stock without par value   See *no-par stock.*

Unissued shares   Capital stock authorized but not yet issued. *466*

Self-Test

True-False

Indicate whether each of the following statements is true or false.

1. A person may favor the corporate form of organization for a risky business enterprise primarily because a corporation's shares can be easily transferred.

2. In the event of corporate liquidation, stockholders whose stock is preferred as to assets are entitled to receive the par value of their shares before any amounts are distributed to creditors or common stockholders.

3. The par value of a share of capital stock is no indication of the market value or book value of the share of stock.

4. When 10,000 shares of $20 par value common stock are issued in payment for a parcel of land with a fair market value of $300,000, the Common Stock account is credited for $200,000, and the Paid-In Capital in Excess of Par Value—Common account is credited for $100,000.

Multiple-Choice

Select the best answer for each of the following questions.

1. Which of the following is not an advantage of the corporate form of organization?
   a. Continuous existence of the entity.
   b. Limited liability of stockholders.
   c. Government regulation.
   d. Easy transfer of ownership.

2. An arbitrary amount assigned by the board of directors to each share of a given class of no-par stock is:
   a. Quasi-par value.
   b. Stated value.
   c. Redemption value.
   d. Liquidation value.

3. Preferred stock that has dividends in arrears is:
   a. Noncumulative preferred stock.
   b. Noncumulative and callable preferred stock.
   c. Noncumulative and convertible preferred stock.
   d. Cumulative preferred stock.

4. Quinn Corporation issued 10,000 shares of $20 par value common stock at $50 per share. The amount that would be credited to Paid-In Capital in Excess of Par Value—Common is:
   a. $200,000.
   b. $300,000.
   c. $500,000.
   d. $700,000.
   e. None of the above.

5. You are given the following information: Capital Stock, $80,000 ($80 par); Paid-In Capital in Excess of Par Value—Common, $200,000; and Retained Earnings, $400,000. Assuming only one class of stock, the book value per share is:
   a. $680.
   b. $280.
   c. $80.
   d. $400.
   e. None of the above.

Now turn to page 493 to check your answers.

Questions

1. Cite the major advantages of the corporate form of business organization and indicate why each is considered an advantage.

2. What is meant by the statement that corporate income is subject to double taxation? Cite several other disadvantages of the corporate form of organization.

3. Why is "Organization Expense" not a good title for the account that records the costs of organizing a corporation? Could you justify leaving the balance of an Organization Costs account intact throughout the life of a corporation?

4. What are the basic rights associated with a share of capital stock if there is only one class of stock outstanding?

5. Explain the purpose or function of: *(a)* the stockholders' ledger, *(b)* the minutes book, *(c)* the stock-transfer agent, and *(d)* the stock registrar.

6. What are the differences between par value stock and no-par value stock?

7. Corporate capital stock is seldom issued for less than par value. Give two reasons why this statement is true.

8. Explain the terms *liquidation value* and *redemption value.*

9. What are the meanings of the terms *stock preferred as to dividends* and *stock preferred as to assets?*

10. What do the terms *cumulative* and *noncumulative* mean in regard to preferred stock?

11. What are *dividends in arrears,* and how should they be disclosed in the financial statements?

12. A corporation has 1,000 shares of 8%, $200 par value, cumulative, preferred stock outstanding. Dividends on this stock have not been declared for three years. Is the corporation legally liable to its preferred stockholders for these dividends? How should this fact be shown in the balance sheet, if at all?

13. Explain why a corporation might issue a preferred stock that is both convertible into common stock and callable.

14. Explain the nature of the account entitled Paid-In Capital in Excess of Par Value. Under what circumstances is this account credited?

15. Blake Corporation issued 5,000 shares of $100 par value common stock at $120 per share. What is the legal capital of Blake Corporation, and why is the amount of legal capital important?

16. What is the general approach of the accountant in determining the dollar amount at which to record the issuance of capital stock for services or property other than cash?

17. What assumptions are made in determining book value?

18. Assuming there is no preferred stock outstanding, how can the book value per share of common stock be determined? Of what significance is the book value per share? What is the relationship of book value per share to market value per share?

Exercises

Exercise 12-1
Determine dividends for common and noncumulative preferred stock (L.O. 3)

Winters Corporation has outstanding 1,000 shares of noncumulative preferred stock and 2,000 shares of common stock. The preferred stock is entitled to an annual dividend of $100 per share before dividends are declared on common stock. What are the total dividends received by each class of stock if Winters Corporation distributes $280,000 in dividends in 2012?

Exercise 12-2
Determine dividends for common and cumulative preferred stock (L.O. 3)

Zeff Corporation has 2,000 shares outstanding of cumulative preferred stock and 6,000 shares of common stock. The preferred stock is entitled to an annual dividend of $18 per share before dividends are declared on common stock. No preferred dividends were paid for last year and the current year. What are the total dividends received by each class of stock if Zeff Corporation distributes $108,000 in dividends?

Gordon Company issued 10,000 shares of common stock for $1,120,000 cash. The common stock has a par value of $100 per share. Give the journal entry for the stock issuance.

Exercise 12-3
Journalize stock
issuance (L.O. 5)

Thore Company issued 30,000 shares of $20 par value common stock for $680,000. What is the journal entry for this transaction? What would the journal entry be if the common stock had no-par or stated value?

Exercise 12-4
Prepare entries for
stock issuance (L.O. 5)

Li & Tu, Inc., needed land for a plant site. It issued 100 shares of $480 par value common stock to the incorporators of their corporation in exchange for land, which cost $56,000 one year ago. Experienced appraisers recently valued the land at $72,000. What journal entry would be appropriate to record the acquisition of the land?

Exercise 12-5
Journalize stock
issuance for property
(L.O. 5)

Smart Corporation owes a trade creditor $30,000 on open account which the corporation does not have sufficient cash to pay. The trade creditor suggests that Smart Corporation issue to him 750 shares of the $24 par value common stock, which is currently selling on the market at $40. Present the entry or entries that should be made on Smart Corporation's books.

Exercise 12-6
Journalize stock
issuance to satisfy
liability (L.O. 5)

Why would a law firm ever consider accepting stock of a new corporation having a total par value of $320,000 as payment in full of a $480,000 bill for legal services rendered? If such a transaction occurred, give the journal entry the issuing company would make on its books.

Exercise 12-7
Journalize stock
issuance for legal
services (L.O. 5)

The stockholders' equity section of Graf Company's balance sheet is as follows:

Exercise 12-8
Compute the book
value and average
price of common stock
(L.O. 6)

```
Stockholders' equity:
  Paid-in capital:
    Common stock—without par value, $12
      stated value; authorized 100,000 shares;
      issued and outstanding, 70,000 shares      $ 840,000
    Paid-in capital in excess of stated value      340,000
      Total paid-in capital                                   $1,180,000
  Retained earnings                                               80,000
      Total stockholders' equity                              $1,260,000
```

Compute the average price at which the 70,000 issued shares of common stock were sold. Compute the book value per share of common stock.

Problems

The outstanding capital stock of Robbins Corporation consisted of 3,000 shares of 10% preferred stock, $250 par value, and 30,000 shares of no-par common stock with a stated value of $250. The preferred was issued at $412, the common at $480 per share. On January 1, 2007, the retained earnings of the company were $250,000. During the succeeding five years, net income was as follows:

Problem 12-1
Determine dividends
for common stock
and cumulative
and noncumulative
preferred stock
(L.O. 3)

2007	$767,500
2008	510,000
2009	48,000
2010	160,000
2011	662,500

No dividends were in arrears as of January 1, 2007, and during the five years 2007–2011, the board of directors declared dividends in each year equal to net income of the year.

Required ➲ Prepare a schedule showing the dividends declared each year on each class of stock assuming the preferred stock is:

    a. Cumulative.
    b. Noncumulative.

Problem 12-2
Journalize stock issuances for cash, services (organization costs), and property; prepare resulting balance sheet (L.O. 5)

On December 27, 2010, Glade Company was authorized to issue 250,000 shares of $24 par value common stock. It then completed the following transactions:

2011
Jan.   14 Issued 45,000 shares of common stock at $30 per share for cash.
         29 Gave the promoters of the corporation 25,000 shares of common stock for their services in organizing the company. The board of directors valued these services at $744,000.
         19 Exchanged 50,000 shares of common stock for the following assets at the indicated fair market values:

Land	$216,000
Building	528,000
Machinery	720,000

Required ➲ **a.** Prepare general journal entries to record the transactions.
    b. Prepare the balance sheet of the company as of March 1, 2011.

Problem 12-3
Post transactions; prepare balance sheets for par value stock, stated value stock, and no-par or stated value stock (L.O. 2, 4, 5)

In the corporate charter that it received on May 1, 2011, Norris Company was authorized to issue 15,000 shares of common stock. The company issued 1,000 shares immediately for $82 per share, cash.

On July 2, the company issued 100 shares of stock to a lawyer to satisfy a $8,400 bill for legal services rendered in organizing the corporation.

On July 5, the company issued 1,000 shares to the principal promoter of the corporation in exchange for a patent. Another 200 shares were issued to this same person for costs incurred and services rendered in bringing the corporation into existence. The market value of the stock was $84 per share.

Required ➲ **a.** Set up T-accounts, and post these transactions. Then prepare a balance sheet for the Norris Company as of July 5, 2011, assuming the authorized stock has a par value of $75 per share.
    b. Repeat part **(a)** for the stockholders' equity accounts, and prepare the stockholders' equity section of the July 5 balance sheet assuming the stock authorized has no par value but has a $30 per share stated value.
    c. Repeat part **(a)** for the stockholders' equity accounts assuming the stock authorized has neither par nor stated value. Prepare the stockholders' equity section of the balance sheet.

Problem 12-4
Journalize stock issuances for cash, property, and services; and prepare resulting stockholders' equity section (L.O. 5)

On May 1, 2011, Farmington Company received a charter that authorized it to issue:

1. 4,000 shares of no-par preferred stock to which a stated value of $12 per share is assigned. The stock is entitled to a cumulative dividend of $9.60, convertible into two shares of common stock, callable at $208, and entitled to $200 per share in liquidation.

2. 1,500 shares of $400 par value, $20 cumulative preferred stock, which is callable at $420 and entitled to $412 in liquidation.
3. 60,000 shares of no-par common stock to which a stated value of $40 is assigned.

May   1   All of the $9.60 cumulative preferred was issued at $204 per share, cash.   ◖ *Transaction*

           2   All of the $20 cumulative preferred was exchanged for merchandise inventory, land, and buildings valued at $128,000, $160,000, and $425,000, respectively.

           3   Cash of $15,000 was paid to reimburse promoters for costs incurred for accounting, legal, and printing services. In addition, 1,000 shares of common stock were issued to the promoters for their services. The value of all of the services (including those paid in cash) was $55,000.

  a. Prepare journal entries for these transactions.   ◖ *Required*

  b. Assume that retained earnings were $200,000. Prepare the stockholders' equity section of the May 31, 2011, balance sheet.

On January 2, 2010, the King Company received its charter. It issued all of its authorized 3,000 shares of no-par preferred stock at $104 and all of its 12,000 authorized shares of no-par common stock at $40 per share. The preferred stock has a stated value of $50 per share, is entitled to a basic cumulative dividend of $6 per share, is callable at $106 beginning in 2012, and is entitled to $100 per share plus cumulative dividends in the event of liquidation. The common stock has a stated value of $10 per share.

Problem 12-5
Prepare stockholders'
equity section;
determine book values
of stock; and determine
dividends for each class
of stock (L.O. 3, 6)

    On December 31, 2011, the end of the second year of operations, retained earnings were $90,000. No dividends have been declared or paid on either class of stock.

  a. Prepare the stockholders' equity section of King Company's December 31, 2011, balance sheet.   ◖ *Required*

  b. Compute the book value of each class of stock.

  c. If $42,000 of dividends were declared as of December 31, 2011, compute the amount paid to each class of stock.

The common stock of Lang Corporation is selling on a stock exchange for $90 per share. The stockholders' equity of the corporation at December 31, 2011, consists of:

Problem 12-6
Compute total market
value for common
stock; compute book
value of common and
preferred stock
(L.O. 6)

Stockholders' equity:
  Paid-in capital:
    Preferred stock—9% cumulative,
      $120 par value, $120 liquidation value,

3,000 shares authorized, issued, and outstanding	$ 360,000	
Common stock—$72 par value, 30,000 shares authorized, issued and outstanding	2,160,000	
Total paid-in capital		$2,520,000
Retained earnings		354,000
Total stockholders' equity		$2,874,000

Assume that in liquidation the preferred stock is entitled to par value plus cumulative unpaid dividends.

  a. What is the total market value of all of the corporation's common stock?   ◖ *Required*

  b. If all dividends have been paid on the preferred stock as of December 31, 2011, what are the book values of the preferred stock and the common stock?

  c. If two years' dividends were due on the preferred stock as of December 31, 2011, what are the book values of the preferred stock and common stock?

Problem 12-7
Compute book values
of a stockholder's
preferred and common
stock (L.O. 6)

Haft Corporation has an agreement with each of its 15 preferred and 30 common stockholders that in the event of the death of a stockholder, it will purchase at book value from the stockholder's estate or heirs the shares of Haft Corporation stock held by the deceased at the time of death. The book value is to be computed in accordance with generally accepted accounting principles.

Following is the stockholders' equity section of the Haft Corporation's December 31, 2011, balance sheet.

Stockholders' equity:
  Paid-in capital:
    Preferred stock—without par value, $50 stated value, $15
      cumulative; 3,000 shares authorized, issued, and outstanding $ 150,000
    Common stock—$62.50 par value, 60,000 shares authorized,
      issued and outstanding   3,750,000
    Paid-in capital in excess of stated value—preferred   840,000
    Paid-in capital in excess of par value—common   30,000
      Total paid-in capital $4,770,000
  Retained earnings   1,800,000
      Total stockholders' equity $6,570,000

The preferred stock is cumulative and entitled to $300 per share plus cumulative dividends in liquidation. No dividends have been paid for 1½ years.

A stockholder who owned 100 shares of preferred stock and 1,000 shares of common stock died on December 31, 2011. You have been employed by the stockholder's executor to compute the book value of each class of stock and to determine the price to be paid for the stock of the deceased stockholder.

Required ➡ Prepare a schedule showing the computation of the amount to be paid for the deceased stockholder's preferred and common stock.

Alternate Problems

Problem 12-1A
Determine dividends
for common stock
and cumulative
and noncumulative
preferred stock (L.O.3)

On January 1, 2007, the retained earnings of Quigley Company were $432,000. Net income for the succeeding five years was as follows:

2007	$288,000
2008	216,000
2009	4,800
2010	48,000
2011	264,000

The outstanding capital stock of the corporation consisted of 2,000 shares of preferred stock with a par value of $480 per share that pays a dividend of $19.20 per year and 8,000 shares of no-par common stock with a stated value of $240 per share. No dividends were in arrears as of January 1, 2007.

Required ➡ Prepare schedules showing how the net income for these five years was distributed to the two classes of stock if in each of the years the entire current net income was distributed as dividends and the preferred stock was:

a. Cumulative.
b. Noncumulative.

On January 1, 2011, Cowling Company was authorized to issue 500,000 shares of $5 par value common stock. It then completed the following transactions:

2011

Jan.   14   Issued 90,000 shares of common stock at $24 per share for cash.

29   Gave the promoters of the corporation 50,000 shares of common stock for their services in organizing the company. The board of directors valued these services at $620,000.

Feb.   19   Exchanged 100,000 shares of common stock for the following assets at the indicated fair market values:

Equipment	$180,000
Building	440,000
Land	600,000

a. Prepare general journal entries to record the transactions.
b. Prepare the balance sheet of the company as of March 1, 2011.

 Required

Problem 12-2A
Journalize stock issuances for cash, services (organization costs), and property; prepare resulting balance sheet (L.O. 5)

On July 3, 2011, Barr Company was authorized to issue 15,000 shares of common stock; 3,000 shares were issued immediately to the incorporators of the company for cash at $320 per share. On July 5 of that year, an additional 300 shares were issued to the incorporators for services rendered in organizing the company. The board valued these services at $96,000. On July 6, 2011, legal and printing costs of $12,000 were paid. These costs related to securing the corporate charter and the stock certificates.

Problem 12-3A
Post transactions; prepare balance sheets for par value stock, stated value stock, and no-par or stated value stock (L.O. 2, 4, 5)

a. Set up T-accounts and post these transactions. Then prepare the balance sheet of the Barr Company as of the close of July 10, 2011, assuming the authorized stock has a $160 par value.
b. Repeat **(a)** for the T-accounts involving stockholders' equity, assuming the stock is no-par stock with a $240 stated value. Prepare the stockholders' equity section of the balance sheet.
c. Repeat **(a)** for the T-accounts involving stockholders' equity, assuming the stock is no-par stock with no stated value. Prepare the stockholders' equity section of the balance sheet.

Required

Tempo Company received its charter on April 1, 2011, authorizing it to issue: (1) 10,000 shares of $400 par value, $32 cumulative, convertible preferred stock; (2) 10,000 shares of $12 cumulative no-par preferred stock having a stated value of $20 per share and a liquidation value of $100 per share; and (3) 100,000 shares of no-par common stock without a stated value.

On April 2, incorporators of the corporation acquired 50,000 shares of the common stock for cash at $80 per share, and 200 shares were issued to an attorney for services rendered in organizing the corporation. On April 3, the company issued all of its authorized shares of $32 convertible preferred stock for land valued at $1,600,000 and a building valued at $4,800,000. The property was subject to a mortgage of $2,400,000. On April 8, the company issued 5,000 shares of the $12 preferred stock in exchange for a patent valued at $1,040,000. On April 10, the company issued 1,000 shares of common stock for cash at $80 per share.

Problem 12-4A
Journalize stock transactions, including conversions; prepare stockholders' equity section (L.O. 3-5)

a. Prepare general journal entries for these transactions.
b. Prepare the stockholders' equity section of the April 30, 2011, balance sheet. Assume retained earnings were $80,000.
c. Assume that each share of the $32 convertible preferred stock is convertible into six shares of common stock and that one-half of the preferred is converted on September 1, 2011. Give the required journal entry.

Required

Problem 12-5A
Prepare stockholders'
equity section;
determine book values
of stock; and determine
dividends for each class
of stock (L.O. 3, 6)

Kane Company issued all of its 5,000 shares of authorized preferred stock on January 1, 2010, at $100 per share. The preferred stock is no-par stock, has a stated value of $5 per share, is entitled to a cumulative basic preference dividend of $6 per share, is callable at $110 beginning in 2011, and is entitled to $100 per share in liquidation plus cumulative dividends. On this same date, Kane also issued 10,000 authorized shares of no-par common stock with a $10 stated value at $50 per share.

On December 31, 2011, the end of its second year of operations, the company's retained earnings amounted to $160,000. No dividends have been declared or paid on either class of stock since the date of issue.

Required ➲
a. Prepare the stockholders' equity section of Kane Company's December 31, 2011, balance sheet.
b. Compute the book value in total and per share of each class of stock as of December 31, 2011.
c. If $110,000 of dividends are to be declared as of December 31, 2011, compute the amount payable to each class of stock.

Problem 12-6A
Determine book value
for each class of stock
(L.O. 6)

The stockholders' equity sections from three different corporations' balance sheets follow.

1) Stockholders' equity:
Paid-in capital:

Preferred stock—7% cumulative, $240 par value,		
500 shares authorized, issued, and outstanding	$ 120,000	
Common stock—$48 par value, 10,000 shares		
authorized, issued and outstanding	480,000	
Total paid-in capital		$ 600,000
Retained earnings		422,400
Total stockholders' equity		$1,022,400

(All dividends have been paid.)

2) Stockholders' equity:
Paid-in capital:

Preferred stock—6% cumulative, $80 par value,		
10,000 shares authorized, issued, and outstanding	$ 800,000	
Common stock—$240 par value, 30,000		
shares authorized, issued and outstanding	7,200,000	
Total paid-in capital		$8,000,000
Retained earnings		88,000
Total stockholders' equity		$8,088,000

(The current year's dividends have not been paid.)

3) Stockholders' equity:
Paid-in capital:

Preferred stock—7% cumulative, $480 par value,		
10,000 shares authorized, issued, and outstanding	$ 4,800,000	
Common stock—$240 par value, 50,000		
shares authorized, issued and outstanding	12,000,000	
Total paid-in capital		$16,800,000
Retained earnings deficit		(1,872,000)
Total stockholders' equity		$14,928,000

(Dividends have not been paid for 2 previous years or the current year.)

Compute the book values per share of the preferred and common stock of each corporation assuming that in a liquidation the preferred stock receives par value plus dividends in arrears.

 Required

Mendell, Inc., is a corporation in which all of the outstanding preferred and common stock is held by the four Lehman brothers. The brothers have an agreement stating that the remaining brothers will, upon the death of a brother, purchase from the estate his holdings of stock in the company at book value.

The stockholders' equity section of the balance sheet for the company on December 31, 2011, the date of the death of James Lehman, shows:

Stockholders' equity:		
Paid-in capital:		
Preferred stock—6%; $320 par value; $320 liquidation value,		
4,000 shares authorized, issued, and outstanding	$1,280,000	
Paid-in capital in excess of par—preferred	64,000	
Common stock—without par value, $16 stated value,		
60,000 shares authorized, issued and outstanding	960,000	
Paid-in capital in excess of par value—common	960,000	
Total paid-in capital		$3,264,000
Retained earnings		128,000
Total stockholders' equity		$3,392,000

No dividends have been paid for the last year on the preferred stock, which is cumulative. At the time of his death, James Lehman held 2,000 shares of preferred stock and 10,000 shares of common stock of the company.

  a. Compute the book value of the preferred stock.
  b. Compute the book value of the common stock.
  c. Compute the amount the remaining brothers must pay to the estate of James Lehman for the preferred and common stock that he held at the time of his death.

 Required

Beyond the Numbers—Critical Thinking

Rudd Company and Clay Company have extremely stable net income amounts of $4,800,000 and $3,200,000, respectively. Both companies distribute all their net income as dividends each year. Rudd Company has 100,000 shares of $80 par value, 6% preferred stock, and 500,000 shares of $8 par value common stock outstanding. Clay Company has 50,000 shares of $40 par value, 8% preferred stock, and 400,000 shares of $8 par value common stock outstanding. Both preferred stocks are cumulative.

  a. Compute the annual dividend per share of preferred stock and per share of common stock for each company.
  b. Based solely on the preceding information, which common stock would you predict to have the higher market price per share? Why?
  c. Which company's stock would you buy? Why?

Required

Jesse Waltrip recently inherited $480,000 cash that he wishes to invest in the common stock of either the West Corporation or the East Corporation. Both corporations have manufactured the same types of products for five years. The stockholders' equity sections of the two corporations' latest balance sheets follow:

WEST CORPORATION

Stockholders' equity:
  Paid-in capital:
    Common stock—$125 par value, 30,000 shares
      authorized, issued and outstanding $3,750,000
    Retained earnings   3,450,000
        Total stockholders' equity $7,200,000

EAST CORPORATION

Stockholders' equity:
  Paid-in capital:
    Preferred stock—8%, $500 par value, cumulative 4,000 shares
      authorized, issued and outstanding $2,000,000
    Common stock—$125 par value, 40,000 shares authorized,
      issued and outstanding   5,000,000 $7,000,000
    Retained earnings   560,000
        Total stockholders' equity $7,560,000

The West Corporation has paid a cash dividend of $6 per share each year since its creation; its common stock is currently selling for $590 per share. The East Corporation's common stock is currently selling for $480 per share. The current year's dividend and three prior years' dividends on the preferred stock are in arrears. The preferred stock has a liquidation value of $600 per share.

Required **a.** What is the book value per share of the West Corporation common stock and the East Corporation common stock? Is book value the major determinant of market value of the stock?

b. Based solely on the previous information, which investment would you recommend to Waltrip? Why?

Annual Report Analysis 12-3
Determine return on average common stockholders' equity (L.O. 7)

Determine the 2010 return on average common stockholders' equity for Wal-Mart Stores, Inc., in the Annual Report Appendix. Explain in writing why this information is important to managers, investors, and creditors.

Refer to the ethics case concerning Joe Morrison on page 477 to answer the following questions:

Ethics Case 12-4
Answer questions regarding the ethics case

a. Which alternative would benefit the company and its management over the next several years?

b. Which alternative would benefit society?

c. If you were Morrison, which side of the argument would you take?

Group Project 12-5
Calculate return on average common stockholders' equity and make investment decision

In teams of two or three students, examine the annual reports of three companies and calculate each company's return on common shareholders' equity for the most recent two years. At least two years are needed to observe any changes. As a team, decide in which of the three companies you would invest. Appoint a spokesperson for the team to explain to the class which company the team would invest in and why.

In a team of two or three students, locate the annual reports of three companies that have preferred stock in their stockholders' equity section. Determine the features of the preferred stock. Analyze the data in the annual report to determine whether dividends have been paid on the preferred stock each year. Are there dividends in arrears? Write a report to your instructor summarizing your findings. Also be prepared to make a short presentation to the class.

Group Project 12-6
Examine annual reports of companies with preferred stock

In a group of one or two students, contact state officials and/or consult library resources to inquire about the incorporation laws in your state. Determine your state laws regarding the issuance of stock at an amount below par value, how legal capital is determined, and the requirements and government fees for incorporating a company in your state. Write a report to your instructor summarizing the results of your investigation and be prepared to make a short presentation to your class.

Group Project 12-7
Investigate incorporation laws of your state

Using the Internet—A View of the Real World

Visit the following website for Adobe Systems Incorporated:
> **http://www.adobe.com**
 Pursue choices on the screen until you locate the consolidated statement of stockholders' equity and comprehensive income. Note the changes that have occurred in the Common Stock, Additional Paid-In Capital, and Retained Earnings accounts. Check out the notes to the financial statements for further information. Write a memo to your instructor summarizing your findings.

Internet Project 12-8
Investigate a consolidated statement of stockholders' equity

Visit the following website for Gartner Group:
> **http://www.gartner.com**
Pursue choices on the screen until you locate the consolidated statement of stockholders' equity. Trace the changes that have occurred in the last three years in the Common Stock account. Check out the notes to the financial statements for further information. Write a memo to your instructor summarizing your findings.

Internet Project 12-9
Investigate a consolidated statement of stockholders' equity

Answers to Self-Test

True-False
  1. **False.** This is not the primary reason a person may prefer the corporate form of business organization in a situation involving considerable risk. The primary reason is that stockholders can lose only the amount of capital they have invested in a corporation.
  2. **False.** The claims of the creditors rank ahead of the claims of the stockholders, even those stockholders whose stock is preferred as to assets.
  3. **True.** Par value is simply the amount per share that is credited to the Capital Stock account for each share issued and is no indication of the market value or the book value of the stock.
  4. **True.** When capital stock is issued for property or services, the transaction is recorded at the fair market value of (1) the property or services received or (2) the stock issued, whichever is more clearly evident.

Multiple-Choice

1. **c.** This feature of corporations is one of the disadvantages of the corporate form of organization.

2. **b.** Stated value is an arbitrary amount assigned by the board of directors to each share of capital stock without a par value.

3. **d.** Dividends in arrears are cumulative unpaid dividends. Only cumulative preferred stock has dividends in arrears.

4. **b.** The amount credited to the Paid-In Capital in Excess of Par Value—Common is computed as follows:

   10,000 shares × ($50 − $20) = $300,000

5. **a.** The book value of common stock is computed as follows:

Total book value of stockholders' equity ($80,000 + $200,000 + $400,000)	$680,000
Total shares	÷ 1,000
Book value per share	$680

Careers in Accounting

The Accountant As A Financial Analyst

The primary purpose of financial reporting is to provide information to investors and creditors. Investors use financial information in the purchasing and selling of stocks, while creditors (such as banks) use financial information in reviewing the credit-worthiness of companies wishing to obtain loans. In making these types of decisions, investors and creditors rely on financial analysts to give them accurate assessments of the value and strength of the company. The role of the financial analysts is to take the financial information reported by a company and translate that into a rating of company performance. It should therefore be no surprise that a successful financial analyst is one that has a deep understanding of financial accounting. Who better to analyze the financial statements than the person who prepared them? Who would have a better understanding of the data and information contained in financial statements than the accountant? Financial statements are becoming ever more complex and difficult to interpret by users. Thus, accountants are becoming increasingly important in assisting others to understand and interpret financial information.

Helping users understand financial information involves such tasks as developing graphs, common-size statements, and performing horizontal and vertical analysis. Analysis could also involve performing data comparisons with relevant financial and nonfinancial data. The Altman Z Model is an example of a tool used by analysts to predict bankruptcy. The model includes such items as retained earnings/total assets and sales/total assets as variables in the calculation. Based upon this test, Cooper Tire & Rubber Company earned a score of 3.00 in a recent year. A score below 1.81 is considered an indication of possible bankruptcy, while a score above 2.99 puts a company in the "safe zone". Therefore, analysts evaluated Cooper as a healthy company that is not likely to go bankrupt in the near term.

Financial analysts make numerous judgments about the financial condition of companies, as in the example above. These services are essential to the decisions of investors and creditors. Thus, financial analysts with a strong accounting background are well compensated for their efforts.

13

Corporations
Paid-In Capital, Retained Earnings, Dividends, and Treasury Stock

As owners of a corporation, stockholders provide much of the capital for its activities. On the balance sheet, we show the stockholders' capital investment in the corporation as paid-in capital under stockholders' equity. Also included in stockholders' equity is the capital accumulated through the retention of corporate earnings (retained earnings). Paid-in capital is a relatively permanent portion of stockholders' equity; the retained earnings balance is a relatively temporary portion of corporate capital and is the source of stockholders' dividends.

The preceding chapter discussed the paid-in capital obtained by issuing shares of stock for cash, property, or services. This chapter describes additional sources of paid-in capital and items affecting retained earnings.

Paid-In (or Contributed) Capital

As you have learned in the preceding chapter, **paid-in capital**, or **contributed capital**, refers to all of the contributed capital of a corporation, including the capital carried in the capital stock accounts. The general ledger does not contain an account titled "Paid-In Capital." Instead, paid-in capital is a category, and companies establish a separate account for each source of paid-in capital.

In Illustration 13.1, we summarize several sources of stockholders' equity and list general ledger account titles used to record increases and decreases in capital from each of these sources. Chapter 12 discussed some of these general ledger accounts. This chapter discusses other general ledger accounts that record sources of stockholders' equity.

The stockholders' equity section of a balance sheet shows the different sources of the corporation's paid-in capital because these sources are important information. For example, these additional sources may be from stock dividends, treasury stock transactions, or donations.

After studying this chapter, you should be able to:

1. Identify the different sources of paid-in capital and describe how to present them on a balance sheet.

2. Account for a cash dividend, a stock dividend, a stock split, and a retained earnings appropriation.

3. Account for the acquisition and reissuance of treasury stock.

4. Describe the proper accounting treatment of discontinued operations, extraordinary items, and changes in accounting principle.

(continued)

Illustration 13.1   Sources of Stockholders' Equity

Sources of Stockholders' Equity	**Illustrative General Ledger Account Titles**
I. Capital paid in (or contributed)	
A. For, or assigned to, shares:	Common Stock
1. Issued to the extent of par or stated value or the amount received for shares without par or stated value.	5% Preferred Stock
	Stock Dividend Distributable—Common (Preferred)
2. To be distributed as a stock dividend.	
3. In addition to par or stated value:	Paid-In Capital in Excess of Par Value—Common (Preferred)
a. In excess of par.	Paid-In Capital in Excess of Stated Value—Common (Preferred)
b. In excess of stated value.	Paid-In Capital—Stock Dividends
c. Resulting from declaration of stock dividends.	Paid-In Capital—Common (Preferred) Treasury Stock Transactions
d. Resulting from reissue of treasury stock at a price above its acquisition price.	
B. Donations (gifts), whether from stockholders or from others.	Paid-In Capital—Donations
II. Capital accumulated by retention of earnings (retained earnings).	
A. Appropriated retained earnings.	Appropriation per Loan Agreement
B. Free and unappropriated retained earnings.	Retained Earnings (Unappropriated)

Objectives

5. Define prior period adjustments and show their proper presentation in the financial statements.

6. Analyze and use the financial results—earnings per share and price-earnings ratio.

Objective 1
Identify the different sources of paid-in capital and describe how to present them on a balance sheet.

Paid-In Capital—Stock Dividends

When it declares a stock dividend, a corporation distributes additional shares of stock (instead of cash) to its present stockholders. A later section discusses and illustrates how the issuance of a stock dividend results in a credit to a Paid-In Capital—Stock Dividends account.

Paid-In Capital—Treasury Stock Transactions

Another source of capital is treasury stock transactions. **Treasury stock** is the corporation's own stock, either preferred or common, that it has issued and reacquired. It is legally available for reissuance. By reacquiring shares of its own outstanding capital stock at one price and later reissuing them at a higher price, a corporation can increase its capital by the difference between the two prices. If the reissue price is *less* than acquisition cost, however, corporate capital decreases. We discuss treasury stock transactions at length later in this chapter.

Paid-In Capital—Donations

Occasionally, a corporation receives a gift of assets, such as a $500,000 building. These donated gifts increase stockholders' equity and are called **donated capital**. The entry to record the gift of a $500,000 building is a debit to Buildings and a credit to Paid-In Capital—Donations. Accountants would make this entry in the amount of the $500,000 fair market value of the gift when received.

Retained Earnings

The **retained earnings** portion of stockholders' equity typically results from accumulated earnings, reduced by net losses and dividends. Like paid-in capital, retained earnings is a source of assets received by a corporation. Paid-in capital is the actual investment by the stockholders; retained earnings is the investment by the stockholders through earnings not yet withdrawn.

The balance in the corporation's Retained Earnings account is the corporation's net income, less net losses, from the date the corporation began to the present, less the sum of dividends paid during this period. Net income increases Retained Earnings, while net losses and dividends decrease Retained Earnings in any given year. Thus, the balance in Retained Earnings represents the corporation's accumulated net income not distributed to stockholders.

When the Retained Earnings account has a debit balance, a **deficit** exists. A company indicates a deficit by listing retained earnings with a negative amount in the stockholders' equity section of the balance sheet. The firm need not change the title of the general ledger account even though it contains a debit balance. The most common credits and debits made to Retained Earnings are for income (or losses) and dividends. Occasionally, accountants make other entries to the Retained Earnings account. We discuss some of these entries later in the chapter.

Paid-In Capital and Retained Earnings on the Balance Sheet

The following stockholders' equity section of a balance sheet presents the various sources of capital in proper form:

Stockholders' equity:			
Paid-in Capital:			
Preferred stock—6%, $100 par value; authorized, issued, and outstanding, 4,000 shares		$ 400,000	
Common stock—no-par value, $5 stated value; authorized, issued, and outstanding, 400,000 shares		2,000,000	$2,400,000
Paid-in capital—			
From preferred stock issuances*		$ 40,000	
From donations		10,000	50,000
Total paid-in capital			$2,450,000
Retained earnings			500,000
Total stockholders' equity			$2,950,000

*This label is not the exact account title but is representative of the descriptions used on balance sheets. The exact account title could be used, but shorter descriptions are often shown.

In their highly condensed, published balance sheets, companies often omit the details regarding the sources of the paid-in capital in excess of par or stated value and replace them by a single item, such as:

Paid-in capital in excess of par (or stated) value $50,000

Dividends are distributions of earnings by a corporation to its stockholders. Usually the corporation pays dividends in cash, but it may distribute additional shares of the corporation's own capital stock as dividends. Occasionally, a company pays dividends in merchandise or other assets. Since dividends are the means whereby the owners of a corporation share in its earnings, accountants charge them against retained earnings.

Before dividends can be paid, the board of directors must declare them so they can be recorded in the corporation's minutes book. Three dividend dates are significant:

1. **Date of declaration**. The date of declaration indicates when the board of directors approved a motion declaring that dividends should be paid. The board action creates the liability for dividends payable (or stock dividends distributable for stock dividends).

> **Dividends**
>
> **Objective 2**
> Account for a cash dividend, a stock dividend, a stock split, and a retained earnings appropriation.

2. **Date of record.** The board of directors establishes the date of record; it determines which stockholders receive dividends. The corporation's records (the stockholders' ledger) determine its stockholders as of the date of record.

3. **Date of payment.** The date of payment indicates when the corporation will pay dividends to the stockholders.

To illustrate how these three dates relate to an actual situation, assume the board of directors of the Allen Corporation declared a cash dividend on May 5, 2012 (date of declaration). The cash dividend declared is $1.25 per share to stockholders of record on July 1, 2012 (date of record), payable on July 10, 2012 (date of payment). Because financial transactions occur on both the date of declaration (a liability is incurred) and on the date of payment (cash is paid), journal entries record the transactions on both of these dates. No journal entry is required on the date of record.

Illustration 13.2 shows the frequencies of dividend payments made by a sample of representative companies for the years 2008 and 2009. Note that cash dividends are far more numerous than stock dividends or dividends in kind (paid in merchandise or other assets).

An Accounting Perspective	**Uses of Technology** After original issuance, investors may trade the stock of a company on secondary markets, such as the New York Stock Exchange. The company makes no entry on its books for these outside trades after issuance. Often, a company engages the services of a company known as a "stock transfer agent" to note trades between shareholders. The stock transfer agent will provide the company with report of the stockholders of record on a particular date. This information allows a company that declares a dividend to be certain that the money or stock goes to the stockholders who own the stock on the date of record rather than to the stockholders who originally purchased the stock.

Cash Dividends

Cash dividends are cash distributions of accumulated earnings by a corporation to its stockholders. To illustrate the entries for cash dividends, consider the following example. On January 21, 2012, a corporation's board of directors declared a 2% quarterly cash dividend on $100,000 of outstanding preferred stock. This dividend is one-fourth of the annual dividend on 1,000 shares of $100 par value, 8% preferred stock. The dividend will be paid on March 1, 2012, to stockholders of record on February 5, 2012. An entry is not needed on the date of record; however, the entries at the declaration and payment dates are as follows:

2012					
Jan.	21	Retained Earnings		2,000	
		Dividends Payable			2,000
		Dividends declared: 2% on $100,000 of outstanding preferred stock, payable March 1, 2012, to stockholders of record on February 5, 2012.			
Mar.	1	Dividends Payable		2,000	
		Cash			2,000
		Paid the dividend declared on January 21, 2012.			

Often a cash dividend is stated as so many dollars per share. For instance, the quarterly dividend could have been stated as $2 per share. When they declare a cash dividend, some companies debit a Dividends account instead of Retained Earnings. (Both methods are acceptable.) The Dividends account is then closed to Retained Earnings at the end of the fiscal year.

Illustration 13.2   Types of Dividends

	Number of Companies	
	2009	2008
Cash Dividends Paid to Common Stock Shareholders		
Per share amount disclosed in retained earnings statements	176	201
Per share amount not disclosed in retained earnings statements	152	145
Total:	328	346
Cash Dividends Paid to Preferred Stock Shareholders		
Per share amount disclosed in retained earnings statements	7	9
Per share amount not disclosed in retained earnings statements	15	19
Total:	22	28
Stock dividends	-	-
Stock Purchase Rights	12	9
Dividends in Kind	3	7

Source: Based on American Institute of Certified Public Accountants, *Accounting Trends & Techniques* (New York: AICPA, 2010), p. 461.

Once a cash dividend is declared and notice of the dividend is given to stockholders, a company generally cannot rescind it unless all stockholders agree to such action.[1] Thus, the credit balance in the Dividends Payable account appears as a current liability on the balance sheet.

Reinforcing Problem
E13-2 Prepare journal entries for cash dividends.

BUSINESS INSIGHT Often investors believe a company that pays dividends is doing well. Therefore, companies try to maintain a record of paying dividends. McDonald's Corporation has raised its dividend every year since paying its first dividend in 1976. Its dividend announcement for 2011 was as follows:

(Reuters, Sept.22)—McDonald's Corp (MCD.N) said on Thursday its board of directors raised the world's biggest hamburger chain's quarterly cash dividend almost 15 percent to 70 cents per share. The dividend will be payable on Dec. 15, to shareholders of record at the close of business on Dec. 1.

A company that lacks sufficient cash for a cash dividend may declare a stock dividend to satisfy its shareholders. Note that in the long run it may be more beneficial to the company and the shareholders to reinvest the capital in the business rather than paying a cash dividend. If so, the company would be more profitable and the shareholders would be rewarded with a higher stock price in the future.

An Accounting Perspective

Stock Dividends

Stock dividends are payable in additional shares of the declaring corporation's capital stock. When declaring stock dividends, companies issue additional shares of the same class of stock as that held by the stockholders.

Corporations usually account for stock dividends by transferring a sum from retained earnings to permanent paid-in capital. The amount transferred for stock dividends depends on the size of the stock dividend. For stock dividends, most states permit corporations to debit Retained Earnings or any paid-in capital accounts other than those representing legal capital. In most circumstances, however, they debit Retained Earnings when a stock dividend is declared.

---

[1]Stockholders might agree to rescind (cancel) a dividend already declared if the company is in difficult financial circumstances and needs to retain cash to pay bills or acquire assets to continue operations.

Stock dividends have no effect on the total amount of stockholders' equity or on net assets. They merely decrease retained earnings and increase paid-in capital by an equal amount. Immediately after the distribution of a stock dividend, each share of similar stock has a lower book value per share. This decrease occurs because more shares are outstanding with no increase in total stockholders' equity.

Stock dividends do not affect the individual stockholder's percentage of ownership in the corporation. For example, a stockholder who owns 1,000 shares in a corporation having 100,000 shares of stock outstanding, owns 1% of the outstanding shares. After a 10% stock dividend, the stockholder still owns 1% of the outstanding shares—1,100 of the 110,000 outstanding shares.

A corporation might declare a stock dividend for several reasons:

1. Retained earnings may have become large relative to total stockholders' equity, so the corporation may desire a larger permanent capitalization.
2. The market price of the stock may have risen above a desirable trading range. A stock dividend generally reduces the per share market value of the company's stock.
3. The board of directors of a corporation may wish to have more stockholders (who might then buy its products) and eventually increase their number by increasing the number of shares outstanding. Some of the stockholders receiving the stock dividend are likely to sell the shares to other persons.
4. Stock dividends may silence stockholders' demands for cash dividends from a corporation that does not have sufficient cash to pay cash dividends.

The percentage of shares issued determines whether a stock dividend is a small stock dividend or a large stock dividend. Firms use different accounting treatments for each category.

Recording Small Stock Dividends   A stock dividend of less than 20 to 25% of the outstanding shares is a small stock dividend and has little effect on the market value (quoted market price) of the shares. Thus, the firm accounts for the dividend at the current market value of the outstanding shares.

Assume a corporation is authorized to issue 20,000 shares of $100 par value common stock, of which 8,000 shares are outstanding. Its board of directors declares a 10% stock dividend (800 shares). The quoted market price of the stock is $125 per share immediately before the stock dividend is announced. Since the distribution is less than 20 to 25% of the outstanding shares, the dividend is accounted for at market value. The entry for the declaration of the stock dividend on August 10, 2012, is:

Aug.	10	Retained Earnings (or Stock Dividends) (800 shares x $125)	100,000	
		Stock Dividend Distributable—Common		
		(800 shares X $100)		80,000
		Paid-In Capital—Stock Dividends		
		(800 shares X $25)		20,000
		To record the declaration of a 10% stock dividend; shares to be distributed on September 20, 2012, to stockholders of record on August 31, 2012.		

This entry records the issuance of the shares:

Sept.	20	Stock Dividends Distributable—Common	80,000	
		Common Stock		80,000
		To record the distribution of 800 shares of common stock as authorized in stock dividends declared on August 10, 2012.		

The **Stock Dividend Distributable—Common account** is a stockholders' equity (paid-in capital) account credited for the par or stated value of the shares distributable when recording the declaration of a stock dividend. Since a stock dividend distributable is not to be paid with assets, it is not a liability. When a balance sheet is prepared between the date the 10% dividend is declared and the date the shares are issued, the proper statement presentation of the effects of the stock dividend is:

Reinforcing Problems
P13-2 and P13-2A Prepare journal entries for cash dividend and small stock dividend.

Stockholders' equity:
  Paid-in Capital:

Common stock—$100 par value; authorized, 20,000 shares; issued and outstanding, 8,000 shares	$ 800,000	
Stock dividend distributable on September 20, 2012, 800 shares at par value	80,000	
Total par value of shares issued and to be issued	$ 880,000	
Paid-in capital from stock dividends	20,000	
Total paid-in capital		$ 900,000
Retained earnings		150,000
Total stockholders' equity		$1,050,000

Suppose, on the other hand, that the common stock in the preceding example is no-par stock and has a stated value of $50 per share. The entry to record the declaration of the stock dividend (when the market value is $125) is:

Retained Earnings (800 shares X $125)	100,000	
Stock Dividends Distributable—Common (800 shares X $50)		40,000
Paid-In Capital—Stock Dividends (800 shares X $75)		60,000
To record the declaration of a stock dividend.		

The entry to record the issuance of the stock dividend is:

Stock Dividend Distributable—Common	40,000	
Common Stock		40,000
To record the issuance of the stock dividend.		

Recording Large Stock Dividends   A stock dividend of more than 20 to 25% of the outstanding shares is a large stock dividend. Since one purpose of a large stock dividend is to reduce the market value of the stock so the shares can be traded more easily, firms do not use the current market value of the stock in the entry. They account for such dividends at their par or stated value rather than at their current market value. The laws of the state of incorporation or the board of directors establish the amounts for stocks without par or stated value.

To illustrate the treatment of a stock dividend of more than 20 to 25%, assume X Corporation has been authorized to issue 10,000 shares of $10 par value common stock, of which 5,000 shares are outstanding. X Corporation declared a 30% stock dividend (1,500 shares) on September 20, 2012, to be issued on October 15, 2012. The required entries are:

Illustration 13.3   Stock Dividends

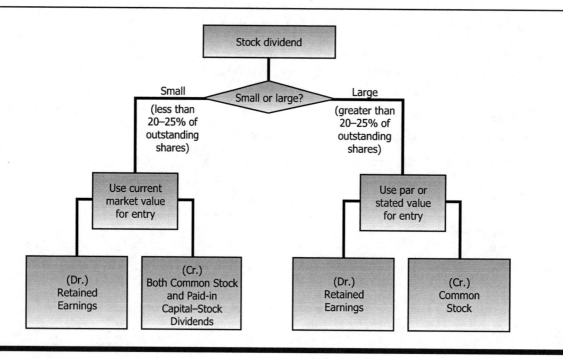

Note to the Student	Sept.	20	Retained Earnings (or Stock Dividends) (1,500 shares X $10)	15,000	
Accountants capitalize			Stock Dividend Distributable—Common		15,000
small stock dividends at the			To declare a 30% stock dividend.		
current market price, while					
they capitalize large stock	Oct.	15	Stock Dividend Distributable—Common	15,000	
dividends at par or stated			Common Stock		15,000
value.			To issue the 30% stock dividend.		

Reinforcing Problem
E13-4 Prepare journal entry for small stock dividend and discuss large stock dividend.

Note that although firms account for the small stock dividend at current market value, they account for the 30% stock dividend at par value (1,500 shares × $10 = $15,000). Because of the differences in accounting for large and small stock dividends, accountants must determine the relative size of the stock dividend before making any journal entries.

To see the effect of small and large stock dividends on stockholders' equity, look at Illustration 13.3.

Stock Splits

Real World Example
Estee Lauder Co., is producer of exclusive cosmetics and perfumes. On November 3, 2011, the Board of Directors announced a two-for-one split of Estee Lauder Co. common stock. The two-for-one split was effected in the form of a 100% stock dividend and was distributed to stockholders of record on January 20, 2012. All Estee Lauder share and per share data reflect this split.

A **stock split** is a distribution of 100% or more of additional shares of the issuing corporation's stock accompanied by a corresponding reduction in the par value per share. The corporation receives no assets in this transaction. A stock split causes a large reduction in the market price per share of the outstanding stock. A two-for-one split doubles the number of shares outstanding, a three-for-one split triples the number of shares, and so on. The split reduces the par value per share at the same time so that the total dollar amount credited to Common Stock remains the same. For instance, a two-for-one split halves the par value per share.[2] If the corporation issues 100% more stock without a reduction in the par value per share, the transaction is a 100% stock dividend rather than a two-for-one stock split.

The entry to record a stock split depends on the particular circumstances. Usually, firms change only the number of shares outstanding and the par or stated

---

[2]If a corporation *reduces* the par value of its stock without issuing more shares, say, from $100 to $60 per share, then $40 per share must be removed from the appropriate capital stock account and credited to Paid-In Capital—Recapitalization. Further discussion of this process, called *recapitalization,* is beyond the scope of this text.

value in the records. (The number of shares authorized may also change.) Thus, they would record a two-for-one stock split in which the par value of the shares decreases from $20 to $10 as follows:

Common Stock—$20 par value	100,000	
Common Stock—$10 par value		100,000
To record a two-for-one stock split; 5,000 shares of $20 par value common stock were replaced by 10,000 shares of $10 par value common stock.		

In Illustration 13.4, we summarize the effects of stock dividends and stock splits. Stock dividends and stock splits have no effect on the total amount of stockholders' equity. In addition, stock splits have no effect on the total amount of paid-in capital or retained earnings. They merely increase the number of shares outstanding and decrease the par value per share. Stock dividends increase paid-in capital and decrease retained earnings by equal amounts.

Reinforcing Problem
E13-5 Prepare journal entries for stock split and small stock dividend.

Illustration 13.4　　Summary of Effects of Stock Dividends and Stock Splits

	Total Stockholders' Equity	Common Stock	Paid-In Capital— Common	Retained Earnings	Number of Shares Outstanding	Par Value per share
Stock dividends:						
Small	No effect	Increases	Increases*	Decreases	Increases	No effect
Large	No effect	Increases	No effect	Decreases	Increases	No effect
Stock Splits	No effect	No effect	No effect	No effect	Increases	Decreases

*Assuming current market value is greater than par value.

Legality of Dividends

The preceding chapter discussed how corporate laws differ regarding the legality of a dividend. State law establishes the *legal* or *stated capital* of a corporation as that portion of the stockholders' equity that must be maintained intact, unimpaired by dividend declarations or other distributions to stockholders. The legal capital often equals the par or stated value of the shares issued or a minimum price per share issued.

The objective of these state corporate laws is to protect the corporation's creditors, whose claims have priority over those of the corporation's stockholders. To illustrate the significance of the legal capital concept, assume a corporation in severe financial difficulty is about to go out of business. If there were no legal capital restrictions on dividends, the stockholders of that corporation might pay themselves a cash dividend or have the corporation buy back their stock, leaving no funds available for the corporation's creditors.

The board of directors of a corporation possesses sole power to declare dividends. The legality of a dividend generally depends on the amount of retained earnings available for dividends—not on the net income of any one period. Firms can pay dividends in periods in which they incurred losses, provided retained earnings and the cash position justify the dividend. And in some states, companies can declare dividends from current earnings despite an accumulated deficit. The financial advisability of declaring a dividend depends on the cash position of the corporation.

Liquidating Dividends

Normally, dividends are reductions of retained earnings since they are distributions of the corporation's net income. However, dividends may be distributions of contributed capital. These dividends are called **liquidating dividends.**

Accountants debit liquidating dividends to a paid-in capital account. Corporations should disclose to stockholders the source of any dividends that are not distributions of net income by indicating which paid-in capital account was debited as a result of the dividend. The legality of paying liquidating dividends depends on the source of the paid-in capital and the laws of the state of incorporation.

An Accounting Perspective

BUSINESS INSIGHT Following a series of large frauds such as Enron and WorldCom, Congress passed major legislation in 2002 called the Sarbanes-Oxley Act (SOX). SOX contained 11 titles with numerous sections pertaining to auditing and financial reporting. It greatly increased the requirements for financial statement disclosures of complex financial transactions. It increased the criminal penalties of white-collar crimes, and it created criminal penalties for the destruction of financial records pertaining to matters under investigation. It also created criminal penalties if the CEO and the CFO of a company fail to certify the financial statements as being in compliance with the Securities Exchange Act of 1934.

Retained Earnings Appropriations

The amount of retained earnings that a corporation may pay as cash dividends may be less than total retained earnings for several contractual or voluntary reasons. These contractual or voluntary restrictions or limitations on retained earnings are **retained earnings appropriations.** For example, a loan contract may state that part of a corporation's $100,000 of retained earnings is not available for cash dividends until the loan is paid. Or a board of directors may decide to use assets resulting from net income for plant expansion rather than for cash dividends. An example of a voluntary restriction was General Electric's annual report statement that cash dividends were limited "to support enhanced productive capability and to provide adequate financial resources for internal and external growth opportunities."

Companies formally record retained earnings appropriations by transferring amounts from Retained Earnings to accounts such as "Appropriation for Loan Agreement" or "Retained Earnings Appropriated for Plant Expansion." Even though some refer to retained earnings appropriations as *retained earnings reserves,* using the term *reserves* is discouraged.

Other reasons for appropriations of retained earnings include pending litigation, debt retirement, and contingencies in general. Such appropriations do not reduce total retained earnings. They merely disclose to balance sheet readers that a portion of retained earnings is not available for cash dividends. Thus, recording these appropriations guarantees that the corporation limits its outflow of cash dividends while repaying a loan, expanding a plant, or taking on some other costly endeavor. *Recording retained earnings appropriations does not involve the setting aside of cash for the indicated purpose; it merely divides retained earnings into two parts—appropriated retained earnings and unappropriated retained earnings.* The establishment of a separate fund would require a specific directive from the board of directors. The only entry required to record the appropriation of $25,000 of retained earnings to fulfill the provisions in a loan agreement is:

Retained Earnings	25,000	
Appropriation per Loan Agreement		25,000
To record restriction on retained earnings.		

Reinforcing Problem
E13-6 Prepare journal entry for appropriation of retained earnings and explain.

When the retained earnings appropriation has served its purpose of restricting dividends and the loan has been repaid, the board of directors may decide to return the appropriation intact to Retained Earnings. The entry to do this is:

Appropriation per Loan Agreement	25,000	
Retained Earnings		25,000
To return balance in Appropriation per Loan Agreement account to Retained Earnings.		

On the balance sheet, retained earnings appropriations appear in the stockholders' equity section as follows:

Reinforcing Problem
E13-1 Prepare stockholders' equity section of balance sheet.

Stockholders' equity:		
Paid-in Capital:		
Preferred stock—8%, $50 par value; 500 shares authorized, issued and outstanding	$25,000	
Common stock—$5 par value; 10,000 shares authorized, issued and outstanding	50,000	
Total paid-in capital		$75,000
Retained Earnings:		
Appropriated:		
Per loan agreement	$25,000	
Unappropriated	20,000	
Total retained earnings		45,000
Total stockholders' equity		$120,000

Note that a retained earnings appropriation does not reduce either stockholders' equity or total retained earnings but merely earmarks (restricts) a portion of retained earnings for a specific reason.

The formal practice of recording and reporting retained earnings appropriations is decreasing. Footnote explanations such as the following are replacing these appropriations:

Note 7. Retained earnings restrictions. According to the provisions in the loan agreement, retained earnings available for dividends are limited to $20,000.

Such footnotes appear after the formal financial statements in "Notes to Financial Statements." The Retained Earnings account on the balance sheet would be referenced as follows: "Retained Earnings (see note 7) . . . $45,000."

Changes in the composition of retained earnings reveal important information about a corporation to financial statement users. A separate formal statement—the *statement of retained earnings*—discloses such changes.

Statement of Retained Earnings

A **statement of retained earnings** is a formal statement showing the items causing changes in unappropriated and appropriated retained earnings during a stated period of time. Changes in unappropriated retained earnings usually consist of the addition of net income (or deduction of net loss) and the deduction of dividends and appropriations. Changes in appropriated retained earnings consist of increases or decreases in appropriations.

Note Ward Corporation's statement of retained earnings in Illustration 13.5. The only new appropriation during 2012 was an additional $35,000 for plant expansion. Ward added this new $35,000 to the $25,000 beginning balance in that account and subtracted that amount from unappropriated retained earnings. An alternative to the statement of retained earnings is the statement of stockholders' equity.

Illustration 13.5   Statement of Retained Earnings

WARD CORPORATION
Statement of Retained Earnings
For Year Ended December 31, 2012

Unappropriated retained earnings:		
January 1, 2012, balance		$180,000
Add: Net income		80,000
		$260,000
Less: Dividends	$15,000	
Appropriation for plant expansion	35,000	50,000
Unappropriated retained earnings, December 31, 2012		$210,000
Appropriated retained earnings:		
Appropriation for plant expansion, January 1, 2012, balance	$25,000	
Add: Increase in 2012	35,000	$ 60,000
Appropriation for contract obligation, January 1, 2012, balance		20,000
Appropriated retained earnings, December 31, 2012		$ 80,000
Total retained earnings, December 31, 2012		$290,000

Statement of Stockholders' Equity

Most corporations include four financial statements in their annual reports: a balance sheet, an income statement, a statement of stockholders' equity (in place of a statement of retained earnings), and a statement of cash flows (discussed in Chapter 16). A **statement of stockholders' equity** is a summary of the transactions affecting the accounts in the stockholders' equity section of the balance sheet during a stated period. These transactions include activities affecting both paid-in capital and retained earnings accounts. Thus, the statement of stockholders' equity includes the information contained in a statement of retained earnings plus some additional information. The columns in the statement of stockholders' equity reflect the major account titles within the stockholders' equity section: the types of stock issued and outstanding, paid-in capital in excess of par (or stated) value, retained earnings, and treasury stock. Each row indicates the effects of major transactions affecting one or more stockholders' equity accounts.

Look at Illustration 13.6, a statement of stockholders' equity. The first row indicates the beginning balances of each account in the stockholders' equity section. This summary shows that Larkin Corporation issued 10,000 shares of common stock, declared a 5% stock dividend on common stock, repurchased 1,200 shares of treasury stock, earned net income of $185,000, and paid cash dividends on both its preferred and common stock. After the transactions' effects are indicated within each row, Larkin added or subtracted each column's components to determine the ending balance in each stockholders' equity account.

Treasury Stock

> **Objective 3**
> Account for the acquisition and reissuance of treasury stock.

Treasury stock is the corporation's own capital stock that it has issued and then reacquired; this stock has not been canceled and is legally available for reissuance. Because it has been issued, we cannot classify treasury stock as unissued stock.

Recall that when a corporation has additional authorized shares of stock that are to be issued after the date of original issue, in most states the preemptive right requires offering these additional shares first to existing stockholders on a pro rata basis. However,

Illustration 13.6   Statement of Stockholders' Equity

LARKIN CORPORATION
Statement of Stockholders' Equity
For the Year Ended December 31, 2012

	$50 Par, Value, 6% Preferred Stock	$20 Par Value Common Stock	Paid-In Capital in Excess of Par Value	Retained Earnings	Treasury Stock	Total
Balance, January 1, 2012	$250,000	$300,000	$200,000	$500,000	$(42,000)	$1,208,000
Issuance of 10,000 shares of common stock		200,000	100,000			300,000
5% stock dividend on common stock, 1,250 shares		25,000	27,500	(52,500)		-0-
Purchase of 1,200 shares of treasury stock					(48,000)	(48,000)
Net income				185,000		185,000
Cash dividends:						
Preferred stock				(15,000)		(15,000)
Common stock				(25,000)		(25,000)
Balance, December 31, 2012	$250,000	$525,000	$327,500	$592,500	$(90,000)	$1,605,000

firms may reissue treasury stock without violating the preemptive right provisions of state laws; that is, treasury stock does not have to be offered to current stockholders on a pro rata basis.

A corporation may reacquire its own capital stock as treasury stock to: (1) cancel and retire the stock; (2) reissue the stock later at a higher price; (3) reduce the shares outstanding and thereby increase earnings per share; or (4) issue the stock to employees. If the intent of reacquisition is cancellation and retirement, the treasury shares exist only until they are retired and canceled by a formal reduction of corporate capital.

For dividend or voting purposes, most state laws consider treasury stock as issued but not outstanding, since the shares are no longer in the possession of stockholders. Also, accountants do not consider treasury shares outstanding in calculating earnings per share. However, they generally consider treasury shares outstanding for purposes of determining legal capital, which includes outstanding shares plus treasury shares.

In states that consider treasury stock as part of legal capital, the cost of treasury stock may not exceed the retained earnings at the date the shares are reacquired. This regulation protects creditors by preventing the corporation in financial difficulty from using funds to purchase its own stock instead of paying its debts. Thus, if a corporation is subject to such a law (as is assumed in this text), the retained earnings available for dividends must exceed the cost of the treasury shares on hand.

Real World Example
At December 31, 2010, General Electric Company reported a balance of $31,938,000,000 in its Treasury Stock account.

When firms reacquire treasury stock, they record the stock at cost as a debit in a stockholders' equity account called *Treasury Stock*.[3] They credit reissuances to the Treasury Stock account at the cost of acquisition. Thus, the Treasury Stock account is debited at cost when shares are acquired and credited at cost when these shares are sold. Any excess of the reissue price over cost represents additional paid-in capital and is credited to **Paid-In Capital—Common (Preferred) Treasury Stock Transactions**.

To illustrate, assume that on February 18, 2012, the Hillside Corporation reacquired 100 shares of its outstanding common stock for $55 each. (The company's stockholders' equity consisted solely of common stock and retained earnings.) On April 18, 2012, the company reissued 30 shares for $58 each. The entries to record these events are:

Acquisition and Reissuance of Treasury Stock

---
[3]Under US GAAP, another acceptable method of accounting for treasury stock transactions is the par value method. However, only the cost method is allowed under IFRS. We leave further discussion of the par value method to intermediate accounting texts.

2012				
Feb.	18	Treasury Stock—Common (100 shares X $55)	5,500	
		Cash		5,500
		Acquired 100 shares of treasury stock at $55.		
Apr.	18	Cash (30 shares X $58)	1,740	
		Treasury Stock—Common (30 shares X $55)		1,650
		Paid-In Capital—Common Treasury Stock Transactions		90
		Reissued 30 shares of treasury stock at $58; cost is $55 per share.		

When the reissue price of subsequent shares is less than the acquisition price, firms debit the difference between cost and reissue price to Paid-In Capital—Common Treasury Stock Transactions. This account, however, never develops a debit balance. By definition, no paid-in capital account can have a debit balance. If Hillside reissued an additional 20 shares at $52 per share on June 12, 2012, the entry would be:

June	12	Cash (20 shares X $52)	1,040	
		Paid-In Capital—Common Treasury Stock Transactions	60	
		Treasury Stock—Common (20 shares X $55)		1,100
		Reissued 20 shares of treasury stock at $52; cost is $55 per share.		

At this point, the credit balance in the Paid-In Capital—Common Treasury Stock Transactions account would be $30. If the remaining 50 shares are reissued on July 16, 2012, for $53 per share, the entry would be:

July	16	Cash (50 shares X $53)	2,650	
		Paid-In Capital—Common Treasury Stock Transactions	30	
		Retained Earnings	70	
		Treasury Stock—Common (50 shares X $55)		2,750
		Reissued 50 shares of treasury stock at $53; cost is $55 per share.		

Notice that Hillside has exhausted the Paid-In Capital—Common Treasury Stock Transactions account credit balance. If more than $30 is debited to that account, it would develop a debit balance. Thus, the remaining $70 of the excess of cost over reissue price is a special distribution to the stockholders involved and is debited to the Retained Earnings account.

Sometimes stockholders donate stock to a corporation. Since donated treasury shares have no cost to the corporation, accountants make only a memo entry when the shares are received.[4] The only formal entry required is to debit Cash and credit the Paid-In Capital—Donations account when the stock is reissued. For example, if donated treasury stock is sold for $5,000, the entry would be:

Cash	5,000	
Paid-In Capital—Donations		5,000
To record the sale of donated treasury stock.		

Reinforcing Problems
E13-7 Prepare journal entries for reacquisition and reissuance of treasury stock.
E13-8 Prepare journal entry(ies) for reissuance of donated stock.
E13-3 Prepare journal entries for cash dividend when treasury stock is held.

Treasury Stock on the Balance Sheet

When treasury stock is held on a balance sheet date, it customarily appears at cost, as a deduction from the sum of total paid-in capital and retained earnings, as follows:

---

[4]The method illustrated here is called the *memo* method. Other acceptable methods of accounting for donated stock are the *cost* method and *par value* method. Intermediate accounting texts discuss these latter two methods.

Stockholders' equity:
  Paid-in Capital:
    Common stock—$10 par value; authorized and issued, 20,000 shares,
      of which 2,000 shares are in the treasury $200,000
    Retained earnings (including $22,000 restricted by acquisition of treasury
      stock) 80,000
        Total paid-in capital and retained earnings $280,000
    Less: Treasury stock at cost, 2,000 shares 22,000
        Total stockholders' equity $258,000

> **BUSINESS INSIGHT** General Mills is a leading producer of ready-to-eat cereals, desserts and baking mixes, snack products, and dinner and side dish mixes. Popular brand names include Cheerios, Green Giant, Pillsbury, Betty Crocker, and Yoplait. For 2011 and 2010, General Mills reported common stock in the treasury (treasury stock) of 109.8 million shares and 98.1 million shares, respectively. General Mills deducted the cost of these shares in the stockholders' equity section of the balance sheet.
>
> **An Accounting Perspective**

Stockholders' Equity on the Balance Sheet

To summarize much of what we have discussed in Chapters 12 and 13, we present the stockholders' equity section of the balance sheet in Illustration 13.7. This partial balance sheet shows: (1) the amount of capital assigned to shares outstanding; (2) the capital contributed for outstanding shares in addition to that assigned to the shares; (3) other forms of paid-in capital; and (4) retained earnings, appropriated and unappropriated.

Illustration 13.7   Stockholders' Equity Section of the Balance Sheet

HYPOTHETICAL CORPORATION
Partial Balance Sheet
December 31, 2012

Stockholder's equity:
  Paid-in capital:
    Preferred stock—8%, $100 par value; 2,000 shares authorized,
      issued, and outstanding .... $ 200,000
    Common stock—$10 par value; authorized, 100,000 shares; issued,
      80,000 shares of which 1,000 are held in the treasury $800,000
    Stock dividend distributable on common stock on January 15,
      2013, 7,900 shares 79,000   879,000

    Paid-in capital—
      From common stock issuances .... $ 40,000
      From stock dividends 60,000
      From treasury stock transactions 30,000
      From donations 50,000   180,000
        Total paid-in capital $1,259,000
  Retained earnings:
    Appropriated:
      Per loan agreement $250,000
    Unappropriated (restricted to the extent of $20,000, the cost
      of treasury shares held) $150,000
        Total retained earnings 400,000
        Total paid-in capital and retained earnings $1,659,000
    Less: Treasury stock, common, 1,000 shares at cost 20,000
        Total stockholders' equity $1,639,000

Reinforcing Problems
E13-1 Prepare stockholders' equity section of balance sheet.

Illustration 13.8   Income Statement

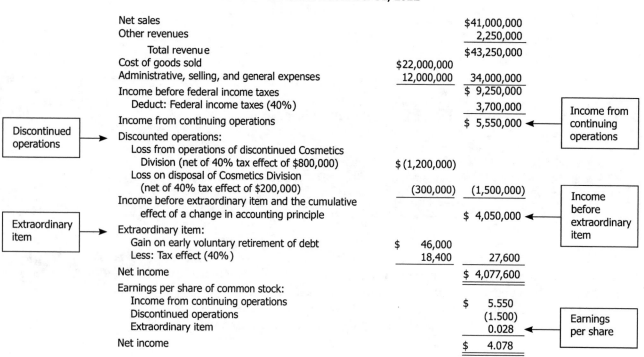

ANSON COMPANY
Income Statement
For the Year Ended December 31, 2012

Net sales		$41,000,000
Other revenues		2,250,000
Total revenue		$43,250,000
Cost of goods sold	$22,000,000	
Administrative, selling, and general expenses	12,000,000	34,000,000
Income before federal income taxes		$ 9,250,000
Deduct: Federal income taxes (40%)		3,700,000
Income from continuing operations		$ 5,550,000
Discounted operations:		
Loss from operations of discontinued Cosmetics Division (net of 40% tax effect of $800,000)	$ (1,200,000)	
Loss on disposal of Cosmetics Division (net of 40% tax effect of $200,000)	(300,000)	(1,500,000)
Income before extraordinary item and the cumulative effect of a change in accounting principle		$ 4,050,000
Extraordinary item:		
Gain on early voluntary retirement of debt	$ 46,000	
Less: Tax effect (40%)	18,400	27,600
Net income		$ 4,077,600
Earnings per share of common stock:		
Income from continuing operations		$ 5.550
Discontinued operations		(1.500)
Extraordinary item		0.028
Net income		$ 4.078

Discontinued operations → (Loss from operations of discontinued Cosmetics Division)

Extraordinary item → (Extraordinary item)

Income from continuing operations ← ($ 5,550,000)

Income before extraordinary item ← ($ 4,050,000)

Earnings per share ← (0.028)

Net Income Inclusions and Exclusions

Objective 4
Describe the proper accounting treatment of discontinued operations, extraordinary items, and changes in accounting principle.

Accounting has long faced the problem of what to include in the net income reported for a period. Should net income include only the revenues and expenses related to normal operations? Or should it include the results of discontinued operations and unusual, nonrecurring gains and losses? And further, should the determination of net income for 2012, for example, include an item that can be clearly associated with a prior year, such as additional federal income taxes for 2011? Or should such items, including corrections of errors, be carried directly to retained earnings? How are the effects of making a change in accounting principle (like a change in depreciation methods) to be reported?

APB Opinion No. 9 (December 1966) sought to provide answers to some of these questions. The *Opinion* directed that unusual and nonrecurring items having an earnings or loss effect are extraordinary items (reported in the income statement) or prior period adjustments (reported in the statement of retained earnings). Extraordinary items are reported separately after net income from regular continuing activities.

In Illustrations 13.8 and 13.10 (p. 517), we show the reporting of discontinued operations, extraordinary items, changes in accounting principle, and prior period adjustments. For Illustrations 13.8 and 13.10, assume that the Anson Company has 1,000,000 shares of common stock outstanding and the company's earnings are taxed at 40%. Also, assume the following:

1. Anson sold its Cosmetics Division on August 1, 2012, at a loss of $500,000. The net operating loss of that division through July 31, 2012, was $2,000,000.
2. Anson had a taxable gain in 2012 of $46,000 from the unusual and infrequent voluntary early retirement of debt (an extraordinary item).
3. In 2012, Anson discovered that the $200,000 cost of land acquired in 2011 had been expensed for both financial accounting and tax purposes. A prior period adjustment was made in 2012.

Next, we explain the effects of these assumptions in greater detail.

Discontinued Operations

A **discontinued operation** occurs when a business sells a component (usually an unprofitable department or division) to another company or abandons it. According to *FASB Statement 144*, "Accounting for the Impairment or Disposal of Long-Lived Assets," a component is a segment, a reporting unit, a subsidiary, or an asset group. When a company discontinues a component, it shows the relevant information in a special section of the income statement immediately after income from continuing operations and before extraordinary items. Two items of information appear:

1. The income or loss (net of tax effect) from the component's operations for the portion of the current year before it was discontinued.
2. The gain or loss (net of tax effect) on disposal of the component.

To illustrate, Anson's sale of its Cosmetics Division on August 1 led to a before-tax loss of $500,000. The after-tax loss was $500,000 × 60% = $300,000. The operating loss before taxes through July 31 was $2,000,000. The after-tax operating loss for that period was $2,000,000 × 60% = $1,200,000. Note this information on the income statement in Illustration 13.8.

Extraordinary Items

Prior to 1973, companies reported a gain or loss as an extraordinary item if it was either unusual in nature or occurred infrequently. As a result, companies were inconsistent in the financial reporting of certain gains and losses. This inconsistency led to the issuance of *APB Opinion No. 30* (September 1973). *Opinion No. 30* redefined **extraordinary items** as those *unusual in nature* and *occurring infrequently.* Note that both conditions must be met—unusual nature and infrequent occurrence. Accountants determine whether an item is unusual and infrequent in light of the environment in which the company operates. Examples of extraordinary items include gains or losses that are the direct result of a major catastrophe (a flood or hurricane where few have occurred before), a confiscation of property by a foreign government, or a prohibition under a newly enacted law. *FASB Statement No. 4* directed that all gains and losses from the voluntary early extinguishment of debt were to be treated as extraordinary items, provided that such transactions are not part of the company's recurring operations. However, *FASB Statement No. 145* rescinded *Statement No. 4* and states that gains and losses from the early extinguishment of debt are to be subject to the same *Opinion No. 4* criteria that pertain to other gains and losses.

Extraordinary items are included in the determination of periodic net income, but are disclosed separately (net of their tax effects) in the income statement below "Income from continuing operations." As shown in Illustration 13.8, Anson reported the extraordinary items after reporting the loss from discontinued operations.

Gains or losses related to ordinary business activities are not extraordinary items regardless of their size. For example, material write-downs of uncollectible receivables, obsolete inventories, and intangible assets are not extraordinary items. However, such items may be separately disclosed as part of income from continuing operations.

Note to the Student
Extraordinary items must be both unusual and infrequent. If an asteroid fell on a building, this clearly would be an extraordinary loss.

International Reporting
Under IFRS, companies are not allowed to present any gains or losses as extraordinary items. Instead, all such items must be included in the operating income and expenses of the income statement.

Illustration 13.9   Extraordinary Items

	2009	2008
Number of Companies		
Presenting extraordinary items	3	2
Not presenting extraordinary items	497	498
Total Companies	500	500

Source: Based on American Institute of Certified Public Accountants, *Accounting Trends & Techniques* (New York: AICPA, 2010), p. 417.

In Illustration 13.9, note that in a sample of 500 companies for the years 2008 and 2009, most companies do not report extraordinary items.

An Accounting Perspective

BUSINESS INSIGHT The terrorist attacks of September 11, 2001, were unique in American history. Losses of property and wealth ran into the tens of billions of dollars. The losses to insurance companies and airlines alone were estimated at more than $50-billion. And, of course, the loss of life was, in a sense, immeasurable.

How were companies that were affected by the 9/11 attacks to report their losses? Should they treat the losses as "extraordinary losses"?

The Emerging Issues Task Force (EITF) of the FASB initially determined that such losses should indeed be reported as extraordinary. However, the EITF reversed itself only a week later and announced that such losses should instead be reported as ordinary. The EITF reasoned that it would be virtually impossible to achieve consistent treatment among affected companies in separating the direct losses incurred by the attacks from the longer-term indirect effects on their profits.

Retained Earnings Adjustments

We have seen that a company sometimes has flexibility when choosing a method of accounting. For instance, a company may decide to use an accelerated depreciation method instead of the straight-line method when preparing its financial statements in accordance with GAAP. As discussed in Chapter 5, once a company chooses a particular accounting method, it should consistently apply that same method in future years.

However, a company may be allowed to voluntarily change from one method of accounting under GAAP to a different method that conforms with GAAP, provided that the newly adopted method is preferable to the previous method. Similarly, new accounting pronouncements might be issued that require a company to replace its existing method of accounting with a new accounting method. How are the effects of these voluntary and involuntary changes reported in the financial statements?

Also, a company might discover that some of its financial statements from earlier years contained significant accounting errors. Further, these prior-year errors might have a continuing effect on the financial statements of the current year. How does a company correct these prior-year errors? How does the company report the correction of such errors in its financial statements for the current year?

The effects of changes in accounting methods and of corrections in errors appear as adjustments in the statement of retained earnings.

Changes in Accounting Principle

Changes in accounting principle can materially alter a company's reported net income and financial position. **Changes in accounting principle** are changes in accounting methods pertaining to items such as inventory. Such changes include a change in inventory method from FIFO to LIFO. Before the issuance of *FASB Statement 154, "Accounting Changes and Error Corrections – a replacement of APB Opinion No. 20 and FASB Statement No. 3,"* a change in depreciation method was also considered a change in accounting principle. Under *FASB Statement 154* changes in depreciation method are considered changes in accounting estimate.

As discussed in Chapter 5, a company should consistently apply the same accounting methods from one period to another. However, a company may make a change if the newly adopted method is preferable and if the change is adequately disclosed in the financial statements. Under *APB Opinion No. 20*, in the period in which the company makes a change in accounting principle, it had to disclose in the financial statements the nature of the change, its justification, and its effect on net income. It also had to disclose on the income statement of the year of change the cumulative effect of the change on prior years' income (net of tax). This treatment was changed under *FASB Statement No. 154.*

In 2007, the FASB and the International Accounting Standards Board agreed to improve international comparability of financial reporting by narrowing differences in their standards. One of the goals of issuing *FASB Statement 154* was to reduce the differences regarding changes in accounting principle between GAAP as applied in the United States and international financial standards.

FASB Statement 154 states that a change in accounting principle should be made only if the change is required by a newly issued accounting pronouncement or the entity can justify the change because it is preferable. The entity is required to report a change in accounting principle through retrospective application to all prior accounting periods unless it is impractical to do so.

Retrospective application involves (1) showing the cumulative effect of the change on prior periods in the carrying amounts of assets and liabilities as of the beginning of the period being reported, (2) making an offsetting adjustment to the opening balance of retained earnings for that period, and (3) presenting financial statements for each individual prior accounting period adjusted to show the period-specific effects of applying the new accounting principle. Illustrations of retrospective application shall be left to intermediate accounting texts.

If it is impractical to determine the cumulative effects of applying a change in accounting principle to any prior period, the new accounting principle should be shown as taking effect as of the earliest date practicable (e.g., the start of the year being currently reported or some earlier year for which the information was available). For instance, assume that a company had used the FIFO method of inventory up to December 31, 2011. On January 1, 2012, it decided to switch to the LIFO method because it was preferable. It determined that it was impractical to determine the effects of the change on all prior years because the records of purchases and sales were no longer available. If these records were available for both beginning and ending inventories on a LIFO basis for 2009 and following years, it would show the adjusted financial statements on a prospective basis for 2009 and beyond. If the data are not available for any prior years, the change should be reported prospectively beginning in 2012.

According to *FASB Statement No. 154* (codified as ASC 250), **prior period adjustments** consist almost entirely of corrections of errors in previously published financial statements. Corrections of abnormal, nonrecurring errors that may have been caused by the improper use of an accounting principle or by mathematical mistakes are prior period adjustments. Normal, recurring corrections and adjustments, which follow inevitably from the use of estimates in accounting practice, are not treated as prior period adjustments. Also, mistakes corrected in the same year they occur are not prior period adjustments. To illustrate a prior period adjustment, suppose that Anson purchased land in 2011 at a total cost of $200,000 and recorded this amount in an expense account instead of in the Land account. Discovery of the error on May 1, 2012, after publication of the 2011 financial statements, would require a prior period adjustment. The adjustment would be recorded directly in the Retained Earnings account. Assuming the error had resulted in an $80,000 underpayment of taxes in 2011, the entry to correct the error would be:

Note to the Student
A change in accounting principle requires that the company show the cumulative effect of the change as an adjustment to the beginning balance of retained earnings for the earliest period presented.

Prior Period Adjustments

Objective 5
Define prior period adjustments and show their proper presentation in the financial statements.

An Ethical Perspective

Ace Chemical Company

Ace Chemical Company is a small, privately held manufacturer that has been operating at a profit for years. The current balance in the Cash account is $8 million, and the balance in Retained Earnings is $4 million. The company's plant assets consist of special purpose equipment that can produce only certain chemicals. The company has long-term debt with a principal balance of $10 million. Its officers (all of whom are stockholders) are concerned about the future prospects of the company. Many similar firms have been sued by customers and employees claiming that toxic chemicals produced by the company caused their health problems. No such suits have yet been filed against Ace, but the officers fully expect them to be filed within the next two years.

The company's stock is not listed on a stock exchange, nor has it recently been traded. The officers hold 70% of the stock and estimate that their total stockholdings have a current market value of about $8 million (although its value would be much lower if all the facts were known). They are worried that if suits are filed and the company loses, there will not even be enough remaining assets to satisfy creditors' claims, and the officers' stock would be worthless. Private legal counsel has informed the officers that the company is likely to lose any suits that are filed.

One of the officers suggested that they could at least receive something for their stock by having the company buy half of the shares held by the officers at a total price of $4 million. Another officer asked if such a treasury stock transaction would be legal. The response was that the transaction would be legal because it did not dip into the present legal capital of the company. Retained earnings would be reduced to a zero balance, but would not develop a debit balance as a result of the transaction.

May	1	Land	200,000	
		Federal Income Taxes Payable		80,000
		Retained Earnings (or Prior Period Adjustment—Land)		120,000
		To correct an accounting error expensing land.		

Prior period adjustments do not appear on the income statements but in the current-year financial statements as adjustments to the opening balance of retained earnings on the statement of retained earnings (Illustration 13.10).

Accounting for Tax Effects

Reinforcing Problems
E13-9 Prepare income statement and statement of retained earnings.
E13-10 Prepare statement of retained earnings.

Most discontinued operations, extraordinary items, changes in accounting principle, and prior period adjustments affect the amount of income taxes a corporation must pay. To report the income tax effect, *FASB Statement No. 109* (codified as ASC 740) requires reporting all of these items *net of their tax effects,* as shown in Illustrations 13.8 and 13.10.[5] **Net-of-tax effect** means that items appear at the dollar amounts remaining after deducting the income tax effects. Thus, the total effect of a discontinued operation, an extraordinary item, a change in accounting principle, or a prior period adjustment appears in one place in the appropriate financial statement. The reference to "Income from continuing operations" on the income statement represents the results of transactions (including income taxes) that are normal for the business and may be expected to recur. Note that the tax effect of an item may appear separately, as it does for the gain on voluntary early retirement of debt in Illustration 13.8. Or the company may mention it parenthetically with only the net amount shown (see loss from discontinued operations in Illustration 13.8 and change in accounting principle and correction of error in Illustration 13.10).

---

[5]FASB, *Statement of Financial Accounting Standards No. 109, "Accounting for Income Taxes"* (Stamford. Conn., 1992). Copyright © by the Financial Accounting Standards Board, High Ridge Park, Stamford, Connecticut 06905, U.S.A.

Illustration 13.10   Statement of Retained Earnings

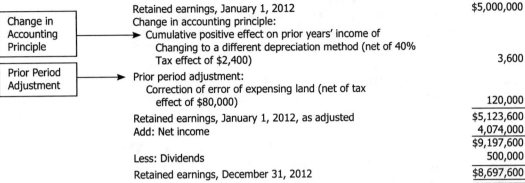

ANSON COMPANY
Statement of Retained Earnings
For the Year Ended December 31, 2012

Change in Accounting Principle

Prior Period Adjustment

Retained earnings, January 1, 2012	$5,000,000
Change in accounting principle:	
Cumulative positive effect on prior years' income of Changing to a different depreciation method (net of 40% Tax effect of $2,400)	3,600
Prior period adjustment:	
Correction of error of expensing land (net of tax effect of $80,000)	120,000
Retained earnings, January 1, 2012, as adjusted	$5,123,600
Add: Net income	4,074,000
	$9,197,600
Less: Dividends	500,000
Retained earnings, December 31, 2012	$8,697,600

1. Income from continuing operations of $5,550,000 (Illustration 13.8) is more representative of the continuing earning power of the company than is the net income figure of $4,077,600.
2. Following income, the special items excluded from continuing operations appear at their actual impact on the company—that is, net of their tax effect.
3. EPS is reported both before ($5.550) and after ($4.078) the discontinued operations, extraordinary item, and the cumulative effect of a change in accounting principle (Illustration 13.8).
4. The correction of the $200,000 error adds only $120,000 to retained earnings (Illustration 13.10). This result occurs because the mistake was included in the 2011 tax return and taxes were underpaid by $80,000. In the 2012 return, the $80,000 of taxes would have to be paid.

Analyzing and Using the Financial Results— Earnings per Share and Price-Earnings Ratio

A major item of interest to investors and potential investors is how much a company earned during the current year, both in total and for each share of stock outstanding. Firms calculate the earnings per share amount only for the common shares of ownership. They compute **earnings per share (EPS)** as net income available to common stockholders divided by the average number of common shares outstanding during that period. **Income available to common stockholders** is net income less any dividends on preferred stock. They deduct the regular preferred dividend on cumulative preferred stock (but not a dividend in arrears) whether or not declared; however, they deduct only declared dividends on noncumulative preferred stock.

To illustrate, Apple Inc. had 936,645,000 weighted-average common shares outstanding with income available to common shareholders of $25,922,000,000 at September 24, 2011. Apple computed EPS as follows:

Objective 6
Analyze and use the financial results—earnings per share and price-earnings ratio.

Apple Inc.
Apple manufactures and markets personal computers, mobile communication devices, and personal digital music players.

$$\text{EPS} = \frac{\text{Income available to common stockholders}}{\text{Weighted-average number of common shares outstanding}}$$

$$= \frac{\$25,922,000,000}{936,645,000}$$

$$= \$27.68 \text{ per share}$$

Firms calculate EPS for each major category on the face of the income statement. In other words, they make an EPS calculation for income from continuing operations, discontinued operations, extraordinary items, and net income. Note in Illustration 13.8 that Anson reports the EPS amounts at the bottom of its income statement.

The **price-earnings ratio** (current market price per share of common stock divided by EPS) provides an index on whether a stock has future high income potential compared to other stocks. Stocks with future high income potential tend to have a high price-earnings ratio.

The market price of Apple Inc.'s common stock at its September 24, 2011, fiscal year-end was $404.30. Earnings per share were $27.68. Apple would compute its price-earnings ratio that day as follows:

$$\text{Price-earnings ratio} = \frac{\text{Current market price per share of common stock}}{\text{EPS}}$$

$$= \frac{\$404.30}{\$27.68}$$

$$= \$14.61$$

This chapter completes the study of stockholders' equity. In Chapter 14, you learn about stock investments and international accounting.

Understanding the Learning Objectives

- Paid-in capital is presented in the stockholders' equity section of the balance sheet. Each source of paid-in capital is listed separately.
- Sources of paid-in capital are:
  1. Common stock.
  2. Preferred stock.
  3. In excess of par value or stated value (common and preferred).
  4. Stock dividends.
  5. Treasury stock transactions.
  6. Donations.

- Cash dividend of $3 on 100,000 of outstanding shares of common stock: declared on July 1 and paid on September 15.

July	1	Retained Earnings		3,000	
		Dividends Payable			3,000
Sept.	15	Dividends Payable		3,000	
		Cash			3,000

Ten percent stock dividend on 10,000 shares of common stock outstanding; par value, $100; market value at declaration, $125 per share (declared on January 1 and paid on February 1).

Jan.	1	Retained earnings (1,000 shares X $125)		125,000	
		Stock Dividends Distributable—Common			
		(1,000 shares X $100)			100,000
		Paid-In Capital—Stock Dividends			
		(1,000 shares X $25)			25,000
Feb.	1	Stock Dividend Distributable—Common		100,000	
		Common Stock			100,000

- Thirty percent stock dividend on 10,000 shares of common stock outstanding: declared on January 1 and payable on February 1; par value, $100.

Jan.	1	Retained Earnings (3,000 shares X $100)	300,000	
		Stock Dividend Distributable—Common		300,000
Feb.	1	Stock Dividend Distributable—Common	300,000	
		Common Stock		300,000

- Stock split: 1,000 shares of $50 par value common stock replaced by 2,000 shares of $25 par value common stock.

Common Stock—$50 par value	50,000	
Common Stock—$25 par value		50,000

- Retained earnings appropriation: $75,000 appropriated for plant expansion.

Retained Earnings	75,000	
Retained Earnings Appropriated for Plant Expansion		75,000

- Treasury stock transactions: 100 shares of common stock were reacquired at $100 each and reissued for $105 each.

Treasury Stock—Common (100 shares X $100)	10,000	
Cash		10,000
Cash (100 shares X $105)	10,500	
Treasury Stock—Common (100 shares X $100)		10,000
Paid-In Capital—Common Treasury Stock Transactions (100 shares X $5)		500

- The income or loss (net of tax effect) from the segment's operations for the portion of the current year before it was discontinued is reported on the income statement below "Income from continuing operations."
- The gain or loss (net of tax effect) on disposal of the segment is also reported in that same section of the income statement.
- Extraordinary items are both unusual in nature and infrequent in occurrence. Extraordinary items appear on the income statement (net of tax effect) below "Income from continuing operations."
- In the period in which a change in accounting principle is made, the nature of the change, its justification, and its effect on beginning retained earnings must be disclosed in the financial statements. Also, the cumulative effect of the change (net of tax effect) must be shown on the statement of retained earnings as an adjustment to beginning retained earnings for the earliest year presented.
- Prior period adjustments consist of errors in previously published financial statements. Prior period adjustments appear (net of tax effect) as a correction to the beginning retained earnings balance on the statement of retained earnings.

Objective 6
Analyze and use the financial results—earnings per share and price-earnings ratio.

• EPS equals the income available to common stockholders divided by the weighted-average number of common shares outstanding. Income available to common stockholders is net income less any dividends on preferred stock. EPS provides information on the return of an investment in common stock.

• The price-earnings ratio equals the current market price per share of common stock divided by EPS. The price-earnings ratio indicates whether a stock has a future high income potential as compared to other stocks.

Demonstration Problem 13–A

Wylie Corporation has outstanding 10,000 shares of $150 par value common stock.

Required Prepare the entries to record:

a. The declaration of a cash dividend of $1.50 per share.

b. The declaration of a stock dividend of 10% at a time when the market value per share is $185.

c. The subsequent declaration of a stock dividend of 40% at a time when the market value per share is $195.

Solution to Demonstration Problem 13–A

a.

Retained Earnings (or Dividends)	15,000	
Dividends Payable		15,000
To record declaration of a cash dividend.		

b.

Retained Earnings (or Stock Dividends).		
(1,000 shares X $185)	185,000	
Stock Dividend Distributable—Common		
(1,000 shares X $150)		150,000
Paid-In Capital—Stock Dividends		35,000
To record declaration of a small stock dividend (10%).		

c.

Retained Earnings (or Stock Dividends) (4,400 shares X $150)	660,000	
Stock Dividend Distributable—Common		660,000
To record declaration of a large stock dividend (40%).		

Demonstration Problem 13–B

Following are selected transactions of Brackett Company:

1. The company reacquired 200 shares of its own $100 par value common stock, previously issued at $105 per share, for $20,600.
2. Fifty of the treasury shares were reissued at $110 per share, cash.
3. Seventy of the treasury shares were reissued at $95 per share, cash.
4. Stockholders of the corporation donated 100 shares of their common stock to the company.
5. The 100 shares of treasury stock received by donation were reissued for $9,000.

Prepare the necessary journal entries to record these transactions.   *Required*

Solution to Demonstration Problem 13–B

1.	Treasury Stock	20,600	
	Cash		20,600
	Acquired 200 shares at $20,600 ($103 per share).		
2.	Cash (50 shares X $110)	5,500	
	Treasury Stock—Common (50 shares X $103)		5,150
	Paid-In Capital—Common Treasury Stock Transactions		350
	Reissued 50 shares at $110 per share; cost is $5,150.		
3.	Cash (70 shares X $95)	6,650	
	Paid-In Capital—Common Treasury Stock Transactions		
	(50 shares X $7)	350	
	Retained Earnings	210	
	Treasury Stock—Common (70 shares X $103)		7,210
	Reissued 70 shares at $95 per share; cost is $7,210.		
4.	Stockholders donated 100 shares of common stock to the company.		
	(Only memo entry is made.)		
5.	Cash	9,000	
	Paid-In Capital—Donations (100 shares X $90)		9,000
	Reissued donated shares at $90 per share.		

Demonstration Problem 13–C

Selected account balances of Nexis Corporation at December 31, 2012, are:

Common Stock (no par value; 100,000 shares authorized, issued, and outstanding; stated value of $20 per share)	$2,000,000
Retained Earnings	570,000
Dividends Payable (in cash, declared December 15 on preferred stock)	16,000
Preferred Stock (8%, par value $200; 1,000 shares authorized, issued, and outstanding)	200,000
Paid-In Capital from Donation of Plant Site	100,000
Paid-In Capital in Excess of Par Value—Preferred	8,000

Required   Present in good form the stockholders' equity section of the balance sheet.

Solution to Demonstration Problem 13–C

NEXIS CORPORATION
Partial Balance Sheet
December 31, 2012

Stockholders' equity:		
Paid-in capital:		
Preferred stock—8%, par value $200; 1,000 shares authorized, issued, and outstanding	$ 200,000	
Common stock—no par value, stated value of $20 per share; 100,000 shares authorized, issued, and outstanding	2,000,000	
Paid-in capital from donation of plant site	100,000	
Paid-in capital in excess of par value--preferred	8,000	
Total paid-in capital		$2,308,000
Retained earnings		570,000
Total stockholders' equity		$2,878,000

New Terms

Cash dividends   Cash distributions of accumulated earnings by a corporation to its stockholders. *500*

Changes in accounting principle   Changes in accounting methods pertaining to such items as inventory. *514*

Contributed capital   See *paid-in capital.*

Date of declaration (of dividends)   The date the board of directors takes action in the form of a motion that dividends be paid. *499*

Date of payment (of dividends)   The date of actual payment of a cash dividend, or issuance of additional shares for a stock dividend. *500*

Date of record (of dividends)   The date of record established by the board that determines the stockholders who will receive dividends. *500*

Deficit   A debit balance in the Retained Earnings account. *499*

Discontinued operation   When a segment of a business is sold to another company or is abandoned. *513*

Dividends   Distribution of earnings by a corporation to its stockholders. *499*

Dividends (cash)   See *cash dividends.*

Dividends (stock)   See *stock dividends.*

Donated capital   Results from donation of assets to the corporation, which increases stockholders' equity. *498*

Earnings per share (EPS)   Earnings to the common stockholders on a per share basis, computed as income available to common stockholders divided by the weighted-average number of common shares outstanding. *517*

Extraordinary items   Items both unusual in nature and infrequent in occurrence; reported in the income statement net of their tax effects, if any. *513*

Income available to common stockholders   Net income less any dividends on preferred stock. *517*

Liquidating dividends   Dividends that are a return of contributed capital, not a distribution chargeable to retained earnings. *505*

Net-of-tax effect   Used for discontinued operations, extraordinary items, changes in accounting principle, and prior period adjustments, whereby items are shown at the dollar amounts remaining after deducting the effects of such items on income taxes, if any, payable currently. *516*

Paid-in capital   All of the contributed capital of a corporation, including that carried in capital stock accounts. When the words *paid-in capital* are included in the account title, the account contains capital contributed in addition to that assigned to the shares issued and recorded in the capital stock accounts. *497*

Paid-In Capital—Common (Preferred) Treasury Stock Transactions   The account credited when treasury stock is reissued for more than its cost; this account is debited to the extent of its credit balance when such shares are reissued at less than cost. *509*

Price-earnings ratio   The current market price per share of common stock divided by EPS. *518*

Prior period adjustments   Consist almost entirely of corrections of errors in previously published financial statements. Prior period adjustments are reported in the statement of retained earnings net of their tax effects, if any. *515*

Retained earnings   That part of stockholders' equity resulting from accumulated earnings; the account to which the results of corporate activity, including prior period adjustments, are carried and to which dividends and certain items resulting from capital transactions are charged. *498*

Retained earnings appropriations   Contractual or voluntary restrictions or limitations on retained earnings that reduce the amount of dividends that may be declared. *506*

Statement of retained earnings   A formal statement showing the items causing changes in unappropriated and appropriated retained earnings during a stated period of time. *507*

Statement of stockholders' equity   A summary of the transactions affecting the accounts in the stockholders' equity section of the balance sheet during a stated period of time. *508*

Stock Dividend Distributable—Common account   The stockholders' equity (paid-in capital) account that is credited for the par or stated value of the shares distributable when recording the declaration of a stock dividend. *503*

Stock dividends   Dividends that are payable in additional shares of the declaring corporation's capital stock. *501*

Stock split   A distribution of 100% or more of additional shares of the issuing corporation's stock, accompanied by a corresponding reduction in the par value per share. The purpose of a stock split is to cause a large reduction in the market price per share of the outstanding stock. *504*

Treasury stock   Shares of capital stock issued and reacquired by the issuing corporation; they have not been formally canceled and are available for reissuance. *498*

Self-Test

True-False

Indicate whether each of the following statements is true or false.

1. The retained earnings balance of a corporation is part of its paid-in capital.
2. The purchase of treasury stock does not affect stockholders' equity.
3. Dividends are expenses since they decrease stockholders' equity.
4. A stock dividend reduces the retained earnings balance and permanently capitalizes the reduced portion of the retained earnings.
5. A retained earnings appropriation reduces the total stockholders' equity shown on the balance sheet.
6. Heavy frost damage suffered by a Florida citrus grower's orange trees would probably be reported as an extraordinary item.

Multiple-Choice

Select the best answer for each of the following questions.

1. Which of the following is not included in paid-in capital?
   a. Common Stock.
   b. Paid-In Capital—Donations.
   c. Stock Dividend Distributable.
   d. Appropriation per Loan Agreement.
2. Bevins Company issued 10,000 shares of $20 par value common stock at $24 per share. Bevins reacquired 1,000 shares of its own stock at a cost of $30 per share. The entry to record the reacquisition is:

a.

Premium on		
Treasury Stock	10,000	
Treasury Stock	20,000	
Cash		30,000

b.

Premium on		
Treasury Stock	6,000	
Treasury Stock	24,000	
Cash		30,000

c.

Treasury Stock	30,000	
Cash		30,000

d.

Treasury Stock	20,000	
Paid-In Capital—		
Treasury Stock		
Transactions	10,000	
Cash		30,000

3. If the company reissues 500 shares of the treasury stock in (2) for $36 per share, the entry is:

a.

Cash	18,000	
Treasury Stock		15,000
Paid-In Capital—		
Treasury Stock		
Transactions		3,000

b.

Cash	18,000	
Treasury Stock		18,000

c.

Cash	18,000	
Treasury Stock		15,000
Retained earnings		3,000

d.

Cash	18,000	
Treasury Stock		10,000
Retained earnings		8,000

4. Treasury stock should be shown on the balance sheet as a:
   a. Reduction of the corporation's stockholders' equity.
   b. Current asset.
   c. Current liability.
   d. Investment asset.
5. An individual stockholder is entitled to receive any dividends declared on stock owned, provided the stock is held on the:
   a. Date of declaration.
   b. Date of record.
   c. Date of payment.
   d. Last day of a fiscal year.
6. ABC Corporation declared the regular quarterly dividend of $2 per share. ABC had issued 12,000

shares and subsequently reacquired 2,000 shares as treasury stock. What would be the total amount of the dividend?

  a. $24,000.
  b. $28,000.
  c. $20,000.
  d. $4,000.

7. Which item is not reported as a separate line item below income from continuing operations, net of tax effects, in the income statement?

  a. Extraordinary items.
  b. Prior period adjustments.
  c. Discontinued operations.
  d. All of the above are shown as separate line items.

Now turn to page 537 to check your answers.

Questions

1. What are the two main elements of stockholders' equity in a corporation? Explain the difference between them.
2. Name several sources of paid-in capital. Would it suffice to maintain one account called *Paid-In Capital* for all sources of paid-in capital? Why or why not?
3. Does accounting for treasury stock resemble accounting for an asset? Is treasury stock an asset? If not, where is it properly shown on a balance sheet?
4. What are some possible reasons for a corporation to reacquire its own capital stock as treasury stock?
5. What is the purpose underlying the statutes that provide for restriction of retained earnings in the amount of the cost of treasury stock? Are such statutes for the benefit of stockholders, management, or creditors?
6. What is the effect of each of the following on the total stockholders' equity of a corporation: (*a*) declaration of a cash dividend, (*b*) payment of a cash dividend already declared, (*c*) declaration of a stock dividend, and (*d*) issuance of a stock dividend already declared?
7. The following dates are associated with a cash dividend of $80,000: July 15, July 31, and August 15. Identify each of the three dates, and give the journal entry required on each date, if any.
8. How should a declared but unpaid cash dividend be shown on the balance sheet? How should a declared but unissued stock dividend be shown?

9. On May 8, the board of directors of Park Corporation declared a dividend, payable on June 5, to stockholders of record on May 17. On May 10, James sold his capital stock in Park Corporation directly to Benton for $20,000, endorsing his stock certificate and giving it to Benton. Benton placed the stock certificate in her safe. On May 30, Benton sent the certificate to the transfer agent of Park Corporation for transfer. Who received the dividend? Why?
10. What are the possible reasons for a corporation to declare a stock dividend?
11. Why is a dividend consisting of the distribution of additional shares of the common stock of the declaring corporation not considered income to the recipient stockholders?
12. What is the difference between a small stock dividend and a large stock dividend?
13. What are liquidating dividends?
14. What is the purpose of a retained earnings appropriation?
15. What is a statement of stockholders' equity?
16. Describe a discontinued operation.
17. What are extraordinary items? Where and how are they reported?
18. Give an example of a change in accounting principle. How are the effects of changes in accounting principle reported?
19. What are prior period adjustments? Where and how are they reported?
20. Why are stockholders and potential investors interested in the amount of a corporation's EPS? What does the EPS amount reveal that total earnings do not?

Exercises

Exercise 13-1
Prepare stockholders'
equity section of
balance sheet (L.O. 1)

The December 31, 2011, trial balance of Yamey Corporation had the following account balances

Common Stock (no-par value; 200,000 shares authorized, issued, and outstanding; stated value of $20 per share)	$4,000,000
Notes Payable (12% due May 1, 2012)	500,000
Retained Earnings, Unappropriated	2,500,000
Dividends Payable in Cash (declared December 15, on preferred stock)	12,000
Appropriation per Loan Agreement	480,000
Preferred Stock (6%, par value $200; 2,000 shares author ized, issued, and outstanding)	400,000
Paid-In Capital in Excess of Stated Value—Common	300,000
Paid-In Capital in Excess of Par Value—Preferred	40,000

Present in proper form the stockholders' equity section of the balance sheet.

Exercise 13-2
Prepare journal entries
for cash dividends
(L.O. 2)

Fogg Company has issued all of its authorized 5,000 shares of $400 par value common stock. On February 1, 2011, the board of directors declared a dividend of $12 per share payable on March 15, 2011, to stockholders of record on March 1, 2011. Give the necessary journal entries.

Exercise 13-3
Prepare journal entries
for cash dividend when
treasury stock is held
(L.O. 2)

The stockholders' equity section of Jay Company's balance sheet on December 31, 2011, shows 100,000 shares of authorized and issued $20 stated value common stock, of which 9,000 shares are held in the treasury. On this date, the board of directors declared a cash dividend of $2 per share payable on January 21, 2012, to stockholders of record on January 10. Give dated journal entries for these.

Exercise 13-4
Prepare journal
entry for small stock
dividend and discuss
large stock dividend
(L.O. 2)

Kevin Company has outstanding 75,000 shares of common stock without par or stated value, which were issued at an average price of $80 per share, and retained earnings of $3,200,000. The current market price of the common stock is $120 per share. Total authorized stock consists of 500,000 shares.

   a. Give the required entry to record the declaration of a 10% stock dividend.
   b. If, alternatively, the company declared a 30% stock dividend, what additional information would you need before making a journal entry to record the dividend?

Exercise 13-5
Prepare journal entries
for stock split and small
stock dividend (L.O. 2)

Grant Corporation's stockholders' equity consisted of 60,000 authorized shares of $30 par value common stock, of which 30,000 shares had been issued at par, and retained earnings of $750,000. The company then split its stock, two for one, by changing the par value of the old shares and issuing new $15 par shares.

a. Give the required journal entry to record the stock split.
b. Suppose instead that the company declared and later issued a 10% stock dividend. Give the required journal entries, assuming that the market value on the date of declaration was $40 per share.

The balance sheet of Willis Company contains the following:

Appropriation per loan agreement $900,000

Exercise 13-6
Prepare journal entry for appropriation of retained earnings and explain (L.O. 2)

a. Give the journal entry made to create this account.
b. Explain the reason for the appropriation's existence and its manner of presentation in the balance sheet.

Kelly Company had outstanding 50,000 shares of $20 stated value common stock, all issued at $24 per share, and had retained earnings of $800,000. The company reacquired 2,000 shares of its stock for cash at book value from the widow of a deceased stockholder.

Exercise 13-7
Prepare journal entries for reacquisition and reissuance of treasury stock (L.O. 3)

a. Give the entry to record the reacquisition of the stock.
b. Give the entry to record the subsequent reissuance of this stock at $50 per share.
c. Give the entry required if the stock is instead reissued at $30 per share and there were no prior treasury stock transactions.

Evan Company received 200 shares of its $200 stated value common stock on December 1, 2011, as a donation from a stockholder. On December 15, 2011, it reissued the stock for $62,400 cash. Give the journal entry or entries necessary for these transactions.

Exercise 13-8
Prepare journal entry(ies) for reissuance of donated stock (L.O. 3)

Vista Company has revenues of $80 million, expenses of $64 million, a tax-deductible earthquake loss (its first such loss) of $4 million, and a tax-deductible loss of $6 million resulting from the voluntary early extinguishment (retirement) of debt. The assumed income tax rate is 40%. The company's beginning-of-the-year retained earnings were $30 million, and a dividend of $2 million was declared.

Exercise 13-9
Prepare income statement and statement of retained earnings (L.O. 2, 4)

a. Prepare an income statement for the year.
b. Prepare a statement of retained earnings for the year.

Conner Company had retained earnings of $56,000 as of January 1, 2011. In 2011, Conner Company had sales of $160,000, cost of goods sold of $96,000, and other operating expenses, excluding taxes, of $32,000. In 2011, Conner Company discovered that it had, in error, depreciated land over the last three years resulting in a balance in the accumulated depreciation account of $40,000. The assumed tax rate for Conner Company is 40%. Present in proper form a statement of retained earnings for the year ended December 31, 2011.

Exercise 13-10
Prepare statement of retained earnings (L.O. 2, 5)

The following information relates to Perry Corporation for the year ended December 31, 2011:

Exercise 13-11
Calculate EPS; present information in income statement format (L.O. 6)

Common stock outstanding	75,000 shares
Income from continuing operations	$1,523,200
Loss on discontinued operations (net of tax)	240,000
Extraordinary gain (net of tax)	144,000

Calculate EPS for the year ended December 31, 2011. Present the information in the same format used in the corporation's income statement.

Exercise 13-12
Calculate EPS;
comment on resulting
amounts (L.O. 6)

Dean Company had an average number of shares of common stock outstanding of 200,000 in 2011 and 215,000 in 2012. Net income for these two years was as follows:

2011	$2,208,000
2012	2,304,000

a. Calculate EPS for the years ended December 31, 2011, and 2012.
b. What might the resulting figures tell a stockholder or a potential investor?

Problems

Problem 13-1
Prepare stockholders'
equity section of
balance sheet (L.O. 1)

The bookkeeper of Hart Company has prepared the following incorrect statement of stockholders' equity for the year ended December 31, 2011:

Stockholders' equity:
  Paid-in Capital:
    Preferred stock—6%, cumulative (8,000 shares) $1,003,200
    Common stock—50,000 shares   2,856,000
      Total paid-in capital $3,859,200
  Retained earnings   1,636,800
      Total stockholders' equity $5,496,000

The authorized stock consists of 12,000 shares of preferred stock with a $120 par value and 75,000 shares of common stock, $48 par value. The preferred stock was issued on two occasions: (1) 5,000 shares at par, and (2) 3,000 shares at $134.40 per share. The 50,000 shares of common stock were issued at $62.40 per share. Five thousand shares of treasury common stock were reacquired for $264,000. The bookkeeper deducted the cost of the treasury stock from the Common Stock account.

Required Prepare the correct stockholders' equity section of the balance sheet at December 31, 2011.

Problem 13-2
Prepare journal entries
for cash dividend and
small stock dividend
(L.O. 2)

The only stockholders' equity items of Jody Company at June 30, 2011, are:

Stockholders' equity:
  Paid-in Capital:
    Common stock—$200 par value, 10,000 shares authorized,
      6,000 shares issued and outstanding $1,200,000
    Paid-in capital in excess of par value   480,000
      Total paid-in capital $1,680,000
  Retained earnings   480,000
      Total stockholders' equity $2,160,000

On August 4, 2011, a 4% cash dividend was declared, payable on September 3. On November 16, a 10% stock dividend was declared. The shares were issued on December 1. The market value of the common stock was $360 per share on November 16 and $354 per share on December 1.

Required Prepare journal entries for these dividend transactions.

Following are selected transactions of White Corporation:

Problem 13-3
Prepare journal entries
for retained earnings
appropriation, asset
acquisition, and stock
dividend (L.O. 2)

2004

Dec.   31   The board of directors authorized the appropriation of $50,000 of retained earnings to provide for the future acquisition of a new plant site and the construction of a new building. (On the last day of each of the next six years, the same action was taken. You need not make entries for these six years.)

2009

Jan.   2   Purchased a new plant site for cash, $100,000.

Mar.   29   Entered into a contract for construction of a new building, payment to be made within 30 days following completion.

2011

Feb.   10   Following final inspection and approval of the new building, Dyer Construction Company was paid in full, $500,000.

Mar.   10   The board of directors authorized release of the retained earnings appropriated for the plant site and building.

Apr.   2   A 5% stock dividend on the 100,000 shares of $50 par value common stock outstanding was declared. The market price on this date was $55 per share.

Prepare journal entries for all of these transactions.

 Required

Following are selected data of Kane Corporation at December 31, 2011:

Problem 13-4
Present statement of
retained earnings
(L.O. 2)

Net income for the year	$512,000
Dividends declared on preferred stock	72,000
Retained earnings appropriated during the year for future plant expansion	240,000
Dividends declared on common stock	64,000
Retained earnings, January 1, unappropriated	720,000
Directors ordered that the balance in the 'Appropriation per loan agreement,' related to a loan repaid on March 31, 2011, be returned to unappropriated retained earnings	480,000

Prepare a statement of retained earnings for the year ended December 31, 2011.

Required

The stockholders' equity of Sayers Company at January 1, 2011, is as follows:

Problem 13-5
Prepare journal
entries for stock
dividend, treasury
stock transactions,
and retained earnings
appropriation
(L.O. 2, 3)

Common stock—no-par value, stated value of $20;	
100,000 shares authorized, 60,000 shares issued	$1,200,000
Paid-in capital in excess of stated value	200,000
Appropriation per loan agreement	75,200
Unappropriated retained earnings	424,000
Treasury stock (3,000 shares at cost)	(72,000)

During 2011, the following transactions occurred in the order listed:

1. Issued 10,000 shares of stock for $368,000.
2. Declared a 4% stock dividend when the market price was $48 per share.
3. Sold 1,000 shares of treasury stock for $43,200.
4. Issued stock certificates for the stock dividend declared in transaction 2.
5. Bought 2,000 shares of treasury stock for $67,200.
6. Increased the appropriation by $43,200 per loan agreement.

Prepare journal entries as necessary for these transactions.

Required

Problem 13-6
Prepare journal entries for treasury stock transactions and for cash dividend; present stockholders' equity section of balance sheet (L.O. 2, 3)

The stockholders' equity of Briar Company on December 31, 2010, consisted of 1,000 authorized, issued, and outstanding shares of $72 cumulative preferred stock, stated value $240 per share, which were originally issued at $1,192 per share; 100,000 shares authorized, issued, and outstanding of no-par, $160 stated value common stock, which were originally issued at $160; and retained earnings of $1,120,000. Following are selected transactions and other data relating to 2011. No previous treasury stock transactions had occurred.

1. The company reacquired 2,000 shares of its common stock at $336.
2. One thousand of the treasury shares were reissued at $288.
3. Stockholders donated 1,000 shares of common stock to the company. These shares were immediately reissued at $256 to provide working capital.
4. The first quarter's dividend of $18 per share was declared and paid on the preferred stock. No other dividends were declared or paid during 2011.

The company suffered a net loss of $224,000 for the year 2011.

Required   a. Prepare journal entries for the preceding numbered transactions.
b. Prepare the stockholders' equity section of the December 31, 2011, balance sheet.

Problem 13-7
Prepare journal entries to close retained earnings appropriation and for treasury stock transactions and cash dividends; present statement of retained earnings and stockholders' equity section of balance sheet (L.O. 2, 3)

The following stockholders' equity section is from Bell Company's October 31, 2010, balance sheet:

Stockholders' equity:
  Paid-in Capital:

Preferred stock—$60 par value, 6%; 1,000 shares authorized;		
350 shares issued and outstanding	$ 21,000	
Common stock—$6 par value; 100,000 shares authorized;		
40,000 shares issued and outstanding	240,000	
Paid-in capital from donation of plant site	15,000	
Total paid-in capital		$276,000
Retained earnings:		
Appropriated:		
Appropriation for contingencies	$ 12,000	
Unappropriated	33,300	
Total retained earnings		45,300
Total stockholders' equity		$321,300

During the ensuing fiscal year, Bell Company entered into the following transactions:

1. The appropriation of $12,000 of retained earnings had been authorized in October 2010 because of the likelihood of an unfavorable court decision in a pending lawsuit. The suit was brought by a customer seeking damages for the company's alleged breach of a contract to supply the customer with certain products at stated prices in 2009. The suit was concluded on March 6, 2011, with a court order directing the company to pay $10,500 in damages. These damages were not deductible in determining the income tax liability. The board ordered the damages paid and the appropriation closed. The loss does not qualify as an extraordinary item.
2. The company acquired 1,000 shares of its own common stock at $9 in May 2011. On June 30, it reissued 500 of these shares at $7.20.
3. Dividends declared and paid during the year were 6% on preferred stock and 18 cents per share on common stock. Both dividends were declared on September 1 and paid on September 30, 2011.

For the fiscal year, the company had net income after income taxes of $11,400, excluding the loss of the lawsuit.

a. Prepare journal entries for the preceding numbered transactions.
b. Prepare a statement of retained earnings for the year ended October 31, 2011.
c. Prepare the stockholders' equity section of the October 31, 2011, balance sheet.

Required

Selected data for Brinks Company for 2011 are given below:

Problem 13-8
Present income statement and statement of retained earnings
(L.O. 2, 4, 5)

Common stock—$20 par value	$2,000,000
Sales, net	1,740,000
Selling and administrative expenses	320,000
Cash dividends declared and paid	120,000
Cost of goods sold	800,000
Depreciation expense	120,000
Interest revenue	20,000
Loss on write-down of obsolete inventory	40,000
Retained earnings (as of 12/31/10)	2,000,000
Operating loss on Candy Division up to point of sale in 2011	40,000
Loss on disposal of Candy Division	200,000
Earthquake loss 1	60,000

Assume the applicable federal income tax rate is 40%. All of the items of expense, revenue, and loss are included in the computation of taxable income. The earthquake loss resulted from the first earthquake experienced at the company's location. In addition, the company discovered that in 2010 it had erroneously charged to expense the $160,000 cost of a tract of land purchased that year and had made the same error on its tax return for 2010.

a. Prepare an income statement for the year ended December 31, 2011.
b. Prepare a statement of retained earnings for the year ended December 31, 2011.

Required

Alternate Problems

The trial balance of Dex Corporation as of December 31, 2011, contains the following selected balances:

Problem 13-1A
Present stockholders' equity section of balance sheet (L.O. 1)

Notes Payable (17%, due May 1, 2013)	$4,000,000
Allowance for Uncollectible Accounts	60,000
Common Stock (without par value, $20 stated value; 300,000 shares authorized, issued, and outstanding)	6,000,000
Retained Earnings, Unappropriated	500,000
Dividends Payable (in cash, declared December 15 on preferred stock)	14,000
Appropriation for Pending Litigation	600,000
Preferred Stock (6%, $200 par value; 3,000 shares authorized, issued, and outstanding)	600,000
Paid-In Capital--Donations	400,000
Paid-In Capital in Excess of Par Value—Preferred	10,000

Present the stockholders' equity section of the balance sheet as of December 31, 2011.

Required

The stockholders' equity section of Carson Company's December 31, 2010, balance sheet follows:

Problem 13-2A
Prepare journal entries for cash dividend and small stock dividend
(L.O. 2)

Stockholders' equity:
Paid-in Capital:
Common stock—$120 par value; authorized, 2,000 shares;

issued and outstanding, 1,000 shares		$120,000	
Paid-in capital in excess of par value		6,000	
Total paid-in capital			$126,000
Retained earnings			48,000
Total stockholders' equity			$174,000

On July 15, 2011, the board of directors declared a cash dividend of $12 per share, which was paid on August 1, 2011. On December 1, 2011, the board declared a stock dividend of 10%, and the shares were issued on December 15, 2011. Market value of the stock was $144 on December 1 and $168 on December 15.

Required ➲ Prepare journal entries for these dividend transactions.

Problem 13-3A
Prepare journal entries for appropriations of retained earnings (L.O. 2)

The ledger of Falcone Company includes the following account balances on September 30 2011:

Appropriation for Contingencies	$210,000
Appropriation for Plant Expansion	392,000
Retained Earnings, Unappropriated	700,000

During October 2011, the company took action to:

1. Increase the appropriation for contingencies by $60,000.
2. Decrease the appropriation for plant expansion by $160,000.
3. Establish an appropriation per loan agreement, with an annual increase of $48,000.
4. Declare a cash dividend of $140,000.

Required ➲ Prepare the journal entries to record these transactions of Falcone Company.

Problem 13-4A
Prepare journal entries for retained earnings appropriation and small stock dividend (L.O. 2)

Following are selected transactions of Taylor Corporation:

2006
Dec. 31 By action of the board of directors, $450,000 of retained earnings was appropriated to provide for future expansion of the company's main building. (On the last day of each of the next four years, the same action was taken. You need not make entries for these years.)

2011
Jan. 3 Obtained, at a cost of $4,500, a building permit to construct a new wing on the main plant building.
July 30 Paid $1,800,000 to Starke Construction Company for completion of the new wing.
Aug. 4 The board of directors authorized the release of the sum appropriated for expansion of the plant building.
4 The board of directors declared a 10% common stock dividend on the 25,000 shares of $500 par value common stock outstanding. The market price on this date was $660 per share.

Required ➲ Prepare journal entries to record all of these transactions.

The following information relates to Dahl Corporation for the year 2011:

Problem 13-5A
Present statement
of retained earnings
(L.O. 2)

Net income for the year	$ 1,680,000
Dividends declared on common stock	235,200
Dividends declared on preferred stock	134,400
Retained earnings, January 1, unappropriated	5,040,000
Appropriation for retirement of bonds	672,000
Balance in "Appropriation for possible loss of a lawsuit," no longer needed on December 31 because of a favorable court decision, is (by directors' order) returned to unappropriated retained earnings	840,000

Prepare a statement of retained earnings for the year ended December 31, 2011.

☛ *Required*

The stockholders' equity of Acorn Company as of December 31, 2010, consisted of 20,000 shares of authorized, issued, and outstanding $50 par value common stock, paid-in capital in excess of par of $240,000, and retained earnings of $400,000. Following are selected transactions for 2011:

Problem 13-6A
Prepare journal entries
for treasury stock
transactions and
for cash dividends;
present stockholders'
equity section
(L.O. 2, 3)

May	1	Acquired 3,000 shares of its own common stock at $100 per share.
June	1	Reissued 500 shares at $120.
	30	Reissued 700 shares at $90.
Oct.	1	Declared a cash dividend of $5 per share.
	31	Paid the cash dividend declared on October 1.

Net income for the year was $80,000. No other transactions affecting retained earnings occurred during the year.

a. Prepare general journal entries for these transactions.
b. Prepare the stockholders' equity section of the December 31, 2011, balance sheet.

☛ *Required*

The stockholders' equity section of Sager Company's December 31, 2010, balance sheet follows:

Problem 13-7A
Prepare journal entries
for stock transactions,
cash dividend, small
stock dividend, and
retained earnings
appropriation;
prepare statement of
retained earnings and
stockholders' equity
section of balance
sheet (L.O. 2, 3)

Stockholders' equity:
Paid-in Capital:

Preferred stock—$60 par value, 5%; authorized, 5,000 shares; issued and outstanding, 2,500 shares		$150,000
Common stock—without par or stated value; authorized, 50,000 shares; issued, 25,000 shares of which 500 are held in treasury		225,000
Paid-in capital in excess of par—preferred		3,000
Total paid-in capital		$378,000
Retained earnings:		
Appropriated:		
For plant expansion	$ 15,000	
Unappropriated (restricted as to dividends to the extent of $6,000, the cost of the treasury stock held)	126,000	
Total retained earnings		141,000
Total paid-in capital and retained earnings		$519,000
Less: Treasury stock, common, at cost (500 shares)		(6,000)
Total stockholders' equity		$513,000

Following are selected transactions that occurred in 2011:

Jan. 13 Cash was received for 550 shares of previously unissued common stock at $13.20.

Feb. 4 A plot of land was accepted as payment in full for 500 shares of common stock, and the stock was issued. Closing market price of the common stock on this date was $12 per share.

Mar. 24 All of the treasury stock was reissued at $14.40 per share.

June 23 The regular semiannual dividend on the preferred stock was declared.
30 The preferred dividend was paid.

July 3 A 10% stock dividend was declared on the common stock. Market price on this date was $16.80.
18 The stock dividend shares were issued.

Oct. 4 The company reacquired 105 shares of its common stock at $14.40.

Dec. 18 The regular semiannual dividend on the preferred stock and a $0.24 per share dividend on the common stock were declared.
31 Both dividends were paid.
31 An additional appropriation of retained earnings of $3,000 for plant expansion was authorized.

Required ➲
a. Prepare journal entries to record the 2011 transactions.
b. Prepare a statement of retained earnings for the year 2011, assuming net income for the year was $25,800.
c. Prepare the stockholders' equity section of the December 31, 2011, balance sheet.

Problem 13-8A
Present income statement and statement of retained earnings (L.O. 2, 4, 5)

Selected data of Ace Company for the year ended December 31, 2011, are:

Sales, net	$1,000,000
Interest expense	90,000
Cash dividends on common stock	150,000
Selling and administrative expenses	245,000
Cash dividends on preferred stock	70,000
Rent revenue	400,000
Cost of goods sold	650,000
Flood loss (has never occurred before)	200,000
Interest revenue	90,000
Other revenue	150,000
Depreciation and maintenance on rental equipment	270,000
Stock dividend on common stock	300,000
Operating income on Plastics Division up to point of sale in 2011	50,000
Gain on disposal of Plastics Division	25,000
Litigation loss (has never occurred before)	320,000

Assume the applicable federal income tax rate is 40%. All of the preceding items of expense, revenue, and loss are included in the computation of taxable income. The litigation loss resulted from a court award of damages for patent infringement on a product that the company produced and sold in 2007 and 2008, but was discontinued in 2008. In addition, the company discovered that in 2010 it had erroneously charged to expense the $250,000 cost of a tract of land purchased that year and had made the same error on its tax return for 2010. Retained earnings as of January 1, 2011, were $5,600,000. Assume there were 10,000 shares of common stock and 5,000 shares of preferred stock outstanding for the entire year.

Required ➲ Prepare an income statement and a statement of retained earnings for 2011.

Beyond the Numbers—Critical Thinking

The stockholders' equity section of the Bates Corporation's balance sheet for June 30, 2011, follows

Stockholders' equity:
Paid-in Capital:
Common stock—$20 par value; authorized 200,000 shares;
issued and outstanding 80,000 shares $1,600,000
Paid-in capital in excess of par value 960,000

Total paid-in capital		$2,560,000
Retained earnings		1,520,000
Total stockholders' equity		$4,080,000

On July 1, 2011, the corporation's directors declared a 10% stock dividend distributable on August 2 to stockholders of record on July 16. On November 1, 2011, the directors voted a $2.40 per share annual cash dividend payable on December 2 to stockholders of record on November 16. For four years prior to 2011, the corporation had paid an annual cash dividend of $2.52.

As of July 1, 2011, Bob Jones owned 8,000 shares of Bates Corporation's common stock, which he had purchased four years earlier. The market value of his stock was $48 per share on July 1, 2011, and $43.64 per share on July 16, 2011.

a. What amount of cash dividends will Jones receive in 2011? How does this amount differ from the amount of cash dividends Jones received in the previous four years?

b. Jones has asked you, his CPA, to explain why the price of the stock dropped from $48 to $43.64 on July 16, 2011. Write a memo to Jones explaining your answer.

c. Do you think Jones is better off as a result of the stock dividend and the $2.40 cash dividend than he would have been if he had just received the $2.52 cash dividend? Write a memo to Jones explaining your answer.

The following journal entries are for Keel Corporation:

1.	Retained Earnings	12,000	
	Reserve for Uncollectible Accounts		12,000
	To record the adjusting entry for uncollectible accounts.		
2.	Retained Earnings	48,000	
	Reserve for Depreciation		48,000
	To record depreciation expense.		
3.	Retained Earnings	120,000	
	Appropriation for Plant Expansion		120,000
	To record retained earnings appropriation.		
4.	Retained Earnings	8,000	
	Stock Dividend Distributable—Common		8,000
	To record 10% stock dividend declaration (100 shares to be distributed—$80 par value, $120 market value).		
5.	Stock Dividend Distributable—Common	8,000	
	Common Stock		8,000
	To record distribution of stock dividend.		

6.	Treasury Stock	32,000	
	Cash		32,000
	To record acquisition of 200 shares of $80 par value common stock at $160 per share.		
7.	Cash	17,600	
	Treasury Stock		17,600
	To record sale of 100 treasury shares at $176 per share.		
8.	Cash	6,800	
	Treasury Stock		6,800
	To record sale of 50 treasury shares at $136 per share.		
9.	Common Stock	16,000	
	Dividends Payable		16,000
	To record declaration of cash dividend.		
10.	Dividends Payable	16,000	
	Cash		16,000
	To record payment of cash dividend.		

Prior to this year, the company had no treasury stock transactions. The management of Keel Corporation has asked you, a CPA, to analyze these journal entries and decide whether each is correct. The explanations are all correct. Wherever a journal entry is incorrect, prepare the journal entry that should have been made.

Annual Report Analysis 13-3
Determine the number of shares of common stock issued and the cost of treasury stock. Compute EPS. (L.O. 3, 7)

The following questions are based on the Coca-Cola Company's annual report. To view the report, go to the Coca-Cola web site at **www.cocacola.com**. After you activate the web site, click on "About the Coca-Cola Company". Go to "Investors" and a menu will drop down that has "Reports & Financial Statements" as an option. Click on "Financial Statements" for the most recent year and then "Balance Sheet". Open it to find the total cost of treasury shares. Then go to Selected Financial Data and open it to find the number of common shares outstanding.

a. Based on the information in the balance sheet and the note, determine the number of common shares outstanding and the total cost of treasury stock shares on hand at the end of the year.
b. In writing, discuss what reasons Coca-Cola might have to acquire treasury stock.
c. Find Coca-Cola's basic EPS for the year listed in its Income Statement. If the common stock was trading at a price-earnings ratio of 15.0, what must have been the stock's market price?

Ethics Case—Writing Experience 13-4
Answer questions based on the ethics case

Based on the ethics case on page 516, answer the following questions concerning Ace Chemical Company in writing:

a. Is this transaction fair to the creditors?
b. Why wouldn't the officers merely declare a $4 million cash dividend? Is the proposed treasury stock transaction fair to the other stockholders?
c. If you were one of the officers, would you feel comfortable in going ahead with this proposed treasury stock transaction?

Group Project 13-5
Library project—
Compare features of accounting software packages

In teams of two to three students, go to the library to find articles evaluating accounting software packages. Use a periodicals index such as the *Accounting and Tax Index* or the *Business Periodicals Index* to locate these articles. Compare the cost and features of three accounting software packages. As a team, prepare a memorandum to the manager of a small retail business. Compare and contrast the three accounting software packages so the manager might decide which package to purchase. In the memorandum, cite the sources used in gathering the data and properly reference any direct quotes or paraphrasing. The heading of the memorandum should contain the date, to whom it is written, from whom, and the subject matter.

With a small group of students, go to the library and locate Statement of Financial Accounting Standards No. 4, "Reporting Gains and Losses from Extinguishing of Debt," published by the Financial Accounting Standards Board. (Note: This statement was rescinded by Statement of Accounting Standards No. 145 in 2002.) Write a report to your instructor giving the highlights of the standard. Why were these gains and losses treated as extraordinary items? Why did the Board act on this topic? Why did one member of the Board dissent?

Group Project 13-6
Library Project—
Investigate accounting treatment for gains and losses from extinguishment of debt

With one or two other students, locate the annual reports of three companies and study their statements of stockholders' equity. Determine why the number of common shares outstanding changed (if at all) during the current year. For instance, the number of outstanding shares may have increased due to new issuances, exercise of stock options, conversion of preferred stock, exercise of warrants, stock dividends, and other causes. The number of shares outstanding may have decreased because of repurchases of stock (treasury stock transactions). Write a report to your instructor presenting your findings. Also be prepared to make a short presentation to your class.

Group Project 13-7
Study statements of stockholders' equity

Using the Internet—A View of the Real World

Visit the following website for the General Electric Company:
  http://www.ge.com.
Pursue choices on the screen until you locate the consolidated balance sheet (labeled "Statement of Financial Position"). What title does GE use for stockholders' equity? What are the various components of GE's stockholders' equity? Trace the changes that have occurred in the last two years in retained earnings and treasury stock to the statement of shareowners' equity. Check out the notes to the financial statements for further information. Write a memo to your instructor summarizing your findings.

Internet Project 13-8
Investigate a consolidated balance sheet

Visit the following website for 3M:
  http://www.3m.com
Pursue choices on the screen until you locate the most recent annual report at the Investor Relations Section. Trace the changes that have occurred in the stockholders' equity section for the most recent two years. Identify the causes of the changes. Check out the notes to the financial statements for further information. Write a memo to your instructor summarizing your findings.

Internet Project 13-9
Investigate a consolidated statement of stockholders' equity

Answers To Self-Test

True-False
1. **False.** The paid-in capital of a corporation only includes capital contributed by stockholders or others. Thus, it does not include retained earnings.

2. **False.** The purchase of treasury stock reduces total stockholders' equity.

3. **False.** Dividends are distributions of earnings in the past and are not expenses.

4. **True.** A stock dividend permanently capitalizes a portion of retained earnings by decreasing retained earnings and increasing paid-in capital by an equal amount.

5. **False.** The purpose of a retained earnings appropriation is to disclose that a portion of retained earnings is not available for cash dividends. Thus, such an appropriation does not reduce total stockholders' equity.

6. **False.** Such damage occurs too frequently to be considered nonrecurring.

Multiple-Choice

1. **d.** Appropriation per Loan Agreement is part of retained earnings.

2. **c.** When treasury stock is reacquired, the stock is recorded at cost in a debit-balance stockholders' equity account, Treasury Stock.

3. **a.** The excess of the reissue price over the cost of treasury stock is recorded in the Paid-In Capital—Treasury Stock Transactions account.

4. **a.** Treasury stock is customarily shown as a deduction from total stockholders' equity.

5. **b.** The date of record determines who is to receive the dividends.

6. **c.** The total amount of dividends is computed as follows:

Total Outstanding shares at declaration:	
(12,000-2,000) shares	10,000
Dividend per share	X $2
Total dividend amount	$20,000

7. **b.** Prior period adjustments are shown as adjustments to the opening balance of retained earnings on the statement of retained earnings.

Careers in Accounting

The Role of Accountants in Business Acquisitions

The number and size of corporate mergers and acquisitions has accelerated at an amazing pace over the last decade. The combination of these sometimes mega-giant corporations, involves complex strategic alliance decisions. The potential rewards of mergers and acquisitions can be enormous – increased market share, broadened product lines, stability for the overall company, strengthened financial position, captured key executive or technical talent, and cost savings. In 1999, Exxon and Mobil merged in an $82 billion deal, which was the largest merger in the world to that point. The companies originally estimated that the merger would save the companies $2.8 billion, but by the end of 2007 that number had risen to nearly $7 billion. Exxon Mobil has earned record profits every year since then.

Not all mergers and acquisitions turn out this well. In fact, many mergers and acquisitions weaken companies. For example, the largest merger in U.S. history took place in January 2000, between AOL and Time Warner. The price of the merger was in excess of $180 billion. However, the merger proved to be a failure, and by the end of 2009, AOL and Time Warner were again operating as separate companies.

When considering the acquisition of a company, the first question is "Do we really want to go into business with this company?" Target companies may misrepresent their financial position or conceal suspicious behavior in an attempt to maximize their purchase price. Accountants are used by acquirers to scope out the full details of a target's financials, operations, and human assets. Accountants are intimately familiar with accounting practices and recording procedures and therefore are best trained to find financial statement misrepresentations. Discoveries by accountants have canceled many giant mergers and acquisitions.

The second question to consider is "What is the target worth?" The acquiring company generally requires the target company to make available its financial statements. Accounting professionals are asked to interpret the financial statements and other financial data to determine the value of the target. Accounting professionals also understand how accounting numbers translate into firm value and which aspects of firm value are not captured by accounting numbers.

Business acquisitions are commonplace in every industry. The role of accounting professionals in business valuation is essential to the success of the company and represents one of the fastest growing areas in accounting.

14

Stock Investments

Often a large company attempts to take over a smaller company by acquiring a controlling interest (more than 50% of the outstanding shares) in that target company. Some of these takeover attempts are friendly (not resisted by the target company), and some are unfriendly (resisted by the target company). If the attempt is successful, the two companies become one business entity for accounting purposes, and consolidated financial statements are prepared. The company that takes over another company is the *parent company;* the company acquired is the *subsidiary company.* This chapter discusses accounting for parent and subsidiary companies.

When a corporation purchases the stock of another corporation, the method of accounting for the stock investment depends on the corporation's motivation for making the investment and the relative size of the investment. A corporation's motivation for purchasing the stock of another company may be as: (1) a short-term investment of excess cash; (2) a long-term investment in a substantial percentage of another company's stock to ensure a supply of a required raw material (for example, when large oil companies invest heavily in, or purchase outright, wildcat oil drilling companies); or (3) a long-term investment for expansion (when a company purchases another profitable company rather than starting a new business operation). On the balance sheet, the first type of investment is a current asset, and the last two types are long-term (noncurrent) investments. As explained in the chapter, the purchaser's level of ownership of the investee company determines whether the investment is accounted for by the cost method or the equity method.

Objectives

5. Prepare consolidated financial statements through the use of a consolidated statement work sheet.

6. Describe the uses and limitations of consolidated financial statements.

7. Analyze and use the financial results— dividend yield on common stock and payout ratio on common stock.

Cost and Equity Methods

Investors in common stock can use two methods to account for their investments— the cost method or the equity method. Under both methods, they initially record the investment at cost (price paid at acquisition). Under the **cost method**, the investor company does not adjust the investment account balance subsequently for its share of the investee's reported income, losses, and dividends. Instead, the investor company receives dividends and credits them to a Dividends Revenue account. Under the **equity method**, the investor company adjusts the investment account for its share of the investee's reported income, losses, and dividends.

The Accounting Principles Board (the predecessor of the Financial Accounting Standards Board) has identified the circumstances under which each method must be used. This chapter illustrates each of those circumstances. The general rules for determining the appropriate method of accounting follow:

Types of Common Stock Investment	Method of Accounting Required by Accounting Principles Board in Most Cases
All short-term investments	Cost
Long-term investments of:	
Less than 20%:	
If no significant influence	Cost
If significant influence	Equity
20%-50%	Equity
More than 50%	Cost or equity

Accounting for Short-Term Stock Investments and for Long-Term Stock Investments of Less Than 20%

Objective 1
Report stock investments and distinguish between the cost and equity methods of accounting for stock investments.

Accountants use the **cost method** to account for all short-term stock investments. When a company owns less than 50% of the outstanding stock of another company as a long-term investment, the percentage of ownership determines whether to use the cost or equity method. A purchasing company that owns less than 20% of the outstanding stock of the investee company and that does not exercise significant influence over it, uses the cost method. A purchasing company that owns from 20% to 50% of the outstanding stock of the investee company or owns less than 20%, but still exercises significant influence over it, uses the **equity method**. Thus, firms use the cost method for all short-term stock investments and almost all long-term stock investments of less than 20%. For investments of more than 50%, they use either the cost or equity method because the application of consolidation procedures yields the same result.

Objective 2
Prepare journal entries to account for short-term stock investments and for long-term stock investments of less than 20%.

Cost Method for Short-Term Investments and for Long-Term Investments of Less Than 20%

When a company purchases stock (equity securities) as an investment, accountants must classify the stock according to management's intent. If management bought the security for the principal purpose of selling it in the near term, the security would be a **trading security**. If the stock will be held for a longer term, it is called an **available-for-sale security**. Trading securities are always current assets. Available-for-sale securities may be either current assets or noncurrent assets, depending on how long management intends to hold them. Each classification is accounted for differently. This topic will be discussed later in this chapter.

Securities can be transferred between classifications; however, there are specific rules that must be met for these transfers to be allowed. These rules will be addressed in intermediate accounting. Under the cost method, investors record stock investments at cost, which is usually the cash paid for the stock. They purchase most stocks from other investors (not the issuing company) through brokers who execute trades in an organized market, such as the New York Stock Exchange. Thus, cost usually consists of the price paid for the shares, plus a broker's commission.

For example, assume that Brewer Corporation purchased as a near-term investment 1,000 shares of Cowen Company's $10 par value common stock at $14.22 per share, plus a $180 broker's commission. Brokers quote most stock prices in dollars and cents. Brewer's entry to record its investment is:

Trading Securities [(1,000 shares X $14.22) + $180 commission]	14,400	
Cash		14,400
Purchased 1,000 shares of Cowen common stock as a near-term investment at 14.22 plus commission.		

Accounting for Cash Dividends Received   Investments in stock provide dividends revenue. As a general rule, investors debit cash dividends to Cash and credit Dividends Revenue. The only exception to this general rule is when a dividend declared in one accounting period is payable in the next. This exception allows a company to record the revenue in the proper accounting period. Assume that Cowen declared a $1 per share cash dividend on December 1, 2012, to stockholders of record as of December 20, payable on January 15, 2013. Brewer should make the following entry in 2012:

2012				
Dec.	1	Dividends Receivable	1,000	
		Dividends Revenue		1,000
		To record $1 per share cash dividend on Cowen common stock, payable January 15, 2007.		

When collecting the dividend on January 15, 2013, Brewer debits Cash and credits Dividends Receivable:

2013				
Jan.	15	Cash	1,000	
		Dividends Receivable		1,000
		To record the receipt of a cash dividend on Cowen common stock.		

Stock Dividends and Stock Splits   As discussed in Chapter 13, a company might declare a stock dividend rather than a cash dividend. An investor does not recognize revenue on receipt of the additional shares from a stock dividend. The investor merely records the number of additional shares received and reduces the cost per share for each share held. For example, if Cowen distributed a 10% stock dividend in February 2013, Brewer, which held 1,000 shares at a cost of $14,400 (or $14.40 per share), would receive another 100 shares and would then hold 1,100 shares at a cost per share of $13.09 (computed as $14,400/1,100 shares). Similarly, when a corporation declares a stock split, the investor would note the shares received and the reduction in the cost per share.

FASB Statement No. 115 (codified as ASC 320) governs the subsequent valuation of **marketable equity securities** accounted for under the fair market value method.[1] Marketable refers to the fact that the stocks are readily saleable; equity securities are common and preferred stocks. The *Statement* also addresses the subsequent valuation of debt securities. The subsequent valuation of debt securities will be addressed in intermediate accounting classes.

Real World Example
One share of JPMorgan Chase & Co. common stock sold for $26.50 per share on December 31, 2001. On December 31, 2011, one share of JPMorgan Chase stock sold for $33.01 per share.

Subsequent Valuation of Stock Investments under the Fair Market Value Method

---

[1]*FASB, Statement of Financial Accounting Standards No. 115*, "Accounting for Certain Marketable Securities" (Stamford, Conn., 1993). Copyright © by the Financial Accounting Standards Board, Stamford, Connecticut 06856, U.S.A. Quoted (or excerpted) with permission. Copies of the complete document are available from the FASB.

Illustration 14.1   Stock Portfolio of Hanson Company

Company	No. of Shares	Cost per Share	Market Price per Share 12/31/12	Total Cost	Total Market 12/31/12	Increase/(Decrease) in Market Value
A	200	$35	$40	$ 7,000	$ 8,000	$ 1,000
B	400	10	15	4,000	6,000	2,000
C	100	90	50	9,000	5,000	(4,000)
				$20,000	$19,000	$ (1,000)

The FASB *Statement* requires that at year-end, companies adjust the carrying value of each of their two portfolios (trading securities and available-for-sale securities) to their fair market value. Fair market value is considered to be the market price of the securities or what a buyer or seller would pay to exchange the securities. An unrealized holding gain or loss will usually result in each portfolio.

Trading Securities   To illustrate the application of the fair market value to trading securities, assume that Hanson Company has the securities shown in Illustration 14.1 in its trading securities portfolio. Applying the fair market value method reveals that the total fair market value of the trading securities portfolio is $1,000 less than its cost. The journal entry required at the end of 2012 is:

2012 Dec.	31	Unrealized Loss on Trading Securities	1,000	
		Trading Securities		1,000
		To record unrealized loss from market decline of trading securities.		

Note that the debit is to the Unrealized Loss on Trading Securities account. This loss is *unrealized* because the securities have not been sold. However, **the loss is reported in the income statement as a deduction in arriving at net income**. The credit in the preceding entry is to the Trading Securities account so as to adjust its balance to its fair market value. (An unrealized holding gain would be an addition to net income.)

If Hanson sold investment C on January 1, 2013, the company would receive $5,000 (assuming no change in market values from the previous day). The loss on the sale results from market changes in 2012 rather than in 2013; the fair market value procedure placed that loss in the proper year. The entry for the sale is:

2013 Jan.	1	Cash	5,000	
		Trading Securities—Company C Stock		5,000
		To record sale of Company C Stock.		

No adjustment needs to be made to the unrealized loss account previously debited because the unrealized loss recorded in 2012 has flowed through the income statement and been closed to retained earnings through the closing process.

Available-for-Sale Securities   Assume a marketable equity security that management does not intend to sell in the near term has a cost of $32,000 and a current market value on December 31, 2012, of $31,000. The treatment of the loss depends on whether it results from a temporary decline in market value of the stock or a permanent decline in the value. Assume first that the loss is related to a "temporary" decline in the market value of the stock. The required entry is:

Note to the Student
Check yesterday's *Wall Street Journal* to determine the current market price of one share of JPMorgan Chase stock. Calculate the gain or loss on 100 shares of JPMorgan Chase stock, if the shares were purchased on December 31, 2011, at $33.01 per share and sold at yesterday's market price. When the stock is sold, there is a realized gain or loss.

Reinforcing Problems
E14-1 Prepare entries for trading securities.
E14-2 Prepare entries for trading securities.

2012				
Dec.	31	Unrealized Loss on Available-for-Sale Securities	1,000	
		Available-for-Sale Securities		1,000
		To record unrealized loss from market decline of		
		available-for-sale securities.		

These accounts would appear on the balance sheet as follows:

HANSON COMPANY
Partial Balance Sheet
December 31, 2012

<u>Investments (or Current Assets)*:</u>	
Available-for-sale securities	<u>$31,000</u>
<u>Stockholders' equity:</u>	
Capital stock	$xxx,xxx
Additional paid-in capital	x,xxx
Total paid-in capital	$xxx,xxx
Retained earnings	xx,xxx
Accumulated Other Comprehensive Income:	
Unrealized loss on available-for-sale securities	(1,000)
Total stockholders' equity	$xxx,xxx

*Depending on the length of time management intends to
hold the securities.

Note that the unrealized loss for available-for-sale securities appears in the balance
sheet as a separate negative component of accumulated other comprehensive income in
stockholders' equity rather than in the income statement (as it does for trading securities).
An unrealized gain would be shown as a separate positive component of accumulated
other comprehensive income. An unrealized loss or gain on available-for-sale securities is not included in the determination of net income because it is **not** expected to be
realized in the near future. These securities will probably not be sold soon.

The sale of an available-for-sale security results in a realized gain or loss and is
reported on the income statement for the period. Any unrealized gain or loss on the balance sheet must be recognized at that time. Assume the stock discussed above is sold on
January 1, 2013, for $31,000 (assuming no change in market value from the previous day)
after the company had held the stock for three years. The entries to record this sale are:

2013				
Jan.	1	Realized Loss on Available-for-Sale Securities	1,000	
		Unrealized Loss on Available-for-Sale Securities		1,000
		Cash	31,000	
		Available-for-Sale Securities		31,000

The account debited in the first entry shows that the unrealized loss has been realized
with the sale of the security; the amount is reported in the income statement. The second
entry writes off the security and records the cash received and is similar to the entry for
the sale of trading securities.

A loss on an individual available-for-sale security that is considered to be "permanent" is recorded as a realized loss and deducted in determining net income. The entry
to record a permanent loss of $1,400 reads:

Realized Loss on Available-for-Sale Securities	1,400	
Available-for-Sale Securities		1,400
To record loss in value of available-for-sale securities.		

Reinforcing Problem
E14-3 Apply fair market value
method to marketable equity
securities

No part of the $1,400 loss is subject to reversal if the market price of the stock recov-
ers. The stock's reduced value is now its "cost." When this stock is later sold, the sale

Note to the Student
If a loss on an available-for-sale security is considered to be permanent, the loss is *realized* even though the security has not been sold. As a realized loss, it appears in the income statement.

will be treated in the same manner as trading securities. The loss or gain has already been recognized on the income statement. Therefore, the entry would simply record the cash received and write off the security sold for its fair market value. If the market value of the security has fluctuated since the last time the account had been adjusted (end of the year), then an additional gain or loss may have to be recorded to account for this fluctuation.

An Accounting Perspective

Business Insight On Pearl Harbor Day, December 7, 1941, the stock market fell from 116.60 to 112.52. The average fell to 92.92 by April 1942. By the end of WW II, the average had risen to 119.40. The average has risen tremendously since that time. For instance, in October 2007 the Dow-Jones Industrial Average broke through the 14,000 barrier. The Dow was back to the 12,000 barrier as of late 2011. Over the last 60 years, investors have averaged about a 10% to 12% return annually by investing in the stock market. No one knows what will happen in the future, but many people invest in stocks to try to stay ahead of inflation. You can visit the DJIA site on the Internet at **http://www.dowjones.com** to learn more about the stock market.

The Equity Method for Long-Term Investments of between 20% and 50%

Objective 3
Prepare journal entries to account for long-term stock investments of 20% to 50%.

When a company (the **investor**) purchases between 20% and 50% of the outstanding stock of another company (the **investee**) as a long-term investment, the purchasing company is said to have significant influence over the investee company. In certain cases, a company may have significant influence even when its investment is less than 20%. In either situation, the investor must account for the investment under the equity method.

When using the **equity method** in accounting for stock investments, the investor company must recognize its share of the investee company's income, regardless of whether or not it receives dividends. The logic behind this treatment is that the investor company may exercise influence over the declaration of dividends and thereby manipulate its own income by influencing the investee's decision to declare (or not declare) dividends.

Thus, when the investee reports income or losses, the investor company must recognize its share of the investee's income or losses. For example, assume that Tone Company (the investor) owns 30% of Dutch Company (the investee) and Dutch reports $50,000 net income in the current year. Under the equity method, Tone makes the following entry as of the end of 2012:

Investment in Dutch Company	15,000	
Income from Dutch Company ($50,000 x 0.30)		15,000
To recognize 30% of Dutch Company's Net Income.		

The $15,000 income from Dutch would be reported on Tone's 2012 income statement. The investment account is also increased by $15,000.

If the investee incurs a loss, the investor company debits a loss account and credits the investment account for the investor's share of the loss. For example, assume Dutch incurs a loss of $10,000 in 2013. Since it still owns 30% of Dutch, Tone records its share of the loss as follows:

Reinforcing Problem
E14-4 Prepare equity method entries for an investment.

Loss from Dutch Company ($10,000 x 0.30)	3,000	
Investment in Dutch Company		3,000
To recognize 30% of Dutch Company's loss.		

Tone would report the $3,000 loss on its 2013 income statement. The $3,000 credit reduces Tone's equity in the investee. Furthermore, because dividends are a distribution of income to the owners of the corporation, if Dutch declares and pays $20,000 in dividends, this entry would also be required for Tone:

Cash	6,000	
Investment in Dutch Company ($20,000 x 0.30)		6,000
To record receipt of 30% of dividends paid by Dutch Company.		

Under the equity method just illustrated, the Investment in the Dutch Company account always reflects Tone's 30% interest in the net assets of Dutch.

Reporting for Stock Investments of More Than 50%

In recent years, many companies have expanded by purchasing a major portion, or all, of another company's outstanding voting stock. The purpose of such acquisitions ranges from ensuring a source of raw materials (such as oil), to desiring to enter into a new industry, or seeking income on the investment. Both corporations remain separate legal entities, regardless of the investment purpose. In this section, you learn how to account for business combinations.

As stated in the introduction to this chapter, a corporation that owns more than 50% of the outstanding voting common stock of another corporation is the **parent company**. The corporation acquired and controlled by the parent company is the **subsidiary company**.

A parent company and its subsidiaries maintain their own accounting records and prepare their own financial statements. However, since a central management controls the parent and its subsidiaries and they are related to each other, the parent company usually must prepare one set of financial statements. These statements, called **consolidated statements**, consolidate the parent's financial statement amounts with its subsidiaries' and show the parent and its subsidiaries as a single enterprise.

According to *FASB Statement No. 94* (codified in ASC 810), consolidated statements must be prepared (1) when one company owns more than 50% of the outstanding voting common stock of another company, and (2) unless control is likely to be temporary or if it does not rest with the majority owner (e.g., the company is in legal reorganization or bankruptcy).[2] Thus, almost all subsidiaries must be included in the consolidated financial statements under *FASB Statement No. 94*. Previously, the consolidated statements did not include subsidiaries in markedly dissimilar businesses than those of the parents.

Parent and Subsidiary Corporations

Objective 4
Describe the nature of parent and subsidiary corporations.

Real World Example
The Walt Disney Company is a parent company; its subsidiaries include the Disney/ABC Television Group, Marvel Entertainment, Walt Disney Parks and Resorts, and The Walt Disney Studio.

BUSINESS INSIGHT The 2011 annual report of The Walt Disney Company includes the following information about presentation of its subsidiaries:
    The consolidated financial statements of the Company include the accounts of The Walt Disney Company and its majority-owned and controlled subsidiaries. Intercompany accounts and transactions have been eliminated in consolidation.

An Accounting Perspective

---

[2] FASB, *Statement of Financial Accounting Standards No. 94*, "Consolidation of All Majority-Owned Subsidiaries" (Stamford, Conn., 1987), p. 5. Copyright © by the Financial Accounting Standards Board, High Ridge Park, Stamford, Connecticut 06905, U.S.A.

Eliminations

Financial transactions involving a parent and one of its subsidiaries or between two of its subsidiaries are **intercompany transactions**. In preparing consolidated financial statements, parent companies eliminate the effects of intercompany transactions by making **elimination entries**. Elimination entries allow the presentation of all account balances as if the parent and its subsidiaries were a single economic enterprise. *Elimination entries appear only on a consolidated statement work sheet, not in the accounting records of the parent or subsidiaries.* After elimination entries are prepared, the parent totals the amounts remaining for each account of the work sheet and prepares the consolidated financial statements.

To illustrate the need for elimination entries, assume Y Company formed the Z Company, receiving all of Z Company's $100,000 par value common stock for $100,000 cash. If the stock of an existing company had been acquired, it would have been purchased from that company's stockholders. The parent records the following entry on its books:

Investment in Z Company	100,000	
Cash		100,000
To record an investment in Z Company. Purchased 100% of Z Company stock.		

Z Company, the subsidiary, records the following entry on its books:

Cash	100,000	
Common Stock		100,000
To record issuance of all of the common stock to Y Company.		

An elimination entry can offset the parent company's subsidiary investment account against the stockholders' equity accounts of the subsidiary. On the consolidated statements work sheet, the required elimination is:

Common Stock (Z Company)	100,000	
Investment in Z Company		100,000

This elimination is required because the parent company's investment in the stock of the subsidiary actually represents an equity interest in the net assets of the subsidiary. Unless the investment is eliminated, the same resources appear twice on the consolidated balance sheet—first as the investment account of the parent and second as the assets of the subsidiary. By eliminating Z Company's common stock, the parent avoids double counting stockholders' equity. Viewing the two companies as if they were one, the Z Company common stock is really not outstanding; it is held within the consolidated group.

Consolidated financial statements present financial data as though the companies were a single entity. Since no entity can owe an amount to itself or be due an amount from itself, Z Company must eliminate intercompany receivables and payables (amounts owed to and due from companies within the consolidated group) during the preparation of consolidated financial statements. For example, assume the parent company purchased $5,000 of bonds issued by its subsidiary company. Because no debt is owed to or due from any entity outside the consolidated enterprise, Y Company would eliminate those balances by an entry like the following that offsets the Investment in Bonds against the Bonds Payable:

Bonds Payable (subsidiary company)	5,000	
Investment in Bonds (parent company)		5,000
To eliminate intercompany bonds and bond investment.		

Illustration 14.2   Consolidated Balance Sheet Work Sheet (stock acquired at book value)

P COMPANY AND SUBSIDIARY S COMPANY
Work Sheet for Consolidated Balance Sheet
January 1, 2012 (date of acquisition)

Assets	P Company	S Company	Eliminations		Consolidated Amounts
			Debit	Credit	
Cash	26,000	12,000			38,000
Notes receivable	5,000			(2) 5,000	
Accounts receivable, net	24,000	15,000			39,000
Merchandise inventory	35,000	30,000			65,000
Investment in S Company	106,000			(1) 106,000	
Equipment, net	41,000	15,000			56,000
Building, net	65,000	35,000			100,000
Land	20,000	10,000			30,000
	322,000	117,000			328,000
Liabilities and Stockholders' Equity					
Accounts payable	18,000	6,000			24,000
Notes payable		5,000	(2) 5,000		
Common stock	250,000	100,000	(1) 100,000		250,000
Paid-in capital excess of par valueÑcommon		4,000	(1) 4,000		-0-
Retained earnings	54,000	2,000	(1) 2,000		54,000
	322,000	117,000	111,000	111,000	328,000

When preparing consolidated statements, the parent would similarly eliminate other intercompany balances.

Consolidated Balance Sheet at Time of Acquisition

A parent company may acquire a subsidiary at its book value or at a cost above or below book value. Also, the parent may acquire 100% of the outstanding voting common stock of the subsidiary or some lesser percentage exceeding 50%.

To consolidate its assets and liabilities with those of its subsidiaries, a parent company prepares a consolidated statement work sheet similar to the one in Illustration 14.2. A **consolidated statement work sheet** is an informal record on which elimination entries are made for the purpose of showing account balances as if the parent and its subsidiaries were a single economic enterprise. The first two columns of the work sheet show assets, liabilities, and stockholders' equity of the parent and subsidiary as they appear on each corporation's balance sheet. The pair of columns labeled Eliminations allows intercompany items to be offset and consequently eliminated from the consolidated statement. The final column shows the amounts that will appear on the consolidated balance sheet.

The work sheet in Illustration 14.2 consolidates the accounts of P Company and its subsidiary, S Company, on January 1, 2012. P Company acquired S Company on January 1, 2012, by purchasing all of its outstanding voting common stock for $106,000 cash, which was the book value of the stock. Book value is equal to stockholders' equity, or net assets (assets minus liabilities). Thus, common stock ($100,000), paid-in capital in excess of par value—common ($4,000), and retained

Acquisition of Subsidiary at Book Value

Objective 5
Prepare consolidated financial statements through the use of a consolidated statement work sheet.

earnings ($2,000) equal $106,000. When P Company acquired the S Company stock, P Company made the following entry in its books:

Investment in S Company	106,000	
Cash		106,000
To record investment in S Company.		

The Investment in S Company account appears as an asset on P Company's balance sheet. By buying the subsidiary's stock, the parent acquired a 100% equity, or ownership, interest in the subsidiary's net assets. Thus, if both the investment account and the subsidiary's assets appear on the consolidated balance sheet, the same resources would be counted twice. The Common Stock and Retained Earnings accounts of the subsidiary also represent an equity interest in the subsidiary's assets. Therefore, P's investment in S Company must be offset against S Company's stockholders' equity accounts so that the subsidiary's assets and the ownership interest in these assets appear only once on the consolidated balance sheet. P Company accomplishes this elimination by entry *(1)* under Eliminations on the work sheet. The entry debits S Company's Common Stock for $100,000, Paid-In Capital in Excess of Par Value—Common for $4,000, and Retained Earnings for $2,000 and credits Investment in S Company for $106,000. In journal entry form, the elimination entry *made only on the consolidated work sheet* is:

Common Stock	100,000	
Paid-In Capital in Excess of Par Value—Common	4,000	
Retained Earnings	2,000	
Investment in S Company		106,000
To eliminate investment account and subsidiary stockholder's equity.		

Entry *(2)* eliminates the effect of an intercompany debt. On the date it acquired S Company, P Company loaned S Company $5,000. The loan is a $5,000 note receivable on P's books and a $5,000 note payable on S's books. If the elimination entry is not made on the work sheet, the consolidated balance sheet would show $5,000 owed to the consolidated enterprise by itself. From the viewpoint of the consolidated equity, neither an asset nor a liability exists. Therefore, entry *2* on the work sheet eliminates both the asset and liability. The entry debits Notes Payable and credits Notes Receivable for $5,000. In general journal form, entry *(2)* is:

Notes Payable	5,000	
Notes Receivable		5,000
To eliminate intercompany payable and receivable.		

Reinforcing Problem
E14-5 Record investment at book value and elimination entry as of acquisition date.

Note that P Company makes elimination entries only on the consolidated statement work sheet; no elimination entries appear in the accounting records of either P Company or S Company. P Company uses the final work sheet column to prepare the consolidated balance sheet

An Accounting Perspective

USES OF TECHNOLOGY Computer applications have greatly simplified the preparation of consolidated work sheets. Spreadsheet programs in particular expedite the process of constructing consolidated financial statements.

In the previous example, P Company acquired 100% of S Company at a cost equal to book value. In some cases, firms acquire subsidiaries at a cost greater than or less than book value. For example, assume P Company purchased 100% of S Company's outstanding voting common stock for $125,000 (instead of $106,000). The book value of this stock is $106,000. Cost exceeds book value by $19,000. P Company's management may have paid more than book value because (1) the subsidiary's earnings prospects justify paying a price greater than book value or (2) the total fair market value of the subsidiary's assets exceeds their total book value.

Where cost exceeds book value because of expected above-average earnings, the investor labels the excess *goodwill* on the consolidated balance sheet. **Goodwill** is an intangible value attached to a business primarily due to above-average earnings prospects (as discussed in Chapter 11). On the other hand, if the excess is attributable to the belief that assets of the subsidiary are undervalued, then the investor increases the asset values on the consolidated balance sheet to the extent of the excess. In Illustration 14.3, $4,000 is due to the undervaluation of land owned by the company, and the remaining $15,000 of the excess of cost over book value is due to expected above-average earnings. As a result, P Company adds $4,000 of the $19,000 excess to Land, and identifies the other $15,000 as Goodwill on the work sheet (Illustration 14.3) and on the balance sheet (Illustration 14.4).

P Company establishes Goodwill as part of the first elimination entry. Elimination entry *(1)* in Illustration 14.3 involves debits to the subsidiary's Common Stock for $100,000, Paid-In Capital in Excess of Par Value—Common for $4,000, Retained Earnings for $2,000, Land for $4,000, and Goodwill for $15,000, and a credit to Investment in S Company for $125,000. In journal form, entry *(1)* is:

Common Stock	100,000	
Paid-In Capital in Excess of Par Value—Common	4,000	
Retained Earnings	2,000	
Land	4,000	
Goodwill	15,000	
Investment in S Company		125,000
To eliminate investment and subsidiary stockholder's equity and to establish increased value of land and goodwill.		

Entry *(2)* is the same as elimination entry *(2)* in Illustration 14.2. Entry *(2)* eliminates the intercompany loan by debiting Notes Payable and crediting Notes Receivable for $5,000.

After these elimination entries are made, the company consolidates and extends the remaining amounts to the Consolidated Amounts column. It uses the amounts in this column to prepare the consolidated balance sheet in Illustration 14.4. Notice that the firm carries the $15,000 debit to Goodwill to the Consolidated Amounts column and lists it as an asset in the consolidated balance sheet.

As noted earlier, a company may purchase all or part of another company at more than book value and create goodwill on the consolidated balance sheet. *FASB Statement No. 142* (2006) (codified as ASC 350) requires goodwill to be recorded at acquisition cost and to remain at this amount until there is evidence of impairment. We leave a discussion of this topic to a more advanced text.

Under some circumstances, a parent company may pay less than book value of the subsidiary's net assets. In such cases, it is highly unlikely that a bargain purchase has been made. The most logical explanation is that some of the subsidiary's assets are overvalued. Firms use the excess of book value over cost to reduce proportionately the value of the noncurrent assets acquired (except long-term investments in marketable securities). If noncurrent assets are reduced to zero, the remaining dollar amount is a deferred credit labeled, "Excess of Fair Value Over Cost of Assets Acquired".

> **Acquisition of Subsidiary at a Cost above or below Book Value**

> **Note to the Student**
> Goodwill is the excess over fair market value of the net assets of the subsidiary. Net assets are total assets less total liabilities, or total stockholders' equity. Thus, a company that pays more than the fair market value of the net assets creates an intangible asset called goodwill on its books but not on the subsidiary's books.

Illustration 14.3   Consolidated Balance Sheet Work Sheet (stock acquired at more than book value)

P COMPANY AND SUBSIDIARY S COMPANY
Work Sheet for Consolidated Balance Sheet
January 1, 2012 (date of acquisition)

Assets	P Company	S Company	Eliminations Debit	Eliminations Credit	Consolidated Amounts
Cash	7,000	12,000			19,000
Notes receivable	5,000			(2) 5,000	
Accounts receivable, net	24,000	15,000			39,000
Merchandise inventory	35,000	30,000			65,000
Investment in S Company	125,000			(1) 125,000	
Equipment, net	41,000	15,000			56,000
Building, net	65,000	35,000			100,000
Land	20,000	10,000	(1) 4,000		34,000
Goodwill			(1) 15,000		15,000
	322,000	117,000			328,000
Liabilities and Stockholders' Equity					
Accounts payable	18,000	6,000			24,000
Notes payable		5,000	(2) 5,000		
Common stock	250,000	100,000	(1) 100,000		250,000
Paid-in capital excess of par value—common		4,000	(1) 4,000		-0-
Retained earnings	54,000	2,000	(1) 2,000		54,000
	322,000	117,000	130,000	130,000	328,000

Acquisition of Less Than 100% of a Subsidiary

Sometimes a parent company acquires less than 100% of the outstanding voting common stock of a subsidiary. For example, assume P Company acquired 80% of S Company's outstanding voting common stock. P Company is the majority stockholder, but another group of stockholders owns the remaining 20% of the stock. Stockholders who own less than 50% of a subsidiary's outstanding voting common stock are *noncontrolling interest stockholders,* and their claim or interest in the subsidiary is the **noncontrolling interest.** These stockholders have an interest in the subsidiary's net assets and share the subsidiary's income or loss with the parent company.

Look at Illustration 14.5, which shows the elimination entries required when P Company purchases 80% of S Company's stock for $90,000. The book value of the stock acquired by P Company is $84,800 (80% of $106,000). Assuming no assets are undervalued, P Company attributes the excess of cost ($90,000) over book value ($84,800) of $5,200 to S Company's above-average earnings prospects (goodwill).

Elimination entry *(1)* eliminates S Company's stockholders' equity by debiting Common Stock for $100,000, Paid-In Capital in Excess of Par Value—Common for $4,000, and Retained Earnings for $2,000. To establish the noncontrolling interest, it credits a Noncontrolling Interest account for $21,200 (20% of $106,000). P Company eliminates the investment account by crediting Investment in S Company for $90,000. The $5,200 debited to Goodwill makes the debits equal the credits. In journal form, the elimination entry *(1)* is:

Illustration 14.4   Consolidated Balance Sheet

P COMPANY AND SUBSIDIARY S COMPANY
Consolidated Balance Sheet
January 1, 2012

Assets

Current assets:
Cash	$ 19,000	
Accounts receivable, net	39,000	
Merchandise inventory	65,000	
Total current assets		$123,000

Property, plant, and equipment:
Equipment, net	$ 56,000	
Building, net	100,000	
Land	34,000	
Total property, plant, and equipment		190,000
Goodwill		15,000
Total assets		$328,000

Liabilities and Stockholders' Equity

Current liabilities:
Account payable		$24,000

Stockholders' equity:
Common stock	$250,000	
Retained earnings	54,000	
Total stockholders' equity		304,000
Total liabilities and stockholders equity		$328,000

Common Stock	100,000	
Paid-In Capital in Excess of Par Value—Common	4,000	
Retained Earnings	2,000	
Goodwill	5,200	
Investment in S Company		90,000
Noncontrolling Interest		21,200
To eliminate investment and subsidiary stockholder's equity and to establish noncontrolling interest and goodwill.		

Reinforcing Problems
E14-6 Determine amount of goodwill.
E14-7 Record investment at more than book value and elimination entry as of acquisition date.
E14-8 Compute difference between cost and book value of common stock investments.
E14-9 Compute book value, difference between cost and book value, and noncontrolling interest of an investment.

Elimination entry *2* is the same as shown in Illustration 14.2. The entry eliminates intercompany debt by debiting Notes Payable and crediting Notes Receivable for $5,000.

On the consolidated balance sheet (Illustration 14.6), noncontrolling interest appears in the stockholders' equity section, but separate from the parent's equity.

Accounting for Income, Losses, and Dividends of a Subsidiary

When a subsidiary is operating profitably, its net assets and retained earnings increase. The subsidiary pays dividends to both the parent company and noncontrolling stockholders. The subsidiary records all transactions in its accounting records in a normal manner.

As noted earlier, two different methods used by an investor to account for investments in common stock are the cost and equity methods. A parent company may use either the cost or equity method of accounting for its investment in a consolidated subsidiary. This choice is allowed because the investment account is eliminated during the consolidation process; therefore, the results are identical after consolidation.

Illustration 14.5   Consolidated Balance Sheet Work Sheet (80% of stock acquired at more than book value)

P COMPANY AND SUBSIDIARY S COMPANY
Work Sheet for Consolidated Balance Sheet
January 1, 2012 (date of acquisition)

| Assets | P Company | S Company | Eliminations | | Consolidated Amounts |
			Debit	Credit	
Cash	42,000	12,000			54,000
Notes receivable	5,000			(2) 5,000	
Accounts receivable, net	24,000	15,000			39,000
Merchandise inventory	35,000	30,000			65,000
Investment in S Company	90,000			(1) 90,000	
Equipment, net	41,000	15,000			56,000
Building, net	65,000	35,000			100,000
Land	20,000	10,000			30,000
Goodwill			(1) 5,200		5,200
	322,000	117,000			349,200
Liabilities and Stockholders' Equity					
Accounts payable	18,000	6,000			24,000
Notes payable		5,000	(2) 5,000		
Common stock	250,000	100,000	(1) 100,000		250,000
Paid-in capital excess of par value—common		4,000	(1) 4,000		-0-
Retained earnings	54,000	2,000	(1) 2,000		54,000
Noncontrolling interest				(1) 21,200	21,200
	322,000	117,000	116,200	116,200	349,200

To illustrate the consolidation process at a date after acquisition, we assume the parent company uses the equity method.

Consolidated Financial Statements at a Date after Acquisition

Under the equity method, the investment account on the parent company's books increases and decreases as the parent records its share of the income, losses, and dividends reported by the subsidiary. Thus, the balance in the investment account differs after acquisition from its balance on the date of acquisition. Consequently, the amounts eliminated on the consolidated statements work sheet differ from year to year. As an illustration, assume the following facts:

1. P Company acquired 100% of the outstanding voting common stock of S Company on January 1, 2012. P Company paid $121,000 for stockholders' equity totaling $106,000. The excess of cost over book value is attributable to (a) an undervaluation of land amounting to $4,000 and (b) the remainder to S Company's above-average earnings prospects.
2. During 2012, S Company earned $20,000 from operations.
3. On December 31, 2012, S Company paid a cash dividend of $8,000.
4. S Company owes P Company $5,000 on a note at December 31.
5. Including its share (100%) of S Company's income, P Company earned $31,000 during 2012.
6. P Company paid a cash dividend of $10,000 during December 2012.
7. P Company uses the equity method of accounting for its investment in S Company.

Illustration 14.6   Consolidated Balance Sheet

P COMPANY AND SUBSIDIARY S COMPANY
Consolidated Balance Sheet
January 1, 2012

Assets

Current assets:		
Cash	$ 54,000	
Accounts receivable, net	39,000	
Merchandise inventory	65,000	
Total current assets		$158,000
Property, plant, and equipment:		
Equipment, net	$ 56,000	
Building, net	100,000	
Land	30,000	
Total property, plant, and equipment		186,000
Goodwill		5,200
Total assets		$349,200

Liabilities and Stockholders' Equity

Current liabilities:		
Account payable		$24,000
Stockholders' equity:		
Common stock	$250,000	
Retained earnings	54,000	
Total P Company stockholders' equity		304,000
Noncontrolling interest		21,200
Total liabilities and stockholders equity		$349,200

The financial statements for the two companies as of December 31, 2012, are in the first two columns of Illustration 14.7.

The work sheet shown in Illustration 14.7 allows us to prepare a consolidated income statement, statement of retained earnings, and balance sheet. Notice that in Illustration 14.7, P Company has a balance of $20,000 in its Income of S Company account and a balance of $133,000 in its Investment in S Company account. These balances are the result of the following journal entries made by P Company in 2012:

2012					
Jan.	1	Investment in S Company		121,000	
		Cash			121,000
		To record 100% investment in subsidiary.			
Dec.	31	Investment in S Company		20,000	
		Income of S Company			20,000
		To record income of subsidiary.			
	31	Cash		8,000	
		Investment in S Company			8,000
		To record dividends received from subsidiary.			

The explanations for the elimination entries on the work sheet in Illustration 14.7 are as follows:

Entry 1: During the year, S Company earned $20,000. P Company increased its investment account balance by $20,000. Entry 1 on the work sheet eliminates the subsidiary's income from the Investment in S Company account and the Income of S Company account ($20,000). This entry reverses the entry made on the books of P Company to recognize the parent's share of the subsidiary's income (the first December 31 journal entry).

Illustration 14.7   Consolidated Work Sheet One Year after Acquisition

P COMPANY AND SUBSIDIARY S COMPANY
Work Sheet for Consolidated Balance Sheet
December 31, 2012

Income Statement	P Company	S Company	Eliminations Debit	Eliminations Credit	Consolidated Amounts
Revenue from sales	397,000	303,000			700,000
Income of S Company	20,000		(1) 20,000		
Cost of goods sold	(250,000)	(180,000)			(430,000)
Expenses (excluding depreciation and taxes)	(100,000)	(80,000)			(180,000)
Depreciation expense	(7,400)	(5,000)			(12,400)
Federal income tax expense	(28,600)	(18,000)			(46,600)
Net income, carried forward	31,000	20,000			31,000*
Statement of Retained Earnings					
Retained earnings—January 1:					
P Company	54,000				54,000
S Company		6,000	(3) 6,000		
Net income brought forward	31,000	20,000			31,000*
	85,000	26,000			85,000*
Dividends:					
P Company	(10,000)				(10,000)
S Company		(8,000)		(2) 8,000	
Retained earnings—Dec. 31 carried forward	75,000	18,000			75,000*
Balance Sheet Assets					
Cash	38,000	16,000			54,000
Notes receivable	5,000			(4) 5,000	
Accounts receivable, net	25,000	18,000			43,000
Merchandise inventory	40,000	36,000			76,000
Investment in S Company	133,000		(2) 8,000	(3) 121,000	
				(1) 20,000	
Equipment, net	36,900	12,000			48,900
Building, net	61,700	33,000			94,700
Land	20,000	10,000	(3) 4,000		34,000
Goodwill			(3) 11,000		11,000
	359,600	125,000			361,600*
Liabilities and Stockholders' Equity					
Accounts payable	19,600	2,000			21,600
Notes payable	15,000	5,000	(4) 5,000		15,000
Common stock	250,000	100,000	(3) 100,000		250,000
Retained earnings	75,000	18,000			75,000*
	359,600	125,000	154,000	154,000	361,600*

* Totals are determined vertically, not horizontally

Entry 2: When S Company paid its cash dividend, P Company debited Cash and credited the investment account for $8,000 (the second December 31 journal entry). *Entry 2* restores the investment account to its balance before the dividends from S Company were deducted. That is, P Company debits its investment account and credits S Company's dividends account for $8,000. On a consolidated basis, a company cannot pay a dividend to itself.

Entry 3: *Entry 3* eliminates the original investment account balance ($121,000) and the subsidiary's stockholders' equity accounts as of the date of acquisition (retained earnings of $6,000 and common stock of $100,000). The entry also establishes goodwill of $11,000 and increases land by $4,000 to account for the excess of acquisition cost over book value.

Entry 4: *Entry 4* eliminates the intercompany debt of $5,000.

After the first three entries have been made, the investment account contains a zero balance from the viewpoint of the consolidated entity.

After making the eliminations, P Company combines the corresponding amounts and places them in the Consolidated Amounts column. Notice that certain totals in the first two columns do not add across to the total in the Consolidated Amounts column. For instance, consolidated net income is $31,000, not $31,000 plus $20,000. The firm carries the net income row in the Income Statement section forward to the net income row in the Statement of Retained Earnings section. Likewise, it carries the ending retained earnings row in the Statement of Retained Earnings section forward to the retained earnings row in the Balance Sheet section. P Company uses the final work sheet column to prepare the consolidated income statement (Illustration 14.8), the consolidated statement of retained earnings (Illustration 14.9), and the consolidated balance sheet (Illustration 14.10).

Reinforcing Problem
E14-10 Compute investment account balance at year-end and noncontrolling interest at beginning and end of year.

Uses and Limitations of Consolidated Statements

Consolidated financial statements are of primary importance to stockholders, managers, and directors of the parent company. The parent company benefits from the income and other financial strengths of the subsidiary. Likewise, the parent company suffers from a subsidiary's losses and other financial weaknesses.

Consolidated financial statements are of limited use to the creditors and noncontrolling interest stockholders of the subsidiary. The subsidiary's creditors have a claim against the subsidiary alone; they cannot look to the parent company for payment. Minority stockholders in the subsidiary do not benefit or suffer from the parent company's operations. Noncontrolling interest stockholders benefit from the subsidiary's income and financial strengths; they suffer from the subsidiary's losses and financial weaknesses. Thus, the subsidiary's creditors and noncontrolling interest stockholders are more interested in the subsidiary's individual financial statements than in the consolidated statements. Because of these factors, annual reports always include the financial statements of the consolidated entity, and sometimes include the financial statements of certain subsidiary companies alone, but never include the parent company's financial statements alone.

Objective 6
Describe the uses and limitations of consolidated financial statements.

Real World Example
Microsoft Corporation reported consolidated net income of $23.15 billion for the 2011 fiscal year.

Analyzing and Using the Financial Results— Dividend Yield on Common Stock and Payout Ratios

Investors often search for stocks that fulfill their needs. To locate this stock, potential stockholders may use the dividend yield on common stock ratio or the payout ratio on common stock. To demonstrate these ratios, consider the 2010 annual report of The Coca-Cola Company.

Objective 7
Analyze and use the financial results—dividend yield on common stock and payout ratio on common stock.

Illustration 14.8   Consolidated Income Statement

P COMPANY AND SUBSIDIARY S COMPANY
Consolidated Income Statement
For the Year Ended December 31, 2012

Revenue from sales		$700,000
Cost of goods sold		430,000
Gross margin		$270,000
Expenses (excluding depreciation and taxes)	$180,000	
Depreciation expense	12,400	
Federal income tax expense	46,600	239,000
Net sales		$ 31,000

Illustration 14.9   Consolidated Statement of Retained Earnings

P COMPANY AND SUBSIDIARY S COMPANY
Consolidated Statement of Retained Earnings
For the Year Ended December 31, 2012

Retained earnings, January 1, 2012	$54,000
Net income	31,000
Subtotal	$85,000
Dividends	10,000
Retained earnings, December 31, 2012	$75,000

Illustration 14.10   Consolidated Balance Sheet (one year after acquisition)

P COMPANY AND SUBSIDIARY S COMPANY
Consolidated Balance Sheet
December 31, 2012

Assets

Current assets:		
Cash	$ 54,000	
Accounts receivable, net	43,000	
Merchandise inventory	76,000	
Total current assets		$173,000
Property, plant, and equipment:		
Equipment, net	$ 48,900	
Building, net	94,700	
Land	34,000	
Total property, plant, and equipment		177,600
Goodwill		11,000
Total assets		$361,600

Liabilities and Stockholders' Equity

Current liabilities:		
Account payable	$ 21,600	
Notes payable	15,000	
Total liabilities		$ 36,600
Stockholders' equity:		
Common stock	$250,000	
Retained earnings	75,000	
Total stockholders' equity		325,000
Total liabilities and stockholders' equity		$361,600

	2010	**2009**
Dividend per share of common stock	$ 1.76	$1.64
Current market price per share	65.77	57.00
Earnings per share	5.12	2.95

Investors use the **dividend yield on common stock ratio** as a tool to compare stocks. Some investors favor stocks with a high dividend yield ratio and a high payout ratio. Other investors would rather have the corporation retain more of the funds and use them to attempt to increase future earnings and the market price of the stock. The formula for the dividend yield on common stock ratio is:

$$\text{Dividend yield on common stock ratio} = \frac{\text{Dividend per share of common stock}}{\text{Current market price per share}}$$

For Coca-Cola, the dividend yield on common stock ratios are:

2010: $1.76/$65.77 = 2.68%
2009: $1.64/$57.00 = 2.88%

To determine the relevance of this ratio, an investor compares these numbers to ratios calculated on other stocks.

Investors calculate the **payout ratio on common stock** as follows:

$$\text{Payout ratio on common stock} = \frac{\text{Dividend per share of common stock}}{\text{Earnings per share (EPS)}}$$

This ratio indicates whether a company pays out a large percentage of earnings as dividends or reinvests most of its earnings. When computing the payout ratio, remember that negative earnings per share result in an invalid calculation. Coca-Cola's payout ratios are:

2010: $1.76/$5.12 = 34.38%
2009: $1.64/$2.95 = 55.59%

Now that you have studied consolidated financial statements, you should realize the importance of presenting a complete picture of the business operations of a company. In Chapter 15 you learn about long-term financing, its advantages and disadvantages, and how bonds differ from stocks.

Understanding the Learning Objectives

- Under the cost method, the investor company records its investment at the price paid at acquisition and does not adjust the investment account balance subsequently. The cost method is used for all short-term investments, long-term investments of less than 20% where the purchasing company does not exercise significant influence over the investee company, and may be used for long-term investments of more than 50%.
- Under the equity method, the investment is also initially recorded at acquisition price but is then adjusted periodically for the investor company's share of the investee's reported income, losses, and dividends. The equity method is used for all long-term investments of between 20% and 50%, and may be used for investments of more than 50%. This method is also used for investments of less than 20% if the purchasing company exercises significant influence over the investee company.

The Coca-Cola Company
The world's largest soft drink company, The Coca-Cola Company has more than 500 brands and 3,500 beverage products that it sells in more than 200 countries worldwide.

Objective 1
Report stock investments and distinguish between the cost and equity methods of accounting for stock investments.

Objective 2
Prepare journal entries to account for short-term stock investments and for long-term stock investments of less than 20%.

- Under the cost method, the initial investment is debited to either Trading Securities or Available-for-Sale Securities, depending on whether the investment is a near-term or longer-term investment.
- At the end of each accounting period, the company must adjust the carrying value of each investment. The fair market value method is applied independently to each of these portfolios.
- Under the cost method, dividends received are credited to Dividend Revenue.
- Under the equity method, the initial investment is debited to an Investment in (Company Name) account. Income, losses, and dividends result in increases or decreases to the investment account.

Objective 3
Prepare journal entries to account for long-term stock investments of 20% to 50%.

- The equity method must be used for long-term investments of 20% to 50% and for long-term investments of less than 20% where significant influence is present.
- The initial investment is debited to an Investment in (Company Name) account. The purchasing company's share of the investee's income is debited to the investment account, and the purchaser's share of the investee's losses and dividends is credited to the investment account as they are reported by the investee.

Objective 4
Describe the nature of parent and subsidiary corporations.

- A corporation that owns more than 50% of the outstanding voting common stock of another corporation is called the *parent company.*
- The corporation acquired and controlled by the parent company is known as the *subsidiary company.*
- A parent company and its subsidiaries maintain their own accounting records and prepare their own financial statements, but the parent company must also prepare consolidated financial statements. The consolidated financial statements consolidate the financial results of the parent and subsidiaries as a single enterprise.
- Consolidated financial statements must be prepared (1) when one company owns more than 50% of the outstanding voting stock of another company and (2) unless control is likely to be temporary or if it does not rest with the majority owner.
- In preparing consolidated financial statements, the effects of intercompany transactions must be eliminated by making elimination entries. Elimination entries are made only on a consolidated statement work sheet, not in the accounting records of either company.
- One elimination entry offsets the parent company's subsidiary investment account against the stockholders' equity accounts of the subsidiary. Intercompany receivables and payables also must be eliminated.

Objective 5
Prepare consolidated financial statements through the use of a consolidated statement work sheet.

- A consolidated financial statements work sheet is an informal record in which elimination entries are made for the purpose of showing account balances as if the parent and its subsidiaries were a single economic enterprise.
- A consolidated balance sheet work sheet is prepared at the time of acquisition. The first two columns of the work sheet show assets, liabilities, and stockholders' equity of the parent and subsidiary as they appear on each corporation's individual balance sheet. The next pair of columns shows the eliminations. The final column shows the amounts that appear on the consolidated balance sheet.

- A consolidated work sheet is prepared at various dates after acquisition. The first two columns show the income statements, statements of retained earnings, and balance sheets of the parent and subsidiary. The next pair of columns shows the eliminations. The final column shows the amounts that appear in the consolidated financial statements.
- Consolidated financial statements are of primary importance to stockholders, managers, and directors of the parent company. On the other hand, consolidated financial statements are of limited use to the creditors and minority stockholders of the subsidiary.

Objective 6
Describe the uses and limitations of consolidated financial statements.

- Dividend yield on common stock ratio $= \dfrac{\text{Dividend per share of common stock}}{\text{Current market price per share}}$

- This ratio helps investors to compare stocks.

- Payout ratio on common stock $= \dfrac{\text{Dividend per share of common stock}}{\text{Earnings per share (EPS)}}$

- This ratio indicates whether a company pays out a large percentage of earnings as dividends or reinvests most of its earnings.

Objective 7
Analyze and use the financial results—dividend yield on common stock and payout ratio on common stock.

Demonstration Problem 14–A

Following are selected transactions and other data for Kelly Company for 2012:

Mar.   21   Purchased 600 shares of Sly Company common stock at $48.75 per share, plus a $450 broker's commission. Also purchased 100 shares of Rob Company common stock at $225 per share, plus a $376. commission. Both investments are expected to be temporary.

June   2   Received cash dividends of $1.50 per share on the Sly common shares and $3 per share on the Rob common shares.

Aug.   12   Received shares representing a 100% stock dividend on the Rob shares.

       30   Sold 100 shares of Rob common stock at $120 per share, less a $360 broker's commission.

Sept.   15   Received shares representing a 10% stock dividend on the Sly common stock. Market price today was $52.50 per share.

Dec.   31   Per share market values for the two investments in common stock are Sly, $45.75, and Rob, $106.50. Both investments are considered temporary.

Prepare journal entries to record these transactions and the necessary adjustments for a December 31 closing.

 Required

Solution to Demonstration Problem 14–A

2012				
Mar.	21	Trading Securities	52,576	
		Cash		52,576
		To record purchase of 600 shares of Sly common stock for $29,700 and 100 of Rob common stock for$22,876		
June	2	Cash	1,200	
		Dividend Revenue		1,200
		To record cash dividends: $900 Sly and $300 Rob.		
Aug.	12	Received 100 shares of Rob common stock as a 100% stock dividend. The new cost per share is $22,876 ÷ 200 shares = $114.38		
	30	Cash	11,640	
		Trading securities		11,438
		Gain on Sale of Trading Securities		202
		To record the sale of trading securities: Proceeds = $12,000 - $360; cost = $114.38 x 100 shares.		
Sept.	15	Received 60 shares of Sly common stock as a 10% stock dividend. New cost per share is $29,700 ÷ 660 shares = $45.		
Dec.	31	Unrealized Loss on Trading Securities	293	
		Trading Securities		293
		To write trading securities down to market value.		

	Cost	Market	Inc. (Dec.) in Market Value
Sly common stock	$29,700	$30,195*	$495
Rob common stock	11,438	10,650†	(788)
Total	$41,138	$40,845	$(293)

* $45.75 x 660 shares = $30,195.
† $106.50 x 100 shares = $10,650.

Demonstration Problem 14–B

Lanford Company acquired all of the outstanding voting common stock of Casey Company on January 2, 2012, for $300,000 cash. After the close of business on the date of acquisition, the balance sheets for the two companies were as follows:

	Landford Company	Casey Company
Assets		
Cash	$ 75,000	$ 30,000
Accounts receivable, net	90,000	37,500
Notes receivable	15,000	7,500
Merchandise inventory	112,500	45,000
Investment in Casey Company	300,000	
Investment in bonds		30,000
Plant and equipment, net	303,000	195,000
Total assets	$895,500	$345,000
Liabilities and Stockholders Equity		
Accounts payable	$ 75,000	$ 45,000
Notes payable	22,500	15,000
Bonds payable	225,000	
Common stock--$7.50 par value	300,000	150,000
Paid-in capital excess of par value—common		60,000
Retained earnings	273,000	75,000
Total liabilities and stockholders' equity	$895,500	$345,000

On January 2, 2012, Casey Company borrowed $15,000 from Lanford Company by giving a note. On that same day, Casey Company purchased $30,000 of Lanford Company's bonds. The excess of cost over book value is attributable to Casey Company's above-average earnings prospects.

Prepare a work sheet for a consolidated balance sheet on the date of acquisition.   *Required*

Solution to Demonstration Problem 14–B

LANDFORD COMPANY AND SUBSIDIARY CASEY COMPANY
Work Sheet for Consolidation Balance Sheet
January 2, 2012 (date of acquisition)

Assets	P Company	S Company	Eliminations Debit	Eliminations Credit	Consolidated Amounts
Cash	75,000	30,000			105,000
Accounts receivable, net	90,000	37,500			127,500
Notes receivable	15,000	7,500		(2) 15,000	7,500
Merchandise inventory	112,500	45,000			157,500
Investment in Casey Company	300,000			(1) 300,000	-0-
Investment in bonds		30,000		(3) 30,000	-0-
Plant and equipment, net	303,000	195,000			498,000
Goodwill			(1) 15,000		15,000
	895,500	345,000			910,500
Liabilities and Stockholders' Equity					
Accounts payable	75,000	45,000			120,000
Notes payable	22,500	15,000	(2) 15,000		22,500
Bonds payable	225,000		(3) 30,000		195,000
Common stock	300,000	150,000	(1) 150,000		300,000
Paid-in capital excess of par value—common		60,000	(1) 60,000		-0-
Retained earnings	273,000	75,000	(1) 75,000		273,000
	895,500	345,000	345,000	345,000	910,500

New Terms

Available-for-sale securities   Securities purchased that will be held for longer than the near term. *542*

Consolidated statements   The financial statements that result from consolidating the parent's financial statement amounts with those of its subsidiaries (after certain eliminations have been made). The consolidated statements reflect the financial position and results of operations of a single economic enterprise. *547*

Consolidated statement work sheet   An informal record on which elimination entries are made to show account balances as if the parent and its subsidiaries were a single economic enterprise. *549*

Cost method   A method of accounting for stock investments in which the investor company does not adjust the investment account balance for its share of the investee's reported income, losses, and dividends. Dividends received are credited to Dividends Revenue. *542*

Dividend yield on common stock ratio   Equal to dividend per share of common stock divided by the current market price per share. Investors use this ratio to compare stocks. *559*

Elimination entries   Entries made on a consolidated statement work sheet to remove certain intercompany items and transactions. Elimination entries allow the presentation of all account balances as if the parent and its subsidiaries were a single economic enterprise. *548*

Equity method   A method of accounting for stock investments where the investment account is adjusted periodically for the investor company's share of the investee's income, losses, and dividends as they are reported by the investee. *542, 546*

Goodwill   An intangible value attached to a business primarily due to above-average earnings prospects. *551*

Intercompany transactions   Financial transactions involving a parent and one of its subsidiaries or between two of the subsidiaries. *548*

Investee   A company that has 20% to 50% of its stock purchased by another company (the investor) as a long-term investment. *546*

Investor   A company that purchases 20% to 50% of another company (the investee) as a long-term investment. *546*

Marketable equity securities   Readily saleable common and preferred stocks of other companies. *543*

Noncontrolling interest   The claim or interest of the stockholders who own less than 50% of a subsidiary's outstanding voting common stock. The noncontrolling interest stockholders have an interest in the subsidiary's net assets and share the subsidiary's earnings with the parent company. *552*

Parent company   A corporation that owns more than 50% of the outstanding voting common stock of another corporation. *547*

Payout ratio on common stock   Calculated by dividing dividend per share of common stock by earnings per share (EPS). The ratio indicates whether a company pays out a large percentage of earnings as dividends or reinvests most of its earnings. *559*

Subsidiary company   A corporation acquired and controlled by a parent corporation; control is established by ownership of more than 50% of the subsidiary's outstanding voting common stock. *547*

Trading securities   Securities bought principally for sale in the near term. *542*

Self-Test

True-False

Indicate whether each of the following statements is true or false.

1. Under the cost method, the investment account is adjusted when dividends are received.
2. The cost method should be used when a corporation makes a long-term investment of less than 20%, and there is no significant control.
3. In a stock split, the investor does not recognize revenue, but reduces the cost per share of stock.
4. Trading securities and available-for-sale securities should be grouped separately in applying the fair market value rules.
5. When making elimination entries, the entries are made only on the consolidated statements work sheet and not on the accounting records of the parent and subsidiary.

Multiple-Choice

Select the best answer for each of the following questions.

1. In which of the following cases is the investor company limited to use of the equity method in accounting for its stock investments?
   a. Short-term investments.
   b. Long-term investments of less than 20%.
   c. Long-term investments of 20%–50%.
   d. Long-term investments of more than 50%.
2. Under the equity method, which of the following is true?
   a. Dividends received reduce the investment account.
   b. Dividends received increase the investment account.
   c. The investor's share of net income decreases the investment account.
   d. The investor's share of net loss increases the investment account.
3. When the fair market value rules are followed, which of the following is true when the market value of the stocks in the Trading Securities account falls below their cost?
   a. The Unrealized Losses on Trading Securities account is credited.
   b. The Recovery of Market Value of Trading Securities account is credited.
   c. The Allowance for Market Decline of Current Marketable Equity Securities is debited.
   d. The Unrealized Loss on Trading Securities is debited.
4. Under the equity method, the investment account always reflects only the:
   a. Dividends paid by the investee corporation.
   b. Investor's interest in the net assets of the investee.
   c. Investor's share of net income.
   d. Historical cost of the investment.
5. The excess of cost over the book value of an investment that is due to expected above-average earnings is labeled on the consolidated balance sheet as:
   a. Goodwill.
   b. Common stock.
   c. Retained earnings.
   d. Loss on investment.

Now turn to page 574 to check your answers.

Questions

1. For what reasons do corporations purchase the stock of other corporations?
2. Explain how marketable securities should be classified in the balance sheet.
3. Describe the valuation bases used for marketable equity securities.
4. Under what circumstances is the equity method used to account for stock investments?
5. Explain briefly the accounting for stock dividends and stock splits from the investor's point of view.
6. Of what significance is par value to the investing corporation?
7. What is the purpose of preparing consolidated financial statements?
8. Under what circumstances must consolidated financial statements be prepared?
9. Why is it necessary to make elimination entries on the consolidated statement work sheet? Are these elimination entries also posted to the accounts of the parent and subsidiary? Why or why not?
10. Why might a corporation pay an amount in excess of the book value for a subsidiary's stock? Why might it pay an amount less than the book value of the subsidiary's stock?
11. The item Noncontrolling interest often appears as one amount in the consolidated balance sheet. What does this item represent?
12. How do a subsidiary's earnings, losses, and dividends affect the investment account of the parent when the equity method of accounting is used?
13. Why are consolidated financial statements of limited usefulness to the creditors and minority stockholders of a subsidiary?

Exercises

On July 1, 2012, Tam Company purchased 200 shares of Del Company capital stock as a temporary investment (trading securities) at $676.80 per share plus a commission of $720. On July 15, a 10% stock dividend was received. Tam received a cash dividend of $3.60 per share on August 12, 2012. On November 1, Tam sold all of the shares for $835.20 per share, less a commission of $720. Prepare entries to record all of these transactions in Tam Company's accounts.

Key Company purchased 200 shares of Franklin Company stock at a total cost of $7,560 on July 1, 2012. At the end of the accounting year (December 31, 2012), the market value for these shares was $6,840. By December 31, 2013, the market value had risen to $7,920. This stock is the only marketable equity security that Key Company owns. The company classifies the securities as trading securities. Give the entries necessary at the date of purchase and at December 31, 2012, and 2013.

Corbit Company has marketable equity securities that have a fair market value at year-end that is $13,440 below their cost. Give the required entry if:

a. The securities are current assets classified as trading securities.
b. The securities are noncurrent assets classified as available-for-sale securities, and the loss is considered to be temporary.
c. The securities are noncurrent assets classified as available-for-sale securities, and the loss is considered to be permanent.

State where each of the accounts debited in **a, b,** and **c** would be reported in the financial statements.

Ruiz Company owns 75% of Sim Company's outstanding common stock and uses the equity method of accounting. Sim Company reported net income of $702,000 for 2012. On December 31, 2012, Sim Company paid a cash dividend of $189,000. In 2013, Sim Company incurred a net loss of $125,000. Prepare entries to reflect these events on Ruiz Company's books.

On February 1, 2012, Larkin Company acquired 100% of the outstanding voting common stock of TRD Company for $8,400,000 cash. The stockholders' equity of the TRD Company consisted of common stock, $6,720,000, and retained earnings, $1,680,000. Prepare (a) the entry to record the investment in TRD Company and (b) the elimination entry on the work sheet used to prepare a consolidated balance sheet as of the date of acquisition.

Given the facts in Exercise 14–5, how much would be recorded as goodwill in each of the following instances? The same amount was paid, but the parent company acquired a—

a. 90% interest.
b. 70% interest.
c. 55% interest.

Heidi Corporation acquired, for cash, 80% of the outstanding voting common stock of Sumpter Company. After the close of business on the date of acquisition, Sumpter Company's stockholders' equity consisted of common stock, $5,880,000, and retained earnings, $2,184,000. The cost of the investment exceeded the book value by $302,400 and was attributable to above-average earnings prospects. Prepare (a) the entry to record the investment in Sumpter Company and (b) the elimination entry on the work sheet used to prepare consolidated financial statements as of the date of acquisition.

On January 1, 2011, Company J acquired 85% of the outstanding voting common stock of Company K. On that date, Company K's stockholders' equity consisted of: Compute the difference between cost and book value in each of the following cases:

Exercise 14-8
Compute difference between cost and book value of common stock investments (L.O. 5)

Stockholders' equity:
Paid-in capital:

Common stock, $90 par; 30,000 shares authorized, issued, and outstanding	$2,700,000
Retained earnings	675,000
Total stockholders' equity	$3,375,000

a. Company J pays $2,868,750 cash for its interest in Company K.
b. Company J pays $3,375,000 cash for its interest in Company K.
c. Company J pays $2,610,000 cash for its interest in Company K.

The January 1, 2012, stockholders' equity section of Saye Company's balance sheet follows:

Exercise 14-9
Compute book value, difference between cost and book value, and noncontrolling interest of an investment (L.O. 5)

Stockholders' equity:
Paid-in capital:

Common stock, $144 par; authorized, 200,000 shares; issued, and outstanding, 150,000 shares	$21,600,000
Paid-in capital in excess of par value	3,600,000
Total paid-in capital	$25,200,000
Retained earnings	2,160,000
Total stockholders' equity	$27,360,000

Ninety percent of Saye Company's outstanding voting common stock was acquired by Tim Company on January 1, 2013, for $24,048,000. Compute (*a*) the book value of the investment, (*b*) the difference between cost and book value, and (*c*) the noncontrolling interest.

Company S purchased 90% of Company T's outstanding voting common stock on January 2, 2012. The investment is accounted for under the equity method. Company S paid $2,790,000 for its proportionate equity of $2,430,000. The difference was due to undervalued land owned by Company T. Company T earned $324,000 during 2012 and paid cash dividends of $108,000.

Exercise 14-10
Compute investment account balance at year-end and noncontrolling interest at beginning and end of year (L.O. 2, 5)

a. Compute the balance in the investment account on December 31, 2012.
b. Compute the amount of the noncontrolling interest on (1) January 2, 2012, and (2) December 31, 2012.

Problems

Paris Company acquired on July 15, 2012, 400 shares of Rome Company $720 par value capital stock at $698.40 per share plus a broker's commission of $1,728. On August 1, 2012, Paris Company received a cash dividend of $8.64 per share. On November 3, 2012, it sold 200 of these shares at $756 per share less a broker's commission of $1,152. On December 1, 2012, Rome Company issued shares comprising a 100% stock dividend declared on its capital stock on November 18.

Problem 14-1
Prepare entries for trading securities (L.O. 1, 2)

On December 31, 2012, the end of Paris Company's calendar-year accounting period, the market quotation for Rome Company's common stock was $331.20 per share. The decline was considered to be temporary.

a. Prepare journal entries to record all of these data assuming the securities are considered temporary investments classified as trading securities. Where should the accounts in the last entry appear in the financial statements?

Required

b. Assume Rome Company has become a major customer so the shares are held for long-term affiliation purposes. Indicate how the investment should be shown in the balance sheet.

568   PART IV   Sources of Equity Capital for Management's Use in Producing Revenues

Problem 14-2
Prepare entries for trading securities; compare entries to those for available-for-sale securities (L.O. 1, 2)

On October 17, 2012, Strong Company purchased the following common stocks (all trading securities) at the indicated per share prices that included commissions:

600 shares of X Company common stock @ $216	$129,600
1,000 shares of Y Company common stock @ $144	144,000
1,600 shares of Z Company common stock @ $72	115,200

On December 31, 2012, the market prices per share of the above common stocks were X, $223.20; Y, $136.80; and Z, $54.

Summarized, the cash dividends per share received in 2013 were X, $14.40; Y, $7.20; and Z, $5.40.

On December 31, 2013, the per share market prices were X, $252.80; Y, $115.20; and Z, $72. All of these changes in market prices are considered temporary.

Required

   a. Prepare journal entries for all of these transactions, including calendar year-end adjusting entries, assuming the shares of common stock acquired are considered trading securities.

   b. If the securities acquired are considered available-for-sale securities, how would the entries made in a differ?

   c. For both parts a and b, give the descriptions (titles) and the dollar amounts of the items that would appear in the income statements for 2012 and 2013.

Problem 14-3
Prepare equity method entries for an investment and eliminating entries for consolidated statements work sheet (L.O. 1, 3, 5)

On January 1, 2012, Long Company acquired 80% of the outstanding voting common stock of Fall Company for $4,032,000 cash. Long Company uses the equity method. During 2012, Fall reported $672,000 of net income and paid $288,000 in dividends. The stockholders' equity section of the December 31, 2011, balance sheet for Fall follows:

Stockholders' equity:	
Paid-in capital:	
Common stock—$42 par	$4,200,000
Retained earnings	840,000
Total stockholders' equity	$5,040,000

Required

   a. Prepare the general journal entries to record the investment and the effect of Fall's income and dividends on Long Company's accounts.

   b. Prepare the elimination entry that would be made on the work sheet for a consolidated balance sheet as of the date of acquisition.

Problem 14-4
Prepare equity method entries for an investment (L.O. 1, 3, 5)

Pearson Company acquired 75% of the outstanding voting common stock of Frost Company for $1,444,800 cash on January 1, 2012. The investment is accounted for under the equity method. During 2012, 2013, and 2014, Frost Company reported the following:

	Net Income (loss)	Dividends Paid
2012	$357,840	$290,640
2013	(45,360)	-0-
2014	108,360	72,240

Required

   a. Prepare general journal entries to record the investment and the effect of the subsidiary's income, losses, and dividends on Pearson Company's accounts.

   b. Compute the balance in the investment account on December 31, 2014.

Problem 14-5
Prepare work sheet and consolidated balance sheet at acquisition (L.O. 5)

Cord Company acquired 100% of the outstanding voting common stock of Thorpe Company on January 2, 2012, for $2,700,000. At the end of business on the date of acquisition, the balance sheets for the two companies were as follows:

	Cord Company	Thorpe Company
Assets		
Cash	$ 315,000	$ 180,000
Accounts receivable, net	234,000	144,000
Notes receivable	360,000	90,000
Merchandise inventory	495,000	234,000
Investment in Thorpe Company	2,700,000	
Equipment, net	648,000	450,000
Building, net	1,890,000	990,000
Land	765,000	405,000
Total assets	$7,407,000	$2,493,000
Liabilities and Stockholders Equity		
Accounts payable	$ 117,000	$ 135,000
Notes payable	90,000	108,000
Common stock—$45 par value	5,400,000	1,800,000
Retained earnings	1,800,000	450,000
Total liabilities and stockholders' equity	$7,407,000	$2,493,000

The excess of cost over book value is attributable to the above-average earnings prospects of Thorpe Company. On the date of acquisition, Thorpe Company borrowed $72,000 from Cord Company by giving a note.

a. Prepare a work sheet for a consolidated balance sheet as of the date of acquisition.
b. Prepare a consolidated balance sheet for January 2, 2012.

 Required

Refer to Problem 14–5. Cord Company uses the equity method. Assume the following are from the adjusted trial balances of Cord Company and Thorpe Company on December 31, 2012:

Problem 14-6
Prepare work sheet for consolidated financial statements (L.O. 5)

	Cord Company	Thorpe Company
Debit Balance Accounts		
Cash	$ 351,000	$ 315,000
Accounts receivable, net	378,000	180,000
Notes receivable	315,000	45,000
Merchandise inventory, December 31	495,000	287,100
Investment in Thorpe Company	2,790,000	
Equipment, net	615,000	427,500
Building, net	1,815,000	950,400
Land	765,000	405,000
Cost of goods sold	1,800,000	630,000
Expense (excluding depreciation and taxes)	720,000	270,900
Depreciation expense	108,000	62,100
Income tax expense	585,000	189,000
Dividends	540,000	108,000
Total of the accounts with debit balances	$11,277,000	$3,870,000
Credit Balance Accounts		
Accounts payable	$ 135,000	$ 180,000
Notes payable	144,000	90,000
Common stock—$45 par value	5,400,000	1,800,000
Retained earnings—January 1	1,800,000	450,000
Revenue from sales	3,600,000	1,350,000
Income from Thorpe Company	198,000	
Total of the accounts with credit balances	$11,277,000	$3,870,000

There is no intercompany debt at the end of the year.

Prepare a work sheet for consolidated financial statements on December 31, 2012.

 Required

Problem 14-7
Prepare consolidated
income statement,
statement of retained
earnings, and balance
sheet (L.O. 5)

Using the work sheet from Problem 14–6, prepare the following items:

a. Consolidated income statement for the year ended December 31, 2012.
b. Consolidated statement of retained earnings for the year ended December 31, 2012.
c. Consolidated balance sheet for December 31, 2012.

Alternate Problems

Problem 14-1A
Prepare entries for
available-for-sale
securities (L.O. 1, 3)

On September 1, 2012, Ramsey Company purchased the following relatively long-term investments classified as available-for-sale securities:

1. Two thousand shares of Lacey Company capital stock at $439.20 plus broker's commission of $5,760.
2. One thousand shares of Membrow Company capital stock at $705.60 plus broker's commission of $5,040.

Cash dividends of $18.00 per share on the Lacey capital stock and $14.40 per share on the Membrow capital stock were received on December 7 and December 10, respectively.
   On December 31, 2012, per share market values are Lacey, $460.80; and Membrow, $655.20.

Required

a. Prepare journal entries to record these transactions.
b. Prepare the necessary adjusting entry(ies) at December 31, 2012, to adjust the carrying values assuming that market price changes are believed to be temporary. Where would the accounts appear in the financial statements?

Problem 14-2A
Prepare entries for
trading securities
(L.O. 1, 2)

Kress, Inc., purchased on July 2, 2012, 240 shares of Baker Company $180 par value common stock as a temporary investment at $288 per share, plus a broker's commission of $432.
   On July 15, 2012, a cash dividend of $7.20 per share was received. On September 15, 2012, Baker Company split its $180 par value common shares two for one.
   On November 2, 2012, Kress sold 200 shares of Baker common stock at $180, less a broker's commission of $288.

Required

a. Prepare journal entries to record all of the above transactions.
b. How would you recommend that the remaining shares be classified in the December 31, 2012, balance sheet if still held at that date?
c. Assume the remaining shares were considered current assets classified as trading securities at the end of 2012, at which time their market value was $128 per share. Prepare any necessary adjusting entries for the end of 2012.

Problem 14-3A
Prepare equity
method entries for
an investment and
eliminating entries
for consolidated
work sheet
(L.O. 1, 3, 5)

Prime Company acquired 90% of the outstanding voting common stock of Orr Company on January 1, 2012, for $7,560,000 cash. Prime Company uses the equity method. During 2012, Orr reported $1,512,000 of net income and paid $504,000 in cash dividends. The stockholders' equity section of the December 31, 2011, balance sheet for Orr follows:

Stockholders' equity:	
Paid-in capital:	
Common stock, $21.00 par	$6,720,000
Retained earnings	1,680,000
Total stockholders' equity	$8,400,000

Required

a. Prepare general journal entries to record the investment and the effect of Orr's earnings and dividends on Prime Company's accounts.
b. Prepare the elimination entry that would be made on the work sheet for a consolidated balance sheet as of the date of acquisition.

Codd Company acquired 70% of the outstanding voting common stock of Snow Company for $8,568,000 on January 1, 2012. The investment is accounted for under the equity method. During the years 2012–2014, Snow Company reported the following:

Problem 14-4A
Prepare equity method entries for an investment
(L.O. 1, 3, 5)

	Net Income (loss)	Dividends Paid
2012	$1,454,880	$871,920
2013	372,960	223,440
2014	(23,520)	55,860

a. Prepare general journal entries to record the investment and the effect of the subsidiary's income, losses, and dividends on Codd Company's accounts.

b. Compute the investment account balance on December 31, 2014.

◖ *Required*

Maple Company acquired all of the outstanding voting common stock of Dodd Company on January 2, 2012, for $4,320,000. On the date of acquisition, the balance sheets for the two companies were as follows:

Problem 14-5A
Prepare work sheet and consolidated balance sheet at acquisition (L.O. 5)

	Maple Company	Dodd Company
Debit Balance Accounts		
Cash	$ 900,000	$ 270,000
Accounts receivable, net	432,000	360,000
Notes receivable	180,000	108,000
Merchandise inventory	1,368,000	864,000
Investment in Dodd Company	4,320,000	
Equipment, net	1,224,000	738,000
Building, net	3,,330,000	1,656,000
Land	1,404,000	450,000
Total assets	$13,158,000	$4,446,000
Liabilities and Stockholders Equity		
Accounts payable	$ 792,000	$ 360,000
Notes payable	216,000	252,000
Common stock—$120 par value	9,540,000	3,564,000
Retained earnings	2,610,000	270,000
Total of the accounts with credit balances	$13,158,000	$4,446,000

The management of Maple Company thinks that the Dodd Company's land is undervalued by $162,000. The remainder of the excess of cost over book value is due to superior earnings potential.

On the date of acquisition, Dodd Company borrowed $180,000 from Maple Company by giving a note.

a. Prepare a work sheet for a consolidated balance sheet as of the date of acquisition.

b. Prepare a consolidated balance sheet for January 2, 2012.

◖ *Required*

Refer back to Problem 14–5A. Maple Company uses the equity method. Assume the following amounts are taken from the adjusted trial balances of Maple Company and Dodd Company on December 31, 2012:

Problem 14-6A
Prepare work sheet for consolidated financial statements (L.O. 5)

	Maple Company	Dodd Company
Debit Balance Accounts		
Cash	$ 864,000	$ 364,296
Accounts receivable, net	553,536	414,000
Notes receivable	342,000	90,000
Merchandise inventory, December 31	1,530,000	1,008,000
Investment in Dodd Company	4,519,356	
Equipment, net	1,174,500	691,860
Building, net	3,136,500	1,573,200
Land	1,404,000	450,000
Cost of goods sold	8,064,000	2,160,000
Expense (excluding depreciation and taxes)	2,160,000	810,000
Depreciation expense	243,000	128,940
Income tax expense	569,664	123,504
Dividends	477,000	178,200
Total of the accounts with debit balances	$25,037,556	$7,992,000
Credit Balance Accounts		
Accounts payable	$ 720,000	$ 378,000
Notes payable	270,000	180,000
Common stock—$90 par value	9,540,000	3,564,000
Retained earnings	2,610,000	270,000
Revenue from sales	11,520,000	3,600,000
Income from Dodd Company	377,556	
Total of the accounts with credit balances	$25,037,556	$7,992,000

There is no intercompany debt at the end of the year.

Required Prepare a work sheet for consolidated financial statements on December 31, 2012.

Problem 14-7A
Prepare consolidated income statement, statement of retained earnings, and balance sheet (L.O. 5)

Using the work sheet from Problem 14–6A, prepare the following items:

a. Consolidated income statement for the year ended December 31, 2012.
b. Consolidated statement of retained earnings for the year ended December 31, 2012.
c. Consolidated balance sheet for December 31, 2012.

Beyond the Numbers—Critical Thinking

Business Decision Case 14-1
Classify a portfolio of marketable equity securities as current or noncurrent investments (L.O. 1)

You are the CPA engaged to audit the records of Quigley Company. You find that your client has a portfolio of marketable equity securities that has a total market value of $300,000 less than the total cost of the portfolio. You ask the vice president for finance if the client expects to sell these securities in the coming year. He answers that he doesn't know. The securities will be sold if additional cash is needed to finance operations. When you ask for a cash forecast, you are told that a forecast has been prepared that covers the next year. It indicates no need to sell the marketable securities.

Required Write a brief statement in which you explain how you would classify the client's portfolio of marketable securities in the balance sheet. Does it really make any difference whether the securities are classified as trading securities or available-for-sale securities? Explain.

Business Decision Case 14-2
Prepare a consolidated balance sheet at acquisition (L.O. 5)

On January 2, 2012, Brown Company acquired 60% of the voting common stock of Cobb Company for $720,000 cash. The excess of cost over book value was due to above-average earnings prospects. Brown has hired you to help it prepare consolidated financial statements and has already collected the following information for both companies as of January 2, 2012:

	Brown Company	Cobb Company
Assets		
Cash	$ 72,000	$ 54,000
Accounts receivable, net	108,000	126,000
Merchandise inventory	288,000	216,000
Investment in Cobb Company	720,000	
Plant and equipment, net	936,000	738,000
Total assets	$2,124,000	$1,134,000
Liabilities and Stockholders Equity		
Accounts payable	$ 144,000	$ 54,000
Common stock	1,440,000	720,000
Retained earnings	540,000	360,000
Total liabilities and stockholders' equity	$2,124,000	$1,134,000

a. Brown believes that consolidated financial statements can be prepared simply by adding together the amounts in the two individual columns. Is this correct? If not, why not?

b. Prepare a consolidated balance sheet for the date of acquisition without preparing a consolidated statement work sheet.

 Required

International Flavors & Fragrances, Inc., is the leading creator and manufacturer of flavors and fragrances used by others to impart or improve flavor or fragrance in a wide variety of consumer products.

Use the following excerpt from International Flavors & Fragrances Inc.'s 2010 annual report to calculate the dividend yield on common stock and the payout ratios. Then comment on the results.

Business Decision Case 14-3
Compute the dividend yield on common stock and the payout ratios. Analyze ratios (L.O. 7)

	2010	2009	2008
Earnings per share	$3.29	$2.48	$2.89
Dividends per share ($)	1.04	1.00	0.96
Stock price per common share ($)	55.59	41.14	22.72

In teams of two or three students, select three companies you believe may be profitable short-term investments. Determine the current market prices for those companies' stocks from today's newspaper and the market prices six months ago. Calculate the gain or loss that your team would have recorded if it had purchased 500 shares of each company's stock six months ago and sold all of the shares today. Write a short memo to your instructor describing why you selected those companies and why you believe the market prices of their stocks increased or decreased. Also, be prepared to describe your analysis to the class.

Group Project 14-4
Determine gain or loss on short-term investments

With one or two other students, go to the library and locate *Statement of Financial Standards No. 94,* "Consolidation of All Majority-Owned Subsidiaries," published by the Financial Accounting Standard Board in 1987. In a report to your instructor answer questions such as: What does the standard require? Why did the FASB act on this topic? Why are "nonhomogeneous" subsidiaries included in the consolidated group? Why did one of the Board members dissent from the statement? Describe some of the important background on this topic as given in the statement.

Group Project 14-5
Library Project— Investigate consolidation standard

In a small group of students, locate the annual reports of three companies with investments in other companies. Compare the accounting and reporting for the investments by the three companies. For instance, by reading the notes to the financial statements, try to determine whether they account for the investments using the cost or equity methods. Is there goodwill on the balance sheets? What else can you determine about the investments? Write a report to your instructor summarizing your findings.

Group Project 14-6
Analyze annual reports of companies with investments in other companies

Using the Internet—A View of the Real World

Internet Project 14-7
Investigate a consolidated balance sheet

Visit the following website for General Electric Company:

http://www.ge.com

Pursue choices on the screen until you locate the consolidated statement of financial position. You will probably go down some "false paths" to get to this financial statement, but you can get there. Check to see if there is a noncontrolling interest listed on the consolidated statement of financial position. Check out the notes to the financial statements for further information. Browse around the site for any other interesting information concerning the company. Write a memo to your instructor summarizing your findings.

Answers to Self-Test

True-False

1. **False.** Under the cost method of accounting for stock investments, the Dividend Revenue account, rather than the investment account, is adjusted.
2. **True.** For long-term investments of less than 20%, the cost method should be used.
3. **True.** Revenue is not recognized when there is a stock split. The new number of shares is recorded, and the cost per share is reduced.
4. **True.** Trading securities should be considered separately from available-for-sale securities in applying the fair market value method.
5. **True.** Eliminating entries are not made on the accounting records of the parent and subsidiary. Only the work sheet is affected by elimination entries made during consolidation.

Multiple-Choice

1. **c.** The Accounting Principles Board has said that investors must use the equity method when accounting for long-term investments of 20% to 50%.
2. **a.** Under the equity method, dividends received reduce the investment account; the other choices are not true.
3. **d.** If the market value of securities falls below their cost, an unrealized loss account is debited.
4. **b.** Under the equity method, the investment account always reflects the investor's interest in the net assets of the investee.
5. **a.** If cost is greater than the book value of an investment because of expected above-average earnings, the excess cost should be labeled goodwill.

Careers in Accounting

The Accountant's Role In Financial Institutions

Companies that require funds to maintain existing operations and expand new operations frequently do not have the necessary cash available within the company. Therefore, these companies are required to obtain long-term financing from banks and other financial institutions. The operations of financial institutions are unique from those of the typical manufacturing or service company. As a result, the accounting measurement and disclosure practices followed by financial institutions can be quite different from those followed in other industries. In addition to the more traditional careers in accounting (auditing, professional services, financial reporting, cost accounting, and taxation), accounting majors with interests in finance may pursue a career in financial institutions.

Accountants in this industry commonly deal with issues related to marketable securities, derivatives, hedging, sale of receivables, foreign currency exchanges, and loan loss provisions and impairments. In addition, accountants in this area are being called upon to play an increasing role in the strategic operations of the financial institution. Not only are accountants needed to account for the institution's transactions, but they are being asked to recommend new opportunities for growth and to advise on financial risk as well. Some of these new areas include issues related to asset/liability management, interest rate risk, present value measurements, capital structure, and key ratio analysis.

Accountants also play a key role in one of the most important decisions of a financial institution - the decision of whether to lend money to a prospective borrower. The decision to lend money hinges on the ability of the prospective borrower to pay interest and repay debt. Since accountants have been trained in financial statement preparation and interpretation, accountants are some of the most sought after professionals for understanding the financial position and risk of a prospective borrower.

15

Long-Term Financing
Bonds

In previous chapters, you learned that corporations obtain cash for recurring business operations from stock issuances, profitable operations, and short-term borrowing (current liabilities). However, when situations arise that require large amounts of cash, such as the purchase of a building, corporations also raise cash from long-term borrowing, that is, by issuing bonds. The issuing of bonds results in a Bonds Payable account.

Bonds Payable

A **bond** is a long-term debt, or liability, owed by its issuer. Physical evidence of the debt lies in a negotiable *bond certificate*. In contrast to long-term notes, which usually mature in 10 years or less, bond maturities often run for 20 years or more.

Generally, a bond issue consists of a large number of $1,000 bonds rather than one large bond. For example, a company seeking to borrow $100,000 would issue one hundred $1,000 bonds rather than one $100,000 bond. This practice enables investors with less cash to invest to purchase some of the bonds.

Bonds derive their value primarily from two promises made by the borrower to the lender or bondholder. The borrower promises to pay (1) the **face value** or principal amount of the bond on a specific maturity date in the future and (2) periodic interest at a specified rate on face value at stated dates, usually semiannually, until the maturity date.

Large companies often have numerous long-term notes and bond issues outstanding at any one time. The various issues generally have different stated interest rates and mature at different points in the future. Companies present this information in the footnotes to their financial statements. Illustration 15.1 shows a portion of the long-term borrowings footnote from Dow Chemical Company's 2010 annual report. Promissory notes, debenture bonds, and foreign notes are shown, with their amounts, maturity dates, and interest rates.

> ### Learning Objectives
>
> After studying this chapter, you should be able to:
>
> **1.** Describe the features of bonds and tell how bonds differ from shares of stock.
>
> **2.** List the advantages and disadvantages of financing with long-term debt and prepare examples showing how to employ financial leverage.
>
> **3.** Prepare journal entries for bonds issued at face value.
>
> **4.** Explain how interest rates affect bond prices and what causes a bond to sell at a premium or a discount.
>
> (continued)

Illustration 15.1   Dow Chemical Company's Long-Term Notes and Bonds (in millions)

Promissory Notes and Debentures at December 31, 2010

	(Millions)	
	2010	**2009**
5.30%, final maturity 2011	$ 1,057	1,054
5.33%, final maturity 2012	2,154	2,280
6.05%, final maturity 2013	389	389
7.27%, final maturity 2014	2,096	1,750
5.90%, final maturity 2015	1,250	1,250
Subtotal	$6,946	$6,723

Dow Chemical Company
Dow Chemical Company is one of the largest chemical companies in the world, with annual sales of more than $50 billion.

Foreign Notes at December 31, 2010

	(Millions)	
	2010	**2009**
5.68%, final maturity 2011, Euro	$ 665	$ 713
Subtotal	$ 665	$ 713

Objectives

5. Apply the concept of present value to compute the price of a bond.

6. Prepare journal entries for bonds issued at a discount or a premium.

7. Prepare journal entries for bond redemptions and bond conversions.

8. Describe the ratings used for bonds.

9. Analyze and use the financial results—times interest earned ratio.

10. Explain future value and present value concepts and make required calculations (Appendix).

Objective 1
Describe the features of bonds and tell how bonds differ from shares of stock.

Comparison with Stock

A bond differs from a share of stock in several ways:

1. A bond is a debt or liability of the issuer, while a share of stock is a unit of ownership.
2. A bond has a maturity date when it must be paid. A share of stock does not mature; stock remains outstanding indefinitely unless the company decides to retire it.
3. Most bonds require stated periodic interest payments by the company. In contrast, dividends to stockholders are payable only when declared; even preferred dividends need not be paid in a particular period if the board of directors so decides.
4. Bond interest is deductible by the issuer in computing both net income and taxable income, while dividends are not deductible in either computation.

Selling (Issuing) Bonds

A company seeking to borrow millions of dollars generally is not able to borrow from a single lender. By selling (issuing) bonds to the public, the company secures the necessary funds.

Usually companies sell their bond issues through an investment company or a banker called an **underwriter.** The underwriter performs many tasks for the bond issuer, such as advertising, selling, and delivering the bonds to the purchasers. Often the underwriter guarantees the issuer a fixed price for the bonds, expecting to earn a profit by selling the bonds for more than the fixed price.

When a company sells bonds to the public, many purchasers buy the bonds. Rather than deal with each purchaser individually, the issuing company appoints a *trustee* to represent the bondholders. The **trustee** usually is a bank or trust company. The main duty of the trustee is to see that the borrower fulfills the provisions of the *bond indenture.* A **bond indenture** is the contract or loan agreement under which the bonds are issued. The indenture deals with matters such as the interest rate, maturity date and maturity amount, possible restrictions on dividends, repayment plans, and other provisions relating to the debt. An issuing company that does not adhere to the bond indenture provisions is in default. Then, the trustee takes action to force the issuer to comply with the indenture.

Bonds may differ in some respects; they may be secured or unsecured bonds, registered or unregistered (bearer) bonds, and term or serial bonds. We discuss these differences next.

Certain bond features are matters of legal necessity, such as how a company pays interest and transfers ownership. Such features usually do not affect the issue price of the bonds. Other features, such as convertibility into common stock, are *sweeteners* designed to make the bonds more attractive to potential purchasers. These sweeteners may increase the issue price of a bond.

Secured Bonds   A **secured bond** is a bond for which a company has pledged specific property to ensure its payment. Mortgage bonds are the most common secured bonds. A **mortgage** is a legal claim (lien) on specific property that gives the bondholder the right to possess the pledged property if the company fails to make required payments.

Unsecured Bonds   An **unsecured bond** is a **debenture bond**, or simply a *debenture*. A debenture is an unsecured bond backed only by the general creditworthiness of the issuer, not by a lien on any specific property. A financially sound company can issue debentures more easily than a company experiencing financial difficulty.

Registered Bonds   A **registered bond** is a bond with the owner's name on the bond certificate and in the register of bond owners kept by the bond issuer or its agent, the registrar. Bonds may be registered as to principal (or face value of the bond) or as to both principal and interest. Most bonds in our economy are registered as to principal only. For a bond registered as to both principal and interest, the issuer pays the bond interest by check. To transfer ownership of registered bonds, the owner endorses the bond and registers it in the new owner's name. Therefore, owners can easily replace lost or stolen registered bonds.

Unregistered (Bearer) Bonds   An **unregistered (bearer) bond** is the property of its holder or bearer because the owner's name does not appear on the bond certificate or in a separate record. Physical delivery of the bond transfers ownership.

Coupon Bonds   A **coupon bond** is a bond not registered as to interest. Coupon bonds carry detachable coupons for the interest they pay. At the end of each interest period, the owner clips the coupon for the period and presents it to a stated party, usually a bank, for collection.

Term Bonds and Serial Bonds   A **term bond** matures on the same date as all other bonds in a given bond issue. **Serial bonds** in a given bond issue have maturities spread over several dates. For instance, one-fourth of the bonds may mature on December 31, 2013, another one-fourth on December 31, 2014, and so on.

Callable Bonds   A **callable bond** contains a provision that gives the issuer the right to call (buy back) the bond before its maturity date. The provision is similar to the call provision of some preferred stocks. A company is likely to exercise this call right when its outstanding bonds bear interest at a much higher rate than the company would have to pay if it issued new but similar bonds. The exercise of the call provision normally requires the company to pay the bondholder a call premium of about $30 to $70 per $1,000 bond. A **call premium** is the price paid in excess of face value that the issuer of bonds must pay to redeem (call) bonds before their maturity date.

Characteristics of Bonds

Note to the Student
Look in *The Wall Street Journal* for announcements of bond issues.

Convertible Bonds   A **convertible bond** is a bond that may be exchanged for shares of stock of the issuing corporation at the bondholder's option. A convertible bond has a stipulated conversion rate of some number of shares for each $1,000 bond. Although any type of bond may be convertible, issuers add this feature to make risky debenture bonds more attractive to investors.

Bonds with Stock Warrants   A **stock warrant** allows the bondholder to purchase shares of common stock at a fixed price for a stated period. Warrants issued with long-term debt may be nondetachable or detachable. A bond with *nondetachable warrants* is virtually the same as a convertible bond; the holder must surrender the bond to acquire the common stock. *Detachable warrants* allow bondholders to keep their bonds and still purchase shares of stock through exercise of the warrants.

Junk Bonds   **Junk bonds** are high-interest rate, high-risk bonds. Many junk bonds issued in the 1980s financed corporate restructurings. These restructurings took the form of management buyouts (called leveraged buyouts or LBOs), hostile takeovers of companies by outside parties, or friendly takeovers of companies by outside parties. In the early 1990s, junk bonds lost favor because many issuers defaulted on their interest payments. Some issuers declared bankruptcy or sought relief from the bondholders by negotiating new debt terms.

Several advantages come from raising cash by issuing bonds rather than stock. First, the current stockholders do not have to dilute or surrender their control of the company when funds are obtained by borrowing rather than issuing more shares of stock. Second, it may be less expensive to issue debt rather than additional stock because the interest payments made to bondholders are tax deductible while dividends are not. Finally, probably the most important reason to issue bonds is that the use of debt may increase the earnings of stockholders through favorable financial leverage.

Favorable Financial Leverage   A company has **favorable financial leverage** when it uses borrowed funds to increase earnings per share (EPS) of common stock. An increase in EPS usually results from earning a higher rate of return than the rate of interest paid for the borrowed money. For example, suppose a company borrowed money at 10% and earned a 15% rate of return. The 5% difference increases earnings.

Illustration 15.2 provides a more comprehensive example of favorable financial leverage. The two companies in the illustration are identical in every respect except in the way they are financed. Company A issued only capital stock, while Company B issued equal amounts of 10% bonds and capital stock. Both companies have $20,000,000 of assets, and both earned $4,000,000 of income from operations. If we divide income from operations by assets ($4,000,000 ÷ $20,000,000), we see that both companies earned 20% on assets employed. Yet B's stockholders fared far better than A's. The ratio of net income to stockholders' equity is 18% for B, while it is only 12% for A.

Assume that both companies issued their stock at the beginning of 2012 at $10 per share. B's $1.80 EPS are 50% greater than A's $1.20 EPS. This EPS difference probably would cause B's shares to sell at a substantially higher market price than A's shares. B's larger EPS would also allow a larger dividend on B's shares.

Company B in Illustration 15.2 is employing financial leverage, or **trading on the equity**. The company is using its stockholders' equity as a basis for securing funds on which it pays a fixed return. Company B expects to earn more from the use of such funds than their fixed after-tax cost. As a result, Company B increases its rate of return on stockholders' equity and EPS.[1]

---

[1]Issuing bonds is only one method of using leverage. Other methods of using financial leverage include issuing preferred stock or long-term notes.

Illustration 15.2   Favorable Financial Leverage

COMPANIES A AND B CONDENSED STATEMENTS
Balance Sheets
December 31, 2012

	Company A	Company B
Total assets	$20,000,000	$20,000,000
Bonds payable, 10%		$10,000,000
Stockholders' equity (capital stock)	$20,000,000	10,000,000
Total equities	$20,000,000	$20,000,000

Income Statements
For the Year Ended December 31, 2012

	Company A	Company B
Income from operations	$ 4,000,000	$ 4,000,000
Interest expense		1,000,000
Income before federal income taxes	$ 4,000,000	$ 3,000,000
Deduct: Federal income taxes (40%)	1,600,000	1,200,000
Net income	$ 2,400,000	$1,800,000
Number of common shares outstanding	2,000,000	1,000,000
Earnings per share (EPS) (Net income ÷ Number of common shares outstanding)	$1.20	$1.80
Rate of return on assets employed (Income from Operations ÷ Total assets; both companies $4,000,000/$20,000,000)	20%	20%
Rate of return on stockholders' equity (Net income ÷ Stockholders' equity):		
Company A ($2,400,000/$20,000,000)	12%	
Company B ($1,800,000/$10,000,000)		18%

Several disadvantages accompany the use of debt financing. First, the borrower has a fixed interest payment that must be met each period to avoid default. Second, use of debt also reduces a company's ability to withstand a major loss. For example, assume that instead of having net income, both Company A and Company B in Illustration 15.2 sustain a net loss in 2012 of $11,000,000. At the end of 2012, Company A will still have $9,000,000 of stockholders' equity and can continue operations with a chance of recovery. Company B, on the other hand, would have negative stockholders' equity of $1,000,000 and the bondholders could force the company to liquidate if B could not make interest payments as they came due. The result of sustaining the loss by the two companies is as follows:

Note to the Student
Financial leverage results from the difference between the cost of borrowed funds and the rate of return earned with those funds.
Favorable financial leverage exists when the rate of return is higher than the cost of the borrowed money.

COMPANIES A AND B
Partial Balance Sheets
December 31, 2012

	Company A	Company B
Stockholders' equity:		
Paid-in capital:		
Common stock	$ 20,000,000	$ 10,000,000
Retained earnings	(11,000,000)	(11,000,000)
Total stockholders' equity	$ 9,000,000	$ (1,000,000)

A third disadvantage of debt financing is that it also causes a company to experience unfavorable financial leverage when income from operations falls below a certain level. **Unfavorable financial leverage** results when the cost of borrowed funds exceeds the revenue they generate; it is the reverse of *favorable financial leverage.* In the previous example, if income from operations fell to $1,000,000, the rates of return on stockholders' equity would be 3% for A and zero for B, as shown in this schedule:

COMPANIES A AND B
Income Statements
For the Year Ended December 31, 2012

	Company A	Company B
Income from operations	$1,000,000	$1,000,000
Interest expense		1,000,000
Income before federal income taxes	$ 1,000,000	$ —0—
Deduct: Federal income taxes (40%)	400,000	—0—
Net income	$ 600,000	$ —0—
Rate of return on stockholders' equity:		
Company A ($600,000/$20,000,000)	3%	
Company B ($0/$10,000,000)		0%

The fourth disadvantage of issuing debt is that loan agreements often require maintaining a certain amount of working capital (Current assets – Current liabilities) and place limitations on dividends and additional borrowings.

Accounting for Bonds Issued at Face Value

When a company issues bonds, it incurs a long-term liability on which periodic interest payments must be made, usually twice a year. If interest dates fall on other than balance sheet dates, the company must accrue interest in the proper periods. The following examples illustrate the accounting for bonds issued at face value on an interest date and issued at face value between interest dates.

Bonds Issued at Face Value on an Interest Date Valley Company's accounting year ends on December 31. On December 31, 2012, Valley issued 10-year, 12% bonds with a $100,000 face value, for $100,000. The bonds are dated December 31, 2012, call for semiannual interest payments on June 30 and December 31, and mature on December 31, 2022. Valley made the required interest and principal payments when due. The entries for the 10 years are as follows:

On December 31, 2012, the date of issuance, the entry is:

2012					
Dec.	31	Cash		100,000	
		Bonds Payable			100,000
		To record bonds issued at face value.			

On each June 30 and December 31 for 10 years, beginning June 30, 2013 (ending June 30, 2022), the entry would be:

Each year June and Dec.	30 31	Bond Interest Expense ($100,000 X 0.12 X 1/2)	6,000	
		Cash		6,000
		To record periodic interest payment.		

On December 31, 2022, the maturity date, the entry would be:

2022				
Dec.	31	Bond Interest Expense	6,000	
		Bonds Payable	100,000	
		Cash		106,000
		To record final interest and bond redemption payment.		

Note that Valley does not need adjusting entries because the interest payment date falls on the last day of the accounting period. The income statement for each of the 10 years 2013–2022 would show Bond Interest Expense of $12,000 ($6,000 × 2); the balance sheet at the end of each of the years 2012–2020 would report bonds payable of $100,000 in long-term liabilities. At the end of 2021, Valley would reclassify the bonds as a current liability because they will be paid within the next year.

The real world is more complicated. For example, assume the Valley bonds were dated October 31, 2012, issued on that same date, and pay interest each April 30 and October 31. Valley must make an adjusting entry on December 31 to accrue interest for November and December. That entry would be:

2012					
Dec.	31	Bond Interest Expense ($100,000 X 0.12 X (2/12))	2,000	
		Bond Interest Payable		2,000
		To accrue two month' interest expense.		

The April 30, 2013, entry would be:

2013					
Apr.	30	Bond Interest Expense ($100,000 X 0.12 X (4/12))	4,000	
		Bond Interest Payable	2,000	
		Cash		6,000
		To record semiannual interest payment.		

The October 31, 2013, entry would be:

2013					
Oct.	31	Bond Interest Expense	6,000	
		Cash		6,000
		To record semiannual interest payment.		

Each year Valley would make similar entries for the semiannual payments and the year-end accrued interest. The firm would report the $2,000 Bond Interest Payable as a current liability on the December 31 balance sheet for each year.

Bonds Issued at Face Value between Interest Dates   Companies do not always issue bonds on the date they start to bear interest. Regardless of when the bonds are physically issued, interest starts to accrue from the most recent interest date. Firms report bonds to be selling at a stated price "plus accrued interest." The issuer must pay holders of the bonds a full six months' interest at each interest date. Thus, investors purchasing bonds after the bonds begin to accrue interest must pay the seller for the unearned interest accrued since the preceding interest date. The bondholders are reimbursed for this accrued interest when they receive their first six months' interest check.

Using the facts for the Valley bonds dated December 31, 2012, suppose Valley issued its bonds on May 31, 2013, instead of on December 31, 2012. The entry required is:

2013					
May	31	Cash	105,000	
		Bonds Payable		100,000
		Bond Interest Payable ($100,000 X 0.12 X (5/12))		5,000
		To record bonds issued at face value plus accrued interest.		

This entry records the $5,000 received for the accrued interest as a debit to Cash and a credit to Bond Interest Payable.

The entry required on June 30, 2013, when the full six months' interest is paid, is:

2013						
June	30	Bond Interest Expense ($100,000 X 0.12 X (1/12))		1,000		
		Bond Interest Payable		5,000		
		Cash				6,000
		To record bond interest payment.				

This entry records $1,000 interest expense on the $100,000 of bonds that were outstanding for one month. Valley collected $5,000 from the bondholders on May 31 as accrued interest and is now returning it to them.

Bond Prices and Interest Rates

The price of a bond issue often differs from its face value. The amount a bond sells for above face value is a **premium.** The amount a bond sells for below face value is a **discount.** A difference between face value and issue price exists whenever the market rate of interest for similar bonds differs from the contract rate of interest on the bonds. The **market interest rate** (also called the *effective rate* or *yield*) is the minimum rate of interest that investors accept on bonds of a particular risk category. The higher the risk category, the higher the minimum rate of interest that investors accept. The **contract rate of interest** is also called the *stated, coupon,* or *nominal rate.* Firms state this rate in the bond indenture, print it on the face of each bond, and use it to determine the amount of cash paid each interest period. The market rate fluctuates from day to day, responding to factors such as the interest rate the Federal Reserve Board charges banks to borrow from it; government actions to finance the national debt; and the supply of, and demand for, money.

Market and contract rates of interest are likely to differ. Issuers must set the contract rate before the bonds are actually sold to allow time for such activities as printing the bonds. Assume, for instance, that the contract rate for a bond issue is set at 12%. If the market rate is equal to the contract rate, the bonds will sell at their face value. However, by the time the bonds are sold, the market rate could be higher or lower than the contract rate. As shown in Illustration 15.3, if the market rate is lower than the contract rate, the bonds will sell for more than their face value. Thus, if the market rate is 10% and the contract rate is 12%, the bonds will sell at a premium as the result of investors bidding up their price. However, if the market rate is higher than the contract rate, the bonds will sell for less than their face value. Thus, if the market rate is 14% and the contract rate is 12%, the bonds will sell at a discount. Investors are not interested in bonds bearing a contract rate less than the market rate unless the price is reduced. Selling bonds at a premium or a discount allows the purchasers of the bonds to earn the market rate of interest on their investment.

Computing long-term bond prices involves finding **present values** using compound interest. The appendix to this chapter explains the concepts of future value and present value. If you do not understand the present value concept, read the appendix before continuing with this section.

Buyers and sellers negotiate a price that yields the going rate of interest for bonds of a particular risk class. The price investors pay for a given bond issue is equal to the present value of the bonds. To compute present value, we discount the promised cash flows from the bonds—principal and interest—using the market, or effective, rate. We use the market rate because the bonds must yield at least this rate or investors are attracted to alternative investments. The life of the bonds is stated in interest (compounding) periods. The interest rate is the effective rate per interest period, which is found by dividing the annual rate by the number of times interest is paid per year. For example, if the annual rate is 12%, the semiannual rate would be 6%.

Illustration 15.3   Bond Premiums and Discounts

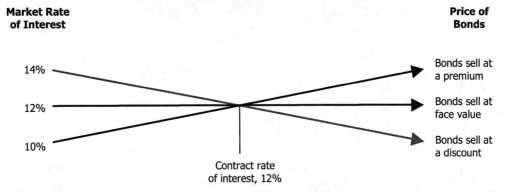

	Market Rate	Contract Rate
Bonds sell at a *premium* if Market rate < Contract rate	10%	12%
Bonds sell at a *face value* if Market rate = Contract rate	12%	12%
Bonds sell at a *discount* if Market rate > Contract rate	14%	12%

Market Rate of Interest

14%

12%

10%

Contract rate of interest, 12%

Price of Bonds

Bonds sell at a premium

Bonds sell at face value

Bonds sell at a discount

Real-World Example
On April 14, 2011, the 30-year Treasury Bond gained $8.50 per $1,000 bond, as the yield rate fell to 4.48% from 4.55%. Thus, when the bond price rises, its yield rate falls.

Issuers usually quote bond prices as percentages of face value—100 means 100% of face value, 97 means 97% of face value, and 103 means 103% of face value. For example, one hundred $1,000 face value bonds issued at 103 have a price of $103,000. Regardless of the issue price, at maturity the issuer of the bonds must pay the investor(s) the face value of the bonds.

Bonds Issued at Face Value   The following example illustrates the specific steps in computing the price of bonds. Assume Carr Company issues 12% bonds with a $100,000 face value to yield 12%. Dated and issued on June 30, 2012, the bonds call for semiannual interest payments on June 30 and December 31 and mature on June 30, 2015.[2] The bonds would sell at face value because they offer 12% and investors seek 12%. Potential purchasers have no reason to offer a premium or demand a discount. One way to prove the bonds would be sold at face value is by showing that their present value is $100,000:

	Cash Flow	X	Present Value Factor	=	Present Value
Principal of $100,000 due in six interest periods multiplied by present value factor for 6% from Table A.3 of the Appendix (end of text)	$100,000	X	0.70496	=	$ 70,496
Interest of $6,000 due at the end of six interest periods multiplied by present value factor for 6% from Table A.4 of the Appendix (end of text)	6,000	X	4.91732	=	29,504
Total price (present value)					$100,000

According to this schedule, investors who seek an effective rate of 6% per six-month period should pay $100,000 for these bonds. Notice that the same number of interest periods and semiannual interest rates occur in discounting both the principal and interest payments to their present values. The entry to record the sale of these bonds on June 30, 2012, debits Cash and credits Bonds Payable for $100,000.

---

[2]Bonds do not normally mature in such a short time; we use a three-year life for illustrative purposes only.

An Accounting Perspective

BUSINESS INSIGHT Some persons estimate that Social Security will be broke by the year 2037 unless changes are made. Therefore, you may want to set aside funds during your working career to provide for retirement.

Over the last 60 years, the inflation rate has averaged about 3.5% per year, treasury bills have averaged a little above 4% per year, corporate bonds have averaged a little over 5% per year, and stocks have averaged a little over 10% per year. Using the tables at the end of the text we can determine how much you would have at age 65 if you invested $2,000 each year for 45 years in treasury bills, corporate bonds, or stocks, beginning at age 20.

To do this calculation for treasury bills, for instance, we would first use Table A.2 to determine the future value of an annuity of $2,000 for 30 periods at 4% ($2,000 × 56.08494 = $112,170). (We would have used 45 periods, but the table only went up to 30 periods.) Then we would use Table A.1 to find the value of this lump sum of $112,170 for another 15 years at 4% ($112,170 × 1.80094 = $202,011). Then we cannot forget that we have another 15 years of $2,000 annuity to consider. Thus, we go back to Table A.2 and calculate the future value of an annuity of $2,000 for 15 periods at 4% ($2,000 × 20.02359 = $40,047). Then we add the $202,011 and the $40,047 to get the total future value of $242,058. (You would have invested $2,000 × 45 years = $90,000.) Would you be pleased? Not when you see what you could have had at age 65 if you invested in stocks.

If you had invested in corporate bonds at 5%, you would have $319,401. However, if you had invested in stocks at 10%, you would have $1,437,810 at age 65. Can you use the tables in the back of the text to verify these amounts?

Bonds Issued at a Discount Assume the $100,000, 12% Carr bonds are sold to yield a current market rate of 14% annual interest, or 7% per semiannual period. Carr computes the present value (selling price) of the bonds as follows:

	Cash Flow	X	Present Value Factor	=	Present Value
Principal of $100,000 due in six interest periods multiplied by present value factor for 7% from Table A.3 of the Appendix (end of text)	$100,000	X	0.66634	=	$66,634
Interest of $6,000 due at the end of six interest periods multiplied by present value factor for 7% from Table A.4 of the Appendix (end of text)	6,000	X	4.76654	=	28,599
Total price (present value)					$95,233

Note that in computing the present value of the bonds, Carr uses the actual $6,000 cash interest payment that will be made each period. The amount of cash the company pays as interest does not depend on the market interest rate. However, Carr uses the market rate per semiannual period—7%— to find interest factors in the tables.

The journal entry to record issuance of the bonds is:

Objective 6
Prepare journal entries for bonds issued at a discount or a premium.

2012				
June	30	Cash	95,233	
		Discount on Bonds Payable	4,767	
		Bonds Payable		100,000
		To record bonds issued at a discount.		

In recording the bond issue, Carr credits Bonds Payable for the face value of the debt. The company debits the difference between face value and price received to Discount on Bonds Payable, a contra account to Bonds Payable. Carr reports the bonds payable and discount on bonds payable in the balance sheet as follows:

Reinforcing Problem
E15-2 Compute bond interest expense; show how bond price was determined.

Long-term liabilities:
Bonds payable, 12%, due June 30, 2015 $100,000
Less: Discount on bonds payable   4,767 $95,233

The $95,233 is the carrying value, or *net liability,* of the bonds. Carrying value is the face value of the bonds minus any unamortized discount or plus any unamortized premium. The next section discusses unamortized premium on bonds payable.

Bonds Issued at a Premium   Assume that Carr issued the $100,000 face value of 12% bonds to yield a current market rate of 10%. The bonds would sell at a premium calculated as follows:

	Cash Flow	X	Present Value Factor	=	Present Value
Principal of $100,000 due in six interest periods multiplied by present value factor for 5% from Table A.3 of the Appendix (end of text)	$100,000	X	0.74622	=	$ 74,622
Interest of $6,000 due at the end of six interest periods multiplied by present value factor for 5% from Table A.4 of the Appendix (end of text)	6,000	X	5.07569	=	30,454
Total price (present value)					$105,076

The journal entry to record the issuance of the bonds is:

2012 June	30	Cash	105,076	
		Bonds Payable		100,000
		Premium on Bonds Payable		5,076
		To record bonds issued at a premium.		

The **carrying value** of these bonds at issuance is $105,076, consisting of the face value of $100,000 and the premium of $5,076. The premium is an adjunct account shown on the balance sheet as an addition to bonds payable as follows:

Long-term liabilities:
Bonds payable, 12%, due June 30, 2011 $100,000
Add: Premium on bonds Payable   5,076 $105,076

When a company issues bonds at a premium or discount, the amount of bond interest expense recorded each period differs from bond interest payments. A discount increases and a premium decreases the amount of interest expense. For example, if Carr issues bonds with a face value of $100,000 for $95,233, the total interest cost of borrowing would be $40,767: $36,000 (which is six payments of $6,000) plus the discount of $4,767. If the bonds had been issued at $105,076, the total interest cost of borrowing would be $30,924: $36,000 less the premium of $5,076. The $4,767 discount or $5,076 premium must be allocated or charged to the six periods that benefit from the use of borrowed money. Two methods are available for amortizing a discount or premium on bonds—the straight-line method and the effective interest rate method.

> **Discount/Premium Amortization**

The straight-line method records interest expense at a *constant amount;* the effective interest rate method records interest expense at a *constant rate. APB Opinion No. 21* states that the straight-line method may be used *only when it does not differ materially from the effective interest rate method.* In many cases, the differences are not material.

An Accounting Perspective

The Straight-Line Method   The **straight-line method of amortization** allocates an equal amount of discount or premium to each month the bonds are outstanding. The issuer calculates the amount by dividing the discount or premium by the total number of months from the date of issuance to the maturity date. For example, if it sells $100,000 face value bonds for $95,233, Carr would charge the $4,767 discount to interest expense at a rate of $132.42 per month (equal to $4,767 ÷ 36). Total discount amortization for six months would be $794.52, computed as follows: $132.42 × 6. Interest expense for each six-month period then would be $6,794.52, calculated as follows: $6,000 + ($132.42 × 6). The entry to record the expense on December 31, 2012, would be:

Reinforcing Problem
E15-3 Calculate interest using straight-line amortization.

2012				
Dec.	31	Bond Interest Expense	6,794.52	
		Cash		6,000.00
		Discount on Bonds Payable ($132.42 X 6)		794.52
		To record interest payment and discount amortization.		

By the maturity date, all of the discount would have been amortized.

To illustrate the straight-line method applied to a premium, recall that earlier Carr sold its $100,000 face value bonds for $105,076. Carr would amortize the $5,076 premium on these bonds at a rate of $141 per month, equal to $5,076 ÷ 36. The entry for the first period's semiannual interest expense on bonds sold at a premium is:

2012				
Dec.	31	Bond Interest Expense	5,154	
		Premium on Bonds Payable ($141 X 6)	846	
		Cash		6,000
		To record interest payable and premium amortization.		

By the maturity date, all of the premium would have been amortized.

The Effective Interest Rate Method   *APB Opinion No. 21* called for an amortization procedure called the **effective interest rate method**, or simply the **interest method**. Under the interest method, interest expense for any interest period is equal to the effective (market) rate of interest on the date of issuance times the carrying value of the bonds at the beginning of that interest period. Using the Carr example of 12% bonds with a face value of $100,000 sold to yield 14%, the carrying value at the beginning of the first interest period is the selling price of $95,233. Carr would record the interest expense for the first semiannual period as follows:

2012				
Dec.	31	Bond Interest Expense ($95,233 X 0.14 X 1/2)	6,666	
		Cash ($100,000 X 0.12 X 1/2)		6,000
		Discount on Bonds Payable		666
		To record discount amortization and interest payment.		

Note that interest expense is the carrying value times the effective interest rate. The cash payment is the face value times the contract rate. The discount amortized for the period is the difference between the two amounts.

After the preceding entry, the carrying value of the bonds is $95,899, or $95,233 + $666. Carr reduced the balance in the Discount on Bonds Payable account by $666 to $4,101, or $4,767 – $666. Assuming the accounting year ends on December 31, the entry to record the payment of interest for the second semiannual period on June 30, 2013, is:

2013				
June	30	Bond Interest Expense ($95,899 X 0.14 X 1/2)	6,713	
		Cash ($100,000 X 0.12 X 1/2)		6,000
		Discount on Bonds Payable		713
		To record discount amortization and interest payment.		

Carr can also apply the effective interest rate method to premium amortization. If the Carr bonds had been issued at $105,076 to yield 10%, the premium would be $5,076. The firm calculates interest expense in the same manner as for bonds sold at a discount. However, the entry would differ somewhat, showing a debit to the premium account. The entry for the first interest period is:

2012				
Dec.	31	Bond Interest Expense ($105,076 X 0.10 X 1/2)	5,254	
		Premium on Bonds Payable	746	
		Cash ($100,000 X 0.12 X 1/2)		6,000
		To record interest payment and premium amortization.		

After the first entry, the carrying value of the bonds is $104,330, or $105,076 – $746. The premium account now carries a balance of $4,330, or $5,076 – $746. The entry for the second interest period is:

2013				
June	30	Bond Interest Expense ($104,330 X 0.10 X 1/2)	5,216*	
		Premium on Bonds Payable	784	
		Cash ($100,000 X 0.12 X 1/2)		6,000
		To record interest payment and premium amortization.		

* Rounded down.

International Reporting
Under IFRS, companies may only use the effective interest method to amortize bond discounts and premiums; the straight-line method of amortization is not allowed. Also, U.S. GAAP requires that any discount or premium be amortized over the contractual life of the bond. However, the amortization period under IFRS is the *expected life* of the bond.

Reinforcing Problem
E15-4 Prepare entry to record interest payment.

An Accounting Perspective

BUSINESS INSIGHT The differences between the straight-line method and effective interest method for amortizing a bond discount can be seen in the following graphic. The carrying values (CV) start at the same point and end at the same point under both methods. The total interest expense is the same under both methods. However, the interest expense and amortization of bond discount are at a constant amount each period under the straight-line method, and they are at a constant rate under the effective interest rate method.

Straight-line — CV — **Effective Interest**

$ — Int Exp. — $

Time
Interest expense:
constant *amount*

Time
Interest expense:
constant *rate*

Discount and Premium Amortization Schedules   A discount amortization schedule (Illustration 15.4) and a premium amortization schedule (Illustration 15.5) aid in preparing entries for interest expense. Usually, companies prepare such schedules when they first issue bonds, often using computer programs designed for this purpose. The companies then refer to the schedules whenever they make journal entries to record interest. Note that in each period the amount of interest expense changes; interest expense gets larger when a discount is involved and smaller when a premium is involved. This fluctuation occurs because the carrying value to which a constant interest rate is applied changes each interest payment date. With a discount, carrying value increases; with a premium, it decreases. However, the actual cash paid as interest is always a constant amount determined by multiplying the bond's face value by the contract rate.

Recall that the issue price was $95,233 for the discount situation and $105,076 for the premium situation. The total interest expense of $40,767 for the discount situation in Illustration 15.4 is equal to $36,000 (which is six $6,000 payments) plus the $4,767 discount. This amount agrees with the earlier computation of total interest expense. In Illustration 15.5, total interest expense in the premium situation is $30,924, or $36,000 (which is six $6,000 payments) less the $5,076 premium. In both illustrations, at the maturity date the carrying value of the bonds is equal to the face value, because the discount or premium has been fully amortized.

Adjusting Entry for Partial Period   Illustrations 15.4 and 15.5 also would be helpful if Carr must accrue interest for a partial period. Instead of a calendar-year accounting period, assume the fiscal year of the bond issuer ends on August 31. Using the information provided in the premium amortization schedule (Illustration 15.5), the adjusting entry needed on August 31, 2012, is:

2012				
Aug.	31	Bond Interest Expense ($5,254 X (2/6))	1,751	
		Premium on Bonds Payable ($746 X (2/6))	249	
		Bond Interest Payable ($6,000 X (2/6))		2,000
		To record two months' accrued interest.		

Illustration 15.4   Discount Amortization Schedule for Bonds Payable

(A) Interest Payment Date	(B) Bond Interest Expense Debit (E X 0.14 X 1/2)	(C) Cash Credit ($100,000 X 0.12 X 1/2)	(D) Discount on Bonds Payable Credit (B – C)	(E) Carrying Value of Bonds Payable (previous balance in E + D)
Issue Price				$ 95,233
12/31/12	$ 6,666	$ 6,000	$ 666	95,899
6/30/13	6,713	6,000	713	96,612
12/31/13	6,763	6,000	763	97,375
6/30/14	6,816	6,000	816	98,191
12/31/14	6,873	6,000	873	99,064
6/30/15	6,936*	6,000	936	100,000
	$40,767	$36,000	$4,767	

* Includes rounding difference.

This entry records interest for two months, July and August, of the six-month interest period ending on December 31, 2012. The first line of Illustration 15.5 shows the interest expense and premium amortization for the six months. Thus, the previous entry records two-sixths (or one-third) of the amounts for this six-month period. Carr would record the remaining four months' interest when making the first payment on December 31, 2012. That entry reads:

Reinforcing Problem
P15-4 Compute price of bonds, prepare amortization schedule, journalize bond issuance, and accrue interest.

2012					
Dec.	31	Bond Interest Payable		2,000	
		Bond Interest Expense ($5,254 X (4/6))		3,503	
		Premium on Bonds Payable ($746 X 4/6)		497	
		Cash			6,000
		To record four months' interest expense and semiannual interest payment			

During the remaining life of the bonds, Carr would make similar entries for August 31 and December 31. The amounts would differ, however, because Carr uses the interest method of accounting for bond interest. The entry for each June 30 would be as indicated in Illustration 15.5.

Redeeming Bonds Payable

Bonds may be (1) paid at maturity, (2) called, or (3) purchased in the market and retired. Bonds may also be retired by being converted into stock. Each action is either a redemption of bonds or the extinguishment of debt. A company that pays its bonds at maturity would have already amortized any related discount or premium and paid the last interest payment. The only entry required at maturity would debit Bonds Payable and credit Cash for the face amount of the bonds as follows:

Objective 7
Prepare journal entries for bond redemptions and bond conversions.

2015					
June	30	Bonds Payable		100,000	
		Cash			100,000
		To pay bonds on maturity date.			

Illustration 15.5   Premium Amortization Schedule for Bonds Payable

(A) Interest Payment Date	(B) Bond Interest Expense Debit (E X 0.10 X 1/2)	(C) Cash Credit ($100,000 X 0.12 X 1/2)	(D) Premium on Bonds Payable Debit (B – C)	(E) Carrying Value of Bonds Payable (previous balance in E - D)
Issue Price				$105,076
12/31/12	$ 5,254	$6,000	$ 746	104,330
6/30/13	5,216*	6,000	784	103,546
12/31/13	5,177	6,000	823	102,723
6/30/14	5,136	6,000	864	101,859
12/31/14	5,093	6,000	907	100,952
6/30/15	5,048	6,000	952	100,000
	$30,924	$36,000	$5,076	

*Rounded down.

Reinforcing Problems
E15-5 Record call of bonds and payment of interest.
E15-6 Record accrued interest and purchase and retirement of bonds.

An issuer may redeem some or all of its outstanding bonds before maturity by calling them. The issuer may also purchase bonds in the market and retire them. In either case, the accounting is the same. Assume that on January 1, 2014, Carr calls bonds totaling $10,000 of the $100,000 face value bonds in Illustration 15.5 at 103, or $10,300. Even though accrued interest would be added to the price, assume that the interest due on this date has been paid. A look at the last column on the line dated 12/31/13 in Illustration 15.5 reveals that the carrying value of the bonds is $102,723, which consists of Bonds Payable of $100,000 and Premium on Bonds Payable of $2,723. Since 10% of the bond issue is being redeemed, Carr must remove 10% from each of these two accounts. The firm incurs a loss for the excess of the price paid for the bonds, $10,300, over their carrying value, $10,272. The required entry is:

2014					
Jan.	1	Bonds Payable		10,000	
		Premium on Bonds Payable ($2,723 ÷ 10)		272	
		Loss on Bond Redemption ($10,272 - $10,300)		28	
		Cash			10,300
		To record bonds redeemed.			

Gains and losses from voluntary early retirement of bonds are usually reported as part of ordinary income. In some cases, the gains and losses are reported as extraordinary items, if material. We report such extraordinary gains and losses in the income statement, net of their tax effects, as described in Chapter 13.

Serial Bonds

To avoid the burden of redeeming an entire bond issue at one time, companies sometimes issue **serial bonds** that mature over several dates. Assume that on June 30, 2007, Jasper Company issued $100,000 face value, 12% serial bonds at 100. Interest is payable each year on June 30 and December 31. A total of $20,000 of the bonds matures each year starting on June 30, 2012. Jasper has a calendar-year accounting period. Entries required for 2012 for interest expense and maturing debt are:

2012				
June	30	Bond Interest Expense ($100,000 X 0.12 X 1/2)	6,000	
		Cash		6,000
		To record interest payment.		
	30	Serial Bonds Payable	20,000	
		Cash		20,000
		To record retirement of serial debt.		
Dec.	31	Bond Interest Expense ($80,000 X 0.12 X 1/2)	4,800	
		Cash		4,800
		To record payment of semiannual interest expense.		

Reinforcing Problem
P15-6A Record serial bond transactions, and show financial reporting.

Note that Jasper calculates the interest expense for the last six months of 2012 only on the remaining outstanding debt ($100,000 original issue less the $20,000 that matured on June 30, 2012). Each year after the bonds maturing that year are retired, interest expense decreases proportionately. Jasper reports the $20,000 amount maturing the next year as a current liability on each year-end balance sheet. The remaining debt is a long-term liability.

Naturally, bond investors are concerned about the safety of their investments. They fear the company may default on paying the entire principal at the maturity date. This concern has led to provisions in some bond indentures that require companies to make periodic payments to a **bond redemption fund,** often called a **sinking fund.** The fund trustee uses these payments to redeem a stated amount of bonds annually and pay the accrued bond interest. The trustee determines which bonds to call and uses the cash deposited in the fund only to redeem these bonds and pay their accrued interest.

To illustrate, assume Hand Company has 12% coupon bonds outstanding that pay interest on March 31 and September 30 and were issued at face value. The bond indenture requires that Hand pay a trustee $53,000 each September 30. The entry for the payment to the trustee is:

Bond Redemption or Sinking Funds

Sept.	30	Sinking Fund	53,000	
		Cash		53,000
		To record payment to trustee of required deposit.		

The trustee calls $50,000 of bonds, pays for the bonds and accrued interest, and notifies Hand. The trustee also bills Hand for its fee and expenses incurred of $325. Assuming no interest has been recorded on these bonds for the period ended September 30, the entries are:

Sept.	30	Bonds Payable	50,000	
		Bond Interest Expense	3,000	
		Sinking Fund		53,000
		To record bond redemption and interest paid by trustee.		
	30	Sinking Fund Expense	325	
		Cash		325
		To record trustee fee and expenses.		

Reinforcing Problem
E15-7 Record sinking fund transactions.

If a balance exists in the Sinking Fund account at year-end, Hand includes it in a category labeled Investments or Other Assets on the balance sheet. Hand would describe the $50,000 of bonds that must be retired during the coming year as "Current maturity of long-term debt" and report it as a current liability on the balance sheet.

The existence of a sinking fund does not necessarily mean that the company has created a retained earnings appropriation entitled "Appropriation for Bonded Indebtedness." A sinking fund usually is contractual (required by the bond indenture), and an appropriation of retained earnings is simply an announcement by the board of directors that dividend payments will be limited over the term of the bonds. The former requires cash to be paid in to a trustee, and the latter restricts retained earnings available for dividends to stockholders. Also, even if the indenture does not require a sinking fund, the corporation may decide to (1) pay into a sinking fund and not appropriate retained earnings, (2) appropriate retained earnings and not pay into a sinking fund, (3) do neither, or (4) do both.

Convertible Bonds

A company may add to the attractiveness of its bonds by giving the bondholders the option to convert the bonds to shares of the issuer's common stock. In accounting for the conversions of **convertible bonds,** a company treats the carrying value of bonds surrendered as the capital contributed for shares issued.

Suppose a company has $10,000 face value of bonds outstanding. Each $1,000 bond is convertible into 50 shares of the issuer's $10 par value common stock. On May 1, when the carrying value of the bonds was $9,800, investors presented all of the bonds for conversion. The entry required is:

Reinforcing Problem
E15-8 Record conversion of bonds into capital stock.

May	1	Bonds Payable	10,000	
		Discount on Bonds Payable		200
		Common Stock ($10,000 ÷ $1,000 = 10 bonds;		
		10 bonds X 50 shares X $10 par)		5,000
		Paid-In Capital in Excess of Par Value—Common		4,800
		To record bonds converted to common stock.		

The entry eliminates the $9,800 book value of the bonds from the accounts by debiting Bonds Payable for $10,000 and crediting Discount on Bonds Payable for $200. It credits Common Stock for the par value of the 500 shares issued (500 shares × $10 par). The excess amount ($4,800) is credited to Paid-In Capital in Excess of Par Value—Common.

An Accounting Perspective

BUSINESS INSIGHT The Securities and Exchange Commission took action to protect the public against abusive telemarketing calls from sellers of municipal bonds. The residence of any person can only be called between 8 a.m. and 9 p.m., without their prior consent. Callers must clearly disclose the purpose of the call. Also, a centralized 'Do-not-call' list of people who do not wish to receive solicitations must be maintained and honored.

Source: 'SEC Approves Rule Governing Calls From Muni-Bond Sellers to Investors,' *The Wall Street Journal*, Friday, December 27, 2001, p. A2.

Bond Rating Services

Two of the leading bond rating services are Moody's Investors Service and Standard & Poor's Corporation. The bonds are rated as to their riskiness. The ratings used by these services are:

Objective 8
Describe the ratings used for bonds.

	Moody's	Standard & Poor's
Highest quality to upper medium	Aaa	AAA
	Aa	AA
	A	A
Medium to speculative	Baa	BBB
	Ba	BB
	B	B
Poor to lowest quality	Caa	CCC
	Ca	CC
	C	C
In default, value is questionable		DDD
		DD
		D

Normally, Moody's rates junk bonds at Ba or below and Standard & Poor's at BB or below. As a company's prospects change over time, the ratings of its outstanding bonds change because of the higher or lower probability that the company can pay the interest and principal on the bonds when due. A severe recession may cause many companies' bond ratings to decline.

Bond prices appear regularly in certain newspapers. For instance, *The Wall Street Journal* quoted IBM's bonds as follows:

Issue	Coupon	Maturity	Yield	Price	Change
IBM	7%	2013	6.6	113	–2

The bonds carry a coupon rate of 7%. The bonds mature in 2013. The current price is $113 per hundred, or $1,130.00 for a $1,000 bond. The price the preceding day was $115, since the change was –2. The current price yields a return to investors of 6.6%. As the market rate of interest changes from day to day, the market price of the bonds varies inversely. Thus, if the market rate of interest increases, the market price of bonds decreases, and vice versa.

Real World Example
A bond issued by Clear Channel Communications that was scheduled to mature on March 15, 2012, had a CCC bond rating according to Standard & Poor's on April 15, 2011.

BUSINESS INSIGHT Companies sometimes invest in the bonds of other companies. According to ASC 320 (covered in Chapter 14), investments in these bonds fall into three categories—trading securities, available-for-sale securities, or held-to-maturity securities. The bonds would be classified as trading securities if they were acquired principally for the purpose of selling them in the near future. If the bonds were to be held for a longer period of time, but not until maturity, they would be classified as available-for-sale securities. Bonds that will be held to maturity are classified as held-to-maturity securities. All trading securities are current assets. Available-for-sale securities are either current assets or long-term assets, depending on how long management intends to hold them. Discounts and premiums on bonds classified as trading and available-for-sale securities are not amortized because management does not know how long they will be held. Held-to-maturity securities are long-term assets. Discounts and premiums on bonds classified as held-to-maturity securities are amortized by the holder of the bonds in the same manner as for the issuer of the bonds. Further discussion of investments in bonds is reserved for an intermediate accounting course.

An Accounting Perspective

Analyzing and Using the Financial Results—Times Interest Earned Ratio

The **times interest earned ratio** (or *interest coverage ratio*) indicates the ability of a company to meet required interest payments when due. We calculate the ratio as follows:

$$\text{Times interest earned ratio} = \frac{\text{Income before interest and taxes (IBIT)}}{\text{Interest expense}}$$

Income before interest and taxes (IBIT), also called "earnings before interest and taxes (EBIT)," is the numerator because there would be no income taxes if interest expense is equal to or greater than IBIT. To find IBIT when the income statement is not complex, take net income and add back interest expense and taxes. However, in complex situations, when there are discontinued operations, changes in accounting principle, extraordinary items, interest revenue, and/or other similar items, analysts often use "operating income" to represent IBIT. The higher the ratio, the more comfortable creditors feel about receiving interest payments in the future.

Objective 9
Analyze and use the financial results—times interest earned ratio.

Reinforcing Problem
E15-9 Calculate times interest earned ratios for a company and comment.

An Ethical Perspective

Rawlings Furniture Company

The Rawlings brothers inherited 300,000 shares (30%) of the common stock of the Rawlings Furniture Company from their father, who had founded the company 55 years earlier. One brother served as president of the company, and the other two brothers served as vice presidents. The company, which produced a line of fine furniture sold nationwide, earned an average of $4 million per year. Located in Jamesville, New York, the company had provided steady employment for approximately 10% of the city's population. The city had benefited from the revenues the company attracted to the area and from the generous gifts provided by the father.

The remainder of the common stock was widely held and was traded in the over-the-counter market. No other stockholder held more than 4% of the stock. The stock had recently traded at $30 per share. The company has $10 million of 10% bonds outstanding, which mature in 15 years.

The brothers enjoyed the money they received from the company, but did not enjoy the work. They also were frustrated by the fact that they did not own a controlling interest (more than 50%) of the company. If they had a controlling interest, they could make important decisions without obtaining the agreement of the other stockholders.

With the assistance of a New York City brokerage house, the brothers decided to pursue a plan that could increase their wealth. The company would offer to buy back shares of common stock at $40 per share. These shares would then be canceled, and the Rawlings brothers would have a controlling interest. The stock buy-back would be financed by issuing 10-year, 14%, high-interest junk bonds. The brokerage house had located some financial institutions willing to buy the bonds. The interest payments on the junk bonds would be $3 million per year. The brothers thought the company could make these payments unless the country entered a recession. If need be, wage increases could be severely restricted or eliminated and the company's pension plan could be terminated. If the junk bonds could be paid at maturity, the brothers would own a controlling interest in what could be an extremely valuable company. If the interest payments could not be met or if the junk bonds were defaulted at maturity, the company could eventually be forced to liquidate. The risks are high, but so are the potential rewards.

If another buyer entered the picture at this point and bid an even higher amount for the stock, the brothers could sell their shares and exit the company. Two of the brothers hoped that another buyer might bid as much as $50 per share so they could sell their shares and pursue other interests. The changes a new buyer might make are unpredictable at this point.

The times interest earned ratios in a recent year for several companies (described in footnotes to the table) were as follows:

Company	Earnings Before Interest and Taxes (Millions)	Interest Expense (Millions)	Times Interest Earned Ratio
Ford Mother Company[a]	$19,136	$10,902	1.76
Proctor & Gamble Company[b]	6,258	722	8.67
AMR Corporation[c]	1,754	467	3.76
Dell Computer Corporation[d]	3,241	47	68.96
Hewlett-Packard Company[e]	4,882	257	19.00

[a]Ford Motor Company is the world's largest producer of trucks and the second largest producer of cars and trucks combined.
[b]Proctor and Gamble markets more than 300 brands to nearly five billion customers in over 140 countries.
[c]AMR's principal subsidiary is American Airlines.
[d]Dell is the world's largest direct computer systems company.
[e]Hewlett-Packard Company designs, manufactures, and services products and systems for measurement, computation, and communications.

You can see from these data that a great deal of variability exists in the times interest earned ratios for real companies. To judge the ability of companies to pay bond interest when due, bondholders would carefully examine other financial data as well.

Some companies that issued high-interest junk bonds in the 1980s defaulted on their interest payments and had to declare Chapter 11 bankruptcy or renegotiate payment terms with bondholders in the 1990s. Other companies with high-interest bonds issued new low-interest bonds and used the proceeds to retire the high-interest bonds.

Chapter 16 discusses the fourth major financial statement—the statement of cash flows, which we mentioned in Chapter 1. This statement shows the cash inflows and outflows from operating, investing, and financing activities.

Understanding the Learning Objectives

- A bond is a liability (with a maturity date) that bears interest that is deductible in computing both net income and taxable income.
- A stock is a unit of ownership on which a dividend is paid only if declared, and dividends are not deductible in determining net income or taxable income.
- Bonds may be secured or unsecured, registered or unregistered, callable, and/or convertible.

Objective 1
Describe the features of bonds and tell how bonds differ from shares of stock.

- Advantages include stockholders retaining control of the company, tax deductibility of interest, and possible creation of favorable financial leverage.
- Disadvantages include having to make a fixed interest payment each period, reduction in a company's ability to withstand a major loss, possible limitations on dividends and future borrowings, and possible reduction in earnings per share caused by unfavorable financial leverage.

Objective 2
List the advantages and disadvantages of financing with long-term debt and prepare examples showing how to employ financial leverage.

- If bonds are issued at face value on an interest date, no accrued interest is recorded.
- If bonds are issued between interest dates, accrued interest must be recorded.

Objective 3
Prepare journal entries for bonds issued at face value.

- If the market rate is lower than the contract rate, bonds sell for more than their face value, and a premium is recorded.
- If the market rate is higher than the contract rate, bonds sell for less than their face value, and a discount is recorded.

Objective 4
Explain how interest rates affect bond prices and what causes a bond to sell at a premium or a discount.

- The present value of the principal plus the present value of the interest payments is equal to the price of the bond.
- The contract rate of interest is used to determine the amount of future cash interest payments.
- The effective rate of interest is used to discount the future payment of principal and of interest back to the present value.

Objective 5
Apply the concept of present value to compute the price of a bond.

- When bonds are issued, Cash is debited, and Bonds Payable is credited. For bonds issued at a discount, Discount on Bonds Payable is also debited. For bonds issued at a premium, Premium on Bonds Payable is also credited. For bonds issued between interest dates, Bond Interest Payable is also credited.
- Any premium or discount must be amortized over the period the bonds are outstanding.
- Under the effective interest rate method, interest expense for any period is equal to the effective (market) rate of interest at date of issuance times the carrying value of the bond at the beginning of that interest period.
- Under the straight-line method of amortization, an equal amount of discount or premium is allocated to each month the bonds are outstanding.

Objective 6
Prepare journal entries for bonds issued at a discount or a premium.

| **Objective 7** |
| Prepare journal entries for bond redemptions and bond conversions. |

- When bonds are redeemed before they mature, a loss or gain on bond redemption may occur.
- A bond sinking fund might be required in the bond indenture.
- Bonds may be convertible into shares of stock. The carrying value of the bonds is the capital contributed for shares of stock issued.

| **Objective 8** |
| Describe the ratings used for bonds. |

- Bonds are rated as to their riskiness.
- The two leading bond rating services are Moody's Investors Services and Standard & Poor's Corporation.
- Each of these services has its own rating scale. For instance, the highest rating is Aaa (Moody's) and AAA (Standard & Poor's).

| **Objective 9** |
| Analyze and use the financial results—times interest earned ratio. |

- The times interest earned ratio indicates a company's ability to meet interest payments when due.
- The ratio is equal to income before interest and taxes (IBIT) divided by interest expense.

| **Objective 10** |
| Explain future value and present value concepts and make required calculations (Appendix). |

- The future value of an investment is the amount to which a sum of money invested today will grow in a stated time period at a specified interest rate.
- Present value is the current worth of a future cash receipt and is the reciprocal of future value. To discount future receipts is to bring them back to their present values.

APPENDIX   Future Value and Present Value

Managers apply the concepts of interest, future value, and present value in making business decisions. Therefore, accountants need to understand these concepts to properly record certain business transactions.

The Time Value of Money

| **Objective 11** |
| Explain future value and present value concepts and make required calculations. |

The concept of the *time value of money* stems from the logical reference for a dollar today rather than a dollar at any future date. Most individuals prefer having a dollar today rather than at some future date because (1) the risk exists that the future dollar will never be received; and (2) if the dollar is on hand now, it can be invested, resulting in an increase in total dollars possessed at that future date.

Most business decisions involve a comparison of cash flows in and out of the company. To be useful in decision making, such comparisons must be in dollars of the same point in time. That is, the dollars held now must be accumulated or rolled forward, or future dollars must be discounted or brought back to the present dollar value, before comparisons are valid. Such comparisons involve future value and present value concepts.

Future Value

The **future value or worth** of any investment is the amount to which a sum of money invested today grows during a stated period of time at a specified interest rate. The interest involved may be simple interest or compound interest. **Simple interest** is interest on principal only. For example, $1,000 invested today for two years at 12% simple interest grows to $1,240 since interest is $120 per year. The principal of $1,000, plus

2 × $120, is equal to $1,240. **Compound interest** is interest on principal and on interest of prior periods. For example, $1,000 invested for two years at 12% compounded annually grows to $1,254.40 as follows:

Principal or present value	$1,000.00
Interest, year 1 = $1,000 X 0.12 =	120.00
Value at end of year 1	$1,120.00
Interest, year 2 = $1,120 X 0.12 =	134.40
Value at end of year 2 (future value)	$1,254.40

In Illustration 15.6, we graphically portray these computations of future worth and show how $1,000 grows to $1,254.40 with a 12% interest rate compounded annually. The effect of compounding is $14.40—the interest in the second year that was based on the interest computed for the first year, or $120 × 0.12 = $14.40.

Interest tables ease the task of computing the future worth to which any invested amount will grow at a given rate for a stated period. An example is Table A.1 in the Appendix at the end of this text. To use the Appendix tables, first determine the number of compounding periods involved. A compounding period may be any length of time, such as a day, a month, a quarter, a half-year, or a year, but normally not more than a year. The number of compounding periods is equal to the number of years in the life of the investment times the number of compoundings per year. Five years compounded annually is five periods, five years compounded quarterly is 20 periods, and so on.

Second, determine the interest rate per compounding period. Interest rates are usually quoted in annual terms; in fact, federal law requires statement of the interest rate in annual terms in some situations. Divide the annual rate by the number of compounding periods per year to get the proper rate per period. Only with an annual compounding period will the annual rate be the rate per period. All other cases involve a lower rate. For example, if the annual rate is 12% and interest is compounded monthly, the rate per period (one month) will be 1%.

To use the tables, find the number of periods involved in the Period column. Move across the table to the right, stopping in the column headed by the Interest Rate per Period, which yields a number called a *factor*. The factor shows the amount to which an investment of $1 will grow for the periods and the rate involved. To compute the future worth of the investment, multiply the number of dollars in the given situation by this factor. For example, suppose your parents tell you that they will invest $8,000 at 12% for four years and give you the amount to which this investment grows if you graduate from college in four years. How much will you receive at the end of four years if the interest rate is 12% compounded annually? How much will you receive if the interest rate is 12% compounded quarterly?

To calculate these amounts, look at the end-of-text Appendix, Table A.1. In the intersection of the 4 period row and the 12% column, you find the factor 1.57352. Multiplying this factor by $8,000 yields $12,588.16, the answer to the first question. To answer the second question, look at the intersection of the 16 period row and the 3% column. The factor is 1.60471, and the value of your investment is $12,837.68. The more frequent compounding would add $12,837.68 – $12,588.16 = $249.52 to the value of your investment. The reason for this difference in amounts is that 12% compounded quarterly is a higher rate than 12% compounded annually.

An **annuity** is a series of equal cash flows (often called *rents*) spaced equally in time. The semiannual interest payments received on a bond investment are a common example of an annuity. Assume that $100 will be received at the end of each of the next three semiannual periods. The interest rate is 6% per semiannual period. Using Table A.1 in the Appendix, we find the future value of each of the $100 receipts as follows:

Future Value of an Annuity

Illustration 15.6   Compound Interest and Future Value

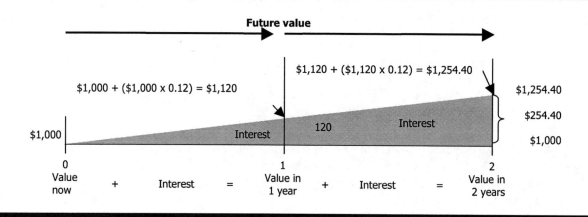

Future value (after three periods) of $100
received at the end of the—

First period: 1.12360 X $100 = $112.36
Second period: 1.06000 X   100 =   106.00
Third period: 1.00000 X   100 =   100.00
Total future value $318.36

Such a procedure would become quite tedious if the annuity consisted of many receipts. Fortunately, tables are available to calculate the total future value directly. See the Appendix, Table A.2. For the annuity just described, you can identify one single factor by looking at the 3 period row and 6% column. The factor is 3.18360 (the sum of the three factors shown above), and when multiplied by $100, yields $318.36, which is the same answer. In Illustration 15.7, we graphically present the future value of an annuity.

Present Value

Present value is the current worth of a future cash receipt and is the reciprocal of future value. In future value, we calculate the future value of a sum of money possessed now. In present value, we calculate the current worth of rights to future cash receipts possessed now. We discount future receipts by bringing them back to their present values.

Reinforcing Problem
E15-10 Determine present value of a lump sum payment (based on appendix).

Assume that you have the right to receive $1,000 in one year. If the appropriate interest rate is 12% compounded annually, what is the present value of this $1,000 future cash receipt? You know that the present value is less than $1,000 because $1,000 due in one year is not worth $1,000 today. You also know that the $1,000 due in one year is equal to some amount, P, plus interest on P at 12% for one year. Thus, $P + 0.12P = $1,000$, or $1.12P = $1,000$. Dividing $1,000 by 1.12, you get $892.86; this amount is the present value of your future $1,000. If the $1,000 was due in two years, you would find its present value by dividing $892.86 by 1.12, which equals $797.20. Portrayed graphically, present value looks similar to future value, except for the direction of the arrows (Illustration 15.8).

Table A.3 (end-of-text Appendix) contains present value factors for combinations of a number of periods and interest rates. We use Table A.3 in the same manner as Table A.1. For example, the present value of $1,000 due in four years at 16% compounded annually is $552.29, computed as $1,000 × 0.55229. The 0.55229 is the present value factor found in the intersection of the 4 period row and the 16% column.

Illustration 15.7   Future Value of an Annuity

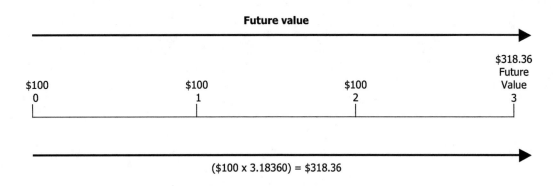

Illustration 15.8   Compound Interest and Present Value

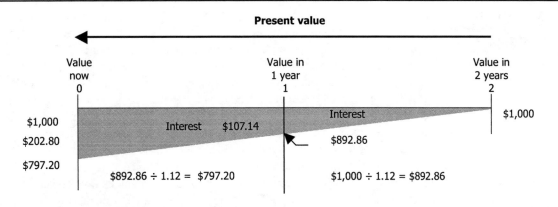

As another example, suppose that you wish to have $4,000 in three years to pay for a vacation in Europe. If your investment increases at a 20% rate compounded quarterly, how much should you invest now? To find the amount, you would use the present value factor found in Table A.3, 12 period row, 5% column. This factor is 0.55684, which means that an investment of about 56 cents today would grow to $1 in 12 periods at 5% per period. To have $4,000 at the end of three years, you must invest 4,000 times this factor (0.55684), or $2,227.36.

The semiannual interest payments on a bond are a common example of an annuity. As an example of calculating the present value of an annuity, assume that $100 is received at the end of each of the next three semiannual periods. The interest rate is 6% per semiannual period. By using Table A.3 (Appendix), you can find the present value of each of the three $100 payments as follows:

Present Value of an Annuity

Present value of $100 due in:
1 period: 0.94340 X $100	=	$ 94.34
2 period: 0.89000 X 100	=	89.00
3 period: 0.83962 X 100	=	83.96
Total present value		$267.30

Illustration 15.9   Present Value of an Annuity

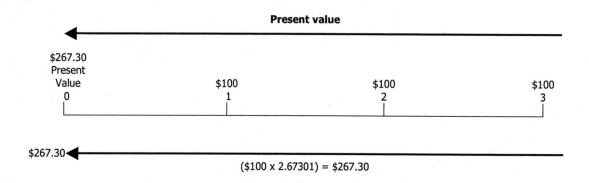

Present value

$267.30
Present
Value
0

$100
1

$100
2

$100
3

$267.30 ◄

($100 x 2.67301) = $267.30

Reinforcing Problems
E15-11 Determine present value for an annuity (based on appendix).
E15-12 Determine present value for lottery winnings (based on appendix).
E15-13 Determine future value of an annuity (based on appendix).

Such a procedure could become quite tedious if the annuity consisted of a large number of payments. Fortunately, tables are also available showing the present values of an annuity of $1 per period for varying interest rates and periods. See the end-of-text Appendix, Table A.4. For the annuity just described, you can obtain a single factor from the table to represent the present value of an annuity of $1 per period for three (semiannual) periods at 6% per (semiannual) period. This factor is 2.67301; it is equal to the sum of the present value factors for $1 due in one period, $1 in two periods, and $1 in three periods found in the Appendix, Table A.3. When this factor is multiplied by $100, the number of dollars in each payment, it yields the present value of the annuity, $267.30. In Illustration 15.9, we graphically present the present value of this annuity and show how to find the present value of the three $100 cash flows by multiplying the $100 by a present value of an annuity factor, 2.67301.

Suppose you won a lottery that awarded you a choice of receiving $10,000 at the end of each of the next five years or $35,000 cash today. You believe you can earn interest on invested cash at 15% per year. Which option should you choose? To answer the question, compute the present value of an annuity of $10,000 per period for five years at 15%. The present value is $33,521.60, or $10,000 × 3.35216. You should accept the immediate payment of $35,000 since it has the larger present value.

Demonstration Problem

Jackson Company issued $100,000 face value of 15%, 20-year junk bonds on April 30, 2012. The bonds are dated April 30, 2012, call for semiannual interest payments on April 30 and October 31, and are issued to yield 16% (8% per period).

Required ➡

a. Compute the amount received for the bonds.

b. Prepare an amortization schedule. Enter data in the schedule for only the first two interest periods. Use the effective interest rate method.

c. Prepare journal entries to record issuance of the bonds, the first six months' interest expense on the bonds, the adjustment needed on December 31, 2012 (assuming Jackson's accounting year ends on that date), and the second six months' interest expense on April 30, 2013.

Solution to Demonstration Problem

a.   Price received:

Present value of principal: $100,000 X 0.04603
(see Appendix, Table A.3, 40 period row, 8% column) $ 4,603
Present value of interest: $7,500 X 11.92461
(see Appendix, Table A.4, 40 period row, 8% column)   89,435
Total $94,038

b.

(A) Interest Payment Date	(B) Bond Interest Expense Debit (E X 0.16 X 1/2)	(C) Cash Credit ($100,000 X 0.15 X 1/2)	(D) Discount on Bonds Payable Credit (B — C)	(E) Carrying Value of Bonds Payable (previous balance in E + D)
Issue price				$94,038
10/31/12	$7,523	$7,500	$23	94,061
4/30/13	7,525	7,500	25	94,086

c.

2012				
Apr.	30	Cash	94,038	
		Discount on Bonds Payable	5,962	
		Bonds Payable		100,000
		Issued $100,000 face value of 20-year, 15% bonds to yield 16%.		
Oct.	31	Bond Interest Expense	7,523	
		Discount on Bonds Payable		23
		Cash		7,500
		Paid semiannual bond interest expense.		
Dec.	31	Bond Interest Expense ($7,525 X (1/3))	2,508	
		Discount on Bonds Payable		8
		Bond Interest Payable ($7,500 X (1/3))		2,500
		To record accrual of two months' interest expense.		
2013				
Apr.	30	Bond Interest Payable	2,500	
		Bond Interest Expense ($7,525 X (2/3))	5,017	
		Discount on Bonds Payable		17
		Cash		7,500
		Paid semiannual bond interest expense.		

New Terms

Annuity   A series of equal cash flows spaced in time. *599*

Bearer bond   See *unregistered bond.*

Bond   A long-term debt, or liability, owed by its issuer. A *bond certificate,* a negotiable instrument, is the formal, physical evidence of the debt owed. *577*

Bond indenture   The contract or loan agreement under which bonds are issued. *578*

Bond redemption (or sinking) fund   A fund used to bring about the gradual redemption of a bond issue. *593*

Callable bond   A bond that gives the issuer the right to call (buy back) the bond before its maturity date. *579*

Call premium   The price paid in excess of face value that the issuer of bonds must pay to redeem (call) bonds before their maturity date. *579*

Carrying value (of bonds)   The face value of bonds minus any unamortized discount or plus any unamortized premium. Sometimes referred to as net liability on the bonds. *587*

Compound interest   Interest calculated on the principal and on interest of prior periods. *599*

Contract rate of interest   The interest rate printed on the bond certificates and specified on the bond indenture; also called the stated, coupon, or nominal rate. *584*

Convertible bond   A bond that may be exchanged for shares of stock of the issuing corporation at the bondholders' option. *580, 594*

Coupon bond   A bond not registered as to interest; it carries detachable coupons that are to be clipped and presented for payment of interest due. *579*

Debenture bond   An unsecured bond backed only by the general creditworthiness of its issuer. *579*

Discount (on bonds)   Amount a bond sells for below its face value. *584*

Effective interest rate method (interest method)   A procedure for calculating periodic interest expense (or revenue) in which the first period's interest is computed by multiplying the carrying value of bonds payable (bond investments) by the market rate of interest at the issue date. The difference between computed interest expense (revenue) and the interest paid (received), based on the contract rate times face value, is the discount or premium amortized for the period. Computations for subsequent periods are based on the carrying value at the beginning of the period. *588*

Face value   Principal amount of a bond. *577*

Favorable financial leverage   An increase in EPS and the rate of return on stockholders' equity resulting from earning a higher rate of return on borrowed funds than the fixed cost of such funds. Unfavorable financial leverage results when the cost of borrowed funds exceeds the income they generate, resulting in decreased income to stockholders. *580, 581*

Future value or worth   The amount to which a sum of money invested today will grow during a stated period of time at a specified interest rate. *598*

Interest method   See *effective interest rate method.*

Junk bonds   High-interest rate, high-risk bonds; many were issued in the 1980s to finance corporate restructurings. *580*

Market interest rate   The minimum rate of interest investors will accept on bonds of a particular risk category. Also called effective rate or yield. *584*

Mortgage   A legal claim (lien) on specific property that gives the bondholder the right to possess the pledged property if the company fails to make required payments. A bond secured by a mortgage is called a mortgage bond. *579*

Premium (on bonds)   Amount a bond sells for above its face value. *584*

Present value   The current worth of a future cash receipt(s); computed by discounting future receipts at a stipulated interest rate. *584, 600*

Registered bond   A bond with the owner's name on the bond certificate and in the register of bond owners kept by the bond issuer or its agent, the registrar. *579*

Secured bond   A bond for which a company has pledged specific property to ensure its payment. *579*

Serial bonds   Bonds in a given bond issue with maturities spread over several dates. *579, 592*

Simple interest   Interest on principal only. *598*

Sinking fund   See Bond redemption fund.

Stock warrant   A right that allows the bondholder to purchase shares of common stock at a fixed price for a stated period of time. Warrants issued with long-term debt may be detachable or nondetachable. *580*

Straight-line method of amortization   A procedure that, when applied to bond discount or premium, allocates an equal amount of discount or premium to each period in the life of a bond. *588*

Term bond   A bond that matures on the same date as all other bonds in a given bond issue. *579*

Times interest earned ratio   Income before interest and taxes (IBIT) divided by interest expense. In complex situations, "operating income" is often used to represent IBIT. *595*

Trading on the equity   A company using its stockholders' equity as a basis for securing funds on which it pays a fixed return. *580*

Trustee   Usually a bank or trust company appointed to represent the bondholders and to enforce the provisions of the bond indenture against the issuer. *578*

Underwriter   An investment company or a banker that performs many tasks for the bond issuer in issuing bonds; may also guarantee the issuer a fixed price for the bonds. *578*

Unfavorable financial leverage   Results when the cost of borrowed funds exceeds the revenue they generate; it is the reverse of favorable financial leverage. *581*

Unregistered (bearer) bond   Ownership transfers by physical delivery. *579*

Unsecured bond   A debenture bond, or simply a debenture. *579*

Self-Test

True-False
Indicate whether each of the following statements is true or false.

1. An unsecured bond is called a debenture bond.
2. Callable bonds may be called at the option of the holder of the bonds.
3. Favorable financial leverage results when borrowed funds are used to increase earnings per share of common stock.
4. If the market rate of interest exceeds the contract rate, the bonds are issued at a discount.
5. The straight-line method of amortization is the recommended method.

Multiple-Choice
Select the best answer for each of the following questions.

1. Harner Company issued $100,000 of 12% bonds on March 1, 2012. The bonds are dated January 1, 2012, and were issued at 96 plus accrued interest. The entry to record the issuance would be:

   a.

Cash	98,000	
Discount on Bonds Payable	4,000	
Bonds Payable		100,000
Bonds Interest Payable		2,000

   b.

Cash	102,000	
Bonds Payable		100,000
Bond Interest Payable		2,000

   c.

Cash	96,000	
Discount on Bonds Payable	4,000	
Bonds Payable		100,000

   d. None of the above.

2. If the bonds in (1) had been issued at 104, the entry to record the issuance would have been:

   a.

Cash	104,000	
Bonds Payable		100,000
Premium on Bonds Payable		4,000

   b.

Cash	102,000	
Bonds Payable		100,000
Bond Interest Payable		2,000

   c.

Cash	106,000	
Bonds Payable		100,000
Premium on Bonds Payable		4,000
Bonds Interest Payable		2,000

   d. None of the above.

3. On January 1, 2012, the Alvarez Company issued $400,000 face value of 8%, 10-year bonds for cash of $328,298, a price to yield 11%. The bonds pay interest semiannually and mature on January 1, 2022. Using the effective interest rate method, the bond interest expense for the first six months of 2012 would be:

   a. $36,113.
   b. $18,056.
   c. $32,000.
   d. $16,000.

4. If the straight-line amortization method had been used in (3), the interest expense for the first six months would have been:
   a. $39,170.
   b. $32,000.
   c. $18,000.
   d. $19,585.

5. Assume a company has net income of $100,000, income tax expense of $40,000, and interest expense of $20,000. The times interest earned ratio is:
   a. 5 times.
   b. 7 times.
   c. 8 times.
   d. 9 times.

Now turn to page 613 to check your answers.

Questions

1. What are the advantages of obtaining long-term funds by the issuance of bonds rather than additional shares of capital stock? What are the disadvantages?
2. What is a bond indenture? What parties are usually associated with it? Explain why.
3. Explain what is meant by the terms coupon, callable, convertible, and debenture.
4. What is meant by the term *trading on the equity?*
5. When bonds are issued between interest dates, why should the issuing corporation receive cash equal to the amount of accrued interest (accrued since the preceding interest date) in addition to the issue price of the bonds?
6. Why might it be more accurate to describe a sinking fund as a bond redemption fund?
7. Indicate how each of the following items should be classified in a balance sheet on December 31, 2011.

   a. Cash balance in a sinking fund.
   b. Accrued interest on bonds payable.
   c. Debenture bonds payable due in 2021.
   d. Premium on bonds payable.
   e. First-mortgage bonds payable, due July 1, 2012.
   f. Discount on bonds payable.
   g. First National Bank—Interest account.
   h. Convertible bonds payable due in 2014.
8. Why is the effective interest rate method of computing periodic interest expense considered theoretically preferable to the straight-line method?
9. Why would an investor whose intent is to hold bonds to maturity pay more for the bonds than their face value?
10. Of what use is the times interest earned ratio?

Exercises

Exercise 15-1
Record issuance of bonds at face value, adjusting entry, and payment of interest
(L.O. 3)

On September 30, 2012, Domingo's Construction Company issued $120,000 face value of 12%, 10-year bonds dated August 31, 2012, at 100, plus accrued interest. Interest is paid semiannually on February 28 and August 31. Domingo's accounting year ends on December 31. Prepare journal entries to record the issuance of these bonds, the accrual of interest at year-end, and the payment of the first interest coupon.

Exercise 15-2
Compute bond interest expense; show how bond price was determined
(L.O. 4-6)

On December 31, 2011, East Lansing Office Equipment Company issued $1,600,000 face value of 8%, 10-year bonds for cash of $1,400,605, a price to yield 10%. The bonds pay interest semiannually and mature on December 31, 2021.

a. State which is higher, the market rate of interest or the contract rate.
b. Compute the bond interest expense for the first six months of 2012, using the interest method.
c. Show how the $1,400,605 price must have been determined.

Exercise 15-3
Calculate interest expense using straight-line amortization (L.O. 6)

Compute the annual interest expense on the bonds in Exercise 15–2, assuming the bond discount is amortized using the straight-line method.

After recording the payment of the interest coupon due on June 30, 2012, the accounts of Myrtle Beach Sailboat, Inc., showed Bonds Payable of $300,000 and Premium on Bonds Payable of $10,572. Interest is payable semiannually on June 30 and December 31. The five-year, 12% bonds have a face value of $300,000 and were originally issued to yield 10%. Prepare the journal entry to record the payment of interest on December 31, 2012. Use the interest method. (Round all amounts to the nearest dollar.)

Exercise 15-4
Prepare entry to record interest payment (L.O. 6)

On June 30, 2012 (a semiannual interest payment date), Holiday Rollerblade Company redeemed all of its $400,000 face value of 10% bonds outstanding by calling them at 106. The bonds were originally issued on June 30, 2008, at 100. Prepare the journal entry to record the payment of the interest and the redemption of the bonds on June 30, 2012.

Exercise 15-5
Record call of bonds and payment of interest (L.O. 7)

On August 31, 2011, as part of the provisions of its bond indenture, Caribbean Cruise Line, Inc., acquired $480,000 of its outstanding bonds on the open market at 96 plus accrued interest. These bonds were originally issued at face value and carry a 12% interest rate, payable semiannually. The bonds are dated November 30, 2004, and pay semiannual interest on May 31 and November 30. Prepare the journal entries required to record the accrual of the interest to the acquisition date on the bonds acquired and the acquisition of the bonds.

Exercise 15-6
Record accrued interest and purchase and retirement of bonds (L.O. 7)

Cleveland Heating Systems, Inc., is required to make a deposit of $18,000 plus semiannual interest expense of $540 on October 31, 2011, to the trustee of its sinking fund so that the trustee can redeem $18,000 of the company's bonds on that date. The bonds were issued at 100. Prepare the journal entries required on October 31 to record the sinking fund deposit, the bond retirement, payment of interest (due on that date), and payment of trustee expenses, assuming the latter is $100.

Exercise 15-7
Record sinking fund transactions (L.O. 7)

After interest was paid on September 30, 2012, $60,000 face value of Miami Video Rentals, Inc., outstanding bonds were converted into 8,000 shares of the company's $5 par value common stock. Prepare the journal entry to record the conversion, assuming the bonds were issued at 100.

Exercise 15-8
Record conversion of bonds into capital stock (L.O. 7)

A recent annual report of Target Corporation showed the following amounts as of the dates indicated

Exercise 15-9
Calculate times interest earned ratios for a company and comment (L.O. 9)

	Year Ended January 31		
	2009	2008	2007
Earnings before interest (and taxes) (millions)	$4,673	$4,402	$5,272
Interest expense (millions)	804	894	668

Calculate the times interest earned ratio for each year and comment on the results.

What is the present value of a lump-sum payment of $20,000 due in five years if the market rate of interest is 10% per year (compounded annually) and the present value of $1 due in five periods at 10% is 0.62092?

Exercise 15-10
Determine present value of a lump-sum payment (based on appendix) (L.O. 10)

What is the present value of a series of semiannual payments of $10,000 due at the end of each six months for the next five years if the market rate of interest is 10% per year and the present value of an annuity of $1 for 10 periods at 5% is 7.72173?

Exercise 15-11
Determine present value of an annuity (based on appendix) (L.O. 10)

Joe Mordino bought a ticket in the Georgia lottery for $1, hoping to strike it rich. To his amazement, he won $4,000,000. Payment was to be received in equal amounts at the end of each of the next 20 years. Mordino heard from relatives and friends he had not heard from in years. They all wanted to renew their relationship with this new millionaire. Federal and state income taxes were going to be about 40% (36% for federal and 4% for state) on each year's income from the lottery check. The discount rate to use in all present value calculations is 12%.

Exercise 15-12
Determine present value of lottery winnings (based on appendix) (L.O. 10)

a. How much will Mordino actually receive after taxes each year?

b. Is Mordino a multimillionaire according to the present value of his cash inflow after taxes?

c. What is the present value of the net amount the state has to pay out? Remember that the state gets part of the money back in the form of taxes.

Exercise 15-13
Determine future value of an annuity (based on appendix) (L.O. 10)

After Joe Mordino won $4,000,000 in the Georgia lottery, he decided to purchase $10,000 of lottery tickets at the end of each year for the next 20 years. He was hoping to hit the lottery again, but he never did. If the state can earn 12% on ticket revenue received, how much will the annuity of $10,000 from Mordino grow to by the end of 20 years?

Problems

Problem 15-1
Record issuance of bonds and payment of interestl (L.O. 3)

On June 1, 2011, Economy Auto Parts, Inc., issued $180,000 of 10-year, 16% bonds dated Apri l1, 2011, at 100. Interest on bonds is payable semiannually on presentation of the appropriate coupon. All of the bonds are of $1,000 denomination. The company's accounting period ends on June 30, with semiannual statements prepared on December 31 and June 30. The interest payment dates are April 1 and October 1.

All of the first coupons on the bonds are presented to the company's bank and paid on October 2, 2011. All but two of the second coupons are similarly received and paid on April 1, 2012.

Required ➲ Prepare all necessary journal entries for these transactions through April 1, 2012, including the adjusting entry needed at June 30, 2011.

Problem 15-2
Compute two prices on bond issue and first periodÕs interest (L.O. 5, 6)

Ecological Water Filtration, Inc., is going to issue $400,000 face value of 10%, 15-year bonds. The bonds are dated June 30, 2011, call for semiannual interest payments, and mature on June 30, 2026.

a. Compute the price investors should offer if they seek a yield of 8% on these bonds. Also, compute the first six months' interest, assuming the bonds are issued at this price. Use the interest method and calculate all amounts to the nearest dollar.

b. Repeat part a, assuming investors seek a yield of 12%.

Problem 15-3
Record bond interest expense and interest accrual for partial period (L.O. 6)

On July 1, 2011, South Carolina Table Company issued $600,000 face value of 10%, 10-year bonds. The bonds call for semiannual interest payments and mature on July 1, 2021. The company received cash of $531,180, a price that yields 12%.

Assume that the company's fiscal year ends on March 31. Prepare journal entries (to the nearest dollar) to record the bond interest expense on January 1, 2012, and the adjustment needed on March 31, 2012, using the interest method. Calculate all amounts to the nearest dollar.

Problem 15-4
Compute price of bonds, prepare amortization schedule, journalize bond issuance, and accrue interest (L.O. 5, 6)

Storall Company issued $200,000 face value of 16%, 20-year junk bonds on July 1, 2012. The bonds are dated July 1, 2012, call for semiannual interest payments on July 1 and January 1, and were issued to yield 12% (6% per period).

a. Compute the amount received for the bonds.

b. Prepare an amortization schedule similar to that in Illustration 15.5. Enter data in the schedule for only the first two interest periods. Use the interest method.

c. Prepare journal entries to record issuance of the bonds, the first six months' interest expense on the bonds, and the adjustment needed on May 31, 2013, assuming the company's fiscal year ends on that date.

Kelly Furniture Company issued $400,000 face value of 18%, 20-year junk bonds on October 1, 2011. The bonds are dated October 1, 2011, call for semiannual interest payments on April 1 and October 1, and are issued to yield 16% (8% per period).

a. Compute the amount received for the bonds.
b. Prepare an amortization schedule similar to that in Illustration 15.5. Enter data in the schedule for only the first two interest periods. Use the interest method and make all calculations to the nearest dollar.
c. Prepare entries to record the issuance of the bonds, the first six months' interest on the bonds, and the adjustment needed on June 30, 2012, assuming the company's fiscal year ends on that date.

Problem 15-5
Compute price of bonds; prepare amortization schedule; journalize bond issuance; payment of first periodŌs interest, and accrual of partial periodŌs interest (L.O. 5, 6)

Houston Clothing Company issued $600,000 of 12% serial bonds on July 1, 2011, at face value. The bonds are dated July 1, 2011; call for semiannual interest payments on July 1 and January 1; and mature at the rate of $120,000 per year, with the first maturity date falling on July 1, 2012. The company's accounting period ends on September 30.

Prepare journal entries to record the interest payment of July 1, 2012; the maturing of $120,000 of bonds on July 1, 2012; and the adjusting entry needed on September 30, 2012. Also, show how the bonds would be presented in the company's balance sheet for September 30, 2012.

Problem 15-6
Record serial bond transactions, and show financial reporting (L.O. 7)

Required

Alternate Problems

On December 1, 2011, New Jersey Waste Management Company issued $300,000 of 10-year, 9% bonds dated July 1, 2011, at 100. Interest on the bonds is payable semiannually on July 1 and January 1. All of the bonds are registered. The company's accounting period ends on March 31. Quarterly financial statements are prepared.

The company deposits a sum of money sufficient to pay the semiannual interest on the bonds in a special checking account in First National Bank and draws interest payment checks on this account. The deposit is made the day before the checks are drawn.

Prepare journal entries to record the issuance of the bonds; the December 31 adjusting entry; the January 1, 2012, interest payment; and the adjusting entry needed on March 31, 2012, to prepare quarterly financial statements.

Problem 15-1A
Record issuance of bonds, payment of bonds, payment of interest, and partial period interest accrual (L.O. 3)

Required

Safe Toy Company is seeking to issue $800,000 face value of 10%, 20-year bonds. The bonds are dated June 30, 2011, call for semiannual interest payments, and mature on June 30, 2031.

a. Compute the price investors should offer if they seek a yield of 8% on these bonds. Also, compute the first six months' interest assuming the bonds are issued at that price. Use the interest method and calculate all amounts to the nearest dollar.
b. Repeat part a assuming investors seek a yield of 12%.

Problem 15-2A
Compute two prices for bond issue and first periodŌs interest (L.O. 5, 6)

On July 1, 2011, Tick-Tock Clock Company issued $100,000 face value of 8%, 10-year bonds. These bonds call for semiannual interest payments and mature on July 1, 2021. The company received cash of $87,538, a price that yields 10%.

Assume that the company's fiscal year ends on March 31. Prepare journal entries to record the bond interest expense on January 1, 2012, and the adjustment needed on March 31, 2012, using the interest method. Calculate all amounts to the nearest dollar.

Problem 15-3A
Record bond interest expense and interest accrual for partial period (L.O. 6)

Creative Web Page issued $600,000 face value of 15%, 20-year bonds on October 1, 2012. The bonds are dated October 1, 2012, call for semiannual interest payments on April 1 and October 1, and are issued to yield 16% (8% per period).

a. Compute the amount received for the bonds.

Problem 15-4A
Compute price of bonds; prepare amortization schedule; journalize bond issuance and accrue interest (L.O. 5, 6)

Required ➡   **b.** Prepare an amortization schedule similar to that in Illustration 15.4. Enter data in the schedule for only the first two interest periods. Use the interest method.

   c. Prepare journal entries to record issuance of the bonds, the first six months' interest expense on the bonds, and the adjustment needed on May 31, 2013, assuming Creative Web Page's fiscal year ends on that date.

Problem 15-5A
Compute price of bonds; prepare amortization schedule; journalize bond issuance, and record two interest payments (L.O. 5, 6)

Goodhew Software Systems, Inc., issued $100,000 face value of 10%, 20-year bonds on July 1, 2011. The bonds are dated July 1, 2011, call for semiannual interest payments on July 1 and January 1, and are issued to yield 12% (6% per period).

➡   **a.** Compute the amount received for the bonds.

   b. Prepare an amortization schedule similar to that in Illustration 15.4. Enter data in the schedule for only the first two interest periods. Use the interest method and calculate all amounts to the nearest dollar.

   c. Prepare entries to record the issuance of the bonds, the first six months' interest on the bonds, and the adjustment needed on June 30, 2012, assuming Goodhew's fiscal year ends on that date.

Problem 15-6A
Record serial bond transactions, and show financial reporting (L.O. 7)

Western Solar Energy Company issued $400,000 of 12% bonds on July 1, 2011, at face value. The bonds are dated July 1, 2011, call for semiannual payments on July 1 and January 1, and mature at the rate of $40,000 per year on July 1, beginning in 2012. The company's accounting period ends on September 30.

Required ➡   **a.** Prepare journal entries to record the interest expense and payment for the six months ending July 1, 2012; the maturing of the bonds on July 1, 2012; and the adjusting entries needed on September 30, 2012.

   b. Show how the bonds would be presented in the company's balance sheet for September 30, 2012.

Beyond the Numbers—Critical Thinking

Business Decision Case 15-1
Analyze two financing proposals; decide whether investment should be made (L.O. 2)

A company is trying to decide whether to invest $2 million on plant expansion and $1 million to finance a related increase in inventories and accounts receivable. The $3 million expansion is expected to increase business volume substantially. Profit forecasts indicate that income from operations will rise from $1.6 million to $2.4 million. The income tax rate will be about 40%. Net income last year was $918,000. Interest expense on debt now outstanding is $70,000 per year. There are 200,000 shares of common stock currently outstanding.

The $3 million needed can be obtained in two alternative ways:

1. Finance entirely by issuing additional shares of common stock at an expected issue price of $75 per share.
2. Finance two-thirds with bonds, one-third with additional stock. The bonds would have a 20-year life, bear interest at 10%, and sell at face value. The issue price of the stock would be $80 per share.

Required ➡   Should the investment be made? If so, explain which financing plan you would recommend. (Hint: Calculate earnings per share for last year and for future years under each of the alternatives.)

Business Decision Case 15-2
Answer questions regarding annual report (L.O. 7)

An annual report of a company contained the following paragraph in the notes to the financial statements:

The 9 7/8% Senior Subordinated Debentures are redeemable at the option of [the company] at 103.635% of the principal amount plus accrued interest if redeemed prior to [a certain date], and at decreasing prices thereafter. Mandatory sinking fund payments of $3,000,000 (which [the company] may increase to $6,000,000 annually) . . . and are intended to retire, at par plus accrued interest, 75% of the issue prior to maturity.

Answer the following questions:

Required

a. What does the term debentures mean?
b. How much is the call premium initially? Does this premium decrease over time?
c. Under what circumstances might the company want to increase the sinking fund payments?

The Wall Street Journal contained a table showing yield comparisons for groups of corporate bonds. The following data have been adapted from the table:

Business Decision Case 15-3
Answer questions regarding bond yields (L.O. 8)

	Yield Percentage			
	As of		52-week	
Risk category	4/28	4/27	High	Low
1-10 year maturities:				
High quality	7.08%	6.94%	7.16%	5.32%
Medium quality	7.41	7.26	7.49	5.76
Over 10 year maturities:				
High quality	7.91	7.81	8.06	6.93
Medium quality	8.36	8.25	8.49	7.29
High-yield bonds	10.45	10.48	10.53	9.25

Standard & Poor's ratings were:
High quality　AAA to AA
Medium quality　A to BBB
High yield　BB to C

Prepare written answers to the following questions.

Required

a. In each column of numbers, why do the yield rates increase from top to bottom?
b. For the high quality and medium quality bonds, what could account for the increase in the yield rates from 4/27 to 4/28? Take into consideration possible economic events.
c. Which risk class of bonds was closest to its 52-week high on 4/28? What could have been the cause?

Refer to the Annual Report Appendix and determine the times interest earned ratio for 2011 for Wal-Mart Stores. Use "operating income" to represent IBIT. Prepare written comments on the results of your analysis.

Annual Report Analysis 15-4
Calculate times interest earned ratio for Wal-Mart and prepare written comments on results (L.O. 9)

A recent annual report of Emhart Corporation contained the following paragraph in its notes to the financial statements:

Annual Report Analysis 15-5
Decide whether to convert or surrender bonds (real world problem) (L.O. 7)

The 6 3/4% convertible subordinated debentures may be converted into shares of common stock at a price of $26.50 per share at any time prior to maturity. They are redeemable at prices decreasing from 105 percent of face amount currently to 100 percent [at a certain future date].

Answer the following questions:

Required

a. If you held one $1,000 bond, how many shares of stock would you receive if you converted the bond into shares of stock? (Hint: You can use the principal amount of the bond to buy shares of stock at the stated price.)
b. Assume you held one $1,000 bond and the bond was called by the company at a price of 105% of the face amount. If the current market price per share of the stock was $29, would you convert the bond into shares of stock or would you surrender the bond? Explain.

Ethics Case—Writing Experience 15-6
Answer questions regarding ethics case

Refer to "An Ethical Perspective" on page 596. Write out the answers to the following questions:

a. What motivates the brothers to pursue this new strategy?
b. Are the brothers the only ones assuming the risks?
c. How will workers, the city, the holders of the original bond issue, and the other present stockholders be affected if the junk bonds are issued and are then defaulted?
d. How might these parties (stakeholders) be affected if a new buyer outbids the management?
e. What ethical considerations are involved?

Group Project 15-7
Write a paper on a specific topic

In groups of two or three students, write a two-page, double-spaced paper on one of the following topics:

The Use of Junk Bonds in the 1980s

Why Market Rates of Interest and Prices of Bonds Are Inversely Related

How a Company Can Force Conversion of Callable, Convertible Bonds

How Bond Sinking Funds Work

Do some library research on your topic and properly cite your sources. Make your analysis convincing. Your paper should be neat, contain no spelling or grammatical errors, and be the result of several drafts. Use a word processing program to prepare your paper if possible. Your paper should have a cover page with the title and the authors' names.

Group Project 15-8
Investigate why effective interest rate method is favored over straight-line method for amortization of premiums and discounts

In a small group of students, locate *Accounting Principles Board Opinion No. 21* (from a faculty member or from the library) relating to the amortization of premiums and discounts on bonds. Investigate why the Board recommended the effective interest rate method over the straight-line method for amortizing bond premiums and discounts. Which method do you favor and why? Summarize the highlights of the APB *Opinion* and your own opinions in a written report to your instructor.

Group Project 15-9
Investigate annual reports of companies with bonds outstanding

With one or two other students, locate the annual reports of three companies with bonds outstanding as part of their long-term debt. You should read the notes to the financial statements to determine the composition of the long-term debt. Identify the bonds (e.g., debentures, serial), their interest rates, and any other information pertaining to them. Compare the bonds outstanding for the three companies. Write a report to your instructor summarizing your findings.

Using the Internet—A View of the Real World

Internet Project 15-10
Analyze types of long-term debt

Visit the following site for The Dow Chemical Company:
        http://www.dow.com
By following the instructions on the screen, locate the notes to the financial statements and find the one pertaining to long-term debt. In your own words, write a short report to your instructor summarizing the types of long-term debt held by the company and some of the details of the arrangements with lenders.

Internet Project 15-11
Investigate long-term borrowings

Visit the following website for Eastman Chemical Company:
        http://www.eastman.com
Pursue choices on the screen until you locate the financial information. Then investigate long-term borrowings. You will probably go down some "false paths" to get to this financial information, but you can get there. Check to determine the composition of the long-term borrowings. Check out the notes to the financial statements for further information. Browse around the site for any other interesting information concerning the company. Write a memo to your instructor summarizing your findings.

Answers To Self-Test

True-False

1. True. These unsecured bonds are called debenture bonds and are backed only by the general creditworthiness of the issuer.
2. False. Callable bonds may be called at the option of the issuer.
3. True. This statement is the definition of favorable financial leverage. However, unfavorable financial leverage can result when favorable financial leverage was planned. Unfavorable financial leverage will result if income before interest and taxes is much lower than anticipated. Then earnings per share for the common stockholders would be lower than they would have been without the borrowing.
4. True. Purchasers will not be willing to pay the face amount if the market rate of interest exceeds the contract rate. By paying less than the face value, purchasers can earn the market rate of interest on the bonds.
5. False. The effective interest rate method is the recommended method. The straight-line method may be used only when the results are not materially different from the interest method.

Multiple-Choice

1. a. The discount of $4,000 must be recorded. Also, the accrued interest must be recognized ($100,000 × 12% × 2/12 = $2,000).
2. c. The premium is $4,000, and the accrued interest is $2,000. Both must be recognized.
3. b. The interest is ($328,298 × 0.11 × 1/2) = $18,056.
4. d. The interest would have been ($400,000 × 0.04) + ($71,702/20) = $19,585.
5. c. Income before interest and taxes is ($100,000 + $40,000 + $20,000) = $160,000. This total of $160,000 divided by interest of $20,000 = 8 times.

Careers in Accounting

A Career In External Auditing

In 1929 the Dow Jones Industrial Average fell 40% over the period from September 3rd to October 29th. The Dow bottomed out in July 1932, after losing 89% of its value. Some blamed accounting for the run-up in prices and the subsequent crash. Stocks may have been overpriced because companies engaged in "window dressing" to enhance their reported income. At the time, accounting practices and reporting procedures were not well-established. As investors began to understand this, confidence fell. Investors panicked and sold stocks in a frenzy. This action contributed to the Great Depression of the 1930's. The Dow did not reach pre-crash levels again until 1954.

In response to the financial crisis, the Securities and Exchange Commission (SEC) was established in 1934 to regulate the filing requirements of firms listed on U.S. stock exchanges. The SEC requires all listed firms in each year to prepare financial statements in accordance with generally accepted accounting principles (GAAP) and to have those financial statements audited by an independent party. This independent verification was meant to restore investor confidence and provide ongoing integrity in the capital market system. If a company fails to follow GAAP, it can be delisted from the stock exchange.

For many reasons, managers have incentives to manipulate income to enhance reported performance. It is the job of auditors to use their understanding of accounting principles and business practices to provide reasonable assurance that financial statements are free from such manipulation. One possible indication of income manipulation occurs when accrual earnings are high relative to cash flows from operating activities, sometimes referred to as "cash earnings." Accrual earnings are typically easier to manipulate because they employ estimates, whereas cash earnings are tied to actual cash receipts and payments from operations. Accrual earnings can be managed upward by recognizing earnings prematurely (or falsely) or by underestimating expenses such as depreciation expense or bad debts expense.

In addition to the challenges of verifying the accuracy of financial statements, a career in auditing provides a variety of options. Students can work for global auditing firms or small local firms, choose to travel frequently or on a limited basis, and decide to live in any geographic area around the world. A career in auditing also provides an excellent springboard for future opportunities. Companies realize that their auditors can be a valuable part of the management team. Auditors have expertise about the firm, its industry, and its accounting practices. Auditors commonly leave the auditing profession to work for one of their many clients.

Analysis Using the Statement of Cash Flows

The income statement, statement of stockholders' equity (or statement of retained earnings), and the balance sheet do not answer all the questions raised by users of financial statements. Such questions include: How much cash was generated by the company's operations? How can the Cash account be overdrawn when my accountant said the business was profitable? Why is such a profitable company able to pay only small dividends? How much was spent for new plant and equipment, and where did the company get the cash for the expenditures? How was the company able to pay a dividend when it incurred a net loss for the year?

In this chapter, you will learn about the statement of cash flows, which answers these questions. The statement of cash flows is another major required financial statement; it shows important information not shown directly in the other financial statements.

Purposes of the Statement of Cash Flows

In November 1987, the Financial Accounting Standards Board issued *Statement of Financial Accounting Standards No. 95,* "Statement of Cash Flows"[1] (codified as ASC 230). The *Statement* became effective for annual financial statements for fiscal years ending after July 15, 1988. Thus, the statement of cash flows is now one of the major financial statements issued by a company. The statement of cash flows replaced the statement of changes in financial position, on which *funds* were generally defined as working capital. **Working capital** is equal to current assets minus current liabilities.

The main purpose of the statement of cash flows is to report on the cash receipts and cash disbursements of an entity during an accounting period. Broadly defined, *cash* includes both cash and cash equivalents, such as short-term investments in Treasury bills, commercial paper, and money market funds. Another purpose

[1] FASB, Statement of Financial Accounting Standards No. 95, "Statement of Cash Flows" (Stamford, Conn., 1987). Copyright by the Financial Accounting Standards Board, High Ridge Park, Stamford, Connecticut 06905. U.S.A. Quoted (or excerpted) with permission. Copies of the complete document are available from the FASB.

Learning Objectives

After studying this chapter, you should be able to:

1. Explain the purposes and uses of the statement of cash flows.

2. Describe the content of the statement of cash flows and where certain items would appear on the statement.

3. Describe how to calculate cash flows from operating activities under both the direct and indirect methods.

4. Prepare a statement of cash flows, under both the direct and indirect methods, showing cash flows from operating activities, investing activities, and financing activities.

(continued)

Objectives

5. Analyze a statement of cash flows of a real company.

6. Analyze and use the financial results—cash flow per share of common stock, cash flow margin, and cash flow liquidity ratios.

7. Use a working paper to prepare a statement of cash flows (appendix).

Management Uses

Objective 1
Explain the purposes and uses of the statement of cash flows.

Investor and Creditor Uses

Objective 2
Describe the content of the statement of cash flows and where certain items would appear on the statement.

of this statement is to report on the entity's investing and financing activities for the period. As shown in Illustration 16.1, the statement of cash flows reports the effects on cash during a period of a company's operating, investing, and financing activities. Firms show the effects of significant investing and financing activities that do not affect cash in a schedule separate from the statement of cash flows.

Uses of the Statement of Cash Flows

The **statement of cash flows** summarizes the effects on cash of the operating, investing, and financing activities of a company during an accounting period; it reports on past management decisions on such matters as issuance of capital stock or the sale of long-term bonds. This information is available only in bits and pieces from the other financial statements. Since cash flows are vital to a company's financial health, the statement of cash flows provides useful information to management, investors, creditors, and other interested parties.

The statement of cash flows presents the effects on cash of all significant operating, investing, and financing activities. By reviewing the statement, management can see the effects of its past major policy decisions in quantitative form. The statement may show a flow of cash from operating activities large enough to finance all projected capital needs internally rather than having to incur long-term debt or issue additional stock. Alternatively, if the company has been experiencing cash shortages, management can use the statement to determine why such shortages are occurring. Using the statement of cash flows, management may also recommend to the board of directors a reduction in dividends to conserve cash.

The information in a statement of cash flows assists investors, creditors, and others in assessing the following:

1. Enterprise's ability to generate positive future net cash flows.
2. Enterprise's ability to meet its obligations.
3. Enterprise's ability to pay dividends.
4. Enterprise's need for external financing.
5. Reasons for differences between net income and associated cash receipts and payments.
6. Effects on an enterprise's financial position of both its cash and noncash investing and financing transactions during the period (disclosed in a separate schedule).

Information in the Statement of Cash Flows

The statement of cash flows classifies cash receipts and disbursements as operating, investing, and financing cash flows. Both inflows and outflows are included within each category. Look at Illustration 16.2 to see how activities can be classified to prepare a statement of cash flows.

   Operating activities generally include the cash effects (inflows and outflows) of transactions and other events that enter into the determination of net income. *Cash inflows* from operating activities affect items that appear on the income statement and include: (1) cash receipts from sales of goods or services; (2) interest received from making loans; (3) dividends received from investments in equity securities; (4) cash received from the sale of trading securities;[2] and (5) other cash receipts that do not arise from transactions defined as investing or financing activities, such

---

[2]The amendment to *FASB Statement No.115*, "Accounting for Certain Investments in Debt and Equity Securities" (Stamford, Conn., 2012), par. 18, states that, cash flows from the purchase and sale of trading securities should be classified based on the nature and purpose for which they were acquired. In this text we will assume they were always acquired for short term purposes and will be classified as operating activities.

Illustration 16.1   Statement of Cash Flows–Basic Content

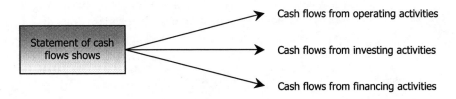

Investing and financing activities that do not affect cash are shown in a separate schedule.

Illustration 16.2   Rules for Classifying Activities in the Statement of Cash Flows

Operating activities   Cash effect of transactions and other events that enter into the determination of net income

Cash inflows from:	Cash outflows for:
Sales of goods or services	Merchandise inventory
Interest	Salaries and wages
Dividends	Interest
Sale of trading securities	Purchase of trading securities
Other sources not related to investing or financing activities (e.g., insurance settlements)	Other expenses
	Other items not related to investing or financing activities (e.g., contributions to charities)

Investing activities   Transactions involving the acquisition or disposal of noncurrent assets

Cash inflows from:	Cash outflows for:
Sale of property, plant, and equipment	Purchase of property, plant, and equipment
Sale of available-for-sale and held-to-maturity securities	Purchase of available-for-sale and held-to-maturity securities
Collection of loans	Making of loans

Financing activities   Transactions with creditors and owners

Cash inflows from:	Cash outflows for:
Issuing capital stock	Purchase of treasury stock
Issuing debt (bonds, mortgages, notes, and other short- or long-term borrowing of cash)	Payment of debt (principal only)
	Cash dividends

as amounts received to settle lawsuits, proceeds of certain insurance settlements, and cash refunds from suppliers.

Cash outflows for operating activities affect items that appear on the income statement and include payments: (1) to acquire inventory; (2) to other suppliers and employees for other goods or services; (3) to lenders and other creditors for interest; (4) for purchases of trading securities; and (5) all other cash payments that do not arise from transactions defined as investing or financing activities, such as taxes and payments to settle lawsuits, cash contributions to charities, and cash refunds to customers.

Investing activities generally include transactions involving the acquisition or disposal of noncurrent assets. Thus, *cash inflows* from investing activities include cash received from: (1) the sale of property, plant, and equipment; (2) the sale of available-for-sale and held-to-maturity securities; and (3) the collection of long-term loans made to others. *Cash outflows* for investing activities include cash paid: (1) to purchase property, plant, and equipment; (2) to purchase available-for-sale and held-to-maturity securities; and (3) to make long-term loans to others.

Note to the Student
Cash flows from operating activities consist of items from the income statement converted to a cash basis. Cash flows from investing activities are the cash inflows and outflows resulting from the acquisition and disposal of noncurrent assets. Cash flows from financing activities are generally the cash inflows and outflows resulting from the noncurrent liabilities and equity sections of the balance sheet.

Financing activities generally include the cash effects (inflows and outflows) of transactions and other events involving creditors and owners. *Cash inflows* from financing activities include cash received from issuing capital stock and bonds, mortgages, and notes, and from other short- or long-term borrowing. *Cash outflows* for financing activities include payments of cash dividends or other distributions to owners (including cash paid to purchase treasury stock) and repayments of amounts borrowed. Payment of interest is not included because interest expense appears on the income statement and is, therefore, included in operating activities. Cash payments to settle accounts payable, wages payable, and income taxes payable are not financing activities. These payments are included in the operating activities section.

A Separate Schedule for Significant Noncash Investing and Financing Activities

Information about all material investing and financing activities of an enterprise that do not result in cash receipts or disbursements during the period appear in a separate schedule, rather than in the statement of cash flows. The disclosure may be in narrative form. For instance, assume a company issued a mortgage note to acquire land and buildings. A separate schedule might appear as follows:

Schedule of noncash financing and investing activities:
Mortgage note issued to acquire land and buildings $35,000

An Accounting Perspective

BUSINESS INSIGHT In a supplemental schedule of noncash investing and financing activities, Johnson & Johnson reported one item as follows:

Treasury stock issued for employee compensation and stock option plans, net of cash proceeds $673 million

The company included the cash proceeds amount from the exercise of stock options ($1,226 million) in the cash flows from financing activities section of the statement of cash flows.

Cash Flows from Operating Activities

Cash flows from operating activities show the net amount of cash received or disbursed during a given period for items that normally appear on the income statement. You can calculate these cash flows using either the direct or indirect method. The **direct method** deducts from cash sales only those operating expenses that *consumed cash*. This method converts each item on the income statement *directly* to a cash basis. Alternatively, the **indirect (addback) method** starts with accrual basis net income and indirectly adjusts net income for items that affected reported net income but did not involve cash.

In ASC 230, the FASB encourages use of the direct method but permits use of the indirect method. Whenever given a choice between the indirect and direct methods in similar situations, accountants choose the indirect method almost exclusively. The American Institute of Certified Public Accountants reports that approximately 98% of all companies choose the indirect method of cash flows.

The direct method converts each item on the income statement to a cash basis. For instance, assume that sales are stated at $100,000 on an accrual basis. If accounts receivable increased by $5,000, cash collections from customers would be $95,000, calculated as $100,000 − $5,000. The direct method also converts all remaining items on the income statement to a cash basis, as we will illustrate later.

The indirect method adjusts net income (rather than adjusting individual items in the income statement) for (1) changes in current assets (other than cash) and current liabilities, and (2) items that were included in net income but did not affect cash.

The most common example of an operating expense that does not affect cash is depreciation expense. The journal entry to record depreciation debits an expense account and credits an accumulated depreciation account. This transaction has no effect on cash and, therefore, should not be included when measuring cash from operations. Because accountants deduct depreciation in computing net income, net income understates cash from operations. Under the indirect method, since net income is a starting point in measuring cash flows from operating activities, depreciation expense must be added back to net income.

Consider the following example. Company A had net income for the year of $20,000 after deducting depreciation of $10,000, yielding $30,000 of positive cash flows. Thus, Company A had $30,000 of positive cash flows from operating activities. Company B had a net loss for the year of $4,000 after deducting $10,000 of depreciation. Although Company B experienced a loss, it had $6,000 of positive cash flows from operating activities, as shown here:

International Reporting
Just like U.S. GAAP, IFRS encourage the use of the direct method when determining cash flows from operating activities. IFRS do allow certain flexibility when classifying activities involving the receipt of interest and dividends. Under U.S. GAAP, such receipts are treated as operating activities; under IFRS, such receipts may be treated as either operating or investing activities. Also, under U.S. GAAP, the payment of interest is an operating activity, while the payment of dividends is a financing activity. However, under IFRS, both types of payments could be treated as either operating activities or as financing activities.

	Company A	Company B
Net income (loss)	$20,000	$(4,000)
Add depreciation expense (which did not require use of cash)	10,000	10,000
Positive cash flows from operating activities	$30,000	$ 6,000

Company B's loss would have had to exceed $10,000 to generate negative cash flows from operating activities.

Companies add other expenses and losses back to net income because they do not actually use company cash; they call these addbacks **noncash charges or expenses.** Besides depreciation, the items added back include amounts of depletion that were expensed, amortization of intangible assets such as patents and goodwill, amortization of discount on bonds payable, and losses from disposals of noncurrent assets.

BUSINESS INSIGHT Jeff Bezos founded Amazon.com, Inc. in 1994. The company began operations in 1995 and held its initial public offering in 1997. However, profits did not come right away. Amazon.com's accumulated deficit at December 31, 2001, was $2,861 million. Also, its operating activities in 2001 used $120 million. However, things began improving in 2002. Amazon.com's operating activities actually provided cash flows of $174 million that year. Then, in 2003, Amazon.com became profitable, reporting a modest net income of $35 million. How do you think Amazon was able to operate and expand during the years that it was unprofitable and its operating activities were using cash?

An Accounting Perspective

To illustrate the addback of losses from disposals of noncurrent assets, assume that Quick Company sold a piece of equipment for $6,000. The equipment had cost $10,000 and had accumulated depreciation of $3,000. The journal entry to record the sale is:

Cash	6,000	
Accumulated Depreciation	3,000	
Loss on Sale of Equipment	1,000	
Equipment		10,000
To record disposal of equipment at a loss.		

Quick would show the $6,000 inflow from the sale of the equipment as a cash inflow from investing activities on its statement of cash flows. Although Quick deducted the loss of $1,000 in calculating net income, it recognized the total $6,000 effect on cash (which reflects the $1,000 loss) as resulting from an investing activity. Thus, Quick must add the loss back to net income in converting net income to cash flows from operating activities to avoid double-counting the loss.

Certain revenues and gains included in arriving at net income do not provide cash; these items are **noncash credits or revenues.** Quick should deduct these revenues and gains from net income to compute cash flows from operating activities. Such items include gains from disposals of noncurrent assets, income from investments carried under the equity method, and amortization of premiums on bonds payable.

To illustrate why we deduct the gain on the disposal of a noncurrent asset from net income, assume that Quick sold the equipment just mentioned for $9,000. The journal entry to record the sale is:

Cash	9,000	
Accumulated Depreciation	3,000	
Equipment		10,000
Gain on Sale of Equipment		2,000
To record disposal of equipment at a gain.		

Quick shows the $9,000 inflow from the sale of the equipment on its statement of cash flows as a cash inflow from investing activities. Thus, it has already recognized the total $9,000 effect on cash (including the $2,000 gain) as resulting from an investing activity. Since the $2,000 gain is also included in calculating net income, Quick must deduct the gain in converting net income to cash flows from operating activities to avoid double-counting the gain.

Steps in Preparing Statement of Cash Flows

Accountants follow specific procedures when preparing a statement of cash flows. We show these procedures using the financial statements and additional data for Welby Company in Illustration 16.3.

After determining the change in cash, the first step in preparing the statement of cash flows is to calculate the cash flows from operating activities, using either the direct or indirect method. The second step is to analyze all of the noncurrent accounts and additional data for changes resulting from investing and financing activities. The third step is to arrange the information gathered in steps 1 and 2 into the proper format for the statement of cash flows.

The direct method converts the income statement from the accrual basis to the cash basis. Accountants must consider changes in balance sheet accounts that are related to items on the income statement. The accounts involved are all current assets or current liabilities. The following schedule shows which balance sheet accounts are related to the items on Welby's income statement:

Income Statement Items	Related Balance Sheet Items	Cash Flows from Operating Activities
Sales	Accounts Receivable	Cash received from customers
Cost of goods sold	Accounts Payable and Merchandise Inventory	Cash paid for merchandise
Operating expenses and taxes	Accrued Liabilities and Prepaid Expenses	Cash paid for operating expenses

For other income statement items, the relationship is often obvious. For instance, salaries payable relates to salaries expense, federal income tax payable relates to federal income tax expense, prepaid rent relates to rent expense, and so on.

The table below shows how income statement items are affected by balance sheet accounts:

Illustration 16.3   Financial Statements and Other Data

WELBY COMPANY
Comparative Balance Sheet
December 31, 2012 and 2011

	2012	2011	Increase/ (Decrease)
Assets			
Cash	$ 21,000	$ 10,000	$11,000
Accounts receivable, net	30,000	20,000	10,000
Merchandise inventory	26,000	30,000	(4,000)
Equipment	70,000	50,000	20,000
Accumulated depreciation—Equipment	(10,000)	(5,000)	(5,000)
Total assets	$137,000	$105,000	$32,000
Liabilities and Stockholders' Equity			
Accounts payable	$ 9,000	$ 15,000	$(6,000)
Accrued liabilities payable	2,000	—0—	2,000
Common stock ($10 par value)	90,000	60,000	30,000
Retained earnings	36,000	30,000	6,000
Total liabilities and stockholders' equity	$137,000	$105,000	$32,000

WELBY COMPANY
Income Statement
For the Year Ended December 31, 2012

Sales		$140,000
Cost of goods sold		100,000
Gross margin		$ 40,000
Operating expenses		
(other than depreciation)	$25,000	
Depreciation expense	5,000	30,000
Net income		$ 10,000

Additional data

1. Equipment purchased for cash during 2012 amounted to $20,000.
2. Common stock with a par value of $30,000 was issued at par for cash.
3. Cash dividends declared and paid in 2012 totaled $4,000.

Accrual Basis		**Cash Basis (Cash Flows from Operating Activities)**
Sales	+ Decrease or − Increase in Accounts Receivable	= Cash received from customers
Cost of goods sold	{ + Increase or − Decrease in Merchandise Inventory *and* + Decrease or − Increase in Accounts Payable	= Cash paid for merchandise
Operating expenses	{ + Decrease or − Increase in related accrued liability *And* + Increase or − Decrease in related prepaid expense	= Cash paid for operating expense

Noncash operating expenses (such as depreciation expense and amortization expense), revenues, gains, and losses are reduced to zero in the cash basis income statement.

Illustration 16.4   Working Paper to Convert Income Statement from Accrual Basis to Cash Basis

WELBY COMPANY
Working Paper to Convert Income Statement from Accrual
Basis to Cash Basis
For the Year Ended December 31, 2012

	Accrual Basis	Add	Deduct	Cash Basis (Cash Flows from Operating Activities)
Sales	$140,000		$10,000*	$130,000
Cost of goods sold	$100,000		4,000 ‡	$102,000
		$6,000 †		
Operating expenses	25,000		2,000§	23,000
Depreciation expense	5,000		5,000	—0—
	$130,000			125,000
Net income	$ 10,000			$ 5,000

* Increase in Accounts Receivable.
† Decrease in Accounts Payable.
‡ Decrease in Merchandise Inventory.
§ Increase in Accrued Liabilities Payable.

As a general rule, an increase in a current asset (other than cash) decreases cash inflow or increases cash outflow. Thus, when accounts receivable increases, sales revenue on a cash basis decreases (some customers who bought merchandise have not yet paid for it). When inventory increases, cost of goods sold on a cash basis increases (increasing cash outflow). When a prepaid expense increases, the related operating expense on a cash basis increases. (For example, a company not only paid for insurance expense but also paid cash to increase prepaid insurance.) The effect on cash flows is just the opposite for decreases in these other current assets.

An increase in a current liability increases cash inflow or decreases cash outflow. Thus, when accounts payable increases, cost of goods sold on a cash basis decreases (instead of paying cash, the purchase was made on credit). When an accrued liability (such as salaries payable) increases, the related operating expense (salaries expense) on a cash basis decreases. (For example, the company incurred more salaries than it paid.) Decreases in current liabilities have just the opposite effect on cash flows.

Welby Company had no prepaid expenses. The current assets and current liabilities affecting the income statement items changed as follows:

Note to the Student
T-accounts could be used for the conversion from the accrual basis to the cash basis.

Reinforcing Problems
E16-2 Calculate the amount of cash paid for merchandise.
E16-3 Show effects of conversion from accrual to cash basis income.

	Increase	Decrease
Accounts receivable	$10,000	
Merchandise inventory		$4,000
Accounts payable		6,000
Accrued liabilities payable	2,000	

Thus, Welby converted its income statement to a cash basis as shown in Illustration 16.4.

Alternate Step 1: Determining Cash Flows from Operating Activities— Indirect Method

The indirect method makes certain adjustments to convert net income to cash flows from operating activities. Welby must analyze the effects of changes in current accounts (other than cash) on cash. The firm should also take into account noncash items such as depreciation that affected net income but not cash. Welby had only one such item—depreciation expense of $5,000. Applying these adjustments to Welby's financial statements and other data in Illustration 16.3 yields the following schedule:

Cash flow from operating activities:		
Net income	$ 10,000	
Adjustments to reconcile net income to net cash provided by operating activities:		
Increase in accounts receivable	(10,000)	
Decrease in merchandise inventory	4,000	
Decrease in accounts payable	(6,000)	
Increase in accrued liabilities payable	2,000	
Depreciation expense	5,000	
Net cash provided by operating activities		$5,000

Real-World Example
For the year ending December 31, 2010, using the indirect method, General Electric Company reported net cash provided by operating activities of $36,123,000,000.

Notice that both the direct and indirect methods result in $5,000 net cash provided by operating activities.

You can use the following table to make the adjustments to net income required by the indirect method for the changes in current assets and current liabilities:

For changes in these current assets and current liabilities:	Make these adjustments to convert accrual basis net income to cash basis net income:	
	Add	**Deduct**
Accounts Receivable	Decrease	Increase
Merchandise Inventory	Decrease	Increase
Prepaid expenses	Decrease	Increase
Accounts Payable	Increase	Decrease
Accrued liabilities payable	Increase	Decrease

Note that you would handle all changes in current asset accounts in a similar manner. All changes in current liability accounts require the opposite treatment of the current asset changes. Use this table in making these adjustments:

For Changes in—	**Add the Changes to Net Income**	**Deduct the Changes from Net Income**
Current assets	Decreases	Increases
Current liabilities		Increases Decreases

In applying the rules in this table, add a decrease in a current asset to net income, and deduct an increase in a current asset from net income. For current liabilities, add increases to net income, and deduct decreases from net income.

Under the indirect method, the amount of cash flows from operating activities is calculated as follows:

Accrual basis net income

+ or − Changes in noncash current asset and current liability accounts

+ Expenses and losses not affecting cash

− Revenues and gains not affecting cash

= Cash flows from operating activities

Reinforcing Problems
E16-4 Compute cash flows from operating activities.
E16-5 Compute cash flows from operating activities.

After analyzing the changes in current accounts for their effect on cash, we examine the noncurrent accounts and additional data. Remember that a change in a noncurrent account usually comes about because cash is received or disbursed.

In the Welby example, we must analyze four noncurrent accounts: Retained Earnings, Equipment, Accumulated Depreciation—Equipment, and Common Stock.

Step 2: Analyzing the Noncurrent Accounts and Additional Data

1. The analysis of the noncurrent accounts can begin with any of the noncurrent accounts; we begin by reviewing the Retained Earnings account. Retained Earnings is the account to which net income or loss for the period was closed. The $6,000 increase in this account consists of $10,000 of net income less $4,000 of dividends paid.

Retained Earnings			
		Beg. bal.	30,000
Dividends	4,000	Net income	10,000
		End. bal.	36,000

The net income amount is in the income statement. We enter both net income and dividends on the statement of cash flows in Illustration 16.5, Part B. The $10,000 net income is the starting figure in determining cash flows from operating activities. Thus, we enter the net income of $10,000 on the statement in the cash flows from operating activities section. The dividends are shown as a deduction in the cash flow from financing activities section.

2. The Equipment account increased by $20,000. The dividends are shown as a deduction in the cash flow from financing activities section. The additional data indicate that $20,000 of equipment was purchased during the period. A purchase of equipment is a deduction in the cash flows from investing activities section.

3. The $5,000 increase in the Accumulated Depreciation—Equipment account equals the amount of depreciation expense in the income statement for the period. As shown earlier, because depreciation does not affect cash, under the indirect (addback) method we add it back to net income on the statement of cash flows to convert accrual net income to a cash basis.

4. The $30,000 increase in common stock resulted from the issuance of stock at par value, as disclosed in the additional data (item 2) in Illustration 16.3. An issuance of stock in the statement of cash flows is a positive amount in the cash flows from financing activities section.

Reinforcing Problem
E16-6 Indicate treatment of a dividend.

Step 3: Arranging Information in the Statement of Cash Flows

Reinforcing Problems
BDC16-1 Prepare a statement of cash flows using the indirect method and answer owner's questions.
BDC16-2 Prepare a schedule showing cash flows from operating activities under the indirect method and decide whether certain goals can be met.

After we have analyzed the noncurrent accounts, we can prepare the statement of cash flows from the information generated. Part A of Illustration 16.5 presents the statement of cash flows for Welby using the direct method. Part B shows the statement of cash flows for Welby using the indirect method. The appendix to this chapter shows how a working paper can be used to assist in preparing a statement of cash flows for the Welby Company under the indirect method. However, we believe you will gain a greater conceptual understanding by not using a working paper.

The statement of cash flows has three major sections: cash flows from operating activities, cash flows from investing activities, and cash flows from financing activities. The format in the operating activities section differs for the direct and indirect methods. The direct method adjusts each item in the income statement to a cash basis. The indirect method makes these same adjustments but to net income rather than to each item in the income statement. Both methods eliminate not only the effects of noncash items, such as depreciation, but also gains and losses on sales of plant assets.

The only item in the cash flows from investing activities section is the cash outflow of $20,000 for the purchase of equipment. In a more complex situation, other items could be included in this category.

Two items are under the cash flows from financing activities section: The issuance of common stock resulted in a cash inflow of $30,000 and the payment of dividends resulted in a cash outflow of $4,000.

The last line of the statement is the $11,000 increase in cash for the year. Other examples could result in a decrease in cash for the year.

If the direct method is used, the reconciliation of net income to net cash flows from operating activities (the indirect method) must be shown in a separate schedule. However, if the indirect method is used and the reconciliation is shown in the statement of cash flows, no such separate schedule is required. Possibly this is one of the reasons why so many companies use the indirect method.

However, if the indirect method is used, the amount of interest and income taxes paid must be provided in related disclosures, usually immediately below the statement

Illustration 16.5   Statement of Cash Flows-Welby Company

A. Direct Method

WELBY COMPANY
Statement of Cash Flows
For the Year Ended December 31, 2012

Cash flows from operating activities:

Cash received from customers	$130,000	
Cash paid for merchandise	(102,000)	
Cash paid for operating expenses	(23,000)	
Net cash provided by operating activities		$ 5,000

Cash flows from investing activities:

Purchase of equipment		(20,000)

Cash flows from financing activities:

Proceeds from issuing common stock	$ 30,000	
Paid cash dividends	(4,000)	
Net cash provided by financing activities		26,000
Net increase (decrease) in cash		$11,000

> This portion differs between the two versions

> This portion is the same in both versions

Indirect

B. ~~Direct~~ Method

WELBY COMPANY
Statement of Cash Flows
For the Year Ended December 31, 2012

Cash flows from operating activities:

Net income	$ 10,000	
Adjustments to reconcile net income to net cash		
Provided by operating activities:		
Increase in accounts receivable	(10,000)	
Decrease in merchandise inventory	4,000	
Decrease in accounts payable	(6,000)	
Increase in accrued liabilities payable	2,000	
Depreciation expense	5,000	
Net cash provided by operating activities		$ 5,000

Cash flows from investing activities:

Purchase of equipment		(20,000)

Cash flows from financing activities:

Proceeds from issuing common stock	$ 30,000	
Paid cash dividends	(4,000)	
Net cash provided by financing activities		26,000
Net increase (decrease) in cash		$11,000

of cash flows. For instance, if Welby Company had paid interest of $200 and income taxes of $8,000, these facts would be reported as follows:

Supplemental cash flow information:	
Interest paid	$ 200
Income taxes paid	8,000

Analysis of the Statement of Cash Flows

Business students will benefit throughout their careers from knowing how to analyze a statement of cash flows. We will use the consolidated statement of cash flows from Synotech, Inc. to illustrate the analysis. This company will be used in the next chapter to illustrate the complete analysis and interpretation of all the financial statements. The example is adapted from a real U.S.A. company's recent annual report.

Illustration 16.6 shows the consolidated statements of cash flows for the years 2012, 2011, and 2010 for Synotech, Inc. We also include portions of Management's Discussion and Analysis of the 2012 statement of cash flows. We will then discuss the statement further, explaining various items and illustrating how the information might be used for decision making.

Liquidity and Capital Resources

Net cash provided by operations increased 13% to $1,101.0 in 2012 compared with $972.3 in 2011 and $995.3 in 2010. The increase in cash generated by operating activities in 2012 reflects the Company's improved profitability and working capital management. Cash generated from operations was used to fund capital spending, reduce debt levels and increase dividends.

During 2012, long-term debt decreased from $3,634.8 to $3,476.6. The Company continued to focus on enhancing its debt portfolio, resulting in the refinancing of a substantial portion of commercial paper and other short-term borrowings to longer term instruments. In 2012, the Company entered into a $595.6 loan agreement and obtained a $487.2 term loan with foreign commercial banks.

As of December 31, 2012, $410.3 of domestic and foreign commercial paper was outstanding. These borrowings carry a Standard & Poor's rating of A1. The commercial paper as well as other short-term borrowings are classified as long-term debt at December 31, 2012, as it is the Company's intent and ability to refinance such obligations on a long-term basis. The Company has additional sources of liquidity available in the form of lines of credit maintained with various banks. At December 31, 2012, such unused lines of credit amounted to $2,142.8.

The ratio of net debt to total capitalization (defined as the ratio of the book values of debt less cash and marketable securities ["net debt"] to net debt plus equity) decreased to 58% during 2012 from 64% in 2011. The decrease is primarily the result of higher Company earnings in 2012 as well as effective working capital management and lower acquisitions than in prior years. The ratio of market debt to market capitalization (defined as above using fair market values) decreased to 17% during 2012 from 23% in 2011. The Company primarily uses market value analyses to evaluate its optimal capitalization.

Capital expenditures were 5.2% of net sales in both 2012 and 2011 and were 5.3% of net sales in 2010. Capital spending continues to be focused primarily on projects that yield high aftertax returns, thereby reducing the Company's cost structure. Capital expenditures for 2013 are expected to continue at the current rate of approximately 5% of net sales.

Other investing activities in 2012, 2011 and 2010 included strategic acquisitions and equity investments worldwide. The aggregate purchase prices of all 2012, 2011 and 2010 acquisitions were $76.2, $1,586.3 and $179.8, respectively.

During 2010, the Company repurchased a significant amount of common shares in the open market and private transactions to provide for employee benefit plans and to maintain its targeted capital structure. Aggregate repurchases for the year approximated 6.9 million shares with a total purchase price of $433.3.

Illustration 16.6   Consolidated Statements of Cash flows for Synotech, Inc.— Indirect Method

($ Millions)	2012	2011	2010
Operating Activities			
Net income	$ 762.0	$ 206.4	$ 696.2
Adjustments to reconcile net income to net cash provided by operations:			
Restructured operations, net	(126.7)	509.9	(46.9)
Depreciation and amortization	379.6	360.4	282.2
Deferred income taxes and other, net	(27.6)	(75.5)	77.6
Cash effects of changes in:			
Receivables	(18.5)	(52.9)	(60.1)
Inventories	(1.4)	(31.3)	(53.4)
Other current assets	–0–	(50.9)	(9.4)
Payables and accruals	133.6	106.2	109.1
Net cash provided by operations	$ 1,101.0	$ 972.3	$ 995.3
Investing Activities			
Capital expenditures	$ (550.8)	$ (518.2)	$ (481.0)
Payment for acquisitions, net of cash acquired	(71.2)	(1,560.5)	(175.7)
Sale of marketable securities and other investments	31.6	7.4	70.1
Other, net	(14.4)	(20.6)	37.3
Net cash used for investing activities	$ (604.8)	$ (2,091.9)	$ (549.3)
Financing Activities			
Principal payments on debt	$ (1,397.5)	$ (20.5)	$ (106.0)
Proceeds from issuance of debt, net	1,292.9	1,464.0	379.7
Proceeds from outside investors	10.3	36.6	18.2
Dividends paid	(355.5)	(331.8)	(296.3)
Purchase of common stock	(32.9)	(10.8)	(429.5)
Proceeds from exercise of stock options and other, net	36.8	33.9	22.2
Net cash (used for) provided by financing activities	$ (445.9)	$ 1,171.4	$ (411.7)
Effect of exchange rate changes on cash and cash equivalents	$ (2.8)	$ (5.2)	$ (3.3)
Net increase in cash and cash equivalents	$ 47.5	$ 46.6	$ 31.0
Cash and cash equivalents at beginning of year	250.5	203.9	172.9
Cash and cash equivalents at end of year	$ 298.0	$ 250.5	$ 203.9
Supplemental Cash Flow Information			
Income taxes paid	$ 304.4	$ 351.0	$ 313.3
Interest paid	274.9	274.3	116.3
Non-cash consideration in payment for acquisitions	–0–	58.7	9.6
Principal payments on ESOP debt, guaranteed by the Company	(6.0)	(5.3)	(4.8)

Dividend payments were $355.5 in 2012, up from $331.8 in 2011 and $296.3 in 2010.

Internally generated cash flows appear to be adequate to support currently planned business operations, acquisitions and capital expenditures. Significant acquisitions would require external financing.

The Company is a party to various superfund and other environmental matters and is contingently liable with respect to lawsuits, taxes and other matters arising out of the normal course of business. Management proactively reviews and manages its exposure to, and the impact of, environmental matters. While it is possible that the Company's cash flows and results of operations in particular quarterly or annual periods could be affected by the one-time impacts of the resolution of such contingencies, it is the opinion of management that the ultimate disposition of these matters, to the extent not previously provided for, will not have a material impact on the Company's financial condition or ongoing cash flows and results of operations.

Refer to Illustration 16.6. First we will discuss the items in the operating activities section of the statement of cash flows, then we will discuss investing activities and financing activities.

Operating Activities   The company used the indirect method of calculating net cash provided by operations. Various adjustments were made to convert accrual based net income to cash basis net income.

The "restructured operations, net" item resulted from the fact that many companies restructured their operations by closing plants and significantly reducing their work forces. Some companies recognized a net loss from restructuring and others recognized a net gain. Apparently, the company recognized a net gain in 2012 because it deducted the item from net income on the statement of cash flows. The actual cash flows from restructuring will occur in a later period.

"Depreciation and amortization" includes depreciation on plant assets and amortization of intangible assets. Depreciation and amortization are noncash charges against revenues and must be added back to net income.

The "deferred income taxes and other, net" item deduction from net income results primarily from the fact that income tax expense on the income statement was lower than the actual income taxes paid in 2012. This phenomenon occurs because of using a different method for tax and accounting purposes for such items as depreciation.

Receivables and inventories increased (causing cash to decrease), while other current assets remained about the same. Payables and accruals increased (causing cash to increase). These changes are net of any amounts related to acquisitions, dispositions, or amounts that are included elsewhere, such as in "restructured operations, net." The changes described may differ from the amounts derived from only analyzing the balance sheets for the last two years because of certain technical "adjustments" that are beyond the scope of this text.

Investing Activities   "Capital expenditures" include the purchase of plant assets, such as new machinery and equipment, to modernize production facilities. Companies normally select those capital expenditures with the highest rate of return. For instance, if funds are limited (and they normally are) and two capital investments (a machine and a mainframe computer) are being considered, one yielding a 20% return and the other yielding a 25% return, the company will normally select the one with the 25% return.

"Payment for acquisitions, net of cash acquired" shows the amount spent in acquiring other companies and segments of other companies, net of the amount of cash held by those companies and obtained as a part of the acquisition.

The company sold "marketable securities and other investments." These securities normally consist of stocks, bonds, and other instruments of other companies. For fiscal years beginning after December 15, 1993, marketable securities must be identified as trading securities, available-for-sale securities, or held-to-maturity securities. Trading securities and available-for-sale securities were discussed in some detail in Chapter 14. Held-to-maturity securities were mentioned briefly in Chapter 15. These held-to-maturity securities are debt securities (such as bonds of other companies) that the company has purchased and has both the intent and ability to hold to maturity. As mentioned earlier, the proceeds from sales and purchases of trading securities must be shown as cash flows from operating activities, and the proceeds from sales and purchases of available-for-sale and held-to-maturity securities must be shown as cash flows from investing activities.

Financing Activities   The company paid off some old debt ($1,397.5 million) and incurred new debt ($1,292.9 million). Recently many companies are substituting new debt with a low interest rate for old debt with a high interest rate, just as homeowners refinance their homes to lower their interest rate.

The "proceeds from outside investors" resulted from the other participants in the formation of certain businesses in which the company holds more than a 50% share.

"Dividends paid" is an item that should be familiar to you. Dividends paid increased each year for the period 2010 through 2012.

The company bought back some of its own stock (treasury stock). Companies often buy back their own shares because they (1) need the shares to issue to employees or officers under stock option plans, (2) want to bolster the market price of the stock, or (3) hope to later sell the stock at a substantially higher price.

"Proceeds from exercise of stock options and other, net" represents the proceeds received from employees and officers who exercised their stock options. Stock options are usually granted to employees to encourage them to work efficiently to increase profitability, which should increase the market price of the stock. Stock options made available to officers are for the same purpose or to attract or retain a talented executive. Normally, an option gives the recipient the right to buy a certain number of shares at a stated price within a given timeframe. For instance, the president of a company may be granted an option to buy 10,000 shares at $40 per share any time after two years from that date and before six years from that date. Assume that the current market price is $38. If the market price of the stock rises to $80 at some time during the option period, the president could buy the shares at $40 and then hold them or sell them at the higher market price. Executives of companies have become multimillionaires by exercising their stock options. The employees and executives of Synotech, Inc., paid the company between $22.2 million and $36.8 million per year to exercise their stock options during the three-year period. The company resissued some of its treasury stock as a result of the exercise of the stock options.

We will discuss some examples of the ways that the information in the statement of cash flows can be used by management, stockholders, and creditors to make decisions. Each of these parties would use more than the statement of cash flows to perform an analysis of the company's performance, but we will restrict ourselves to the statement of cash flows. The next chapter shows a more complete analysis of the company's performance.

Use of the Cash Flow Information for Decision Making

Management   Management is the first to see the information contained in the statement of cash flows. You have already read portions of "Management's Discussion and Analysis" concerning the information contained in that statement. Management concluded that the amount of internally generated cash flows (net cash provided by operations) appears adequate to support currently planned business operations, acquisitions, and capital expenditures. Thus, unless the company engages in a significant acquisition it will not have to sell more stock or borrow more funds in the foreseeable future. Also, the company apparently replaced some of its high interest rate debt ($1,397.5 million) with lower interest rate debt ($1,292.9 million). Many companies are doing this same thing recently to take advantage of the low interest rates available.

Reinforcing Problems
P16–3A Analyze Drexler, Inc.'s statement of cash flows.
P16–4A Analyze Procter & Gamble's 2011 statement of cash flows.

Stockholders   Stockholders can see that dividend payments ($355.5 million) are comfortably covered by net cash provided by operations ($1,101.0 million). Stockholders are undoubtedly pleased that the per share dividend rate has increased each year during 2010 through 2012. The company continues to invest in its future by making capital expenditures ($550.8 million) to modernize its productive facilities. The repurchase of its own stock ($32.9 million) decreases the number of shares outstanding, although some of the stock will undoubtedly be reissued in the future as employees and executives exercise their stock options. Any net reduction in the number of shares outstanding will tend to increase earnings per share and help to increase the market price per share in the future. Also, the company may decide to increase dividends per share in the

A Broader Perspective

Johnson & Johnson

JOHNSON & JOHNSON AND SUBSIDIARIES
CONSOLIDATED STATEMENTS OF CASH FLOWS
(Dollars in Millions)

	2010	2009	2008
Cash flows from operating activities			
Net earnings	$ 13,334	$ 12,266	$ 12,949
Adjustments to reconcile net earnings to cash flows from operating activities:			
Depreciation and amortization of property and intangibles	2,939	2,774	2,832
Stock based compensation	614	628	627
Purchased in-process research and development	—	—	181
Deferred tax provision	356	(436)	22
Accounts receivable allowances	12	58	86
Changes in assets and liabilities, net of effects from acquisitions:			
(Increase)/decrease in accounts receivable	(207)	453	(736)
(Increase)/decrease in inventories	(196)	95	(101)
Increase/(decrease) in accounts payable and accrued liabilities	20	(507)	(272)
(Increase)/decrease in other current and non-current assets	(574)	1,209	(1,600)
Increase in other current and non-current liabilities	87	31	984
Net cash flows from operating activities	**16,385**	**16,571**	**14,972**
Cash flows from investing activities			
Additions to property, plant and equipment	(2,384)	(2,365)	(3,066)
Proceeds from the disposal of assets	524	154	785
Acquisitions, net of cash acquired	(1,269)	(2,470)	(1,214)
Purchases of investments	(15,788)	(10,040)	(3,668)
Sales of investments	11,101	7,232	3,059
Other (primarily intangibles)	(38)	(109)	(83)
Net cash used by investing activities	**(7,854)**	**(7,598)**	**(4,187)**
Cash flows from financing activities			
Dividends to shareholders	(5,804)	(5,327)	(5,024)
Repurchase of common stock	(2,797)	(2,130)	(6,651)
Proceeds from short-term debt	7,874	9,484	8,430
Retirement of short-term debt	(6,565)	(6,791)	(7,319)
Proceeds from long-term debt	1,118	9	1,638
Retirement of long-term debt	(32)	(219)	(24)
Proceeds from the exercise of stock options/excess tax benefits	1,226	882	1,486
Net cash used by financing activities	**(4,980)**	**(4,092)**	**(7,464)**
Effect of exchange rate changes on cash and cash equivalents	(6)	161	(323)
Increase in cash and cash equivalents	3,545	5,042	2,998
Cash and cash equivalents, beginning of year	15,810	10,768	7,770
Cash and cash equivalents, end of year	**$ 19,355**	**$ 15,810**	**$ 10,768**

future. These favorable factors might induce present stockholders to retain their stock or even increase their holdings. Potential stockholders might also be attracted to the stock.

Creditors   An encouraging factor is the increasing amount of net cash provided by operations in 2012. Also comforting to creditors is the information in Management's Discussion and Analysis that the company has access to $2,142.8 million in lines of credit.

The preceding discussions are merely examples of how the information contained in the statement of cash flows might be analyzed to make decisions. The next section describes three ratios that can provide further analyses of cash flows.

Analyzing and Using the Financial Results—Cash Flow per Share of Common Stock, Cash Flow Margin, and Cash Flow Liquidity Ratios

The information in the statement of cash flows provides a basis for analyzing financial results. However, further analysis is possible through the use of three ratios relating to cash flow: the cash flow per share of common stock, cash flow margin, and cash flow liquidity ratios. The ratios shown below are results for Synotech, Inc. and recent results for other companies. All dollar amounts are rounded to the nearest million.

The **cash flow per share of common stock ratio** is equal to the net cash provided by operations divided by the average number of shares of common stock outstanding. This ratio indicates the company's ability to pay dividends and liabilities. The higher the ratio, the greater the ability to pay. The cash flow per share of common stock ratios for the companies were:

> **Objective 6**
> Analyze and use the financial results—cash flow per share of common stock, cash flow margin, and cash flow liquidity ratios.

Company	Net Cash Provided by Operating Activities (millions)	Average Shares of Common Stock Outstanding* (millions)	Cash Flow per Share
Synotech, Inc.	$1,101	183	$6.02
J. C. Penney, Inc.	592	236	2.51
The Walt Disney Company	6,994	1,878	3.72
General Electric Company	36,123	10,661	3.39

*To determine the average number of shares, add the beginning and ending numbers outstanding and divide by two.

The **cash flow margin ratio** is equal to net cash provided by operating activities divided by net sales. This ratio is a measure of a company's ability to turn sales revenue into cash. The higher the ratio, the better. The cash flow margin ratios for the companies were:

Company	Net Cash Provided by Operating Activities (millions)	Net Sales (millions)	Cash Flow Margin
Synotech, Inc.	$ 1,101	10,499	10.49%
J. C. Penney, Inc.	592	17,759	3.33%
The Walt Disney Company	6,994	40,893	17.10%
General Electric Company	36,123	150,211	24.05%

The **cash flow liquidity ratio** is equal to the total of cash, marketable securities, and net cash provided by operating activities divided by current liabilities. This ratio is a test of a company's short-term, debt-paying ability. The higher the ratio, the better. The cash flow liquidity ratios for the companies were:

Company	Cash, Marketable Securities, and Net Cash Provided by Operating Activities (millions)	Current Liabilities (millions)	Cash Flow Liquidity Ratio
Synotech, Inc.	$1,470	$2,285	.64 times
J. C. Penney, Inc.	3,214	2,647	1.21 times
The Walt Disney Company	10,179	12,088	.84 times
General Electric Company	159,019	627,018	.25 times

On the first of these measures, Synotech, Inc., seems to be in the strongest position, although all of the companies are financially sound. On the second measure, General Electric and Walt Disney have the highest cash flow margin ratios. On the third measure, J. C. Penney seems to be in the strongest position. However, a more valid comparison on each of these measures would be made if each of these companies was compared with other companies in its industry. Dun & Bradstreet's Industry Norms and Key Business Ratios can be used for this purpose. (This source could also be used for comparisons of ratios in the next chapter.) A complete analysis using the techniques described in the next chapter would provide additional information about the strengths and weaknesses of each of these companies.

Understanding the Learning Objectives

Objective 1
Explain the purposes and uses of the statement of cash flows.

- The statement of cash flows summarizes the effects on cash of the operating, financing, and investing activities of a company during an accounting period.
- Management can see the effects of its past major policy decisions in quantitative form.
- Investors and creditors can assess the entity's ability to generate positive future net cash flows, to meet its obligations, and to pay dividends, and can assess the need for external financing.

Objective 2
Describe the content of the statement of cash flows and where certain items would appear on the statement.

- Operating activities generally include the cash effects (inflows and outflows) of transactions and other events that enter into the determination of net income. The cash flows from operating activities can be measured in two ways. The direct method deducts from cash sales only those operating expenses that consumed cash. The indirect method starts with net income and adjusts net income for items that affected reported net income but did not involve cash.
- Investing activities generally include transactions involving the acquisition or disposal of noncurrent assets.
- Financing activities generally include the cash effects (inflows and outflows) of transactions and other events involving creditors and owners.

Objective 3
Describe how to calculate cash flows from operating activities under both the direct and indirect methods.

- The direct method deducts from cash sales only those operating expenses that consumed cash. The FASB recommends use of the direct method.
- The indirect method starts with accrual basis net income and indirectly adjusts net income for items that affected reported net income but did not involve cash. A large majority of companies use the indirect method.

Objective 4
Prepare a statement of cash flows, under both the direct and indirect methods, showing cash flows from operating activities, investing activities, and financing activities.

- The first step is to determine the cash flows from operating activities. Either the direct or indirect method may be used.
- The second step is to analyze all the noncurrent accounts for changes in cash resulting from investing and financing activities.
- The third step is to arrange the information gathered in steps 1 and 2 into the format required for the statement of cash flows.

Objective 5
Analyze a statement of cash flows of a real company.

- Business students will benefit throughout their careers from knowing how to analyze a statement of cash flows.
- "Management's Discussion and Analysis" in the annual report provides part of the analysis.

- Inspection of the statement of cash flows together with "Management's Discussion and Analysis" will provide the most insight as to the cash flow situation.
- The cash flow per share of common stock ratio tests a company's ability to pay dividends and liabilities and is equal to net cash provided by operating activities divided by the average number of shares of common stock outstanding.
- The cash flow margin ratio measures a company's ability to turn sales revenue into cash and is equal to net cash provided by operating activities divided by net sales.
- The cash flow liquidity ratio tests a company's short-term, debt-paying ability and is equal to the total of cash, marketable securities, and net cash provided by operating activities divided by current liabilities.
- A work sheet can be used to assist in preparing a statement of cash flows.
- A company's comparative balance sheets, income statement, and additional data are used to prepare the work sheet.
- The work sheet technique makes the recording of the effects of transactions on cash flows almost a mechanical process.

Objective 6
Analyze and use the financial results—cash flow per share of common stock, cash flow margin, and cash flow liquidity ratios.

Objective 7
Use a working paper to prepare a statement of cash flows (Appendix).

Use of a Working Paper to Prepare a Statement of Cash Flows

APPENDIX

This appendix shows how a work sheet could be used to assist in preparing a statement of cash flows. We use the comparative balance sheets, income statement, and additional data for the Welby Company, shown on page 621, as the basis for this example.

Objective 7
Use a working paper to prepare a statement of cash flows (Appendix).

Look at the working paper in Illustration 16.7 for Welby Company, which we use to analyze the transactions and prepare the statement of cash flows. While discussing the steps in preparing the working paper, we describe the items and trace their effects in the entries.

1. Enter the beginning account balances of all balance sheet accounts in the first column and the ending account balances in the fourth column. Notice that the debit items precede the credit items.
2. Total the debits and credits in the first and fourth columns to make sure that debits equal credits in each column.
3. Write "Cash Flows from Operating Activities" immediately below the total of the credit items. Skip sufficient lines for recording adjustments to convert accrual net income to cash flows from operating activities. Then write "Cash Flows from Investing Activities" and allow enough space for those items. Finally, write "Cash Flows from Financing Activities" and allow enough space for those items.
4. Enter entries for analyzing transactions in the second and third columns. The entries serve two functions: (*a*) they explain the change in each account; and (*b*) they classify the changes into operating, investing, and financing activities. We discuss these entries individually in the next section.
5. Total the debits and credits in the second and third columns; they should be equal. You will have one pair of totals for the balance sheet items and another pair for the bottom portion of the working paper. We use the bottom portion of the working paper to prepare the statement of cash flows.

Completing the Working Paper

To complete the working paper in Illustration 16.7, we must analyze the change in each noncash balance sheet account. The focus of this working paper is on cash, and every change in cash means a change in a noncash balance sheet account. After we have made the proper entries to analyze all changes in noncash balance sheet accounts, the working paper shows all activities affecting cash flows. The following explanations are keyed to the entry numbers on the working paper:

Entry 0: In comparing the beginning and ending cash balances, we determine the change in the Cash account during the year is an $11,000 increase. An entry on the working paper6 debits Cash for $11,000 and credits Increase in Cash for Year near the bottom of the schedule. This *0* entry does not explain the change in cash but is the "target" of the analysis. The entry sets out the change in cash that the statement seeks to explain. No further attention need be paid to cash in completing the working paper.

We now direct our attention toward changes in other balance sheet accounts. These accounts can be dealt with in any order; first, we record the net income for the period and analyze the current assets (other than cash) and the current liabilities. Second, we analyze the changes in the noncurrent accounts.

Entry 1: The income statement shows a net income for 2012 of $10,000. Entry *1* records the $10,000 as the starting point in measuring cash flows from operating activities and credits Retained Earnings as a partial explanation of the change in that account.

The next task is to analyze changes in current accounts other than Cash. The current accounts of Welby Company are closely related to operations, and their changes are included in converting net income to cash flows from operating activities.

Entry 2: We deduct the $10,000 increase in accounts receivable from net income when converting it to cash flows from operating activities. If accounts receivable increased, sales to customers exceeded cash received from customers. To convert net income to a cash basis, we must deduct the $10,000.

The working paper technique makes the recording of these effects almost mechanical. By debiting Accounts Receivable for $10,000, we increase it from $20,000 to $30,000. If Accounts Receivable is debited, we must credit an item that can be entitled "Increase in Accounts Receivable." We deduct the increase from net income in converting it to cash flows from operating activities.

Entry 3: is virtually a duplicate of entry *2,* except it involves merchandise inventory rather than receivables and is a decrease rather than an increase.

Entry 4: records the effect of a decrease in accounts payable on net income in converting it to cash flows from operating activities.

Entry 5: records the effect of an increase in accrued liabilities payable in converting net income to cash flows from operating activities.

Next, we analyze the changes in the noncurrent balance sheet accounts.

Entry 6: We add the $5,000 depreciation back to net income and credit the respective accumulated depreciation account. You can find the depreciation expense (1) on the income statement, or (2) by solving for the credit needed to balance the accumulated depreciation account on the balance sheet.

Illustration 16.7   Working Paper for Statement of Cash Flows

WELBY COMPANY
Working Paper for Statement of Cash Flows
For the Year Ending December 31, 2012

	Account Balances 12/31/11	Analysis of Transactions for 2012		Account Balances 12/31/12
		Debit	Credit	
Debits				
Cash	10,000	(0) 11,000		21,000
Accounts Receivable, Net	20,000	(2) 10,000		30,000
Merchandise Inventory	30,000		(3) 4,000	26,000
Equipment	50,000	(7) 20,000		70,000
Totals	110,000			147,000
Credits				
Accumulated Depreciation—Equipment	5,000		(6) 5,000	10,000
Accounts Payable	15,000	(4) 6,000		9,000
Accrued Liabilities Payable	—0—		(5) 2,000	2,000
Common Stock ($10 par value)	60,000		(8) 30,000	90,000
Retained Earnings	30,000	(9) 4,000	(1) 10,000	36,000
Totals	110,000	51,000	51,000	147,000
Cash Flows from Operating Activities				
Net Income		(1) 10,000		
Increase in Accounts Receivable			(2) 10,000	
Decrease in Merchandise Inventory		(3) 4,000		
Decrease in Accounts Payable			(4) 6,000	
Increase in Accrued Liabilities Payable		(5) 2,000		
Depreciation Expense		(6) 5,000		
Cash Flows from Investing Activities:				
Purchase of Equipment			(7) 20,000	
Cash Flows from Financing Activities:				
Proceeds from Issuing Common Stock		(8) 30,000		
Payment of Cash Dividends			(9) 4,000	
Increase in Cash for Year			(0) 11,000	
		51,000	51,000	

Accumulated Depreciation—Equipment

Beg. bal.	5,000	
(6)	5,000	
End. bal.	10,000	

Entry 7: We debit the Equipment account and credit "Purchase of Equipment" in the investing activities section for the $20,000 cash spent to acquire new plant assets (equipment).

Entry 8: We show the $30,000 cash received from sale of common stock as a financing activity. The entry also explains the change in the Common Stock account. If stock had been sold for more than its stated value of $50 per share, we would record the excess in a separate Paid-In Capital in Excess of Stated Value account. However, we would report the total amount of cash received from the issuance of common stock as a single figure on the statement of cash flows. Only this total amount received is significant to creditors and other users of the financial statements trying to judge the solvency of the company.

Entry 9: We debit Retained Earnings and credit Payment of Cash Dividends for the $4,000 dividends declared and paid. The entry also completes the following explanation of the change in Retained Earnings. Notice that on the statement of cash flows, the dividends must be paid to be included as a cash outflow from financing activities.

Retained Earnings			
		Beg. bal.	30,000
(9)	4,000	(1)	10,000
		End. bal.	36,000

Preparing the Statement of Cash Flows

Using the data in the lower section of the working paper, we would prepare the statement of cash flows under the indirect method shown in Illustration 16.5 (Part B) on page 625.

Demonstration Problem

The following comparative balance sheets are for Dells Corporation as of June 30, 2012, and June 30, 2011. Also provided is the statement of income and retained earnings for the year ended June 30, 2012, with additional data.

DELLS COMPANY
Comparative Balance Sheet
June 30, 2012 and 2011

Assets	2012	2011	Increase (Decrease)
Current assets:			
Cash	$ 30,000	$ 80,000	$ (50,000)
Accounts receivable, net	160,000	100,000	60,000
Merchandise inventory	100,000	70,000	30,000
Prepaid rent	20,000	10,000	10,000
Total current assets	$310,000	$260,000	$ 50,000
Property, plant, and equipment:			
Equipment	$400,000	$200,000	$200,000
Accumulated depreciation—equipment	(60,000)	(50,000)	(10,000)
Total property, plant, and equipment	$340,000	$150,000	$190,000
Total assets	$650,000	$410,000	$240,000

Liabilities and Stockholders' Equity	2012	2011	Increase (Decrease)
Current liabilities:			
Accounts payable	$ 50,000	$ 40,000	$ 10,000
Notes payable—bank	—0—	50,000	(50,000)
Salaries payable	10,000	20,000	(10,000)
Federal income taxes payable	30,000	20,000	10,000
Total current liabilities	$ 90,000	$130,000	$ (40,000)
Stockholders' equity:			
Common stock, $10 par	$300,000	$100,000	$200,000
Paid-in capital in excess of par	50,000	—0—	50,000
Retained earnings	210,000	180,000	30,000
Total stockholders' equity	$560,000	$280,000	$280,000
Total liabilities and stockholders' equity	$650,000	$410,000	$240,000

DELLS CORPORATION
Statement of Income and Retained Earnings
For the Year Ended June 30, 2012

Sales		$1,000,000
Cost of goods sold	$600,000	
Salaries and wages expense	200,000	
Rent expense	40,000	
Depreciation expense	20,000	
Interest expense	3,000	
Loss on sale of equipment	7,000	870,000
Income before federal income taxes		$ 130,000
Deduct: Federal income taxes		60,000
Net income		$ 70,000
Retained earnings, July 1, 2011		180,000
		$ 250,000
Deduct: Dividends		40,000
Retained earnings, June 30, 2012		$ 210,000

⬤ *Additional data*

1. Equipment with a cost of $20,000, on which $10,000 of depreciation had been recorded, was sold for $3,000 cash. Additional equipment was purchased for $220,000.
2. Stock was issued for $250,000 cash.
3. The $50,000 bank note was paid.

Using the data given for Dells Corporation:

⬤ *Required*

a. Prepare a statement of cash flows—indirect method.
b. Prepare a working paper to convert net income from an accrual basis to a cash basis. Then prepare a partial statement of cash flows—direct method, showing only the cash flows from operating activities section.

Solution to Demonstration Problem

a.

DELLS COMPANY
Statement of Cash Flows
For the Year Ended June 30, 2012

Cash flows from operating activities:		
Net income	$ 70,000	
Adjustments to reconcile net income to net cash provided by operating activities:		
Increase in accounts receivable	(60,000)	
Increase in merchandise inventory	(30,000)	
Increase in prepaid rent	(10,000)	
Increase in accounts payable	10,000	
Decrease in salaries payable	(10,000)	
Increase in federal income taxes payable	10,000	
Loss on sale of equipment	7,000	
Depreciation expense	20,000	
Net cash provided by operating activities		$7,000
Cash flows from investing activities:		
Proceeds from sale of equipment	$ 3,000	
Purchase of equipment	(220,000)	
Net cash used by investing activities		(217,000)
Cash flows from financing activities:		
Proceeds from issuing common stock	$250,000	
Repayment of bank note	(50,000)	
Dividends paid	(40,000)	
Net cash provided by financing activities		160,000
Net increase (decrease) in cash		$(50,000)

b.

DELLS CORPORATION
Working Paper to Convert Income Statement
from Accrual Basis to Cash Basis
For the Year Ended June 30, 2012

	Accrual Basis	Add	Deduct	Cash Basis (Cash Flows from Operating Activities)
Sales	$1,000,00		$60,000[a]	$940,000
Cost of goods sold	$600,000	$30,000[b]	10,000[c]	$620,000
Salaries and wages expense	200,000	10,000[d]		210,000
Rent expense	40,000	10,000[e]		50,000
Depreciation expense	20,000		20,000	—0—
Interest expense	3,000			3,000
Loss on sale of equipment	7,000		7,000	—0—
Federal income taxes	60,000		10,000[f]	50,000
		930,000		933,000
Net income		$ 70,000		$ 7,000

[a]Increase in Accounts Receivable.
[b]Increase in Merchandise Inventory.
[c]Increase in Accounts Payable.
[d]Decrease in Salaries Payable.
[e]Increase in Prepaid Rent.
[f]Increase in Federal Income Taxes Payable.

DELLS CORPORATION
Partial Statement of Cash Flows—Direct Method
For the Year Ended June 30, 2012

Cash flows from operating activities:	
Cash received from customers	$ 940,000
Cash paid for merchandise	(620,000)
Salaries and wages paid	(210,000)
Rent paid	(50,000)
Interest paid	(3,000)
Federal income taxes paid	(50,000)
Net cash provided by operating activities	$ 7,000

New Terms

Cash flow liquidity ratio Cash and marketable securities plus net cash provided by operating activities divided by current liabilities. *631*

Cash flow margin ratio Net cash provided by operating activities divided by net sales. *631*

Cash flow per share of common stock ratio Net cash provided by operating activities divided by the average number of shares of common stock outstanding. *631*

Cash flows from operating activities The net amount of cash received or disbursed during a given period on items that normally appear on the income statement. *618*

Direct method Deducts from cash sales only those operating expenses that consumed cash. *618*

Financing activities Generally include the cash effects of transactions and other events involving creditors and owners. Cash payments made to settle current liabilities such as accounts payable, wages payable, and income taxes payable are not financing activities. These payments are operating activities. *618*

Indirect method A method of determining cash flows from operating activities that starts with net income and indirectly adjusts net income for items that do not involve cash. Also called the addback method. *618*

Investing activities Generally include transactions involving the acquisition or disposal of noncurrent assets. Examples include cash received or paid from the sale or purchase of property, plant, and equipment; available-for-sale and held-to-maturity securities; and loans made to others. *617*

Noncash charges or expenses Expenses and losses that are added back to net income because they do not actually use cash of the company. The items added back include amounts of depreciation on plant assets, depletion that was expensed, amortization of intangible assets such as patents and goodwill, amortization of discount on bonds payable, and losses from disposals of noncurrent assets. *619*

Noncash credits or revenues   Revenues and gains included in arriving at net income that do not provide cash; examples include gains from disposals of noncurrent assets, income from investments carried under the equity method, and amortization of premium on bonds payable. *620*

Operating activities   Generally include the cash effects of transactions and other events that enter into the determination of net income. *616*

Statement of cash flows   A statement that summarizes the effects on cash of the operating, investing, and financing activities of a company during an accounting period. Both inflows and outflows are included in each category. The statement of cash flows must be prepared each time an income statement is prepared. *616*

Working capital   Equal to current assets minus current liabilities. *615*

Self-Test

True-False

Indicate whether each of the following statements is true or false.

1. The requirement for a statement of cash flows was preceded by the requirement for the statement of changes in financial position.
2. The statement of cash flows is one of the major financial statements.
3. Investing activities are transactions with creditors and owners.
4. The direct method of calculating cash flows from operations is encouraged by the FASB and is the predominant method used.
5. Issuance of capital stock and the subsequent reacquisition of some of those shares would both be financing activities.

Multiple-Choice

Select the best answer for each of the following questions.

1. Which of the following statements is true?
   a. The direct method of calculating cash flows from operations starts with net income and adjusts for noncash revenues and expenses and changes in current assets and current liabilities.
   b. The indirect method of calculating cash flows from operations adjusts each item in the income statement to a cash basis.
   c. The descriptions in (a) and (b) should be reversed.
   d. The direct method is easier to use than the indirect method.
2. Investing activities include all of the following except:
   a. Payment of debt.
   b. Collection of loans.
   c. Making of loans.
   d. Sale of available-for-sale and held-to-maturity securities.
3. If sales on an accrual basis are $500,000 and accounts receivable increased by $30,000, the cash received from customers would be:
   a. $500,000.
   b. $470,000.
   c. $530,000.
   d. Cannot be determined.
4. Assume cost of goods sold on an accrual basis is $300,000, accounts payable increased by $20,000, and inventory increased by $50,000. Cash paid for merchandise is:
   a. $370,000.
   b. $230,000.
   c. $270,000.
   d. $330,000.
5. Assume net income was $200,000, depreciation expense was $10,000, accounts receivable increased by $15,000, and accounts payable increased by $5,000. The amount of cash flows from operating activities is:
   a. $200,000.
   b. $180,000.
   c. $210,000.
   d. $190,000.

Now turn to page 658 to check your answers.

Questions

1. What are the purposes of the statement of cash flows?
2. What are some of the uses of the statement of cash flows?
3. What information is contained in the statement of cash flows?
4. Which activities are generally included in operating activities?
5. Which activities are included in investing activities?
6. Which activities are included in financing activities?
7. Where should significant investing and financing activities that do not involve cash flows be reported?
8. Explain the difference between the direct and indirect methods for computing cash flows from operating activities.
9. What are noncash expenses? How are they treated in computing cash flows from operating activities?
10. Describe the treatment of a gain on the sale of equipment in preparing a statement of cash flows under the indirect method.
11. Depreciation is sometimes referred to as a source of cash. Is it a source of cash? Explain.
12. Why is it unlikely that cash flows from operating activities will be equal to net income for the same period?
13. If the net income for a given period is $25,000, does this mean there is an increase in cash of the same amount? Why or why not?
14. Why might a company have positive cash flows from operating activities even though operating at a net loss?

15. Indicate the type of activity each of the following transactions represents (operating, investing, or financing) and whether it is an inflow or an outflow.
    a. Sold goods.
    b. Purchased building.
    c. Issued capital stock.
    d. Received cash dividends.
    e. Paid cash dividends.
    f. Purchased treasury stock.
    g. Sold available-for-sale securities.
    h. Made a loan.
    i. Paid interest on loan.
    j. Paid bond principal.
    k. Received proceeds of insurance settlement.
    l. Made contribution to charity.
16. Refer to "A Broader Perspective" on page 630. Answer the following questions:
    a. What was the major investing activity in 2010?
    b. Was there a net negative or positive cash flow from investing activities?
    c. Was the positive cash flow from operating activities large enough to pay the cash dividends?

17. **Real World Question**
    Refer to the Wal-Mart Stores, Inc. financial statements Appendix. Does it use the direct method or indirect method of reporting cash flows from operating activities?

Exercises

Exercise 16-1
Report specific items on statement of cash flows (L.O. 2, 4)

Indicate how the following data should be reported in a statement of cash flows. A company paid $500,000 cash for land. A building was acquired for $2,500,000 by assuming a mortgage on the building.

Exercise 16-2
Calculate the amount of cash paid for merchandise (L.O. 3)

Cost of goods sold in the income statement for the year ended 2012 was $260,000. The balances in Merchandise Inventory and Accounts Payable were:

	January 1, 2012	December 31, 2012
Merchandise Inventory	$160,000	$180,000
Accounts Payable	44,000	36,000

Calculate the amount of cash paid for merchandise for 2012.

Fill in the following chart, showing how increases and decreases in these accounts affect the conversion of accrual basis income to cash basis income:

Exercise 16-3
Show effects of
conversion from accrual
to cash basis income
(L.O. 3)

	Add	**Deduct**
Accounts Receivable		
Merchandise Inventory		
Prepaid Expenses		
Accounts Payable		
Accrued Liabilities Payable		

The income statement of a company shows net income of $200,000; merchandise inventory on January 1 was $76,500 and on December 31 was $94,500; accounts payable for merchandise purchases were $57,000 on January 1 and $68,000 on December 31. Compute the cash flows from operating activities under the indirect method.

Exercise 16-4
Compute cash flows
from operating
activities (L.O. 3)

The operating expenses and taxes (including $80,000 of depreciation) of a company for a given year were $600,000. Net income was $350,000. Prepaid insurance decreased from $18,000 to $14,000 during the year, while wages payable increased from $22,000 to $36,000 during the year. Compute the cash flows from operating activities under the indirect method.

Exercise 16-5
Compute cash flows
from operating activities
(L.O. 3)

Dividends payable increased by $20,000 during a year in which total dividends declared were $120,000. What amount appears for dividends paid in the statement of cash flows?

Exercise 16-6
Indicate treatment of a
dividend (L.O. 2, 4)

Following are balance sheet data for Quality Merchandise, Inc.:

Exercise 16-7
Compute cash used to
purchase plant assets
(L.O. 2, 4)

	December 31	
	2013	**2012**
Cash	$ 47,000	$ 26,000
Accounts receivable, net	141,000	134,000
Merchandise inventory	83,000	102,000
Prepaid expenses	9,000	11,000
Plant assets (net of accumulated depreciation)	235,000	230,000
Accounts payable	122,000	127,000
Accrued liabilities payable	40,000	41,000
Capital stock	300,000	300,000
Retained earnings	53,000	35,000

Assume that the depreciation recorded in 2013 was $15,000. Compute the cash spent to purchase plant assets, assuming no assets were sold or scrapped in 2013.

Use the data in Exercise 16–7. Assume the net income for 2013 was $24,000, depreciation was $15,000, and dividends declared and paid were $6,000. The company paid interest of $2,000 and income taxes of $14,000. Prepare a statement of cash flows—indirect method. Also prepare any necessary supplemental schedule(s).

Exercise 16-8
Prepare statement of
cash flows (L.O. 4)

The following data are from a company's Automobile and the Accumulated Depreciation—Automobile accounts:

Exercise 16-9
Report specific items
on statement of cash
flows (L.O. 2, 4)

Automobile

Date		**Debit**	**Credit**	**Balance**
Jan. 1	Balance brought forward			16,000
July 1	Traded for new auto		16,000	-0-
	New auto	31,000		31,000

Accumulated Depreciation—Automobile

Date		**Debit**	**Credit**	**Balance**
Jan. 1	Balance brought forward			12,000
July 1	One-half year's depreciation		2,000	14,000
	Auto traded	14,000		-0-
Dec. 31	One-half year's depreciation		4,000	4,000

The old auto was traded for a new one, with the difference in values paid in cash. The income statement for the year shows a loss on the exchange of autos of $1,200.

Indicate the dollar amounts, the descriptions of these amounts, and their exact locations in a statement of cash flows—indirect method.

Problems

Problem 16-1
Prepare working paper to convert income statement to cash basis; prepare cash flows from operating activities under both methods (L.O. 2, 3)

The income statement and other data of Dunbar Carpet Outlet, Inc., follow:

DUNBAR CARPET OUTLET, INC.
Income Statement
For the Year Ended December 31, 2012

Sales		$920,000
Cost of goods sold		380,000
Gross margin		$540,000
Operating expenses (other than depreciation)	$140,000	
Depreciation expense	40,000	180,000
Net income		$360,000

Changes in current assets (other than cash) and current liabilities during the year were:

	Increase	Decrease
Accounts receivable		$20,000
Merchandise inventory	$16,000	
Prepaid insurance	8,000	
Accounts payable	28,000	
Accrued liabilities payable	4,000	

Depreciation was the only noncash item affecting net income.

Required ➡

a. Prepare a working paper to calculate cash flows from operating activities under the direct method.

b. Prepare the cash flows from operating activities section of the statement of cash flows under the direct method.

c. Prove that the same cash flows amount will be obtained under the indirect method by preparing the cash flows from operating activities section of the statement of cash flows under the indirect method. You need not prepare a working paper.

Problem 16-2
Prepare statement of cash flows under the indirect method (L.O. 4)

The following comparative balance sheets and other data are for Cellular Telephone Sales, Inc.:

CELLULAR TELEPHONE SALES, INC.
Comparative Balance Sheets
December 31, 2013 and 2012

	2013	2012
Assets		
Cash	$ 76,105	$51,000
Accounts receivable, net	26,075	24,250
Merchandise inventory	30,000	35,000
Supplies on hand	1,750	2,550
Prepaid expenses	1,400	1,200
Land	180,000	142,500
Equipment	270,000	300,000
Accumulated depreciation—equipment	(75,000)	(67,500)
Total assets	$510,330	$489,000
Liabilities and Stockholders' Equity		
Accounts payable	$ 45,330	$ 76,300
Salaries payable	4,000	2,000
Accrued liabilities payable	2,000	8,250
Long-term note payable	150,000	150,000
Common stock ($5 par)	185,000	165,000
Paid-in capital in excess of par	32,500	—0—
Retained earnings	91,500	87,450
Total liabilities and stockholders' equity	$510,330	$489,000

1. Land was bought for $37,500 cash. The company intends to build a building on the land. *Additional data*
   Currently the company leases a building for its operations.
2. Equipment costing $50,000 with accumulated depreciation of $30,000 was sold for $23,500 (a gain of $3,500), and equipment costing $20,000 was purchased for cash.
3. Depreciation expense for the year was $37,500.
4. Common stock was issued for $52,500 cash.
5. Dividends declared and paid in 2013 totaled $32,950.
6. Net income was $37,000.
7. The company paid interest of $3,000 and income taxes of $17,000.

Prepare a statement of cash flows under the indirect method. Also prepare any necessary supplemental schedule(s).   *Required*

CA, Inc., is leading independent enterprise information technology (IT) management software and solutions company. It has a broad portfolio of software solutions that address customer needs, including mainframe; service assurance; security (identity and access management); project and portfolio management; service management; virtualization and service automation; and cloud computing.

Problem 16-3
Analyze CA Inc.'s statement of cash flows (L.O. 5, 6)

The company's statements of cash flows for the years 2009 through 2011 follow. Then the relevant portion of Management's Discussion and Analysis of the statement of cash flows is provided.

CA, Inc. and Subsidiaries
Consolidated Statements of Cash Flows

(In Millions)	Year Ended March,31,		
	2011	2010	2009
Operating activities:			
Net income	$ 827	$ 771	$ 671
Income from discontinued operations	(4)	(12)	(10)
Income from continuing operations	823	759	661
Adjustments to reconcile income from continuing operations to net cash provided by operating activities:			
Depreciation and amortization	379	292	259
Provision for deferred income taxes	140	68	(56)
Provision for bad debts	6	6	15
Share based compensation expense	80	102	92
Amortization of discount on convertible debt	—	29	37
Asset impairments and other non-cash activities	2	13	2
Foreign currency transaction losses (gains)	4	(10)	67
Changes in other operating assets and liabilities, net of effect of acquisitions:			
Decrease in trade and current installment accounts receivable, net	140	8	195
(Decrease) increase in deferred revenue	(128)	94	(49)
Increase (decrease) in taxes payable, net	(8)	(18)	34
Increase (decrease) in accounts payable, accrued expenses and other	23	(21)	(73)
(Decrease) increase in accrued salaries, wages, and commissions	(16)	25	(29)
Decrease in restructuring liabilities	(63)	(12)	(13)
Changes in other operating assets and liabilities	(5)	1	42
Net cash provided by operating activities — continuing operations	1,377	1,336	1,184
Investing activities:			
Acquisitions of businesses, net of cash acquired, and purchased software	(252)	(617)	(76)
Purchases of property and equipment	(92)	(79)	(83)
Proceeds from sale and divestiture of assets	13	—	6
Capitalized software development costs	(170)	(188)	(129)
Purchases of marketable securities	(209)	—	—
Proceeds from the sale of marketable securities	9	—	—
Maturities of marketable securities	19	—	—
Other investing activities	(18)	(4)	(2)
Net cash used in investing activities — continuing operations	(700)	(888)	(284)

Financing activities:

Dividends paid	(82)	(83)	(83)
Purchases of common stock	(235)	(227)	(4)
Debt borrowings	260	744	1
Debt repayments	(273)	(1,205)	(680)
Debt issuance costs	—	(6)	—
Proceeds from call spread option	—	61	—
Exercise of common stock options and other	10	11	7
Net cash used in financing activities — continuing operations	(320)	(705)	(759)
Net change in cash and cash equivalents before effect of exchange rate changes on cash — continuing operations	357	(257)	141
Effect of exchange rate changes on cash	89	104	(252)
Cash provided by operating activities — discontinued operations	4	24	28
Cash provided by investing activities — discontinued operations	16	—	—
Net effect of discontinued operations on cash and cash equivalents	20	24	28
Increase (decrease) in cash and cash equivalents	466	(129)	(83)
Cash and cash equivalents at beginning of period	2,583	2,712	2,795
Cash and cash equivalents at end of period	$3,049	$2,583	$2,712

Management's Discussion and Analysis

Liquidity and capital resources

Our cash and cash equivalent balances are held in numerous locations throughout the world, with 47% held in our subsidiaries outside the United States at March 31, 2011. Cash, cash equivalents and marketable securities totaled $3,228 million at March 31, 2011, representing an increase of $645 million from the March 31, 2010 balance of $2,583 million. The increase in cash was primarily due to the decrease in cash used in investing and financing activities for fiscal 2011, compared with fiscal 2010. The decrease in cash used in investing activities was primarily due to the reduction of cash paid for acquisitions, partially offset by our investment in marketable securities in order to enhance the yield of our investments while maintaining the safety of our portfolio. The decrease in cash used in financing activities was primarily due to the cash utilized during fiscal 2010 to repay our debt outstanding, which enhanced our capital structure and financial flexibility. During fiscal 2011, there was an $89 million favorable translation effect from foreign currency exchange rates on cash held outside the United States in currencies other than the U.S. dollar.

We expect that existing cash and cash equivalents, the availability of borrowings under existing and renewable credit lines, and cash expected to be provided from operations will be sufficient to meet ongoing cash requirements.

We expect to use existing cash, cash equivalents and marketable securities balances and future cash generated from operations to fund capital spending, financing activities such as the repayment of our debt balances as they mature, the payment of dividends, and the potential repurchase of shares of common stock in accordance with any plans approved by our Board of Directors, as well as our continued investment in our enterprise resource planning implementation and future acquisitions.

Debt arrangements

We have entered into interest rate swaps to convert $500 million of our 6.125% Notes into floating interest rate payments through December 1, 2014. Under the terms of the swaps, we will pay quarterly interest at an average rate of 2.88% plus the three-month LIBOR rate, and will receive payment at 5.625%. The LIBOR based rate is set quarterly three months prior to the date of the interest payment. At March 31, 2011, the fair value of these derivatives was $15 million, of which $11 million is included in "Other current assets" and $4 million is included in "Other noncurrent assets, net" in the Consolidated Balance Sheet. The carrying value of the 6.125% Notes was adjusted by an amount that is equal and offsetting to the fair value of the swaps.

At March 31, 2011, $250 million of our Revolving Credit Facility due August 2012, was reclassified from long-term debt to current debt and was repaid in April 2011.

At March 31, 2011, our senior unsecured notes were rated Baa2 (stable) by Moody's Investor Services, BBB (positive) by Standard and Poor's, and BBB+ (stable) by Fitch Ratings. At April 11, 2011 Standard and Poor's upgraded our credit rating to BBB+ (stable), resulting in a decrease in the interest rate applicable to incremental borrowings from 0.66% to 0.58%.

Stock repurchases

On May 12, 2010, our Board of Directors approved a stock repurchase program that authorizes us to acquire up to $500 million of our common stock. During fiscal 2011, we entered into brokerage arrangements with third-party financial institutions to purchase our common stock in the open market on our behalf. We acquired 10. 5million shares of our common stock for $218 million under these arrangements during fiscal 2011. At March 31, 2011, we were authorized to purchase an aggregate amount of up to $282 million of additional shares of common stock under our current stock repurchase program.

On May 12, 2011, our Board of Directors approved a stock repurchase program that authorized us to acquire up to an additional $500 million of our common stock, in addition to the previous program approved on May 12, 2010. We will fund the program with available cash on hand and repurchase shares on the open market from time to time based on market conditions and other factors.

Dividends

We have paid cash dividends each year since July 1990. For fiscal 2011, 2010 and 2009, we paid annual cash dividends of $0.16 per share, which have been paid out in quarterly installments of $0.04 per share as and when declared by our Board of Directors. Total cash dividends paid was $82 million, $83 million and $83 million for fiscal 2011, 2010 and 2009, respectively.

On May 12, 2011, we announced an increase of the Company's regular quarterly dividend to $0.05 per share as and when declared by the Board of Directors.

Contractual obligations and commitments

We have commitments under certain contractual arrangements to make future payments for goods and services. These contractual arrangements secure the rights to various assets and services to be used in the future in the normal course of business. For example, we are contractually committed to make certain minimum lease payments for the use of property under operating lease agreements. In accordance with current accounting rules, the future rights and related obligations pertaining to such contractual arrangements are not reported as assets or liabilities on our Consolidated Balance Sheets. We expect to fund these contractual arrangements with cash generated from operations in the normal course of business.

a. Explain why depreciation and amortization were added to income from continuing operations when calculating net cash provided by operating activities. Why was the provision for bad debts added to income from continuing operations each year?

b. How does the Company plan to use the future cash generated by operating activities?

c. Why would the upgrade of the Company's credit rating by Standard and Poor's result in a decrease in the interest rate applicable to the Company's incremental borrowings?

d. What information would normally appear immediately below the statement of cash flows that seems to be missing?

e. Does the amount of cash provided by operating activities seem large enough to continue the present dividend payments?

f. Given the following data, calculate the cash flow per share of common stock ratio, the cash flow margin ratio, and cash flow liquidity ratio.

Required

	(in millions)
Average number of shares of common stock outstanding	507
Net sales	4,429
Cash and marketable securities	3,124
Current liabilities	3,924

Mechan Systems Company develops, manufactures, markets, installs and supports a wide range of standards-based LAN and WAN connectivity hardware and software products. The company's statements of cash flow for the years 2010–2012 follow. Then the relevant portion of Management's Discussion and Analysis of the statement of cash flows is provided.

Problem 16-4
Analyze Mechan Systems Company's statement of cash flows
(L.O. 5, 6)

CONSOLIDATED STATEMENTS OF CASH FLOWS
Years Ended February 29, 2012, and February 28, 2011 and 2010
(in thousands)

	2012	2011	2010
Cash flows from operating activities:			
Net income	$ 164,418	$ 161,974	$ 119,218
Adjustments to reconcile net income to net cash provided by operating activities:			
Depreciation and amortization	32,061	26,832	17,335
Provision for losses on accounts receivable	356	72	1,734
Loss on disposals of property, plant and equipment	93	174	113
Deferred taxes	(38,766)	(4,434)	(6,151)
Changes in assets and liabilities:			
Accounts receivables	(55,101)	(27,698)	(17,707)
Inventories	(50,483)	(23,080)	(8,758)
Prepaid expenses and other assets	(18,844)	(3,123)	1,211
Accounts payable and accrued expenses	62,908	11,336	22,003
Income taxes payable	3,705	10,476	(3,924)
Net cash provided by operating activities	$ 100,347	$ 152,529	$ 125,074
Cash flows from investing activities:			
Capital expenditures	$ (65,035)	$ (63,091)	$ (39,399)
Purchase of available-for-sale securities	(79,427)	(71,598)	(30,097)
Purchase of held-to-maturity securities	(205,852)	(282,712)	(258,517)
Maturities of marketable securities	208,922	323,682	197,406
Net cash used in investing activities	$(141,392)	$ (93,719)	$(130,607)
Cash flows from financing activities:			
Repayment of notes receivable from stockholders	$ 174	$ 131	$ 66
Repurchase of common stock	(1,173)	(13,070)	—
Tax benefit of options exercised	7,215	5,712	6,980
Common stock issued to employee stock purchase plan	3,323	2,287	1,637
Proceeds from stock option exercise	16,021	4,887	7,185
Net cash provided by (used for) financing activities	$ 25,560	$ (53)	$ 15,868
Effect of exchange rate changes on cash	$ 166	$ 712	$ 161
Net increase (decrease) in cash and cash equivalents	$ (15,319)	$ 59,469	$ 10,496
Cash and cash equivalents, beginning of year	114,032	54,563	44,067
Cash and cash equivalents, end of year	$ 98,713	$ 114,032	$ 54,563
Cash paid during the year for:			
Income taxes	$ 105,233	$ 68,420	$ 67,263

Management's Discussion and Analysis

Net cash provided by operating activities was $100.3 million in fiscal 2012, compared to $152.5 million in fiscal 2011 and $125.1 million in fiscal 2010.

Capital investment for fiscal 2012 of $65.0 million included $9.8 million for building costs of which $3.4 was for the purchase of an engineering building, $21.4 million for engineering computer and computer related software and equipment, $5.5 million for manufacturing and related equipment and $19.0 million for expanding global sales operations. During fiscal 2011, capital expenditures of $63.1 million included approximately $8.2 million for building costs related to expanding manufacturing and distribution capacities and enlarging worldwide sales operations, $12.5 million for manufacturing and manufacturing support equipment and $15.0 million for engineering computer and computer related equipment. Another $15.0 million was spent in support of expanded global sales activities. During fiscal 2010, capital expenditures of $39.4 million included $3.9 million on buildings, $10.1 million on engineering equipment, $7.8 million on manufacturing capacity expansions and $2.0 million to equip new sales offices.

Cash, cash equivalents and marketable securities increased during fiscal 2012 to $407.0 million, from $345.9 million in the prior fiscal year. State and local municipal bonds of approximately $264.2 million, maturing in approximately 1.5 years, were being held by the Company at February 29, 2012.

At February 29, 2012, the Company did not have any short or long term borrowing or any significant financial commitments outstanding, other than those required in the normal course of business.

In the opinion of management, internally generated funds from operations and existing cash, cash equivalents and marketable securities will be adequate to support the Company's working capital and capital expenditures requirements for both short and long term needs.

a. Which method did the company use in arriving at net cash flows from operating activities? ◖ *Required*

b. Did current assets other than cash increase or decrease during the year ended February 29, 2012?

c. Did current liabilities increase or decrease during the year ended February 29, 2012?

d. What were the main investing activities during this three-year period?

e. What was the main source of cash from financing activities during the three-year period?

f. Did the company pay any interest expense during the year ended February 19, 2012?

g. Given the following data, calculate the cash flow per share of common stock ratio, the cash flow margin ratio, and the cash flow liquidity ratio. How do these ratios compare with the ratios shown for other companies in the chapter?

	(in thousands)
Average number of shares of common stock outstanding	71,839
Net sales	$1,069,715
Cash and marketable securities	253,540
Current liabilities	164,352

The following comparative balance sheets and other data are for Dayton Tent & Awning Sales, Inc.:

Problem 16-5
Prepare working paper and statement of cash flows under the indirect method (Appendix) (L.O. 7)

DAYTON TENT & AWNING SALES, INC.
Comparative Balance Sheets
June 30, 2013 and 2012

	2013	2012
Assets		
Cash	$ 441,800	$ 332,600
Accounts receivable, net	750,750	432,900
Merchandise inventory	819,000	850,200
Prepaid insurance	3,900	5,850
Land	312,000	351,000
Buildings	2,184,000	1,209,000
Machinery and tools	858,000	468,000
Accumulated depreciation—machinery and tools	(809,250)	(510,900)
Total assets	$ 4,560,200	$ 3,138,650
Liabilities and Stockholders' Equity		
Accounts payable	$ 226,750	$ 275,500
Accrued liabilities payable	185,800	111,700
Bank loans (due in 2016)	56,550	66,300
Mortgage bonds payable	382,200	185,250
Common stock—$100 par	1,755,000	585,000
Paid-in capital in excess of par	58,500	—0—
Retained earnings	1,895,400	1,914,900
Total liabilities and stockholders' equity	$ 4,560,200	$ 3,138,650

◖ *Additional data*

1. Net income for the year was $128,000.
2. Depreciation for the year was $356,850.
3. There was a gain of $7,800 on the sale of land. The land was sold for $46,800.
4. The additional mortgage bonds were issued at face value as partial payment for a building valued at $975,000. The amount of cash paid was $778,050.
5. Machinery and tools were purchased for $448,500 cash.
6. Fully depreciated machinery with a cost of $58,500 was scrapped and written off.
7. Additional common stock was issued at $105 per share. The total proceeds were $1,228,500.
8. Dividends declared and paid were $147,500.
9. A payment was made on the bank loan, $9,750.
10. The company paid interest of $9,000 and income taxes of $75,000. ◖ *Required*
    a. Prepare a working paper for a statement of cash flows.
    b. Prepare a statement of cash flows under the indirect method. Also prepare any necessary supplemental schedule(s).

Alternate Problems

Problem 16-1A
Prepare working paper
to convert income
statement to cash
basis; prepare cash
flows from operating
activities under both
methods (L.O. 2, 3)

The following income statement and other data are for Kennesaw Auto Glass Specialists, Inc.:

KENNESAW AUTO GLASS SPECIALISTS, INC.
Income Statement
For the Year Ended December 31, 2012

Sales		$450,000
Cost of goods sold		125,000
Gross margin		$325,000
Operating expenses (other than depreciation)	$60,000	
Depreciation expense	20,000	80,000
Net income		$245,000

Changes in current assets (other than cash) and current liabilities during the year were:

	Increase	Decrease
Accounts receivable	$15,000	
Merchandise inventory		$25,000
Prepaid insurance	8,000	
Accounts payable		15,000
Accrued liabilities payable	4,000	

Depreciation was the only noncash item affecting net income.

Required ➡

a. Prepare a working paper to calculate cash flows from operating activities under the direct method.

b. Prepare the cash flows from operating activities section of the statement of cash flows under the direct method.

c. Prove that the same cash flows amount is obtained under the indirect method by preparing the cash flows from operating activities section of the statement of cash flows under the indirect method. You need not prepare a working paper.

Problem 16-2A
Prepare statement of
cash flows under the
indirect method
(L.O. 4)

The following information relates to Dunwoody Nursery & Garden Center, Inc. The company leases a building adjacent to its land.

DUNWOODY NURSERY & GARDEN CENTER, INC.
Comparative Balance Sheets
December 31, 2013 and 2012

	2013	2012
Assets		
Cash	$ 44,500	$ 52,000
Accounts receivable, net	59,000	60,000
Merchandise inventory	175,000	120,000
Equipment	412,500	315,000
Accumulated depreciation—equipment	(120,000)	(105,000)
Land	75,000	15,000
Total assets	$646,000	$457,000
Liabilities and Stockholders' Equity		
Accounts payable	$ 43,750	$40,750
Accrued liabilities payable	2,250	3,750
Capital stock—common—$10 par	375,000	300,000
Paid-in capital in excess of par	150,000	75,000
Retained earnings	75,000	37,500
Total liabilities and stockholders' equity	$646,000	$457,000

1. Net income was $97,500 for the year.
2. Fully depreciated equipment costing $15,000 was sold for $3,750 (a gain of $3,750), and equipment costing $112,500 was purchased for cash.
3. Depreciation expense for the year was $30,000.
4. Land was purchased, $60,000.
5. An additional 7,500 shares of common stock were issued for cash at $20 per share (total proceeds, $150,000).
6. Cash dividends of $60,000 were declared and paid.

◗ *Additional data*

The company paid interest of $6,000 and income taxes of $65,000. Prepare a statement of cash flows under the indirect method. Also prepare any necessary supplemental schedule(s).

◗ *Required*

Drexler, Inc., is an independent service organization that markets and services electronic credit card authorization and payment systems to small retail, wholesale, and professional businesses located throughout the United States. Prior to installing the company's electronic system, most of these businesses have used manual, paper-based systems to process credit card transactions or did not accept credit cards at all. As the use of credit cards has significantly expanded, electronic processing has proved more convenient by accelerating customer purchases, lowering processing expenses, and reducing losses from fraudulent cards.

Problem 16-3A
Analyze Drexler, Inc.'s
statement of cash flows
(L.O. 5, 6)

The company's account portfolio has grown through the purchase of account portfolios as well as through the internal development of accounts using telemarketing and field sales. With approximately 90,000 accounts at July 31, 2012, the company is one of the largest independent service organizations in the country.

The company's statements of cash flows for the years 2010–2012 follow. Then the relevant portion of Management's Discussion and Analysis of the statement of cash flows is provided.

Consolidated Statement of Cash Flows

	2010	2011	2012
Cash flows from operating activities:			
Net cash received from merchants	$ 19,657,687	$ 34,353,326	$ 67,313,124
Cash paid to vendors and employees	(14,758,040)	(28,467,472)	(49,128,150)
Interest received	22,262	310,136	1,672,714
Interest paid	(268,586)	(198,485)	(505,856)
Income taxes paid	(994,969)	(1,600,405)	(5,630,881)
Net cash provided by operating activities	$ 3,658,354	$ 4,397,100	$ 13,720,951
Cash flows from investing activities:			
Purchase of merchant portfolios	$ (8,415,055)	$(24,576,426)	$(31,787,725)
Purchase of property and equipment	(1,465,984)	(1,917,395)	(1,777,955)
Net cash used in investing activities	$ (9,881,039)	$(26,493,821)	$(33,565,680)
Cash flows from financing activities:			
Proceeds from issuance of long-term debt	$ 7,650,000	$ 16,450,000	$ 305,000
Payments on long-term debt	(1,163,170)	(12,828,503)	(16,545,500)
Proceeds from issuance of common stock	—	17,098,894	140,963,115
Payments to repurchase treasury stock	(45,000)	(32,500)	(12,000)
Proceeds from noncontrolling shareholder contribution	—	—	120,000
Net cash provided by financing activities	$ 6,441,830	$ 20,687,891	$124,830,615
Net increase (decrease) in cash and cash equivalents	$ 219,145	$ (1,408,830)	$104,985,886
Cash and cash equivalents at beginning of year	1,664,830	1,883,975	475,145
Cash and cash equivalents at end of year	$ 1,883,975	$ 475,145	$105,461,031

Supplemental schedule of noncash activities:
In connection with the purchase of merchant portfolios in fiscal years 2010 and 2011, the Company issued promissory notes totaling $5,061,804 and $80,500, respectively.
The company recognized a tax benefit of $318,517 for the year ended July 31, 2012 for the excess of the fair market value at the exercise date over that at the award date for stock options exercised.
In connection with the purchase of merchant portfolio in March 2010, the Company issued 312,500 shares of common stock.
In connection with an agreement between the Company and a processing back entered into simultaneously with the purchase of a merchant portfolio in March 2010, the Company issued warrants to purchase 120,000 shares of common stock.

Reconciliation of net income to net cash provided by operating activities:

Net income	$ 2,592,444	$ 3,640,155	$ 8,625,376
Fiscal year conversion of acquisition	—	—	(356,914)
Adjustments:			
Depreciation and amortization expense	1,648,023	3,517,852	7,509,630
Provision for merchant losses	484,993	483,245	654,705
Stock award compensation and other	239,659	241,477	120,395
Deferred income taxes	(453,658)	35,982	(761,705)
Changes in assets and liabilities:			
Accounts receivable	(1,562,961)	(1,459,799)	(2,125,510)
Inventory	(50,235)	(157,087)	(186,289)
Other assets	(1,716,464)	(1,895,097)	(501,353)
Accounts payable	1,557,611	44,106	587,784
Accrued liabilities	975,065	(223,411)	210,064
Deferred revenues	(56,123)	169,677	(55,232)
Net cash provided by operating activities	$ 3,658,354	$ 4,397,100	$ 13,720,951

Management's Discussion and Analysis

Capital Expenditures and Investing Activities

Capital expenditures were approximately $1.8 million for fiscal year 2012 as compared to $1.9 million for fiscal year 2011 and $1.5 million for fiscal year 2010. The increase in capital expenditures was primarily the result of additional expenditures related to the Company's management information system, the purchase of additional credit card terminals, the Company's relocation of its office facilities and the purchase of peripheral equipment for lease to merchants. In addition to the increase in capital expenditures, the Company used $8.4 million, $24.6 million and $31.8 million for the purchase of merchant portfolios in fiscal years 2010, 2011 and 2012, respectively. The Company purchased five merchant portfolios in fiscal 2010, nine merchant portfolios in fiscal year 2011 and five in fiscal year 2012.

Financing Activities

The significant increase in cash provided by financing activities for fiscal year 2011 resulted from the consummation of the Company's initial public offering in August 2010. Cash provided by financing activities for fiscal year 2011 was $20.7 million which reflects the net proceeds of the initial public offering after retirement of the Company's outstanding indebtedness. Additionally, the Company issued $15.3 million of long-term debt in connection with three of the nine merchant portfolios purchased in fiscal year 2011.

The cash provided by financing activities for fiscal 2012 reflects the Company's consummation of its second and third public offerings in October 2011 and April 2012, respectively. Net cash provided by financing activities was $124.8 million in fiscal 2012 which reflects the net proceeds from the offerings after retirement of the Company's outstanding bank indebtedness.

Future Capital Needs

Management believes that significant expenditures for the purchase of additional merchant portfolios may be required for the Company to sustain its growth in the future. Management expects to fund such purchases primarily through cash generated from operations and additional bank borrowings. Management believes the combination of these sources will be sufficient to meet the Company's anticipated liquidity needs and its growth plans through fiscal year 2013. The Company, however, may pursue additional expansion opportunities, including purchases of additional merchant portfolios, which may require additional capital, and the Company may incur, from time to time, additional short-term and long-term indebtedness or issue, in public or private transactions, equity or debt securities, the availability and terms of which will depend upon then prevailing market and other conditions.

The Company's revolving credit facility was amended and restated during fiscal year 2011 to increase the line of credit to $17.5 million. The Company repaid all outstanding debt related to this credit facility with the proceeds from its second public offering during fiscal year 2012. The amended agreement expires November 1, 2012 with all amounts then outstanding under the agreement due on November 1, 2012, unless the agreement is extended or the outstanding amounts have been converted to a term loan requiring equal monthly payments for 48 months.

Borrowings under the amended revolving credit facility are used to finance purchases of merchant portfolios and equipment and for working capital purposes. Borrowings are secured by substantially all the Company's assets and life insurance policies on the lives of two of the Company's executive officers.

a. Which method is the company using to determine net cash provided by operating activities?
b. Why does the company show the indirect method below the statement of cash flows?
c. What is the trend of net cash provided by operating activities over the three years?
d. How has the company increased its merchant portfolios?
e. What items of property and equipment were acquired during the three-year period?
f. What was the major source of the huge increase in cash and cash equivalents over the three-year period? How were the proceeds used?
g. How does the company expect to finance future expenditures to acquire additional merchant portfolios?
h. How are amounts secured that are borrowed under the line of credit?
i. Given the following data, calculate the cash flow per share of common stock ratio, the cash flow margin ratio, and the cash flow liquidity ratio. (Round the net cash provided from operating activities to the nearest thousand before you calculate the ratios.) How do the ratios compare with the ones for companies illustrated in the chapter?

	(in thousands)
Average number of shares of common stock outstanding	28,539
Net sales	$149,840
Cash and marketable securities	105,461
Current liabilities	6,862

Founded in 1837, The Procter & Gamble Company is a world leader in the production of beauty products, male grooming products, health care products, fabric and home care products, and baby and family care products. Its leading brands include Pantene, Gillette, Tide, Crest, Pampers, Vicks, and Bounty. Many of its products are marketed worldwide, with twenty-four of its brands each achieving more than $1 billion in worldwide sales in 2011.

The company's statements of cash flows for the years 2009–2011 follow. Then the relevant portion of Management's Discussion and Analysis of the statement of cash flows is provided.

Problem 16-4A
Analyze The Procter & Gamble Company's 2011 statement of cash flows (L.O. 5, 6)

The Procter & Gamble Company
Consolidated Statements of Cash Flow

Amounts in millions; Years ended June 30	2011	2010	2009
Cash and cash equivalents, beginning of year	$ 2,879	$ 4,781	$ 3,313
Operating activities			
Net earnings	11,797	12,736	13,436
Depreciation and amortization	2,838	3,108	3,082
Share-based compensation expense	414	453	516
Deferred income taxes	128	36	596
Gain on sale of businesses	(203)	(2,670)	(2,377)
Change in accounts receivable	(426)	(14)	415
Change in inventories	(501)	86	721
Change in accounts payable, accrued and other liabilities	358	2,446	(742)
Change in other operating assets and liabilities	(1,190)	(305)	(758)
Other	16	196	30
Total operating activities	13,231	16,072	14,919
Investing activities			
Capital expenditures	(3,306)	(3,067)	(3,238)
Proceeds from asset sales	225	3,068	1,087
Acquisitions, net of cash acquired	(474)	(425)	(368)
Change in investments	73	(173)	166
Total investing activities	(3,482)	(597)	(2,353)

Financing activities

Dividends to shareholders	**(5,767)**	(5,458)	(5,044)
Change in short-term debt	**151**	(1,798)	(2,420)
Additions to long-term debt	**1,536**	3,830	4,926
Reductions of long-term debt	**(206)**	(8,546)	(2,587)
Treasury stock purchases	**(7,039)**	(6,004)	(6,370)
Impact of stock options and other	**1,302**	721	681
Total financing activities	**(10,023)**	(17,255)	(10,814)
Effect of exchange rate changes on cash and cash equivalents	**163**	(122)	(284)
Change in cash and cash equivalents	**(111)**	(1,902)	1,468
Cash and cash equivalent, end of year	**$ 2,768**	$ 2,879	$ 4,781

SUPPLEMENTAL DISCLOSURE

Cash payments for:

Interest	$ **806**	$ 1,184	$ 1,226
Income taxes	**2,992**	4,175	3,248
Assets acquired through non-cash capital leases	**13**	20	8
Divestiture of coffee business in exchange for shares of P&G stock	**—**	—	2,466

Management's Discussion and Analysis*

Financial Condition

We believe our financial condition continues to be of high quality, as evidenced by our ability to generate substantial cash from operations and ready access to capital markets at competitive rates.

Operating cash flow provides the primary source of funds to finance operating needs and capital expenditures. Excess operating cash is used first to fund shareholder dividends. Other discretionary uses include share repurchases and tack-on acquisitions to complement our portfolio of brands and geographies. As necessary, we may supplement operating cash flow with debt to fund these activities. The overall cash position of the Company reflects our strong business results and a global cash management strategy that takes into account liquidity management, economic factors and tax considerations.

Operating Activities

Operating cash flow was $13.2 billion in 2011, an 18% decrease versus the prior year. Operating cash flow resulted primarily from net earnings adjusted for non-cash items (depreciation and amortization, stock-based compensation, deferred income taxes and gain on the sale of businesses), partially offset by an increase in working capital. The net of accounts receivable, inventory and accounts payable consumed $569 million of operating cash flow in 2011 mainly due to increases in inventories and accounts receivables. Inventory consumed $501 million driven by higher commodity costs, business growth and increased stock levels in advance of initiatives and sourcing changes. Inventory days on hand increased by five days due to the impact of foreign exchange, higher commodity costs and increased safety stock levels. Accounts receivable used $426 million primarily to support business growth. Accounts receivable days sales outstanding were up three days due to timing of sales and the impact of foreign exchange. Inventory and accounts receivable increases were partially offset by accounts payable, accrued and other liabilities, which increased to support business growth. Other operating assets and liabilities were also a significant use of operating cash flow due primarily to net reductions in reserves for uncertain tax positions and an increase in the amount of value added taxes due from various governmental authorities. In the prior year, working capital was a net source of cash.

Free Cash Flow. We view free cash flow as an important measure because it is one factor impacting the amount of cash available for dividends and discretionary investment. It is defined as operating cash flow less capital expenditures and is one of the measures used to evaluate senior management and determine their at-risk compensation. Free cash flow was $9.9 billion in 2011, a decrease of 24% versus the prior year. Free cash flow decreased due to lower operating cash flow and higher capital spending. Free cash flow productivity, defined as the ratio of free cash flow to net earnings, was 84% in 2011.

Investing Activities

Net investing activities consumed $3.5 billion of cash in 2011 and $597 million in 2010 mainly due to capital spending and acquisitions, partially offset by proceeds from asset sales, including $3.0 billion in cash received from the sale of our global pharmaceuticals business in 2010.

Capital Spending. We view capital spending efficiency as a critical component of our overall cash management strategy. We manage capital spending to support our business growth plans and have cost controls to deliver our cash generation targets. Capital expenditures, primarily to support capacity expansion, innovation and cost savings, were $3.3 billion in 2011 and $3.1 billion in 2010. The increase in capital spending resulted primarily from capacity expansions. Capital spending as a percentage of net sales increased 10 basis points to 4.0% in 2011. Capital spending as a percentage of net sales decreased 30 basis points to 3.9% in 2010 behind the scale leverage of net sales growth and a reduction in capital spending.

Acquisitions. Acquisitions used $474 million of cash in 2011 primarily for the acquisition of Ambi Pur, an air freshener business. In 2010, acquisitions used $425 million of cash primarily for the acquisition of Natura, a leading producer and distributor of branded premium natural pet foods.

Proceeds from Asset Sales. Proceeds from asset sales contributed $225 million to cash in 2011 mainly due to the sale of our Infasil brand in Western Europe and Zest brand in North America. In 2010, proceeds from asset sales contributed $3.1 billion to cash mainly due to the sale of our global pharmaceuticals business.

Financing Activities

Dividend Payments. Our first discretionary use of cash is dividend payments. Dividends per common share increased 9% to $1.97 per share in 2011. Total dividend payments to common and preferred shareholders were $5.8 billion in 2011 and $5.5 billion in 2010. The increase in dividend payments resulted from increases in our quarterly dividends per share, partially offset by a reduction in the number of shares outstanding. In April 2011, the Board of Directors declared an increase in our quarterly dividend from $0.4818 to $0.525 per share on Common Stock and Series A and B ESOP Convertible Class A Preferred Stock. This represents a 9% increase compared to the prior quarterly dividend and is the 55th consecutive year that our dividend has increased. We have paid a dividend in every year since our incorporation in 1890.

Long-Term and Short-Term Debt. We maintain debt levels we consider appropriate after evaluating a number of factors, including cash flow expectations, cash requirements for ongoing operations, investment and financing plans (including acquisitions and share repurchase activities) and the overall cost of capital. Total debt was $32.0 billion in 2011 and $29.8 billion in 2010. Our total debt increased in 2011 mainly due to net debt issuances to fund general corporate purposes.

Treasury Purchases. Total share repurchases were $7.0 billion in 2011 and $6.0 billion in 2010.

Liquidity

Our current liabilities exceeded current assets by $5.3 billion, largely due to our commercial paper program. We anticipate being able to support our short-term liquidity and operating needs largely through cash generated from operations. We utilize short- and long-term debt to fund discretionary items such as acquisitions and share repurchases. We have strong short- and long-term debt ratings which have enabled and should continue to enable us to refinance our debt as it becomes due at favorable rates in commercial paper and bond markets. In addition, we have agreements with a diverse group of financial institutions that, if needed, should provide sufficient credit funding to meet short-term financing requirements.

On June 30, 2011, our short-term credit ratings were P-1 (Moody's) and A-1+ (Standard & Poor's), while our long-term credit ratings are Aa3 (Moody's) and AA- (Standard & Poor's), both with a stable outlook.

We maintain bank credit facilities to support our ongoing commercial paper program. These facilities can be extended for certain periods of time as specified in, and in accordance with, the terms of each credit agreement. The current facility is an $11.0 billion facility split between a $7.0 billion 5-year facility and a $4.0 billion 364-day facility, which expire in August 2016 and August 2012, respectively. We anticipate that these facilities will remain largely undrawn for the foreseeable future. These credit facilities do not have cross-default or ratings triggers, nor do they have material adverse events clauses, except at the time of signing. In addition to these credit facilities, we have an automatically effective registration statement on Form S-3 filed with the SEC that is available for registered offerings of short- or long-term debt securities.

Guarantees and Other Off-Balance Sheet Arrangements

We do not have guarantees or other off-balance sheet financing arrangements, including variable interest entities, which we believe could have a material impact on financial condition or liquidit

*Source: The Procter & Gamble Company's 2011 annual report, p. 45.

a. Does the company use the direct or indirect method of calculating net cash provided by operating activities?   ⌐ *Required*

b. Determine whether each of the current assets (other than cash) and current liabilities increased or decreased during 2011.

c. How is the company expanding its asset base?

d. What is the likelihood that the company will be able to pay at least the current level of dividends in the future?

e. Do you expect to see purchases of treasury stock increase or decrease in the future?

f. Given the following data, calculate the cash flow per share of common stock ratio, the cash flow margin ratio, and the cash flow liquidity ratio. (Round the net cash provided by operating activities to the nearest million before you calculate the ratios.) How do the ratios compare with the ones for companies illustrated in the chapter?

Required ➡

	(in millions)
Average number of shares of common stock outstanding	2,804
Net sales	82,559
Cash and marketable securities	2,768
Current liabilities	27,293

Problem 16-5A
Prepare working paper and statement of cash flows under the indirect method (Appendix) (L.O. 7)

The following information is from the accounting records of Wescott Office Supplies, Inc., for the fiscal years 2013 and 2012:

	2013	2012
Assets		
Cash	$ 66,250	$ 61,000
Accounts receivable, net	84,000	42,000
Merchandise inventory	42,000	48,250
Prepaid expenses	7,875	12,125
Land	94,500	78,750
Buildings	199,500	147,000
Accumulated depreciation—buildings	(31,500)	(26,250)
Equipment	257,250	210,000
Accumulated depreciation—equipment	(78,750)	(63,000)
Total assets	$641,125	$509,875
Liabilities and Stockholders' Equity		
Accounts payable	$ 73,500	$ 47,250
Accrued liabilities payable	50,500	55,750
Five-year note payable	52,500	—0—
Capital stock—$50 par	420,000	367,500
Retained earnings	44,625	39,375
Total liabilities and stockholders' equity	$641,125	$509,875

Additional data ➡

1. Net income for year ended June 30, 2013, was $56,250.
2. Additional land was acquired for cash, $15,750.
3. No equipment or building retirements occurred during the year.
4. Equipment was purchased for cash, $47,250.
5. The five-year note for $52,500 was issued to pay for a building erected on land leased by the company.
6. Stock was issued at par for cash, $52,500.
7. Dividends declared and paid were $51,000.
8. The company paid interest of $10,000 and income taxes of $40,000.

a. Prepare a working paper for a statement of cash flows.
b. Prepare a statement of cash flows under the indirect method. Also prepare any necessary supplemental schedule(s).

Beyond the Numbers—Critical Thinking

Business Decision Case 16-1
Prepare a statement of cash flows using the indirect method and answer president's questions (L.O. 1, 2, 4)

National Sports, Inc., is a sports equipment sales company. During 2013, the company replaced $18,000 of its fully depreciated equipment with new equipment costing $23,000. Although a midyear dividend of $5,000 was paid, the company found it necessary to borrow $5,000 from its bank on a two-year note. Further borrowing may be needed since the Cash account is dangerously low at year-end.

Following are the income statement and "cash flow statement," as the company's accountant calls it, for 2013.

NATIONAL SPORTS, INC.
Income Statement
For the Year Ended December 31, 2013

Sales		$195,000
Cost of goods sold	$140,000	
Operating expense and taxes	49,700	189,700
Net income		$ 5,300

NATIONAL SPORTS, INC.
Cash Flow Statement
For the Year Ended December 31, 2013

Cash received:		
From operations:		
Net income		$ 5,300
Depreciation		5,000
Total cash from operations		$10,300
Note issued to bank		5,000
Mortgage note issued		16,000
Total funds provided		$31,300
Cash paid:		
New equipment	$23,000	
Dividends	5,000	28,000
Increase in cash		$ 3,300

The company's president is very concerned about what he sees in these statements and how it relates to what he knows has actually happened. He turns to you for help. Specifically, he wants to know why the cash flow statement shows an increase in cash of $3,300 when he knows the cash balance decreased from $15,000 to $500 during the year. Also, why is depreciation shown as providing cash?

You believe you can answer the president's questions after receiving the following condensed balance sheet data:

NATIONAL SPORTS, INC.
Comparative Balance Sheets
December 31, 2013 and 2012

	December 31	
	2013	**2012**
Assets		
Current assets:		
Cash	$ 500	$ 15,000
Accounts receivable, net	17,800	13,200
Merchandise inventory	28,500	17,500
Prepaid expenses	700	300
Total current assets	$ 47,500	$ 46,000
Property, plant, and equipment:		
Equipment	$ 40,000	$ 35,000
Accumulated depreciation—equipment	(11,000)	(24,000)
Total property, plant, and equipment	$ 29,000	$ 11,000
Total assets	$ 76,500	$ 57,000
Liabilities and Stockholders' Equity		
Current liabilities:		
Accounts payable	$ 8,700	$ 10,000
Accrued liabilities payable	600	1,100
Total current liabilities	$ 9,300	$ 11,100
Long-term liabilities:		
Notes payable	5,000	—0—
Mortgage note payable	16,000	—0—
Total liabilities	$ 30,300	$ 11,100
Stockholders' equity:		
Common stock	$ 40,000	$ 40,000
Retained earnings	6,200	5,900
Total stockholders' equity	$ 46,200	$ 45,900
Total liabilities and stockholders' equity	$ 76,500	$ 57,000

Required ➲ Prepare a correct statement of cash flows using the indirect method that shows why National Sports, Inc., is having such a difficult time keeping sufficient cash on hand. Also, answer the president's questions. The company paid interest of $400 and income taxes of $3,000.

Business Decision Case 16-2
Prepare a schedule showing cash flows from operating activities under the indirect method and decide whether certain goals can be met (L.O. 4)

Following are comparative balance sheets for Hardiplank Siding, Inc.:

HARDIPLANK SIDING, INC.
Comparative Balance Sheets
December 31, 2013 and 2012

	2013	2012
Assets		
Cash	$ 80,000	$ 57,500
Accounts receivable, net	60,000	45,000
Merchandise inventory	90,000	52,500
Land	67,500	60,000
Buildings	90,000	90,000
Accumulated depreciation—buildings	(30,000)	(27,000)
Equipment	285,000	225,000
Accumulated depreciation—equipment	(52,500)	(48,000)
Goodwill	120,000	150,000
Total assets	$710,000	$605,000
Liabilities and Stockholders' Equity		
Accounts payable	$ 95,000	$ 65,000
Accrued liabilities payable	30,000	22,500
Capital stock	315,000	300,000
Paid-in capital—stock dividends	75,000	67,500
Paid-in capital—land donations	15,000	—0—
Retained earnings	180,000	150,000
Total liabilities and stockholders' equity	$710,000	$605,000

An analysis of the Retained Earnings account for the year reveals the following:

Balance, January 1, 2013		$150,000
Add: Net income for the year		107,500
		$257,500
Less: Cash dividends	$55,000	
Stock dividends	22,500	77,500
Balance, December 31, 2013		$180,000

Additional data ➲

a. Equipment with a cost of $30,000 on which $27,000 of depreciation had been accumulated was sold during the year at a loss of $1,500. Included in net income is a gain on the sale of land of $9,000.

b. The president of the company has set two goals for 2014: (1) increase cash by $40,000 and (2) increase cash dividends by $35,000. The company's activities in 2014 are expected to be quite similar to those of 2013, and no new fixed assets will be acquired.

Required ➲ Prepare a schedule showing cash flows from operating activities under the indirect method for 2013. Can the company meet its president's goals for 2014? Explain.

Annual Report Analysis 16-3
Decide whether Wal-Mart can maintain its current dividend (real world problem) (L.O. 1)

Refer to the Annual Report Appendix. Evaluate the ease with which Wal-Mart Stores, Inc. will be able to maintain its dividend payments in the future at 2011 amounts. (Hint: Compare current dividend amount with net cash provided by operating activities.)

Refer to "A Broader Perspective" on page 630 and answer the following questions:

Annual Report Analysis 16-4
Analyze a company's statement of cash flows and answer questions (L.O. 5)

   a. Over the last three years from which major activities (operations, investing, financing) has Johnson & Johnson received net cash inflows and on which major activities have they spent the funds?
   b. What relationship do you see between "Depreciation and amortization of property and intangibles" and "Additions of property, plant, and equipment"?
   c. What were the two major sources of cash outflows to stockholders and which was larger?
   d. By how much did the investments in marketable securities grow or shrink over the three-year period?
   e. By how much did long-term debt grow or shrink over the three-year period?
   f. If you were a stockholder, would you feel uncertain or confident that this company will be able to pay future dividends at the same rate as in the past?
   g. For what reason or reasons might the company be buying back its own stock?
   h. For the latest year, did the current assets (other than cash) and current liabilities go up or down?
   i. From the information that is available, does it appear that the company is performing well or poorly?

In groups of two or three students write a two-page, double-spaced paper on one of the following topics:

Group Project 16-5
Write a paper on a specific topic

   Which Is Better, the Direct or Indirect Method (of calculating net cash provided by operating activities)?

   Analysis of the Johnson & Johnson Cash Flow Statement (shown in "A Broader Perspective" in this chapter)

   Analysis of Cash Flow Statement for Wal-Mart Stores, Inc. (shown in the Annual Report Appendix)

Your analysis should be convincing and have no spelling or grammatical errors. Your paper should be neat and the result of several drafts. The paper should have a cover page with the title and the authors' names. Use a word processing program if possible.

In a group of one or two other students, go to the library and locate *Statement of Financial Accounting Standards No. 95,* "Statement of Cash Flows," published by the Financial Accounting Standards Board. Write a report to your instructor answering the following questions:

Group Project 16-6
Perform library project on aspects of Statement of Financial Accounting Standards No. 95

   1. Why did the Board settle on cash flows instead of working capital flows?
   2. Why did the Board strongly recommend use of the direct method?
   3. Why did some members of the Board dissent from the final statement?

In a group of one or two other students, go to the library and locate *Statement of Financial Accounting Standards No. 95,* "Statement of Cash Flows," published by the Financial Accounting Standards Board. Write a report to your instructor covering the following points:

Group Project 16-7
Perform library project on aspects of Statement of Financial Accounting Standards No. 95

   1. Describe the controversy over how to treat interest and dividends received.
   2. What is the Board's position on reporting cash flow per share? Why did they take that position?
   3. What is the Board's position on noncash transactions? Why did they take that position?

Using the Internet—A View of the Real World

Internet Project 16-8
Analyze statement of cash flows

Visit the following website for the Apple Inc.:
> **http://www.apple.com**

Search "Investor Relations" and follow the instructions on the screen to locate the latest statement of cash flows and then print it. Analyze the statement and write a report to your instructor summarizing your analysis.

Internet Project 16-9
Analyze statement of cash flows

Visit the following website for Verizon:
> **http://www.verizon.com**

By following the information on the screen, locate the latest statement of cash flows and then print it. Analyze the statement and then write a report to your instructor summarizing your analysis.

Answers to Self-Test

True-False

1. **True.** Before July 1988, the statement of changes in financial position was required. This statement emphasized changes in working capital rather than changes in cash.
2. **True.** The statement of cash flows must be published every time an income statement is published.
3. **False.** Investing activities are transactions involving the acquisition or disposal of noncurrent assets. Transactions with creditors and owners are financing activities.
4. **False.** While the direct method is the method encouraged by the FASB, it is not the predominant method in use. In a recent study, only about 3% of the companies surveyed used the direct method.
5. **True.** Both of these transactions are with owners and, therefore, would be financing activities.

Multiple-Choice

1. **c.** The descriptions in (a) and (b) would be correct if they were reversed. The indirect method is easier to use, and this characteristic is probably the main reason why it is used by most companies.
2. **a.** Payment of debt is a financing activity because it is a transaction with creditors. All of the others are investing activities because they are transactions involving the acquisition or disposal of noncurrent assets.
3. **b.** Sales of $500,000 minus the increase in accounts receivable of $30,000 = $470,000.
4. **d.** Cost of goods sold of $300,000, less the increase in accounts payable of $20,000, plus the increase in inventory of $50,000 = $330,000.
5. **a.** Net income of $200,000, plus depreciation of $10,000, less the increase in accounts receivable of $15,000, plus the increase in accounts payable of $5,000 = $200,000.

Careers in Accounting

Accountants as Investment Analysts

More than ever, accounting students are being hired as securities analysts, portfolio managers, strategists, consultants, or other investment specialists. Duties in these fields involve understanding the operations of the company, assessing the value of the company, and predicting its future performance. These fields can be enormously exciting and may reap tremendous monetary rewards to those who are successful. For example, Monster Beverage Corporation (formerly known as Hansen Natural) was one of the highest performing stocks in the decade following the terrorist attacks on September 11, 2001. An initial investment of $1,000 in Monster Beverage would have grown to $18,194 by September 11, 2011. Apple Inc. was another strong performer during that decade. A $1,000 investment in Apple would have grown to $5,186. What accounting information could have been used to predict the amazing performance of Monster Beverage and Apple?

Failure to understand the relationship between financial accounting information and company value can result in negative consequences as well. For example, Amazon.com saw its stock price soar from $10 in June 1998 to $100 by January 1999, despite having never reported positive earnings in any year of the company's existence. Investors then realized that the company could not meet expected earnings projections in the near term and that the company was highly overvalued. The stock price retreated to its previous level of $10 by the end of 2000. However, when Amazon.com became profitable in 2006, demand for its stock returned. At the end of 2011, a share of Amazon.com stock was worth $182. In the area of investing, what accounting information can be used to separate the winners from the losers?

This is the goal of investment analysts -- to understand the current value of a company and then use available information in predicting future performance. Investment analysts rely heavily on financial statements as a source of information in predicting stock price movements. Since financial statements are prepared by accountants, it is no surprise that accountants are being hired for purposes of interpreting financial information and making predictions. Given the complexity of business organizations and business transactions in today's global markets, accounting professionals no longer are solely responsible for preparing financial statements, but are being asked to interpret these statements as well.

17

Analysis and Interpretation of Financial Statements

The two primary objectives of every business are *solvency and profitability*. *Solvency* is the ability of a company to pay debts as they come due; it is reflected on the company's balance sheet. *Profitability* is the ability of a company to generate income; it is reflected on the company's income statement. Generally, all those interested in the affairs of a company are especially interested in solvency and profitability.

This chapter discusses several common methods of analyzing and relating the data in financial statements and, as a result, gaining a clear picture of the solvency and profitability of a company. Internally, management analyzes a company's financial statements as do external investors, creditors, and regulatory agencies. Although these users have different immediate goals, their overall objective in financial statement analysis is the same—to make predictions about an organization as an aid in decision making.

Objectives of Financial Statement Analysis

Management's analysis of financial statements primarily relates to parts of the company. Using this approach, management can plan, evaluate, and control operations within the company. Management obtains any information it wants about the company's operations by requesting special-purpose reports. It uses this information to make difficult decisions, such as which employees to lay off and when to expand operations. Our primary focus in this chapter, however, is not on the special reports accountants prepare for management. Rather, it is on the information needs of persons outside the firm.

Investors, creditors, and regulatory agencies generally focus their analysis of financial statements on the company as a whole. Since they cannot request special-purpose reports, external users must rely on the general-purpose financial statements that companies publish. These statements include a balance sheet, an income statement, a statement of stockholders' equity, a statement of cash flows, and the explanatory notes that accompany the financial statements.

Learning Objectives

After studying this chapter, you should be able to:

1. Describe and explain the objectives of financial statement analysis.

2. Describe the sources of information for financial statement analysis.

3. Calculate and explain changes in financial statements using horizontal analysis, vertical analysis, and trend analysis.

4. Perform ratio analysis on financial statements using liquidity ratios, long-term solvency ratios, profitability tests, and market tests.

5. Describe the considerations used in financial statement analysis.

**Financial Statement
Analysis**

Users of financial statements need to pay particular attention to the explanatory notes, or the financial review, provided by management in annual reports. This integral part of the annual report provides insight into the scope of the business, the results of operations, liquidity and capital resources, new accounting standards, and geographic area data. Moreover, this section provides an economic outlook that an analyst may find very helpful when considering the possible future profitability of the company.

Financial statement analysis consists of applying analytical tools and techniques to financial statements and other relevant data to obtain useful information. This information reveals significant relationships between data and trends in those data that assess the company's past performance and current financial position. The information shows the results or consequences of prior management decisions. In addition, analysts use the information to make predictions that may have a direct effect on decisions made by users of financial statements.

Present and potential investors are interested in the future ability of a company to earn profits—its profitability. These investors wish to predict future dividends and changes in the market price of the company's common stock. Since both dividends and price changes are likely to be influenced by earnings, investors may predict earnings. The company's past earnings record is the logical starting point in predicting future earnings.

Some outside parties, such as creditors, are more interested in predicting a company's solvency than its profitability. The **liquidity** of the company affects its short-term solvency. The company's liquidity is its state of possessing liquid assets, such as cash and other assets easily converted to cash. Because companies must pay short-term debts soon, liquid assets must be available for their payment. For example, a bank asked to extend a 90-day loan to a company would want to know the company's projected short-term liquidity. Of course, the company's predicted ability to repay the 90-day loan is likely to be based at least partially on its past ability to pay off debts.

Long-term creditors are interested in a company's long-term solvency, which is usually determined by the relationship of a company's assets to its liabilities. Generally, we consider a company to be solvent when its assets exceed its liabilities so that the company has a positive stockholders' equity. The larger the assets are in relation to the liabilities, the greater the long-term solvency of the company. Thus, the company's assets could shrink significantly before its liabilities would exceed its assets and destroy the company's solvency.

Investors perform several types of analyses on a company's financial statements. All of these analyses rely on comparisons or relationships of data that enhance the utility or practical value of accounting information. For example, knowing that a company's net income last year was $100,000 may or may not, by itself, be useful information. Some usefulness is added when we know that the prior year's net income was $25,000. And even more useful information is gained if we know the amounts of sales and assets of the company. Such comparisons or relationships may be expressed as:

1. Absolute increases and decreases for an item from one period to the next.
2. Percentage increases and decreases for an item from one period to the next.
3. Percentages of single items to an aggregate total.
4. Trend percentages.
5. Ratios.

Earlier chapters have discussed and illustrated many of these analysis techniques. However, in this chapter we apply all of these techniques in analyzing Synotech, Inc.'s performance. This was the company introduced in Chapter 16.

Items 1 and 2 make use of comparative financial statements. **Comparative financial statements** present the same company's financial statements for one or two successive periods in side-by-side columns. The calculation of dollar changes or percentage changes in the statement items or totals is **horizontal analysis.** This analysis detects changes in a company's performance and highlights trends.

Analysts also use vertical analysis of a single financial statement, such as an income statement. **Vertical analysis** (item 3) consists of the study of a single financial statement in which each item is expressed as a *percentage of a significant total.* Vertical analysis is especially helpful in analyzing income statement data such as the percentage of cost of goods sold to sales.

Financial statements that show only percentages and no absolute dollar amounts are **common-size statements.** All percentage figures in a common-size balance sheet are percentages of total assets while all the items in a common-size income statement are percentages of net sales. The use of common-size statements facilitates vertical analysis of a company's financial statements.

Trend percentages (item 4) are similar to horizontal analysis except that comparisons are made to a selected base year or period. Trend percentages are useful for comparing financial statements over several years because they disclose changes and trends occurring through time.

Ratios (item 5) are expressions of logical relationships between items in the financial statements of a single period. Analysts can compute many ratios from the same set of financial statements. A ratio can show a relationship between two items on the same financial statement or between two items on different financial statements (e.g., balance sheet and income statement). The only limiting factor in choosing ratios is the requirement that the items used to construct a ratio have a logical relationship to one another.

Sources of Information

Financial information about publicly owned corporations can come from different sources such as published reports, government reports, financial service information, business publications, newspapers, and periodicals.

Public corporations must publish annual financial reports. The Annual Report Appendix gives such data for Wal-Mart Stores, Inc. The major sections of an annual report are (not necessarily in this order):

Published Reports

1. Consolidated financial statements   Consolidated financial statements include a balance sheet containing two years of comparative data; an income statement containing three years of comparative data; a statement of cash flows containing three years of comparative data; and a statement of shareholders' equity containing three years of comparative data. For examples of each statement, refer to the Annual Report Appendix.

Objective 2
Describe the sources of information for financial statement analysis.

2. Notes to consolidated financial statements   Notes to consolidated financial statements provide an in-depth look into the numbers contained in the financial statements. The notes usually contain sections on significant accounting policies, long-term debt, leases, stock option plans, etc. These explanations allow stockholders to look beyond the numbers to the events that triggered the dollar amounts recorded in the financial statements.

3. Letters to stockholders   Most annual reports are introduced with a letter to the stockholders. The letter often includes information about the company's past history, its mission, current year operating results, and the company's future goals. In the 2010

Gaylord Entertainment Company
Gaylord Entertainment owns and operates hotels in major U.S. cities. It also owns and operates a variety of entertainment holdings, including the Grand Ole Opry.

letter to shareholders, management of Gaylord Entertainment Company had to explain the effect that a major flood had on the company's operations and indicate that the future would be brighter.

What an extraordinary year 2010 turned out to be, but the work we put into our company in earlier years and the strong people culture we have created carried us through a 1,000 year flood and a recession that's been described as once in a generation. These challenges have been met head on, and I believe today we are a stronger and more decisive company that is poised for a very exciting future.

The first four months of 2010 had us believing that we had turned a corner. After more than two years of adverse economic conditions that had significant implications across the hospitality, travel and tourism sectors, we began to see signs that people were flying, booking rooms, planning meetings and vacationing once again.

But on May 2nd the world changed for us. The result of the nearly 14 inches of rain that fell on Nashville over the course of those two days in early May has been referred to by experts as a "once in a thousand year flood." For others, because it garnered relatively little media attention outside Tennessee, it was also described as the "forgotten flood." I can assure you, however, that the devastation has not been forgotten by anyone who witnessed it firsthand. It is still difficult to describe how I felt when I first saw the extent of the flooding at the Gaylord Opryland, the legendary Grand Ole Opry House, and throughout this fine city at daybreak on Monday, May 3rd. Yet despite the shock that morning, I never had any doubt that our resiliency would enable us to overcome this horrific event.

Across the board, every single person in this organization committed to doing everything in their power to assist our recovery, and to rebuild our assets better than they were before. The reaction from our loyal customers was similar. Almost universally, the response from groups and meeting planners was to ask how they could help, a testament to the deep relationships we have cultivated over the years across our properties.

In the end, our teams worked tireless hours to meet the herculean task of rebuilding head on, as we reopened the Grand Ole Opry House on September 28th and the Gaylord Opryland on November 15th, on time, on budget, and to rave reviews. We are confident that 2011 will be a great year for these businesses and they will once again be a significant contributor to our success.

4. Reports of independent accountants   The Securities and Exchange Commission (SEC) requires the financial statements of certain companies to be audited. The report of independent accountants, found at the end of the financial statements, provides assurance that the financial statements prepared by the company have been audited and are free of material misstatements. The report also may include a paragraph highlighting the significant accounting policies that the company has changed recently.

5. Management discussion and analysis   The management discussion and analysis section of the annual report provides management's view of the performance of the company. The analysis is based on the financial statements, the conditions of the industry, and ratios.

Government Reports

Publicly held companies must file detailed annual reports (Form 10–K), quarterly reports (Form 10–Q), and special events reports (Form 8–K) with the Securities and Exchange Commission. These reports are available to the public online and sometimes contain more detailed information than the published reports.

Financial Service Information, Business Publications, Newspapers, and Periodicals

Financial statement information is often more meaningful when users compare it with industry norms. Two firms that provide information on individual companies and industries are Moody's Investors Service and Standard & Poor's. Dun & Bradstreet Companies, Inc., publishes *Key Business Ratios* and Robert Morris Associates publishes *Annual Statement Studies;* both provide information for specific industries. Standard & Poor's *Industry Surveys* contains background descriptions and the economic outlook for different industries.

Business publications such as *The Wall Street Journal, Barron's, Forbes,* and *Fortune* also report industry financial news. Because financial statement users must be knowledgeable about current developments in business, the information in financial newspapers and periodicals is very valuable to them.

Horizontal Analysis and Vertical Analysis: an Illustration

The comparative financial statements of Synotech, Inc., will serve as a basis for an example of horizontal analysis and vertical analysis of a balance sheet and a statement of income and retained earnings. Recall that horizontal analysis calculates changes in comparative statement items or totals, whereas vertical analysis consists of a comparison of items on a single financial statement.

Imagine that you are a prospective investor interested in Synotech, Inc.. You have acquired the 2012 Annual Report of the company and want to perform some horizontal and vertical analyses of the financial statements.

First, we begin with the balance sheets. Illustration 17.1 shows the comparative balance sheets for 2012 and 2011 in Columns (1) and (2). Take a few minutes to study the balance sheets. Then review Columns (3) and (4), which show the horizontal analysis that would be performed on the comparative balance sheets.

Column (3) shows the change that occurred in each item between December 31, 2011, and December 31, 2012. If the change between the two dates is an increase from 2011 to 2012, the change is a positive figure. If the change is a decrease, the change is a negative figure and is shown in parentheses. Column (4) shows the percentage change in each item. You can calculate the percentage change by dividing the dollar change by the dollar balance of the earlier year (2011). While examining the horizontal analysis in Illustration 17.1 note that:

1. Total current assets have increased $14.3 million, consisting largely of increases in cash, marketable securities, and other current assets despite a $63.0 million decrease in net receivables, while total current liabilities have increased $181.4 million, largely as a result of increases in the current portion of long-term debt and other accruals.
2. Total liabilities have decreased $114.1 million, while total assets increased by $311.0 million.

Next, study Column (4), which expresses as a percentage the dollar change in Column (3). Frequently, these percentage increases are more informative than absolute amounts, as illustrated by the current asset and current liability changes. Although the absolute amount of current liabilities has increased tremendously over the amount of current assets, the percentages reveal that current assets increased .5%, while current liabilities increased 8.6%. Thus, current liabilities are increasing at a faster rate than current assets. Current assets still exceed current liabilities. This fact indicates that the company will be able to pay its debts as they come due.

Studying the percentages in Column (4) could lead to several other observations. For instance, the 6.9% decrease in long-term debt indicates that interest charges will be lower in the future, having a positive effect on future net income. The 14.2% increase in retained earnings could be a sign of increased dividends in the future; in addition, the increase in cash of 19% could support this conclusion.

Now examine Columns (5) and (6) to see the vertical analysis that would be performed. A vertical analysis of the company's balance sheet discloses each account's significance to total assets or total equities. This comparison aids in assessing the importance of the changes in each account. Columns (5) and (6) in Illustration 17.1 express the dollar amount of each item in Columns (1) and (2) as a percentage of total assets or equities. For example, although other assets declined $6.3 million in 2012, the decrease of 1.4% in the account represents only approximately 4.8% of total assets and, therefore, probably does not have great significance. Vertical analysis also shows that total debt financing decreased from 78.0% of total equities (liabilities and stockholders' equity) in 2011, to 74.3% in 2012. At the same time, the percentage of stockholder financing to total assets of the company increased from 22.0% to 25.7%.

Illustration 17.1   Comparative Balance Sheets

SYNOTECH, INC.
Comparative Balance Sheets
December 31, 2012 and 2011
($ millions)

	December 31		Horizontal Analysis Increase or (Decrease) 2012 over 2011		Vertical Analysis Percent of Total Assets	
	(1)	**(2)**	**(3)**	**(4)**	**(5)**	**(6)**
	2012	**2011**	**Dollars***	**Percent***	**2012**	**2011**
Assets						
Current Assets						
Cash and cash equivalents	$ 298.0	$ 250.5	$47.5	19.0%	3.1 %	2.7 %
Marketable securities	71.3	57.5	13.8	24.0	0.8	0.6
Receivables, net	1,277.3	1,340.3	(63.0)	(4.7)	13.5	14.6
Inventories	924.8	929.8	(5.0)	(0.5)	9.8	10.1
Other current assets	275.3	254.3	21.0	8.3	2.9	2.8
Total current assets	$2,846.7	$2,832.4	$14.3	0.5	30.0	30.9
Property, plant and equipment, net	2,914.7	2,586.2	328.5	12.7	30.7	28.2
Goodwill and other intangibles, net	3,264.5	3,290.0	(25.5)	(0.8)	34.4	35.9
Other assets	455.9	462.2	(6.3)	(1.4)	4.8	5.0
Total assets	$9,481.8	$9,170.8	$311.0	3.4	100.0	100.0
Liabilities and Shareholders' Equity						
Current Liabilities						
Notes and loans payable	$ 206.8	$ 245.3	$ (38.5)	(15.7)	2.2	2.7
Current portion of long-term debt	132.5	44.4	88.1	198.4	1.4	0.5
Accounts payable	902.0	886.4	15.6	1.8	9.5	9.7
Accrued income taxes	111.7	92.1	19.6	21.3	1.2	1.0
Other accruals	932.2	835.6	96.6	11.6	9.8	9.1
Total current liabilities	$2,285.2	$2,103.8	$181.4	8.6	24.1	22.9
Long-term debt	3,344.2	3.590.4	(246.2)	(6.9)	35.3	39.2
Deferred income taxes	281.2	284.8	(3.6)	(1.3)	3.0	3.1
Other liabilities	1,130.4	1,176.1	(45.7)	(3.9)	11.9	12.8
Total liabilities	$7,041.0	$7,155.1	$(114.1)	(1.6)	74.3	78.0
Shareholders' Equity						
Preferred stock	$ 471.2	$ 484.2	$ (13.0)	(2.7)	5.0	5.3
Common stock, $1.20 par value (500,000,000 shares authorized, 183,213,295 shares issued)	219.9	219.9	0.0	0.0	2.3	2.4
Additional paid-in capital	1,321.9	1,240.4	81.5	6.6	13.9	13.5
Retained earnings	3,277.1	2,870.6	406.5	14.2	34.6	31.3
Cumulative translation adjustments	(641.6)	(615.6)	(26.0)	4.2	-6.8	-6.7
	$4,648.5	$4,199.5	$449.0	10.7	49.0	45.8
Unearned compensation	(445.1)	(453.6)	8.5	(1.9)	-4.7	-4.9
Treasury stock, at cost	(1,762.6)	(1,730.2)	(32.4)	1.9	-18.6	-18.9
Total shareholders' equity	$2,440.8	$2,015.7	$425.1	21.1	25.7	22.0
Total liabilities and stockholders equity	$9,481.8	$9,170.8	$311.0	3.4	100.0	100.0

*Dollars = (1) — (2); Percent = (3)/(2)

Analysis of Statement of Income and Retained Earnings

Illustration 17.2 provides the information needed to analyze Synotech's comparative statements of income and retained earnings. Such a statement merely combines the income statement and the statement of retained earnings. Columns (7) and (8) in Illustration 17.2 show the dollar amounts for the years 2012 and 2011, respectively. Study these statements for a few minutes. Then examine Columns (9) and (10) which show the horizontal analysis that would be performed on the company's comparative

Illustration 17.2   Comparative Statements of Income and Retained Earnings

SYNOTECH, INC.
Comparative Statements of Income and Retained Earnings
For the years ended December 31, 2012 and 2011
($ millions)

			Horizontal Analysis		Vertical Analysis	
	Year Ended, December 31		Increase or (Decrease) 2012 over 2011		Percent of Net Sales	
	(7)	(8)	(9)	(10)	(11)	(12)
	2012	2011	Dollars*	Percent*	2012	2011
Net Sales	$10,498.8	$10,029.8	$469.0	4.7%	100.0%	100.0%
Cost of goods sold	5,341.3	5,223.7	117.6	2.3	50.9	52.1
Gross Profit	$5,157.5	$4,806.1	$351.4	7.3	49.1	47.9
Selling, general and administrative expenses	3,662.5	3,455.5	207.0	6.0	34.9	34.5
Provision for restructured operations	—	552.6	(552.6)	(100.0)	0.0	
						5.5
Other expense, net	112.6	115.3	(2.7)	(2.3)	1.1	
						1.1
Interest expense, net of interest income of $41.2 and $36.7, respectively	236.9	246.5	(9.6)	(3.9)	2.3	2.5
Income before income taxes	$1,145.5	$436.2	$709.3	162.6	10.9	4.3
Provision for income taxes	383.5	229.8	153.7	66.9	3.7	2.3
Net income	$762.0	$206.4	$555.6	269.2	7.3	2.1
Retained earnings, January 1	2,870.6	2,996.0	(125.4)	(4.2)		
Total	$3,632.6	$3,202.4	$430.2	13.4		
Dividends declared:						
Series B Convertible Preference Stock, net of income taxes	25.1	25.3	(0.2)	(0.8)		
Preferred stock	0.6	0.6	0.0	0.0		
Common stock	329.8	305.9	23.9	7.8		
Retained Earnings, December 31	$3,277.1	$2,870.6	$406.5	14.2		

*Dollars = (7) - (8); Percent = (9)/(8)

statements of income and retained earnings. Columns (9) and (10) show the absolute and percentage increase or decrease in each item from 2011 to 2012. The absolute change is determined by deducting the 2011 amount from the 2012 amount. If the change between two dates is an increase from 2011 to 2012, the change is a positive figure. If the change is a decrease, the change is a negative figure and is shown in parentheses. You calculate the percentage change by dividing the dollar change by the dollar amount for 2011.

The horizontal analysis shows that sales increased a total of $469.0 million, an increase of 4.7%. Since cost of goods sold increased by a much smaller amount ($117.6 million), gross profit increased by $351.4, or 7.3%. The $552.6 million expense in 2011 was the result of a provision for restructured operations. Although this is not a recurring expense, it does not classify as an extraordinary expense and is treated as part of income from continuing operations.

Now look at Columns (11) and (12) to see the vertical analysis that would be performed. Columns (11) and (12) express the dollar amount of each item in Columns (7) and (8) as a percentage of net sales. Even though cost of goods sold increased in 2012, it remained a fairly constant percentage of net sales. Therefore, gross profit as a percentage of net sales increased only slightly. The percentage of expenses to net sales decreased somewhat, thus yielding an increase in income before income taxes as a percentage of net sales.

Having completed the horizontal analysis and vertical analysis of Synotech's balance sheet and statement of income and retained earnings, you are ready to study trend percentages and ratio analysis. The last section in this chapter discusses some final considerations in financial statement analysis. Professional financial statement analysts use several tools and techniques to determine the solvency and profitability of companies.

Trend Percentages

Trend percentages, also referred to as *index numbers,* help you to compare financial information over time to a base year or period. You can calculate trend percentages by:

1. Selecting a base year or period.
2. Assigning a weight of 100% to the amounts appearing on the base-year financial statements.
3. Expressing the corresponding amounts on the other years' financial statements as a percentage of base-year or period amounts. Compute the percentages by dividing nonbase-year amounts by the corresponding base-year amounts and then multiplying the result by 100.

The following information for Synotech illustrates the calculation of trend percentages:

($ millions)	2010	2011	2012
Net Sales	$ 9,105.5	$10,029.8	$10,498.8
Cost of goods sold	4,696.0	5,223.7	5,341.3
Gross profit	$ 4,409.5	$ 4,806.1	$ 5,157.5
Operating expenses	3,353.6	4,369.9	4,012.0
Income before income taxes	$ 1,055.9	$ 436.2	$ 1,145.5

If 2010 is the base year, to calculate trend percentages for each year divide net sales by $9,105.5 million; cost of goods sold by $4,696.0 million; gross profit by $4,409.5 million; operating expenses by $3,353.6 million; and income before income taxes by $1,055.9 million. After all divisions have been made, multiply each result by 100. The resulting percentages reflect trends as follows:

	2010	2011	2012
Net sales	100.0%	110.2%	115.3%
Cost of goods sold	100.0	111.2	113.7
Gross profit	100.0	109.0	117.0
Operating expenses	100.0	130.3	119.6
Income before income taxes	100.0	41.3	108.5

These trend percentages indicate the changes taking place in the organization and highlight the direction of these changes. For instance, the percentage of sales is increasing each year compared to the base year. Cost of goods sold increased at a lower rate than net sales in 2012, causing gross profit to increase at a higher rate than net sales. Operating expenses in 2011 increased due to the provision for restructured operations, causing a significant decrease in income before income taxes. Percentages provide clues to an analyst about which items need further investigation or analysis. In reviewing trend percentages, a financial statement user should pay close attention to the trends in related items, such as the cost of goods sold in relation to sales. Trend analysis that shows a constantly declining gross margin (profit) rate may be a signal that future net income will decrease.

As useful as trend percentages are, they have one drawback. Expressing changes as percentages is usually straightforward as long as the amount in the base year or period is positive—that is, not zero or negative. Analysts cannot express a $30,000 increase in notes receivable as a percentage if the increase is from zero last year to $30,000 this year. Nor can they express an increase from a loss last year of $10,000 to income this year of $20,000 in percentage terms.

Proper analysis does not stop with the calculation of increases and decreases in amounts or percentages over several years. Such changes generally indicate areas worthy of further investigation and are merely clues that may lead to significant findings. Accurate predictions depend on many factors, including economic and political conditions; management's plans regarding new products, plant expansion, and promotional outlays; and the expected activities of competitors. Considering these factors along with horizontal analysis, vertical analysis, and trend analysis should provide a reasonable basis for predicting future performance.

Reinforcing Problems
P17-2 Perform trend analysis and comment on the results.
P17-2A Perform trend analysis and comment on the results.

Ratio Analysis

Logical relationships exist between certain accounts or items in a company's financial statements. These accounts may appear on the same statement or on two different statements. We set up the dollar amounts of the related accounts or items in fraction form called *ratios*. These ratios include: (1) liquidity ratios; (2) equity, or long-term solvency, ratios; (3) profitability tests; and (4) market tests.

Objective 4
Perform ratio analysis on financial statements using liquidity ratios, long-term solvency ratios, profitability tests, and market tests.

Liquidity ratios indicate a company's short-term debt-paying ability. Thus, these ratios show interested parties the company's capacity to meet maturing current liabilities.

Liquidity Ratios

Current (or Working Capital) Ratio   Working capital is the excess of current assets over current liabilities. The ratio that relates current assets to current liabilities is the **current (or working capital) ratio**. The current ratio indicates the ability of a company to pay its current liabilities from current assets and, thus, shows the strength of the company's working capital position.

You can compute the current ratio by dividing current assets by current liabilities:

$$\text{Current ratio} = \frac{\text{Current assets}}{\text{Current liabilities}}$$

The ratio is usually stated as a number of dollars of current assets to one dollar of current liabilities (although the dollar signs usually are omitted). Thus, for Synotech in 2012, when current assets totaled $2,846.7 million and current liabilities totaled $2,285.2 million, the ratio is 1.25:1, meaning that the company has $1.25 of current assets for each $1.00 of current liabilities.

The current ratio provides a better index of a company's ability to pay current debts than does the absolute amount of working capital. To illustrate, assume that we are comparing Synotech to Company B. For this example, use the following totals for current assets and current liabilities:

	Synotech	Company B
Current assets (a)	$ 2,846.7	$120.0
Current liabilities (b)	2,285.2	53.2
Working capital (a - b)	$ 561.5	$ 66.8
Current ratio (a/b)	1.25:1	2.26:1

Synotech has eight times as much working capital as Company B. However, Company B has a superior debt-paying ability since it has $2.26 of current assets for each $1.00 of current liabilities.

Short-term creditors are particularly interested in the current ratio since the conversion of inventories and accounts receivable into cash is the primary source from which the company obtains the cash to pay short-term creditors. Long-term creditors are also interested in the current ratio because a company that is unable to pay short-term debts may be forced into bankruptcy. For this reason, many bond indentures, or contracts, contain a provision requiring that the borrower maintain at least a certain minimum current ratio. A company can increase its current ratio by issuing long-term debt or capital stock or by selling noncurrent assets.

A company must guard against a current ratio that is too high, especially if caused by idle cash, slow-paying customers, and/or slow-moving inventory. Decreased net income can result when too much capital that could be used profitably elsewhere is tied up in current assets.

Refer to Illustration 17.1. The Synotech data in Column (4) indicate that current liabilities are increasing more rapidly than current assets. We could also make such an observation directly by looking at the change in the current ratio. Synotech's current ratios for 2012 and 2011 follow:

($ millions)	December 31 2012	2011	Amount of Increase
Current assets (a)	$2,846.7	$2,832.4	14.3
Current liabilities (b)	2,285.2	2,103.8	181.4
Working capital (a − b)	$ 561.5	$ 728.6	$(167.1)
Current ratio (a/b)	1.25:1	1.35:1	

Synotech's working capital decreased by $167.1 million, or 22.9% ($167.1/$728.6), and its current ratio decreased from 1.35:1 to 1.25:1. Together, these figures reflect that its current liabilities increased faster than its current assets.

Acid-Test (Quick) Ratio   The current ratio is not the only measure of a company's short-term debt-paying ability. Another measure, called the **acid-test (quick) ratio**, is the ratio of quick assets (cash, marketable securities, and net receivables) to current liabilities. Analysts exclude inventories and prepaid expenses from current assets to compute quick assets because they might not be readily convertible into cash. The formula for the acid-test ratio is:

$$\text{Acid-test ratio} = \frac{\text{Quick assets}}{\text{Current liabilities}}$$

Short-term creditors are particularly interested in this ratio, which relates the pool of cash and immediate cash inflows to immediate cash outflows.

The acid-test ratios for 2012 and 2011 for Synotech are:

($ millions)	December 31 2012	2011	Amount of Increase or (Decrease)
Quick assets (a)	$1,646.6	$1,648.3	$ (1.7)
Current liabilities (b)	2,285.2	2,103.8	181.4
Net quick assets (a − b)	$ (638.6)	$ (455.5)	$(183.1)
Acid-test ratio (a/b)	.72:1	.78:1	

In deciding whether the acid-test ratio is satisfactory, investors consider the quality of the marketable securities and receivables. An accumulation of poor-quality marketable securities or receivables, or both, could cause an acid-test ratio to appear deceptively favorable. When referring to marketable securities, poor quality means securities likely to generate losses when sold. Poor-quality receivables may be uncollectible or not collectible until long past due. The quality of receivables depends primarily on their age, which can be assessed by preparing an aging schedule or by calculating the accounts receivable turnover. (Covered in Chapter 9.)

Cash Flow Liquidity Ratio   Another approach to measuring short-term liquidity is the **cash flow liquidity ratio**. The numerator, as an approximation of cash resources, consists of (1) cash and marketable securities, or liquid current assets, and (2) net cash provided by operating activities, or the cash generated from the company's operations. This reflects the company's ability to sell inventory and collect accounts receivable. The formula for the cash flow liquidity ratio is:

$$\frac{\text{Cash and marketable securities} + \text{Net cash provided by operating activities}}{\text{Current liabilities}}$$

For 2012, Synotech has $298.0 million in cash and cash equivalents, $71.3 million in marketable securities, $2,285.2 million in current liabilities, and $1,101.0 million in cash provided by operating activities (taken from the statement of cash flows in its annual report). Its cash flow liquidity ratio is:

$$\frac{\$298.0 + \$71.3 + \$1,101.0}{\$2,285.2} = .64 \text{ times}$$

This indicates that the company is going to have to rely on some other sources of funding to pay its current liabilities. The company's liquid current assets will only cover about two-thirds of the current liabilities. Possibly net cash provided by operations will be substantially higher in 2013.

Accounts Receivable Turnover   **Turnover** is the relationship between the amount of an asset and some measure of its use. **Accounts receivable turnover** is the number of times per year that the average amount of receivables is collected. To calculate this ratio, divide net credit sales (or net sales) by average net accounts receivable; that is, accounts receivable after deducting the allowance for uncollectible accounts:

$$\frac{\text{Accounts receivable}}{\text{turnover}} = \frac{\text{Net credit sales (or net sales)}}{\text{Average net accounts receivable}}$$

When a ratio compares an income statement item (like net credit sales) with a balance sheet item (like net accounts receivable), the balance sheet item should be an average. Ideally, analysts calculate average net accounts receivable by averaging the end-of-month balances or end-of-week balances of net accounts receivable outstanding during the period. The greater the number of observations used, the more accurate the resulting average. Often, analysts average only the beginning-of-year and end-of-year balances because this information is easily obtainable from comparative financial statements. Sometimes a formula calls for the use of an average balance, but only the year-end amount is available. Then the analyst must use the year-end amount.[1]

In theory, the numerator of the accounts receivable turnover ratio consists of only net credit sales because those are the only sales that generate accounts receivable. However, if cash sales are relatively small or their proportion to total sales remains fairly constant, analysts can obtain reliable results by using total net sales. In most cases, the analyst may have to use total net sales because the separate amounts of cash sales and credit sales are not reported on the income statement.

Synotech's accounts receivable turnover ratios for 2012 and 2011 follow. Net accounts receivable on January 1, 2010, totaled $1,259.5 million.

---

[1]These general comments about the use of averages in a ratio apply to the other ratios involving averages discussed in this chapter.

($ millions)	December 31 2012	December 31 2011	Amount of Increase
Net sales (a)	$10,498.8	$10,029.8	$469.0
Net accounts receivable:			
January 1	$ 1,340.3	$ 1,259.5	$ 80.8
December 31	1,277.3	1,340.3	(63.0)
Total (b)	$ 2,617.6	$ 2,599.8	$ 17.8
Average net receivables (c) (b/2 = c)	$ 1,308.8	$1,299.9	
Turnover of accounts receivable (a/c)	8.02	7.72	

The accounts receivable turnover ratio provides an indication of how quickly the company collects receivables. The accounts receivable turnover ratio for 2012 indicates that Synotech collected, or turned over, its accounts receivable slightly more than eight times. The ratio is better understood and more easily compared with a company's credit terms if we convert it into a number of days, as is illustrated in the next ratio.

Number of Days' Sales in Accounts Receivable

The **number of days' sales in accounts receivable** ratio is also called the *average collection period for accounts receivable*. Calculate it as follows:

$$\text{Number of days' sales in accounts receivable (average collection period for accounts receivable)} = \frac{\text{Number of days in year (365)}}{\text{Accounts receivable turnover}}$$

The turnover ratios for Synotech show that the number of days' sales in accounts receivable decreased from about 47 days (365/7.72) in 2011 to 46 days (365/8.02) in 2012. The change means that the average collection period for the company's accounts receivable decreased from 47 to 46 days.

Reinforcing Problems
E17-3 Compute average number of days receivables are outstanding; determine effect of increase in turnover. BDC17-2 Compute turnover ratios for four years and number of days' sales in accounts receivable; evaluate effectiveness of company's credit policy.

An Accounting Perspective

BUSINESS INSIGHT The number of days' sales in accounts receivable ratio measures the average liquidity of accounts receivable and indicates their quality. Generally, the shorter the collection period, the higher the quality of receivables. However, the average collection period varies by industry; for example, collection periods are short in utility companies and much longer in some retailing companies. A comparison of the average collection period with the credit terms extended customers by the company provides further insight into the quality of the accounts receivable. For example, receivables with terms of 2/10, n/30 and an average collection period of 75 days need to be investigated further. It is important to determine why customers are paying their accounts much later than expected.

Reinforcing Problem
E17-5 Compute inventory turnover.

Inventory Turnover

A company's inventory turnover ratio shows the number of times its average inventory is sold during a period. You can calculate **inventory turnover** as follows:

$$\text{Inventory turnover} = \frac{\text{Cost of goods sold}}{\text{Average inventory}}$$

When comparing an income statement item and a balance sheet item, measure both in comparable dollars. Notice that we measure the numerator and denominator in cost rather than sales dollars. (Earlier, when calculating accounts receivable turnover, we measured both numerator and denominator in sales dollars.) Inventory turnover relates a measure of sales volume to the average amount of goods on hand to produce this sales volume.

Synotech's inventory on January 1, 2011, was $856.7 million. The following schedule shows that the inventory turnover decreased slightly from 5.85 times per year in 2011 to 5.76 times per year in 2012. To convert these turnover ratios to the number of days it takes the company to sell its entire stock of inventory, divide 365 by the inventory turnover. Synotech's average inventory sold in about 63 and 62 (365/5.76 and 365/5.85) in 2012 and 2011, respectively.

($ millions)	December 31 2012	December 31 2011	Amount of Increase or (Decrease)
Cost of goods sold (a)	$5,341.3	$5,223.7	$117.6
Merchandise inventory:			
January 1	$929.8	$856.7	$ 73.1
December 31	924.8	929.8	(5.0)
Total (b)	$1,854.6	$1,786.5	$ 68.1
Average inventory (c) (b/2 = c)	$927.3	$893.3	
Turnover of inventory (a/c)	5.76	5.85	

Other things being equal, a manager who maintains the highest inventory turnover ratio is the most efficient. Yet, other things are not always equal. For example, a company that achieves a high inventory turnover ratio by keeping extremely small inventories on hand may incur larger ordering costs, lose quantity discounts, and lose sales due to lack of adequate inventory. In attempting to earn satisfactory income, management must balance the costs of inventory storage and obsolescence and the cost of tying up funds in inventory against possible losses of sales and other costs associated with keeping too little inventory on hand.

BUSINESS INSIGHT Cabletron Systems develops, manufactures, installs, and supports a wide range of standards-based LAN and WAN connectivity hardware and software products. For the year ended March 3, 2006, both its number of day's sales in accounts receivable and its inventory turnover rate increased as compared to the prior year. In its 2006 annual report, the company explained these increases as follows:

Accounts receivable, net of allowance for doubtful accounts, were $210.9 million, or 66 days of sales outstanding, at March 3, 2006 compared to $228.4 million at February 29, 2005, or 54 days sales outstanding. The increase in days of sales outstanding was a result of the timing of sales and related collections.

Worldwide inventories were $98.1 million at March 3, 2006 or 63 days of inventory, compared to $85.0 million, or 37 days of inventory, at February 29, 2005. The increase of days in inventory was due to the increase in finished goods inventory purchased to protect against an anticipated shortage of supply components.

An Accounting Perspective

Total Assets Turnover   **Total assets turnover** shows the relationship between the dollar volume of sales and the average total assets used in the business. We calculate it as follows:

$$\text{Total assets turnover} = \frac{\text{Net sales}}{\text{Average total assets}}$$

This ratio measures the efficiency with which a company uses its assets to generate sales. The larger the total assets turnover, the larger the income on each dollar invested in the assets of the business. For Synotech, the total asset turnover ratios for 2012 and 2011 follow. Total assets as of January 1, 2011, were $7,370.9 million.

($ millions)	2012	2011	Amount of Increase
Net sales (a)	$ 10,498.8	$ 10,029.8	$ 469.0
Total assets:			
January 1	$9,170.8	$7,370.9	$1,799.9
December 31	9,481.8	9,170.8	311.0
Total (b)	$18,652.6	$16,541.7	$2,110.9
Average total assets (c) (b/2 = c)	$9,326.3	$8,270.9	
Turnover of total assets (a/c)	1.13:1	1.21:1	

Each dollar of total assets produced $1.21 of sales in 2011 and $1.13 of sales in 2012. In other words, between 2011 and 2012, the company had a decrease of $.08 of sales per dollar of investment in assets.

Equity, or long-term solvency, ratios show the relationship between debt and equity financing in a company.

Equity (Stockholders' Equity) Ratio   The two basic sources of assets in a business are owners (stockholders) and creditors; the combined interests of the two groups are *total equities*. In ratio analysis, however, the term *equity* generally refers only to stockholders' equity. Thus, the **equity (stockholders' equity) ratio** indicates the proportion of total assets (or total equities) provided by stockholders (owners) on any given date. The formula for the equity ratio is:

$$\text{Equity ratio} = \frac{\text{Stockholders' equity}}{\text{Total assets (or total equities)}}$$

Synotech's liabilities and stockholders' equity from Illustration 17.1 follow. The company's equity ratio increased from 22.0% in 2011 to 25.7% in 2012. Illustration 17.1 shows that stockholders increased their proportionate equity in the company's assets due largely to the retention of earnings (which increases retained earnings).

($millions)	December 31, 2012 Amount	December 31, 2012 Percent	December 31, 2011 Amount	December 31, 2011 Percent
Current liabilities	$2,285.2	24.1%	$2,103.8	22.9%
Long-term liabilities	4,755.8	50.2	5,051.3	55.1
Total liabilities	$7,041.0	74.3	$7,155.1	78.0
Total stockholders' equity	2,440.8	25.7	2,015.7	22.0
Total equity (equal to total assets)	$9,481.8	100.0%	$9,170.8	100.0%

The equity ratio must be interpreted carefully. From a creditor's point of view, a high proportion of stockholders' equity is desirable. A high equity ratio indicates the existence of a large protective buffer for creditors in the event a company suffers a loss. However, from an owner's point of view, a high proportion of stockholders' equity may or may not be desirable. If the business can use borrowed funds to generate income in excess of the net after-tax cost of the interest on such funds, a lower percentage of stockholders' equity may be desirable.

To illustrate the effect of higher leveraging (i.e., a larger proportion of debt), assume that Synotech could have financed an increase in its productive capacity with $40 million of 6% bonds instead of issuing 5 million additional shares of common stock. The effect on income for 2012 would be as follows, assuming a federal income tax rate of 40%:

Net income as presently stated (Illustration 17.2)	$762,000,000
Deduct additional interest on debt (0.06 × $40 million)	2,400,000
	$759,600,000
Add reduced taxes due to interest deduction (.4 × 2,400,000)	960,000
Adjusted net income	$760,560,000

As shown, increasing leverage by issuing bonds instead of common stock reduces net income. However, there are also fewer shares of common stock outstanding. Assume the company has 183 million shares of common stock outstanding. Earnings per share (EPS) with the additional debt would be $4.16 (or $760,560,000/183 million shares), and EPS with the additional stock would be $4.05 (or $762,000,000/188 million shares).

Since investors place heavy emphasis on EPS amounts, many companies in recent years have introduced large portions of debt into their capital structures to increase EPS, especially since interest rates have been relatively low in recent years.

We should point out, however, that too low a percentage of stockholders' equity (too much debt) has its dangers. Financial leverage magnifies losses per share as well as EPS since there are fewer shares of stock over which to spread the losses. A period of business recession may result in operating losses and shrinkage in the value of assets, such as receivables and inventory, which in turn may lead to an inability to meet fixed payments for interest and principal on the debt. As a result, the company may be forced into liquidation, and the stockholders could lose their entire investments.

Stockholders' Equity to Debt (Debt to Equity) Ratio   Analysts express the relative equities of owners and creditors in several ways. To say that creditors held a 74.3% interest in the assets of Synotech on December 31, 2012, is equivalent to saying stockholders held a 25.7% interest. Another way of expressing this relationship is the **stockholders' equity to debt ratio**:

$$\frac{\text{Stockholders' equity}}{\text{to debt ratio}} = \frac{\text{Stockholders' equity}}{\text{Total debt}}$$

Such a ratio for Synotech would be .28:1 (or $2,015.7 million/$7,155.1 million) on December 31, 2011, and .35:1 (or $2,440.8 million/$7,041.0 million) on December 31, 2012. This ratio is often inverted and called the **debt to equity ratio.** Some analysts use only long-term debt rather than total debt in calculating these ratios. These analysts do not consider short-term debt to be part of the capital structure since it is paid within one year.

Profitability is an important measure of a company's operating success. Generally, we are concerned with two areas when judging profitability: (1) relationships on the income statement that indicate a company's ability to recover costs and expenses, and (2) relationships of income to various balance sheet measures that indicate the company's relative ability to earn income on assets employed. Each of the following ratios utilizes one of these relationships.

Profitability Tests

Rate of Return on Operating Assets   The best measure of earnings performance without regard to the sources of assets is the relationship of net operating income to operating assets, the **rate of return on operating assets**. This ratio shows the earning power of the company as a bundle of assets. By disregarding both nonoperating assets and nonoperating income elements, the rate of return on operating assets measures the profitability of the company in carrying out its primary business functions. We can break the ratio down into two elements—the operating margin and the turnover of operating assets.

Operating margin reflects the percentage of each dollar of net sales that becomes net operating income. Net operating income excludes **nonoperating income elements** such as extraordinary items, cumulative effect on prior years of changes in accounting principle, losses or gains from discontinued operations, interest revenue, and interest expense. Another name for **net operating income** is "income before interest and taxes" (IBIT). The formula for operating margin is:

$$\text{Operating margin} = \frac{\text{Net operating income}}{\text{Net sales}}$$

Reinforcing Problems
P17-5 and P17-5A Compute rate of return on operating assets and demonstrate effects of various transactions on this rate of return.

Turnover of operating assets shows the amount of sales dollars generated for each dollar invested in operating assets. **Operating assets** are all assets actively used in producing operating revenues. Typically, we use year-end operating assets, even though in theory an average would be better. **Nonoperating assets** are owned by a company but not used in producing operating revenues, such as land held for future use, a factory building rented to another company, and long-term bond investments.

Analysts do not use these nonoperating assets in evaluating earnings performance. Nor do they use total assets that include nonoperating assets not contributing to the generation of sales. The formula for the turnover of operating assets is:

$$\text{Turnover of operating assets} = \frac{\text{Net sales}}{\text{Operating assets}}$$

The rate of return on operating assets of a company is equal to its operating margin multiplied by turnover of operating assets. The more a company earns per dollar of sales and the more sales it makes per dollar invested in operating assets, the higher is the return per dollar invested. To find the rate of return on operating assets, use the following formulas:

$$\begin{array}{c}\text{Rate of return on} \\ \text{operating assets}\end{array} = \begin{array}{c}\text{Operating} \\ \text{margin}\end{array} \times \begin{array}{c}\text{Turnover of} \\ \text{operating assets}\end{array}$$

or

$$\begin{array}{c}\text{Rate of return on} \\ \text{operating assets}\end{array} = \frac{\text{Net operating income}}{\text{Net sales}} \times \frac{\text{Net sales}}{\text{Operating assets}}$$

Note to the Student
Use any annual report and calculate the profitability ratios.

Because net sales appears in both ratios (once as a numerator and once as a denominator), we can cancel it out, and the formula for rate of return on operating assets becomes:

$$\begin{array}{c}\text{Rate of return on} \\ \text{operating assets}\end{array} = \frac{\text{Net operating income}}{\text{Operating assets}}$$

Reinforcing Problem
E17-6 Compute rate of return on operating assets.

For analytical purposes, the formula should remain in the form that shows margin and turnover separately, since it provides more information.

The rates of return on operating assets for Synotech for 2012 and 2011 are:

($ millions)	2012	2011	Amount of Increase or (Decrease)
Net operating income (a)*	$1,382.4	$ 682.7	$699.7
Net sales (b)	$10,498.8	$10,029.8	$469.0
Operating assets (c)†	$9,481.8	$ 9,170.8	$311.0
Operating margin (a/b)	13.17%	6.81%	
Turnover of operating assets (b/c)	1.11 times	1.09 times	
Rate of return on operating assets (a/c)	14.58%	7.44%	

*Calculated as income before income taxes plus net interest expense. This method excludes nonoperating items.

†When companies have no nonoperating assets, total assets are used in the calculation.

Net Income to Net Sales (Return on Sales) Ratio   Another measure of a company's profitability is the **net income to net sales** ratio, calculated as follows:

$$\text{Net income to net sales} = \frac{\text{Net income}}{\text{Net sales}}$$

This ratio measures the proportion of the sales dollar that remains after deducting all expenses. The computations for Synotech for 2012 and 2011 are:

Business Insight Companies that are to survive in the economy must attain some minimum rate of return on operating assets. However, they can attain this minimum rate of return in many different ways. To illustrate, consider a grocery store and a jewelry store, each with a rate of return of 8% on operating assets. The grocery store normally would attain this rate of return with a low margin and a high turnover, while the jewelry store would have a high margin and a low turnover, as shown here:

	Margin	×	Turnover	=	Rate of Return on Operating Assets
Grocery store	1%	×	8.0 times	=	8%
Jewelry store	20	×	0.4	=	8

($ millions)	2012	2011	Amount of Increase or (Decrease)
Net income (a)	$ 762.0	$206.4	$555.6
Net sales (b)	$10,498.8	$10,029.8	$469.0
Ratio of net income to net sales (a/b)	7.26%	2.06%	

Although the ratio of net income to net sales indicates that the net amount of profit increased on each sales dollar, exercise care in using and interpreting this ratio. The net income includes all nonoperating items that may occur only in a particular period; therefore, net income includes the effects of such things as extraordinary items, changes in accounting principle, effects of discontinued operations, and interest charges. Thus, a period that contains the effects of an extraordinary item is not comparable to a period that contains no extraordinary items. Also, since interest expense is deductible in the determination of net income while dividends are not, the methods used to finance a company's assets affect net income.

Return on Average Common Stockholders' Equity   From the stockholders' point of view, an important measure of the income-producing ability of a company is the relationship of **return on average common stockholders' equity,** also called *rate of return on average common stockholders' equity,* or simply the **return on equity (ROE).** Although stockholders are interested in the ratio of operating income to operating assets as a measure of management's efficient use of assets, they are even more interested in the return the company earns on each dollar of stockholders' equity. The formula for return on average common stockholders' equity if no preferred stock is outstanding is:

$$\text{Return on average common stockholders' equity} = \frac{\text{Net income}}{\text{Average common stockholders' equity}}$$

When a company has preferred stock outstanding, the numerator of this ratio becomes net income minus the annual preferred dividends, and the denominator becomes the average book value of common stock. As described in Chapter 12, the book value of common stock is equal to total stockholders' equity minus (1) the liquidation value (usually equal to par value) of preferred stock and (2) any dividends in arrears on cumulative preferred stock. Thus, the formula becomes:

$$\text{Return on average common stockholders' equity} = \frac{\text{Net income} - \text{Preferred stock dividends}}{\text{Average book value of common stock}}$$

Reinforcing Problem
E17-7 Compute return on common stockholders' equity.

Synotech has preferred stock outstanding. The ratios for the company follow. Total common stockholders' equity on January 1, 2011, was $1,697.4 million. Preferred dividends were $25.7 million in 2012 and $25.9 million in 2011.

($ millions)	2012	2011	Amount of Increase or (Decrease)
Net income – Preferred stock dividends (a)	$ 736.3	$ 180.5	$ 555.8
Total common stockholders' equity (book value of common stock):*			
January 1	$1,531.5	$1,697.4	$(165.9)
December 31	1,969.6	1,531.5	438.1
Total (b)	$3,501.1	$3,228.9	$ 272.2
Average common stockholders' equity: (c) (b/2 =c)	$1,750.6	$1,614.5	
Return on common stockholders' equity (a/c)	42.06%	11.18%	

*Total stockholders' equity – Par value of preferred stock

The stockholders would regard the increase in the ratio from 11.18% to 42.06% favorably. This ratio indicates that for each dollar of capital invested by a common stockholder, the company earned approximately 42 cents in 2012.

An Accounting Perspective

BUSINESS INSIGHT Sometimes, two companies have the same return on assets but have different returns on stockholders' equity, as shown here:

	Company 1	Company 2
Return on assets	12.0%	12.0%
Return on stockholders' equity	6.4	8.0

The difference of 1.6% in Company 2's favor is the result of Company 2's use of borrowed funds, particularly long-term debt, in its capital structure. Use of these funds (or preferred stock with a fixed return) is called trading on the equity. When a company is trading profitably on the equity, it is generating a higher rate of return on its borrowed funds than it is paying for the use of the funds. The excess, in this case 1.6%, is accruing to the benefit of the common stockholders, because their earnings are being increased.

Companies that magnify the gains from this activity for the stockholders are using leverage. Using leverage is a risky process because losses also can be magnified, to the disadvantage of the common stockholders. We discussed trading on the equity and *leverage* in Chapter 15.

Reinforcing Problem
E17-4 Compute cash flow margin.

Cash Flow Margin   The cash flow margin measures a company's overall efficiency and performance. The **cash flow margin** indicates the ability of a company to translate sales into cash. Measuring the amount of cash a company generates from every dollar of sales is important because a company needs cash to service debt, pay dividends, and invest in new capital assets. The formula for the cash flow margin is:

$$\text{Cashflow margin} = \frac{\text{Net cash provided by operating activities}}{\text{Net sales}}$$

Thus, we calculate Synotech's 2012 cash flow margin as follows:

$$\frac{\$1{,}101.0 \text{ million net cash provided by operating activities}}{\$10{,}498.8 \text{ million net sales}} = 10.49\%$$

Reinforcing Problems
E17-8 Compute EPS.
E17-10 Compute EPS for current and prior year.

Earnings per Share of Common Stock   Probably the measure used most widely to appraise a company's operations is **earnings per share (EPS)** of common stock. EPS is equal to earnings available to common stockholders divided by the weighted-average number of shares of common stock outstanding. The financial press regularly publishes actual and forecasted EPS amounts for publicly traded corporations, together with period-to-period comparisons. The Accounting Principles Board noted the significance attached to EPS by requiring that such amounts be reported on the face of the income statement.[2] (Chapter 13 illustrates how earnings per share should be presented on the income statement.)

The calculation of EPS may be fairly simple or highly complex depending on a corporation's capital structure. A company has a simple capital structure if it has no outstanding securities (e.g., convertible bonds, convertible preferred stocks, warrants, or options) that can be exchanged for common stock. If a company has such securities outstanding, it has a complex capital structure. Discussion of EPS for a corporation with a complex capital structure is beyond the scope of this text.

A company with a simple capital structure reports a single basic EPS amount, which is calculated as follows:

$$\text{EPS of common stock} = \frac{\text{Earnings available to common stockholders}}{\text{Weighted-average number of common shares outstanding}}$$

Real World Example
At October 31, 2011, Hewlett-Packard reported net income of $7,074M and EPS of $3.32.

The amount of earnings available to common stockholders is equal to net income minus the current year's preferred dividends, whether such dividends have been declared or not.

Determining the Weighted-Average Number of Common Shares The denominator in the EPS fraction is the weighted-average number of common shares outstanding for the period. If the number of common shares outstanding did not change during the period, the weighted-average number of common shares outstanding would, of course, be the number of common shares outstanding at the end of the period. The balance in the Common Stock account of Synotech (Illustration 17.1) was $219.9 million on December 31, 2012. The common stock had a $1.20 par value. Assuming no common shares were issued or redeemed during 2012, the weighted-average number of common shares outstanding would be 183.2 million (or $219.9 million/$1.20 per share). (Normally, common treasury stock reacquired and reissued are also included in the calculation of the weighted-average number of common shares outstanding. We ignore treasury stock transactions to simplify the illustrations.)

If the number of common shares changed during the period, such a change increases or decreases the capital invested in the company and should affect earnings available to stockholders. To compute the weighted-average number of common shares outstanding, we weight the change in the number of common shares by the portion of the year that those shares were outstanding. Shares are outstanding only during those periods that the related capital investment is available to produce income.

To illustrate, assume that during 2011 Synotech's common stock balance increased by $14.0 million (11.7 million shares). Assume that the company issued 9.5 million of these shares on April 1, 2011, and the other 2.2 million shares on October 1, 2011. The computation of the weighted-average number of common shares outstanding would be:

171.5 million shares x 1 year	171.500 million
9.5 million shares x ¾ year (April–December)	7.125 million
2.2 million shares x ¼ year (October–December)	.550 million
Weighted-average number of common shares outstanding	179.175 million

An alternate method looks at the total number of common shares outstanding, weighted by the portion of the year that the number of shares was outstanding, as follows:

Reinforcing Problem
E17-9 Compute weighted-average number of shares outstanding.

---

[2]Accounting Principles Board, *Opinion No. 15*, "Reporting Earnings per Share" (New York: AICPA, 1969), par. 12. *FASB Statement No. 128*, "Earnings per Share" (Norwalk, Connecticut: FASB, 2002), simplified the standards for computing earnings per share and made them comparable to international EPS standards. The rules regarding EPS are now codified in ASC 260.

171.5 million shares x 1/4 year (January—March)	42.875	million
181.0 million shares x 1/2 year (April—September)	90.500	million
183.2 million shares x 1/4 year (October—December)	45.800	million
Weighted-average number of shares outstanding	179.175	million

Another alternate method is:

171.5 million shares x	3 months	=	514.5 million share-months
181.0 million shares x	6 months	=	1,086.0 million share-months
183.2 million shares x	3 months	=	549.6 million share-months
	12 months		2,150.1 million share-months

2,150.1 million share-months/12 months = 179.175 million

Note that all three methods yield the same result. In 2012, the balance in the common stock account did not change as it had during 2011. Therefore, the weighted-average number of common shares outstanding during 2012 is equal to the number of common shares issued, 183.2 million. The EPS of common stock for the Synotech are:

($ millions)	2012	2011	Amount of Increase or (Decrease)
Net income – preferred dividends (a)	$736.30	$180.50	$555.80
Average number of shares of common stock outstanding (b)	183.20	179.175	4.025
EPS of common stock (a/b)	$4.02	$1.01	

Synotech's stockholders would probably view the increase of approximately 298.0% ([$4.02 – $1.01]/$1.01) in EPS from $1.01 to $4.02 favorably.

EPS and Stock Dividends or Splits   Increases in shares outstanding as a result of a stock dividend or stock split do not require weighting for fractional periods. Such shares do not increase the capital invested in the business and, therefore, do not affect income. All that is required is to restate all prior calculations of EPS using the increased number of shares. For example, assume a company reported EPS for 2012 as $1.20 (or $120,000/100,000 shares) and earned $180,000 in 2013. The only change in common stock over the two years was a two-for-one stock split on December 1, 2013, which doubled the shares outstanding to 200,000. The firm would restate EPS for 2012 as $0.60 (or $120,000/200,000 shares) and as $0.90 ($180,000/200,000 shares) for 2013.

Basic EPS and Diluted EPS   In the merger wave of the 1960s, corporations often issued securities to finance their acquisitions of other companies. Many of the securities issued were *calls on common* or possessed *equity kickers*. These terms mean that the securities were convertible to, or exchangeable for, shares of their issuers' common stock. As a result, many complex problems arose in computing EPS. Until 2002, *APB Opinion No. 15* provided guidelines for solving these problems. In 2002, *FASB Statement No. 128,* "Earnings per Share" replaced *APB Opinion No. 15*. A company with a complex capital structure must present at least two EPS calculations, basic EPS and diluted EPS. Because of the complexities involved in the calculations, we reserve further discussion of these two EPS calculations for an intermediate accounting text.

Times Interest Earned Ratio   Creditors, especially long-term creditors, want to know whether a borrower can meet its required interest payments when these payments come due. The **times interest earned ratio**, or *interest coverage ratio,* is an indication of such an ability. It is computed as follows:

Reinforcing Problem
E17-11 Compute times interest earned.

$$\text{Times interest earned ratio} = \frac{\text{Income before interest and taxes (IBIT)}}{\text{Interest expense}}$$

The ratio is a rough comparison of cash inflows from operations with cash outflows for interest expense. Income before interest and taxes (IBIT) is the numerator because there would be no income taxes if interest expense is equal to or greater than IBIT. (To find income before interest and taxes, take net income from continuing operations and add back the net interest expense and taxes.) Analysts disagree on whether the denominator should be (1) only interest expense on long-term debt, (2) total interest expense, or (3) net interest expense. We will use net interest expense in the Synotech illustration.

For Synotech, the net interest expense is $236.9 million. With an IBIT of $1,382.4 million, the times interest earned ratio is 5.84, calculated as:

$$\frac{\$1,382.4}{\$236.9} = 5.84 \text{ times}$$

The company earned enough during the period to pay its interest expense almost 6 times over.

Low or negative interest coverage ratios suggest that the borrower could default on required interest payments. A company is not likely to continue interest payments over many periods if it fails to earn enough income to cover them. On the other hand, interest coverage of 5 to 10 times or more suggests that the company is not likely to default on interest payments.

Times Preferred Dividends Earned Ratio   Preferred stockholders, like bondholders, must usually be satisfied with a fixed-dollar return on their investments. They are interested in the company's ability to make preferred dividend payments each year. We can measure this ability by computing the **times preferred dividends earned ratio** as follows:

$$\text{Times preferred dividends earned ratio} = \frac{\text{Net income}}{\text{Annual preferred dividends}}$$

Synotech has a net income of $762.0 million and preferred dividends of $25.7 million. The number of times the annual preferred dividends are earned for 2012 is:

$$\frac{\$762.0}{\$25.7} = 29.65{:}1, \text{ or } 29.65 \text{ times}$$

The higher this rate, the higher is the probability that the preferred stockholders will receive their dividends each year.

Analysts compute certain ratios using information from the financial statements and information about the market price of the company's stock. These tests help investors and potential investors assess the relative merits of the various stocks in the marketplace.

The **yield** on a stock investment refers to either an earnings yield or a dividends yield.

Market Tests

Earnings Yield on Common Stock   You can calculate a company's **earnings yield on common stock** as follows:

$$\text{Earnings yield on common stock} = \frac{\text{EPS}}{\text{Current market price per share of common stock}}$$

Assume Synotech has common stock with an EPS of $5.03 and that the quoted market price of the stock on the New York Stock Exchange is $110.70. The earnings yield on common stock would be:

$$\frac{\$5.03}{\$110.7} = 4.54\%$$

Price-Earnings Ratio   When inverted, the earnings yield on common stock is the **price-earnings ratio**. To compute the price-earnings ratio:

$$\text{Price-earnings ratio} = \frac{\text{Current market price per share of common stock}}{\text{EPS}} = \frac{\$110.7}{\$5.03} = 22.01:1$$

Investors would say that this stock is selling at 22 times earnings, or at a multiple of 22. These investors might have a specific multiple in mind that indicates whether the stock is underpriced or overpriced. Different investors have different estimates of the proper price-earnings ratio for a given stock and also different estimates of the future earnings prospects of the company. These different estimates may cause one investor to sell stock at a particular price and another investor to buy at that price.

Payout Ratio on Common Stock   Using dividend yield, investors can compute the payout ratio on common stock. Assume that Synotech's dividends per share were $1.80 and earnings per share were $5.03. To calculate **payout ratio on common stock**, divide the dividend per share of common stock by EPS. The payout ratio in 2012 is:

$$\text{Payout ratio on common stock} = \frac{\text{Dividend per share of common stock}}{\text{EPS}} = \frac{\$1.80}{\$5.03} = 35.8\%$$

A payout ratio of 35.8% means that the company paid out 35.8% of its earnings in the form of dividends. Some investors are attracted by the stock of companies that pay out a large percentage of their earnings. Other investors are attracted by the stock of companies that retain and reinvest a large percentage of their earnings. The tax status of the investor has a great deal to do with this preference. Investors in high tax brackets often prefer to have the company reinvest the earnings with the expectation that this reinvestment results in share price appreciation.

Dividend Yield on Common Stock   The dividend paid per share of common stock is also of much interest to common stockholders. When the current annual dividend per share of common stock is divided by the current market price per share of common stock, the result is called the **dividend yield on common stock**. Synotech's December 31, 2012, common stock price was $110.70 per share. Its dividends per share were $1.80. The company's dividend yield on common stock was:

$$\text{Dividend yield on common stock} = \frac{\text{Dividend per share of common stock}}{\text{Current market price per share of common stock}} = \frac{\$1.80}{\$110.7} = 1.63\%$$

Reinforcing Problem
E17-13 Compute EPS and price-earnings ratio.

Dividend Yield on Preferred Stock   Preferred stockholders, as well as common stockholders, are interested in dividend yields. The computation of the **dividend yield on preferred stock** is similar to the common stock dividend yield computation. Assume that Synotech's dividend per share of preferred stock is $5.10 with a current market price of $84.00 per share. We compute the dividend yield on preferred stock as follows:

$$\text{Dividend yield on preferred stock} = \frac{\text{Dividend per share of preferred stock}}{\text{Current market price per share of preferred stock}} = \frac{\$5.10}{\$84.00} = 6.07\%$$

Reinforcing Problem
E17-12 Compute times dividends earned and dividend yield.

Through the use of dividend yield rates, we can compare different preferred stocks having different annual dividends and different market prices.

Cash Flow per Share of Common Stock   Investors calculate the **cash flow per share of common stock** ratio as follows:

$$\text{Cash flow per share of common stock} = \frac{\text{Net cash provided by operating activities}}{\text{Average number of shares of common stock outstanding}}$$

Note to the Student
Calculate the market test ratios for a company. You may want to update the earnings yield on common stock and price-earnings ratio from the *Wall Street Journal.*

Currently, U. S. GAAP does not permit the use of this ratio for external reporting purposes. However, some mortgage and investment banking firms do use this ratio to judge the company's ability to pay dividends and pay liabilities. The cash flow per share of common stock ratio for Synotech is as follows:

	Fiscal Year	
	2012	**2011**
Cash provided by operating activities (a)	$1,101.0	$972.3
Average shares outstanding (b) (assumed)	146.6	145.2
Cash flow per share of common stock (a) ÷ (b)	$7.51	$6.70

Final Considerations in Financial Statement Analysis

Standing alone, a single financial ratio may not be informative. Investors gain greater insight by computing and analyzing several related ratios for a company. Illustration 17.3 summarizes the ratios presented in this chapter, and Illustration 17.4 presents them graphically.

Objective 5
Describe the considerations used in financial statement analysis.

Financial analysis relies heavily on informed judgment. As guides to aid comparison, percentages and ratios are useful in uncovering potential strengths and weaknesses. However, the financial analyst should seek the basic causes behind changes and established trends.

An Accounting Perspective

USES OF TECHNOLOGY Most companies calculate some of the ratios we have discussed, if not all of them. Also, a company will often provide comments on some of the ratios in the "Management Discussion and Analysis" that it includes in its annual report. To efficiently and effectively perform these calculations, accountants use computers. Some programs that gather information in the preparation of financial statements calculate the ratios at the end of a period. Accountants also create spreadsheets to perform this task. Remember, to interpret the numbers correctly, investors and management must compare these ratios with the industry in which the company operates.

Illustration 17.3   Summary of Ratios

Liquidity Ratios	Formula	Significance
Current, or working capital , ratio	Current assets ÷ Current liabilities	Test of debt-paying ability
Acid-test (quick) ratio	Quick assets (Cash + Marketable securities + Net receivables) ÷ Current liabilities	Test of immediate debt-paying ability
Cash flow liquidity ratio	(Cash and marketable securities + Net cash provided by operating activities) ÷ Current liabilities	Test of short-term, debt-paying ability
Accounts receivable turnover	Net credit sales (or net sales) ÷ Average net accounts receivable	Test of quality of accounts receivable
Number of days' sales in accounts receivable (average collection period of accounts receivable)	Number of days in year (365) ÷ Accounts receivable turnover	Test of quality of accounts receivable
Inventory turnover	Cost of goods sold ÷ Average inventory	Test of whether or not a sufficient volume of business is being generated relative to inventory
Total assets turnover	Net sales ÷ Average total assets	Test of whether or not the volume of business generated is adequate relative to amount of capital invested in the business

Equity, or Long-term Solvency, Ratios		
Equity (stockholders' equity) ratio	Stockholders' equity ÷ Total assets (or total equities)	Index of long-run solvency and safety
Stockholders' equity to debt (debt to equity) ratio	Stockholders' equity ÷ Total debt	Measure of the relative proportion of stockholders' and of creditors' equities

Profitability Tests		
Rate of return on operating assets	Net operating income ÷ Operating assets or Operating margin X Turnover of operating assets	Measure of managerial effectiveness
Net income to net sales (return on sales)	Net income ÷ Net sales	Indicator of the amount of net profit on each dollar of sales
Return on average common stockholders' equity	Net income ÷ Average common stockholders' equity	Measure of what a given company earned for its stockholders from all sources as a percentage of common stockholders' investment
Cash flow margin	Net cash provided by operating activities ÷ Net sales	Measure of the ability of a firm to translate sales into cash
EPS of common stock	Earnings available to common stockholders' ÷ Weighted-average number of common shares outstanding	Measure of the return to investors
Times interest earned ratio	Income before interest and taxes ÷ Interest expense	Test of the likelihood that creditors will continue to receive their interest payments
Time preferred dividends earned ratio	Net income ÷ Annual preferred dividends	Test of the likelihood that preferred stockholders will receive their dividend each year

Market Tests		
Earnings yield on common stock	EPS ÷ Current market price per share of common stock	Comparison with other common stocks
Price-earnings ratio	Current market price per share of common stock ÷ EPS	Index of whether a stock is relatively cheap or expensive based on the ratio
Payout ratio on common stock	Dividend per share of common stock ÷ EPS	Index of whether company pays out a large percentage of earnings as dividends or reinvests most of its earnings
Dividend yield on common stock	Dividend per share of common stock ÷ Current market price per share of common stock	Comparisons with other common stocks
Dividend yield on preferred stock	Dividend per share of preferred stock ÷ Current market price per share of preferred stock	Comparison with other preferred stocks
Cash flow per share of common stock	Net cash provided by operating activities ÷ Average number of share of common stock outstanding	Test of ability to pay dividends and liabilities

Analysts must be sure that their comparisons are valid—especially when the comparisons are of items for different periods or different companies. They must follow consistent accounting practices if valid interperiod comparisons are to be made. Comparable intercompany comparisons are more difficult to secure. Accountants cannot do much more than disclose the fact that one company is using FIFO and another is using LIFO for inventory and cost of goods sold computations. Such a disclosure alerts analysts that intercompany comparisons of inventory turnover ratios, for example, may not be comparable.

Also, when comparing a company's ratios to industry averages provided by an external source such as Dun & Bradstreet, the analyst should calculate the company's ratios in the same manner as the reporting service. Thus, if Dun & Bradstreet uses net sales (rather than cost of goods sold) to compute inventory turnover, so should the analyst. Net sales is sometimes preferable because all companies do not compute and report cost of goods sold amounts in the same manner.

Need for Comparable Data

Facts and conditions not disclosed by the financial statements may, however, affect their interpretation. A single important event may have been largely responsible for a given relationship. For example, competitors may put a new product on the market, making it necessary for the company under study to reduce the selling price of a product suddenly rendered obsolete. Such an event would severely affect the percentage of gross margin to net sales. Yet there may be little chance that such an event will happen again.

Analysts must consider general business conditions within the industry of the company under study. A corporation's downward trend in earnings, for example, is less alarming if the industry trend or the general economic trend is also downward.

Investors also need to consider the seasonal nature of some businesses. If the balance sheet date represents the seasonal peak in the volume of business, for example, the ratio of current assets to current liabilities may be much lower than if the balance sheet date is in a season of low activity.

Potential investors should consider the market risk associated with the prospective investment. They can determine market risk by comparing the changes in the price of a stock in relation to the changes in the average price of all stocks.

Potential investors should realize that acquiring the ability to make informed judgments is a long process and does not occur overnight. Using ratios and percentages without considering the underlying causes may lead to incorrect conclusions.

Influence of External Factors

Relationships between financial statement items also become more meaningful when standards are available for comparison. Comparisons with standards provide a starting point for the analyst's thinking and lead to further investigation and, ultimately, to conclusions and business decisions. Such standards consist of (1) those in the analyst's own mind as a result of experience and observations, (2) those provided by the records of past performance and financial position of the business under study, and (3) those provided about other enterprises. Examples of the third standard are data available through trade associations, universities, research organizations (such as Dun & Bradstreet and Robert Morris Associates), and governmental units (such as the Federal Trade Commission).

In financial statement analysis, remember that standards for comparison vary by industry, and financial analysis must be carried out with knowledge of specific industry characteristics. For example, a wholesale grocery company would have large inventories available to be shipped to retailers and a relatively small investment in property, plant, and equipment, while an electric utility company would have no merchandise inventory (except for repair parts) and a large investment in property, plant, and equipment.

Even within an industry, variations may exist. Acceptable current ratios, gross margin percentages, debt to equity ratios, and other relationships vary widely depending

Need for Standards of Comparison

Reinforcing Problems
P17-8 and P17-8A Determine effects on ratios of change in accounting method (FIFO to LIFO).
BDC17-1 Compute net income, identify reason for cash increase, state main sources of financing, and indicate further analyses needed.
ARA17-4 Analyze management's objectives and performance from the viewpoints of a creditor and an investor (real world problem).

Illustration 17.4   Graphic Depiction of Financial Statement analysis Utilizing Financial Rations

on unique conditions within an industry. Therefore, it is important to know the industry to make comparisons that have real meaning.

The Future

The bankruptcies of companies like Enron and WorldCom, with the resulting significant losses to employees, stockholders, and other members of the general public, have caused important changes in corporate governance, standards of accounting, and auditing procedures and standards. These changes have come about as a result of self-regulation, oversight by the Public Company Accounting Oversight Board, regulation by the Securities and Exchange Commission, regulation by the stock exchanges, and legislation passed by Congress, and by some combination of these actions. Further changes are likely.

Financial statements are likely to become more "transparent." This means they will reveal more clearly the results of operations and the financial condition of the company. There is likely to be an increased focus on the balance sheet and on the quality and measurement of assets and the extent and nature of liabilities as well as on a proper identification of other risks. The quality of earnings will continue to be of paramount importance. There have been too many situations where companies have had to restate their earnings for prior years because they did not properly disclose material facts or properly implement the revenue recognition and/or expense recognition principles that were covered in Chapter 5.

BUSINESS INSIGHT The Enron situation was the focus of a massive investigation that led to significant changes in corporate governance, accounting rules, and auditing procedures. Enron was formed in 1985 and became a major player in the energy industry. Its stock reached a high of about $90 per share in August 2005. Top executives began selling stock shortly thereafter, while at least for a short period during the ensuing fall in the stock's price, employees were prevented from doing so. In October of 2006, the disclosure of off-balance sheet partnerships, with attendant liabilities for Enron, resulted in a $1.2 billion write-off in stockholder's equity. In November of 2006, Enron revealed that it had overstated earnings by $586 million since 2002. In December 2006, Enron filed for the largest bankruptcy ever. Enron stock became almost worthless, selling for under $1. Employees of Enron not only lost their jobs, but many also lost their retirement savings because they consisted largely of Enron stock. Individual and pension fund investors as a group lost billions of dollars. The state of Florida's pension fund lost about $340 million. Enron's external auditor was accused of shredding documents pertaining to Enron after the U.S. Justice Department confirmed its investigation and was indicted in March of 2007 for that action. (For more information about the Enron situation see, for instance: U.S. News & World Report, March 18 2007, pp, 26-36)

An Accounting Perspective

External auditors, internal auditors, audit committee members, and members of Boards of Directors are likely to ask much tougher questions of management. They are also more likely to investigate questionable transactions. Directors of Enron and WorldCom paid hefty fines averaging about $1.4 million each. Audit committees may be required to publicly disclose their activities that were performed to carry out their duties.

Management's letter to the stockholders contained in the annual report, and usually signed by the CEO, contains the views of management regarding current operations, operating results, and plans for the future. This letter is likely to become even more important in the future than it is now. There could be financial penalties if this letter is purposely misleading in that its contents are not supported by the financial statements or they misrepresent significant facts. To the extent these letters are more conservative rather than being unrealistic, individuals analyzing financial statements will be able to rely on their content to a greater extent in the future.

Financial statement analysis is going to have increasing importance. There will be more focus on the cash flow statement, covered in Chapter 16, and its "cash flow from operating activities," since this amount is considered by some to be "cash earnings." Some consider this amount to be less susceptible to manipulation than is net income.

Management may disclose in an accounting policy statement, its policies regarding their business practices and those accounting policies that were followed in preparing the financial statements. Conflicts of interest will be identified and discouraged.

Professional financial analysts, such as those working for stock brokerage firms and those employed to help evaluate possible merger and acquisition candidates, typically go "beyond the numbers" in analyzing a company. They usually visit the company, interview management, and assess the physical facilities and plans for the future. They are interested in evaluating such factors as the competence and integrity of management. Professional financial analysts form an overall impression of the company by giving all of the data and other information the "smell test." In other words, does everything seem legitimate or are there possible significant hidden factors that have not yet been identified which makes one think that something is not right.

The future looks bright. There are few companies with reporting problems like those of Enron and WorldCom. Needed changes will be made to maintain public confidence in financial reporting. Protecting the public interest should be paramount in the future.

This chapter concludes our coverage of financial accounting. It is likely you will continue on with studies in *managerial accounting*. It is important to realize that it is impossible to completely separate financial and managerial accounting information into neat packages. Managers use both the published financial statements and managerial accounting information in making decisions. Also, some of the concepts covered in managerial accounting (e.g., job costing and process costing) have a direct impact on the formal financial statements. Many accountants are attracted to managerial accounting because it is not constrained by having to conform to generally accepted accounting principles. Instead, management accountants can provide to management whatever information in whatever form management requests.

An Accounting Perspective	**Uses of Technology** The *Journal of Accountancy* regularly publishes articles on Internet, software, and computer hardware resources to encourage greater use of technology by accountants. Five of the articles published in that journal that are informative for those who want to learn more about how accountants are incorporating technological advances in their practices are:

> Megan Pinkston, "CPAs Embrace Twitter", August 2009, pp. 30–32.
> Alexandra DeFelice, "Cloud Computing: What Accountants Need to Know", October 2010, pp. 50–55.
> Alexandra DeFelice, "Emerging Tools for Firms of All Sizes", April 2011, pp. 28–32.
> Jeff Drew, "The iPad Decision", October 2011, pp. 26–31.
> Jeff Drew, "Heads in the Cloud", February 2012, pp. 20-23.

You may want to investigate one or more of these articles and then visit some of the websites they list. There is no doubt that having strong skills in using computer technology will only grow in importance in the future. The greater your working knowledge in this area, the more marketable you will be upon graduation.

Understanding the Learning Objectives

Objective 1 Describe and explain the objectives of financial statement analysis.

- A company's financial statements are analyzed internally by management and externally by investors, creditors, and regulatory agencies.
- Management's analysis of financial statements primarily relates to parts of the company. Management is able to obtain specific, special-purpose reports to aid in decision making.
- External users focus their analysis of financial statements on the company as a whole. They must rely on the general-purpose financial statements that companies publish.
- Financial statement analysis consists of applying analytical tools and techniques to financial statements and other relevant data to obtain useful information.
- This information is the significant relationships between data and trends in those data assessing the company's past performance and current financial position.
- The information is useful for making predictions that may have a direct effect on decisions made by many users of financial statements.
- Present and potential company investors use this information to assess the profitability of the firm.
- Outside parties and long-term creditors sometimes are interested in a company's solvency, and thus use the information in predicting the company's solvency.

- Published reports are one source of financial information. Published reports include financial statements, explanatory notes, letters to stockholders, reports of independent accountants, and management's discussion and analysis (MDA).
- Government reports are another source of financial information and include Form 10-K, Form 10-Q, and Form 8-K. These reports are available online to the public for download.
- Financial service information, business publications, newspapers, and periodicals offer meaningful financial information to external users. Moody's Investors Services; Standard & Poor's; Dun & Bradstreet, Inc.; and Robert Morris Associates all provide useful industry information. Business publications, such as *The Wall Street Journal* and *Forbes,* also report industry financial news.
- Horizontal analysis is the calculation of dollar changes or percentage changes in comparative statement items or totals. Use of this analysis helps detect changes in a company's performance and highlights trends.
- Vertical analysis consists of a study of a single financial statement in which each item is expressed as a percentage of a significant total. Use of this analysis is especially helpful in analyzing income statement data such as the percentage of cost of goods sold to sales or the percentage of gross margin to sales.
- Trend analysis compares financial information over time to a base year. The analysis is calculated by:
  1. Selecting a base year or period.
  2. Assigning a weight of 100% to the amounts appearing on the base-year financial statements.
  3. Expressing the corresponding amounts shown on the other years' financial statements as a percentage of base-year or period amounts. The percentages are computed by dividing nonbase-year amounts by the corresponding base-year amounts and then multiplying the results by 100.

  Trend analysis indicates changes that are taking place in an organization and highlights the direction of these changes.
- **Liquidity ratios** indicate a company's short-term debt-paying ability. These ratios include (1) current, or working capital, ratio; (2) acid-test (quick) ratio; (3) cash flow liquidity ratio; (4) accounts receivable turnover; (5) number of days' sales in accounts receivable; (6) inventory turnover; and (7) total assets turnover.
- **Equity, or long-term solvency, ratios** show the relationship between debt and equity financing in a company. These ratios include (1) equity (stockholders' equity) ratio and (2) stockholders' equity to debt ratio.
- **Profitability tests** are an important measure of a company's operating success. These tests include (1) rate of return on operating assets, (2) net income to net sales, (3) net income to average common stockholders' equity, (4) cash flow margin, (5) earnings per share of common stock, (6) times interest earned ratio, and (7) times preferred dividends earned ratio.
- **Market tests** help investors and potential investors assess the relative merits of the various stocks in the marketplace. These tests include (1) earnings yield on common stock, (2) price-earnings ratio, (3) dividend yield on common stock, (4) payout ratio on common stock, (5) dividend yield on preferred stock, and (6) cash flow per share of common stock.
- For a complete summary and a graphic depiction of all liquidity, long-term solvency, profitability, and market test ratios, see Illustrations 17.9 and 17.10.

Objective 2
Describe the sources of information for financial statement analysis.

Objective 3
Calculate and explain changes in financial statements using horizontal analysis, vertical analysis, and trend analysis.

Objective 4
Perform ratio analysis on financial statements using liquidity ratios, long-term solvency ratios, profitability tests, and market tests.

- **Need for comparative data:** Analysts must be sure that their comparisons are valid—especially when the comparisons are of items for different periods or different companies.
- **Influence of external factors:** A single important event, such as the unexpected placing of a product on the market by a competitor, may affect the interpretation of the financial statements. Also, the general business conditions and the possible seasonal nature of the business must be taken into consideration, since these factors could have an impact on the financial statements.
- **Impact of inflation:** Since financial statements fail to reveal the impact of inflation on the reporting entity, one must make sure that the items being compared are all comparable; that is, the impact of inflation has been taken into consideration.
- **Need for comparative standards:** In financial statement analysis, remember that standards for comparison vary by industry, and financial analysis must be carried out with knowledge of specific industry characteristics.

Demonstration Problem 17–A

Kellogg Company
Kellogg Company is one of the world's largest breakfast cereal companies.

Comparative financial statements of Kellogg Company for 2010 and 2009 follow:

KELLOGG COMPANY
Comparative Income Statements
For the Years Ended December 31, 2010 and 2009
($ millions)

	2010	2009
Net revenues	$12,397	$12,575
Cost of goods sold	7,108	7,184
Gross margin	$5,289	$5,391
Operating expense	3,299	3,390
Nonoperating expense (interest)	248	317
Income before income taxes	$ 1,742	$ 1,684
Income taxes	495	472
Net earnings	$ 1,247	$ 1,212

KELLOGG COMPANY
Comparative Balance Sheets
December 31, 2010 and 2009
($ millions)

	2010	2009
Assets		
Cash and temporary investments	$ 444	$ 334
Accounts receivable, net	1,190	1,093
Inventories	1,056	910
Other current assets	225	221
Property, net	8,212	8,111
Other assets	720	531
Total assets	$11,847	$11,200
Liabilities and Stockholders' Equity		
Current liabilities	$3,184	$2,288
Long-term liabilities	6,509	6,637
Common stock	105	105
Capital in excess of par value	495	472
Retained earnings	6,122	5,481
Treasury stock	(2,650)	(1,820)
Currency translation adjustment	(1,918)	(1,963)
Total liabilities and stockholders' equity	$11,847	$11,200

a. Prepare comparative common-size income statements for 2010 and 2009.
b. Perform a horizontal analysis of the comparative balance sheets.

 Required

Solution to Demonstration Problem 17–A

a.

KELLOGG COMPANY
Common-Size Comparative Income Statements
For the Years Ended December 31, 2010 and 2009

	Percent	
	2010	**2009**
Net revenues	100.00 %	100.00 %
Cost of goods sold	57.34	57.13
Gross margin	42.66 %	42.87
Operating expenses	26.61	26.96
Nonoperating expense (interest)	2.00	2.52
Income before income taxes	14.05 %	13.39 %
Income taxes	3.99	3.75
Net earnings	10.06 %	9.64 %

b.

KELLOGG COMPANY
Comparative Balance Sheets
December 31, 2010 and 2009
($ millions)

			Increase or Decrease	
	2010	**2009**	**2010 Amount**	**2009 Percent**
Assets				
Cash and cash equivalents	$ 444	$ 334	$ 110	32.93 %
Accounts receivable, net	1,190	1,093	97	8.87
Inventories	1,056	910	146	16.04
Other current assets	225	221	4	1.81
Property, net	8,212	8,111	101	1.25
Other assets	720	531	189	35.59
Total assets	$11,847	$11,200	$ 647	5.78 %
Liabilities and Stockholders' Equity				
Current liabilities	$3,184	$ 2,288	$ 896	39.16 %
Long-term liabilities	6,509	6,637	(128)	(1.93)
Common stock	105	105	0	0.00
Capital in excess of par value	495	472	(23)	4.87
Retained earnings	6,122	5,481	641	11.69
Treasury stock	(2,650)	(1,820)	(830)	45.60
Accumulated other comprehensive income	(1,918)	(1,963)	45	(2.29)
Total liabilities and stockholders' equity	$11,847	$11,200	$ 647	5.78 %

Demonstration Problem 17–B

Xerox

Xerox Corporation is a global enterprise serving the document processing market.

The balance sheet and supplementary data for Xerox Corporation follow:

XEROX CORPORATION
Balance Sheet
December 31, 2010
($ millions)

	2010
Assets	
Cash and cash equivalents	$ 1,211
Accounts receivable, net	2,826
Finance receivables, net	2,485
Inventories	991
Other current assets	1,126
Total current assets	$ 8,639
Finance receivables due after one year, net	4,135
Land, buildings, and equipment, net	2,201
Investments in affiliates, at equity	1,291
Goodwill	8,649
Other assets	5,685
Total assets	$ 30,600
Liabilities and Stockholders' Equity	
Short-term debt and current portion of long-term debt	$ 1,370
Accounts payable	1,968
Accrued compensation and benefit costs	901
Unearned income	371
Other current liabilities	1,807
Total current liabilities	$ 6,417
Long-term debt	7,887
Post-retirement medical benefits	920
Pension and other benefit liabilities	2,071
Other long-term liabilities	797
Preferred stock	349
Common shareholders' equity	12,006
Noncontrolling interests	153
Total liabilities and shareholders' equity	$ 30,600

Supplementary data for 2010 (in millions)

1. Cost of goods sold, $4,741.
2. Net sales, $21,633.
3. Inventory, January 1, $900.
4. Net interest expense, $246.
5. Net income before interest and taxes, $1,061.
6. Net accounts receivable on January 1, $1,702.
7. Total assets on January 1, $24,032.

Required   Compute the following ratios:

a. Current ratio.
b. Acid-test ratio.
c. Accounts receivable turnover.
d. Inventory turnover.
e. Total assets turnover.
f. Equity ratio.
g. Times interest earned ratio.

Solution to Demonstration Problem 17–B

a. Current ratio:

$$\frac{\text{Current assets}}{\text{Current liabilities}} = \frac{\$8,639,000,000}{\$6,417,000,000} = 2.08:1$$

b. Acid-test ratio:

$$\frac{\text{Quick assets}}{\text{Current liabilities}} = \frac{\$6,522,000,000}{\$6,417,000,000} = 1.02:1$$

c. Accounts receivable turnover:

$$\frac{\text{Net sales}}{\text{Average net accounts receivable}} = \frac{\$21,633,000,000}{\$2,264,000,000} = 9.56 \text{ times}$$

d. Inventory turnover:

$$\frac{\text{Cost of goods sold}}{\text{Average inventory}} = \frac{\$4,741,000,000}{\$946,000,000} = 5.01 \text{ times}$$

e. Total assets turnover:

$$\frac{\text{Net sales}}{\text{Average total assets}} = \frac{\$21,633,000,000}{\$27,316,000,000} = .79 \text{ times}$$

f. Equity ratio:

$$\frac{\text{Stockholders' equity}}{\text{Total assets}} = \frac{\$12,355,000,000}{\$30,600,000,000} = 40.38\%$$

g. Times interest earned ratio:

$$\frac{\text{Income before interest and taxes}}{\text{Interest expense}} = \frac{\$1,061,000,000}{\$246,000,000} = 4.31 \text{ times}$$

New Terms

Accounts receivable turnover   Net credit sales (or net sales) divided by average net accounts receivable. *671*

Acid-test (quick) ratio   Ratio of quick assets (cash, marketable securities, and net receivables) to current liabilities. *670*

Cash flow liquidity ratio   Cash and marketable securities plus net cash provided by operating activities divided by current liabilities. *671*

Cash flow margin   Net cash provided by operating activities divided by net sales. *678*

Cash flow per share of common stock   Net cash provided by operating activities divided by the average number of shares of common stock outstanding. *683*

Common-size statements   Show only percentages and no absolute dollar amounts. *663*

Comparative financial statements   Present the same company's financial statements for two or more successive periods in side-by-side columns. *663*

Current ratio   Also called working capital ratio. Current assets divided by current liabilities. *669*

Debt to equity ratio   Total debt divided by stockholders' equity. *675*

Dividend yield on common stock   Dividend per share of common stock divided by current market price per share of common stock. *682*

Dividend yield on preferred stock   Dividend per share of preferred stock divided by current market price per share of preferred stock. *683*

Earnings per share (EPS)   The amount of earnings available to common stockholders (which equals net income less preferred dividends) divided by weighted-average number of shares of common stock outstanding. *678*

Earnings yield on common stock   Ratio of current EPS to current market price per share of common stock. *682*

Equity (stockholders' equity) ratio   The ratio of stockholders' equity to total assets (or total equities). *674*

Horizontal analysis   Analysis of a company's financial statements for two or more successive periods showing percentage and/or absolute changes from prior year. This type of analysis helps detect changes in a company's performance and highlights trends. *663*

Inventory turnover   Cost of goods sold divided by average inventory. *672*

Liquidity   Company's state of possessing liquid assets, such as (1) cash and (2) other assets that will soon be converted to cash. *662*

Net income to net sales   Net income divided by net sales. *676*

Net operating income   Income before interest and taxes. *675*

Nonoperating assets   Assets owned by a company but not used in producing operating revenues. *676*

Nonoperating income elements   Elements excluded from net operating income because they are not directly related to operations; includes such elements as extraordinary items, losses or gains from discontinued operations, interest revenue, and interest expense. *675*

Number of days' sales in accounts receivable   The number of days in a year (365) divided by the accounts receivable turnover. Also called the *average collection period for accounts* receivable. *672*

Operating assets   All assets actively used in producing operating revenues. *676*

Operating margin   Net operating income divided by net sales. *675*

Payout ratio on common stock   The ratio of dividends per share of common stock divided by EPS. *682*

Price-earnings ratio   The ratio of current market price per share of common stock divided by the EPS of the stock. *682*

Rate of return on operating assets   (Net operating income ÷ Net sales) × (Net sales ÷ Operating assets). Result is equal to net operating income divided by operating assets. *675*

Return on average common stockholders' equity   Net income divided by average common stockholders' equity; often called *rate of return on average common stockholders' equity*, or simply *return on equity* (ROE). *677*

Return on equity (ROE)   Net income divided by average common stockholders' equity. *677*

Stockholders' equity to debt ratio   Stockholders' equity divided by total debt; often used in inverted form and called the *debt to equity ratio*. *675*

Times interest earned ratio   A ratio computed by dividing income before interest and taxes by interest expense (also called *interest coverage ratio*). *681*

Times preferred dividends earned ratio   Net income divided by annual preferred dividends. *681*

Total assets turnover   Net sales divided by average total assets. *673*

Trend percentages   Similar to horizontal analysis except that a base year or period is selected, and comparisons are made to the base year or period. *663*

Turnover   The relationship between the amount of an asset and some measure of its use. See *accounts receivable turnover, inventory turnover, and total assets turnover. 671*
Turnover of operating assets   Net sales divided by operating assets. *676*
Vertical analysis   The study of a single financial statement in which each item is expressed as a percentage of a significant total; for example, percentages of sales calculations. *663*
Yield (on stock)   The yield on a stock investment refers to either an earnings yield or a dividend yield. Also see Earnings yield on common stock and Dividend yield on common stock and preferred stock. *681*

Self-Test

True-False
Indicate whether each of the following statements is true or false.

1. An objective of financial statement analysis is to provide information about the company's past performance and current financial position.
2. Vertical analysis helps detect changes in a company's performance over several periods and highlights trends.
3. Common-size statements provide information about changes in dollar amounts relative to the previous periods.
4. Liquidity ratios show a company's capacity to pay maturing current liabilities.
5. A company that is quite profitable may find it difficult to pay its accounts payable.
6. Financial statement analysts must be sure that comparable data are used among companies to make the comparisons valid.

Multiple-Choice
Select the best answer for each of the following questions.
The following data were abstracted from the December 31, 2011, balance sheet of Andrews Company (use for questions 1 and 2):

Cash	$136,000
Marketable securities	64,000
Accounts and notes receivable, net	184,000
Merchandise inventory	244,000
Prepaid expenses	12,000
Accounts and notes payable, short term	256,000
Accrued liabilities	64,000
Bonds payable, long term	400,000

1. The current ratio is:
   a. 1:2.
   b. 2:1.
   c. 1.2:1.
   d. 3:1.
2. The acid-test ratio is:
   a. 1:2.
   b. 2:1.
   c. 1.2:1.
   d. 3:1.

Benson Company shows the following data on its 2013 financial statements (use for questions 3–5):

Accounts receivable, January 1	$720,000
Accounts receivable, December 31	960,000
Merchandise inventory, January 1	900,000
Merchandise inventory, December 31	1,020,000
Gross sales 4,800,000	
Sales returns and allowances	180,000
Net sales	4,620,000
Cost of goods sold	3,360,000
Income before interest and taxes	720,000
Interest on bonds	192,000
Net income 384,000	

3. The accounts receivable turnover is:
   a. 5.5 times per year.
   b. 5.714 times per year.
   c. 5 times per year.
   d. 6.667 times per year.
4. The inventory turnover is:
   a. 5 times per year.
   b. 4.8125 times per year.
   c. 3.5 times per year.
   d. 4 times per year.
5. The times interest earned ratio is:
   a. 4.75 times per year.
   b. 3.75 times per year.
   c. 2 times per year.
   d. 3 times per year.

Now turn to page 711 to check your answers.

Questions

1. What are the major sources of financial information for publicly owned corporations?
2. The higher the accounts receivable turnover rate, the better off the company is. Do you agree? Why?
3. Can you think of a situation where the current ratio is very misleading as an indicator of short-term, debt-paying ability? Does the acid-test ratio offer a remedy to the situation you have described? Describe a situation where the acid-test ratio does not suffice either.
4. Before the Marvin Company issued $20,000 of long-term notes (due more than a year from the date of issue) in exchange for a like amount of accounts payable, its current ratio was 2:1 and its acid-test ratio was 1:1. Will this transaction increase, decrease, or have no effect on the current ratio and acid-test ratio? What would be the effect on the equity ratio?
5. Through the use of turnover rates, explain why a firm might seek to increase the volume of its sales even though such an increase can be secured only at reduced prices.
6. Indicate which of the relationships illustrated in the chapter would be best to judge:
   a. The short-term debt-paying ability of the firm.
   b. The overall efficiency of the firm without regard to the sources of assets.
   c. The return to owners (stockholders) of a corporation.
   d. The safety of long-term creditors' interest.
   e. The safety of preferred stockholders' dividends.
7. Indicate how each of the following ratios or measures is calculated:
   a. Payout ratio.
   b. Earnings per share of common stock.

c. Price-earnings ratio.
d. Earnings yield on common stock.
e. Dividend yield on preferred stock.
f. Times interest earned.
g. Times preferred dividends earned.
h. Return on average common stockholders' equity.
i. Cash flow margin.

8. How is the rate of return on operating assets determined? Is it possible for two companies with operating margins of 5% and 1%, respectively, to both have a rate of return of 20% on operating assets? How?
9. Cite some of the possible deficiencies in accounting information, especially regarding its use in analyzing a particular company over a 10-year period.

10. **Real World Question** From the Consolidated Statements of Income of Wal-Mart Stores, Inc., in the Annual Report Appendix, determine the percentage change in operating income from 2010 to 2011.

11. **Real World Question** From the Consolidated Statements of Income of Wal-Mart Stores, Inc., in the Annual Report Appendix, recompute the 2011 net income per common share.

12. **Real World Question** From the financial statements of Wal-Mart Stores, Inc., in the Annual Report Appendix, determine the 2011 cash dividends per common share.

13. **Real World Question** From the financial statements of Wal-Mart Stores, Inc., in the Annual Report Appendix, determine the 2011 cash flow margin.

Exercises

Exercise 17-1
Perform horizontal and vertical analysis (L.O 3)

Income statement data for Boston Company for 2013 and 2012 follow:

	2013	2012
Net sales	$2,610,000	$1,936,000
Cost of goods sold	1,829,600	1,256,400
Selling expenses	396,800	350,000
Administrative expenses	234,800	198,400
Federal income taxes	57,600	54,000

Prepare a horizontal and vertical analysis of the income data in a form similar to Illustration 17.2. Comment on the results of this analysis.

A company engaged in the following three independent transactions:

Exercise 17-2
Determine effects of
various transactions on
the current ratio
(L.O 4)

1. Merchandise purchased on account, $2,400,000.
2. Machinery purchased for cash, $2,400,000.
3. Capital stock issued for cash, $2,400,000.
a. Compute the current ratio after each of these transactions assuming current assets were $3,200,000 and the current ratio was 1:1 before the transactions occurred.
b. Repeat part a assuming the current ratio was 2:1.
c. Repeat part a assuming the current ratio was 1:2.

A company has sales of $3,680,000 per year. Its average net accounts receivable balance is $920,000.

Exercise 17-3
Compute average
number of days' sales
in accounts receivable
are outstanding;
determine effect of
increase in turnover
(L.O 4)

a. What is the average number of days' sales in accounts receivable are outstanding?
b. By how much would the capital invested in accounts receivable be reduced if the turnover could be increased to 6 without a loss of sales?

Columbia Corporation had the following selected financial data for December 31, 2011:
Net cash provided by operating activities

Exercise 17-4
Compute cash flow
margin (L.O 4)

Net sales	$1,800,000
Cost of goods sold	1,080,000
Operating expenses	315,000
Net income 195,000	
Total assets 1,000,000	
Net cash provided by operating activities	25,000

Compute the cash flow margin.

From the following partial income statement, calculate the inventory turnover for the period.

Exercise 17-5
Compute inventory
turnover (L.O 4)

Net Sales		$2,028,000
Cost of goods sold:		
Beginning inventory	$ 324,000	
Purchases	1,236,000	
Cost of goods available for sale	$1,560,000	
Less: Ending inventory	265,200	
Cost of goods sold		1,294,800
Gross margin		$ 733,200
Operating expenses		327,600
Net operating income		$ 405,600

Eastern, Inc., had net sales of $3,520,000, gross margin of $1,496,000, and operating expenses of $904,000. Total assets (all operating) were $3,080,000. Compute Eastern's rate of return on operating assets.

Exercise 17-6
Compute rate of return
on operating assets
(L.O 4)

Nelson Company began the year 2012 with total stockholders' equity of $2,400,000. Its net income for 2012 was $640,000, and $106,800 of dividends were declared. Compute the rate of return on average stockholders' equity for 2012. No preferred stock was outstanding.

Exercise 17-7
Compute return on
common stockholders'
equity (L.O 4)

Rogers Company had 60,000 shares of common stock outstanding on January 1, 2012. On April 1, 2012, it issued 20,000 additional shares for cash. The amount of earnings available for common stockholders for 2012 was $600,000. What amount of EPS of common stock should the company report?

Exercise 17-8
Compute EPS (L.O 4)

Smith Company started 2013 with 800,000 shares of common stock outstanding. On March 31, it issued 96,000 shares for cash, and on September 30, it purchased 80,000 shares of its own stock for cash. Compute the weighted-average number of common shares outstanding for the year.

Exercise 17-9
Compute weighted-
average number of
shares outstanding
(L.O 4)

Exercise 17-10
Compute EPS for current and prior year (L.O 4)

A company reported EPS of $2 (or $2,400,000/1,200,000 shares) for 2011, ending the year with 1,200,000 shares outstanding. In 2012, the company earned net income of $7,680,000, issued 320,000 shares of common stock for cash on September 30, and distributed a 100% stock dividend on December 31, 2012. Compute EPS for 2012, and compute the adjusted earnings per share for 2011 that would be shown in the 2012 annual report.

Exercise 17-11
Compute times interest earned (L.O 4)

A company paid interest of $32,000, incurred federal income taxes of $88,000, and had net income (after taxes) of $112,000. How many times was interest earned?

Exercise 17-12
Compute times dividends earned and dividend yield (L.O 4)

John Company had 20,000 shares of $600 par value, 8% preferred stock outstanding. Net income after taxes was $5,760,000. The market price per share was $720.

a. How many times were the preferred dividends earned?
b. What was the dividend yield on the preferred stock assuming the regular preferred dividends were declared and paid?

Exercise 17-13
Compute EPS and price-earnings ratio (L.O 4)

A company had 80,000 weighted-average number of shares of $320 par value common stock outstanding. The amount of earnings available to common stockholders was $800,000. Current market price per share is $720. Compute the EPS and the price-earnings ratio.

Problems

Problem 17-1
Perform horizontal and vertical analysis and comment on the results (L.O 3)

Loom's comparative statements of income and retained earnings for 2012 and 2011 are given below.

LOOM
Consolidated Statement of Earnings
For the Years Ended December 31, 2012 and 2011
($ Thousands, except per data share)

	(1) 2012	(2) 2011
Net sales	$ 2,403,100	$ 2,297,800
Cost of sales	1,885,700	1,651,300
Gross earnings	$ 517,400	$ 646,500
Selling, general and administrative expenses	429,700	376,300
Goodwill amortization	37,300	35,200
Impairment writedown of goodwill	158,500	0
Operating earnings (loss)	$ (108,100)	$235,000
Interest expense	(116,900)	(95,400)
Other expense-net	(21,700)	(6,100)
Earnings (loss) before income tax (benefit) expense and discontinued operations	$ (246,700)	$133,500
Income tax (benefit) expense	(19,400)	73,200
Earnings (loss) before discontinued operations	$ (227,300)	$60,300
Discontinued Operations		
Loss from disposal of weaving operations	(5,200)	0
Net earnings (loss)	$ (232,500)	$60,300
Retained earnings, January 1	680,600	620,300
	$ 448,100	$680,600
Dividends	0	0
Retained earnings, December 31	$ 448,100	$680,600

LOOM
Consolidated Balance Sheet
As of December 31, 2012 and 2011
($ Thousands)

	December 31	
	(1) 2012	(2) 2011
Assets		
Current Assets		
Cash and cash equivalents	$ 26,500	$ 49,400
Notes and accounts receivable (less allowance for possible losses of $26,600 and $20,700, respectively)	261,000	295,600
Inventories		
Finished goods	522,300	496,200
Work in process	132,400	141,500
Materials and supplies	44,800	39,100
Other	72,800	54,800
Total current assets	$ 1,059,800	$ 1,076,600
Property, Plant, and Equipment		
Land	$ 20,100	$ 19,300
Buildings, structures and improvements	486,400	435,600
Machinery and equipment	1,076,600	1,041,300
Construction in progress	24,200	35,200
Total property, plant and equipment	$ 1,607,300	$ 1,531,400
Less accumulated depreciation	578,900	473,200
Net property, plant and equipment	$ 1,028,400	$ 1,058,200
Other Assets		
Goodwill	$ 771,100	$ 965,800
Other	60,200	62,900
Total other assets	$ 831,300	$ 1,028,700
Total assets	$ 2,919,500	$ 3,163,500
Liabilities and Stockholders' Equity		
Current Liabilities		
Current maturities of long-term debt	$ 14,600	$ 23,100
Trade accounts payable	60,100	113,300
Accrued insurance obligations	38,800	23,600
Accrued advertising and promotion	23,800	23,400
Interest payable	16,000	18,300
Accrued payroll and vacation pay	15,300	33,100
Accrued pension	11,300	19,800
Other accounts payable and accrued expenses	123,900	77,200
Total current liabilities	$ 303,800	$ 331,800
Noncurrent Liabilities		
Long-term debt	1,427,200	1,440,200
Net deferred income taxes	0	43,400
Other	292,900	222,300
Total noncurrent liabilities	$ 1,720,100	$ 1,705,900
Total liabilities	$ 2,023,900	$ 2,037,700
Common Stockholders' Equity		
Common stock and capital in excess of par value, $.01 par value; authorized, Class A, 200,000,000 shares, Class B, 30,000,000 shares; issued and outstanding:		
Class A Common Stock, 69,268,701 and 69,160,349 shares, respectively	$ 465,600	$ 463,700
Class B Common Stock, 6,690,976 shares	4,400	4,400
Retained earnings	448,100	680,600
Currency translation and minimum pension liability adjustments	(22,500)	(22,900)
Total common stockholders' equity	$ 895,600	$ 1,125,800
Total liabilities and stockholders' equity	$ 2,919,500	$ 3,163,500

Required

a. Perform a horizontal and vertical analysis of Loom's financial statements in a manner similar to those illustrated in this chapter.
b. Comment on the results of the analysis in a.

Problem 17-2
Perform trend analysis and comment on the results (L.O 3)

Deere & Company manufactures, distributes, and finances a full range of agricultural equipment; a broad range of industrial equipment for construction, forestry, and public works; and a variety of lawn and grounds care equipment. The company also provides credit, health care, and insurance products for businesses and the general public. Consider the following information from the Deere & Company 2011 Annual Report:

(in millions)	2008	2009	2010	2011
Sales	$28,438	$23,112	$26,005	$32,013
Cost of goods sold	19,575	16,255	17,399	21,919
Gross margin	8,863	6,857	8,606	10,094
Operating expenses	6,810	5,984	6,741	7,294
Net operating income	$ 2,053	$ 873	$ 1,865	$ 2,800

Required

a. Prepare a statement showing the trend percentages for each item using 2008 as the base year.
b. Comment on the trends noted in part a.

Problem 17-3
Compute working capital, current ratio, and acid-test ratio (L.O 4)

The following data are for Toy Company:

	December 31	
	2013	**2012**
Allowance for uncollectible accounts	$72,000	$57,000
Prepaid expenses	34,500	45,000
Accrued liabilities	210,000	186,000
Cash in Bank A	1,095,000	975,000
Wages payable	-0-	37,500
Accounts payable	714,000	585,000
Merchandise inventory	1,342,500	1,437,000
Bonds payable, due in 2015	615,000	594,000
Marketable securities	217,500	147,000
Notes payable (due in six months)	300,000	195,000
Accounts receivable	907,500	870,000
Cash flow from operating activities	192,000	180,000

a. Compute the amount of working capital at both year-end dates.
b. Compute the current ratio at both year-end dates.
c. Compute the acid-test ratio at both year-end dates.
d. Compute the cash flow liquidity ratio at both year-end dates.
e. Comment briefly on the company's short-term financial position.

Problem 17-4
Determine effects of various transactions on working capital and current ratio (L.O 4)

On December 1, 2013, Energy Company's current ratio was 3:1 before the following transactions were completed in December:

1. Purchased merchandise on account.
2. Paid a cash dividend declared on November 15, 2013.
3. Sold equipment for cash.
4. Temporarily invested cash in trading securities.
5. Sold obsolete merchandise for cash (at a loss).
6. Issued 10-year bonds for cash.
7. Wrote off goodwill to retained earnings.
8. Paid cash for inventory.
9. Purchased land for cash.
10. Returned merchandise that had not been paid for.
11. Wrote off an account receivable as uncollectible. Uncollectible amount is less than the balance in the Allowance for Uncollectible Accounts.
12. Accepted a 90-day note from a customer in settlement of customer's account receivable.
13. Declared a stock dividend on common stock.

Consider each transaction independently of all the others.

Required

a. Indicate whether the amount of working capital will increase, decrease, or be unaffected by each of the transactions.
b. Indicate whether the current ratio will increase, decrease, or be unaffected by each of the transactions.

Digital Company has net operating income of $500,000 and operating assets of $2,000,000. Its net sales are $4,000,000.

The accountant for the company computes the rate of return on operating assets after computing the operating margin and the turnover of operating assets.

Problem 17-5
Compute rate of return on operating assets and demonstrate effects of various transactions on this rate of return (L.O 4)

a. Show the computations the accountant made.
b. Indicate whether the operating margin and turnover increase or decrease after each of the following changes. Then determine what the actual rate of return on operating assets would be. The events are not interrelated; consider each separately, starting from the original earning power position. No other changes occurred.
  (1) Sales increased by $160,000. There was no change in the amount of operating income and no change in operating assets.
  (2) Management found some cost savings in the manufacturing process. The amount of reduction in operating expenses was $40,000. The savings resulted from the use of less materials to manufacture the same quantity of goods. As a result, average inventory was $16,000 lower than it otherwise would have been. Operating income was not affected by the reduction in inventory.
  (3) The company invested $80,000 of cash (received on accounts receivable) in a plot of land it plans to use in the future (a nonoperating asset); income was not affected.
  (4) The federal income tax rate increased and caused income tax expense to increase by $20,000. The taxes have not yet been paid.
  (5) The company issued bonds and used the proceeds to buy $400,000 of machinery to be used in the business. Interest payments are $20,000 per year. Net operating income increased by $100,000 (net sales did not change).

Amazon.com, Inc., is a multinational E-commerce company that earns revenues from the sale of books, e-books, music, software, electronics, and other consumer goods. The following information is taken from the 2011 annual report for Amazon.com:

Problem 17-6
Compute EPS, rate of return on sales and stockholders' equity, and number of times interest earned for two years (L.O 4)

(in millions)	2011	2010
Net sales	$48,077	$34,204
Income before interest and taxes	1,042	1,563
Net income	631	1,152
Interest expense	108	66
Stockholders' equity (on December 31, 2009, $5,257)	7,757	6,864
Common stock, par value $0.01, December 31	5	5

Compute the following for both 2011 and 2010. Then compare and comment.

Required

a. EPS of common stock.
b. Net income to net sales.
c. Net income to average common stockholders' equity.
d. Times interest earned ratio.

The Walt Disney Company operates several ranges of products from theme parks and resorts to broadcasting and other creative content. The following balance sheet and supplementary data are for The Walt Disney Company for 2011.

Problem 17-7
Compute numerous standard ratios (L.O 4)

THE WALT DISNEY COMPANY
Consolidated Balance Sheet
For September 30, 2011
($ millions)
Assets

Cash and cash equivalents		$ 3,185
Receivables		6,182
Inventories		1,595
Television costs		2,121
Other		674
Total current assets		$13,757
Film and television costs		4,357
Investments		2,435
Theme Parks, Resorts, and other property, at cost		
Attractions, buildings and equipment	$35,515	
Accumulated depreciation	(19,572)	
		15,943
Projects in process		2,625
Land		1,127
Intangible Assets, net		29,266
Other Assets		2,614
Total Assets		$72,214

Liabilities and Stockholders' Equity

Accounts Payable and other accrued liabilities		$ 6,362
Current portion of borrowings		3,055
Unearned royalties and other advances		2,671
Total current liabilities		$12,088
Borrowings		10,922
Deferred Income Taxes		2,866
Other long-term liabilities		6,795
Common shareholders' equity		
Common shares ($.01 par value)	$30,296	
Retained Earnings	38,375	
Accumulated other comprehensive loss	(2,630)	
Treasury shares	(28,656)	
Noncontrolling interests	2,068	39,453
Total Liabilities and Stockholders' Equity		$72,124

Supplementary data required for 2011 (in millions)

1. Net income, $4,807.
2. Income before interest and taxes, $8,386.
3. Cost of goods sold, $33,112.
4. Net sales, $40,893.
5. Inventory on September 30, 2011, $1,442.
6. Total interest expense for the year, $343.

Required ➲ Calculate the following ratios and show your computations. For calculations normally involving averages, such as average stockholders' equity, use year-end amounts unless the necessary information is provided.

a. Current ratio.
b. Net income to average common stockholders' equity.
c. Inventory turnover.
d. Number of days' sales in accounts receivable (assume 365 days in fiscal year 2011).
e. EPS of common stock (ignore treasury stock).
f. Times interest earned ratio.
g. Equity ratio.
h. Net income to net sales.
i. Total assets turnover.
j. Acid-test ratio.

Cooper Company currently uses the FIFO method to account for its inventory but is considering a switch to LIFO before the books are closed for the year. Selected data for the year are:

Problem 17-8
Determine effects on
ratios of change in
accounting method
(FIFO to LIFO) (L.O 4)

Merchandise inventory, January 1	$1,430,000
Current assets	3,603,600
Total assets (operating)	5,720,000
Cost of goods sold (FIFO)	2,230,800
Merchandise inventory, December 31 (LIFO)	1,544,400
Merchandise inventory, December 31 (FIFO)	1,887,600
Current liabilities	1,144,000
Net sales	3,832,400
Operating expenses	915,200

a. Compute the current ratio, inventory turnover ratio, and rate of return on operating assets assuming the company continues using FIFO. ◖ *Required*

b. Repeat part a assuming the company adjusts its accounts to the LIFO inventory method.

Alternate Problems

Steel Corporation's comparative statements of income and retained earnings and consolidated balance sheet for 2012 and 2011 follow.

Problem 17-1A
Perform horizontal and
vertical analysis and
comment on
the results
(L.O 3)

STEEL CORPORATION
Consolidated Statement of Earnings
For the Years Ended December 31, 2012 and 2011
($ thousands)

	December 31	
	(1) **2012**	**(2)** **2011**
Net sales	$4,867.5	$4,819.4
Costs and Expenses:		
Cost of sales	$4,302.8	$4,287.3
Depreciation	184.0	261.1
Estimated restructuring losses	111.8	137.4
Total Costs	$4,598.6	$4,685.8
Income from operations	$ 268.9	$ 133.6
Financing income (expense):		
Interest and other income	7.7	7.1
Interest and other financing costs	(60.0)	(46.2)
Loss before Income Taxes	$ 216.6	$ 94.5
Benefit (Provision) for Income Taxes	(37.0)	(14.0)
Net earnings	$ 179.6	$ 80.5
Retained Earnings, January 1	(859.4)	(939.9)
	$ (679.8)	$ (859.4)
Dividends	0.0	0.0
Retained Earnings, December 31	$ (679.8)	$ (859.4)

STEEL CORPORATION
Consolidated Balance Sheet
As of December 31, 2012 and 2011

	December 31	
	(1) **2012**	**(2)** **2011**
Assets		
Current Assets		
Cash and cash equivalents	$ 180.0	$ 159.5
Receivables	374.6	519.5
Total	$ 554.6	$ 679.0
Inventories		
Raw materials and supplies	$ 335.5	$ 331.9
Finished and semifinished products	604.9	534.9
Contract work in process less billings of $10.9 and $2.3	17.8	16.1
Total inventories	$ 958.2	$ 882.9
Other current assets	$ 13.0	$ 7.2
Total current assets	$ 1,525.8	$ 1,569.1
Property, Plant and Equipment less accumulated depreciation of $4329.5 and $4167.8	$ 2,714.2	$ 2,759.3
Investments and Miscellaneous Assets	112.3	124.2
Deferred Income Tax Asset – net	885.0	903.2
Intangible Asset – Pensions	463.0	426.6
Total Assets	$ 5,700.3	$ 5,782.4
Liabilities and Stockholders' Equity		
Current Liabilities		
Accounts payable	$ 381.4	$ 387.0
Accrued employment costs	208.0	165.8
Postretirement benefits other than pensions	150.0	138.0
Accrued taxes	72.4	67.6
Debt and capital lease obligations	91.5	88.9
Other current liabilities	146.3	163.9
Total current liabilities	$ 1,049.6	$ 1,011.2
Pension Liability	$ 1,115.0	$ 1,117.1
Postretirement Benefits Other Than Pensions	1,415.0	1,441.4
Long-term Debt and Capital Lease Obligations	546.8	668.4
Other	335.6	388.5
Total noncurrent liabilities	$ 3,412.4	$ 3,615.4
Total Liabilities	$ 4,462.0	$ 4,626.6
Common Stockholders' Equity		
Preferred Stock—at $1 per share par value (aggregate liquidation preference of $481.2); Authorized 20,000,000 shares	$ 11.6	$ 11.6
Preference Stock—at $1 per share par value (aggregate liquidation preference of $88.2); Authorized 20,000,000 shares	2.6	2.6
Common Stock—at $1 per share par value/Authorized 250,000,000 and 150,000,000 shares; Issued 112,699,869 and 111.882,276 shares	112.7	111.9
Held in Treasury, 1,992,189 and 1,996,715 shares at cost	(59.4)	(59.5)
Additional Paid-in Capital	1,850.6	1,948.6
Accumulated Deficit	(679.8)	(859.4)
Total common stockholders' equity	$ 1,238.3	$ 1,155.8
Total liabilities and stockholders' equity	$ 5,700.3	$ 5,782.4

Required   a. Perform a horizontal and vertical analysis of Steel's financial statements in a manner similar to Illustrations 17.1 and 17.2.

b. Comment on the results obtained in part a.

Ford Motor Company is is a worldwide producer of cars and trucks and ranks among the largest providers of financial services in the United States. The following information pertains to Ford:

Problem 17-2A
Perform trend analysis and comment on the results
(L.O 3)

(in millions)	2008	2009	2010
Sales	$143,584	$116,283	$128,954
Cost of goods sold	126,620	98,866	104,451
Gross margin	$ 16,964	$ 17,417	$ 24,503
Operating expenses	15,065	13,029	11,909
Net operating income	$ 1,899	$ 4,388	$ 12,594

a. Prepare a statement showing the trend percentages for each item, using 2008 as the base year.   ⬤ *Required*
b. Comment on the trends noted in part a.

The following data are for Clock Company:
Allowance for uncollectible accounts

Problem 17-3A
Compute working capital, current ratio, and acid-test ratio
(L.O 4)

	December 31	
	2013	2012
Notes payable (due in 90 days)	$75,200	$60,000
Merchandise inventory	240,000	208,000
Cash	100,000	128,000
Marketable securities	49,600	30,000
Accrued liabilities	19,200	22,000
Accounts receivable	188,000	184,000
Accounts payable	112,000	72,000
Allowance for uncollectible accounts	24,000	15,200
Bonds payable, due 2010	156,000	160,000
Prepaid expenses	6,400	7,360
Cash flow from operating activities	60,000	40,000

a. Compute the amount of working capital at both year-end dates.   ⬤ *Required*
b. Compute the current ratio at both year-end dates.
c. Compute the acid-test ratio at both year-end dates.
d. Compute the cash flow liquidity ratio at both year-end dates.
e. Comment briefly on the company's short-term financial position.

Tulip Products, Inc., has a current ratio on December 31, 2012, of 2:1 before the following transactions were completed in December:

Problem 17-4A
Determine effects of various transactions on working capital and current ratio (L.O 4)

1. Sold a building for cash.
2. Exchanged old equipment for new equipment. (No cash was involved.)
3. Declared a cash dividend on preferred stock.
4. Sold merchandise on account (at a profit).
5. Retired mortgage notes that would have matured in 2016.
6. Issued a stock dividend to common stockholders.
7. Paid cash for a patent.
8. Temporarily invested cash in government bonds.
9. Purchased inventory for cash.
10. Wrote off an account receivable as uncollectible. Uncollectible amount is less than the balance of the Allowance for Uncollectible Accounts.
11. Paid the cash dividend on preferred stock that was declared earlier.
12. Purchased a computer and gave a two-year promissory note.
13. Collected accounts receivable.
14. Borrowed from the bank on a 120-day promissory note.
15. Discounted a customer's note. Interest expense was involved.

Consider each transaction independently of all the others.

Required ➡

a. Indicate whether the amount of working capital will increase, decrease, or be unaffected by each of the transactions.
b. Indicate whether the current ratio will increase, decrease, or be unaffected by each of the transactions.

Problem 17-5A
Compute rate of return on operating assets and demonstrate effects of various transactions on this rate of return (L.O 4)

The following selected data are for three companies:

	Net Operating Assets	Operating Income	Net Sales
Company 1	$ 1,404,000	$ 187,200	$ 2,059,200
Company 2	8,424,000	608,400	18,720,000
Company 3	37,440,000	4,914,000	35,100,000

Required ➡

a. Determine the operating margin, turnover of operating assets, and rate of return on operating assets for each company.
b. In the subsequent year, the following changes took place (no other changes occurred):

Company 1 bought some new machinery at a cost of $156,000. Net operating income increased by $12,480 as a result of an increase in sales of $249,600.

Company 2 sold some equipment it was using that was relatively unproductive. The book value of the equipment sold was $624,000. As a result of the sale of the equipment, sales declined by $312,000, and operating income declined by $6,240.

Company 3 purchased some new retail outlets at a cost of $6,240,000. As a result, sales increased by $9,360,000, and operating income increased by $499,200.

1. Which company has the largest absolute change in:
   a. Operating margin ratio?
   b. Turnover of operating assets?
   c. Rate of return on operating assets?
2. Which one realized the largest dollar change in operating income? Explain this change in relation to the changes in the rate of return on operating assets.

Problem 17-6A
Compute EPS, rate of return on sales and stockholders' equity, and number of times interest earned for two years (L.O 4)

One of the largest spice companies in the world, McCormick & Company, Inc., produces a diverse array of specialty foods. The following information is for McCormick & Company, Inc.:

($ thousands)	2011	2011
Net sales	$3,697,600	$3,336,800
Income before interest and taxes	540,300	509,800
Net income	348,800	344,700
Interest expense	51,200	49,300
Stockholders' equity	1,618,500	1,462,700
Common stock, no par value, November 30	821,900	756,500

Assume average common shares outstanding for 2011 and 2010 are 132,900 and 133,100 (in thousands), respectively.

Required ➡

Compute the following for both 2011 and 2010. Then compare and comment. Assume stockholders' equity for 2009 was $1,343,500.

a. EPS of common stock.
b. Net income to net sales.
c. Return on average common stockholders' equity.
d. Times interest earned ratio.

Problem 17-7A
Compute numerous standard ratios (L.O 4)

Parametric Technology Corporation is in the CAD/CAM/CAE industry and is the top supplier of software tools used to automate a manufacturing company. The following consolidated balance sheet and supplementary data are for Parametric for 2011:

PARAMETRIC TECHNOLOGY CORPORATION
Consolidated Balance Sheet
September 30, 2011 (in thousands)
Assets

Current Assets
Cash and cash equivalents	$ 167,878
Accounts Receivable, net of allowances for doubtful accounts of $ 3,902	230,220
Other current assets	194,166
Total Current Assets	$ 592,264
Property and equipment, net	62,569
Goodwill	613,394
Other Assets	361,455
Total Assets	$ 1,629,682

Liabilities and Stockholders' Equity

Current Liabilities
Accounts payable and accrued expenses	$ 77,141
Accrued compensation	95,980
Deferred revenue	279,935
Income taxes	16,335
Total Current Liabilities	$ 469,391
Long-term liabilities	337,601

Stockholders' Equity
Preferred stock, $.01 par value; 5,000 shares authorized; none issued
Common stock, $.01 par value; 500,000 shares authorized; 116,937 (2011)
and 115,826 (2010) shares issued	1,169
Additional paid-in capital	1,805,021
Accumulated deficit	(918,736)
Accumulated other comprehensive loss	(64,764)
Total Liabilities and Stockholders' Equity	$ 1,629,682

1. Net income, $85,424.
2. Income before interest and taxes, $117,114.
3. Cost of goods sold, $356,768.
4. Net sales, $1,166,949.
5. Total interest expense for the year, $3,310.
6. Weighted-average number of shares outstanding, 117,579.

*Supplementary data
for 2011 (in millions)*

Calculate the following ratios and show your computations. For calculations normally involv- *Required*
ing averages, such as average accounts receivable or average stockholders' equity, use year-end
amounts if the information is not available to use averages.

a. Current ratio.
b. Net income to average common stockholders' equity.
c. Number of days' sales in accounts receivable (assume 365 days in 2011).
d. EPS of common stock.
e. Times interest earned ratio.
f. Equity ratio.
g. Net income to net sales.
h. Total assets turnover.
i. Acid-test ratio.

Paper Company is considering switching from the FIFO method to the LIFO method of
accounting for its inventory before it closes its books for the year. The January 1 merchandise
inventory was $864,000. Following are data compiled from the adjusted trial balance at the
end of the year:

Problem 17-8A
Determine effects on
ratios of change in
accounting method
(FIFO to LIFO) (L.O 4)

Merchandise inventory, December 31 (FIFO)	$1,008,000
Current liabilities	720,000
Net sales	2,520,000
Operating expenses	774,000
Current assets	1,890,000
Total assets (operating)	2,880,000
Cost of goods sold	1,458,000

If the switch to LIFO takes place, the December 31 merchandise inventory would be $900,000.

Required ➲

a. Compute the current ratio, inventory turnover ratio, and rate of return on operating assets assuming the company continues using FIFO.

b. Repeat a assuming the company adjusts its accounts to the LIFO inventory method.

Beyond the Numbers—Critical Thinking

Business Decision Case 17-1
Compute net income, identify reason for cash increase, state main sources of financing, and indicate further analyses needed (L.O 3, 4)

The comparative balance sheets of the Darling Corporation for December 31, 2013, and 2012 follow:

DARLING CORPORATION
Comparative Balance Sheets
December 31, 2013 and 2012
($ millions)

	2013	2012
Assets		
Cash	$ 480,000	$ 96,000
Accounts receivable, net	86,400	115,200
Merchandise inventory	384,000	403,200
Plant and equipment, net	268,800	288,000
Total assets	$1,219,200	$902,400
Liabilities and Stockholders' Equity		
Accounts payable	$ 96,000	$ 96,000
Common stock	672,000	672,000
Retained earnings	451,200	134,400
Total liabilities and stockholders' equity	$1,219,200	$902,400

Based on your review of the comparative balance sheets, determine the following:

a. What was the net income for 2013 assuming there were no dividend payments?

b. What was the primary source of the large increase in the cash balance from 2012 to 2013?

c. What are the two main sources of assets for Darling Corporation?

d. What other comparisons and procedures would you use to complete the analysis of the balance sheet?

Business Decision Case 17-2
Compute turnover ratios for four years and number of days' sales in accounts receivable; evaluate effectiveness of company's credit policy (L.O 4)

As Miller Manufacturing Company's internal auditor, you are reviewing the company's credit policy. The following information is from Miller's annual reports for 2010, 2011, 2012, and 2013:

	2010	2011	2012	2013
Net accounts receivable	$ 1,080,000	$ 2,160,000	$ 2,700,000	$ 3,600,000
Net sales	10,800,000	13,950,000	17,100,000	19,800,000

Management has asked you to calculate and analyze the following in your report:

a. If cash sales account for 30% of all sales and credit terms are always 1/10, n/60, determine all turnover ratios possible and the number of days' sales in accounts receivable at all possible dates. (The number of days' sales in accounts receivable should be based on year-end accounts receivable and net credit sales.)

b. How effective is the company's credit policy?

Wendy Prince has consulted you about the possibility of investing in one of three companies (Apple Company, Baker Company, or Cookie Corp.) by buying its common stock. The companies' shares are selling at about the same price. The long-term capital structures of the companies are as follows:

**Business Decision
Case 17-3**
Analyze investment
alternatives (L.O 3, 4)

	Apple Company	Baker Company	Cookie Corp.
Bonds with a 10% interest rate			$2,400,000
Preferred stock with a 8% dividend rate		$2,400,000	
Common stock, $10 par value	$4,800,000	2,400,000	2,400,000
Retained earnings	384,000	384,000	384,000
Total long-term equity	$5,184,000	$5,184,000	$5,184,000
Number of common shares outstanding	480,000	240,000	240,000

Prince has already consulted two investment advisers. One adviser believes that each of the companies will earn $300,000 per year before interest and taxes. The other adviser believes that each company will earn about $960,000 per year before interest and taxes. Prince has asked you to write a report covering these points:

a. Compute each of the following, using the estimates made by the first and second advisers.
   (1) Earnings available for common stockholders assuming a 40% tax rate.
   (2) EPS of common stock.
   (3) Rate of return on total stockholders' equity.
b. Which stock should Prince select if she believes the first adviser?
c. Are the stockholders as a group (common and preferred) better off with or without the use of long-term debt in the companies?

The following selected financial data excerpted from the annual report of Appliance Corporation represents the summary information which management presented for interested parties to review:

**Annual Report
Analysis 17-4**
Analyze management's
objectives and
performance from the
viewpoints of a creditor
and an investor
(L.O 3, 4)

APPLIANCE CORPORATION
Selected Financial Data
($ thousands except per share data)

	2012	2011	2010	2009	2008
Net sales	$3,039,524	$3,372,515	$2,987,054	$ 3,041,223	$2,970,626
Cost of sales	2,250,616	2,496,065	2,262,942	2,339,406	2,254,221
Income taxes	74,800	90,200	38,600	15,900	44,400
Income (loss) from continuing operations	(14,996)	151,137	51,270	(8,354)	79,017
Percent of income (loss) from continuing operations to net sales	(0.5%)	4.5%	1.7%	(0.3%)	2.7%
Income (loss) from continuing operations per share	$ (0.14)	$ 1.42	$ 0.48	$ (0.08)	$ 0.75
Dividends paid per share	0.515	0.50	0.50	0.50	0.50
Average shares outstanding (in thousands)	107,062	106,795	106,252	106,077	105,761
Working capital	$ 543,431	$ 595,703	$ 406,181	$ 452,626	$ 509,025
Depreciation of property, plant and equipment	102,572	110,044	102,459	94,032	83,352
Additions to property, plant and equipment	152,912	84,136	99,300	129,891	143,372
Total assets	2,125,066	2,504,327	2,469.498	2,501,490	2,535,068
Long-term debt	536,579	663,205	724,695	789,232	809,480
Total debt to capitalization	45.9%	50.7%	60.0%	58.7%	45.9%
Shareowners' equity per share of common stock	$ 6.05	$ 6.82	$ 5.50	$ 5.62	$ 9.50

Required ➲   **a.** As a creditor, what do you believe management's objectives should be? Which of the preceding items of information would assist a creditor in judging management's performance?

b. As an investor, what do you believe management's objectives should be? Which of the preceding items of information would assist an investor in judging management's performance?

c. What other information might be considered useful?

Group Project 17-5
Analyze an annual report

Choose a company the class wants to know more about and obtain its annual report. In groups of two or three students, calculate either the liquidity, equity, profitability, or market test ratios. Each group should select a spokesperson to tell the rest of the class the results of the group's calculations. Finally, the class should decide whether or not to invest in the corporation based on the ratios they calculated.

Group Project 17-6
Analyze a company's performance against industry norms

In a group of two or three students, go to the library and attempt to locate Dun & Bradstreet's Industry Norms and Key Business Ratios. You may have to ask the reference librarian for assistance to see if this item is available at your institution. If it is not available at your institution, ask if it is available through an interlibrary loan. (Obviously, if you cannot obtain this item, you cannot do this project.) Then select and obtain the latest annual report of a company of your choice. Determine the company's SIC Code (a code that indicates the industry in which that company operates). SIC Codes for specific companies are available on COMPACT DISCLOSURE, an electronic source that may be available at your library. As an alternative, you could call the company's home office to inquire about its SIC Code. The annual report often contains the company's phone number. From the annual report, determine various ratios for the company, such as the current ratio, debt to equity ratio, and net income to net sales. Then compare these ratios to the industry norms for the company's SIC Code as given in the Dun & Bradstreet source. Write a report to your instructor summarizing the results of your investigation.

Group Project 17-7
Analyze the major sections of an annual report

In a group of two or three students, obtain the annual report of a company of your choice Identify the major sections of the annual report and the order in which they appear. Would you recommend the order be changed to emphasize the most useful and important information? If so, how? Then describe some specific useful information in each section. Comment on your perceptions of the credibility that a reader of the annual report could reasonably assign to each section of the report. For instance, if such a discussion appears in the annual report you select, would you assign high credibility to everything that appears in the Letter to Stockholders regarding the company's future prospects? Write a report to your instructor summarizing the results of your investigation.

Using the Internet—A View of the Real World

Internet Project 17-8
Analyze an annual report retrieved on the Internet

Visit the following website for Apple, Inc.:

    http://www.apple.com

By following choices on the screen, locate the income statements and balance sheets for the latest two years. Calculate all of the ratios illustrated in the chapter for which the data are available. Compare the ratios to those shown for Synotech as presented in the chapter. Write a report to your instructor showing your calculations and comment on the results of your comparison of the two companies.

**Internet Project
17-9**
Analyze an annual
report retrieved on the
Internet

Visit the following website for General Electric Company:

http://www.ge.com

By following choices on the screen, locate the income statements and balance sheets for the latest two years. Calculate all of the ratios illustrated in the chapter for which the data are available. Compare the ratios to those shown for Synotech as presented in the chapter. Write a report to your instructor showing your calculations and comment on the results of your comparison of the two companies.

Answers to Self-Test

True-False

1. **True.** Financial statement analysis consists of applying analytical tools and techniques to financial statements and other relevant data to obtain useful information.
2. **False.** Horizontal analysis provides useful information about the changes in a company's performance over several periods by analyzing comparative financial statements of the same company for two or more successive periods.
3. **False.** Common-size statements show only percentage figures, such as percentages of total assets and percentages of net sales.
4. **True.** Liquidity ratios such as the current ratio and acid-test ratio indicate a company's short-term debt-paying ability.
5. **True.** The accrual net income shown on the income statement is not cash basis income and does not indicate cash flows.
6. **True.** Analysts must use comparable data when making comparisons of items for different periods or different companies.

Multiple-Choice

1. **b.** Current assets:
   $136,000 + $64,000 + $184,000 + $244,000 + $12,000 = $640,000
   Current liabilities:
   $256,000 + $64,000 = $320,000
   Current ratio:
   $640,000/$320,000 = 2:1
2. **c.** Quick assets:
   $136,000 + $64,000 + $184,000 = $384,000
   Current liabilities:
   256,000 + $64,000 = $320,000
   Acid-test ratio:
   $384,000/$320,000 = 1.2:1
3. **a.** Net sales:
   $4,620,000
   Average accounts receivable:
   ($720,000 + $960,000)/2 = $840,000
   Accounts receivable turnover:
   $4,620,000/$840,000 = 5.5
4. **c.** Cost of goods sold:
   $3,360,000
   Average inventory:
   ($900,000 + $1,020,000)/2 = $960,000
   Inventory turnover:
   $3,360,000/$960,000 = 3.5
5. **b.** Income before interest and taxes, $720,000
   Interest on bonds, 192,000
   Times interest earned ratio:
   $720,000/$192,000 = 3.75 times
   Average accounts receivable:
   ($720,000 + $960,000)/2 = $840,000
   Accounts receivable turnover:
   $4,620,000/$840,000 = 5.5

Check Figures

P6-3A	(d) Net income, $162,144
P6-4A	(c) Trial balance total, $997,898
P6-5A	(b) Net income, $302,560
BDC6-1	(a) Net income, 2006, $49,500
BDC6-2	No check figure
ARA6-3	No check figure
EC6-4	No check figure

Chapter 7

E7-1	Corrected income, 2007, $418,784
E7-2	No check figure
E7-3	Ending inventory, $170,220
E7-4	Ending inventory, $162,480
E7-5	Ending inventory, $5,600
E7-6	(a) Weighted average ending inventory, $18,141.12
E7-7	Sept. 20, Dr. to Cost of Goods Sold, $2,016
E7-8	(6) Dr. to Cost of Goods Sold, $18,816
E7-9	(5) Dr. to Cost of Goods Sold, $4,835
E7-10	Ending inventory, $2,952
E7-11	Paper profits, $3,000
E7-12	No check figure
E7-13	Carrying amount for used auto, $72,000
E7-14	Dr. Loss Due to Decline in Market Value of Inventory, $240
E7-15	Lower of cost or market, $50,640
E7-16	Lower of cost or market, $51,360
E7-17	Estimated inventory, $201,600
E7-18	Estimated inventory, $684,000
E7-19	Estimated inventory at cost, $30,175
P7-1	Corrected income, 2007, $345,000
P7-2	(a) Corrected income, 2004, $644,000
P7-3	(a) Gross margin, $100,920
P7-4	Mar. 31, Dr. Cost of Goods Sold, $388
P7-5	(a) (2) LIFO-perpetual, ending inventory, $117,600
	(b) (2) LIFO-periodic, ending inventory, $112,400
P7-6	(a) Mar. 25, Dr. Cost of Goods Sold, $80,100
P7-7	(a) (1) FIFO-perpetual, ending inventory, $8,712 (same as FIFO-periodic)
P7-8	(a) Gross margin, $374,400
P7-9	Lower of cost or market, $88,848
P7-10	(b) Net income, first quarter, $36,800
P7-11	Estimated ending inventory at cost, $47,880
P7-1A	Corrected income, 2007, $304,800
P7-2A	(a) Corrected income, 2004, $270,000
P7-3A	(a) Gross margin, $80,500

P7-4A	(a) Cost of Goods Sold, $1,776.24
P7-5A	(a) (2) LIFO-perpetual, ending inventory, $32,160
	(b) (2) LIFO-periodic, ending inventory, $22,680
P7-6A	(a) Oct. 15, Dr. Cost of Goods Sold, $25,800
P7-7A	(a) (1) FIFO-perpetual, ending inventory, $46,950 (same as FIFO-periodic)
P7-8A	(a) Gross margin, $808,000
P7-9A	Lower of cost or market, $189,056
P7-10A	(b) Estimated inventory, $802,882
P7-11A	Estimated ending inventory at cost, $126,000
BDC7-1	(a) Green, net income, $6,100
BDC7-2	Estimated inventory, $70,400
ARA7-3	No check figure
EC7-4	No check figure

Chapter 8

E8-1	No check figure
E8-2	No check figure
E8-3	Adjusted cash balance, $14,915
E8-4	Adjusted cash balance, $14,070
E8-5	Cr. Cash, $126
E8-6	Checks outstanding at March 31, $24,000
E8-7	Deposits in transit, $4,740
E8-8	Adjusted cash balance, $4,401
E8-9	Cr. cash, $340
E8-10	No check figure
E8-11	Dec. 2, Dr. Petty Cash, $900
P8-1	Adjusted cash balance, $30,626.39
P8-2	Adjusted cash balance, $53,821
P8-3	Dec. 31, Cr. Petty Cash, $97.95
P8-4	Apr. 30, Cr. Cash, $156.93
P8-1A	Adjusted cash balance, $28,935
P8-2A	Adjusted cash balance, $136,350
P8-3A	Mar. 31, Cr. Cash, $258.50
P8-4A	June 30, Cr. Cash Short and Over, $2.10
BDC8-1	No check figure
BDC8-2	No check figure
BDC8-3	(b) Corrected cash balance, $23,003.80
ARA8-4	No check figure
ARA8-5	No check figure
EC8-6	No check figure

Chapter 9

E9-1	(b) Dr. Uncollectible Accounts Expense, $4,750
E9-2	Required allowance balance, $42,075
E9-3	No check figure
E9-4	(a) Dr. Credit Card Expense, $2,400
E9-5	Sales tax payable, $20,000

E9-6	Full amount, $32M
E9-7	No check figure
E9-8	Crawford, Inc., Dr. Interest Expense, $800
E9-9	Dunston, Inc., Dr. Accounts Receivable—Crawford, Inc., $20,800
E9-10	(a) Dr. Discount on Notes Payable, $400
E9-11	(a) Dr. Interest Expense, $400
E9-12	No. of days' sales in accounts receivable, 132.73 days
P9-1	(b) Dr. Uncollectible Accounts Expense, $2,450
P9-2	Dr. Cash, $3,880
P9-3	(a) Jan. 2, Cr. Sales Tax Payable, $4,000
P9-4	(a) Estimated product warranty payable, $114,000
P9-5	Sept. 29, Dr. Dishonored Notes Receivable, $104,000
P9-6	Dec. 31, Dr. Interest Expense, $450
P9-1A	(b) Dr. Uncollectible Accounts Expense, $16,750
P9-2A	Dr. Credit Card Expense, $500
P9-3A	(a) July 1, Cr. Sales Tax Payable, $1,200
P9-4A	(a) Estimated product warranty payable, $12,000
P9-5A	July 14, Cr. Interest Revenue, $5,400
P9-6A	(a) Nov. 1, Dr. Discount on Notes Payable, $4,500
BDC9-1	(a) Total benefit, $96,600
BDC9-2	No check figure
ARA9-3	No check figure

Chapter 10

E10-1	Total cost of land, $702,400
E10-2	Total cost of land, $522,000
E10-3	Total cost of machine, $734,400
E10-4	Cost of machine, $20,000
E10-5	2006, Dec. 31, Dr. Depreciation Expense—Office Furniture, $6,000
E10-6	Double-declining balance, 2006, $180,000
E10-7	Asset cost, $144,000
E10-8	(a) 2007, Depreciation, SOYD method, $20,400
E10-9	Depreciation expense, first year, $2,000
E10-10	Depreciation for 2009, $11,200
E10-11	No check figure
E10-12	Depreciation for 2007, $20,400
E10-13	Depreciation for 2008, $11,200
E10-14	Net income overstated in 2007, $1,000
E10-15	Net income overstated in 2006, $96,000
P10-1	Total cost of machine, $123,840
P10-2	Total cost of land, $209,832
P10-3	(c) Dr. Depreciation Expense—Machinery, $39,583

P10-4	(a) Total cost of building, $254,080
P10-5	(c) SOYD depreciation in 2006, $192,000
P10-6	(c) DDB depreciation in 2007, $23,438
P10-1A	Total cost of machine, $460,400
P10-2A	Total cost of land, $1,374,240
P10-3A	(a) Total cost of truck, $32,160
P10-4A	(a) Total cost of land, $318,000
P10-5A	(c) SOYD depreciation expense, $24,444
P10-6A	(c) DDB depreciation expense, 2007, $10,200
BDC10-1	(a) Cost of land, $771,600
BDC10-2	(a) (4) DDB depreciation, $50,400
BDC10-3	No check figure
BDC10-4	No check figure
ARA10-5	No check figure

Chapter 11

E11-1	(a) Dr. Loss on Disposal of Plant Assets, $2,700
E11-2	Cr. Gain on Disposal of Plant Assets, $2,700
E11-3	(b). Dr. Fire Loss, $7,500
E11-4	Dr. Loss on Disposal of Plant Assets, $4,050
E11-5	(e) Dr. Loss on Disposal of Plant Assets, $30,000
E11-6	Depletion per ton, $1.08
E11-7	Depletion per ton, $0.72
E11-8	Depreciation for year, $112,500
E11-9	Amortization each year 2003–2008, $5,850
E11-10	Dr. Franchise Amortization Expense, $1,350
E11-11	Dec. 31, Dr. Rent Expense, $54,000
E11-12	Goodwill, $180,000
P11-1	Dr. Loss on Disposal of Plant Assets, $900
P11-2	(a) Book Value, $42,750
P11-3	Dr. Moving Vans (new), $30,025
P11-4	Dec. 31, Dr. Depreciation Expense—Buildings, $124,020
P11-5	(b) Depreciation for 2006, $10,000
P11-6	2007, Dec. 31, Dr. Patent Amortization Expense, $22,200
P11-7	(c) Dr. Rent Expense, $28,800
P11-1A	(b) Dr. Loss on Disposal of Plant Assets, $2,880
P11-2A	(a) Book value of truck, $24,300
P11-3A	Dr. Loss on Disposal of Plant Assets, $540
P11-4A	Oct. 1, Dr. Trucks (D), $106,680
P11-5A	Dr. Depletion, $246,000
P11-6A	Patent amortization expense,

	2007, $14,400
P11-7A	(a) Dr. Patent Amortization Expense, $19,200
BDC11-1	(a) Cr. Gain on Disposal of Plant Assets, $33,000
BDC11-2	(a) (2) Goodwill, $750,000
ARA11-3	No check figure
EC11-4	No check figure

Chapter 12

E12-1	Preferred dividends, $100,000
E12-2	Preferred dividends, $72,000
E12-3	Dr. Cash, $1,120,000
E12-4	Dr. Cash, $680,000
E12-5	Dr. Land, $72,000
E12-6	Cr. Common Stock, $18,000
E12-7	Dr. Organization Costs, $480,000
E12-8	Book value, $18 per share
P12-1	2005 (Assumption A) Preferred dividend, $102,000
P12-2	(a) Jan. 29, Dr. Organization Costs, $744,000
P12-3	(a) Total assets, $191,200
P12-4	(b) Total stockholders' equity, $1,769,000
P12-5	(b) Total book value of common stock, $546,000
P12-6	(b) Total book value of common stock, $2,514,600
P12-7	Book value of preferred stock, $967,500
P12-1A	2006 (Assumption A) Preferred dividend, $62,400
P12-2A	(b) Total assets, $4,000,000
P12-3A	(a) Total assets, $1,056,000
P12-4A	(b) Total stockholders' equity, $9,216,000
P12-5A	(b) Total book value of common stock, $615,000
P12-6A	(1) Total book value of common stock, $902,400
P12-7A	(c) Total cash payment, $1,017,600
BDC12-1	(a) Rudd Co., common stock dividends, $4,320,000
BDC12-2	(a) East Corporation, Book value per share of common, $113
ARA12-3	No check figure
EC12-4	No check figure

Chapter 13

E13-1	Total stockholders' equity, $7,720,000
E13-2	Feb. 1, Cr. Dividends Payable, $60,000
E13-3	Dec. 31, Cr. Dividends Payable, $182,000
E13-4	(a) Cr. Stock Dividends Distributed—Common, $900,000
E13-5	(b) Cr. Paid-In Capital—Stock Dividend, $30,000
E13-6	(a) Dr. Retained Earnings, $900,000
E13-7	(a) Book value per share, $40
E13-8	Cr. Paid-in Capital—Donations, $62,400

E13-9	(a) Net income, $3,600,000
E13-10	Retained earnings, Dec. 31, $99,200
E13-11	Net income per share, $19.03
E13-12	(a) Earnings per share, 2007, $10.72
P13-1	Total stockholders' equity, $5,496,000
P13-2	Nov. 16, Cr. Paid-In Capital—Stock Dividend, $96,000
P13-3	2006, Apr. 2, Cr. Paid-In Capital—Stock Dividend, $25,000
P13-4	Unappropriated retained earnings, Dec. 31, $1,336,000
P13-5	(3) Cr. Paid-In Capital—Common Treasury Stock Transactions, $19,200
P13-6	(b) Total stockholders' equity, $17,942,000
P13-7	(b) Retained earnings, Oct 31, 2006, $36,930
P13-8	(a) Net income, $48,000
P13-1A	Total paid-in capital, $7,010,000
P13-2A	Dec. 1, Cr. Paid-In Capital—Stock Dividend, $2,400
P13-3A	(4) Cr. Dividends Payable, $140,000
P13-4A	Aug. 4, Cr. Paid-In Capital—Stock Dividend, $400,000
P13-5A	Unappropriated retained earnings, $6,518,400
P13-6A	(b) Total stockholders' equity, $1,452,000
P13-7A	(b) Appropriated retained earnings, $18,000
P13-8A	Net loss, $36,000
BDC13-1	(a). Cash dividends Jones will receive, $21,120
BDC13-2	No check figure
ARA13-3	No check figure
EC13-4	No check figure

Chapter 14

E14-1	Nov. 1, Cr. Realized Gain on Trading Securities, $46,944
E14-2	Dec. 31, 2007, Dr. Unrealized Loss on Trading Securities, $720
E14-3	(c) Dr. Realized Loss on Available-for-Sale Securities, $13,440
E14-4	Dr. Loss from Sim Company, $93,750
E14-5	(b) Dr. Common Stock (TRD Company), $6,720,000
E14-6	(a) Goodwill = $840,000
E14-7	(b) Dr. Goodwill, $302,400
E14-8	(b) Excess of cost over book value, $506,250
E14-9	(a) Book value of investment, $24,624,000
E14-10	(a) Dec. 31, 2007, balance in investment account, $2,984,400
P14-1	(a) Nov. 3, Realized Gain on Trading Securities, $9,504
P14-2	(a) Dec. 31, 2007, Dr. Unrealized Loss on Trading Securities, $31,680

P14-3	(b) Jan. 1, 2007, Cr. Minority Interest, $1,008,000
P14-4	(b) Dec. 31, 2009, Investment account balance, $1,488,270
P14-5	(b) Total assets, $7,578,000
P14-6	Goodwill, $450,000
P14-7	(a) Net income, $585,000
P14-1A	(b) Dec. 31, Dr. Unrealized Loss on Market Decline of Available-for-Sale Securities, $18,000
P14-2A	(a) Nov. 2, Cr. Realized Gain on Sale of Trading Securities, $6,732
P14-3A	(b) Jan. 1, 2007, Cr. Minority Interest, $840,000
P14-4A	(b) Dec. 31, 2009, Investment account balance, $9,025,170
P14-5A	(b) Total assets, $13,590,000
P14-6A	Goodwill, $324,000
P14-7A	(a) Net income, $860,892
BDC14-1	No check figure
BDC14-2	(b) Total assets, $2,610,000
BDC14-3	No check figure

Chapter 15

E15-1	Sept. 30, 2007, Cr. Bond Interest Payable, $1,200
E15-2	(c) Total price, $1,400,605
E15-3	Bond interest expense, $147,940
E15-4	Dr. Premium on Bonds Payable, $2,471
E15-5	Dr. Loss on Bond Redemption, $24,000
E15-6	Cr. Gain on Bond Redemption, $19,200
E15-7	Dr. Bond Interest Expense, $540
E15-8	Cr. Paid-in Capital in Excess of Par—Common, $20,000
E15-9	No check figure
E15-10	Present value, $12,418.40
E15-11	Present value, $77,217.30
E15-12	(c) Present value, $1,434,132
E15-13	Future value, $720,524
P15-1	June 1, 2006, Cr. Bond Interest Payable, $4,800
P15-2	(a) Price to be offered, $469,169
P15-3	Jan. 1 Cr. Discount on Bonds Payable, $1,871
P15-4	(a) Price received, $260,185
P15-5	(a) Price received, $447,698

P15-6	July 1, 2007, Dr. Bond Interest Expense, $36,000
P15-1A	Dec. 1, 2006, Cr. Bond Interest Payable, $11,250
P15-2A	(a) Price to be offered, $958,343
P15-3A	Jan. 1, Cr. Discount on Bonds Payable, $377
P15-4A	(a) Price received, $564,225
P15-5A	(a) Price received, $84,954
P15-6A	(a) July 1, 2007, Dr. Bond Interest Expense, $24,000
BDC15-1	Alternative (1), EPS, $5.83
BDC15-2	No check figure
BDC15-3	No check figure
ARA15-4	No check figure
ARA15-5	No check figure
EC15-6	No check figure

Chapter 16

E16-1	No check figure
E16-2	Cost of goods sold, cash basis, $288,000
E16-3	No check figure
E16-4	Net cash provided by operating activities, $193,000
E16-5	Net cash provided by operating activities, $448,000
E16-6	No check figure
E16-7	Purchase of plant assets, $20,000
E16-8	Net cash provided by operating activities, $47,000
E16-9	No check figure
P16-1	(b) Net cash provided by operating activities, $428,000
P16-2	Net cash provided by operating activities, $39,555
P16-3	No check figure
P16-4	(g) Cash flow per share of common stock ratio, $1.40
P16-5	(b) Net cash provided by operating activities, $217,700
P16-1A	(b) Net cash provided by operating activities, $256,000
P16-2A	Net cash provided by operating activities, $71,250
P16-3A	(i) Cash flow liquidity ratio, 17.37 times
P16-4A	No check figure
P16-5A	(b) Net cash provided by operating activities, $66,750
BDC16-1	Net cash provided by operating activities, $(7,500)

BDC16-2	Net cash provided by operating activities, $149,500
ARA16-3	No check figure
ARA16-4	No check figure
ARA16-5	No check figure

Chapter 17

E17-1	Net income increase, 18.1%
E17-2	(a) (3) Current ratio, 1.75:1
E17-3	(a) 91.25 days
E17-4	Cash flow margin, 1.39%
E17-5	Inventory turnover, 5.2 times
E17-6	Rate of return on operating assets, 19.2%
E17-7	Return on average common stockholders' equity, 24%
E17-8	EPS, $8 per share
E17-9	Weighted-average no. of shares, 852,000
E17-10	EPS for 2006, $1
E17-11	No. of times interest earned, 7.25 times
E17-12	(a) Times preferred dividend earned, 6 times
E17-13	P-E ratio, 72
P17-1	(a) Net earnings decrease, 456.6%
P17-2	No check figure
P17-3	(b) Current ratio, 2008, 2.88:1
P17-4	No check figure
P17-5	(a) Rate of return on operating assets, 25%
P17-6	No check figure
P17-7	No check figure
P17-8	(a) Rate of return on operating assets, 12%
P17-1A	(a) Net sales increase, 1.0%
P17-2A	No check figure
P17-3A	(c) Acid-test ratio, 2008, 1.52:1
P17-4A	No check figure
P17-5A	(a) Co. 1, Rate of return on operating assets, 13.38%
P17-6A	No check figure
P17-7A	No check figure
P17-8A	(a) Inventory turnover, 1.56 times
BDC17-1	(a) Net income, $316,800
BDC17-2	(a) No. of days' sales in accounts receivable, 2005, 52.14 days
BDC17-3	(a) (2) Apple, Inc., EPS using first advisor's estimate, $0.38
ARA17-4	No check figure

Appendix
Annual Report
Wal-Mart Stores, Inc.

Note: The following pages contain excerpts from the 2011 Annual Report of Wal-Mart Stores, Inc. The complete annual report, including all of the notes to the financial statements, is available for download at http://www.walmartstores.com/sites/annualreport/2011/financials/Walmart_2011_Annual_Report.pdf

Walmart
2011 Annual Report

Building
the Next
Generation
Walmart

Executive Officers

Eduardo Castro-Wright
Vice Chairman, responsible for
Global eCommerce and
Global Sourcing

M. Susan Chambers
Executive Vice President,
People Division

Brian C. Cornell
Executive Vice President,
President and Chief Executive Officer,
Sam's Club

Leslie A. Dach
Executive Vice President,
Corporate Affairs

Michael T. Duke
President and Chief Executive Officer

Rollin L. Ford
Executive Vice President,
Chief Information Officer

Jeffrey J. Gearhart
Executive Vice President,
General Counsel and Corporate Secretary

Charles M. Holley, Jr.
Executive Vice President and
Chief Financial Officer

C. Douglas McMillon
Executive Vice President,
President and Chief Executive Officer,
Walmart International

William S. Simon
Executive Vice President,
President and Chief Executive Officer,
Walmart U.S.

S. Robson Walton
Chairman of the Board of Directors

Steven P. Whaley
Senior Vice President and Controller

Walmart ✳.
2011
Financial Report

2011 Financial Review

Five-Year Financial Summary

(Dollar amounts in millions, except per share and unit count data)

As of and for the Fiscal Years Ended January 31,	2011	2010	2009	2008	2007
		As Adjusted			
Operating Results [1]					
Net sales	$418,952	$405,132	$401,087	$373,821	$344,759
Net sales increase	3.4%	1.0%	7.3%	8.4%	11.6%
Comparable sales in the United States [2]	-0.6%	-0.8%	3.5%	1.6%	2.0%
Walmart U.S.	-1.5%	-0.7%	3.2%	1.0%	1.9%
Sam's Club	3.9%	-1.4%	4.9%	4.9%	2.5%
Gross profit margin	24.7%	24.9%	24.2%	24.0%	23.4%
Operating, selling, general and administrative expenses, as a percentage of net sales	19.3%	19.7%	19.3%	19.0%	18.5%
Operating income	$ 25,542	$ 24,002	$ 22,767	$ 21,916	$ 20,552
Income from continuing operations attributable to Walmart	15,355	14,449	13,235	12,841	12,224
Net income per share of common stock:					
Diluted net income per common share from continuing operations attributable to Walmart	$ 4.18	$ 3.73	$ 3.35	$ 3.15	$ 2.93
Dividends declared per common share	1.21	1.09	0.95	0.88	0.67
Financial Position					
Inventories	$ 36,318	$ 32,713	$ 34,013	$ 34,690	$ 33,235
Property, equipment and capital lease assets, net	107,878	102,307	95,653	96,867	88,287
Total assets	180,663	170,407	163,096	163,200	151,274
Long-term debt, including obligations under capital leases	43,842	36,401	34,549	33,402	30,735
Total Walmart shareholders' equity	68,542	70,468	64,969	64,311	61,298
Unit Counts					
Walmart U.S. segment	3,804	3,755	3,703	3,595	3,488
Walmart International segment	4,557	4,099	3,595	3,093	2,733
Sam's Club segment	609	605	611	600	588
Total units	8,970	8,459	7,909	7,288	6,809

[1] *Effective May 1, 2010, the Company implemented a new financial system for its operations in the United States, Canada and Puerto Rico. Concurrent with this implementation and the increased system capabilities, the Company changed the level at which we apply the retail method of accounting for inventory in these operations. The retrospective application of this accounting change impacted both segment and consolidated operating income, as well as consolidated net income for all comparable periods presented. See "Notes to Consolidated Financial Statements," Note 2. "Accounting Change."*

In addition, we reclassified certain revenue and expense items within our Consolidated Statements of Income for financial reporting purposes. The reclassifications did not impact consolidated operating income or consolidated net income attributable to Walmart. The changes were effective February 1, 2009 and have been reflected for fiscal 2010, 2009 and 2008.

[2] *Comparable store and club sales include fuel. Fiscal 2008 and fiscal 2007 comparable sales include all stores and clubs that have been open for at least the previous 12 months. Additionally, for those fiscal years, stores and clubs that are relocated, expanded or converted are excluded from comparable sales for the first 12 months following the relocation, expansion or conversion. Fiscal 2011, 2010 and 2009 comparable sales include sales from stores and clubs open for the previous 12 months, including remodels, relocations and expansions. Fiscal 2008 and fiscal 2007 comparable store and club sales do not reflect reclassifications effective February 1, 2009, as noted above.*

Consolidated Statements of Income

(Amounts in millions except per share data)	2011	Fiscal Years Ended January 31, 2010 As Adjusted	2009 As Adjusted
Revenues:			
Net sales	$418,952	$405,132	$401,087
Membership and other income	2,897	2,953	3,167
	421,849	408,085	404,254
Costs and expenses:			
Cost of sales	315,287	304,444	303,941
Operating, selling, general and administrative expenses	81,020	79,639	77,546
Operating income	25,542	24,002	22,767
Interest:			
Debt	1,928	1,787	1,896
Capital leases	277	278	288
Interest income	(201)	(181)	(284)
Interest, net	2,004	1,884	1,900
Income from continuing operations before income taxes	23,538	22,118	20,867
Provision for income taxes:			
Current	6,703	7,643	6,564
Deferred	876	(487)	569
	7,579	7,156	7,133
Income from continuing operations	15,959	14,962	13,734
Income (loss) from discontinued operations, net of tax	1,034	(79)	146
Consolidated net income	16,993	14,883	13,880
Less consolidated net income attributable to noncontrolling interest	(604)	(513)	(499)
Consolidated net income attributable to Walmart	$ 16,389	$ 14,370	$ 13,381
Basic net income per common share:			
Basic income per common share from continuing operations attributable to Walmart	$ 4.20	$ 3.74	$ 3.36
Basic income (loss) per common share from discontinued operations attributable to Walmart	0.28	(0.02)	0.04
Basic net income per common share attributable to Walmart	$ 4.48	$ 3.72	$ 3.40
Diluted net income per common share:			
Diluted income per common share from continuing operations attributable to Walmart	$ 4.18	$ 3.73	$ 3.35
Diluted income (loss) per common share from discontinued operations attributable to Walmart	0.29	(0.02)	0.04
Diluted net income per common share attributable to Walmart	$ 4.47	$ 3.71	$ 3.39
Weighted-average number of common shares:			
Basic	3,656	3,866	3,939
Diluted	3,670	3,877	3,951
Dividends declared per common share	$ 1.21	$ 1.09	$ 0.95

See accompanying notes.

Consolidated Balance Sheets

	As of January 31,	
(Amounts in millions except per share data)	**2011**	2010 As Adjusted
ASSETS		
Current assets:		
Cash and cash equivalents	$ **7,395**	$ 7,907
Receivables, net	**5,089**	4,144
Inventories	**36,318**	32,713
Prepaid expenses and other	**2,960**	3,128
Current assets of discontinued operations	**131**	140
Total current assets	**51,893**	48,032
Property and equipment:		
Land	**24,386**	22,591
Buildings and improvements	**79,051**	73,657
Fixtures and equipment	**38,290**	34,035
Transportation equipment	**2,595**	2,355
Construction in process	**4,262**	5,210
Property and equipment	**148,584**	137,848
Less accumulated depreciation	**(43,486)**	(38,304)
Property and equipment, net	**105,098**	99,544
Property under capital leases:		
Property under capital leases	**5,905**	5,669
Less accumulated amortization	**(3,125)**	(2,906)
Property under capital leases, net	**2,780**	2,763
Goodwill	**16,763**	16,126
Other assets and deferred charges	**4,129**	3,942
Total assets	**$180,663**	$170,407
LIABILITIES AND EQUITY		
Current liabilities:		
Short-term borrowings	$ **1,031**	$ 523
Accounts payable	**33,557**	30,451
Accrued liabilities	**18,701**	18,734
Accrued income taxes	**157**	1,347
Long-term debt due within one year	**4,655**	4,050
Obligations under capital leases due within one year	**336**	346
Current liabilities of discontinued operations	**47**	92
Total current liabilities	**58,484**	55,543
Long-term debt	**40,692**	33,231
Long-term obligations under capital leases	**3,150**	3,170
Deferred income taxes and other	**6,682**	5,508
Redeemable noncontrolling interest	**408**	307
Commitments and contingencies		
Equity:		
Preferred stock ($0.10 par value; 100 shares authorized, none issued)	**—**	—
Common stock ($0.10 par value; 11,000 shares authorized, 3,516 and 3,786 issued and outstanding at January 31, 2011 and January 31, 2010, respectively)	**352**	378
Capital in excess of par value	**3,577**	3,803
Retained earnings	**63,967**	66,357
Accumulated other comprehensive income (loss)	**646**	(70)
Total Walmart shareholders' equity	**68,542**	70,468
Noncontrolling interest	**2,705**	2,180
Total equity	**71,247**	72,648
Total liabilities and equity	**$180,663**	$170,407

See accompanying notes.

Consolidated Statements of Shareholders' Equity

(Amounts in millions)	Number of Shares	Common Stock	Capital in Excess of Par Value	Retained Earnings	Accumulated Other Comprehensive Income (Loss)	Total Walmart Shareholders' Equity	Noncontrolling Interest	Total Equity
Balances — February 1, 2008 (As Adjusted)	3,973	$397	$3,028	$ 57,022	$ 3,864	$ 64,311	$1,939	$ 66,250
Consolidated net income	—	—	—	13,381	—	13,381	499	13,880
Other comprehensive income	—	—	—	—	(6,552)	(6,552)	(371)	(6,923)
Cash dividends ($0.95 per share)	—	—	—	(3,746)	—	(3,746)	—	(3,746)
Purchase of Company stock	(61)	(6)	(95)	(3,315)	—	(3,416)	—	(3,416)
Other	13	2	987	2	—	991	(273)	718
Balances — January 31, 2009 (As Adjusted)	3,925	393	3,920	63,344	(2,688)	64,969	1,794	66,763
Consolidated net income (excludes redeemble noncontrolling interest)	—	—	—	14,370	—	14,370	499	14,869
Other comprehensive income	—	—	—	—	2,618	2,618	64	2,682
Cash dividends ($1.09 per share)	—	—	—	(4,217)	—	(4,217)	—	(4,217)
Purchase of Company stock	(145)	(15)	(246)	(7,136)	—	(7,397)	—	(7,397)
Purchase of redeemable noncontrolling interest	—	—	(288)	—	—	(288)	—	(288)
Other	6	—	417	(4)	—	413	(177)	236
Balances — January 31, 2010 (As Adjusted)	3,786	378	3,803	66,357	(70)	70,468	2,180	72,648
Consolidated net income (excludes redeemable noncontrolling interest)	—	—	—	16,389	—	16,389	584	16,973
Other comprehensive income	—	—	—	—	716	716	162	878
Cash dividends ($1.21 per share)	—	—	—	(4,437)	—	(4,437)	—	(4,437)
Purchase of Company stock	(280)	(28)	(487)	(14,319)	—	(14,834)	—	(14,834)
Other	10	2	261	(23)	—	240	(221)	19
Balances — January 31, 2011	3,516	$352	$3,577	$ 63,967	$ 646	$ 68,542	$2,705	$ 71,247

Comprehensive Income

(Amounts in millions)	2011	2010 As Adjusted	2009 As Adjusted
Consolidated net income:			
Consolidated net income [1]	$16,993	$14,883	$13,880
Other comprehensive income:			
Currency translation [2]	1,137	2,854	(6,860)
Net change in fair values of derivatives	(17)	94	(17)
Minimum pension liability	(145)	(220)	(46)
Total comprehensive income	17,968	17,611	6,957
Less amounts attributable to the noncontrolling interest:			
Consolidated net income [1]	(604)	(513)	(499)
Currency translation [2]	(259)	(110)	371
Amounts attributable to the noncontrolling interest	(863)	(623)	(128)
Comprehensive income attributable to Walmart	$17,105	$16,988	$ 6,829

[1] Includes $20 million and $14 million in fiscal 2011 and 2010, respectively, that is related to the redeemable noncontrolling interest.

[2] Includes $97 million and $46 million in fiscal 2011 and 2010, respectively, that is related to the redeemable noncontrolling interest.

See accompanying notes.

Consolidated Statements of Cash Flows

(Amounts in millions)	2011	2010 As Adjusted	2009 As Adjusted
Cash flows from operating activities:			
Consolidated net income	$ 16,993	$ 14,883	$ 13,880
Loss (income) from discontinued operations, net of tax	(1,034)	79	(146)
Income from continuing operations	15,959	14,962	13,734
Adjustments to reconcile income from continuing operations to net cash provided by operating activities:			
Depreciation and amortization	7,641	7,157	6,739
Deferred income taxes	651	(504)	581
Other operating activities	1,087	318	752
Changes in certain assets and liabilities, net of effects of acquisitions:			
Accounts receivable	(733)	(297)	(101)
Inventories	(3,086)	2,213	(184)
Accounts payable	2,557	1,052	(410)
Accrued liabilities	(433)	1,348	2,036
Net cash provided by operating activities	23,643	26,249	23,147
Cash flows from investing activities:			
Payments for property and equipment	(12,699)	(12,184)	(11,499)
Proceeds from disposal of property and equipment	489	1,002	714
Proceeds from disposal of certain international operations, net	—	—	838
Investments and business acquisitions, net of cash acquired	(202)	—	(1,576)
Other investing activities	219	(438)	781
Net cash used in investing activities	(12,193)	(11,620)	(10,742)
Cash flows from financing activities:			
Net change in short-term borrowings	503	(1,033)	(3,745)
Proceeds from issuance of long-term debt	11,396	5,546	6,566
Payments of long-term debt	(4,080)	(6,033)	(5,387)
Dividends paid	(4,437)	(4,217)	(3,746)
Purchase of Company stock	(14,776)	(7,276)	(3,521)
Purchase of redeemable noncontrolling interest	—	(436)	—
Payment of capital lease obligations	(363)	(346)	(352)
Other financing activities	(271)	(396)	267
Net cash used in financing activities	(12,028)	(14,191)	(9,918)
Effect of exchange rates on cash and cash equivalents	66	194	(781)
Net increase (decrease) in cash and cash equivalents	(512)	632	1,706
Cash and cash equivalents at beginning of year	7,907	7,275	5,569
Cash and cash equivalents at end of year	$ 7,395	$ 7,907	$ 7,275
Supplemental disclosure of cash flow information			
Income tax paid	$ 6,984	$ 7,389	$ 6,596
Interest paid	2,163	2,141	1,787
Capital lease obligations incurred	49	61	284

Fiscal Years Ended January 31,

See accompanying notes.

Notes to Consolidated Financial Statements

1 Summary of Significant Accounting Policies

General

Wal-Mart Stores, Inc. ("Walmart," the "Company" or "we") operates retail stores in various formats around the world, aggregated into three reportable segments: (1) the Walmart U.S. segment; (2) the Walmart International segment; and (3) the Sam's Club segment. We are committed to saving people money so they can live better. We earn the trust of our customers every day by providing a broad assortment of quality merchandise and services at every day low prices ("EDLP") while fostering a culture that rewards and embraces mutual respect, integrity and diversity. EDLP is our pricing philosophy under which we price items at a low price every day so our customers trust that our prices will not change under frequent promotional activity. Our fiscal year ends on January 31.

Principles of Consolidation

The consolidated financial statements include the accounts of Wal-Mart Stores, Inc. and its subsidiaries. All material intercompany accounts and transactions have been eliminated in consolidation. Investments in unconsolidated affiliates, which are 50% or less owned and do not meet the consolidation criteria of Topic 810 of the Financial Accounting Standards Codification ("ASC") are accounted for using the equity method. These investments are immaterial to our consolidated financial statements.

The Company's operations in Argentina, Brazil, Chile, China, Costa Rica, El Salvador, Guatemala, Honduras, India, Japan, Mexico, Nicaragua and the United Kingdom are consolidated using a December 31 fiscal year-end, generally due to statutory reporting requirements. There were no significant intervening events during January 2011 which materially affected the consolidated financial statements. The Company's operations in the United States and Canada are consolidated using a January 31 fiscal year-end.

Use of Estimates

The consolidated financial statements have been prepared in conformity with accounting principles generally accepted in the United States. Those principles require management to make estimates and assumptions that affect the reported amounts of assets and liabilities. Management's estimates and assumptions also affect the disclosure of contingent assets and liabilities at the date of the financial statements and the reported amounts of revenues and expenses during the reporting period. Actual results may differ from those estimates.

Cash and Cash Equivalents

The Company considers investments with a maturity of three months or less when purchased to be cash equivalents. All credit card, debit card and EBT transactions that process in less than seven days are classified as cash and cash equivalents. The amounts due from banks for these transactions classified as cash totaled $1.2 billion and $2.6 billion at January 31, 2011 and 2010, respectively. In addition, cash and cash equivalents includes restricted cash related to cash collateral holdings from various counterparties as required by certain derivative and trust agreements of $504 million and $469 million at January 31, 2011 and 2010, respectively.

Receivables

Receivables consist primarily of amounts due from:
- insurance companies resulting from our pharmacy sales;
- banks for customer credit card, debit card and electronic bank transfers that take in excess of seven days to process;
- suppliers for marketing or incentive programs;
- consumer financing programs in certain international subsidiaries; and
- real estate transactions.

We establish a reserve for uncollectible receivables based on historical trends in collection of past due amounts and write-off history. Our overall reserve for uncollectible receivables was $252 million and $298 million at January 31, 2011 and 2010, respectively.

Our Walmart International segment offers a limited amount of consumer credit products, principally through our subsidiaries in Chile, Canada and Mexico. At January 31, 2011, the balance of these receivables was $673 million, net of its reserve for doubtful accounts of $83 million, and is included in receivables, net on the accompanying consolidated balance sheet.

Inventories

The Company values inventories at the lower of cost or market as determined primarily by the retail method of accounting, using the last-in, first-out ("LIFO") method for substantially all of the Walmart U.S. segment's merchandise inventories. The retail method of accounting results in inventory being valued at the lower of cost or market since permanent markdowns are currently taken as a reduction of the retail value of inventory. The Sam's Club segment's merchandise is valued based on the weighted-average cost using the LIFO method. Inventories for the Walmart International operations are primarily valued by the retail method of accounting and are stated using the first-in, first-out ("FIFO") method. At January 31, 2011 and 2010, our inventories valued at LIFO approximate those inventories as if they were valued at FIFO.

As discussed in Note 2, effective May 1, 2010, the Company changed the level at which it applies the retail method for valuing inventory for its operations in the United States, Canada, and Puerto Rico. The retrospective application of this accounting change impacted both segment and consolidated operating income, as well as consolidated net income for all comparable periods presented.

Property and Equipment

Property and equipment are stated at cost. Gains or losses on disposition are recognized as earned or incurred. Costs of major improvements are capitalized, while costs of normal repairs and maintenance are charged to expense as incurred. Property and equipment are generally depreciated over the following estimated useful lives on a straight-line basis:

Buildings and improvements	3–40 years
Fixtures and equipment	3–25 years
Transportation equipment	4–15 years

Leasehold improvements are depreciated over the shorter of the estimated useful life of the asset or the remaining expected lease term. If significant expenditures are made for leasehold improvements late in the expected term of a lease and renewal is reasonably assured, the useful life of the leasehold improvement is limited to the end of the renewal period or economic life of the asset, whichever is shorter. Depreciation expense, including amortization of property under capital leases, for fiscal years 2011, 2010 and 2009 was $7.6 billion, $7.2 billion and $6.7 billion, respectively.

Notes to Consolidated Financial Statements

Capitalized Interest

The interest costs associated with construction projects are capitalized and included as part of the cost of the project. When no debt is incurred specifically for a project, interest is capitalized on amounts expended on the project using our weighted-average cost of borrowing. Capitalization of interest ceases when the project is substantially complete. Interest costs capitalized on construction projects were $63 million, $85 million and $88 million in fiscal 2011, 2010 and 2009, respectively.

Long-Lived Assets

Long-lived assets are stated at cost. Management reviews long-lived assets for indicators of impairment whenever events or changes in circumstances indicate that the carrying amount may not be recoverable. The evaluation is performed at the lowest level of identifiable cash flows, which is at the individual store level or in certain circumstances a market group of stores. Undiscounted cash flows expected to be generated by the related assets are estimated over the asset's useful life based on updated projections. If the evaluation indicates that the carrying amount of the asset may not be recoverable, any potential impairment is measured based upon the fair value of the related asset or asset group as determined by an appropriate market appraisal or other valuation technique.

Goodwill and Other Acquired Intangible Assets

Goodwill represents the excess of the purchase price over the fair value of net assets acquired in business combinations and is allocated to the appropriate segment when acquired. Other acquired intangible assets are stated at the fair value acquired as determined by a valuation technique commensurate with the intended use of the related asset. Goodwill and indefinite-lived intangible assets are not amortized; rather, they are evaluated for impairment annually during our fourth fiscal quarter or whenever events or changes in circumstances indicate that the value of the asset may be impaired. Definite-lived intangible assets are considered long-lived assets and are amortized on a straight-line basis over the periods that expected economic benefits will be provided.

Goodwill is evaluated for impairment by determining the fair value of the related reporting unit. Fair value is measured based on the discounted cash flow method and relative market-based approaches. The analyses require significant management judgment to evaluate the capacity of an acquired business to perform within projections. The Company has not recorded impairment charges related to goodwill.

The following table reflects goodwill activity, by operating segment, for fiscal years 2011 and 2010:

(Amounts in millions)	Walmart U.S.	Walmart International	Sam's Club	Total
February 1, 2009	$207	$14,740	$313	$15,260
Currency translation and other	—	866	—	866
January 31, 2010	207	15,606	313	16,126
Currency translation and other	—	605	—	605
Acquisitions	32	—	—	32
January 31, 2011	**$239**	**$16,211**	**$313**	**$16,763**

During fiscal 2011, Walmart U.S. completed an immaterial business acquisition that resulted in the recognition of $32 million in goodwill.

Indefinite-lived intangible assets are included in other assets and deferred charges on the accompanying Consolidated Balance Sheets. These assets are evaluated for impairment based on their fair values using valuation techniques which are updated annually based on the most recent variables and assumptions. There were no impairment charges related to indefinite-lived intangible assets recorded during the fiscal years ended January 31, 2011, 2010 and 2009.

Self-Insurance Reserves

The Company uses a combination of insurance, self-insured retention and self-insurance for a number of risks, including, but not limited to, workers' compensation, general liability, vehicle liability, property and the Company's obligation for employee-related health care benefits. Liabilities relating to these claims associated with these risks are estimated by considering historical claims experience, including frequency, severity, demographic factors, and other actuarial assumptions. In estimating our liability for such claims, we periodically analyze our historical trends, including loss development, and apply appropriate loss development factors to the incurred costs associated with the claims. See Note 6.

Income Taxes

Income taxes are accounted for under the liability method. Deferred tax assets and liabilities are recognized for the estimated future tax consequences attributable to differences between the financial statement carrying amounts of existing assets and liabilities and their respective tax bases. Deferred tax assets and liabilities are measured using enacted tax rates in effect for the year in which those temporary differences are expected to be recovered or settled. The effect on deferred tax assets and liabilities of a change in tax rate is recognized in income in the period that includes the enactment date. Valuation allowances are established when necessary to reduce deferred tax assets to the amounts more likely than not to be realized.

The Company records a liability for unrecognized tax benefits resulting from uncertain tax positions taken or expected to be taken in a tax return. The Company records interest and penalties related to unrecognized tax benefits in interest expense and operating, selling, general and administrative expenses, respectively, in the Company's Consolidated Statements of Income.

Revenue Recognition

The Company recognizes sales revenue net of sales taxes and estimated sales returns at the time it sells merchandise to the customer. Customer purchases of shopping cards are not recognized as revenue until the card is redeemed and the customer purchases merchandise by using the shopping card. The Company also recognizes revenue from service transactions at the time the service is performed. Generally, revenue from services is classified as a component of net sales on our Consolidated Statements of Income.

Notes to Consolidated Financial Statements

Sam's Club Membership Fee Revenue Recognition

The Company recognizes Sam's Club membership fee revenue both in the United States and internationally over the term of the membership, which is 12 months. The following table summarizes membership fee activity for each of the fiscal years 2011, 2010 and 2009.

(Amounts in millions)	Fiscal Years Ended January 31,		
	2011	2010	2009
Deferred membership fee revenue, beginning of year	**$ 532**	$ 541	$ 551
Cash received from members	**1,074**	1,048	1,044
Membership fee revenue recognized	**(1,064)**	(1,057)	(1,054)
Deferred membership fee revenue, end of year	**$ 542**	$ 532	$ 541

Sam's Club membership fee revenue is included in membership and other income in the revenues section of the accompanying Consolidated Statements of Income. The deferred membership fee is included in accrued liabilities on the accompanying Consolidated Balance Sheets.

Cost of Sales

Cost of sales includes actual product cost, the cost of transportation to the Company's warehouses, stores and clubs from suppliers, the cost of transportation from the Company's warehouses to the stores and clubs and the cost of warehousing for our Sam's Club segment and import distribution centers.

Payments from Suppliers

Walmart receives money from suppliers for various programs, primarily volume incentives, warehouse allowances and reimbursements for specific programs such as markdowns, margin protection and advertising. Substantially all payments from suppliers are accounted for as a reduction of inventory purchases and recognized in our Consolidated Statements of Income when the related inventory is sold.

Operating, Selling, General and Administrative Expenses

Operating, selling, general and administrative expenses include all operating costs of the Company, except those costs related to the transportation of products from the supplier to the warehouses, stores or clubs, the costs related to the transportation of products from the warehouses to the stores or clubs and the cost of warehousing for our Sam's Club segment and import distribution centers. As a result, the majority of the cost of warehousing and occupancy for our Walmart U.S. and Walmart International segments' distribution facilities is included in operating, selling, general and administrative expenses. Because we do not include most of the cost of our Walmart U.S. and Walmart International segments' distribution facilities in cost of sales, our gross profit and gross profit as a percentage of net sales (our "gross profit margin") may not be comparable to those of other retailers that may include all costs related to their distribution facilities in cost of sales and in the calculation of gross profit.

Advertising Costs

Advertising costs are expensed as incurred and were $2.5 billion, $2.4 billion and $2.1 billion in fiscal 2011, 2010 and 2009, respectively. Advertising costs consist primarily of print, television and digital advertisements.

Advertising reimbursements received from suppliers are generally accounted for as a reduction of purchases and recognized in our Consolidated Statements of Income when the related inventory is sold.

Leases

The Company estimates the expected term of a lease by assuming the exercise of renewal options where an economic penalty exists that would preclude the abandonment of the lease at the end of the initial non-cancelable term and the exercise of such renewal is at the sole discretion of the Company. This expected term is used in the determination of whether a store or club lease is a capital or operating lease and in the calculation of straight-line rent expense. Additionally, the useful life of leasehold improvements is limited by the expected lease term or the economic life of the asset, whichever is shorter. If significant expenditures are made for leasehold improvements late in the expected term of a lease and renewal is reasonably assured, the useful life of the leasehold improvement is limited to the end of the renewal period or economic life of the asset, whichever is shorter.

Rent abatements and escalations are considered in the calculation of minimum lease payments in the Company's capital lease tests and in determining straight-line rent expense for operating leases.

Pre-Opening Costs

The costs of start-up activities, including organization costs, related to new store openings, store remodels, expansions and relocations are expensed as incurred and included in operating, selling, general and administrative expenses on our Consolidated Statements of Income. Pre-opening costs totaled $320 million, $227 million and $289 million for the years ended January 31, 2011, 2010 and 2009, respectively.

Currency Translation

The assets and liabilities of all international subsidiaries are translated from the respective local currency to the U.S. dollar using exchange rates at the balance sheet date. The income statements of international subsidiaries are translated from the respective local currencies to the U.S. dollar using average exchange rates for the period covered by the income statements. Related translation adjustments are recorded as a component of accumulated other comprehensive income (loss).

Reclassifications

In connection with the Company's finance transformation project, we reviewed and adjusted the classification of certain revenue and expense items within our Consolidated Statements of Income for financial reporting purposes. The reclassifications did not impact operating income or consolidated net income attributable to Walmart. The changes were effective February 1, 2010 and have been reflected in all periods presented.

Recent Accounting Pronouncements

A new accounting standard, effective for and adopted by the Company on February 1, 2010, changes the approach to determining the primary beneficiary of a variable interest entity ("VIE") and requires companies to assess more frequently whether they must consolidate VIEs. The adoption of this new standard did not have a material impact on our consolidated financial statements.

Report of Independent Registered Public Accounting Firm

**The Board of Directors and Shareholders
of Wal-Mart Stores, Inc.**

We have audited the accompanying consolidated balance sheets of
Wal-Mart Stores, Inc. as of January 31, 2011 and 2010, and the related
consolidated statements of income, shareholders' equity, and cash flows
for each of the three years in the period ended January 31, 2011. These
financial statements are the responsibility of the Company's management. Our responsibility is to express an opinion on these financial
statements based on our audits.

We conducted our audits in accordance with the standards of the Public
Company Accounting Oversight Board (United States). Those standards
require that we plan and perform the audit to obtain reasonable assurance
about whether the financial statements are free of material misstatement.
An audit includes examining, on a test basis, evidence supporting the
amounts and disclosures in the financial statements. An audit also includes
assessing the accounting principles used and significant estimates made
by management, as well as evaluating the overall financial statement
presentation. We believe that our audits provide a reasonable basis for
our opinion.

In our opinion, the financial statements referred to above present fairly,
in all material respects, the consolidated financial position of Wal-Mart
Stores, Inc. at January 31, 2011 and 2010, and the consolidated results of
its operations and its cash flows for each of the three years in the period
ended January 31, 2011, in conformity with U.S. generally accepted
accounting principles.

As discussed in Note 2 to the consolidated financial statements,
effective May 1, 2010, the Company has elected to change its method
of accounting for inventory under the retail inventory method.

We also have audited, in accordance with the standards of the Public
Company Accounting Oversight Board (United States), Wal-Mart Stores,
Inc.'s internal control over financial reporting as of January 31, 2011,
based on criteria established in *Internal Control – Integrated Framework*
issued by the Committee of Sponsoring Organizations of the Treadway
Commission and our report dated March 30, 2011 expressed an
unqualified opinion thereon.

Ernst & Young LLP

Rogers, Arkansas
March 30, 2011

Report of Independent Registered Public Accounting Firm on Internal Control Over Financial Reporting

The Board of Directors and Shareholders of Wal-Mart Stores, Inc.

We have audited Wal-Mart Stores, Inc.'s internal control over financial reporting as of January 31, 2011, based on criteria established in *Internal Control – Integrated Framework* issued by the Committee of Sponsoring Organizations of the Treadway Commission (the COSO criteria). Wal-Mart Stores, Inc.'s management is responsible for maintaining effective internal control over financial reporting, and for its assessment of the effectiveness of internal control over financial reporting included in the accompanying "Management's Report to Our Shareholders." Our responsibility is to express an opinion on the Company's internal control over financial reporting based on our audit.

We conducted our audit in accordance with the standards of the Public Company Accounting Oversight Board (United States). Those standards require that we plan and perform the audit to obtain reasonable assurance about whether effective internal control over financial reporting was maintained in all material respects. Our audit included obtaining an understanding of internal control over financial reporting, assessing the risk that a material weakness exists, testing and evaluating the design and operating effectiveness of internal control based on the assessed risk, and performing such other procedures as we considered necessary in the circumstances. We believe that our audit provides a reasonable basis for our opinion.

A company's internal control over financial reporting is a process designed to provide reasonable assurance regarding the reliability of financial reporting and the preparation of financial statements for external purposes in accordance with generally accepted accounting principles. A company's internal control over financial reporting includes those policies and procedures that (1) pertain to the maintenance of records that, in reasonable detail, accurately and fairly reflect the transactions and dispositions of the assets of the company; (2) provide reasonable assurance that transactions are recorded as necessary to permit preparation of financial statements in accordance with generally accepted accounting principles, and that receipts and expenditures of the company are being made only in accordance with authorizations of management and directors of the company; and (3) provide reasonable assurance regarding prevention or timely detection of unauthorized acquisition, use or disposition of the company's assets that could have a material effect on the financial statements.

Because of its inherent limitations, internal control over financial reporting may not prevent or detect misstatements. Also, projections of any evaluation of effectiveness to future periods are subject to the risk that controls may become inadequate because of changes in conditions, or that the degree of compliance with the policies or procedures may deteriorate.

In our opinion, Wal-Mart Stores, Inc. maintained, in all material respects, effective internal control over financial reporting as of January 31, 2011, based on the COSO criteria.

We also have audited, in accordance with the standards of the Public Company Accounting Oversight Board (United States), the consolidated balance sheets of Wal-Mart Stores, Inc. as of January 31, 2011 and 2010, and related consolidated statements of income, shareholders' equity and cash flows for each of the three years in the period ended January 31, 2011 and our report dated March 30, 2011 expressed an unqualified opinion thereon.

Ernst & Young LLP

Rogers, Arkansas
March 30, 2011

Management's Report to Our Shareholders

Management of Wal-Mart Stores, Inc. ("Walmart", the "company" or "we") is responsible for the preparation, integrity and objectivity of Walmart's Consolidated Financial Statements and other financial information contained in this Annual Report to Shareholders. Those Consolidated Financial Statements were prepared in conformity with accounting principles generally accepted in the United States. In preparing those Consolidated Financial Statements, management was required to make certain estimates and judgments, which are based upon currently available information and management's view of current conditions and circumstances.

The Audit Committee of the Board of Directors, which consists solely of independent directors, oversees our process of reporting financial information and the audit of our Consolidated Financial Statements. The Audit Committee stays informed of the financial condition of Walmart and regularly reviews management's financial policies and procedures, the independence of our independent auditors, our internal control over financial reporting and the objectivity of our financial reporting. Both the independent auditors and the internal auditors have free access to the Audit Committee and meet with the Audit Committee periodically, both with and without management present.

Acting through our Audit Committee, we have retained Ernst & Young LLP, an independent registered public accounting firm, to audit our Consolidated Financial Statements found in this Annual Report to Shareholders. We have made available to Ernst & Young LLP all of our financial records and related data in connection with their audit of our Consolidated Financial Statements. We have filed with the Securities and Exchange Commission ("SEC") the required certifications related to our Consolidated Financial Statements as of and for the year ended January 31, 2011. These certifications are attached as exhibits to our Annual Report on Form 10-K for the year ended January 31, 2011. Additionally, we have also provided to the New York Stock Exchange the required annual certification of our Chief Executive Officer regarding our compliance with the New York Stock Exchange's corporate governance listing standards.

Report on Internal Control Over Financial Reporting

Management has responsibility for establishing and maintaining adequate internal control over financial reporting. Internal control over financial reporting is a process designed to provide reasonable assurance regarding the reliability of financial reporting and the preparation of financial statements for external reporting purposes in accordance with accounting principles generally accepted in the United States. Because of its inherent limitations, internal control over financial reporting may not prevent or detect misstatements. Management has assessed the effectiveness of the Company's internal control over financial reporting as of January 31, 2011. In making its assessment, management has utilized the criteria set forth by the Committee of Sponsoring Organizations ("COSO") of the Treadway Commission in *Internal Control – Integrated Framework*. Management concluded that based on its assessment, Walmart's internal control over financial reporting was effective as of January 31, 2011. The Company's internal control over financial reporting as of January 31, 2011, has been audited by Ernst & Young LLP as stated in their report which appears in this Annual Report to Shareholders.

Evaluation of Disclosure Controls and Procedures

We maintain disclosure controls and procedures designed to provide reasonable assurance that information required to be timely disclosed is accumulated and communicated to management in a timely fashion. Management has assessed the effectiveness of these disclosure controls and procedures as of January 31, 2011, and determined they were effective as of that date to provide reasonable assurance that information required to be disclosed by us in the reports we file or submit under the Securities Exchange Act of 1934, as amended, was accumulated and communicated to management, as appropriate, to allow timely decisions regarding required disclosure and were effective to provide reasonable assurance that such information is recorded, processed, summarized and reported within the time periods specified by the SEC's rules and forms.

Report on Ethical Standards

Our Company was founded on the belief that open communications and the highest standards of ethics are necessary to be successful. Our long-standing "Open Door" communication policy helps management be aware of and address issues in a timely and effective manner. Through the open door policy all associates are encouraged to inform management at the appropriate level when they are concerned about any matter pertaining to Walmart.

Walmart has adopted a Statement of Ethics to guide our associates in the continued observance of high ethical standards such as honesty, integrity and compliance with the law in the conduct of Walmart's business. Familiarity and compliance with the Statement of Ethics is required of all associates who are part of management. The Company also maintains a separate Code of Ethics for our senior financial officers. Walmart also has in place a Related-Party Transaction Policy. This policy applies to Walmart's senior officers and directors and requires material related-party transactions to be reviewed by the Audit Committee. The senior officers and directors are required to report material related-party transactions to Walmart. We maintain a global ethics office which oversees and administers an ethics helpline. The ethics helpline provides a channel for associates to make confidential and anonymous complaints regarding potential violations of our statements of ethics, including violations related to financial or accounting matters.

Michael T. Duke
President and Chief Executive Officer

Charles M. Holley, Jr.
Executive Vice President and Chief Financial Officer

Corporate and Stock Information

Corporate Information

Stock Registrar and Transfer Agent:
Computershare Trust Company, N.A.
P.O. Box 43069
Providence, Rhode Island 02940-3069 USA
Worldwide 1-800-438-6278
TDD for hearing-impaired inside the U.S. 1-800-952-9245
Internet: http//www.computershare.com

Listing

New York Stock Exchange
Stock Symbol: WMT

Annual Meeting

Our Annual Meeting of Shareholders will be held on Friday, June 3, 2011,
at 7:00 a.m. (Central time) in Bud Walton Arena on the University of Arkansas
campus, Fayetteville, Arkansas.

Communication With Shareholders

Wal-Mart Stores, Inc. periodically communicates with shareholders
and other members of the investment community about our operations.
For further information regarding our policy on shareholder and investor
communications, refer to our website, www.walmartstores.com/investors.

Independent Registered Public Accounting Firm

Ernst & Young LLP
5414 Pinnacle Point Dr., Suite 102
Rogers, Arkansas 72758 USA

The following reports are available without charge upon request by writing
the company c/o Investor Relations or by calling 1-479-273-8446. These
reports are also available via the corporate website.
• Annual Report on Form 10-K
• Quarterly Reports on Form 10-Q
• Earnings Releases
• Current Reports on Form 8-K
• Copy of Annual Shareholders' Meeting Proxy Statement
• Supplier Standards Report
• Global Responsibility Report

Market Price of Common Stock

The high and low market price per share for the company's common stock
in fiscal 2011 and 2010 were as follows:

	2011		2010	
	High	Low	High	Low
1st Quarter	$56.27	$52.66	$54.57	$46.25
2nd Quarter	54.95	47.77	51.75	47.35
3rd Quarter	54.82	50.00	52.56	48.73
4th Quarter	57.90	53.14	55.20	49.52

For the first quarter of fiscal 2012, year ended January 31,

	2012	
	High	Low
1st Quarter*	$56.73	$50.97

*Through March 21, 2011

Dividends Payable Per Share

For fiscal 2012 dividends will be paid based on the following schedule:

April 4, 2011	$0.3650
June 6, 2011	$0.3650
September 6, 2011	$0.3650
January 3, 2012	$0.3650

Dividends Paid Per Share

For fiscal 2011, dividends were paid on the following schedule:

April 5, 2010	$0.3025
June 1, 2010	$0.3025
September 7, 2010	$0.3025
January 3, 2011	$0.3025

For fiscal 2010, dividends were paid on the following schedule:

April 6, 2009	$0.2725
June 1, 2009	$0.2725
September 8, 2009	$0.2725
January 4, 2010	$0.2725

Stock Performance Chart

This graph compares the cumulative total shareholder return on
Walmart's common stock during the five fiscal years ending with fiscal 2011
to the cumulative total returns on the S&P 500 Retailing Index and the S&P
500 Index. The comparison assumes $100 was invested on February 1, 2006
in shares of our common stock and in each of the indices shown and
assumes that all of the dividends were reinvested.

Comparison of 5-Year Cumulative Total Return
Among Wal-Mart Stores, Inc., S&P 500 Index and S&P 500 Retailing Index

Assumes $100 invested on February 1, 2006.
Assumes dividends reinvested.
Fiscal year ending January 31, 2011.

Shareholders

As of March 21, 2011, there were 283,633 holders of record of Walmart's
common stock.

Building the Next Generation Walmart Responsibly

Along with visiting our interactive annual report at walmartstores.com/investors, please also visit walmartstores.com to see how we are becoming a more globally responsible company. Our shareholders can continue to help Walmart become a more sustainable company by registering to receive Annual Shareholders Meeting materials and other company information electronically by registering for electronic delivery of materials at www.walmartstores.com/investors. Please also consider voting your shares electronically. Instructions are included in your shareholders package.

50% reduction
Walmart has reduced paper usage for the annual report and proxy over the last five years.

Helping the environment through a more responsible annual report

The minimized environmental footprint of this report is the result of an extensive, collaborative effort of Walmart and its supply chain partners. The environmental and social impact continues to be an important consideration. It is printed on FSC®-certified responsibly forested paper containing recycled PCW fiber that is Elementally Chlorine Free (ECF). It is printed using 100% renewable wind power (RECs), along with environmental manufacturing principles that were utilized in the printing process. These practices include environmentally responsible procurement, lean manufacturing, green chemistry principles, the recycling of residual materials and reduced volatile organic compound inks and coatings.

5.33 acres
of forest land preserved via managed forestry

1,431.34 fewer
trees consumed via recycling

289,812 kWh
less energy – the same used by 11 homes for a year

638.5 metric tons
of greenhouse gas offset – the equivalent of taking 128 cars off the road for a year

65,767.5 kWh
converted to clean renewable sources (printing plant using RECs)

520,616.58 fewer
gallons of water consumed

Savings baselines were developed using the U.S. national averages of similar coated papers and printing practices by EarthColor Printing.

Appendix
Compound Interest
and Annuity Tables

Table A.1

Future Value of $1 at Compounding Interest: 1%-20% $FV = (1 + i)^n$

Period	1%	2%	3%	4%	5%	6%	7%	8%	9%	10%
1	1.01000	1.02000	1.03000	1.04000	1.05000	1.06000	1.07000	1.08000	1.09000	1.10000
2	1.02010	1.04040	1.06090	1.08160	1.10250	1.12360	1.14490	1.16640	1.18810	1.21000
3	1.03030	1.06121	1.09273	1.12486	1.15762	1.19102	1.22504	1.25971	1.29503	1.33100
4	1.04060	1.08243	1.12551	1.16986	1.21551	1.26248	1.31080	1.36049	1.41158	1.46410
5	1.05101	1.10408	1.15927	1.21665	1.27628	1.33823	1.40255	1.46933	1.53862	1.61051
6	1.06152	1.12616	1.19405	1.26532	1.34010	1.41852	1.50073	1.58687	1.67710	1.77156
7	1.07214	1.14869	1.22987	1.31593	1.40710	1.50363	1.60578	1.71382	1.82804	1.94872
8	1.08286	1.17166	1.26677	1.36857	1.47746	1.59385	1.71819	1.85093	1.99256	2.14359
9	1.09369	1.19509	1.30477	1.42331	1.55133	1.68948	1.83846	1.99900	2.17189	2.35795
10	1.10462	1.21899	1.34392	1.48024	1.62889	1.79085	1.96715	2.15892	2.36736	2.59374
11	1.11567	1.24337	1.38423	1.53945	1.71034	1.89830	2.10485	2.33164	2.58043	2.85312
12	1.12683	1.26824	1.42576	1.60103	1.79586	2.01220	2.25219	2.51817	2.81266	3.13843
13	1.13809	1.29361	1.46853	1.66507	1.88565	2.13293	2.40985	2.71962	3.06580	3.45227
14	1.14947	1.31948	1.51259	1.73168	1.97993	2.26090	2.57853	2.93719	3.34173	3.79750
15	1.16097	1.34587	1.55797	1.80094	2.07893	2.39656	2.75903	3.17217	3.64248	4.17725
16	1.17258	1.37279	1.60471	1.87298	2.18287	2.54035	2.95216	3.42594	3.97031	4.59497
17	1.18430	1.40024	1.65285	1.94790	2.29202	2.69277	3.15882	3.70002	4.32763	5.05447
18	1.19615	1.42825	1.70243	2.02582	2.40662	2.85434	3.37993	3.99602	4.71712	5.55992
19	1.20811	1.45681	1.75351	2.10685	2.52695	3.02560	3.61653	4.31570	5.14166	6.11591
20	1.22019	1.48595	1.80611	2.19112	2.65330	3.20714	3.86968	4.66096	5.60441	6.72750
21	1.23239	1.51567	1.86029	2.27877	2.78596	3.39956	4.14056	5.03383	6.10881	7.40025
22	1.24472	1.54598	1.91610	2.36992	2.92526	3.60354	4.43040	5.43654	6.65860	8.14027
23	1.25716	1.57690	1.97359	2.46472	3.07152	3.81975	4.74053	5.87146	7.25787	8.95430
24	1.26973	1.60844	2.03279	2.56330	3.22510	4.04893	5.07237	6.34118	7.91108	9.84973
25	1.28243	1.64061	2.09378	2.66584	3.38635	4.29187	5.42743	6.84848	8.62308	10.83471
26	1.29526	1.67342	2.15659	2.77247	3.55567	4.54938	5.80735	7.39635	9.39916	11.91818
27	1.30821	1.70689	2.22129	2.88337	3.73346	4.82235	6.21387	7.98806	10.24508	13.10999
28	1.32129	1.74102	2.28793	2.99870	3.92013	5.11169	6.64884	8.62711	11.16714	14.42099
29	1.33450	1.77584	2.35657	3.11865	4.11614	5.41839	7.11426	9.31727	12.17218	15.86309
30	1.34785	1.81136	2.42726	3.24340	4.32194	5.74349	7.61226	10.06266	13.26768	17.44940

Period	11%	12%	13%	14%	15%	16%	17%	18%	19%	20%
1	1.11000	1.12000	1.13000	1.14000	1.15000	1.16000	1.17000	1.18000	1.19000	1.20000
2	1.23210	1.25440	1.27690	1.29960	1.32250	1.34560	1.36890	1.39240	1.41610	1.44000
3	1.36763	1.40493	1.44290	1.48154	1.52088	1.56090	1.60161	1.64303	1.68516	1.72800
4	1.51807	1.57352	1.63047	1.68896	1.74901	1.81064	1.87389	1.93878	2.00534	2.07360
5	1.68506	1.76234	1.84244	1.92541	2.01136	2.10034	2.19245	2.28776	2.38635	2.48832
6	1.87041	1.97382	2.08195	2.19497	2.31306	2.43640	2.56516	2.69955	2.83976	2.98598
7	2.07616	2.21068	2.35261	2.50227	2.66002	2.82622	3.00124	3.18547	3.37932	3.58318
8	2.30454	2.47596	2.65844	2.85259	3.05902	3.27841	3.51145	3.75886	4.02139	4.29982
9	2.55804	2.77308	3.00404	3.25195	3.51788	3.80296	4.10840	4.43545	4.78545	5.15978
10	2.83942	3.10585	3.39457	3.70722	4.04556	4.41144	4.80683	5.23384	5.69468	6.19174
11	3.15176	3.47855	3.83586	4.22623	4.65239	5.11726	5.62399	6.17593	6.77667	7.43008
12	3.49845	3.89598	4.33452	4.81790	5.35025	5.93603	6.58007	7.28759	8.06424	8.91610
13	3.88328	4.36349	4.89801	5.49241	6.15279	6.88579	7.69868	8.59936	9.59645	10.69932
14	4.31044	4.88711	5.53475	6.26135	7.07571	7.98752	9.00745	10.14724	11.41977	12.83918
15	4.78459	5.47357	6.25427	7.13794	8.13706	9.26552	10.53872	11.97375	13.58953	15.40702
16	5.31089	6.13039	7.06733	8.13725	9.35762	10.74800	12.33030	14.12902	16.17154	18.48843
17	5.89509	6.86604	7.98608	9.27646	10.76126	12.46768	14.42646	16.67225	19.24413	22.18611
18	6.54355	7.68997	9.02427	10.57517	12.37545	14.46251	16.87895	19.67325	22.90052	26.62333
19	7.26334	8.61276	10.19742	12.05569	14.23177	16.77652	19.74838	23.21444	27.25162	31.94800
20	8.06231	9.64629	11.52309	13.74349	16.36654	19.46076	23.10560	27.39303	32.42942	38.33760
21	8.94917	10.80385	13.02109	15.66758	18.82152	22.57448	27.03355	32.32378	38.59101	46.00512
22	9.93357	12.10031	14.71383	17.86104	21.64475	26.18640	31.62925	38.14206	45.92331	55.20614
23	11.02627	13.55235	16.62663	20.36158	24.89146	30.37622	37.00623	45.00763	54.64873	66.24737
24	12.23916	15.17863	18.78809	23.21221	28.62518	35.23642	43.29729	53.10901	65.03199	79.49685
25	13.58546	17.00006	21.23054	26.46192	32.91895	40.87424	50.65783	62.66863	77.38807	95.39622
26	15.07986	19.04007	23.99051	30.16658	37.85680	47.41412	59.26966	73.94898	92.09181	114.47546
27	16.73865	21.32488	27.10928	34.38991	43.53531	55.00038	69.34550	87.25980	109.58925	137.37055
28	18.57990	23.88387	30.63349	39.20449	50.06561	63.80044	81.13423	102.96656	130.41121	164.84466
29	20.62369	26.74993	34.61584	44.69312	57.57545	74.00851	94.92705	121.50054	155.18934	197.81359
30	22.89230	29.95992	39.11590	50.95016	66.21177	85.84988	111.06465	143.37064	184.67531	237.37631

Table A.2
Future Value of an Ordinary Annuity of $1 per Period: 1%-20%

$$FV_A = \frac{(1+i)^n - 1}{i}$$

Period	1%	2%	3%	4%	5%	6%	7%	8%	9%	10%
1	1.00000	1.00000	1.00000	1.00000	1.00000	1.00000	1.00000	1.00000	1.00000	1.00000
2	2.01000	2.02000	2.03000	2.04000	2.05000	2.06000	2.07000	2.08000	2.09000	2.10000
3	3.03010	3.06040	3.09090	3.12160	3.15250	3.18360	3.21490	3.24640	3.27810	3.31000
4	4.06040	4.12161	4.18363	4.24646	4.31012	4.37462	4.43994	4.50611	4.57313	4.64100
5	5.10101	5.20404	5.30914	5.41632	5.52563	5.63709	5.75074	5.86660	5.98471	6.10510
6	6.15202	6.30812	6.46841	6.63298	6.80191	6.97532	7.15329	7.33593	7.52333	7.71561
7	7.21354	7.43428	7.66246	7.89829	8.14201	8.39384	8.65402	8.92280	9.20043	9.48717
8	8.28567	8.58297	8.89234	9.21423	9.54911	9.89747	10.25980	10.63663	11.02847	11.43589
9	9.36853	9.75463	10.15911	10.58280	11.02656	11.49132	11.97799	12.48756	13.02104	13.57948
10	10.46221	10.94972	11.46388	12.00611	12.57789	13.18079	13.81645	14.48656	15.19293	15.93742
11	11.56683	12.16872	12.80780	13.48635	14.20679	14.97164	15.78360	16.64549	17.56029	18.53117
12	12.68250	13.41209	14.19203	15.02581	15.91713	16.86994	17.88845	18.97713	20.14072	21.38428
13	13.80933	14.68033	15.61779	16.62684	17.71298	18.88214	20.14064	21.49530	22.95338	24.52271
14	14.94742	15.97394	17.08632	18.29191	19.59863	21.01507	22.55049	24.21492	26.01919	27.97498
15	16.09690	17.29342	18.59891	20.02359	21.57856	23.27597	25.12902	27.15211	29.36092	31.77248
16	17.25786	18.63929	20.15688	21.82453	23.65749	25.67253	27.88805	30.32428	33.00340	35.94973
17	18.43044	20.01207	21.76159	23.69751	25.84037	28.21288	30.84022	33.75023	36.97370	40.54470
18	19.61475	21.41231	23.41444	25.64541	28.13238	30.90565	33.99903	37.45024	41.30134	45.59917
19	20.81090	22.84056	25.11687	27.67123	30.53900	33.75999	37.37896	41.44626	46.01846	51.15909
20	22.01900	24.29737	26.87037	29.77808	33.06595	36.78559	40.99549	45.76196	51.16012	57.27500
21	23.23919	25.78332	28.67649	31.96920	35.71925	39.99273	44.86518	50.42292	56.76453	64.00250
22	24.47159	27.29898	30.53678	34.24797	38.50521	43.39229	49.00574	55.45676	62.87334	71.40275
23	25.71630	28.84496	32.45288	36.61789	41.43048	46.99583	53.43614	60.89330	69.53194	79.54302
24	26.97346	30.42186	34.42647	39.08260	44.50200	50.81558	58.17667	66.76476	76.78981	88.49733
25	28.24320	32.03030	36.45926	41.64591	47.72710	54.86451	63.24904	73.10594	84.70090	98.34706
26	29.52563	33.67091	38.55304	44.31174	51.11345	59.15638	68.67647	79.95442	93.32398	109.18177
27	30.82089	35.34432	40.70963	47.08421	54.66913	63.70577	74.48382	87.35077	102.72313	121.09994
28	32.12910	37.05121	42.93092	49.96758	58.40258	68.52811	80.69769	95.33883	112.96822	134.20994
29	33.45039	38.79223	45.21885	52.96629	62.32271	73.63980	87.34653	103.96594	124.13536	148.63093
30	34.78489	40.56808	47.57542	56.08494	66.43885	79.05819	94.46079	113.28321	136.30754	164.49402

Period	11%	12%	13%	14%	15%	16%	17%	18%	19%	20%
1	1.00000	1.00000	1.00000	1.00000	1.00000	1.00000	1.00000	1.00000	1.00000	1.00000
2	2.11000	2.12000	2.13000	2.14000	2.15000	2.16000	2.17000	2.18000	2.19000	2.20000
3	3.34210	3.37440	3.40690	3.43960	3.47250	3.50560	3.53890	3.57240	3.60610	3.64000
4	4.70973	4.77933	4.84980	4.92114	4.99337	5.06650	5.14051	5.21543	5.29126	5.36800
5	6.22780	6.35285	6.48027	6.61010	6.74238	6.87714	7.01440	7.15421	7.29660	7.44160
6	7.91286	8.11519	8.32271	8.53552	8.75374	8.97748	9.20685	9.44197	9.68295	9.92992
7	9.78327	10.08901	10.40466	10.73049	11.06680	11.41387	11.77201	12.14152	12.52271	12.91590
8	11.85943	12.29969	12.75726	13.23276	13.72682	14.24009	14.77325	15.32700	15.90203	16.49908
9	14.16397	14.77566	15.41571	16.08535	16.78584	17.51851	18.28471	19.08585	19.92341	20.79890
10	16.72201	17.54874	18.41975	19.33730	20.30372	21.32147	22.39311	23.52131	24.70886	25.95868
11	19.56143	20.65458	21.81432	23.04452	24.34928	25.73290	27.19994	28.75514	30.40355	32.15042
12	22.71319	24.13313	25.65018	27.27075	29.00167	30.85017	32.82393	34.93107	37.18022	39.58050
13	26.21164	28.02911	29.98470	32.08865	34.35192	36.78620	39.40399	42.21866	45.24446	48.49660
14	30.09492	32.39260	34.88271	37.58107	40.50471	43.67199	47.10267	50.81802	54.84091	59.19592
15	34.40536	37.27971	40.41746	43.84241	47.58041	51.65951	56.11013	60.96527	66.26068	72.03511
16	39.18995	42.75328	46.67173	50.98035	55.71747	60.92503	66.64885	72.93901	79.85021	87.44213
17	44.50084	48.88367	53.73906	59.11760	65.07509	71.67303	78.97915	87.06804	96.02175	105.93056
18	50.39594	55.74971	61.72514	68.39407	75.83636	84.14072	93.40561	103.74028	115.26588	128.11667
19	56.93949	63.43968	70.74941	78.96923	88.21181	98.60323	110.28456	123.41353	138.16640	154.74000
20	64.20283	72.05244	80.94683	91.02493	102.44358	115.37975	130.03294	146.62797	165.41802	186.68800
21	72.26514	81.69874	92.46992	104.76842	118.81012	134.84051	153.13854	174.02100	197.84744	225.02560
22	81.21431	92.50258	105.49101	120.43600	137.63164	157.41499	180.17209	206.34479	236.43846	271.03072
23	91.14788	104.60289	120.20484	138.29704	159.27638	183.60138	211.80134	244.48685	282.36176	326.23686
24	102.17415	118.15524	136.83147	158.65862	184.16784	213.97761	248.80757	289.49448	337.01050	392.48424
25	114.41331	133.33387	155.61956	181.87083	212.79302	249.21402	292.10486	342.60349	402.04249	471.98108
26	127.99877	150.33393	176.85010	208.33274	245.71197	290.08827	342.76268	405.27211	479.43056	567.37730
27	143.07864	169.37401	200.84061	238.49933	283.56877	337.50239	402.03234	479.22109	571.52237	681.85276
28	159.81729	190.69889	227.94989	272.88923	327.10408	392.50277	471.37783	566.48089	681.11162	819.22331
29	178.39719	214.58275	258.58338	312.09373	377.16969	456.30322	552.51207	669.44745	811.52283	984.06797
30	199.02088	241.33268	293.19922	356.78685	434.74515	530.31173	647.43912	790.94799	966.71217	1181.88157

Compound Interest and Annuity Tables

Table A.3

Present Value of \$1 at Compounding Interest: 1%-20%

$$PV = \frac{1}{(1+i)^n}$$

Period	1%	2%	3%	4%	5%	6%	7%	8%	9%	10%
1	0.99010	0.98039	0.97087	0.96154	0.95238	0.94340	0.93458	0.92593	0.91743	0.90909
2	0.98030	0.96117	0.94260	0.92456	0.90703	0.89000	0.87344	0.85734	0.84168	0.82645
3	0.97059	0.94232	0.91514	0.88900	0.86384	0.83962	0.81630	0.79383	0.77218	0.75131
4	0.96098	0.92385	0.88849	0.85480	0.82270	0.79209	0.76290	0.73503	0.70843	0.68301
5	0.95147	0.90573	0.86261	0.82193	0.78353	0.74726	0.71299	0.68058	0.64993	0.62092
6	0.94205	0.88797	0.83748	0.79031	0.74622	0.70496	0.66634	0.63017	0.59627	0.56447
7	0.93272	0.87056	0.81309	0.75992	0.71068	0.66506	0.62275	0.58349	0.54703	0.51316
8	0.92348	0.85349	0.78941	0.73069	0.67684	0.62741	0.58201	0.54027	0.50187	0.46651
9	0.91434	0.83676	0.76642	0.70259	0.64461	0.59190	0.54393	0.50025	0.46043	0.42410
10	0.90529	0.82035	0.74409	0.67556	0.61391	0.55839	0.50835	0.46319	0.42241	0.38554
11	0.89632	0.80426	0.72242	0.64958	0.58468	0.52679	0.47509	0.42888	0.38753	0.35049
12	0.88745	0.78849	0.70138	0.62460	0.55684	0.49697	0.44401	0.39711	0.35553	0.31863
13	0.87866	0.77303	0.68095	0.60057	0.53032	0.46884	0.41496	0.36770	0.32618	0.28966
14	0.86996	0.75788	0.66112	0.57748	0.50507	0.44230	0.38782	0.34046	0.29925	0.26333
15	0.86135	0.74301	0.64186	0.55526	0.48102	0.41727	0.36245	0.31524	0.27454	0.23939
16	0.85282	0.72845	0.62317	0.53391	0.45811	0.39365	0.33873	0.29189	0.25187	0.21763
17	0.84438	0.71416	0.60502	0.51337	0.43630	0.37136	0.31657	0.27027	0.23107	0.19784
18	0.83602	0.70016	0.58739	0.49363	0.41552	0.35034	0.29586	0.25025	0.21199	0.17986
19	0.82774	0.68643	0.57029	0.47464	0.39573	0.33051	0.27651	0.23171	0.19449	0.16351
20	0.81954	0.67297	0.55368	0.45639	0.37689	0.31180	0.25842	0.21455	0.17843	0.14864
21	0.81143	0.65978	0.53755	0.43883	0.35894	0.29416	0.24151	0.19866	0.16370	0.13513
22	0.80340	0.64684	0.52189	0.42196	0.34185	0.27751	0.22571	0.18394	0.15018	0.12285
23	0.79544	0.63416	0.50669	0.40573	0.32557	0.26180	0.21095	0.17032	0.13778	0.11168
24	0.78757	0.62172	0.49193	0.39012	0.31007	0.24698	0.19715	0.15770	0.12640	0.10153
25	0.77977	0.60953	0.47761	0.37512	0.29530	0.23300	0.18425	0.14602	0.11597	0.09230
26	0.77205	0.59758	0.46369	0.36069	0.28124	0.21981	0.17220	0.13520	0.10639	0.08391
27	0.76440	0.58586	0.45019	0.34682	0.26785	0.20737	0.16093	0.12519	0.09761	0.07628
28	0.75684	0.57437	0.43708	0.33348	0.25509	0.19563	0.15040	0.11591	0.08955	0.06934
29	0.74934	0.56311	0.42435	0.32065	0.24295	0.18456	0.14056	0.10733	0.08215	0.06304
30	0.74192	0.55207	0.41199	0.30832	0.23138	0.17411	0.13137	0.09938	0.07537	0.05731
31	0.73458	0.54125	0.39999	0.29646	0.22036	0.16425	0.12277	0.09202	0.06915	0.05210
32	0.72730	0.53063	0.38834	0.28506	0.20987	0.15496	0.11474	0.08520	0.06344	0.04736
33	0.72010	0.52023	0.37703	0.27409	0.19987	0.14619	0.10723	0.07889	0.05820	0.04306
34	0.71297	0.51003	0.36604	0.26355	0.19035	0.13791	0.10022	0.07305	0.05339	0.03914
35	0.70591	0.50003	0.35538	0.25342	0.18129	0.13011	0.09366	0.06763	0.04899	0.03558
36	0.69892	0.49022	0.34503	0.24367	0.17266	0.12274	0.08754	0.06262	0.04494	0.03235
37	0.69200	0.48061	0.33498	0.23430	0.16444	0.11579	0.08181	0.05799	0.04123	0.02941
38	0.68515	0.47119	0.32523	0.22529	0.15661	0.10924	0.07646	0.05369	0.03783	0.02673
39	0.67837	0.46195	0.31575	0.21662	0.14915	0.10306	0.07146	0.04971	0.03470	0.02430
40	0.67165	0.45289	0.30656	0.20829	0.14205	0.09722	0.06678	0.04603	0.03184	0.02209

Table A.3 (cont.)

Present Value of $1 at Compounding Interest: 1%-20% (continued)

Period	11%	12%	13%	14%	15%	16%	17%	18%	19%	20%
1	0.90090	0.89286	0.88496	0.87719	0.86957	0.86207	0.85470	0.84746	0.84034	0.83333
2	0.81162	0.79719	0.78315	0.76947	0.75614	0.74316	0.73051	0.71818	0.70616	0.69444
3	0.73119	0.71178	0.69305	0.67497	0.65752	0.64066	0.62437	0.60863	0.59342	0.57870
4	0.65873	0.63553	0.61332	0.59208	0.57175	0.55229	0.53365	0.51579	0.49867	0.48225
5	0.59345	0.56743	0.54276	0.51937	0.49718	0.47611	0.45611	0.43711	0.41905	0.40188
6	0.53464	0.50663	0.48032	0.45559	0.43233	0.41044	0.38984	0.37043	0.35214	0.33490
7	0.48166	0.45235	0.42506	0.39964	0.37594	0.35383	0.33320	0.31393	0.29592	0.27908
8	0.43393	0.40388	0.37616	0.35056	0.32690	0.30503	0.28478	0.26604	0.24867	0.23257
9	0.39092	0.36061	0.33288	0.30751	0.28426	0.26295	0.24340	0.22546	0.20897	0.19381
10	0.35218	0.32197	0.29459	0.26974	0.24718	0.22668	0.20804	0.19106	0.17560	0.16151
11	0.31728	0.28748	0.26070	0.23662	0.21494	0.19542	0.17781	0.16192	0.14757	0.13459
12	0.28584	0.25668	0.23071	0.20756	0.18691	0.16846	0.15197	0.13722	0.12400	0.11216
13	0.25751	0.22917	0.20416	0.18207	0.16253	0.14523	0.12989	0.11629	0.10421	0.09346
14	0.23199	0.20462	0.18068	0.15971	0.14133	0.12520	0.11102	0.09855	0.08757	0.07789
15	0.20900	0.18270	0.15989	0.14010	0.12289	0.10793	0.09489	0.08352	0.07359	0.06491
16	0.18829	0.16312	0.14150	0.12289	0.10686	0.09304	0.08110	0.07078	0.06184	0.05409
17	0.16963	0.14564	0.12522	0.10780	0.09293	0.08021	0.06932	0.05998	0.05196	0.04507
18	0.15282	0.13004	0.11081	0.09456	0.04081	0.06914	0.05925	0.05083	0.04367	0.03756
19	0.13768	0.11611	0.09806	0.08295	0.07027	0.05961	0.05064	0.04308	0.03670	0.03130
20	0.12403	0.10367	0.08678	0.07276	0.06110	0.05139	0.04328	0.03651	0.03084	0.02608
21	0.11174	0.09256	0.07680	0.06383	0.05313	0.04430	0.03699	0.03094	0.02591	0.02174
22	0.10067	0.08264	0.06796	0.05599	0.04620	0.03819	0.03162	0.02622	0.02178	0.01811
23	0.09069	0.07379	0.06014	0.04911	0.04017	0.03292	0.02702	0.02222	0.01830	0.01509
24	0.08170	0.06588	0.05323	0.04308	0.03493	0.02838	0.02310	0.01883	0.01538	0.01258
25	0.07361	0.05882	0.04710	0.03779	0.03038	0.02447	0.01974	0.01596	0.01292	0.01048
26	0.06631	0.05252	0.04168	0.03315	0.02642	0.02109	0.01687	0.01352	0.01086	0.00874
27	0.05974	0.04689	0.03689	0.02908	0.02297	0.01818	0.01442	0.01146	0.00912	0.00728
28	0.05382	0.04187	0.03264	0.02551	0.01997	0.01567	0.01233	0.00971	0.00767	0.00607
29	0.04849	0.03738	0.02889	0.02237	0.01737	0.01351	0.01053	0.00823	0.00644	0.00506
30	0.04368	0.03338	0.02557	0.01963	0.01510	0.01165	0.00900	0.00697	0.00541	0.00421
31	0.03935	0.02980	0.02262	0.01722	0.01313	0.01004	0.00770	0.00591	0.00455	0.00351
32	0.03545	0.02661	0.02002	0.01510	0.01142	0.00866	0.00658	0.00501	0.00382	0.00293
33	0.03194	0.02376	0.01772	0.01325	0.00993	0.00746	0.00562	0.00425	0.00321	0.00244
34	0.02878	0.02121	0.01568	0.01162	0.00864	0.00643	0.00480	0.00360	0.00270	0.00203
35	0.02592	0.01894	0.01388	0.01019	0.00751	0.00555	0.00411	0.00305	0.00227	0.00169
36	0.02335	0.01691	0.01228	0.00894	0.00653	0.00478	0.00351	0.00258	0.00191	0.00141
37	0.02104	0.01510	0.01087	0.00784	0.00568	0.00412	0.00300	0.00219	0.00160	0.00118
38	0.01896	0.01348	0.00962	0.00688	0.00494	0.00355	0.00256	0.00186	0.00135	0.00098
39	0.01708	0.01204	0.00851	0.00604	0.00429	0.00306	0.00219	0.00157	0.00113	0.00082
40	0.01538	0.01075	0.00753	0.00529	0.00373	0.00264	0.00187	0.00133	0.00095	0.00068

Table A.4

Present Value of an Ordinary Annuity of $1 per Period: 1%–20%

$$PV_A = \frac{1 - \dfrac{1}{(1+i)^n}}{i}$$

Period	1%	2%	3%	4%	5%	6%	7%	8%	9%	10%
1	0.99010	0.98039	0.97087	0.96154	0.95238	0.94340	0.93458	0.92593	0.91743	0.90909
2	1.97040	1.94156	1.91347	1.88609	1.85941	1.83339	1.80802	1.78326	1.75911	1.73554
3	2.94099	2.88388	2.82861	2.77509	2.72325	2.67301	2.62432	2.57710	2.53129	2.48685
4	3.90197	3.80773	3.71710	3.62990	3.54595	3.46511	3.38721	3.31213	3.23972	3.16987
5	4.85343	4.71346	4.57971	4.45182	4.32948	4.21236	4.10020	3.99271	3.88965	3.79079
6	5.79548	5.60143	5.41719	5.24214	5.07569	4.91732	4.76654	4.62288	4.48592	4.35526
7	6.72819	6.47199	6.23028	6.00205	5.78637	5.58238	5.38929	5.20637	5.03295	4.86842
8	7.65168	7.32548	7.01969	6.73274	6.46321	6.20979	5.97130	5.74664	5.53482	5.33493
9	8.56602	8.16224	7.78611	7.43533	7.10782	6.80169	6.51523	6.24689	5.99525	5.75902
10	9.47130	8.98259	8.53020	8.11090	7.72173	7.36009	7.02358	6.71008	6.41766	6.14457
11	10.36763	9.78685	9.25262	8.76048	8.30641	7.88687	7.49867	7.13896	6.80519	6.49506
12	11.25508	10.57534	9.95400	9.38507	8.86325	8.38384	7.94269	7.53608	7.16073	6.81369
13	12.13374	11.34837	10.63496	9.98565	9.39357	8.85268	8.35765	7.90378	7.48690	7.10336
14	13.00370	12.10625	11.29607	10.56312	9.89864	9.29498	8.74547	8.24424	7.78615	7.36669
15	13.86505	12.84926	11.93794	11.11839	10.37966	9.71225	9.10791	8.55948	8.06069	7.60608
16	14.71787	13.57771	12.56110	11.65230	10.83777	10.10590	9.44665	8.85137	8.31256	7.82371
17	15.56225	14.29187	13.16612	12.16567	11.27407	10.47726	9.76322	9.12164	8.54363	8.02155
18	16.39827	14.99203	13.75351	12.65930	11.68959	10.82760	10.05909	9.37189	8.75563	8.20141
19	17.22601	15.67846	14.32380	13.13394	12.08532	11.15812	10.33560	9.60360	8.95011	8.36492
20	18.04555	16.35143	14.87747	13.59033	12.46221	11.46992	10.59401	9.81815	9.12855	8.51356
21	18.85698	17.01121	15.41502	14.02916	12.82115	11.76408	10.83553	10.01680	9.29224	8.64869
22	19.66038	17.65805	15.93692	14.45112	13.16300	12.04158	11.06124	10.20074	9.44243	8.77154
23	20.45582	18.29220	16.44361	14.85684	13.48857	12.30338	11.27219	10.37106	9.58021	8.88322
24	21.24339	18.91393	16.93554	15.24696	13.79864	12.55036	11.46933	10.52876	9.70661	8.98474
25	22.02316	19.52346	17.41315	15.62208	14.09394	12.78336	11.65358	10.67478	9.82258	9.07704
26	22.79520	20.12104	17.87684	15.98277	14.37519	13.00317	11.82578	10.80998	9.92897	9.16095
27	23.55961	20.70690	18.32703	16.32959	14.64303	13.21053	11.98671	10.93516	10.02658	9.23722
28	24.31644	21.28127	18.76411	16.66306	14.89813	13.40616	12.13711	11.05108	10.11613	9.30657
29	25.06579	21.84438	19.18845	16.98371	15.14107	13.59072	12.27767	11.15841	10.19828	9.36961
30	25.80771	22.39646	19.60044	17.29203	15.37245	13.76483	12.40904	11.25778	10.27365	9.42691
31	26.54229	22.93770	20.00043	17.58849	15.59281	13.92909	12.53181	11.34980	10.34280	9.47901
32	27.26959	23.46833	20.38877	17.87355	15.80268	14.08404	12.64656	11.43500	10.40624	9.52638
33	27.98969	23.98856	20.76579	18.14765	16.00255	14.23023	12.75379	11.51389	10.46444	9.56943
34	28.70267	24.49589	21.13184	18.41120	16.19290	14.36814	12.85401	11.58693	10.51784	9.60857
35	29.40858	24.99862	21.48722	18.66461	16.37419	14.49825	12.94767	11.65457	10.56682	9.64416
36	30.10751	25.48884	21.83225	18.90828	16.54685	14.62099	13.03521	11.71719	10.61176	9.67651
37	30.79951	25.96945	22.16724	19.14258	16.71129	14.73678	13.11702	11.77518	10.65299	9.70592
38	31.48466	26.44064	22.49246	19.36786	16.86789	14.84602	13.19347	11.82887	10.69082	9.73265
39	32.16303	26.90259	22.80822	19.58448	17.01704	14.94907	13.26493	11.87858	10.72552	9.75696
40	32.83469	27.35548	23.11477	19.79277	17.15909	15.04630	13.33171	11.92461	10.75736	9.77905

Table A.4 (cont.)

Present Value of an Ordinary Annuity of $1 per Period: 1%-20% (continued)

Period	11%	12%	13%	14%	15%	16%	17%	18%	19%	20%
1	0.90090	0.89286	0.88496	0.87719	0.86957	0.86207	0.85470	0.84746	0.84034	0.83333
2	1.71252	1.69005	1.66810	1.64666	1.62571	1.60523	1.58521	1.56564	1.54650	1.52778
3	2.44371	2.40183	2.36115	2.32163	2.28323	2.24589	2.20958	2.17427	2.13992	2.10648
4	3.10245	3.03735	2.97447	2.91371	2.85498	2.79818	2.74324	2.69006	2.63859	2.58873
5	3.69590	3.60478	3.51723	3.43308	3.35216	3.27429	3.19935	3.12717	3.05763	2.99061
6	4.23054	4.11141	3.99755	3.88867	3.78448	3.68474	3.58918	3.49760	3.40978	3.32551
7	4.71220	4.56376	4.42261	4.28830	4.16042	4.03857	3.92238	3.81153	3.70570	3.60459
8	5.14612	4.96764	4.79877	4.63886	4.48732	4.34359	4.20716	4.07757	3.95437	3.83716
9	5.53705	5.32825	5.13166	4.94637	4.77158	4.60654	4.45057	3.30302	4.16333	4.03097
10	5.88923	5.65022	5.42624	5.21612	5.01877	4.83323	4.65860	4.49409	4.33893	4.19247
11	6.20652	5.93770	5.68694	5.45273	5.23371	5.02864	4.83641	4.65601	4.48650	4.32706
12	6.49236	6.19437	5.91765	5.66029	5.42062	5.19711	4.98839	4.79322	4.61050	4.43922
13	6.74987	6.42355	6.12181	5.84236	5.58315	5.34233	5.11828	4.90951	4.71471	4.53268
14	6.98187	6.62817	6.30249	6.00207	5.72448	5.46753	5.22930	5.00806	4.80228	4.61057
15	7.19087	6.81086	6.46238	6.14217	5.84737	5.57546	5.32419	5.09158	4.87586	4.67547
16	7.37916	6.97399	6.60388	6.26506	5.95423	5.66850	5.40529	5.16235	4.39770	4.72956
17	7.54879	7.11963	6.72909	6.37286	6.04716	5.74870	5.47461	5.22233	4.98966	4.77463
18	7.70162	7.24967	6.83991	6.46742	6.12797	5.81785	5.53385	5.27316	5.03333	4.81219
19	7.83929	7.36578	6.93797	6.55037	6.19823	5.87746	5.58449	5.31624	5.07003	4.84350
20	7.96333	7.46944	7.02475	6.62313	6.25933	5.92884	5.62777	5.35275	5.10086	4.86958
21	8.07507	7.56200	7.10155	6.68696	6.31246	5.97314	5.66476	5.38368	5.12677	4.89132
22	8.17574	7.64465	7.16951	6.74294	6.35866	6.01133	5.69637	5.40990	5.14855	4.90943
23	8.26643	7.71843	7.22966	6.79206	6.39884	6.04425	5.72340	5.43212	5.16685	4.92453
24	8.34814	7.78432	7.28288	6.83514	6.43377	6.07263	5.74649	5.45095	5.18223	4.93710
25	8.42174	7.84314	7.32998	6.87293	6.46415	6.09709	5.76623	5.46691	5.19515	4.94759
26	8.48806	7.89566	7.37167	6.90608	6.49056	6.11818	5.78311	5.48043	5.20601	4.95632
27	8.54780	7.94255	7.40856	6.93515	6.51353	6.13636	5.79753	5.49189	5.21513	4.96360
28	8.60162	7.98442	7.44120	6.96066	6.53351	6.15204	5.80985	5.50160	5.22280	4.96967
29	8.65011	8.02181	7.47009	6.98304	6.55088	6.16555	5.82039	5.50983	5.22924	4.97472
30	8.69379	8.05518	7.49565	7.00266	6.56598	6.17720	5.82939	5.51681	5.23466	4.97894
31	8.73315	8.08499	7.51828	7.01988	6.57911	6.18724	5.83709	5.52272	5.23921	4.98245
32	8.76860	8.11159	7.53830	7.03498	6.59053	6.19590	5.84366	5.52773	5.24303	4.98537
33	8.80054	8.13535	7.55602	7.04823	6.60046	6.20336	5.84928	5.53197	5.24625	4.98781
34	8.82932	8.15656	7.57170	7.05985	6.60910	6.20979	5.85409	5.53557	5.24895	4.98984
35	8.85524	8.17550	7.58557	7.07005	6.61661	6.21534	5.85820	5.53862	5.25122	4.99154
36	8.87859	8.19241	7.59785	7.07899	6.62314	6.22012	5.86171	5.54120	5.25312	4.99295
37	8.89963	8.20751	7.60872	7.08683	6.62881	6.22424	5.86471	5.54339	5.25472	4.99412
38	8.91859	8.22099	7.61833	7.09371	6.63375	6.22779	5.86727	5.54525	5.25607	4.99510
39	8.93567	8.23303	7.62684	7.09975	6.63805	6.23086	5.86946	5.54682	5.25720	4.99592
40	8.95105	8.24378	7.63438	7.10504	6.64178	6.23350	5.87133	5.54815	5.25815	4.99660

New Terms Index

Subject Index

Noncash charges or expenses, 389–390, 619–620
Noncash credits or revenues, 620
Noncumulative preferred stock, 468
Nonoperating assets, 676
Nonoperating expenses, 231
Nonoperating income elements, 678
Nonoperating revenues, 231
No-par stock, 465
    issuance for cash, 471–473
    with stated value, 465, 472
Normal balances, 54
Notes, 52, 152, 360–361
    dishonored, 363
    interest accrual and, 364–365
    interest-bearing, 366
    interest calculation for, 361
    maturity date of, 361–362
    noninterest-bearing, 366–367
    in normal business transactions, 362–363
    renewal of, 364
    short-term financing though, 366–367
Notes payable, 18, 154
Notes Payable account
    acquisitions and, 553
    discounting notes payable and, 366–367
Notes Receivable account
    acquisitions and, 553
    dishonored notes and, 363–364
Not-for-profit accounting, 5–6
NSF (Not Sufficient Funds) check, 319–320
Number of days' sales in accounts receivable, 369
Number of days' sales in accounts turnover ratio, 672

Obsolescence, 391
Office equipment, 153
Office furniture, 153
"One write" system, 146
Operating activities, 18, 19, 616, 618–620, 628
    cash flows from. *See* Cash flows from operating activities
Operating assets, 676
    rate of return on, 406–407, 675
    turnover of, 676
Operating budgets. *See* Flexible operating budgets; Planned operating budgets
Operating cycles, 151, 355
Operating expenses, 231
Operating leases, 438
Operating margin, 675
Operating revenues, 230
Organization costs, 462
Other expenses, 231
Other revenues, 231
Outstanding checks, 322
Outstanding stock, 466–467
Owners
    of corporations, 460. *See also* Stockholders
    distributions to, technical definition of, 195
    investments by, technical definition of, 195
    as users of accounting information, 6

Pacioli, Luca, 1, 49
Paid-in capital, 154, 470, 497–498
    on balance sheet, 499
    in excess of par (or stated) value, 472
Paid-In Capital—Common (Preferred) Treasury Stock Transactions account, 509, 510
Paid-in Capital—Donations account, 390, 498, 510
Paid-In Capital in Excess of Par Value account, 472, 474, 551, 552
    bond redemption and, 594
Paid-In Capital in Excess of Stated Value account, 474–475
Paid-In Capital—Stock Dividends account, 498
Paper profits, 272
Parent companies, 541, 547
    financial statements of.
      See Consolidated balance sheet; Consolidated financial statements
Partners, skills needed by, 148
Partnerships, 14
Par value, 465
Par value stock, issuance for cash, 471–472
Passage of title, 225
Patents, 153, 436
Payables, 345
Payees, 305, 318, 344, 360
Payout ratio on common stock, 557–559, 682, 689
Payroll, service bureaus for processing of, 357
Payroll liabilities, 357–358
Pegboard system, 146
Percentage-of-completion method, 185–186
Percentage-of-receivables method, 349–351
Percentage-of-sales method, 347–348
Performance measures.
Period costs, 186
Periodicals, 664
Periodic inventory procedure, 221, 222
    inventory methods under, 265–268
    for inventory valuation, 264–268
    journal entries under, 264
    lack of control under, 238–239
Periodicity concept, 21, 179
Permanent accounts, 58
Perpetual inventory procedure, 221, 222
    inventory methods under, 269–271
    for inventory valuation, 262–265, 269–271, 276–277
    journal entries under, 264
Petty Cash account, 325–326
Petty cash custodians (cashiers), 325
Petty cash funds, 325–327
    Cash Short and Over account and, 327
    establishing, 325
    operating, 325
    replenishing, 325–326
Petty cash vouchers, 325
Physical deterioration, 391
Physical inventories, 226–227
Plant and equipment, 385
Plant assets. *See* Property, plant, and equipment
Pollution, clean-up costs for, 359
Post-closing trial balance, 145

Posting, 60, 68, 70, 72–74
Posting Reference column, in general journal, 58, 68–70
Predictive value, 191
Preemptive rights, 462
Preferred stock, 467–470
    callable, 469–470
    convertible, 469
    cumulative, 468
    noncumulative, 468
    preference as to assets and, 469
    preference as to dividends and, 468
Premium(s)
    bonds issued at, 584, 587
    call, 470, 579
Premium on Bonds Payable account, 592
Prepaid expenses, 104, 152
    adjusting entries for, 104–110
Prepaid insurance, 104–105
Prepaid Insurance account, 63, 104
Prepaid rent, 106
Prepaid Rent account, 62, 106, 438
Present value, 584, 600–602
    tables of, A–6–A–9
Price(s)
    of bonds.
    inventory valuation and, 222
Price-earnings ratio, 518, 682
Principal (of a note), 361
Prior period adjustments, 515
Private Securities Litigation Reform Act, 506
    joint. *See* Joint product *entries*
Product costs, 186
Production decisions, managerial accounting information for, 7
Product Warranty Expense account, 358–359
Profit(s)
    gross, 231
    inventory (paper), 272
Profitability, 16
Profitability tests, 675–681
Project selection. *See* Capital budgeting
Promissory notes, 360. *See also* Notes
Property, capital stock issued for, 473
Property, plant, and equipment, 152–153, 385–408, 425–432
    depreciation of. *See* Depreciation
    destruction of, 428
    exchanges of, 428–431
    gifts of, 390
    group purchases of, 388
    initial recording of, 386–390
    rate of return on, 406–407
    retirement without sale, 427–428
    sale of, 426
    self-constructed, 389
    subsequent expenditures on, 401–404
    subsidiary records used to control, 404–406
Proxies, 463
Public, as users of accounting information, 7
Public accounting firms. *See* Accounting firms
Purchase(s)
    of low-cost items, 403
    net, 224
    net cost of, 225
    of plant assets, 386–390

Chart of Accounts

ACCOUNT NUMBER/ ACCOUNT TITLE		ACCOUNT NUMBER/ ACCOUNT TITLE	

Asset Accounts

100	Cash
101	Petty Cash
103	Accounts Receivable
104	Allowance for Uncollectible Accounts
105	Merchandise Inventory
106	Repair Parts Inventory
107	Supplies on Hand
108	Prepaid Insurance
109	Store Supplies on Hand
110	Prepaid Advertising
111	Prepaid Printing Expense
112	Prepaid Rent
113	Receivables from Employees
114	Receivable from Insurance Company
115	Rent Receivable
120	Notes Receivable
121	Interest Receivable
125	Salvaged Materials
130	Land
140	Buildings
141	Accumulated Depreciation–Buildings
150	Trucks
151	Accumulated Depreciation–Trucks
152	Automobiles
153	Accumulated Depreciation–Automobiles
160	Office Furniture
161	Accumulated Depreciation–Office Furniture
165	Furniture and Fixtures
166	Accumulated Depreciation–Furniture and Fixtures
170	Equipment
171	Accumulated Depreciation–Equipment
172	Office Equipment
173	Accumulated Depreciation–Office Equipment
174	Store Fixtures
175	Accumulated Depreciation–Store Fixtures
180	Machinery
181	Accumulated Depreciation–Machinery
190	Ore Deposits
191	Accumulated Depreciation–Ore Deposits
192	Land Improvements
193	Accumulated Depreciation–Land Improvements
194	Leasehold
195	Leasehold Improvements

Asset Accounts (concluded)

196	Franchises
197	Patents
198	Copyrights
199	Goodwill

Liability Accounts

200	Accounts Payable
201	Notes Payable
202	Discount on Notes Payable
203	Loan Payable
204	Interest Payable
205	Vouchers Payable
206	Salaries Payable (or Wages Payable)
207	Sales Salaries Payable
208	Office Salaries Payable
209	Officers' Salaries Payable
210	Unearned Delivery Fees
211	Unearned Subscriptions
212	Unearned Ticket Fees
213	Unearned Laundry Fees
214	Unearned Management Fees
215	Unearned Rent
216	Unearned Service Fees
217	Unearned Commissions
218	Mortgage Note Payment
219	Travel Expenses Payable
220	Employees' Federal Income Taxes Payable
221	FICA Taxes Payable
222	Medical Insurance Premiums Payable
223	Employees' State Income Taxes Payable
224	Federal Unemployment Taxes Payable
225	State Unemployment Taxes Payable
226	Sales Tax Payable
227	Federal Excise Tax Payable
230	Estimated Product Warranty Payable
232	Estimated Property Taxes Payable
235	Other Liabilities
240	Commissions Payable

Stockholder's Equity Accounts

300	Capital Stock
310	Retained Earnings
320	Dividends

ACCOUNT NUMBER/ ACCOUNT TITLE		ACCOUNT NUMBER/ ACCOUNT TITLE	

Revenue and Gain Accounts

400	Service Revenue
401	Ticket Revenue
402	Horse Boarding Fees Revenue
403	Concessions Revenue
404	Riding and Lesson Fees Revenue
405	Tennis Lesson Revenue
406	Campsite Rental Revenue
407	Rental Revenue
408	Commissions Revenue
409	Legal Fees Revenue
410	Sales
411	Sales Discounts
412	Sales Returns and Allowances
413	Membership and Lesson Revenue
414	Management Fee Revenue
415	Subscriptions Revenue
418	Interest Revenue
420	Miscellaneous Revenue
421	Gain on Disposal of Plant Assets
422	Other Revenue

Cost of Goods Sold, Operating Expense, and Loss Accounts

500	Purchases
501	Purchase Discounts
502	Purchase Returns and Allowances
503	Transportation–In
504	Cost of Goods Sold
505	Advertising Expense
506	Gas and Oil Expense
507	Salaries Expense (or Wage Expense)
508	Sales Salaries Expense
509	Office Salaries Expense
510	Officers' Salaries Expense
511	Utilities Expense
512	Insurance Expense
513	Feed Expense
515	Rent Expense
516	Supplies Expense
518	Store Supplies Expense
519	Delivery Expense
520	Depreciation Expense–Buildings
521	Depreciation Expense–Trucks
522	Depreciation Expense–Automobiles
523	Depreciation Expense–Office Furniture
524	Depreciation Expense–Equipment

Cost of Goods Sold, Operating Expense, and Loss Accounts (continued)

525	Depreciation Expense–Office Equipment
526	Depreciation Expense–Store Fixtures
527	Depreciation Expense–Machinery
528	Depreciation Expense–Land Improvements
529	Depreciation Expense–Furniture and Fixtures
530	Repairs Expense
531	Entertainment Expense
532	Travel Expense
533	Property Tax Expense
534	Uncollectible Accounts Expense
535	Product Warranty Expense
536	Legal and Accounting Expense
537	Cleaning Expense
538	Payroll Tax Expense
539	Printing Expense
540	Interest Expense
541	Commissions Expense
542	Credit Card Expense
543	Discounts Lost
544	Bank Service Charge Expense
545	Postage Expense
546	Cash Short and Over
547	Franchise Amortization Expense
548	Patent Amortization Expense
549	Research and Development Expense
550	Copyright Amortization Expense
551	Goodwill Amortization Expense
552	Telephone Expense
557	Miscellaneous Selling Expense
567	Miscellaneous Administrative Expense
568	Miscellaneous Expense
570	Loss from Inventory Shortage
571	Loss from Disposal of Plant Asset
572	Losses During Construction from Damage and Injuries
573	Fire Loss
574	Loss on Accident
575	Loss on Theft of Truck
576	Loss on Sale of Assets

Other Accounts

| 580 | Depletion |
| 600 | Income Summary |